PRINCIPLES AND PRACTICE OF

DISINFECTION, PRESERVATION AND STERILIZATION

PRINCIPLES AND PRACTICE OF

DISINFECTION, PRESERVATION AND STERILIZATION

EDITED BY

A.D. RUSSELL
BPharm, DSc, PhD, FRPharmS, FRCPath
Professor of Pharmaceutical Microbiology,
University of Wales College of Cardiff

W.B. HUGO
BPharm, PhD, FRPharmS
Formerly Reader in
Pharmaceutical Microbiology,
University of Nottingham

G.A.J. AYLIFFE
BSc, MD, FRCPath
Emeritus Professor of Medical Microbiology,
University of Birmingham;
Honorary Director,
Hospital Infection Research Laboratory,
Dudley Road Hospital,
Birmingham

SECOND EDITION

OXFORD
BLACKWELL SCIENTIFIC PUBLICATIONS
LONDON EDINBURGH BOSTON
MELBOURNE PARIS BERLIN VIENNA

Editorial Offices:
Osney Mead, Oxford OX2 0EL
25 John Street, London WClN 2BL
23 Ainslie Place, Edinburgh EH3 6AJ
3 Cambridge Center, Cambridge
Massachusetts 02142, USA
54 University Street, Carlton
Victoria 3053, Australia

Other Editorial Offices:
Librairie Arnette SA
2, rue Casimir-Delavigne
75006 Paris
France

Blackwell Wissenschafts-Verlag
Meinekestrasse 4
D-1000 Berlin 15
Germany

Blackwell MZV
Feldgasse 13
A-1238 Wien
Austria

First published 1982
Second edition 1992

Set by Setrite Typesetters, Hong Kong
Printed in Great Britain by The Alden Press,
Oxford and bound by Hartnolls Ltd, Bodmin, Cornwall

DISTRIBUTORS

Marston Book Services Ltd
PO Box 87
Oxford OX2 0DT
(*Orders*: Tel: 0865 791155
Fax: 0865 791927
Telex: 837515)

USA
Blackwell Scientific Publications, Inc.
3 Cambridge Center
Cambridge, MA 02142
(*Orders*: Tel: 800 759–6102
617 225–0401)

Canada
Times Mirror Professional Publishing, Ltd
5240 Finch Avenue East
Scarborough, Ontario M1S 5A2
(*Orders*: Tel: 800 268–4178
416 298–1588)

Australia
Blackwell Scientific Publications
(Australia) Pty Ltd
54 University Street
Carlton, Victoria 3053
(*Orders*: Tel: 03 347–0300)

British Library
Cataloguing in Publication Data

Principles and practice of
disinfection, preservation and
sterilization – 2nd. ed.
1. Microorganisms. Control
I. Russell, A.D. II. Hugo, W.B.
III. Ayliffe, G.A.J.
616.01

ISBN 0–632–02625–1

Contents

List of Contributors

V.G. ALDER *Formerly Microbiology Department, Bristol Royal Infirmary, Bristol, UK.* Present Address: *17 Bowood, Harford Drive, Frenchay, Bristol BS16 1NS, UK*

M.C. ALLWOOD *Medicines Research Unit, District Pharmacy Office, Derbyshire Royal Infirmary, London Road, Derby DE1 2QY, UK*

G.A.J. AYLIFFE *Hospital Infection Research Laboratory, Dudley Road Hospital, Birmingham B18 7QH, UK*

SALLY F. BLOOMFIELD *Chelsea Department of Pharmacy, Kings College London, University of London, Manresa Road, London SW3 6LX, UK*

A.F. BRAVERY *Building Research Establishment, Garston, Watford WD2 7JR, UK*

M.A. BRIGGS *Paint Research Association, Teddington, Middlesex TW11 8LD, UK*

F.F. BUSTA *Department of Food Science and Nutrition, University of Minnesota, 1334 Eckles Avenue, St Paul, Minnesota 55108, USA*

R.E. CHILD *Welsh Folk Museum, St Fagans, Cardiff CF5 6XB, Wales, UK*

E.A. CHRISTENSEN *Control Department, Statens Seruminstitut, Amager Boulevard 80, DK 2300 Copenhagen, Denmark*

B.J. COLLINS (deceased) *Formerly Hospital Infection Research Laboratory, Dudley Road Hospital, Birmingham B18 7QH, UK*

M.J. DAY *School of Pure and Applied Biology, University of Wales College of Cardiff, Cardiff CF1 3TL, Wales, UK*

S.P. DENYER *Department of Pharmacy, Brighton Polytechnic, Moulsecoomb, Brighton BN7 4GJ, UK*

R. ELSMORE *Coalite Chemicals, PO Box 152, Buttermilk Lane, Bolsover, Chesterfield SH4 6A2, UK*

G.W. GOULD *Unilever Research Laboratory, Colworth House, Sharnbrook, Bedford MK44 1LQ, UK*

V.W. GREENE *Epidemiology Unit, Medical School, Ben Gurion University, Beer Sheva, Israel*

E.A. HILDITCH *Cuprinol Limited, Adderwell, Frome, Somerset BA11 1NL, UK*

E.C. HILL *ECHA Microbiology Limited, Cardiff Workshops, Lewis Road, East Moors, Cardiff CF1 5EG, Wales, UK*

W.B. HUGO *Formerly Department of Pharmacy, University of Nottingham, Nottingham NG7 2RD, UK.* Present Address: *618 Wollaton Road, Nottingham NG8 2AA, UK*

E.L. JARROLL *Department of Biology, Cleveland State University, Cleveland, Ohio 44115–2403, USA*

J.B. KING *School of Pure and Applied Biology, University of Wales College of Cardiff, Cardiff CF1 3TL, Wales, UK*

H. KRISTENSEN *Control Department, Statens Seruminstitut, Amager Boulevard 80, DK 2300 Copenhagen, Denmark*

E.J.L. LOWBURY *Formerly MRC Industrial Injuries and Burns Unit, Accident Hospital, Birmingham, UK.* Present Address: *79 Vernon Road, Edgbaston, Birmingham B16 9SQ, UK*

P. MANN *Formerly Microbiology Department, Bristol Royal Infirmary, Bristol, UK.* Present Address: *The Old Vicarage, Southstoke, Bath BA2 7DU, UK*

B.J. McCARTHY *Biotechnology Department, British Textile Technology Group, Shirley Towers, 856 Wilmslow Road, Didsbury, Manchester M20 8RX, UK*

A. MILLER *Environmental Science and Technology Department, Riso National Laboratory, DK-4000, Roskilde, Denmark*

G. MOLIN *Department of Applied Microbiology, Chemical Center, University of Lund, PO Box 124, S-22100 Lund, Sweden*

M.S. PARKER *Formerly School of Pharmacy, Brighton Polytechnic, Moulsecoomb, Brighton BN2 4GJ, UK.* Present Address: *56 Rowan Way, Rottingdean, Brighton BN2 7FP, UK*

JANE PEAR *Formerly Process Unit, Pira Paper and Board Division, Randalls Road, Leatherhead, Surrey KT22 7RU, UK.* Present Address: *Outdowns Lodge, Effingham, Surrey KT24 5QN, UK*

P.J. QUINN *Department of Veterinary Microbiology and Parasitology, Faculty of Veterinary Medicine, Ballsbridge, Dublin 4, Ireland*

G. REYBROUCK *Public Health Laboratory, School of Public Health, Katholieke Universiteit Leuven, B-3000 Leuven, Belgium*

A.D. RUSSELL *Welsh School of Pharmacy, University of Wales College of Cardiff, PO Box 13, Cardiff CF1 3XF, Wales, UK*

ROSEMARY A. SIMPSON *Division of Hospital Infection, Central Public Health Laboratory, Colindale Avenue, Colindale, London NW9 5HT, UK*

J.N. SOFOS *Department of Animal Sciences, Colorado State University, Fort Collins, Colorado 80523, USA*

W.R. SPRINGLE *Paint Research Association, Teddington, Middlesex TW11 8LD, UK*

D.J. STICKLER *School of Pure and Applied Biology, University of Wales College of Cardiff, Cardiff CF1 3TL, Wales, UK*

D.M. TAYLOR *AFRC & MRC Neuropathogenesis Unit, Institute for Animal Health, Ogston Building, West Mains Road, Edinburgh EH9 3JF, Scotland, UK*

ELAINE UNDERWOOD *Wyeth Laboratories, New Lane, Havant, Hampshire PO9 2NG, UK*

BRENDA WEIR *Formerly Pira Paper and Board Division. Currently BBC London.* Present Address: *6 Whitelands, Hook End, Brentwood, Essex CM15 OQG, UK*

Preface to the Second Edition

Since the publication of the first edition, the emergence of human immunodeficiency virus (HIV) infections has been associated with an increased interest in decontamination of equipment and the testing of antiviral agents. These topics are dealt with in the relevant chapters. Two other diseases have assumed public prominence—legionnaires' disease and bovine spongiform encephalitis. We have been fortunate in obtaining the services of experts to deal with disinfection in relation to these two conditions. In addition, chapters have been added on antifungal agents, mycobacteria and protozoa. Methicillin-resistant *Staphylococcus aureus* (MRSA) strains have been causing outbreaks of infections in hospitals all over the world. Our knowledge of the problem of resistance has been strengthened by the inclusion of a chapter on the effects of biocides on these MRSA strains. The remaining chapters have been updated and revised.

We would like to thank all our authors for their help and co-operation, and our publishers for their continued support.

A.D.R.
W.B.H.
G.A.J.A.

Preface to the First Edition

Sterilization, disinfection and preservation, all designed to eliminate, prevent or frustrate the growth of micro-organisms in a wide variety of products, were incepted empirically from the time of man's emergence and remain a problem today. The fact that this is so is due to the incredible ability of the first inhabitants of the biosphere to survive and adapt to almost any challenge. This ability must in turn have been laid down in their genomes during their long and successful sojourn on this planet.

It is true to say that of these three processes, sterilization is a surer process than disinfection, which in turn is a surer process than preservation. It is in the latter field that we find the greatest interactive play between challenger and challenged. The microbial spoilage of wood, paper, textiles, paints, stonework, stored foodstuffs, to mention only a few categories at constant risk, costs the world many billions of pounds each year and if it were not for considerable success in the preservative field this figure would rapidly become astronomical. Disinfection processes do not suffer quite the same failure rate and one is left with the view that failure here is due more to uninformed use and naive interpretation of biocidal data. Sterilization is an infinitely more secure process and, provided that the procedural protocol is followed, controlled and monitored, it remains the most successful of the three processes.

In the field of communicable bacterial diseases and some virus infections, there is no doubt that these have been considerably reduced, especially in the wealthier industrial societies, by improved hygiene, more extensive immunization and possibly by availability of antibiotics. However, hospital-acquired infection remains an important problem and is often associated with surgical operations or instrumentation of the patient. Although heat sterilization processes at high temperatures are preferred whenever possible, medical equipment is often difficult to clean adequately, and components are sometimes heat-labile. Disposable equipment is useful and is widely used if relatively cheap, but is obviously not practicable for the more expensive items. Ethylene oxide is often used in industry for sterilizing heat-labile products, but has a limited use for reprocessing medical equipment. Low-temperature steam with or without formaldehyde has been developed as a possible alternative to ethylene oxide in the hospital.

Although aseptic methods are used for surgical techniques, skin disinfection is still necessary and a wider range of non-toxic antiseptic agents suitable for application to tissues is required. Older antibacterial agents have been re-introduced, e.g. silver nitrate for burns, alcohol for hand disinfection in the general wards, and less corrosive hypochlorites for disinfection of medical equipment.

Nevertheless, excessive use of disinfectants in the environment is undesirable and may change the hospital flora, selecting naturally antibiotic-resistant organisms, such as *Pseudomonas aeruginosa*, which are potentially dangerous to highly susceptible patients. Chemical disinfection of the hospital environment is therefore reduced to a minimum and is replaced where applicable by good cleaning methods or by physical methods of disinfection or sterilization.

A.D.R.
W.B.H.
G.A.J.A.

PART 1
DISINFECTION AND ANTISEPSIS

Chapter 1
Historical Introduction

1 EARLY CONCEPTS

In any account dealing with the history of microbiology, it is necessary to keep in mind the watershed between the empirical and the theoretical. This historical divide is marked by a period concerning both the discovery of bacteria and their later implication in disease, putrefaction and spoilage.

Throughout the empiric era it is quite amazing the extent to which hygienic precepts were being applied. These may be read in, for example, the literature of the Near and Middle East when written records became available and readable and no doubt these records were preceded by an oral code. An interesting example of early written codes of hygiene may be found in the Bible, especially in the book of Leviticus, chapters 11–15. This in turn reflects the accumulating wisdom of western asiatic medicine.

The process of flaming, used every day in bacteriological laboratories, was recorded in the book of Numbers where the passing of metal objects, especially cooking vessels, through fire was declared to cleanse them. Again it may be inferred that there was an awareness that something more than mechanical cleanness was required, and this represents an early empirical example of heat sterilization.

Chemical disinfection of a sort could be seen in the practice recorded at the time of Persian imperial expansion, *c.* 450 BC, of storing water in vessels of copper or silver to keep it potable. Water stored in pottery vessels soon acquired a foul odour and taste. Aristotle recommended to Alexander the Great the practice of boiling the water to be drunk by his armies.

Wine, vinegar and honey were used on dressings and as cleansing agents for wounds and it is interesting to note that diluted acetic acid has been recommended comparatively recently for the topical treatment of wounds and surgical lesions infected by *Pseudomonas aeruginosa*.

The art of mummification, which so obsessed the Egyptian civilization (although it owed its success largely to desiccation in the dry atmosphere of the country), also employed a variety of balsams which contained natural preservatives. Natron, a crude native sodium carbonate, was also used to preserve the bodies of human and animal alike.

Not only in hygiene but in the field of food preservation were practical procedures discovered. Thus tribes which had not progressed beyond the status of hunter-gatherers discovered that meat and fish could be preserved by drying, salting or mixing with natural spices. As the great civilizations of the Mediterranean and Near and Middle East receded, so arose the European high cultures and, whether through reading or independent discovery, precepts of empirical hygiene were also developed.

There was, of course, a continuum of contact between Europe and the Middle and Near East through the Arab and Ottoman incursions into Europe, but it is difficult to find early European writers acknowledging the heritage of these empires.

An early account of procedures to try and combat the episodic scourge of the plague may be found in the writings of the 14th century where one Joseph of Burgundy recommended the burning of juniper branches in rooms where the plague sufferers had lain. Sulphur, too, was burned in the hope of removing the cause of this terrible disease.

The association of malodour with disease and the belief that matter floating in the air might be responsible for diseases, a Greek concept, led to these procedures. If success was achieved it may be due to the elimination of rats later to be shown as the bearers of the causal organism. In Renaissance Italy at the turn of the 15th century a poet, philosopher and physician, Girolamo Fracastoro, who was professor of logic at the University of Padua, recognized possible causes of disease, mentioning contagion and airborne infection; he thought there must exist 'seeds of disease' as indeed there did! Robert Boyle, the sceptical chemist, writing in the mid-17th century, wrote of a possible relationship between fermentation and the disease process. In this he foreshadowed the views of Louis Pasteur. There is no evidence in the literature that Pasteur even read the opinions of Robert Boyle or Fracastoro.

The next landmark in this history was the discovery by Antonie van Leeuwenhoek of small living creatures in a variety of habitats such as tooth scrapings, pond water and vegetable infusions. His drawings, seen under his simple microscopes (× 300), were published in the *Philosophical Transactions of the Royal Society* in 1677 and also in a series of letters to the Society before and after this date. Some of his illustrations are thought to represent bacteria, although the greatest magnification he is said to have achieved was 300 times. When considering Leeuwenhoek's great technical achievement in microscopy and his painstaking application of it to original investigation, it should be borne in mind that bacteria in colony form must have been seen from the beginning of man's existence. A very early report of this was given by the Greek historian Siculus who, writing of the siege of Tyre in 332 BC, states how bread, distributed to the Macedonians, had a bloody look. This was probably attributable to infestation by *Serratia marcescens*; this phenomenon must have been seen, if not recorded, from time immemorial.

Turning back to Europe, it is also possible to find other examples of workers who believed, but could not prove scientifically, that some diseases were caused by invisible living agents, *contagium animatum*. Amongst these were Kircher (1658), Lange (1659), Lancisi (1718) and Marten (1720).

By observation and intuition, therefore, we see that the practice of heat and chemical disinfection, the inhibitory effect of desiccation and the implication of invisible objects with the cause of some diseases were known or inferred from early times.

Before passing to a more rationally supported history it is necessary to report on a remarkable quantification of chemical preservation published in 1775 by Joseph Pringle. Pringle was seeking to evaluate preservation by salting and he added pieces of lean meat to glass jars containing solutions of different salts; these he incubated, and judged his end point by the presence or absence of smell. He regarded his standard 'salt' as sea salt and expressed the results in terms of the relative efficiency as compared with sea salt; nitre, for example, had a value of 4 by this method. One hundred and fifty-three years later, Rideal and Walker were to use a similar method with phenolic disinfectants and *Salmonella typhi*; their standard was phenol.

2 CHEMICAL DISINFECTION

Now, newer and purer chemical disinfectants began to be used. Mercuric chloride, corrosive sublimate, found use as a wound dressing; it had been used since the Middle Ages and was introduced by Arab physicians. In 1798 bleaching powder was first made and a preparation of it was employed by Alcock in 1827 as a deodorant and disinfectant. Lefevre introduced chlorine water in 1843. In 1839 Davies had suggested iodine as a wound dressing. Semmelweis was to use chlorine water in his work on childbed fever occurring in the obstetrics division of the Vienna General Hospital. He achieved a sensational reduction in the incidence of the infection by insisting that all attending the birth washed their hands in chlorine water; later (in 1847) he substituted chlorinated lime.

Wood and coal tar were used as wound dressings in the early 19th century and in a letter to the *Lancet* Smith (1836–37) describes the use of creosote (Gr. *Kreas*=flesh, *sotes*=saviour) as a wound dressing. In 1850 Le Beuf, a French pharmacist, prepared an extract of coal tar by using the natural saponin of quillaia bark as a dispersing agent. Le Beuf asked a well-known surgeon, Jules Lemair, to evaluate his product. It proved to be highly efficacious. Küchenmeister was to use pure phenol in solution as a wound dressing in 1860 and Joseph Lister also used phenol in his great studies on antiseptic surgery during the 1860s. It is also of interest to record that a number of chemicals were being used as wood preservatives. Wood tar had been used in the 1700s to preserve the timbers of ships, and mercuric chloride was used for the same purpose in 1705. Copper sulphate was introduced in 1767 and zinc chloride in 1815. Many of these products are still in use today.

Turning back to evaluation, Bucholtz (1875) determined what is called today the minimum inhibitory concentration of phenol, creosote and benzoic and salicylic acids to inhibit the growth of bacteria. Robert Koch made measurements of the inhibitory power of mercuric chloride against anthrax spores but overvalued the product as he failed to neutralize the substance carried over in his tests. This was pointed out by Geppert who, in 1889, used ammonium sulphide as a neutralizing agent for mercuric chloride and obtained much more realistic values for the antimicrobial powers of mercuric chloride.

It will be apparent that, parallel with these early studies, an important watershed already alluded to in the opening paragraphs of this brief history had been passed. That is the scientific identification of a microbial species with a specific disease. Credit for this should go to an Italian, Agostino Bassi, a lawyer from Lodi (a small town near Milan). Although not a scientist or medical man, he performed exacting scientific experiments to equate a disease of silkworms with a fungus. Bassi identified plague and cholera as being of microbial origin and also experimented with heat and chemicals as antimicrobial agents. His work anticipated the great names of Pasteur and Koch in the implication of microbes with certain diseases, but because it was published locally in Lodi and in Italian it has not found the place it deserves in many textbooks.

Two other chemical disinfectants still in use today were early introductions. Hydrogen peroxide was first examined by Traugott in 1893, and Dakin reported on chlorine-releasing compounds in 1915. Quaternary ammonium compounds were introduced by Jacobs in 1916.

In 1897, Kronig and Paul, with the acknowledged help of the Japanese physical chemist Ikeda, introduced the science of disinfection dynamics; their pioneering publication was to give rise to innumerable studies on the subject lasting through to the present day.

3 STERILIZATION

As has been stated above, heat sterilization has been known since early historical times as a cleansing and purifying agent. In 1832 William Henry, a Manchester physician, studied the effect of heat on contagion by placing contaminated material, i.e. clothes worn by sufferers from typhus and scarlet fever, in air heated by water sealed in a pressure vessel. He realized that he could achieve temperatures higher than 100°C by using a closed vessel fitted with a proper safety valve. He found that garments so treated could be worn with impunity by others who did not then contract the diseases. Louis Pasteur also used a pressure vessel with safety valve for sterilization.

Sterilization by filtration has been observed from early times. Foul-tasting waters draining from ponds and percolating through soil or gravel were sometimes observed on emerging, spring-like, at a lower part of the terrain to be clear and potable (drinkable), and artificial filters of pebbles were constructed. Later, deliberate construction of tubes of unglazed porcelain or compressed Kieselguhr, the so-called Chamberland or Berkefeld filters, made their appearance in 1884 and 1891, respectively. After this time the science of sterilization and disinfection followed a more ordered pattern of evolution, culminating in the new technology of radiation sterilization. However, mistakes—often fatal—still occur and the discipline must at all times be accompanied by vigilance and critical monitoring and evaluation.

4 REFERENCES

4.1 General references

Brock, T.D. (Ed.) (1961) *Milestones in Microbiology*. London: Prentice Hall.

Bullock, W. (1938) *The History of Bacteriology*. Oxford: Oxford University Press.

Collard, P. (1976) *The Development of Microbiology*. Cambridge: Cambridge University Press.

Hugo, W.B. (1991) A brief history of heat and chemical preservation and disinfection. *Journal of Applied Bacteriology*, **71**, 9–18.

Medical Research Council (1930) *A System of Bacteriology in Relation to Medicine*. Vol. 1. Chapter 1. London: HMSO.

Reid, R. (1974) *Microbes and Men*. London: British Broadcasting Corporation.

4.2 Special references

Crellin, J.K. (1966) The problem of heat resistance of micro-organisms in the British spontaneous generation controversies of 1860–1880. *Medical History*, **10**, 50–59.

Gaughran, E.R. and Goudie, A.J. (1975). Heat sterilisation methods. *Acta Pharmaceutica Suecica*, **12** Suppl., 15–25.

Hugo, W.B. (1978) Early studies in the evaluation of disinfectants. *Journal of Antimicrobial Chemotherapy*, **4**, 489–494.

Hugo, W.B. (1978) Phenols: a review of their history and development as antimicrobial agents. *Microbios*, **23**, 83–85.

Selwyn, S. (1979) Early experimental models of disinfection and sterilization. *Journal of Antimicrobial Chemotherapy*, **5**, 229–238.

Smith, Sir F. (1836–7) External employment of creosote. *Lancet*, **ii**, 221–222.

Chapter 2
Types of Antimicrobial Agents

1 INTRODUCTION

Many different types of antimicrobial agents are now available and serve a variety of purposes in the medical, veterinary, dental and other fields (Russell *et al.* 1984; Gorman & Scott, 1985; Gardner & Peel, 1986, 1991; Russell & Hugo, 1987; Russell, 1990a,b, 1991a,b; Russell & Chopra, 1990). Subsequent chapters will discuss the factors influencing their activity and their role as disinfectants and antiseptics and as preservatives in a wide range of products or materials (Akers, 1984; Fels *et al.*, 1987). Additional information is provided on their mechanism of action and on the ways in which micro-organisms show resistance.

The present chapter will concentrate on the antimicrobial properties and uses of the various types of antimicrobial agents. Cross-references to other chapters are made where appropriate. A comprehensive summary of inhibitory concentrations, toxicity and uses is provided by Wallhäusser (1984).

2 PHENOLS

The historical introduction (Chapter 1) and the papers by Hugo (1979) and Marouchoc (1979) showed that phenol and natural-product distillates containing phenols shared, with chlorine and iodine, an early place in the armoury of antiseptics. Today they enjoy a wide use as general disinfectants and as preservatives for a variety of manufactured products. The main general restriction is that they should not be used where they can contaminate foods.

As a result of their long history, a vast literature has accumulated dealing with phenol and its analogues with bactericidal and bacteriostatic indices and phenol coefficient values measured against a large array of micro-organisms. Unfortunately, many different parameters have been used to express their biocidal and biostatic power but the phenol coefficient (Chapter 4) has probably been the most widely employed and serves as a reasonable cross-referencing cipher for the many hundreds of papers and reports written.

A feature of the work in the 1930s is the frequent exclusion of *Pseudomonas* species from the list of test organisms. At that time the pseudomonads were not regarded with the same degree of apprehension as they are today.

The purpose of this section is not to repeat the mass of data but to take advantage of the passage of time and the present position to consider those phenolic derivatives which are likely to be found in common usage. The same accumulation of biological data has, however, enabled a reasonable assessment of the relationship between structure and activity in the phenol series to be compiled (Suter, 1941).

The main conclusions from this survey were:

1 *para*-Substitutions of an alkyl chain up to six carbon atoms in length increases the antibacterial action of phenols, presumably by increasing the surface activity and ability to orientate at an interface. Activity falls off after this due to decreased water-solubility. Again, due to the conferment of polar properties, straight chain *para*-substituents confer greater activity than branched-chain substituents containing the same number of carbon atoms.

2 Halogenation increases the antibacterial activity of phenol. The combination of alkyl and halogen substitution which confers the greatest antibacterial activity is that where the alkyl group is *ortho* to the phenolic group and the halogen *para* to the phenolic group. Russell *et al.* (1987) compared the activity of phenol, cresol and chlorocresol on wild-type and envelope mutant strains of *Escherichia coli* and found that chlorocresol was the most active against all strains and especially against deep rough mutants.

3 Nitration, while increasing the toxicity of phenol towards bacteria, also increases the systemic toxicity and confers specific biological properties on the molecule enabling it to interfere with oxidative phosphorylation. This has now been shown to be due to the ability of nitrophenols to act as uncoupling agents. Studies (Hugo & Bowen, 1973) have shown that the nitro group is not a prerequisite for uncoupling as ethylphenol is an uncoupler. Nitrophenols have now been largely superseded as plant protection chemicals, where at one time they enjoyed a large vogue, although 4-nitrophenol is still used as a preservative in the leather industry.

4 In the bis-phenol series, activity is found with a direct bond between the two C_6H_5— groups or if they are separated by —CH_2—, —S— or —O—. If a —CO—, —SO— or —CH(OH)— group separates the phenyl groups, activity is low. In addition maximum activity is found with the hydroxyl group at the 2,2′ position of the bis-phenol. Halogenation of the bis-phenols confers additional biocidal activity.

2.1 Sources of phenols—the coal tar industry

Most of the phenols which are used to manufacture disinfectants are obtained from the tar obtained as a by-product in the destructive distillation of coal. This process was carried out primarily until the advent of North Sea gas, to produce coal gas, and is still used to produce coke and other smokeless fuels. Coal is heated in the absence of air and the volatile products, one of which is tar, condensed. The tar is fractionated to yield a group of products which include phenols (called tar acids), organic bases and neutral products such as alkyl naphthalenes, and known in the industry as neutral oils. Phenols may be separated by extraction with alkali from which they are regenerated by reaction with acid, e.g. carbon dioxide from flue gas.

The yield of tar acids from tar depends on the type of oven or retort used, the type of coal and the temperature of carbonization. Coal heated in a coke oven yields a tar with about 2% tar acid content; in the low-temperature process used to produce smokeless fuels, some 25% of the weight of tar consists of tar acids.

A typical but abridged analysis of the 50 or more phenolic substances produced is shown in Table 2.1. These figures are based on a low-temperature carbonization process.

The cresols consist of a mixture of 2-, 3- and 4-cresol. The 'xylenols' consist of the six isomeric dimethylphenols plus ethylphenols. The combined fraction, cresols and xylenols, is also available as a commercial product which is known as cresylic acid. High-boiling tar acids consist of higher alkyl homologues of phenol, e.g. the diethylphenols, tetramethylphenols, methylethylphenols, together with methylindanols, naphthols and methylresorcinols, the latter being known as dihydrics. There may be traces of 2-phenylphenol. The chemical constituents of some of the phenolic components are shown in Fig. 2.1. Extended information on coal tars and their constituents is given in the *Coal Tar Data Book* (1965).

Table 2.1 Typical analysis of a coal tar produced by the low-temperature carbonization process

Phenol	Boiling range (°C)	Percentage
Phenol	182	7
Cresols	189–205	15
Xylenols	210–230	22
High-boiling tar acids	230–310	16

As tar distillation is a commercial process, it should be realized that there will be some overlap between fractions. Phenol is obtained at 99% purity. Cresol, of the *British Pharmacopoeia* (1988) (2-, 3- and 4-cresols) must contain less than 2% of phenol. Cresol of the *European Pharmacopoeia* (1976) is 2-cresol (*o*-cresol). This chemical is available commercially and contains 98% of 2-cresol. A commercially mixed xylenol fraction contains no phenols or cresols but may contain 22 of the higher-boiling phenols. High-boiling tar acids may contain some of the higher-boiling xylenols, i.e. 3,4-xylenol (b.p. 227°C).

Mention must be made of the neutral oil fraction which has an adjuvant action in some of the formulated disinfectants to be considered below. It is devoid of biocidal activity and consists mainly of hydrocarbons such as methyl and dimethyl naphthalenes, *n*-dodecane, naphthalene, tetramethyl benzene, dimethylindenes and tetrahydronaphthalene. Some tar distillers offer a neutral oil, boiling range 205–296°C for blending with phenolics destined for disinfectant manufacture (see also Section 2.4.3).

2.2 Properties of phenolic fractions

The passage from phenol (b.p. 182°C) to the higher boiling phenols (b.p.s up to 310°C) is accompanied by a well-defined gradation in properties as follows: water-solubility decreases, tissue trauma decreases, bactericidal activity increases, inactivation by organic matter increases. The ratio of activity against G−ves to activity against G+ves however, remains fairly constant although in the case of pseudo-

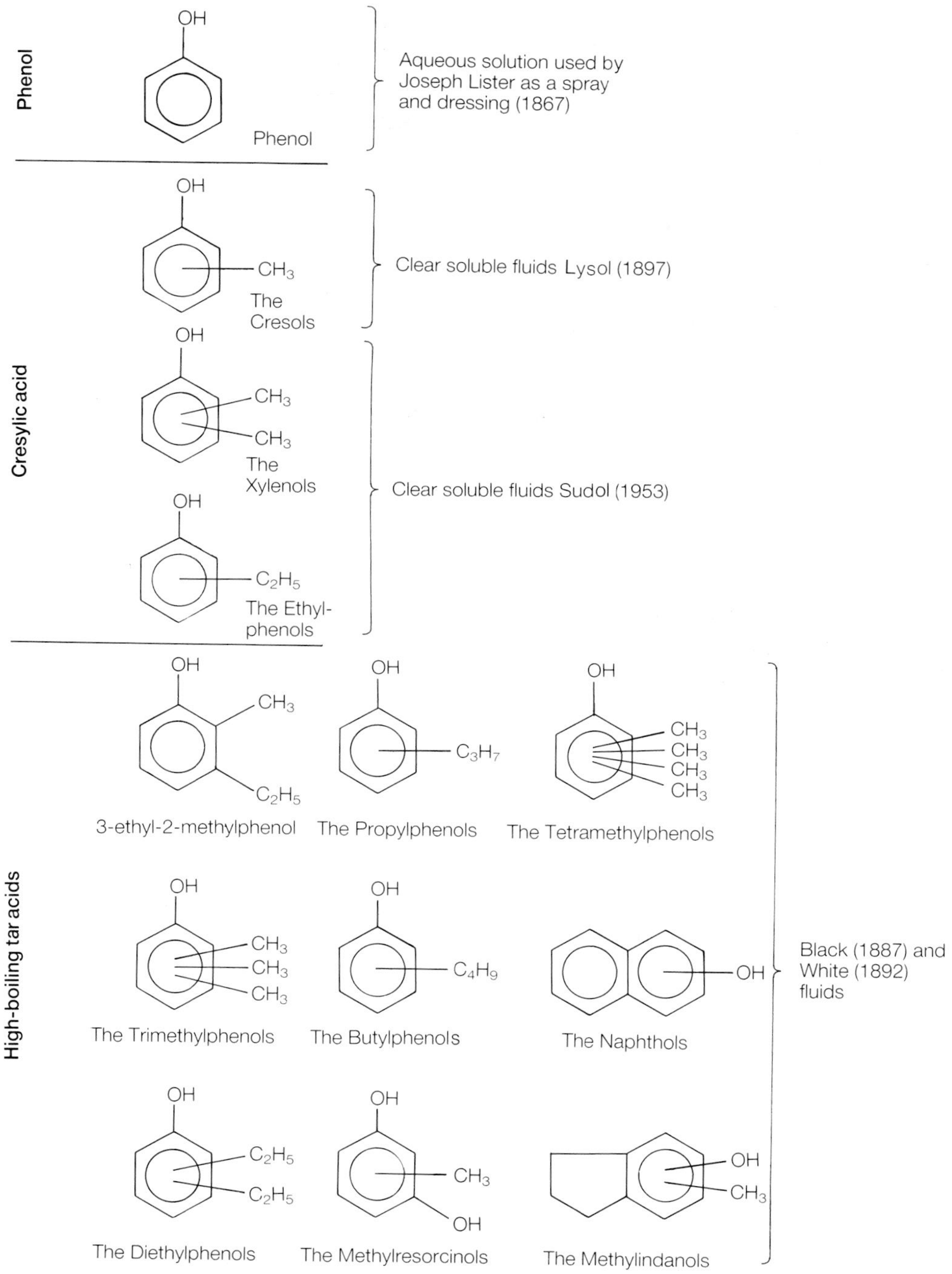

Fig. 2.1 Phenol, cresols, xylenols, ethyl phenols and high-boiling tar acids.

monads, activity tends to decrease with decreasing water solubility; see also Table 2.2.

2.3 Formulation of coal-tar disinfectants

It will be seen from the above data that the progressive increase in desirable biological properties of the coal-tar phenols with increasing boiling point is accompanied by a decrease in water-solubility. This presents formulation problems and part of the story of the evolution of the present-day products is found in the evolution of formulation devices.

The antiseptic and disinfectant properties of coal tar had been noted as early as 1815, and in 1844 a Frenchman called Bayard made an antiseptic powder of coal tar, plaster, ferrous sulphate and clay, an early carbolic powder. Other variations on this theme appeared during the first half of the 19th century.

In 1850, a French pharmacist, Ferdinand Le Beuf, living in Bayonne, prepared an emulsion of coal tar using the bark of a South American tree, the quillaia. This bark contained a triterpenoid glycoside with soap-like properties belonging to the class of natural products called saponins. By emulsifying coal tar, Le Beuf made a usable liquid disinfectant which in the hands of the French surgeon, Lemaire, proved a very valuable aid to surgery. A 'solution' of coal tar prepared with quillaia bark is still described in the *Pharmaceutical Codex* (1979); it would be interesting to know how many people attribute this formula to Le Beuf who developed it 130 years ago. Quillaia is replaced by polysorbate 80 in formulae for coal-tar 'solutions' in the *British Pharmacopoeia* (1988).

In 1887 the use of soap and coal tar was first promulgated, and in 1889 a German experimenter, T. Damman, patented a product which was prepared from coal tar, creosote and soap and which involved the principle of solubilization. Thus, between 1850 and 1887, the basis for the formulation of coal-tar disinfectants had been laid and subsequent discoveries were either rediscoveries or modifications of these two basic themes of emulsification and solubilization. Better-quality tar acid fractions and products with clearer-cut properties aided the production of improved products.

In 1887 John Jeyes of Northampton patented a coal-tar product, the well-known Jeyes fluid, by solubilizing coal-tar acids with a soap made from the resin of pine trees and alkali. It is difficult, from the written history of the Jeyes Company (Palfreyman, 1977), to learn how John acquired the background knowledge for his product but his brother, Philadelphus, was apprenticed to a pharmacist and might have supplied information on formulation.

In 1897, Engler and Pieckhoff in Germany pre-

Table 2.2 Phenol coefficients of coal tar products against *Sal. typhi* and *Staph. aureus*

Product and m.p., m. range (°C)	Phenol coefficient		Water-solubility (g/100 ml)
	Sal. typhi	*Staph. aureus*	
Phenol 182	1	1	6.6
Cresols 190–203	2.5	2.0	2.0
4-Ethylphenol 195	6	6	Slightly
Xylenols 210–230	5	4.5	Slightly
High-boiling tar acids 230–270	40	25	Insoluble
High-boiling tar acids 250–275	60	40	Insoluble

pared the first Lysol by solubilizing cresol with soap.

2.4 The modern range of solubilized and emulsified phenolic disinfectants

Black fluids are essential coal-tar fractions solubilized with soaps: white fluids are prepared by emulsifying tar fractions. Their composition as regards phenol content is shown in Fig. 2.1. The term 'clear soluble fluid' is also used to describe the solubilized products Lysol and Sudol.

2.4.1 Cresol and Soap Solution BP 1963 (Lysol)

This consists of cresol (a mixture of 2-, 3- and 4-cresols) solubilized with a soap prepared from linseed oil and potassium hydroxide; it forms a clear solution on dilution. Most vegetative pathogens, including mycobacteria, are killed in 15 min by dilutions of Lysol ranging from 0.3% to 0.6%. Bacterial spores are much more resistant and there are reports of the spores of *Bacillus subtilis* surviving in 2% Lysol for nearly 3 days. Even greater resistance has been encountered among clostridial spores. Lysol still retains the corrosive nature associated with the phenols and should be used with care. Both the method of manufacture and the nature of the soap used have been found to affect the biocidal properties of the product (Tilley & Schaffer, 1925; Berry & Stenlake, 1942). Rideal–Walker coefficients (BS541: 1985; see Chapter 4) are of the order of 2.

2.4.2 Xylenol-rich cresylic acid and Soap Solution (Sudol: Tenneco Organics Ltd, Avonmouth, Bristol)

By using a coal tar fraction devoid of cresols but rich in xylenols and ethylphenols, a much more active but less corrosive product (Sudol) is obtained. Rideal–Walker coefficients as high as 7 gave been reported for this product. Sudol has a Chick–Martin coefficient (BS808: 1986; see Chapter 4) of 3.9 and is thus seen to be quite potent in the presence of organic matter; in fact, this phenol fraction seems to be the best of those normally used for disinfectant manufacture in retaining activity in the presence of organic debris. Other solubilized phenolics products in this category include Printol and Clearsol (also produced by Tenneco).

Sudol is active against *Mycobacterium tuberculosis* (phenol coefficient 6.3) and *Staphylococcus aureus* (phenol coefficient 6). The phenol coefficient against *Pseudomonas aeruginosa* is 4. It also possesses sporicidal activity: a 2% solution killed a suspension of *Clostridum perfringens* spores in 4 h; however, a suspension of *B. subtilis* spores needed 6 h in a 66% solution for inactivation. A full bacteriological protocol of activity against non-sporing organisms is given by Finch (1953).

Printol and Clearsol are similar to Sudol in general properties (all from Tenneco Organics, Avonmouth, BS11 0YT). Another is Stericol (Sterling Health, Sheffield, S30 4YP).

2.4.3 Black fluids

These are defined in a British Standard (BS 2462: 1961). They consist of a solubilized crude phenol fraction prepared from tar acids, of the boiling range 250–310°C (Fig. 2.1, Table 2.1).

The solubilizing agents used to prepare the black fluids of commerce include soaps prepared from the interaction of sodium hydroxide with resins (which contain resin acids) and with the sulphate and sulphonate mixture prepared by heating castor oil with sulphuric acid (called sulphonated castor oil or Turkey red oil).

Additional stability is conferred by the presence of coal-tar hydrocarbon neutral oils. These have already been referred to in Section 2.1, and comprise such products as the methylnaphthalenes, indenes and naphthalenes. The actual mechanism whereby they stabilize the black fluids has not been adequately explained; however they do prevent crystallization of naphthalene present in the tar acid fraction. Klarmann & Shternov (1936) made a systematic study of the effect of the neutral oil fraction and also purified methyl and dimethylnaphthalenes on the bactericidal efficiency of a coal-tar disinfectant. They prepared mixtures of cresol and soap solution (Lysol type) of the *United States Pharmacopoeia* with varying concentrations of neutral oil. They found, using a phenol coefficient type test and *Salmonella typhi* as test organism, that a product containing 30% cresols and 20% neutral oil was twice as active as a similar product containing 50% cresols alone. However, the replacement of cresol by neutral oil caused a progressive decrease in phenol coefficient when a haemolytic streptococcus and *M. tuberculosis* were used as test organisms. The results were further checked using a pure 2-methylnaphthalene in place of neutral oil and similar findings were obtained. It is worth noting in parenthesis that because of these divergent organism-dependent results, the authors argued against the use of *Sal. typhi* as the sole test organism in disinfectant testing.

Depending on the phenol fraction used and its proportion of cresylic acids to high-boiling tar acid, black fluids of varying Rideal–Walker coefficients reaching as high as 30 can be produced; however, as shown in Section 2.2, increasing biocidal activity is accompanied by an increasing sensitivity to inactivation by organic debris.

To obtain satisfactory products the method of manufacture is critical and a considerable expertise is required to produce active and reproducible batches.

Black fluids give either clear solutions or emulsions on dilution with water, those containing greater proportions of higher phenol homologues giving emulsions. They are partially inactivated by the presence of electrolytes.

2.4.4 *White fluids*

These are also defined in BS 2462: 1961. They differ from the foregoing formulations in being emulsified, as distinct from solubilized, phenolic compounds. The emulsifying agents used include animal glue, casein and the carbohydrate extractable from the seaweed called Irish moss. Products with a range of Rideal–Walker coefficients may be manufactured by the use of varying tar-acid constituents.

As they are already in the form of an oil-in-water emulsion they are less liable to have their activity reduced on further dilution as might happen with black fluids if dilution is carried out carelessly. They are much more stable in the presence of electrolytes. As might be expected from a metastable system — the emulsion — they are less stable on storage than the black fluids which are solubilized systems. As with the black fluids, products of varying Rideal–Walker coefficients may be obtained by varying the composition of the phenol. Neutral oils from coal tar may be included in the formulation.

An interesting account of the methods and pitfalls of manufacture of black and white fluids is given by Finch (1958).

2.5 Non-coal-tar phenols

As has been seen, the coal-tar (and to a lesser extent the petrochemical) industry yields a large array of phenolic products; phenol itself, however, is now made in large quantities by a synthetic process, as are some of its derivatives. Three such phenols, which are used in a variety of roles, are 4-tertiary octylphenol, 2-phenylphenol and 4-hexylresorcinol (Fig. 2.2).

2.5.1 *4-Tertiary octylphenol*

This phenol (often referred to as octylphenol) is a white crystalline substance, m.p. 83°C. The cardinal property in considering its application as a preservative is its insolubility in water, 1 in 60 000 (1.6×10^{-3}%). The sodium and potassium derivatives are more soluble. It is soluble in 1 in 1 of 95% ethanol and proportionally less soluble in ethanol containing varying proportions of water. It has been shown by animal-feeding experiments to be less toxic than phenol or cresol.

Alcoholic solutions of the phenol are 400–500 times as effective as phenol against Gram-positive organisms but against Gram-negative bacteria the factor is only one-fiftieth. Octylphenol is also fungistatic, and has been used as a preservative for proteinaceous products such as glues and non-food gelatines. Its activity is reduced in the presence of some emulgents, a property that might render it unsuitable for the preservation of soaps and cutting oils.

2.5.2 *2-Phenylphenol (2-phenylphenoxide)*

This occurs as a white crystalline powder melting at 57°C. It is much more soluble than octylphenol, 1

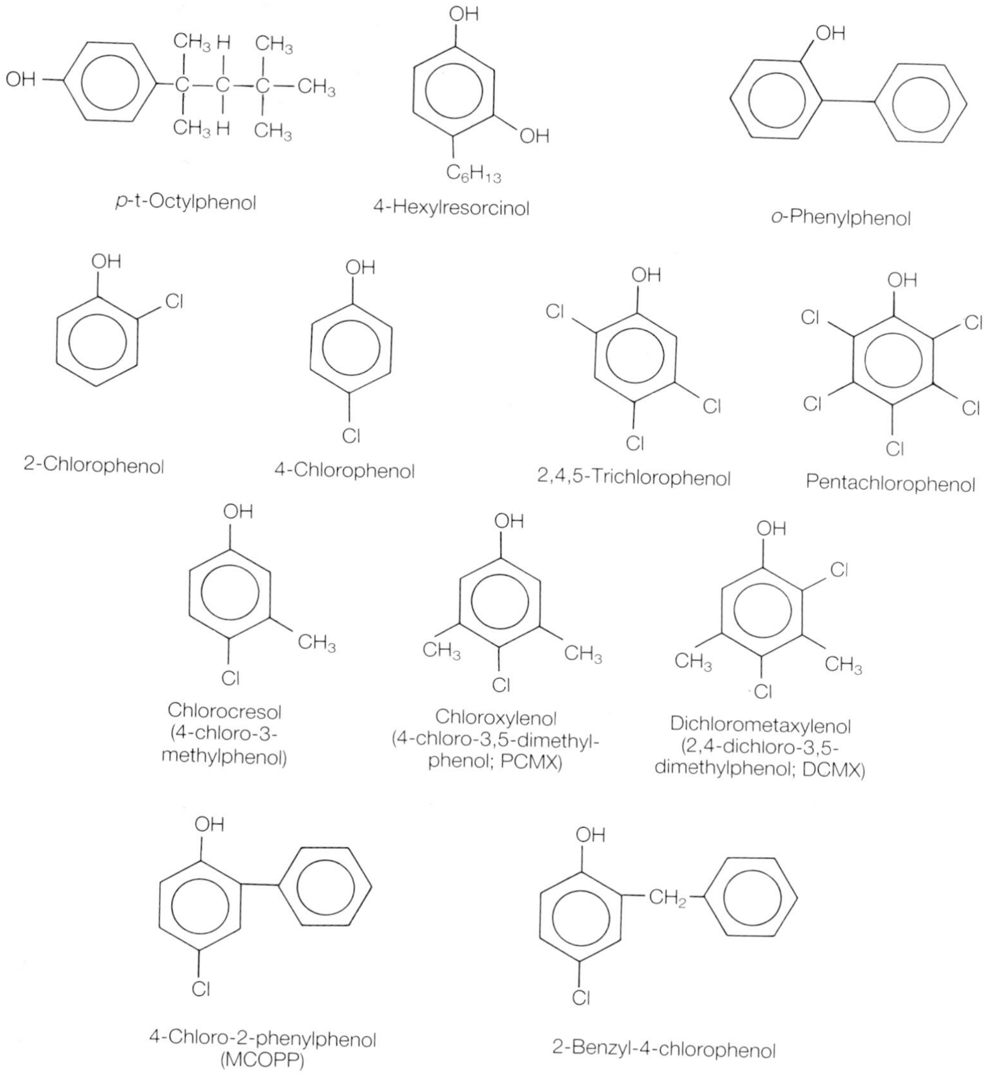

Fig. 2.2 Examples of phenolic compounds.

part dissolving in 1000 parts of water, while the sodium salt is readily soluble in water. It is both antibacterial and antifungal and is used as a preservative, especially against fungi, in a wide variety of applications. Typical inhibitory concentrations (m.i.c.s., μg/ml) for the sodium salt are *E. coli*, 32; *Staph. aureus*, 32; *B. subtilis*, 16; *Pseudomonas fluorescens*, 16; *Aspergillus niger*, 4; *Epidermophyton* spp., 4; *Myrothecium verrucaria*, 2; *Trichophyton interdigitale*, 8. Many strains of *Ps. aeruginosa* are more resistant, requiring higher concentrations than those listed above for their inhibition.

Its main applications have been as ingredients in disinfectants of the pine type, as preservatives for cutting oils and as a general agricultural disinfectant. It has been particularly useful as a slimicide and fungicide in the paper and cardboard industry, and as an addition to paraffin wax in the preparation of waxed paper and liners for bottle and jar caps.

2.5.3 4-Hexylresorcinol

This occurs as white crystalline needles (m.p. 67°C). It is soluble 0.5% in water but freely soluble in organic solvents, glycerol and glycerides (fixed oils). It is of low oral toxicity having been used for the treatment of round and whip worm infections in humans. It is used as a 0.1% solution in 30% glycerol as a skin disinfectant and in lozenges and medicated sweets for the treatment of throat infections.

2.6 Halo- and nitrophenols

The general effect of halogenation (Fig. 2.2) upon the antimicrobial activity of phenols is to increase their activity but reduce their water-solubility (Section 2.1). There is also a tendency for them to be inactivated by organic matter. The work on substituted phenols dates from the early 20th century and was pioneered by Ehrlich and studied extensively by Klarmann *et al.* (1929, 1932, 1933).

To illustrate the effect of chlorination on the biocidal activity of phenols, Rideal–Walker coefficients are as follows: 2-chlorophenol, 3.6; 4-chlorophenol, 4; 3-chlorophenol, 7.4; 2,4-dichlorophenol, 13; 2,4,6-trichlorophenol, 22; 4-chloro-3-methylphenol, 13; 4-chloro-3,5-dimethylphenol, 30.

Chlorophenols are made by the direct chlorination of the corresponding phenol or phenol mixture using either chlorine or sulphuryl chloride.

2.6.1 2,4,6-Trichlorophenol

This is a white or off-white powder which melts at 69.5°C and boils at 246°C. It is a stronger acid than phenol with a pK_a of 8.5 at 25°C. It is almost insoluble in water but soluble in alkali and organic solvents. This phenol has been used as a bactericidal, fungicidal and insecticidal agent. It has found application in textile and wood preservation, as a preservative for cutting oils and as an ingredient in some antiseptic formulations. Its phenol coefficient against *Sal. typhi* is 22 and against *Staph. aureus* is 25.

2.6.2 Pentachlorophenol (2-phenylphenoxide)

A white to cream-coloured powder, m.p. 174°C. It can crystallize with a proportion of water, and is almost insoluble in water but soluble in organic solvents. Pentachlorophenol or its sodium derivative is used as a preservative for adhesives, textiles, wood, leather, paper and cardboard. It has been used for the in-can preservation of paints but it tends to discolour in sunlight. As with other phenols, the presence of iron in the products which it is meant to preserve can also cause discoloration.

2.6.3 4-Chloro-3-methylphenol (chlorocresol)

Chlorocresol is a colourless crystalline compound which melts at 65°C and is volatile in steam. It is soluble 0.38% in water and readily soluble in ethanol, ether and terpenes. It is also soluble in alkaline solutions. Its pK_a at 25°C is 9.5. Chlorocresol is used as a preservative in pharmaceutical products and an adjunct in a former UK pharmacopoeial sterilization process called 'heating with a bactericide' in which a combination of heat, 98–100°C, and a chemical biocide enabled a sterilization process to be conducted at a lower temperature than the more usual 121°C (see Chapter 3). Its Rideal–Walker coefficient in aqueous solution is 13 and nearly double this value when solubilized with castor oil soap. It has been used as a preservative for industrial products such as glues, paints, sizes, cutting oils and drilling muds.

2.6.4 4-Chloro-3,5-dimethylphenol (chloroxylenol; PCMX)

Chloroxylenol is a white crystalline substance melting at 155°C. It is soluble in water at 0.03% and readily soluble in ethanol, ether, terpenes and alkaline solutions. Its pK_a at 25°C is 9.7. It is used chiefly as a topical antiseptic solubilized in a suitable soap solution and often in conjunction with terpineol or pine oil. Phenol coefficients for the pure compound were: *Sal. typhi*, 30; *Staph. aureus*, 26; *Streptococcus pyogenes*, 28; *Trichophyton rosaceum*, 25; *Ps. aeruginosa*, 11. It is not sporicidal and has little activity against the tubercle bacillus (in other words it is a narrow-spectrum bactericide).

It is also inactivated in the presence of organic matter. Its formulation into a solubilized, clear, liquid disinfectant will be considered below (Section 2.8).

2.6.5 2,4-Dichloro-3,5-dimethylphenol (dichloroxylenol; DCMX)

This is a white powder melting at 94°C. It is volatile in steam and soluble in water at 0.02%. Although it is slightly less soluble than PCMX it has similar properties and antimicrobial spectrum. It is used as an ingredient in pine-type disinfectants and in medicated soaps and hand scrubs.

2.6.6 Monochloro-2-phenylphenol

This is obtained by the chlorination of 2-phenylphenol and the commercial product contains 80% of 4-chloro-2-phenylphenol and 20% of 6-chloro-2-phenylphenol. The mixture is a pale straw-coloured liquid which boils over the range 250–300°C. It is almost insoluble in water but may be used in the formulation of pine disinfectants where solubilization is effected by means of a suitable soap.

2.6.7 2-Benzyl-4-chlorophenol

This occurs as a white to pink powder which melts at 49°C. It has a slight phenolic odour and is almost insoluble in water. Suitably formulated by solubilization with vegetable oil soaps, it has a wide biocidal spectrum, being active against Gram-positive and Gram-negative bacteria, viruses, protozoa and fungi.

2.6.8 Mixed chlorinated xylenols

A mixed chlorinated xylenol preparation can be obtained for the manufacture of household disinfectants by chlorinating a mixed xylenols fraction from coal tar.

2.6.9 Other halophenols

Brominated and fluorinated monophenols have been made and tested but they have not found extensive application.

2.6.10 Nitrophenols

Nitrophenols in general are more toxic than the halophenols. 3,5-Dinitro-*o*-cresol was used as an ovicide in horticulture but the nitrophenol most widely used today is 4-nitrophenol which is amongst a group of preservatives used in the leather manufacturing industry at concentrations of 0.1–0.5%. For a general review on the use and mode of action of the nitrophenols see Simon (1953).

2.6.11 Formulated disinfectants containing chlorophenols

It will be seen from the solubility data recounted above that some formulation device such as solubilization, already applied successfully to the more insoluble phenols, might be used to prepare liquid antiseptics and disinfectants based on the good activity and the low level of systemic toxicity and of the likelihood of tissue damage shown by chlorinated cresols and xylenols. Indeed, such a formula was patented in Germany in 1927 although the use of chlorinated phenols as adjuncts to the already existent coal tar products had been mooted in England in the early 1920s.

In 1933, Rapps compared the Rideal–Walker coefficients of an aqueous solution and a castor-oil–soap solubilized system of chlorocresol and chloroxylenol and found the solubilized system to be superior by a factor of almost two. This particular disinfectant recipe received a major advance (also in 1933) when two gynaecologists seeking a safe and effective product for midwifery and having felt that Lysol, one of the few disinfectants available to medicine at the time, was too caustic, made an extensive evaluation of the chloroxylenol–castor oil product; their recipe also contained terpineol (Colebrook & Maxted, 1933). It was fortunate that this preparation was active against β-haemolytic streptococci which are a hazard in childbirth giving rise to puerperal fever. A chloroxylenol–terpineol–soap preparation was the subject of a monograph in the *British Pharmacopoeia* up to 1958 and thereafter in the *British Pharmaceutical Codex* (1973), the *British National Formulary* (1978) and the *Pharmaceutical Codex* (1979).

The bacteriology of this formulation has turned

out to be controversial; the original appraisal indicated good activity against β-haemolytic streptococci and *E. coli* with retained activity in the presence of pus, but subsequent bacteriological examinations by experienced workers gave divergent results. Thus Colebrook in 1941 cast doubt upon the ability of solubilized chloroxylenol–terpineol to destroy staphylococci on the skin, a finding which was refuted by Beath (1943). Ayliffe *et al.* (1966) indicated that the product was more active against *Ps. aeruginosa* than *Staph. aureus*. As so often happens, however, *Ps. aeruginosa* was subsequently shown to be resistant and Lowbury (1951) found that this organism would actually multiply in dilutions of chloroxylenol–soap.

Although still an opportunistic organism, *Ps. aeruginosa* was becoming a dangerous pathogen, especially as more and more patients received radiotherapy or radiomimetic drugs, and attempts were made to potentiate the disinfectant and to widen its spectrum so as to embrace the pseudomonads. It had been well known that ethylenediaminetetra-acetic (EDTA) acid affected the permeability of pseudomonads and some enterobacteria to drugs to which they were normally resistant (for a review see Russell, 1971b) and both Dankert & Schut (1976) and Russell & Furr (1977) were able to demonstrate that chloroxylenol solutions with EDTA were most active against pseudomonads. Hatch & Cooper (1948) had shown a similar potentiating effect with sodium hexametaphosphate. This phenomenon may be worth bearing in mind when formulating hospital disinfectants.

2.6.12 *Phenol*

The parent compound C_6H_5OH (Fig. 2.1) is a white crystalline solid, m.p. 39–40°C, which becomes pink and finally black on long standing. It is soluble in water 1:13 and is a weak acid, pK_a 10. Its biological activity resides in the undissociated molecule (see Section 3.2, p. 23). Phenol is effective against both Gram-positive and Gram-negative vegetative bacteria but is only slowly effective towards bacterial spores and acid-fast bacteria.

It is the reference standard for the Rideal–Walker and Chick–Martin tests for disinfectant evaluation (Chapter 4). As has been mentioned (Chapter 1) it was used by Lister and others in pioneering work on antiseptic surgery. It finds limited application in medicine today, but is used as a preservative in such products as animal glues.

Although first obtained from coal tar, it is now largely obtained by synthetic processes which include the hydrolysis of chlorobenzene of the high-temperature interaction of benzene sulphonic acid and alkali.

2.7 Pine disinfectants

As long ago as 1876, Kingzett took out a patent in Germany for a disinfectant deodorant made from oil of turpentine and camphor and which had been allowed to undergo oxidation in the atmosphere. This was marketed under the trade name 'Sanitas'. Later, Stevenson (1915) described a fluid made from pine oil solubilized by a soap solution. This had a pine oil content of over 60%.

The chief constituent of turpentine is the cyclic hydrocarbon pinene (Fig. 2.3). The odour of pinene, whether in turpentine or from pine oils made by distilling wood chips or leaves (needles) from various coniferous trees, has long held an association in the public's mind with freshness, cleanliness and a safe, disinfected environment, but the terpene hydrocarbons, of which pinene is but one example, have little or no biocidal activity.

The terpene alcohol terpineol (Fig. 2.3), which may be produced synthetically from pinene or turpentine via terpin hydrate, or in 80% purity by steam distilling pine-wood fragments, is another ingredient of pine disinfectants and has already been exploited as an ingredient of the Colebrook

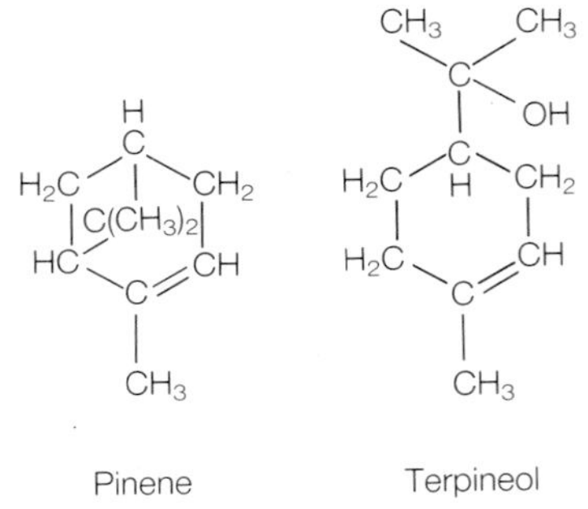

Fig. 2.3 Pinene and terpineol.

& Maxted (1933) chloroxylenol formulation. Unlike pinene, it possesses antimicrobial activity in its own right and it shares with pinene the property of modifying the action of phenols in solubilized disinfectant formulations, although not in the same way for all microbial species. An interesting experiment by Moore & Walker (1939) showed how the inclusion of varying amounts of pine oil in a PCMX/soap formulation modified the phenol coefficient of the preparation depending on the test organism used.

Pine-oil concentrations of from 0% to 10% caused a steady increase in the phenol coefficient from 2.0 to 3.6 when the test organism was *Sal. typhi*. With *Staph. aureus* the value was 0% pine oil, 0.6; 2.5% pine oil, 0.75; thereafter the value fell, having a value of only 0.03 with 10% oil, a pine-oil concentration which gave the maximum *Sal. typhi* coefficient. In this respect, pinene and terpineol may be compared with the neutral oils used in the coal-tar phenol products (Section 2.4.3) but it should be remembered that terpineol possesses intrinsic biocidal activity.

Terpineol is a colourless oil which tends to darken on storing. It has a pleasant hyacinth odour and is used in perfumery, especially for soap products, as well as in disinfectant manufacture. A series of solubilized products has been marketed with 'active' incredients ranging from pine oil, pinene through terpineol to a mixture of pine oil and/or terpineol and a suitable phenol or chlorinated phenol. This gave rise to a range of products extending from those which are really no more than deodorants to effective disinfectants.

Unfortunately there has been a tendency to ignore or be unaware of the above biocidal trends when labelling these varied products, and preparations containing small amount of pine oil or pinene have been described as disinfectants. Attempts to remedy this situation have been made through the publication of a British Standard entitled '*Aromatic disinfectant fluids*' (BS 5197: 1976). The standard makes it clear that it specifies the requirements for a general-use disinfectant and does not imply use in hospitals or in other situations where there is a risk of infectious disease. The active ingredients, as stated in the standard, are substituted phenols together with pine oil or related terpenes and aromatic oils. A typical recipe for such a product would contain 4-chloro-3,5-xylenol, monochloro-2-phenylphenol, 2-phenylphenol, pine oil, terpineol and lime oil solubilized in water by means of potassium ricinoleate. Products with RW coefficients ranging from 3 to 10 may be produced depending on the phenol content.

A further important requirement set out in the standard is that none of the products should be used at a use dilution more than 20 times the RW value, i.e. a product of RW 5 should never be used at dilutions greater than 1:100. Unrealistic use dilutions have contributed as much as uninformed formulation to the unreliability of some of these products.

It is very important that the labelling of this group of products should be carefully scrutinized before use and the mere possession of pine odour not used as the sole and final assessment for disinfectant potential.

2.8 Theory of solubilized systems

It will be apparent from the foregoing account that the art of obtaining aqueous solutions of relatively water-insoluble substances with the aid of soaps has been known since the late 19th century, when this technique was certainly applied to antiseptic systems.

Solubilization is achieved when anionic or cationic soaps aggregate in solution to form multiple particles of micelles which may contain up to 300 molecules of the constituent species. These micelles are so arranged in an aqueous solution that the charged group is on the outside of the particle and the rest of the molecule is within the particle. It is in this part, often a hydrocarbon chain, that the phenols are dissolved, and hence solubilized, in an aqueous milieu.

The nature and antibacterial action of solubilized systems have intrigued many workers, notably Berry and his school, and Alexander and Tomlinson. The relationship between solubilization and antimicrobial activity was explored in detail by Bean & Berry (1950, 1951, 1953) who used a system consisting of 2-benzyl-4-chlorophenol (Section 2.6.7.) and potassium laurate, and of 2,4-dichloro-3,5-dimethylphenol (Section 2.6.5) and potassium laurate. The advantage to a fundamental understanding of the system is that potassium laurate can be prepared in a pure state and its physical properties have been well documented. 2-Benzyl-4-chlorophenol is almost insoluble in water and the antimicrobial activity of a solubilized system containing it will be uncomplicated by a residual water-solubility. The concepts were then extended to chlorocresol.

A plot of weight of solubilized substance per unit weight of solubilizer against the concentration of solubilizer at a given ratio of solubilized substance to solubilizer usually shows the type of curve illustrated in Fig. 2.4, curve OXYZ. Above the line OXYZ a two-phase system is found; below the curve a one-phase system consequent upon solubilization is obtained. Upon this curve has been superimposed a curve (O′ABC) which illustrates the change in bactericidal activity of such a system which is found if the solubilized substance possesses antibacterial activity. Such data give some indication of the complex properties of solubilized systems such as Lysol and Roxenol. Bactericidal activity at O′ is no more than that of the aqueous solution of the bactericide. The increase (O′−A) is due to potentiation of the action of the bactericide by unassociated soap molecules. At A, micelle formation and solubilization begin and thereafter (A−B) activity declines because, it has been suggested, the size of the micelle increases; the amount of drug per micelle decreases, and this is accompanied by a corresponding decrease in the toxicity of the system. However, at B an increase in activity is again found, reaching a maximum at C. This has been explained by the fact that at B, although increase in micellar size no longer occurs, increase in micellar number does, hence the gradual increase in activity.

The lethal event at cell level has been ascribed to an adsorption of the micelles by the bacterial cell and a passage of the bactericide from the micelle on to and into the bacterial cell. In short, this theory postulates that the bactericidal activity is a function of the concentration of the drug in the micelle and not its total concentration in solution. This was held to be the case for both the highly insoluble benzylchlorophenol and the more water-soluble chlorocresol (Bean & Berry, 1951, 1953).

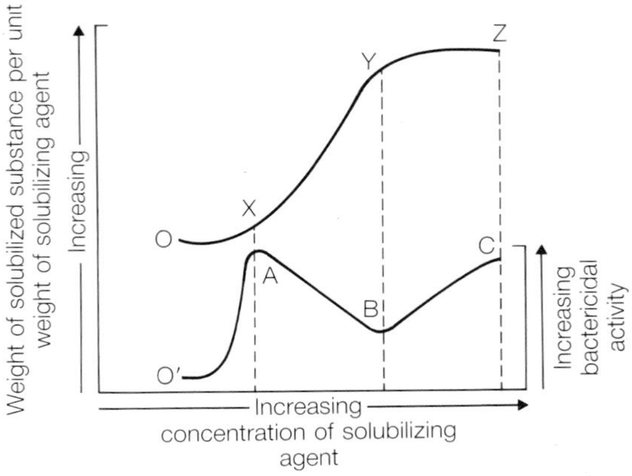

Fig. 2.4 The relationship between solubilization and antibacterial activity in a system containing a constant ratio of solubilized substance to solubilizer and where the solubilized substance possesses low water solubility. *Curve OXYZ*, weight of solubilized substance per unit weight of solubilizing agent plotted against the concentration of solubilizing agent. *Curve O′ABC*, bactericidal activity of the system.

Alexander & Tomlinson (1949), albeit working with a different system, suggest a possible alternative interpretation. They agree that the increase, culminating at A, is due to the potentiation of the action of phenol by the solubilizing agent, which because it possesses detergent properties acts by disrupting the bacterial membrane, thereby permitting more easy access of the drug into the cell. The decline (A−B), however, was thought to be due to the removal of drug from the aqueous milieu into the micelles, thereby decreasing the amount available for reacting with the cell. They reject the notion that a drug-bearing micelle is lethal and capable itself of adsorption on the cell and passing its drug load to the cell, and declare that the activity of this system is a function of the concentration of bactericide in the aqueous phase. It must also be pointed out that high concentrations of soaps may themselves be bactericidal (reviewed by Kabara, 1978) and that this property could explain the increase in activity noted between B and C.

The above is only an outline of one experimental system in a very complex family. For a very complete appraisal together with further patterns of interpretation of experimental data of the problem the papers of Berry *et al.* (1956) and Berry & Briggs (1956) should be consulted. Opinion, however, seems to be settling in favour of the view that activity is a function of the concentration of the bactericide in the aqueous phase. Indeed Mitchell (1964), studying the bactericidal activity of chloroxylenol in aqueous solutions of cetomacrogol, has shown that the bactericidal activity here is related to the amount of chloroxylenol in the aqueous phase of the system. Thus a solution which contained, as a result of adding cetomacrogol, one hundred times as much of the bactericide as a saturated aqueous solution was no more bactericidal than the saturated aqueous solution. Here again, this picture is complicated by the fact that non-ionic surface-active agents, of which cetomacrogol is an example, are known to inactive phenols (Beckett & Robinson, 1958).

2.9 The bis-phenols

Hydroxy halogenated derivatives (Fig. 2.5) of diphenyl methane, diphenyl ether and diphenyl sulphide have provided a number of useful biocides active against bacteria, fungi and algae. They all seem to have low activity against *Ps. aeruginosa* however, i.e. they show the 'pseudomonas gap'; they also have low water-solubility and share the property of the mono-phenols in that they are inactivated by non-ionic surfactants.

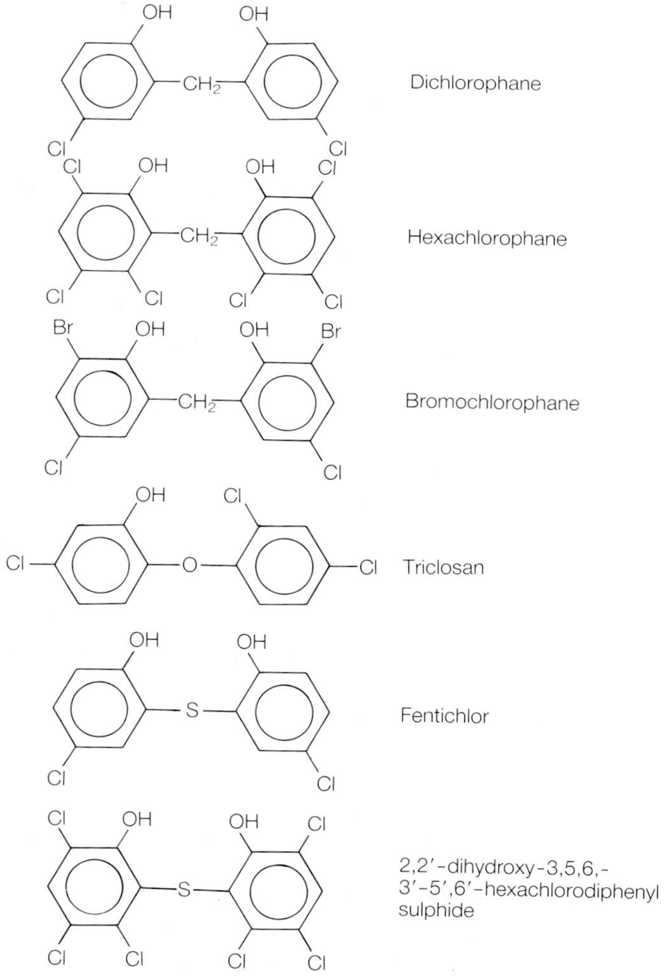

Fig. 2.5 Bis-phenols.

Ehrlich and co-workers were the first to investigate the microbiological activity of the bis-phenols and published their work in 1906. Klarmann and Dunning and colleagues described the preparation and properties of a number of these compounds (Klarmann & von Wowern, 1929; Dunning *et al.*, 1931). A useful summary of this early work has been made by Suter (1941). Later Gump & Walter (1960, 1963, 1964) and Walter & Gump (1962) made an exhaustive study of the biocidal properties of many of these compounds especially with a view to their use in cosmetic formulations.

2.9.1 Derivatives of dihydroxydiphenylmethane

1 Dichlorophane, G-4,5,5′-dichloro-2,2′-dihydroxydiphenylmethane (Panacide[R]: registered, BDH, Poole, England). This compound is active to varying degrees against bacteria, fungi and algae. It is soluble in water at 30 μg/ml but more soluble (45–80 g/100 ml) in organic solvents. The pK_a values at 25°C for the two hydroxyl groups are 7.6 and 11.6.

Typical killing concentrations in μg/ml in broth for bacteria at 25°C after 24 h incubation were: *Staph. aureus*, 2.5; *Streptococcus faecalis*, 7.5; *B. subtilis*, 7.5; *E. coli*, 10; *Sal. typhi*, 7.5; *Ps. aeruginosa*, 80; *Proteus mirabilis*, 50. The toxicity of the compound is low and it has been used for the treatment of tapeworm in man and domestic animals at dose levels of 6 g on two successive days. It has also been used in the treatment of athlete's foot, indicating low skin-irritancy.

It has found application as a preservative for toiletries, textiles and cutting oils and to prevent the growth of bacteria in water-cooling systems and humidifying plants. It is used as a slimicide in paper manufacture. It may be added to papers and other packing materials to prevent microbial growth and has been used to prevent algal growth in greenhouses.

2 Hexachlorophane, 2,2′-dihydroxy-3,5,6,3′,5′,6′-hexachlorodiphenylmethane, G11. This compound is almost insoluble in water but soluble in ethanol, ether and acetone and in alkaline solutions. The pK_a values re 5.4 and 10.9. Its mode of action has been studied in detail by Gerhardt, Corner and colleagues (Corner *et al.*, 1971; Joswick *et al.*, Silvernale *et al.*, 1971; Frederick *et al.*, 1974; Lee & Corner, 1975).

It is used mainly for its antibacterial activity but it is much more active against Gram-positive than Gram-negative organisms. Typical minimum inhibitory (bacteriostatic) concentrations in μg/ml are: *Staph. aureus*, 0.9; *B. subtilis*, 0.2; *Proteus vulgaris*, 4; *E. coli*, 28; *Ps. aeruginosa*, 25.

It has found chief application as an active ingredient in surgical scrubs and medicated soaps and has also been used to a limited extent as a preservative for cosmetics. Its use is limited by its insolubility in water, its somewhat narrow antibacterial spectrum and by the fact that in the United Kingdom it is restricted by a control order made in 1973. In general, this order restricted the use of this product to 0.1% in human medicines and 0.75% in animal medicines. Its toxicity has restricted its use in cosmetic products, and the maximum concentration allowed is 0.1% with the stipulation that it is not to be used in products for children or personal hygiene products.

3 Bromochlorophane, 3,3′-dibromo-5,5′-dichlor-2,2′-dihydroxydiphenylmethane. This product is soluble in water at 100 μg/ml and is markedly more active against Gram-positive organisms than bacteria. Strains of *Staph. aureus* are inhibited at from 8 to 11 μg/ml whereas one hundred times these concentrations are required for *E. coli* and *Ps. aeruginosa*. It has been used as the active ingredient in deodorant preparations and toothpastes.

2.9.2 Derivatives of hydroxydiphenylether

1 Triclosan, 2,4,4′-trichlor-2′-hydroxydiphenylether (Irgasan[R], registered Ciga-Geigy Ltd, Basle, Switzerland). This derivative is only sparingly soluble in water but soluble in solutions of dilute alkalis and organic solvents. It inhibits staphylococci at concentrations ranging from 0.1 to 0.03 μg/ml. Paradoxically, a number of *E. coli* strains are inhibited over a similar concentration range. Most strains of *Ps. aeruginosa* require concentrations varying from 100 to 1000 μg/ml for inhibition. It inhibits the growth of several species of mould at from 1 to 30 μg/ml. It has a similar use potential to other bis-phenols and was the most widely used phenolic preservative reported in the survey by Richardson (1981), appearing in 52 formulations. It is used in some medicated soaps and hand-cleansing gels.

2.9.3 Derivatives of diphenylsulphide

1 Fentichlor, 2,2′-dihydroxy-5,5′-dichlorodiphenyl-sulphide. This chemical is a white powder, soluble in water at 30 μg/ml, but is much more soluble in organic solvents and oils. In common with its bis-phenol cogeners, it shows more activity against Gram-positive organisms and a 'pseudomonas gap'. Typical inhibitory concentrations (μg/ml) are *Staph. aureus*, 2; *E. coli*, 100; *Ps. aeruginosa*, 1000. Typical inhibitory concentrations (μg/ml) for some fungi are: *Candida* spp., 12; *Epidermophyton interdigitale*, 0.4; *Trichophyton granulosum*, 0.4.

Fentichlor has found chief application in the treatment of dermatophytic conditions. It can cause photosensitization and this might limit its use as a cosmetic preservative. Its low water-solubility and narrow spectrum are further disadvantages but it has potential as a fungicide. Its mode of action was described by Hugo & Bloomfield (1971a, b and c) and Bloomfield (1974).

2 Chlorinated analogue of Fentichlor, 2,2′-dihydroxy-3,4,6,3′,4′,6′-hexachloro-diphenylsulphide; 2,2′-thiobis (3,4,6-trichlorophenol). This is a more highly chlorinated analogue of Fentichlor. It is almost insoluble in water. In a field test it proved to be an effective inhibitor of microbial growth in cutting oil emulsions.

An exhaustive study of the antifungal properties of hydroxydiphenylsulphides was made by Pflеger *et al.* (1949).

3 ORGANIC AND INORGANIC ACIDS: ESTERS AND SALTS

3.1 Introduction

A large family of organic acids (see Fig. 2.6), both aromatic and aliphatic, and one or two inorganic acids, have found application as preservatives, more especially in the food industry. Some, for example benzoic acid, are also used in the preservation of pharmaceutical products; others (salicylic, undecylenic and again benzoic) have been used, suitably formulated, for the topical treatment of fungal infections of the skin.

Vinegar, containing acetic acid (ethanoic acid), has been known as long as alcohol, from which it would be formed by natural oxidation, and early on it had been found to act as a preservative. It was also used as a wound dressing. This application has recently been revived in the use of dilute solutions of acetic acid as a wound dressing where pseudomonal infections have occurred.

Hydrochloric and sulphuric acids are two mineral acids sometimes employed in veterinary disinfection. Hydrochloric acid at high concentrations is sporicidal and has been used for disinfecting hides and skin contaminated with anthrax spores. Sulphuric acid, even at high concentrations, is not sporicidal, but in some countries it is used, usually in combination with phenol, for the decontamination of floors, feed boxes and troughs (Russell & Hugo, 1987).

Citric acid is an approved disinfectant against foot-and-mouth virus. It also appears, by virtue of its chelating properties, to increase the permeability of the outer membrane of Gram-negative bacteria (Shibasaki & Kato, 1978) and this would seem to be an area worthy of additional experimentation.

3.2 Physical factors governing the antimicrobial activity of acids

At first sight it might be thought that the special ability of acids to generate protons (hydrogen ions) when dissolved in water underlies their general toxicity; it is well known that acid conditions are inimical to the growth of many micro-organisms. However, many successful antimicrobial acids are weak acids, i.e. they have dissociation constants between 10^{-3} and 10^{-5}; see below.

If an acid is represented by the symbol AH, then its ionization will be represented by A^-H^+. Complete ionization, as seen in aqueous solutions of mineral acids such as hydrogen chloride (where AH = ClH), is not found in the weaker organic acids and their solutions will contain three components: A^-, H^+ and AH. The ratio of the concentration of these three components is called the ionization constant of that acid, K_a, and K_a =

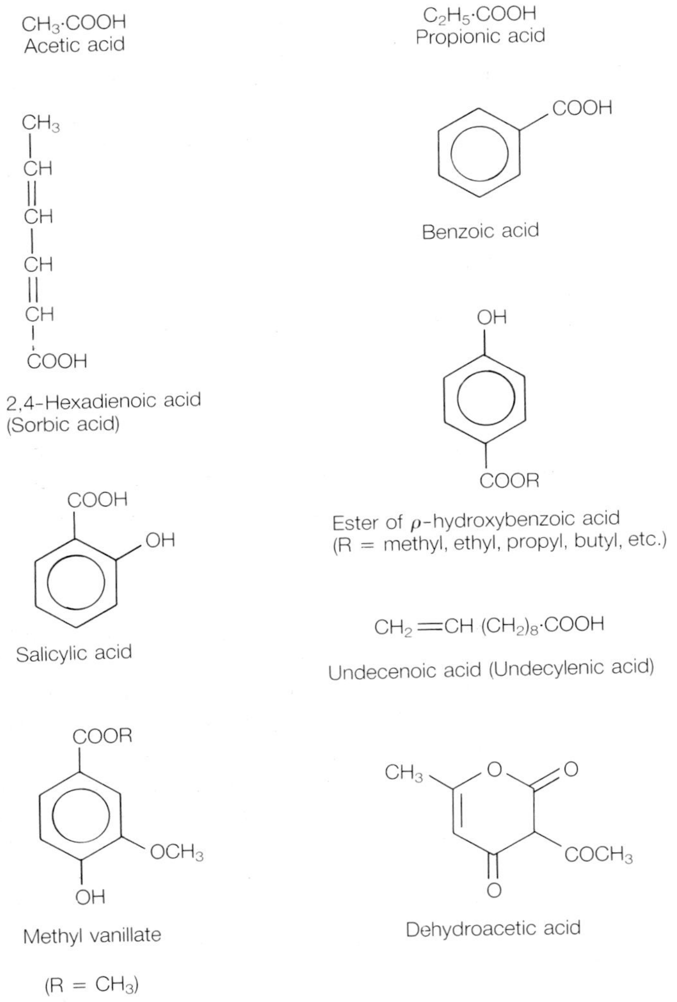

Fig. 2.6 Organic acids and esters.

$A^- \times H^+/AH$. By analogy with the mathematical device used to define the pH scale, if the negative logarithm of K_a is taken a number is obtained, running from about 0 to about 14, called pK_a. Some typical pK_a values are shown in Table 2.3.

An inspection of the equation defining K_a shows that the ratio A^-/AH must depend on the pH of the solution in which it is dissolved, and Henderson and Hasselbalch derived a relationship between this ratio and pH as follows:

$$\log \frac{A^-}{AH} = \text{pH} - \text{p}K_a$$

The application of this equation to the relative proportions of C_6H_5OOH and $C_6H_5COO^-$ in solutions of benzoic acid dissolved in buffers of varying pH is shown in Table 2.4. An inspection of the formula will also show that at the pH value equal to the pK_a value the product is 50% ionized. These data enable an evaluation of the effect of pH on the toxicity of organic acids to be made.

Typically it has been found that a marked toxic effect is seen only when the conditions of pH ensure the presence of the unionized molecular species AH. As the pH increases or, to put it in another way, the equilibrium $HA = HA^- + A^+$

Table 2.3 pK_a values of acids and esters used as antimicrobial agents

Acid or ester	pK_a
Acetic (ethanoic) acid	4.7
Propionic (propanoic acid)	4.8
Sorbic acid (2,4-hexadienoic acid)	4.8
Lactic acid	3.8
Benzoic acid	4.2
Salicylic acid	3.0
Dehydroacetic acid	5.4
Sulphurous acid	1.8, 6.9
Methyl *p*-hydroxybenzoic acid	8.5
Propyl *p*-hydroxybenzoic acid	8.1

Table 2.4 Effect of pH on ionization of benzoic acid, pK_a 4.19

pH	Molecular form (C_6H_5COOH) (%)	Ionic form ($C_6H_5COO^-$) (%)
3.24	90	10
3.59	80	20
3.82	70	30
4.01	60	40
4.19	50	50
4.36	40	60
4.55	30	70
4.79	20	80
5.14	10	90

moves to the right, the concentration of HA falls and the toxicity of the system falls; this may be indicated by a higher minimum inhibitory concentration, longer death time or higher mean single-survivor time, depending on the criterion of toxicity (i.e. antimicrobial activity) chosen.

An inspection of Fig. 2.7 would suggest that HA is more toxic than A^-. However, an altering pH can alter the intrinsic toxicity of the environment. This is due to H^+ alone, the ionization of the cell surface, the activity of transport and metabolizing enzymes and the degree of ionization of the cell surface and hence sorption of the ionic species on the cell. Too simplistic a view, therefore, of the undoubted pH effect on the activity of weak acids must not be assumed. The ideal test organism would be one which is insensitive to changes in pH over a wide range.

Some few pages have been devoted to the above but in the authors' experience predictions for preservative ability of acids validated at one pH are rendered meaningless when such a preservative is added without further consideration to a formulation at a higher pH. The pK_a of the acid preservative should always be ascertained and any pH shift of 1.5 units or more on the alkaline side of this can be expected to cause progressive loss of activity quite sufficient to invalidate the originally determined performance. That pH modifies the antimicrobial effect of benzoic acid has been known for a long time (Cruess & Richert, 1929). For more detailed accounts of the effect of pH on the intensity of action of a large number of ionizable biocides, the papers of Simon & Blackman (1949) and Simon & Beevers (1952a and b) should be consulted.

3.3 Mode of action

The mode of action of acids used as food preservatives has been studied by Freese *et al.* (1973). They produced convincing evidence that many acid preservatives act by preventing the uptake of substrates which depend on a protonmotive force for their entry into the cell, in other words they act as uncoupling agents (Chapter 9). In addition to acids such as benzoic, acetic and propionate, the esters of *p*-hydroxybenzoic acid (the parabens) were also included in the above study; they too acted as uncoupling agents, but also inhibited electron transport.

Equally interesting were experiments on the pH dependence of the substrate uptake effect. The intensity of uptake inhibition by propionate, sorbate and benzoate declined between pH 5 and 7, while that induced by propyl *p*-hydroxybenzoic (pK_a 8.5) remained constant over the same pH range. As has been stated, the growth inhibitory effect of ionizable biocides shows pH dependence and this, as might be expected, is applicable to a biochemical effect upon which growth in turn depends. The total complement of compounds investigated by Freese *et al.* (1973) were acetic, benzoic, propionic, sorbic, caprylic and sulphurous acids, and the methyl, propyl and heptyl esters of *p*-hydroxybenzoic acid. This work has been extended and collated in a review (Freese & Levin,

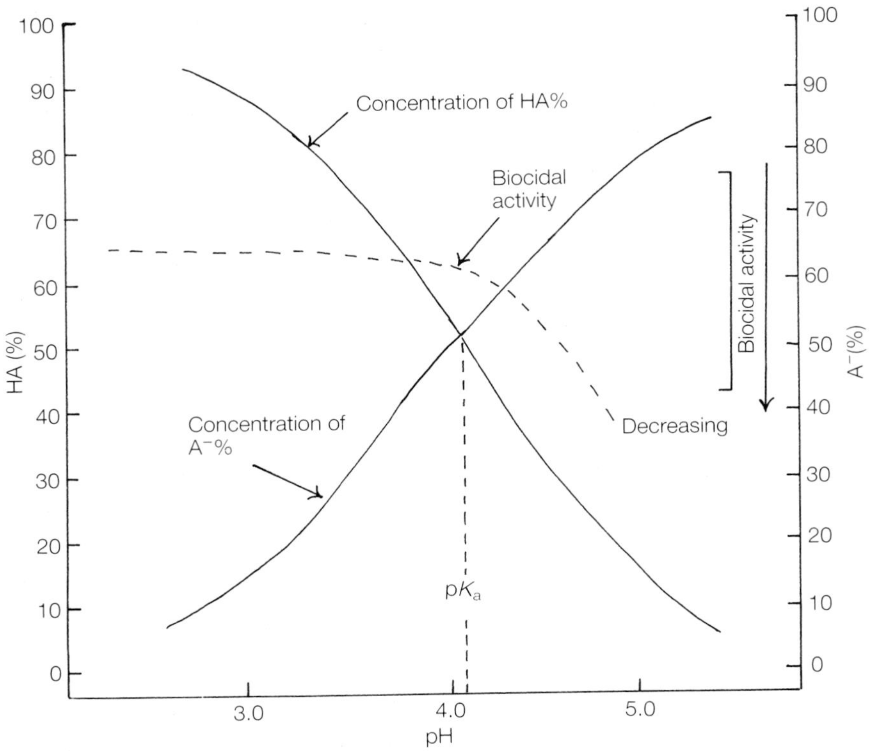

Fig. 2.7 A generalized diagram of the effect of pH on the ionization and biocidal activity of an acid (HA) of pK_a 4.1.

1978). Krebs *et al.* (1983), Salmond *et al.* (1984) Eklund (1985) and Cherrington *et al.* (1990) have contributed further to this area.

3.4 Individual compounds

3.4.1 Acetic acid (ethanoic acid)

This acid, as a diluted petrochemically produced compound or as the natural product vinegar, is used primarily as a preservative for vegetables of which the onion (pickled onions) is the most familiar example. It is an ingredient of many sauces, pickles and salad creams although the latter may need additional preservation. As it is a weak acid (pK_a 4.7) it is not likely to destroy the intracellular pectin of plant tissue thus causing unsightly fragmentation.

Vinegars vary in strength but a wine vinegar may contain 8% of acetic acid. Vinegars made from acetic acid contain not less than 4% of acid, may be artificially coloured brown with caramel and must be clearly labelled as artificial. The toxicity of vinegars and diluted acetic acid must rely to an extent on the inhibitory activity of the molecule itself, as solutions of comparable pH made from mineral acid do not exhibit the same preservative activity. A 5% solution of acetic acid contains 4.997% CH_3COOH and 0.003% H^+. As might be expected from the pK_a value, 4.7, the activity is rapidly lost at pH values above this value. This suggests that the acetate ion is less toxic than the undissociated molecule, although as has been said, the concomitant reduction in hydrogen ion concentration must play some part in the reduction of toxicity. As has been stated, diluted 1–5% acetic acid has been used as a wound dressing where infection with *Pseudomonas* has occurred (Phillips *et al.*, 1968).

3.4.2 *Propionic acid*

This acid is employed almost exclusively as the sodium, and to a lesser extent the calcium, salt in the baking industry where it is used to inhibit mould and bacterial growth in breads and cakes. It is particularly useful in inhibiting the growth of the spore-forming aerobe *Bacillus macerans* which gives rise to an infestational phenomenon called ropy bread.

Manufacturers give explicit directions as to the amount to be used in different products but in general 0.15–0.4% is added to the flour before processing. Other products that have been successfully preserved with propionates include cheeses and malt extract. In addition to foods, wrapping materials for foods have also been protected from microbial damage with the propionates.

3.4.3 *Undecanoic acid (undecylenic acid)*

This has been used either as such or as the calcium or zinc salt in the treatment of superficial dermatophytoses. It is usually applied in ointment form at concentrations of 2–15%.

3.4.4 *2,4-Hexadienoic acid (sorbic acid)*

This unsaturated carboxylic acid, which is also available as its potassium salt, is assimilated by mammals as food. It is effective against a wide range of micro-organisms (Bell *et al.*, 1959) and has been used as the acid itself, or its potassium salt, a concentrations of 0.01–0.1% to preserve bakery products, soft drinks, alcoholic beverages, cheeses, dried fruits, fish, pickles, wrapping materials and pharmaceutical products. As with all acids, there is a critical pH, in this case 6.5, above which activity begins to decline. Again it is the undissociated acid which is the active antimicrobial species (Gooding *et al.*, 1955; Beneke & Fabian, 1955). Sorbic acid was believed to act by interfering with the functioning of the citric acid cycle (York & Vaughan, 1955; Palleroni & de Prinz, 1960), but, as stated. Freese *et al.* (1973) have now shown that it inhibits the uptake of those substances which depend on a protonmotive force to transport them into the cell, and the findings of the other workers mentioned may be as a result of this more fundamental action. Recently, a combination of sorbic acid with monolaurin has been shown to be often more active than parabens or sorbic acid alone (Kabara, 1980).

3.4.5 *Lactic acid*

Lactic acid shares with some other hydroxyacids the interesting property of being able to destroy airborne micro-organisms (Lovelock *et al.*, 1944: see also Section 19). Later a careful study of hydroxyacids, including lactic acid as air disinfectant, was made by Lovelock (1948). Lactic acid was found to be a cheap, efficient aerial bactericide when sprayed into the area to be sterilized. It has, however, a slight irritant action on the nasal mucosa which tends to limit its use. It could be used in emergencies for sterilizing glove boxes or hoods if other means of sterilization are not provided (see also Section 19).

3.4.6 *Benzoic acid*

This organic acid occurs naturally in many natural balsams and gums and these were used as preservatives early in man's history. Benzoic acid, first shown to be antifungal in 1875, is a white crystalline powder which is soluble 1:350 in water. It is used as a preservative for foods and pharmaceutical products, but is rapidly inactivated at pH values above 5.0. As with other preservatives, its activity may also be modified by the milieu in which it acts (Anderson & Chow, 1967; Beveridge & Hope, 1967). Resistance may develop (Ingram, 1959) and the acid may be metabolized by a contaminant it is meant to inhibit (Hugo & Beveridge, 1964; Stanier *et al.*, 1950; Stanier & Orston, 1973). In addition to its use as a preservative, benzoic acid has been combined with other agents for the topical treatment of fungal infections. Its mode of action is discussed in Chapter 9.

3.4.7 *Salicylic acid*

This is often used in combination with benzoic acid and other antifungal agents, for the topical treatment of fungal infections. Salicylic acid has keratinolytic activity and in addition affects metabolic processes. For an account of the action of benzoic and salicylic acids on the metabolism of micro-organisms, see Bosund (1962) and Freese *et al.* (1973).

3.4.8 Dehydroacetic acid (DHA)

Wolf (1950), looking at a general relationship between the structures of organic molecules possessing antimicrobial properties, noticed activity in a group of compounds containing an α,β unsaturated ketone residue. Wolf selected for study a series of 1,2 and 1,4 pyrones (Wolf & Westveer, 1950). Of these, 3-acetyl-6-methyl-1,2-H-pyran-2,4(3H)-dione (3-acetyl-4-hydroxy-6-methyl-2-acetyl-5-hydroxy-3-oxo-4-hexanoic acid-γ-lactone) or dehydroacetic acid showed especial promise.

Dehydroacetic acid is a white or light yellow, odourless, crystalline compound which is soluble at less than 0.1% in water; the sodium salt is soluble to the extent of 33%. Typical inhibitory concentrations (%) of the latter for selected micro-organisms are: *Aerobacter aerogenes*, 0.3; *Bacillus cereus*, 0.3; *Lactobacillus plantarum*, 0.1; *Staph. aureus*, 0.3; *Ps. aeruginosa*, 0.4; *A. niger*, 0.05; *Penicillium expansum*, 0.01; *Rhizopus nigricans*, 0.05; *T. interdigitale*, 0.005; *Saccharomyces cerevisiae*, 0.1. Extensive toxicological studies have indicated that the product is acceptable as a preservative for foods, cosmetics and medicines. The pK_a value of DHA is 5.4 but an inspection of pH/activity data suggests that activity loss above the pK_a value is not as great as with other preservative acids (propionic, benzoic) and indeed in Wolf's 1950 paper, the minimum inhibitory concentration against *Staph. aureus* remained at 0.3% from pH 5 to 9. Loss of activity at alkaline pH values was, however, noted by Bandelin (1950) in his detailed study of the effect of pH on the activity of antifungal compounds, as would be predicted by the pK_a value.

Little was known about its mode of action, although Seevers *et al.* (1950) produced evidence that DHA inhibited succinoxidase activity in mammalian tissue, while Wolf & Westveer (1950) showed that it did not react with microbial–SH enzymes.

DHA has found application in the preservation of foods, food wrappings, pharmaceuticals and toiletries. In the survey made by Richardson (1981) of the preservatives used in 18 500 cosmetic formulas, sodium dehydroacetate was used in 73 and dehydroacetic acid in 145.

3.4.9 Sulphur dioxide, sulphites, bisulphites

The fumes of burning sulphur, generating sulphur dioxide, have been used by the Greeks and Egyptians as fumigants for premises and food vessels to purify and deodorize. Lime sulphur, an aqueous suspension of elementary sulphur and calcium hydroxide, was introduced as a horticultural fungicide in 1803. Later the salts, chiefly sodium, potassium and calcium, of sulphurous acid were used in wine and food preservation.

In addition to their antimicrobial properties members of this group also act as antioxidants helping to preserve the colour of food products.

A pH-dependent relationship exists in solution between the species SO_2, HSO_3^- and SO_3^{2-}. As the pH moves from acid to alkaline, the species predominance moves from SO_2, the toxic species, through HSO_3^- to SO_3^{2-}. Above pH 3.6 the concentration of SO_2 begins to fall, and with it the microbicidal power of the solution. It is postulated that SO_2 can penetrate cells much more readily than can the other two chemical species.

Yeasts and moulds can grow at low pH values, and hence the value of sulphites as inhibitors of fungal growth in acid environments such as fruit juices. For reviews on the antimicrobial activity of sulphur dioxide, see Hammond & Carr (1976) and Wedzicha (1984).

3.4.10 Esters of p-*hydroxybenzoic acid (parabens)*

The marked pH-dependence of acids for their activity and the fact that the biocidal activity lay in the undissociated form led to the notion that esterification of an aromatic hydroxy carboxylic acid might give rise to compounds in which the phenolic group was less easily ionized.

Sabalitschka (1924) prepared a series of alkyl esters of *p*-hydroxybenzoic acid and tested their antimicrobial activity (Sabalitschka & Dietrich,

1926; Sabalitschka *et al.*, 1926). This family of biocides, which may be regarded as either phenols or esters of aromatic hydroxy carboxylic acids, has stood the test of time and is today amongst the most widely used group of preservatives (Richardson, 1977).

As might be imagined for compounds which have been in use for 56 years, there is an extensive literature. The esters usually used are the methyl, ethyl, propyl, butyl and benzyl compounds and are active over a wider pH range (4–8) than acid preservatives (Sokol, 1952) as has also been shown in biochemical experiments. Their pK_a values (8–8.5) compare with around 4 for preservative acids (Table 2.3). They have low water-solubility which decreases in the order methyl–benzyl (Table 2.5). A paper which gives extensive biocidal data is that of Aalto *et al.* (1953). Table 2.5 shows typical data from the literature. Again it can be seen that activity increases from the methyl to the benzyl ester. The compounds show low systemic toxicity (Mathews *et al.*, 1956). Russell & Furr (1986a,b, 1987) and Russell *et al.* (1985, 1987) studied the effects of parabens against wild-type and envelope mutants of *E. coli* and *Salmonella typhimurium*, and found that as the homologous series was ascended solubility decreased but activity became more pronounced, especially against the deep rough strains.

In summary, it can be said that the parabens are generally more active against Gram-positive bacteria and fungi, including yeasts, than against Gram-negative bacteria and in the latter *Ps. aeruginosa* is, as is so often seen, more resistant, especially to the higher homologues. This fact is considered in more detail below.

Hugo & Foster (1964) showed that a strain of *Ps. aeruginosa* isolated from a human eye lesion could metabolize the esters in dilute solution, 0.0343%, a solution strength originally proposed

Table 2.5 Chemical and microbiological properties of esters of *p*-hydroxybenzoic acid

Property*	Ester: Methyl	Ethyl	Propyl	Butyl
Molecular weight	152	166	180	194
Solubility in water (g/100 g) at 15°C	0.16	0.08	0.023	0.005
K_w^o (arachis oil)	2.4	13.4	38.1	239.6
Log *P* (octanol:water)	1.96	2.47	3.04	3.57
MIC values (molar basis)†				
E. coli (wild type)	3.95×10^{-3}	2.7×10^{-3}	1.58×10^{-3}	1.03×10^{-3}
E. coli (deep rough)	2.63×10^{-3}	1.2×10^{-3}	2.78×10^{-4}	1.03×10^{-4}
MIC values (μg/ml)‡				
E. coli	800	560	350	160
Ps. aeruginosa	1000	700	350	150
Concentration (mM) giving 50% inhibition of growth and uptake process in§				
E. coli	5.5	2.2	1.1	0.4
Ps. aeruginosa	3.6	2.8	> 1.0	> 1.0
B. subtilis	4.3	1.3	0.9	0.46

* K_w^o, partition coefficient, oil:water; *P*, partition coefficient, octanol:water.
† Russell *et al.* (1985).
‡ El-Falaha *et al.* (1983).
§ Eklund (1980).

as a preservative vehicle for medicinal eye-drops. Beveridge & Hart (1970) verified that the esters could serve as a carbon source for a number of Gram-negative bacterial species. Rosen *et al.* (1977) studied the preservative action of a mixture of methyl (0.2%) and propyl (0.1%) *p*-hydroxy benzoic acid in a cosmetic lotion. Using a challenge test they found that this concentration of esters failed to kill *Ps. aeruginosa*. It was part of their work indicating that these esters + imidazolindyl urea (Section 17.3.2) were ideal to provide a broad-spectrum preservative system, pseudomonads being successfully eliminated.

It has been traditional to use these esters in mixtures, as for example in Rosen's experiments recounted above. The rationale for those might be seen in the preservation of water-in-oil emulsion systems, where the more water-soluble methyl ester protected the aqueous phase while the propyl or butyl esters might preserve the oil phase. This point is discussed by O'Neill *et al.* (1979).

Another factor which must be borne in mind when using parabens is that they share the property found with other preservatives containing a phenolic group of being inactivated by non-ionic surface agents. Hydrogen bonding between the phenolic hydrogen atom and oxygen residues in polyoxyethylated non-ionic surfactants is believed to be responsible for the phenomenon. Experiments to support this inactivation are described by Patel & Kostenbauder (1958), Pisano & Kostenbauder (1959) and Blaug & Ahsan (1961).

As has been stated, methyl and propyl parabens topped the league table of cosmetic preservatives (Richardson, 1981) and, provided their limitations are borne in mind, they form a very useful set of preservatives.

The mode of action of the parabens has been studied by Furr & Russell (1972a,b and c), Freese *et al.* (1973) and Freese & Levin (1978).

3.4.11 Vanillic acid esters

The methyl, ethyl, propyl and butyl esters of vanillic acid (4-hydroxy-3-methoxy benzoic acid) possess antifungal properties when used at concentrations of 0.1–0.2%. These esters are not very soluble in water and are inactivated above pH 8.0. The ethyl ester has been shown to be less toxic than sodium benzoate and it has been used in the preservation of foods and food packaging materials against fungal infestation.

3.5 Regulations for the use of preservatives in foods

Certain of the foregoing substances described are used as food preservatives. The use of food preservatives is controlled by law in this and many other countries. In the UK, *Preservatives in Foods Regulations* (SI, 1975, No. 1487) should be consulted; for Scotland, SI, 1975, No. 1598 applies. A general treatment, with toxicological data, is to be found in the *Food Additive Series, World Health Organization* (1974) No. 5, while Lloyd & Drake (1975) discuss problems associated with the addition of preservatives to foodstuffs.

The special problems of food preservation are dealt with in Chapter 16 and of pharmaceutical products in Chapter 15. Lueck (1980) has published a detailed monograph on food preservatives which includes a consideration of their history, uses, health aspects and regulatory status, while Tilbury (1980) discusses developments in food preservatives.

4 AROMATIC DIAMIDINES

Diamidines are a group of organic compounds of which a typical structure is shown in Fig. 2.8. They were first introduced into medicine in the 1920s as possible insulin substitutes, as they lowered blood sugar levels in humans. Because of these lowered levels, the notion was sustained that they might possess antitrypanosomal activity because of the exogenous requirement for glucose of this parasite. Later they were found to possess an intrinsic trypanocidal activity not related to their action on blood sugar, and from this arose an investigation into their antimicrobial activity (Thrower & Valentine, 1943; Wien *et al.*, 1948). From these studies two compounds, propamidine and dibromopropamidine, emerged as useful antimicrobial compounds, being active against both bacteria and fungi.

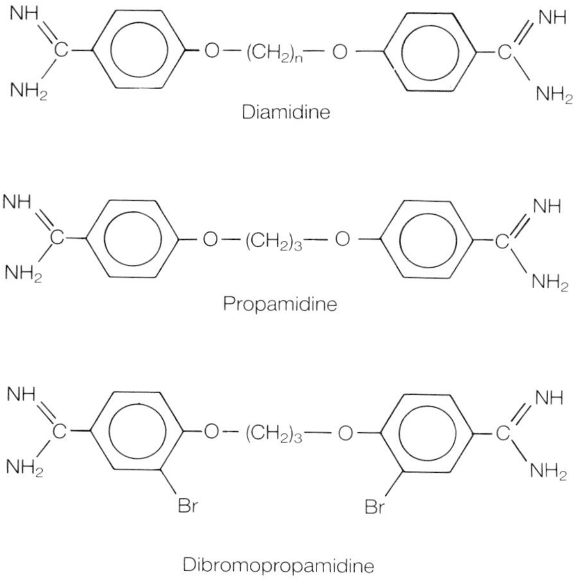

Fig. 2.8 Typical structure of a diamidine; propamidine; dibromopropamidine.

4.1 Propamidine

Propamidine is 4,4′-diamidinophenoxypropane; in order to confer solubility on this molecule it is usually supplied as the di(2-hydroxyethane-sulphate), the isethionate. This product is a white hygroscopic powder which is soluble in water, 1 in 5. Antimicrobial activity and clinical applications are described by Thrower & Valentine (1943). A summary of its antibacterial and antifungal activity is given in Table 2.6. Its activity is reduced by serum, by blood and by low pH values. Micro-organisms exposed to propamidine quickly acquire a resistance to it by serial subculture in the presence of increasing doses. Methicillin-resistant *Staph. aureus* (MRSA) strains may show appreciable resistance to propamidine (see Chapter 10F). It is chiefly used in the form of a cream containing 0.15% as a topical application for wounds.

4.2 Dibromopropamidine

Dibromopropamidine is 2,2′-dibromo-4,4′-diamidinodiphenoxypropane which is again usually supplied as the isethionate. It occurs as white crystals which are readily soluble in water. Dibromopropamidine is active against Gram-positive, non-spore-forming organisms; it is less active against Gram-negative organisms and spore formers but is active against fungi (Table 2.6). Resistance is acquired by serial subculture and resistant organisms so induced also show a resistance to propamidine. Russell & Furr (1986b, 1987) found that Gram-negative bacteria present a permeability barrier to dibromopropamidine isethionate, and MRSA strains may be resistant to the diamidine (Chapter 10F). Its activity is reduced in acid environments and in the presence of blood and serum. It is usually administered as an oil-in-water cream emulsion containing 0.15% of the isethionate.

A more detailed review on this group of compounds will be found in Hugo (1971).

5 BIGUANIDES

5.1 Chlorhexidine

Chlorhexidine (Fig. 2.9) is one of a family of N^1, N^5-substituted biguanides which has emerged from extensive synthetic and screening studies primarily by research workers at Imperial Chemical Industries (Curd & Rose, 1946; Davies *et al.*, 1954; Rose & Swain, 1956). It is available as a dihydrochloride, diacetate and gluconate. At 20°C the solubilities of the dihydrochloride and diacetate are 0.06 and 1.9% w/v, respectively; the digluconate is freely soluble.

Chlorhexidine and its salts occur as white or faintly cream-coloured powders and are available in a number of pharmaceutical formulations. It is widely used combined with cetyltrimethylammonium bromide as a topical antiseptic ('Savlon', ICI Ltd., Alderley Park, Macclesfield, Cheshire, England).

Chlorhexidine has a wide spectrum of antibacterial activity against both Gram-positive and Gram-negative bacteria. Some bacteria, notably strains of *Proteus* and *Providencia* spp., may be highly resistant to the biguanide (Stickler *et al.* 1983; Baillie, 1987; Ismaeel *et al.* 1986a,b; Russell, 1986; Chapter 10A). It is not sporicidal (Shaker *et al.* 1986, 1988; Russell, 1990a,b, 1991b; Russell

Table 2.6 Antimicrobial properties of propamidine and dibromopropamidine

Micro-organism	MIC (μg/ml) of Propamidine*	MIC (μg/ml) of Dibromopropamidine[†]
Staphylococcus aureus	1–16	1
Staphylococcus albus	6	
Streptococcus pyogenes	0.24–4	1
Streptococcus viridans	1–4	2
Streptococcus faecalis	25	
Pseudomonas aeruginosa	250–400	32 (64)
Proteus vulgaris	125–400	128 (256)
Escherichia coli	64–100	4 (32)
Clostridium perfringens	3–32	512
Clostridium histolyticum	256	256
Shigella flexneri	32	8
Salmonella enteriditis	256	65
Salmonella typhimurium	256	64
Actinomyces kimberi	100	10
Actinomyces madurae	100	50
Actinomyces hominis	1000	1000
Trichophyton tonsurans	100	25
Epidermophyton floccosum	250	
Achorion schoenleinii	3.5	
Blastomyces dermatitidis	3.5	
Geotrichum dermatitidis	3.5	200
Hormodendron langevonii		500

* Data from various sources, including Wein *et al.* (1948).
[†] Data from Wein *et al.* (1948).
Figures in parentheses denote bactericidal concentrations.

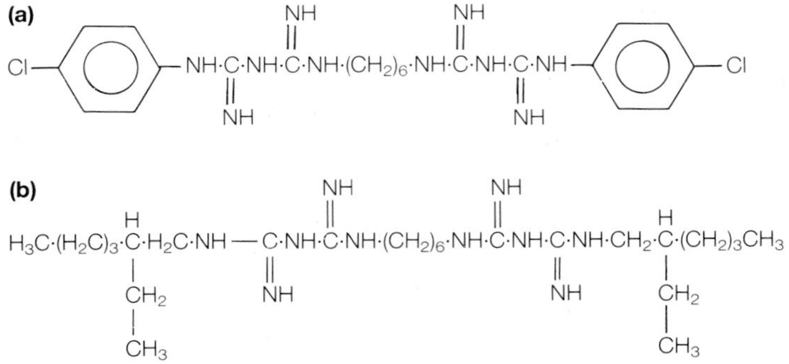

Fig. 2.9 Chlorhexidine (a) and alexidine (b).

& Chopra 1990), and is not lethal to acid-fast organisms (although it shows a high degree of bacteriostasis: Table 2.7) or generally viruses. It has low activity against fungal spores, many being resistant. The drug, is, however, tuberculocidal in ethanolic solution, and sporicidal at 98–100°C. A range of bacteriostatic and bactericidal values against a variety of bacterial species is shown in Tables 2.7 and 2.8, respectively.

Activity is reduced in the presence of serum, blood, pus and other organic matter. Because of its cationic nature its activity is also reduced in the

Table 2.7 Bacteriostatic activity of chlorhexidine against various bacterial species

Organism	Concentration of chlorhexidine (1 in) necessary for inhibition of growth
Streptococcus lactis	2 000 000
Streptococcus pyogenes	2 000 000
Streptococcus pneumoniae	1 000 000
Streptococcus faecalis	1 000 000
Staphylococcus aureus	1 000 000
Corynebacterium diphtheriae	1 000 000
Salmonella typhi	600 000
Salmonella pullorum	300 000
Salmonella dublin	300 000
Salmonella typhimurium	200 000
Proteus vulgaris	200 000
Pseudomonas aeruginosa (1)	300 000
Pseudomonas aeruginosa (2)	300 000
Pseudomonas aeruginosa (3)	80 000
Enterobacter aerogenes	100 000
Escherichia coli	100 000
Vibrio cholerae	300 000
Bacillus subtilis	2 000 000
Clostridium welchii	100 000
Mycobacterium tuberculosis	2 000 000
*Candida albicans**	200 000

Inoculum: one loopful of 24-h broth culture per 10 ml Difco heart–brain infusion medium.
Incubation: 24 h at 37°C.
* Yeast.

presence of soaps and other anionic compounds. Another cause of activity loss is due to the low solubility of the phosphate, borate, citrate, bicarbonate, carbonate or chloride salts. Any system which contains these anions will precipitate chlorhexidine.

Its main use is in medical and veterinary antisepsis. An alcoholic solution is a very effective skin disinfectant (Lowbury & Lilley, 1960). It is used in catheterization procedures, bladder irrigation and in obstetrics and gynaecology. It is one of the recommended bactericides for inclusion in eyedrops. In the veterinary context (Russell & Hugo, 1987), chlorhexidine fulfils the major functions for the application of a disinfectant to cows' teats after milking and can also be used as an antiseptic wound application. Chlorhexidine is also widely employed in the dental field (Gorman & Scott, 1985).

Its mode of action has been studied by Hugo & Longworth (1964a,b, 1965, 1966). At low concentrations, up to 200 μg/ml, it inhibits membrane enzymes and promotes leakage of cellular constituents; this is probably associated with bacteriostasis. As the concentration increases above this value, cytoplasmic constituents are coagulated and a bactericidal effect is seen. Its oral toxicity is low and it may be administered for throat medication in the form of lozenges. Extensive details on uses and application, together with relevant biocidal data, will be found in the booklet *Hibitane*, published by Imperial Chemical Industries (Pharmaceutical Division; address as above).

5.2 Alexidine

Alexidine (Fig. 2.9) is a bisbiguanide that possesses

Table 2.8 Bactericidal activity of chlorhexidine against various bacterial species

Organism	Concentration of chlorhexidine (1 in)		
	To effect 99% kill	To effect 99.9% kill	To effect 99.99% kill
Staphylococcus aureus	125 000	70 000	40 000
Streptococcus pyogenes	—	—	20 000
Escherichia coli	160 000	100 000	50 000
Pseudomonas aeruginosa	40 000	30 000	17 500
Salmonella typhi	200 000	—	125 000

Inoculum: 10^5 in distilled water.
Contact time: 10 min at room temperature.
Neutralizer: egg yolk medium.

ethylhexyl end-groups as distinct from the chlorophenol end-groups found in chlorhexidine. Alexidine is considerably more active than chlorhexidine in inducing cell leakage from *E. coli* and concentrations of alexidine (but not of chlorhexidine) above the MIC induce cell lysis (Chawner & Gilbert, 1989a,b). Alexidine has been recommended for use as an oral antiseptic and antiplaque compound (Gjermo *et al.*, 1973).

6 SURFACE-ACTIVE AGENTS

Surface-active agents (surfactants) have two regions in their molecular structure, one being a hydrocarbon water-repellent (hydrophobic) group, and the other a water-attracting (hydrophilic or polar) group. Depending on the basis of the charge or absence of ionization of the hydrophilic group, surface-active agents are classified into anionic, cationic, non-ionic and ampholytic (amphoteric) compounds.

6.1 Cationic agents

Cationic surfactants possess strong bactericidal, but weak detergent, properties. The term 'cationic detergent' usually signifies a quaternary ammonium compound (QAC, onium compound) but this is not strictly accurate, as the smallest concentration at which a QAC is microbicidal is so low that its detergent activity is negligible (Davis, 1960).

Lawrence (1950) and D'Arcy & Taylor (1962a,b) have reviewed the surface-active quaternary ammonium germicides, and useful data about their properties and activity are provided by Wallhäusser (1984) and about their uses by Gardner & Peel (1986). Early references to their use are found in Jacobs (1916), Jacobs *et al.* (1916a,b) and Domagk (1935).

6.1.1 Chemical aspects

The QACs may be considered as being organically substituted ammonium compounds in which the nitrogen atom has a valency of five, and four of the substituent radicals (R^1-R^4) are alkyl or heterocyclic radicals and the fifth (X^-) is a small anion (Fig. 2.10: general structure). The sum of the carbon atoms in the four R groups is more than 10. For a QAC to have a high antimicrobial activity, at least one of the R groups must have a chain length in the range C_8 to C_{18} (Domagk, 1935). Three of the four covalent links may be satisfied by nitrogen in a pyridine ring, as in the pyridinium compounds such as cetylpyridinium chloride. This and the other important QACs are listed in Fig. 2.10. The cationic onium group may be a simple aliphatic ammonium, a pyridinium or piperidinium or other heterocyclic group (D'Arcy & Taylor, 1962b).

Apart from the monoquaternary compounds, monoquaternary derivatives of 4-aminoquinaldine (e.g. laurolinium) are potent antimicrobial agents, as are the bisquaternary compounds, such as hedaquinium chloride and dequalinium. These are considered in more detail in Section 10 (see also Fig. 2.20).

In addition to the compounds mentioned above, polymeric QACs are used as industrial biocides. One such compound is poly[oxyethylene(dimethylimino)ethylene]dichloride.

Organosilicon-substituted (silicon-bonded) quaternary ammonium salts, organic amines or amine salts have been introduced recently. Compounds with antimicrobial activity in solution are also highly effective on surfaces. One such compound, 3-(trimethoxysily) propyloctadecyldimethyl ammonium chloride, demonstrates powerful antimicrobial activity whilst chemically bonded to a variety of surfaces (Malek & Speier, 1982; Speier & Malek, 1982). Schaeufele (1986) has pointed out that fatty alcohols and/or fatty acids, from both natural and synthetic sources, form the basis of the production of modern QACs which have improved organic soil, and increased hard water tolerance.

6.1.2 Antimicrobial activity

As stated above, the antimicrobial properties of the QACs were first recognized in 1916, but they did not attain prominence until the work of Domagk in 1935. Early workers claimed that the QACs were markedly sporicidal, but the fallacy of this hypothesis has been demonstrated by improved testing methods. In particular, the experimental procedures devised by Davies (1949) are of considerable importance. He found that suspensions

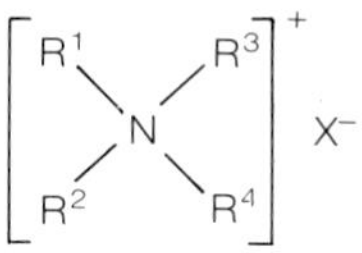

General structure

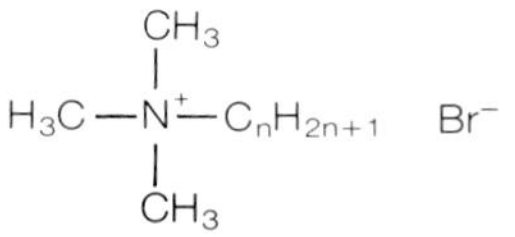

(n = 12,14 or 16)
Cetrimide

(a mixture of dodecyl-, tetradecyl- and hexadecyl-trimethylammonium bromide)

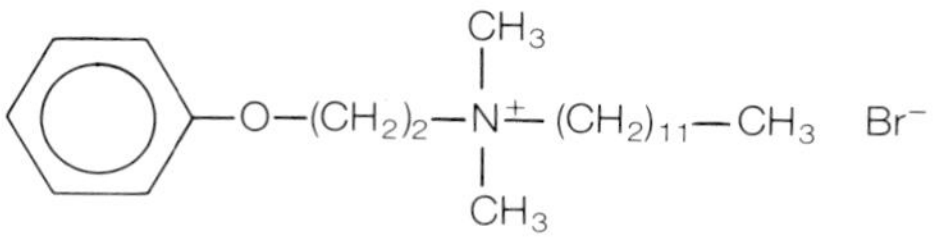

Domiphen bromide

(dodecyldimethyl-2-phenoxyethyl-ammonium bromide)

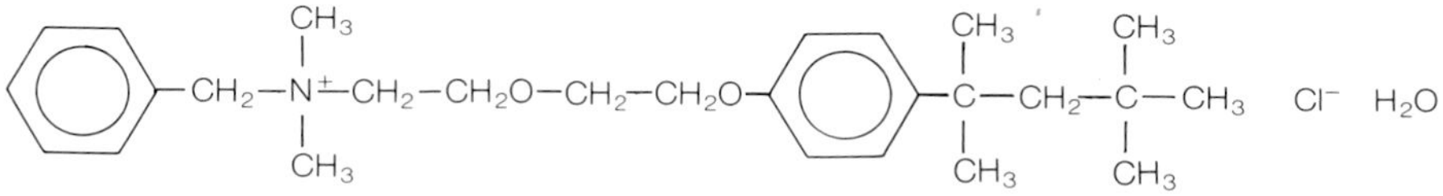

Benzethonium chloride

(benzyldimethyl-2-{2-[4-(1,1,3,3-tetramethylbutyl)-phenoxy]ethoxy}-ethylammonium chloride)

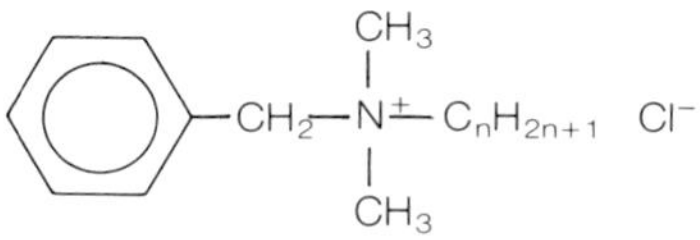

(n = 8 to 18)
Benzalkonium chloride

(a mixture of alkyldimethylbenzyl-ammonium chlorides)

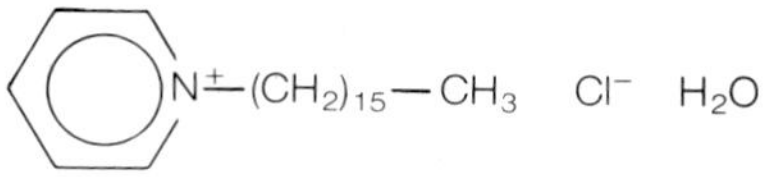

Cetylpyridinium chloride

(1-hexadecylpyridinium chloride)

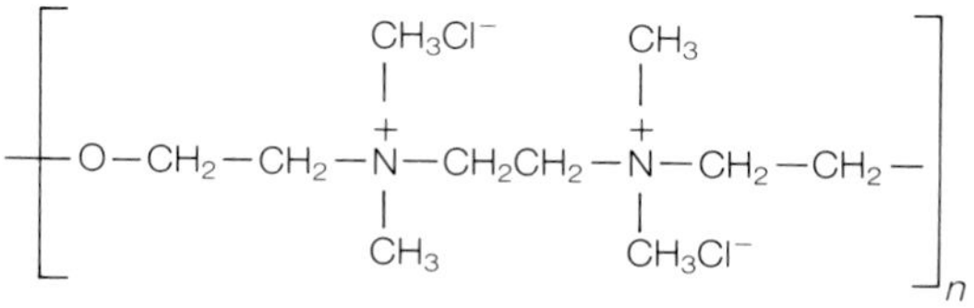

Polymeric QAC

Fig. 2.10 General structure and examples of quaternary ammonium compounds (QACs).

of *B. subtilis* spores were apparently sterilized after 1 h by various QACs when no precautions were made to prevent bacteriostasis in the recovery medium; however, the inclusion in the recovery medium of Lubrol W (see Bergan & Lystad, 1972; Mackinnon, 1974) showed the lack of sporicidal activity (Russell, 1971a). Weber & Black (1948) had earlier recommended the use of lecithin as an inactivator for QACs. Lawrence (1948) showed that soaps and anionic detergents failed to inactivate QACs, and suggested suramin sodium for this purpose. British Standard 3286 (1960) recommends lecithin (2%) solubilized with Lubrol W (3%), although Lubrol W itself may be toxic to streptococci, a point discussed more fully by Russell *et al.* (1979).

The QACs are primarily active against Gram-positive bacteria with concentrations as low as 1 in 200000 (0.005%) being lethal; higher concentrations (*c.* 1 in 30000 or 0.0033%) are lethal to Gram-negative bacteria (Hamilton, 1971) although *Ps. aeruginosa* tends to be highly resistant (Davis, 1962). Nevertheless, cells of this organism which are highly resistant to benzalkonium chloride (1 mg per ml, 0.1%) may still show ultrastructural changes when grown in its presence (Hoffman *et al.*, 1973). The QACs have a trypanocidal activity (reviewed by D'Arcy & Taylor, 1962b) but are not mycobactericidal (Sykes, 1965; Smith, 1968; presumably because of the lipid, waxy coat of these organisms. Gram-negative bacteria, such as *E. coli*, *Ps. aeruginosa* and *Sal. typhimurium*, exclude QACs, but deep rough mutants are sensitive (El-Falaha *et al.*, 1983; Russell & Furr, 1986a,b; Russell *et al.* 1986; Russell & Chopra, 1990). Contamination of solutions of QACs with Gram-negative bacteria has often been reported (Frank & Schaffner, 1976; Kaslow *et al.* 1976).

Viruses are more resistant than bacteria or fungi to the QACs. This is clearly shown in the excellent review of Grossgebauer (1970) who points out that the QACs have a high protein defect, and that whereas they are active against lipophilic viruses (such as herpes simplex, vaccinia, influenza and adenoviruses) they have only a poor effect against viruses (enteroviruses, e.g. polio, coxsackie and ECHO) that show hydrophilic properties.

The QACs possess antifungal properties, although they are fungistatic rather than fungicidal (for a review see D'Arcy, 1971). This applies not only to the monoquaternary compounds, but also to the bisonium compounds, such as hedaquinium and dequalinium (Section 10).

The Ferguson principle stipulates that compounds with the same thermodynamic activity will exert equal effects on bacteria. Weiner *et al.* (1965) studied the activity of three QACs (dodecyltrimethylammonium chloride, dodecyldimethylammonium chloride and dodecylpyridinium chloride) against *E. coli*, *Staph. aureus* and *Candida albicans*, and correlated these results with the surface properties of these agents. A clear relationship was found between the thermodynamic activity (expressed as a ratio of the surface concentration produced by a solution and the surface concentration at the critical micelle concentration (CMC)) and antibacterial activity.

Because most QACs are mixtures of homologues, Laycock & Mulley (1970) studied the antibacterial activity of mono- and multi-component solutions using the homologous series *n*-dodecyl, *n*-tetradecyl and *n*-hexadecyl trimethylammonium bromides individually, binary systems containing C_{12}/C_{14} or C_{14}/C_{16} mixtures, and a ternary mixture (centrimide) of the $C_{12}/C_{14}/C_{16}$ compounds. Antibacterial activity was measured as the concentrations needed to produce survivor levels of 1.0 and 0.01%; CMC was measured by the surface-tension method. In almost every instance the thermodynamic activity (CMC/concentration to produce a particular survivor level) producing an equivalent biological response was reasonably constant, thereby supporting the Ferguson principle for these micelle-forming QACs.

The QACs are incompatible with a wide range of chemical agents, including anionic surfactants (Richardson & Woodford, 1964), non-ionic surfactants, such as lubrols and tweens, and phospholipids, such as lecithin and other fat-containing substances. Benzalkonium chloride has been found to be incompatible with the ingredients of some commercial rubber mixes, but not with silicone rubber; this is important when benzalkonium chloride is employed as a preservative in multiple-dose eye-drop formulations (*Pharmaceutical Codex*, 1979; *British Pharmacopoeia*, 1988).

Although non-ionic surfactants are stated above to inactivate QACs, presumably as a consequence of micellar formation (see Elworthy, 1976, for a useful description of micelles), nevertheless potentiation of the antibacterial activity of the QACs by means of low concentrations of non-ionic agents has been reported (Schmolka, 1973), possibly as a result of increased cellular permeability induced by the non-ionic surfactant (see Chapter 3 for a more detailed discussion).

The antimicrobial activity of the QACs is affected greatly by organic matter, including milk, serum and faeces, which may limit their usefulness in practice. The uses of the QACs are considered below (Section 6.1.3) and also in more general terms in Section 20. They are more effective at alkaline and neutral pH than under acid conditions. The action of benzalkonium chloride on *Ps. aeruginosa* is potentiated by aromatic alcohols, especially 3-phenylpropanol (Richards & McBride, 1973).

6.1.3 Uses

The QACs have many and varied uses. They have been recommended for use in food hygiene in hospitals (Kelsey & Maurer, 1972). Benzalkonium chloride has been employed for the pre-operative disinfection of unbroken skin (0.1–0.2%), for application to mucous membranes (up to 0.1%) and for bladder and urethra irrigation (0.005%); creams are used in treating napkin (diaper) rash caused by ammonia-producing organisms, and lozenges for the treatment of superficial mouth and throat infections. In the United Kingdom, benzalkonium chloride (0.01%) is one of four antimicrobial agents officially recognized as being suitable preservatives for inclusion in eye-drop preparations (*Pharmaceutical Codex*, 1979; *British Pharmacopoeia*, 1988). Benzalkonium chloride is also widely used (at a concentration of 0.001–0.01%) in hard contact-lens soaking (disinfecting) solutions; EDTA (see Section 13) at a concentration of 0.1% may be included to enhance its action (Kay, 1980). The QAC is too irritant to be used with hydrophilic soft (hydrogel) contact-lenses because it can bind to the lens surface, be held within the water present in hydrogels and then be released into the eye (Davies, 1980).

Benzethonium chloride is applied to wounds as an aqueous solution (0.1%) and as a solution (0.2%) in alcohol and acetone for pre-operative skin disinfection and for controlling algal growth in swimming pools.

Cetrimide is used for cleaning and disinfecting burns and wounds and for pre-operative cleansing of the skin. For general disinfecting purposes, a mixture ('Savlon') of cetrimide with chlorhexidine is often employed. At pH 6, but not at pH 7.2, this product may be liable to contamination with *Ps. aeruginosa* (Bassett, 1971). Solutions containing 1–3% of cetrimide are employed as hair shampoos (e.g. 'Cetavlon P.C.', a concentrate to be diluted with water before use) for seborrhoea capitis and seborrhoeic dermatitis.

Cetylpyridinium chloride is employed pharmaceutically, for skin disinfection and for antiseptic treatment of small wound surfaces (0.1–0.5% solutions), as an oral and pharyngeal antiseptic (e.g. lozenges containing 1–2 mg of the QAC) and as a preservative in emulsions. Cosmetically (see also Quack, 1976), it is used at a concentration of between 0.1 and 0.5% in hair preparations and in deodorants; lower concentrations (0.05–0.1%) are incorporated into face and shaving lotions.

Several investigations have been made of the use of QACs in the disinfection of bedding and blankets (Schwabacher *et al.*, 1958; Gillespie & Robinson, 1959; Thomas *et al.*, 1959; Crewther & McQuade, 1964). Blankets and bedding comprise an important source of cross-infection in hospital wards. The bacteria associated with this cross-infection are usually non-sporing, and *Staph. aureus* is a particularly troublesome organism. Contamination of the air in a ward is very marked when beds are being made. The QACs were one of the first methods of disinfecting hospital woollen blankets, which however are now rarely used.

In the veterinary context the QACs have been used for the disinfection of automatic calf feeders and have been incorporated into sheep dips for controlling microbial growth in fleece and wool. They are not, however, widely used on farm sites because of the large amount of organic debris they are likely to encounter.

In general, then, the QACs are very useful disinfectants and pharmaceutical and cosmetic preservatives. Further information on their uses and antimicrobial properties is considered in Section 20 and in Chapters 3 and 15; see also BS6471: 1984 and BS6424: 1984.

6.2 Anionic agents

Anionic surface-active agents are compounds which, in aqueous solution, dissociate into a large complex anion, responsible for the surface activity, and a smaller cation. Examples of anionic surfactants are the alkali-metal and metallic soaps, amine soaps, lauryl ether sulphates (e.g. sodium lauryl sulphate) and sulphated fatty alcohols.

They usually have strong detergent but weak antimicrobial properties, except in high concentrations, when they induce lysis of Gram-negative bacteria (Salton, 1968). Fatty acids are active against Gram-positive but not Gram-negative bacteria (Galbraith *et al.*, 1971). More recent information will be found by consulting Kabara (1984).

6.3 Non-ionic agents

These consist of a hydrocarbon chain attached to a non-polar water-attracting group, which is usually a chain of ethylene oxide units, e.g. cetomacrogols. The properties of non-ionic surfactants depend mainly on the proportions of hydrophilic and hydrophobic groups in the molecule. Other examples include the sorbitan derivatives, such as the polysorbates (Tweens).

The non-ionic surfactants are considered to have no antimicrobial properties. However, low concentrations of polysorbates are believed to affect the permeability of the outer envelopes of Gram-negative cells (Brown, 1975) which are thus rendered more sensitive to various antimicrobial agents. High concentrations of Tweens overcome the activity of QACs: this is considered in more detail in Chapter 3.

6.4 Amphoteric (ampholytic) agents

Amphoteric agents are compounds of mixed anionic–cationic character. They combine the detergent properties of anionic compounds with the bactericidal properties of the cationic. Their bactericidal activity remains virtually constant over a wide pH range (Barrett, 1969) and they are less readily inactivated than QACs by proteins (Clegg, 1970). Examples of amphoteric agents are dodecyl-β-alanine, dodecyl-β-aminobutyric acid and dodecyl-di(aminoethyl)-glycine (Davis, 1960). The last-named belongs to the 'Tego' series of compounds, the name 'Tego' being a trade name (Goldschmidt, Essen).

The Tego compounds are bactericidal to Gram-positive and Gram-negative bacteria, and, unlike the QACs, anionic and non-ionic agents, this includes the mycobacteria (James, 1965; Croshaw, 1971), although the rate of kill of these organisms is less than that of the others (Block, 1977). Compounds based on dodecyl-di(aminoethyl)-glycine find use as disinfectants in the food industry (Kornfeld, 1966).

7 ALDEHYDES

Two aldehydes are currently of considerable importance as disinfectants, viz, glutaraldehyde and formaldehyde, although others have been studied and shown to possess antimicrobial activity. Glyoxal (ethanedial), malonaldehyde (propanedial), succinaldehyde (butanedial) and adipaldehyde (hexanedial) all possess some sporicidal action, with aldehydes beyond adipaldehyde having virtually no sporicidal effect (Pepper & Chandler, 1963). Thus, this section on aldehydes will deal mainly with glutaraldehyde and formaldehyde.

7.1 Glutaraldehyde (pentanedial)

7.1.1 Chemical aspects

Glutaraldehyde is a saturated 5-carbon dialdehyde with an empirical formula of $C_5H_8O_2$ and a molecular weight of 100.12. Its industrial production (Fig. 2.11) involves a two-step synthesis via an ethoxy dihydropyran. Glutaraldehyde is usually obtained commercially as a 2, 25 or 50% solution of acidic pH, although for disinfecting purposes a 2% solution is normally supplied, which must be 'activated' (made alkaline) before use.

The two aldehyde groups may react singly or together to form bisulphite complexes, oximes, cyanohydrins, acetals and hydrazones. Polymerization of the glutaraldehyde molecule occurs by means of the following possible mechanisms:

1 the dialdehyde exists as a monomer, with an equilibrium between the open-chain molecule and the hydrated ring structure [Fig. 2.12(a) and (b)];

2 ring formation occurs by an intramolecular mechanism, so that aqueous solutions of the aldehyde consist of free glutaraldehyde, the cyclic hemiacetal of its hydrate and oligomers of this in equilibrium [Fig. 2.12(c)];

3 different types of polymers may be formed at different pH values, and it is considered that polymers in the alkaline range are unable to revert to the monomer, whereas those in the neutral and acid range revert easily (Boucher, 1974; see Fig. 2.13).

Polymerization increases with a rise in pH and above pH 9 there is an extensive loss of aldehyde groups. Glutaraldehyde is more stable at acid than alkaline pH; solutions at pH 8 and above generally lose activity within four weeks. Novel formulations have been produced, and continue to be designed, to overcome the problems of loss of stability (Babb *et al.*, 1980; Gorman *et al.*, 1980).

7.1.2 Interactions of glutaraldehyde

Glutaraldehyde is a highly reactive molecule. It reacts with various enzymes (but does not sterically alter them to lose all activity) and with proteins; the rate of reaction is pH dependent, increasing considerably over the pH range 4–9, and the reaction product is highly stable (Hopwood *et al.*, 1970). Glutaraldehyde prevents dissociation of free ribosomes (see Russell & Hopwood, 1976), but under the normal conditions of fixation (Hopwood, 1975) little reaction appears to occur between nucleic acids and glutaraldehyde. There is little published information on the possible reactions of glutaraldehyde and lipids (Russell & Hopwood, 1976).

7.1.3 Microbicidal activity

Glutaraldehyde possesses high microbicidal activity against bacteria and their spores, mycelial and spore forms of fungi and various types of viruses (Borick, 1968; Borick & Pepper, 1970). Although

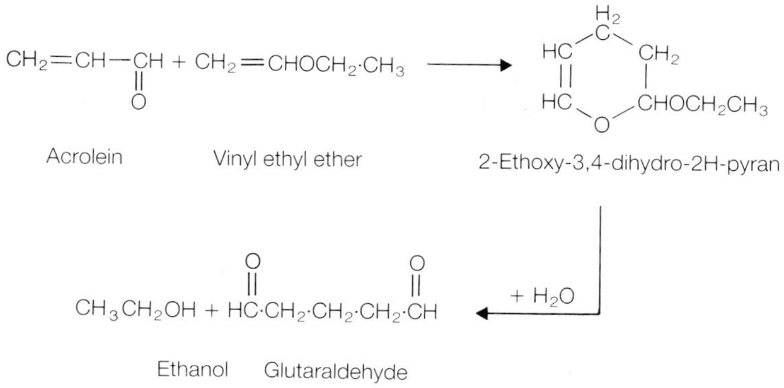

Fig. 2.11 Industrial production of glutaraldehyde.

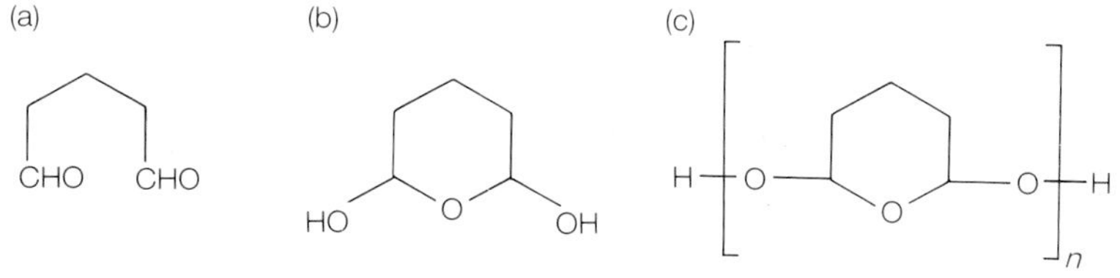

Fig. 2.12 (a) Free glutaraldehyde; (b) hydrated ring structure (cyclic hemiacetal of its hydrate); (c) oligomer.

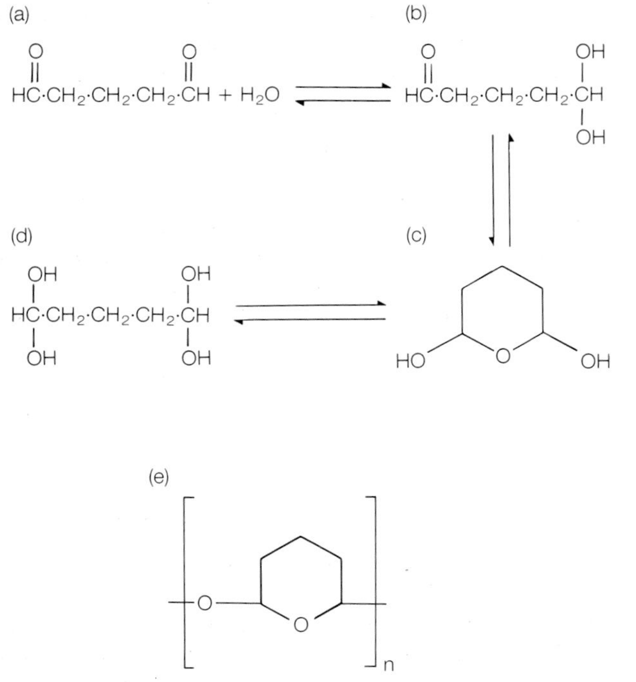

Fig. 2.13 (a) Open-chain molecule of glutaraldehyde; (b), (c) and (d) formation of several more stable 'polymers' (hydrated) in aqueous alkaline solution; (e) polymer with an acetal-like structure, in neutral and acid ranges (after Boucher, 1974).

there was some doubt about its mycobactericidal potency, glutaraldehyde is now considered to be an effective antimycobacterial agent (Collins, 1986: see also Chapter 10D). A summary of its antimicrobial efficacy is presented in Table 2.9, which demonstrates the effect of pH on its activity. The exact mechanism of action of the dialdehyde is unknown, but the fact that its rate of interaction with proteins and enzymes increases with increasing pH (Hopwood *et al.*, 1970; Russell & Munton, 1974) is undoubtedly of importance. The cross-linking mechanism is also influenced by time, concentration and temperature (Eager *et al.*, 1986). Acid glutaraldehyde is a markedly inferior disinfectant to alkaline glutaraldehyde, but this discrepancy disappears with increasing temperature. Resistance development to glutaraldehyde is a late event in sporulation (Power *et al.*, 1988) and sodium hydroxide-induced revival of spores of *Bacillus* spp. has been demonstrated (Dancer *et al.*, 1989; Power *et al.*, 1989, 1990).

Organic matter is considered to have no effect

Table 2.9 Microbicidal activity of glutaraldehyde*

Form of glutaraldehyde	Approximate pH value	Fungicidal activity†	Virucidal activity	Bactericidal activity†	Sporicidal activity†
Acid	4–5	Low	Low to high	Low	Low to very high
Alkaline	8	High	High	High	Reasonable to very high

* See also Gorman *et al.* (1980).
† Use of low dialdehyde concentrations (0.01–0.02%); 2% solutions of acid and alkaline glutaraldehyde are both highly active against bacteria and probably viruses.
† Activity of acid glutaraldehyde increases markedly with temperature and at *c.* 37°C its activity approaches that of alkaline glutaraldehyde.

on the antimicrobial activity of the aldehyde. In view of the interaction of glutaraldehyde with the amino groups in proteins, this would appear to be a rather unusual finding. It is, however, true to state that it retains a considerable degree of activity in the presence of high levels of organic matter, such as 20% serum (Russell, unpublished data).

Dried spores are considerably more resistant to chemical disinfectants than are spores in suspension, and it would appear that glutaraldehyde is no exception. The use of the Association of Official Analytical Chemists (AOAC) test with dried spores of *B. subtilis* has shown that 2% alkaline glutaraldehyde may require up to 10 h to achieve sterilization at 20°C (Rubbo *et al.*, 1967).

The antimicrobial activity of glutaraldehyde has been reviewed by Gorman *et al.* (1980).

7.1.4 Uses of glutaraldehyde

The uses of glutaraldehyde as a fixative in electron microscopy, in leather tanning and biochemically have been discussed by Russell & Hopwood (1976). In a microbiological context, glutaraldehyde has been recommended for the disinfection/sterilization of certain types of medical equipment, notably cystoscopes and anaesthetic equipment. Glutaraldehyde has been employed in the veterinary field for the disinfection of utensils and of premises (Russell & Hugo, 1987) but its potential mutagenic and carcinogenic effects (Quinn 1987) make these uses hazardous to personnel. The main advantages claimed for glutaraldehyde are as follows: it has a broad spectrum of activity with a rapid microbicidal action, and it is non-corrosive to metals, rubber and lenses.

7.2 Formaldehyde

Formaldehyde is used as a disinfectant as a liquid or vapour. Gaseous formaldehyde is referred to briefly in Section 18 and in more detail in Chapter 20. The liquid form will be considered mainly in this section.

The Health and Safety Executive of the UK has indicated that the inhalation of formaldehyde vapour may be presumed to pose a carcinogenic risk to humans. This indication must have considerable impact on the consideration of the role and use of formaldehyde and formaldehyde releasers in sterilization and disinfection processes.

7.2.1 Chemical aspects

Formaldehyde occurs as formaldehyde solution (formalin), an aqueous solution containing *c.* 34–38% w/w CH_2O. Methyl alcohol is present to delay polymerization. Formaldehyde displays many typical chemical reactions, combining with amines to give methylolamines, carboxylic acids to give esters of methylene glycol, phenols to give methylphenols and sulphides to produce thiomethylene glycols.

7.2.2 Interactions of formaldehyde

Formaldehyde interacts with protein molecules by attaching itself to the primary amide and amino groups, whereas phenolic moieties bind little of the aldehyde (Fraenkel-Conrat *et al.*, 1945). Subsequently, it was shown that formaldehyde gave an intermolecular cross-linkage of protein or amino groups with phenolic or indole residues.

In addition to interacting with many terminal groups in viral proteins, formaldehyde can also react extensively with the amino groups of nucleic acid bases, although it is much less reactive with DNA than with RNA (Staehelin, 1958).

7.2.3 Microbicidal activity

Formaldehyde is a microbicidal agent, with lethal activity against bacteria and their spores, fungi and many viruses. Its first reported use as a disinfectant was in 1892. Its sporicidal action is, however, slower than that of glutaraldehyde (Rubbo *et al.*, 1967). Formaldehyde combines readily with proteins (Section 7.2.2) and is less effective in the presence of protein organic matter. Plasmid-mediated resistance to formaldehyde has been described, presumably due to aldehyde degradation (Heinzel, 1988). Formaldehyde vapour may be released by evaporating formalin solutions, by adding potassium permanganate to formalin or alternatively by heating, under controlled conditions, the polymer paraformaldehyde $[(CH_2O)_nH]$ or urea formaldehyde or melamine formaldehyde (Tulis, 1973). The activity of the vapour depends on aldehyde concentration, temperature and relative humidity (r.h.) (Section 18.2).

7.2.4 Formaldehyde-releasing agents

Noxythiolin [oxymethylenethiourea; Fig. 2.14(a)] is a bactericidal agent (Kingston, 1965; Wright & McAllister, 1967; Browne & Stoller, 1970) that apparently owes its antibacterial activity to the release of formaldehyde (Kingston, 1965; Pickard, 1972; cf. Gucklhorn, 1970):

$$CH_3{\cdot}NH{\cdot}CS{\cdot}NH{\cdot}CH_2OH \rightarrow CH_3{\cdot}NH{\cdot}CS{\cdot}NH_2{\cdot}H{+}CHO$$

Noxythiolin has been found to protect animals from lethal doses of endotoxin (Wright & McAllister, 1967; Haler, 1974) and is claimed to be active against all bacteria including those resistant to other types of antibacterial agents (Browne & Stoller, 1970).

Noxythiolin has been widely used both topically and in accessible body cavities, notably as an irrigation solution in the treatment of peritonitis (Pickard, 1972). Unfortunately, solutions are rather unstable (after preparation they should be stored at 10°C and used within seven days). Commercially, noxythiolin is available as 'Noxyflex S' and 'Noxyflex' (Geistlich Ltd, Chester, UK), the latter containing amethocaine hydrochloride as well as noxythiolin. Solutions of 'Noxyflex' (containing 1 or 2.5% noxythiolin) are employed where local discomfort is experienced.

More recently, the amino acid taurine has been selected as the starting point in the design of a new antibacterial agent, taurolin [Fig. 2.14(b)] which is a condensate of two molecules of taurine and three molecules of formaldehyde. Taurolin [bis-(1,1-dioxoperhydro-1,2,4-thiazinyl-4)methane] is

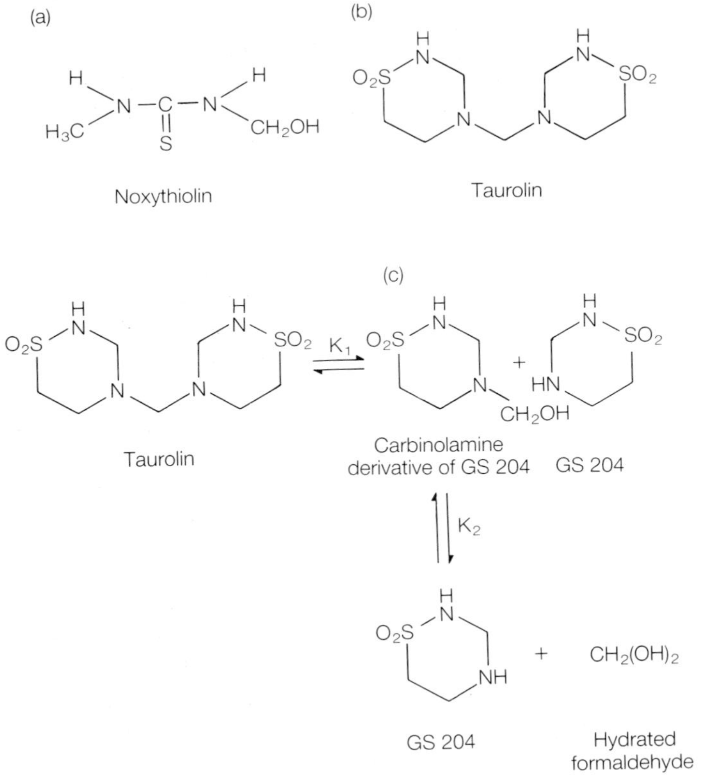

Fig. 2.14 (a) Noxythiolin; (b) taurolin; (c) postulated equilibrium of taurolin in aqueous solution (after Myers *et al.*, 1980).

water-soluble and is stable in aqueous solution. It has a wide spectrum of antimicrobial activity *in vitro* and *in vivo* (Reeves & Schweitzer, 1973; Browne *et al.*, 1976, 1977, 1978).

Taurine is considered to act as a non-toxic formaldehyde carrier, donating methylol groups to bacterial protein and endotoxin (Browne *et al.*, 1976). According to these authors, taurine has a lower affinity for formaldehyde than bacterial protein, but a greater affinity than animal protein, the consequence of which is a selective lethal effect. Taurolin has been shown to protect experimental animals from the lethal effects of *E. coli* and *Bacteroides fragilis* endotoxin (Pfirrman & Leslie, 1979).

This viewpoint that the activity of taurolin results from a release of formaldehyde that is adsorbed by bacterial cells is, however, no longer tenable. When taurolin is dissolved in water (Myers *et al.*, 1980), an equilibrium is established [Fig. 2.14(c)] to release two molecules of the monomer [1,1-dioxo-perhydro-1,2,4-thiadizine (GS 204)] and its carbinolamine derivative. The antibacterial activity of taurolin is considerably greater than that of free formaldehyde (Myers *et al.*, 1980; Allwood & Myers, 1981) and these authors thus concluded that the activity of taurolin was not due entirely to bacterial adsorption of free formaldehyde but also to a reaction with a masked (or latent) formaldehyde. Since GS204 has only a low antibacterial effect, then the carbinolamine must obviously play an important role.

Clinically, the intraperitoneal administration of taurolin has been shown to bring about a significant reduction of morbidity in peritonitis (Browne *et al.*, 1978).

A third formaldehyde-releasing agent is hexamine (methenamine); hexamine itself is inactive but it breaks down by acid hydrolysis to release formaldehyde. It has been reviewed by Allwood & Myers (1981). Derivatives of hexamine are considered in Section 17.5, and other formaldehyde-releasing agents in Sections 17.3 (imidazole derivatives), 17.6 (triazines) and 17.7 (oxazolo-oxazoles). Table 2.18 should also be consulted, as well as Section 18.2 (which deals with release of gaseous formaldehyde) and Paulus (1976).

7.2.5 *Uses of formaldehyde*

Formaldehyde is employed as a disinfectant in both the liquid and gaseous states. Vapour-phase formaldehyde is used in the disinfection of sealed rooms: the vapour can be produced as described above, or alternatively an equal volume of industrial methylated spirits (IMS) can be added to formaldehyde and the mixture used as a spray. Other uses of formaldehyde vapour have been summarized by Russell (1976). These include the following: low-temperature steam plus formaldehyde vapour for the disinfection/sterilization of heat-sensitive medical materials (see also Chapter 18A); hospital bedding and blankets; and fumigation of poultry houses, of considerable importance in hatchery hygiene (Anon., 1970).

Formaldehyde in liquid form has been used as a virucidal agent in the production of certain types of viral vaccines, e.g. polio (inactivated) vaccine. Formaldehyde solution has also been employed for the treatment of warts, as an antiseptic mouthwash, for the disinfection of membranes in dialysis equipment, and as a preservative in hair shampoos. Formaldehyde-releasing agents were considered in Section 7.2.4. Formaldehyde and formaldehyde condensates have been reviewed in depth by Rossmore & Sondossi (1988).

7.3 Other aldehydes

Other aldehydes have been studied but results have sometimes been conflicting, and have thus been re-investigated (Power & Russell, 1990). Sporicidin™, used undiluted and containing 2% glutaraldehyde plus 7% phenol and 1.2% phenate, is slightly more active against spores than is 2% activated, alkaline glutaraldehyde. Gigasept™, containing butan-1,4-dial, dimethoxytetrahydrofuran and formaldehyde, and used at 5% and 10% v/v dilutions, is considerably less active. It is essential that adequate procedures are employed to ensure residual glutaraldehyde (and phenol/phenate, if present) or other aldehyde in determining survivor levels. This has not always been appreciated (Pepper, 1980; Leach, 1981; Isenberg, 1985). 2% glyoxal is weakly sporicidal, and butyraldehyde has no activity.

8 ANTIMICROBIAL DYES

There are three groups of dyes which find application because of their antimicrobial activity: the acridines, the triphenylmethane group and the quinones.

8.1 Acridines

8.1.1 Chemistry

The acridines (Fig. 2.15) are heterocyclic compounds which have proved to be of some value as antimicrobial agents. Acridine itself is feebly basic, but two of the five possible mono-aminoacridines are strong bases, and these (3-aminoacridine and 9-aminoacridine) exist as the resonance hybrid of two canonical formulae. Both these mono-acridines are well ionized as the cation at pH 7.3, and this has an important bearing on their antimicrobial activity (see below and Table 2.10). Further information on the chemistry of the acridines can be found in Albert's excellent book (Albert, 1966).

8.1.2 Antimicrobial activity

The acridines are of considerable interest because they illustrate how small changes in the chemical structure of the molecule cause significant changes in antibacterial activity. The most important limiting factor governing this activity is the degree of ionization, although this must be cationic in nature (Table 2.10). Acridine derivatives that form anions or zwitterions are only poorly antibacterial in comparison to those that form cations. In general terms, if the degree of ionization is less than 33% there is only feeble antibacterial activity, whereas above about 50% there is little further increase in activity (Albert, 1966).

In contrast to the triphenylmethane dyes (Section 8.2), the acridines do not display a selective action against Gram-positive organisms, nor are they inactivated by serum. Acridines compete with H^+ ions for anionic sites on the bacterial cell and are more effective at alkaline than acid pH (Browning *et al.*, 1919–1920). They are relatively slow in their action and are not sporicidal (Foster & Russell, 1971). Resistance to the acridines develops as a result of mutation and indirect selection (Thornley & Yudkin, 1959a,b). Interestingly, acridines can eliminate ('cure') resistance in R^+ strains (see Watanabe, 1963 for an early review).

8.1.3 Uses

For many years, the acridines have held a valuable place in medicine. However, with the advent of antibiotics and other chemotherapeutic agents, they are now used infrequently. Their major use has been the treatment of infected wounds. The first compound to be used medically was acriflavine (a mixture of 3,6-diaminoacridine hydrochloride and 3,6-diamino-10-methylacridinium hydrochloride, the former component being better known as proflavine). Proflavine hemisulphate and 9-aminoacridine (aminacrine) have found use in treating wounds; aminacrine is particularly useful as it is non-staining.

8.2 Triphenylmethane dyes

The most important members of this group are

Table 2.10 Dependence of antibacterial activity of acridines on cationic ionization*

Substance	Predominant type (and percentage) of ionization at pH3 and 37°C	Inhibitory activity
9-Aminoacridine	Cation (99%)	High
9-Aminoacridine-2-carboxylic acid	Zwitterion (99.8%)	Low
Acridine	Neutral molecule (99.7%)	Low
Acridine-9-carboxylic acid	Anion (99.3%)	Low

* Based on the work of Albert and his colleagues (see Albert, 1966).

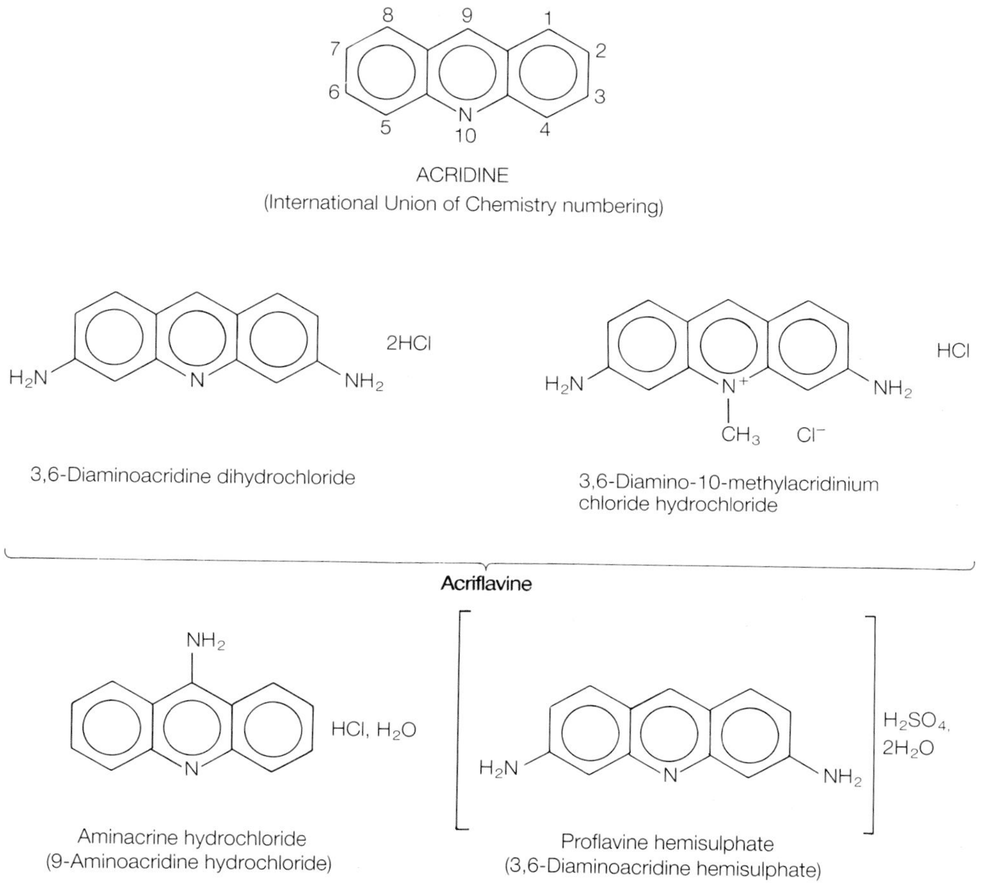

Fig. 2.15 Acridine compounds.

crystal violet, brilliant green and malachite green (Fig. 2.16). These were used as local antiseptics for application to wounds and burns, but were limited in being effective against Gram-positive bacteria (inhibitory concentrations 1 in 750 000 to 1 in 5 000 000) but much less so against Gram-negative organisms, and in suffering a serious decrease in activity in the presence of serum. Their selective activity against Gram-positive bacteria has a practical application in the formulation of selective media for diagnostic purposes, e.g. Crystal Violet Lactose Broth in water filtration control work.

The activity of the triphenylmethane dyes is a property of the pseudobase, the formation which is established by equilibrium between the cation and the base; thus, both the ionization and the equilibrium constants will affect the activity (Albert, 1966). Antimicrobial potency depends on external pH, being more pronounced at alkaline values (Moats & Maddox, 1978).

For an extensive account of the antibacterial dyestuffs see Browning (1976).

8.3 Quinones

Some members of this group of dyes are important agricultural fungicides. The quinones are natural dyes which give colour to many forms of plant and animal life. Chemically (Fig. 2.17), they are diketocyclohexadienes; the simplest member is 1,4-benzoquinone. In terms of toxicity to bacteria, moulds and yeast, naphthaquinones are the most

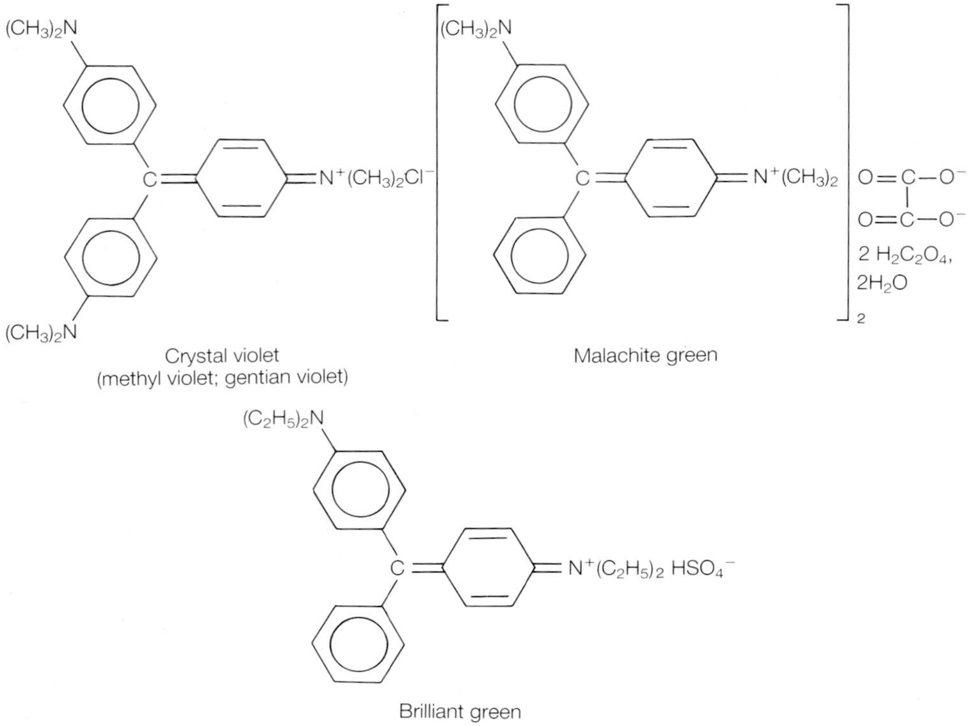

Fig. 2.16 Triphenylmethane dyes.

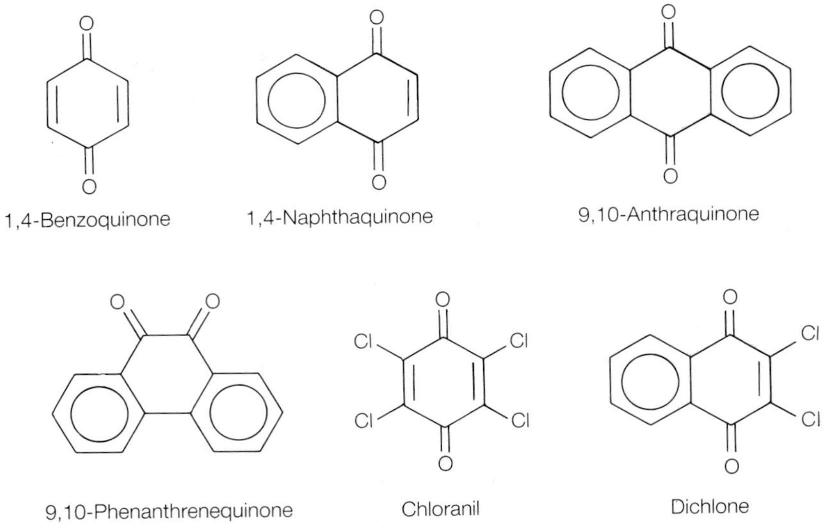

Fig. 2.17 Quinones.

toxic, followed (in this order) by phenanthrenequinones, benzoquinones and anthraquinones.

Antimicrobial activity is increased by halogenation, and two powerful agricultural fungicides are chloranil (tetrachloro-1,4-benzoquinone) and dichlone (2,3-dichloro-1,4-naphthaquinone): see D'Arcy, 1971 and Owens, 1969.

9 HALOGENS

The most important microbicidal halogens are iodine compounds, chlorine compounds and bromine. Fluorine is far too toxic, irritant and corrosive for use as a disinfectant (Trueman, 1971) although, interestingly, fluoride ions have been shown to induce bacterial lysis (Lesher *et al.*, 1977). This section will deal predominantly with iodine, iodophors and chlorine-releasing compounds (those which are bactericidal by virtue of 'available chlorine'), but bromine, iodoform and (considered here for convenience) chloroform will be considered briefly.

9.1 Iodine compounds

9.1.1 Free iodine

Iodine was first employed in the treatment of wounds some 140 years ago and has been shown to be an efficient microbicidal agent with rapid lethal effects against bacteria and their spores, moulds, yeasts and viruses (Gershenfeld, 1956; Anon, 1965; Sykes, 1965; Russell, 1971a; Kelsey & Maurer, 1972). It is normally used in aqueous or alcoholic solution; it is only sparingly soluble in cold water but solutions can be made with potassium iodide. Iodine is less reactive chemically than chlorine, and is less affected by the presence of organic matter than is the latter; however, it must be added that whereas the activity of high concentrations of iodine is little affected by organic matter that of low concentrations is significantly lowered. The activity of iodine is greater at acid than at alkaline pH; see Table 2.11. Unfortunately, iodine solutions stain fabric and tend to be toxic.

9.1.2 Iodophors

Certain surface-active agents can solubilize iodine to form compounds (the iodophors) which retain the germicidal action, but not the undesirable properties of iodine. The uses of the iodophors as detergent-sterilizers have been described by Blatt & Maloney (1961) and Davis (1962). The term iodophor itself means, literally, iodine-carrier. It must be noted that different concentrations of iodophors are used for antiseptic and disinfectant purposes, and that the lower concentrations employed in antisepsis are not claimed to be sporicidal (Favero, 1985).

Gershenfeld (1962) has shown that povidone-iodine is sporicidal, and Lowbury *et al.* (1964) found that povidone-iodine compresses reduced the numbers of viable spores of *Bacillus globigii* on the skin by >99% in 1 h, suggesting that this iodophor had a part to play in removing transient sporing organisms from operation sites. More recently, the importance of povidone-iodine in preventing wound infection has been re-emphasized as a result of the studies of Galland *et al.* (1977) and Lacey (1979).

Table 2.11 Effect of pH on the antimicrobial activity of iodine compounds*

pH	Active form	Comment
Acid and neutral	I_2 (diatomic iodine) Hypo-iodous acid	Highly bactericidal Less bactericidal
Alkaline	Hypo-iodite ion Iodate (IO_3^-), iodide (I^-) and tri-iodide (I_3^-) ions	Even less bactericidal All inactive

* Based on Trueman (1971).

The concentration of free iodine in aqueous or alcoholic iodine solutions is responsible for microbicidal activity. Likewise, the concentration of free iodine in an iodophor is responsible for its activity: this was proved by Allawala & Riegelman (1953), who made a log–log plot of the killing time against the amount of free iodine, and who showed that the 99% killing time against *B. cereus* spores was a function of the concentration of free iodine in the presence or absence of added surface-active agent.

In most iodophor preparations the carrier is usually a non-ionic surfactant in which the iodine is present as micellar aggregates. When an iodophor is diluted with water, dispersion of the micelles occurs and most (80–90%) of the iodine is slowly liberated. Dilution below the critical micelle concentration (c.m.c.) of the non-ionic surface-active agent results in iodine being in simple aqueous solution. A paradoxical effect of dilution on the activity of povidone-iodine has been observed (Gottardi; 1985; Rackur 1985). As the degree of dilution increases, then beyond a certain point bactericidal activity also increases. An explanation of this arises from consideration of physicochemical studies which demonstrate that, starting from a 10% commercially available povidone-iodine solution, the concentration of non-complexed iodine (I_2) initially increases as dilution increases. This reaches a maximum value at about 0·1% and then falls. In contrast, the content of other iodine species, e.g. I^- and I_3^- decreases continuously. These properties affect the sporicidal activity of iodine solutions (Williams & Russell, 1991).

The iodophors, as stated above, are microbicidal, with activity over a wide pH range. The presence of a surface-active agent as carrier improves the wetting capacity. Iodophors may be used in the dairy industry (when employed in the cleansing of dairy plant it is important to keep the pH on the acid side to ensure adequate removal of milkstone) and for skin and wound disinfection. Iodophors such as Betadine, in the form of alcoholic solutions, are widely used in the USA for disinfection of hands for operation sites (see also Chapter 13). Pseudobacteraemia (false-positive blood cultures) has been found to result from the use of contaminated antiseptics. Craven *et al.* (1981) have described such an outbreak of pseudobacteraemia caused by a 10% povidone-iodine solution contaminated with *Pseudomonas cepacia*.

9.1.3 Iodoform

When applied to tissues, iodoform (CHI_3) slowly releases elemental iodine. It thus has some weak antimicrobial activity. It is not often used in practice, and thus will not be considered further.

9.2 Chlorine compounds

9.2.1 Chlorine-releasing compounds

Until the development of Chlorinated Soda Solution, Surgical (Dakin's Solution) in 1916, the commercial chlorine-releasing disinfectants then in use were not of constant composition and contained free alkali and sometimes free chlorine. The stability of free available chlorine in solution is dependent on a number of factors, especially the following (Dychdala 1983):

1 chlorine concentration;
2 pH of the solution;
3 presence of organic matter;
4 light.

These factors are considered below.

The types of chlorine compounds that are most frequently used are the hypochlorites and *N*-chloro compounds (Trueman, 1971; Dychdala, 1983; Gardner & Peel, 1986).

Hypochlorites. These have a wide antibacterial spectrum, although they are less active against spores than against non-sporulating bacteria and have been stated to be of low activity against mycobacteria (Anon, 1965; Croshaw, 1971). Recent studies have suggested that chlorine compounds are among the most potent sporicidal agents (Kelsey *et al.*, 1974; Coates & Death, 1979; Death & Coates, 1979). The hypochlorites show activity against lipid and non-lipid viruses (Morris & Darlow, 1971).

Two factors which can affect quite markedly their antimicrobial action are organic matter, since chlorine is a highly reactive chemical, and pH, the hypochlorites being more active at acid than at alkaline pH (Table 2.12). The former problem can,

Table 2.12 Factors influencing activity of hypochlorites

Factor	Result
pH	Activity decreased by increasing pH (see text and use of NaOH, also)
Concentration of hypochlorite (pH constant)	Activity depends on concentration of available chlorine
Organic matter	Antimicrobial activity reduced considerably
Other agents	Potentiation may be achieved by **1** addition of ammonia **2** 1.5–4% sodium hydroxide* **3** addition of small amounts of bromide†

* Cousins & Allan (1967).
† In the presence of bromide, hypochlorite also has an enhanced effect in bleaching cellulosic fibres.

to some extent, be overcome by increasing the hypochlorite concentration, and it has been shown that the sporicidal activity of sodium hypochlorite (200 parts/10^6 available chlorine) can be potentiated by 1.5–4% sodium hydroxide, notwithstanding the above comment about pH (see Russell, 1971a, 1982). The sporicidal activity can also be potentiated by low concentrations of ammonia (Weber & Levine, 1944) and in the presence of bromine (Farkas-Himsley, 1964): chlorine-resistant bacteria have been found to be unaffected by bromine but to be readily killed by chlorine–bromine solutions (Farkas-Himsley, 1964). Such mixtures could be of value in the disinfection of natural waters.

Organic chlorine compounds. *N*-chloro compounds, which contain the =N—Cl group, show microbicidal activity. Examples of such compounds, the chemical structures of which are shown in Fig. 2.18, are chloramine-T, dichloramine-T, halazone, halane, dichloroisocyanuric acid, sodium and potassium dichloroisocyanurates and trichloroisocyanuric acid. All appear to hydrolyse in water to produce an imino (=NH) group. Their action is claimed to be slower than that of the hypochlorites, although this can be increased under acidic conditions (Cousins & Allen, 1967). A series of imidazolidinone *N,N'*-dihalamine disinfectants has been described (Williams *et al*., 1987, 1988; Worley *et al*., 1987). The dibromo compound (Fig. 2.18) was the most rapidly acting bactericide, particularly under halogen demand-free conditions, with the mixed (bromo-chloro-compound, Fig. 2.18) occupying an intermediate position. However, when stability of the compounds in the series was also taken into account, it was concluded that the mixed product was the most useful as an aqueous disinfectant solution.

Coates (1985) found that solutions of sodium hypochlorite (NaClO) and sodium dichloroisocyanurate (NaDCC) containing the same levels of available chlorine had similar bactericidal activity despite significant differences in their pH. NaDCC solutions are less susceptible than NaClO to inactivation by organic matter (Bloomfield & Miles, 1979a,b; Bloomfield & Uso, 1985; Coates, 1985, 1988).

Uses of chlorine-releasing compounds. Chlorinated Soda Solution (Dakin's Solution) which contains 0.5–0.55% (5000–5500 parts/10^6) available chlorine, and Chlorinated Lime and Boric Acid Solution (Eusol), which contains 0.25% (2500 parts/10^6) available chlorine, are chlorine disinfectants which contain chlorinated lime and boric acid. Dakin's Solution is used as a wound disinfectant or, when appropriately diluted, as an irrigation solution for bladder and vaginal infections. Eusol is used as a wound disinfectant but Morgan (1989) has suggested that chlorinated solutions delay wound healing.

Chlorine gas has been employed to disinfect public water supplies. Sodium hypochlorite is

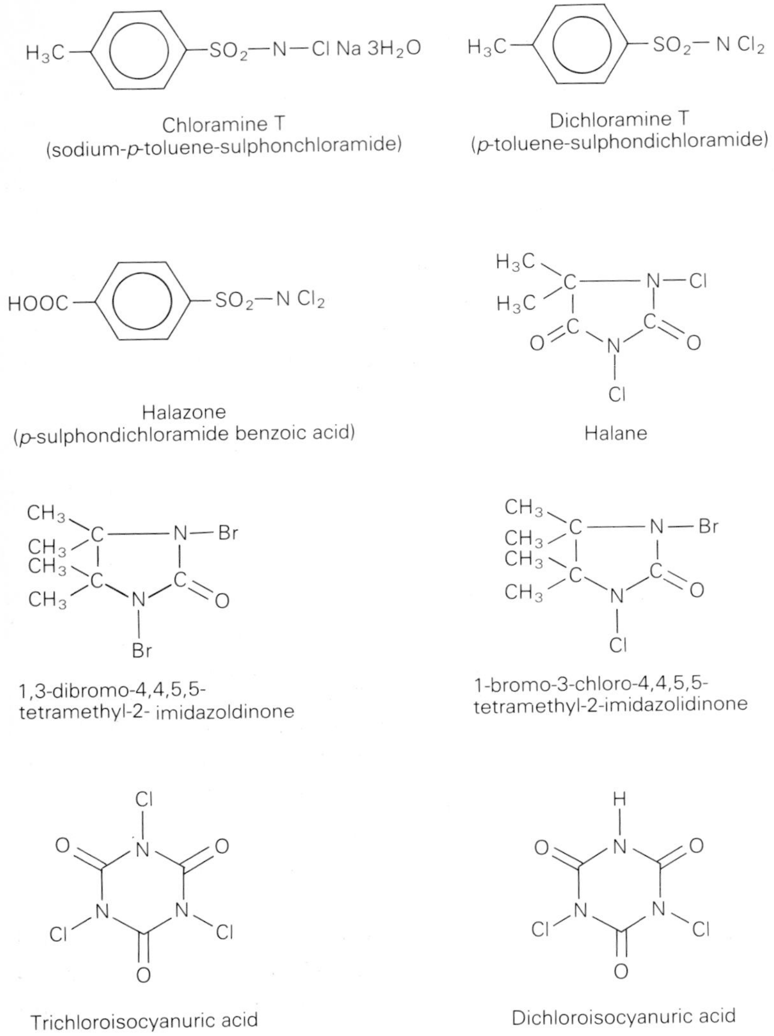

Fig. 2.18 Organic chlorine compounds.

normally used for the disinfection of swimming pools.

Blood spillages containing human immunodeficiency virus (HIV) or hepatitis B virus (HBV) can be disinfected with NaOCl solutions containing 10 000 ppm available chlorine (Working Party, 1985). NaDCC as powder or granules added directly to the spillage is also effective, may give a larger margin of safety because a higher concentration of available chlorine is achieved and is also less susceptible to inactivation by organic matter, as pointed out above (Coates, 1988). Furthermore, only a very short contact time (2–3 min) is necessary before the spill can be removed safely (Coates & Wilson, 1989). Chlorine-releasing powder formulations with high available chlorine concentrations are particularly useful for this purpose (Bloomfield & Miller, 1989; Bloomfield *et al.*, 1990).

9.2.2 Chloroform

Chloroform ($CHCl_3$) has been used as a preservative in many pharmaceutical products intended for internal use, for more than a century. In recent years, with the object of minimizing microbial contamination, this use has been extended. Various authors, notably Westwood & Pin-Lim (1972) and Lynch & Wilson (1977), have shown chloroform to be a bactericidal agent, although it is not sporicidal and its high volatility means that a fall in concentration could result in microbial growth. For details of its antibacterial activity in aqueous solutions and in mixtures containing insoluble powders and the losses, through volatilization, under 'in-use' conditions, the paper by Lynch & Wilson (1977) should certainly be consulted.

The present position is that chloroform may be used in oral pharmaceutical products at concentrations of no greater than 0.5%; in cosmetic products its use (at a maximum concentration of 4%) will be restricted to toothpaste. It is totally banned in the USA.

10 QUINOLINE AND ISOQUINOLINE DERIVATIVES

There are three main groups of derivatives: 8-hydroxyquinoline derivatives, 4-aminoquinaldinium derivatives and isoquinoline derivatives. They are described in Figs 2.19 and 2.20.

10.1 8-Hydroxyquinoline derivatives

8-Hydroxyquinoline (oxine) possesses antibacterial activity against Gram-positive bacteria, but much less against Gram-negative organisms. It also has antifungal activity, although this occurs at a slower rate. Other useful compounds are depicted in Fig. 2.19(b). Like oxine, clioquinol, chlorquinandol and halquinol have very low water-solubilities, and are generally employed as applications to the skin. An interesting feature of their activity (discussed in more detail in Chapter 9) is the fact that they are chelating agents which are active only in the presence of certain metal ions.

10.2 4-Aminoquinaldinium derivatives

These are QACs (see Fig. 2.20) which also fall into this grouping. The most important members are laurolinium acetate and dequalinium chloride (a bis-QAC). Both compounds possess antibacterial activity, especially against Gram-positive bacteria (Collier *et al.*, 1959; Cox & D'Arcy, 1962), as well as significant activity against many species of yeasts and fungi (Frier, 1971; D'Arcy. 1971). Their activity is decreased in the presence of lecithin; serum decreases the effectiveness of laurolinium but not of dequalinium. Dequalinium chloride is used as lozenges or paint in the treatment of infections of the mouth and throat. Laurolinium has been used as a pre-operative skin disinfectant, although this was never widely adopted.

10.3 Isoquinoline derivatives

The most important isoquinoline derivative is hedaquinium chloride [Fig. 2.19(c)], another bis-quaternary salt. This possesses antibacterial and antifungal activity (Collier *et al.*, 1959; D'Arcy, 1971), and is regarded as one of the most active antifungal QAC agents (D'Arcy, 1971).

11 ALCOHOLS

Several alcohols have been shown to possess antimicrobial properties. Generally, the alcohols have rapid bactericidal activity (Morton, 1950) including acid-fast bacilli, but are not sporicidal and have poor activity against many viruses. Their chemical structures are shown in Fig. 2.21.

11.1 Ethyl alcohol (ethanol)

Ethanol is rapidly lethal to non-sporulating bacteria, destroys mycobacteria (Croshaw, 1971) but is ineffective at all concentrations against bacterial spores (Russell, 1971a). The presence of water is essential for its activity, but concentrations below 30% have little action. The most effective concentration is about 60–70% (Price, 1950; see also Croshaw, 1977; Morton, 1977; Scott & Gorman, 1987). Solutions of iodine or chlorhexidine in 70%

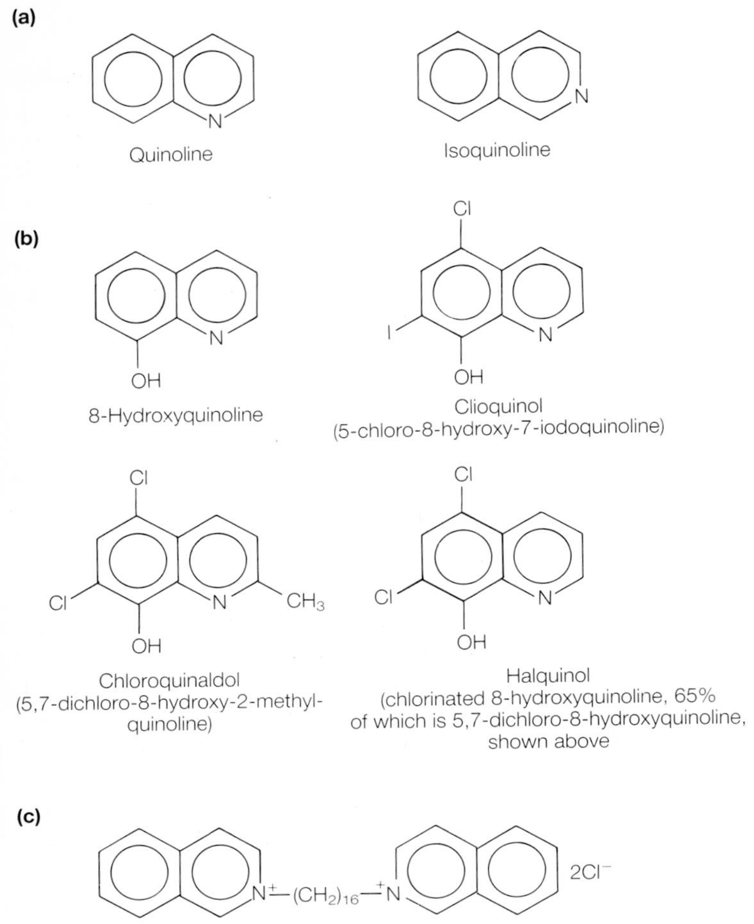

Fig. 2.19 (a) Structures of quinoline and isoquinoline; (b) 8-hydroxyquinoline derivatives with antimicrobial properties; (c) hedaquinium chloride.

alcohol may be employed for the pre-operative disinfection of the skin. Ethanol is the alcohol of choice in cosmetic products because of its relative lack of odour and irritation (Bandelin, 1977).

11.2 Methyl alcohol (methanol)

Methyl alcohol has poor antibacterial activity and is not sporicidal (Russell, 1971a; Bandelin, 1977; Coates & Death, 1978; Death & Coates, 1979). Furthermore, it is potentially toxic, and is thus little used. However, freshly prepared mixtures of alcohols (especially methanol) and sodium hypochlorite are highly sporicidal (Coates & Death, 1978).

11.3 Isopropyl alcohol (isopropanol)

Isopropyl and *n*-propyl alcohols are more effective bactericides than ethanol (Anon, 1965; Kelsey & Maurer, 1972), but are not sporicidal. They are miscible with water in all proportions, but isopropanol has a less objectionable odour than *n*-propanol, and is considered as a suitable alternative to ethanol in various cosmetic products, either as a solvent or as a preservative (Bandelin, 1977).

11.4 Benzyl alcohol

In addition to having antimicrobial properties, benzyl alcohol is also a weak local anaesthetic. It

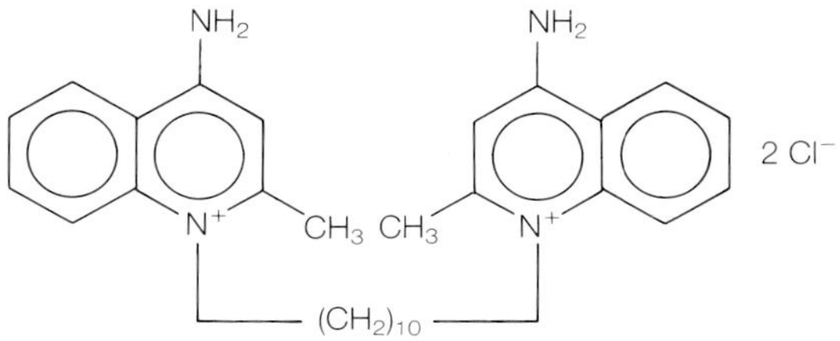

Dequalinium chloride

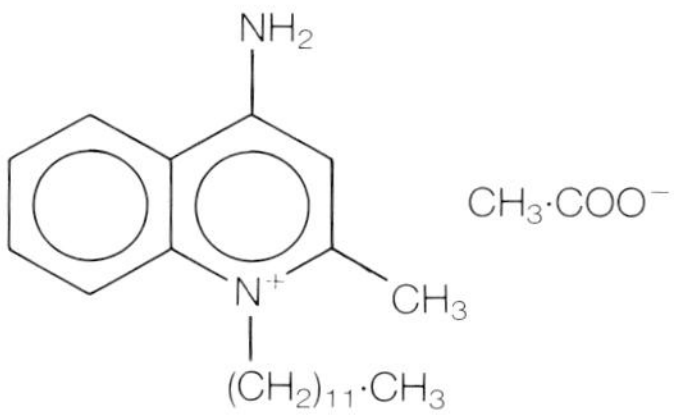

Laurolinium acetate

Fig. 2.20 4-Aminoquinaldinium derivatives with antimicrobial properties.

has activity against Gram-positive and Gram-negative bacteria and against moulds (D'Arcy, 1971).

11.5 Phenylethanol (phenylethyl alcohol)

Phenylethyl alcohol is an antimicrobial agent with selective activity against various bacteria (especially Gram-negative: Lilley & Brewer, 1953) and which has been recommended for use as a preservative in ophthalmic solutions, often in conjunction with another microbicide. Because of its higher activity against Gram-negative bacteria, phenylethyl alcohol may be incorporated into culture media for isolating Gram-positive bacteria from mixed flora, e.g. Phenylethyl Alcohol Agar.

11.6 Bronopol

Bronopol, 2-bromo-2-nitropropan-1,3-diol, is an aliphatic halogenonitro compound with antibacterial and antifungal activity, although bacterial spores are unaffected. It is effective against *Ps. aeruginosa*. Its activity is reduced somewhat by 10% serum and to a greater extent by sulphydryl compounds, but is unaffected by 1% polysorbate or 0.1% lecithin. It has a half-life of about 96 days at pH 8 and 25°C (Toler, 1985).

Bronopol is most stable under acid conditions; the initial decomposition appears to involve the liberation of formaldehyde and the formulation of bromonitroethanol (Fig. 2.22(a)). A second-order

$CH_3{\cdot}CH_2{\cdot}OH$

Ethanol

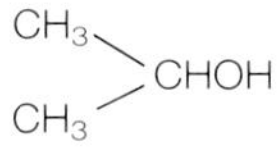

Isopropanol
(Propan-2-ol)

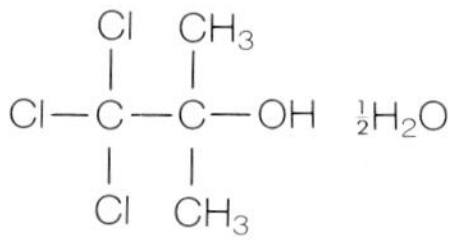

Chlorbutanol
(trichloro-t-butanol)

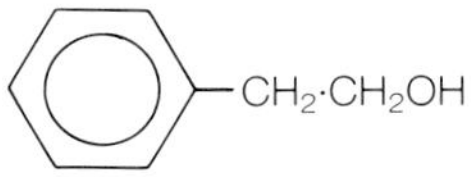

2-Phenylethanol

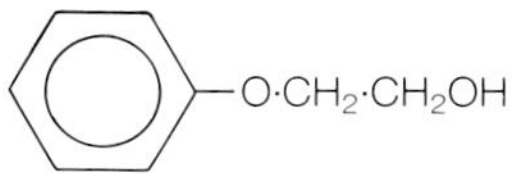

2-Phenoxyethanol

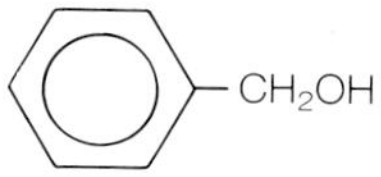

Benzyl alcohol
(Phenylmethanol)

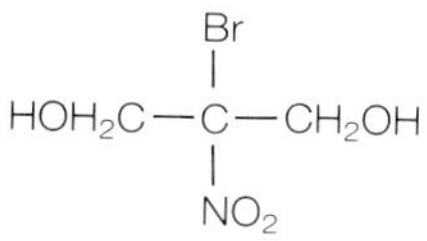

Bronopol
(2-bromo-2-nitropropan-1,3-diol)

Fig. 2.21 Alcohols.

reaction involving bronopol and formaldehyde occurs simultaneously to produce 2-hydroxymethyl-2-nitro-1,3-propanediol [Fig. 2.22(b)] which itself decomposes with the loss of formaldehyde.

Details of the microbiological activity, chemical stability, toxicology and uses of Bronopol are documented by Bryce *et al.* (1978), Croshaw (1984), Toler (1985) and Rossmore & Sondossi (1988).

11.7 Phenoxyethanol

The antimicrobial activity of phenoxyethanol and other preservatives has been reviewed by Gucklhorn (1970, 1971). Phenoxyethanol was shown by Berry (1944) to possess significant activity against *Ps. aeruginosa*, but it has less activity against other Gram-negative organisms or against Gram-positive bacteria.

11.8 Chlorbutanol (chlorbutol)

Chlorbutol is an antibacterial and antifungal agent. It has been used, at a concentration of 0.5% w/v, as a bactericide in injections. One drawback to its employment is its instability, since at acid pH it decomposes at the high temperature used in sterilization processes into hydrochloric acid, and at alkaline pH it is unstable at room temperature.

11.9 2,4-Dichlorobenzyl alcohol

This substance is a white powder, soluble in water to 1% and readily soluble in alcohols. Its ionization is negligible for all practical purposes and it is thus active over a wide pH range. It has a broad spectrum of activity, but both pseudomonads and *Staph. aureus* show some resistance to it (Toler, 1985).

12 PEROXYGENS

12.1 Hydrogen peroxide

Hydrogen peroxide (H_2O_2) is a familiar household antiseptic. It was discovered in 1818 and was early recognized as possessing antibacterial properties. These were extensively investigated in 1893 by Traugott.

Hydrogen peroxide is available as a solution designated as 20- or 10-volume, a means of indicating its strength by describing the volume (20 or 10, respectively) of oxygen evolved from 1 volume of the peroxide solution. Strengths for industrial use of 35, 50 or 90% are available. Hydrogen peroxide solutions are unstable, and benzoic acid or other suitable substance is added as a stabilizer.

Hydrogen peroxide solutions possess disinfectant, antiseptic and deodorant properties. When in contact with living tissue and many metals they decompose, evolving oxygen. Hydrogen peroxide is bactericidal and sporicidal (Russell, 1982, 1990a,b, 1991a,b; Baldry, 1983; Baldry & Fraser, 1988) and is believed to act as a generator of free hydroxyl radicals that can cause DNA strand breakage. It is an oxidizing agent and reacts with oxidizable material, for example alkali nitrites used in anti-corrosion solutions. It is environmentally

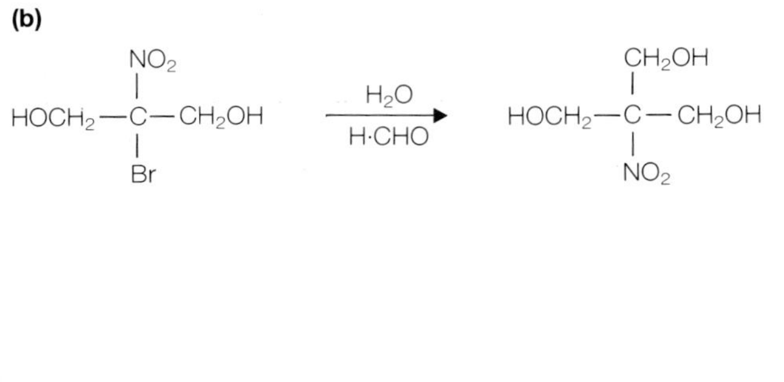

Fig. 2.22 (a) Initial process in the decomposition of bronopol; (b) second-order reaction involving bronopol and formaldehyde.

friendly because its decomposition products are oxygen and water.

Hydrogen peroxide has been used in aseptic packaging technology.

12.2 Peracetic acid

Peracetic acid, $CH_3{\cdot}COOOH$, was introduced as an antibacterial agent in 1955. It is available commercially as a 15% aqueous solution in which an equilibrium exists between peracetic acid and its decomposition products acetic acid ($CH_3{\cdot}COOOH$) and hydrogen peroxide.

Peracetic acid solution has a broad spectrum of activity, including bacteria and their spores, moulds, yeasts, algae and viruses. It finds extensive use in the food industry and for disinfecting sewage sludge. It is a powerful oxidizing agent and in certain situations can be corrosive. The great advantage of peracetic acid is that its final decomposition products, oxygen and water, are innocuous.

More comprehensive data on peracetic acid are provided by Baldry (1983), Baldry & Fraser (1988), and Fraser (1986).

13 CHELATING AGENTS

This section will deal briefly with chelating agents based on ethylenediamine tetraacetic acid (EDTA). EDTA has been the subject of intensive investigation in recent years, and its antibacterial activity has been reviewed by Russell (1971b), Leive (1974) and Wilkinson (1975). The chemical nature of its complexation with metals has been well considered by West (1969).

The chemical structures of EDTA, ethylenedioxybis [ethyliminodi(acetic acid)] (EGTA), *N*-hydroxyethylethylenediamine-*N,N′N′*-triacetic acid (HDTA), *trans*-1,2-diaminocyclohexane-*NNN′ N′*-tetraacetic acid (CDTA), iminodiacetic acid (IDA) and nitrilotriacetic acid (NTA) are provided in Fig. 2.23. Table 2.13 lists their chelating and antibacterial activities.

13.1 EDTA

In medicine, EDTA is commonly employed as the sodium or calcium–sodium salts. Sodium calcium edetate is used in the treatment of chronic lead poisoning, and the sodium salts are used clinically to chelate calcium ions, thereby decreasing serum calcium. EDTA is also used as a stabilizing agent in certain injections and eye-drop preparations (Russell *et al.*, 1967).

The most important early findings, in a microbiological context, were made by Repaske (1956, 1958) who showed that certain Gram-negative bacteria became sensitive to the enzyme lysozyme in the presence of EDTA in tris buffer and that EDTA alone induced lysis of *Ps. aeruginosa*. The importance of tris itself has also been recognized (Leive & Kollin, 1967; Neu 1969) since it appears to affect the permeability of the wall of various Gram-negative bacteria, as well as the nucleotide pool and RNA, which may be degraded. A lysozyme–tris–EDTA system in the presence

Table 2.13 Properties of chelating agents

Property	EDTA	EGTA	HDTA	CDTA	IDA	NTA
Log stability constant*						
Ba	7.76	8.41	5.54	7.99	1.67	4.82
Ca	10.70	11.0	8.0	12.5	2.59	6.41
Mg	8.69	5.21	5.2	10.32	2.94	5.41
Zn	16.26	14.5	14.5	18.67	7.03	10.45
Antibacterial activity†						
Alone	Good		Good	Good	Low	Low
As a potentiating agent for disinfectants	Yes		Yes	Yes	Somewhat	Somewhat

* Abstracted from the information supplied by West (1969).
† Based on the activity against *Ps. aeruginosa* described by Roberts *et al.* (1970) and Haque & Russell (1974a,b).

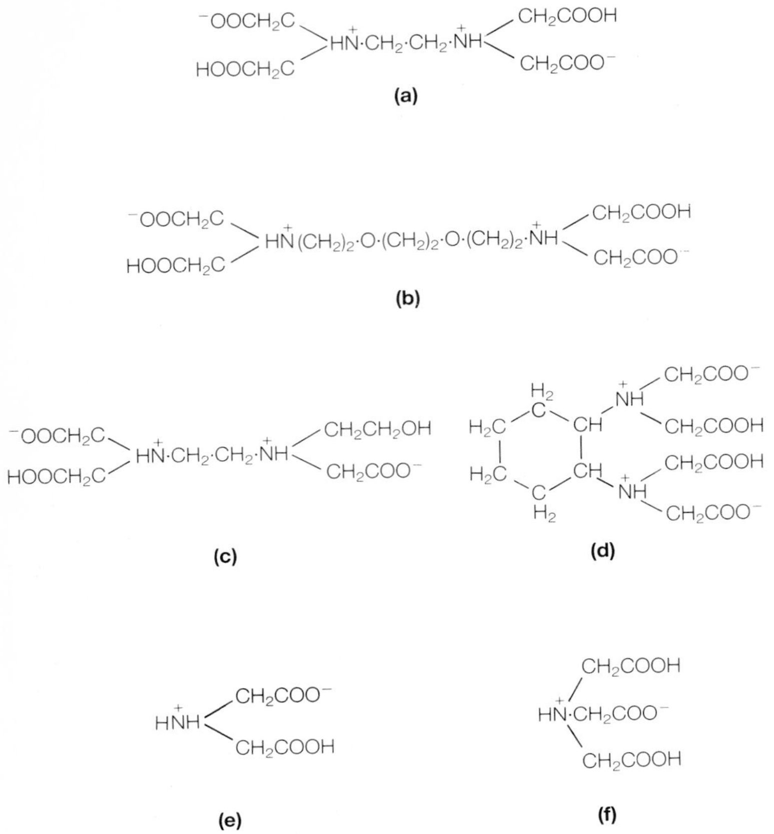

Fig. 2.23 Chelating agents
(a) Ethylenediamine tetraacetic acid (EDTA): (b) ethylenedioxybis [ethylimino-di-(acetic acid)] (EGTA): (c) *N*-hydroxyethyl-ethylenediamine-*N,N'N'*-triacetic acid (HDTA): (d) *trans*-1,2-diaminocyclohexane-*NNN' N'*-tetraacetic acid (CDTA):
(e) iminodiacetic acid (IDA):
(f) nitrilotriacetic acid (NTA).

of sucrose is a standard technique for producing spheroplasts/protoplasts in Gram-negative bacteria (McQuillen, 1960). During this conversion, several enzymes are released into the surrounding medium. A technique known as 'cold shock', which involves treating *E. coli* with EDTA + tris in hypertonic sucrose followed by rapid dispersion in cold magnesium chloride—thus producing a sudden osmotic shift—again results in the release of enzymes but without destroying the viability of the cells.

In the context of disinfection, EDTA is most important in that it will potentiate the activity of many antibacterial agents against many types of Gram-negative but not Gram-positive bacteria. This was clearly shown by Gray & Wilkinson (1965) and has since been confirmed and extended (Russell, 1971b; Wilkinson, 1975). An interesting off-shoot was the development of 'Dettol Chelate', which consists of chloroxylenol and EDTA in a suitable formulation; unlike chloroxylenol alone, this new product has significant activity against *Ps. aeruginosa* strains (Russell & Furr, 1977). EDTA induces a non-specific increase in the permeability of the outer envelope of Gram-negative cells (Leive, 1974), thereby allowing more penetration of non-related agents.

The mechanism of action of EDTA is dealt with in Chapter 9.

13.2 Other chelating agents

Chelating agents other than EDTA are described chemically in Fig. 2.23, and some of their properties (based in part on the excellent book of West, 1969) are listed in Table 2.13. EGTA forms a stronger complex with Ca than does EDTA, whereas for most other metals, except Ba and Hg, it is a weaker complexing agent than EDTA. Notably, there is a divergency of 5.79 log K units between the stability constants of the Ca and Mg complexes with EGTA (West, 1969). CDTA has superior complexing powers over EDTA and is better than all the other chelating agents listed in complexing Mg^{2+} ions. From a microbiological point of view, CDTA was found by Roberts *et al.* (1970) and Haque & Russell (1974a,b) to be the most toxic compound to *Ps. aeruginosa* and other Gram-negative bacteria in terms of leakage, lysis and loss of viability and in extracting metal ions from isolated cell envelopes (Haque & Russell, 1976).

HDTA corresponds to EDTA, one acetic acid of the latter molecule being replaced by a hydroxyethyl group. Its complexes are invariably less stable than those of EDTA. In a microbiological context, HDTA was found (Haque & Russell, 1976) to be rather less effective than EDTA.

IDA forms weak complexes with most metal ions, whereas NTA is more reactive. Both have little activity against *Ps. aeruginosa* although both, to some extent, potentiate the activity of other agents (disinfectants) against this organism.

14 PERMEABILIZERS

Permeabilizers (permeabilizing agents) are chemicals that increase bacterial permeability to biocides. Such chemicals include chelating agents, described above in Section 13, polycations, lactoferrin and transferrin.

14.1 Polycations

Polycations such as poly-L-lysine (lysine$_{20}$; PLL) induce LPS release from the outer membrane of Gram-negative bacteria. PLL-treated organisms show greatly increased sensitivity to hydrophobic antibiotics (Vaara & Vaara, 1983a,b; Viljanen, 1987) but responses to biocides do not appear to have been studied.

14.2 Lactoferrin

Lactoferrin is an iron-binding protein that acts as a chelator, inducing partial LPS loss from the outer membrane of Gram-negative bacteria (Ellison *et al.*, 1988).

14.3 Transferrin

This iron-binding protein is believed to have a similar effect to lactoferrin (Ellison *et al.* 1988). Both are worthy of further studies as potentially important permeabilizers.

15 HEAVY METAL DERIVATIVES

The historical introduction (Chapter 1) has already described the early use of high concentrations of salt employed empirically in the salting process as a preservative for meat, and the use of copper and silver vessels to prevent water from becoming fouled by microbial growth. Salting is still used in some parts of the world as a meat preservative and salts of heavy metals, especially silver, mercury, copper and, more recently, organotin, are still used as antimicrobial agents. The metal derivatives of copper, mercury, silver and tin which find use as antiseptics and preservatives will be discussed in this chapter. Kushner (1971) has reviewed the action of solutes other than heavy metal derivatives on micro-organisms.

In addition to possessing antimicrobial activity in their own right, many metal ions are necessary for the activity of other drugs. A typical example is 8-hydroxyquinoline (Section 10.1) which needs Fe^{2+} for activity. The interesting relationship between antimicrobial compounds and metal cations has been reviewed by Weinberg (1957).

15.1 Copper compounds

Although the pharmacopoeias list a number of recipes containing copper salts (sulphate, actetate, citrate) as ingredients of antiseptic astringent lotions, the main antimicrobial use of copper derivatives is in algicides and fungicides. Cu^{2+} is pre-eminently an algicidal ion and at a final concentration of 0.5–2.9 μg/ml, as copper sulphate, it has been used to keep swimming pools free from algae. Copper is thought to act by the poisoning effect of the copper(II) ion on thiol enzymes and possibly other thiol groups in microbial cells.

Copper sulphate and copper sulphate mixed with lime, Bordeaux mixture, introduced in 1885, are used as fungicides in plant protection. The latter formulation proved especially efficacious as it formed a slow-release copper complex which was not easily washed from foliage. It was said to be first used as a deterrent to human predators of the grape crop and its antifungal properties emerged later. Copper metal, in powder form, finds an interesting application as an additive to cements and concretes. Its function is to inhibit microbial attack on the ingredients of these artificial products. The uses of copper metal here, and as vessels for drinking water in the ancient world, illustrate a phenomenon which has been called the oligodynamic action of metals (Langwell, 1932). Metals are slightly soluble in water and in the case of copper, and also silver (*q.v.*), a sufficient concentration of ions in solution is achieved to inhibit microbial growth. Copper complexes, e.g. copper naphthenate and copper-7-hydroxyquinolate, have been particularly successful in the preservation of cotton fabrics. Wood, paper and paint have also been successfully preserved with copper compounds. As the preservation of paints, timber etc. will be dealt with elsewhere in this volume (see Chapter 17) this chapter will merely summarize, by means of Table 2.14, some copper compounds and their application.

Table 2.14 Copper compounds used as preservatives and some examples of their application.

Compound	Example(s) of application
Copper metal	Concrete
Copper sulphate	Wood, water
Cuprammonium hydroxide	
Cuprammonium carbonate	
Cuprammonium fluoride	Fabrics especially cellulosics
Copper chromate	
Copper borate	
Cuprous oxide	Paints, dark shades
Copper acetoarsenite	Paints, green shades
Copper oleate	
Copper stearate	Fabrics
Copper formate	
Copper naphthenate	Wood, fabric
Copper-8-hydroxyquinolate	Paint, papers
Copper phenylsalicylate	
Copper pentachlorphenate	Fabric

15.2 Silver compounds

Silver and its compounds have found a place in antimicrobial application from ancient times to the present day. Apart from the use of silver vessels to maintain water in a potable state the first systematic use of a silver compound in medicine was its use in the prophylaxis of ophthalmia neonatorum by the installation of silver nitrate solution into the eyes of newborn infants. Silver compounds have been used in recent years in the prevention of infection in burns, but are not very effective in treatment. An organism frequently associated with such infections is *Ps. aeruginosa*, and Brown & Anderson (1968) have discussed the effectiveness of Ag^+ in the killing of this organism. Amongst the Enterobacteriaceae, plasmids may carry genes specifying resistance to antibiotics and to metals. Plasmid-mediated resistance to silver salts is of particular importance in the hospital environment because silver nitrate and silver sulphadiazine (AgSu) may be used topically for preventing infections in severe burns (Russell, 1985).

As might be imagined, silver nitrate is a somewhat astringent compound, below 10^{-4} M a protein precipitant, and attempts to reduce this undesirable propensity while maintaining antimicrobial potency have been made. A device much used in pharmaceutical formulation to promote slow release of a potent substance is to combine it with a high molecular weight polymer. By mixing silver oxide or silver nitrate with gelatin or albumen a water-soluble adduct is obtained which slowly releases silver ions but lacks the caustic astringency of silver nitrate. A similar slow-release compound has been prepared by combining silver with disodiumdinaphthylmethane disulphate (Goldberg *et al.*, 1950).

The oligodynamic action of silver (see Langwell, 1932), already referred to in the historical introduction (Chapter 1) and above, has been exploited in a water purification system employing what is called katadyn silver. Here, metallic silver is coated onto sand used in filters for water purification. Silver-coated charcoal has been used in a similar fashion (Bigger & Griffiths, 1933; Brandes, 1934; Gribbard, 1933; Moiseev, 1934).

15.3 Mercury compounds

Mercury, long a fascination for early technologists (alchemists, medical practitioners, etc.) was used in medicine by the Arabian physicians. In the 1850s mercury salts comprised, with phenol, the hypochlorites and iodine, the complement of topical antimicrobial drugs at the physician's disposal. Mercuric chloride was used and evaluated by Robert Koch and by Geppert. Nowadays its use in medicine has decreased, although a number of organic derivatives of mercury (Fig. 2.24) are used as bacteriostatic and fungistatic agents and as preservatives and bactericides in injections; examples include mercurochrome, nitromersol, thiomersal and phenylmercuric nitrate (Fig. 2.24). Salts such as the stearate, oleate and naphthenate were, until much more recently, extensively employed in the preservation of wood, textiles, paints and leather to quote a few examples (see Table 2.15). With the advent of a major health disaster in Japan due to mercury waste, feeling is hardening all over the world against the use of mercury in any form where it might pollute the environment, and it is unlikely that the inclusion of mercury in any product where environmental pollution may ensue will be countenanced by regulatory authorities.

Mercury resistance is inducible and is not the result of training or tolerance. Plasmids conferring resistance are of two types: (i) 'narrow spectrum', encoding resistance to Hg(II) and to a few specified organomercurials; (ii) 'broad spectrum', encoding resistance to those in (i) plus other organomercury compounds (Foster, 1983). In (i) there is enzymatic reduction of mercury to Hg metal and its vaporization, and in (ii) enzymatic hydrolysis of an organomercurial to inorganic mercury and its subsequent

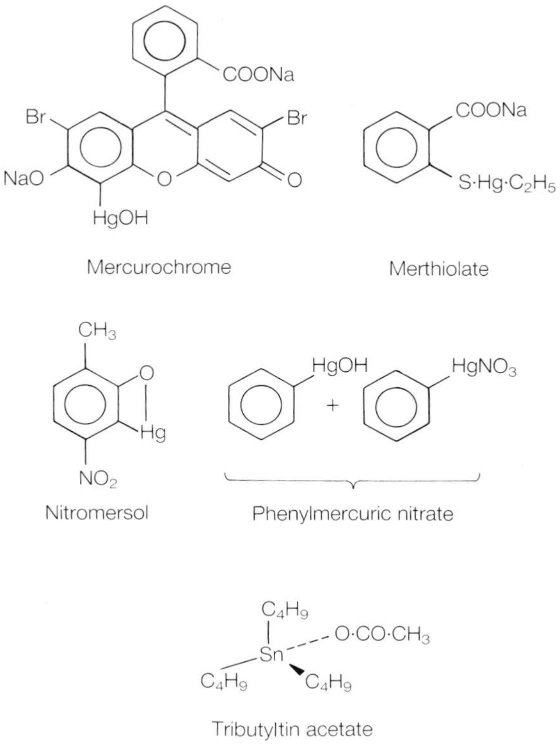

Fig. 2.24 Mercurochrome, merthiolate (thiomersal, sodium ethylmercurithiosalicylate), nitromersol, phenylmercuric nitrate and tributyltin acetate.

reduction as in (i) (Silver & Misra, 1988). Further details are provided in Chapter 10B.

15.3.1 Mercurochrome (disodium-2,7-dibromo-4-hydroxymercurifluorescein)

This is now only of historical interest; it was the first organic mercurial to be used in medicine and

Table 2.15 Derivatives of mercury and their uses as preservatives.

Compound	Use(s)
Phenylmercuric stearate	Leather
Phenylmercuric oleate	Leather
Mercuric naphthenate	Paint
Phenylmercuric acetate	Papers, textiles, pharmaceuticals*
Phenylmercuric nitrate	Pharmaceuticals*

* For additional information, see Chapter 15.

an aqueous solution enjoyed a vogue as a substitute for iodine solutions as a skin disinfectant.

15.3.2 Nitromersol (anhydro-2-hydroxymercuri-6-methyl-3-nitrophenol)

A yellow powder, it is not very soluble in water or organic solvents but will dissolve in aqueous alkali, and is used as a solution of the sodium salt. It is active against vegetative micro-organisms but ineffective against spores and acid-fast bacteria. It is mostly used in the USA.

*15.3.3 Thiomersal (merthiolate; sodium-*o*-(ethylmercurithio)-benzoate)*

This derivative was used as a skin disinfectant, and is now employed as a fungicide and as a preservative (0.01–0.02%) for biological products, for example, bacterial and viral vaccines. It possesses antifungal properties but is without action on spores.

15.3.4 Phenylmercuric nitrate

This organic derivative is used as a bactericide in multi-dose containers of parenteral injections and as an adjunct to heat in the former pharmacopoeial sterilization process heating with a bactericide, at a concentration of 0.001–0.002% w/v, and as a preservative for eye-drops at 0.002% w/v (Brown & Anderson, 1968). It is also employed in the treatment of vaginal candidiasis.

Phenylmercuric nitrate solutions at room temperatures are ineffective against bacterial spores but possess antifungal activity, and are used as antifungal agents in the preservation of paper, textiles and leather. Voge (1947) has discussed this compound in a short review. An interesting formulation of phenylmercuric nitrate with sodium dinaphthylmethanedisulphonate has been described, in which enhanced activity and greater skin penetration is claimed (Goldberg *et al.*, 1950).

15.4 Tin and its compounds (organo-tins)

Tin, stannic or tin (IV) oxide was at one time used as an oral medicament in the treatment of superficial staphylococcal infections. Tin was claimed to be excreted via sebaceous glands and thus concentrated at sites of infection. More recently, organic tin derivatives (Table 2.16, Fig. 2.24) have been used as fungicides and bactericides and as textile and wood preservatives (Smith & Smith, 1975). The organo-tin compounds which find use as biocides are derivatives of tin(IV). They have the general structure R_3SnX where R is butyl or phenyl and X is acetate, benzoate, fluoride, oxide or hydroxide. In structure–activity studies, activity has been shown to reside in the R group; the nature of X determines physical properties such as solubility and volatility (Rose & Lock, 1970; Van der Kerk & Luitjen, 1954). R_3SnX compounds, with R = butyl or phenyl, combine high biocidal activity with low mammalian toxicity. Samples of the range of R_3SnX compounds and their use as biocides are shown in Tables 2.16 and 2.17. Tin differs significantly from copper, silver and mercury salts in being intrinsically much less toxic. It is used to coat cans and vessels used to prepare food or boil water. Organo-tin compounds have some effect on oxidative phosphorylation (Aldridge & Threlfall, 1961) and act as ionophores for anions (Chapter 9). Possible environmental toxicity should be borne in mind when tin compounds are used.

16 ANILIDES

Anilides (Fig. 2.25) have the general structure $C_6H_5.NH.COR$. Two derivatives—salicylanilide, where $R = C_6H_4OH$ and diphenylurea, carbanilide, where $R = C_6H_5.NH$—have formed the basis for antimicrobial compounds.

16.1 Salicylanilide

The parent compound, salicylanilide, was introduced in 1930 as a fungistat for use on textiles (Fargher *et al.*, 1930). It occurs as white or slightly pink crystals, m.p. 137°C, which are soluble in water and organic solvents. It has also been used in ointment form for the treatment of ringworm, but concentrations above 5% should not be used in medicinal products because of skin irritancy. Minimum inhibitory concentrations (μg/ml) for a number of fungi were: *Trichophyton mentagrophytes* 12; *T. tonsurans*, 6; *T. rubrum*, 3; *Epider-*

Table 2.16 Tin compounds used as preservatives and some examples of their uses

Compound	Chemical formula	Use(s)
Tributyltin oxide	$[(C_4H_9)_3\ Sn]_2O$	Antifouling paints Wallpaper adhesives Wood preservatives Antislime agents
Tributyltin fluoride	$(C_4H_9)_3\ SnF$	Antifouling paints
Tributyltin acetate	$(C_4H_9)_3\ SnOCOCH_3$	Antifouling paints
Tributylin benzoate	$(C_4H_9)_3\ SnOCOC_6H_5$	Germicide: usually used with formaldehyde or a QAC
Triphenyltin acetate	$(C_6H_5)_3\ SnOCOCH_3$	Agricultural fungicides
Triphenyltin hydroxide	$(C_6H_5)_3\ SnOH$	Agricultural pesticides Disinfectants

Table 2.17 Minimum inhibitory concentrations (MICs) of tributyltin oxide towards a range of micro-organisms

Organism	MIC (μg/ml)
Aspergillus niger	0.5
Chaetomium globosum	1.0
Penicillium expansum	1.0
Aureobasidium pullulans	0.5
Trichoderma viride	1.0
Candida albicans	1.0
Bacillus mycoides	0.1
Staphylococcus aureus	1.0
Bacterium ammoniagenes	1.0
Pseudomonas aeruginosa	>500
Enterobacter aerogenes	>500

mophyton floccosum, 6; *Microsporum adovini*, 1.5. Despite the effectiveness of the parent compound attempts were made to improve on its performance by the usual device of adding substituents, notably halogens, to the benzene residues; these are considered below.

16.1.1 Substituted salicylanilides

Lemaire *et al.* (1961) investigated 92 derivatives of salicylanilide and related compounds, i.e. benzanilides and salicylaldehydes. The intrinsic antimicrobial activity was obtained from literature values and was usefully summarized as follows. One ring substituent would give an MIC value for

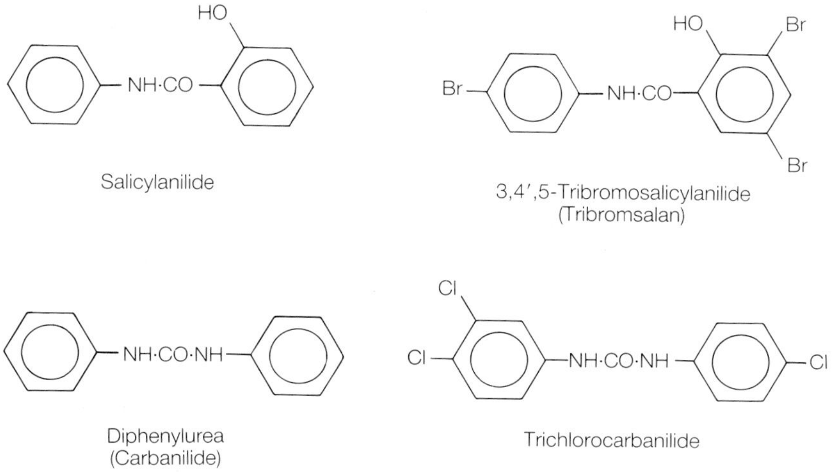

Fig. 2.25 Anilides.

Staph. aureus of 2 μg/ml, but this value could be decreased to 1 μg/ml if substitution occurred in both rings.

The researchers were particularly interested in the role of these compounds as antiseptics for addition to soaps, and went on to evaluate them in this role. They were also interested to find to what extent they remained on the skin (skin substantivity) after washing with soaps containing them. They found that di- to penta-chlorination or bromination with more or less equal distribution of the substituent halogen in both rings gave the best results both for antimicrobial activity and skin substantivity. However, it was also found that skin photosensitization was caused by some analogues.

Of the many compounds tested, the 3,4′,5-tribromo, 2,3,5,3′ and 3,5,3′,4′, tetrachloro salicylanilides have been the most widely used as antimicrobial agents; however, their photosensitizing properties have tended to restrict their use in any situation where they may come in contact with human skin.

Over and above this, many workers who have investigated germicidal soaps, i.e. ordinary soap products with the addition of a halogenated salicylanilide, carbanilide, or for that matter phenolic compounds such as hexachlorophane (2.9.1) or DCMX (2.6.5), have doubted their value in this role, although some may act as deodorants by destroying skin organisms which react with sweat to produce body odour.

16.2 Diphenylureas (carbanilides)

16.2.1 3,4,4′-Trichlorocarbanilide (TCC, triclocarban)

From an extensive study by Beaver *et al.* (1957) the above emerged as one of the most potent of this family of biocides. It inhibits the growth of many Gram-positive bacteria at concentrations from 0.1 to 1.0 μg/ml. Fungi were found to be more resistant, since 1000 μg/ml failed to inhibit *Aspergillus niger*, *Penicillium notatum*, *Candida albicans* and *Fusarium oxysporium*. *Trichophyton gypseum* and *T. inguinale* were inhibited at 50 μg/ml.

It occurs as a white powder, m.p. 250°C; it is very slightly soluble in water.

Like the salicylanilides, it has not found favour in products likely to come in contact with human skin, despite the fact that it had been extensively evaluated as the active ingredient of some disinfectant soaps.

16.3 Mode of action

The mode of action of salicylanilides and carbanilides (diphenylureas) has been studied in detail by Woodroffe & Wilkinson (1966a,b) and Hamilton (1968). The compounds almost certainly owe their bacteriostatic action to their ability to discharge part of the protonmotive force, thereby inhibiting processes dependent upon it, i.e. active transport and energy metabolism.

17 MISCELLANEOUS PRESERVATIVES

17.1 Polymeric biguanides

A novel compound, a polymer of hexamethylene biguanide (Fig. 2.26) with a molecular weight of approximately 3000 (weight average) has found particular use as a cleansing agent in the food industry. Its properties have been described by Davies *et al.* (1968) under the trade name Vantocil 1B (Imperial Chemical Industries Ltd, Blackley, Manchester M9 3DA, England). It is soluble in water and is usually supplied as a 20% aqueous solution. It is also soluble in glycols and alcohols but is insoluble in non-polar solvents such as petroleum ethers or toluene. It inhibits the growth of most bacteria at between 5 and 25 μg/ml but 100 μg/ml is required to inhibit *Ps. aeruginosa* while *P. vulgaris* requires 250 μg/ml. It is less active against fungi; for example *Cladosporium resinae*, which has been implicated as a spoilage organism in pharmaceutical products, requires 1250 μg/ml to prevent growth. Its mode of action has been studied extensively (see Chapter 9).

Because of the residual positive charges on the polymer it is precipitated from aqueous solutions by anionic compounds which include soaps and detergents based on alkyl sulphates. It is also precipitated by detergent constituents such as sodium

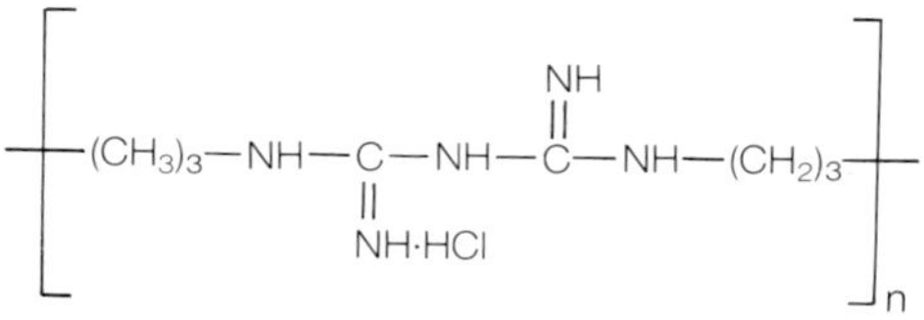

Fig. 2.26 Vantocil 1B (a polymeric biguanide). Mean n is 5.5.

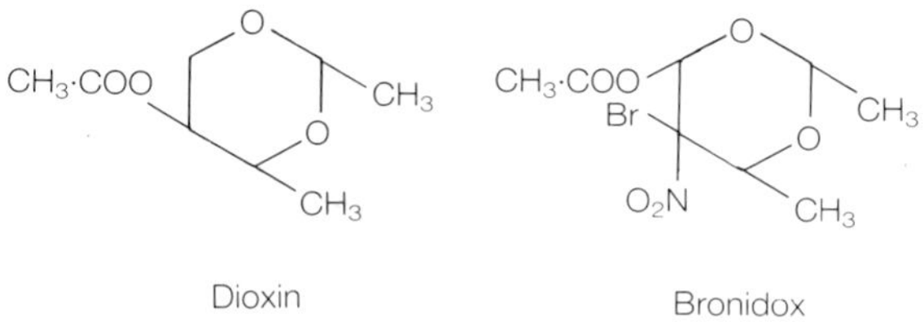

Fig. 2.27 Dioxanes: Dioxin and Bronidox.

hexametaphosphate and in a strongly alkaline environment.

It finds use as a general sterilizing agent in the food industry provided the surfaces to which it is applied are free from occlusive debris, a stricture which applies in all disinfection procedures. Because it is not a surface-active agent it can be used in the brewing industry as it does not affect head retention on ales and beers. Contact should be avoided with one commonly used material in food manufacture, anionic caramel, as this will, like other anionic compounds, inactivate the polymer. It has also been used very successfully for the disinfection of swimming pools. Apart from copper, which it tarnishes, this polymeric biguanide has no deleterious effect on most materials it might encounter in use.

17.2 Derivatives of 1,3-dioxane

17.2.1 6-Acetoxy-2,4-dimethyl-1,3-dioxane (dimethoxane) (Dioxin: Registered Trade Mark, Sindar Corporation, New York, USA)

Dioxin (Fig. 2.27) is a liquid, colourless when pure and soluble in water and organic solvents. It has a marked odour. It is active against a wide range of micro-organisms at concentrations ranging from 300 or 2500 μg/ml (Anon., 1962). It should be noted that the name 'dioxin' is also used for a reaction product, 2,3,7,8-tetrachlorodibenzo-*p*-dioxin (TCDD) which may be formed during the manufacture of trichlorophenol. MIC values (μg/ml) for representative micro-organisms are: *Sacch. cerevisiae*, 2500; *A. niger*, 1250; *Staph. aureus*, 1250; *Ps. aeruginosa*, 625; *Salmonella choleraesuis*, 312.

Dimethoxane is not affected by changes in pH but it is slowly hydrolysed in aqueous solution producing ethanal (acetaldehyde). It is compatible with non-ionic surface-active agents but may cause discoloration in formulations which contain amines or amides.

Dimethoxane finds application as a preservative for cosmetics, emulsion paints and cutting oils. A detailed study of the components of the commercial preparation Giv Gard DXN (Givaudan & Co. Ltd, Whyteleafe, Surrey, UK), showed that the acetoxy group may be either 6-α (74%) or 6-β (22%) to the 1,3-dioxane ring. Small amounts of acetaldehyde may also be present (Woolfson & Woodside, 1976). Later, in a bacteriological study, Woolfson (1977) attributed the action of the commercial product partially to its aldehyde content and partially to the 1,3-dioxane components.

17.2.2 5-Bromo-5-nitro-1,3-dioxane (Bronidox: Henkel Chemicals Ltd, Tretol House, London NW9 OHT, UK)

This nitro bromo derivative of dioxane is available as a 10% solution in propylene glycol as Bronidox L. It is used as a preservative for toiletries and has been described in some detail by Potokar *et al.* (1976) and Lorenz (1977). Its stability at various pH values is tabulated by Croshaw (1977).

It is active against bacteria and fungi and does not show a pseudomonas gap. Minimum inhibitory concentrations of active ingredient μ/ml were: *E. coli*, 50; *Ps. aeruginosa*, 50; *Pr. vulgaris*, 50; *Ps. fluorescens*, 50; *Sal. typhi*, 50; *Serr. marcescens*, 25; *Staph. aureus*, 75; *Str. faecalis*, 75; *Candida albicans*, 25; *Sacch. cerevisiae*, 10; *A. niger*, 10.

Its activity is not affected between pH 5 and 9 and it probably acts as an oxidizing agent oxidizing

—SH to —S—S— groups in essential enzymes. It does not act as a formaldehyde releaser.

It is recommended for use as a preservative for a variety of toiletries including shampoos and hand lotions.

17.3 Derivatives of imidazole

Imidazolines (Fig. 2.28) are 2,3-dihydroimidazoles; 2-heptadecyl-2-imidazoline was introduced as an agricultural fungicide as far back as 1946. Other derivatives containing the imidazole ring have recently found successful application as preservatives. Two are derivatives of 2,4-dioxo-tetrahydroimidazole, the imidazolidones; the parent diketone is hydantoin.

17.3.1 1,3-Di(hydroxymethyl)-5,5-dimethyl-2,4-dioxoimidazole; 1,3-Di(hydroxymethyl)-5,5-dimethylhydantoin (Dantoin)

A 55% solution of this compound (Fig. 2.28) is available commercially as Glydant (Glyco Chemicals Inc., Greenwich, Conn., USA). This product is water-soluble, stable and non-corrosive, with a slight odour of formaldehyde. It is active over a wide range of pH and is compatible with most ingredients used in cosmetics. It has a wide spectrum of activity against bacteria and fungi, being active at concentrations of between 250 and 500 μg/ml. The moulds *Microsporum gypseum* and *Trichophyton asteroides*, however, are particularly susceptible, being inhibited at 32 μg/ml. Its mode of action is attributed to its ability to release formaldehyde, the rate of release of which is more rapid at high pH values, 9–10.5, than low, 3–5. Its optimum stability lies in the range pH 6–8. It has an acceptable level of toxicity and can be used as a preservative over a wide field of products. It has been evaluated by Schanno *et al.* (1980).

17.3.2 NN″-methylene bis [5′-[1-hydroxymethyl]-2,5-dioxo-4-imidazolidinyl urea] (Germall 115: Sutton Laboratories Inc., Roselle, N.J., USA)

In 1970 a family of imidazolidinyl ureas for use as preservatives was described (Berke & Rosen, 1970). One of these under the name Germall 115 has been studied extensively (Rosen & Berke, 1973; Berke & Rosen, 1978). Germall 115 is a white powder very soluble in water, and hence tends to remain in the aqueous phase of emulsions. It is non-toxic, non-irritating and non-sensitizing. It is compatible with emulsion ingredients and with proteins.

A claimed property of Germall 115 has been its ability to act synergistically with other preservatives (Jacobs *et al.*, 1975; Rosen *et al.*, 1977; Berke & Rosen, 1980). Intrinsically it is more active against bacteria than fungi. Most of the microbiological data are based on challenge tests in cosmetic for-

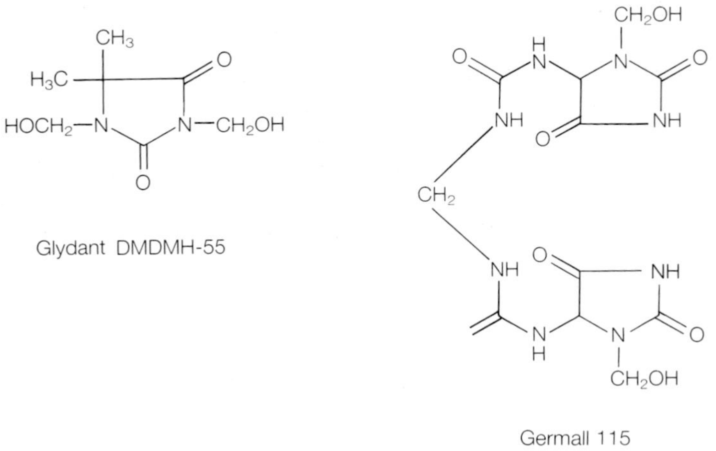

Fig. 2.28 Dantoin or Glydant DMDMH-55 and Germall 115.

mulations, data which are of great value to the cosmetic microbiologist. An investigation of its activity against a series of *Pseudomonas* species and strains (Berke & Rosen, 1978) showed that in a challenge test 0.3% of the compound cleared all species but *Ps. putida* and *Ps. aureofaciens* in 24 h. The latter species were killed between 3 and 7 days. In an agar cup plate test 1% solution gave the following size inhibition zones (mm): *Staph. aureus*, 7,6; *Staph. aureus*, penicillin sensitive, 15.5; *S. albus*, 9.0; *B. subtilis*, 15.0; *Cy. acne*, 5,0; *E. coli*, 3,6; *Ps. ovale*, 2.0.

17.4 Isothiazolones

Ponci *et al.* (1964) studied the antifungal activity of a series of 5-nitro-1,2-dibenzisothiazolones and found many of them to possess high activity. Since this publication a number of isothiazolones (Fig. 2.29) have emerged as antimicrobial preservatives. They are available commercially, usually as suspensions rather than as pure compounds, and find use in a variety of industrial situations.

17.4.1 5-Chloro-2-methyl-4-isothiazolin-3-one

17.4.2 2-Methyl-4-isothiazolin-3-one

A mixture of these two derivatives known as Kathon 886 MW (Rohm and Haas (UK) Ltd, Croydon. CR9 3NB) containing about 14% of active ingredients is available as a preservative for cutting oils and as an in-can preservative for emulsion paints. This mixture is active at concentrations of 2.25–9 μg/ml active ingredient against a wide range of bacteria and fungi and does not show a pseudomonas gap. It is also a potent algastat. Kathon CG, containing 1.5% active ingredients and magnesium salts, has been suggested as a preservative for cosmetic products up to a final concentration of 25 μg/ml active ingredients.

It possesses the additional advantage of being biodegradable to non-toxic metabolites and is non-irritating at normal in-use concentrations. It is water-soluble and compatible with most emulgents. The stability of Kathon 886 at various pH values is described by Croshaw (1977).

17.4.3 2-n-Octyl-4-isothiazolin-3-one (Skane M8: ICI)

This is available as a 45% solution in propylene glycol and is active against bacteria over a range of 400–500 μg/ml active ingredient. To inhibit the growth of one strain of *Ps. aeruginosa* required 500 μg/ml. Fungistatic activity was shown against a wide number of species over the range 0.3–8.0 μg/ml. It is also effective at preventing algal growth at concentrations of 0.5–5.0 μg/ml. It is biodegradable but shows skin and eye irritancy. As might be expected from its *n*-octyl side-chain it is not soluble in water.

17.4.4 1,2-Benzisothiazolin-3-one (Proxel CRL, GXL, AB: Imperial Chemical Industries Ltd, Blackley, Manchester M9 3DA)

This is available commercially in various formulations and is recommended as a preservative for industrial emulsions, adhesives, polishes, glues and paper products. It possesses a low mammalian toxicity but is not recommended for medicinal and cosmetic use for it exhibits marked skin irritancy.

17.5 Derivatives of hexamine

Hexamine (hexamethylene tetramine; 1,3,5,7-triaza-1-azonia-adamantane) has been used as a urinary antiseptic since 1894. Its activity is attributed to a slow release of formaldehyde. Other formaldehyde-releasing compounds are considered in Sections 7.2.4, 17,3, 17.6 and 17.7. Wohl in

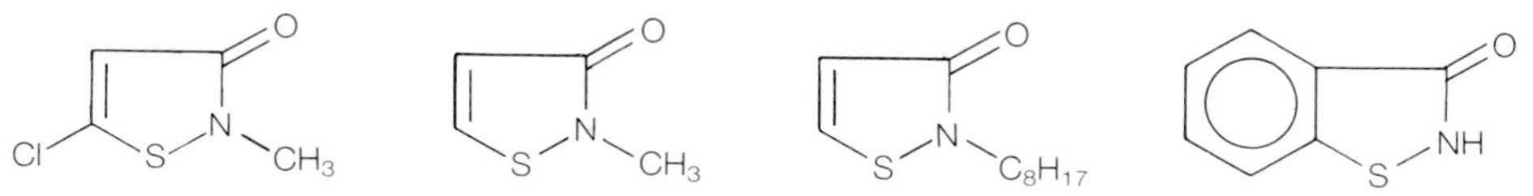

Fig. 2.29 Isothiazolones.

1886 was the first to quaternize hexamine, and in 1915–16 Jacobs and co-workers attempted to extend the antimicrobial range of hexamine by quaternizing one of its nitrogen atoms with halohydrocarbons (Jacobs & Heidelberger, 1915a,b; Jacobs *et al.* 1916a,b). These workers did not consider that their compounds acted as formaldehyde releasers but that activity resided in the whole molecule.

The topic was taken up again by Scott & Wolf (1962). These workers re-examined quaternized hexamine derivatives with a view to using them as preservatives for toiletries, cutting oils and other products. They looked at 31 such compounds and compared their activity also with hexamine and formaldehyde. As well as determining their inhibitory activity towards a staphylococcus, enterobacteria and a pseudomonad they also assessed inhibitory activity towards *Desulphovibrio desulphuricans*, a common contaminant of cutting oils.

Polarographic and spectroscopic studies of formaldehyde release were made on some of the derivatives; this release varied with the substituent used in forming the quaternary salt. A typical set of data for the antimicrobial activity (MIC) of one derivative compared with hexamine and formaldehyde is shown in Table 2.18. In general, the quaternized compounds were found to be more active w/w than hexamine but less active than formaldehyde. Although chemically they contain a quaternized nitrogen atom, unlike the more familiar antimicrobial quaternized compounds (Section 6.1), they are not inactivated by lecithin or protein. The compounds are not as surface-active as conventional QACs. Thus an average figure for the surface tension, dyne cm^{-1}, for 0.1% solutions of the quaternized hexamines was 54; that for 0.1% cetrimide (Section 6.1) was 34.

One of these derivatives of hexamine, i.e. that quaternized with *cis*-1,3-dichloropropene, is being used as a preservative under the name Dowicil 200 (Dow Chemical Co., Wilmslow, Cheshire). *Cis*-1-(3-cischloroallyl)-3,5,7-triaza-1-azonia-admantane chloride *N*-(3-chloroallyl) hexamine (Dowicil 200; Fig. 2.30) is a highly water-soluble hygroscopic white powder; it has a low oil solubility. It is active against bacteria and fungi. Typical minimum inhibitory concentrations (μg/ml) were: *E. coli*, 400; *Pr. vulgaris*, 100; *Sal. typhi*, 50; *Alcaligenes faecalis*, 50; *Ps. aeruginosa*, 600; *Staph. aureus*, 200; *B. subtilis*, 200; *A. niger*, 1200; *T. interdigitale*, 50.

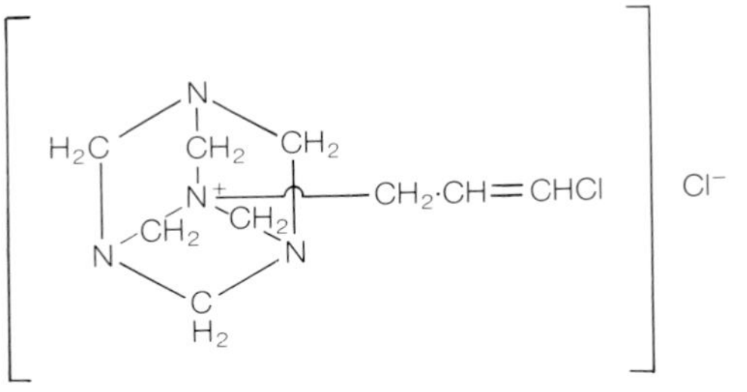

Fig. 2.30 Dowicil 200 [*N*-(3-*cis*-chloroallyl)hexamine].

It is recommended for use as a preservative for cosmetic preparations at concentrations of from 0.1 to 0.2%. Because of its high solubility it does not tend to concentrate in the oil phase of these products, but remains in the aqueous phase where contamination is likely to arise. It is not inactivated by the usual ingredients used in cosmetic manufacture. Its activity is not affected over the usual pH ranges found in cosmetic or cutting oil formulations. For further information, see Rossmore & Sondossi (1988).

17.6 Triazines

The product, theoretically from the condensation of three molecules of ethylamine with three of formaldehyde, is hexahydro-1,3,5-triethyl-*s*-triazine (Bactocide THT: Cochrane and Keene (Chemicals), Rochdale, UK; Fig. 2.31). This is a clear white or slightly yellow viscous liquid readily soluble in water, acetone, ethanol and ether. It is bactericidal and fungicidal and inhibits most bacteria including *Ps. aeruginosa* and *D. desulphuricans* at concentrations of 0.3 mg/ml. Fungi such as *A. niger*, *Penicillium glaucum* and *P. notatum* are inhibited at 0.1 mg/ml, and *Sacch. cerevisiae* at 0.05 mg/ml. It owes its activity to a release of formaldehyde. It has been used as a preservative for cutting oils, for the 'in-can' preservation of emulsion paints for proteinaceous adhesives and to control slime in paper and cardboard manufacture, and to prevent the growth of micro-organisms in water-cooling systems. It has a low intrinsic toxicity and at use dilutions is not irritant to the skin.

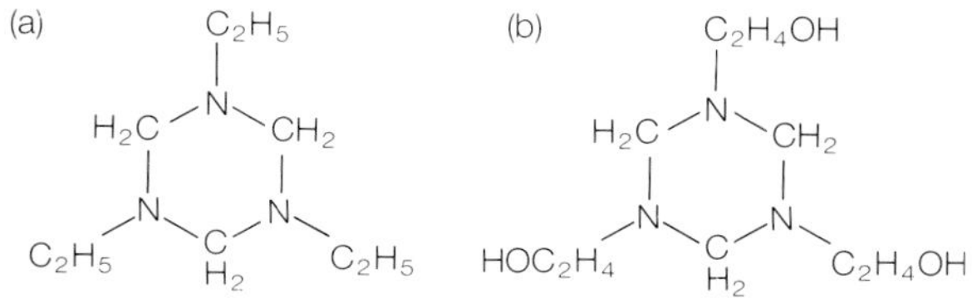

Fig. 2.31 (a) Hexahydro-1,3,5-triethyl-*s*-triazine ('Bactocide THT'); (b) 1,3,5-tris(2-hydroxyethyl)-*s*-triazine ('Grotan').

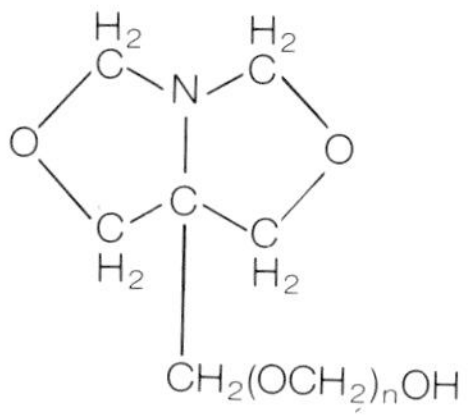

Fig. 2.32 Nuosept 95 ($n = 0 - 5$).

If formaldehyde is reacted with ethanolamine the compound 1,3,5-tris(2-hydroxyethyl)-s-triazine can be formed (Grotan: Stirling Industrial, Sheffield, UK). This has both antibacterial and antifungal activity and is recommended as a preservative for cutting oils. Despite the figures for fungal inhibition it is often found, in practical preservation situations, that although this triazine will inhibit microbial growth, a fungal superinfection is often established; a total preservation system which includes a triazine might well have to contain an additional antifungal compound (Rossmore *et al.*, 1972; Paulus, 1976). This situation may be compared with that found with imidazole derivatives (Section 17.3).

Rossmore (1979) has discussed the uses of heterocyclic compounds as industrial biocides, and Rossmore & Sondossi (1988) have reviewed formaldehyde condensates in general.

17.7 Oxazolo-oxazoles

By reacting formaldehyde with tris (hydroxymethyl) methylamine, a series of derivatives is obtained. The commercial product (Nuosept 95: Tenneco Organics Ltd. Avonmouth, Bristol; Fig. 2.32) contains the molecules species: 5-hydroxymethoxymethyl-1-aza-3,7-dioxabicyclo (3.3.0) octane, 24.5%; 5-hydroxymethyl-1-aza-3,7-dioxabicyclo (3.3.0) octane, 17.7%; 5-hydroxypoly methylenoxy (74% C_2, 21% C_3, 4% C_4, 1% C_5) methyl-1-aza-3,7-dioxabicyclo (3.3.0) octane, 7.8%, and acts as a biostat by virtue of being a formaldehyde releaser.

It is obtained as a clear, pale-yellow liquid which is miscible with water, methanol, ethanol, chloroform and acetone in all proportions, and is recommended as a preservative for cutting oils, water treatment, plants, emulsion (Latex) paints, industrial slurries and starch and cellulose-based products. It is slightly irritant to intact and abraded skin and is a severe eye irritant.

17.8 Methylene bisthiocyanate

This is available commercially as a 10% solution and is recommended for the control of slime in paper manufacture, where it provides a useful alternative to mercurials. The compound (Fig. 2.33) is a skin and eye irritant and thus care is required in its use. Its toxicity is low enough to enable it to be used in the manufacture of papers destined for the packaging of food. At use-dilutions it is unlikely to cause corrosion of materials used in the construction of paper manufacturing equipment.

17.9 Captan

Captan is *N*-(trichloromethylthio)cyclohex-4-ene-1,2-dicarboximide (Fig. 2.34). It is a white crystalline solid, insoluble in water and only slightly soluble in organic solvents. It is decomposed in alkaline solution. Despite its low solubility it can be shown to be an active biocide, being active against both Gram-negative and Gram-positive bacteria, yeasts and moulds. It has been used as an agricultural fungicide, being primarily employed against diseases of fruit trees. It has also been used

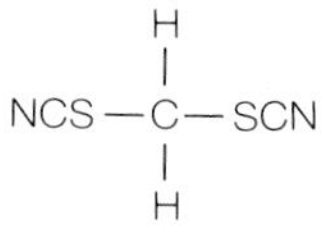

Fig. 2.33 Methylene bisthiocyanate.

Table 2.18 Inhibitory concentrations for hexamine quaternized with $—CH_2Cl{=}CHCl$ compared with values for hexamine and formaldehyde

	MIC* against					
Inhibitor	*Staph. aureus*	*Sal. typhi*	*K. aerogenes*	*Ps. aeruginosa*	*B. subtilis*	*D. desulphuricans*
Hexamine quaternized with $—CH_2—CH{=}CHCl$	4×10^{-4} (100)	2×10^{-4} (50)	2×10^{-4} (50)	2×10^{-3} (500)	4×10^{-4} (100)	2.9×10^{-2} (7250)
Hexamine	3.5×10^{-2} (5000)	3.5×10^{-3} (500)	—	—	—	5.3×10^{-2} (7500)
Formaldehyde	1.6×10^{-3} (50)	3.3×10^{-3} (100)	1.6×10^{-3} (50)	—	—	—

* Molar values (in parentheses μg/ml).

Table 2.19 Properties of the most commonly used gaseous disinfectants

Gaseous disinfectant	Molecular weight	Boiling point (°C)	Solubility in water	Sterilizing concn (mg/l)	Relative humidity requirements (%)	Penetration of materials	Microbidical activity*	Best application as gaseous disinfectant†
Ethylene oxide	44	10.4	Complete	400–1000	Non-desiccated 30–50; large load 60	Moderate	Moderate	Sterilization of plastic medical supplies
Propylene oxide	58	34	Good	800–2000	Non-desiccated 30–60	Fair	Fair	Decontamination
Formaldehyde	30	90°C/ Formalin†	Good	3.10	75	Poor (surface sterilant)	Excellent	Surface sterilant for rooms
β-Propiolactone	72	162	Moderate	2–5	>70	None (surface sterilant)	Excellent	Surface sterilant for rooms
Methyl bromide	95	4.6	Slight	3500	30–50	Excellent	Poor	Decontamination

* Based on an equimolar comparison.
† Formalin contains formaldehyde plus methanol.
† See later also; Chapter 20.

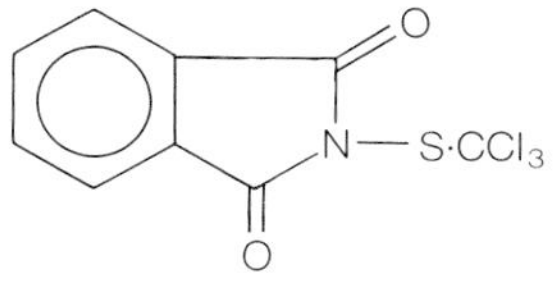

Fig. 2.34 Captan.

to prevent spoilage of stored fruit and in the treatment of skin infections due to fungi in humans and animals.

17.10 Essential oils

Essential oils have been used empirically throughout history as preservatives. Their re-examination as antimicrobial agents has received attention from many workers recently as their use as natural preservatives has contemporary appeal. Their antibacterial properties have been reviewed by Deans & Ritchie (1987).

17.11 General statement

Many of these compounds are relatively new in the preservation field and much of the information concerning their properties and uses is found in the manufacturers' information brochures. Any person wishing to explore their use should consult the manufacturers. An ever-present problem with cosmetics preservation is that of contact sensitization. This is discussed in some detail by Marzulli & Maiback (1973) and is a point which must be carefully checked before a preservative is committed to a product. Another hazard which may arise is that of an induced change in the skin microflora during continuous use of products containing antimicrobial preservatives; this is discussed by Marples (1971).

18 VAPOUR-PHASE DISINFECTANTS

Gaseous sterilization is the subject of a later paper (Chapter 15) and thus only a few comments will be made here. It is only comparatively recently that a scientific basis for using gases as sterilizing or disinfecting agents has been established. Factors influencing the activity of gaseous formaldehyde were described by Nordgren (1939), and more recently by a Committee on Formaldehyde Disinfection (Anon., 1958). The possible uses of gaseous formaldehyde in the disinfection of hospital bedding and blankets and, in conjunction with low-temperature steam, for disinfection of heat-sensitive material, are considered in Section 18.2.1 (see also Chapter 20).

Phillips & Kaye (1949) reviewed the earlier work which had taken place with ethylene oxide, which has bactericidal, mycobactericidal, sporicidal, fungicidal and virucidal activity (Ernst, 1974). A more recent review is by Richards *et al.* (1984).

Other gases of possible value include β-propiolactone, propylene oxide, ozone, methyl bromide and glycidaldehyde (Russell, 1976). Physical and chemical properties of these and the two most important ones (ethylene oxide and formaldehyde) are listed in Table 2.19, and their chemical structures in Fig. 2.35.

18.1 Ethylene oxide

This is discussed in detail later (Chapter 20) and will not be considered here. Useful reviews are those by Hoffman (1971), Phillips (1977) and Richards *et al.* (1984).

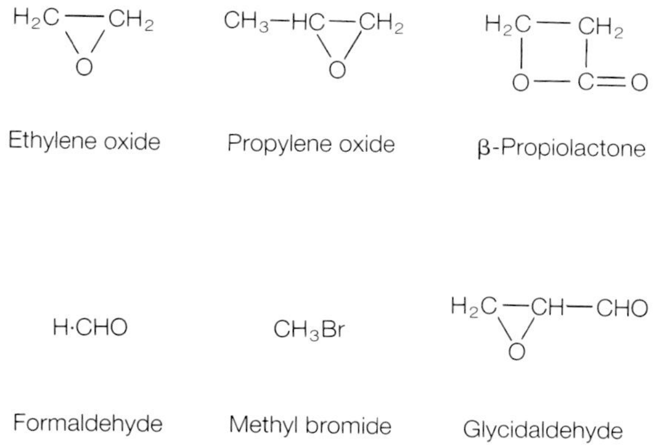

Fig. 2.35 Chemical structures of gaseous disinfectants.

18.2 Formaldehyde-releasing agents

Paraformaldehyde [$HO(CH_2O)_n \cdot H$, where n = 8–100] is a polymer of formaldehyde and is produced by evaporating aqueous solutions of formaldehyde. Although it was considered originally to be of little practical use (Nordgren, 1939) paraformaldehyde has since been shown to depolymerize rapidly when heated, to produce formaldehyde (Taylor *et al.*, 1969). Paraformaldehyde is considered by Tulis (1973) to be an excellent source of monomeric formaldehyde gas, because it can be produced in a temperature-controlled reaction, and there are no contaminating residues (methanol and formic acid) produced during evaporation of formalin solutions, in contrast to the method of evaporating formalin solutions containing 10% methanol to prevent polymerization.

Other formaldehyde-releasing agents are melamine formaldehyde and urea formaldehyde (Fig. 2.36). The former is produced from formaldehyde and melamine under alkaline conditions and the latter is a mixture of mono-methyloyl urea and di-methyloyl urea. When exposed to elevated temperatures these agents release potentially sterilizing amounts of gaseous formaldehyde, the rate of release being a function of time and temperature. These formaldehyde-releasing agents are, however, much less effective as disinfecting or sterilizing sources than paraformaldehyde. The reason for this is that there is a much greater release of formaldehyde from paraformaldehyde than from the resins at various temperatures, and the microbicidal process is strictly a function of the available formaldehyde gas.

Applications and mode of action of formaldehyde condensate biocides have been reviewed by Rossmore & Sondossi (1988).

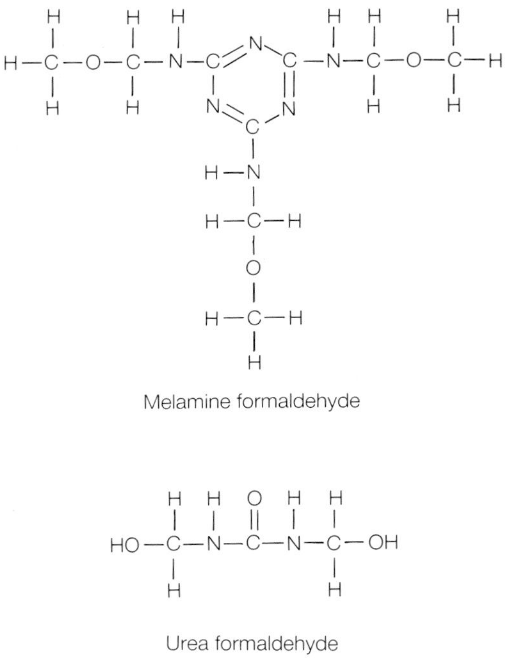

Fig. 2.36 Melamine formaldehyde and urea formaldehyde.

18.2.1 Uses of formaldehyde vapour

Formaldehyde vapour has found use as a disinfectant in the following situations (Russell, 1976):

1 in combination with low-temperature steam (70–90°C) as a method for disinfecting heat-sensitive materials (Alder *et al.*, 1971, 1990). This will be discussed later (Chapter 18A);

2 rarely, in the disinfection of hospital bedding and blankets, when formaldehyde solutions are used in the penultimate rinse of laundering blankets to give a residual bactericidal activity because of the slow evolution of formaldehyde vapour (Dickinson & Wagg, 1967; Alder *et al.*, 1971, 1990);

3 in the terminal disinfection of premises, although this is considered to be of limited value (Kelsey, 1967);

4 as a fumigant in poultry houses after emptying, and before new stock is introduced (Nicholls *et al.*, 1967; Anon., 1970) and in the hatcher to prevent bacterial contamination of shell eggs (Harry, 1963);

5 in the disinfection of safety cabinets.

18.3 *β*-Propiolactone

β-Propiolactone (BPL) requires heating to produce the vapour form, has weak penetrating powers (Table 2.19) and hydrolyses readily in water to give hydracrylic acid (β-hydroxypropionic acid). Its antimicrobial activity depends primarily on its concentration and the temperature and r.h. at which it is used. Its antibacterial activity is maximal at r.h.

levels of 75–85%, although, as with ethylene oxide, it is not so much the environmental moisture content that is important but the content and location of water within the bacterial cell (Hoffman & Warshowsky, 1958). The possibility of BPL being carcinogenic (Walpole *et al.*, 1954), has obviously limited its applications, although BPL vapour may have a use in the decontamination of premises (Spiner & Hoffman, 1960).

18.4 Propylene oxide

Propylene oxide requires only mild heating to produce the vapour form and has a fair penetration of materials (Table 2.19). It hydrolyses slowly in the presence of only a small amount of moisture to give the non-toxic propylene glycol (Kereluk, 1971) and there is no need to remove it from exposed materials (Sykes, 1965). Antibacterial activity decreases with an increase in r.h. (Bruch & Koesterer, 1961), although with desiccated organisms the reverse applies (Himmelfarb *et al.*, 1962). Propylene oxide has been shown to be suitable for treating powdered or flaked foods (Bruch & Koesterer, 1961).

18.5 Methyl bromide

Methyl bromide is a gas at normal temperatures. It is considerably less active as an antibacterial agent than ethylene oxide (Kelsey, 1967; Kereluk, 1971) or propylene oxide (Kelsey, 1967) but has good penetrative ability (Table 2.19). Methyl bromide is listed by Kereluk (1971) as being suitable for some types of fumigation.

18.6 Glycidaldehyde

Glycidaldehyde vapour inactivates sporing and non-sporing bacteria; the inactivation rate depends on concentration, temperature and inversely on r.h. (Dawson, 1962). There is little information as to its possible usefulness as a disinfecting or sterilizing agent.

18.7 Ozone

Ozone, O_3, is an allotropic form of oxygen. It has powerful oxidizing properties, inhibits bacterial growth (Ingram & Haines, 1949; Baird-Parker & Holbrook, 1971) and is bactericidal, virucidal and sporicidal, although spores are 10–15 times more resistant than non-sporing bacteria (Gurley, 1985; Rickloff, 1985). Gaseous ozone reacts with amino acids, RNA and DNA. It is unstable chemically in water, but activity persists because of the production of free radicals, including OH°. A synergistic effect has been shown with the simultaneous use of sonication (Burleson *et al.*, 1975).

18.8 Carbon dioxide

Carbon dioxide in soft drinks inhibits the development of various types of bacteria (Dunn, 1968). The growth of psychrotolerant, slime-producing bacteria is markedly inhibited by CO_2 gas in the atmosphere (Clark & Lentz, 1969).

18.9 Mechanism of action

Only a few brief comments will be made, and the interested reader is directed to the reviews of Bruch & Bruch (1970), Hoffman (1971), Russell (1976) and Richards *et al.* (1984) for further information. It is sufficient to note here that ethylene oxide reacts with proteins and amino acids, and with nucleic acid guanine [to give 7-(2′-hydroxyethyl) guanine] with alkylation of phosphated guanine possibly being responsible for its activity (Michael & Stumbo, 1970). The N-7 guanine position may also be a primary reaction site for BPL (Troll *et al.*, 1969). Formaldehyde is an extremely reactive chemical which interacts with cell protein, RNA and DNA (see Russell & Hopwood, 1976).

19 AERIAL DISINFECTANTS

An early procedure for aerial disinfection was the employment of sulphur dioxide, obtained by burning sulphur, or of chlorine for fumigating sickrooms.

An effective aerial disinfectant should be capable of being dispersed in the air so that complete and rapid mixing of infected air and disinfectant ensues. Additionally, an effective concentration should be maintained in the air, and the disinfectant must be highly and rapidly effective against airborne micro-organisms at different relative humidities. To these microbiological properties must be added the property of no toxicity or irritancy.

The most important means of using aerial disinfectants is by aerosol production. Aerosols consist of a very fine dispersed liquid phase in a gaseous (air) disperse phase. The lethal action of aerosols is believed to be due to condensation of the disinfectant on to the microbial cell (Sykes, 1965). Thus, the disinfectant must be nebulized in a fine spray to enable it to remain airborne and thereby come into contact, by random collision, with any micro-organisms present in the air. Aerosol droplets of <1 μm tend to be the accepted standard. Relative humidity has an important bearing on activity and at low r.h. inadequate condensation of disinfectant on to the microbial cell occurs. This means that dust-borne organisms are less susceptible to aerial disinfectants than are those enclosed in droplets; the optimum r.h. is usually 40–60%. In practice, chemical aerosols may be generated by spraying liquid chemicals into the air from an atomizer; solids may be vaporized by heat from a thermostatically controlled hotplate or dissolved in an appropriate solid and atomized.

Various chemicals have been employed for disinfecting air, including the following:

1 Hexylresorcinol: this phenolic substance is active against a wide range of bacteria, but not spores, in air. It is vaporized from a thermostatically controlled hotplate, and the vapour is odourless and non-toxic.

2 Lactic acid: this is an effective bactericidal aerial agent, but is unfortunately irritant at high concentrations.

3 Propylene glycol: this may be employed as a solvent for dissolving a solid disinfectant prior to atomization, but is also a fairly effective and non-irritating anti-microbial agent in its own right (Baird-Parker & Holbrook, 1971).

4 Formaldehyde: in summary of previous information, formaldehyde gas may be generated by: (a) evaporating commercial formaldehyde solution (formalin); (b) adding formalin to potassium permanganate; (c) volatilizing paraformaldehyde (Taylor *et al.*, 1969); (d) exposing certain organic resins or polymers, such as melamine formaldehyde or urea formaldehyde, to elevated temperatures (Tulis, 1973; see Russell, 1976). Fumigation by formaldehyde has found considerable use in poultry science (Anon, 1970).

20 DISINFECTANTS IN THE FOOD, DAIRY, PHARMACEUTICAL AND COSMETIC INDUSTRIES

The effectiveness of many disinfectants is reduced in the presence of organic matter in its various forms such as blood, serum, pus, dirt, earth, milkstone, food residues and faecal material (Chapter 3). This decreased activity has an important bearing on disinfectant use in the cosmetic (Davis, 1972a), pharmaceutical (Bean, 1967), food (Kornfeld, 1966; Goldenberg & Relf, 1967; Olivant & Shapton, 1970) and dairy (Clegg, 1967, 1970; Davis, 1972b; Anon., 1977) industries. The principles in all cases are the same, viz. either adequate pre-cleaning before use of the disinfectant or a combination of the disinfectant with a suitable detergent.

Organic matter may reduce activity either as a result of a chemical reaction between it and the compound, thus leaving a smaller antimicrobial concentration for attacking micro-organisms, or through a protection of the organisms from attack (Sykes, 1965). Phospholipids in serum, milk and faeces will reduce the antimicrobial activity of QACs.

The nature of the surface being disinfected and the protection afforded by soiling film are of considerable importance, and invisible milkstone in the dairy industry may protect micro-organisms against disinfection (Clegg, 1967). Rapid removal of soiling film may be achieved by use of high pH, for example the use of a combined hypochlorite-detergent at pH 11 (Clegg, 1967). Notwithstanding the lower activity of chlorine disinfectants at alkaline pH, an enhanced effect is observed because of the greater contact between micro-organisms and disinfectant. Of course, under certain circumstances caustic soda solutions are themselves sporicidal (Clegg, 1970). Detergents themselves have a killing effect on some micro-organisms and are frequently, if not invariably, used hot. Some disinfectants may exert a detergent action.

Cosmetic and pharmaceutical creams may pose several problems, since remnants of production batches may remain in relatively inaccessible orifices and crevices in apparatus and machinery used in their preparation. Such remnants could form foci for the infection of future production batches, which in turn could influence the activity of the preservative selected for incorporation into the product. Bean (1967) recommends cleaning of apparatus and machinery, after use, with hot water and detergent, followed by an appropriate disinfectant or steam.

Davis (1972a) recommends four ways of chemically sterilizing/disinfecting equipment in the cosmetic industry:

1 detergent, such as alkali, followed by a hypochlorite or a QAC;

2 cleaning by a stronger concentration of detergent–disinfectant and then sterilization/disinfection by a weaker concentration;

3 cleaning and sterilizing/disinfecting with a detergent–disinfectant (such as alkali and QAC), followed by a 'sterile rinse' with a QAC or a hypochlorite;

4 using a single substance, such as sodium hydroxide or nitric acid, which has powerful cleaning and sterilizing properties, followed by a sterile rinse.

A publication by the British Standards Institute (Anon., 1977) is worthy of comment. This deals with recommended methods for sterilizing plant and equipment used in the dairy industry; the term 'sterilization' as used in this report means 'a process which reduces the number of bacteria in dairy plant and utensils to a level consistent with acceptable quality control and hygienic standards'. Thus, whilst some of the processes recommended might achieve sterilization in the normally accepted sense of the word, the present authors consider that the terms 'disinfection' and 'disinfectant' are more logical. The chemical agents described are: chlorine (see Section 9.2 in the present chapter); iodophors (Section 9.1.2); QACs (Section 6.1); amphoteric surface-active agents (Section 6.4); anionic surface-active agents (Section 6.2) with an inorganic acid, usually phosphoric acid, to give highly acid solutions for removing and preventing milkstone; sodium hydroxide; and formaldehyde (Section 7.2). The report provides useful information on the inclusion of detergents into the formulation to provide balanced products which clean, which are microbicidal and which can be employed below 60°C. At temperatures of 70°C and above, the detergents alone are able to kill most spoilage and pathogenic bacteria. Of prime importance are the compatibility of the two ingredients (in particular the fact that activity of a microbicidal agent may be enhanced or reduced by a detergent: see Chapter 3) and the need to avoid an increase in the risk of corrosion of the plant or equipment. In the latter context it is of interest to note that the incorporation of suitable alkaline agents reduces the risks of corrosion induced by chlorine-releasing agents.

Ultrahigh temperature (UHT) plant in the dairy industry requires true sterilization (as opposed to disinfection above) and for this pressurized hot water at 140–150°C is recommended in the report.

Finally, mention should be made of some studies by Muys *et al.* (1978) who investigated hydrochloric acid vapour as a sterilizing agent for heat-sensitive food containers. The aim of this work was to obtain a rapid low-temperature method in which no toxic residues remained, as occurred with other vapour-phase chemicals such as ethylene oxide, hydrogen peroxide, methyl bromide and propylene oxide. Such residues are unacceptable because they could contaminate food packed in the treated containers. The sporicidal activity of hydrochloric acid vapour in this investigation suggests that it is worthy of further study.

21 DISINFECTANTS IN RECREATIONAL WATERS

The growing popularity of public and private swimming pools has led to the inevitable problems of maintaining adequate hygienic standards, notably in relation to the possible transmission of infective micro-organisms from one person to another. At the same time, control measures must ensure that the swimming-pool water has no toxic or irritant effects on the users of the pool. Various micro-organisms have been associated with infections arising from hydrotherapy pools, swimming pools and whirlpools but the most frequently implicated organism is *Ps. aeruginosa*, the source of which is often the pool pumps (Friend & Newsom,

1986; Aspinall & Graham, 1989). For many years, chlorine disinfectants have been employed as a sanitary control measure. In 1959, the effectiveness of iodine in the disinfection of swimming pool water was described (Black *et al.*, 1959) and since then two important papers which compare the relative effectiveness of chlorine and iodine have been published by Black and his colleagues (Black *et al.*, 1970a,b). Iodine scores over chlorine in the following ways: free chlorine and iodine are effective pool sanitizers, but chlorine is more expensive, and iodine is more stable in dilute aqueous solution. Chlorine employment involves the drawback of maintaining adequate residual concentrations when the pool is heavily used, and its eye toxicity is another factor that must be considered; in contrast, its instability can be considered advantageous in terms of keeping a pool free from organic matter and free available chlorine is active in controlling algae. Iodine is ineffective against algae, and thus cannot be recommended for the disinfection of swimming-pool water until suitable formulations can be developed which overcome this disadvantage. Another useful agent used for the disinfection of swimming pools is the polymeric biguanide, Baquacil SB (Imperial Chemical Industries, Manchester M9 3DA). The properties of this type of compound have been described in Section 17.1.

Warren *et al.* (1981) have published a comparative assessment of swimming-pool disinfectants. Problems arising from the increasing use of whirlpools are referred to in Report (1989).

22 OTHER USES OF ANTIMICROBIAL AGENTS

Antimicrobial agents are used widely as disinfectants and antiseptics in the hospital and domestic environments, as preservatives or bactericides in sterile or non-sterile pharmaceutical or cosmetic products, and as preservatives in certain foodstuffs. Additionally, they are employed in certain specialized areas such as cutting oils, fuels, paper, wood, paint, textiles and the construction industry. These aspects are considered in detail in later chapters.

23 WHICH ANTIMICROBIAL AGENT?

23.1 Regulatory requirements

The Federal Drug Administration in the United States, the EEC for the European community and most other countries publish information on the permitted use and concentration of preservatives. Current regulations should be consulted and complied with when manufacturing in these countries and exporting to them.

The situation from the American point of view has been reviewed by Eirmann (1984). Greenwood (1990) has provided a very comprehensive overview for preservative use over a wide range of countries.

23.2 Which preservative?

Because of the many variables which affect the activity of antimicrobial agents it is almost impossible from a mere scrutiny of the literature to select a preservative which will be optimal in a particular product. Legislation passed in the United States of America by the FDA required the manufacturers of cosmetics to declare the ingredients in their products and to state their function or purpose. This information was computerized and the data relating to declared preservatives published (Richardson, 1981). In this survey 19 584 formulae from 902 companies were included. This list of the 10 most used antimicrobial agents with the number of times they appeared in the 19 584 submissions processed was as follows:

methyl *p*-hydroxybenzoate	6785
propyl *p*-hydroxybenzoate	6174
imidazolidinyl urea	1684
N-(3-*cis*-chlorallyl)hexamine	1001
formaldehyde	874
butyl *p*-hydroxybenzoate	668
2-bromo-2-nitro-propan, 1,3-diol	566
sorbic acid	393
sodium dehydroacetate	191
ethyl *p*-hydroxybenzoate	159

Although this is a statistical, rather than a scientific, survey, it does represent the combined expertise of a large number of organizations. Unfortunately this list did not indicate if and where combinations of preservatives were used.

As regards combinations, an appraisal of the literature seems to suggest that a combination of one of the more water-soluble esters of *p*-hydroxybenzoic acid, probably the methyl ester, together with one of the water-soluble urea derivatives or a sulphydryl reactive compound, might be a good combination to start with. Denyer *et al.* (1985) have discussed synergy in preservative combinations.

If the product is a water-in-oil emulsion, and it is felt that the oily phase needs protection especially from mould infestation, then a third component, one of the oil-soluble esters of *p*-hydroxybenzoic acid, e.g. the butyl ester, or an oil-soluble phenol such as *o*-phenylphenol might well be added. Over and above this there remains the question-begging proviso 'providing other criteria such as compatibility, stability, toxicity and regulatory requirements are satisfied'.

ACKNOWLEDGEMENT

We thank Dr F.C. Cooper and Mr H. Williams, FRSC, for useful discussions on some chemical aspects associated with this chapter.

24 REFERENCES

Aalto, T.R., Firman, M.C. & Rigler, N.E. (1953) *p*-Hydroxybenzoic acid esters as preservatives. I. Uses, antibacterial and antifungal studies, properties and determination. *Journal of the American Pharmaceutical Association*, **42**, 449–457.

Akers, M.J. (1984) Considerations in selecting antimicrobial preservative agents for parenteral product development. *Pharmaceutical Technology*, **8**, 36–46.

Albert, A. (1966) *The Acridines: Their Preparation, Properties and Uses*. 2nd Ed. London: Edward Arnold.

Albert, A. (1979) *Selective Toxicity: The Physico-Chemical Basis of Therapy*. 6th Ed. London: Chapman and Hall.

Alder, V.G., Brown A.M. & Gillespie, W.A. (1990) Disinfection of heat-sensitive material by low-temperature steam and formaldehyde. *Journal of Clinical Pathology*, **19**, 83–89.

Alder, V.G., Boss, E., Gillespie, W.A. & Swann, A.J. (1971) Residual disinfection of wool blankets treated with formaldehyde. *Journal of Applied Bacteriology*, **34**, 757–763.

Aldridge, W.N. & Threlfall, C.J. (1961) Trialkyl tins and oxidative phosphorylation. *Biochemical Journal*, **79**, 214–219.

Alexander, A.E. & Tomlinson, A.J.H. (1949) *Surface Activity*, p. 317. London: Butterworth.

Allawala, N.A. & Riegelman, S. (1953) The properties of iodine in solutions of surface-active agents. *Journal of the American Pharmaceutical Association, Scientific Edition*, **42**, 396–401.

Allwood, M.C. & Myers, E.R. (1981) Formaldehyde-releasing agents. *Society for Applied Bacteriology Technical Series 16*, pp. 69–76. London: Academic Press.

Anderson, R.A. & Chow, C.E. (1967) The distribution and activity of benzoic acid in some emulsified systems. *Journal of the Society of Cosmetic Chemists*, **18**, 207–214.

Anon (1958) Disinfection of fabrics with gaseous formaldehyde. Committee on formaldehyde disinfection. *Journal of Hygiene, Cambridge*, **56**, 488–515.

Anon (1962) Dimethoxane, a new preservative effective with non-ionic agents. *American Perfumer and Cosmetics*, **77**, 32–38.

Anon (1965) Report of the Public Health Laboratory Service Committee on the Testing and Evaluation of Disinfectants. *British Medical Journal*, **i**, 408–413.

Anon (1970) *The Disinfection and Disinfestation of Poultry Houses*. Ministry of Agriculture, Fisheries and Food: Advisory Leaflet 514, revised 1970. London: HMSO.

Anon (1977) Recommendations for sterilisation of plant and equipment used in the dairying industry. BS 5305. London: British Standards Institution.

Aspinall, S.T. & Graham, R. (1989) Two sources of contamination of a hydrotherapy pool by environmental organisms. *Journal of Hospital Infection*, **14**, 285–292.

Ayliffe, G.A.J., Collins, B.J. & Lowbury, E.J.L. (1966) Cleansing and disinfection of hospital floors. *British Medical Journal*, **ii**, 442–445.

Babb, J.R., Bradley, C.R. & Ayliffe, G.A.J. (1980) Sporicidal activity of glutaraldehyde and hypochlorites and other factors influencing their selection for the treatment of medical equipment. *Journal of Hospital Infection*, **1**, 63–75.

Baillie, L. (1987) Chlorhexidine resistance among bacteria isolated from urine of catheterized patients. *Journal of Hospital Infection*, **10**, 83–86.

Baird-Parker, A.C. & Holbrook, R. (1971) The inhibition and destruction of cocci. In *Inhibition and Destruction of the Microbial Cell* (ed. Hugo, W.B.) pp. 369–397. London: Academic Press.

Baldry, M.G.C. (1983) The bactericidal, fungicidal and sporicidal properties of hydrogen peroxide and peracetic acid. *Journal of Applied Bacteriology*, **54**, 417–423.

Baldry, M.G.C. & Fraser, J.A.L. (1988) Disinfection with peroxygens. In *Industrial Biocides* (ed. Payne, K.R.) Critical Reports on Applied Chemistry, Vol. 22, pp. 91–116. Chichester: John Wiley & Sons.

Bandelin, F.J. (1950) The effects of pH on the efficiency of various mould inhibiting compounds. *Journal of the American Pharmaceutical Association, Scientific Edition*,

47, 691–694.

Bandelin, F.J. (1977) Antibacterial and preservative properties of alcohols. *Cosmetics and Toiletries*, **92**, 59–70.

Barrett, M. (1969) Biocides for food plant. *Process Biochemistry*, **4**, 23–24.

Bassett, D.C.J. (1971) The effect of pH on the multiplication of a pseudomonad in chlorhexidine and cetrimide. *Journal of Clinical Pathology*, **24**, 708–711.

Bean, H.S. (1967) The microbiology of topical preparations in pharmaceutical practice. 2. Pharmaceutical aspects. *Pharmaceutical Journal*, **199**, 289–292.

Bean, H.S. & Berry, H. (1950) The bactericidal activity of phenols in aqueous solutions of soap. Part I. The solubility of water-insoluble phenol in aqueous solutions of soap. *Journal of Pharmacy and Pharmacology*, **2**, 484–490.

Bean, H.S. & Berry, H. (1951) The bactericidal activity of phenols in aqueous solutions of soap. Part II. The bactericidal activity of benzylchlorophenol in aqueous solutions of potassium laurate. *Journal of Pharmacy and Pharmacology*, **3**, 639–655.

Bean, H.S. & Berry, H. (1953) The bactericidal activity of phenols in aqueous solutions of soap. Part III. The bactericidal activity of chloroxylenol in aqueous solutions of potassium laurate. *Journal of Pharmacy and Pharmacology*, **5**, 632–639.

Beath, T. (1943) The suppression of infection in recent wounds by the use of antiseptics. *Surgery*, **13**, 667–676.

Beaver, D.J., Roman, D.P. & Stoffel, P.J. (1957) The preparation and bacteriostatic activity of substituted ureas. *Journal of the American Chemical Society*, **79**, 1236–1245.

Beckett, A.H. & Robinson, A.E. (1958) The inactivation of preservatives by non-ionic surface active agents. *Soap, Perfumery and Cosmetics*, **31**, 454–459.

Bell, T.A., Etchells, J.L. & Borg, A.F. (1959) Influence of sorbic acid on the growth of certain species of bacteria, yeasts and filamentous fungi. *Journal of Bacteriology*, **77**, 573–580.

Beneke, E.S. & Fabian, F.W. (1955) Sorbic acid as a fungistatic agent at different pH levels for moulds isolated from strawberries and tomatoes. *Food Technology*, **9**, 486–488.

Bergan, T. & Lystad, A. (1972) Evaluation of disinfectant inactivators. *Acta Pathologica et Microbiologica Scandinavica, Section B*, **80**, 507–510.

Berke, P.A. & Rosen, W.E. (1970) Germall, a new family of antimicrobial preservatives for cosmetics. *American Perfumer and Cosmetics*, **85**, 55–60.

Berke, P.A. & Rosen, W.E. (1978) Imidazolidinyl urea activity against *Pseudomonas*. *Journal of the Society of Cosmetic Chemists*, **29**, 757–766.

Berke, P.A. & Rosen, W.E. (1980) Are cosmetic emulsions adequately preserved against *Pseudomonas*? *Journal of the Society of Cosmetic Chemists*, **31**, 37–40.

Berry, H. (1944) Antibacterial values of ethylene glycol monophenyl ether (phenoxetol). *Lancet*, **ii**, 175–176.

Berry, H. & Briggs, A. (1956) The influence of soaps on the bactericidal activity of sparingly water soluble phenols. *Journal of Pharmacy and Pharmacology*, **8**, 1143–1154.

Berry, H. & Stenlake, J.B. (1942) Variations in the bactericidal value of Lysol BP. *Pharmaceutical Journal*, **148**, 112–113.

Berry, H., Cook, A.M. & Wills, B.A. (1956) Bactericidal activity of soap–phenol mixtures. *Journal of Pharmacy and Pharmacology*, **8**, 425–441.

Beveridge, E.G. & Hauta, A. (1970) The utilisation for growth and the degradation of *p*-hydroxybenzoate esters by bacteria. *International Biodeterioration Bulletin*, **6**, 9–12.

Bigger, J.W. & Griffiths, L.I. (1933) The disinfection of water by the Katadyn system. *Irish Journal of Medical Sciences*, **85**, 17–25.

Black, A.P., Lackey, J.B. & Lackey, E.W. (1959) Effectiveness of iodine for the disinfection of swimming pool water. *American Journal of Public Health*, **49**, 1061–1068.

Black, A.P., Kinman, R.N., Keirn, M.A., Smith, J.J. & Harlan, W.E. (1970a) The disinfection of swimming pool water. Part 1. Comparison of iodine and chlorine as swimming pool disinfectants. *American Journal of Public Health*, **60**, 535–545.

Black, A.P., Keirn, M.A., Smith, J.J., Dykes, G.M. & Harlan, W.E. (1970b) The disinfection of swimming pool water. Part II. A field study of the disinfection of public swimming pools. *American Journal of Public Health*, **60**, 740–750.

Blatt, R. & Maloney, J.V. (1961) An evaluation of the iodophor compounds as surgical germicides. *Surgery, Gynaecology & Obstetrics*, **113**, 699–704.

Blaug, S.M. & Ahsan, S.S. (1961) Interaction of parabens with non-ionic macromolecules. *Journal of Pharmaceutical Sciences*, **50**, 441–443.

Block, S.S. (1983) Surface-active agents: amphoteric compounds. In *Disinfection, Sterilisation and Preservation* (ed. Block, S.S.) 3rd Ed. pp. 335–345. Philadelphia; Lea & Febiger.

Bloomfield, S.F. (1974) The effect of the antibacterial agent Fentichlor on energy coupling in *Staphylococcus aureus*. *Journal of Applied Bacteriology*, **37**, 117–131.

Bloomfield, S.F. & Miles, G.A. (1979a) The antibacterial properties of sodium dichloroisocyanurate and sodium hypochlorite formulations. *Journal of Applied Bacteriology*, **46**, 65–73.

Bloomfield, S.F. & Miles, G.A. (1979b) The relationship between residual chlorine and disinfection capacity of sodium hypochlorite and sodium dichloroisocyanurate solutions in the presence of *Escherichia coli* and of milk. *Microbios Letters*, **10**, 33–43.

Bloomfield, S.F. & Miller, E.A. (1989) A comparison of hypochlorite and phenolic disinfectants for disinfection of clean and soiled surfaces and blood spillages. *Journal of Hospital Infection*, **13**, 231–239.

Bloomfield, S.F. & Uso, E.E. (1985) The antibacterial properties of sodium hypochlorite and sodium dichloroisocyanurate as hospital disinfectants. *Journal of Hospital Infection*, **6**, 20–30.

Bloomfield, S.F., Smith-Burchnell, C.A. & Dalgleish, A.G.

(1990). Evaluation of hypochlorite-releasing agents against the human immunodeficiency virus (HIV). *Journal of Hospital Infection*, **15**, 273–278.

Borick, P.M. (1968) Chemical sterilizers (Chemosterilizers). *Advances in Applied Microbiology*, **10**, 291–312.

Borick, P.M. & Pepper, R.E. (1970) The spore problem. In *Disinfection* (ed. Benarde, M.) pp. 85–102. New York: Marcel Dekker.

Bosund, I. (1962) The action of benzoic and salicylic acids on the metabolism of microorganisms. *Advances in Food Research*, **11**, 331–353.

Boucher, R.M.G. (1974) Potentiated acid 1,5-pentanedial solution—a new chemical sterilizing and disinfecting agent. *American Journal of Hospital Pharmacy*, **31**, 546–557.

Brandes, C.H. (1934). Ionic silver sterilisation. *Industrial and Engineering Chemistry*, **26**, 962–964.

British Pharmacopoeia (1988) London: HMSO.

British Standards relating to disinfectants:

(1946) '*Disinfectant and sanitary powders*'. BS 1013: 1946.

(1961) '*Specification for black and white disinfectants*'. BS 2462: 1961.

(1976) '*Glossary of terms relating to disinfectants*'. BS 5283: 1976.

(1976) '*Aromatic disinfectant fluids*'. BS 5197: 1976.

(1984) '*Method for determination of the antimicrobial activity of QAC disinfectant formulations*'. BS 6471: 1984.

(1984) '*Specification for QAC based aromatic disinfectant fluids*'. BS 6424: 1984.

(1985) '*Method for determination of the Rideal–Walker coefficient of disinfectants*'. BS 541: 1985.

(1986) '*Method for assessing the efficacy of disinfectants by the modified Chick–Martin test*: BS 808:1986.

Brown, M.R.W. (1975) The role of the cell envelope in resistance. In *Resistance of Pseudomonas aeruginosa* (ed. Brown, M.R.W.) pp. 71–107. London: John Wiley & Sons.

Brown, M.R.W. & Anderson, R.A. (1968) The bacterial effect of silver ions on *Pseudomonas aeruginosa*. *Journal of Pharmacy and Pharmacology*, **20**, 1S–3S.

Browne, M.K. & Stoller, J.L. (1970) Intraperitoneal noxythiolin in faecal peritonitis. *British Journal of Surgery*, **57**, 525–529.

Browne, M.K., Leslie, G.B. & Pfirrman, R.W. (1976) Taurolin, a new chemotherapeutic agent. *Journal of Applied Bacteriology*, **41**, 363–368.

Browne, M.K., Leslie, G.B., Pfirrman, R.W. & Brodhage, H. (1977) The *in vitro* and *in vivo* activity of Taurolin against anaerobic pathogenic organisms. *Surgery, Gynaecology & Obstetrics*, **145**, 842–846.

Browne, M.K., MacKenzie, M. & Doyle, P.J. (1978) A controlled trial of Taurolin in establishing bacterial peritonitis. *Surgery, Gynaecology and Obstetrics*, **146**, 721–724.

Browning, C.H. (1964) Chemotherapy of antibacterial dyestuffs. In *Experimental Chemotherapy*. Vol. 2 (eds Schnitzer, R.T. & Hawking, F.) pp. 1–136. London: Academic Press.

Browning, C.H., Gulbransen, R. & Kennaway, E.L. (1919–1920) Hydrogen-ion concentration and antiseptic potency, with special references to the action of acridine compounds. *Journal of Pathology & Bacteriology*, **23**, 106–108.

Bruch, C.W. & Bruch, M.K. (1970) Gaseous disinfection. In *Disinfection* (ed. Benarde, M.) pp. 149–206. New York: Marcel Dekker.

Bruch, C.W. & Koesterer, M.G. (1961) The microbicidal activity of gaseous propylene oxide and its application to powdered or flaked foods. *Journal of Food Science*, **26**, 428–435.

Bryce, D.M., Croshaw, B., Hall, J.E., Holland, V.R. & Lessel, B. (1978) The activity and safety of the antimicrobial agent bronopol (2-bromo-2-nitropropan-1,3-diol). *Journal of the Society of Cosmetic Chemists*, **29**, 3–24.

Burleson, G.R., Murray, T.M. & Pollard, M. (1975) Inactivation of viruses and bacteria by ozone, with and without sonication. *Applied Microbiology*, **29**, 340–344.

Chawner, J.A. & Gilbert, P. (1989a). A comparative study of the bactericidal and growth inhibitory activities of the bisbiguanides alexidine and chlorhexidine. *Journal of Applied Bacteriology*, **66**, 243–252.

Chawner, J.A. & Gilbert, P. (1989b). Interaction of the bisbiguanides chlorhexidine and alexidine with phospholipid vesicles: evidence for separate modes of action. *Journal of Applied Bacteriology*, **66**, 253–258.

Cherrington, C.A., Hinton, M. & Chopra, I. (1990). Effect of short-chain organic acids on macromolecular synthesis in *Escherichia coli*. *Journal of Applied Bacteriology*, **68**, 69–74.

Clark, D.S. & Lentz, C.P. (1969) The effect of carbon dioxide on the growth of slime producing bacteria on fresh beef. *Canadian Institute of Food Technology Journal*, **2**, 72–75.

Clegg, L.F.L. (1967) Disinfectants in the dairy industry. *Journal of Applied Bacteriology*, **30**, 117–140.

Clegg, L.F.L. (1970) Disinfection in the dairy industry. In *Disinfection* (ed. Bernarde, M.A.) pp. 311–375. New York: Marcel Dekker.

Coal Tar Data Book (1965) 2nd Ed. Leeds: The Coal Tar Research Association.

Coates, D. (1985) A comparison of sodium hypochlorite and sodium dichloroisocyanurate products. *Journal of Hospital Infection*, **6**, 31–40.

Coates, D. (1988) Comparison of sodium hypochlorite and sodium dichloroisocyanurate disinfectants: neutralization by serum. *Journal of Hospital Infection*, **11**, 60–67.

Coates, D. & Death, J.E. (1978) Sporicidal activity of mixtures of alcohol and hypochlorite. *Journal of Clinical Pathology*, **31**, 148–152.

Coates, D. & Wilson, M. (1989) Use of sodium dichloroisocyanurate granules for spills of body fluids. *Journal of Hospital Infection*, **13**, 241–251.

Colebrook, L. (1941) Disinfection of the skin. *Bulletin of War Medicine*, **2**, 73–79.

Colebrook, L. & Maxted, W.R. (1933) Antiseptics in midwifery. *Journal of Obstetrics and Gynaecology of the British Empire*, **40**, 966–990.

Collier, H.O.J., Cox, W.A., Huskinson, P.L. & Robinson, F.A. (1959) Further observations on the biological properties of dequalinium (Dequadin) and hedaquinium (Teoquil). *Journal of Pharmacy and Pharmacology*, **11**, 671–680.

Collins, J. (1986) The use of glutaraldehyde in laboratory discard jars. *Letters in Applied Microbiology*, **2**, 103–105.

Corner, T.R., Joswick, H.L., Silvernale, J.N. & Gerhardt, P. (1971) Antimicrobial actions of hexachlorophane: lysis and fixation of bacterial protoplases. *Journal of Bacteriology*, **108**, 501–507.

Cousins, C.M. & Allan, C.D. (1967) Sporicidal properties of some halogens. *Journal of Applied Bacteriology*, **30**, 168–174.

Cox, W.A. & D'Arcy, P.F. (1962) A new cationic antimicrobial agent, *N*-dodecyl-4-amino quinaldinium acetate (Laurolinium acetate). *Journal of Pharmacy and Pharmacology*, **15**, 129–137.

Craven, D.E., Moody, B., Connolly, M.G., Kollisch, N.R., Stottmeier, K.D. & McCabe, W.R. (1981) Pseudobacteremia caused by povidone-iodine solution contaminated with *Pseudomonas cepacia*. *New England Journal of Medicine*, **305**, 621–623.

Crewther, W.G. & McQuade, A.B. (1964) Disinfection of woollen blankets. *Journal of Hygiene, Cambridge*, **62**, 29–37.

Croshaw, B. (1971) The destruction of mycobacteria. In *Inhibition and Destruction of the Microbial Cell* (ed. Hugo, W.B.) pp. 419–449. London: Academic Press.

Croshaw, B. (1977) Preservatives for cosmetics and toiletries. *Journal of the Society of Cosmetic Chemists*, **28**, 3–16.

Croshaw, B. & Holland, V.R. (1984) Chemical preservatives: use of bronopol as a cosmetic preservative. In *Cosmetic and Drug Preservation. Principles and Practice* (ed. Kabara, J.J.) pp. 31–62. New York: Marcel Dekker.

Cruess, W.V. & Richert, P. (1929) Effects of hydrogen ion concentration on the toxicity of sodium benzoate to microorganisms. *Journal of Bacteriology*, **17**, 363–371.

Curd, F.H.S. & Rose, F.L. (1946) Synthetic antimalarials. Part X. Some aryl-diaguanide ('-biguanide') derivatives. *Journal of the Chemical Society*, 729–737.

Dancer, B.N., Power, E.G.M. & Russell, A.D. (1989). Alkali-induced revival of *Bacillus* spores after inactivation by glutaraldehyde. *FEMS Microbiology Letters*, **57**, 345–348.

Dankert, J. & Schut, I.K. (1976) The antibacterial activity of chloroxylenol in combination with ethylenediamine tetraacetic acid. *Journal of Hygiene, Cambridge*, **76**, 11–22.

D'Arcy, P.F. (1971) Inhibition and destruction of moulds and yeasts. In *Inhibition and Destruction of the Microbial Cell* (ed. Hugo, W.B.) pp. 613–686. London: Academic Press.

D'Arcy, P.F. & Taylor, E.P. (1962a) Quaternary ammonium compounds in medicinal chemistry. I. *Journal of Pharmacy and Pharmacology*, **14**, 129–146.

D'Arcy, P.F. & Taylor E.P. (1962b) Quaternary ammonium compounds in medicinal chemistry. II. *Journal of Pharmacy and Pharmacology*, **14**, 193–216.

Davies, A., Bentley, M. & Field, B.S. (1968) Comparison of the action of Vantocil, cetrimide and chlorhexidine on *Escherichia coli* and the protoplasts of Gram-positive bacteria. *Journal of Applied Bacteriology*, **31**, 448–461.

Davies, D.J.G. (1980) Manufacture and supply of contact lens products. I. An academic's view. *Pharmaceutical Journal*, **225**, 343–345.

Davies, G.E. (1949) Quaternary ammonium compounds. A new technique for the study of their bactericidal action and the results obtained with Cetavlon (Cetyltrimethyl ammonium bromide). *Journal of Hygiene, Cambridge*, **47**, 271–277.

Davies, G.E., Francis, J., Martin, A.R., Rose, F.L. & Swain, G. (1954) 1:6-di-4′-chlorophenyl-diguanidinohexane ('Hibitane'): a laboratory investigation of a new antibacterial agency of high potency. *British Journal of Pharmacology*, **9**, 192–196.

Davis, J.G. (1960) Methods for the evaluation of the antibacterial activity of surface active compounds: technical aspects of the problem. *Journal of Applied Bacteriology*, **23**, 318–344.

Davis, J.G. (1962) Idophors as detergent-sterilizers. *Journal of Applied Bacteriology*, **25**, 195–201.

Davis, J.G. (1972a) Fundamentals of microbiology in relation to cleansing in the cosmetics industry. *Journal of the Society of Cosmetic Chemists*, **23**, 45–71.

Davis, J.G. (1972b) Problems of hygiene in the dairy industry. Parts 1 and 2. *Dairy Industries*, **37**, 212–215:(5) 251–256.

Dawson, F.W. (1962) Glycidaldehyde vapour as a disinfectant. *American Journal of Hygiene*, **76**, 209–215.

Deans, S.G. & Ritchie, G. (1987) Antibacterial properties of plant essential oils. *International Journal of Food Microbiology*, **5**, 165–180.

Death, J.E. & Coates, D. (1979) Effect of pH on sporicidal and microbicidal activity of buffered mixtures of alcohol and sodium hypochlorite. *Journal of Clinical Pathology*, **32**, 148–153.

Denyer, S.P., Hugo, W.B. & Harding, V.D. (1985) Synergy in preservative combinations. *International Journal of Pharmaceutics*, **25**, 245–253.

Dickinson, J.C. & Wagg, R.E. (1967) Use of formaldehyde for the disinfection of hospital woollen blankets on laundering. *Journal of Applied Bacteriology*, **33**, 566–573.

Domagk, G. (1935) Eine neue Klasse von Disinfektionsmitteln. *Deutsche Medizinische Wochenschrift*, **61**, 829–932.

Dunn, C.G. (1968) Food preservatives. In *Disinfection, Sterilization and Preservation* (ed. Lawrence, C.A. & Block, S.S.) pp. 632–651. Philadelphia: Lea & Febiger.

Dunning, F., Dunning, B. & Drake, W.E. (1931) Preparation and bacteriological study of some symmetrical organic sulphides. *Journal of the American Chemical Society*, **53**, 3466–3469.

Dychdala, G.R. (1983) Chlorine and chlorine compounds. In *Disinfection, Sterilization and Preservation* (ed. Block, S.S.) 3rd Ed. pp. 157–182. Philadelphia: Lea & Febiger.

Eager, R.C., Leder, J. & Theis, A.B. (1986) Glutaraldehyde: factors important for microbicidal efficacy. *Proceedings of the 3rd Conference on Progress in Chemical Disinfection*, pp. 32–49. Binghamton, New York.

Eirmann, H.J. (1984) Cosmetic product preservation. Safety and regulatory issues. In *Cosmetic and Drug Preservation: Principles and Practice* (ed. Kabara, J.J.) pp. 559–569. New York: Marcel Dekker.

Eklund, T. (1983) Inhibition of growth and uptake processes in bacteria by some chemical food preservatives. *Journal of Applied Bacteriology*, **48**, 423–432.

Eklund, T. (1985) Inhibition of microbial growth at different pH levels by benzoic and propionic acids and esters of *p*-hydroxybenzoic acid. *International Journal of Food Microbiology*, **2**, 159–167.

El-Falaha, B.M.A., Russell, A.D. & Furr, J.R. (1983) Sensitivities of wild-type and envelope-defective strains of *Escherichia coli* and *Pseudomonas aeruginosa* to antibacterial agents. *Microbios*, **38**, 99–105.

Ellison, R.T., Giehl, T.J. & LaForce, F.M. (1988) Damage of the outer membrane of enteric Gram-negative bacteria by lactoferrin and transferrin. *Infection and Immunity*, **56**, 2774–2781.

Elworthy, P.H. (1976) The increasingly clever micelle. *Pharmaceutical Journal*, **217**, 566–570.

Ernst, R.R. (1974) Ethylene oxide sterilization kinetics. *Biotechnology and Bioengineering Symposium* No. 4, pp. 865–878.

Fargher, R.G., Galloway, L.O. & Roberts, M.E. (1930) The inhibitory action of certain substances on the growth of mould fungi. *Journal of Textile Chemistry*, **21**, 245–260.

Farkas-Himsley, H. (1964) Killing of chlorine-resistant bacteria by chlorine-bromide solutions. *Applied Microbiology*, **12**, 1–6.

Favero, M.S. (1985) Sterilization, disinfection and antisepsis in the hospital. In *Manual of Clinical Microbiology* (ed. Lennette, E.H., Balows, A., Hausler, W.J., Jr. & Shadomy, H.J.) 4th edn., pp. 129–137. Washington, D.C.: American Society for Microbiology.

Fels, P., Gay, M., Kabay, A. & Urban, S. (1987) Antimicrobial preservation. Manufacturers' experience with pharmaceuticals in the efficacy test and in practice. *Pharmaceutical Industry*, **49**, 631–637.

Finch, W.E. (1953) A substitute for Lysol. *Pharmaceutical Journal*, **170**, 59–60.

Finch, W.E. (1958) *Disinfectants—Their Value and Uses*. London: Chapman & Hall.

Foster, J.H.S. & Russell, A.D. (1971) Antibacterial dyes and nitrofurans. In *Inhibition and Destruction of the Microbial Cell* (ed. Hugo, W.B.) pp. 185–208. London: Academic Press.

Foster, T.J. (1983) Plasmid-determined resistance to antimicrobial drugs and toxic metal ions in bacteria. *Microbiological Reviews*, **47**, 361–409.

Fraenkel-Conrat, H., Cooper, M. & Alcott, H.S. (1945) The reaction of formaldehyde with proteins. *Journal of the American Chemical Society*, **67**, 950–954.

Frank, M.J. & Schaffner, W. (1976) Contaminated aqueous benzalkonium chloride: an unnecessary hospital infection hazard. *Journal of the American Medical Association*, **236**, 2418–2419.

Fraser, J.A.L. (1986) Novel applications of peracetic acid. *Chemspec '86: BACS Symposium*, pp. 65–69.

Frederick, J.F., Corner, T.R. & Gerhardt, P. (1974) Antimicrobial actions of hexachlorophane: inhibition of respiration in *Bacillus megaterium*. *Antimicrobial Agents and Chemotherapy*, **6**, 712–721.

Freese, E. & Levin, B.C. (1978) Action mechanisms of preservatives and antiseptics. *Developments in Industrial Microbiology*, **19**, 207–227.

Freese, E., Sheu, W. & Galliers, E. (1973) Function of lipophilic acids as antimicrobial food additives. *Nature, London*, **241**, 321–325.

Friend, P.A. & Newsom, S.W.B. (1986) Hygiene for hydrotherapy pools. *Journal of Hospital Infection*, **8**, 213–216.

Frier, M. (1971) Derivatives of 4-amino-quinaldinium and 8-hydroxyquinoline. In *Inhibition and Destruction of the Microbial Cell* (ed. Hugo, W.B.) pp. 107–120. London: Academic Press.

Furr, J.R. & Russell, A.D. (1972a) Some factors influencing the activity of esters of *p*-hydroxybenzoic acid against *Serratia marcescens*. *Microbios*, **5**, 189–198.

Furr, J.R. & Russell, A.D. (1972b) Uptake of esters of *p*-hydroxy benzoic acid by *Serratia marcescens* and by fattened and non-fattened cells of *Bacillus subtilis*. *Microbios*, **5**, 237–346.

Furr, J.R. & Russell, A.D. (1972c) Effect of esters of *p*-hydroxybenzoic acid on spheroplasts of *Serratia marcescens* and protoplasts of *Bacillus megaterium*. *Microbios*, **6**, 47–54.

Galbraith, H., Miller T.B., Paton, A.M. & Thompson, J.K. (1971) Antibacterial activity of long chain fatty acids and the reversal with calcium, magnesium, ergocalciferol and cholesterol. *Journal of Applied Bacteriology*, **34**, 803–813.

Galland, R.B. Saunders, J.H., Mosley, J.G. & Darrell, J.C. (1977) Prevention of wound infection in abdominal operations by per-operative antibiotics or povidone-iodine. *Lancet*, **ii**, 1043–1045.

Gardner, J.F. & Peel, M.M. (1986) *Introduction to Sterilization and Disinfection*. Edinburgh: Churchill Livingstone.

Gardner, J.F. & Peel, M.M. (1991) *Introduction to Sterilization, Disinfection and Infection Control*. Edinburgh: Churchill Livingstone.

Gershenfeld, L. (1956) A new iodine dairy sanitizer. *American Journal of Pharmacy*, **128**, 335–339.

Gershenfeld, L. (1962) Povidone-iodine as a sporicide. *American Journal of Pharmacy*, **134**, 78–81.

Gillespie, E.H. & Robinson, W. (1959) Blanket laundering

and sterilization. *Journal of Clinical Pathology*, **12**, 351.

Gjermo, P., Rolla, G. & Arskaug, L. (1973) The effect on dental plaque formation and some in vitro properties of 12 bis-biguanides. *Journal of Periodontology*, **8**, 81–88.

Goldberg, A.A., Shapero, M. & Wilder, E. (1950). Antibacterial colloidal electrolytes: the potentiation of the activities of mercuric, phenylmercuric and silver ions by a colloidal and sulphonic anion. *Journal of Pharmacy and Pharmacology*, **2**, 20–26.

Goldenberg, N. & Relf, C.J. (1967) Use of disinfectants in the food industry. *Journal of Applied Bacteriology*, **30**, 141–147.

Gooding, C.M., Melnick, D., Lawrence, R.L. & Luckmann, F.H. (1955) Sorbic acid as a fungistatic agent for foods. IX. Physico-chemical considerations in using sorbic acid to protect foods. *Food Research*, **20**, 639–648.

Gorman, S.P. & Scott, E.M. (1985) A comparative evaluation of dental aspirator cleansing and disinfectant solutions. *British Dental Journal*, **158**, 13–16.

Gorman, S.P., Scott, E.M. & Russell, A.D. (1980) Antimicrobial activity, uses and mechanism of action of glutaraldehyde. *Journal of Applied Bacteriology*, **48**, 161–190.

Gottardi, W. (1985) The influence of the chemical behaviour of iodine on the germicidal action of disinfectant solutions containing iodine. *Journal of Hospital Infection*, **6**, *Supplement A*, 1–11.

Gray, G.W. & Wilkinson, S.G. (1965) The action of ethylenediamine tetraacetic acid on *Pseudomonas aeruginosa*. *Journal of Applied Bacteriology*, **28**, 153–164.

Greenwood, R.K. (1990) Preservatives: registration and regulatory affairs. In *Guide to Microbiology Control in Pharmaceuticals* (eds Denyer, S.P. & Baird, R.M.) pp. 313–340. Chichester: Ellis Horwood.

Gribbard, J. (1933) The oligodynamic action of silver in the treatment of water. *Canadian Journal of Public Health*, **24**, 96–97.

Grossgebauer, K. (1970) Virus disinfection. In *Disinfection* (ed. Benarde, M.) pp. 103–148. New York: Marcel Dekker.

Gucklhorn, I.R. (1970) Antimicrobials in cosmetics. Parts 1–7. *Manufacturing Chemist and Aerosol News*, **41** (6) 44–45; (7) 51–52; (8) 28–29: (10) 49–50: (11) 48–49: (12) 50–51.

Gucklhorn, I.R. (1971) Antimicrobials in cosmetics. Parts 8 and 9. *Manufacturing Chemist and Aerosol News*, **42** (1) 35–37; (2) 35–39.

Gump, W.S. & Walter, G.R. (1960) Chemical and antimicrobial activity of bis phenols. *Journal of the Society of Cosmetic Chemists*, **11**, 307–314.

Gump, W.S. & Walter, G.R. (1963) Chemical structure and antimicrobial activity of bis phenols. III. Broad spectrum evaluation of hexachlorophane and its isomers. *Journal of the Society of Cosmetic Chemists*, **14**, 269–276.

Gump, W.S. & Walter, G.R. (1964) Chemical structure and antimicrobial activity of bis phenols. IV. Broad spectrum evaluation of 2,2′-methylene bis (dichlorophenols). *Journal of the Society of Cosmetic Chemists*, **15**, 717–725.

Gurley, B. (1985) Ozone: pharmaceutical sterilant of the future? *Journal of Parenteral Science and Technology*, **39**, 256–261.

Haler, D. (1974) The effect of 'Noxyflex' (Noxythiolin), on the behaviour of animals which have been infected intraperitoneally with suspensions of faeces. *International Journal of Clinical Pharmacology*, **9**, 160–164.

Hamilton, W.A. (1968) The mechanism of the bacteriostatic action of tetrachlorosalicylanide: a membrane-active antibacterial compound. *Journal of General Microbiology*, **50**, 441–458.

Hamilton, W.A. (1971) Membrane-active anti-bacterial compounds. In *Inhibition and Destruction of the Microbial Cell* (ed. Hugo, W.B.) pp. 77–106. London: Academic Press.

Hammond, S.M. & Carr, J.G. (1976) The antimicrobial activity of SO_2. In *Inhibition and Inactivation of Vegetative Microbes* (eds Skinner, F.A. & Hugo, W.B.) Society for Applied Bacteriology Symposium Series No. 5, pp. 89–110. London: Academic Press.

Haque, H. & Russell, A.D. (1974a) Effect of ethylenediamine tetraacetic acid and related chelating agents on whole cells of Gram-negative bacteria. *Antimicrobial Agents & Chemotherapy*, **5**, 447–452.

Haque, H. & Russell, A.D. (1974b) Effect of chelating agents on the susceptibility of some strains of Gram-negative bacteria to some antibacterial agents. *Antimicrobial Agents & Chemotherapy*, **6**, 200–206.

Haque, H. & Russell, A.D. (1976) Cell envelopes of Gram-negative bacteria: composition, response to chelating agents and susceptibility of whole cells to antibacterial agents. *Journal of Applied Bacteriology*, **40**, 89–99.

Harry, E.G. (1963) The relationship between egg spoilage and the environment of the egg when laid. *British Poultry Science*, **4**, 91–100.

Hatch, E. & Cooper, P. (1948) Sodium hexametaphosphate in emulsions of Dettol for obstetric use. *Pharmaceutical Journal*, **161**, 198–199.

Heinzel, M. (1988) The phenomena of resistance to disinfectants and preservatives. In *Industrial Biocides* (ed. Payne, K.R.) Critical Reports on Applied Chemistry, Vol. 22, pp. 52–67. Chichester: John Wiley & Sons.

Hilbert, G.C. & Johnson, T.B. (1929) Germicidal activity of diarylsulphide phenols. *Journal of the American Chemical Society*, **51**, 1526–1536.

Himmelfarb, P., El-Bis, H.M., Read, R.B. & Litsky, W. (1962) Effect of relative humidity on the bactericidal activity of propylene oxide vapour. *Applied Microbiology*, **10**, 431–435.

Hoffman, H.-P., Geftic, S.M., Gelzer, J., Heymann, H. & Adaire, F.W. (1973) Ultrastructural alterations associated with the growth of resistant *Pseudomonas aeruginosa* in the presence of benzalkonium chloride. *Journal of Bacteriology*, **113**, 409–416.

Hoffman, R.K. (1971) Toxic gases. In *Inhibition and Destruction of the Microbial Cell* (ed. Hugo, W.B.)

pp. 225–258. London: Academic Press.

Hoffman, R.K. & Warshowsky, B. (1958) Beta-propiolactone vapour as a disinfectant. *Applied Microbiology*, **6**, 358–362.

Holloway, P.M., Bucknall, R.A. & Denton, G.W. (1986) The effects of sub-lethal concentrations of chlorhexidine on bacterial pathogenicity. *Journal of Hospital Infection*, **8**, 39–46.

Hopwood, D. (1975) The reactions of glutaraldehyde with nucleic acids. *Histochemical Journal*, **7**, 267–276.

Hopwood, D., Allen, C.R. & McCabe, M. (1970) The reactions between glutaraldehyde and various proteins. An investigation of their kinetics. *Histochemical Journal*, **2**, 137–150.

Hugo, W.B. (1971) Amidines. In *Inhibition and Destruction of the Microbial Cell*. (ed. Hugo, W.B.) pp. 121–136. London: Academic Press.

Hugo, W.B. (1978) Membrane-active antimicrobial drugs—a reappraisal of their mode of action in the light of the chemiosmotic theory. *International Journal of Pharmaceutics*, **1**, 127–131.

Hugo, W.B. (1979) Phenols: a review of their history and development as anti-microbial agents. *Microbios*, **23**, 83–85.

Hugo, W.B. & Beveridge, E.G. (1964) The resistance of gallic acid and its alkyl esters to attack by bacteria able to degrade aromatic ring compounds. *Journal of Applied Bacteriology*, **27**, 304–311.

Hugo, W.B. & Bloomfield, S.F. (1971a) Studies on the mode of action of the phenolic antibacterial agent Fentichlor against *Staphylococcus aureus* and *Escherichia coli*. I. The absorption of Fentichlor by the bacterial cell and its antibacterial activity. *Journal of Applied Bacteriology*, **34**, 557–567.

Hugo, W.B. & Bloomfield, S.F. (1971b) Studies on the mode of action of the phenolic antimicrobial agent Fentichlor against *Staphylococcus aureus* and *Escherichia coli*. II. The effects of Fentichlor on the bacterial membrane and the cytoplasmic constituents of the cell. *Journal of Applied Bacteriology*, **34**, 569–578.

Hugo, W.B. & Bloomfield, S.F. (1971c) Studies on the mode of action on the antibacterial agent Fentichlor on *Staphylococcus aureus* and *Escherichia coli*. III. The effect of Fentichlor on the metabolic activities of *Staphylococcus aureus* and *Escherichia coli*. *Journal of Applied Bacteriology*, **34**, 579–591.

Hugo, W.B. & Bowen, J.G. (1973) Studies on the mode of action of 4-ethylphenol. *Microbios*, **8**, 189–197.

Hugo, W.B. & Foster, J.H.S. (1964) Growth of *Pseudomonas aeruginosa* in solutions of esters of *p*-hydroxy benzoic acid. *Journal of Pharmacy and Pharmacology*, **16**, 209.

Hugo, W.B. & Longworth, A.R. (1964a) Some aspects of the mode of action of chlorhexidine. *Journal of Pharmacy and Pharmacology*, **16**, 655–662.

Hugo, W.B. & Longworth, A.R. (1964b) Effect of chlorhexidine on 'protoplasts' and spheroplasts of *Escherichia coli*, protoplasts of *Bacillus megaterium* and the Gram staining reaction of *Staphylococcus aureus*. *Journal of Pharmacy and Pharmacology*, **16**, 751–758.

Hugo, W.B. & Longworth, A.R. (1965) Cytological aspects of the mode of action of chlorhexidine. *Journal of Pharmacy and Pharmacology*, **17**, 28–32.

Hugo, W.B. & Longworth, A.R. (1966) The effect of chlorhexidine on the electrophoretic mobility, cytoplasmic constituents, dehydrogenase activity and cell walls of *Escherichia coli* and *Staphylococcus aureus*. *Journal of Pharmacy and Pharmacology*, **18**, 569–578.

Imperial Chemical Industries. *'Hibitane'/Chlorhexidine*. Manufacturer's Handbook.

Ingram, M. (1959) Benzoate-resistant yeasts. *Journal of Applied Bacteriology*, **22**, vi.

Ingram, M. & Haines, R.B. (1949) Inhibition of bacterial growth by pure ozone in the presence of nutrients. *Journal of Hygiene, Cambridge*, **47**, 146–168.

International Wool Secretariat (1961) The sterilisation of hospital wool blankets. *Wool Science Review*, No. 19 and No. 20, pp. 1–34.

Isenberg, H.D. (1985) Clinical laboratory studies of disinfection with sporicidin. *Journal of Clinical Microbiology*, **22**, 735–739.

Ismaeel, N., El-Moug, T., Furr, J.R. & Russell, A.D. (1986a) Resistance of *Providencia stuartii* to chlorhexidine: A consideration of the role of the inner membrane. *Journal of Applied Bacteriology*, **60**, 361–367.

Ismaeel, N., Furr, J.R. & Russell, A.D. (1986b) Reversal of the surface effects of chlorhexidine diacetate on cells of *Providencia stuartii*. *Journal of Applied Bacteriology*, **61**, 373–381.

James, A.M. (1965) The modification of the bacterial surface by chemical and enzymic treatment. In *Cell Electrophoresis* (ed. Ambrose, E.J.) pp. 154–170. London: J. & A. Churchill.

Jacobs, G., Henry, S.M. & Cotty, Y.F. (1975) The influence of pH, emulsifier and accelerated ageing upon preservative requirements of o/w emulsions. *Journal of the Society of Cosmetic Chemists*, **26**, 105–117.

Jacobs, W.A. (1916) The bactericidal properties of the quaternary salts of hexamethylenetetramine. I. The problem of the chemotherapy of experimental bacterial infections. *Journal of Experimental Medicine*, **23**, 563–568.

Jacobs, W.A. & Heidelberger, M. (1915a) The quaternary salts of hexamethylenetetramine. I. Substituted benzyl halides and the hexamethylene tetramine salts derived therefrom. *Journal of Biological Chemistry*, **20**, 659–683.

Jacobs, W.A. & Heidelberger, M. (1915b) The quaternary salts of hexamethylenetetramine. VIII. Miscellaneous substances containing aliphatically bound halogen and the hexamethylenetetramine salts derived therefrom. *Journal of Biological Chemistry*, **21**, 465–475.

Jacobs, W.A., Heidelberger, M. & Amoss, H.L. (1916a) The bactericidal properties of the quaternary salts of hexamethylenetetramine. II. The relation between constitution and bactericidal action in the substituted benzylhexamethylenetetraminium salts. *Journal of Experimental Medicine*, **23**, 569–576.

Jacobs, W.A., Heidelberger, M. & Bull, C.G. (1916b). The bactericidal properties of the quaternary salts of hexamethylenetetramine. III. The relation between constitution and bactericidal action in the quaternary salts obtained from halogenacetyl compounds. *Journal of Experimental Medicine*, **23**, 577–599.

Joswick, H.L., Corner, T.R., Silvernale, J.N. & Gerhardt, P. (1971) Antimicrobial actions of hexachlorophane: release of cytoplasmic materials. *Journal of Bacteriology*, **168**, 492–500.

Kabara, J.J. (1978) Fatty acids and derivatives as antimicrobial agents—a review. In *The Pharmacological Effects of Lipids* (ed. Kabara, J.J.) pp. 1–14. Champaign, Illinois: The American Oil Chemists' Society.

Kabara, J.J. (1980) GRAS antimicrobial agents for cosmetic products. *Journal of the Society of Cosmetic Chemists*, **31**, 1–10.

Kabara, J.J. (1984) Medium chain fatty acids and esters as antimicrobial agents. In *Cosmetic and Drug Preservation: Principles and Practice* (ed. Kabara, J.J.) pp. 275–304. New York: Marcel Dekker.

Kaslow, R.A., Mackel, D.C. & Mallison, G.F. (1976) Nosocomial pseudobacteraemia: positive blood cultures due to contaminated benzalkonium antiseptic. *Journal of the American Medical Association*, **236**, 2407–2409.

Kay, J.B. (1980) Manufacture and supply of contact lens products. 2. An industrial view. *Pharmaceutical Journal*, **225**, 345–348.

Kelsey, J.C., (1967) Use of gaseous antimicrobial agents with special reference to ethylene oxide. *Journal of Applied Bacteriology*, **30**, 92–100.

Kelsey, J.C. & Maurer, I.M. (1972) *The Use of Chemical Disinfectants in Hospitals*. Public Health Laboratory Service Monograph Series No. 2. London: HMSO.

Kelsey, J.C., Mackinnon, I.H. & Maurer, I.M. (1974) Sporicidal activity of hospital disinfectants. *Journal of Clinical Pathology*, **27**, 632–638.

Kereluk, K. (1971) Gaseous sterilization: methyl bromide, propylene oxide and ozone. In *Progress in Industrial Microbiology* (ed. Hockenhull, D.J.D.) Vol. 10, pp. 105–128. Edinburgh: Churchill Livingstone.

Kingston, D. (1965) Release of formaldehyde from polynoxyline and noxythiolin. *Journal of Clinical Pathology*, **18**, 666–667.

Klarmann, E.G. & Shternov, V.A. (1936) Bactericidal value of coal-tar disinfectants. Limitation of the *B. typhosus* phenol coefficient as a measure. *Industrial and Engineering Chemistry. Analytical Edition*, **8**, 369–372.

Klarmann, E.G. & von Wowern, J. (1929) The preparation of certain chloro- and bromo-derivatives of 2,4-dihydroxydiphenylmethane and ethane and their germicidal action. *Journal of the American Chemical Society*, **51**, 605–610.

Klarmann, E.G., Gates, L.W. & Shternov, U.A. (1932) Halogen derivatives of monohydroxydiphenyl-methane and their antibacterial activity. *Journal of the American Chemical Society*, **54**, 3315–3328.

Klarmann, E.G., Shternov, V.A. & Gates, L.W. (1933) The alkyl derivatives of halogen phenols and their bactericidal action. I. Chlorphenols. *Journal of the American Chemical Society*, **55**, 2576–2589.

Klarmann, E.G., Shternov, V.A. & von Wowern, J. (1929) The germicidal action of halogen derivatives of phenol and resorcinol and its impairment by organic matter. *Journal of Bacteriology*, **17**, 423–442.

Kornfeld, F. (1966) Properties and techniques of application of biocidal ampholytic surfactants. *Food Manufacture*, **41**, 39–46.

Krebs, H.A., Wiggins, D., Stubbs, M., Sols, A. & Bedoya, F. (1983) Studies on the mechanism of the antifungal action of benzoate. *Biochemical Journal*, **214**, 657–663.

Kushner, D.J. (1971) Influence of solutes and ions on microorganisms. In *Inhibition and Destruction of the Microbial Cell* (ed. Hugo, W.B.) pp. 259–283. London: Academic Press.

Lacey, R.W. (1979) Antibacterial activity of povidone iodine towards non-sporing bacteria. *Journal of Applied Bacteriology*, **46**, 443–449.

Langwell, H. (1932) Oligodynamic action of metals. *Chemistry and Industry*, **51**, 701–702.

Lawrence, C.A. (1948) Inactivation of the germicidal action of quaternary ammonium compounds. *Journal of the American Pharmaceutical Association, Scientific Edition*, **37**, 57–61.

Lawrence, C.A. (1950) *Surface-Active Quaternary Ammonium Germicides*. London and New York: Academic Press.

Laycock, H.H. & Mulley, B.A. (1970) Application of the Ferguson principle to the antibacterial activity of mono- and multi-component solutions of quaternary ammonium surface-active agents. *Journal of Pharmacy and Pharmacology*, **22**, 157S–162S.

Leach, E.D. (1981) A new synergized glutaraldehyde-phenate sterilizing solution and concentrated disinfectant. *Infection Control*, **2**, 26–30.

Lee, C.R. & Corner, T.R. (1975) Antimicrobial actions of hexachlorophane: iron salts do not reverse inhibition. *Journal of Pharmacy and Pharmacology*, **27**, 694–696.

Leive, L. (1974) The barrier function of the Gram-negative envelope. *Annals of the New York Academy of Sciences*, **235**, 109–127.

Leive, L. & Kollin, V. (1967) Controlling EDTA treatment to produce permeable *E. coli* with normal metabolic process. *Biochemical and Biophysical Research Communications*, **28**, 229–236.

Lemaire, H.C., Schramm, C.H. & Cahn, A. (1961) Synthesis and germicidal activity of halogenated salicylanilides and related compounds. *Journal of Pharmaceutical Sciences*, **50**, 831–837.

Lesher, R.J., Bender, G.R. & Marquis, R.E. (1977) Bacteriolytic action of fluoride ions. *Antimicrobial Agents and Chemotherapy*, **12**, 339–345.

Lilley, B.D. & Brewer, J.H. (1953) The selective antibacterial activity of phenylethyl alcohol. *Journal of the American Pharmaceutical Association, Scientific Edition*, **42**, 6–8.

Lloyd, A.G. & Drake, J.J.P. (1975) Problems posed by essential food preservatives. *British Medical Journal*, **iii**, 214–219.

Lorenz, P. (1977) 5-bromo-5-nitro-1, 3-dioxane: A preservative for cosmetics. *Cosmetics and Toiletries*, **92**, 89–91.

Lovelock, J.E. (1948) Aliphatic-hydroxycarboxylic acids as air disinfectants. In *Studies in Air Hygiene*, Medical Research Council Special Report Series No. 262, 1948, pp. 89–104. London: HMSO.

Lovelock, J.E., Lidwell, O.M. & Raymond, W.F. (1944) Aerial disinfection. *Nature, London*, **153**, 20–21.

Lowbury, E.J.L. (1951) Contamination of cetrimide and other fluids with *Pseudomonas aeruginosa. British Journal of Industrial Medicine*, **8**, 22–25.

Lowbury, E.J.L. & Lilley, H.A. (1960) Disinfection of the hands of surgeons and nurses. *British Medical Journal*, **i**, 1445–50.

Lowbury, E.J.L., Lilley, H.A. & Bull, J.P. (1964) Methods of disinfection of hands. *British Medical Journal*, **ii**, 531–536.

Lueck, E. (1980) *Antimicrobial Food Additives*. Berlin: Springer-Verlag.

Lynch, M., Lund, W. & Wilson, D.A. (1977) Chloroform as a preservative in aqueous systems. Losses under 'in-use' conditions and antimicrobial effectiveness. *Pharmaceutical Journal*, **219**, 507–510.

Mackinnon, I.H. (1974) The use of inactivators in the evaluation of disinfectants. *Journal of Hygiene, Cambridge*, **73**, 189–195.

Malek, J.R. & Speier, J.L. (1982) Development of an organosilicone antimicrobial agent for the treatment of surfaces. *Journal of Coated Fabrics*, **12**, 38–45.

Marouchoc, S.R. (1979) Classical phenol derivatives and their uses. *Developments in Industrial Microbiology*, **20**, 15–24.

McQuillen, K. (1960) Bacterial protoplasts. In *The Bacteria*. Vol. I (eds Gunsalus, I.C. & Stanier, R.Y.) pp. 249–349. London: Academic Press.

Marples, R.R. (1971) Antibacterial cosmetics and the microflora of human skin. *Developments in Industrial Microbiology*, **12**, 178–187.

Marzulli, F.N. & Maibach, H.J. (1973) Antimicrobials: experimental contact sensitization in man. *Journal of the Society of Cosmetic Chemists*, **24**, 399–421.

Mathews, C., Davidson, J., Bauer, E., Morrison, J.L. & Richardson, A.P. (1956) *p*-Hydroxybenzoic acid esters as preservatives. II. Acute and chronic toxicity in dogs, rats and mice. *Journal of the American Pharmaceutical Association*, **45**, 260–267.

Michael, G.T. & Stumbo, C.R. (1970) Ethylene oxide sterilisation of *Salmonella senftenberg* and *Escherichia coli*: death kinetics and mode of action. *Journal of Food Science*, **35**, 631–634.

Mitchell, A.G. (1964) Bactericidal activity of chloroxylenol in aqueous solutions of cetomacrogol. *Journal of Pharmacy and Pharmacology*, **16**, 533–537.

Moats, W.A. & Maddox, S.E., Jr (1978) Effect of pH on the antimicrobial activity of some triphenylmethane dyes. *Canadian Journal of Microbiology*, **24**, 658–661.

Moiseev, S. (1934) Sterilization of water with silver coated sand. *Journal of the American Water Works Association*, **26**, 217–222.

Moore, O. & Walker, J.N. (1939) Selective action in germicidal preparations containing chlorinated phenols. *Pharmaceutical Journal*, **143**, 507–509.

Morgan, D.A. (1989) Chlorinated solutions: E (useful) or (E) useless? *Pharmaceutical Journal*, **243**, 219–220.

Morris, E.J. & Darlow, H.M. (1971) Inactivation of viruses. In *Inhibition and Destruction of the Microbial Cell* (ed. Hugo, W.B.) pp. 687–702. London: Academic Press.

Morton, H.E. (1950) Relationship of concentration and germicidal efficiency of ethyl alcohol. *Annals of the New York Academy of Sciences*, **53**, 191–196.

Morton, H.E. (1977) Alcohols. In *Disinfection, Sterilization and Preservation* (ed. Block, S.S.) 2nd Ed. pp. 301–308. Philadelphia: Lea & Febiger.

Muys, G.T., Van Rhee, R. & Lelieveld, H.L.M. (1978) Sterilization by means of hydrochloric acid vapour. *Journal of Applied Bacteriology*, **45**, 213–217.

Myers, J.A., Allwood, M.C., Gidley, M.J. & Sanders, J.K.M. (1980) The relationship between structure and activity of Taurolin. *Journal of Applied Bacteriology*, **48**, 89–96.

Neu, H.C. (1969) The role of amine buffers in EDTA toxicity and their effect on osmotic shock. *Journal of General Microbiology*, **57**, 215–220.

Newcastle Regional Hospital Board Working Party (1962) Blankets and air hygiene: a report of a trial of blanket disinfection. *Journal of Hygiene, Cambridge*, **60**, 85–94.

Nichols, A.A., Leaver, C.W.E. & Panes, J.J. (1967) Hatchery hygiene evaluation as measured by microbiological examination of samples of fluff. *British Poultry Science*, **8**, 297.

Nordgren, C. (1939) Investigations on the sterilising efficacy of gaseous formaldehyde. *Acta Pathologica et Microbiologica Scandinavica, Supplement* XL, pp. 1–165.

Olivant, D.J. & Shapton, D.A. (1970) Disinfection in the food processing industry. In *Disinfection* (ed. Benarde, M.A.) pp. 393–428. New York: Marcel Dekker.

O'Neill, J.J., Peelor, P.L., Peterson, A.F. & Strube, C.H. (1979) Selection of parabens as preservatives for cosmetics and toiletries. *Journal of the Society of Cosmetic Chemists*, **30**, 25–39.

Owens, R.G. (1969) Organic sulphur compounds. In *Fungicides* (ed. Torgeson, D.C.) Vol. 2, pp. 147–301. New York: Academic Press.

Palfreyman, D. (1977) John Jeyes... the making of a household name. Thetford: Jeyes.

Palleroni, N.J. & de Prinz, M.J.R. (1960) Influence of sorbic acid on acetate oxidation by *Saccharomyces cerevisae* var. *ellipsoideus. Nature. London*, **185**, 688–689.

Patel, W.K. & Kostenbauder, H.B. (1958) Binding of *p*-hydroxybenzoic acid esters by polyoxyethylene 21 sorbitan mono-oleate. *Journal of the American Pharmaceutical Association*, **47**, 289–293.

Paulus, W. (1976) Problems encountered with formaldehyde-releasing compounds used as preservatives in aqueous systems, especially lubricoolants—possible solutions to the problems. In *Proceedings of the 3rd International Biodegradation Symposium* (eds Shaply, J.M. & Kaplan, A.M.) pp. 1075–1082. London: Applied Science Publishers.

Pepper, R.E. (1980) Comparison of the activities and stabilities of alkaline glutaraldehyde sterilizing solutions. *Infection Control*, **1**, 90–92.

Pepper, R.E. & Chandler, V.L. (1963) Sporicidal activity of alkaline alcoholic saturated dialdehyde solutions. *Applied Microbiology*, **11**, 384–388.

Pfirrman, R.W. & Leslie, G.B. (1979) The anti-endotoxic activity of Taurolin in experimental animals. *Journal of Applied Bacteriology*, **46**, 97–102.

Pfleger, R., Schraufstatter, E., Gehringer, F. & Sciuk, J. (1949) Zur Chemotherapie der Pilzimfektionen. I. Mitteilung: *In vitro* Untersuchungen aromatischer sulphide. *Zeitschrift für Naturforschung*, **4b**, 344–350.

Pharmaceutical Codex (1979) London: Pharmaceutical Press.

Phillips, C.R. (1977) Gaseous sterilization. In *Disinfection, Sterilization and Preservation* (ed. Block, S.S.) 2nd Ed. pp. 529–611. Philadelphia: Lea & Febiger.

Phillips, C.R. & Kaye, S. (1949) The sterilizing action of gaseous ethylene oxide. I. Review. *American Journal of Hygiene*, **50**, 270–279.

Phillips, I., Lobo, A.Z., Fernandes, R. & Gundara, N.S. (1968) Acetic acid in the treatment of superficial wounds infected by *Pseudomonas aeruginosa*. *Lancet*, **i**, 11–12.

Pickard, R.G. (1972) Treatment of peritonitis with per- and post-operative irrigation of the peritoneal cavity with noxythiolin solution. *British Journal of Surgery*, **59**, 642–648.

Pisano, F.D. & Kostenbauder, H.B. (1959) Correlation of binding data with required preservative concentrations of *p*-hydroxybenzoates in the presence of Tween 80. *Journal of the American Pharmaceutical Association*, **48**, 310–314.

Ponci, R., Baruffini, A. & Gialdi, F. (1964) Antifungal activity of 2′,2′-dicarbamino-4′,4-dinitrodiphenyldisulphides and 5-nitro-1,2-benzisothiazolones. *Farmaco, Edizione Scientifica*, **19**, 121–136.

Potokar, M., Greb, W., Ippen, H., Maibach, H.I., Schulz, K.H. & Gloxhuber, C. (1976) Bronidox, ein neues Konservierungsmittel fur die Kosmetic Eigenschaften und toxikologisch-dermatologische Prufergebnisse. *Fette, Seife, Anstrichmittel*, **78**, 269–276.

Power, E.G.M. & Russell, A.D. (1989) Glutaraldehyde: its uptake by sporing and non-sporing bacteria, rubber, plastic and an endoscope. *Journal of Applied Bacteriology*, **67**, 329–342.

Power, E.G.M. & Russell, A.D. (1990) Sporicidal action of alkaline glutaraldehyde: factors influencing activity and a comparison with other aldehydes. *Journal of Applied Bacteriology*, **69**, 261–268.

Power, E.G.M., Dancer, B.N. & Russell, A.D. (1988) Emergence of resistance to glutaraldehyde in spores of *Bacillus subtilis* 168. *FEMS Microbiology Letters*, **50**, 223–226.

Power, E.G.M., Dancer, B.N. & Russell, A.D. (1989) Possible mechanisms for the revival of glutaraldehyde-treated spores of *Bacillus subtilis* NCTC 8236. *Journal of Applied Bacteriology*, **67**, 91–98.

Power, E.G.M., Dancer, B.N. & Russell, A.D. (1990) Effect of sodium hydroxide and two proteases on the revival of aldehyde-treated spores of *Bacillus subtilis*. *Letters in Applied Microbiology*, **10**, 9–13.

Price, P.B. (1950) Re-evaluation of ethyl alcohol as a germicide. *Archives of Surgery*, **60**, 492–502.

Quack, J.M. (1976) Quaternary ammonium compounds in cosmetics. *Cosmetics and Toiletries*, **91** (2), 35–52.

Quinn, P.J. (1987) Evaluation of veterinary disinfectants and disinfection processes. In *Disinfection in Veterinary and Farm Animal Practice* (eds Linton, A.H., Hugo, W.B. & Russell, A.D.) pp. 66–116. Oxford: Blackwell Scientific Publications.

Rackur, H. (1985) New aspects of the mechanism of action of povidone-iodine. *Journal of Hospital Infection*, **6**, *Supplement A*, 13–23.

Rapps, N.F. (1933) The bactericidal efficiency of chlorocresol and chloroxylenol. *Journal of the Society of Chemical Industry*, **52**, 175T–176T.

Reeves, D.S. & Schweitzer, F.A.W. (1973) Experimental studies with an antibacterial substance, Taurolin. *Proceedings of the 8th International Congress of Chemotherapy* (Athens) pp. 583–586. Greece: Hellenic.

Repaske, R. (1956) Lysis of Gram-negative bacteria by lysozyme. *Biochimica et Biophysica Acta*, **22**, 189–191.

Repaske, R. (1958) Lysis of Gram-negative organisms and the role of versene. *Biochimica et Biophysica Acta*, **30**, 225–232.

Report (1989) Expert Advisory Committee on Biocides, page 32. London: HMSO.

Richards, C., Furr, J.R. & Russell, A.D. (1984) Inactivation of micro-organisms by lethal gases. In *Cosmetic and Drug Preservation: Principles and Practice* (ed. Kabara, J.J.) pp. 209–222. New York: Marcel Dekker.

Richards, R.M.E. & McBride, R.J. (1973) Enhancement of benzalkonium chloride and chlorhexidine acetate activity against *Pseudomonas aeruginosa* by aromatic alcohols. *Journal of Pharmaceutical Sciences*, **62**, 2035–2037.

Richardson, E.L. (1981) Update: frequency of preservative use in cosmetic formulas as disclosed to FDA. *Cosmetics and Toiletries*, **96**, 91–92.

Richardson, G. & Woodford, R. (1964) Incompatibility of cationic antiseptics with sodium alginate. *Pharmaceutical Journal*, **192**, 527–528.

Rickloff, J.R. (1985) An evaluation of the sporicidal activity of ozone. *Applied and Environmental Microbiology*, **53**, 683–686.

Roberts, N.A., Gray, G.W. & Wilkinson, S.G. (1970) The bactericidal action of ethylenediamine tetraacetic acid on *Pseudomonas aeruginosa. Microbios*, **2**, 189–208.

Rose, F.L. & Swain, G. (1956) Bisguanides having antibacterial activity. *Journal of the Chemical Society*. 4422–4425.

Rose, M.S. & Lock, E.A. (1970) The interaction of triethyltin with a component of guinea-pig liver supernatant. *Biochemical Journal*, **190**, 151–157.

Rosen, W.E. & Berke, P.A., (1973) Modern concepts of cosmetic preservation. *Journal of the Society of Cosmetic Chemists*, **24**, 663–675.

Rosen, W.E., Berke, P.A., Matzin, T. & Peterson, A.F. (1977) Preservation of cosmetic lotions with imidazolidinyl urea plus parabens. *Journal of the Society of Cosmetic Chemists*, **28**, 83–87.

Rossmore, H.W. (1979) Heterocyclic compounds as industrial biocides. *Developments in Industrial Microbiology*, **20**, 41–71.

Rossmore, H.W., DeMare, J. & Smith, T.H.F. (1972) Anti- and pro-microbial activity of hexahydro-1,3,5-tris(2-hydroxyethyl)-s-triazine in cutting fluid emulsion. In *Biodeterioration of Materials* (eds Walters, A.H. & Hueck-van der Plas, E.H.) Vol. 2, pp. 266–293. London: Applied Science Publishers.

Rossmore, H.W. & Sondossi, M. (1988) Applications and mode of action of formaldehyde condensate biocides. *Advances in Applied Microbiology*, **33**, 223–277.

Rubbo, S.D., Gardner, J.F. & Webb, R.L. (1967) Biocidal activities of glutaraldehyde and related compounds. *Journal of Applied Bacteriology*, **30**, 78–87.

Russell, A.D. (1971a) The destruction of bacterial spores. In *Inhibition and Destruction of the Microbial Cell* (ed. Hugo, W.B.) pp. 451–612. London: Academic Press.

Russell, A.D. (1971b) Ethylenediamine tetraacetic acid. In *Inhibition and Destruction of the Microbial Cell* (ed. Hugo, W.B.) pp. 209–224. London: Academic Press.

Russell, A.D. (1976) Inactivation of non-sporing bacteria by gases. *Society for Applied Bacteriology Symposium No. 5: Inactivation of Vegetative Micro-organisms* (eds Skinner, F.A. & Hugo, W.B.) pp. 61–88. London: Academic Press.

Russell, A.D. (1982) *The Destruction of Bacterial Spores*. London: Academic Press.

Russell, A.D. (1985) The role of plasmids in bacterial resistance to antiseptics, disinfectants and preservatives. *Journal of Hospital Infection*, **6**, 9–19.

Russell, A.D. (1986) Chlorhexidine: antibacterial action and bacterial resistance. *Infection*, **14**, 212–215.

Russell, A.D. (1990a) The bacterial spore and chemical sporicides. *Clinical Microbiology Reviews*, **3**, 99–119.

Russell, A.D. (1990b) The effects of chemical and physical agents on microbes: Disinfection and sterilization. In *Topley & Wilson's Principles of Bacteriology, Virology and Immunity* (eds Dick H.M. & Linton A.H.) 8th Ed., Vol. 1, pp. 71–103. London: Edward Arnold.

Russell, A.D. (1991a) Principles of antimicrobial activity. In *Disinfection, Sterilization and Preservation* (ed. Block, S.S.) 4th Ed. Philadelphia: Lea & Febiger.

Russell, A.D. (1991b) Chemical sporicidal and sporistatic agents. In *Disinfection, Sterilization and Preservation* (ed. Block, S.S.) 4th Ed. Philadelphia: Lea & Febiger.

Russell, A.D. & Chopra, I. (1990) *Understanding Antibacterial Action and Resistance*. Chichester: Ellis Horwood.

Russell, A.D. & Furr, J.R. (1977) The antibacterial activity of a new chloroxylenol preparation containing ethylenediamine tetraacetic acid. *Journal of Applied Bacteriology*, **43**, 253–260.

Russell, A.D. & Furr, J.R. (1986a) The effects of antiseptics, disinfectants and preservatives on smooth, rough and deep rough strains of *Salmonella typhimurium. International Journal of Pharmaceutics*, **34**, 115–123.

Russell, A.D. & Furr, J.R. (1986b) Susceptibility of porin- and lipopolysaccharide-deficient strains of *Escherichia coli* to some antiseptics and disinfectants. *Journal of Hospital Infection*, **8**, 47–56.

Russell, A.D. & Furr, J.R. (1987) Comparative sensitivity of smooth, rough and deep rough strains of *Escherichia coli* to chlorhexidine, quaternary ammonium compounds and dibromopropamide isethionate. *International Journal of Pharmaceutics*, **36**, 191–197.

Russell, A.D. & Hopwood, D. (1976) The biological uses and importance of glutaraldehyde. In *Progress in Medicinal Chemistry* (eds Ellis, G.P. & West, G.B.) Vol. 13, pp. 271–301. Amsterdam: North-Holland Publishing Company.

Russell, A.D. & Hugo, W.B. (1987) Chemical disinfectants. In *Disinfection in Veterinary and Farm Animal Practice* (eds Linton, A.H., Hugo, W.B. & Russell, A.D.) pp. 12–42. Oxford: Blackwell Scientific Publications.

Russell, A.D. & Munton, T.J. (1974) Bactericidal and bacteriostatic activity of glutaraldehyde and its interaction with lysine and proteins. *Microbios*, **11**, 147–152.

Russell, A.D., Ahonkhai, I. & Rogers, D.T. (1979) Microbiological applications of the inactivation of antibiotics and other antimicrobial agents. *Journal of Applied Bacteriology*, **46**, 207–245.

Russell, A.D., Furr, J.R. & Pugh, W.J. (1985) Susceptibility of porin- and lipopolysaccharide-deficient mutants of *Escherichia coli* to a homologous series of esters of *p*-hydroxybenzoic acid. *International Journal of Pharmaceutics*, **27**, 163–173.

Russell, A.D., Furr, J.R. & Pugh, W.J. (1987) Sequential loss of outer membrane lipopolysaccharide and sensitivity of *Escherichia coli* to antibacterial agents. *International Journal of Pharmaceutics*, **35**, 227–232.

Russell, A.D., Hammond, S.A. & Morgan, J.R. (1986) Bacterial resistance to antiseptics and disinfectants. *Journal of Hospital Infection*, **7**, 213–225.

Russell, A.D., Jenkins, J. & Harrison, I.H. (1967) Inclusion of antimicrobial agents in pharmaceutical products. *Advances in Applied Microbiology*, **9**, 1–38.

Russell, A.D., Yarnych, V.S. & Koulikouskii, A.U. (1984) *Guidelines on Disinfection in Animal Husbandry for Prevention and Control of Zoonotic Diseases*. WHO/UPH/84.4. Geneva: World Health Organization.

Sabalitschka, T. (1924) Chemische Konstitution und Konservierungsvermögen. *Pharmazeutisch Monatsblatten*, **5**, 235–327.

Sabalitschka, T. & Dietrich, R.K. (1926) Chemical constitution and preservative properties. *Disinfection*, **11**, 67–71.

Sabalitschka, T., Dietrich, K.R. & Bohm, E. (1926) Influence of esterification of carbocyclic acids on inhibitive action with respect to micro-organisms. *Pharmazeutische Zeitung*, **71**, 834–836.

Salmond, C.V., Kroll, R.H. & Booth, I.R. (1984) The effect of food preservatives on pH homeostasis in *Escherichia coli*. *Journal of General Microbiology*, **130**, 2845–2850.

Salton, M.R.J. (1986) Lytic agents, cell permeability and monolayer penetratability. *Journal of General Physiology*, **52**, 2275–2825.

Schanno, R.J., Westlund, J.R. & Foelsch, D.H. (1980) Evaluation of 1,3-dimethylol-5,5-dimethylhydantoin as a cosmetic preservative. *Journal of the Society of Cosmetic Chemists*, **31**, 85–96.

Schaeufele, P.J. (1986) Advances in quaternary ammonium biocides. *Proceedings of the 3rd Conference on Progress in Chemical Disinfection*, pp. 508–519. Binghamton, New York.

Schmolka, I.R. (1973) The synergistic effects of non ionic surfactants upon cationic germicidal agents. *Journal of the Society of Cosmetic Chemists*, **24**, 577–592.

Schwabacher, H., Salsburgy, A.J. & Fincham, W.J. (1958). Blankets and infection: Wool, terylene or cotton? *Lancet*, **ii**, 709–712.

Scott, C.R. & Wolf, P.A. (1962) The antibacterial activity of a series of quaternaries prepared from hexamethylene tetramine and halohydrocarbons. *Applied Microbiology*, **10**, 211–216.

Scott, E.M. & Gorman, S.P. (1987) Chemical disinfectants, antiseptics and preservatives. In *Pharmaceutical Microbiology* (eds Hugo, W.B. & Russell, A.D.) 4th Ed. pp. 226–252. Oxford: Blackwell Scientific Publications.

Seevers, H.M., Shideman, F.E., Woods, L.A.A., Weeks, J.R. & Kruse, W.T. (1950) Dehydroacetic acid (DHA). II. General pharmacology and mechanism of action. *Journal of Pharmacology and Experimental Therapeutics*, **99**, 69–83.

Shaker, L.A., Furr, J.R. & Russell, A.D. (1988) Mechanism of resistance of *Bacillus subtilis* spores to chlorhexidine. *Journal of Applied Bacteriology*, **64**, 531–539.

Shaker, L.A., Russell, A.D. & Furr, J.R. (1986) Aspects of the action of chlorhexidine on bacterial spores. *International Journal of Pharmaceutics*, **34**, 51–56.

Shaker, L.A., Dancer, B.N., Russell, A.D. & Furr, J.R. (1988) Emergence and development of chlorhexidine resistance during sporulation of *Bacillus subtilis* 168. *FEMS Microbiology Letters*, **51**, 73–76.

Sheu, C.W., Salomon, J.L., Simmons, J.L., Sreevalsan, T. & Freese, E. (1975) Inhibitory effect of lipophilic fatty acids and related compounds on bacteria and mammalian cells. *Antimicrobial Agents and Chemotherapy*, **7**, 349–363.

Shibasaki, I. & Kato, N. (1978) Combined effects on antibacterial activity of fatty acids and their esters against Gram-negative bacteria. In *The Pharmacological Effects of Lipids* (ed. Kabara, J.J.) pp. 15–24. Champaign, Illinois. The American Oil Chemists' Society.

Silver, S., Misra, S. (1988) Plasmid-mediated heavy metal resistances. *Annual Review of Microbiology*, **42**, 717–743.

Silvernale, J.N., Joswick, H.L., Corner, T.R. & Gerhardt, P. (1971) Antimicrobial action of hexachlorophene: cytological manifestations. *Journal of Bacteriology*, **108**, 482–491.

Simon, E.W. (1953) Mechanisms of dinitrophenol toxicity. *Biological Reviews*, **28**, 453–479.

Simon, E.W. & Beevers (1952a) The effect of pH on the biological activities of weak acids and bases. I. The most usual relationship between pH and activity. *New Phytologist*, **51**, 163–190.

Simon, E.W. & Beevers, H. (1952b) The effect of pH on the biological activities of weak acids and bases. II. Other relationships between pH and activity. *New Phytologist*, **51**, 191–197.

Simon, E.W. & Blackman, G.E. (1949) *The significance of hydrogen ion concentration in the study of toxicity*. Symposium of the Society of Experimental Biology No. 3, pp. 253–265. Cambridge: Cambridge University Press.

Smith, C.R. (1968) Mycobactericidal agents. In *Disinfection, Sterilization and Preservation* (eds Lawrence, C.A. & Block, S.S.) 2nd Ed. pp. 504–514. Philadelphia: Lea & Febiger.

Smith, P.J. & Smith, L. (1975) Organotin compounds and applications. *Chemistry in Britain*, **11**, 208–212, 226.

Sofos, J.N., Pierson, M.D., Blocher, L.C. & Busta, F.F. (1986) Mode of action of sorbic acid on bacterial cells and spores. *International Journal of Food Microbiology*, **3**, 1–17.

Sokol, H. (1952) Recent developments in the preservation of pharmaceuticals. *Drug Standards*, **20**, 89–106.

Speier, J.L. & Malek, J.R. (1982) Destruction of micro-organisms by contact with solid surfaces. *Journal of Colloid and Interfacial Science*, **89**, 68–76.

Spiner, D.R. & Hoffman, R.K. (1960) Method of disinfecting large enclosures with BPL vapour. *Applied Microbiology*, **8**, 152–155.

Staehelin, M. (1958) Reaction of tobacco mosaic virus nucleic acid with formaldehyde. *Biochimica et Biophysica Acta*, **29**, 410–417.

Stanier, R.Y. & Orston, L.N. (1973) The ketoadipic pathway. In *Advances in Microbial Physiology* (eds Rose, A.H. & Tempest, D.W.) Vol. 9. pp. 89–151. London: Academic Press.

Stanier, R.Y., Sleeper, B.P., Tsuchida, M. & Macdonald,

D.L. (1950) The bacterial oxidation of aromatic compounds. III. The enzymic oxidation of catechol and proto-catechuic acid to β-ketoadipic acid. *Journal of Bacteriology*, **59**, 137–151.

Stevenson, A.F. (1915) *An efficient liquid disinfectant*. Public Health Reports 30, pp. 3003–3008. Washington, DC: US Public Health Service.

Stickler, D.J., Thomas, B., Clayton, C.L. & Chawla, J.C. (1983) Studies on the genetic basis of chlorhexidine resistance. *British Journal of Clinical Practice*, Symposium No. 25, pp. 23–28.

Suter, G.M. (1941) Relationships between the structure and bactericidal properties of phenols. *Chemical Reviews*, **28**, 269–299.

Sykes, G. (1965) *Disinfection and Sterilization* 2nd Ed. London: E. & F.N. Spon Ltd.

Taylor, L.A., Barbeito, M.S. & Gremillion, G.G. (1969) Paraformaldehyde for surface sterilization and detoxification. *Applied Microbiology*, **17**, 614–618.

Thomas, C.G.A., West, B. & Besser, H. (1959) Cleansing and sterilization of hospital blankets. *Guy's Hospital Reports*, **108**, 446–463.

Thornley, M.J. & Yudkin, J. (1959b) The origin of bacterial resistance to proflavine. I. Training and reversion in *Escherichia coli. Journal of General Microbiology*, **20**, 355–364.

Thornley, M.J. & Yudkin, J. (1959b) The origin of bacterial resistance to proflavine. 2. Spontaneous mutation to proflavine resistance in *Escherichia coli. Journal of General Microbiology*, **20**, 365–372.

Thrower, W.R. & Valentine, F.C.O. (1943) Propamidine in chronic wound sepsis. *Lancet*, **i**, 133.

Tilbury, R. (ed.) (1980) *Developments in Food Preservatives*. London: Applied Science Publishers.

Tilley, F.W. & Schaffer, J.M. (1925) Germicidal efficiency of coconut oil and linseed oil soaps and their mixtures with cresol. *Journal of Infectious Diseases*, **37**, 359–367.

Toler, J.C. (1985) Preservative stability and preservative systems. *International Journal of Cosmetic Sciences*, **7**, 157–164.

Troll, W., Rinde, E. & Day, P. (1969) Effect on N-7 and C-8 substitution of guanine in DNA on T_m buoyant density and RNA polymerase primary. *Biochimica et Biophysica Acta*, **174**, 211–219.

Trueman, J.R. (1971) The halogens. In *Inhibition and Destruction of the Microbial Cell* (ed. Hugo, W.B.) pp. 135–183. London: Academic Press.

Tulis, J.J. (1973) Formaldehyde gas as a sterilant. In *Industrial Sterilization*: International Symposium, Amsterdam, 1972 (eds Phillips, G.B. & Miller, W.S.) pp. 209–238. Durham, North Carolina: Duke University Press.

Van Der Kerk, H.J.M. & Luijten, J.G.A. (1954) Investigations on organo-tin compounds. III. The biocidal properties of organo-tin compounds. *Journal of Applied Chemistry*, **4**, 314–319.

Vaara, M. & Vaara, T. (1983a) Polycations sensitise enteric bacteria to antibiotics. *Antimicrobial Agents and Chemotherapy*, **24**, 107–113.

Vaara, M. & Vaara, T. (1983b) Polycations as outer membrane-disorganizing agents. *Antimicrobial Agents and Chemotherapy*, **24**, 114–122.

Viljanen, P. (1987) Polycations which disorganize the outer membrane inhibit conjugation in *Escherichia coli. Journal of Antibiotics*, **40**, 882–886.

Voge, C.I.B. (1947) Phenylmercuric nitrate and related compounds. *Manufacturing Chemist and Manufacturing Perfumer*, **18**, 5–7.

Wallhäusser, K.H. (1984) Antimicrobial preservatives used by the cosmetic industry. In *Cosmetic and Drug Preservation: Principles and Practice* (ed. Kabara, J.J.) pp. 605–745. New York: Marcel Dekker.

Walpole, A.L., Roberts, D.C., Rose, F.L., Hendry, J.A. & Homer, R.F. (1954) Cytotoxic agents. IV. The carcinogenic actions of some monofunctional ethylene amine derivatives. *British Journal of Pharmacology*, **9**, 306–323.

Walter, G.R. & Gump. W.S. (1962) Chemical structure and antimicrobial activity of bisphenols. II. Bactericidal activity in the presence of an anionic surfactant. *Journal of the Society of Cosmetic Chemists*, **13**, 477–482.

Warren, I.C., Hutchinson, M. & Ridgway, J.W. (1981) Comparative assessment of swimming pool disinfectants. In *Disinfectants: Their Use and Evaluation of Effectiveness* (eds Collins, C.H., Allwood, M.C., Bloomfield, S.F. & Fox, A.) Society for Applied Bacteriology Technical Series No. 16, pp. 123–139. London: Academic Press.

Watanabe, T. (1963) Infective heredity of multiple drug resistance in bacteria. *Bacteriological Reviews*, **27**, 87–115.

Weber, G.R. & Black, L.A. (1948) Laboratory procedure for evaluating practical performance of quaternary ammonium and other germicides proposed for sanitizing food utensils. *American Journal of Public Health*, **38**, 1405–1417.

Weber, G.R. & Levine, M. (1944) Factors affecting germicidal efficiency of chlorine and chloramine. *American Journal of Public Health*, **32**, 719–728.

Wedzicha, B.C. (1984) *Chemistry of Sulphur Dioxide in Foods*. London: Elsevier Applied Science Publishing.

Weinberg, E.D. (1957) The mutual effect of antimicrobial compounds and metallic cations. *Bacteriological Reviews*, **21**, 46–68.

Weiner, N.D., Hart, F. & Zografi, G. (1965) Application of the Ferguson principle to the antimicrobial activity of quaternary ammonium salts. *Journal of Pharmacy and Pharmacology*, **17**, 350–355.

West, T.S. (1969) *Complexometry with EDTA and Related Agents*. 3rd Ed. Poole: BDH Chemicals Ltd.

Westwood, N. & Pin-Lim, B. (1972) Survival of *E. coli*, *Staph. aureus*, *Ps. aeruginosa* and spores of *B. subtilis* in BPC mixtures. *Pharmaceutical Journal*, **208**, 153–154.

Wien, R., Harrison, J. & Freeman, W.A. (1948) Diamidines as antibacterial compounds. *British Journal of Pharmacology*, **3**, 211–218.

Wilkinson, S.G. (1975) Sensitivity to ethylenediamine tetra-acetic acid. In *Resistance of Pseudomonas aeruginosa* (ed.

Brown, M.R.W.) pp. 145–188. London: John Wiley & Sons.

Williams, D.E., Elder, E.D. & Worley, S.D. (1988) Is free halogen necessary for disinfection? *Applied and Environmental Microbiology*, **54**, 2583–2585.

Williams, D.E., Worley, S.D., Barnela, S.B. & Swango, L.J. (1987) Bactericidal activities of selected organic *N*-halamines. *Applied and Environmental Microbiology*, **53**, 2082–2089.

Williams, N.D. & Russell, A.D. (1991) The effects of some halogen-containing compounds on *Bacillus subtilis* endospores. *Journal of Applied Bacteriology*, **70**, 427–436.

Wolf, P.A. (1950) Dehydroacetic acid, a new microbiological inhibitor. *Food Technology*, **4**, 294–297.

Wolf, P.A. & Westveer, W.M. (1950) The antimicrobial activity of several substituted pyrones. *Archives of Biochemistry*, **28**, 201–206.

Woodroffe, R.C.S. & Wilkinson, B.E. (1966a) The antibacterial action of tetrachlorosalicylanilide. *Journal of General Microbiology*, **44**, 343–352.

Woodroffe, R.C.S. & Wilkinson, B.E. (1966b) Location of the tetrachlorosalicylanilide taken in by *Bacillus megaterium*. *Journal of General Microbiology*, **244**, 353–358.

Woolfson, A.D. (1977) The antibacterial activity of dimethoxane. *Journal of Pharmacy and Pharmacology*, **29**, 73P.

Woolfson, A.D. & Woodside, W. (1976) Analysis of the constituents of commercial dimethoxane. *Journal of Pharmacy and Pharmacology*, **28**, 28P.

Working Party (1985) Acquired immune deficiency syndrome: recommendations of a Working Party of the Hospital Infection Society. *Journal of Hospital Infection*, **6** (*Supplement C*), 67–80.

Worley, S.D., Williams, D.E. & Barnela, S.B. (1987) The stabilities of new *N*-halamine water disinfectants. *Water Research*, **21**, 983–988.

Wright, C.J. & McAllister, T.A. (1967) Protective action of noxythiolin in experimental endotoxaemia. *Clinical Trials Journal*, **4**, 680–681.

York, G.K. & Vaughan, R.H. (1955) Site of microbial inhibition by sorbic acid. *Bacteriological Proceedings*, **55**, 20.

Chapter 3
Factors Influencing the Efficacy of Antimicrobial Agents

1 INTRODUCTION

The activity of biocides (antiseptics, disinfectants and preservatives) against micro-organisms depends on:

1 the external physical environment;
2 the nature, structure and composition, and condition of the organism itself;
3 the ability of the organism to degrade or inactivate the particular substance converting it to an inactive form Russell (1991a).

It has long been known that a modification of the concentration of the antimicrobial agent, or the temperature or pH at which it is acting, can have profound influence on activity. The practical value of a knowledge of these effects in terms of antisepsis, disinfection or preservation, or as an aid in certain thermal sterilization processes may be considerable. However, many other parameters must also be considered. Whilst many of these may be of academic value only, taken *in toto* they may lead to a better understanding of the reasons for the sensitivity or resistance of micro-organisms to biocides, as well as to possible means of improving, or potentiating, the activity of such agents.

For these reasons as many factors as possible will be considered, but those antimicrobial substances which will be dealt with will be biocides (disinfectants, antiseptics and preservatives) and not antibiotics, which are outside the scope of this chapter. Antibiotics were considered in an earlier paper (Russell, 1974).

Three main aspects will be examined, viz. how pre-treatment, in-treatment and post-treatment factors influence activity. Wherever possible, practical implications as well as theoretical ones will be discussed; in this context, Rutala (1990) and Russell & Gould (1988, 1991) should be considered for further information.

As pointed out above, the activity of an antimicrobial compound depends on the external environment and on the organism itself; additionally, its ability to degrade or inactivate the particular compound by converting it to an inactive form must also be considered. Whilst there is much evidence for the enzymatic inactivation of antibiotics there is far less information available as to the inactivation of biocides (Beveridge, 1987; Hugo, 1991). This aspect will be considered briefly later (Section 3.7). Of increasing importance is the existence of bacteria as biofilms and the possible decreased susceptibility to biocides and antibiotics. This is discussed in Section 5.

2 PRE-TREATMENT CONDITIONS

Investigators have, over the years, used a variety of techniques with the result that a considerable amount of useful information has accrued. Basically, techniques of growing bacteria have been either by means of continuous, or of batch, culture, with the latter predominating. The main criticism of batch culture is, of course, that cells of different physiological age will be present, whereas continuous cultures, e.g. those grown in a chemostat, overcome this criticism. Farewell & Brown (1971) have reviewed pre-treatment procedures on subsequent sensitivity of microbes to inimical treatments.

2.1 Chemostat-grown cultures

Bacterial cell walls are highly variable structures which can change in response to the growth environment. Chemostat cultures of *Aerobacter aerogenes* grown under conditions of Mg^{2+}, glycerol or phosphate limitation produce cells with wide variation in wall composition (Tempest & Ellwood, 1969). Cells of a *Bacillus subtilis* suspension showed differing responses to the enzyme lysozyme, which acts on peptidoglycan, depending on whether they had been chemostat grown under conditions of Mg^{2+}, phosphate or ammonia limitation. Thus, phenotypic variation in bacterial cell walls is achieved under a rigidly controlled chemical environment in the chemostat. Investigations into the effect of antibacterial agents on chemostat-grown cultures have been made by Melling *et al.* (1974) and Dean *et al.* (1976) who showed that *Ps. aeruginosa* exhibited different degrees of sensitivity, when grown under magnesium-limited conditions and at varying dilution rates, to EDTA and various antibiotics.

2.2 Batch-grown cultures

Far more extensive investigations have been undertaken with batch-grown cultures, and thus these will be examined in greater detail.

2.2.1 Growth medium

Growth medium composition may markedly influence the subsequent sensitivity of cells to antibacterial agents, e.g. the leakage of 260-nm-absorbing material from hexachlorophane-treated *Bacillus megaterium* (Joswick *et al.*, 1971).

'Fattened' cells of Gram-positive bacteria are produced when cultures are grown in glycerol-containing broth. Alteration in the cell-wall lipid of these cells may profoundly affect their sensitivity to antibacterial agents (Vaczi, 1973), notably phenols (Hugo & Franklin, 1968) and esters of *p*-hydroxbenzoic acids (Furr & Russell, 1972). Growth of an *E. coli* strain in a medium containing L-alanine or L-cystine resulted in cells which differed greatly from broth-grown cells in their response to biocides (Hugo & Ellis, 1975). The

L-alanine-grown cells had a structural deformity which rendered them more permeable, and hence more susceptible, to these antibacterial agents, whereas the comparative response of L-cystine-grown and broth-grown cells could be correlated with the differences in the composition of the cell walls.

Magnesium-limited batch cultures of *Ps. aeruginosa* produce cells which are highly resistant to ethylenediamine tetraacetic acid (EDTA; Brown & Melling, 1969), to chloroxylenol (Cowen, 1974) and to a combination of chloroxylenol and EDTA (Dankert & Schut, 1976). Profound changes occur in the walls of Mg^{2+}-limited cells of this organism (Eagon *et al.*, 1975) and these alterations are intimately linked with sensitivity and resistance of the whole cells to antiseptics and other antibacterial agents.

It seems likely that in the envelopes of Mg-limited cells, the normal outer membrane-stabilizing Mg^{2+} bridges are replaced by polyamides, thereby reducing sensitivity to ion chelators and to biocides that promote their own uptake by displacing cations (Gilbert & Wright, 1987).

There is little published information which deals with the effect of changes in sporulation medium on the subsequent sensitivity of bacterial spores to antibacterial agents. Chlorocresol has been found (Purves & Parker, 1973) to have a greater inhibitory effect on the germination of spores produced on a complex medium, where absorption of spore coats occurred, than on the germination of those produced on a synthetic medium, where emergence was by rupture of the coats.

It has been recommended that, since the composition of the sporulation medium can influence the response of spores to antibacterial agents, spores should be prepared in chemically defined media (Hodges *et al.*, 1980). This is obviously of importance where standardization of test methods is concerned. However, in determining factors influencing spore resistance, variations in conditions form a useful tool for associating changes in spores with response to biocides.

2.2.2 *pH of culture medium*

There is surprisingly little information as to the effect of variations in the pH of the culture medium on subsequent sensitivity of bacteria to antimicrobial agents. Differences in the phospholipid contents of batch-grown cells of *B. megaterium* and *Staphylococcus aureus* grown at different pH values have been observed, but cell-wall changes have not been examined (Houtsmuller & Van Deenen, 1964; Op den Kamp *et al.*, 1965).

Changes in cell walls of bacteria grown in media of different pH values might be expected to lead to variations in response of the organisms to biocides. It must, however, be added that changes in pH value of the medium will occur during growth of the organism as a result of its metabolic activity.

2.2.3 *Temperature of incubation*

Again, there is surprisingly little information on the effect of incubation temperature of the culture medium in which the cells are grown and their sensitivity when later exposed to a non-antibiotic antimicrobial agent. Studies have been carried out with antibiotics, e.g. the effect of antibiotics on methicillin-resistant *Staph. aureus*, or the effect of nystatin on the yeast, *Saccharomyces cerevisiae*, grown at different temperatures. Quite significant changes may occur in cells grown at different temperatures, notably the phospholipid content (de Siervo, 1969).

There is no doubt that a comparison of the response to antimicrobial agents of micro-organisms grown at different temperatures could provide much useful information, especially if quantitative studies on cell-wall composition are made simultaneously.

Changes in sporulation conditions have been shown to influence not only the composition of spores but also their responses to heat and radiation (Russell, 1971a, 1982). *B. subtilis* spores produced at 37°C are rather more sensitive to inhibition by chlorocresol of their germination than are spores produced at 50°C (Bell & Parker, 1975). However, there is a dearth of information in this area, and no conclusions can as yet be reached.

2.2.4 *Anaerobiosis*

Data about the effect of antibacterial agents on

bacteria grown under anaerobic conditions are sparse. In a review of those factors influencing the antimicrobial activity of phenols, Bennett (1959) pointed out that aerobic organisms were more resistant than anaerobes, and that facultative aerobes were sensitive under aerobic, but much less so under anaerobic, conditions. The basis of this response is unknown.

2.3 Condition of organism

2.3.1 Gaseous disinfectants

The state of hydration of the micro-organisms under test may be an important factor in determining their sensitivity or resistance to an antimicrobial agent. Pre-treatment equilibration of bacterial spores, *E. coli* and *Staph. aureus* to low relative humidity (r.h.) values, 1%, increases their resistance to ethylene oxide at 33% r.h., whereas under 'optimum' conditions, i.e. with 'naked' spores placed on filter paper, the antibacterial activity is most rapid at this r.h. (Gilbert *et al.*, 1964). Once bacterial cells have been dried beyond a certain critical point, they must be physically wetted or placed in an environment of 100% r.h. to become rehydrated. This factor is of paramount importance in ensuring sterilization by ethylene oxide.

It has also been shown that organisms pre-dried from different media vary in their subsequent sensitivity to ethylene oxide. Bacterial spores dried from saline, serum and broth are more resistant than those dried from water or methanol, and those dried from saline always have a small proportion of cells which are not killed even after prolonged exposure to the gas (Beeby & Whitehouse, 1965). Bacteria trapped inside crystals are protected from the action of ethylene oxide, which is unable to penetrate crystalline materials. *Staph. aureus* cells, grown in tryptose broth, washed with water, placed on filter discs and exposed to ethylene oxide at 'optimum' (33%) r.h. are more readily killed than similarly grown but unwashed cells of this organism (Gilbert *et al.*, 1964). Adsorption of organic matter represented by tryptose broth to the cells is the probable reason for the reduced effect of the gas.

The nature of the surface on which organisms are dried before exposure to ethylene oxide may have a considerable effect on response to the gas. Bacteria dried on hard or non-hygroscopic surfaces are more resistant on subsequent exposure than are the same organisms dried on absorbent or hygroscopic surfaces (Kereluk *et al.*, 1970).

The inactivation of micro-organisms by ethylene oxide and other gases has been the subject of several reviews, notably those by Hoffman (1971), Ernst (1974), Russell (1976) and Richards *et al.* (1984). Chapter 20 in the present volume should also be consulted.

2.3.2 Liquid biocides

Dried bacteria are considerably more resistant than bacteria in liquid suspension. In experiments with glutaraldehyde, Russell (unpublished data) found that concentrations of 50 times those needed to kill liquid suspensions of non-sporulating bacteria were necessary to kill the same strains dried onto syringe needles. This is by no means an isolated occurrence. In practice bacteria are frequently found in dry conditions, and simulated tests can provide useful information. In this context, the publication detailing the Association of Analytical Chemists' (AOAC) test methods for evaluating disinfectant activity is a valuable document (AOAC, 1984).

2.4 Pre-treatment with chemical agents

Some significant findings, especially from an understanding of the nature of bacterial permeability or impermeability to biocides, have resulted from investigations involving pre-exposure of micro-organisms to chemical agents before treatment of cells with antimicrobial compounds. This section will thus deal with the following pre-treatment environments:

1 growth of micro-organisms in a specified medium containing a specified chemical agent;
2 growth in a specified medium, followed by washing the cells, and exposing them to a specified chemical agent;
3 exposure of cells to a specified mutagen.

2.4.1 *Pre-treatment with polysorbate*

Polysorbates (Tweens) are non-ionic surface-active agents which find importance in the formulation of certain pharmaceutical products (see Chapter 15). Polysorbate 80-treated *Ps. aeruginosa* cells in which organisms were grown in broth containing up to 0.175% polysorbate, became permeable to the dye, anilino-naphthalene-8-sulphonate (Brown & Winsley, 1969). It is possible that polysorbate alters the permeability of the cells since it has been found that polysorbate 80-treated bacteria leak intracellular constituents and become susceptible to changes in pH, temperature or sodium chloride concentration (Brown & Winsley, 1969; see also Brown, 1975). Support for this comes from the findings (Brown & Richards, 1964) that pre-treatment of *Ps. aeruginosa* with polysorbate 80 renders the cells more sensitive to benzalkonium chloride and chlorhexidine diacetate.

2.4.2 *Pre-treatment with cationic surface-active agents*

Pre-treatment of *Ps. aeruginosa* with benzalkonium chloride produced cells sensitive to polysorbate 80, which adversely affected the cell envelope, and to phenethyl alcohol, which had an enhanced effect on the membrane (Hoffman *et al.*, 1973; Richards & Cavill, 1976). In this context it is of interest to note that the cationic agent, cetyltrimethylammonium bromide (CTAB), is believed to unmask a sub-unit of the carrier protein in the outer layer of the cytoplasmic membrane, thereby allowing the transport of β-galactoside into permease-less *E. coli* mutants (Ulitzer, 1970). However, pre-treatment of *Proteus* spp. with cationic agents did not increase their sensitivity to unrelated agents (Chapman & Russell, 1978).

2.4.3 *Pre-treatment with permeabilizers*

Permeabilizers are chemical agents that increase bacterial permeability to antimicrobial agents. To date, permeabilizers have been most widely studied with Gram-negative bacteria and include chelating agents, polycations, lactoferrin and transferrin, triethylene tetramine and specific cationic compounds (Smith, 1975; Vaara & Vaara, 1983a,b; Hukari *et al.*, 1986; Viljanen, 1987; Modha *et al.*, 1989; Russell & Chopra, 1990).

Leive (1965) found that whereas *E. coli* cells were normally insensitive to the antibiotic actinomycin D, pre-treatment of the cells with ethylenediamine tetraacetic acid (EDTA) rendered them susceptible to the antibiotic. This is probably the result of a non-specific increase in permeability as a consequence of treatment with the chelating agent, since cells of many Gram-negative strains pre-treated with EDTA or a related chelating agent become sensitive to many unrelated antibacterial agents, including chlorhexidine, benzalkonium chloride and cetrimide (for reviews, see Russell, 1971b; Wilkinson, 1975; Hart, 1984; Russell & Gould, 1988; Russell & Chopra, 1990; Russell, 1990a, 1991a).

EDTA is believed to remove cations, especially Mg^{2+} and Ca^{2+}, from the outer envelope layers of Gram-negative bacteria. Additionally, a considerable amount of lipopolysaccharide is removed, although generally the cells remain viable.

In some experiments, permeabilizers are included with test inhibitor in the growth medium. Properties of these permeabilizing agents are considered in Table 3.1. Other permeabilizers used in the laboratory for increasing bacterial spore sensitivity to biocides include urea in combination with dithiothreitol and sodium lauryl sulphate (UDS; Russell, 1990b, 1991b). Few, if any, significant studies have been made about ways of increasing the permeability to biocides of mycobacteria or fungi.

2.4.4 *Pre-treatment with cross-linking agents*

Pre-treatment of Gram-negative bacteria with glutaraldehyde (Munton & Russell, 1972; Russell & Haque, 1975) or other cross-linking agents (Schmalreck & Teuber, 1976) renders the cells more resistant to lysis by osmotic shock, EDTA-lysozyme or sodium lauryl sulphate. Glutaraldehyde-treated cells of *Staph. aureus* became more resistant to lysis by lysostaphin (Russell & Vernon, 1975). Such findings are of potential value in studying the mechanism of action of cross-linking agents, which appear to act on the bacterial cell wall or envelope.

Table 3.1 Permeabilizing agents*

Type of agent	Example	Action
Chelating agent	EDTA (and similar agents)	Leakage (and lysis in *Ps. aeruginosa*); removal of some outer membrane Mg^{2+} and LPS
Polycations	Polylysine	Displacement of outer membrane Mg^{2+} and release of LPS
Iron-binding proteins	Lactoferrin, transferrin	Partial LPS loss

* Based on Russell & Chopra (1990).

Pre-treatment of bacterial spores with glutaraldehyde reduces the permeabilizing-induced sensitivity to lysozyme (Thomas & Russell, 1974), providing evidence for a binding of the aldehyde at the spore surface but not ruling out penetration into the spore.

2.4.5 *Exposure of cells to mutagenic agents*

Methods of using mutagenic agents, such as *N*-methyl-*N'*-nitro-*N*-nitrosoguanidine (NTG) to produce mutants of bacteria of fungi have been described by Adelberg *et al.* (1965) and Hopwood (1970). Novobiocin-supersensitive (NS) mutants of *E. coli* have been produced by exposure of the parent cells to NTG (Tamaki *et al.*, 1971; Ennis & Bloomstein, 1974). These NS mutants were more sensitive than the parent cells to EDTA, lysozyme and tris, as well as to deoxycholate (Singh & Reithmeier, 1975), and were shown to be heptose-deficient mutants with associated alterations in the protein component of the outer membrane.

The response of antibiotic-supersensitive strains of *Ps. aeruginosa* and *E. coli* to biocides has been studied (El-Falaha *et al.*, 1983; Russell & Furr, 1986; Russell, Furr & Pugh, 1985, 1987; Russell *et al.*, 1986). All *E. coli* strains showed a similar degree of sensitivity to chlorhexidine, but deep rough mutants were much more sensitive to QACs and parabens.

2.4.6 *Induction of spheroplasts, protoplasts and mureinoplasts*

Spheroplasts (sphaeroplasts) are osmotically fragile forms of bacteria which retain at least some of their outer envelope material. They are usually induced in hypertonic media by antibiotics such as penicillins, cephalosporins or D-cycloserine which inhibit a specific stage in the biosynthesis of the bacterial cell wall, or by exposure of cells to ethylenediamine tetraacetic acid (EDTA), tris, lysozyme and sucrose. If the latter treatment is used, however, it is pertinent to note that the outer membrane of stationary-phase cells may be more resistant to 'destabilizers' such as tris and EDTA than are exponentially growing cells, i.e. the outer membrane of the former may be more stable than that of the latter cells (Witholt *et al.*, 1976).

Protoplasts are osmotically fragile forms of bacteria which contain no cell-wall material. Sensitive bacteria such as *Micrococcus lysodeikticus*, *Sarcina lutea* and *B. megaterium* can be converted into protoplasts by means of the enzyme lysozyme.

Mureinoplasts are osmotically fragile forms of Gram-negative bacteria which have lost the outer lipoprotein and lipopolysaccharide layers by repeated washing of the cells with hypertonic sucrose (Gorman & Scott, 1977; see also Weiss, 1976). Mureinoplasts, which retain the original peptidoglycan may be converted to protoplasts by treatment with lysozyme.

Treatment of spheroplasts, protoplasts or mureinoplasts with biocides may be of value in assessing the influence of the outer cell layers on the penetration of the antibacterial compounds. It must, however, be recognized that in these forms there may be stretching of the remaining outside layers, as in spheroplasts, or of the cytoplasmic membrane itself (as in all three forms) which could distort the conclusions reached.

3 FACTORS DURING TREATMENT

Several parameters influence the in-use activity of biocides. These include the concentration of agent; the number, type and location of micro-organisms; the temperature and pH of treatment and the presence of extraneous material such as organic or other interfering matter. These have important effects on the actual performance of disinfectants, antiseptics and preservatives, and consequently will be considered at some length.

3.1 Concentration of biocide

Kinetic studies involving the effect of concentration on the lethal activity of microbicidal substances have employed a symbol, η, termed the concentration exponent (dilution coefficient) which is a measure of the effect of changes in concentration (or dilution) on cell death rate. To determine η, it is necessary to measure the time necessary to produce a comparable degree of death of a bacterial suspension at two different concentrations of the antimicrobial agent. Death rates may be determined in different ways, including an assessment of D-values (decimal reduction times: Hurwitz & McCarthy, 1985).

Then, if C_1 and C_2 represent the two concentrations and t_1 and t_2 the respective times to reduce the viable population to a similar degree

$$C_1^{\eta}t_1 = C_2^{\eta}t_2 \qquad (3.1)$$

or

$$\eta = \frac{\log t_2 - \log t_1}{\log C_1 - \log C_2} \qquad (3.2)$$

A decrease in concentration of substances with high η values results in a marked increase in the time necessary to achieve a comparable kill, other conditions remaining constant. In contrast, compounds with low η values are much less influenced (Table 3.2).

A knowledge of the effect of concentration on antimicrobial activity is essential in the following situations:

1 in the evaluation of biocidal activity;
2 in the sterility testing of pharmaceutical and medical products;
3 in ensuring adequate preservative levels in pharmaceutical products;
4 in deciding what dilution instructions are reasonable in practice.

Other factors, which will be considered later, may also influence the effective ('free') available concentration of an antimicrobial agent.

3.2 Numbers and location of micro-organisms

It is obviously easier for an antimicrobial agent to be effective when there are few micro-organisms against which it has to act. This is particularly important in the production of various types of pharmaceutical and cosmetic products, and is discussed in detail later (Chapter 15). Likewise, the location of micro-organisms must be considered in assessing activity (Scott & Gorman, 1987). An example of this occurs in the cleaning of equipment used in the large-scale production of creams (Bean, 1967) where difficulties may arise in the penetration of a disinfectant to all parts of the equipment.

Table 3.2 Concentration exponents (η values) of various antimicrobial agents*

Substance(s)	η Value	Increased time factor (x...) when concentration reduced to: One-half	One-third
Phenolics	6	2^6, i.e. $64x$	3^6, i.e. $729x$
Alcohol	10	2^{10}, i.e. $1024x$	3^{10}, i.e. $59\,000x$
Parabens	2.5	$2^{2.5}$, i.e. $5.7x$	3^{2-5}, i.e. $15.6x$
Chlorhexidine	2	$4x$	$8x$
Mercury compounds	1	$2x$	$3x$
Quaternary ammonium compounds	1	$2x$	$3x$
Formaldehyde	1	$2x$	$3x$

* Based, in part, on Bean (1967).

Table 3.3 Possible relationship between concentration exponents and mechanisms of action of biocides*

Group	Examples	Mechanism of action
A (η 1–2)	Chlorhexidine	Membrane disrupter
	QACs	Membrane disrupter
	Mercury components	–SH reactors
	Glutaraldehyde	$-NH_2$ groups and nucleic acids
B (η 2–4)	Parabens	Concentration-dependent effects: transport inhibited (low), membrane integrity affected (high)
	Sorbic acid	Transport inhibitor (effect on protonmotive force); another unidentified mechanism?
C (η > 4)	Aliphatic alcohols	Membrane disrupters
	Phenolics	

* Based on Hugo & Denyer (1987) and Russell & Chopra (1990).

3.3 Temperature

The activity of a disinfectant or preservative is usually increased when the temperature at which it acts is increased. Useful formulae to measure the effect of temperature on activity are given by

$$\theta^{(T_2-T_1)} = k_2/k_1 \quad (3.3)$$

or

$$\theta^{(T_2-T_1)} = t_1/t_2 \quad (3.4)$$

in which k_2 and k_1 are the rate (velocity) constants at temperatures T_2 and T_1, respectively (Equation 3.3) or t_2 and t_1 are the respective times to bring about a complete kill at T_2 and T_1 (Equation 3.4).

The temperature coefficient, θ, refers to the effect of temperature per 1°C rise, and is nearly always between 1.0 and 1.5 (Bean, 1967). Consequently, it is more usual to specify the θ^{10} (or Q_{10}) value, which is the change in activity per 10°C rise in temperature (Table 3.4).

The relationship between θ and Q_{10} is given by

$$\theta = \sqrt[10]{Q_{10}} \quad (3.5)$$

i.e. θ is the 10th root of Q_{10} (or θ^{10}).

The activity of isoascorbic acid increases markedly at elevated temperatures (Mackey & Seymour, 1990).

The potent microbicidal agent, glutaraldehyde, shows a very marked temperature-dependent activity. The alkalinized, or 'potentiated', form of this dialdehyde is a far more powerful agent at 20°C than the more stable acid formulation (Section 3.4). However, at temperatures of about 40°C and above there is little, if any, difference in activity (Boucher, 1975), although the alkaline formulation is less stable at higher temperatures (Gorman *et al.*, 1980).

3.4 Environmental pH

pH can influence biocidal activity in the following ways.

1 Changes may occur in the molecule. Substances such as phenol, benzoic acid, sorbic acid and dehydroacetic acid are effective only or mainly in the unionized form (see also Chapter 2) and as the pH rises an increase takes place in their degree of dissociation. Glutaraldehyde is more stable at acid pH but is considerably more potent at alkaline pH, and it has been postulated that its interaction with amino groups, which occurs most rapidly above pH 7, may be responsible for its lethal effect (Russell & Hopwood, 1976; Gorman *et al.*, 1980; Power & Russell, 1990).

2 Changes may occur in the cell surface. As pH increases, the number of negatively charged groups on the bacterial cell surface increases, with the result that positively charged molecules have an enhanced degree of binding, e.g. QACs (Hugo, 1965, 1981) and dyes such as crystal violet and ethyl violet (Moats & Maddox, 1978) which remain essentially in their ionized form over the pH range 5–9.

Table 3.4 Temperature coefficient (Q_{10} values) of various antimicrobial agents*

Substance(s)	Q_{10} Value	Special application
Phenols and cresols	3–5	Bactericides in some injections†
Formaldehyde	1.5	
Aliphatic alcohols	30–50	
Ethylene oxide	2.7	Sterilization (may be used at 60°C)
β-Propiolactone	2–3	Sterilization (but carcinogenic?)

* Based, in part, on Bean (1967).
† Heating with a bactericide, a process no longer official (*British Pharmacopoeia*, 1988).

3 Partitioning of a compound between a product in which it is present and the microbial cell may be influenced by pH (Bean, 1972).

Table 3.5 summarizes the effects of pH on antimicrobial activity and lists some postulated reasons for these modifications. The sporicidal activity of sodium hypochlorite is potentiated in the presence of alcohols, especially methanol (Coates & Death, 1978) although there is no simple explanation between activity, stability and pH change of the mixture. Maximal sporicidal activity and stability are achieved by buffering hypochlorite alone or a hypochlorite/methanol mixture to within a pH range of 7.6–8.1 (Death & Coates, 1979).

3.5 Interfering substances

3.5.1 Organic matter

Organic matter occurs in various forms: serum, blood, pus, earth, food residues, milkstone (dried residues of milk), faecal material. Organic matter may interfere with the microbicidal activity of disinfectants and other antimicrobial compounds. This interference generally takes the form of a 'reaction' between the biocide and the organic matter, thus leaving a reduced concentration of antimicrobial agent for attacking micro-organisms. This reduced activity is notably seen with highly reactive compounds such as chlorine disinfectants. An alternative possibility is that organic material protects micro-organisms from attack.

Organic soil (as yeast) has been incorporated into various testing procedures, such as the Chick–Martin procedure and the 'dirty conditions' of the Modified Kelsey–Sykes test (Kelsey & Maurer, 1974; Coates, 1977; Cowen, 1978) which at least give some indication of the likely usefulness of the disinfectant in actual practice.

Organic matter decreases the effect of hypochlorites against bacteria (including mycobacteria and spores), viruses and fungi (Grossgebauer, 1970; Russell, 1971a: Trueman, 1971; Croshaw, 1977; Scott & Gorman, 1987; Russell & Hugo, 1987). Because of their lower chemical reactivity, iodine and iodophors are influenced to a rather lesser extent (Sykes, 1965). Phenols may also show a reduced activity in the presence of organic matter, although Lysol will retain much of its activity in the presence of faeces and sputum. Because of its reactivity with $-NH_2$ groups, it would be expected that the antimicrobial activity of glutaraldehyde would be reduced in the presence of serum: this does not, however, appear to be the case (Borick, 1968; Russell, unpublished) although conflicting data have been reported (Bergan & Lystad, 1971a,b).

Disinfectant use in the cosmetic, pharmaceutical, food and dairy industries is influenced by the reduction of activity that may occur in the presence of organic soil (Bean, 1967; Clegg, 1967; Goldenberg & Relf, 1967; Davis, 1972a,b). Adequate pre-cleaning before employment of a disinfectant or a combination of disinfectant with a suitable detergent may overcome the problem. The nature of the surface and the protection afforded by soiling film are of considerable importance; in the dairy industry, invisible milkstone may protect micro-organisms against disinfection. For further information, Chapter 2 should be consulted.

Detergents themselves may have a lethal effect on micro-organisms and are frequently, if not in-

Table 3.5 Effect of pH on antimicrobial activity

Activity as environmental pH increases	Comments
Decreased activity	
Phenols Organic acids (e.g. benzoic, sorbic)*	Increase in degree of dissociation of molecule
Hypochlorites	Active factor is undissociated hypochlorous acid (see Chapter 2)
Iodine	Most active form is diatomic iodine, I_2 (see Chapter 2)
Increased activity	
Quaternary ammonium compounds Biguanides Diaminidines	Increase in degree of ionization of bacterial surface groups
Acridines Triphenylmethane dyes	Basic nature; competition with H^+ ions
Glutaraldehyde	Interaction with $-NH_2$ groups? (Increases with increasing pH)

* It is now considered that the anion also plays some role in antimicrobial activity: see Eklund (1980, 1983, 1985a,b), Salmond *et al.* (1984) and Sofos *et al.* (1986).

variably, used hot. Some disinfectants may exert a detergent action. Cosmetic and pharmaceutical creams may pose a disinfection problem, since remnants of production batches may remain in relatively inaccessible orifices and crevices in apparatus and machinery used for their preparation; the likely outcome is that such remnants would form foci for the infection of future production batches. Cleaning of all apparatus with hot water and detergent, followed by an appropriate disinfectant or steam, has been recommended (Bean, 1967).

3.5.2 Surface-active agents

The antimicrobial activity of methyl and propyl *p*-hydrozybenzoates and of quaternary ammonium compounds is reduced markedly by macromolecular polymers and by non-ionic agents. Significant increases in concentration of these antimicrobial compounds are needed to inhibit growth of micro-organisms in the presence of polysorbates (tweens) (Patel & Kostenbauder, 1958; Evans & Dunbar, 1965; Kostenbauder, 1983). Nevertheless, although the *total* inhibitory concentration increases with increasing polysorbate concentration, the concentration of *free* preservative required for microbial inhibition is a constant which is independent of the polysorbate concentration, and which is considerably less than the total concentration (Figs 3.1 and 3.2).

The amount of preservative bound to a non-ionic surfactant may be obtained from the following equation:

$$R = SC + 1 \qquad (3.6)$$

in which R is the ratio of total to free preservative concentration, S is the surfactant concentration and C is a constant which has a unique value for each surfactant–preservative mixture and which increases in value as the lipid solubility of the preservative increases.

The interaction (considered briefly below) of preservatives with non-ionic surface active agents has important repercussions in the preservation of various types of pharmaceutical and cosmetic products, notably creams and emulsions. This aspect is considered in detail in Chapter 15. Interaction of preservatives with non-ionic surfactants could be the result of either micellar solubilization or complex formation between the two molecules.

Interaction between a preservative and a macromolecule does not necessarily mean that the preservative has no effect. Provided that compensation is made for the amount of bound preservative, an appropriate preservative concentration may be included in a product. This implies that an adequate concentration of free preservative exists in the

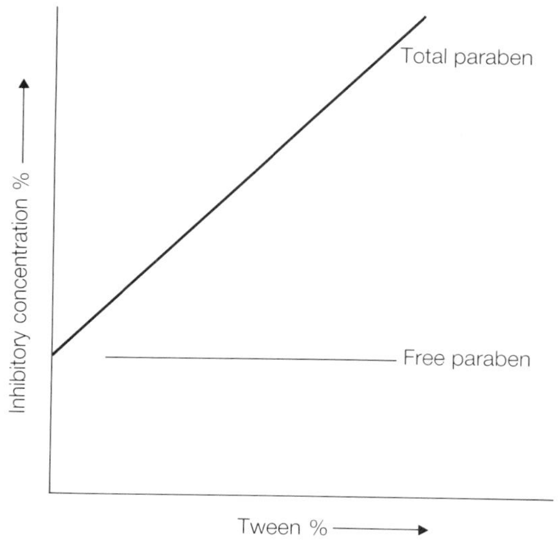

Fig. 3.1 Effect of polysorbate (tween) 80 concentration on the inhibitory concentration of methyl *p*-hydroxybenzoate (methyl paraben).

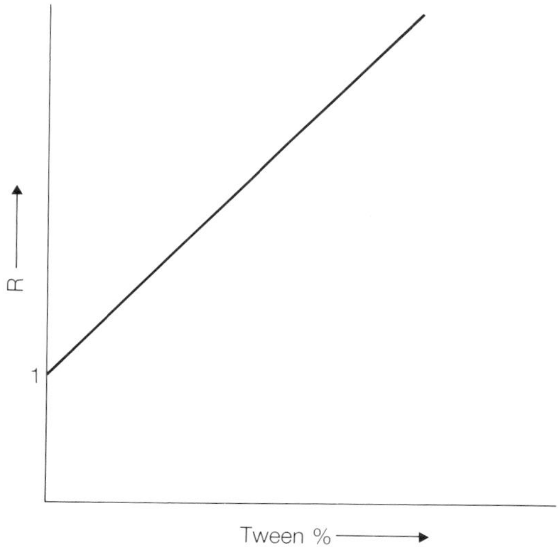

Fig. 3.2 Relationship between polysorbate (Tween) 80 concentration and *R* (ratio of total: free drug).

aqueous phase outside the micelle or complex. However, other problems could also arise, including possible difficulties in formulation and toxicity to the user.

A seemingly paradoxical result is the observation that non-ionic surfactants can increase the efficacy of antimicrobial agents. Low concentrations of polysorbates, tritons and tergitols have been shown to increase the microbicidal potency of esters of *p*-hydroxybenzoic acid and of benzalkonium chloride and chlorhexidine (Allwood, 1973). The antagonistic and synergistic effects of non-ionic surfactants on the antibacterial activity of cationic surface-active agents have been well documented by Schmolka (1973). Below the critical micelle concentration (CMC) of the non-ionic agent, it is believed that potentiation occurs by an effect of this agent on the surface layers of the bacterial cell resulting in an increased cellular permeability to the antimicrobial compound; above the CMC of the non-ionic agent, the germicide is distributed between the aqueous and micellar phases, or complexes with the non-ionic surfactant. However, it is only the concentration of germicide in the aqueous phase that is available for attacking microorganisms.

Because of their inactivation of various types of antimicrobial preservatives, non-ionic surfactants are frequently employed as neutralizing agents (Russell *et al.*, 1979; Russell, 1981) and this aspect is considered in more detail in Section 4.1.

Other surface-active agents which influence the activity of antimicrobial compounds include the soaps. Soap is employed as a solubilizing agent whereby 'solutions' of phenols with a low aqueous solubility may be prepared. Several phenols have a low aqueous solubility; however, bactericidal activity depends on the proportion of soap to phenol. A considerable amount of research has been carried out on the effect of the anionic agent, potassium laurate, on the bactericidal potency of benzylchlorphenol (Cook, 1960). Below the CMC of the soap, there is only low solubility of the phenol; at the CMC solubility increases rapidly. There is an initial rapid increase in bactericidal activity until just beyond the CMC. As the soap concentration increases, the solubility of the phenol increases until a second critical concentration is reached and then remains constant. The bactericidal activity decreases until this second critical point is reached and subsequently increases. Several interpretations of these findings are possible and have been put forward by various authors. However, three important points that must be considered in any final analysis are:

1 low soap concentrations modify the bacterial surface, whose permeability is thereby modified with a resultant increased entry of the phenol;

2 high soap concentrations are themselves bactericidal;

3 it is the concentration of benzychlorphenol in the aqueous (non-micellar) phase that is responsible for the bactericidal effect.

It is generally agreed that in concentrated solutions of Lysol (solution of cresol with soap) the cresol is solubilized within the micelles and that dilution below the CMC releases the cresol to produced a highly active solution. Further information has been provided in Chapter 2.

3.5.3 Partitioning between oil and water

A problem encountered in the formulation of pharmaceutical and cosmetic creams is that whereas the preservatives employed may have a good antimicrobial activity in aqueous conditions, their biological activity may be decreased considerably when an oil is present. The reason for this is that the preservative is partitioned between the oil and aqueous phases of the cream; since micro-organisms may live and multiply in the aqueous phase, it is necessary that an adequate preservative concentration should be maintained in this phase.

Bean and his co-workers (see Bean, 1972) have derived the following equation whereby the concentration of preservative in the aqueous phase may be obtained:

$$C_w = C(\Psi + 1)/(K_w^o \Psi + 1) \qquad (3.7)$$

In this equation, C_w represents the concentration of preservative in the aqueous phase, C the total preservative concentration and Ψ the oil/water ratio. The partition coefficient, K_w^o, may vary widely for a single preservative, depending on the type of oil used. If K_w^o is high, then an adequate aqueous phase concentration of preservative can be achieved only by means of an excessive total concentration.

Other significant contributions in this field have been made by Mitchell & Kazmi (1975; Kazmi & Mitchell, 1978a,b) and Parker (1978), and these are considered in greater detail in Chapter 15.

It does not necessarily follow that the total amount of preservative in the aqueous phase is available for attacking micro-organisms, because the nature of the emulgent must be taken into account (Section 3.5.2). Likewise, the pH of the cream must be considered, since pH may affect the partition coefficient, may cause dissociation of the preservative molecule or may, in its own right, inhibit growth.

3.5.4 Partitioning between rubber and water

Two important types of sterile pharmaceutical products are injections and eye-drops. Multiple-dose formulations are prepared with rubber closures for the former, and with silicone rubber closures for the latter. Such formulations require the presence of suitable antimicrobial agents which act as preservatives and (in some instances in Britain) as an aid to the sterilization process. A major problem, however, is the partitioning of the antimicrobial agent that occurs between the rubber closure and the aqueous product (Wiener, 1955; Wing, 1955, 1956a,b). The distribution between rubber and water for phenol is 25:75; for chlorocresol 85:15; chlorbutanol 80–90:10–20; phenylmercuric nitrate 95:5.

This problem, and the means of at least partially overcoming it, are described in greater detail by Allwood (1978).

3.5.5 Metal ions

The activity of antimicrobial agents may be reduced or enhanced or remain unchanged in the presence of cations. Mn^{2+} and Zn^{2+} ions reduce and enhance, respectively, the anti-pseudomonal activity of salicylaldehyde, whereas Ca^{2+} and Mg^{2+} have no effect. The anti-staphylococcal potency of anionic surfactants is increased in the presence of low concentrations of divalent cations, whereas the bactericidal activity of long-chain fatty acids is diminished greatly in the presence of Mg^{2+}, Ca^{2+} or Ba^{2+} ions (Galbraith & Miller, 1973).

The antibacterial activity of many antibacterial compounds is potentiated against Gram-negative bacteria when EDTA is present (Russell, 1971b;

Wilkinson, 1975; Hart, 1984), and one disinfectant/antiseptic product incorporated chloroxylenol and EDTA in a suitable formulation. The antibacterial activity of this product against *Ps. aeruginosa* is reduced in the presence of Mg^{2+} or Ca^{2+} ions (Dankert & Schut, 1976) or of artificial hard water, prepared to the specifications of the World Health Organization, at various pH levels (Dankert & Schut, 1976; Russell & Furr, 1977). Obviously, hard water should be widely employed in microbicidal tests on disinfectants and antiseptics.

3.6 Humidity

Ideally, relative humidity (r.h.) should be considered from two points of view, *viz.* the effect of pre-humidification of the cells, and the effect of humidity during treatment. Pre-humidification was discussed earlier (Section 2.3.1) and thus only humidity during treatment will be dealt with here, since the subject is considered in depth later (Chapter 20).

R.h. has a profound influence on the activity of gaseous disinfectants such as ethylene oxide, β-propiolactone and formaldehyde (Anon., 1958; Hoffman, 1971; Russell, 1976, 1982, 1990b). With bacterial spores dried on cotton patches as test pieces, ethylene oxide is most active at r.h. of 28–32%, β-propiolactone at r.h. above 70% and formaldehyde at about 60%. This is, in fact, an oversimplification of the effect of r.h., which is the single most important factor influencing the activity of vapour-phase disinfectants (Chapter 20).

3.7 Type of organism

This section will consider the effects of biocides on bacterial cells and spores, moulds and yeasts, viruses and prions. Information on the efficacy of such compounds against rickettsiae, chlamydia and mycoplasma is often lacking, although Quinn (1987) has provided some preliminary data.

3.7.1 Gram-positive bacteria

This sub-section deals with Gram-positive bacteria other than mycobacteria and bacterial spores, which are considered in Sections 3.7.2 and 3.7.4, respectively. As well as being important pathogens. Gram-positive bacteria may also be associated with spoilage of pharmaceutical and cosmetic products. Generally, however, they are more sensitive to biocides than are Gram-negative bacteria. Probably the main reason for this difference in sensitivity resides in the relative composition of the cell envelope. In general terms, the cell wall of Gram-positive bacteria is composed basically of peptidoglycan which forms a thick, fibrous layer. Interspersed with this basal structure may be other molecules such as teichoic and teichuronic acids (Rogers *et al.*, 1978) and lipids, although the latter usually occur to a much smaller extent than in the wall of Gram-negative bacteria. Many antibacterial agents (see Chapter 9) must penetrate the outer and cytoplasmic membranes to reach their site of action. It is unlikely that the wall of Gram-positive bacteria presents a barrier to entry of antibacterial substances as does the lipid-rich envelope of Gram-negative organisms.

The effects of various disinfectants, antiseptics and preservatives on Gram-positive bacteria have been well documented (Baird-Parker & Holbrook, 1971). Cocci are readily killed by halogens, but staphylococci are generally more resistant than streptococci to alcohols and glycols; staphylococci tend to be less susceptible than other non-sporing bacteria to ethylene oxide. Cocci are generally sensitive to phenols, especially the bisphenols. Gram-positive bacteria are considerably more sensitive than Gram-negative bacteria to quaternary ammonium compounds and salicylanilides (Hamilton, 1971).

Although resistance to antibiotics, notably the β-lactam group, is frequently associated with the ability of the organism to destroy the drug, the development of resistance to a biocide, i.e. during 'training' of an organism by repeated exposure to gradually increasing concentrations of that agent, is not necessarily associated with any increased destruction of the compound. Chaplin (1951) was the first to associate this type of resistance with the increased lipid content found in Gram-negative bacteria, and it thus seems likely that this extra lipid acts as an additional barrier to the entry of an antibacterial compound. Staphylococcal walls normally have a low wall lipid content; however, an increase in this wall lipid leads to an enhanced resistance of staphylococci (or of vegetative cells of *B. subtilis*) to phenols and to other agents (Hugo & Franklin, 1968; Hugo & Davidson, 1973). Conversely, a decrease in the lipid content of wall of staphylococci renders the cells more sensitive to antibacterial agents (Hugo & Davidson, 1973). Vaczi (1973) provides an excellent account of the role of lipid in bacterial resistance.

A particular problem might be found with methicillin-resistant *Staph. aureus* (MRSA) strains which, in addition to being antibiotic-resistant, may also be less sensitive than methicillin-sensitive (MSSA) strains to some biocides. This aspect is covered more fully in Chapter 10F.

3.7.2 Mycobacteria

For convenience, mycobacteria are considered separately from other Gram-positive bacteria.

Reliable information on the mycobactericidal activity of chemical disinfectants is still lacking (Croshaw, 1971). The resistance of acid-fast bacteria to disinfectants is considered as being intermediate between vegetative bacteria and bacterial spores (Spaulding *et al.*, 1977).

Resistance of mycobacteria to many disinfectants is undoubtedly linked to the composition of the cell walls of these organisms: an excellent review of the structure of mycobacterial cell walls has been written by Petit & Lederer (1978). The cell walls of mycobacteria always contain alanine, glutamic acid and *meso*-diaminopimelic acid (DAP) and the monosaccharides, galactose and arabinose. The muramic acid is *N*-glycolated and not *N*-acetylated; a characteristic property of the walls of these organisms is the presence of long-chain fatty acids (mycolic acids) which exist in ester linkage with arabinose; see Chapter 10D.

Mycobacteria possess an unusually high wall lipid content, and the resultant hydrophobic nature of the wall may be responsible, at least in part, for their high resistance, which is more or less proportional to the content of waxy material (Croshaw, 1971). Quaternary ammonium compounds and dyes are inhibitory to *M. tuberculosis* but are not tuberculocidal, and this organism is also resistant to chlorhexidine, acids and alkalis but moderately sensitive to ampholytic surface-active agents including the 'Tego' compounds. Of the phenols, *o*-phenylphenol is particularly effective, but the bisphenols are inactive. Alcohols, formaldehyde (liquid and vapour forms), formaldehyde-alcohol, iodine-alcohol and ethylene oxide are tuberculocidal agents (Newman *et al.*, 1955; Anon., 1958; Spaulding, 1977; Rubin, 1983). Glutaraldehyde is generally considered to be a good mycobactericidal agent (see review by Russell & Hopwood, 1976) although slow tuberculocidal action has also been observed (Bergan & Lystad, 1971a,b). F.M. Collins (1986) and J. Collins (1986) have now confirmed that glutaraldehyde is mycobactericidal.

3.7.3 Gram-negative bacteria

Gram-negative bacteria, especially *E. coli*, *Klebsiella* spp., *Proteus* spp., *Ps. aeruginosa* and *Serr. marcescens*, appear to be increasingly implicated as hospital pathogens. *Ps. aeruginosa*, in particular, has long been considered as being an extremely troublesome organism with above-average resistance to many antibiotics and other antibacterial agents (Brown, 1975). Russell *et al.* (1986) have examined the responses of hospital isolates of Gram-negative bacteria to various biocides.

Gram-negative are often less sensitive than Gram-positive bacteria to biocides (Baird-Parker & Holbrook, 1971). This may reflect the considerable differences in the composition, notably the lipid content, of the cell envelopes of the two types of organisms. Envelope permeability to antibacterial substances will be considered in detail in Chapter 10A. The response of legionellae to biocides is discussed in Report (1989) and in Chapter 10E.

Resistance of Gram-negative bacteria to many antibiotics is linked to R-plasmid mediated enzymatic inactivation or to intrinsic resistance. Likewise, R^+ strains of Gram-negative bacteria may destroy mercury compounds (Smith, 1967; Summers & Silver, 1972; Foster, 1983; Silver & Misra, 1988). Some R-plasmids may be associated with sensitivity and resistance to sodium deoxycholate (Hesslewood & Smith, 1974). The role of plasmids in bacterial resistance to biocides was considered by Russell (1985); see also Chapter 10B.

3.7.4 Bacterial spores

A comprehensive review of the resistance of spores to chemical and physical agents has been published (Russell, 1971a). Many antibacterial substances may not be sporicidal but may be sporostatic, e.g. phenols, quaternary ammonium compounds, mercury compounds, biguanides, alcohols, parabens.

There is surprisingly little information on the effects of non-antibiotic antibacterial agents on the sporulation process, whereas several studies have been made of the effects of such compounds on the germination and outgrowth processes. Depending on its concentration, phenol will retard or inhibit germination, as will glutaraldehyde, whereas ethylene oxide and quaternary ammonium compounds allow germination to proceed but inhibit outgrowth (Parker, 1969; Marletta & Stumbo, 1970).

Comparatively few substances are actively sporicidal. Examples of sporicides include glutaraldehyde, formaldehyde, halogens, ethylene oxide and acid alcohol (Anon., 1958; Sykes, 1970; Hoffman, 1971; Russell, 1971a: Trueman, 1971; Kelsey *et al.*, 1974; Russell & Hopwood, 1976). Details of spore sensitivity and resistance and mechanisms of sporicidal action have been published (Russell, 1983, 1990b, 1991b).

The subject of resistance of bacterial spores will be dealt with in more detail in Chapter 10C.

3.7.5 Moulds and yeasts

Several species of moulds and yeasts are pathogenic. Others are important spoilage organisms of foods and pharmaceutical and cosmetic products. Thus, a brief discussion of their sensitivity and resistance will be made.

Many compounds show both antibacterial and antifungal activity. These include phenolics (notably the halogenated members and hexachlorophane), quaternary ammonium compounds (D'Arcy, 1971), oxine, diamidines, organic mercury derivatives (including penotrane) and esters of *p*-hydroxybenzoic acids, the parabens. Sorbic acid shows significant antifungal activity at low pH values, when it occurs in solution mainly in the undissociated form. At higher pH values it dissociates and activity is lost.

The antifungal activity of biocides is discussed in detail in Chapter 5.

3.7.6 Viruses

Several bactericidal agents possess virucidal properties, although antibacterial activity does not necessarily imply antiviral potency. For a comprehensive treatise of virus disinfection, the excellent review of Grossgebauer (1970) should be consulted. Mechanisms of antiviral activity of biocides are well discussed by Thurman & Gerba (1988, 1989) and Stagg (1982) has considered methods of estimating virucidal activity. Morphological changes in viruses sometimes occur following exposure to biocides (Taylor & Butler, 1982).

Some antimicrobial agents are much less active in destroying non-lipid-enveloped viruses (e.g. enteroviruses such as polio, coxsackie and ECHO) than lipid-enveloped ones. On the other hand, the latter are quite sensitive to disinfectants with a lipophilic character. Into this category come certain phenol derivatives, such as *o*-phenylphenol, isopropanol, cationic detergents (although viruses are more resistant to these compounds than are bacteria or fungi), ether and chloroform (Grossgebauer, 1970; Klein & Deforest, 1983). Chlorine disinfectants are considered to be effective in killing all virus types (Dychdala, 1983) and to be useful in preventing the spread of foot-and-mouth disease (Trueman, 1971). Mercury compounds are inactive against viruses.

Formaldehyde, which is often used in the preparation of viral vaccines, may require an extensive period in order to be virucidal (Grossgebauer, 1970) and in the vapour state it has a low power of penetration. β-Propiolactone vapour acts similarly, but the liquid form is strongly virucidal. Ethylene oxide is virucidal when employed in both the liquid and gaseous states (Sykes, 1965).

Glutaraldehyde is a compound with considerable activity against most types of micro-organisms (Chapter 2). It is, in addition, a virucidal agent with activity against many types of viruses.

Viruses that have, in recent years, caused a

considerable degree of concern are hepatitis B virus (HBV) and human immunodeficiency virus (HIV). The former is now believed to be less resistant than at first thought, and both it and HIV (Spire *et al.*, 1984) can be readily inactivated by glutaraldehyde and chlorine-releasing agents (Bloomfield *et al.*, 1990; Committee, 1990; see also Russell, 1990b). The responses of various animal viruses to biocides were discussed by Russell & Hugo (1987); see also Chapter 6.

3.7.7 Prions

Unconventional agents are believed to be highly resistant to many chemical disinfection and physical sterilization processes (Committee, 1986), including ultraviolet and ionizing radiations, high temperatures, glutaraldehyde and chlorine. Sodium hydroxide is, however, considered to be an effective decontaminant (Brown *et al.*, 1984). The subject is discussed in more detail later (Chapter 7).

3.7.8 Protozoa

An increasing amount of information has become available about the sensitivity of protozoa to biocides (see Chapter 8), with considerable attention said to the trophozoite and cyst forms of organisms belonging to the genus *Giardia*. An excellent review on the sensitivity of *Giardia* cysts has been published by Jarroll (1988).

4 POST-TREATMENT FACTORS

Several factors influence the recovery of micro-organisms exposed to antimicrobial compounds. These include the composition and pH of the recovery medium, removal of the antimicrobial agent, the temperature and period of incubation and the composition of the diluent used for serial dilution in the carrying out of viable counts. However, there is very little information as to the actual repair of injury suffered by damaged but still-alive micro-organisms (in contrast to the increasingly interesting data pertaining to the repair of bacteria damaged by exposure to ionizing or ultraviolet radiation or to heat). This point will be returned to later.

4.1 Neutralization of biocides

To prevent an inhibitory concentration of an antimicrobial agent from being transferred to the recovery medium, it is essential that the activity of the antimicrobial compound be nullified. This may be achieved by means of an inactivating agent (inactivator, neutralizing agent, antidote) which overcomes the activity of the inhibitory (antimicrobial) agent. The antidote must itself be non-toxic to micro-organisms and any product resulting from neutralization must likewise be non-toxic. Examples of suitable antidotes are provided in Table 3.6.

Disinfectants which have high dilution coefficients (Section 3.1) rapidly lose their activity on dilution and this may be sufficient to overcome any residual activity, i.e. dilution to a sub-inhibitory value in the recovery medium. Inactivating agents such as Tweens may, however, provide a suitable alternative (Table 3.6). Inactivating agents may be included in the first diluent tube (Section 4.2) or recovery medium (Section 4.3) or both.

A third technique is one involving membrane filtration. In this the mixture of disinfectant plus micro-organisms is filtered through a membrane filter; this is then washed *in situ*, so that the organisms are retained on the membrane and traces of antimicrobial agent are removed. Transfer of the membrane to an appropriate agar medium enables any surviving cells to produce colonies. This method was originally devised for sterility testing and has since been applied to disinfectant evaluation (Prince *et al.*, 1975).

The microbiological importance of overcoming the activity of various classes of antibiotics and other antimicrobial compounds has been discussed in detail by Russell *et al.* (1979) and Russell (1981).

4.2 Diluent in viable counting procedures

Sterile glass distilled water, one-quarter-strength Ringer's solution, 0.9% w/v saline, peptone water and nutrient broth have been employed as diluents by various investigators: for their possible toxic effects, see King & Hurst (1963). Some bacteria, e.g. *Ps. aeruginosa* (Brown, 1975) and some strains of *Proteus* spp. are affected by water, and viable

Table 3.6 Inactivating agents for some antimicrobial agents*

Antimicrobial agent	Possible inactivating agent(s)	Comments
Phenols and cresols	None (dilution) Tweens (polysorbates)	High dilution coefficient (Table 3.2)
Parabens	None (dilution) Tweens	
Iodine and related compounds	Sodium thiosulphate	Sodium thiosulphate may be inhibitory to some bacteria, e.g. staphylococci
Chlorine and hypochlorites	Nutrient media Sodium thiosulphate	See Kelsey *et al.* (1974) Also, sodium thiosulphate may be toxic to some bacterial species
Glutaraldehyde	Sodium sulphite Glycine Dilution	Sodium sulphite is not recommended because of toxicity
Quaternary ammonium compounds, chlorhexidine	Lubrol + lecithin Lecithin + tween (Letheen)	
Mercury compounds	–SH compounds	Thioglycollate may be toxic to bacteria
Organic arsenicals	–SH compounds	
Bronopol	–SH compounds	

* For further details, see Russell *et al.* (1979) and Russell (1981). Note that non-ionic surface-active agents may themselves adversely affect micro-organisms.

counts in which water is the diluent may be lower than when another diluent is employed. It must be remembered that bacteria exposed to a chemical agent may already be in a stressed state (if not already dead) before a viable count on survivors as undertaken. Use of an 'incorrect' diluent could exacerbate this condition and lead to inaccurate conclusions as to the potency of the bactericide.

4.3 Recovery media

The composition of the recovery medium may influence the counts of cells exposed to chemical antimicrobial compounds. Surprisingly, the subject has been comparatively little studied. It is, however, known that nutrient broth containing activated charcoal (Norit) or various cations will reduce both the rate and extent of damage of phenol-treated bacteria (Harris, 1963). Likewise, there is a death of information as to the effects of recovery medium pH on viable counts.

The possible value of varying the composition of the recovery medium when studies of the mechanism of action of a chemical agent are being carried out is demonstrated clearly in Table 3.7, which is based on the studies of Michael & Stumbo (1970). An interesting finding was that of Durant & Higdon (1987) who showed that the numbers of colonies from *Ps. aeruginosa* cells previously treated with bronopol were several-hundredfold higher on recovery media containing catalase than on unsupplemented agar. This was attributed to the presence of sublethally injured bacteria, but the mechanism of this repair has not been elucidated.

4.4 Incubation temperature

Bacteria which survive an inimical treatment may recover better at a temperature below the optimum for undamaged bacteria. Harris (1963) has shown that the optimum temperature for phenol-damaged

Table 3.7 Growth of *Salmonella senftenberg* after exposure to ethylene oxide*

Cells	Recovery medium	Result
Unexposed	1 TSY broth	Growth
	2 MS broth	Growth (rate less than TSY)
EO-exposed	1 TSY broth	Slight lag, then growth
	2 MS broth	Very long lag
EO-exposed	1 MS broth + guanine	Repair and reproduction
	2 MS broth + GTP	Repair and reproduction
	3 MS broth + other supplements†	No repair or reproduction
	4 MS broth + EO-exposed guanine	Repair and reproduction
	5 MS broth + EO-exposed GTP	No repair or reproduction

* After Michael & Stumbo (1970).
† Other supplements tested: amino acids, organic acids, base components of DNA and RNA, vitamins, nucleic-acid sugars.
Abbreviations: EO, ethylene oxide; TSY broth, trypticase soy broth + 0.5% yeast extract; MS broth, a minimal salts + glucose liquid medium; GTP, guanosine triphosphate.

bacteria is 28°C. This may be analogous to the minimal medium repair (MMR) sometimes found with heat-stressed bacteria (Pierson *et al.*, 1978), although there is no evidence that MMR occurs with bactericide-injured cells.

Chemical-treated spores may require long incubation periods before germination and growth occur. In such instances a heat-shocking process after incubation for a specific number of days may be necessary to induce germination.

4.5 Repair of injury

Studies on the repair of thermally injured organisms have been made by several investigators, notably Ordal and his colleagues (see Tomlins & Ordal, 1976). One aspect which has yielded much useful information is to determine colony formation of aliquots of heated suspensions of *Staph. aureus* on an agar medium and on the same medium containing sodium chloride to which the thermally injured cells are susceptible; for further information see Busta (1978).

The principles of this method can certainly be adopted to a study of cells stressed after treatment with an antimicrobial compound. Following exposure the cells are transferred to a suitable liquid medium and incubated; during intervals thereafter, the surviving cells do not increase in numbers, as shown by the constancy of viable counts on 'optimal composition' agar. Counts on agar containing a high concentration of NaCl (or any other appropriate medium to which the stressed cells become sensitive; see Corry *et al.*, 1977) increase until they reach the level attained on the 'optimal composition' agar. At this point repair of injury is considered to be complete. This method has been adopted by M.C. Allwood and colleagues (personal communication) for studying the repair of chlorhexidine-injured *E. coli* cells, and by Corry *et al.* (1977) who investigated the repair of damage of bacteria following treatment with some antibiotics and other antimicrobial agents. Table 3.7 should also be consulted in this context.

Further information on revival after chemical injury or in general can be obtained by consulting Gilbert (1984) and Andrew & Russell (1984), respectively. An interesting concept of repair would be to consider the sensitivity and revival of well-defined DNA repair mutants so widely employed in studies of ultraviolet and ionizing radiation.

5 BACTERIAL BIOFILMS

The interaction of bacteria with surfaces is initially reversible but eventually irreversible. Such irreversible adhesion is initiated by bacteria binding by means of expolysaccharide glycocalyx polymers

(Costerton *et al.*, 1987). The sister cells produced as a result of cell division are then bound within this matrix and eventually there is a continuous biofilm on the colonized surface. Bacteria enclosed in this biofilm exist in a specific micro-environment that differs from cells grown in batch culture under ordinary laboratory conditions.

Bacteria within biofilms are much more resistant to antibacterial agents (both biocides and antibiotics) than are batch-grown cells, e.g. to chlorine (LeChevalier *et al.*, 1988), chlorhexidine (Marrie & Costerton, 1981) and iodine (Pyle & McFeters, 1990). Interestingly, hydrogen peroxide, at concentrations well below those required for total disinfection, has been found to remove biofilms (Christensen *et al.*, 1990).

Biofilms associated with legionellae are discussed in Chapter 10E and in a wider context in Chapter 10A.

6 REFERENCES

Adelberg, E.A., Mandel, M. & Chen, G.C.C. (1965) Optimal conditions for mutagenesis by *N*-methyl-*N'*-*N*-nitrosoguanidine in *Escherichia coli*. *Biochemical and Biophysical Research Communications*, **18**, 788–795.

Allwood, M.C. (1973) Inhibition of *Staphylococcus aureus* by combinations of non-ionic surface-active agents and anti-bacterial substances. *Microbios*, **7**, 209–214.

Allwood, M.C. (1978) Antimicrobial agents in single- and multi-dose injections. *Journal of Applied Bacteriology*, **44**, Svii–Sxvii.

Andrew, M.H.E. & Russell, A.D. (1984) Editors, *The Revival of Injured Microbes*. Society for Applied Bacteriology Symposium Series No. 12. London: Academic Press.

Anon (1958) Disinfection of fabrics with gaseous formaldehyde. Committee on Formaldehyde Disinfection *Journal of Hygiene, Cambridge*, **56**, 488–515.

AOAC (1984) *Official Methods of Analysis of the Association of Official Analytical Chemists*, 14th Ed. Part 4: Disinfectants. Washington: Association of Official Analytical Chemists.

Baird-Parker, A.C. & Holbrook, R. (1971) The inhibition and destruction of cocci. In *Inhibition and Destruction of the Microbial Cell* (ed. Hugo, W.B.) pp. 369–397. London: Academic Press.

Bean, H.S. (1967) Types and characteristics of disinfectants. *Journal of Applied Bacteriology*, **30**, 6–16.

Bean, H.S. (1972) Preservatives for pharmaceuticals. *Journal of the Society of Cosmetic Chemists*, **23**, 703–720.

Beeby, M.M. & Whitehouse, C.E. (1965) A bacterial spore test piece for the control of ethylene oxide sterilization. *Journal of Applied Bacteriology*, **28**, 349–360.

Bell, N.D.S. & Parker, M.S. (1975) The effect of sporulation temperature on the resistance of *Bacillus subtilis* to a chemical inhibitor. *Journal of Applied Bacteriology*, **38**, 295–299.

Bennett, E.O. (1959) Factors affecting the antimicrobial activity of phenols. *Advances in Applied Microbiology*, **1**, 123–140.

Bergan, T. & Lystad, A. (1971a) Disinfectant evaluation by a capacity use-dilution test. *Journal of Applied Bacteriology*, **34**, 741–750.

Bergan, T. & Lystad, A. (1971b) Antitubercular action of disinfectants. *Journal of Applied Bacteriology*, **34**, 751–756.

Beveridge, E.G. (1987) Microbial spoilage and preservation of pharmaceuâical products. In *Pharmaceutical Microbiology* 4th Edn. (eds Hugo, W.B. & Russell, A.D.) pp. 360–380. Oxford: Blackwell Scientific Publications.

Bloomfield, S.F., Smith-Burchnell, C.A. & Dalgleish, A.G. (1990) Evaluation of hypochlorite-releasing disinfectants against the human immunodeficiency virus. *Journal of Hospital Infection*, **15**, 273–278.

Borick, P.M. (1968) Chemical sterilizers (Chemosterilizers). *Advances in Applied Microbiology*, **10**, 291–312.

Boucher, R.M.G. (1975) On biocidal mechanisms in the aldehyde series. *Canadian Journal of Pharmaceutical Sciences*, **10**, 1–7.

Brown, M.R.W. (1975) The role of the cell envelope in resistance. In *Resistance of Pseudomonas aeruginosa* (ed. Brown, M.R.W.) pp. 71–107. London: John Wiley & Sons.

Brown, M.R.W. & Melling, J. (1969) Loss of sensitivity to EDTA by *Pseudomonas aeruginosa* grown under conditions of Mg-limitation. *Journal of General Microbiology*, **54**, 439–444.

Brown, M.R.W. & Richards, R.M.E. (1964) Effect of polysorbate (Tween) 80 on the resistance of *Pseudomonas aeruginosa* to chemical inactivation. *Journal of Pharmacy and Pharmacology*, **16**, (Supplement), 51T-55T.

Brown, M.R.W. & Winsley, B.E. (1969) Effect of polysorbate 80 on cell leakage and viability of *Pseudomonas aeruginosa* exposed to rapid changes of pH, temperature and toxicity. *Journal of General Microbiology*, **56**, 99–107.

Brown, P., Rohwer, R.G. & Gajdusek, D.C. (1984) Sodium hydroxide decontamination of Creutzfeldt-Jakob disease virus. *New England Journal of Medicine*, **310**, 727.

Busta, F.F. (1978) Introduction to injury and repair of microbial cells. *Advances in Applied Microbiology*, **20**, 185–201.

Chaplin, C.E. (1951) Observations on quaternary ammonium disinfectants. *Canadian Journal of Botany*, **29**, 373–382.

Chapman, D.G. & Russell, A.D. (1978) Pretreatment with colistin and *Proteus* sensitivity to other agents. *Journal of Antibiotics*, **31**, 124–130.

Christensen, B.E., Trønnes, H.N., Vollan, K., Smidsrød, O. & Bakke, R. (1990) Biofilm removal by low concentrations of hydrogen peroxide. *Biofouling*, **2**, 165–175.

Clegg, L.F.L. (1967) Disinfectants in the dairy industry. *Journal of Applied Bacteriology*, **30**, 117–140.

Coates, D. (1977) Kelsey–Sykes capacity test: origin, evolution and current status. *Pharmaceutical Journal*, **219**, 402–403.

Coates, D. & Death, J.E. (1978) Sporicidal activity of mixtures of alcohol and hypochlorite. *Journal of Clinical Pathology*, **31**, 148–152.

Collins, F.M. (1986) Kinetics of the tuberculocidal response by alkaline glutaraldehyde in solution and on an inert surface. *Journal of Applied Bacteriology*, **61**, 87–93.

Collins, J. (1986) The use of glutaraldehyde in laboratory discard jars. *Letters in Applied Microbiology*, **2**, 103–105.

Committee (1986) Committee on Health Care Issues, American Neurological Association. Precautions in handling tissues, fluids and other contaminated materials from patients with documented or suspected Creutzfeldt-Jakob disease. *Annals of Neurology*, **19**, 75–77.

Committee (1990) Advisory Committee on Dangerous Pathogens. HIV—the causative agent of AIDS and related conditions.

Cook, A.M. (1960) Phenolic disinfectants. *Journal of Pharmacy & Pharmacology*, **12**, 19T–28T.

Corry, J.E.L., Van Doornf, H. & Mossel, D.A.A. (1977) Recovery and revival of microbial cells, especially those from environments containing antibiotics. In *Antibiotics and Antibiosis in Agriculture* (ed. Woodbine, M.) pp. 174–196. London: Butterworth.

Costerton, J.W., Cheng, K.-J., Geesey, G.G., Ladd, T.I., Nickel, J.C., Dasgupta, M. & Marrie, T.J. (1987) Bacterial biofilms in nature and disease. *Annual Review of Microbiology*, **41**, 435–464.

Cowen, R.A. (1974) Relative merits of 'in use' and laboratory methods for the evaluation of antimicrobial products. *Journal of the Society of Cosmetics Chemists*, **25**, 307–323.

Cowen, R.A. (1978) Kelsey–Sykes capacity test: a critical review. *Pharmaceutical Journal*, **220**, 202–204.

Croshaw, B. (1971) The destruction of mycobacteria. In *Inhibition and Destruction of the Microbial Cell* (ed. Hugo, W.B.) pp. 419–449. London: Academic Press.

Croshaw, B. (1977) Preservatives for cosmetics and toiletries *Journal of the Society of Cosmetic Chemists*, **28**, 3–16.

Dankert, J. & Schut, I.K. (1976) The antibacterial activity of chloroxylenol in combination with ethylenediamine tetraacetic acid. *Journal of Hygiene, Cambridge*, **76**, 11–22.

D'Arcy, P.F. (1971) Inhibition and destruction of moulds and yeasts. In *Inhibition and Destruction of the Microbial Cell* (ed. Hugo, W.B.) pp. 613–686. London: Academic Press.

Davis, J.G. (1972a) Fundamentals of microbiology in relation to cleansing in the cosmetic industry. *Journal of the Society of Cosmetic Chemists*, **23**: 45–71.

Davis, J.G. (1972b) Problems of hygiene in the dairy industry. Parts 1 and 2. *Dairy Industries*, **37**,(4), 212–215; (5) 251–256.

Dean, A.C.R., Ellwood, D.C., Melling, J. & Robinson, A. (1976) The action of antibacterial agents on bacteria grown in continuous culture. In *Continuous Culture—Applications and New Techniques* (eds Dean, A.C.R., Ellwood, D.C., Evans, C.G.T. & Melling, J.) pp. 251–261. London: Ellis Horwood.

Death, J.E. & Coates, D. (1979) Effect of pH on sporicidal and microbicidal activity of buffered mixtures of alcohol and sodium hypochlorite. *Journal of Clinical Pathology*, **32**, 148–153.

Durant, C. & Higdon, P. (1987) Preservation of cosmetic and toiletry products. In *Preservatives in the Food, Pharmaceutical and Environmental Industries* (eds Board, R.G., Allwood, M.C. & Banks, J.G.) Society for Applied Bacteriology Technical Series No. 22, pp. 231–253. Oxford: Blackwell Scientific Publications.

Dychdala, G.R. (1983) Chlorine and chlorine compounds. In *Disinfection, Sterilization and Preservation* (ed. Block, S.S.) 3rd Ed. pp. 157–182. Philadelphia: Lea & Febiger.

Eagon, R.G., Stinnett, J.D. & Gilleland, H.E. (1975) Ultrastructure of *Pseudomonas aeruginosa* as related to resistance. In *Resistance of Pseudomonas aeruginosa* (ed. Brown, M.R.W.) pp. 109–143. London: John Wiley & Sons.

Eklund, T. (1980) Inhibition of growth and uptake processes in bacteria by some chemical food preservatives. *Journal of Applied Bacteriology*, **48**, 423–432.

Eklund, T. (1983) The antimicrobial effect of dissociated and undissociated sorbic acid at different pH levels. *Journal of Applied Bacteriology*, **54**, 383–389.

Eklund, T. (1985a) The effect of sorbic acid and esters of *p*-hydroxybenzoic acid on the protonmotive force in *Escherichia coli* membrane vesicles. *Journal of General Microbiology*, **131**, 73–76.

Eklund, T. (1985b) Inhibition of microbial growth at different pH levels by benzoic and propionic acids and esters of *p*-hydroxybenzoic acid. *International Journal of Food Microbiology*, **2**, 159–167.

El-Falaha, B.M.A., Russell, A.D. & Furr, J.R. (1983) Sensitivities of wild-type and envelope-defective strains of *Escherichia coli* and *Pseudomonas aeruginosa* to antibacterial agents. *Microbios*, **38**, 99–105.

Ennis, H.L. & Bloomstein, M.I. (1974) Antibiotic-sensitive mutants of *Escherichia coli* possess altered outer membranes. *Annals of the New York Academy of Sciences*, **235**, 593–600.

Ernst, R.R. (1974) Ethylene oxide sterilisation kinetics. *Biotechnology and Bioengineering Symposium No. 4*, pp. 858–878.

Evans, W.F. & Dunbar, S.F. (1965) The effect of surfactants on germicides and preservatives. *Society of Chemical Industry: Symposium, Surface Activity and the Microbial Cell*. London: Society of Chemical Industry.

Farewell, J.A. & Brown, M.R.W. (1971) The influence of inoculum history on the response of micro-organisms to inhibitory and destructive agents. In *Inhibition and Destruction of the Microbial Cell* (ed. Hugo, W.B.) pp. 703–752. London: Academic Press.

Foster, T.J. (1983) Plasmid-determined resistance to antimicrobial drugs and toxic metal ions in bacteria. *Microbiological Reviews*, **47**, 361–409.

Furr, J.R. & Russell, A.D. (1972) Uptake of esters of *p*-hydroxybenzoic acid by *Serratia marcescens* and by fattened and non-fattened cells of *Bacillus subtilis*, *Microbios*, **5**, 237–246.

Galbraith, H. & Miller, T.B. (1973) Effect of metal cations and pH on the antibacterial activity and uptake of long chain fatty acids. *Journal of Applied Bacteriology*, **36**, 635–646.

Gilbert, G.L., Gambill, D.M., Spiner, D.R., Hoffman, R.K. & Phillips, C.R. (1964) Effect of moisture on ethylene oxide sterilization. *Applied Microbiology*, **12**, 496–503.

Gilbert, P. (1984) The revival of micro-organisms sublethally injured by chemical inhibitors. In *The Revival of Injured Microbes* (eds Andrew, M.H.E. & Russell, A.D.) Society for Applied Bacteriology Symposium Series No. 12, pp. 175–197. London: Academic Press.

Gilbert, P. & Wright, N. (1987) Non-plasmidic resistance towards preservatives of pharmaceutical products. In *Preservatives in the Food, Pharmaceutical and Environmental Industries* (eds Board, R.G., Allwood, M.C. & Banks, J.G.) Society for Applied Bacteriology Technical Series No. 22, pp. 255–279. Oxford: Blackwell Scientific Publications.

Goldenberg, N. & Relf, C.J. (1967) Use of disinfectants in the food industry. *Journal of Applied Bacteriology*, **30**, 141–147.

Gorman, S.P. & Scott, E.M. (1977) Preparation and stability of mureinoplasts of *Escherichia coli*. *Microbios*, **18**, 123–130.

Gorman, S.P., Scott, E.M. & Russell, A.D. (1980) Antimicrobial activity, uses and mechanism of action of glutaraldehyde. *Journal of Applied Bacteriology*, **48**, 161–190.

Grossgebauer, K. (1970) Virus disinfection. In *Disinfection* (ed. Benarde, M.A.) pp. 103–148. New York; Marcel Dekker.

Hamilton, W.A. (1971) Membrane-active antibacterial compounds. In *Inhibition and Destruction of the Microbial Cell* (ed. Hugo, W.B.) pp. 77–93. London: Academic Press.

Harris, N.D. (1963) The influence of recovery medium and incubation temperature on the survival of damaged bacteria. *Journal of Applied Bacteriology*, **26**, 387–397.

Hart, J.R. (1984) Chelating agents as preservative potentiators. In *Cosmetic and Drug Preservation: Principles and Practice* (ed. Kabara, J.J.) pp. 323–337. New York: Marcel Dekker.

Hesslewood, S.R. & Smith, J.T. (1974) Envelope alterations produced by R-factors in *Proteus mirabilis*. *Journal of General Microbiology*, **85**, 146–152.

Hodges, N.A., Melling, J. & Parker, S.J. (1980) A comparison of chemically defined and complex media for the production of *Bacillus subtilis* spores having reproducible resistance and germination characteristics. *Journal of Pharmacy and Pharmacology*, **32**, 126–130.

Hoffman, H.P., Geftic, S.G., Gelzer, J., Heyman, H. & Adair, F.W. (1973) Ultrastructural observations associated with the growth of resistant *Pseudomonas aeruginosa* in the presence of benzalkonium chloride. *Journal of Bacteriology*, **113**, 409–416.

Hoffman, R.K. (1971) Toxic gases. In *Inhibition and Destruction of the Microbial Cell* (ed. Hugo, W.B.) pp. 225–258. London: Academic Press.

Hopwood, D.A. (1970) The isolation of mutants. In *Methods of Microbiology* (eds Norris, J.R. & Ribbons, D.W.) Vol. 3A, pp. 363–433. London: Academic Press.

Houtsmuller, U.M.T. & Van Deenen, L.L.M. (1965) Identification of a bacterial phospholipid as an *O*-ornithine ester of phosphatidyl glycerol. *Biochimica et Biophysica Acta*, **70**, 211–213.

Hugo, W.B. (1965) Some aspects of the action of cationic surface-active agents on microbial cells with special reference to their action on enzymes. *Surface Activity and the Microbial Cell*. SCI Monograph 19, pp. 67–82. London: Society of Chemical Industry.

Hugo, W.B. (1991) The degradation of preservatives by microorganisms. *International Biodeterioration*, **27**, 185–194.

Hugo, W.B. & Davidson, J.R. (1973) Effect of cell lipid depletion in *Staphylococcus aureus* upon its resistance to antimicrobial agents. II. A comparison of the response of normal and lipid depleted cells of *S. aureus* to antibacterial drugs. *Microbios*, **8**, 63–72.

Hugo, W.B. & Denyer, S.P. (1987) The concentration exponent of disinfectants and preservatives (biocides). In *Preservatives in the Food, Pharmaceutical and Environmental Industries* (eds Board, R.G., Allwood, M.C. & Banks, J.G.) Society for Applied Bacteriology Technical Series No. 22, pp. 281–291. Oxford: Blackwell Scientific Publications.

Hugo, W.B. & Ellis, J.D. (1975) Cell composition and drug resistance in *Escherichia coli*. In *Resistance of Microorganisms to Disinfectants* (ed. Kedzia, W.B.) 2nd International Symposium. pp. 43–45. Poznan, Poland: Polish Academy of Sciences.

Hugo, W.B. & Franklin, I. (1968) Cellular lipid and the antistaphylococcal activity of phenols. *Journal of General Microbiology*, **52**, 365–373.

Hukasi, R., Helander, I.M. & Vaara, M. (1986) Chain length heterogeneity of lipopolysaccharide released from *Salmonella typhimurium* by ethylene-diaminetetraacetic acid or polycations. *Journal of Biological Chemistry*, **154**, 673–676.

Hurwitz, S.J. & McCarthy, T.J. (1985) Dynamics of disinfection of selected preservatives against *Escherichia coli*. *Journal of Pharmaceutical Sciences*, **74**, 892–894.

Jacobs, S.E. (1960) Some aspects of the dynamics of disinfection. *Journal of Pharmacy & Pharmacology*, **12**, 9T–18T.

Jarroll, E.L. (1988) Effect of disinfectants on *Giardia* cysts. *CRC Critical Review in Environmental Control*, **18**, 1–28.

Joswick, H.L., Corner, T.R., Silvernale, J.N. & Gerhardt,

P. (1971) Antimicrobial actions of hexachorophane: release of cytoplasmic materials. *Journal of Bacteriology*, **108**, 492–500.

Kazmi, S.J.A. & Mitchell, A.G. (1978a) Preservation of solubilized and emulsified systems. I. Correlation of mathematically predicted preservative availability with antimicrobial activity. *Journal of Pharmaceutical Sciences*, **7**, 1260–1266.

Kazmi, S.J.A. & Mitchell, A.G. (1978b) Preservation of solubilized and emulsified systems. II. Theoretical development of capacity and its role in antimicrobial activity of chlorocresol in cetomacrogol-stabilized systems. *Journal of Pharmaceutical Sciences*, **67**, 1266–1271.

Kelsey, J.C. & Maurer, I.M. (1974) An improved Kelsey–Sykes test for disinfectants. *Pharmaceutical Journal*, **213**, 528–530.

Kelsey, J.C., Mackinnon, I.H. & Maurer, I.M. (1974) Sporicidal activity of hospital disinfectants. *Journal of Clinical Pathology*, **27**, 632–638.

Kereluk, K., Gammon, R.A. & Lloyd, R.S. (1970) Microbiological aspects of ethylene oxide sterilization. II. Microbial resistance to ethylene oxide. *Applied Microbiology*, **19**, 152–156.

King, W.L. & Hurst, A. (1963) A note on the survival of some bacteria in different diluents. *Journal of Applied Bacteriology*, **26**, 504–506.

Klein, M. & Deforest, A. (1983) Principles of viral inactivation. In *Disinfection, Sterilization and Preservation* (ed. Block, S.S.), 3rd Ed., pp. 422–434. Philadelphia: Lea & Febiger.

Kostenbauder, H.B. (1983) Physical factors influencing the activity of antimicrobial agents. In *Disinfection, Sterilization and Preservation* (ed. Block S.S.), 3rd Ed., pp. 811–828. Philadelphia: Lea & Febiger.

LeChevalier, M.W., Cawthorn, C.D. & Lee, R.G. (1988) Inactivation of biofilm bacteria. *Applied and Environmental Microbiology*, **54**, 2492–2499.

Leive, L. (1965) A non-specific increase in permeability in *Escherichia coli* produced by EDTA. *Proceedings of the National Academy of Sciences, USA*, **53**, 745–750.

Mackey, B.M. & Seymour, D.A. (1990) The bactericidal effect of isoascorbic acid combined with mild heat. *Journal of Applied Bacteriology*, **67**, 629–638.

Marletta, J. & Stumbo, C.R. (1970) Some effects of ethylene oxide on *Bacillus subtilis*. *Journal of Food Science*, **35**, 627–631.

Marrie, T.J. & Costerton, J.W. (1981). Prolonged survival of *Serratia marcescens* in chlorhexidine. *Applied and Environmental Microbiology*, **42**, 1093–1102.

Melling, J., Robinson, A. & Ellwood, D.C. (1974) Effect of growth environment in a chemostat on the sensitivity of *Pseudomonas aeruginosa* to polymyxin B sulphate. *Proceedings of the Society for General Microbiology*, **1**, 61.

Michael, G.I. & Stumbo, C.R. (1970) Ethylene oxide sterilization of *Salmonella senftenberg* and *Escherichia coli*: death kinetics and mode of action. *Journal of Food Science*, **35**, 631–634.

Mitchell, A.G. & Kazmi, S.J.A. (1975) Preservative availability in emulsified systems. *Canadian Journal of Pharmaceutical Sciences*, **10**, 67–68.

Moats, W.A. & Maddox, S.E., Jr. (1978) Effect of pH on the antimicrobial activity of some triphenylmethane dyes. *Canadian Journal of Microbiology*, **24**, 658–661.

Moats, W.A., Kinner, J.A. & Maddox, S.E., Jr. (1974) Effect of heat on the antimicrobial activity of brilliant green dye. *Applied Microbiology*, **27**, 844–847.

Modha, J., Berrett-Bee, K.J. & Rowbury, R.J. (1989) Enhancement by cationic compounds of the growth inhibitory effect of novobiocin on *Escherichia coli*. *Letters in Applied Microbiology*, **8**, 219–222.

Munton, T.J. & Russell, A.D. (1972) Effect of glutaraldehyde on the outer layers of *Escherichia coli*. *Journal of Applied Bacteriology*, **35**, 193–199.

Newman, L.B., Colwell, C.A. & Jameson, A.L. (1955) Decontamination of articles made by tuberculous patients in physical medicine and rehabilitation. *American Review of Tuberculosis and Pulmonary Diseases*, **71**, 272–278.

Op Den Kamp, J.A.F., Houtsmueller, U.M.T. & Van Deenen, L.L.M. (1963) On the phospholipids of *Bacillus megaterium*. *Biochimica et Biophysica Acta*, **106**, 438–441.

Parker, M.S. (1969) Some effects of preservatives on the development of bacterial spores. *Journal of Applied Bacteriology*, **32**, 322–328.

Parker, M.S. (1978). The preservation of cosmetic and pharmaceutical creams. *Journal of Applied Bacteriology*, **44**, Sxxix–Sxxxiv.

Patel, N.K. & Kostenbauder, H.B. (1958) Interaction of preservatives with macromolecules. I. *Journal of the American Pharmaceutical Association, Scientific Edition*, **47**, 289–293.

Petit, J.F. & Lederer, E. (1978) Structure and immunostimulant properties of mycobacterial cell walls. In *Relation between Structure and Function in the Prokaryotic Cell* (eds Stanier, R.Y., Rogers, H.J. & Ward, J.B.) 28th Symposium of the Society for General Microbiology, pp. 178–199. Cambridge: Cambridge University Press.

Pierson, M.D., Gomez, R.F. & Martin, S.E. (1978) The involvement of nucleic acids in bacterial injury. *Advances in Applied Microbiology* (ed. Perlman, D.) Vol. 23, pp. 263–284. New York: Academic Press.

Power, E.G.M. & Russell, A.D. (1990) Uptake of L-(^{14}C)-alanine by glutaraldehyde-treated and untreated spores of *Bacillus subtilis*. *FEMS Microbiology Letters*, **66**, 271–276.

Prince, J., Deverill, C.E.A. & Ayliffe, G.A.J. (1975) A membrane filter technique for testing disinfectants. *Journal of Clinical Pathology*, **28**, 71–76.

Purves, J. & Parker, M.S. (1973) The influence of sporulation and germination media on the development of spores of *Bacillus megaterium* and their inhibition by chlorocresol. *Journal of Applied Bacteriology*, **36**, 39–45.

Pyle, B.H. & McFeters, G.A. (1990) Iodine susceptibility of pseudomonads grown attached to stainless steel surfaces. *Biofouling*, **2**, 113–120.

Quinn, P.J. (1987) Evaluation of veterinary disinfectants

and veterinary processes. In *Disinfection in Veterinary and Farm Animal Practice* (eds Linton, A.H., Hugo, W.B. & Russell, A.D.) pp. 66–116. Oxford: Blackwell Scientific Publications.

Report (1989) *Report of the Expert Advisory Committee on Biocides*. Department of Health. London: HMSO.

Richards, C., Furr, J.R. & Russell, A.D. (1984) Inactivation of micro-organisms by lethal gases. In *Cosmetic and Drug Preservation: Principles and Practice* (ed. Kabara, J.J.) pp. 209–222. New York: Marcel Dekker.

Richards, R.M.E. & Cavill, R.H. (1976) Electron microscope study of effect of benzalkonium chloride and edetate disodium on cell envelope of *Pseudomonas aeruginosa*. *Journal of Pharmaceutical Sciences*, **65**, 76–80.

Rogers, H.J., Ward, J.B. & Burdett, I.D.J. (1978) Structure and growth of the walls of Gram-positive bacteria. In *Relations between Structure and Function in the Prokaryotic Cell* (eds Stanier, R.Y., Rogers, H.J. & Ward, J.B.) 28th Symposium of the Society for General Microbiology, pp. 139–175. Cambridge: Cambridge University Press.

Rubin, J. (1983) Agents for disinfection and control of tuberculosis. In *Disinfection, Sterilization and Preservation* (ed. Block, S.S.) 3rd Ed., pp. 414–421. Philadelphia: Lea & Febiger.

Russell, A.D. (1971a) The destruction of bacterial spores. In *Inhibition and Destruction of the Microbial Cell* (ed. Hugo, W.B.) pp. 451–612. London: Academic Press.

Russell, A.D. (1971b) Ethylenediamine tetraacetic acid. In *Inhibition and Destruction of the Microbial Cell* (ed. Hugo, W.B.) pp. 209–225. London: Academic Press.

Russell, A.D. (1974) Factors influencing the activity of antimicrobial agents: An appraisal. *Microbios*, **10**, 151–174.

Russell, A.D. (1976) Inactivation of non-sporing bacteria by gases. In *The Inactivation of Vegetative Bacteria* (eds Skinner, F.A. & Hugo, W.B.) pp. 61–88. Society for Applied Bacteriology Symposium Series No. 5. London: Academic Press.

Russell, A.D. (1981) Neutralization procedures in the evaluation of bactericidal activity. Society for Applied Bacteriology. Technical Series No. 15. London: Academic Press.

Russell, A.D. (1982) *The Destruction of Bacterial Spores* London: Academic Press.

Russell, A.D. (1983) Mechanism of action of chemical sporicidal and sporistatic agents. *International Journal of Pharmaceutics*, **16**, 127–140.

Russell, A.D. (1985) The role of plasmids in bacterial resistance to antiseptics, disinfectants and preservatives. *Journal of Hospital Infection*, **6**, 9–19.

Russell, A.D. (1990a) The bacterial spore and chemical sporicidal agents. *Clinical Microbiology Reviews*, **3**, 99–119.

Russell, A.D. (1990b) The effect of chemical and physical agents on microbes: disinfection and sterilization. In *Topley & Wilson's Principles of Bacteriology and Immunity* (eds Dick, H.M. & Linton, A.H.) 8th edn., pp. 71–103. London: Edward Arnold.

Russell, A.D. (1991a) Principles of antimicrobial activity. In *Disinfection, Sterilization and Preservation* (ed. Block, S.S.) 4th Ed. (In press.) Philadelphia: Lea & Febiger.

Russell, A.D. (1991b) Chemical sporicidal and sporistatic agents. In *Disinfection, Sterilization and Preservation* (ed. Block, S.S.) 4th Ed. (In press.) Philadelphia: Lea & Febiger.

Russell, A.D. & Chopra, I. (1990) *Understanding Antibacterial Action and Resistance*. Chichester: Ellis Horwood.

Russell, A.D. & Furr, J.R. (1977) The antibacterial activity of a new chloroxylenol preparation containing ethylenediamine tetraacetic acid. *Journal of Applied Bacteriology*, **45**, 253–260.

Russell, A.D. & Furr, J.R. (1986) The effects of antiseptics, disinfectants and preservatives on smooth, rough and deep rough strains of *Salmonella typhimurium*. *International Journal of Pharmaceutics*, **34**, 115–123.

Russell, A.D. & Gould, G.W. (1988) Resistance of Enterobacteriaceae to preservatives and disinfectants. *Journal of Applied Bacteriology, Symposium Supplement*, **65**, 167S–195S.

Russell, N.J. & Gould, G.W. (1991) Factors affecting growth and survival. In *Food Preservatives* (eds Russell, N.J. & Gould, G.W.) pp.13–21. Glasgow & London: Blackie.

Russell, A.D. & Haque, H. (1975) Inhibition of EDTA-lysozyme lysis of *Pseudomonas aeruginosa* by glutaraldehyde. *Microbios*, **13**, 151–153.

Russell, A.D. & Hopwood, D. (1976) The biological uses and importance of glutaraldehyde. In *Progress in Medicinal Chemistry* (eds Ellis, G.P. & West, G.B.) Vol. 13, pp. 271–301. Amsterdam: North-Holland Publishing Company.

Russell, A.D. & Hugo, W.B. (1987) Chemical disinfectants. In *Disinfection in Veterinary and Farm Animal Practice* (eds Linton, A.H., Hugo, W.B. & Russell, A.D.) pp. 12–42. Oxford: Blackwell Scientific Publications.

Russell, A.D. & Vernon, G.N. (1975) Inhibition by glutaraldehyde of lysostaphin-induced lysis of *Staphylococcus aureus*. *Microbios*, **13**, 147–149.

Russell, A.D., Ahonkhai, I. & Rogers, D.T. (1979) Microbiological applications of the inactivation of antibiotics and other antimicrobial agents. *Journal of Applied Bacteriology*, **46**, 207–245.

Russell, A.D., Furr, J.R. & Pugh, W.J. (1985) Susceptibility of porin- and lipopolysaccharide-deficient mutants of *Escherichia coli* to a homologous series of esters of *p*-hydroxybenzoic acid. *International Journal of Pharmaceutics*, **27**, 163–173.

Russell, A.D., Furr, J.R. & Pugh, W.J. (1987) Sequential loss of outer membrane lipopolysaccharide and sensitivity of *Escherichia coli* to antibacterial agents. *International Journal of Pharmaceutics*, **35**, 227–232.

Russell, A.D., Hammond, S.A. & Morgan, J.R. (1986) Bacterial resistance to antiseptics and disinfectants. *Journal of Hospital Infection*, **7**, 213–225.

Rutala, W.A. (1990) APIC guideline for selection and use of disinfectants. *American Journal of Infection Control*, **18**, 99–117.

Salmond, C.V., Kroll, R.G. & Booth, I.R. (1984) The effect of food preservatives on pH homeostasis in *Escherichia coli*. *Journal of General Microbiology*, **130**, 2845–2850.

Schmolka, I.R. (1973) The synergistic effects of non-ionic surfactants upon cationic germicidal agents. *Journal of the Society of Cosmetic Chemists*, **24**, 577–592.

Schmalreck, A.F. & Teuber, M. (1976) Effect of chemical modification by (di)imidoesters on cells and cell envelopes components of *Escherichia coli and Salmonella typhimurium*. *Microbios*, **17**, 93–101.

Scott, E.M. & Gorman, S.P. (1987) Chemical disinfectants, antiseptics and preservatives. In *Pharmaceutical Microbiology* (eds Hugo, W.B. & Russell, A.D.) 4th Ed., pp. 226–252. Oxford: Blackwell Scientific Publications.

De Siervo, A.J. (1969) Alterations in the phospholipid composition of *Escherichia coli* during growth at different temperatures. *Journal of Bacteriology*, **100**, 1342–1349.

Silver, S. & Misra, S. (1988) Plasmid-mediated heavy metal resistances. *Annual Review of Microbiology*, **42**, 717–743.

Singh, A.P. & Reithmeier, A.F. (1975) Leakage of periplasmic enzymes from cells of heptose-deficient mutants of *Escherichia coli* associated with alterations in the protein component of the outer membrane. *Journal of General and Applied Microbiology*, **21**, 109–118.

Smith, D.H. (1967) R-factors mediate resistance to mercury, nickel and cobalt. *Science*, **156**, 1114–1115.

Smith, G. (1975) Triethylene tetramine, a new potentiator of antibiotic activity. *Experientia*, **31**, 84–85.

Sofos, J.N., Pierson, M.D., Blocher, J.C. & Busta, F.F. (1986) Mode of action of sorbic acid on bacterial cells and spores. *International Journal of Food Microbiology*, **3**, 1–17.

Spaulding, E.H., Cundy, K.R. & Turner, F.J. (1977) Chemical disinfection of medical and surgical materials. In *Disinfection, Sterilization and Preservation* (ed. Block, S.S.) 2nd Ed., pp. 654–684. Philadelphia: Lea & Febiger.

Spire, B., Barré-Sinoussi, F., Montagnier, L. & Chermann, J.C. (1984) Inactivation of lymphadenopathy associated virus by chemical disinfectants. *Lancet*, **ii**, 899–901.

Stagg, C.H. (1982) Evaluating chemical disinfectants for virucidal activity. In *Methods in Environmental Virology* (eds Gerba, C.P. & Goyal, S.M.) pp. 331–348. New York: Marcel Dekker.

Summers, A.O. & Silver, S. (1972) Mercury resistance in a plasmid-bearing strain of *Escherichia coli*. *Journal of Bacteriology*, **112**, 1228–1236.

Sykes, G. (1965) *Disinfection and Sterilization*. 2nd Ed. London: E. & F.N. Spon.

Sykes, G. (1970) The sporicidal properties of chemical disinfectants *Journal of Applied Bacteriology*, **33**, 147–156.

Tamaki, S., Sato, T. & Matsuhashi, M. (1971). The role of lipopolysaccharides in antibiotic resistance and bacteriophage adsorption of *Escherichia coli* K-12. *Journal of Bacteriology*, **105**, 968–975.

Taylor, G.R. & Butler, M. (1982) A comparison of the virucidal properties of chlorine, chlorine dioxide, bromine chloride and iodine. *Journal of Hygiene, Cambridge*, **89**, 321–328.

Tempest, D.W. & Ellwood, D.C. (1969) The influence of growth conditions on the composition of some cell wall components of *Aerobacter aerogenes*, *Biotechnology and Bioengineering*, **11**, 775–783.

Thomas, S. & Russell, A.D. (1974) Temperature-induced changes in the sporicidal activity and chemical properties of glutaraldehyde. *Applied Microbiology*, **28**, 331–335.

Thurman, R.B. & Gerba, C.P. (1988) Molecular mechanisms of viral inactivation by water disinfectants. *Advances in Applied Microbiology*, **33**, 75–105.

Thurman, R.B. & Gerba, C.P. (1989) The molecular mechanisms of copper and silver ion disinfection of bacteria and viruses. *CRC Critical Reviews in Environmental Control*, **18**, 295–315.

Tomlins, R.I. & Ordal, Z.J. (1976) Thermal injury and inactivation in vegetative bacteria. In *The Inactivation of Vegetative Bacteria* (eds Skinner, F.A. & Hugo, W.B.) pp. 153–190. Society for Applied Bacteriology Symposium Series No. 5. London: Academic Press.

Trueman, J.R. (1971) The halogens. In *Inhibition and Destruction of the Microbial Cell* (ed. Hugo, W.B.) pp. 135–183. London: Academic Press.

Tyler, R. & Ayliffe, G.A.J. (1987) A surface test for virucidal activity of disinfectants: preliminary study with herpes virus. *Journal of Hospital Infection*, **9**, 22–29.

Ulitzer, S. (1970) The transport of β-galactosides across the membrane of permeaseless *Escherichia coli* ML 35 cells after treatment with cetyltrimethylammonium bromide. *Biochimica et Biophysica Acta*. **211**, 533–541.

Vaara, M. & Vaara, T. (1983a) Polycations sensitize enteric bacteria to antibiotics. *Antimicrobial Agents and Chemotherapy*, **24**, 107–113.

Vaara, M. & Vaara, T. (1983b) Polycations as outer membrane disorganizing agents. *Antimicrobial Agents and Chemotherapy*, **24**, 114–122.

Vaczi, L. (1973) *The Biological Role of Bacterial Lipids*. Budapest: Akademiai Kiadó.

Vaughan, J.M., Chen, Y.S., Lindburg, K. & Morales, D. (1987) Inactivation of human and simian rotaviruses by ozone. *Applied and Environmental Microbiology*, **53**, 2218–2221.

Viljanen, P. (1987) Polycations which disorganize the outer membrane inhibit conjugation in *Escherichia coli*. *Journal of Antibiotics*, **40**, 882–886.

Weiss, R.L. (1976) Protoplast formation in *Escherichia coli*. *Journal of Bacteriology*, **128**, 668–670.

Wiener, S. (1955) The interference of rubber with the bacteriostatic action of thiomersalate. *Journal of Pharmacy and Pharmacology*, **7**, 118–125.

Wilkinson, S.G. (1975). Sensitivity to ethylene diaminetetraacetic acid. In *Resistance of Pseudomonas aeruginosa* (ed. Brown, M.R.W.) pp. 145–188. London: John Wiley & Sons.

Wing, W.T. (1955) An examination of rubber used as a closure for containers of injectable solutions. Part I. Factors affecting the absorption of phenol. *Journal of Pharmacy and Pharmacology*, **7**, 648–658.

Wing, W.T. (1956a) An examination of rubber used as a closure for containers of injectable solutions. Part II. The absorption of chlorocresol. *Journal of Pharmacy and Pharmacology*, **8**, 734–737.

Wing, W.T. (1956b) An examination of rubber used as a closure for containers of injectable solutions. Part III. The effect of the chemical composition of the rubber mix on phenol and chlorocresol absorption. *Journal of Pharmacy and Pharmacology*, **7**, 738–743.

Witholt, B., Van Heerikhuizen, H. & De Leij, L. (1976) How does lysozyme penetrate through the bacteria outer membrane? *Biochimica et Biophysica Acta*, **443**, 534–544.

Chapter 4
Evaluation of the Antibacterial and Antifungal Activity of Disinfectants

1 INTRODUCTION

One of the more recent definitions of disinfection is as follows: 'disinfection is the selective elimination of certain undesirable micro-organisms in order to prevent their transmission, and is achieved by action on their structure or metabolism, irrespective of their functional state' (Reber *et al.*, 1972). Although there are other definitions of disinfection, it is common to all that the main purpose is the elimination of the hazard of contamination or infection. In consequence, the purpose of testing disinfectants is to check if these products fulfil their objective, or more usually, to determine whether micro-organisms are killed or eliminated by the action of the disinfectant. The principle of evaluation of disinfectants is simple: microbial cells are added to the test dilution of the disinfectant, and, after a specified exposure period, it is then checked to determine whether they have been killed. Developing tests of this kind, however, is difficult and complex because many factors have to be incorporated: choice of the test organisms, preparation of the cell suspensions, neutralization of the disinfectant residues in the subculture (Chapter 3), determination of the endpoint, etc. The most logical way would be to start with a consideration of the requirements that have to be fulfilled by a disinfectant, i.e. what is expected from a disinfectant in a particular field of application, and to elaborate the testing method in relation to these requirements. Only the Swiss Microbiological Society (Reber *et al.*, 1972) and, to a lesser extent, the International Colloquium on the Evaluation of Disinfectants in Europe (Schmidt, 1973) have pursued this line of reasoning. Progress has been slow and definitions, requirements, and certainly testing methods have to be discussed on an international or even a European basis. Although antiseptics and disinfectants have been tested early in the history of microbiology even before the 'golden age' of bacteriology (Hugo, 1978), a general, internationally accepted test scheme does not exist. On the contrary, the microbicidal activity of disinfectants is determined by test methods that vary in different countries and are based upon different principles (Reybrouck, 1975, 1986). Different results are often obtained, and a preparation can be registered in one country but not accepted in another.

In recent years there has been a change in the approach to disinfectant testing. Originally, experiments were directed mainly towards the kinetics of disinfection. It was considered sufficient to examine whether micro-organisms were killed by a disinfectant in terms of a stated concentration (or a range of concentrations) or times of exposure, in suspension tests, such as the determination of the phenol coefficient, or in carrier tests. A more practical approach has appeared recently. Capacity tests and practical tests were developed in order to simulate real-life situations, and the results give more precise information on the effective use-dilution for a given field of application. According to the specific purpose for which the product is used, other test organisms and other exposure times are tested, and the influence of water hardness and other factors can be included. In some European countries, it was realized that not only disinfectants themselves, but also their use in a given field of application or disinfection procedure should be tested (Borneff *et al.*, 1975).

Nevertheless, the present situation is that every country has its own testing methods, and different professions (food, medicine, veterinary, water) within a country also use different techniques. It is unusual for a manual to describe a complete test scheme with detailed testing methods which have to be followed rigorously for registration purposes, or are at least generally accepted. The best known examples are those of the American Association of Official Analytical Chemists (AOAC), the German Society for Hygiene and Microbiology (Deutsche Gesellschaft für Hygiene und Mikrobiologie, DGHM) and the French Association of Normalization (Association française de normalisation, AFNOR). The American association publishes the *Official Methods of Analysis* (AOAC, 1984), in which one chapter is concerned with disinfectants. From 1959 the German society edited the *Richtinien für die Prüfung chemischer Desinfektionsmittel* (Guidelines for the Evaluation of Chemical Disinfectants) (Kliewe *et al.*, 1959). These were revised several times, and the last edition, which is still incomplete, is based on the *Empfehlungen für die Prüfung und Bewertung der Wirksamkeit chemischer Desinfektionsverfahren* (Recommendations for the Testing and the Evaluation of the Efficacy of Chemical Disinfectant Procedures) produced by a working group of German hygienists (Beck *et al.*, 1977). The present edition will be further named *DGHM Guidelines* (Borneff *et al.*, 1981). AFNOR has collected the official methods into a bilingual booklet (French–English); the last edition appeared recently (AFNOR, 1989). Also the German Veterinary Society (Deutsche Veterinärmedizinische Gesellschaft) (DVG, 1988), and the British Standards Institution (BSI) have published some test methods. Most other testing methods are found in scientific journals. There also exists an almost incalculable number of other methods, some of which are more or less successful, but most are only of local importance. In this survey an attempt will be made to make some sense out of the present multiplicity of methods and to discuss the problems as clearly as possible. However, only the more widely used techniques will be considered, omitting those which have not yet been subjected to the criteria of wide use and critique. Attention will be drawn especially to the techniques followed in the evaluation of disinfectants for use in hospitals and medicine. More detailed reviews may be found elsewhere (Collins *et al.*, 1981; Crémieux & Fleurette, 1983; Ayliffe, 1989; Reuter, 1989).

2 THE CLASSIFICATION OF DISINFECTANT TESTS

Although all disinfectant tests have the same final purpose, namely measuring the antimicrobial activity of a chemical substance or preparation, a large number of testing methods have been described. In order to clarify these tests, it is helpful to subdivide them, and this can be done in different ways (Table 4.1).

First, the antimicrobial efficiency of a disinfectant can be examined at three stages of testing. The first stage concerns laboratory tests in which it is verified whether a chemical compound or a preparation possesses antimicrobial activity. These are the pre-

Table 4.1 Classification of disinfectant tests.

A	Classification according to test organism
	1 Determination of antibacterial activity:
	non-acid-fast vegetative bacteria: bactericidal tests
	acid-fast bacteria: tuberculocidal tests
	bacterial spores: sporicidal tests
	2 Determination of antifungal activity: fungicidal tests
	3 Determination of antiviral activity: virucidal tests
B	Classification according to the type of action: -static versus -cidal tests: bacteriostatic and bactericidal, tuberculostatic and tuberculocidal, sporistatic and sporicidal, fungistatic and fungicidal, virustatic and virucidal tests
C	Classification according to the test structure
	1 *In-vitro* tests:
	test cells in suspension: suspension tests
	several additions of cell suspension: capacity tests
	test organisms on carrier: carrier tests
	2 Practical tests:
	tests determining the efficacy of the disinfection of surfaces, rooms, instruments, fabrics, excreta, the hands, the skin
	3 In-use tests
D	Classification according to the aim of the test
	1 First testing stage: preliminary tests, screening tests:
	tests determining whether a chemical substance or preparation possesses antibacterial properties
	tests determining the relationship between exposure periods and disinfectant dilutions
	tests determining the influence of organic matter, serum, etc.
	2 Second testing stage: tests determining the use-dilution of a disinfectant for a specific application
	3 Third testing stage:
	tests in the field *in loco* or *in situ* determining the usability of the disinfectant in practice
	clinical effectiveness studies

liminary screening tests. The second stage is still carried out in the laboratory but in conditions simulating real-life situations. In these tests, disinfection procedures and not disinfectants are examined. It is determined in which conditions and at which use-dilution the preparation is active. The last stage takes place in the field, and comprises the *in-loco* or *in-situ* tests. These are less popular since complete standardization is impossible in the field. Variants of these *in-loco* tests are in-use tests, which examine whether, after a normal period of use, germs in the disinfectant solution are still killed.

Most simple tests such as suspension and phenol coefficient tests are preliminary tests of the first stage. The use-dilution of the disinfectant is determined by another method, usually a more practical test, but in some instances the use-dilutions of surface disinfectants are determined by simple tests. In the United Kingdom the Kelsey–Sykes test, which is a capacity test, and in the USA the AOAC use-dilution method, which is a carrier test, are the recommended or official tests. For convenience we shall designate as an *in-vitro* test all methods with a simple structure that are not carried out under practical conditions or in the field. Schematically they may be divided into suspension, capacity and carrier tests. The main second-stage tests are the practical tests, which are also carried out in the laboratory. If a disinfectant is intended for floor disinfection, its activity is determined on different kinds of surface which may be encountered in a hospital, such as tiles, stainless-steel surfaces, PVC sheets, etc. These are contaminated artificially and after exposure to the product they are examined for surviving micro-organisms. This is a 'practical' test, whereas an in-use test is carried out in the hospital environment.

Hence we shall distinguish between *in-vitro*, practical and in-use tests. This classification is followed in the examination of disinfectants active against vegetative bacteria (bactericidal tests), bacterial spores (sporicidal), mycobacteria (tuberculocidal) and fungi (fungicidal). Virucidal testing methods are considered in Chapter 6. The suffix *static* means that the growth of the micro-organisms is only inhibited, whereas *-cidal* refers to killing of the organisms.

3 TESTS DETERMINING THE ACTIVITY OF DISINFECTANTS AGAINST VEGETATIVE BACTERIA

3.1 *In-vitro* tests

No chemical substance or preparation can be regarded as a disinfectant if it is not active against vegetative bacteria; this is the first and main requirement. Therefore, disinfectant testing always starts with the determination of antibacterial activity. There are several types of tests, which can be classified as suspension tests, capacity tests or carrier tests. Bacterial cells exposed to the action of the disinfectant are, as the name implies, suspended in a medium or diluent in suspension tests, whereas in carrier tests they are fixed and dried on a vehicle. In capacity tests the test dilution of the disinfectant is loaded with several additions of a bacterial suspension, and after each addition the reaction mixture is subcultured for survivors to determine whether the capacity of the agent has been exhausted by successive additions of bacteria. Tests for the determination of bacteriostatic properties will be treated separately.

3.1.1 Tests for determining bacteriostatic activity

The bacteriostatic activity of a disinfectant is determined by an evaluation of the minimum inhibitory concentration (MIC). This is the simplest method of measuring inhibition of bacterial growth, and is similar to the test-tube serial dilution method for determining susceptibility to antibiotics. The disinfectant is mixed with nutrient broth in decreasing concentrations, the tubes are inoculated with a culture of the bacterium to be tested and after a suitable period of incubation, the lowest concentration which inhibits the growth of the organisms is the MIC value. It is important to ensure the absence of any antagonist (neutralizer or inactivator) which might inhibit further bacteriostatic activity of the disinfectant or its residues in the subculture. The structure of such a test is shown in Fig. 4.1. These tests are rarely used in the evaluation of disinfectants, since a disinfectant is required to have bactericidal rather than bacteriostatic activity. Nevertheless, in the *DGHM Guide-*

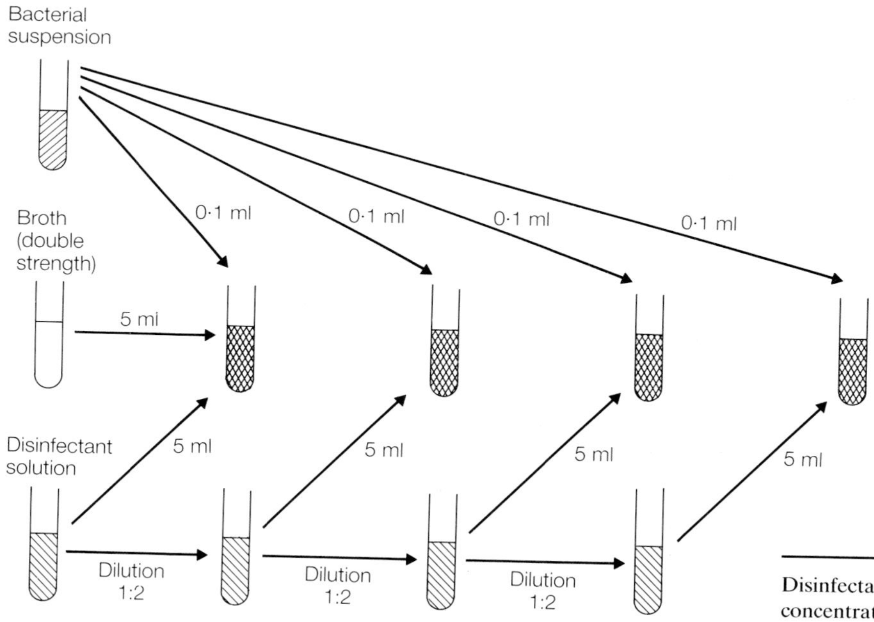

Disinfectant concentration (%)	Growth
0.25	+
0.5	–
1.0	–
2.0	–

Minimum bacteristatic (inhibitory) concentration: 0.5%: presence, +; absence, –.

Fig. 4.1 A test for the determination of the minimum inhibitory concentration: the DGHM test.

lines (Borneff *et al.*, 1981) and the *DVG Guidelines* (DVG, 1988) this technique is used for determining the efficacy of the neutralizer used in bactericidal tests, and Kelsey and Sykes (Kelsey & Maurer, 1974) apply it for the selection of the most resistant test organism for inclusion in their capacity test.

3.1.2 Suspension tests

Suspension tests have the following features in common: an appropriate volume of bacterial suspension, the inoculum, is added to the disinfectant in the concentration to be tested and after a predetermined exposure (reaction, disinfection, medication) time, an aliquot is examined to determine whether the inoculum is killed or not. This can be done in a qualitative way (presence or absence of growth in the subculture) or quantitatively (counting the number of surviving organisms in order to compare them to the original inoculum size). The simple structure enables the test to be easily extended: several concentrations or additional exposure periods can be examined, potentially inhibitory substances such as organic matter or soap can be added, and the influence of water hardness or other factors can be determined. The influence of such interfering substances is determined separately in the French test schedule by the AFNOR tests NF T 72–170 and NF T 72–171 (determination of bactericidal activity in presence of specific interfering substances; dilution–neutralization method, membrane filtration method respectively) (AFNOR, 1989), whereas most other prescriptions include these substances in the basic tests (e.g. the European suspension test, the Kelsey–Sykes test) or in the practical tests (e.g. the *DGHM Guidelines*).

Qualitative suspension tests. The procedure in a qualitative suspension test is as follows: after a fixed exposure period a sample is withdrawn from the disinfectant/bacterial cell mixture and added to nutrient broth: the presence of macroscopically observable growth after incubation indicates a failure of the disinfectant activity. An example is given in Fig. 4.2. The main disadvantage of these extinction tests is that survival of a single bacterial cell gives the same final result as an inoculum that is not affected at all by the disinfectant. Results are reproducible as long as completely active or completely inactive use-dilutions are tested, but in the critical concentration both negative and positive cultures will appear. The difficulty of interpreting such results can be partially overcome by subculturing more samples: if only a small number of cells survive, not all subculture tubes will show growth and the proportion of negative cultures gives a semi-quantitative indication of the activity of the disinfectant.

Qualitative suspension tests are still found in the German prescriptions. Four test organisms are used in the *DGHM Guidelines* (Borneff *et al.*, 1981); they are *Staphylococcus aureus* ATCC 6538, *Escherichia coli* ATCC 11229, *Proteus mirabilis* ATCC 14153, and *Pseudomonas aeruginosa* ATCC 15442. The *DVG Guidelines* (DVG, 1988) use the same organisms, but *E. coli* is substituted by *Enterococcus faecium* DSM 2918. Several exposure periods between 5 min (in former editions 2 min) and 60 min (or 30 s, 1, 2 and 5 min for hand disinfectants) are examined. The results show the concentration/time relationship of a disinfectant, as demonstrated in Fig. 4.2, but, although it is possible to quantify the germicidal activity from extinction data, if multiple tubes are inoculated (Reybrouck, 1975), these tests remain without any practical value.

Determination of the phenol coefficient. Tests for determining the phenol coefficient are essentially qualitative suspension tests in which the activity of the disinfectant under test is compared with that of phenol. By introducing this standard disinfectant in the same experiment, Rideal and Walker in 1903 tried to resolve the major difficulty of reproducibility: all casual factors influencing the resistance of the organisms were thus eliminated, since the same test suspension was used for the standard and the unknown disinfectant. Originally the test organism was *Sal. typhi*, which is rather sensitive to phenolics. More exposure times, e.g. 2½, 5, 7½ and 10 min, were included and dividing the highest dilution of the test disinfectant showing a negative culture after 7½ min but growth after 5 min by the phenol dilution, gives the phenol coefficient, as shown in Fig. 4.3. The Rideal–Walker test was

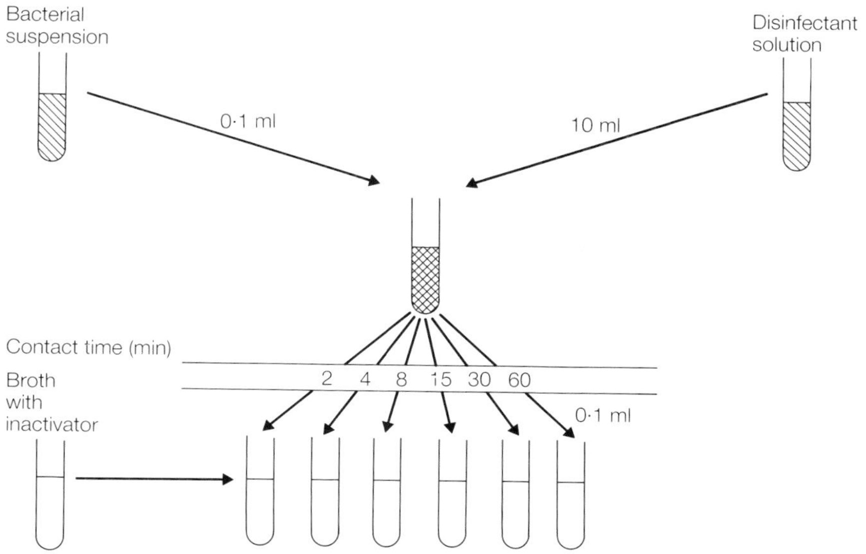

Disinfectant concentration (%)	Growth in subculture after:					
	2 min	4 min	8 min	15 min	30 min	60 min
1.0	+	−	−	−	−	−
0.5	+	+	+	−	−	−
0.25	+	+	+	+	+	−

Presence, +; absence, −.

Fig. 4.2 A qualitative suspension test: the DGHM test.

adapted by the British Standards Institution (BSI, 1985). In the modification by Chick & Martin (BSI, 1986) the bacterial cells are mixed with a yeast suspension before exposure to the disinfectant, thereby increasing the organic load. The manual of the *Official Methods of Analysis* (AOAC, 1984) also describes a very detailed test procedure for the Rideal–Walker test, using *Sal. typhi* ATCC 6539, *Staph. aureus* ATCC 6538 and *Ps. aeruginosa* ATCC 15442 as test organisms. The phenol coefficient is applicable only to phenolic preparations and has the same defects as the qualitative tests, especially the presence of skips or wild plusses (Croshaw, 1981). Although these tests are still used extensively in all parts of the world, it would be better if they were replaced by quantitative suspension tests.

Quantitative suspension tests. Many quantitative suspension tests have been described in the last four decades (Reybrouck, 1977, 1980). After the exposure of bacterial cells to the disinfectant, surviving organisms can be counted by two techniques, either by direct culture or by membrane filtration.

The basic principle of the quantitative suspension tests using direct culture is as follows: after contact with the disinfectant a sample of the reaction mixture is inoculated on a solid nutrient medium; after incubation the number of survivors is counted and compared with the initial inoculum size. The decimal log reduction rate, microbicidal effect (ME) or germicidal effect (GE) can be calculated, using the formula GE = log N_C − log N_D (N_C being the number of colony-forming units developed in the control series in which the disinfectant is replaced

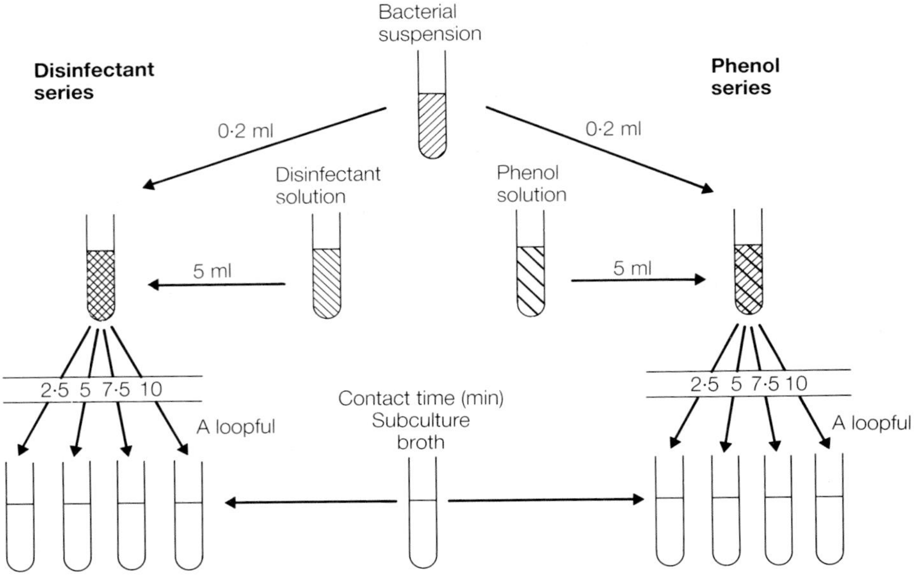

Disinfectant concentration	Growth in subculture after: 2.5 min	5 min	7.5 min	10 min
1/1000	−	−	−	−
1/1100	+	−	−	−
1/1200	+	+	−	−
1/1300	+	+	+	−
Phenol control 1/100	+	+	−	−

Phenol coefficient $= \frac{1200}{100} = 12.0.$

Presence, +; absence, −.

Fig. 4.3 A test for the determination of the phenol coefficient: the Rideal–Walker test.

by distilled water, and N_D being the number of colony-forming units counted after exposure to the disinfectant). The pour-plate technique as well as surface plates may also be used for subculturing (Reybrouck, 1977). Fig. 4.4 shows the basic structure of such a test.

Most of the bactericidal tests used for routine, as well as research purposes are quantitative suspension tests in which the number of survivors is determined by direct culture. One of the first tests to be published was the *Method for Laboratory Evaluation of Disinfectant Activity of Quaternary Ammonium Compounds* (BSI, 1960). It describes only the outline of the testing procedure, however, and omits details of type of culture media, fixed reaction times, etc. These different elements can be varied depending on the aim of the test, e.g. as a test for the influence of organic matter or as a test in presence of milk. The AOAC test for the determination of the sanitizing action of germicidal and

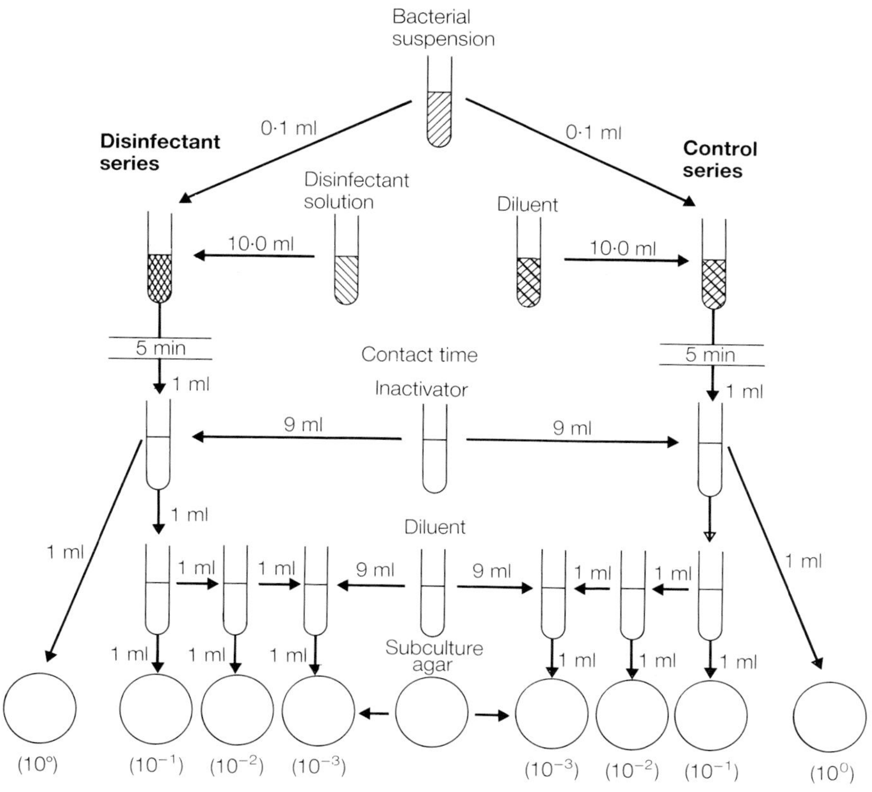

Dilution of the subculture	Number of colony-forming units (cfu)			
	In control series		In disinfectant series	
	Number	Log	Number	Log
10^0	tntc*	—	tntc	—
10^{-1}	tntc	—	88	1.94
10^{-2}	tntc	—	6	0.78
10^{-3}	tntc	—	0	—
10^{-4}	110	2.04	0	—

* Too numerous to count.

Germicidal effect $= \log N_C - \log N_D$
$= (4 + 2.04) - (1 + 1.94)$
$= 3.10$ (after 5 min)

where N_C is number of cfu in control series, and N_D is number in disinfectant series.

Fig. 4.4 A quantitative suspension test: the *in-vitro* test.

detergent disinfectants for food-contact surfaces (AOAC, 1984) is, on the contrary, more detailed.

Several tests with detailed methods are now widely in use in Europe. The Dutch standard suspension test (Van Klingeren *et al.*, 1977) is based on a modification of the technique by Mossel (1963) in the Central Institute for Nutrition Research and the Committee on Phytopharmacy (Reybrouck, 1975). Originally this test was designed for the food industry, which explains why the bacterial cells are suspended in an albumin solution before exposure to the disinfectant. The organic load renders the test more severe than other similar tests. The exposure period is 5 min, pour plates are used for culturing after exposure to disinfectants, and the incubation temperature is 32°C. There are separate versions for hospitals, the food industry and for veterinary use, which differ only in details, e.g. the choice of test organisms. The common name for the standard suspension test is the 5-5-5 test, because 5 test organisms (*Ps. aeruginosa*, *E. coli*, *Staph. aureus*, *B. cereus* and *Sacch. cerevisiae*) were originally tested, the exposure time was 5 min, and the criterion for activity was a germicidal effect of 5 logarithms. In the last version of the hospitals test, the bacteria are *Ps. aeruginosa* ATCC 15442, *Pr. mirabilis* ATCC 14153, *Sal. typhimurium* ATCC 13311 and *Staph. aureus* ATCC 6538.

A new test was developed on the basis of the food industry edition of the standard suspension test: it is the so-called European suspension test (Council of Europe, 1987). The test organisms are *Staph. aureus* ATCC 6538, *Enterococcus* (*Streptococcus*) *faecium* DVG 8582, *Ps. aeruginosa* ATCC 15442, *P. mirabilis* ATCC 14153 and *Sacch. cerevisiae* ATCC 9763. The disinfectant concentration is prepared in hard water. The version for clean conditions prescribes an organic load of 0.03% bovine albumin in the preparation of the bacterial suspension; the organic load for dirty conditions is 1.0% bovine albumin. The criterion is a reduction of at least 5 log after 5 min.

The other widely propagated quantitative suspension tests are those of the AFNOR and the DGHM (Reybrouck, 1980). The criterion of the French AFNOR test NF T 72–150 (determination of bactericidal activity; dilution–neutralization method) (AFNOR, 1989) is also a reduction of 5 log after a reaction time of 5 min. The following test organisms are proposed: *Ps. aeruginosa* CIP A 22, *E. coli* ATCC 10536, *Staph. aureus* ATCC 9144 and *Enterococcus faecium* ATCC 10541; the incubation temperature is 37°C and also the pour-plate technique is followed. Under the auspices of the Committee of the International Colloquium on the Evaluation of Disinfectants in Europe a new *in-vitro* test was developed in 1975 (Reybrouck & Werner, 1977; Reybrouck *et al.*, 1979) which served as a basis for the quantitative suspension test of the *DGHM Guidelines* (Borneff *et al.*, 1981). It is not surprising that all these quantitative suspension tests differ only in details; their structure and most of the items (test organisms, nutrient media, diluents, etc.) are identical (Reybrouck, 1980).

Sporadically, the membrane filtration technique has been applied for determining the number of survivors after disinfection. In this case the reaction mixture is filtered through the membrane filter, which retains the bacteria on its surface, whereafter it is rinsed with large volumes of sterile physiological saline to remove all disinfectant residues. The main advantage of this procedure is that neutralization by inactivators becomes unnecessary. Nevertheless, this technique is rather sensitive and some disinfectants as surface-active agents are difficult to remove. The AFNOR Test NF T 72–151 (AFNOR, 1989) is the only test using membrane filtration that is currently applied.

3.1.3 Capacity tests

Each time a mop is soaked in a bucket containing a disinfectant solution, or a soiled instrument placed in a container of disinfectant, a certain quantity of dirt and bacteria is added to the solution. The ability to retain activity in the presence of an increasing load is the capacity of the disinfectant. Capacity tests simulate the practical situations of housekeeping and instrument disinfection. The scheme is as follows (Fig. 4.5): a predetermined volume of bacterial suspension is added to the use-dilution of the agent, and after a given exposure time the mixture is sampled for survivors, mostly in a semi-quantitative way by inoculating several culture broths. After a certain period a second addition

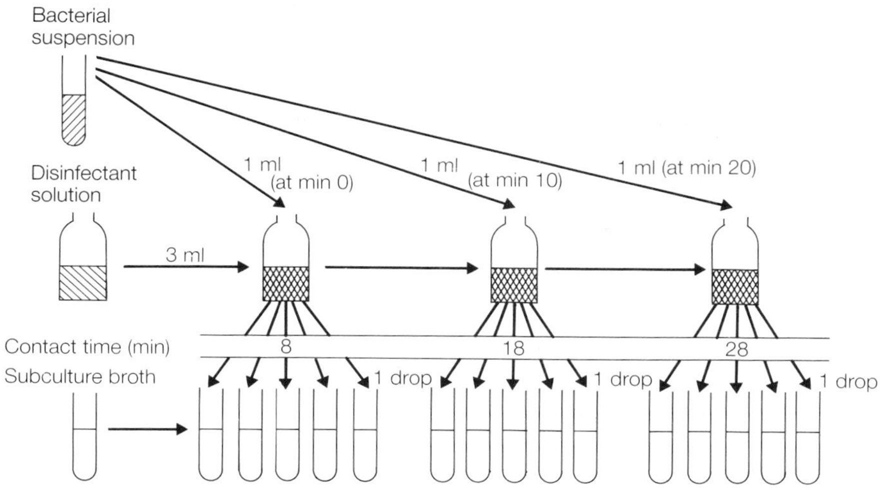

Disinfectant concentration (%)	Number of subculture broths (out of 5) showing growth after:		
	8 min	18 min	28 min
2.0	0	0	3
1.0	0	2	5
0.5	1	4	5
0.25	5	5	5

Use-dilution: 1.0%.

Fig. 4.5 A capacity test: the Kelsey–Sykes test.

of the bacterial suspension is made and a new subculture is made after the same reaction time; several additions with subcultures are carried out. Although capacity tests are *in-vitro* tests they closely resemble real-life situations, and in most instances are used as tests confirming the use-dilution. The most widely used capacity test, not only in the UK, but also elsewhere in Europe, is the Kelsey–Sykes test: the original method of 1965 (Kelsey *et al.*, 1965) was modified in 1969 (Kelsey & Sykes, 1969) and improved in 1974 (Kelsey & Maurer, 1974). The bacteria in these tests are suspended in standard hard water for the test under clean conditions, and in a yeast suspension for the test under dirty conditions. The latter is now revised as a British standard (BSI, 1987) to estimate the concentration of disinfectants which may be recommended for use under dirty conditions in hospitals. This version is as follows: there are four test organisms, *Ps. aeruginosa* NCTC 6749, *P. vulgaris* NCTC 4635, *E. coli* NCTC 8196 and *Staph. aureus* NCTC 4163; the bacteria are suspended in a yeast suspension; the disinfectant is diluted in hard water, the initial volume being 3 ml. The reaction time is 8 min and a new addition of 1 ml of bacterial suspension is carried out 2 min after the subculture of the preceding addition; subculture is done by transferring a 0.02 ml aliquot portion to each of five subculture tubes. Generally this test is more severe for disinfectants than suspension tests, and is affected by organic matter or by the hardness of the water (Reybrouck, 1975); it does, however, give a valuable evaluation of the efficacy of agents for floor disinfection (Croshaw, 1981). Another well-known capacity test was published by the International Dairy Federation (Internationaler Milchwirtschaftsverband, 1963); in this technique 0.5 ml bacterial suspension is added to 100 ml of disinfectant solution; 10 additions are carried out with an exposure time of 1 min and each addition is made 30 seconds after the preceding subculture. The AOAC test for the determination of the chlorine germicidal equivalent concentration (AOAC, 1984) is also a capacity test.

3.1.4 *Carrier tests*

It seems logical that for evaluating the efficacy of preparations intended for instrument disinfection, pieces of metal or catheters should be contaminated artificially and then immersed in the use-dilution; thereafter it is checked to determine whether all germs are killed. In tests on pieces of cloth or other textiles, they can be soaked in the disinfectant. Although such techniques may be considered to be practical tests, the situation is different when the carriers to be disinfected are abstracted and standardized into non-realistic objects, e.g. a porcelain cylinder, or when conclusions are applied to other fields. Therefore, these tests are treated as *in-vitro* tests. The structure of a carrier test is very simple (Fig. 4.6): the carrier is transferred to the use-dilution of the disinfectant, and after a fixed reaction time it is transferred to nutrient broth for subculture; usually a minimum of 10 carriers are used in a test. The most widely reported carrier tests are those of the German Society for Hygiene and Microbiology and the use-dilution method of the AOAC. In the carrier test of the *DGHM Guidelines* (Borneff *et al.*, 1981) the carriers, pieces of a standard cotton cloth each 1 cm^2, are contaminated by soaking for 15 min in a suspension of one of the five test bacteria; the wet pieces of cloth are placed in a dish, and 10 ml of the disinfectant solution is added. After each exposure time, ranging from 5 to 120 min, one carrier is transferred to broth with neutralizer for rinsing and then into another for final culture. This German carrier test serves only as an *in vitro* test, giving an indication of potentially active concentration–time relationships. In the use-dilution method of the AOAC (AOAC, 1984) the test organisms are *Sal. choleraesuis* ATCC 10708, *Staph. aureus* ATCC 6538 and *Ps. aeruginosa* ATCC 15442; in each test 10 stainless-steel penicillin cups are contaminated and immersed for 10 min in 10 ml of use-dilution of the disinfectant under test, and then they are subcultured. This test confirms the phenol-coefficient results and determines the maximum dilution that is still 'effective for practical disinfection'. In this sense it is also an *in vitro* test, although it is much more severe than the suspension tests or the Kelsey–Sykes test (Reybrouck & Van de Voorde, 1975). Recent studies at the University of North Carolina brought out clearly the extreme variability of the test results obtained by the use-dilution method among different laboratories, especially in the case of *Ps. aeruginosa*, even when the methodology was modified and more standardized in 32 instances (Cole *et al.*, 1988). It is now planned to develop a quantitative carrier method, or to abandon it in favour of a suspension test, although other groups will retain the use-dilution method with new pass–fail criteria (Alfano *et al.*, 1988; Beloian, 1989).

3.2 Practical tests

The practical tests under real-life conditions belong to the second testing stage. After measuring the time–concentration relationship of the disinfectant in the *in vitro* test, these practical tests are performed to verify if the proposed use-dilution is still adequate in these real-life conditions. In this way these tests are adapted to present a picture of the microbicidal efficacy of a preparation in the conditions under which it would be used, but have the advantage that the experiments still take place in the laboratory, and can be better standardized.

The formulation and elaboration of such tests is not difficult, but most of them have a limited application since they are found to be poorly reproducible. Factors influencing the resistance of the test bacteria to a disinfectant are more easily recognized in *in vitro* tests, but in the practical tests it can be difficult, if not impossible, to standardize some of them. Drying of organisms on carriers, hands or fabrics results not only in a decrease in the number of test bacteria, but probably also in the viability of the cell. The changes

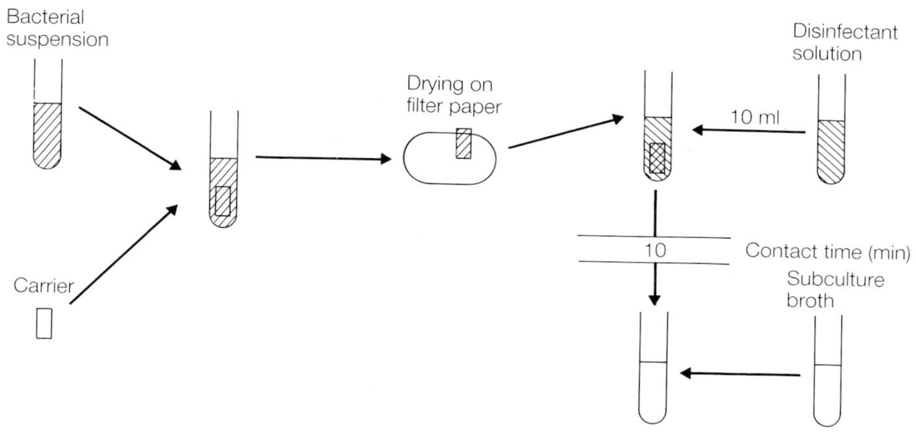

Disinfectant concentration %	Number of subculture broths (out of 10) showing growth
0.25	10
0.5	2
1.0	0
2.0	0

Use-dilution: 1.0%.

Fig. 4.6 A carrier test: the AOAC use-dilution test.

will be influenced by many factors such as the drying time, the temperature and relative humidity of the air, the intrinsic humidity of the carrier itself, the suspending medium of the cells and the growth phase of the organisms. Although repeatability in one laboratory may be reasonable, collaborative trials in different laboratories show that reproducibility is not attained easily. That is the reason why in some countries (e.g. United Kingdom) the use-dilution is determined in tests classified as *in vitro* tests.

In the countries where these tests are used several tests are described for each field of application and include the assessment of disinfection of instruments and surfaces, of cubicles and rooms, of the air, of sputum and faeces, of hands and skin, of swimming pools, effluents and others. The most elaborate and complete review can be found in the methods of the German Society for Hygiene and Microbiology. This chapter deals only with those fields of application for which typical tests are described and that are generally accepted and practised in the countries concerned.

3.2.1 Tests for instrument disinfection

The technique that is most likely to be followed for the assessment of instrument disinfection is a carrier test with standardised pieces of metal or of catheters. Such a test is the use-dilution method of the AOAC (AOAC, 1984). In the *DGHM Guidelines* (DGHM, 1982) specific instrument disinfection tests, which are different from the carrier tests, are described: a broth culture of the same test organisms as used in the suspension tests is mixed with bovine blood to a final concentration of 20% and the disinfectant is diluted in standard hard water to which 0.5% bovine albumin is added; rubber hoses of standardized composition and dimensions are soaked in the culture–blood mixture and then dried for 4 h at 37°C; thereafter they are immersed in the disinfectant solution for 15, 30, 45 and 60 min, respectively. After this exposure period, one carrier is withdrawn, rinsed in a culture broth with neutralizer and subcultured in another tube of broth for 7 days. In this way the lower limit of the active concentration is determined. These tests differ from the carrier tests mainly by the higher load of organic matter and the dilution of the disinfectant in hard water.

3.2.2 Tests for surface disinfection

The assessment of disinfectants for surface disinfection is done in some countries by methods that have been classified under the *in-vitro* tests: in the Netherlands by the standard suspension test, in the United Kingdom by the Kelsey–Sykes test, and in the USA by the use-dilution method of the AOAC. In Germany particularly, preparations for surface disinfection are evaluated by a test under practical conditions. These tests are based on the work of Heicken (1949), who studied the efficacy of different agents on suspensions of *Sal. paratyphi* and on infected stools dried on different carriers such as wood, laquered or painted wood, glass, linoleum, etc. These tests were modified several times; the most recent *DGHM Guidelines* (DGHM, 1984) are based on the technique of the Hygiene Institute of Mainz (Borneff & Werner, 1977). The test schedule is as follows (Fig. 4.7): a 30 × 30 mm area of the standard operating-theatre tiles measuring 50 × 50 mm is contaminated with a standardized inoculum of the following test bacteria: *Staph. aureus* ATCC 6538, *E. coli* ATCC 11229 and *Ps. aeruginosa* ATCC 15442; after a drying time of 90 min at room temperature, a definite volume of the disinfectant solution is distributed over the carrier; exposure lasts for 15 min, 30 min, 1 h and 4 h; the number of survivors is determined by impression on 'Rodac' plates or by a rinsing technique, in which the carrier is rinsed in a diluent, and the number of bacteria is determined in the rinsing fluid. This technique overcomes the difficulty of a large number of colonies, which are too numerous to count on impression plates. In order to determine the spontaneous dying rate of the organisms caused by drying on the carrier a control series is included, and from the comparison of the survivors in this with the test series, the reduction is determined quantitatively.

Another practical test for surface disinfection is the AFNOR test NF T 72–190 (determining bactericidal, fungicidal and sporicidal action, germ-carrier method) (AFNOR, 1989). In this test skim milk is added to the bacterial suspension (*Ps. aeruginosa* CIP A 22, *E. coli* ATCC 10536, *Staph. aureus* ATCC 9144, *Enterococcus faecium* ATCC 10541); the mixture is spread over the carrier (watch glasses, stainless steel, plastic supports), and dried on it; disinfection is performed by spreading 0.2 ml disinfectant solution over the carrier; after the chosen contact time the support is immersed in a rinsing fluid; after shaking, the carrier is withdrawn, put on a solid nutrient medium and covered by a thin layer of melted agar; the rinsing fluid is cultured by membrane filtration.

It is logical that the above-mentioned testing techniques that differ, not only in details, but in essential and important elements, must give varying results (Reybrouck, 1986, 1990).

3.2.3 Tests for textile disinfection

The assessment of preparations for laundry disinfection exemplifies clearly that the three stages of disinfectant testing are necessary. By a suspension test it can be stated whether the laundry additive possesses bactericidal properties. A carrier test using fabrics which are treated in an experimental washing machine at the same temperature and with the same disinfectant concentration as in the washing cycle is used in the second stage. In such tests it can be proven that some preparations act on the washing fluid but not the textile, whereas others show the reverse phenomenon. These differences cannot be demonstrated by an *in-vitro* test. In practice it is found that the third testing stage is also necessary, since the peculiarities of a washing system cannot necessarily be reproduced on a laboratory scale. This is particularly true for the continuous-washing machines.

The practical tests for textile disinfection of the *DGHM Guidelines* (DGHM, 1982) are the most detailed. The test for chemical laundry disinfection differs basically from the carrier test in two items:

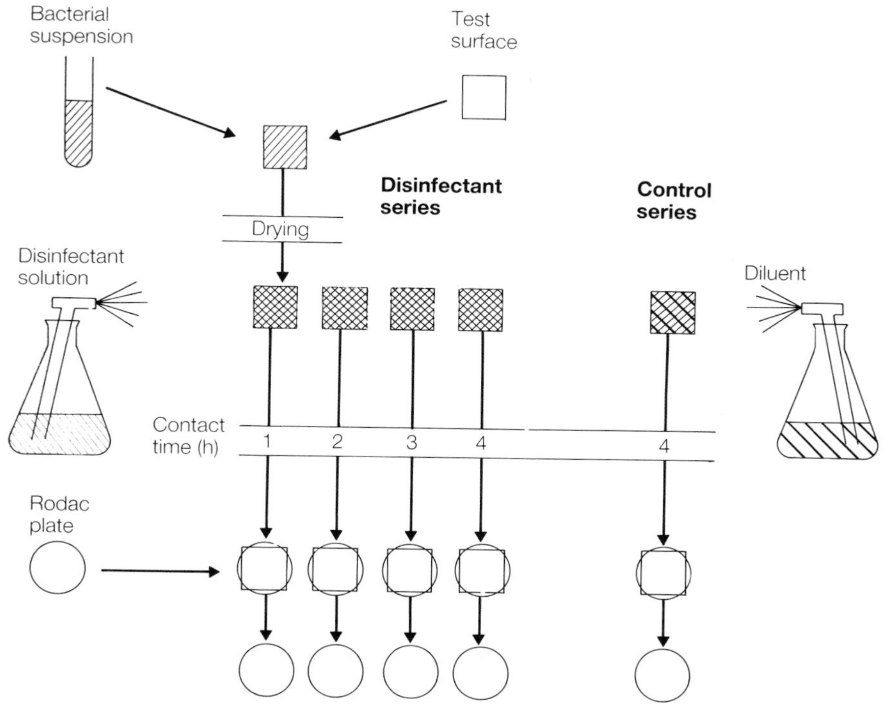

	Number of colony-forming units on Rodac plate after:			
	1 h	2 h	3 h	4 h
Disinfectant	tntc*	350	20	0
control series (dilution 10^5)				250

* Too numerous to count.

$$\begin{aligned}\text{Germicidal effect} &= \log N_C - \log N_D \\ &= (\log 10^5 + \log 250) - \log 350 \\ &= (5 + 2.40) - 2.54 \\ &= 4.86 \text{ (after 2 h) [or } 7.40 - 1.30 \\ &= 6.10 \text{ (after 3 h)]}\end{aligned}$$

(for abbreviations see Fig. 4.4).

Fig. 4.7 A practical test: the DGHM surface disinfection test.

the disinfectant is diluted in standard hard water to which 0.2% bovine albumin is added, and the exposure lasts 4, 6 and 12 h at 12–14°C. This test gives only a clear picture of the disinfection of fabrics by immersion at room temperature and for a long time. In another test for chemothermal laundry disinfection, the contaminated test pieces are washed with other hospital laundry in a washing machine at 90°C. Thereafter, the test pieces as well as 500 ml of the washing fluid are examined qualitatively for survivors. If the disinfectant is adopted for continuous-washing machines, then a washing cycle in such machines has to be performed, i.e. an *in-loco* test.

The International Scientific and Technical Committee on Laundering (ISTCL, 1976) proposed a technique using 12.5 cm diam. discs of fabric contaminated by a suspension in horse serum of *Str. faecalis* var. *zymogenes* NCTC 10927 and dried overnight. After the cycle in the washing machine, a 12 × 12 mm piece is cut from the disc and is treated in a homogenizer with 5 ml of diluent; this fluid is then examined for survivors. In the USA there are some methods which in addition determine the bacteriostatic activity of laundry additives (Lashen, 1971; AOAC, 1984). This again reflects the difference in philosophy: in Europe the bactericidal effect of the washing procedure is taken into consideration, whereas in the USA fabrics are also treated to reduce bacterial recontamination.

3.2.4 *Other practical tests*

Since, in most countries, preparations for hand and skin disinfection are regulated by the legislation on drugs, their testing is performed mostly in other laboratories, and often not by those dealing with the other fields of disinfection. Antiseptics are not treated in, for example, the manual of the AOAC. Tests for hand and skin disinfection will be considered in the chapter on antisepsis (Chapter 13). In addition to the above-mentioned practical tests there exist tests for many other fields of application, e.g. for swimming-pool water in the manual of the AOAC (1984). The discussion of all such tests is beyond the scope of this chapter and most are not generally acceptable outside the country of origin.

3.3 In-use tests

The only valid test of a bactericidal product is its evaluation in the field under actual conditions of use, and preferably by assessing its performance in the prevention of the transmission of infection (or contamination). Nevertheless, today it is practically impossible to evaluate the effectiveness of a disinfectant using this criterion. The occurrence of infection is influenced by many factors, of which only a few are identified and can be evaluated. We are now unable to measure the value of hand antisepsis by a decrease of the infection rate as did Semmelweis more than a century ago.

An indirect method of measuring the efficacy of a disinfectant is by a microbiological monitoring of the environment. Although a decrease in bacterial contamination in the environment does not result automatically in a drop of the infection rate, the inverse relationship is more likely, i.e. no decrease in the number of infections might be expected without improved hygiene measures. In this sense the degree of contamination of the surfaces after disinfection can be used to assess the effectiveness of the procedure. A technique that can detect the failure of a disinfection procedure in a more direct way is the in-use test. This type of test is based on the principle that the use-dilution of an effective preparation for surface or instrument disinfection should not retain surviving bacteria after use; the solution should be sufficiently bactericidal so that, despite the load by dirt, blood or serum, it continues to kill the germs within a short time. An in-use test is performed in the following way (Kelsey & Maurer, 1966; Prince & Ayliffe, 1972): a sample is taken from bucket contents after cleaning, from liquid wrung from mops, from containers for contaminated instruments, etc. It is diluted 1 to 10 in an inactivating solution to neutralize the action of the disinfectant and 5 or 10 drops of this dilution are placed on to the surface of an agar plate: if after incubation growth of non-sporulating bacteria occurs, then the use-dilution of the disinfectant tested was certainly too low. The membrane filtration technique can also be applied for isolation of survivors in the disinfectant solution (Prince & Ayliffe, 1972). Another technique consists in the monitoring of the disinfected and cleaned surfaces by means of culture on Rodac plates (Scott *et al.*, 1984). In-use tests are very helpful in the monitoring of disinfection practice in a hospital, but they are not usually applied routinely.

4 TESTS DETERMINING THE ACTIVITY OF DISINFECTANTS AGAINST MYCOBACTERIA

Tuberculocidal tests are considered separately from the methods for the determination of the general bactericidal properties of disinfectants. Mycobacteria are more resistant to the influence of external factors such as desiccation and chemical disinfection than are other vegetative bacteria (Chapter 3). Although comparatively few substances show tuberculocidal characteristics, this property is not absolutely necessary for all areas of application (Reber *et al.*, 1972). Furthermore, most pathogenic mycobacteria grow slowly so that definitive results are only available after months. Rapid-growing mycobacteria such as *Mycobacterium smegmatis* are therefore taken as test organisms, certainly for preliminary tests. As with the other bactericidal tests, a distinction can be drawn between suspension tests, capacity tests, carrier tests and tests under practical conditions. Some of the above-mentioned *in vitro* tests have been adapted as tuberculocidal tests. Most AFNOR tests can be performed using *M. smegmatis* CIP 7326 as the test organism.

The *Official Methods of Analysis* (AOAC, 1984) only mentions carrier tests, namely a presumptive screening test using *M. smegmatis* PRD 1 and a confirmative test using *M. bovis* (BCG). The carriers are porcelain penicylinders, 10 of which are tested per trial. After contamination they are submitted to the action of the disinfectant under test for 10 min. In the confirmatory test, each carrier is transferred to a tube with 10 ml of serum or neutralizer, followed by transfer of the cylinder and two 2-ml amounts of serum to subculture broth. The maximum dilution of the disinfectant which kills the test organisms in the 10 carriers and shows no growth in each of the two additional subcultures, represents the maximum safe use-dilution for practical tuberculocidal disinfection. As in the case of other carrier tests, a revision of this test has been undertaken, since it lacks precision and accuracy (Ascenzi *et al.*, 1986).

The most extensive test schedule is found in the methods of the German Society for Hygiene and Microbiology (Borneff *et al.*, 1981; DGHM, 1982). The first-stage tests are qualitative suspension tests and carrier tests using small pieces of cotton cloth as described in the bactericidal tests; the test organism is *M. tuberculosis* ATCC 25618. The contaminated carriers are submerged in the disinfectant solution for times ranging from 5 to 120 min; they are then rinsed twice in a neutralizer and transferred to the surface of a Loewenstein–Jensen agar plate for subculture. The second-stage tests are practical tests for the disinfection of fabrics and instruments. Since the strain *M. tuberculosis* ATCC 25618 has at least two variants that differ in resistance towards disinfectants, it is now usual to use *M. terrae* for determining the tuberculocidal potential of disinfectants (Gundermann, 1987; Van Klingeren & Pullen, 1987).

5 TESTS DETERMINING THE ACTIVITY OF DISINFECTANTS AGAINST BACTERIAL SPORES

The determination of the sporicidal properties of disinfectants is very important. Since bacterial spores are more resistant to the action of chemical substances than any other living organisms (Chapters 3 and 10C), a disinfectant possessing sporicidal activity is by definition a sterilant. In this sense the procedure of a sporicidal test should be so stringent that in practice the most resistant spores should be used and, after the exposure to the disinfectant, surviving spores should be capable of resuscitation under optimal conditions.

Some bactericidal suspension tests have been modified to a sporicidal test. In the Dutch standard suspension test (Van Klingeren *et al.*, 1977) *B. cereus* ATCC 9139 is taken as the test organism: the spores are suspended in distilled water and heated up at 80°C for 60 s. Whereas the general criterion for a bactericidal disinfectant is a lethal effect of 5 logarithms within 5 min, in this case a microbicidal effect of only 1 log after the same reaction period is required. This criterion does not correspond to any realistic condition, and it is imposed on every disinfectant; in this context the test does not determine sporicidal properties of any practical value.

The most famous (probably the most prominent) sporicidal test is the carrier test of the AOAC (AOAC, 1984). The carriers are porcelain penicylinders or silk suture loops. Spores of *B. subtilis* ATCC 19659 or *Clostridium sporogenes* ATCC 3584 are standardized with regard to their resistance towards a 2.5 M solution of hydrochloric acid; in each experiment 30 carriers are tested and the exposure period is not fixed. A preparation is considered to be sporicidal if at least 59 out of 60 replicates do not show growth. This test is also suitable for testing the sporicidal or sterilizing activity of a gas.

The tests proposed in France, AFNOR tests NF T 72–230 and NF T 72–231 (determination of sporicidal activity; dilution–neutralization method, membrane filtration method respectively) (AFNOR, 1989), are quantitative suspension tests. It is worth mentioning that none of the German scientific societies describes any sporicidal test, although their range of tests is the most extensive; recently some of the existing German techniques have been modified to, and proposed as, a sporicidal test (Stockinger *et al.*, 1989). Some other sporicidal tests have been described (Borick, 1973; Beloian, 1983), but one is doubtful of attaching the designation 'sporicidal' to a disinfectant, and such tests are less frequently made.

Since the consequences of the use of sterile objects in medicine, and in the pharmaceutical and food industries, are so far-reaching (Chapters 18C, D) the user is unlikely to be satisfied by a single sporicidal test applied to the proposed chemosterilizing procedure. Regular sterility controls are needed to monitor the technique and the preparation (Beloian, 1983). These, as well as the biological sterilization control procedures using test spores, are in fact *in-loco* tests.

6 TESTS DETERMINING THE ACTIVITY OF DISINFECTANTS AGAINST FUNGI

Since, in clinical microbiology, mycology is possibly less important than bacteriology or virology, there is little medical interest in fungicidal tests. In most instances they are confined to an adaptation of the bactericidal test, using *Candida albicans* ATCC 10231 as the test organism. An example of such an adaptation is the Dutch standard suspension test for hospital disinfectants (Van Klingeren *et al.*, 1977), although in the original description (Mossel, 1963), and in the version for the food industry, *Sacch. cerevisiae* is taken as test organism. The *DGHM Guidelines* (Borneff *et al.*, 1981) also use *C. albicans* ATCC 10231 in both the fungistatic and the fungicidal suspension tests and in the practical tests for textile and instrument disinfection. In the test for surface disinfection, *C. albicans* ATCC 10231 and *Trichophyton mentagrophytes* ATCC 9533 are used as test organisms (DGHM, 1984); small pieces of beech wood measuring 5 × 20 × 2 mm are contaminated by a suspension of these organisms; exposure lasts 15 and 30 min, and 1, 2 and 4 h; after disinfection and neutralization the wooden pieces are inoculated on Sabouraud nutrient agar, and growth is assessed semi-quantitatively.

The best known and probably the most widely used fungicidal test is that of the AOAC (1984), which is an adaptation of the phenol-coefficient test and is thus a qualitative suspension test. The organism used is *T. mentagrophytes*. After exposure of the standardized suspension to the disinfectant solution for 5, 10 and 15 min, a sample is taken and after neutralization is inoculated into glucose broth. The highest dilution that kills the test cells in 10 min is considered to be the highest dilution that could be expected to disinfect rapidly inanimate surfaces contaminated with pathogenic fungi. Both French tests, the AFNOR tests NF T 72–200 and NF T 72–201 (determination of fungicidal activity; dilution–neutralization method, membrane filtration method respectively) (AFNOR, 1989) are quantitative suspension tests; the test organisms are *Absidia corymbifera*, *Cladosporium cladosporioides*, *Penicillium verrucosum* var. *cyclopium* and *C. albicans* ATCC 2091. Other fungicidal tests have been published (Czerkowicz, 1983), and different varieties of testing methods are followed in the preservation of wood and paints (see Chapter 15).

Generally, it can be stated that in medicine tests with *C. albicans* serve as fungicidal tests, and that even an extension of the test strains to *Trichophyton* spp. does not make the test of representative value. Other fungi, e.g. the conidiospores of *Aspergillus* species, can be more resistant (Lensing & Oei, 1985). In addition to this it should be remembered that tests on inanimate surfaces, and clinical studies with preparations for medical or veterinary use, are two different aspects, and that today the interest in antifungal drugs is greater than in antifungal disinfectants. In this sense it appears difficult to prove the fungicidal properties of a disinfectant in an accepted scientific way.

7 CONCLUSION

It may cause some surprise that the evaluation of the microbiological activity of disinfectants cannot be summarized in a few pages. In theory, disinfectant testing is very easy: test organisms (bacteria, spores, fungi or viruses) in suspension, fixed on carriers, or dried on test surfaces for the practical tests, are exposed to the disinfectant solution under test and after a predetermined exposure period it is checked to determine whether and to what extent the micro-organisms are killed. The number of tests described and their diversity show that there is a lack of agreement among workers on the standardization of all the components of a testing method, and that all these factors influence the resistance, the survival and the recovery of test organisms. Since the performance of different testing procedures yields such a diversity of results for the same disinfectant, it is not surprising that some preparations are applied at a lower use-concentration in one country than in another. Agreement can probably be more easily reached as to the requirements a disinfectant should satisfy for a certain field of application; deciding on criteria of reduction rates after a given exposure is even more difficult. Disagreement is still apparent on the testing methods themselves; even the necessity to test disinfectants in three stages is not generally accepted. So long as there is absence of agreement on such principles, different testing methods will be used, and varying results will be obtained. In this sense, harmonization of the testing schedule and of disinfectant tests will not occur in the immediate future.

8 REFERENCES

AFNOR, Association Française de Normalisation (1989) *Recueil de Normes françaises. Antiseptiques et Désinfectants*. 2nd Ed. Paris La Défense: Association Française de Normalisation.

Alfano, E.M., Cole, E.C. & Rutala, W.A. (1988) Quantitative evaluation of bacteria washed from stainless steel penicylinders during AOAC use-dilution method. *Journal of the Association of Official Analytical Chemists*, **71**, 868–871.

AOAC, Association of Official Analytical Chemists (1984) *Official Methods of Analysis*. 14th Ed. Arlington: Association of Official Analytical Chemists.

Ascenzi, J.M., Ezzell, R.J. & Wendt, T.M. (1986) Evaluation of carriers used in the test methods of the Association of Official Analytical Chemists. *Applied and Environmental Microbiology*, **51**, 91–94.

Ayliffe, G.A.J. (1989) Standardization of disinfectant testing. *Journal of Hospital Infection*, **13**, 211–216.

Beck, E.G., Borneff, J., Grün, L., Gundermann, K.-O., Kanz, E., Lammers, T., Mülhens, K., Primavesi, C.A., Schmidt, B., Schubert, R., Weinhold, E. & Werner, H.-P. (1977) Empfehlungen für die Prüfung und Bewertung der Wirksamkeit chemischer Desinfektionsverfahren. *Zentralblatt für Bakteriologie, Parasitenkunde, Infektionskrankheiten und Hygiene, I. Abteilung Originale, Reihe B*, **165**, 335–380.

Beloian, A. (1983) Methods of testing for sterility: efficacy of sterilizers, sporicides, and sterilizing processes. In *Disinfection, Sterilization, and Preservation* (ed. Block, S.S.) 3rd Ed. pp. 885–917. Philadelphia: Lea & Febiger.

Beloian, A. (1989) General Referee Reports: Committee on pesticide formulations and disinfectants. Disinfectants. *Journal of the Association of Official Analytical Chemists*, **72**, 62.

Borick, P.M. (ed.) (1973) *Chemical Sterilization*. Stroudsburg: Dowden, Hutchinson & Ross.

Borneff, J. & Werner, H.-P. (1977) Entwicklung einer neuen Prüfmethode für Flächendesinfektionsverfahren. VII. Mitteilung: Vorschlag der Methodik. *Zentralblatt für Bakteriologie, Parasitenkunde, Infektionskrankheiten und Hygiene, I. Abteilung Originale, Reihe B*, **165**, 97–101.

Borneff, J., Werner, H.-P., Van De Voorde, H. & Reybrouck, G. (1975) Kritische Beurteilung der Prüfmethoden für chemische Desinfektionsmittel und Verfahren. *Zentralblatt für Bakteriologie, Parasitenkunde, Infektionskrankheiten und Hygiene. I. Abteilung, Originale, Reihe B*, **160**, 590–600.

Borneff, J., Eggers, H.-J., Grün, L., Gundermann, K.-O., Kuwert, E., Lammers, T., Primavesi, C.A., Rotter, M., Schmidt-Lorenz, W., Schubert, R., Sonntag, H.-G:, Spicher, G., Teuber, M., Thofern, E., Weinhold, E., & Werner, H.-P. (1981) *Richtlinien für die Prüfung und Bewertung chemischer Desinfektionsverfahren*. Erster Teilabschnitt, Stuttgart: Gustav Fischer Verlag.

BSI, British Standard Institution (1960) *Method for laboratory evaluation of disinfectant activity of quaternary ammonium compounds*. BS 3286: 1960.

BSI, British Standard Institution (1985) *Determination of the Rideal–Walker Coefficient of Disinfectants*. BS 541: 1985.

BSI, British Standard Institution (1986) *Assessing the Efficacy of Disinfectants by the Modified Chick–Martin Test*. BS 808: 1986.

BSI, British Standard Institution (1987) *Estimation of Concentration of Disinfectants used in 'Dirty' Conditions in*

Hospitals by the Modified Kelsey–Sykes Test. BS 6905: 1987.

Cole, E.C., Rutala, W.A. & Samsa, G.P. (1988) Disinfectant testing using a modified use-dilution method: collaborative study. *Journal of the Association of Official Analytical Chemists*, **71**, 1187–1194.

Collins, C.H., Allwood, M.C., Bloomfield, S.F. & Fox, A. (1981) *Disinfectants: their Use and Evaluation of Effectiveness*. Society for Applied Bacteriology, Technical Series No. 16. London: Academic Press.

Council of Europe (1987) *Test Methods for the Antimicrobial Activity of Disinfectants in Food Hygiene*. Strasbourg: Council of Europe.

Crémieux, A. & Fleurette, J. (1983) Methods of testing disinfectants. In *Disinfection, Sterilization and Preservation* (ed. Block, S.S.) 3rd Ed. pp. 918–945. Philadelphia: Lea & Febiger.

Croshaw, B. (1981) Disinfectant testing—with particular reference to the Rideal–Walker and Kelsey–Sykes tests. In *Disinfectants: their Use and Evaluation of Effectiveness* (eds Collins, C.H., Allwood, M.C., Bloomfield, S.F. & Fox, A.) pp. 1–15. London: Academic Press.

Czerkowicz, T.J. (1983) Methods of testing fungicides. In *Disinfection, Sterilization, and Preservation* (ed. Block, S.S.) 3rd Ed. pp. 998–1008. Philadelphia: Lea & Febiger.

DGHM, Deutsche Gesellschaft für Hygiene und Mikrobiologie (1982) Prüfung und Bewertung chemischer Desinfektionsverfahren—Anforderungen für die Aufnahme in die VII. Liste. *Hygiene + Medizin*, **7**, 453–455.

DGHM, Deutsche Gesellschaft für Hygiene und Mikrobiologie (1984) Prüfung und Bewertung chemischer Desinfektionsverfahren—Anforderungen für die Aufnahme in die VII. Liste. *Hygiene + Medizin*, **9**, 41–46.

DVG, Deutsche Veterinärmedizinische Gesellschaft (1988) *Richtlinien für die Prüfung chemischer Desinfektionsmittel*. 2nd Ed. Giessen: Deutsche Veterinärmedizinische Gesellschaft.

Gundermann, K.O. (1987) Zur Frage der Empfindlichkeit der verschiedenen Mykobakterienstämme gegen Desinfektionsmittel unterschiedlicher Zusammensetzung. *Das Arztliche Laboratorium*, **33**, 327–330.

Heicken, K. (1949) Die Prüfung und Wertbestimmung chemischer Desinfektionsmittel für die Zimmerdesinfektion. *Zeitschrift für Hygiene*, **129**, 538–569.

Hugo, W.B. (1978) Early studies in the evaluation of disinfectants. *Journal of Antimicrobial Chemotherapy*, **4**, 489–494.

Internationaler Milchwirtschaftsverband (1963) Standard-Kapazitätstest für die Bestimmung der Desinfektionswirkung von Desinfektionsmitteln in der Milchwirtschaft (Internationaler Standard FIL/IDF 18–1962). *Milchwissenschaft*, **18**, 406–410.

ISTCL, International Scientific and Technical Committee on Laundering (1976) ISTCL method for testing disinfection in laundry machines.

Kelsey, J.C. & Maurer, I.M. (1966) An in-use test for hospital disinfectants. *Monthly Bulletin of the Ministry of Health and the Public Health Laboratory Service*, **25**, 180–184.

Kelsey, J.C. & Maurer, I.M. (1974) An improved (1974) Kelsey-Sykes test for disinfectants. *Pharmaceutical Journal*, **207**, 528–530.

Kelsey, J.C. & Sykes, G. (1969) A new test for the assessment of disinfectants with particular reference to their use in hospitals. *Pharmaceutical Journal*, **202**, 607–609.

Kelsey, J.C., Beeby, M.M. & Whitehouse, C.W. (1965) A capacity use-dilution test for disinfectants. *Monthly Bulletin of the Ministry of Health and the Public Health Laboratory Service*, **24**, 152–160.

Kliewe, H., Heicken, K., Schmidt, B., Wagener, K., Wüstenberg, J., Ostertag, H., Grün, L., Lammers, T. & Mülhens, K. (1959) *Richtlinien für die Prüfung chemischer Desinfektionsmittel*. Deutsche Gesellschaft für Hygiene und Mikrobiologie. Stuttgart: Gustav Fischer Verlag.

Lashen, E.S. (1971) New method for evaluating antibacterial activity directly on fabric. *Applied Microbiology*, **21**, 771–773.

Lensing, H.H. & Oei, H.L. (1985) Investigations on the sporicidal and fungicidal activity of disinfectants. *Zentralblatt für Bakteriologie, Parasitenkunde, Infektionskrankheiten und Hygiene, I. Abteilung Originale, Reihe B*, **181**, 487–495.

Mossel, D.A.A. (1963) The rapid evaluation of disinfectants intended for use in food processing plants. *Laboratory Practice*, **12**, 898–890.

Prince, J. & Ayliffe, G.A.J. (1972) In-use testing of disinfectants in hospitals. *Journal of Clinical Pathology*, **25**, 586–589.

Reber, H., Fleury, C., Gaschen, M., Hess, E., Regamey, R., Ritter, P., Tanner, F. & Vischer, W. (1972) *Bewertung und Prüfung von Desinfektionsmitteln und -verfahren*. Basel: Schweizerische Mikrobiologische Gesellschaft.

Reuter, G. (1989) Anforderungen an die Wirksamkeit von Desinfektionsmitteln für den lebensmittelverarbeitenden Bereich. *Zentralblatt für Bakteriologie, Parasitenkunde, Infektionskrankheiten und Hygiene, I. Abteilung Originale, Reihe B*, **187**, 564–577.

Reybrouck, G. (1975) A theoretical approach of disinfectant testing. *Zentralblatt für Bakteriologie, Parasitenkunde, Infektionskrankheiten und Hygiene, I. Abteilung Originale, Reihe B*, **160**, 342–367.

Reybrouck, G. (1977) Factors influencing the assessment of the pseudomonacidal activity of disinfectants by a quantitative suspension test. II. The post-disinfection recovery of surviving organisms. *Zentralblatt für Bakteriologie, Parasitenkunde, Infektionskrankheiten und Hygiene, I. Abteilung Originale, Reihe B*, **165**, 113–125.

Reybrouck, G. (1980) A comparison of the quantitative suspension tests for the assessment of disinfectants. *Zentralblatt für Bakteriologie, Parasitenkunde, Infektionskrankheiten und Hygiene, I. Abteilung Originale, Reihe B*, **170**, 449–456.

Reybrouck, G. (1986) Uniformierung der Prüfung von Desinfektionsmitteln in Europa. *Zentralblatt für Bakterio-*

logie, Parasitenkunde, Infektionskrankheiten und Hygiene, I. Abteilung Originale, Reihe B, **182**, 485–498.

Reybrouck, G. (1990) The assessment of the bactericidal activity of surface disinfectants. I. A comparison of three tests under practical conditions. *Zentralblatt für Hygiene und Umweltmedizin*, **190**, 479–491.

Reybrouck, G. & Van De Voorde, H. (1975) Aussagekraft der Ergebnisse von vier nationalen Methoden zur Wertbestimmung von Desinfektionsmitteln. *Zentralblatt für Bakteriologie, Parasitenkunde, Infektionskrankheiten und Hygiene, I. Abteilung Originale, Reihe B*, **160**, 541–550.

Reybrouck, G. & Werner, H.-P. (1977) Ausarbeitung eines neuen quantitativen *in-vitro*-Tests für die bakteriologische Prüfung chemischer Desinfektionsmittel. *Zentralblatt für Bakteriologie, Parasitenkunde, Infektionskrankheiten und Hygiene, I. Abteilung Originale, Reihe B*, **165**, 126–137.

Reybrouck, G., Borneff, J., Van De Voorde, H. & Werner, H.-P. (1979) A collaborative study on a new quantitative suspension test, the *in vitro* test, for the evaluation of the bactericidal activity of chemical disinfectants. *Zentralblatt für Bakteriologie, Parasitenkunde, Infektionskrankheiten und Hygiene, I. Abteilung Originale, Reihe B*, **168**, 463–479.

Schmidt, B. (1973) Das 2. Internationale Colloquium über die Wertbestimmung von Desinfektionsmitteln in Europa. *Zentralblatt für Bakteriologie, Parasitenkunde, Infektionskrankheiten und Hygiene, I. Abteilung Originale, Reihe B*, **157**, 411–420.

Scott, E., Bloomfield, S.F. & Barlow, C.G. (1984) Evaluation of disinfectants in the domestic environment under 'in use' conditions. *Journal of Hygiene, Cambridge*, **92**, 193–203.

Stockinger, H., Böhm, R. & Strauch, D. (1989) Die vergleichende experimentelle Prüfung zweier verschiedener Desinfektionsmittelwirkstoffe auf Sporozidie im Modellversuch mit Sporen pathogener und apathogener Clostridienarten sowie von *Bacillus cereus*. *Zentralblatt für Hygiene und Umweltmedizin*, **188**, 166–178.

Van Klingeren, B. & Pullen, W. (1987) Comparative testing of disinfectants against *Mycobacterium tuberculosis* and *Mycobacterium terrae* in a quantitative suspension test. *Journal of Hospital Infection*, **10**, 292–298.

Van Klingeren, B., Leussink, A.B. & Van Wijngaarden, L.J. (1977) A collaborative study on the repeatability and the reproducibility of the Dutch Standard-Suspension-Test for the evaluation of disinfectants. *Zentralblatt für Bakteriologie, Parasitenkunde, Infektionskrankheiten und Hygiene, I. Abteilung Originale, Reihe B*, **164**, 521–548.

Chapter 5
Antifungal Activity of Biocides

1 INTRODUCTION

Yeasts and moulds comprise important groups of micro-organisms that are responsible for various types of infections and for causing spoilage of foods, pharmaceutical products and cosmetic products. Some fungal species are of agricultural and industrial importance and many cause disease in plants. Yeasts are unicellular ovoid or spherical cells that reproduce by bud formation, sexual spores not being formed. Moulds grow as branching filaments or hyphae that form a mass of intertwining strands, the mycelium. Yeast-like fungi grow as round or ovoid cells or as non-branching filaments (pseudohyphae) that, unlike true hyphae, do not form spores but reproduce by budding. The best-known example of a yeast-like fungus is *Candida*, with *C. albicans* a particularly important organism because of its association with oral thrush in infants and with intestinal and vaginal candidiasis. *C. glabrata* is one type of *Candida* that does not produce pseudohyphae.

Fungal infections (mycoses) in humans or animals are essentially of two types: superficial, involving skin, nails or hair and readily transmissible, and deep (or systemic). It is noticeable that comparatively few chemotherapeutic drugs are available for treating deep mycoses; the most important drugs are polyenic antibiotics, imidazoles and flucytosine, with griseofulvin suitable for superficial mycoses. These will not be described *per se*, except in so far as to consider how studies with such drugs could point the way for investigations with biocides.

The effects of biocides on bacteria and bacterial spores have been widely studied. A vast literature provides information about sensitivity and mechanisms of action and, to some extent, of resistance. This is not true with fungi. Data are comparatively sparse and scattered throughout many types of publication, and there have been few advanced studies of the modes of antifungal action of biocides or of the mechanisms of fungal resistance. Some of these aspects will be considered here, and suggestions made about possible ways of obtaining additional information.

Reviews that deal, in part, with antifungal activity of antiseptics, disinfectants and preservatives have been published by Torgeson (1969), D'Arcy (1971), Hugo (1971), Russell (1971), Trueman (1971), Dawes (1976), Lueck (1980), Croshaw

& Holland (1984), Haag & Loncrini (1984), Hall (1984), Kabara (1984), Report (1984), Wallhäusser (1984), Gardner & Peel (1986), Chapman (1987), Quinn (1987), Baldry & Fraser (1988), Eigener (1988), Heinzel (1988), Lehmann (1988) Woodcock (1988), and Russell & Gould (1991).

2 FUNGI: COMPOSITION AND STRUCTURE

Fungi, as distinct from bacteria, are classified as eukaryotic organisms. They differ from bacteria, the prokaryotes, in many important respects (Wilkinson, 1986). Chiefly, fungi possess a nuclear membrane and mitochondria and contain more than the one chromosome characteristic of bacteria. Their cell wall chemistry also differs profoundly. These facts must be borne in mind when conducting mode of action studies. Fungal structure will now be considered in more detail.

The outermost region, as in bacteria, is the cell wall. This surrounds the delicate plasma (cytoplasmic) membrane internal to which is the cytoplasm. The fungal cell wall demonstrates mechanical strength and a close relationship exists between wall composition and taxonomic classification (Bartnicki-Garcia, 1968; Table 5.1). Some 80–90% of the dry weight of fungal cell walls is made up of polysaccharides. Skeletal polysaccharides consist of chitin, cellulose and glucans, and are composed mainly of glucose and *N*-acetylglucosamine (GlcNAc), as demonstrated in Fig. 5.1. Chitin and β-glucans are responsible for the mechanical strength of the wall. Other sugars, often in chemical complexes with proteins, consist of homo- and hetero-polysaccharides that act as cementing substances (Farkas, 1979). In *Saccharomyces cerevisiae* the glucan is composed mainly of a high molecular weight β(1–3) fraction containing a small proportion of β(1–6) linkages (Bálint *et al.*, 1976). Ballou (1976) has described the structure and biosynthesis of the mannan component of fungal cell walls. A small amount of lipid may also be present. For comprehensive details of *Candida* spp. see Odds (1988).

Differences have been noted in the appearance of fungal cell walls in cells of different ages (Farkas, 1979). An interesting aspect of this has been the finding that stationary-phase cells of *C. albicans* are several orders more resistant to the polyene antibiotic, amphotericin, than are exponential-phase cells (Gale *et al.*, 1980; Notario *et al.*, 1982). The walls of the former are thicker and more likely, therefore, to act as a barrier to the antibiotic. This aspect, and its possible significance to biocide resistance, is considered more fully on p. 144.

Table 5.1 Chemical composition of fungal cell walls.

Principal cell wall polymers	Taxonomic class	Example
Chitin, chitosan	Zygomycetes	*Mucor rouxii*
Chitin, glucan	Ascomycetes (mycelial forms)	*Neurospora crassa*
	Deuteromycetes (mycelial forms)	*Aspergillus niger*
Glucan, mannan	Ascomycetes (yeast forms)	*Saccharomyces cerevisiae*
	Deuteromycetes (yeast forms)	*Candida utilis*

The fungal cell wall should not, however, be regarded as a compact structure, since some large molecules can pass through the wall in both directions. This suggests that a certain number of pores must be present (Farkas, 1979) or that a reorganization of the wall structure occurs to produce openings that will allow the passage of these molecules (Scherrer *et al.*, 1974).

Beneath, and protected by, the cell wall is the plasma membrane (cytoplasmic membrane), which is lipoprotein in nature and in which sterols, notably ergosterol, are present, interrelated with phospholipids. The nucleus and other internal organelles (the mitochondria and chloroplasts) are enclosed in membranes within the cytosol, and ribosomes are 80S (40S and 60S subunits) as opposed to the 70S (30S and 50S) found in prokaryotes.

3 FUNGAL SENSITIVITY TO BIOCIDES

The chemical and biological properties of a range of antimicrobial agents were considered earlier. In

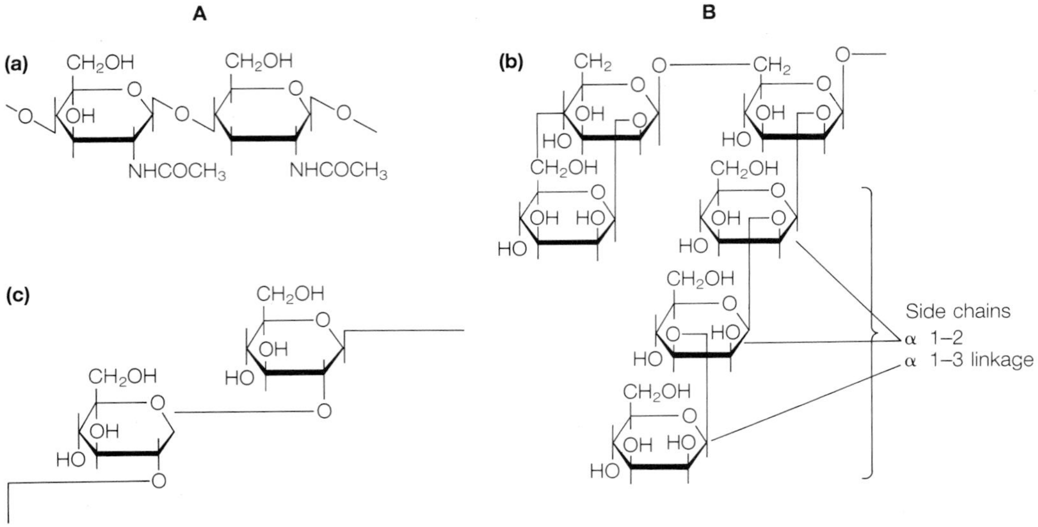

Fig. 5.1 Polysaccharides found in fungal cell walls: (a) chitin; (b) mannan; (c) glucan.

this section the inhibitory and lethal effects of some of those compounds on fungi will be assessed and a comparison made, where possible, with activity against bacteria and their spores.

3.1 Inhibitory and lethal effects of biocides

Tables 5.2 and 5.3 provide a list of minimum inhibitory concentrations (MICs) and minimum fungicidal concentrations of some antiseptics, disinfectants and preservatives against some commonly found or medically important fungi. From these tables it is possible to reach the following conclusions:

1 fungicidal concentrations are often much higher than those needed to inhibit growth;

2 moulds are sometimes, but not invariably, more resistant than yeasts; see, for example, data on chlorhexidine and the organomercury compounds;

3 the parabens show the classical response of increasing activity with ascension of the homologous series from methyl to butyl ester.

More quantitative data with some of these biocides have been published by Brown & Bullock (1960), Gerrard *et al.* (1960), Chauhan & Walters (1961, 1962), Chauhan *et al.* (1963) and Rivers & Walters (1966). As would be expected, activity depended on concentration, time of exposure and temperature. For example, a 99% kill of *Penicillium notatum* spores at 20°C was achieved in 20 min by 1.125% and in 80 min by 1% phenol (Chauhan & Walters, 1961); as temperature increased, the time to produce this 2-log kill cycle was reduced, being 1 min at 45°C (Chauhan & Walters, 1962). Inhibition of oxygen uptake does not provide a quantitative measure of the fungicidal activity of phenol (Chauhan *et al.*, 1963; Rivers & Walters, 1966) or of other inhibitors (Rivers & Walters, 1966). Fungicidal test methods are described by Czerkowicz (1983) and in Chapter 4.

Chlorhexidine salts are less active against yeasts and moulds than non-sporing bacteria. Inactivation of *C. albicans*, *C. glabrata* and *Sacch. cerevisiae* depends on chlorhexidine concentration with a tailing-off in the rate of kill noted at lower biguanide concentrations (S. Hiom and A.D. Russell, unpublished data).

Glutaraldehyde is a bactericidal, sporicidal and virucidal agent (Gorman *et al.*, 1980). It also shows fungistatic (Dabrowa *et al.*, 1972) and fungicidal activity (Stonehill *et al.*, 1963; Dabrowa *et al.*,

Table 5.2 Inhibitory concentrations of biocides towards some common fungi*. Figures in μg/ml except for ethanol (% v/v).

	Yeasts		Moulds		
Antimicrobial agent	*C. albicans*	*Sacch. cerevisiae*	*Trichophyton* spp.	*Penicillium* spp.	*Aspergillus* spp.
Organic acids					
Benzoic	500–1000	750		500–1000	500–1000
Dehydroacetic		300			
Propionic	2000			2000	2000
Sorbic	25–50	200–500		200–500	200–500
Parabens					
Methyl	1000	1000	160	500	600
Ethyl	800	500	80	250	400
Propyl	250	125	40	125	200
Butyl	125	63	20	100	150
QACs					
Benzalkonium chloride		20		50	50
Cetrimide/CTAB	12.5	50		100	50
Dequalinium chloride	0.63–5				
Biguanides					
Chlorhexidine	10–20	20		200	200
Phenols					
Chlorocresol	2500	2500			2500
Chloroxylenol	2000	1000			2000
Alcohols					
Benzyl alcohol	2500				5000
Bronopol	200–1000		50–200	200–1000	200–1000
Chlorbutanol		2000			
Ethanol	10%			10%	10%
Phenoxyethanol	5000	5000			5000
Phenylethanol	2500	5000		5000	5000
Mercurials					
PMN/PMA	8	8		16	16
Thiomersal	32	32		128	128

* Based on data in Wallhäusser (1984) and D'Arcy (1971).
CTAB, cetyltrimethylammonium bromide; PMA, phenylmercuric acetate; PMN, phenylmercuric nitrate.

1972; Gorman & Scott, 1977; Gorman *et al.*, 1980; Gray, 1980). Formaldehyde is equally effective in killing *C. albicans* as vegetative Gram-negative bacteria; the conidia of *Aspergillus niger* are more resistant but not more so than *Staph. aureus* (Spicher & Peters, 1976).

Various organic acids, e.g. benzoic, sorbic (Bandelin, 1950; Gooding *et al.*, 1955; Bell *et al.*, 1959; Balatsouras & Polymenacos, 1963; Hunter & Segal, 1973; Krebs *et al.*, 1983; Kabara, 1984; Cole & Keenan, 1987) and the esters of *para*(4)-hydroxybenzoic acid (Aalto *et al.*, 1953; Maddox,

Table 5.3 Lethal concentration of biocides towards some fungi*

Group	Antimicrobial agent	Yeast	Moulds	
		C. albicans	*P. chrysogenum*	*A. niger*
Organic acids	Benzoic	1200	1000	1000
Parabens	Methyl	5000	5000	5000
	Ethyl	2500	2500	5000
	Propyl	625	1250	2500
	Butyl	625	1250	1250
QACs	Benazalkonium chloride	10	100–200	100–200
	Cetrimide/CTAB	25	100	250
Biguanides	Chlorhexidine	20–40	400	200
Alcohols	Chlorbutanol	2500		5000
Mercurials	Thiomersal	128	2048	4096

* Derived from information provided by Wallhäusser (1984).

1982; Haag & Loncrini, 1984; Report, 1984) are effective antifungal agents. Environmental pH markedly affects the activity of the former, but not the antifungal efficacy of the latter.

Peracetic acid is an excellent bactericide, sporicide and fungicide (Baldry, 1983; Baldry & Fraser, 1988), but its activity decreases with increasing pH.

Pospisil (1989) has examined the efficacy of various antiseptic and disinfectant preparations against potentially pathogenic micromycetes, and Berger *et al.* (1976) have described the antifungal properties of electrically generated metallic ions.

The antimicrobial properties of sulphur dioxide, SO_2, depend upon the degree of ionization of the molecule and on pH (Hammond & Carr, 1976; Babich & Stotzky, 1978). When dissolved in water, SO_2 or its salts (sulphite, bisulphite and metabisulphite) set up a pH-dependent equilibrium mixture and SO_2 activity is maximal at acid pH. At these low pH values the proportion of sulphite (SO^{2-}) ions decreases, and of SO_2 molecules increases at the expense of bisulphate (HSO_3^-) ions. The active principle is the unbound (free) SO_2 concentration, and molecular SO_2, i.e. the molecules of SO_2 existing in aqueous solution at low pH (Hammond & Carr, 1976) is *ca.* 100 and 500 times more active against *A. niger* and yeasts, respectively, than sulphite or bisulphite ions.

Organic sulphur compounds such as dithiocarbamates, for plant disease control, and thiram (tetramethylthiuram disulphide) are highly active fungicides, but mercaptans and alkyl sulphides have a low order of fungicidal activity (Owens, 1969). Bent (1979) has described the wide variety of chemical structures that are used as agricultural fungicides.

3.2 Comparative responses of bacteria and fungi

Spaulding (1972) has listed the following categories of biocidal activity:

(a) high-level—a biocide inactivating bacterial spores, vegetative bacteria, fungi, lipid enveloped and non-lipid enveloped viruses;

(b) intermediate level—a biocide inactivating all those listed in (a) except bacterial spores;

(c) low level—a biocide inactivating vegetative bacteria, lipid enveloped viruses and fungi only.

From this it can be seen that antifungal activity is perceived as being of a low level, i.e. that fungi are not particularly resistant to biocides. This point of view is substantiated in Favero's (1985) important contribution. Nevertheless, instances abound where activity of a biocide is shown to be considerably less against yeasts and moulds than against non-sporulating bacteria. Some examples are provided in Table 5.4, from which it can be seen that

Table 5.4 Kinetic approach: *D*-values at 20°C of biocides against bacteria and fungi*

Antimicrobial agent	pH	Concn. (%)	*D*-values (hours) vs. *A. niger*	*C. albicans*	*E. coli*	*Ps. aeruginosa*	*Staph. aureus*
Phenol	5.1	0.5	20	13.5	0.94	—†	0.66
	6.1	0.5	32.4	18.9	1.72	0.166	1.9
Benzyl alcohol	5.0	1.0	28.8	39	0.37	0.16	5.48
	6.1	1.0	76.8	92.1	8.53	1.48	7.2
Benzalkonium chloride	6.1	0.001	—‡	9.66	0.06	3.01	3.12
	6.1	0.002	—‡	5.5	—†	0.054	0.67
Ethanol	7.1	20	58	1.31	0.03	—†	1.05

* Abstracted from the work of Karabit *et al.* (1985, 1986, 1988, 1989).
† Inactivation so rapid that *D*-values could not be measured.
‡ No inactivation: fungistatic effect only.

C. albicans and (especially) *A. niger* are much more resistant than *E. coli*, *Ps. aeruginosa* and *Staph. aureus* (surprisingly the most resistant bacterial strain) to phenol, two alcohols and a QAC. QACs have also been found to be less effective vs. *C. albicans* by Weiner *et al.* (1965).

The kinetic approach to the testing of preservative efficacy is a useful one, since it provides important information about the rate of kill, often measured as the *D*-value. This is the time of exposure necessary for a specific concentration at defined pH and temperature to reduce the viable population by one log cycle. This is the approach adopted in Table 5.4, and thereby enables a direct comparison to be made with different organisms. This procedure is based on the work of Orth (1979, 1980, 1984), who developed this method for evaluating preservative efficacy in cosmetics, but it is equally applicable to pharmaceutical products. It is noticeable that Orth pointed out the much higher resistance of *A. niger* and *A. flavus* to several preservatives than that shown by non-sporulating bacteria. This kinetic assessment can be used to determine the time necessary to inactivate an appropriate fraction of a microbial inoculum added to a test pharmaceutical (or other) product, e.g. as exemplified in the British (1988) and United States XXI (1985) pharmacopoeias. Table 5.5 compares the requirements of these two official volumes; whilst there are differences between the compendia, it is again clear that inactivation of bacteria is more rapid than that of yeasts and moulds.

3.3 Uses of antifungal agents

Fungal infections are not usually life-threatening, although some can be serious, particularly in patients with depressed immunity. Chemotherapeutic considerations are outside the scope of this chapter, but it is important to discuss biocides predominantly as (a) preservatives to prevent contamination or spoilage of formulated products, (b) disinfectants for those occasions where yeasts and moulds might prove to be an environmental problem or hazard, (c) as industrial and agricultural fungicides.

Fungal contamination of food, pharmaceutical and cosmetic products can be a problem, particularly if these are of high water activity (A_w) and stored in warm conditions. Apart from such obvious measures as quality control of all raw materials, including water, the inclusion of a suitable preservative may be necessary. This aspect is covered more fully in Chapters 15 and 16.

Disinfectants specifically for use against yeasts and moulds are not often required, although it is as well to re-emphasize that fungi are often more resistant than non-sporulating bacteria but less so than bacterial spores. Hypochlorites are very effective fungicidal agents.

Table 5.5 Pharmacopoeial requirements in antimicrobial agent tests for preservative efficiency.

	BP (1988)		USP (XXI)	
Pharmaceutical	Bacteria	Yeasts and moulds	Bacteria	Yeasts and moulds
Sterile products	Not less than a 3-log reduction in 6 h, and no survivors at 24 h	Not less than a 2-log reduction in 7 days, and no increase thereafter	A 3-log reduction in 14 days	No increase after 14 and 28 days

Agricultural fungicides make up 10–15% of total pesticide sales in the United States. Such fungicides include the most widely used type, the dithiocarbamates (see also Owens, 1969), heterocyclic nitrogen compounds, e.g. captan, quinones such as chloranil and dichlone, and heavy metals, in particular Bordeaux mixture, a copper salt mixed with lime which is the most widely used fungicide for control of foliar disease (Bent, 1979; Lukens, 1983). Properties of these were considered in Chapter 2. Industrially important products that may require the presence of an appropriate antifungal-type preservative include wool, cotton, wood and leather (Block, 1983). Further aspects of these are dealt with in the various sections of Chapter 17; see also Lyr (1987a,b).

Benzoic and salicylic acids are used for treating skin infections, and copper 8-quinolonate for treating room surfaces following outbreaks of *Aspergillus* in immunocompromised patients (Barnes & Rogers, 1989). Sulphur dioxide, in the form of appropriate salts, is often applied to foods (Hammond & Carr, 1976).

4 MECHANISMS OF ANTIFUNGAL ACTION

Comparatively little is known about the ways in which fungi are killed by biocides. It is often assumed that they are inactivated in a similar or identical fashion to vegetative bacteria. Whilst such a proposition has undoubted attractions, the different structural and chemical properties of bacteria and fungi mean that this concept may not necessarily or always be true. Nevertheless, it is probably correct to state that in both the prokaryotic (bacterial) and eukaryotic (fungal) cells the first interaction between biocide and organisms occurs at the cell surface, followed by passage of the biocide across the cell wall (or outer membrane) to reach its target site(s) within the cell. Some biocides are likely to have a predominant effect on the outer layers (Section 4.1). In Gram-positive cocci, simple diffusion across the cell wall is likely to occur; in Gram-negative bacteria, passage occurs either via the hydrophilic or hydrophobic routes, or possibly via a self-promoted entry mechanism (Hancock, 1984). The obvious question arises as to how biocides enter yeasts and moulds, but at present there is little information available. It would be presumptuous to speculate upon the relative importance of diffusion, passage through pores or possible self-promoted entry mechanisms. Interestingly, Gerston *et al.* (1966) considered that pores in fungal cell walls were too small for the entrance of very large molecules.

Adsorption of biocides by yeasts and moulds has not been widely studied, although, as with bacteria, it is a phenomenon that has been known for several years. Knaysi & Gordon (1930), for example, described the adsorption of iodine by yeast, and this was later examined in greater detail (Hugo & Newton, 1964). An unusual pattern of uptake, Z-curve adsorption, was noted by Gilbert *et al.* (1978) in their studies on the uptake of 2-phenoxyethanol by *E. coli* and *Candida lipolytica*; interestingly, a C-type adsorption uptake pattern was observed

Table 5.6 Postulated mechanisms of action of antifungal agents

Target	Antifungal	Comment
Fungal cell wall	Glutaraldehyde	Cross-linking agent
Plasma membrane	Chlorhexidine QACs	Leakage of intracellular constituents; probably cause generalized increase in permeability
	Organic acids	Undissociated form is most active Intracellular shift in pH
	Parabens	Not fully understood

with *Ps. aeruginosa*. The Z-pattern is interpreted as being produced by a concentration of phenoxyethanol that promotes a breakdown in structure of the adsorbing species, i.e. the micro-organism, leading to the production of new adsorption sites, whereas the C-pattern is believed to indicate a more ready penetration of biocide into the adsorbate (here the micro-organism) than of the solvent. Adsorption of dyes by fixed yeast cells was described by Giles & Mackay (1965).

Chlorhexidine binds strongly to whole cells and isolated cell walls of *Sacch. cerevisiae*; furthermore, it causes a reduction in electrophoretic mobility at biguanide concentrations up to 50 μg/ml, but much higher concentrations (>700 μg/ml) cause reversal of net surface charge (Walters *et al*., 1983). Norris & Kelley (1979), Gadd & White (1989) and Gadd (1990) have described the accumulation of metals by yeasts and other organisms.

Useful though they are, however, adsorption studies and effects on electrophoretic mobility (surface charge changes) provide only preliminary data about the site and mechanism of action of a biocide acting on bacteria or fungi. Whilst it would be inadvisable to omit studies on adsorption from any investigation, it would be equally irresponsible to base conclusions about the mode of action solely on whole-cell interactions. Large numbers of microbes are invariably needed (but may be reduced if a radioactive compound is available) and, certainly with some bacterial studies, it may be difficult to relate adsorption of a biocide with cellular sensitivity or resistance. Insufficient is known about adsorption by fungi of differing sensitivities to reach a similar conclusion.

A most interesting paper dealing with mechanisms for fungitoxicants reaching their site of action was published more than 20 years ago by Miller (1969). Other important reviews are those of Somers (1962), Owens (1963, 1969). Owens & Hayes (1964), Lukens (1971, 1983), Bent (1979) and Lyr (1987a). Hansch & Lien (1971) have surveyed structure–activity relationships in antifungal agents, and information on selective toxicity mechanisms can be obtained from Albert's (1979) extensive work. Lyr (1987b) has edited a comprehensive work on the mechanisms of action of modern selective fungicides.

4.1 Fungal cell walls as targets

Few antimicrobial agents are likely to have the fungal cell wall as a major, or sole, target. Compounds that would be assumed to have at least some effect include cross-linking agents such as glutaraldehyde and formaldehyde, and cationic biocides such as QACs and chlorhexidine. It was shown above that biocides do, indeed, adsorb to yeasts, although this in itself does not necessarily explain their mechanism of action.

Glutaraldehyde is an important 'chemosterilizing' agent that combines strongly with $-NH_2$ groups at the microbial cell surface and elsewhere within the cell (Gorman *et al*., 1980). Glutaraldehyde inhibits spore germination and sporulation, and the presence of polymers (e.g.

chitin) in the cell walls of fungi that resemble bacterial peptidoglycan demonstrates a potentially reactive site (Gorman & Scott, 1977). As would be expected from antibacterial studies, the activity of the dialdehyde on *C. lipolytica* increases with concentration, pH and period of contact (Navarro & Monsan, 1976). These authors demonstrated that glutaraldehyde agglutinated the cells of this organism, of *Sacch. carlsbergensis* and of some bacterial species and increased their settling rate, as a consequence of an effect on the outer cell layers.

Chlorhexidine was described above as binding strongly to whole cells and to isolated cell walls (Walters *et al*. 1983) but it is not known whether such adsorption contributes to the overall fungicidal effect. Chlorhexidine is considered to be a membrane-active agent (Section 4.2).

4.2 Membrane-active biocides

The plasma membrane is likely to be a major target site for many antifungal agents, as it is for several antibacterial agents (Russell & Hugo, 1988). This section will concentrate on the known activity towards fungi of chlorhexidine, QACs and organic acids.

4.2.1 Chlorhexidine

Only few studies of any significance have been made about the mechanism of action of chlorhexidine against yeasts. Elferink & Booij (1974) described the effects of chlorhexidine on baker's yeast and found that the biguanide induced the rapid release of K^+ ions, indicative of membrane damage. Similar findings were made by Walters *et al*. (1983), who observed that pentose release from *Sacch. cerevisiae* was induced maximally at a concentration of 50 μg/ml (exposure time 3 h, temperature 30°C) as opposed to a minimal inhibitory concentration of 7 μg/ml. There was no evidence of lysis, but the highest chlorhexidine level (1000 μg/ml) induced some clumping.

Bobichon & Bouchet (1987) investigated the action of chlorhexidine, at a sublethal concentration, on the ultrastructure of budding *C. albicans* and observed a loss of cytoplasmic components, indicative of plasma membrane damage, together with coagulation of 'nucleoproteins' and wall modification.

4.2.2 Quaternary ammonium compounds

Like chlorhexidine, QACs are known to induce leakage of intracellular material from yeasts (Armstrong, 1957, 1958; Scharff & Beck, 1959; Elferink & Booij, 1974). Armstrong (1957, 1958) studied the effects of six cationic compounds on baker's yeast with a view to exploring any relationship between cytolytic damage, as determined by phosphorus release from treated cells, and metabolism (measured by the conversion of glucose to acid and carbon dioxide). He concluded that the initial toxic effect on the cell was a disorganization of the cell membrane followed by inactivation of cell enzymes. One QAC, cetyltrimethylammonium bromide (CTAB), has been suggested as disrupting organized lipid structures in lipid bilayers and in the yeast membrane (Elferink & Booij, 1974).

Low concentrations of benzalkonium chloride stimulated oxygen consumption in baker's yeasts whilst inhibiting the Pasteur effect, but without causing an appreciable alteration in membrane permeability; higher concentrations, however, induced K^+ loss (Scharff & Beck, 1959). Sevag & Ross (1944), studying the effect of QACs on enzyme systems in yeast, noted an inhibition of glucose oxidation.

4.2.3 Organic acids and esters

Organic acids, such as benzoic and sorbic acids, are rapidly taken up by yeasts (Macris, 1974; Krebs *et al*., 1983; Warth, 1977, 1985, 1986, 1988). They act as lipophilic acids that damage the plasma membrane, and at the acid pH at which they are employed the anion is concentrated in the cytoplasm. Hunter & Segal (1973) provided evidence for an inhibition of active transport in *Penicillium chrysogenum*. Cole & Keenan (1987) proposed that *Zygosaccharomyces bailii* increased its cytoplasmic buffering capacity and secreted organic acids during normal metabolism, and thus concluded that acid tolerance in this organism was based on an ability to withstand large falls in intracellular pH. Krebs *et al*. (1983) showed that, in

Sacch. cerevisiae, benzoic acid enters the cell in its undissociated form and that the neutralization of the acid within the cell causes an intracellular pH shift of more than one pH unit.

Mitchell's chemiosmotic theory (considered in greater detail in Chapter 9) is a mechanism whereby, during metabolism, protons are extruded with acidification of the external environment. Hunter & Segal (1973), in their studies on the effects of weak acids on amino acid transport in *P. chrysogenum*, have demonstrated the existence of a proton or charge gradient as the driving force. Organic acids and esters produce inhibition of Δ pH across the bacterial cytoplasmic membrane, and a similar effect might be produced in fungi.

4.2.4 *Other agents*

Heavy metals, e.g. copper salts and organomercury compounds, may act by binding to key functional groups of enzymes in fungi (Lukens, 1983). Quinones, such as chloranil and dichlone, may produce alkylation of $-NH_2$ groups in enzymes. Simon (1953a,b,c) found that 3,5-dinitro-*o*-cresol acted as an uncoupling agent in yeast, stimulating oxygen uptake. Ethylenediamine tetraacetate (EDTA) affects fungal membranes (Indge, 1968a,b), inducing K^+ leakage (Elferink, 1974) and decreasing protoplast resistance to osmotic lysis (Diamond & Rose, 1970). Sulphur dioxide interacts with enzyme systems (Hammond & Carr, 1976).

4.3 Other target sites

Other potential target sites in fungi include the ribosomes, nucleic acids and structural and functional (enzymes) proteins. It is difficult to state the role of ribosomes, structural protein, RNA and DNA as targets for fungicidal attack since so few relevant studies have been made.

In contrast, some investigations (considered in Section 4.2) have examined effects of antifungal agents on specific enzyme systems, at least some of which are associated with the plasma membrane. However, as pointed out by Hugo (1981), it is difficult to envisage a situation in which inhibition and/or cell death can be accounted for by inhibition of a specific enzyme, unless this reaction is essential for the metabolism of the cell. Thus enzyme inactivation must be considered as being only one of many inhibited reactions, and is unlikely to be the primary mechanism of action of an antifungal agent.

Sulphur dioxide interacts with disulphide bridges in proteins, e.g. cystine sulphitolysis is responsible for cleavage of the disulphide bond in cystine, producing cysteine and cysteine sulphonate. Interaction of sulphur dioxide with nucleic acids is responsible for mutagenic effects in yeasts (Hammond & Carr, 1976).

5 POSSIBLE MECHANISMS OF FUNGAL RESISTANCE TO BIOCIDES

5.1 Theoretical concepts

Two basic mechanisms of fungal resistance to biocides can be envisaged. In the first, natural (intrinsic) resistance is associated with the innate ability of a fungal cell to present a permeability barrier to one or more biocides, or to inactivate a biocide by virtue of constitutively present enzymes. In the second, acquired resistance to a biocide could ensue as a result of mutation or via the acquisition of genetic material. Whilst a considerable amount of information is available about these two major aspects of bacterial resistance to antibiotics, and a steadily accumulating fund of knowledge of resistance to biocides (Russell & Chopra, 1990), data on the mechanisms of fungal resistance to non-antibiotic agents are sparse. Fungal resistance to agricultural fungicides is discussed by Dekker (1987) and Georgopoulos (1987).

5.2 Intrinsic biocide resistance

The structure of the fungal cell wall (Table 5.1, Fig. 5.1) suggests that there is ample opportunity for a cell to exclude biocide molecules. No significant investigations have been made to date with biocides, but some evidence accumulated from studies on sensitivity of *C. albicans* to the polyenic antibiotic, amphotericin (Gale, 1986; Kerridge, 1986) points the way towards a more fundamental approach. It should be possible to determine the component(s) of cell walls responsible for limiting biocide entry by the use of appropriate cell wall-degrading enzymes and specific wall-acting antibiotics or other drugs by using cells of different physiological ages, and by the utilization of mutant strains that are defective in a cell wall component. Such studies are currently under way in the author's laboratory.

Production of hydrogen sulphide by micro-organisms can reduce heavy metal toxicity, because H_2S combines with heavy metals to form insoluble sulphides. Consequently H_2S-producing microbes may demonstrate tolerance to such metals. For example, strains of *Sacch. cerevisiae* that produce H_2S are more tolerant to copper and mercury than are non-tolerant strains, because in the tolerant strains the metals are precipitated as insoluble sulphides (Gadd & Griffiths, 1978; Gadd, 1990). Inactivation of an organomercury compound, phenylmercuric acetate, by *Penicillium roqueforti* Thom has been observed (Russell, 1955), although reduced permeability to the phenylmercury ion has also been proposed as being a mechanism of resistance or tolerance (Greenaway, 1972; Greenaway *et al.*, 1978). Tolerance to organomercury has been found in *Pyrenophora avenae* (Crosier *et al.*, 1970).

Inactivation of other fungitoxic agents has also been described. Yanagita (1980), Kato *et al.* (1982, 1983) and Heinzel (1988) have all reported the role of formaldehyde dehydrogenase in resistance to formaldehyde, and noted the degradation of potassium sorbate by a *Penicillium* species has also been observed. The ability of certain fungi to reduce toxic metallic arsenic derivatives to the volatile and dispersible arsine has been known from the time when these compounds were used as wallpaper colourants.

5.3 Acquired biocide resistance

There appears to be no evidence linking the presence of plasmids in fungal cells and the ability of the organisms to acquire resistance to fungicidal or fungistatic agents. However, acquired resistance to organic acids has been described. Starved cells of *Sacch. bailii* concentrate benzoic and sorbic acids intracellularly, whereas in the presence of glucose their intracellular concentration is reduced considerably. The effect of glucose can be quenched by means of metabolic inhibitors (Warth, 1977). Pitt (1974) had previously shown that growth of this organism in the presence of subinhibitory concentrations of a preservative greatly increased its resistance when exposed to higher concentrations, higher resistance levels being found in the presence of higher glucose levels. Thus, this organism possesses an inducible preservative elimination system. In subsequent studies, Warth (1985, 1986, 1988) demonstrated that a major effect of benzoic acid on yeasts of various levels of susceptibility in the presence of glucose was the energy requirement for the reduction in cytoplasmic benzoate concentration and the maintenance of internal pH (pH_i). Hydrogen ions arising from the dissociation of benzoic acid inside the cell must be exported, hence the need for the energy requirement to maintain the alkaline pH. Benzoate in energized cells is considered to be eliminated by flowing down the electrochemical gradient (Warth, 1988). A similar model may apply to explain the resistance of acid-tolerant yeasts to acetate (Moon, 1983). However, Cole & Keenan (1987) consider that resistance of *Zygosacc. bailii* to weak acids is not the consequence of a simple pH_i-independent extrusion pumping mechanism, but that it includes an ability of the cell to tolerate significant pH_i falls with a consequent compensation by a re-establishment of a 'normal' pH_i value. Warth (1989a,b,c) has since demonstrated that organic acids, but not methyl paraben, are continuously removed from the cell. The prime permeability barrier to propanoic acid in *Zygosacch. bailii* is the plasma membrane and not the cell wall (Warth, 1989a).

Yeasts grown under different conditions show different levels of sensitivity to ethanol. Cells with linoleic acid-enriched membranes are more resistant than are cells with oleic acid-enriched membranes, from which it has been inferred (Gomez & Herrero, 1983; Rose, 1987) that a more fluid membrane enhances ethanol resistance.

6 CONCLUSIONS

A considerable variation exists in the response of various yeasts and moulds to biocides. Generally, fungi are more resistant than non-sporulating bacteria (except mycobacteria) to these agents, but more susceptible than bacterial spores. Consequently, sporicidal compounds such as glutaraldehyde and chlorine-based disinfectants will also be fungicidal. The mechanisms of action of fungitoxic compounds are often poorly understood, as are reasons for differing sensitivities shown by fungi.

Antifungal agents are important in product preservation, as disinfectants and as agricultural and industrial fungicides. Bent's (1979) review describes the range of chemical compounds investigated for use as agricultural fungicides, and illustrates the chemical structure of many of them.

7 REFERENCES

Aalto, T.R., Firman, M.C. & Rigler, N.E. (1953) *p*-Hydroxybenzoic acid esters as preservatives. I. Uses, antibacterial and antifungal studies, properties and determination. *Journal of the American Pharmaceutical Association, Scientific Edition*, **42**, 449–457.

Albert, A. (1979) *Selective Toxicity: The Physico-chemical Basis of Therapy*. 6th Ed. London: Chapman & Hall.

Armstrong, W.M. (1957) Surface-active agents and cellular metabolism. I. The effect of cationic detergents on the production of acid and carbon dioxide by baker's yeast. *Archives of Biochemistry and Biophysics*, **71**, 137–147.

Armstrong, W.M. (1958) The effect of some synthetic dyestuffs on the metabolism of baker's yeast. *Archives of Biochemistry and Biophysics*, **73**, 153–160.

Babich, H.L. & Stotzky, S. (1978) Influence of pH on inhibition of bacteria, fungi and coliphages by bisulphite and sulphite. *Environmental Research*, **15**, 405–417.

Balatsouras, G.D. & Polymenacos, N.G. (1963) Chemical preservatives as inhibitors of yeast growth. *Journal of Food Science*, **28**, 267–275.

Baldry, M.G.C. (1983) The bactericidal, fungicidal and sporicidal properties of hydrogen peroxide and peracetic acid. *Journal of Applied Bacteriology*, **54**, 417–423.

Baldry, M.G.C. & Fraser, J.A.L. (1988) Disinfection with peroxygens. In *Industrial Biocides* (ed. Payne, K.R.) Critical Reports on Applied Chemistry, Vol. 22, pp. 91–116. Chichester: John Wiley & Sons.

Balint, S., Farkas, V. & Bauer, S. (1976) Biosynthesis of β-glucans catalyzed by a particulate enzyme preparation from yeast. *FEBS Letters*, **64**, 44–47.

Ballou, C.E. (1976) Structure and biosynthesis of the mannan component of the yeast cell envelope. *Advances in Microbial Physiology*, **14**, 93–158.

Bandelin, F.J. (1950) The effects of pH on the efficiency of various mould inhibiting compounds. *Journal of the American Pharmaceutical Association, Scientific Edition*, **47**, 691–694.

Barnes, R.A. & Rogers, T.R.F. (1989) Control of an outbreak of nosocomial aspergillosis by laminar air-flow isolation. *Journal of Hospital Infection*, **14**, 89–94.

Bartnicki-Garcia, S. (1968) Cell wall chemistry, morphogenesis and taxonomy of fungi. *Annual Review of Microbiology*, **22**, 87–208.

Bell, T.A., Etchells, J.L. & Borg, A.F. (1959) Influence of sorbic acid on the growth of certain species of bacteria, yeasts and filamentous fungi. *Journal of Bacteriology*, **77**, 573–580.

Bent, K.J. (1979) Fungicides in perspective: 1979. *Endeavour*, **3**(1), 7–14.

Berger, T.J., Spadaro, J.A., Bierman, R., Chapin, S.E. & Becker, R.O. (1976) Antifungal properties of electrically generated metallic ions. *Antimicrobial Agents and Chemotherapy*, **10**, 856–860.

Block, S.S. (1983) Preservatives for industrial products. In *Disinfection, Sterilization and Preservation* (ed. Block, S.S.) 3rd Ed. pp. 608–655. Philadelphia: Lea & Febiger.

Bobichon, H. & Bouchet, P. (1987) Action of chlorhexidine on budding *Candida albicans*: scanning and transmission electron microscopic study. *Mycopathologia*, **100**, 27–35.

Brown, M.R.W. & Bullock, K. (1960) Mould spore suspensions and powders for use in fungicidal kinetic studies. Part I. Preliminary experiments with *Rhizopus nigricans* and *Penicillium digitatum*. *Journal of Pharmacy and Pharmacology*, **12**, 119T–126T.

British Pharmacopoeia (1988) London: HMSO.

Chapman, D.G. (1987) Preservatives available for use. In *Preservatives in the Food, Pharmaceutical and Environmental Industries* (eds Board, R.G., Allwood, M.C. & Banks, J.G.) Society for Applied Bacteriology Technical Series No. 22, pp. 177–195. Oxford: Blackwell Scientific Publications.

Chauhan, N.M. & Walters, V. (1961) Studies on the kinetics of fungicidal action. Part I. The effect of concentration and time on the viability of *Penicillium notatum* spores in solutions of phenol. *Journal of Pharmacy and Pharmacology*, **13**, 470–478.

Chauhan, N.M. & Walters, V. (1962) Studies on the kinetics of fungicidal action. Part II. The effect of temperature on the viability of *Penicillium notatum* spores in water and solutions of phenol. *Journal of Pharmacy and Pharmacology*, **14**, 605–610.

Chauhan, N.M., Rivers, S.M. & Walters, V. (1963) On the relationship between the effect of phenol on the oxygen uptake and the viability of *Penicillium notatum* spores. *Journal of Pharmacy & Pharmacology*, **15**, 143T–147T.

Cole, M.B. & Keenan, M.H.J. (1987) Effects of weak acids and external pH on the intracellular pH of *Zygosaccharomyces bailii*, and its implications in weak-acid resistance. *Yeast*, **3**, 23–32.

Croshaw, B. & Holland, V.R. (1984) Chemical preservatives: use of bronopol as a cosmetic preservative. In *Cosmetic and Drug Preservation. Principles and Practice* (ed. Kabara, J.J.) pp. 31–62. New York, Marcel Dekker.

Crosier, W.F., Waters, E.C. & Crosier, D.C. (1970) Development of tolerance to organic mercurials by *Pyrenophora avenae*. *Plant Disease Reporter*, **54**, 783–785.

Czerkowicz, T.J. (1983) Methods of testing fungicides. In *Disinfection, Sterilization and Preservation* (ed. Block, S.S.) 3rd Ed. pp. 998–1008. Philadelphia: Lea & Febiger.

Dabrowa, N., Landau, J.W. & Newcomer, V.D. (1972) Antifungal activity of glutaraldehyde *in vitro*. *Archives of Dermatology*, **105**, 555–557.

D'Arcy, P.F. (1971) Inhibition and destruction of moulds and yeasts. In *Inhibition and Destruction of the Microbial Cell* (ed. Hugo, W.B.) pp. 613–686. London: Academic Press.

Dawes, I.W. (1976) The inactivation of yeasts. In *Inhibition and Inactivation of Vegetative Microbes* (eds Skinner, F.A. & Hugo, W.B.) Society for Applied Bacteriology Symposium Series No. 5, pp. 279–304. London: Academic Press.

Dekker, J. (1987) Development of resistance to modern fungicides and strategies for its avoidance. In *Modern Selective Fungicides* (ed. Lyr, H.) pp. 39–52. Harlow, Essex: Longman.

Diamond, R.J. & Rose, A.H. (1970) Osmotic properties of spheroplasts from *Saccharomyces cerevisiae* grown at different temperatures. *Journal of Bacteriology*, **102**, 311–319.

Eigener, U. (1988) Disinfectant testing and relevance in practical application. In *Industrial Biocides* (ed. Payne, K.R.) Critical Reports on Applied Chemistry, Vol. 22, pp. 37–51. Chichester: John Wiley & Sons.

Elferink, J.G.R. (1974) The effect of ethylenediaminetetraacetic acid on yeast cell membranes. *Protoplasma*, **80**, 261–268.

Elferink, J.G.R. & Booij, H.L. (1974) Interaction of chlorhexidine with yeast cells. *Biochemical Pharmacology*, **23**, 1413–1419.

Farkas, V. (1979) Biosynthesis of cell walls of fungi. *Microbiological Reviews*, **43**, 117–144.

Favero, M.S. (1985) Sterilization, disinfection and antisepsis in the hospital. In *Manual of Clinical Microbiology* (eds Lennette, E.H., Balows, A., Hausler, W.J., jr. & Shadomy, H.J.) 4th Ed. pp. 129–137. Washington, DC: American Society for Microbiology.

Gadd, G.M. (1990) Metal tolerance. In *Microbiology of Extreme Environments* (ed. Edwards, C.) pp. 178–210. Milton Keynes: Open University Press.

Gadd, G.M. & Griffiths, A.J. (1978) Microorganisms and heavy metal toxicity. *Microbial Ecology*, **4**, 303–317.

Gadd, G.M. & White, C. (1989) Heavy metal and radionuclide accumulation and toxicity in fungi and yeasts. In *Metal–Microbe Interactions* (eds Poole, R.K. & Gadd, G.M.) Special Publications of the Society for General Microbiology, No. 26, pp. 19–38. Oxford: Oxford University Press.

Gale, E.F. (1986) Nature and development of phenotypic resistance to amphotericin B in *Candida albicans*. *Advances in Microbial Physiology*, **27**, 277–320.

Gale, E.F., Ingram, H., Kerridge, D., Notario, V. & Wayman, F. (1980) Reduction of amphotericin resistance in stationary phase cultures of *Calbica albicans* by treatment with enzymes. *Journal of General Microbiology*, **117**, 383–391.

Gardner, J.F. & Peel, M.M. (1986) *Introduction to Sterilization and Disinfection*. Edinburgh and London: Churchill Livingstone.

Georgopoulos, S.G. (1987) The genetics of fungicide resistance. In *Modern Selective Fungicides* (ed. Lyr, H.) pp. 53–63. Harlow, Essex: Longman.

Gerrard, H.N., Harkiss, A.V. & Bullock, K. (1960) Mould spore suspensions and powders for use in fungicidal kinetic studies. Part II. Preparations using *Penicillium spinulosum*. *Journal of Pharmacy and Pharmacology*, **12**, 127T–133T.

Gerston, H., Parmegiana, R., Weiner, A. & D'Ascoli, R. (1966) Fungal spore walls as a possible barrier against potential antifungal agents of the group copper (II) complexes of 5-halogeno- and 5-nitro-8-quinolinols. *Contributions of the Boyce Thompson Institute*, **23**, 219–228.

Gilbert, P., Beveridge, E.G. & Sissons, I. (1978) The uptake of some membrane-active agents by bacteria and yeast: possible microbiological examples of Z-curve adsorption. *Journal of Colloid and Interfacial Science*, **64**, 377–379.

Giles, C.H. & McKay, R.B. (1965) The adsorption of cationic (basic) dyes by fixed yeast cells. *Journal of Bacteriology*, **89**, 390–397.

Gomez, R.F. & Herrero, A.A. (1983) Chemical preservation of foods. In *Economic Microbiology* (ed. Rose, A.H.) Vol. 8: Food Microbiology, pp. 77–116. London: Academic Press.

Gooding, C.M., Melnick, D., Lawrence, R.L. & Luckmann, F.H. (1955) Sorbic acid as a fungistatic agent for foods. IX. Physico-chemical considerations in using sorbic acid to protect foods. *Food Research*, **20**, 639–648.

Gorman, S.P. & Scott, E.M. (1977) A quantitative evaluation of the antifungal properties of glutaraldehyde. *Journal of Applied Bacteriology*, **43**, 83–89.

Gorman, S.P., Scott, E.M. & Russell, A.D. (1980) Antimicrobial activity, uses and mechanism of action of glutaraldehyde. *Journal of Applied Bacteriology*, **48**, 161–190.

Gray, K.G. (1980) The microbiology of glutaraldehyde. *Australian Journal of Hospital Pharmacy*, **10**, 139–141.

Greenaway, W. (1972) Permeability of phenyl-Hg^+-resistant and phenyl-Hg^+-susceptible isolates of *Pyrenophora avenae* to the phenyl-Hg^+ ion. *Journal of General Microbiology*, **73**, 251–255.

Greenaway, W., Ward, S., Rajan, A.K. & Whatley, F.R. (1978). A spectrophotometric technique for recording uptake of an organomercurial by mycelial fungi. *Journal of General Microbiology*, **107**, 31–35.

Haag, T.E. & Loncrini, D.F. (1984) Esters of *para*-hydroxybenzoic acid. In *Cosmetic and Drug Preservation, Principles and Practice* (ed. Kabara, J.J.) pp. 63–67. New

York: Marcel Dekker.

Hall, A.L. (1984) Cosmetically acceptable phenoxyethanol. In *Cosmetic and Drug Preservation. Principles and Practice* (ed. Kabara, J.J.) pp. 79–108. New York: Marcel Dekker.

Hammond, S.M. & Carr, J.G. (1976) The antimicrobial activity of SO_2^- with particular reference to fermented and non-fermented fruit juices. In *Inhibition and Inactivation of Vegetative Microbes* (eds Skinner, F.A. & Hugo, W.B.) Society for Applied Bacteriology Symposium Series No. 5, pp. 89–110. London: Academic Press.

Hancock, R.E.W. (1984) Alterations in outer membrane permeability. *Annual Review of Microbiology*, **38**, 237–264.

Hansch, C. & Lien, E.J. (1971) Structure–activity relationships in antifungal agents: a survey. *Journal of Medicinal Chemistry*, **14**, 653–669.

Heinzel, M. (1988) The phenomena of resistance to disinfectants and preservatives. In *Industrial Biocides* (ed. Payne, K.R.) Critical Reports on Applied Chemistry, Vol. 22, pp. 52–67. Chichester: John Wiley & Sons.

Hugo, W.B. (1971) Amidines. In *Inhibition and Destruction of the Microbial Cell* (ed. Hugo, W.B.) pp. 121–136. London: Academic Press.

Hugo, W.B. (1981) The mode of action of antiseptics. In *Handbuch der Antiseptik* (ed. Weuffen, W., Kramer, A., Gröschel, D., Berencsi, G. & Bulka, E.) Band I, Teil 2, pp. 39–77. Berlin: VEB Verlag Volk und Gesundheit.

Hugo, W.B. & Newton, J.M. (1964) The adsorption of iodine from solution by microorganisms and by serum. *Journal of Pharmacy and Pharmacology*, **16**, 48–55.

Hunter, D.R. & Segal, I.H. (1973) Effect of weak acids on amino acid transport by *Penicillium chrysogenum*: evidence for a proton or charge gradient as the driving force. *Journal of Bacteriology*, **113**, 1184–1192.

Indge, K.J. (1968a) The effect of various anions and cations on the lysis of yeast protoplasts by osmotic shock. *Journal of General Microbiology*, **41**, 425–432.

Indge, K.J. (1968b) Metabolic lysis of yeast protoplasts. *Journal of General Microbiology*, **41**, 433–440.

Kabara, J.J. (1984) Composition and structure of microorganisms. In *Cosmetic and Drug Preservation. Principles and Practice* (ed. Kabara, J.J.) pp. 21–27. New York: Marcel Dekker.

Karabit, M.S., Juneskans, O.T. & Lundgren, P. (1985) Studies on the evaluation of preservative efficacy. I. The determination of antimicrobial characteristics of phenol. *Acta Pharmaceutica Suecica*, **22**, 281–290.

Karabit, M.S., Juneskans, O.T. & Lundgren, P. (1986) Studies on the evaluation of preservative efficacy. II. The determination of antimicrobial characteristics of benzyl alcohol. *Journal of Clinical and Hospital Pharmacy*, **11**, 281–289.

Karabit, M.S., Juneskans, O.T. & Lundgren, P. (1988) Studies on the evaluation of preservative efficacy. III. The determination of antimicrobial characteristics of benzalkonium chloride. *International Journal of Pharmaceutics*, **46**, 141–147.

Karabit, M.S., Juneskans, O.T. & Lundgren, P. (1989) Factorial designs in the evaluation of preservative efficacy. *International Journal of Pharmaceutics*, **56**, 169–174.

Kato, N., Miyawaki, N. & Sakasawa, C. (1982) Oxidation of formaldehyde by resistant yeasts *Debaryomyces vanriji* and *Trichosporon penicillatum*. *Agricultural and Biological Chemistry*, **46**, 655–661.

Kato, N., Miyawaki, N. & Sakasawa, C. (1983) Formaldehyde dehydrogenase from formaldehyde-resistant *Debaryomyces vanriji* FT-1 and *Pseudomonas putida* F61. *Agricultural and Biological Chemistry*, **47**, 415–416.

Kerridge, D. (1986) Mode of action of clinically important antifungal drugs. *Advances in Microbial Physiology*, **27**, 1–72 and 321.

Knaysi, G. & Gordon, M. (1930) The manner of death of certain bacteria and yeast when subjected to mild chemical and physical agents. *Journal of Infectious Diseases*, **47**, 303–317.

Krebs, H.A., Wiggins, D., Stubbs, M., Sols, A. & Bedoya, F. (1983) Studies on the antifungal action of benzoate. *Biochemical Journal*, **214**, 657–663.

Lehmann, R.H. (1988) Synergisms in disinfectant formulations. In *Industrial Biocides* (ed. Payne, K.R.) Critical Reports on Applied Chemistry, Vol. 22, pp. 68–90. Chichester: John Wiley & Sons.

Leuck, E. (1980) *Antimicrobial Food Additives*, New York: Springer-Verlag.

Lukens, R.J. (1971) *Chemistry of Fungicidal Action*. Molecular Biology, Biochemistry and Biophysics. No. 10. London: Chapman & Hall.

Lukens, R.J. (1983) Antimicrobial agents in crop production. In *Disinfection, Sterilization and Preservation* (ed. Block, S.S.) 3rd Ed. pp. 695–713. Philadelphia: Lea & Febiger.

Lyr, H. (1987a) Selectivity in modern fungicides and its basis. In *Modern Selective Fungicides* (ed. Lyr, H.) pp. 31–88. Harlow, Essex: Longman.

Lyr, H. (1987b) *Modern Selective Fungicides*. Harlow, Essex: Longman.

Marth, E.H., Capp, C.M., Hasenzahl, L., Jackson, H.W. & Hussong, R.V. (1966) Degradation of potassium sorbate by *Penicillium* species. *Journal of Dairy Science*, **49**, 1197–1205.

Macris, B.J. (1974) Mechanism of benzoic acid uptake by *Saccharomyces cerevisiae*. *Applied Microbiology*, **30**, 503–506.

Maddox, D.N. (1982) The role of *p*-hydroxybenzoates in modern cosmetics. *Cosmetics & Toiletries*, **97** (11), 85–88.

Miller, L.P. (1969) Mechanisms for reaching the site of action. In *Fungicides. An Advanced Treatise* (ed. Torgeson, D.C.) Vol. 2, pp. 1–58. New York: Academic Press.

Moon, N.J. (1983) Inhibition of the growth of acid tolerant yeasts by acetate, lactate and propionate and their synergistic mixtures. *Journal of Applied Bacteriology*, **55**, 453–460.

Navarro, J.M. & Monsan, P. (1976) Etude du mécanisme d'interaction du glutaraldéhyde avec les microorganismes.

Annales Microbiologie (Institut Pasteur), **127B**, 295–307.

Norris, P.R. & Kelley, D.P. (1979) Accumulation of metals by bacteria and yeasts. *Developments in Industrial Microbiology*, **20**, 299–308.

Notario, V., Gale, E.F., Kerridge, D. & Wayman, F. (1982) Phenotypic resistance to amphotericin B in *Candida albicans*: relationship to glucan metabolism. *Journal of General Microbiology*, **128**, 761–777.

Odds, F.C. (1988) *Candida and Candidosis. A Review and Bibliography*. London: Baillière Tindall.

Orth, D.S. (1979) Linear regression method for rapid determination of cosmetic preservative efficacy. *Journal of the Society of Cosmetic Chemists*, **30**, 321–332.

Orth, D.S. (1980) Establishing cosmetic preservative efficacy by use of D-values. *Journal of the Society of Cosmetic Chemists*, **31**, 165–172.

Orth, D.S. (1984) Evaluation of preservatives in cosmetic products. In *Cosmetic and Drug Preservation. Principles and Practice* (ed. Kabara, J.J.) pp. 403–421. New York: Marcel Dekker.

Owens, R.G. (1963) Chemistry and physiology of fungicidal action. *Annual Review of Phytopathology*, **1**, 77–100.

Owens, R.G. (1969) Organic sulfur compounds. In *Fungicides. An advanced Treatise* (ed. Torgeson, D.C.) Vol. 2, pp. 147–301. New York: Academic Press.

Owens, R.G. & Hayes, A.D. (1964) Biochemical action of thiram and some dialkyl dithiocarbamates. *Contributions of the Boyce Thompson Institute*, **22**, 227–240.

Pitt, J.I. (1974) Resistance of some food spoilage yeasts to preservatives. *Food Technology in Australia*, **26**, 238–241.

Pospisil, J. (1989) Efficacy of selected disinfectants and antiseptic preparations against potentially pathogenic micromycetes. *Cs. Epidemiologie, Mikrobiologie, Immunologie*, **38**, 180–187.

Quinn, P.J. (1987) Evaluation of veterinary disinfectants and disinfection processes. In *Disinfection in Veterinary and Farm Animal Practice* (eds Linton, A.H., Hugo, W.B. & Russell, A.D.) pp. 66–116. Oxford: Blackwell Scientific Publications.

Report (1984) Final report on the safety assessment of methylparaben, ethylparaben, propylparaben and butylparaben. *Journal of the American College of Toxicology*, **3**, 147–209.

Rivers S.M. & Walters, V. (1966) The effect of benzoic acid, phenol and hydroxybenzoates on the oxygen uptake and growth of some lipolytic agents. *Journal of Pharmacy and Pharmacology*, **18**, 45S–51S.

Rose, A.H. (1987) Responses to the chemical environment. In *The Yeasts* (ed. Rose, A.H. & Harrison, J.S.) 2nd Edn., Vol. 2: *Yeasts and the Environment*, pp. 5–40. London: Academic Press.

Russell, A.D. (1971) Ethylenediaminetetra-acetic acid. In *Inhibition and Destruction of the Microbial Cell* (ed. Hugo, W.B.) pp. 209–224. London: Academic Press.

Russell, A.D. & Chopra, I. (1990) *Understanding Antibacterial Action and Resistance*. Chichester: Ellis Horwood.

Russell, A.D. & Hugo, W.B. (1988) Perturbation of homeostatic mechanisms in bacteria by pharmaceuticals. *FEMS Symposium No. 44*, pp. 206–219. Bath: Bath University Press.

Russell, N.J. & Gould, G.W. (1991) (Eds) *Food Preservatives*. Glasgow & London: Blackie.

Russell, P. (1955) Inactivation of phenylmercuric acetate in ground wood pulp by a mercury-resistant strain of *Penicillium roqueforti* Thom. *Nature, London*, **176**, 1123–1124.

Scharff, T.G. & Beck, J.L. (1959) Effects of surface-active agents on carbohydrate metabolism in yeast. *Proceedings of the Society of Experimental Biology and Medicine*, **100**, 307–311.

Scherer, R., Loudon, L. & Gerhardt, P. (1974) Porosity of the yeast cell wall and membrane. *Journal of Bacteriology*, **118**, 534–540.

Sevag, M.G. & Ross, O.A. (1944) Studies on the mechanism of the inhibitory action of zephiran on yeast cells. *Journal of Bacteriology*, **48**, 677–682.

Simon, E.W. (1953a) The action of nitrophenols in respiration and glucose assimilation in yeast. *Journal of Experimental Botany*, **4**, 377–392.

Simon, E.W. (1953b) Dinitrocresol, cyanide and the Pasteur effect in yeast. *Journal of Experimental Botany*, **4**, 393–402.

Simon, E.W. (1953c) Mechanisms of dinitrophenol toxicity. *Biological Reviews*, **28**, 453–479.

Somers, E. (1962) Mechanisms of toxicity of agricultural fungicides. *Science Progress*, **198**, 218–234.

Spaulding, E.H. (1972) Chemical disinfection and antisepsis in the hospital. *Journal of Hospital Research*, **9**, 5–31.

Spicher, G. & Peters, J. (1976) Microbial resistance to formaldehyde. I. Comparative quantitative studies in some selected species of vegetative bacteria, bacterial spores, fungi, bacteriophages and viruses (in German). *Zentralblatt für Bakteriologie, Parasitenkunde, Infektionskrankheiten und Hygiene, I. Abteilung Originale Reihe B*, **163**, 486–508.

Splittstoesser, D.F., Queale, D.T. & Mattick, L.R. (1978) Growth of *Saccharomyces bisporus* var. *bisporus*, a yeast resistant to sorbic acid. *American Journal of Enology and Viticology*, **29** 272–276.

Stonehill, A.A., Krop, S. & Borick, P.M. (1963) Buffered glutaraldehyde, a new chemical sterilizing solution. *American Journal of Hospital Pharmacy*, **20**, 458–465.

Tadeusiak, B. (1976) Fungicidal activity of glutaraldehyde. *Roczniki Panstwowego Zakladu Higieny* (Poland), **27**, 689–695.

Torgeson, D.C. (1969) Ed., *Fungicides. An advanced Treatise*. Vol. 2. London: Academic Press.

Trueman, J.R. (1971) The halogens. In *Inhibition and Destruction of the Microbial Cell*. (ed. Hugo, W.B.) pp. 137–183. London: Academic Press.

United States Pharmacopoeia (1985) Edition XXI. Easton, Pennsylvania: Mack Publishing Co.

Wallhäusser, K.H. (1984) Antimicrobial preservatives used by the cosmetic industry. In *Cosmetic and Drug Preser-*

vation. Principles and Practice (ed. Kabara, J.J.) pp. 605–745. New York: Marcel Dekker.

Walters, T.H., Furr, J.R. & Russell, A.D. (1983) Antifungal action of chlorhexidine. *Microbios*, **38**, 195–204.

Warth, A.D. (1977) Mechanism of resistance of *Saccharomyces bailii* to benzoic, sorbic and other weak acids used as food preservatives. *Journal of Applied Bacteriology*, **43**, 215–230.

Warth, A.D. (1985) Resistance of yeast species to benzoic and sorbic acids and to sulfur dioxide. *Journal of Food Protection*, **48**, 564–569.

Warth, A.D. (1986) Effect of nutrients and pH on the resistance of *Zygosaccharomyces bailii* to benzoic acid. *International Journal of Food Microbiology*, **3** 263–271.

Warth, A.D. (1988) Effect of benzoic acid on growth yield of yeasts differing in their resistance to preservatives. *Applied and Environmental Microbiology*, **54**, 2091–2095.

Warth, A.D. (1989a) Transport of benzoic and propanoic acids by *Zygosaccharomyces bailii*. *Journal of General Microbiology*, **135**, 1383–1390.

Warth, A.D. (1989b) Relationships among cell size, membrane permeability and preservative resistance in yeast species. *Applied and Environmental Microbiology*, **55**, 2995–2999.

Warth, A.D. (1989c) Relationships between the resistance of yeasts to acetic, propanoic and benzoic acids and to methyl paraben and pH. *International Journal of Food Microbiology*, **8**, 343–349.

Weiner, N.D., Hart, F. & Zografi, G. (1965) Application of the Ferguson principle to the antimicrobial activity of quaternary ammonium salts. *Journal of Pharmacy and Pharmacology*, **17**, 350–355.

Wilkinson, J.F. (1986) *Introduction to Microbiology*, 3rd Ed. Oxford: Blackwell Scientific Publications.

Woodcock, P.M. (1988) Biguanides as industrial biocides. In *Industrial Biocides* (ed. Payne, K.R.) Critical Reports on Applied Chemistry, Vol. 22, pp. 19–36. Chichester: John Wiley & Sons.

Yanagita, T. (1980) Studies on the formaldehyde resistance of *Aspergillus* fungi attacking the silkworm larvae. II. Aldehyde dehydrogenase of *Aspergillus* spp. *Journal of Sericultural Science of Japan*, **49**, 45–50.

Chapter 6
Virucidal Activity of Disinfectants

1 INTRODUCTION

The control of viral infections relies on specific measures appropriate for each virus family. Decisions relating to individual viruses are usually determined by their importance in human or animal populations, their mode of spread and their disease-producing capacity. Measures which may be applied for the prevention or control of viral disease are listed in Table 6.1. Whether based on vaccination, disinfection or control of arthropod vectors, these measures are aimed at lessening the chance of infection in susceptible populations.

Viruses of different families vary greatly in their resistance to disinfection procedures, enveloped viruses usually being more sensitive than non-enveloped viruses. Each type of chemical disinfectant has a characteristic range of antiviral activity. Efficiency, however, may be influenced by many factors, some relating to the number and accessibility of the viruses and others relating to the presence of organic matter or interfering compounds in the environment. Standard procedures for the evaluation of chemical disinfectants in virucidal tests are not yet agreed internationally, and in many instances the ability of chemical compounds to inactivate viruses is either inferred from bactericidal test procedures or not reported. Assessing the virucidal activity of disinfectants is more demanding and expensive than bactericidal testing procedures, since chemical disinfectants are usually toxic for tissue at concentrations active against viruses.

Physical methods of inactivating viruses are generally more readily standardized than chemical ones, although ultraviolet (UV) radiation of biological materials presents certain difficulties and low-pressure mercury vapour lamps used to generate UV light gradually lose their efficiency. Filtration is used mainly to remove bacterial and fungal cells from fluids or gases, but ultrafilters can also be used to remove viruses. Membrane filters can be manufactured from various polymers to precise pore sizes but the porosity of depth filters cannot be accurately determined.

2 CULTIVATION OF VIRUSES

Viruses replicate only within living cells. Some viruses are restricted in the kinds of cells in which they replicate *in vitro* and a few have not yet been cultivated under laboratory conditions. The host cell must provide the energy and synthetic machinery for the production of viral proteins and nucleic acid. Most viruses can be grown in cultured cells, embryonated hens' eggs or in laboratory animals. In veterinary virology the natural host animal can also be used for the cultivation of viruses. *In vitro* cultivation of viruses in cell cultures is essential for the study of their mode of replication, for diagnostic virology and, in many instances, for the evaluation of virucides. Many types of cells undergo only a few divisions *in vitro* before dying off, while others can survive for many generations and some can be propagated indefinitely. There are three basic types of cell culture: primary cultures, diploid cell lines and continuous cell lines. Primary cultures are made by dispersing cells, often from foetal organs or tissues, with trypsin. Although they are unable to grow for more than a few passages in culture, they contain several cell types and are thus very sensitive to many animal viruses. Diploid cell lines are secondary cultures which have undergone a change that allows their limited culture that roughly correlates to the life span of the species of origin — up to 50 passages for foetal human cells and approximately 10 for foetal cells from cattle or horses. Continuous cell lines are cells of a single type that are capable of indefinite propagation *in vitro*. They often originate from malignant tissues or by spontaneous transformation of a diploid cell line. The type of cell culture used for virus cultivation depends on the sensitivity of the cells to a particular virus.

Avian embryos have been used for more than half a century for the cultivation of many viruses. Although largely replaced by tissue culture methods, developing chick embryos are still used for isolation and cultivation of many avian viruses. They are also used for vaccine production and for producing high yields of certain viruses, notably influenza virus and Newcastle disease virus. Eggs for virological investigations should, ideally, be selected from specific pathogen-free (SPF) poultry to ensure freedom from salmonellosis, avian leukosis, Marek's disease, mycoplasma agents and adenovirus infection. The vaccination programme applied in flocks used to supply eggs for virology should be known, since passive antibody transmission via the yolk sac may interfere with isolation of some poultry viruses.

Animals are still essential for many procedures in virology. They are used for virus isolation, to study virus pathogenicity and to evaluate experimental vaccines. They are also used extensively for production of antisera and, in recent years, mice have been commonly used for implantation of hybridomas which secrete monoclonal antibodies.

3 ASSAY OF VIRUS PARTICLES IN SUSPENSION AND VIRAL INFECTIVITY

The number of virus particles in suspension can be counted directly by electron microscopy. Several methods may be used. The viral suspension can be mixed with a known concentration of latex particles to provide an easily recognizable marker and the ratio of virus particles to latex beads can be determined. Viruses can be deposited on the grid by ultracentrifugation or allowed to diffuse into agar on the underside of an ultrathin carbon-coated plastic film on a copper grid, thereby allowing enumeration of the number in a known volume.

A relatively concentrated preparation of virus is necessary for these procedures, and infectious virus particles cannot be distinguished from non-infectious ones.

In a method analogous to bacterial colony counts, virus numbers can be estimated using monolayers of cultured cells. A series of 10-fold dilutions of a viral suspension is inoculated onto monolayers of cultured cells, the virions allowed time to absorb to the cell and then overlaid with agar or methylcellulose gel. This ensures that viral progeny are restricted to the immediate vicinity of the infected cells. Each infectious virus unit produces a plaque, a localized focus of infected cells, which is visible after staining of the monolayer. Some viruses such as herpesviruses and poxviruses will produce plaques even in cell monolayers maintained in liquid medium. As infection with a single virus particle can form a plaque, the infectivity titre of the original virus suspension is expressed in terms of plaque-forming units (PFU) per ml.

When inoculated onto the chorioallantoic membrane of an embryonated egg, some viruses such as vaccinia form pocks. Such viruses can be quantitated by relating the number of pocks counted to the virus dilution inoculated.

Another type of assay, referred to as a quantal assay, is used to determine the effect of a particular dilution of viral suspension on cell cultures, embryonated eggs or experimental animals. The data produced by this method relate to changes induced by the dilution of virus that results in visible changes such as death of a chick embryo or infection in an experimental animal. The number of infectious virus particles in the inoculum is not determined by this procedure. The endpoint of a quantal titration is taken to be that dilution of virus which infects or kills 50% of the inoculated hosts (ID_{50} for animals, or $TCID_{50}$ in tissue culture).

4 DETECTION OF VIRAL GROWTH IN CELL CULTURE

The growth of viruses in cell culture can be monitored by a number of biochemical procedures which demonstrate intracellular increase in viral macromolecules, or by simpler methods that demonstrate degenerative changes.

The most easily recognized effects of infection with lytic viruses are cytopathic effects (CPE), which can be observed both macroscopically and microscopically. Virus-induced cytopathic effects include cell lysis or necrosis and formation of inclusion bodies or syncytia. Most viruses produce some obvious cytopathic effects in infected cells that are characteristic of the virus group. Cells infected with viruses which bud from cytoplasmic membranes, such as orthomyxoviruses and paramyxoviruses, acquire the ability to adsorb suitable erythrocytes to their cell membranes. This phenomenon is referred to as haemadsorption, and in some cases occurs in the absence of cytopathic effects. Haemagglutination is a different but related phenomenon, in which erythrocytes are agglutinated by free virus such as influenza virus. Although haemagglutination is not a sensitive indicator of small numbers of virions, its simplicity provides a convenient assay if large amounts of virus are present.

Some viruses replicate in cell culture without producing CPE. These viruses can be detected by interference, i.e. the ability of a non-cytopathic virus to prevent the entry and CPE of other cytopathic strains of the same virus which are added later. Oncogenic viruses may induce morphological transformation, accompanied by loss of contact inhibition and piling up of cells into discrete foci.

Newly synthesized viral antigen can be detected by staining the fixed cell monolayer with antibody that has been labelled or conjugated with material that can be visualized with either the light or electron microscope. Antibody labelled with fluorescein or peroxidase is commonly used for light microscopy. For electron microscopy, antibody tagged with large particles such as ferritin is often used.

Virus growth in embryonated eggs may, depending on the virus used, result in dwarfing of the embryo, pocks on the chorioallantoic membrane, development of haemagglutinins in the embryonic fluids, or death of the embryo.

5 VIRUCIDAL TESTS

Inactivation of viruses can be achieved by a number of physical or chemical methods (Table 6.1). There

Table 6.1 Methods of removing, inactivating, preventing the spread or limiting the impact of viruses or unconventional infectious agents in susceptible populations

Biological methods	Physical methods	Chemical or biochemical methods
Isolation of infected or suspect groups	Cleaning	Disinfectants
	Sonication	Detergents
Vaccination of susceptible population	Desiccation	pH changes
	Filtration	Photodynamic inactivation
Chemotherapy, immunomodulation	Heat (moist, dry)	Lipid solvents
		Enzymes
Control of wildlife reservoirs of infection	Centrifugation	
Prevention of animal access to contaminated pasture and water	Radiation (ionizing, non-ionizing)	
Control of insect vectors		
Removal of suspect animal material from food chain		

is great variation, however, in the susceptibility of different viruses to pH and temperature changes, solvents, enzymes and detergents. Virucidal tests with chemical compounds present many challenges because of the diversity of viral agents encountered, and also because of the many different systems required to demonstrate survival or inactivation of such a heterogeneous group of infectious agents. Much of the published data on virucidal compounds has been obtained under a variety of experimental conditions and results are, accordingly, often difficult to compare. To add further to the difficulty of interpretation, standardization of virucidal tests usually assumes that virus particles are in an unaggregated state and used at a given concentration. Because of their natural association with tissue cells in which they are usually grown, both of these conditions are often difficult to achieve.

5.1 Evaluation of chemical disinfectants

Chemical disinfectants cannot be reliably evaluated on the basis of the amount of active chemical agent present in the formulation, since this does not necessarily correlate with virucidal activity. The spectrum of activity of a given virucidal disinfectant cannot be predicted from its formulation alone. Alterations arising from dilution, pH changes and interaction with organic matter or other interfering substances must also be considered.

Chemical disinfectants usually have a characteristic virucidal action and individual disinfectants vary in their mode of action, rate of killing and in accordance with prevailing test conditions. Disinfectants are not selectively toxic for microorganisms, they also kill mammalian cells and must be removed, diluted to non-toxic levels or neutralized before treated viruses are added to test systems to determine virus survival or inactivation. Among the more important variables in evaluation of virucides are: the characteristics of the virus selected, number of virions present, concentration of virucide, hydrogen ion concentration, temperature, duration of exposure and the methods used to avoid cytotoxic effects of the chemical virucide (Table 6.2).

Table 6.2 Factors influencing virucide evaluation

1	Characteristics of the virus selected, particularly those relating to its cytopathic effects in tissue culture, changes induced in chick embryos or its ability to produce disease in susceptible animals
2	Concentrations of virucide used
3	Concentration of virus added to virucide and, if in suspension, presence or absence of aggregates
4	Contact time between virus and disinfectant
5	Methods employed to avoid cytotoxic effects of virucide
6	Temperature at which experiment was conducted
7	Presence of organic matter or other interfering substances
8	pH of buffer employed and its ionic concentration
9	Sensitivity of test method for assessing virus survival
10	Reproducibility of test procedure
11	Type of controls employed to evaluate toxic effects of disinfectants or inactivators in test procedure
12	Reduction in virus titre compared to untreated virus control taken as evidence of effectiveness

6 MECHANISMS OF VIRAL INACTIVATION

Most viruses pathogenic for humans and animals have limited tolerance to extreme variations in their physical environment. They also have limited survival ability away from host cells unless protected from adverse influences by the local microenvironment or by adsorption to particulate matter. In their natural environment many viruses tend to be associated with solids such as cellular debris or organic matter and are, therefore, not in a 'free' state (Berg, 1973). The presence of organic matter, particularly in aggregated form, may afford protection to viruses against physical or chemical inactivation.

Inactivation of viruses implies that, as a consequence of treatment, there is permanent loss of infectivity. Released nucleic acid must also be destroyed before a virus can be considered truly inactivated. The exposure of a population of virions to physical or chemical inactivating procedures for a limited time results in the inactivation of a proportion of the virions, while others retain infectivity. The proportion of virions that is inactivated is related to the *dose* (product of time × concentration or intensity). When a microbial population is exposed to a lethal agent such as a disinfectant, the kinetics of inactivation are usually exponential, especially when dealing with bacteria. With viruses, the shape of the survival curve can be used to evaluate the mechanism of inactivation and the dose of the agent required to achieve a certain degree of inactivation. The inactivation dose is inversely related to the complexity of the organism and viruses are about 10,000 times more resistant than man to the lethal effects of radiation (Shay *et al.*, 1988).

The rate of killing of bacteria following exposure to lethal agents such as heat or chemical disinfectants follows the kinetics of a first-order reaction in which the logarithm of the number of survivors decreases as a linear function of time of exposure (Fig. 6.1). Inactivation of viruses should, ideally, follow a similar pattern. For this to happen viruses should occur as discrete units equally susceptible to the disinfection procedure, both viruses and disinfectant should be uniformly dispersed in the fluid phase, the disinfectant should be stable in its chemical composition and organic matter or other interfering substances should be absent from the reaction (Thurman & Gerba, 1988). Survival curves for viruses may follow a linear pattern (single-hit curve), exhibiting the kinetics of a first-order reaction, or they may exhibit multiple-hit or multicomponent patterns which are non-linear (Davis & Dulbecco, 1980). Errors in interpretation may occur when the survival curve is of either the multiple-hit or multicomponent type. In virucidal tests, any aggregation of virus, alteration in disinfectant stability or change in the experimental methodology which alters the kinetics of disinfection is likely to cause deviation from ideal linear inactivation.

Different types of viruses have varying susceptibilities to disinfectants in general and, in addition, the susceptibility of a given virus will vary with the type of disinfectant employed. Inactivation may result from changes in virus conformation, damage to the envelope, capsid proteins, or the nucleic acid. Other changes may relate to alteration in the overall charge of virus particles or alteration in the surface components at, or adjacent to the attachment site, which interacts with the receptor on the surface of a host cell. Virus clumping or aggregation may prevent contact with disinfectant as some

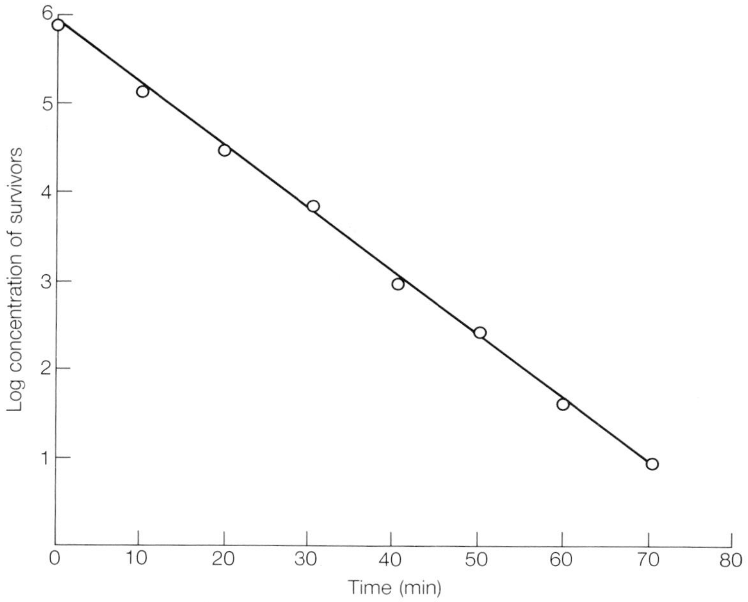

Fig. 6.1 Diagrammatic representation of exponential killing of bacteria by a chemical disinfectant.

virions in the centre of aggregated masses may not be acted on by the disinfectant.

6.1 Thermal inactivation of viruses

The effect of temperature on viruses is more readily evaluated than chemical methods of inactivation, because procedures to eliminate the cytotoxic effects of chemicals are not required. All types of micro-organisms can be killed by moist or dry heat at a temperature appropriate to their level of resistance. There is considerable variation in the heat stability of different viruses. Mechanisms of thermal injury vary from denaturation and coagulation of protein to damage to nucleic acid. Heat also causes a loss of functional integrity of some viruses such as human rotavirus, with evidence of morphological damage at lower temperatures and disintegration of virions at higher temperatures (Rodgers *et al.*, 1985).

6.2 Ultraviolet radiation

The effectiveness of UV light as a virucidal agent correlates with the shorter wavelengths of the UV spectrum, from 250 to 260 nm. The mechanism of UV radiation injury is attributed to absorption by, and resultant damage to nucleic acid. Alteration in genetic information through the formation of pyrimidine dimers or other induced changes in nucleic acid may inactivate some viruses or lead to mutational changes (Thurman & Gerba, 1988). The effects of UV light seem to be dose-related and may vary from interference with virus uncoating to disintegration of the virion. Rapid morphological changes have been observed in some viruses with loss of the outer capsid coat evident in rotaviruses after short exposure (Rodgers *et al.*, 1985). The survival curves of viruses and bacteria following exposure to UV light are similar, but some viruses exhibit much greater resistance to UV irradiation than bacteria (Chang *et al.*, 1985).

The disinfectant action of sunlight is due primarily to its content of UV light, most of which is screened out by the ozone layer or glass. For disinfection purposes, UV light can be produced artificially by mercury vapour lamps. Unlike ionizing radiation, the energy of UV radiation is low and its power of penetration is poor. It does not penetrate solids but will affect organisms in thin layers of water, in air or on flat surfaces. Surface disinfection by UV radiation is useful in laboratory safety cabinets and in small rooms where aseptic manipulations are carried out. UV light is readily absorbed by organic matter and its virucidal activity is lowered by a dusty atmosphere or by thin layers of protein on surfaces being treated.

6.3 Ionizing radiations

Ionizing radiations are classified according to their physical properties and can be divided into two major categories: (a) those that have mass and that may be charged or uncharged, and (b) those that occur as a form of energy only. Particulate ionizing radiations are composed of particles moving at high velocities such as cathode rays, which are streams of artificially accelerated electrons. Some of the ionizing radiations are products of radioactive decay (α-, β- and γ-rays), others are produced by X-ray apparatus and by nuclear reactors. The ionizing radiations that are of greatest practical value for destruction of micro-organisms are the electromagnetic X-rays, γ-rays and particulate cathode rays. These radiations have a much higher energy content than UV radiation, and consequently have a greater capacity to produce lethal effects. The penetrating power of ionizing radiations contributes to their effectiveness as sterilizing agents.

The effect of ionizing radiations on micro-organisms depends on the amount of energy absorbed by the material being treated. Various changes take place in material exposed to ionizing radiations and these changes are attributed to ionization, radical formation and biochemical alterations. Water is ionized; when oxygen is present superoxide radicals may be formed, and damage to DNA results from the release of highly active radicals. The inactivation dose for micro-organisms is inversely related to the complexity of the organisms, bacterial spores and viruses being among the most resistant structures (Shay *et al.*, 1988).

6.4 Inactivation of viruses by chemical methods

A wide range of chemicals—including acids, alcohols, alkalis, alkylating agents, some dyes, detergents, halogens, heavy metals, solvents, phenolic compounds and surface-active compounds—are capable of inactivating viruses. Individual viruses vary in their susceptibility to chemical inactivation. The presence or absence of an outer envelope on a virus has an important bearing on its susceptibility to chemical disinfection. In general, chemical substances such as ether, alcohol or detergent which react with the envelope of lipophilic viruses inactivate them, whereas non-enveloped viruses are resistant to such compounds. Virucidal compounds may bring about their effect by denaturing protein, lipid, nucleic acid or specific enzymes.

Minor morphological changes have been observed in poliovirus treated with halogen disinfectants, and iodine inactivation was accompanied by defined structural changes (Taylor & Butler, 1982). Viruses are usually stable at pH values close to 7. Some, such as the virus of foot-and-mouth disease, are rapidly inactivated in acid conditions but in common with other picornaviruses are resistant to phenolic and quaternary ammonium disinfectants. Principles of viral inactivation have been reviewed by Klein & Deforest (1983).

7 VIRUCIDAL TESTING PROCEDURES

The virucidal activity of chemical disinfectants may be determined by tube suspension methods, carrier methods, plaque-formation techniques *in vitro* and by evaluating virus survival in susceptible laboratory animals. Some viruses such as Norwalk virus, which lack an animal model and cannot be grown readily in cell culture systems, may require human volunteers to assess their survival.

Before virucidal tests can be standardized to an acceptable level, several technical problems have to be resolved. The number of infectious virus particles in the test system should be known, and the number required to initiate infection in host cells or susceptible animals should be determined. The natural association of viruses with tissue cells or debris often interferes with the reproducibility of such procedures. Factors which may influence the evaluation of virucides are listed in Table 6.2.

7.1 Toxicity of disinfectants for tissue culture

A serious difficulty in evaluating the inactivation of viruses by disinfectants is the cytotoxicity of many chemical compounds for mammalian cells. Dilution may be used to overcome this effect when the virus titre is high and the compound has low toxicity. This may lead to erroneous conclusions, however, if surviving viruses are in low numbers in the reaction mixture and if high numbers of viruses are required to initiate infection or induce demonstrable changes in the test system. Neutralization of the disinfectant is an alternative to dilution but neutralizing compounds must also be free of cytotoxic effects. Virucidal tests employing neutralizing compounds require the following controls: (a) virus alone; (b) virus and disinfectant; (c) disinfectant alone; (d) virus, disinfectant and neutralizer; (e) neutralizer alone and (f) virus and neutralizer. Samples from each control should be used for chick embryo or cell culture inoculation, and any cytopathic effects should be interpreted with reference to the changes induced by disinfectant or neutralizer alone or in combination with virus.

Dialysis has been proposed as a method of removing or reducing the concentration of disinfectant in virucidal tests to a level that would not interfere with the growth of cell cultures. Gel filtration using a cross-linked dextran gel has been employed for the separation of virus and disinfectant (Blackwell & Chen, 1970). By this means diluent and disinfectant are absorbed into the gel, while high molecular weight particles such as viruses are excluded.

Ultrafiltration has been employed as a method of overcoming the limitations of dilution of the disinfectant (Boudouma *et al.*, 1984). In this procedure the virus suspension and disinfectant are mixed, and after specified incubation intervals the mixture is sampled. The sample aliquot is diluted in phosphate-buffered saline to stop the reaction, concentrated at 4°C by ultrafiltration and titrated for virus survival. The disinfectant is removed during ultrafiltration and its possible cytotoxic effects on cell cultures thus avoided.

Other possible methods of separating virus from disinfectant include density-gradient ultracentrifugation, preparative isoelectric focusing and a range of electrophoretic procedures using support media of large pore size. Figure 6.2 illustrates methods of testing virucides, and includes methods which can be employed to overcome the cytotoxic effects of disinfectants.

7.2 Virucidal assays

Methods of testing virucides include suspension tests, carrier methods, plaque suppression tests with animal viruses, and bacteriophage test systems (Quinn, 1987). Detailed descriptions of virucidal assays have been published by Chen & Koski (1983).

7.2.1 Suspension methods

Some viruses may be inactivated by drying, and suspension tests are appropriate for such viruses. These tests usually employ a virus suspension of specified concentration and dilutions of disinfectant. Serum or other sources of organic matter may be added to simulate practical conditions of use. The virus–disinfectant mixture is usually incubated at room temperature for fixed intervals and residual virus infectivity is determined in cell cultures, embryonated eggs or susceptible animals. Appropriate controls for each reagent used should be included in each test. The cytotoxicity produced by some chemical compounds can be eliminated by the methods outlined in Fig. 6.2. It is recommended that the virus titre used in suspension experiments be at least 10^4, and that the protocol should allow for replicate sampling. Test results should be reported as the reduction in virus titre, expressed as $\log_{10}$, attributed to the activity of disinfectant and should be calculated by an accepted statistical method. Suspension tests generally only furnish the minimum requirements for virus inactivation, and for practical recommendations carrier methods should be employed.

Establishing the number of infective units in suspension tests is hampered by the possibility of aggregate formation. Clusters of more than 100 infective virions, which are not uncommon in enterovirus preparations, may represent only a single infective unit after 99% infectivity reduction (Moldenhauer, 1984). Aggregation may even be

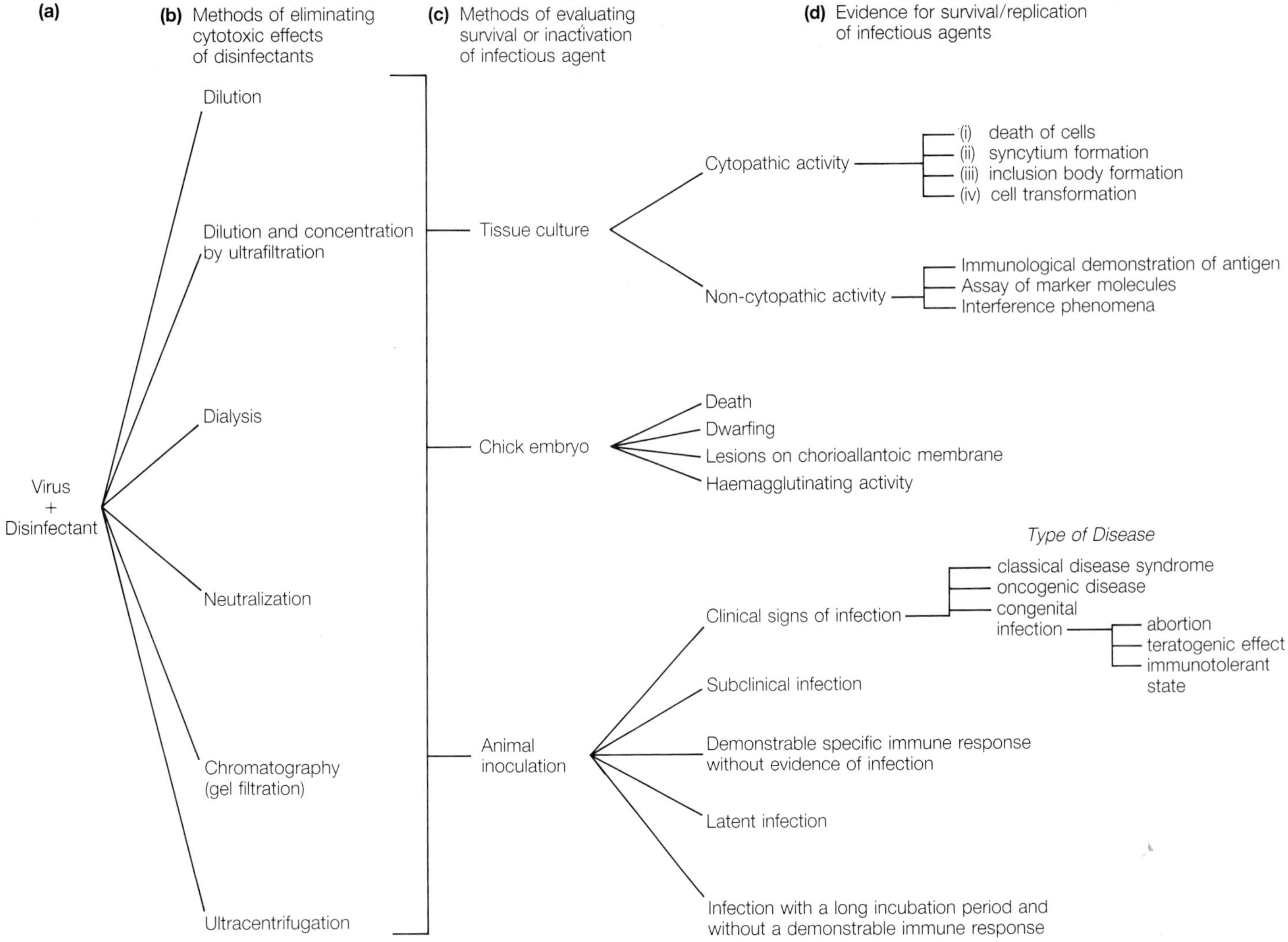

Fig. 6.2 Methods of testing virucides and chemical compounds active against unconventional infectious agents (such as the agent of bovine spongiform encephalopathy). Following treatment of the infectious agent with disinfectant (a), the cytotoxic effects of disinfectant are eliminated by appropriate procedures (b). The final steps (c) and (d) indicate the biological testing methods which may be used to determine survival or inactivation of the infectious agent.

caused by the disinfectant used, especially if it precipitates protein.

7.2.2 Carrier methods

Virucides that are intended for use on dry environmental surfaces should be tested under simulated-use conditions. Carrier methods are used to test the activity of disinfectants against viruses dried on surfaces. A particular difficulty with this method is that some viruses may be inactivated by drying.

Carrier rings, cylinders, discs of stainless steel, glass, plastic and the surface of hands of a volunteer have been used in carrier experiments. To simulate in-use conditions the virus being tested is inoculated onto hard, non-porous surfaces, allowed to dry and then treated with the disinfectant at different dilutions. Alternatively, the carriers may be immersed in virus suspension and then dried. It is generally recommended that a recoverable virus titre of at least 10^4 be used on the test surface and at least a 3-log reduction in viral titre, without cytotoxicity, be obtained.

Lorenz & Jann (1964) described a carrier method using Newcastle disease virus (NDV), a paramyxovirus. Carrier rings are immersed in virus suspensions and then dried. They are then transferred to dilutions of disinfectant and subsequently to broth. Ten-day-old embryonated eggs are inoculated with a small aliquot (0.1 ml) of this broth into the allantoic sac. If none of the inoculated embryos die within 5 days after inoculation the disinfectant is judged to be effective at the dilution tested. An obvious limitation of this method is its restriction to viruses causing death of the chick embryo.

Slavin (1973) described a surface disinfectant test (carrier test) using stainless-steel discs suitable for both bacteria and viruses. A 15% solution of gelatin containing 2.5% yeast suspension, Tween 80 and the test virus at a suitable density (sufficient to allow a 4-log drop) was placed in a cavity on the disc and cooled at 4°C. Three viruses—a bovine herpesvirus, a bovine myxovirus and a porcine enterovirus—were used. The discs were placed in disinfectant for the required time, transferred to distilled water and then into nutrient broth containing 5% horse serum. The nutrient broth was held at 37°C to allow the gelatine to liquefy and titrations of the virus were added to cell cultures. The effective concentration of disinfectant was taken as that which gave a 4-log drop in virus titre.

A suspension test using 11 viruses was compared with a carrier test using the surface of both hands and the individual fingertips of a single volunteer, by Schürmann & Eggers (1983). They concluded that the hand test was a useful model and the suspension test yielded optimistic data.

Discs of stainless-steel, glass and two types of plastic were used to evaluate the virucidal activity of 27 disinfectants against human rotavirus (HRV) (Lloyd-Evans *et al.*, 1986). A volume of 20 μl of HRV containing 10^7 PFU was air-dried on each disc, an equal volume of disinfectant was applied over the surface of each virus-contaminated disc and after 1 min the reaction was stopped by the addition of tryptose phosphate broth. Virus was eluted from the discs using a sonic bath, diluted in Earle's balanced salt solution and plaque-assayed. A disinfectant was considered effective if it reduced the plaque titre by 3-$\log_{10}$ or greater. A carrier method employing virus dried on coverslips under vacuum in the cold was developed by Allen *et al.* (1988). Virus titres remained high for up to 3 weeks at −70°C. Coverslips with dried virus were exposed to disinfectant in a cuvette. Cytotoxicity of disinfectant was determined by exposing the coverslip without virus to disinfectant, then placing it in medium with indicator cells.

Stainless-steel discs contaminated with coxsackievirus, adenovirus and parainfluenza virus were air-dried under ambient conditions and treated with 16 disinfectant formulations for 1 min, eluted into tryptose phosphate broth and plaque assayed (Sattar *et al.*, 1989). A 3-$\log_{10}$ or greater reduction in virus infectivity was considered effective for the virucides used.

A number of workers have found that some carriers, such as porcelain and stainless-steel penicylinders, fail to carry sufficient titre of virus for virucidal tests (Chen & Koski, 1983). In addition, considerable variation in virus titres recovered can be attributed to washing-off of virus by disinfectant. This variation appears to be inherent in this type of testing procedure (Allen *et al.*, 1988).

7.2.3 Plaque suppression tests

The principle of this method is that a layer of host cells on a suitable agar medium is infected with virus. Small discs of filter paper treated with disinfectant are applied, and after a designated incubation period the discs are removed and then the agar is stained with a suitable dye to observe plaque suppression and also possible toxicity to host cells (Sykes, 1965). This method can be applied to a range of viruses including vaccinia, herpes and Newcastle disease viruses (Tyler & Ayliffe, 1987; Tyler *et al.*, 1990).

7.3 Assessment of virucidal activity with bacteriophages

Bacteriophages have been used in place of animal and human viruses to test the virucidal activity of disinfectants. The coliphages T2, MS2 and ΦX 174 were used by Lepage & Romond (1984) to test the virucidal activity of iodophor, aldehyde, hypochlorite, quaternary ammonium and amphoteric compounds. The coliphage ΦX 174 has been used in suspension and carrier tests to determine the virucidal activity of disinfectants (Bydžovská & Kneiflová, 1983). Bacteriophages, particularly coliphages, have been used as indicators for enteroviruses in wastewater and polluted water, but they are more resistant than enteroviruses to adverse environmental conditions and to disinfection (Kott, 1981).

7.4 Approved tests for virucidal activity

A limited number of tests for approval of virucides are recognized by professional groups or governments. The German Society for Veterinary Medicine (DVG) has issued a defined protocol for testing the virucidal activity of disinfectants (Schliesser, 1979). The test procedure employs a virus suspension of $10^6 ID_{50}$ in 20% bovine serum. Four test viruses, two enveloped and two non-enveloped, are used: (a) enteric cytopathogenic bovine orphan virus (picornavirus); (b) infectious canine hepatitis virus (adenovirus); (c) Newcastle disease virus (paramyxovirus) and (d) vaccinia virus (pox-virus). A suspension test in the presence and absence of 20% bovine serum is used, and a carrier test using wood and gauze is also specified (virus dried at 37°C for 90 min). Appropriate dilutions of disinfectant are added for 15, 30, 60 and 120 min; samples are inoculated into cell cultures and chick embryos. Toxicity of the disinfectant alone for the cell cultures and embryonated eggs must be assessed. Disinfectants are rated according to their effective concentration which achieves complete inactivation or limited virucidal activity.

In the UK, the Ministry of Agriculture, Fisheries and Food (1970) has published the protocol of a test for approval of disinfectants for use against fowl pest (Newcastle disease virus and fowl plague virus—avian influenza). Two separate tests are used: (a) a toxicity test, to determine if the disinfectant under test is toxic for embryonated eggs; and (b) a virus test system to assess the degree of inactivation of the test virus (Newcastle disease virus), using 9-day-old embryonated eggs inoculated into the allantoic cavity. The disinfectant under test must give a reduction of at least 10^4 in virus titre.

8 VIRUS SURVIVAL OR INACTIVATION

Confirmation of virus inactivation or survival requires either tissue culture, chick embryo or animal inoculation. A number of human viral pathogens, such as Norwalk virus, present particular difficulties due to the absence of suitable cell culture systems or susceptible laboratory animals.

Where animal inoculation is employed it is essential that the animals used are (a) susceptible to the virus or infectious agent, (b) immunologically naive, and (c) in the appropriate age category to show clinical signs of the replicating agent. For diseases with long incubation periods the life span of the animal selected is another important consideration. Some infectious agents of animals such as the agents of scrapie and of bovine spongiform encephalopathy (see Chapter 7) apparently elicit no immune response and have exceptionally long incubation periods. Diagnosis of these spongiform encephalopathies is based on clinical signs, pathognomonic lesions in the brain and demonstration of scrapie-associated fibrils.

The appropriate method for assessing survival or inactivation of a virus or unconventional infectious agent must be based on its characteristics and its ability to produce a cytopathic effect or induce either clinical or subclinical disease in a susceptible animal. In the absence of a recognizable clinical disease a strong specific immune response to the agent, either cell-mediated or humoral, may indicate evidence of survival of the infectious agent. An inactivated infectious agent may also stimulate a weak immune response, but the extent and duration of the response is usually easily distinguished from that induced by a live agent. For the demonstration of a latent infection it may be necessary to immunosuppress the host with suitable drugs such as corticosteroids. To demonstrate the survival of some infectious agents which attack the developing foetus, pregnant animals are required. Re-isolation of infectious agent is a necessary part of laboratory procedure. Virus concentration is one of the important limiting factors in the animal inoculation model (Fig. 6.2) as there is a minimal infective dose for most viruses and the amount of virus surviving following chemical treatment may determine the outcome of experimental challenge. *In vitro* culture of hepatitis B virus (HBV) has not yet been accomplished, but chimpanzees and gibbons are highly susceptible to experimental infection with human HBV (see also Murray *et al.*, 1991). Animals for HBV investigations should be kept in quarantine for at least three months and their health status monitored. Their transaminase values should be in the normal range and, if necessary, liver biopsy can be carried out. It may be necessary to monitor exposed animals for at least six months as the incubation period may vary with virus content of the challenge dose. The lack of an animal model or a readily available cell culture system for Norwalk virus presents obvious experimental difficulties, and human volunteers are required.

For tissue culture procedures, several dilution series of the recovered virus should be employed and, in addition, a number of subpassages should be carried out before final interpretation of the data. A range of immunodetection systems can be applied to demonstrate virus replication in cell cultures. Where appropriate, DNA probing, with or without amplification, may be used. Assay of marker molecules may also be employed, and virus replication may be detected by *in situ* hybridization using a radioactive probe of the genome.

Direct and indirect tests are available for HIV, and these include reverse transcriptase assay, viral antigen enzyme-linked immunosorbent assays, radioimmunoassay, indirect immunofluorescence and *in situ* hybridization (Levy, 1988). HIV can also be cultured in PHA-stimulated leucocytes from seronegative donors. In some human T-cell lines, HIV will induce plaque and syncytium formation.

9 INACTIVATION OF VIRUSES BY PHYSICAL AND CHEMICAL METHODS: PUBLISHED REPORTS

9.1 Ultraviolet inactivation

The effect of UV irradiation on human rotavirus and simian rotavirus was investigated by Meng *et al.* (1987). Both simian and human isolates were rapidly inactivated under conditions achieved in a biological safety cabinet.

The survival curves of poliovirus and simian rotavirus following UV irradiation were similar (Chang *et al.*, 1985). These viruses were three to four times more resistant to UV light than vegetative bacteria. Rodgers *et al.* (1985) investigated the morphological damage induced in human rotavirus by UV irradiation. As early as 1 min after exposure the smooth capsid layer was damaged, and by 120 min no intact virus particles were observed. The effect of UV irradiation on HIV was evaluated using a reverse transcriptase assay (Spire *et al.*, 1985). High doses were required to inactivate the virus, which proved resistant to the doses normally employed in laminar hoods.

Considerable variation was observed in the sensitivity of selected animal RNA viruses to UV irrradiation (Watanabe *et al.*, 1989). The infectivity of canine distemper virus and Sendai virus was reduced by 10^6PFU after 5 min treatment, but Theiler's murine encephalomyelitis virus and a reovirus proved highly resistant. The virucidal efficacy of UV irradiation against three coronaviruses and two parvoviruses of animals was investigated by Saknimit *et al.* (1988). All five viruses were inactivated within 15 min.

The susceptibility of viruses pathogenic for fish was examined to determine the usefulness of UV-water treatment units for the control of fish diseases (Sako & Sorimachi, 1985; Yoshimizu *et al.*, 1986). Susceptibility of infectious pancreatic necrosis virus was low, but infectious haemopoietic necrosis virus and oncorhynchus masou virus were inactivated by the treatment.

9.2 Heat inactivation

Heat treatment of plasma products for human use was introduced to reduce the risk of transmission of viral agents, notably hepatitis B virus and HIV virus. The thermal inactivation patterns of selected human viruses are shown in Fig. 6.3.

9.2.1 *Inactivation of human immunodeficiency virus*

The stability of HIV (HTLV-III) virus was studied at room temperature (23–27°C) and at 56°C (Resnick *et al.*, 1986). Infectious virus was detected after 15 days at room temperature in an aqueous environment and at 11 days at 37°C. Virus recovery was reduced at a rate of approximately 1-$\log_{10}$ per 20 min at 54–56°C and infectious virus was detected after 3 h exposure. The authors also point out that the level of viral transcriptase activity decreased rapidly to below detectable levels within 30 min, whereas infectivity assays detected virus for a much longer period of time. An earlier publication (Martin *et al.*, 1985) suggested that HTLV-III virus dropped from $10^{5.15}$ to undetectable levels within 10 min at 56°C, using an antigen capture assay. In the lyophilized state the time required to reduce virus titre 1-log at 60°C was 32 min compared with 24 s in the liquid state (McDougal *et al.*, 1985).

In antihaemophilic cryoprecipitate, the time needed for inactivation of 5-$\log_{10}$ tissue culture infective doses of virus was 30 min at 60°C (Hilfenhaus *et al.*, 1986). Longer periods of heat treatment were required to inactivate the virus in plasma protein preparations containing high concentrations of the stabilizers glycine and sucrose than had been observed in previous experiments.

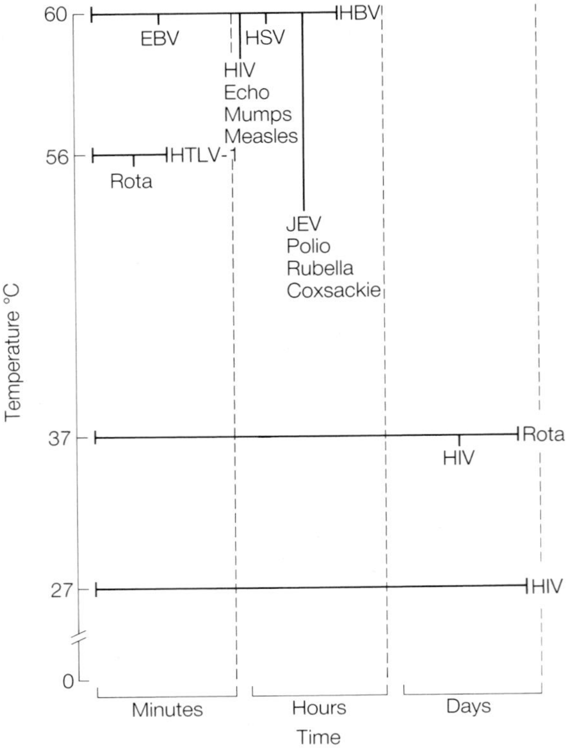

Fig. 6.3 Thermal inactivation patterns of viruses of human origin. The published data on which this figure is based are referred to in relevant sections of the text. EBV: Epstein–Barr virus; Echo: echoviruses; HBV: hepatitis B virus; HIV: human immunodeficiency virus; HSV: herpes simplex virus; HTLV-1: human T-lymphotropic virus-1; JEV: Japanese encephalitis virus; Rota: human rotavirus.

Factor VIII concentrates required heat treatment at 60°C for 1 h. Heat treatment of plasma proteins for 1 h at 60°C was shown to reliably inactivate HIV virus (Mauler *et al.*, 1987). Other workers (Uemura *et al.*, 1989) have used heat treatment at 60°C for 10 h to render human IgG free of viral agents, but HIV virus was inactivated within 1 h at 60°C.

9.2.2 *Inactivation of hepatitis B virus*

A number of methods of interrupting transmission of hepatitis B virus (HBV) have been developed, and these include screening blood donors to exclude known carriers and heat treatment of blood products. When human factor VIII concentrate containing 300 or 30 000 chimpanzee infectious doses of HBV was heated at 60°C in a lyophilized state for more than 10 h none of the test chimpanzees developed hepatitis (Hollinger *et al.*, 1984). Heating plasma proteins at 60°C for 10 h inactivated a broad spectrum of viruses including HBV, although some virus might survive the treatment in samples containing exceptionally high concentrations of HBV (Mauler *et al.*, 1987).

9.2.3 *Inactivation of other human viruses by heat*

Heat treatment of human rotavirus at 100°C (wet) or 60°C (dry) resulted in a rapid loss of outer capsid shell followed by disintegration of virions (Rodgers *et al.*, 1985). Human and simian rotavirus retained infectivity at room temperature for 14 days but were completely inactivated after 14 days at 37°C (Meng *et al.*, 1987). Both viruses were inactivated after 90 min at 56°C.

When liquid samples of antihaemophilic cryoprecipitate and factor VIII concentrates containing cytomegalovirus, Epstein–Barr virus, herpes simplex virus, poliovirus and vaccinia virus were heated at 60°C for 10 h, each was efficiently inactivated with the exception of vaccinia virus which retained some infectivity after 10 h (Hilfenhaus *et al.*, 1986). The effect of heat at 60°C on variola virus, mumps virus, measles virus, chikungunya virus, Japanese encephalitis virus, rubella virus, poliovirus, coxsackievirus and an echovirus was assessed by Higashi *et al.* (1977). Mumps, measles and variola viruses were readily inactivated after 1 h of treatment. Chikungunya virus, Japanese encephalitis virus, rubella virus, poliovirus, coxsackievirus and the echovirus retained some infectivity after 1 h, but were completely inactivated after 5 h of treatment. Uemura *et al.* (1989) heated mumps, vaccinia, chikungunya, Sindbis and an echovirus in a solution of human IgG at 60°C. Although heating continued for 10 h, all viruses tested were inactivated after 1 h.

Human T-lymphotropic virus-1 (HTLV-1) was inactivated by heating at 56°C for 30 min, based on the disappearance of reverse transcriptase from the supernatant culture fluid after heating (Yamato *et al.*, 1986).

9.2.4 *Inactivation of animal viruses and unconventional infectious agents by heat*

The thermal inactivation patterns of selected animal viruses and unconventional infectious agents are shown in Fig. 6.4.

The thermolability of mouse hepatitis virus, canine coronavirus, Kilham rat virus and canine parvovirus was investigated by Saknimit *et al.*, (1988). Both coronaviruses, mouse hepatitis virus and canine coronavirus, were inactivated by heating at 60°C for 15 min. Neither parvovirus was inactivated by heating at 80°C for 30 min and a temperature of 100°C was required for 1 min for inactivation of both viruses.

Four animal RNA viruses, Sendai virus, canine distemper virus, Theiler's murine encephalomyelitis virus and a reovirus, were heated at different temperatures for different time intervals (Watanabe *et al.*, 1989). The Sendai virus and canine distemper virus were labile, both losing their infectivity after 3 min at 60°C. The reovirus and Theiler's murine encephalomyelitis virus survived treatment at 60°C for 120 min and a temperature of 80°C was required for their inactivation. Vesicular stomatitis virus proved to be heat-labile, requiring less than 1 h at 60°C for its inactivation (Higashi *et al.*, 1977). Swine vesicular disease virus suspended in milk was inactivated in 2 min at 60°C and suspended in pig slurry it was inactivated in 2 min at 64°C (Herniman *et al.*, 1973). A bovine enterovirus and a bovine parvovirus seeded into liquid manure were heated at 70°C for 30 min (Monteith *et al.*, 1986). The enterovirus was inactivated but the parvovirus was not inactivated by this treatment.

Foot-and-mouth disease virus can survive pasteurization at 72°C for 15 s in milk and 93°C for 15 s in cream (Blackwell & Hyde, 1976). The virus can be reliably inactivated at 148°C for 3 s (Cunliffe *et al.*, 1979b; Walker *et al.*, 1984).

The agents associated with transmissible spongiform encephalopathies have a number of features in common, and one of their most remarkable attributes is their degree of thermostability (Chatigny & Prusiner, 1980; Brown *et al.*, 1986). Scrapie is one of the best-known of these unconventional infectious agents and at least 20 strains of

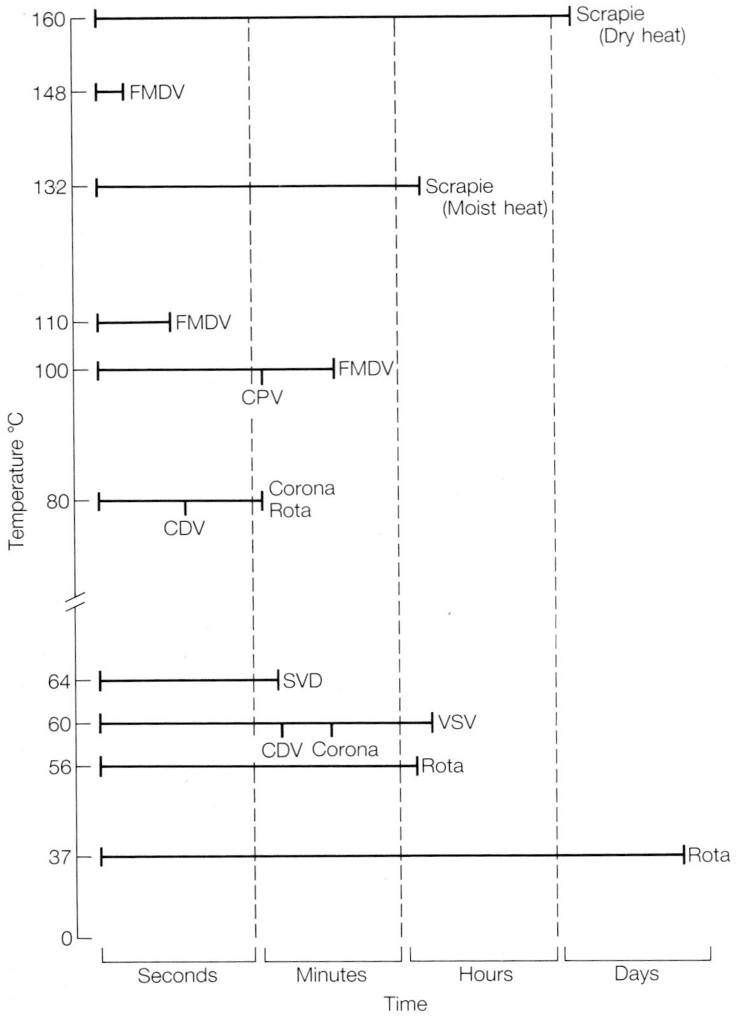

Fig. 6.4 Thermal inactivation patterns of viruses of animal origin based on published data referred to in the text. CDV: canine distemper virus; Corona: coronavirus; CPV: canine parvovirus; FMDV: foot-and-mouth disease virus; Rota: rotavirus; SVD: swine vesicular disease virus; VSU: vesicular stomatitis virus.

this agent exist (Bradley, 1990). Bovine spongiform encephalopathy (BSE) probably resulted from the use of commercial diets containing scrapie-contaminated ingredients. Physical decontamination of the agents of scrapie and BSE present many problems (Taylor, 1989). Smears of mouse brain infected with the ME7 strain of scrapie exposed to dry heat at 160°C for 24 h still retained infectivity (Dickinson & Taylor, 1978).

9.3 Inactivation by γ-irradiation

Gamma-irradiation has been used for many years to inactivate micro-organisms for a variety of purposes. Some workers have examined the sensitivity of selected animal viruses to γ-irradiation under conditions most favourable for virus survival. Swine vesicular disease virus, vesicular stomatitis virus and bluetongue virus were irradiated in tissues from experimentally infected animals using a ^{60}Co source (Thomas *et al.*, 1982). Pseudorabies virus, fowl plague virus, swine vesicular disease virus and vesicular stomatitis virus were irradiated in liquid animal faeces. All viruses were tested for survival in animals and *in vitro*. Swine vesicular disease was one of the most resistant viruses to γ-irradiation, but none of the viral preparations was infectious for their appropriate host animal after 6.0 Mrad.

A bovine enterovirus and a bovine parvovirus seeded into liquid manure were irradiated using ^{60}Co (Monteith *et al.*, 1986). The enterovirus was inactivated by a γ-irradiation dose of 1.0 Mrad, but the parvovirus survived this dose.

9.4 Inactivation of viruses by chemical methods

9.4.1 HIV inactivation

The effect of time and concentration of disinfectants on HIV was investigated by Spire *et al.* (1984). Sodium hypochlorite, β-propiolactone, glutaraldehyde, sodium hydroxide and ethanol were used at different concentrations and for different time intervals. The disinfectants were incubated with whole virus, and reverse transcriptase activity was assayed. A concentration of 0.2% sodium hypochlorite reduced reverse transcriptase production to low levels. Glutaraldehyde, sodium hydroxide and ethanol were effective at specified concentrations. Formalin at 0.1% slowly inactivated the virus and required 48 h to halt reverse transcriptase production, while β-propiolactone at 0.25% gave complete inactivation. Alcohols, hypochlorite, the detergent NP-40, hydrogen peroxide, phenolic disinfectants and paraformaldehyde inactivated HIV at concentrations below those used in routine disinfection (Martin *et al.*, 1985). HIV-1, air-dried on tonometer tips, was completely inactivated by 3% hydrogen peroxide or 70% isopropyl alcohol (Pepose *et al.*, 1989). Contact lenses experimentally contaminated with HTLV-III were readily disinfected with commercially available cleaning solutions (Vogt *et al.*, 1986).

Infectivity of HIV (HTLV-III) was undetectable within 1 min of treatment with 0.5% sodium hypochlorite, 70% alcohol, or 0.5% nonidet-P40, and within 10 min of treatment with 0.08% quaternary ammonium chloride or with a 1:1 mixture of acetone–alcohol (Resnick *et al.*, 1986). Chlorine-releasing agents are effective disinfectants against HIV (Hanson *et al.*, 1989; Bloomfield *et al.*, 1990).

A solution of povidone-iodine at 0.25% concentration completely inhibited reverse transcriptase production by HIV after a short time interval (Kaplan *et al.*, 1987).

The organic solvent tri(*n*-butyl) phosphate (TNBP) has been used in recent years for the inactivation of viruses in labile blood derivatives. Laboratory and animal investigations indicate that HIV, HBV, and non-A, non-B hepatitis viruses can be inactivated by TNBP in blood derivatives (Horowitz, 1989). The virucidal ability of naturally occurring fatty acids was investigated in labile blood derivatives (Horowitz *et al.*, 1988). Some inactivation of HIV and other enveloped viruses was observed, but the degree of inactivation depended on the sample composition.

9.4.2 Inactivation of hepatitis B virus

HBV in dried human plasma was exposed for 10 min at 20°C to five disinfectants: sodium hypochlorite, 22% aqueous glutaraldehyde, 2% glutaraldehyde with 7% phenol, 70% aqueous isopropyl alcohol and an iodophor detergent–disinfectant (Bond *et al.*, 1983). Chimpanzees injected with the treated material showed no signs of infection over nine months of observation. Kobayashi *et al.* (1984) have studied the susceptibility of HBV to disinfectants.

9.4.3 Inactivation of other human viruses

Chlorine dioxide, bromine chloride, iodine and chlorine were active against poliovirus at micromolar concentrations (Taylor & Butler, 1982). The activity of these disinfectants was influenced by pH; chlorine was most effective against poliovirus at pH 7, bromine chloride at pH 5 and chlorine dioxide and iodine at pH 9. Ozone inactivation of cell-associated poliovirus and coxsackievirus was investigated by Emerson *et al.* (1982). Unassociated viral controls were rapidly inactivated by low concentrations, whereas cell-associated poliovirus required a high concentration of ozone for 2 min to achieve inactivation. The coxsackievirus required 5 min exposure for complete inactivation. The rate of inactivation of coxsackievirus by glutaraldehyde was investigated by Saitanu & Lund (1975). A solution of 2% glutaraldehyde at pH 7.4 and 25°C reduced the titre of infectious virus by 2-$\log_{10}$ in

1 min and the reaction was not adversely affected by high concentrations of organic matter. The virucidal activity of sodium hypochlorite, chlorhexidine, phenolic disinfectants, cetrimide-chlorhexidine, 2% alkaline glutaraldehyde and ethanol combined with methanol, against a coxsackievirus, echovirus, poliovirus and rotavirus was evaluated by Narang & Codd (1983). Sodium hypochlorite, alkaline glutaraldehyde and ethanol combined with methanol were completely virucidal for all four viruses. The phenolic disinfectants had limited effect while chlorhexidine and cetrimide-chlorhexidine had no virucidal activity. The virucidal effects of a series of five alcohols on rotavirus, astrovirus and echovirus were reported by Kurtz *et al.* (1980). With a reaction time of 1 min 40% concentrations of the higher alcohols caused at least a 10^4-fold drop in rotavirus titre. Although not as effective against rotavirus, methanol and ethanol reduced the titres of the more resistant astrovirus and echovirus when used at high concentrations. The infectivity of human and simian rotaviruses was lost after treatment with 8% formaldehyde for 5 min, 70% ethanol for 30 min and 2% phenol and 1% hydrogen peroxide for 1 h (Meng *et al.*, 1987).

Sodium hypochlorite, cetrimide and 70% ethanol induced a rapid loss of the outer capsid layer in human rotavirus (Rodgers *et al.*, 1985). The effect of chlorhexidine and phenol on virus structure was evident only after extended periods of exposure. Of 27 disinfectants tested against human rotavirus only one-third proved effective, and these included halogens, glutaraldehyde, some acids and some bases (Lloyd-Evans *et al.*, 1986).

9.4.4 Animal viruses

Only five of 13 compounds exhibited virucidal activity against swine vesicular disease virus (Blackwell *et al.*, 1975). Sodium hydroxide, tincture of iodine, a mixture of sodium hydroxide and iodine, formaldehyde and sodium hypochlorite completely inactivated the virus after 30 min at 25°C. Acids, alkalis, oxidizing agents, detergents and other chemicals were tested for their activity against swine vesicular disease virus by Herniman *et al.* (1973). Virus diluted in hard water was inactivated by nitric, sulphuric, acetic and formic acids, and by sodium hydroxide, sodium metasilicate, benzene sulphonic acid, formalin, ethyl alcohol, iodophor disinfectants, and disinfectants containing formic or acetic acids and by sodium hypochlorite. Swine vesicular disease virus was inactivated by 0.2% glutaraldehyde during an interval of 11 days at 22–26°C (Cunliffe *et al.*, 1979a). Of 10 commercially available disinfectants tested for their ability to inactivate the virus of African swine fever, only one, containing *o*-phenylphenol, had virucidal activity when the virus–disinfectant mixtures were tested in pigs (Stone and Hess, 1973).

The virucidal activity of 10 disinfectants was tested against Talfan virus (a porcine enterovirus) and a porcine adenovirus (Derbyshire & Arkell, 1971). Sodium hypochlorite and ethyl alcohol inactivated the virus most efficiently; formaldehyde inactivated the viruses slowly at 4°C, while chlorhexidine and an ampholytic surface-active agent had little activity against these viruses.

The virus of foot-and-mouth disease was rapidly inactivated in the presence of acid, alkali or sodium hypochlorite (Sellers, 1968). The presence of organic matter reduced the activity of sodium hypochlorite. The rate of virus inactivation was slow in the presence of phenolic disinfectants.

Fourteen disinfectants were evaluated for their virucidal activity against porcine parvovirus, pseudorabies virus (a herpesvirus) and transmissible gastroenteritis virus (a coronavirus) by Brown (1981). Only sodium hypochlorite and sodium hydroxide inactivated porcine parvovirus after 5 min incubation. Pseudorabies and transmissible gastroenteritis viruses were inactivated after 5 min by all of the disinfectants tested. When the incubation time was extended to 20 min, both 2% glutaraldehyde and 8% formaldehyde inactivated porcine parvovirus.

Porcine enterovirus and porcine adenovirus seeded into pig slurry were inactivated by treatment of the slurry with calcium hydroxide at pH 11.5 (Derbyshire & Brown, 1979).

A total of 12 test compounds were used against San Miguel sea-lion virus and vesicular exanthema of swine virus (Blackwell, 1978). These two caliciviruses were inactivated rapidly by a number of chemical formulations including sodium hypochlorite, sodium carbonate, sodium hydroxide, citric acid and acetic acid. The test iodophor compound inactivated the San Miguel sea-lion virus completely, but had only minimal virucidal activity against vesicular exanthema of swine virus.

The efficacy of nine disinfectants against eight virus groups was assessed by a comparison of titres of the viruses before and after exposure to each disinfectant (Evans *et al.*, 1977). Formalin, glutaraldehyde, hypochlorite and peracetic acid were effective against all the viruses selected.

Thirty-five commonly used commercial disinfectants were evaluated for their virucidal activity against feline viral rhinotracheitis (a herpesvirus), feline calicivirus and feline panleukopenia (a parvovirus) (Scott, 1980). Of 22 tested against feline viral rhinotracheitis, all were virucidal; 11 of 35 were virucidal for feline calicivirus, but only three of 27 were effective against feline panleukopenia.

The virucidal activity of nine disinfectants against Aleutian disease virus of mink was investigated by Shen *et al.* (1981). Formalin took 30 min to inactivate the virus, but sodium hypochlorite, an iodophor, glutaraldehyde and a phenolic disinfectant inactivated 4-$\log_{10}$ of virus within 10 min at 23°C. Twelve disinfectants in the presence of 10% bovine serum were tested against equine infectious anaemia virus (Shen *et al.*, 1977). All the compounds inactivated 4-$\log_{10}$ of virus within 5 min at 23°C. Sodium hydroxide, formalin and glutaraldehyde took longer to inactivate the virus than phenolic disinfectants, halogen derivatives and 70% ethanol.

Coronaviruses of laboratory animals were inactivated by ethanol, isopropanol, halogen disinfectants and quaternary ammonium compounds, but parvoviruses proved more resistant (Saknimit *et al.*, 1988).

The virucidal properties of an iodophor, sodium hypochlorite, formalin, thiomersal, malachite green and acriflavine were tested against infectious pancreatic necrosis virus, isolated from rainbow trout (Elliott & Amend, 1978). Iodine and chlorine compounds showed good activity, but efficacy depended on the concentration of virus, the presence of organic matter and water pH. The virus was not inactivated by exposure to 0.2% formalin for 60 min, by thiomersal or malachite green.

10 CONCLUDING REMARKS

Many technical problems have to be overcome in the development of satisfactory tests for virucidal compounds. The diversity of viruses encountered in animals and man renders standardization of testing procedures difficult. Nevertheless, harmonization of testing procedures for virucides should be attempted so that valid comparisons of efficacy, based on published reports, can be made. Much reliance is still placed on virucidal compounds for the control and prevention of viral diseases in human and animal populations. With the emergence of new diseases of animals, such as BSE, even greater reliance is now being placed on methods of decontaminating food for animal and human consumption. It would be reassuring for those concerned with the control of viral diseases in general if more scientific data were available on the spectrum of activity and efficacy of the many virucidal disinfectants available commercially. In the absence of approved tests for virucidal activity, decisions will have to be based on independent published reports until these are superseded by standardized scientific procedures.

ACKNOWLEDGEMENTS

I wish to thank Mrs L. Doggett for typing the manuscript, Mrs D. Maguire for preparing the illustrations, the library staff for assistance with database searches, and my colleagues for constructive criticism.

11 REFERENCES

Allen, L.B., Kehoe, M.J., Hsu, S.C., Barfield, R., Holland, C.S. & Dimitrijevich, S.D. (1988) A simple method of drying virus on inanimate objects for virucidal testing. *Journal of Virological Methods*, **19**, 239–248.

Berg, G. (1973) Removal of viruses from sewage, effluents, and waters. *Bulletin of the World Health Organization*, **49**, 451–460.

Blackwell, J.H. (1978) Comparative resistance of San Miguel sea-lion virus and vesicular exanthema of swine virus to chemical disinfectants. *Research in Veterinary Science*, **25**, 25–28.

Blackwell, J.H. & Chen, J.H.S. (1970) Effects of various germicidal chemicals on H.Ep.2 cell cultures and *Herpes simplex* virus. *Journal of the Association of Official Ana-*

lytical Chemists, **53**, 1229–1236.

Blackwell, J.H. & Hyde, J.L. (1976) Effect of heat on foot-and-mouth disease virus (FMDV) in the components of milk from FMDV-infected cows. *Journal of Hygiene (Cambridge)*, **77**, 77–83.

Blackwell, J.H., Graves, J.H. & McKercher, P.D. (1975) Chemical inactivation of swine vesicular disease virus. *British Veterinary Journal*, **131**, 317–322.

Bloomfield, S.F., Smith-Burchnell, C.A. & Dalgleish, A.G. (1990) Effect of hypochlorite-releasing disinfectants against the human immunodeficiency virus (HIV). *Journal of Hospital Infection*, **15**, 273–278.

Bond, W.W., Favero, M.S., Petersen, N.J. & Ebert, J.W. (1983) Inactivation of hepatitis B virus by intermediate-to-high level disinfectant chemicals. *Journal of Clinical Microbiology*, **18**, 535–538.

Boudouma, M., Enjalbert, L. and Didier, J. (1984) A simple method for the evaluation of antiseptic and disinfectant virucidal activity. *Journal of Virological Methods*, **9**, 271–276.

Bradley, R. (1990) Bovine spongiform encephalopathy: the need for knowledge, balance, patience and action. *Journal of Pathology*, **160**, 283–285.

Brown, P., Rohwer, R.G. & Gajdusek, D.C. (1986) Newer data on the inactivation of scrapie virus or Creutzfeldt-Jakob disease virus in brain tissue. *Journal of Infectious Diseases*, **153**, 1145–1148.

Brown, T.T. (1981) Laboratory evaluation of selected disinfectants as virucidal agents against porcine parvovirus, pseudorabies virus and transmissible gastroenteritis virus. *American Journal of Veterinary Research*, **42**, 1033–1036.

Bydžovská, O. & Kneiflová, J. (1983) Assessment of viral disinfection by means of bacteriophage ΦX 174. *Journal of Hygiene, Epidemiology, Microbiology and Immunology*, **27**, 60–68.

Chang, J.C., Ossoff, S.F., Lobe, D.C., Dorfman, M.H., Dumais, C.M., Qualls, R.G. & Johnson, J.D. (1985) UV inactivation of pathogenic and indicator microorganisms. *Applied and Environmental Microbiology*, **49**, 1361–1365.

Chatigny, M.A. & Prusiner, S.B. (1980) Biohazards of investigations on the transmissible spongiform encephalopathies. *Reviews of Infectious Diseases*, **2**, 713–724.

Chen, J.H.S. & Koski, T.A. (1983) Methods of testing virucides. In *Disinfection, Sterilization and Preservation* (ed. Block, S.S.) 3rd Ed. pp. 981–997. Philadelphia: Lea & Febiger.

Cunliffe, H.R., Blackwell, J.H. & Walker, J.S. (1979a) Glutaraldehyde inactivation of exotic animal viruses in swine heart tissue. *Applied and Environmental Microbiology*, **37**, 1044–1046.

Cunliffe, H.R., Blackwell, J.H., Dors, R. and Walker, J.S. (1979b) Inactivation of milkborne foot-and-mouth disease virus at ultra-high temperatures. *Journal of Food Protection*, **42**, 135–137.

Davis, B.D. and Dulbecco, R. (1980) Sterilization and disinfection. In *Microbiology*, (eds Davis, B.D., Dulbecco, R., Eisen, H.E., and Ginsberg, H.S.) 3rd Ed. pp. 1264–1274. Philadelphia: Harper & Row.

Derbyshire, J.B. & Arkell, S. (1971) The activity of some chemical disinfectants against Talfan virus and porcine adenovirus type 2. *British Veterinary Journal*, **127**, 137–142.

Derbyshire, J.B. & Brown, E.G. (1979) The inactivation of viruses in cattle and pig slurry by aeration or treatment with calcium hydroxide. *Journal of Hygiene, Cambridge*,

Dickinson, A.G. and Taylor, D.M. (1978) Resistance of scrapie agent to decontamination. *New England Journal of Medicine*, **299**, 1413–1414.

Elliott, D.G. & Amend, D.F. (1978) Efficacy of certain disinfectants against infectious pancreatic necrosis virus. *Journal of Fish Biology*, **12**, 277–286.

Emerson, M.A., Sproul, O.J. & Buck, C.E. (1982) Ozone inactivation of cell-associated viruses. *Applied and Environmental Microbiology*, **43**, 603–608.

Evans, D.H., Stuart, P. & Roberts, D.H. (1977) Disinfection of animal viruses. *British Veterinary Journal*, **133**, 356–359.

Hanson, P.J.V., Gor, D., Jeffries, D.J. & Collins, J.V. (1989) Chemical inactivation of HIV on surfaces. *British Medical Journal*, **298**, 862–864.

Herniman, K.A.J., Medhurst, P.M., Wilson, J.N. & Sellers, R.F. (1973) The action of heat, chemicals and disinfectants on swine vesicular disease virus. *Veterinary Record* **93**, 620–624.

Higashi, N., Arimura, H. & Ishikawa, H. (1977) Inactivation of viruses intentionally added to urokinase samples by heat-treatment. *Chemical Pharmaceutical Bulletin* (Tokyo), **25**, 3366–3369.

Hilfenhaus, J., Herrmann, A., Mauler, R. & Prince, A.M. (1986) Inactivation of the AIDS-causing retrovirus and other human viruses in antihaemophilic plasma protein preparations by pasteurization. *Vox Sanguinis*, **50**, 208–211.

Hollinger, F.B., Dolana, G., Thomas, W. & Gyorkey, F. (1984) Reduction in risk of hepatitis transmission by heat-treatment of a human Factor VIII concentrate. *Journal of Infectious Diseases*, **150**, 250–262.

Horowitz, B. (1989) Virus sterilization by treatment with tri (*n*-butyl) phosphate/detergent mixtures. *Colloque INSERM*, **175**, 365–372.

Horowitz, B., Piët, M.P.J., Prince, A.M., Edwards, C.A., Lippin, A. & Walakovits, L.A. (1988) Inactivation of lipid-enveloped viruses in labile blood derivatives by unsaturated fatty acids. *Vox Sanguinis*, **54**, 14–20.

Kaplan, J.C., Crawford, D.C., Durno, A.G. & Schooley, R.T. (1987) Inactivation of human immunodeficiency virus by Betadine. *Infection Control*, **8**, 412–414.

Klein, M. & Deforest, A. (1983) Principles of viral inactivation. In *Disinfection, Sterilization and Preservation* (ed. Block, S.S.) 3rd Ed. pp. 422–434. Philadelphia: Lea & Febiger.

Kobayashi, H., Tsuzuki, M., Koshimizu, K., Toyama, H., Yoshihara, N., Shikata, T., Abe, K., Mizuno, K., Otomo, N. & Oda, T. (1984) Susceptibility of hepatitis B virus to disinfectants or heat. *Journal of Clinical Microbiology*, **20**, 214–216.

Kott, Y. (1981) Viruses and bacteriophages. *Science of the Total Environment*, **18**, 13–23.

Kurtz, J.B., Lee, T.W. & Parsons, A.J. (1980) The action of alcohols on rotavirus, astrovirus and enterovirus. *Journal of Hospital Infection*, **1**, 321–325.

Lepage, Ch. & Romond, Ch. (1984) Détermination de l'activité virucide intérêt du bactériophage comme modèle viral. *Pathologie Biologie*, **32**, 631–635.

Levy, J.A. (1988) Retroviridae: Human immunodeficiency virus. In *Laboratory Diagnosis of Infectious Diseases* (eds Lennette, E.H., Halonen, P. and Murphy, F.A.) Vol. II, pp. 677–691. New York: Springer-Verlag.

Lloyd-Evans, N., Springthorpe, V.S. & Sattar, S.A. (1986) Chemical disinfection of human rotavirus-contaminated inanimate surfaces. *Journal of Hygiene, Cambridge*, **97**, 163–173.

Lorenz, D.E. & Jann, G.J. (1964) Use-dilution test and Newcastle disease virus. *Applied Microbiology*, **12**, 24–26.

Martin, L.S., McDougal, J.S. & Loskoski, S.L. (1985) Disinfection and inactivation of the human T lymphotropic virus Type III/lymphadenopathy-associated virus. *Journal of Infectious Disease* **152**, 400–403.

Mauler, R., Merkle, W. & Hilfenhaus, J. (1987) Inactivation of HTLV-III/LAV, hepatitis B and non-A/non B viruses by pasteurization in human plasma protein preparations. *Developments in Biological Standardization*, **67**, 337–351.

McDougal, J.S., Martin, L.S., Cort, S.P., Mozen, M., Heldebrant, C.M. & Evatt, B.L. (1985) Thermal inactivation of acquired immunodeficiency syndrome virus, human T Lymphotropic Virus-III/Lymphadenopathy-associated virus, with special reference to antihemophilic factor. *Journal of Clinical Investigation*, **76**, 875–877.

Meng, Z-D., Birch, C., Heath, R. & Gust, I. (1987) Physicochemical stability and inactivation of human and simian rotaviruses. *Applied and Environmental Microbiology*, **53**, 727–730.

Ministry of Agriculture, Fisheries and Food (1970) *Protocol of Test for Approval of Disinfectants for Use Against Fowl Pest (Newcastle Disease Virus, Fowl Plague Virus)*. MAFF, Central Veterinary Laboratory, Weybridge.

Moldenhauer, D. (1984) Quantitative evaluation of the effects of disinfectants against viruses in suspension experiments. *Zentralblatt für Bakteriologie und Hygiene, I Abteilung Originale*, **B179**, 544–554.

Monteith, H.D., Shannon, E.E. & Derbyshire, J.B. (1986) The inactivation of a bovine enterovirus and a bovine parvovirus in cattle manure by anaerobic digestion, heat treatment, gamma irradiation, ensilage and composting. *Journal of Hygiene, Cambridge*, **97**, 175–184.

Murray, S.M., Freiman, J.S., Vickery, K., Lim, D., Cossart, Y.E. & Whiteley, R.K. (1991) Duck hepatitis B virus: a model to assess efficacy of disinfectants against hepadnavirus activity. *Epidemiology and Infection*, **106**, 435–443.

Narang, H.K. & Codd, A.A. (1983) Action of commonly used disinfectants against enteroviruses. *Journal of Hospital Infection*, **4**, 209–212.

Pepose, J.S., Linette, G., Lee, S.F. & MacRae, S. (1989) Disinfection of Goldmann tonometers against human immunodeficiency virus type I. *Archives of Ophthalmology*, **107**, 983–985.

Quinn, P.J. (1987) Evaluation of veterinary disinfectants and disinfection processes. In *Disinfection in Veterinary and Farm Animal Practice* (eds Linton, A.H., Hugo, W.B. and Russell, A.D.) pp. 66–116. Oxford: Blackwell Scientific Publications.

Resnick, L., Veren, K., Salahuddin, S.Z., Tondreau, S. & Markham, P.D. (1986) Stability and inactivation of HTLV-III/LAV under clinical and laboratory environments. *Journal of the American Medical Association*, **255**, 1887–1891.

Rodgers, F.G., Hufton, P., Kurzawska, E., Molloy, C. & Morgan, S. (1985) Morphological response of human rotavirus to ultra-violet radiation, heat and disinfectants. *Journal of Medical Microbiology*, **20**, 123–130.

Saitanu, K. & Lund, E. (1975) Inactivation of enterovirus by glutaraldehyde. *Applied Microbiology*, **29**, 571–574.

Saknimit, M., Inatsuki, I., Sugiyama, Y. & Yagami, K. (1988) Virucidal efficacy of physico-chemical treatments against coronaviruses and parvoviruses of laboratory animals. *Experimental Animals*, **37**, 341–345.

Sako, H. & Sorimachi, M. (1985) Susceptibility of fish pathogenic viruses, bacteria and a fungus to ultraviolet irradiation and the disinfectant effect of UV-ozone water sterilizer on the pathogens in water. *Bulletin of the National Research Institute in Aquaculture*, No. 8, 51–58.

Sattar, S.A., Springthorpe, V.S., Karim, Y. & Loro, P. (1989) Chemical disinfection of non-porous inanimate surfaces experimentally contaminated with four human pathogenic viruses. *Epidemiology and Infection*, **102**, 493–505.

Schliesser, Th. (1979) Testing of chemical disinfectants for veterinary medicine. *Hygiene und Medizin*, **4**, 51–56.

Schürmann, W. & Eggers, H.J. (1983) Antiviral activity of an alcoholic hand disinfectant. Comparison of the *in vitro* suspension test with the *in vivo* experiments on hands, and on individual fingertips. *Antiviral Research*, **3**, 25–41.

Scott, F.W. (1980) Virucidal disinfectants and feline viruses. *American Journal of Veterinary Research*, **41**, 410–414.

Sellers, R.F. (1968) The inactivation of foot-and-mouth disease virus by chemicals and disinfectants. *Veterinary Record*, **83**, 504–506.

Shay, B.J., Egan, A.F. and Wills, P.A. (1988) The use of irradiation for extending the storage life of fresh and processed meats. *Food Technology in Australia*, **40**, 310–313.

Shen, D.T., Crawford, T.B., Gorham, J.R. & McGuire, T.C. (1977) Inactivation of equine infectious anemia virus by chemical disinfectants. *American Journal of Veterinary Research*, **38**, 1217–1219.

Shen, D.T., Leendertsen, L.W. & Gorham, J.R. (1981) Evaluation of chemical disinfectants for Aleutian disease virus of mink. *American Journal of Veterinary Research*, **42**, 838–840.

Slavin, G. (1973) A reproducible surface contamination method for disinfectant tests. *British Veterinary Journal*,

129, 13–18.

Spire, B., Barré-Sinoussi, F., Dormont, D., Montagnier, L. and Chermann, J.C. (1985) Inactivation of lymphadenopathy-associated virus by heat, gamma rays and ultraviolet light. *Lancet*, **1**, 188–189.

Spire, B., Montagnier, L., Barré-Sinoussi, F. & Chermann, J.C. (1984) Inactivation of lymphadenopathy associated virus by chemical disinfectants. *Lancet*, **2**, 899–901.

Stone, S.S. & Hess, W.R. (1973) Effects of some disinfectants on African swine fever virus. *Applied Microbiology*, **25**, 115–122.

Sykes, G. (1965) *Disinfection and Sterilization*, pp. 291–308. London: Chapman & Hall.

Taylor, D.M. (1989) Scrapie agent decontamination: implications for bovine spongiform encephalopathy. *Veterinary Record*, **24**, 291–292.

Taylor, G.R. & Butler, M. (1982) A comparison of the virucidal properties of chlorine, chlorine dioxide, bromine chloride and iodine. *Journal of Hygiene, Cambridge*, **89**, 321–328.

Thomas, F.C., Ouwerkerk, T. & McKercher, P. (1982) Inactivation by gamma irradiation of animal viruses in simulated laboratory effluent. *Applied and Environmental Microbiology*, **43**, 1051–1056.

Thurman, R.B. & Gerba, C.P. (1988) Molecular mechanisms of viral inactivation by water disinfectants. *Advances in Applied Microbiology*, **33**, 75–105.

Tyler, R. & Ayliffe, G.A.J (1987) A surface test for virucidal activity: preliminary study with herpes virus. *Journal of Hospital Infection*, **9**, 22–29.

Tyler, R., Ayliffe, G.A.J. & Bradley, C.R. (1990) Virucidal activity of disinfectants. *Journal of Hospital Infection*, **15**, 339–345.

Uemura, Y., Uriyu, K., Hirao, Y., Takechi, K., Ishikawa, H., Nakajima, T., Kagitani, Y., Yokoyama, K., Funakoshi, S., Nishida, M., Yabushita, S., Furuta, K., Hamamoto, Y., Tochikura, T.S. & Yamamoto, N. (1989) Inactivation and elimination of viruses during the fractionation of an intravenous immunoglobulin preparation: liquid heat treatment and polyethylene glycol fractionation. *Vox Sanguinis*, **56**, 155–161.

Vogt, M.W., Ho, D.D., Bakar, S.R., Gilbard, J.P., Schooley, R.T. & Hirsch, M.S. (1986) Safe disinfection of contact lenses after contamination with HTLV-III. *Ophthalmology*, **93**, 771–774.

Walker, J.S., de Leeuw, P.W., Callis, J.J. & van Bekkum, J.G. (1984) The thermal death time curve for foot-and-mouth disease virus contained in primarily infected milk. *Journal of Biological Standardization*, **12**, 185–189.

Watanabe, Y., Miyata, H. & Sato, H. (1989) Inactivation of laboratory animal RNA-viruses by physicochemical treatment. *Experimental Animals*, **38**, 305–311.

Yamato, K., Taguchi, H., Yoshimoto, S., Fujishita, M., Yamashita, M., Ohtsuki, Y., Hoshino, H. & Miyoshi, I. (1986) Inactivation of lymphocyte-transforming activity of human T-cell leukaemia virus Type I by heat. *Japanese Journal of Cancer Research* (Gann) **77**, 13–15.

Yoshimizu, M., Takizawa, H. & Kimura, T. (1986) UV susceptibility of some fish pathogenic viruses. *Fish Pathology*, **21**, 47–52.

Chapter 7
Inactivation of Unconventional Agents of the Transmissible Degenerative Encephalopathies

1 INTRODUCTION

1.1 Terminology

The term 'slow virus disease' has been applied traditionally to a miscellany of infections which share one common feature, i.e. prolonged incubation periods compared with conventional virus infections. A number of these are now known to constitute a distinct group of unusual neurological diseases (Section 1.2) caused by unconventional transmissible agents (Section 1.3), and are referred to as transmissible degenerative encephalopathies (TDE).

1.2 Disease characteristics

The TDE (Table 7.1) share many unusual features (Table 7.2) but their incidence and geographic distribution vary. Creutzfeldt–Jakob disease (CJD), including the familial form Gerstmann–Straussler–Scheinker disease (GSS), affects humans worldwide at a frequency of only around 1 per million (Masters, 1987), whereas scrapie affects sheep in many but not all areas of the world inflicting losses of up to 30% in affected flocks (Palsson, 1979). Transmissible mink encephalopathy (TME) has occurred sporadically in North America and Europe (Eckroade *et al.*, 1979). Kuru is confined to Papua New Guinea (Alpers, 1987), chronic wasting disease (CWD) is confined to North America (Williams & Young, 1980), and bovine spongiform encephalopathy (BSE) has occurred only in cattle born in Eire or the UK, although its aetiology (Section 1.3.3) suggests the potential for a wider distribution.

Scrapie has existed for at least 250 years, whereas other TDE have been recognized for much shorter periods. More is known about scrapie as a natural disease in sheep and as an experimental disease in rodents, and it is the model for the group.

A feature of all TDE is that a normal sialoglycoprotein which is expressed predominantly in neurons converts to a protease-resistant protein (PrP) as a consequence of infection (Carp *et al.*, 1985) and accumulates in the central nervous sys-

Table 7.1 The transmissible degenerative encephalopathies (TDE)

Disease	Recognized hosts
Scrapie	Sheep, goats
Transmissible mink encephalopathy (TME)	Mink
Chronic wasting disease (CWD)	Elk, mule-deer
Bovine spongiform encephalopathy (BSE)	Cattle
Creutzfeldt–Jakob disease (CJD)	Humans
Gerstmann–Straussler–Scheinker disease (GSS)	Humans
Kuru	Humans

Table 7.2 Characteristics of the TDE

Long incubation	Afebrile
No antibody response	Fatal
Neuronal vacuolation	No inflammatory response
Protein (PrP) accumulation	Unconventional causal agents

tem. This is associated topographically with neuronal vacuolation (Bruce *et al.*, 1989), the principal lesion detectable by histological examination, and is thought to cause the fatal neurological dysfunction which is a clinical hallmark for the TDE.

1.3 Agent characteristics

Among the striking features of the TDE is the unconventional properties of their causal agents (Table 7.3).

1.3.1 Nature of the agents

Although the unconventional nature of scrapie agent has long been recognized (Stamp *et al.*, 1959) no agent-specific nucleic acid has been detected for the TDE. Because PrP co-purifies with infectivity it has been suggested that the transmissible agent is solely a protein devoid of nucleic acid (Prusiner, 1982) but the known hydrophobic nature of PrP could encourage adventitious association with an unidentified agent which would co-purify. The idea of an infectious protein clashes with fundamental biological dogma, and a more comfortable hypothesis is that the infectious agent is a novel, quasi-viral hybrid with a nucleic acid genome but with a coat of host-derived protein (Dickinson & Outram, 1979) which may be PrP. This 'virino' model invokes the need for only a very small nucleic acid which would be difficult to detect; the hypothesis argues that nucleic acid is essential in explaining the diversity of strains and the mutations which are known to occur with scrapie agent (Dickinson *et al.*, 1989).

1.3.2 Resistance to inactivation

The agents of the TDE are remarkably resistant to inactivation. Because they have not been purified it is difficult to know to what degree their resistance is intrinsic and how much it is influenced by the protective effect of host tissue to which they are intimately bound (Section 3.1.2); the hydrophobic nature of the cell membrane domains with which infectivity is associated encourages the formation of aggregates in homogenized tissue preparations (Rohwer & Gajdusek, 1980). The protective effect of such aggregates is recognized for conventional

Table 7.3 Properties of the TDE agents

No antibody response	Not detected by electron microscopy
Slow replication in tissue culture	Not purified or characterized
No inflammatory response	Pathological lesions confined to central nervous system
Modify a normal host protein	Resistance to inactivation

viruses (Salk & Gori, 1960) and may at least partly explain the resistance of TDE agents (Sections 3.1.1. and 3.2.6).

Survival of these agents under harsh conditions could explain outbreaks of scrapie in sheep grazed on pastures which had been unoccupied by sheep for several years (Palsson, 1979), and the rare, sporadic cases of CJD of unknown aetiology. CJD agent remains highly infectious after 28 months at room temperature (Tateishi *et al.*, 1987), and scrapie agent survives in a desiccated state for at least 30 months (Wilson *et al.*, 1950).

1.3.3 Accidental transmission

The difficulty of inactivating TDE agents became apparent when several hundred out of 14 000 sheep, vaccinated against louping-ill, developed scrapie. Sheep tissue used to prepare the vaccine was infected unsuspectedly with scrapie agent, which survived an exposure to 0.35% formalin that inactivated the louping-ill virus (Gordon *et al.*, 1940).

CJD has also been transmitted accidentally through using decontamination methods recognized retrospectively as being inappropriate. Brain electrodes disinfected with ethanol and then 'sterilized' with formaldehyde vapour were implicated on one occasion (Bernoulli *et al.*, 1977). On another a standard hot-air sterilization process was considered to have failed to decontaminate CJD-infected surgical instruments (Foncin *et al.*, 1980).

Circumstantial evidence suggests that BSE which affected 460 cattle per week by March 1990 (Anon., 1990) was caused by the unnatural transmission of scrapie agent to bovines via foodstuff (Dickinson & Taylor, 1988; Wilesmith *et al.*, 1988). Prior to July 1988 commercial diets contained meat and bone meal derived from animals including sheep (Statutory Instrument 1039, 1988). The emergence of BSE coincided with the introduction of less rigorous cooking procedures to produce the meal (Morgan, 1988).

2 PRACTICAL CONSIDERATIONS IN DECONTAMINATION STUDIES

No standard methods exist. Experiments have involved various tissue preparations, e.g. crude macerates, unspun 20% homogenates, 10% tissue supernates, biochemically processed and ultracentrifuged material. Exposure times have been varied and the temperature for chemical treatment has been generally either 4°C or room temperature, occasionally with mechanical stirring. These variables undoubtedly contribute to the equivocal results sometimes obtained (Section 3.2).

The assumption is sometimes made that procedures effective for partially purified infectivity are applicable equally for dealing with crude tissue contamination, but this is unwarranted (Taylor, 1986a). Decontamination experiments should mimic the most adverse conditions, thus enhancing the prospect of detecting residual infectivity after exposure to partially-inactivating procedures, especially since bioassay is the only available procedure for detection of TDE infectivity.

Unlike other TDE, distinct strains of scrapie agent have been cloned, and those have reproducible biological characteristics (Dickinson *et al.*, 1989). Because high titres of infectivity in brain tissue combined with a short incubation period are a feature of the 263K strain of scrapie agent in hamsters it has been regarded as the optimal model for decontamination studies (Rosenberg *et al.*, 1986); this is reasonable for chemical studies where there is little evidence that TDE agent isolates or strains differ in susceptibility. However, the 22A strain of scrapie agent in mice is relatively thermostable (Dickinson & Taylor, 1978; Kimberlin *et al.*, 1983) and is the most appropriate model for studying thermal destruction of the TDE agents even though infectivity titres in brain are lower than for 263K (Taylor, 1986a).

Little has been done to validate chemical procedures for decontaminating the surfaces of equipment, benches, etc., but preliminary evidence suggests that it may be inadvisable to extrapolate from 'test-tube' studies involving tissue homogenates (Asher *et al.*, 1987).

Decontamination studies have usually involved brain tissue. Reticuloendothelial tissues are also infected, although at a lower level, but it is unknown whether there are differences in the degree of protection afforded to the TDE agents by different tissues.

Under well-defined experimental conditions,

specific strains of scrapie in rodents display highly reproducible inverse relationships between dose of infectivity administered and subsequent incubation period before the onset of clinical signs (Outram, 1976). For any given model the amount of infectivity present in an inoculum can be calculated by comparing the incubation period of the recipients with an 'incubation period assay' graph, without the need for titration. Unfortunately this procedure cannot be applied to infectivity exposed to chemical or physical treatments because these can radically alter dose–response curves (e.g. Dickinson & Fraser, 1969; Somerville & Carp, 1983), and require that recipient animals are observed for extended periods (Outram, 1976).

3 INACTIVATION METHODS

Inactivation studies on TDE agents are conducted either to obtain clues regarding their molecular nature or to establish meaningful decontamination standards. The former generally utilize partially purified materials, whereas the latter involve crude preparations and will be considered here.

3.1 Physical methods

3.1.1 Radiation

When CJD, kuru and scrapie agents are exposed to doses of γ (150 kGy) or germicidal UV irradiation (254 nm wavelength; 100 kJ/m^{-2}) representing gross overkill for conventional viruses, infectivity is recoverable (Latarjet, 1979); TME agent is equally resistant (Marsh & Hanson, 1969). Resistance may be attributable at least partially to protective mechanisms afforded by the intimate association of these agents with cell membranes (Millson *et al.*, 1976) and the tendency of infected tissue fragments to form aggregates which would need to receive as many radiation 'single-hits' as there are infectious units to achieve inactivation (Rohwer, 1983); interpretation of irradiation data has caused considerable debate (Alper, 1987). These methods are inappropriate for inactivating TDE agents.

3.1.2 Heat

Thermal studies involving the transfer of heat from water to samples in glass containers have shown that at temperatures up to 100°C there is only a small effect on CJD (Tateishi *et al.*, 1987) and scrapie agents (Stamp *et al.*, 1959). Exposure of 5 mg smears of scrapie-infected brain tissue (ME7 strain) to hot-air 'sterilization' at 160°C for 24 h also failed to eliminate infectivity (Dickinson & Taylor, 1978), and the 22A strain is known to be even more thermostable (see below). In the more energy-abundant medium of steam above atmospheric pressure, i.e. autoclaving, significant to complete inactivation is achieved. Gravity-displacement autoclaving at 126°C for 2 h inactivates the 139A strain of scrapie agent but not the more thermostable strain 22A (Kimberlin *et al.*, 1983) which is inactivated after 4 h exposure (Dickinson, 1976); a CJD isolate and the 263K strain of scrapie were inactivated at 132°C for 1 h (Brown *et al.*, 1986b) which has been adopted as a standard for CJD agent decontamination in the USA (Rosenberg *et al.*, 1986). Porous-load autoclaving at 136°C for 3 min inactivates both the 139A and 22A strains of scrapie agent (Kimberlin *et al.*, 1983); these data form the basis for the UK steam sterilization standard for CJD agent, i.e. 134–138°C for 18 min (DHSS, 1984). Because of the greater efficiency of porous-load autoclaving the UK standard is considered to be more rigorous (Taylor, 1987).

Autoclaving studies have confirmed that the presence of tissue impedes inactivation of scrapie agent (Section 1.3.2). Gravity-displacement autoclaving of infected brain macerate (22A strain) at 126°C for 30 min resulted in a loss of 2.1-$\log_{10}$ ID_{50} (Kimberlin *et al.*, 1983). When autoclaved at 100°C or 105°C as a 10% homogenate (i.e. 10-fold less tissue and infectivity per unit volume), the titre losses were 2.5- and 3.5-logs respectively (Taylor & Dickinson, unpublished data).

3.2 Chemical methods

3.2.1 Acids and bases

Little inactivation of scrapie infectivity occurs over

the pH range 2–10 (Mould *et al.*, 1965) but CJD and scrapie (263K) agents exposed to 1 M sodium hydroxide (pH 14) for 1 h were found to be completely inactivated (Brown *et al.*, 1986b). However, residual infectivity has been detected following treatment of 263K scrapie agent with 1 M sodium hydroxide (Diringer & Braig, 1989) even for periods up to 24 h (Prusiner *et al.*, 1984). CJD infectivity has also been reported to survive exposure to 1 M (Tamai *et al.*, 1988) or 2 M sodium hydroxide (Tateishi *et al.*, 1988). The data of Brown *et al.* (1986b) show that the material was diluted before injection, thus reducing the sensitivity of the assays. It seems likely that further work will show that sodium hydroxide treatment results in considerable but not complete inactivation.

In contrast, there is minimal inactivation of CJD agent exposed to 1 M hydrochloric acid (pH 0.1) for 1 h (Brown *et al.* 1986b).

3.2.2 Alkylating agents

Viability of scrapie agent exposed to 0.35% formalin has been mentioned (Section 1.3.3) but it can survive even more rigorous treatments, e.g. immersion of infected brain tissue for 974 days in 20% formol saline (Taylor & Dickinson, unpublished data). CJD and TME agents are equally resilient, the former surviving at least a year in 10% formol saline (Tateishi *et al.*, 1980); the latter survives formol fixation for at least 6 years (Burger & Gorham, 1977).

Scrapie infectivity survived an exposure to 12.5% unbuffered glutaraldehyde (pH 4.5) for 16 h (Dickinson & Taylor, 1978); CJD agent was not inactivated by a 14-day exposure to 5% buffered histological glutaraldehyde at pH 7.3 (Amyx *et al.*, 1981). However, 2% glutaraldehyde buffered to pH8 is recognized as being more active microbiologically, but has yet to be tested.

Acetylethyleneimine (Stamp *et al.*, 1959) and β-propiolactone (Haig & Clarke, 1968) have little effect on scrapie agent. Ethylene oxide exposure causes very little loss of CJD (Brown *et al.*, 1982a) or scrapie infectivity (Dickinson, 1976).

3.2.3 Detergents

Mild detergents have little effect on TDE agents (Millson *et al.*, 1976) but sodium dodecyl sulphate has some effect on CJD (Walker *et al.*, 1983) and scrapie infectivity (Millson *et al.*, 1976) which is enhanced by heat (Kimberlin *et al.*, 1983).

3.2.4 Halogens

Sodium hypochlorite solutions containing up to 2.5% available chlorine have inactivated CJD and scrapie infectivity (Brown *et al.*, 1986b). An extended study with scrapie demonstrated that a solution containing 1.4% available chlorine is effective in 30 min, leading to the recommendation that 2% be used in practice (Kimberlin *et al.*, 1983). Unfortunately such strong solutions are corrosive to metals. The less corrosive chlorine-releasing compound sodium dichloroisocyanurate is equally effective for bacterial inactivation (Coates, 1985) but has not been tested with TDE agents.

Only a modest reduction in scrapie infectivity was obtained using 2% iodine in sodium iodide for 4 h (Brown *et al.*, 1982b). Similar results were observed with scrapie and CJD agents using an iodophor containing 0.8% iodine (Asher *et al.*, 1981).

3.2.5 Organic solvents

Numerous studies, particularly with scrapie, show that organic solvents generally have little effect on TDE infectivity. Experimental exposures have included 1 h with acetone (Hunter & Millson, 1964), 2 weeks with 5% chloroform (Wilson, 1955), 16 h with ether (Gajdusek & Gibbs, 1968), 2 weeks with 4% phenol (Wilson, 1955), and 2 weeks with ethanol (Dickinson & Taylor, 1978).

3.2.6 Oxidizing agents

Exposure of scrapie agent to chlorine dioxide (50 ppm for 24 h) inactivated only a small proportion of infectivity (Brown *et al.*, 1982b). Treatment of scrapie agent with 3% hydrogen peroxide for 24 h caused little inactivation (Brown *et al.*, 1982a).

Scrapie-infected brain homogenates were not inactivated by concentrations of up to 18% peracetic acid, but 2% inactivated intact brain tissue (Taylor, unpublished data). These apparently anomalous results are considered to demonstrate the protective effect of aggregation which occurs in homogenized preparations (Section 1.3.2).

3.2.7 Salts and urea

Oxidizing salts and urea have been tested for their effect on TDE agents with conflicting results. For example, the report that sodium metaperiodate has a considerable effect on scrapie infectivity (Hunter *et al.*, 1969) is contradicted by several other studies (Adams *et al.*, 1972; Dickinson, 1972; Brown *et al.*, 1982b). Similarly, a claim that potassium permanganate inactivates all CJD and scrapie infectivity in homogenates of brain tissue (Asher *et al.*, 1981) is challenged by data from other experiments (Brown *et al.*, 1982a; Kimberlin *et al.*, 1983; Brown *et al.*, 1986b). The claim that urea is an effective scrapiecide (Millson *et al.*, 1976) is not supported by other studies which have been reviewed (Brown *et al.*, 1986b).

4 LABORATORY EXPOSURE TO TDE

4.1 Human TDE

CJD and GSS collectively have an incidence of around $1{:}10^6$, suggesting that natural horizontal transmission does not occur readily. However, iatrogenic transmission has occurred; to the incidents described in Section 1.3.3 can be added infections linked to therapy with growth hormone derived from human pituitary glands (Brown, 1988), corneal grafting (Duffy *et al.*, 1974) and the use of human dura mater in surgical reconstruction (Prichard *et al.*, 1987; Nisbet, 1989; Masullo *et al.*, 1989).

Medical and paramedical personnel had been considered to be no more at risk of developing CJD than are the general population (Miller, 1987) until, in addition to a report of CJD in a neurosurgeon (Schoene *et al.*, 1981) three cases were reported among histology technicians (Brown *et al.*, 1987; Miller, 1988; Sitwell *et al.*, 1988). Infectivity is known to survive the rigours of histological tissue processing (Brown *et al.*, 1986a), and procedures have been recommended for making CJD tissues safe to handle in the histology laboratory. A proposal to autoclave formol-fixed tissues at 132°C for 1 h is inappropriate (Taylor, 1986b); although the microscopic architecture of formol-fixed scrapie brain remains acceptable even after autoclaving at 138°C (Taylor & McBride, 1987), very little infectivity is lost by autoclaving at 134°C for 18 min (Taylor & McConnell, 1988). Enhanced resistance to further inactivating procedures following sublethal exposure to formalin is a recognized phenomenon for conventional viruses (Gard & Maaloe, 1959). The use of 15% phenol in formalin has been suggested as a means of inactivating CJD infectivity in tissue, but there are no supportive data (Taylor, 1989a). A suggestion that a mixture of sodium hypochlorite and formalin is effective (Armbrustmacher, 1989) must be ruled out, since the carcinogen bis-(chloromethyl)-ether may be produced by their interaction. Safe handling of fixed CJD tissues depends on containment and good working practices (Chatigny & Prusiner, 1979).

4.2 Animal TDE

Scrapie is relatively common in some countries, e.g. France, UK and USA, but numerous studies have failed to demonstrate any association with human disease (Taylor, 1989b). The occurrence of an epidemic of scrapie in a new host, i.e. BSE in cattle, gave rise to increased concern, but it is considered that there is little risk to human health (DOH:MAFF, 1989; Taylor, 1989b). As with CJD, scrapie (Brown *et al.*, 1982b) and TME infectivity (Burger & Gorham, 1977) are known to survive routine histological processing.

There are no mandatory standards for laboratory work with the animal TDE agents, but good laboratory practice dictates that protective clothing should be used and that containment of aerosol, e.g. from high-titre tissue homogenates, is achieved using safety cabinets.

5 REFERENCES

Adams, D.H., Field, E.J. & Joyce, G. (1972) Periodate—an inhibitor of the scrapie agent? *Research in Veterinary Science*, **13**, 195–198.

Alper, T. (1987) Radio- and photobiological techniques in the investigation of prions. In *Prions: Novel Infectious Pathogens Causing Scrapie and Creutzfeldt–Jakob Disease* (eds Prusiner, S.B. & McKinley, M.P.) pp. 113–146. London: Academic Press.

Alpers, M. (1987) Epidemiology and clinical aspects of kuru. In *Prions: Novel Infectious Pathogens Causing Scrapie and Creutzfeldt–Jakob Disease* (eds Prusiner, S.B. & McKinley, M.P.) pp. 451–465. London: Academic Press.

Amyx, H.L., Gibbs, C.J., Kingsbury, D.T. & Gajdusek, D.C. (1981) Some physical and chemical characteristics of a strain of Creutzfeldt–Jakob disease in mice. *Abstracts of the Twelfth World Congress of Neurology*, Kyoto, 20–25 September, p. 255.

Anon (1990) BSE scare tactics accusation. *Veterinary Record*, **126**, 252–253.

Armbrustmacher, V.M. (1989) Personal communication cited by Titford & Bastian (1989)

Asher, D.M., Gibbs, C.J., Diwan, A.R., Kingsbury, D.T., Sulima, M.P. & Gajdusek, D.C. (1981) Effects of several disinfectants and gas sterilization on the infectivity of scrapie and Creutzfeldt–Jakob disease. *Abstracts of the Twelfth World Congress of Neurology*, Kyoto, 20–25 September, p. 225.

Asher, D.M., Pomeroy, K.L., Murphy, L., Gibbs, C.J. & Gajdusek, D.C. (1987) Attempts to disinfect surfaces contaminated with etiological agents of the spongiform encephalopathies. *Abstracts of the VIIth International Congress of Virology*, Edmonton, 9–14 August, p. 147.

Bernoulli, C., Siegfried, J., Baumgartner, G., Regli, F., Rabinowicz, T., Gajdusek, D.C. & Gibbs, C.J. (1977) Danger of accidental person-to-person transmission of Creutzfeldt–Jakob disease by surgery. *Lancet*, **i**, 478–479.

Brown, P. (1988) The decline and fall of Creutzfeldt–Jakob disease associated with human growth hormone therapy. *Neurology*, **38**, 1135–1137.

Brown, P., Gibbs, C.J., Amyx, H.L., Kingsbury, D.T., Rohwer, R.G., Sulima, M.P. & Gajdusek, D.C. (1982a) Chemical disinfection of Creutzfeldt–Jakob disease virus. *New England Journal of Medicine*, **306**, 1279–1282.

Brown, P., Rohwer, R.G., Green, E.M. & Gajdusek D.C. (1982b) Effect of chemicals, heat and histopathological processing on high-infectivity hamster-adapted scrapie virus. *Journal of Infectious Diseases*, **145**, 683–687.

Brown, P., Gibbs, C.J. & Gajdusek, D.C. (1986a) Transmission of Creutzfeldt–Jakob disease from formalin-fixed, paraffin-embedded human brain tissue. *New England Journal of Medicine*, **315**, 1614–1615.

Brown, P., Rohwer, R.G. & Gajdusek, D.C. (1986b) Newer data on the inactivation of scrapie virus or Creutzfeldt–Jakob disease virus in brain tissue. *Journal of Infectious Diseases*, **153**, 1145–1148.

Brown, P., Cathala, F., Raubertas, R.F., Gajdusek, D.C. & Castaigne, P. (1987). The epidemiology of Creutzfeldt–Jakob disease: conclusion of a 15-year investigation in France and review of the world literature. *Neurology*, **37**, 895–904.

Bruce, M.E., McBride, P.A. & Farquhar, C.F. (1989) Precise targeting of the pathology of the sialoglycoprotein, PrP, and vacuolar degeneration in mouse scrapie. *Neuroscience Letters*, **102**, 1–6.

Burger, D. & Gorham, J.R. (1977) Observation on the remarkable stability of transmissible mink encephalopathy virus. *Research in Veterinary Science*, **22**, 131–132.

Carp, R.I., Merz, P.A., Kascsak, R.J., Merz, G. & Wisniewski, H.M. (1985) Nature of the scrapie agent: current status of facts and hypotheses. *Journal of General Virology*, **66**, 1357–1368.

Chatigny, M.A. & Prusiner, S.B. (1979) Biohazards and risk assessment of laboratory studies on the agents causing the spongiform encephalopathies. In *Slow Transmissible Diseases of the Nervous System* (eds Prusiner, S.B. & Hadlow, W.J.) Vol. 1, pp. 491–514. London: Academic Press.

Coates, D. (1985) A comparison of sodium hypochlorite and sodium dichloroisocyanurate products. *Journal of Hospital Infection*, **6**, 31–40.

DHSS (1984) Management of patients with spongiform encephalopathy [Creutzfeldt–Jakob disease (CJD)]. DHSS Circular DA (84) 16.

Dickinson, A.G. (1972) Private communication cited by Hunter *et al.* (1972).

Dickinson, A.G. (1976) Scrapie in sheep and goats. In *Slow Virus Diseases of Animals and Man* (ed. Kimberlin, R.H.) pp. 209–241. Amsterdam: North-Holland.

Dickinson, A.G. & Fraser, H. (1969) Modification of the pathogenesis of scrapie in mice by treatment of the agent. *Nature, London*, **222**, 892–893.

Dickinson, A.G. & Outram, G.W. (1979) The scrapie replication-site hypothesis and its implications for pathogenesis. In *Slow Transmissible Diseases of the Nervous System* (eds Prusiner, S.B. & Hadlow, W.J.) Vol. 2, pp. 13–21. London: Academic Press.

Dickinson, A.G. & Taylor, D.M. (1978) Resistance of scrapie agent to decontamination. *New England Journal of Medicine*, **229**, 1413–1414.

Dickinson, A.G. & Taylor, D.M. (1988). Options for the control of scrapie in sheep and its counterpart in cattle. *Proceedings of the Third World Congress on Sheep and Beef Cattle Breeding*, Vol 1, 19–23 June, Paris, pp. 553–564.

Dickinson, A.G., Outram, G.W., Taylor, D.M. & Foster, J.D. (1989) Further evidence that scrapie agent has an independent genome. In *Unconventional Virus Diseases of the Central Nervous System* (eds Court, L.A., Dormont, D., Brown, P. & Kingsbury, D.T.) pp. 446–460. Moisdon la Riviere: Abbaye de Melleray.

Diringer, H. & Braig, H.R. (1989) Infectivity of unconventional viruses in dura mater. *Lancet*, **i**, 439–440.

DOH:MAFF (1989) *Report of the Working Party on Bovine Spongiform Encephalopathy*. HMSO.

Duffy, P., Wolf, J., Collins, G., De Voe, A.G., Streeten, B. & Cowen, D. (1974) Possible person-to-person transmission of Creutzfeldt–Jakob disease. *New England Journal of Medicine*, **290**, 692.

Eckroade, R.J., ZuRhein, G.M. & Hanson, R.P. (1979) Experimental transmissible mink encephalopathy: brain lesions and their sequential development in mink. In *Slow Transmissible Diseases of the Nervous System*, (eds Prusiner, S.B. & Hadlow W.J.) Vol. 1, pp. 409–449. London: Academic Press.

Foncin, J.F., Gaches, J., Cathala, F., El Sherif, E. & Le Beau (1980) Transmission iatrogene interhumaine possible de maladie de Creutzfeldt–Jakob avec alteinte des grains du cervulet. *Revue Neurologique*, **136**, 280.

Gajdusek, D.C. & Gibbs, C.J. (1968) Slow, latent and temperate virus infections of the central nervous system. In *Infections of the Nervous System* (ed. Zimmerman, H.M.) pp. 254–280. Baltimore: Williams & Wilkins.

Gard, S. & Maaloe, O. (1959) Inactivation of viruses. In *The Viruses* (eds Burnet, F.M. & Stanley, W.M.) Vol. 1, pp. 359–427. New York: Academic Press.

Gordon, W.S., Brownlee, A. & Wilson, D.R. (1940) Studies in louping-ill, tick-borne fever and scrapie. *Report of the Proceedings of the Third International Congress for Microbiology*, pp. 362–363. Baltimore: Waverley.

Haig, D.A. & Clarke, M.C. (1968) The effect of β-propiolactone on the scrapie agent. *Journal of General Virology*, **3**, 281–283.

Hunter, G.D. & Millson, G.C. (1964) Further experiments on the comparative potency of tissue extracts from mice infected with scrapie. *Research in Veterinary Science*, **5**, 149–153.

Hunter, G.D., Gibbons, R.A., Kimberlin, R.H. & Millson, G.C. (1969) Further studies of the infectivity and stability of extracts and homogenates derived from scrapie affected mouse brains. *Journal of Comparative Pathology*, **79**, 101–108.

Hunter, G.D., Millson, G.C. & Heitzman, R.J. (1972) The nature and biochemical properties of the scrapie agent. *Annales de Microbiologie. Institut Pasteur*, **123**, 571–583.

Kimberlin, R.H., Walker, C.A., Millson, G.C., Taylor, D.M., Robertson, P.A., Tomlinson, A.H. & Dickinson, A.G. (1983) Disinfection studies with two strains of mouse-passaged scrapie agent. *Journal of the Neurological Sciences*, **59**, 355–369.

Latarjet, R. (1979) Inactivation of the agents of scrapie, Creutzfeldt–Jakob disease, and kuru by radiations. In *Slow Transmissible Diseases of the Nervous System* (eds Prusiner, S.B. & Hadlow, W.J.) Vol. 2, pp. 387–407. London: Academic Press.

Marsh, R.F. & Hanson, R.P. (1969) Physical and chemical properties of the transmissible mink encephalopathy agent. *Journal of Virology*, **3**, 176–180.

Masters, C.L. (1987) The epidemiology of Creutzfeldt–Jakob disease: studies on the natural mechanisms of transmission. In *Prions: Novel Infectious Proteins Causing Scrapie and Creutzfeldt–Jakob Disease* (eds Prusiner, S.B. & McKinley, M.P.) pp. 511–522. Orlando: Academic Press.

Masullo, C., Pocchiari, M., Maachi, G., Alema, G., Piazza, G. & Panzera, M.A. (1989) Transmission of Creutzfeldt–Jakob disease by dural cadaveric graft. *Journal of Neurosurgery*, **71**, 954–955.

Miller, D.C. (1987) Precautions against Creutzfeldt–Jakob disease. *Nursing*, **17**, 65.

Miller, D.C. (1988) Creutzfeldt–Jakob disease in histopathology technicians. *New England Journal of Medicine*, **318**, 853–854.

Millson, G.C., Hunter, G.D. & Kimberlin, R.H. (1976) The physico-chemical nature of the scrapie agent. In *Slow Virus Diseases of Animals and Man* (ed. Kimberlin, R.H.) pp. 243–266. Amsterdam: North-Holland.

Morgan, K.L. (1988) Bovine spongiform encephalopathy: time to take scrapie seriously. *Veterinary Record*, **122**, 445–446.

Mould, D.L., Dawson, A.McL. & Smith, W. (1965) Scrapie in mice. The stability of the agent to various suspending media, pH and solvent extraction. *Research in Veterinary Science*, **6**, 151–154.

Nisbet, T.J. (1989) Update: Creutzfeldt–Jakob disease in a second patient who received a cadaveric dura mater graft. *Morbidity and Mortality Weekly Review*, **38**, 37–38, 43.

Outram, G.W. (1976) The pathogenesis of scrapie in mice. In *Slow Virus Diseases of Animals and Man* (ed Kimberlin, R.H.) pp. 325–357. Amsterdam: North-Holland.

Palsson, P.A. (1979) Rida (scrapie) in Iceland and its epidemiology. In *Slow Transmissible Disease of the Nervous System* (eds Prusiner, S.B. & Hadlow, W.J.) Vol. 1, pp. 357–366. London: Academic Press.

Prichard, J., Thadani, V., Kalb, R. & Manuelidis, E. (1987) Rapidly progressive dementia in a patient who received a cadaveric dura mater graft. *Morbidity and Mortality Weekly Review*, **36**, 49–50, 55.

Prusiner, S.B. (1982) Novel proteinaceous infectious particles cause scrapie. *Science*, **216**, 136–144.

Prusiner, S.B., McKinley, M.P., Bolton, D.C., Bowman, K.A., Groth, D.F., Cochran, S.P., Hennessey, E.M., Braunfeld, M.B., Baringer, J.R. & Chatigny, M.A. (1984) Prions: methods for assay, purification, and characterization. In *Methods in Virology* (eds Maramorosch, K. & Koprowski, H.) Vol. VIII, pp. 293–345.

Rohwer, R.G. (1983) Scrapie inactivation kinetics—an explanation for scrapie's apparent resistance to inactivation—a reevaluation of estimates of its small size. In *Virus non Conventionnels et Affections du Système Nerveux Central* (eds Court, L.A. & Cathala, F.) pp. 84–113. Paris: Masson.

Rohwer, R.G. & Gajdusek, D.C. (1980) Scrapie, virus or viroid: the case for a virus. In *Search for the Cause of Multiple Sclerosis and Other Chronic Diseases of the CNS* (Proceedings of the 1st International Symposium of the Hertie Foundation in Frankfurt, September 1979) pp. 335–355. Weinheim: Verlag Chemie.

Rosenberg, R.N., White, C.L., Brown P., Gajdusek, D.C., Volpe, J.J., Posner, J. & Dyck, P.J. (1986) Precautions in handling tissues, fluids, and other contaminated materials from patients with documented or suspected Creutzfeldt–Jakob disease. *Annals of Neurology*, **19**, 75–77.

Salk, J.E. & Gori, J.B. (1960) A review of theoretical, experimental, and practical considerations in the use of formaldehyde for the inactivation of poliovirus. *Annals of the New York Academy of Sciences*, **83**, 609–637.

Schoene, W.C., Masters, C.L., Gibbs, C.J., Gajdusek, D.C., Tyler, H.R., Moore, F.D., Dammin, G.J. (1981) Transmissible spongiform encephalopathy (Creutzfeldt–Jakob disease). *Archives of Neurology*, **38**, 473–477.

Sitwell, L., Lach, B., Atack, E., Atack, D. & Izukawa, D. (1988) Creutzfeldt–Jakob disease in histopathology technicians. *New England Journal of Medicine*, **318**, 854.

Somerville, R.A. & Carp. R.I. (1983) Altered scrapie infectivity estimates by titration and incubation period in the presence of detergents. *Journal of General Virology*, **64**, 2045–2050.

Stamp, J.T., Brotherston, J.C., Zlotnik, I., McKay, J.M.K. & Smith, W. (1959) Further studies on scrapie. *Journal of Comparative Pathology*, **69**, 268–280.

Statutory Instrument (1988) *The Bovine Spongiform Encephalopathy Order*, 1988. HMSO.

Tamai, Y., Taguchi, F. & Miura, S. (1988) Inactivation of the Creutzfeldt–Jakob disease agent. *Annals of Neurology*, **24**, 466.

Tateishi, J., Koga, M., Sato, Y. & Mori, R. (1980) Properties of the transmissible agent derived from chronic spongiform encephalopathy. *Annals of Neurology*, **7**, 390–391.

Tateishi, J., Hikita, K., Kitamoto, T. & Nagara, H. (1987) Experimental Creutzfeldt–Jakob disease: induction of amyloid plaques in rodents. In *Prions: Novel Infectious Pathogens Causing Scrapie and Creutzfeldt–Jakob Disease* (eds Prusiner, S.B. & McKinley, M.P.) pp. 415–426. New York: Academic Press.

Tateishi, J., Tashima, T. & Kitamoto, T. (1988) Inactivation of the Creutzfeldt–Jakob disease agent. *Annals of Neurology*, **24**, 466.

Taylor, D.M. (1986a) Decontamination of Creutzfeldt–Jakob disease agent. *Annals of Neurology*, **20**, 749.

Taylor, D.M. (1986b). Decontamination of formaldehyde-fixed tissues of Creutzfeldt–Jakob disease. *Journal of Neuropathology and Experimental Neurology*, **45**, 760–761.

Taylor, D.M. (1987) Autoclaving standards for Creutzfeldt–Jakob disease agent. *Annals of Neurology*, **22**, 557–558.

Taylor, D.M. (1989a) Phenolized formalin may not inactivate Creutzfeldt–Jakob disease infectivity. *Neuropathology and Applied Neurobiology*, **15**, 585–586.

Taylor, D.M. (1989b) Bovine spongiform encephalopathy and human health. *Veterinary Record*, **125**, 413–415.

Taylor, D.M. & McBride, P.A. (1987) Autoclaved, formol-fixed scrapie brain is suitable for histopathological examination but may still be infective. *Acta Neuropathologica*, **74**, 194–196.

Taylor, D.M. & McConnell, I. (1988). Autoclaving does not decontaminate formol-fixed scrapie tissues. *Lancet*, **i**, 1463–1464.

Titford, M. & Bastian, F.O. (1989) Handling Creutzfeldt–Jakob disease tissues in the laboratory. *Journal of Histotechnology*, **12**, 214–217.

Walker, A.S., Inderlied, C.B. & Kingsbury, D.T. (1983) Conditions for the chemical and physical inactivation of the K.Fu. strain of the agent of Creutzfeldt–Jakob disease. *American Journal of Public Health*, **73**, 661–665.

Wilesmith, J.W., Wells, G.A.J., Cranwell, M.P. & Ryan, J.B.M. (1988) Bovine spongiform encephalopathy: epidemiological studies. *Veterinary Record*, **123**, 638–644.

Williams, E.S. & Young, S. (1980) Chronic wasting disease of captive mule deer: a spongiform encephalopathy. *Journal of Wildlife Diseases*, **16**, 89–98.

Wilson, D.R. (1955) Unpublished work cited by Dickinson, A.G. (1976).

Wilson, D.R. Anderson, R.D. & Smith, W. (1950) Studies in scrapie. *Journal of Comparative Pathology*, **60**, 267–282.

Chapter 8
Sensitivity of Protozoa to Disinfectants

1 INTRODUCTION

This chapter deals with the effect of disinfectants on a variety of protozoa: *Giardia lamblia*, a flagellated parasite of the human small intestine, causes giardiasis, the most frequently reported waterborne parasitic disease in the United Kingdom and the United States (Meyer & Jarroll, 1980; Craun, 1986); *Entamoeba histolytica*, a parasitic amoeba inhabiting the human large intestine, is the aetiological agent of amoebiasis (Albach & Booden, 1978); *Cryptosporidium*, a coccidian parasite of the intestinal and respiratory epithelium of vertebrates, can cause cryptosporidiosis (Fayer & Ungar, 1986); *Naegleria fowleri*, a free-living amoeboflagellate, can cause a rapidly fatal primary amoebic meningoencephalitis (Griffin, 1978); and *Acanthamoeba culbertsoni*, a free-living amoeba, which occasionally infects humans (Griffin, 1978).

These distinctly different protozoa are considered together here because all: (1) are potentially pathogenic to humans, (2) may be acquired from water, (3) are controlled environmentally by filtration, sterilization or disinfection, and (4) have a resistant cyst stage in their life cycle.

2 WATSON'S LAW

Watson's Law, published in 1908 (Watson, 1908) has recently been applied to protozoan disinfection studies. Watson's Law simply put is as follows:

$$k = C^{\eta}t$$

where k is a constant for a given micro-organism exposed to a disinfectant under a fixed set of pH and temperature conditions, C is the disinfectant concentration in milligrams per litre, η is the coefficient of dilution (see also Chapter 3), and t is the contact time required to achieve a fixed percentage of inactivation. Plotting C and t values, respectively, on a logarithmic ordinate and abscissa will result in a straight line whose slope is η. If values of η are <1, then contact time is more important than concentration; if values of η are >1, then the converse is true. However, if $\eta = 1$, then the concentration of the disinfectant and the contact time are equally important, with the Ct product being independent of the actual disinfectant concentration used. Hoff (1986) concluded that the major advantage of using Ct products for establishing disinfectant concentrations and contact times was that they were based on experimental data. The major problem, in his opinion, was that when the data used to calculate Ct products were limited, extrapolation of the data was required. This is especially disconcerting with respect to pH variations in environmental water, since pH influences are far less predictable in their effects on chlorine than are the influences of temperature. Nonetheless, *Ct* products provide a convenient way of comparing the efficacy of disinfectants on protozoan cysts under a given set of conditions. In some of the older literature where *Ct* products were not calculated, η will be taken to be 1 for the purpose of calculating estimates used in this chapter.

3 EFFECT OF DISINFECTANTS ON PROTOZOA

The reader is cautioned that controversy exists regarding the most appropriate method for determining cyst viability (or cyst death) when conducting disinfection experiments on protozoans. Most of the data presented in this chapter will be based either on data obtained using *in vitro* excystation (*Giardia*, *Entamoeba*, *Cryptosporidium*), animal infectivity (*Giardia*, *Cryptosporidium*), or plaque assays (*Naegleria*, *Acanthamoeba*) as the criterion of cyst viability. A caveat regarding the *Ct* products for the *Cryptosporidium* data presented here is that these products were computed in a limited number of disinfectant concentrations, and should be regarded only as estimates.

It is impossible to include all of the historical studies on protozoan disinfection in this chapter. Studies on *Giardia*, for example, far exceed those on the other four parasites, and these have been reviewed elsewhere (Jarroll *et al.*, 1984; Jarroll, 1988).

3.1 Chlorine

Jarroll *et al.* (1981) showed that *G. lamblia* cysts were completely inactivated (>99.8%) by 2 mg chlorine/l in 60 min at pH 6 and 5°C. At this same temperature and chlorine concentration the percentage of cyst inactivation deteriorated as the pH rose to 8; 4 mg/l inactivated >99.8% of the cysts at pH values of 6 and 7, but not at pH 8. A chlorine concentration of 8 mg/l killed >99.8% of the cysts within 10 min at pH 6 and 7, but required 30 min to achieve the same results at pH 8. As the water temperature increased, the concentration of chlorine and the contact time required for cyst inactivation decreased. Rice *et al.* (1982) confirmed the low-temperature data presented by Jarroll *et al.* (1981), and further showed that *Giardia muris* cysts are approximately 1.5 times more resistant to chlorine than those of *G. lamblia*. With that information came the idea of using *G. muris* cysts as surrogates for *G. lamblia* cysts in future disinfection studies on *Giardia*.

Leahy *et al.* (1987) examined the dynamics of *G. muris* inactivation by chlorine. As was true for *G. lamblia*, decreasing the temperature at a given contact time, pH value and chlorine concentration decreased the efficacy of chlorine against *G. muris*; the *Ct* product at 25°C and pH 7 ranged from 25.5 to 44.8 mg·min/l. At pH 7 and 5°C the range was 449–1012 mg·min/l. It is generally accepted that increasing the pH decreases the efficacy of the halogen as a disinfectant. However, in the case of *G. muris*, the greater killing with respect to free chlorine occurred at pH 7, followed by pH 5 and pH 9. Plotting these same data with respect to hypochlorous acid (HOCl) concentration yielded results exactly opposite to those one would expect, i.e. killing was best at pH 9 > pH 7 > pH 5. While far too little is known of *Giardia* cyst wall biochemistry (Jarroll *et al.*, 1989) and cyst physiology to make strong statements concerning the reasons for these contradictions, Leahy *et al.* (1987) speculated that these surprising results could be due to: (1) pH-induced changes in the surface of the organism affecting the cyst's sensitivity to HOCl, or (2) an alteration in the mechanism of action of the disinfectant allowing for greater sensitivity to the hypochlorite ion (ClO^-) than was believed previously.

Because animal sources of human type *Giardia* cysts are preferable to human sources for providing consistent supplies of cysts for research, baseline data have been collected using *G. lamblia* cysts from the Mongolian gerbil (Belosevic *et al.*, 1983) for comparison to those from humans. Based on the results of Rubin *et al.* (1989) using *in vitro* excystation as the criterion of cyst viability, the *Ct* products for *G. lamblia* cysts from gerbils ranged from 120 mg·min/l (at pH 7 and 15°C) to nearly 1500 mg·min/l (at pH 9 and 15°C). Data from Jarroll *et al.* (1981), who also used *in-vitro* excystation but cysts from humans, equated to a *Ct* value of 120 mg·min/l at pH 7 and 5°C. The difference in these two values might be due to the differences in excystation methods used, difference in host sources of the cysts, or differences in the *Giardia* strains themselves. Hibler *et al.* (1987), using *G. lamblia* cysts and gerbil infectivity as the criterion of viability, determined that, between 0.5°C and 5°C, *Ct* values for chlorine ranging from 157 to 425 mg·min/l were required to render cysts incapable of infecting gerbils.

Stringer *et al.* (1975) used *in vitro* excystation (Stringer, 1972) as the sole criterion for *E. histolytica* cyst viability in studies on halogen disinfectants. In these studies, cysts were obtained from infected monkeys, rather than *in vitro* cultured cysts, because Stringer *et al.* (1975) believed that the latter were less resistant to disinfection than the former. Since this work is most directly comparable to that for *Giardia* and the soil amoeba, it will be discussed in the greatest detail. Estimating from the data generated by Stringer *et al.* (1975), the mean *Ct* product for chlorine disinfection of *E. histolytica* cysts (99% kill) at pH 7 and 30°C is approximately 20 mg·min/l in buffered water. This estimate suggests that *E. histolytica* cysts are approximately as resistant to chlorine as those of *G. muris*.

Korich *et al.* (1990), using excystation and animal infectivity, reported that *Cryptosporidium* oocyst viability dropped from 80% to 0% after 2 h in 80 mg chlorine/l at pH 7 and 25°C; inactivation after 90 min was at least 99%. The *Ct* product based on these results was about 7200 mg·min/l.

Several authors have reported the effect of chlorine on *Naegleria fowleri* (pathogenic) and *N. gruberi* (non-pathogenic) (De Jonckheere & van de Voorde, 1976; Chang, 1978; Cursons *et al.*, 1980; Rubin *et al.*, 1983). However, the data collected by Rubin and his colleagues (1983) are more easily compared to those reported for *Giardia* and *Entamoeba*, and thus will be presented here. The criterion of viability used was a plaque assay which is based on counting the number of plaques appearing on a bacterial lawn as a result of excysted amoebae, from cysts remaining viable after exposure to the disinfectant, feeding on the bacteria. The plates inoculated with cysts previously exposed to a disinfectant are compared to control plates inoculated with untreated cysts. The mean *Ct* product for free chlorine for 99% inactivation of *N. gruberi* is 12.1 mg·min/l at 25°C and pH 7; the mean *Ct* value for HOCl is 9.34 mg·min/l at 25°C and pH 7 (Rubin *et al.*, 1983). The *Ct* value for *N. fowleri* appears to be about twice that for *N. gruberi* (Chang, 1978; Rubin *et al.*, 1983) suggesting that *N. fowleri* cysts are no more resistant to chlorine than those of *E. histolytica*. When cyanuric acid acid is present, the normal killing effect of chlorine on *N. gruberi* is inhibited, but with or without cyanuric acid, HOCl appears to be the major cysticidal agent (Engel *et al.*, 1983).

The data available for the efficacy of the halogens against *Acanthamoeba* cysts are difficult to interpret because the criterion of viability was not quantitative. Rather, De Jonckheere & van de Voorde (1976) exposed *Acanthamoeba* cysts to disinfectants and recorded the contact time required to result in negative cultures of amoebae. In the case of *Acanthamoeba* sp. (strain 4A), the condition required to produce a negative culture was a 24 h exposure to an initial chlorine concentration of 8 mg/l with a 6 mg/l residual. *A. culbertsoni* cysts (A-1) (a pathogenic amoeba) exposed for 24 h to an initial chlorine level of 4 mg/l or 1.75 mg/l residual, yielded negative cultures. Because cultures were not initiated, except at 3 and 24 h, the exact length of exposure required to effect killing is not known. The results suggest that *Acanthamoeba* cysts are more resistant to chlorine than are those of *Naegleria* (De Jonckheere & van de Voorde, 1976; Cursons *et al.*, 1980).

3.2 Chloramines

Chloramines such as NH_2Cl, $NHCl_2$, and NCl_3 are chemically more complex than other commonly used chemical water disinfectants, and generally are less effective against protozoan cysts than are other halogens. Often it requires 25–100 times more chloramines than free chlorine to achieve similar results. In practice, chloramines are formed by the addition of chlorine and ammonia independently to water; thus, there is a time when a transient, but detectable, level of free chlorine exists. Such a transient level of free chlorine undoubtedly enhances the cysticidal nature of chloramine treatment of water.

Most of the literature dealing with the effect of

chloramines on protozoan cysts is confined to their effect on *Giardia* (Rubin, 1987). Meyer *et al.* (1989) added chlorine (as sodium hypochlorite) and ammonia (as ammonium sulphate) to water under conditions that simulated field conditions with a Cl_2:N ratio of approximately 7:1; the *Ct* values for >99% kills ranged from a low of 185 mg·min/l at 18°C to a high of 650 mg·min/l at 3°C. These authors suggested that temperature exerts a major effect on the efficacy of chloramines against *Giardia* cysts, and to a lesser extent increasing pH decreases chloramine efficiency as a cysticide.

Since the transient nature of the free chlorine in solution is difficult to control, some laboratory experiments assessing the efficacy of chloramines against *Giardia* used preformed chloramines with a Cl_2:N ratio of 1:4. One study showed that, at pH 7 and 15°C, the mean *Ct* product for preformed chloramines was approximately 850 mg·min/l (Hoff, 1986).

A comparison of these studies suggests that chloramines generated under field conditions do appear to be somewhat more cysticidal than those that are preformed. Controlled laboratory testing with preformed chloramines does yield more conservative and perhaps more consistent estimates of the efficacy of chloramines. Nonetheless, it is clear that within the neutral pH range chloramines, preformed or not, are less cysticidal than free chlorine.

Preformed monochloramine exhibited results similar to those for free chlorine against *Cryptosporidium* oocysts, i.e. a *Ct* product of 7200 mg·min/l at 25°C (Korich *et al.* 1990).

3.3 Chlorine dioxide

Chlorine dioxide as a disinfectant offers advantages over chloramines or free chlorine: (1) in the pH range from 6 to 9 its efficacy increases threefold, (2) it does not disproportionate like free chlorine over the pH range normally encountered in water treatment, and (3) it is less reactive with demand substances than free or combined chlorine (Hoff, 1986). It is, however, not without its disadvantages, which include (1) easy loss from solution due to volatilization and (2) disproportionation above pH 10 into non-cysticidal chlorate and chlorite ions.

At present the only data available on the efficacy of ClO_2 show that it is much superior to free chlorine or to chloramines as a *Giardia* cysticide. The mean *Ct* value for ClO_2 at pH 7 and 5°C was 11.9 mg·min/l; this dropped to 5.2 at pH 7 and 25°C. The best performance for ClO_2 was at pH 9 and 25°C, which yielded a *Ct* product of 2.8 mg·min/l (Rubin, 1989).

Chlorine dioxide appears to be more efficacious against *Cryptosporidium* oocysts than either free chlorine or monochloramine. Exposure of oocysts to 1.3 mg ClO_2/l at pH 7 reduced excystation from 87% to 5% in an hour at 25°C. Based on these results, a *Ct* product of 78 mg·min/l has been calculated (Korich *et al.*, 1990).

A comparison of the efficacy of ClO_2 to that of free chlorine against *N. gruberi* shows that, at pH 7 and 25°C, the *Ct* products are 12.1 and 5.51 mg·min/l, respectively. As with other disinfectants, increasing the temperature decreased the *Ct* value, suggesting improved cysticidal action. Increasing the pH unexpectedly decreased the *Ct* value from a high of 6.35 mg·min/l at pH 5 to low of 2.91 mg·min/l at pH 9 (Sproul *et al.*, 1983; Chen *et al.*, 1985; Rubin, 1989).

3.4 Iodine

Few reports deal with the efficacy of iodine against *Giardia*. In most of these studies iodine was tested for its efficacy as a small-quantity water disinfectant (Jarroll *et al.*, 1980a,b). However, the kinetics of iodine disinfection against *G. muris* have been examined (Rubin & Chen, unpublished; Rubin, 1987). Rubin (1987) reported *Ct* products for elemental iodine ranging from a low of 76.6 mg·min/l at pH 7 and 25°C to a high of 392.7 mg·min/l at pH 7 and 5°C for the inactivation of *G. muris* cysts. These data suggest that iodine is a slightly more effective cysticide against *G. muris* than chlorine, especially at low temperatures.

The *Ct* product for iodine against *E. histolytica* cysts (99% kill) under the conditions used by Stringer *et al.* (1975) was considerably higher than that for chlorine. At pH 7 and 30°C, a *Ct* value of 70 mg·min/l is an approximation of the data. While iodine was the least effective of the three halogens tested in buffered water against *E. histolytica*, it was the most effective halogen tested in sewage effluent at pH values below 8.

Parenthetically, iodine (2–5 mg/l) failed to inactivate *A. culbertsoni* cysts after a 24-h exposure in artificially made swimming-pool water (DeJonckheere & van de Voorde, 1976).

3.5 Bromine

Stringer *et al.* (1975) observed that bromine was superior to iodine or chlorine as an *E. histolytica* cysticide in buffered water. They reported that at pH 4 only 1.5 mg bromine/l were required to produce 99.9% cyst destruction in 10 min at 30°C. These data translate into a *Ct* product of approximately 15 mg·min/l. At this same pH and temperature, iodine exhibited a *Ct* value of 50 while chlorine exhibited a value of 20 mg·min/l. As the pH increased to 10, the *Ct* value for bromine increased to only 40 mg·min/l, while the *Ct* products for chlorine and iodine rose to 120 and 200 mg·min/l, respectively.

De Jonckheere & van de Voorde (1976) were unable to inactivate *A. culbertsoni* cysts in artificially made swimming-pool water with a 24-h exposure of cysts to bromine at 0.4–1 mg/l.

3.6 Ozone

The data of Wickramanayake *et al.* (1984a,b) leave little doubt that ozone is the most effective *Giardia* cysticide tested to date. While *G. lamblia* cysts were at least an order of magnitude more resistant to ozone than *E. coli* (*Ct* = 0.02 mg·min/l at pH 7.2 and 1°C; Katzenelson *et al.*, 1974) and approximately twice as resistant to ozone as polio-virus 1 (*Ct* = 0.22 mg·min/l at pH 7.2 and 5°C; Roy *et al.*, 1982), these protozoan cysts exhibited *Ct* products of only 0.17 mg·min/l at pH 7 and 25°C, and 0.53 mg·min/l at pH 7 and 5°C. At pH 7 and 5°C, *G. muris* cysts exhibited *Ct* values approximately fourfold higher than *G. lamblia* cysts under comparable conditions. The effect of temperature on the efficacy of ozonation is obvious from the data above, and as one would expect the effectiveness of ozonation increases as the temperature increases. The effect of pH on ozonation showed that cyst killing was greatest at pH 9 followed by pH 5 and pH 7, respectively. One can speculate that this effect is related to the structural and physiological changes in the parasite's cyst wall altering the permeability to ozone.

Newton & Jones (1949) reported that >98% of the *E. histolytica* cysts examined were inactivated following a 5-min exposure to from 0.7 to 1.1 mg/l ozone at pH 7.5–8 in tap water at 19°C. These same authors observed little, if any, difference in destruction of *E. histolytica* cysts from 10 to 27°C.

Korich *et al.* (1990) reported that *Cryptosporidium* oocysts, like the other protozoan cysts examined, are quite sensitive to ozone. These workers calculated a *Ct* value of between 5 and 10 mg·min/l from the observation that excystation decreased from 84% to 0% after 5 min in 1 mg ozone/l at 25°C.

Wickramanayake *et al.* (1984a) showed that *N. gruberi* cysts are more resistant to ozone than are *G. muris* cysts. In fact at pH 7 and 25°C, the average *Ct* product was 1.29 mg·min/l for *N. gruberi* versus 0.27 mg·min/l for *G. muris*. Lowering the water temperature to 5°C increased the *Ct* product to 1.94 mg·min/l against *G. muris*, while that value for *N. gruberi* rose to 4.23 mg·min/l under the same conditions. No difference in sensitivity to ozone was detected between *Naegleria* and *Acanthamoeba* (Cursons *et al.*, 1980).

3.7 Ultraviolet radiation

Rice & Hoff (1981) demonstrated that *G. lamblia* cysts were more resistant to ultraviolet (UV) radiation than *E. coli*. In their studies, *E. coli* viability was reduced by nearly 3-log cycles at 3 milliwatts per second per square centimetre (mW s/cm^2), but *G. lamblia* cyst survival was not reduced by 1-log at 43–63 mW s/cm^2. It has been suggested, however, that these results were due to low UV exposure dose, since Carlson *et al.* (1985) were able to reduce *G. muris* cyst viability by approximately 99% in 20 min using laser-generated UV at 109.7 mW s/cm^2. The addition of colour with absorbance at 254 nm, regardless of the source, appeared to increase cyst survival; whereas small organic or inorganic particles, 5 μm in diameter or less, did not adversely affect UV inactivation of cysts; larger particles may provide shielding from UV. Short-circuiting and the collection of air bubbles in commercial UV disinfection units can also decrease the effectiveness of UV.

De Jonckheere (1982) compared the microbiological quality of hospital hydrotherapy pools treated with either halogens (chlorine or bromine) or UV. He reported that the halogenated pools as a rule were not highly contaminated with coliforms or pseudomonads unless poorly managed, but that the irradiated pools often had poor bacteriological quality with high numbers of *Pseudomonas aeruginosa* and thermophilic *Naegleria*. The above results are consistent with those of Rice & Hoff (1981), who showed the ineffectiveness of UV against *Giardia* cysts.

Chang *et al.* (1985) examined the survival of *Escherichia coli*, *Salmonella typhi*, *Shigella sonnei*, *Streptococcus faecalis*, *Staphylococcus aureus*, *Bacillus subtilis* spores, poliovirus type 1, simian rotavirus SA11, and *Acanthamoeba castellani* cysts exposed to UV. *A. castellani* cysts were much more resistant to UV than were any of the other organisms tested; 15 times more resistant than *E. coli*. Nevertheless, *A. castellani* cysts appear to be much less resistant to UV than *G. lamblia* cysts, which were approximately 68 times more resistant to UV than *E. coli* at the −0.6-log survival level (Chang *et al.*, 1985).

4 SUMMARY

It is generally the rule, with respect to protozoans examined to date, that ozone is the most effective cysticide; chlorine dioxide is superior to iodine and chlorine. Iodine, at least against *Giardia*, seems to be a slightly better cysticide than chlorine, but chlorine is generally much superior to chloramines. The effectiveness of ozone and the halogens is temperature- and pH-dependent. Higher temperatures normally enhance the efficacy of these disinfectants while lower temperatures have an opposite effect, requiring additional contact time or disinfectant. Halogens that would normally be expected to exhibit decreasing efficacy with increasing pH have shown, quite surprisingly, opposite results in the case of several of these protozoans.

Experimental evidence exists showing that ultraviolet radiation, to be cysticidal for most protozoans, requires much higher dosages (perhaps an order of magnitude larger) than those required to be bactericidal.

Virtually all disinfection studies to date have shown that protozoa resist chemical disinfection and UV radiation better than most bacteria or viruses. One implication of this is that the absence of viable coliform organisms in treated water cannot be considered as an absolute indicator of the absence of viable protozoans.

An impressive amount of laboratory data has been collected in the past 10 years on the efficacy of water disinfection methods against *Giardia*, *Entamoeba* and *Naegleria*. Information concerning the treatment of water for *Cryptosporidium* is beginning to appear, but the paucity of information on this potential pathogen makes it imperative that this work be expanded (Campbell *et al.*, 1982).

5 REFERENCES

Albach, R. & Booden, T. (1978) Amoebae. In *Parasitic Protozoa* (ed. Kreier, J.) Vol. 2, pp. 455–506. New York: Academic Press.

Belosevic, M., Faubert, G., MacLean, J., Law, C. & Croll, N. (1983) *Giardia lamblia* infections in Mongolian gerbils: an animal model. *Journal of Infectious Diseases*, **147**, 222–226.

Campbell, I., Tzipori, S., Hutchison, G. & Angus, K. (1982) Effect of disinfectants on survival of *Cryptosporidium* oocysts. *Veterinary Record*, **111**, 414–415.

Carlson, D., Seabloom, R., DeWalle, F., Wetzler, T., Engeset, J., Butler, R., Wangsuphachart, S. & Wang, S. (1985) Ultra-violet disinfection of water for small water supplies. United States Environmental Protection Agency Project Summary No. 600/S2–85/092, September.

Chang, J., Ossoff, S., Lobe, D., Dorfman, M., Dumais, C., Qualls, R. & Johnson, J. (1985) UV inactivation of pathogenic and indicator microorganisms. *Applied and Environmental Microbiology*, **49**, 1361–1365.

Chang, S. (1978) Resistance of pathogenic *Naegleria* to some common physical and chemical agents. *Applied and Environmental Microbiology*, **35**, 368–375.

Chen, Y., Sproul, O. & Rubin, A. (1985) Inactivation of *Naegleria gruberi* cysts by chlorine dioxide. *Water Research*, **19**, 783–789.

Craun, G. (1986) Waterborne giardiasis in the United States 1965–84. *Lancet*, **ii**, 513.

Cursons, R., Brown, T. & Keys, E. (1980) Effect of disinfectants on pathogenic free-living amoebae: in axenic conditions. *Applied and Environmental Microbiology*, **40**, 62–66.

De Jonckheere, J. (1982) Hospital hydrotherapy pools treated with ultra violet light: bad bacteriological quality and presence of thermophilic *Naegleria*. *Journal of Hygiene, Cambridge*, **88**, 205–214.

De Jonckheere, J. & van de Voorde, H. (1976) Differences in destruction of cysts of pathogenic and nonpathogenic *Naegleria* and *Acanthamoeba* by chlorine. *Applied and Environmental Microbiology*, **31**, 294–297.

Engel, J., Rubin, A. & Sproul, O. (1983) Inactivation of *Naegleria gruberi* cysts by chlorinated cyanurates. *Applied and Environmental Microbiology*, **46**, 1157–1162.

Fayer, R. & Ungar, B. (1986) *Cryptosporidium* spp. and cryptosporidiosis. *Microbiological Reviews*, **50**, 458–483.

Griffin, J. (1978) Pathogenic free-living amoebae. In *Parasitic Protozoa* (ed. Kreier, J.) pp. 507–549. New York: Academic Press.

Hibler, C., Hancock, C., Perger, L., Wegryzn, J. & Swabby, K. (1987) Inactivation of *Giardia* cysts with chlorine at 0.5°C to 5.0°C. American Water Works Association Research Report. Denver, CO.

Hoff, J. (1986) Strengths and weakness of using Ct values to evaluate disinfection practice. Water Quality Technology Conference Presentation (AWWA), Portland, OR, November.

Jarroll, E. (1988) Effect of disinfectants on *Giardia* cysts. *CRC Reviews in Environmental Control*, **18**, 1–28.

Jarroll, E., Bingham, A. & Meyer, E. (1980a) *Giardia* cyst destruction: effectiveness of six small quantity water disinfection methods. *American Journal of Tropical Medicine and Hygiene*, **29**, 8–11.

Jarroll, E., Bingham, A. & Meyer, E. (1980b) Inability of an iodination method to destroy completely *Giardia* cysts in cold water. *Western Journal of Medicine*, **132**, 567–569.

Jarroll, E., Bingham, A. & Meyer, E. (1981) Effect of chlorine on *Giardia lamblia* cyst viability. *Applied and Environmental Microbiology*, **41**, 483–487.

Jarroll, E., Hoff, J. & Meyer, E. (1984) Resistance of cysts to disinfection agents. In *Giardia and Giardiasis* (eds Erlandsen, S. & Meyer, E.) pp. 311–328. New York: Plenum Press.

Jarroll, E., Manning, P., Lindmark, D., Coggins, J. & Erlandsen, S. (1989) *Giardia* cyst wall specific carbohydrate: evidence for the presence of galactosamine. *Molecular and Biochemical Parasitology*, **32**, 121–132.

Katzenelson, E., Kletter, B. & Shuval, H. (1974) Inactivation kinetics of viruses and bacteria in water by use of ozone. *Journal of the American Water Works Association*, **66**, 725–729.

Korich, D.G., Mead, J.R., Madore, M.S., Sinclair, N.A. & Sterling, C.R. (1990) Effects of ozone, chlorine dioxide, chlorine and monochloramine on *Cryptosporidium parvum* oocyst viability. *Applied and Environmental Microbiology*, **56**, 1423–1428.

Leahy, J., Rubin, A. & Sproul, O. (1987) Inactivation of *Giardia muris* cysts by free chlorine. *Applied and Environmental Microbiology*, **53**, 1448–1453.

Meyer, E. & Jarroll, E. (1980) Giardiasis. *American Journal of Epidemiology*, **111**, 1–12.

Meyer, E., Glicker, J., Bingham, A. & Edwards, R. (1989) Inactivation of *Giardia muris* cysts by chloramines. *Water Resources Bulletin*, **25**, 335–340.

Newton, W. & Jones, M. (1949) Effect of ozone in water on cysts of *Entamoeba histolytica*. *American Journal of Tropical Medicine*, **29**, 669.

Rice, E. & Hoff, J. (1981) Inactivation of *Giardia lamblia* cysts by ultraviolet irradiation. *Applied and Environmental Microbiology*, **42**, 546–547.

Rice, E., Hoff, J. & Schaefer, F. (1982) Inactivation of *Giardia* cysts by chlorine. *Applied and Environmental Microbiology*, **43**, 250–251.

Roy, D., Engelbrecht, R. & Chian, E. (1982) Comparative inactivation of six enteroviruses by ozone. *Journal of the American Water Works Association*, **74**, 660–664.

Rubin A. (1987) Factors affecting the inactivation of *Giardia* cysts by monochloramines and comparison with other disinfectants. Conference on Current Research in Drinking Water Treatment (presentation). US Environmental Protection Agency and American Water Works Association Research Foundation (sponsors). Cincinnati, OH, March.

Rubin, A. (1989) Control of protozoan cysts in water by disinfection with chlorine dioxide. In *Environmental Quality and Ecosystems Stability*: Vol. IV-A: *Environmental Quality*. (eds Luria, M., Steinberger, Y. & Spanier, E.) pp. 391–400. Jerusalem, Israel: ISEEQS Publications.

Rubin, A., Engel, J & Sproul, O. (1983) Disinfection of amoebic cysts in water with free chlorine. *Journal of the Water Pollution Control Federation*, **55**, 1174–1182.

Rubin, A., Evers, D., Eyman, C. & Jarroll E. (1989) Inactivation of gerbil-cultured *Giardia lamblia* cysts by free chlorine. *Applied and Environmental Microbiology*, **55**, 2592–2594.

Sproul, O., Chen, Y., Engel, J. & Rubin, A. (1983) Comparison of chlorine and chlorine dioxide for the inactivation of amoebic cysts. *Environmental Technology Letter*, **4**, 335–342.

Stringer, R. (1972) New bioassay system for evaluating per cent survival of *Entamoeba histolytica* cysts. *Journal of Parasitology*, **58**, 306–310.

Stringer, R., Cramer, W. & Kruse, C. (1975) Comparison of bromine, chlorine and iodine as disinfectants for amoebic cysts. In *Disinfection — Water and Wastewater* (ed. Johnson, J.) pp. 193–209. Ann Arbor MI: Ann Arbor.

Watson, H. (1908) A note on the variation of the rate of disinfection with change in the concentration of the disinfectant. *Journal of Hygiene*, **8**,. 536–542.

Wickramanayake, G., Rubin, A. & Sproul, O. (1984a) Inactivation of *Naegleria* and *Giardia* cysts in water by ozonation. *Journal of the Water Pollution Control Federation*, **56**, 983–988.

Wickramayanake, G., Rubin, A. & Sproul, O. (1984b) Inactivation of *Giardia lamblia* cysts with ozone. *Applied and Environmental Microbiology*, **48**, 671–672.

Chapter 9
Disinfection Mechanisms

1 INTRODUCTION

Three areas may be recognized in studies of disinfection mechanisms, and resistance and revival of microbes therefrom:

1 studies of the kinetics of disinfection;
2 biochemical and biophysical studies of the basic mechanisms of chemical stress and its reversal;
3 methods of evaluating disinfectants.

Only the kinetic and the biochemical and biophysical studies concerning the effects of chemical stress and their reversal will be dealt with here. Part 3, above, is dealt with in Chapter 4. Interactions of chemicals with whole cells, cell walls, membranes and the cytoplasm will be considered in turn, followed by suggestions on the possible mechanism of survival to chemical disinfectant attack (for reviews see Hugo, 1976a,b, 1980 and Russell & Hugo, 1988).

A compilation of experimental methods used to elucidate mechanisms of action has been published by Denyer & Hugo (1991).

2 THE KINETIC APPROACH

In an exemplary paper by Kronig & Paul, published in 1897, and reprinted in English in Brock (1961), the foundation was laid for the kinetic approach to chemical sterilization and the fundamental conditions to be observed in chemical studies of the process. Having codified rules which included the notion that comparative toxicity studies should be carried out at equimolecular proportions, with known numbers of bacteria in pure culture at constant temperature and under similar conditions of culture, Kronig & Paul (1897) went on to apply the emerging rules of chemical kinetics to the disinfection process, a procedure they stated was valid because the process must be a chemical one. They were the first to plot the logarithm of the surviving organisms against time, which they found gave a linear response.

The theme of linear log survival/time was developed by Madsen & Nyman (1907) and survival investigated by many other workers, notably Chick (1908), Knaysi (1930), Knaysi & Morris (1930), Jordan & Jacobs (1944), Rahn (1945), Berry & Michaels (1947), Eddy (1953), Jacobs (1960) and Prokop & Humphrey (1970).

Departures from true linearity were often encountered, and Madsen & Nyman (1907) concluded that the different rates of destruction of bacteria under the influence of lethal agents were determined essentially by variability of resistance among the cells in a population. Rahn & Schroeder (1941) thought that in each bacterial species there was a single vulnerable molecule the destruction of which was lethal. Such an hypothesis is not supported by our present knowledge of the varied mode of action of lethal chemicals.

Eddy & Hinshelwood (Eddy, 1953) investigated the death rate of *Klebsiella aerogenes* under chemical stress induced by 3,6-diaminoacridine, *m*-cresol and acid. No satisfactory evidence was found that cells in a given culture possessed variable resistance, and indeed Eddy showed that survivors in a disinfection process gave rise to a population no more resistant than the originals. The often-observed lag phase, before decrease in viability proceeded logarithmically, suggests that a number of events must occur before a significant number of cells begin to die: the number of these events may be the variable factor.

Eddy (1953) believed that at first certain essential metabolic capabilities were impaired. This phase was not considered lethal but gave rise to the initial lag phase. In the light of other evidence it is probable that this represents bacteriostasis as it is reversible, at least if the contact time is not prolonged. As time proceeds the cells die according to the logarithmic law. The slowing-up of the death rate after a further lapse of time was taken as indicative of an adaptive (?phenotypic) process, enabling the cells which had survived by chance to adjust to the chemical stress. However, these adapted cells show the same death pattern as in the original experiment when they are subcultured and re-challenged.

The significance of the variation in survival curves continues to be the subject of research, and Casolari (1981) has described a mathematical model in which functions derived from it can describe the varying shapes of survival curves whether concave, convex, sigmoid or linear. It also claims to explain the tailing-off effect.

A factor which can be calculated from survival data is known as the concentration exponent, η, which measures the effect of dilution on the activity of a stressing agent. It may be calculated from the following expression: (log death time at concentration C_2) − (log death time at concentration C_1)/log C_1 − log C_2. Typical values of η for phenol are 6, for mercuric chloride and formaldehyde, 1 and for ethanol, 9 (see also Chapter 3). There is an exponential relationship between loss of activity and dilution. Thus in the case of phenol, where $\eta = 6$, a threefold dilution will mean a decrease in activity by a factor of 3^6 or 729. In practical terms, rapid dilution of a solution of a chemical antimicrobial agent with a high value of η will nullify the stress and the survivor level amongst the remaining population will stabilize. Can we learn anything from the vast array of such data? Very little, it is feared, about mechanisms of disinfection, for the curves represent interactions of chemicals having differing cellular targets and modes of action with highly complex micro-organisms at different stages of growth, and with different structures and chemical compositions. The subject has been reviewed by Hugo and Denyer (1987).

3 INTERACTIONS WITH THE WHOLE CELL

However organelle- or enzyme-selective a drug may finally turn out to be, its first apparent interaction is with the whole cell, and this may be examined as an adsorption process or by micro-electrophoresis.

3.1 Adsorption

As early as 1911, Herzog & Betzel realized the importance of adsorption in the disinfection process, in their studies with baker's yeast, and since then many others have measured the uptake of drugs by cells. The technique consists essentially of adding a suspension of cells to a solution of the drug and at suitable time intervals removing a sample, centrifuging it, and determining the residual amount of drug in the cell-free supernatant solution. If the cells have removed drug from solution, the concentration of the drug in the supernatant fluid will have diminished. From these data, adsorption isotherms may be plotted and information concerning rate and total amount of uptake may be computed. Furthermore, by a consideration of the nature of the isotherm, some notion of the adsorptive mechanism may be inferred (Giles *et al.*, 1960, 1974). These authors considered five main patterns of adsorption which they called S, L, H, C and Z. (Fig. 9.1).

3.1.1 S (S-shaped) pattern

The 'S' pattern is found when the solute molecule is monofunctional, has moderate intermolecular attraction, causing it to orientate vertically, and meets strong competition for substrate sites from molecules of the solvent or by another adsorbed species. Monohydric phenols when adsorbed on a polar substrate from water usually give this pattern.

3.1.2 L (Langmuir) pattern

In the 'L' pattern, as more sites are filled it becomes increasingly difficult for a bombarding solute to find a vacant site. The adsorbed solute molecule is either not orientated vertically or there is strong competition from the solvent. If vertical orientation does occur there is a strong intramolecular attraction between the adsorbed molecules. Amongst the phenols, resorcinol shows this type of behaviour.

3.1.3 H (high-affinity) pattern

The 'H' pattern is obtained when the solute is almost completely adsorbed. Sometimes the process is accompanied by ion exchange, as in many bacteriological staining procedures. It is also shown by the uptake of iodine from an iodophor by yeast (Hugo & Newton, 1964).

3.1.4 C (constant partition) pattern

The 'C' pattern is obtained when the solutes penetrate more readily into the adsorbate than does

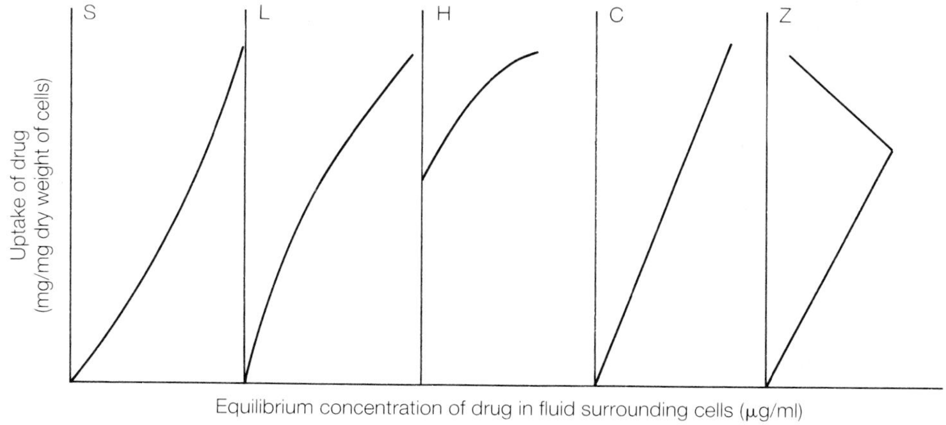

Fig. 9.1 Pattern of adsorption isotherms.

the solvent. It has been shown to occur when aqueous solutions of phenols are adsorbed by synthetic polypeptides, and it might also be expected to occur when phenols are adsorbed from an aqueous solution by bacteria containing a high proportion of lipid in their cell wall.

3.1.5 Z pattern

In the 'Z' pattern a sharp break in the isotherm is seen, accompanied thereafter by an increased uptake; this is interpreted as being caused by that concentration of adsorbed species which promotes a breakdown in the structure of the adsorbing species and the generation of new adsorbing sites. This was first seen by Giles & Tolia (1974) when studying the uptake of *p*-nitrophenol from organic solvents by cellulose fibres.

3.1.6 Examples of adsorption studies

More recent studies on the adsorption of antibacterial substances by micro-organisms include the uptake of cetyltrimethylammonium bromide (CTAB) by bacteria (Salton, 1951), the adsorption of hexylresorcinol by *E. coli* (Beckett *et al.*, 1959), of iodine by *E. coli*, *Staph. aureus* and *Sacch. cerevisiae* (Hugo & Newton, 1964), of chlorhexidine by *Staph. aureus*, *E. coli* and *Clostridium perfringens* (Hugo & Longworth, 1964; Hugo & Daltrey, 1974), of basic dyes by fixed yeast cells (Giles & McKay, 1965), of phenols by *E. coli* (Bean & Das, 1966) and *Micrococcus lysodeikticus* (Judis, 1966), of dequalinium by *E. coli* and *Staph. aureus* (Hugo & Frier, 1969) of Fentichlor by *E. coli* and *Staph. aureus* (Hugo & Bloomfield, 1971a), of glutaraldehyde by *E. coli* (Munton & Russell, 1970; Gorman & Scott, 1977), of parabens by *Serratia marcescens* (Furr & Russell, 1972), and of polyhexamethylene biguanides by *E. coli* (Broxton *et al.*, 1984c). Resistant cells may take up less of a biocide, e.g. a benzalkonium chloride-resistant strain of *Ps. aeruginosa* took up less than a eudomoras-sensitive strain (Sakazami *et al.*, 1989). This is not always true, however.

Gilbert *et al.* (1978) report a most interesting example of the 'Z' pattern referred to above. In studies of the mode of action of 2-phenoxyethanol and some of its analogues on *E. coli*, these workers found very similar isotherms to the cellulose *p*-nitrophenol type.

Extending this work (Gilbert *et al.*, 1978), it was found that a similar pattern was given with the yeast *Candida lipolytica*. When, however, *Ps. aeruginosa* was the test organism no such inflexion was obtained, a 'C'-type pattern being observed. This is a finding which might well be of significance in explaining, at the cellular level, the greater resistance of *Pseudomonas* to a wide variety of antimicrobial compounds.

Information on the site of adsorption may be obtained by studying the process at different pH values, but it should be borne in mind that the ionization of the disinfectant as well as receptor sites on the cell surfaces may be affected by changes in pH.

Adsorption studies of a different nature involving the uptake of drugs by nucleic acids have been used extensively to study actions on this molecule, and will be dealt with later.

The action of such substances as serum and organic debris in reducing the stress caused by some chemical bactericides may be due to their ability to compete with the bacterial cell for some of the active agent. In some cases, drugs may be desorbed from the cell after initial adsorption, thereby decreasing the stress.

3.2 Changes in electrophoretic mobility

Bacterial cells are normally negatively charged and, if suspended in water or a suitable electrolyte solution containing electrodes to which a potential has been applied, the cells will migrate to the positively charged electrode. This phenomenon may be placed on a quantitative basis by observing the rate of migration of a single cell to the electrode by timing over a measured distance using a microscope and calibrated eyepiece micrometer. Once the system has been standardized, the effect of drugs on mobility may be studied, and from the data so obtained some notion of the drug–cell interaction and the effect of drugs on the charged bacterial cell surface may be deduced. The subject of bacterial cell electrophoresis has been reviewed in detail by Lerch (1953), James (1965, 1972) and

Richmond & Fisher (1973). In general, it can be said that while providing an exact tool for studying drug–cell interactions, electrophoresis has not provided much insight into the mechanisms of death.

Electrophoretic studies using antimicrobial compounds include CTAB and *Staph. aureus* (McQuillen, 1950), phenol and *E. coli* (Haydon, 1956), chlorhexidine and *E. coli* and *Staph. aureus* (Hugo & Longworth, 1966) and polyhexamethylene biguanides and *E. coli* (Broxton *et al.*, 1984c).

4 INTERACTIONS WITH THE CELL WALL AND OTHER STRUCTURES EXTERNAL TO THE CYTOPLASMIC MEMBRANE

Antibiotics which have the cell wall as their target include penicillins, cephalosporins, cycloserine, vancomycin and ristocetin. In addition, Pulvertaft & Lumb (1948) showed that *E. coli*, streptococci and staphylococci lysed almost completely when rapidly growing cultures were exposed to low concentrations of antiseptics such as formalin (0.012%), phenol (0.032%), mercuric chloride (0.0008%), sodium hypochlorite (0.005%) and merthiolate (0.0004%). They presumed that the autolytic enzymes were not inhibited at the low concentrations of antiseptic used, and compared this with the action of penicillin. The involvement of autolytic enzymes in penicillin action has been postulated (see Rogers & Forsburg, 1971, Tomasz, 1979). Washed suspensions of *E. coli*, obtained from stationary-phase cultures, are not, however, lysed by low or high phenol concentrations.

Thiomersalate has been shown to increase the susceptibility of *Bacillus anthracis* to lysis, and the observation has been confirmed with *B. cereus*. Low concentrations of some mercury compounds, which include mercuric chloride, phenylmercuric acetate and merthiolate, can lyse growing cultures of *E. coli*.

Sodium lauryl sulphate can lyse non-respiring (cyanide-treated) cells of *E. coli*. The organisms enlarged into globular forms and then lysed rapidly, although actively metabolizing cells were not susceptible. Anionic detergents can cause disaggregation of isolated walls of Gram-negative bacteria due to their action upon the lipid-containing compounds of the wall, rather than to lytic enzymes. The lytic effect of anionic detergents on walls of wild-type and envelope mutants of *E. coli* and *Ps. aeruginosa* has recently been studied by El-Falaha *et al.* (1989). Sodium deoxycholate interferes with the flagellation and mobility of *E. coli* and *Proteus vulgaris* (D'Mello & Yotis, 1987).

Phenol (0.5%) caused lysis of cell pairs of *E. coli* only at the time of separation, i.e. when the cytoplasmic membrane was weak and exposed and its phospholipid content minimal.

Evidence of cell-wall damage may be inferred from the phenomenon of drug-induced long forms of bacteria (Hughes, 1956). Thus, long forms may be induced in *Pr. vulgaris* by treatment with 1–2% phenol: a similar effect has been observed with *m*-cresol acting on *K. aerogenes*. Methyl violet, methyl green, fuchsin and methylene blue can induce long forms in *Salmonella typhi*. The involvement of lytic enzymes in long-form induction cannot be excluded.

Other chemicals that have an effect on outer cellular components include glutaraldehyde (Gorman *et al.*, 1980), which combines strongly with amino groups in amino acids and proteins, and permeability agents, e.g. ethylenediamine tetraacetic acid (EDTA), polycations such as poly-L-lysine and the iron-binding proteins lactoferrin and transferrin (Vaara & Vaara, 1983a,b; Ellison *et al.*, 1988; Russell & Chopra, 1990; see also Chapter 3). Glutaraldehyde also acts elsewhere in the cell, e.g. at the site of the cytoplasmic membrane (Section 5.1) and at cytoplasmic sites (Russell & Chopra, 1990), and EDTA can affect ribosomal stability (Section 6.4).

5 INTERACTIONS WITH THE CYTOPLASMIC MEMBRANE

Early work in this area was concerned with drug-induced leakage of material, and there is little doubt that this contributes to stasis or death according to the time and intensity of exposure to the chemical stress concerned. More recently, reactions at the molecular level have been revealed, and it is these reactions which are currently the most exciting. They include uncoupling of oxidative phosphorylation and inhibition of energy-dependent transport.

5.1 Leakage of cell constituents and modification of cell permeability

Kuhn & Bielig (1940) made the suggestion that cationic detergents of the quaternary ammonium compound (QAC) class might act on the bacterial cell membrane by dissociating conjugated proteins and, in a manner analogous to haemolysis, damage it so much that death would ensue. Hotchkiss (1944) proved that membrane damage was occurring, by demonstrating that nitrogen- and phosphorus-containing compounds leaked from staphylococci treated with a QAC or the polypeptide antibiotic, tyrocidin.

Phenol, *p*-chloro-*m*-xylenol, *p*-chloro-*m*-cresol, *p*-chloro-*o*-cresol, 2,4-dichlorophenol, 2,4,6-trichlorophenol and 2,4,-dichloro-*m*-xylenol, CTAB and chlorhexidine all promote a concentration-dependent leakage of cell contents from microbial cells.

In the case of chlorhexidine-induced leakage of intracellular material from *E. coli* and *Staph. aureus*, a diphasic leakage/concentration pattern is found. The first part of the curve represents increasing leakage with increasing concentration of antiseptic, but a high concentrations the protoplasmic contents or cytoplasmic membrane became gradually coagulated so that the leakage became progressively less. Electron micrographs of thin sections of bacteria taken after suitable dose treatments confirmed this view (Fig. 9.2). A similar pattern is found with hexachlorophene and *B. megaterium*. However, Hugo & Bloomfield (1971a,b,c) in their studies on the mode of action of 2,2′-thiobis (4-chlorophenol), Fentichlor, found a close correlation between bactericidal action on *E. coli* and *Staph. aureus* and ability to promote leakage of material absorbing at 260 nm. Bacteriostatic concentrations of the drug did not cause leakage.

Many solvents including butanol, ethanol, toluene and phenylethanol cause the release of intracellular constituents. The phenylethanol/*E. coli* interaction is reversible, suggesting that the structural integrity of the membrane is not seriously impaired.

Anionic detergents such as dodecyl sulphate (SDS) are generally less toxic to bacteria, although their target is also the cytoplasmic membrane. This may be due to the fact that in SDS and other anionic detergents the active ion is negatively charged and may be repelled by the negatively charged bacterial surface.

Non-ionic, surface-active agents are practically non-toxic to bacteria: indeed some, e.g. nonidet, are useful biochemical tools for preparing enzymically active bacterial membranes. Non-ionic agents have been shown to act synergistically when combined with various antibacterial compounds but also protect cells from phenols (Chapter 3).

Ion-specific electrodes have allowed very accurate determinations of ion efflux from bacterial cells treated with membrane-active antimicrobial agents. Lambert & Hammond (1973) have concluded that the order of release of cell constituents from *E. coli* treated with 0.2 mM cetrimide was K^+, then PO_4^{3-}, followed by material absorbing at 260 nm. The release of K^+ was complete in 30 min.

It is clear that solvents and certain antibacterial agents promote leakage of ions, labile nucleic acids and their component purines, pyrimidines, pentoses and inorganic phosphorus, and detection of all these substances is used to determine membrane damage. It is unlikely that this is a rapidly fatal process, and it is probably associated with bacteriostasis. As might be expected, this type of damage is often reparable.

Salton (1968) has reviewed the mode of action of detergents on bacteria, and he concluded that the sequence of events following exposure of microbes was:

1 adsorption onto the cell followed by a penetration into the largely porous cell wall;
2 reactions with lipid/protein complexes of the cytoplasmic membrane leading to its disorganization;
3 leakage of low-molecular-weight components from the cytoplasm;
4 degradation of proteins and nucleic acids;
5 wall lysis caused by autolytic enzymes.

It is very important, when considering these propositions and any other interaction of drugs with micro-organisms, to bear in mind the difference in structure of walls of Gram-positive and

Gram-negative bacteria, and especially the role of the outer layers of the walls of the latter group (Section 9; Chapter 10A).

Glutaraldehyde (pentanedial) $CHO\cdot(CH_2)_3\cdot CHO$, which first found use as a tanning agent for leather and later as a fixative for tissue prior to embedding and sectioning for electron microscopy, was introduced as an antibacterial agent in 1962 and has been extensively studied (for comprehensive reviews see Russell & Hopwood, 1976; Gorman *et al.*, 1980).

As might be imagined from a molecule containing two reactive groups, glutaraldehyde has widespread chemical reactivity, combining with $-NH_2$, $-COOH$ and $-SH$ groups and with many components of the cell which contain these groups. Wall, wall lipopolysaccharide, protein, nucleic acid and lipid have all been implicated and it is hard to decide, to date, which is the reaction (if there is only one), which causes the fatal lesion.

The fact that glutaraldehyde reacts with the ε-amino group of lysine, thus forming an internal protein cross-link, might mean that the function of membrane transport proteins and porins could be impaired. Larger concentrations must kill by a generalized reaction with the many reactive groups of structural and functional components of the cell.

Other examples of work showing disinfectant-induced leakage of cell constituents include CTAB (Salton, 1951), tetrachlorosalicylanilide and *Staph. aureus* (Woodroffe & Wilkinson, 1956), chlorhexidine and *E. coli* and *Staph. aureus* (Hugo & Longworth, 1965; Chawner & Gilbert, 1989a,b; Fitzgerald *et al.*, 1989), phenol and *Serratia marcescens* (Kroll & Anagnostopoulos, 1981), polyhexamethylene biguanides and *E. coli* (Broxton *et al.*, 1984a,b) and phenoxyethanol and *E. coli* and *Ps. aeruginosa* (Fitzgerald *et al.*, to be published).

5.2 Inhibition of energy processes

Any discussion on this topic must be linked with both uncoupling of oxidative phosphorylation and the chemiosmotic theory of membrane transport (Mitchell, 1968, 1970, 1972). Mitchell proposed that oxidative phosphorylation, ATP synthesis, active transport and the maintenance of intracellular solute levels are powered by a protonmotive force, generated by metabolic oxido-reductions, which are apparent as chemical and electrical gradients or potential differences across the cytoplasmic membrane. It may be expressed in mathematical terms thus:

$$\Delta p = \Delta\Psi - Z\Delta\text{pH},$$

where Δp is the protonmotive force, $\Delta\Psi$ is the membrane electrical potential in mV and ΔpH is the trans-membrane pH gradient. Z is a factor converting pH values to mV, and at 37°C has a value of 62. The expression $-Z\Delta$pH, therefore, is a pH difference expressed in mV. Typical reported experimental values of these potentials in bacteria at 37°C are 120 mV for $\Delta\Psi$ and -62 mV for $Z\Delta$pH. Thus

$$\Delta p = 182 \text{ mV}.$$

ΔpH may be measured by a pH meter or by measuring the distribution of a weak acid, such as dimethyloxazolidinedione, aspirin or benzoic acid, across the membrane; $\Delta\Psi$ may be measured by the distribution of ions such as K^+, dibenzyldimethylammonium or triphenylmethylphosphonium by the application of the Nernst equation; ion distribution is measured spectroscopically or with ion specific electrodes.

It will be recalled that the protonmotive force ($\Delta\Psi - Z\Delta$pH) is said to be responsible for the synthesis of adenosine triphosphate (ATP) as part of the process of oxidative phosphorylation.

It has been known almost from the beginning of this century that nitrophenols, especially 2,4-dinitrophenol (DNP), interfered with oxidative phosphorylation without inhibiting other metabolic processes. The name 'uncoupling agent' was coined for DNP, and later was applied to other compounds of similar activity because they, like DNP, uncoupled oxidation from phosphorylation.

Mitchell showed that 2,4-dinitrophenol caused a backflow of protons across the bacterial and mitochondrial membrane which resulted in a partial or total collapse of the protonmotive force. It was thought that the molecular properties associated with the ability to promote uncoupling was that of a weak acid with lipid solubility. The molecule dissolved in the lipid bilayer of the membrane and acted as a proton-conductor by virtue of its ionizability. Since the discovery of this special property other substances, some of them used as antibacterial agents, have been found to act in a similar manner; examples include Fentichlor and tetrachlorosalicylanilide.

Reviewing the above data it is possible to see a general pattern of behaviour. The nitrophenols short-circuit the membrane, as it were, causing a rapid backflow of protons into the cell and hence the collapse of Δp; they do not cause leakage of cellular constituents and are active at concentrations of 10^{-6} M. Such compounds are now also called proton ionophores.

Certain other phenolic compounds cause both leakage and collapse of Δp; it is often found that concentrations of 10^{-5} M cause Δp collapse whereas leakage is promoted by concentrations of the order of 10^{-4} M.

It seemed worthwhile to examine the effect of a membrane-active, non-phenolic substance such as a cationic detergent which possesses antibacterial activity and promotes leakage of cytoplasmic constituents. Such a compound is cetyltrimethylammonium bromide, and Denyer & Hugo (1977) examined the effect of this extensively investigated compound on its ability to modify Δp.

Using *Staph. aureus* it was shown that 18 μg/ml (5.3×10^{-5} M) cetrimide caused the discharge of the pH component of Δp; 18 μg/ml was also the bacteriostatic concentration and the concentration which caused the maximum leakage of material absorbing at 260 nm. The results indicated that discharge of all or part of the protonmotive force was not the sole prerogative of coupling agents, and it became clear that this biochemical effect might be part of the general action of detergents.

From this it followed that studies on the mode of action of those antibacterial agents which show evidence of membrane activity by traditional techniques, i.e. leakage of cell constituents, must be extended to investigate whether components of the protonmotive force are modified. These experimental systems are more difficult to set up, but to omit them and the results they may produce must always leave a doubt in the mind that the fundamental biochemical lesion has been missed (Hugo, 1978). Organic acids, such as sorbic acid, affect the protonmotive force and inhibit transport across the membrane, but might also possess an additional, as yet unidentified, mechanism of action (Eklund, 1985; Sofos *et al.*, 1986; Russell & Hugo, 1988; Cherrington *et al.*, 1990; Russell & Chopra, 1990).

5.2.1 Interference with membrane enzymes

Chlorhexidine has been claimed to be an inhibitor of both membrane-bound and soluble adenosine triphosphate (ATPase) and also of net K^+ uptake in *Strep. faecalis* while hexachlorophene inhibits part of the membrane-bound electron transport chain in *Bacillus megaterium*. However, it is now believed that inhibition of membrane-bound ATPase is not a primary target of chlorhexidine action, since activity is inhibited only at high biguanide concentrations (Chopra *et al.*, 1987). One explanation of the phenomenon is that chlorhexidine phosphate is very insoluble and may have acted as an ATPase inhibitor by precipitating its substrate!

Mercuric salts act at low concentrations (10^{-6} M), by combining with membrane enzymes containing thiol groups. At such concentrations this action can be reversed by addition of thiol compounds, e.g. thioglycollate or cysteine to the reaction system. Bronopol (2-bromo-2-nitropropanl,3-diol) oxidizes thiol groups to disulphides in bacteria; this action may be reversed by thiol compounds. These compounds also cause membrane damage as indicated by leakage of material which absorbs at 260 nm.

6 INTERACTIONS WITH THE CYTOPLASM

There are four targets for antibacterial drugs: the cytoplasm itself, cytoplasmic enzymes, the nucleic acids and the ribosomes. Hugo (1965a, 1967) has reviewed the first two of these aspects in considerable detail, but a few of the main points are given below.

6.1 Irreversible coagulation of cytoplasmic constituents

This drastic lesion is usually seen at drug concentrations far higher than those causing general lysis or leakage. It was the first cytological effect to be reported and so most antiseptics were classified as general protoplasmic poisons or as protein precipitants. Indeed, at concentrations used in many practical disinfection procedures this is undoubtedly the mechanism of rapid killing, the more subtle and more slowly fatal effects being completely masked.

The cytoplasmic components most likely to be coagulated or denatured are proteins and nucleic acids; most studies have been made on the former. Functionally, proteins are of two main kinds in living cells, structural and enzymic. The high specificity of enzymes is due to their unique surface contours and to the distribution of charges on this surface. The latter arise from residual charges, on the carboxylic acid or amino groups of the constituent amino acids, that are left after peptide-bond formation. It is not difficult to imagine that a derangement of this uniquely contoured and electrically charged unit can upset its function.

As early as 1901, Meyer showed that the degree of antibacterial action of phenols was proportional to their distribution between water and protein, thus suggesting that protein was a prime target. Cooper (1912) came to a similar conclusion and decided that phenols destroy the protein structure within the cell. Bancroft & Richter (1931) actually observed a coagulation of cell protein in *B. megaterium* and *K. aerogenes* using ultraviolet microscopy.

Three main methods are available for studying protoplasmic coagulation—light and electron microscopy, light scattering and direct observation of cytoplasm obtained from smashed cells. Examples of studies by electron microscopy include those of Salton *et al.* (1951) and Dawson *et al.* (1953) (with CTAB) on whole cells treated with antibacterial compounds, and those of Hugo & Longworth (1966) (with chlorhexidine), and Bringmann (1953) (with chlorine, bromine, iodine, Cu^{2+}, Ag^{+} and hydrogen peroxide) on thin sections. Hugo and Longworth found a correlation between the appearance of thin sections and cytoplasmic leakage. Thus at the concentration which caused maximum leakage, electron micrographs of thin sections showed a significant loss of electron-dense material; at higher concentrations, which promoted no leakage due to a general coagulation and sealing-in of labile protoplasmic constituents, the electron micrographs showed a dense granular cytoplasm differing markedly in appearance from that seen in untreated cells (Fig. 9.2).

An interesting technique for studying protoplasmic coagulation is based upon protoplast formation and the fact that rod-shaped cells yield globular protoplasts in isotonic media. If this operation is carried out on cells which have been treated with a coagulant or fixative, then a rod-shaped protoplast is produced which, if coagulation is severe, does not undergo lysis or osmotic explosion on subsequent dilution of the medium (Tomcsik, 1955; Hugo & Longworth, 1964; Daltrey & Hugo, 1974). Coagulation of protein may affect the light-scattering properties of cells, and this is a sensitive method of assessing changes in treated bacteria.

Yet another method consists of disrupting the cells and investigating the action of antiseptic on cell-free extracts. Although this system is an artificial one, and the relative concentrations of the protoplasmic constituents change and suffer enzymatic degradation, it gives some indication of the order of concentration required to produce coagulation. Thus, Hugo & Longworth (1966) found that protein and nucleic acid were precipitated from cell-free preparations of *E. coli* at concentrations of chlorhexidine far higher than those causing leakage.

6.2 Effects on metabolism and enzymes

Despite the large volume of work stretching over many years, and still being prosecuted, the general conclusion is that enzyme inactivation is only one of many events caused by chemical stress and is not likely to be a prime mechanism for death. In some circumstances, however, it may be a cause of bacteriostasis. The reviews of Rahn & Schroeder (1941) and Roberts & Rahn (1946) are worth reading for a discussion of this topic. Early work was reviewed by Hugo (1957).

6.3 Effects on nucleic acids

There are a number of antibiotics which affect the biosynthesis and functioning of nucleic acids. How-

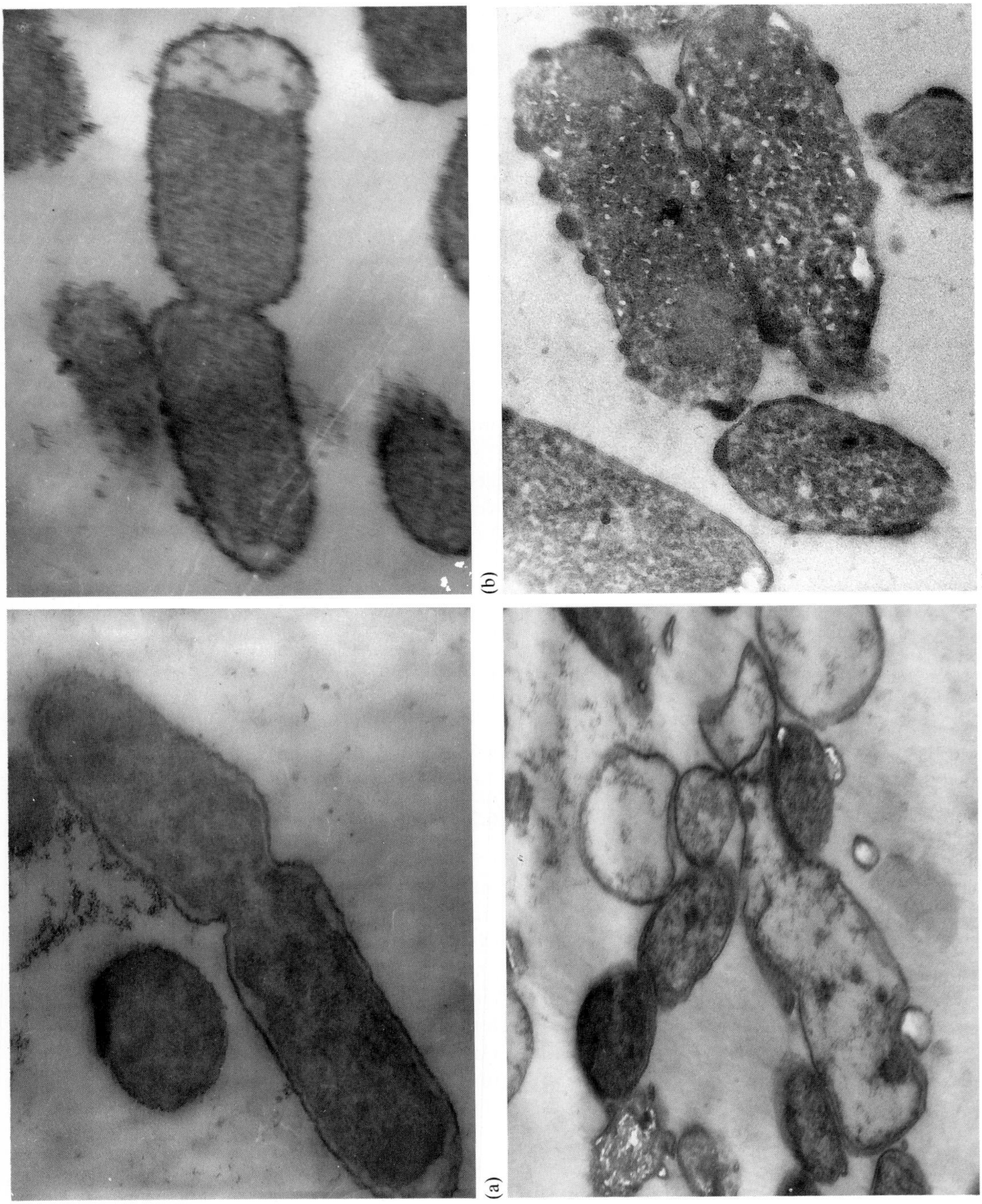

Fig. 9.2 Electron micrographs of thin sections of *Escherichia coli* in phosphate buffer (0.013 M, pH 7.3) after treatment for 6 h with chlorhexidine diacetate at concentrations of: (a) 0 μg/ml; (b) 20 μg/ml; (c) 90 μg/ml; (d) 500 μg/ml (from Hugo & Longworth, 1965).

ever, amongst the non-antibiotic antibacterial drugs, only three main compounds affecting these targets have been identified: these are the acridine dyes, formaldehyde and phenylethanol.

6.3.1 Acridine dyes

Acridine dyes, first introduced into medicine as trypanocidal agents, have been used extensively as antibacterial agents and a large amount of work has been carried out on their mode of action. As with the TPM (triphenylmethane) dyes, it was realized early that the cation was the active ion. McIlwain (1941) showed that nucleic acids antagonized the antibacterial action of acridine dyes, and Ferguson & Thorne (1946), after studying the effect of a series of acridine compounds on growth and respiration of *E. coli*, concluded that they inhibited reactions closely connected with synthetic processes. It emerged that if acridine dyes were only 33% ionized as a cation, there was very little antibacterial action, and for really high activity 98–100% of the molecule should exist in the cationic form. Other studies showed that the flat area of the molecule should be from 0.38 to 0.48 nm^2. Albert (1966) has reviewed acridine chemistry comprehensively.

Studies of DNA binding with proflavine showed a first-order reaction which equilibrated with one molecule of proflavine binding to every four or five nucleotides. There was also a slower reaction of higher order in which a 1:1 binding occurred (Peacocke & Skerrett, 1956; Waring, 1965; Blake & Peacock, 1968). These interactions also involved marked spectral, viscosity and melting-temperature changes.

From a review of available binding data, Lerman proposed (1961), and later elaborated (1964a,b), an intercalation model in which it was suggested that proflavine was bound by DNA, through the two primary amino groups, being held by ionic links to two phosphoric acid residues, and the flat acridine ring system being linked on the purine and pyrimidine residues by Van der Waals forces. Pritchard *et al.* (1966) and Blake & Peacocke (1968) have suggested an alternative mechanism in which the acridine ring lies between two adjacent bases on the same polynucleotide with the primary amino groups now lying close to the phosphoric acid residues of the DNA. The intercalation theory is compatible with the finding of McIlwain (1941) that nucleic acids antagonize the action of acridines; and with the observation, summarized in Albert (1966), that molecular size and shape are of importance in determining the relative potency of acridines. Pritchard *et al.* (1966) and Blake & Peacocke (1968) the observation that acridines inhibit synthetic processes (Ferguson & Thorne, 1946).

Ribonucleic acid polymerase has also been identified as a target for acridines in cell-free preparations from *E. coli*. Nicholson & Peacocke (1965) suggested that inhibitory acridine molecules, which included proflavine and 9-aminoacridine, occupy sites on the polymerase which normally bind nucleoside triphosphates or the bases in the DNA molecule during copying. Waring (1965) discussed the ability of 23 drugs, including proflavine, to inhibit incorporation of adenosine monophosphate into RNA.

Although the main site of activity of acridines is DNA and RNA polymerase it is possible that other, possibly secondary, lesions may be induced in bacterial cells under the influence of these compounds. Such secondary sites are discussed by Foster & Russell (1971).

6.3.2 Formaldehyde

Grossman *et al.* (1961) have shown a reasonably specific reaction to occur between nucleotides and formaldehyde. The amino groups of the purine and pyrimidine rings have been cited as likely sites for the interaction. Collins & Guild (1968) have shown that formaldehyde binding to DNA at 100°C and pH 8 is irreversible. However, Staehelin (1958) found that binding with RNA was reversible if it had not proceeded for longer than 2 h; after 2 h the reaction was slowly reversible only after dialysis. The first reaction was thought to be due to formation of stable methylene bridges, $-NH \cdot CH_2NH-$, between bases containing amino groups. Clearly reactions of this type could occur with cellular amino groups other than those in the nucleic acid molecule.

6.3.3 *Phenylethanol*

Phenylethanol has already been referred to as a membrane-active compound, but it has also been shown to inhibit initiation of replication at high concentrations (Lark & Lark, 1966). Richardson & Leach (1969) re-examined the action of phenylethanol on *B. subtilis*. They concluded that any effects of the drug on DNA function were secondary to its effects on membrane integrity and transport of RNA and DNA precursors into the cells.

6.4 Ribosomes

Ribosomes are associated with the formation of peptides from amino acids ordered by messenger RNA and assembled by transfer RNA. This process is a singular target for many antibiotics and there are some non-antibiotic antibacterial agents whose target lies here.

Treatment of cells with toluene releases ribosomes (Jackson & De Moss, 1965) but this may be taken as a manifestation of the extent of membrane damage by this compound such that a unit the size of a ribosome could be released.

Ethylenediamine tetraacetic acid (EDTA) is a specific chelator of certain metals, including Mg^{2+}, necessary for the integrity of the 50S and 30S ribosome units in prokaryotes. EDTA is not regarded as a primary antibacterial agent although it is used in conjunction with certain antiseptics to enhance their activity, especially against Gram-negative organisms (Russell, 1971; Leive, 1974). Its possible action on ribosome structure must be borne in mind when it is present in antibacterial systems.

Hydrogen peroxide dissociates the 30S and 50S subunits of the 70S ribosome in *E. coli* (Nakamura & Tamaoki, 1968). This process is 80% reversible upon adding to 10 mM Mg^{2+}, providing the concentration of hydrogen peroxide has not exceeded 0.1%. *p*-Chloromercuribenzoate (0.5 mM) dissociates the 100S ribosomes of *E. coli* into 70S monomers (Wang & Matheson, 1967). This reaction can be reversed by 2-mercaptoethanol but not by Mg^{2+}.

The ribosome cannot be considered a prime target for the specific selective action of any known non-antibiotic antibacterial agent although it may be destroyed by some chemical agents.

7 GENOTYPIC RESISTANCE TO DISINFECTANTS

Resistance to certain metal ions has been discovered in the penicillinase plasmid of *Staph. aureus* by Novick & Roth (1968) who found that the resistance markers conferred an increase in resistance ranging from 3- to 100-fold depending on the ion involved. Separate genetic loci for resistance to arsenate, arsenite, lead, cadmium, mercuric and bismuth ions were demonstrated. These workers did not attempt to identify the biochemical mechanisms associated with this resistance, but it is interesting to note that a common target for all the resistant ions listed is the thiol group.

A most interesting mechanism for mercury-resistant, plasmid-bearing strains of *E. coli*, *Staph. aureus* and *Ps. aeruginosa* involves the biochemical conversion of Hg^{2+} into a volatile organomercury compound (Summers & Lewis, 1973). These workers and Vaituzis *et al.* (1975) have summarized other examples of micro-organisms which can produce volatile mercury compounds from Hg^{2+}. Further investigation might reveal that other volatile organometallic compounds are produced by strains of microbes resistant to metal ions. Recent reviews have been published by Foster (1983), Russell (1985), Lyon & Skurray (1987), Chopra (1988), Russell & Gould (1988) and Russell & Chopra (1990).

Thornley & Yudkin (1959a,b) and Sinai & Yudkin (1959a,b,c) studied the origin of bacterial resistance to proflavine. They concluded that no single factor determines drug resistance for a single species/single drug combination.

Russell (1972) showed that strains of *Ps. aeruginosa* with or without R-factors 1822 and 3425 were equally resistant to glutaraldehyde, chloroxylenol solution, Lysol, chlorhexidine, CTAB and phenylmercuric nitrate, suggesting that transferable drug resistance was not occurring with these non-antibiotic antimicrobial agents. Plasmid $(P)^+$ strains of *Ps. aeruginosa* have shown transferable drug resistance to antibiotics (Roe *et al.*, 1971). This aspect is discussed in more detail in Chapter 10B.

8 CONVERSION OF A TOXIC SUBSTANCE TO A NON-TOXIC DERIVATIVE

Many organisms are able to decompose aromatic compounds many of which are used as disinfectants (Rogoff, 1961; Evans, 1963; Ribbons, 1965; Hugo, 1965b; Gibson, 1968; Beveridge, 1975; Sleat & Robinson, 1984). Beveridge & Hugo (1964) examined the ability of some Gram-negative, non-sporing rods, mainly pseudomonads, to use aromatic compounds, many of them disinfectants, as a sole carbon source. *p*-Cresol, phenol, benzoic acid, *p*-hydroxybenzoic acid and salicylic acid were readily attacked. The metabolic versatility of *Vibrio* 01, an organism now thought to be *Acinetobacter calcoaceticus*, in decomposing many compounds, including some traditional disinfectants, is amply demonstrated in the papers of Fewson (1967) and Beveridge & Tall (1969). Hugo & Foster (1964) found a strain of *Ps. aeruginosa* able to utilize methyl and propyl-*p*-hydroxybenzoates as sole sources of carbon. Grant (1967) showed a similar capability with *K. aerogenes*. It is clear that this pattern of resistance can be of practical significance, for the hydroxybenzoates were once used as preservatives in eye-drops.

9 CHANGES IN ACCESS TO THE VULNERABLE SITE: A POSSIBLE INVOLVEMENT OF LIPID

The role of cellular lipid in resistance has attracted considerable interest in recent years. The first hint that bacterial lipid was involved in determining the relative resistance of bacteria to detergents was provided by an experiment of Dyar & Ordal (1946). A strain of *Staph. aureus* with a high lipid content showed exceptional sensitivity to changes in electrophoretic mobility, induced by cetylpyridinium chloride, and acquired a greater apparent negative charge in the presence of sodium dodecylsulphate

Following serial subculture, Chaplin (1951) obtained a 43-fold increase in the resistance of a strain of *E. coli* and a 200-fold increase in the resistance of *Serr. marcescens* to a series of QACs. He was unable to demonstrate resistance in *Staph. aureus*. Fischer & Larose (1952) found the adaptive process to be dependent on pH. Thus greater resistance was acquired more rapidly if the serial subcultures were performed at pH 6.8 rather than at pH 7.7. The effect of pH was thought to be on ionization of QAC and hence on drug uptake. In a further paper Chaplin (1952) stained cells with Sudan Black B, carried out electrophoretic mobility studies and showed an increase in the lipid content of the resistant cells of *Serr. marcescens*. Strong support for the existence of this lipid and its involvement in resistance came when lipase-treated cells lost their resistance.

Lowick & James (1957) trained *K. aerogenes* to grow in the presence of crystal violet and demonstrated by electrophoretic techniques that the surface of the resistant cells was predominantly lipid whereas in the case of untrained cells the surface was predominantly polysaccharide. Hugo & Stretton (1966) grew micro-organisms in nutrient broth containing glycerol and increased their lipid content. These organisms showed an increased resistance to penicillins. Hugo & Franklin (1968) studied the effect of this lipid enhancement on the resistance to phenols of the Oxford strain of *Staph. aureus*. They used a series of 4-*n*-alkylphenols from phenol to hexylphenol. Enhanced cellular lipid protected the cells from the inhibitory action of only pentylphenol and *n*-hexylphenol. This protection conferred a non-specific blanketing mechanism in which the amyl- and hexyphenols are locked at the interface between the cellular lipid and the aqueous environment. In a similar study, Hamilton (1968) found no significant increase in resistance to tetrachlorosalicylanilide, tribromosalicylanilide, trichloroacetanilide, monochlorophenoxysalicylanilide or hexachlorophene in a glycerol-grown cuture of the same organism.

Lipid depletion in *Staph. aureus* and *E. coli* was achieved by Hugo *et al.* (1971) by growing biotin-deficient organisms. Only a slight decrease in resistance to a series of phenols and alkyl trimethylammonium bromides was found in both organisms.

Vaczi has published a monograph on the biological role of bacterial lipids which includes a comprehensive review on lipid content and resistance to both antibiotic and non-antibiotic antimicrobial agents (Vaczi, 1973): see also Chapter 10A.

9.1 Special role of the Gram-negative cell wall in resistance

Gram-negative, rod-shaped bacteria possess lipoprotein and lipopolysaccharide layers outside the peptidoglycan layer which afford protection to antimicrobial agents. The lipopolysaccharide may be partly removed by EDTA which results in an increased susceptibility to both antibiotic and non-antibiotic drugs (Russell, 1971; Leive, 1974; Haque & Russell, 1974a,b).

Sanderson *et al.* (1974) and Nikaido (1976) have produced evidence using mutants of *Sal. typhimurium* deficient in the carbohydrate components of the lipopolysaccharide that carbohydrate may play a role in selective exclusions: see also Chapter 10A.

For further reviews see Hancock (1984), Nikaido & Vaara (1985) and Russell & Chopra (1990).

10 SUMMARY

A summary of the data presented in this chapter is provided as a table (Table 9.1) and diagrammatically (Fig. 9.3).

11 APPENDIX

The treatment in the foregoing chapter has been to examine the action of drugs on each defined structure in the cell and also to examine the role of the structures in resistance. When the mode of action of a new antimicrobial drug is to be elucidated the approaches as outlined in the main chapter are followed systematically to seek the prime target or targets. In this appendix, selected examples of such studies on individual compounds or families of compounds are given to illustrate the experimental approaches used. The references are given in an abbreviated form and may duplicate some given in the main section of the chapter, but are included for completion for those interested in individual compounds.

The subject of mechanisms of antibacterial action has recently been published as a Technical Series Monograph No. 27 by The Society of Applied

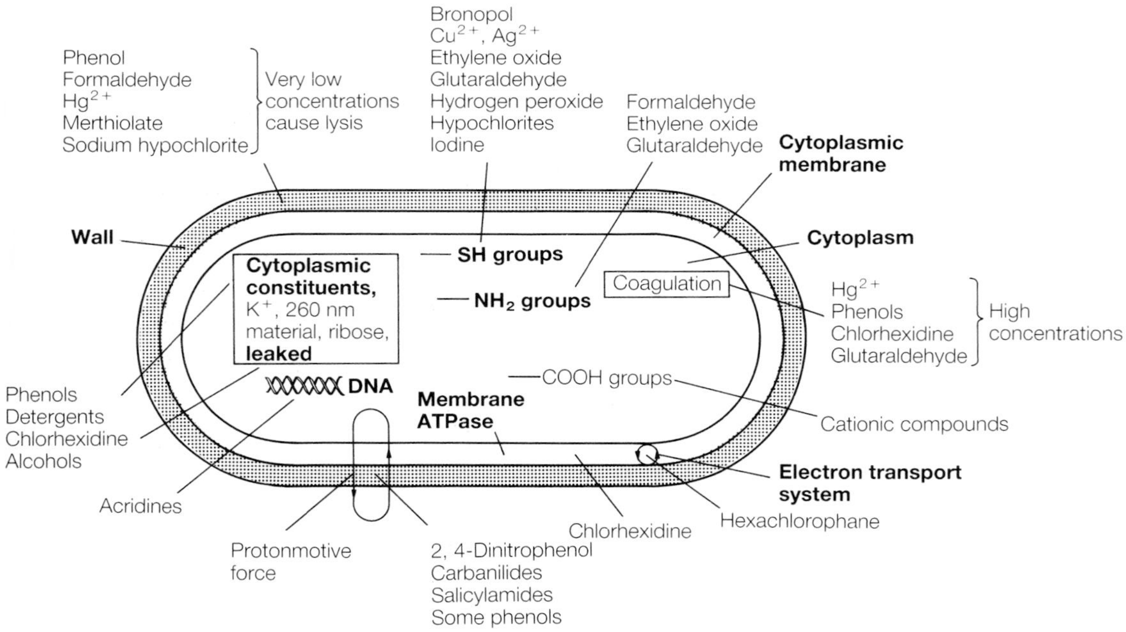

Fig. 9.3 Diagram showing main targets for non-antibiotic antibacterial agents.

Table 9.1 Cellular targets for non-antibiotic antibacterial drugs

Target or reaction attacked	Acridine dyes	Alcohols	Anilides (TCS, TCC)	Bronopol	Chlorhexidine	Copper (II) salts	Ethylene oxide	Formaldehyde	Glutaraldehyde	Hexachlorophane	Hydrogen peroxide	Hypochlorites, chlorine releasers	Iodine	Mercury (II) salts, organic mercurials	Phenols	β-Propiolactone	Quaternary ammonium compounds	Silver (I) salts	Sulphur dioxide, sulphites
1 Cell wall								+				+		+	+				
2 Cytoplasmic membrane																			
2.1 Action on membrane potentials			+							+					+				
2.2 Action on membrane enzymes																			
2.2.1 Electron transport chain										+									
2.2.2 Adenosine triphosphatase					+	+	+												
2.2.3 Enzymes with thiol groups				+			+		+		+	+	+	+		+		+	+
2.3 Action on general membrane permeability		+	+		+										++		+		
3 Cytoplasm																			
3.1 General coagulation					+++	+++			++	+++				+++	+++		+++	+++	
3.2 Ribosomes											+			+					
3.3 Nucleic acids	+																		
3.4 Thiol groups				+		+	+		+		+	+	+	+		+		+	
3.5 Amino groups							+	++	+			+				+			+
4 Highly reactive compounds							+		+			+				+			

Non-antibiotic antimicrobial agents (column headings).

Crosses indicating activity, which appear in several columns for a given compound, demonstrate the multiple actions for the compound concerned. This activity is nearly always concentration dependent, and the number of crosses indicate the order of concentration at which the effect is elicited, i.e. +, elicited at low concentrations: +++, elicited at high concentrations.

When a cross appears in only one target column, this is the only known site of action of the drug.

Bacteriology (Denyer & Hugo, 1991) and a theoretical discussion provided by Russell & Chopra (1990).

Acids

Acids: liphophilic, acetic, benzoic, propionate, sorbate, caprylic: a review. Freese, E., Sheu, C.W. & Galliers, E. (1973) *Nature, London*, **241**, 321–325.

Acridines

Albert, A. (1966) *The Acridines: Their Preparation, Physical, Chemical and Biological Properties and Uses.* 2nd Ed. London: Edward Arnold; Waring, M.J. (1966) Cross linking and intercalation in nucleic acids. In *Biochemical Studies of Antimicrobial Drugs* 16th Symposium of the Society for General Microbiology, p. 235. Cambridge: Cambridge University Press; Albert, A. (1973) *Selective Toxicity*. 5th Ed., p. 282. London: Chapman & Hall.

Alexidine

Chawner, J.A. & Gilbert, P. (1989) *Journal of Applied Bacteriology*, **66**, 243, 253.

Alcohols

Ingram, L.O. & Buttke, T.M. (1984) *Advances in Microbial Physiology*, **25**, 253.

Benzalkonium chloride

Brown, M.R.W. & Tomlinson, E. (1979) *Journal of Pharmaceutical Sciences*, **68**, 146; Lang, M. & Rye, R.M. (1972) *Journal of Pharmacy and Pharmacology*, **24**, 219.

Benzoic acid

Bosund, I. (1962) *Advances in Food Research*, **11**, 331–353. (A review); Krebs, H.A. *et al.* (1983) *Biochemical Journal*, **214**, 657.

Bronopol,2-bromo-2-nitropropan-1,3-diol

Stretton, R.J. & Manson, T.W. (1973) *Journal of Applied Bacteriology*, **36**, 61; Bowman, W.H. & Stretton, R.J. (1972) *Antimicrobial Agents and Chemotherapy*, **2**, 504.

Cetrimide, cetavlon

Salton, M.R.J. (1950) *Australian Journal of Scientific Research*, **3**, 45; (1951) *Journal of General Microbiology*, **5**, 391; Salton, M.R.J. *et al.* (1981) *Journal of General Microbiology*, **5**, 405; Hugo, W.B. & Denyer, S.P. (1977) *Journal of Pharmacy and Pharmacology*, **29**, 66P; McQuillen, K. (1950) *Biochimica et Biophysica Acta*, **5**, 463; Lambert, P.A. & Hammond, S.M. (1973) *Biochemical and Biochemical Research Communications*, **54**, 796; Smith, A.R. *et al.* (1975) *Journal of Applied Bacteriology*, **38**, 143; Salt, W.G. & Wiseman, D. (1968) *Journal of Pharmacy and Pharmacology*, **20**, 145; (1970) **22**, 261, 767; Dawson *et al.* (1953) *Journal of Pathology and Bacteriology*, **66**, 513.

Chlorhexidine ('Hibitane')

Hugo, W.B. & Longworth, A.R. (1964) *Journal of Pharmacy and Pharmacology*, **16**, 62, 751; (1965) **17**, 28; (1966) **18**, 569; Hugo, W.B. & Daltrey, Diana C. (1974) *Microbios*, **11**, 119, 131; Elferink, J.G.R. & Booij, H.L. (1974) *Biochemical Pharmacology*, **23**, 1413; Davies, A. *et al.* (1968) *Journal of Applied Bacteriology*, **31**, 448; Harold, F.M. *et al.* (1969) *Biochimica et Biophysica Acta*, **183**, 129; Rye, R.M. & Wiseman, D. (1964/5) *Journal of Pharmacy and Pharmacology*, **16**, 516; **17**, 295.

Dequalinium, dequadin

Hugo, W.B. & Frier, M. (1969) *Applied Microbiology*, **17**, 18.

Dodecyldiethanolamine

Lambert, P.A. & Smith, A.R.W. (1974) *Proceedings of the Society of General Microbiology*, **1**, 49; (1976) *Microbios*, **15**, 191; **17**, 35.

Fatty acids

Galbraith, H. & Miller, T.B. (1973) *Journal of Applied Bacteriology*, **36**, 635, 647, 659.

Fentichlor

Hugo, W.B. & Bloomfield, Sally F. (1971) *Journal of Applied Bacteriology*, **34**, 557, 569, 579; Bloomfield, Sally F. (1974) *Journal of Applied Bacteriology*, **37**, 117.

Formaldehyde

Neely, W.B. (1963) *Journal of Bacteriology*, **85**, 1028, 1420;

86, 445; (1966) *Journal of General Microbiology*, **45**, 187; Müller, A. (1900) *Archives of Hygiene*, **89**, 363; Rossmore, H.W. & Sondossi, M. (1988) *Advances in Applied Microbiology*, **33**, 223 (includes condensates).

Glutaraldehyde

Russell, A.D. & Hopwood, D. (1976) *Progress in Medicinal Chemistry*, **13**, 271 (A review); Gorman, S.P., Scott, E.M. & Russell, A.D. *Journal of Applied Bacteriology*, 1980, **48**, 161–190 (A review.).

Hexachlorophane

Gerhart, P. *et al.* (1971) *Journal of Bacteriology*, **108**, 482, 492, 501; *Antimicrobial Agents and Chemotherapy (1974)* **6**, 712; Lee, C.R. & Garner, T.R. (1975) *Journal of Pharmacy and Pharmacology*, **27**, 694.

8-Hydroxyquinoline, oxine

Rubbo, S.D. *et al.* (1950) *British Journal of Experimental Pathology*, **31**, 425; Albert, A. *et al.* (1953) *British Journal of Experimental Pathology*, **34**, 119; (1954), **34**; Albert, A. (1959) Metal binding agents in chemotherapy: the activation of metals by chelation. In *The Strategy of Chemotherapy*. 8th Symposium of the Society for General Microbiology, p. 112. (A review.) Cambridge: Cambridge University Press.

Isothiazolines

Collier, J.B. *et al.* (1990) *Journal of Applied Bacteriology*, **69**, 569, 578.

Parabens

Furr, J.R. & Russell, A.D. (1972) *Microbios*, **5**, 189, 237; **6**, 47; Freese, E. *et al.* (1973) *Nature, London*, **241**, 321; Freese, E. & Levin, B.C. *Developments in Industrial Microbiology*, **19**, 207; Eklund, T. (1985) *Journal of General Microbiology*, **131**, 73; Ness, I.F. & Eklund, T. (1983) *Journal of Applied Bacteriology*, **54**, 237; Russell, A.D. *et al.* (1985) *International Journal of Pharmaceutics*, **27**, 263.

Peroxygens (Hydrogen peroxide, peracetic acid)

Baldry, M.G.C. (1983) *Journal of Applied Bacteriology*, **54**, 417; (1984), **57**, 499; (1985), **58**, 315; Davis, B.D. *et al.* (1990) *Microbiology* 4th Ed. London: Harper & Row.

Phenols

Hugo, W.B. (1956) *Journal of General Microbiology*, **15**, 315; Judis, J. *et al.* (1962) *Journal of Pharmaceutical Sciences*, **51**, 261; (1963) **52**, 126; (1964) **53**, 196; (1965) **54**, 417, 1436; James, A.T. *et al.* (1964) *Biochimica et Biophysica Acta*, **79**, 351; Bean, H.S. & Das, A. (1966) *Journal of Pharmacy and Pharmacology*, **18**, 1075; Pullman, J.E. & Reynolds, B.L. (1965) *Australasian Journal of Pharmacy*, **46**, 580; Hugo, W.B. & Bowen, J.G. (1973) *Microbios*, **8**, 139; Beckett, A.H. *et al.* (1959) *Journal of Pharmacy and Pharmacology*, **11**, 360; Gilbert, P. & Brown, M.R.W. (1978) *Journal of Bacteriology*, **133**, 1066; Suter, C.M. (1941) *Chemical Reviews*, **28**, 269; Kroll, R.G. & Anagnostopoulos, G.D. (1981) *Journal of General Microbiology*, **50**, 139.

2-Phenoxyethanol, phenoxetol

Hugo, W.B. (1956) *Journal of General Microbiology*, **15**, 315; Gilbert, P., Beveridge, E.G. & Crone, P.B. (1977) *Microbios*, **19**, 17, 125; **20**, 29.

Phenylethanol

Silver, S. & Wendt, L. (1976) *Journal of Bacteriology*, **93**, 560; Richardson, A.G. & Leach, F.R. (1969) *Biochimica et Biophysica Acta*, **174**, 264, 276; Lang, M. & Rye, R.M. (1972) *Journal of Pharmacy and Pharmacology*, **24**, 219.

Polyethoxyalkyl phenols, tritons

Allwood, M.C. & Lamikanra, A. (1976) *Microbios Letters*, **3**, 131; *Journal of Applied Bacteriology (1977)* **42**, 379, 387.

Polyhexamethylene biguanides

Davies, A. *et al.* (1968) *Journal of Applied Bacteriology*, **31**, 448; Ikeda, T. *et al.* (1983) *Biochimica et Biophysica Acta*, **735**, 380; Broxton, P. *et al.* (1983) *Journal of Applied Bacteriology*, **54**, 345; (1984), **57**, 115; *Microbios*, **40**, 187; **41**, 15; Gilbert, P. *et al.* (1990) *Journal of Applied Bacteriology*, **69**, 585, 593.

Sorbic acid

Bell, T.A. *et al.* (1959) *Journal of Bacteriology*, **77**, 573; Gooding, C.M. *et al.* (1955) *Food Research*, **20**, 639; Palleroni, N.J. & de Prinz, M.R.J. (1960) *Nature, London*, **185**, 688; York, G.K. & Vaughn, R.H. (1955) *Bacteriological Proceedings*, **55**, 20; Eklund, T. (1985) *Journal of General Microbiology*, **131**, 73; Salmond, C.Y. *et al.* (1984) *Journal of General Microbiology*, **130**, 2845.

Sulphur dioxide, sulphites and bisulphites

Hammond, S.M. & Carr, J.G. (1976) The antimicrobial activity of SO_2. In *Inhibition and Inactivation of Vegetative Micro-organisms* (eds Skinner, F.A. & Hugo, W.B.) Society for Applied Bacteriology Symposium Series No. 5. pp. 89–110. London: Academic Press. (A review.)

iso-Thiazolones

Fuller, S.J. (1986) *Ph.D. Thesis*, University of Nottingham; Fuller, S.J. *et al.* (1985) *Letters in Applied Microbiology*, **1**, 13; Collier, P.J. *et al.* (1990) *Journal of Applied Bacteriology*, **69**, 569, 578.

Tetrachlorosalicylanilide (TCS)

Hamilton, W.A. (1968) *Journal of General Microbiology*, **50**, 441.

Triclosan

Regos, J. & Hitz, H.R. (1974) *Zeitschrifte für Bakteriologie*, **A 226**, 390.

12 REFERENCES

Albert, A. (1966) *The Acridines*. 2nd Ed. London: Edward Arnold.

Albert, A., Gibson, M. & Rubbo, S. (1953) The influence of chemical constitution on antibacterial activity. VI. The bactericidal action of 8-hydroxyquinoline (oxine). *British Journal of Experimental Pathology*, **34**, 119–130.

Armstrong, W. McD. (1958) The effect of some synthetic dyestuffs on the metabolism of baker's yeast. *Archives of Biochemistry and Biophysics*, **73**, 153–160.

Baker, Z., Harrison, R.W. & Miller, B.F. (1941b) The bactericidal action of synthetic detergents. *Journal of Experimental Medicine*, **74**, 611–620.

Bancroft, W.D. & Richter, G.H. (1931) The chemistry of disinfection. *Journal of Physical Chemistry*, **35**, 511–530.

Bean, H.S. & Das, A. (1966) The adsorption by *Escherichia coli* of phenols and their bactericidal activity. *Journal of Pharmacy and Pharmacology*, **18**, 107S–113S.

Beckett, A.H., Vahora, A.A. & Robinson, A.E. (1958) The interactions of chelating agents with bacteria. I. 8-Hydroxyquinoline (oxine) and *Staphylococcus aureus*. *Journal of Pharmacy and Pharmacology*, **10**, 160T–169T.

Beckett, A.H., Das, R.N. & Robinson, A.E. (1959) Metallic cations and the antibacterial action of oxine. *Journal of Pharmacy and Pharmacology*, **11**, 195T–197T.

Beckett, A.H., Patki, S.J. & Robinson, A. (1959) The interaction of phenolic compounds with bacteria. I. Hexylresorcinol and *Escherichia coli*. *Journal of Pharmacy and Pharmacology*, **11**, 360–366.

Bennett, E.O. (1959) Factors affecting the antimicrobial activity of phenols. *Advances in Applied Microbiology*, **1**, 123–140.

Berry, H. & Michaels, I. (1947) The evaluation of the bactericidal activity of ethylene glycol and some of its monoalkylethers against *Bacterium coli*. *Quarterly Journal of Pharmacy and Pharmacology*, **20**, 331–347.

Beveridge, E.G. (1975) The microbial spoilage of pharmaceutical products. In *Microbial Aspects of the Deterioration of Materials* (eds Lovelock, D.W. & Gilbert, R.J.) pp. 213–235. London: Academic Press.

Beveridge, E.G. & Hugo, W.B. (1964) The resistance of gallic acid and its alkyl esters to attack by bacteria able to degrade aromatic ring structures. *Journal of Applied Bacteriology*, **27**, 304–311.

Beveridge, E.G. & Tall, D. (1969) The metabolic availability of phenol analogues to bacterium NCIB 8250. *Journal of Applied Bacteriology*, **32**, 304–311.

Blake, A. & Peacocke, A.R. (1968) The interaction of amino acridines with nucleic acids. *Biopolymers*, **6** 1225–1253.

Bolle, A. & Kellenberger, E. (1958) The action of sodium lauryl sulphate on *E. coli*. *Schweizerische Zeitschrift für Pathologie und Bakteriologie*, **21**, 714–740.

Bringmann, G. (1953) Electron microscope findings on the action of chlorine, bromine, iodine, copper, silver and hydrogen peroxide on *Escherichia coli*. *Zeitschrift für Hygiene und Infectionskrankheiten*, **138**, 155–166.

Brock, T.D. (1961) *Milestones in Microbiology*. Englewood Cliffs: Prentice-Hall.

Broxton, P., Woodcock, P.M. & Gilbert, P. (1983) A study of the antibacterial activity of some polyhexamethylene biguanides towards *Escherichia coli* ATCC 8739. *Journal of Applied Bacteriology*, **54**, 345–353.

Broxton, P., Woodcock, P.M. & Gilbert, P. (1984a) Interaction of some polyhexamethylene biguanides and membrane phospholipids in *Escherichia coli*. *Journal of Applied Bacteriology*, **57**, 115–124.

Broxton, P., Woodcock, P.M. & Gilbert, P. (1984b) Injury and recovery of *Escherichia coli* ATCC 8739 from treatment with some polyhexamethylene biguanides. *Microbios*, **40**, 187–193.

Broxton, P., Woodcock, P.M. & Gilbert, P. (1984c) Binding of some polyhexamethylene biguanides to the cell envelope of *Escherichia coli* ATCC 8739. *Microbios*, **41**, 15–22.

Casolari, A. (1981) A model describing microbial inactivation and growth kinetics. *Journal of Theoretical Biology*, **88**, 1–34.

Chaplin, C.E. (1951) Observations on quaternary ammonium disinfectants. *Canadian Journal of Botany*, **29**, 373–382.

Chaplin, C.E. (1952) Bacterial resistance to quaternary ammonium disinfectants. *Journal of Bacteriology*, **63**, 453–458.

Chawner, J.A. & Gilbert, P. (1989a) A comparative study of

the bactericidal and growth inhibitory activities of the bisbiguanides alexidine and chlorhexidine. *Journal of Applied Bacteriology*, **66**, 243–252.

Chawner, J.A. & Gilbert, P. (1989b) Interaction of the bisbiguanides chlorhexidine and alexidine with phospholipid vesicles: evidence for separative modes of action. *Journal of Applied Bacteriology*, **66**, 253–258.

Cherrington, C.A., Hinton, M.H. & Chopra, I. (1990) Effects of short-chain organic acids on macromolecular synthesis in *Escherichia coli. Journal of Applied Bacteriology*, **68**, 69–71.

Chick, H. (1908) An investigation of the laws of disinfection. *Journal of Hygiene, Cambridge*, **8**, 92–99.

Chopra, I. (1988) Mechanisms of resistance to antibiotics and other chemo-therapeutic agents. *Journal of Applied Bacteriology*, Symposium Supplement, **65**, 149S–166S.

Chopra, I., Johnson, S.C. & Bennett, P.M. (1987) Inhibition of *Providencia stuartii* cell envelope enzymes by chlorhexidine. *Journal of Antimicrobial Chemotherapy*, **19**, 743–751.

Collins, C.A. & Guild, W.R. (1968) Irreversible effects of formaldehyde on DNA. *Biochimica et Biophysica Acta*, **157**, 107–113.

Cooper, E.A. (1912) On the relationship of phenol and *m*-cresol to proteins: a contribution to our knowledge of the mechanism of disinfection. *Biochemical Journal*, **6**, 362–387.

Costerton, J.W., Ingram, J.M. & Cheng, K.J. (1974) Structure and function of the cell envelope of Gram-negative bacteria. *Journal of Bacteriology*, **38**, 87–110.

Cowan, S.T. & Rowatt, E. (1958) *The Strategy of Chemotherapy*. Symposia of the Society of General Microbiology. Vol. 8. London: Cambridge University Press.

Cross, R.J., Taggart, J.V., Covo, G.A. & Green, D.E. (1949) Studies on the cyclophorase system. VI. The coupling of oxidation and phosphorylation. *Journal of Biological Chemistry*, **177**, 655–678.

Daltrey, D.L. & Hugo, W.B. (1974) Studies on the mode of action and the antibacterial agent chlorhexidine on *Clostridium perfringens* 2. Effect of chlorhexidine on metabolism and the cell membrane. *Microbios*, **11**, 131–146.

Dawson, I.A., Lominski, I. & Stern, H. (1953) An electron microscope study of the action of cetyltrimethylammonium bromide (CTAB) on *Staphylococcus aureus. Journal of Pathology and Bacteriology*, **66**, 513–526.

Denyer, S.P. & Hugo, W.B. (1977) The mode of action of cetyltrimethylammonium bromide (CTAB) on *Staphylococcus aureus. Journal of Pharmacy and Pharmacology*, **29**, 66P.

Denyer, S.P. & Hugo, W.B. (1990) Eds. *Mechanisms of Action of Chemical Biocides, Their Study and Exploitation*. Society for Applied Bacteriology Technical Series No. 27. Oxford: Blackwell Scientific Publications.

D'Mello, A. & Yotis, W.W. (1987) The action of sodium deoxycholate on *Escherichia coli. Applied and Environmental Microbiology*, **53**, 1944–1946.

Dobrogosz, W.J. & De Moss, R.D. (1963) Induction and repression of L-arabinose isomerase in *Pedicoccus pentosaceus. Journal of Bacteriology*, **85**, 1350–1364.

Dyar, M.T. & Ordal, E.J. (1946) Electrokinetic studies of bacterial surfaces. I. The effects of surface-active agents on the electrophoretic mobilities of bacteria. *Journal of Bacteriology*, **51**, 149–167.

Eddy, A.A. (1953) Death rate of populations of *Bact. lactis aerogenes*. III. Interpretation of survival curves. *Proceedings of the Royal Society of London, Series B*, **141**, 137–145.

Eklund, P. (1985) The effect of sorbic acid and esters of *p*-hydroxybenzoic acid on the protonmotive force in *Escherichia coli. Journal of General Microbiology*, **313**, 73–76.

El-Falaha, B.M.A., Furr, J.R. & Russell, A.D. (1989) Effect of anionic detergents on wild-type and envelope mutants of *Escherichia coli* and *Pseudomonas aeruginosa. Letters in Applied Microbiology*, **8**, 15–19.

Ellison, R.T., Giehl, T.J. & La Force, F.M. (1988) Damage of the outer membrane of entire Gram-negative bacteria by lactoferrin and transferrin. *Infection and Immunity*, **56**, 2774–2781.

Evans, W.C. (1963) The microbiological degradation of aromatic compounds. *Journal of General Microbiology*, **32**, 177–184.

Ferguson, T.B. & Thorne, S. (1946) The effects of some acridine compounds on the growth and respiration of *Escherichia coli. Journal of Pharmacology and Experimental Therapeutics*, **86**, 258–263.

Fewson, C.A. (1967) The growth and metabolic versatility of the Gram-negative bacterium NC1B 8250 *('Vibrio 01'). Journal of General Microbiology*, **46**, 255–266.

Fischer, R. & Larose, P. (1952) Factors governing the adaption of bacteria against quaternaries. *Nature, London*, **170**, 715–716.

Foster, J.H.S. & Russell, A.D. (1971) Antibacterial dyes and nitrofurans. In *Inhibition and Destruction of the Microbial Cell* (ed. Hugo, W.B.) London: Academic Press.

Furr, J.R. & Russell, A.D. (1972) Uptake of esters of *p*-hydroxybenzoic acid by *Serratia marcescens* and by fattened and non-fattened cells of *Bacillus subtilis. Microbios*, **5**, 237–246.

Ghuysen, J.M. (1968) Use of bacteriolytic enzymes in determining of wall structure and their role in cell metabolism. *Bacteriological Reviews*, **32**, 425–464.

Gibson, D.T. (1968) Microbial degradation of aromatic compounds. *Science, Washington*, **161**, 1093–1097.

Gilbert, P., Beveridge, E.G. & Crone, B.P. (1977) The lethal action of 2-phenoxyethanol and its analogues upon *Escherichia coli* NCTC 5933. *Microbios*, **19**, 125–141.

Gilbert, P., Beveridge, E.G. & Sissons, I. (1978) The uptake of some membrane-active drugs by bacteria and yeast: possible microbiological examples of Z-curve adsorption. *Journal of Colloid and Interfacial Science*, **64**, 377–379.

Giles, C.H., MacEwan, T.H., Nakhwa, S.N. & Smith, D. (1960) Studies in adsorption. XI. A system of classification of solution adsorption mechanisms and measurement of specific surface areas of solids. *Journal of the Chemical Society*, 3973–3993.

Giles, C.H. & McKay, R.B. (1965) The adsorption of cationic (basic) dyes by fixed yeast cells. *Journal of Bacteriology*, **89**, 390–397.

Giles, C.H. & Tolia, A.H. (1974) Studies in adsorption. XIX. Measurement of external specific surface of fibres by solution adsorption. *Journal of Applied Chemistry*, **14**, 186–195.

Giles, C.H., Smith, D. & Huitson, A. (1974) A general treatment and classification of the solute adsorption isotherm 1. Theoretical. *Journal of Colloid and Interfacial Science*, **47**, 755–765.

Gorman, S.P. & Scott, E.M. (1977) Uptake and media reactivity of glutaraldehyde solutions related to structure and biocidal activity. *Microbios Letters*, **5**, 163–169.

Gorman, S.P., Scott, E.M. & Russell, A.D. (1980) Antimicrobial activity, uses and mechanism of action of glutaraldehyde. *Journal of Applied Bacteriology*, **48**, 161–190.

Grant, D.J.W. (1967) Kinetic aspects of the growth of *Klebsiella aerogenes* with some benzenoid carbon sources. *Journal of General Microbiology*, **46**, 213–224.

Grossman, L., Levine, S.S. & Allison, W.S. (1961) The reaction of formaldehyde with nucleotides and T2 bacteriophage DNA. *Journal of Molecular Biology*, **3**, 47–60.

Hamilton, W.A. (1968) The mechanism of the bacteriostatic action of tetrachlorosalicyanilide. *Journal of General Microbiology*, **50**, 441–458.

Hamilton, W.A. (1975) Energy coupling in microbial transport. *Advances in Microbial Physiology*, **12**, 1–53.

Hancock, R.E.W. (1984) Alterations in membrane permeability. *Annual Review of Microbiology*, **38**, 237–264.

Haque, H. & Russell, A.D. (1974a) Effect of chelating agents on the susceptibility of some strains of Gram-negative bacteria to some antibacterial agents. *Antimicrobial Agents and Chemotherapy*, **6**, 200–206.

Haque, H. & Russell, A.D. (1974b) Effect of ethylenediamine-tetraacetic acid and related chelating agents on whole cells of Gram-negative bacteria. *Antimicrobial Agents and Chemotherapy*, **6**, 447–452.

Harold, F.M. (1972) Conservation and transformation of energy by bacterial membranes. *Bacteriological Reviews*, **36**, 172–230.

Harold, F.M., Pavlasova, E. & Baarda, J.R. (1970) A transmembrane pH gradient in *Streptococcus faecalis;* origin and dissipation by proton conductors and *N,N'*-dicyclohexylcarbodiimide. *Biochimica et Biophysica Acta*, **196**, 235–244.

Haydon, D.A. (1956) Surface behaviour of *Bacterium coli*. II. The interaction with phenol. *Proceedings of the Royal Society*, **145B**, 383–391.

Herzenberg, L.A. (1959) Studies in the induction of β-galactosidase in a cryptic strain of *Escherichia coli*. *Biochimica et Biophysica Acta*, **31**, 525–538.

Herzog, R.A. & Betzel, R. (1911) Zür Theorie der Dissinfektion. *Physiologische Chemie*, **74**, 221–226.

Hotchkiss, R.D. (1944) Greamicidin, tyrocidin and tyrothricin. *Advances in Enzymology*, **4**, 153–199.

Hughes, W.H. (1956) The structure and development of the induced long forms of bacteria. *Symposia of the Society for General Microbiology*, **6** (eds Spooner, E.T.C. & Stocker, B.A.D.) pp. 341–360. Cambridge: Cambridge University Press.

Hugo, W.B. (1957) The mode of action of antiseptics. *Journal of Pharmacy and Pharmacology*, **9**, 145–161.

Hugo, W.B. (1965a) Some aspects of the action of cationic surface active agents in microbial cells with special reference to their action on enzymes. In *Surface, Activity and the Microbial Cell: SCI Monograph*, **19**, pp. 67–82. London: Society of Chemical Industry.

Hugo, W.B. (1965b) The degradation of preservatives by micro-organisms. In *Scientific and Technical Symposium. 112th Annual Meeting, American Pharmaceutical Association, Detroit*, CIII. pp. 1–7.

Hugo, W.B. (1967) The mode of action of antibacterial agents. *Journal of Applied Bacteriology*, **30**, 17–50.

Hugo, W.B., Ed. (1971) *Inhibition and Destruction of the Microbial Cell.* London: Academic Press.

Hugo, W.B. (1976a) Survival of microbes exposed to chemical stress. In *The Survival of Vegetative Microbes.* (eds Gray, T.G.R. & Postgate, J.R.) 26th Symposium, Society for General Microbiology. Cambridge: Cambridge University Press.

Hugo, W.B. (1976b) The inactivation of vegetative bacteria by chemicals. In *Inhibition and Inactivation of Vegetative Microbes* (eds Skinner, F.A. & Hugo, W.B.) Society for Applied Bacteriology Symposium Series No. 5. London: Academic Press.

Hugo, W.B. (1978) Membrane-active antimicrobial compounds — a reappraisal of their mode of action in the light of the chemi-osmotic theory. *International Journal of Pharmaceutics*, **1**, 127–131.

Hugo, W.B. (1980) The mode of action of antiseptics. In *Handbuch der Antiseptik* (eds. Wigert H. und Weifen W.) pp. 39–77. Berlin: VEB Verlag.

Hugo, W.B. (1991) The degradation of preservatives by microorganisms. *International Biodeterioration*, **27**, 185–194.

Hugo, W.B. & Bloomfield, S.F. (1971a) Studies on the mode of action of the phenolic antibacterial agent Fentichlor against *Staphylococcus aureus* and *Escherichia coli*. I. The adsorption of Fentichlor by the bacterial cell and its antibacterial activity. *Journal of Applied Bacteriology*, **34**, 557–567.

Hugo, W.B. & Bloomfield, S.F. (1971b) Studies on the mode of action of the phenolic antibacterial agent Fentichlor against *Staphylococcus aureus* and *Escherichia coli*. II. The effects of Fentichlor on the bacterial membrane and the cytoplasmic constituents of the cell. *Journal of Applied Bacteriology*, **34**, 569–578.

Hugo, W.B. & Bloomfield, S.F. (1971c) Studies on the mode of action of the phenolic antibacterial agent Fentichlor against *Staphylococcus aureus* and *Escherichia coli*. III.

The effect of Fentichlor on the metabolic activities of *Staphylococcus aureus* and *Escherichia coli*. *Journal of Applied Bacteriology*, **34**, 579–591.

Hugo, W.B. & Daltrey, D.C. (1974) Studies on the mode of action of the antibacterial agent chlorhexidine on *Clostridium perfringens*. I. Adsorption of chlorhexidine on the cell, its antibacterial activity and physical effects. *Microbios*, **11**, 119–129.

Hugo, W.B. & Davidson, J.R. (1973) Effect of cell lipid depletion in *Staphylococcus aureus* upon its resistance to antimicrobial agents. II. A comparison of the response of normal and lipid depleted cells of *S. aureus* to antibacterial drugs. *Microbios*, **8**, 63–72.

Hugo, W.B. & Denyer, S.P. (1987) The concentration exponent of disinfectants and preservatives (Biocides). In *Preservatives in the Food, Pharmaceutical and Environmental Industries*. (eds Board, R.G., Allwood, M.C. & Banks, J.G.) Society for Applied Bacteriology Technical Series No. 22, pp. 281–291. Oxford: Blackwell Scientific Publications.

Hugo, W.B. & Foster, J.H.S. (1964) Growth of *Pseudomonas aeruginosa* in solutions of esters of *p*-hydrobenzoic acid. *Journal of Pharmacy and Pharmacology*, **16**, 209.

Hugo, W.B. & Franklin, I. (1968) Cellular lipid and the antistaphylococcal action of phenols. *Journal of General Microbiology*, **52**, 365–373.

Hugo, W.B. & Frier, M. (1969) Mode of action of the antibacterial compound dequalinium acetate. *Applied Microbiology*, **17**, 118–127.

Hugo, W.B. & Longworth, A.R. (1964) Some aspects of the mode of action of chlorhexidine. *Journal of Pharmacy and Pharmacology*, **16**, 655–662.

Hugo, W.B. & Longworth, A.R. (1965) Cytological aspects of the mode of action of chlorhexidine. *Journal of Pharmacy and Pharmacology*, **17**, 28–32.

Hugo, W.B. & Longworth, A.R. (1966) The effect of chlorhexidine on the electrophoretic mobility, cytoplasmic content, dehydrogenase activity and cell walls of *Escherichia coli* and *Staphylococcus aureus*. *Journal of Pharmacy and Pharmacology*, **18**, 569–578.

Hugo, W.B. & Newton, J.M. (1964) The adsorption of iodine from solution by microorganisms and by serum. *Journal of Pharmacy and Pharmacology*, **16**, 48–55.

Hugo, W.B. & Stretton, R.J. (1966) The role of cellular lipid in the resistance of Gram-positive bacteria to penicillins. *Journal of General Microbiology*, **42**, 133–138.

Hugo, W.B., Bowen, J.G. & Davidson, J.R. (1971) Lipid depletion in bacteria induced by biotin deficiency and its relation to resistance to antibacterial agents. *Journal of Pharmacy and Pharmacology*, **23**, 69–70.

Jackson, R.W. & De Moss, J.A. (1965) Effect of toluene on *Escherichia coli*. *Journal of Bacteriology*, **90**, 1420–1425.

Jacobs, S.E. (1960) Some aspects of the dynamics of disinfection. *Journal of Pharmacy and Pharmacology*, **12**, 9T–18T.

James, A.M. (1965) The modification of the bacterial surface by chemical and enzymatic treatment. In *Cell Electrophoresis* (ed. Ambrose E.J.) pp. 154–170. London: J. & A. Churchill.

James, A.M. (1972) *The Electrochemistry of Bacterial Surfaces*. Inaugural Lecture. University of London: Bedford College.

Jordan, R.C. & Jacobs, S.E. (1944) Studies on the dynamics of disinfection. I. New data on the reaction between phenol and *Bact. coli* using an improved technique, together with an analysis of the distribution of resistance amongst the cells of the bacterial population studied. *Journal of Hygiene, Cambridge*, **43**, 275–289.

Judis, J. (1966) Factors affecting binding of phenol derivatives to *Micrococcus lysodeikticus* cells. *Journal of Pharmaceutical Sciences*, **53**, 803–817.

Knayi, G. (1930) Disinfection I. The development of our knowledge of disinfection. *Journal of Infectious Diseases*, **47**, 293–302.

Knaysi, G. & Morris, G. (1930) The manner of death of certain bacteria and yeast when subjected to mild chemical and physical agents. *Journal of Infectious Diseases*, **47**, 303–317.

Knox, W.E., Stumph, P.K., Green, D.E. & Auerbach, V.H. (1948) The inhibition of sulphydryl enzymes as the basis of the bacterial action of chlorine. *Journal of Bacteriology*, **55**, 451–458.

Kroll, R.G. & Anagnostopoulos, G.D. (1981) Potassium leakage as a lethality index of phenol and the effect of solute and water activity. *Journal of General Microbiology*, **50**, 139–147.

Kuhn, R. & Bielig, H.J. (1940) Uber Invertseifen. I. Die Einwirkung von Invertseifen auf Eiweiss-Stoffe. *Berichte der Deutschen Chemischen Gesellschaft*, **73**, 1080–1091.

Lambert, P.A. & Hammond, S.M. (1973) Potassium fluxes. First indications of membrane damage in microorganisms. *Biochemical and Biophysical Research Communications*, **54**, 796–799.

Lark, K.G. & Lark, C. (1966) Regulation of chromosome replication in *Escherichia coli* a comparison of the effects of phenylethyl alcohol treatment with those of amino acid starvation. *Journal of Molecular Biology*, **20**, 9–19.

Leive, L. (1974) The barrier function of the Gram-negative envelope. *Annals of the New York Academy of Sciences*, **235**, 109–127.

Lerch, C. (1953) Electrophoresis of *Micrococcus pyogenes* var. *aureus*. *Acta Pathologica et Microbiologica Scandinavica*, **98**, *Supplement*, 1–94.

Lerman, L.S. (1961) Structural considerations in the interaction of DNA and acridines. *Journal of Molecular Biology*, **3**, 18–30.

Lerman, L.S. (1964a) Acridine mutagens and DNA structure. *Journal of Cellular and Comparative Physiology*, **64**, *Supplement*, 1–18.

Lerman, L.S. (1964b) Amino acid group reactivity in DNA-aminoacridine complexes. *Journal of Molecular Biology*, **10**, 367–380.

Levinthal, C., Singer, E.R. & Fetherhol, K. (1962) Reactivation and hybridization of reduced alkaline phosphatase.

Proceedings of the National Academy of Sciences, U.S.A., **48**, 1230–1237.

Lowick, J.H.B. & James, A.M. (1957) The electrokinetic properties of *Aerobacter aerogenes*. A comparison of the properties of normal and crystal violet-trained cells. *Biochemical Journal*, **65**, 431–438.

Lyon, B.R. & Skurray, R.A. (1987) Antimicrobial resistance of *Staphylococcus aureus*: genetic basis. *Microbiological Reviews*, **51**, 88–137.

McQuillen, K. (1950) The bacterial surface I. The effect of cetyltrimethylammonium bromide on the electrophoretic mobility of certain Gram-positive bacteria. *Biochimica et Biophysica Acta*, **5**, 463–471.

Madsen, T. & Nyman, M. (1907) Zur Theorie der Desinfektion. I. *Zeitschrift für Hygiene und Infektionskrankheiten*, **57**, 388–395.

McIlwain, H. (1941) A nutritional investigation of the antibacterial action of acriflavine. *Biochemical Journal*, **35**, 1311–1319.

Meyer, H. (1901) Zur Theorie der Alkoholnarkose. III. Der Einfluss Wechselnder Temperatur auf Wirkungstark und Narcotics. *Archiv für Experimentielle Pathologie und Pharmakologie*, **46**, 388–342.

Mickelson, M.N. (1974) Effect of uncoupling agents and respiratory inhibitors on the growth of *Streptococcus agalactiae*. *Journal of Bacteriology*, **120**, 733–740.

Mitchell, P. (1961) Coupling of phosphorylation to electron and hydrogen transfer by a chemiosmotic type of mechanism. *Nature, London*, **191**, 144–148.

Mitchell, P. (1968) *Chemiosmotic Coupling and Energy Transduction*. Bodmin: Glyn Research Ltd.

Mitchell, P. (1970) Membranes of cells and organelles. In *Symposia of the Society for General Microbiology*, **20**, (eds Charles, H.P. & Knight, B.C.J.G.) pp. 121–166. Cambridge: Cambridge University Press.

Mitchell, P. (1972) Chemiosmotic coupling in energy transduction: a logical development of biochemical knowledge. *Journal of Bioenergetics*, **3**, 5–24.

Mitchell, P. & Moyle, J. (1967) Acid-base titration across the membrane system of rat-liver mitochondria: catalysis by uncouplers. *Biochemical Journal*, **104**, 588–600.

Munton, T.J. & Russell, A.D. (1970) Aspects of the action of glutaraldehyde on *Escherichia coli*. *Journal of Applied Bacteriology*, **33**, 410–419.

Nakamura, K. & Tamaoki, T. (1968) Reversible dissociation of *Escherichia coli* ribosomes by hydrogen peroxide. *Biochimica et Biophysica Acta*, **161**, 368–376.

Newton, B.A. & Reynolds, P.E. (1966) *Biochemical Studies of Antimicrobial Drugs*. Symposia of the Society for General Microbiology, Vol. 16. Cambridge: Cambridge University Press.

Nicholson, B.H. & Peacocke, A.R. (1965) The inhibition of ribonucleic acid polymerase by acridines. *Biochemical Journal*, **100**, 50–58.

Nikaido, H. (1976) Outer membrane of *Salmonella typhimurium*: transmembrane diffusion of some hydrophobic substances. *Biochimica et Biophysica Acta*, **433**, 118–132.

Nikaido, H. & Vaara, M. (1955) Molecular basis of bacterial outer membrane permeability. *Microbiological Reviews*, **49**, 1–32.

Niven, D.F. & Hamilton, W.A. (1974) Mechanisms of energy coupling to the transport of amino acids in *Staphylococcus aureus*. *European Journal of Biochemistry*, **37**, 244–248.

Novick, R.P. & Roth, C. (1968) Plasmid-linked resistance to inorganic salts in *Staphylococcus*. *Journal of Bacteriology*, **95**, 1335–1342.

Peacocke, A.R. & Skerrett, J.N.H. (1956) The interaction of aminoacridines with nucleic acids. *Transactions of the Faraday Society*, **52**, 261–279.

Pritchard, N.J., Blake, A. & Peacocke, A.R. (1966) Modified intercalation model for the interaction of amino acridines and DNA. *Nature, London*, **272**, 1360–1361.

Prokop, A. & Humphrey, A.E. (1970) Kinetics of disinfection. In *Disinfection* (ed. Bernarde, M.A.) pp. 61–83. New York: Marcel Dekker.

Pulvertaft, R.J.V. & Lumb, G.D. (1948) Bacterial lysis and antiseptics. *Journal of Hygiene, Cambridge*, **46**, 62–64.

Rahn, O. (1945) Factors affecting the rate of disinfection. *Bacteriological Reviews*, **9**, 1–47.

Rahn, O. & Schroeder, W.R. (1941) Inactivation of enzymes as the cause of death in bacteria. *Byodynamica*, **3**, 199–208.

Ribbons, D.W. (1965) The microbial degradation of aromatic compounds. *Annual Reports on the Progress of Chemistry*, **62**, 455–468.

Richardson, A.G. & Leach, F.R. (1969) The effect of phenylethyl alcohol on *Bacillus subtilis* transformation. I. Characterisation of the effect. *Biochimica et Biophysica Acta*, **174**, 264–275.

Richardson, A.G., Pierson, D.L. & Leach, F.R. (1969) The effect of phenylethanol on *Bacillus subtilis* transformation. II. Transport of DNA and precursors. *Biochimica et Biophysica Acta*, **174**, 276–281.

Richmond, D.V. & Fisher, D.J. (1973) The electrophoretic mobility of microorganisms. *Advances in Microbial Physiology*, **9**, 1–29.

Roberts, M.H. & Rahn, O. (1946) The amount of enzyme inactivation at bacteriostatic and bactericidal concentrations of disinfectants. *Journal of Bacteriology*, **52**, 639–644.

Roe, E., Jones, R.J. & Lowbury, E.J.L. (1971) Transfer of antibiotic resistance between *Pseudomonas aeruginosa* and other Gram-negative bacilli in burns. *Lancet*, **6**, 149–152.

Rogers, H.J. & Forsberg, C.W. (1971) Role of autolysins in killing of bacteria by some bactericidal antibiotics. *Journal of Bacteriology*, **108**, 1235–1243.

Rogoff, M.H. (1961) The oxidation of aromatic compounds by bacteria. *Advances in Applied Microbiology*, **3**, 193–221.

Russell, A.D. (1971) Ethylenediaminetetraacetic acid. In *Inhibition and Destruction of the Microbial Cell* (ed. Hugo, W.B.) pp. 209–224. London: Academic Press.

Russell, A.D. (1972) Comparative resistance of R^+ and other strains of *Pseudomonas aeruginosa* to non-antibiotic antibacterials. *Lancet*, **ii**, 332.

Russell, A.D. (1974) Factors influencing the activity of antimicrobial agents: an appraisal. *Microbios*, **10**, 151–174.

Russell, A.D. (1985) The role of plasmids in bacterial resistance to antiseptics, disinfectants and preservatives. *Journal of Hospital Infection*, **6**, 9–19.

Russell, A.D. (1986) Chlorhexidine: antibacterial action and bacterial resistance. *Infection*, **14**, 212–215.

Russell, A.D. & Chopra, I. (1990) *Understanding Antibacterial Action and Resistance*. Chichester: Ellis Horwood.

Russell, A.D. & Gould, G.W. (1988) Resistance of Enterobacteriaceae to preservatives and disinfectants. *Journal of Applied Bacteriology, Symposium Supplement*, **65**, 167S–195S.

Russell, A.D. & Hopwood, D. (1976) The biological uses and importance of glutaraldehyde. *Progress in Medicinal Chemistry*, **13**, 271–301.

Russell, A.D. & Hugo, W.B. (1988) Perturbation of homeostatic mechanisms in bacteria by pharmaceuticals. In *Homeostatic Mechanisms in Microorganisms.*: FEMS Symposium no 44 (eds. Whittenbury, R, Gould, G.W. & Board, R.G.) pp. 206–219. Bath: Bath University.

Sakagami, Y, Yokagama, H., Nishimura, H., Ose, Y. & Tashima, T. (1989) Mechanism of resistance to benzalkonium chloride by *Pseudomonas aeruginosa*. *Applied and Environmental Microbiology*, **55**, 2036–2040.

Salton, M.R.J. (1951) The adsorption of cetyltrimethylammonium bromide by bacteria, its action in releasing cellular constituents and its bacterial effect. *Journal of General Microbiology*, **5**, 391–404.

Salton, M.R.J. (1968) Lytic agents, cell permeability and monolayer penetratability. *Journal of General Physiology*, **52**, 277S–252S.

Salton, M.R.J., Horne, R.W. & Coslett, V.E. (1951) Electron microscopy of bacteria treated with cetyltrimethylammonium bromide. *Journal of General Microbiology*, **5**, 405–407.

Sanderson, K.E., MacAlistair, T., Costerton, J.W. & Cheng, K.-J. (1974) Permeability of lipopolysaccharide-deficient (rough) mutants of *Salmonella typhinurium* to antibiotics, lysozyme and other agents. *Canadian Journal of Microbiology*, **20**, 1135–1145.

Silver, S. & Misra, S. (1988) Plasmid-mediated heavy metal resistances. *Annual Review of Microbiology*, **42**, 717–743.

Simon, E.W. (1953) Mechanism of dinitrophenol toxicity. *Biological Review*, **28**, 453–479.

Sinai, J. & Yudkin, J. (1959a) The origin of bacterial resistance to proflavine. III. The alleged rapid adaptation to proflavine resistance in *Bacterium lactis aerogenes* (syn. *Aerobacter aerogenes, Klebsiella pneumoniae*). *Journal of General Microbiology*, **20**, 373–383.

Sinai, J. & Yudkin, J. (1959b) The origin of bacterial resistance to proflavine. IV. Cycles of resistance in *Escherichia coli* and their bearing on variations in resistance in cultures. *Journal of General Microbiology*, **20**, 384–399.

Sinai, J. & Yudkin, J. (1959c) The origin of bacterial resistance to proflavine. V. Transformation of proflavine resistance in *Escherichia coli. Journal of General Microbiology*, **20**, 400–413.

Sleat, R. & Robinson, J.P. (1984) The bacteriology of anaerobic degradation of aromatic compounds. *Journal of Applied Bacteriology*, **57**, 381–394.

Smith, A.R.W., Lambert, P.A., Hammond, S.M. & Jessup, Carol. (1975) The differing effects of cetyltrimethylammonium bromide and cetrimide B.P. upon growing cultures of *Escherichia coli*. NCIB 8277. *Journal of Applied Bacteriology*, **38**, 143–149.

Sofos, J.N., Pierson, M.D., Blocher, J.C. & Busta, F.F. (1986) Mode of action of sorbic acid on bacterial cells and spores. *International Journal of Food Microbiology*, **3**, 1–17.

Staehelin, M. (1958) Reactions of tobacco mosaic virus nucleic acid with formaldehyde. *Biochimica et Biophysica Acta*, **29**, 410–417.

Stretton, R.J. & Manson, T.W. (1973) Some aspects of the mode of action of the antibacterial compound Bronopol (2-bromo-2-nitropropan-1,3-diol). *Journal of Applied Bacteriology*, **36**, 61–76.

Summers, A.O. & Lewis, E. (1973) Volatilization of mercuric chloride by mercury-resistant plasmid-bearing strains of *Escherichia coli, Staphylococcus aureus* and *Pseudomonas aeruginosa. Journal of Bacteriology*, **113**, 1070–1072.

Thornley, M.J. & Yudkin, J. (1959a) The origin of bacterial resistance to proflavine. I. Training and reversion in *Escherichia coli. Journal of General Microbiology*, **20**, 355–364.

Thornley, M.J. & Yudkin, J. (1959b) The origin of bacterial resistance in *Escherichia coli. Journal of General Microbiology*, **20**, 365–372.

Tomasz, A. (1979) The mechanism of the irreversible antimicrobial effects of penicillins: how the β-lactum antibiotics kill and lyse bacteria. *Annual Review of Microbiology*, **33**, 113–137.

Tomcsik, J. (1955) Effects of disinfectants and of surface active agents on bacterial protoplasts. *Proceedings of the Society of Experimental Biology and Medicine*, **89**, 459–463.

Vaara, M. & Vaara, T. (1983a) Polycations sensitise enteric bacteria to antibiotics. *Antimicrobial Agents and Chemotherapy*, **24**, 107–113.

Vaara, M. & Vaara, T. (1983b) Polycations as outer membrane-disorganizing agents. *Antimicrobial Agents and Chemotherapy*, **24**, 112–122.

Vaczi, L. (1973) *The Biological Role of Bacterial Lipids*. Budapest: Akademiai Kiado.

Vaituzis, Z., Nelson, J.D. Jr, Wan, L.W. & Colwell, R.R. (1975) Effects of mercuric chloride on growth and morphology of selected strains of mercury-resistant bacteria. *Applied Microbiology*, **29**, 275–286.

Walsh, C.T. & Kaback, H.R. (1973) Vinylglycolic acid. An inactivator of the phosphoenolpyruvate-phosphate transferase system in *Escherichia coli. Journal of Biological*

Chemistry, **248**, 5456–5462.

Wang, J.H. & Matheson, A.T. (1967) The possible role of sulphydryl groups in the dimerization of 70S ribosomes from *Escherichia coli*. *Biochemical and Biophysical Research Communications*, **23**, 740–744.

Waring, M.J. (1965) The effects of antimicrobial agents on ribonucleic acid polymerase. *Molecular Pharmacology*, **1**, 1–13.

Weinbach, E.C. (1957) Biochemical basis for the toxicity of pentachlorophenol. *Proceedings of the National Academy of Sciences, USA*, **43**, 393–397.

Williamson, R.L. & Metcalfe, R.L. (1967) Salicylanilides: a new group of active uncouplers of oxidative phosphorylation. *Science, Washington*, **158**, 1694–1695.

Woldringh, C.L. (1973) Effects of toluene and phenylethyl alcohol on the ultrastructure of *Escherichia coli*. *Journal of Bacteriology*, **114**, 1359–1361.

Woodroffe, R.C.S. & Wilkinson, B.E. (1966) The antibacterial activity of tetrachlorosalicylanilide. *Journal of General Microbiology*, **44**, 343–352.

Chapter 10
Bacterial Sensitivity and Resistance
A · INTRINSIC RESISTANCE

1 INTRODUCTION

The response of a natural community of microbes to a challenge from a non-antibiotic antibacterial agent will depend on a variety of factors. The pH, temperature, presence of organic debris and other chemical inactivators, the mode and rate of growth of the organisms can all profoundly influence the outcome. In addition many studies have revealed considerable variation in the innate sensitivity of the vegetative cells of different groups of bacteria to antiseptics, disinfectants and preservatives (Table 10.1). Generally Gram-negative organisms are more resistant than Gram-positive species. Special problems of resistance are also posed by *Pseudomonas aeruginosa* and *Mycobacterium tuberculosis*. This resistance phenomenon is consistently demonstrated by natural isolates of these groups of organisms, and it has been described as *intrinsic*, implying that it is due to some inherent feature of the cells and to distinguish it from *acquired* resistance which occurs when resistant strains emerge from previously sensitive species after exposure to antibacterial agents.

Predictably, it has been proposed that the basic features of the Gram-negative cell which prevent the penetration of crystal violet and result in its accessibility to extraction with alcohol or acetone in the classical Gram-staining procedure, also tend to exclude many antibacterials and prevent them reaching their biochemical or structural targets within the cell. Before examining this in more detail it is important to point out that Gram-negativity is not always correlated with greater resistance to antibacterials. There are a number of exceptions: chlorine, for example, is more active against *Ps. aeruginosa* and *Proteus mirabilis* than against *Staph. aureus* (Trueman, 1971), and similar findings have been reported for phenoxyethanol (Berry, 1944) and silver salts (Sykes, 1958).

2 THE ENTEROBACTERIACEAE

Many of the antibacterial agents that are less active against Gram-negative cells are believed to exert their effect by inducing metabolic or structural lesions in the cytoplasmic membrane (Hugo, 1967). Hamilton (1971) proposed that the actual cytoplasmic membranes of Gram-positive and Gram-negative cells are equally sensitive to the action of these agents, and that layers of the Gram-negative cell envelope external to the membrane may either constitute a non-absorbing barrier or may absorb and retain the agent, in both cases protecting the underlying sensitive membrane.

The molecular organization of the surface layers of bacteria is now known in some detail. In Gram-positive cells the cytoplasmic membrane is closely

Table 10.1 Comparative responses of *Staphylococcus aureus*, *Pseudomonas aeruginosa* and some Enterobacteriaceae to antiseptics, disinfectants and preservatives*†

	MIC (μg/ml) versus			
Antimicrobial agent	*Staphylococcus aureus*	*Pseudomonas aeruginosa*	*Escherichia coli*	*Klebsiella pneumoniae*
Bronopol	62.5	31.25	31.25	62.5
Phenylethanol	1250	2500–5000	2500	
Propionic acid	2000	3000	2000	1250
Sorbic acid (pH 6)	50–100	100–300	50–100	50–100
Benzoic acid (pH 6)	50–100	200–500	100–200	100–200
Methyl paraben	800	1000	800	800
Ethyl paraben	500	800	600	600
Propyl paraben	150	400	300	300
Butyl paraben	120	175	150	100
Chlorocresol	625	1250	1250	625
Chloroxylenol	250	1000	1000	500
o-Phenylphenol	100	1000	500	500
Hexachlorophane	0.5	250	12.5	12.5
Triclosan	0.1	>300	5	5
Propamidine isethionate	2	256	64	256
Dibromopropamidine isethionate	1	32	4	
Hexetidine	5	>10000	1250	>10000
8-Hydroxyquinoline	4	128	64	64
Chlorhexidine	0.5–1	5–60	1	5–10
Benzethonium chloride	0.5	250	32	
Cetrimide	4	64–128	16	16
Thiomersal	0.2	8	4	4
Phenylmercuric nitrate	0.1	1–5	0.5	0.5

* Inoculum size *ca.* 10^6 cfu/ml.
† Based on Wallhäusser (1984).

encased within a thick fibrous layer of peptidoglycan interspersed by teichoic and teichuronic acids and lipids (Rogers *et al.*, 1978). The envelope of Gram-negative cells (Fig. 10.1) is a more complex and sophisticated structure (Hammond *et al.*, 1984). The cell-wall peptidoglycan is less substantial and not as intimately associated with the cytoplasmic membrane. An important additional feature is the presence of an outer membrane external to the peptidoglycan. Although in electron micrographs this outer membrane appears similar to the cytoplasmic membrane, its biochemical composition is quite different. It contains less phospholipid, fewer types of proteins and a unique component, lipopolysaccharide (LPS). In *Escherichia coli* and *Salmonella typhimurium*, at least, there is an asymmetric organization of these components. The LPS molecules are entirely located at the outer surface of the membrane (Muhlradt & Golecki, 1975) and the phospholipid molecules are almost exclusively found at the inner face (Kamio & Nikaido, 1976; Nikaido *et al.*, 1977). There are four or five major outer membrane proteins (OMP) and they are exposed at the cell surface (Verkleij *et al.*, 1977). The protein molecules are so arranged as to span the membrane and are assembled in such a way as to produce water-filled channels or 'porins' (Nakae, 1976). DiRienzo *et al.* (1978) have proposed that the porins are produced by three molecules of protein, each held in place by the triple-coiled structure of a special lipoprotein molecule, which extends through the outer membrane and is covalently linked to the underlying peptidoglycan.

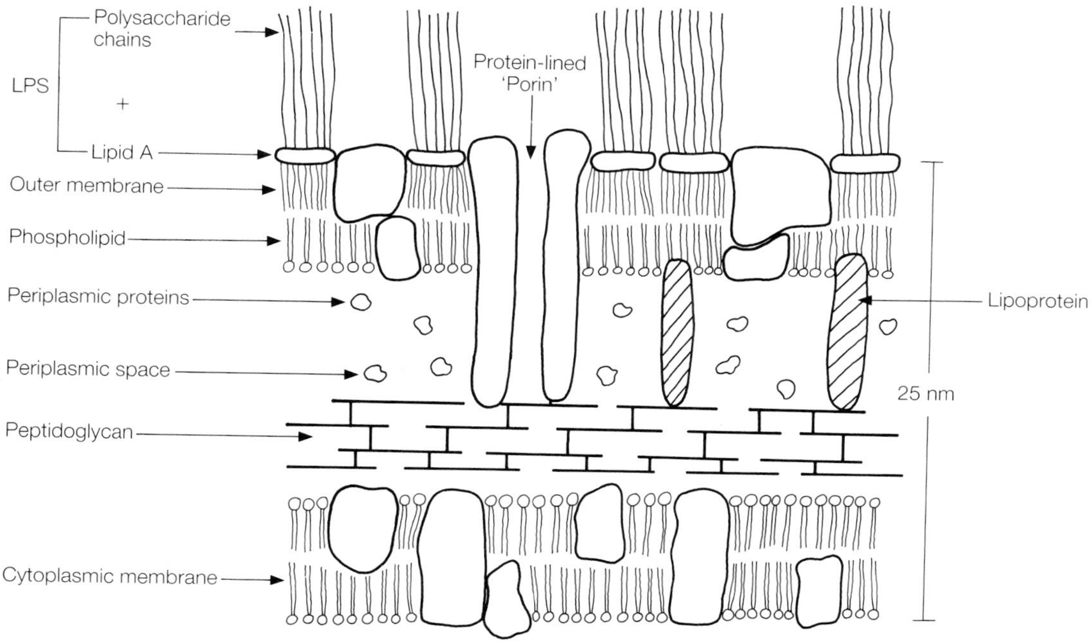

Fig. 10.1 The Gram-negative cell envelope.

These pores are believed to be 1.5–2.0 nm in diameter and normally allow the passage of low-molecular-weight nutrients such as amino acids, sugars and salts into the periplasmic space from where they are subsequently actively transported into the cytoplasm. The data from studies in which the penetration of oligosaccharides into vesicles reconstituted from the components of the outer membrane and into plasmolysed cells has been observed (Nakae & Nikaido, 1975; Decad & Nikaido, 1976; Nixdorf *et al.*, 1977) indicate that porins impose a sharp exclusion limit in terms of molecular size. The outer membranes of the enteric bacteria *E. coli*, *Sal. typhimurium*, *P. mirabilis* and *P. morganii* appear, therefore, to constitute a permeability barrier for hydrophilic compounds with molecular weights greater than 550–650.

The Gram-negative cell thus confronts the challenge of an antibacterial agent with an exposed outer surface composed essentially of the LPS polysaccharide chains and the protein-lined diffusion pores. There is now considerable evidence that this layer provides a formidable barrier to the penetration of many types of antibacterial agents (Russell & Gould, 1988). A number of different approaches have been taken in an attempt to clarify the precise nature of the protection afforded by the outer membrane. These have involved the modification of the membrane by genetic, phenotypic or chemical means and observing the effect of these manipulations on sensitivity to various antibacterial agents.

The availability of a comprehensive collection of mutants of *Sal. typhimurium* having well-defined alterations in their LPS polysaccharide chains has facilitated an examination of how variations in these structures affect the sensitivity to antibacterials. The results of this approach (Roantree *et al.*, 1969, 1977; Schlecht & Westphal, 1970) indicate that shortening the sugar chains of the LPS has little effect on the antibacterial sensitivity until 80–90% of the chain is deleted. Loss of the next few sugar residues, however, produced cells with greatly increased sensitivity towards some antibiotics and to crystal violet, malachite green and phenol. The sensitivity of these 'deep rough' mutants to a number of other antibiotics was, however, unaffected.

Nikaido (1976) put forward an explanation of these changes. He showed that those agents whose activity was increased in deep rough mutants as against the wild strain were generally hydrophobic. Those agents whose activity was unaffected by LPS alteration were mainly small hydrophilic molecules (mol. wt <600). He then proposed that these changes were not a direct result of the alterations in the LPS structure but were due to an extensive reorganization of the outer membrane. The loss of a crucial glucose residue from the LPS blocks the incorporation of many protein molecules into the outer membrane (Ames *et al.*, 1974) and this results in a compensatory reorientation of phospholipid molecules at the outer surface (Smit *et al.*, 1975). These exposed phospholipid bilayer regions then allow the rapid penetration of hydrophobic molecules like phenol, by dissolution and diffusion in the lipid (Nikaido & Nakae, 1979).

The so-called *omp* mutants of *Sal. typhimurium*, which have a normal wild-type LPS composition but reduced levels of outer membrane proteins, are sensitive to crystal violet and deoxycholate (Ames *et al.*, 1974) and also allow the rapid penetration of a number of hydrophobic antibiotics (Nikaido, 1976). These observations emphasize the integrated nature of the components of the outer membrane and confirm that membrane reorganization, with phospholipid replacing protein at the outer surface, rather than alteration of the LPS structure itself, is the cause of increased hydrophobic permeability in the rough mutants (Nikaido & Vaara, 1985).

In *E. coli*, Tamaki & Matsuhashi (1973) showed that rough mutants with extensive LPS effects were unusually sensitive to the hydrophobic antibiotic novobiocin and hypersensitive to the enzyme lysozyme. Gustafsson *et al.* (1973) studied the uptake of gentian violet into a wild type and a collection of envelope mutants of *E. coli*. They found that all strains they tested bound the dye instantaneously to the outer envelope. The mutants then, however, continued to absorb the dye and permitted its penetration through to the ribosomal fraction of the cytoplasm. The rate of uptake of this second phase increased with increasing deficiency of LPS. However, it was again clear that LPS is not the only important factor as *env* A mutants, with some unknown envelope defect but with normal LPS composition, took up the dye extremely rapidly at a rate equivalent to that observed with spheroplasts.

More recently, the observations of Russell *et al.* (1985, 1987) and Russell & Furr (1986a,b, 1987) on rough and deep rough mutants of *E. coli* and *Sal. typhimurium* also suggest that extensive loss of the LPS chain has to occur before sensitivity increases to esters of *para*-(4)-hydroxybenzoic acid, benzalkonium chloride and cetylpyridinium chloride. Deep rough mutants of *E. coli*, however, showed no increase in sensitivity to chlorhexidine, an observation which suggests that this antiseptic has a different cell-entry mechanism from the quaternary ammonium compounds.

The exposure of *E. coli* cells to 0.2 mM ethylenediamine-tetraacetic acid (EDTA) in 0.12 M tris buffer (pH 8.0) for just 2 min at 37°C results in their sensitization to a wide range of antibacterial agents, including many which are active against the cytoplasmic membrane (Leive, 1968). The cells also release periplasmic enzymes (Neu & Chou, 1967) and become sensitive to lysozyme (Repaske, 1956). These observations indicate that EDTA exerts an effect on a permeability barrier in the cell which is external to the peptidoglycan. The evidence on the precise mode of action has been reviewed by Russell (1971) and Wilkinson (1975). The first stage of the EDTA sensitization process involves the chelation of metal cations which are bound to the polyanionic polysaccharide chains of LPS. These cations are believed to have a structural function in forming stabilizing cross-bridges between the LPS chains. Dissociation of the outer membrane follows with the loss of LPS, protein and lipid. The layer is not totally disrupted, however, the amount of LPS released not exceeding 50% of the total present. The remaining LPS fraction, which is still located at the outer surface of the membrane, cannot be removed by raising the EDTA concentration or by re-treating the cells with EDTA (Leive, 1974). These observations have led Nikaido (1976) to suggest that the EDTA-induced loss of protein and LPS results in a reorganization of the outer membrane, similar to that which occurs in the deep rough mutants, phospholipid molecules replacing the lost components, thus producing exposed phospholipid bilayer regions with all the consequences that this has for permeability. Whatever the subsequent reorganizations are, this EDTA effect shows that an intact outer membrane provides the cell with a useful protective barrier.

Phenotypic modifications in envelope composition can be achieved by variation in the growth conditions (Ellwood & Tempest, 1972). For example, when *Klebsiella aerogenes* was grown in chemostat culture with glycerol as the limiting nutrient in the medium, the wall LPS content increased markedly with increasing growth rate (Tempest & Ellwood, 1969). Working with the same species, Robinson & Tempest (1973) showed that sulphate-limited organisms contained less protein in their envelope than did glucose-limited cells. This use of continuous culture has not yet been exploited in the study of how the outer membranes of the Enterobacteriaceae provide cells with protective barriers. Gilbert & Brown (1978a), however, found that carbon-depleted batch cultures of *E. coli* were significantly more sensitive to chlorophenols than were magnesium- or phosphate-depleted cultures. Unfortunately, analysis of cell phospholipid and LPS from these cultures could not explain the increased sensitivity of the carbon-depleted cells. Klemperer *et al.* (1980) reported that phosphate depleted (P−) *E. coli* were less susceptible to chlorhexidine than were carbon depleted (C−) cultures and that the (P−) cells contained less phospholipid than (C−) cultures. Wright & Gilbert (1987), however, reported that while the sensitivity of *E. coli* to chlorhexidine increased with nitrogen and carbon limitation, magnesium and phosphate limitation decreased sensitivity, and it was not possible to explain these changes in sensitivity in terms of alteration in cell envelope composition.

The concept that has emerged from the work on the surface layers of the Enterobacteriaceae, therefore, is that the protein-lined pores in the outer membrane are the only non-specific permeation pathway to the periplasmic space. Hydrophobic molecules and large hydrophilic ones (>650 daltons) are impeded or denied access to the vulnerable cytoplasmic membrane. In their natural habitat this undoubtedly provides essential protection for the organism from the toxic effects of fatty acids and bile salts that abound in the gut. The lesson from this work for those interested in the rational design of antibacterial agents is that the addition of hydrophobic substituents to a molecule would be likely to inhibit its cellular penetration, while alterations which make the compound more hydrophilic are likely to facilitate its passage to the cellular target.

3 *PSEUDOMONAS AERUGINOSA*

The properties of *Ps. aeruginosa* that have allowed it to become an important cause of hospital-acquired infections include abilities to grow in dilute aqueous environments, to resist most antibiotics and to survive in the presence of many antiseptics and disinfectants (Lowbury, 1975). This latter capacity has even been used in formulating selective media for the isolation of the organism, e.g. cetrimide agar (Brown & Lowbury, 1965). The intrinsic resistance of *Ps. aeruginosa* warrants a separate consideration as it has a number of features distinctive from those propounded for the enterobacteria above. With the possible exception of *Providencia stuartii* (Thomas *et al.*, 1978), *Ps. aeruginosa* is significantly more resistant than the Enterobacteriaceäe to many antiseptics; it is also characteristically more sensitive to EDTA and to the antibiotic polymyxin, than most other Gram-negative rods.

As with the Enterobacteriaceae, the evidence strongly implicates the cell envelope in resistance to chemical agents. Hamilton (1970), for example, showed that conversion of *Ps. aeruginosa* to spheroplasts rendered the organisms sensitive to cytoplasmic membrane-active agents such as cetyltrimethylammonium bromide (CTAB). It is now well established that the primary reason for the intrinsic resistance of *Ps. aeruginosa* is the low permeation rates of hydrophilic substances across the outer membrane (Angus *et al.*, 1982; Yoshimura & Nikaido, 1982; Nicas & Hancock, 1983).

The *Ps. aeruginosa* envelope appears to differ significantly from that of *E. coli* or *Sal. typhi-*

murium. Meadow (1975) proposed a structure which has a number of unique features. While it consists essentially of two lipoprotein layers separated by a sheet of peptidoglycan and a periplasmic space, the outer membrane appears to have phospholipid and LPS at both faces. Protein porins occur in the outer membrane, but the data of Decad & Nikaido (1976) from work with plasmolysed cells suggest that the exclusion limit for these pores is significantly higher than that for the enteric Gram-negative rods. Hancock & Nikaido (1978) have succeeded in reconstituting vesicles from outer membrane components of *Ps. aeruginosa* and such vesicles only retained saccharides of molecular weight >9000, indicating a pore size much larger than those of *E. coli*, *Sal. typhimurium* or *P. mirabilis*. It appears, then, that the outer membrane of *Ps. aeruginosa* has areas of phospholipid bilayers and large protein pores which allow the passage of hydrophilic molecules up to 9000 daltons in size. It is difficult to explain how such a layer affords special protection to the cytoplasmic membrane against hydrophilic antiseptic molecules.

This paradox was resolved when Benz & Hancock (1981) and Yoshimura *et al.* (1983), demonstrated that the permeability to small sugars in vesicles produced by reconstituting a given amount of *Ps. aeruginosa* porin protein with phospholipids was about 40-fold lower than that obtained in vesicles prepared from the same amount of *E. coli* porin protein. It seems that very few of the protein molecules in the *Ps. aeruginosa* outer membrane form the large channels. Thus while the exclusion limit is large due to the presence of a few large pores, the surface area of channels available for the diffusion of large hydrophilic molecules is small. The experiments of Woodruff *et al.* (1986) incorporating *Ps. aeruginosa* porin protein into black lipid bilayers and measuring pore size as a function of electrical conductance across the membranes, confirmed the heterogeneity of the porins. The large channels comprised less than 1% of the total, the predominant channels were of a much smaller bore and thus probably impenetrable to molecules as large as the hydrophilic antiseptics.

A major source of evidence that the outer membrane endows *Ps. aeruginosa* with its refractility to antibacterials comes from observations on the reaction of the species to EDTA. *Ps. aeruginosa* is, in fact, extremely sensitive to EDTA (see also Boggis *et al.*, 1979; Kenwood *et al.*, 1979) and concentrations of the agent which have little effect on other Gram-negative rods, produce rapid lysis of the pseudomonad (Gray & Wilkinson, 1965). At low temperature, or in low concentrations of EDTA, *Ps. aeruginosa* will survive exposure, but the loss of the LPS, protein and lipid resulting from the chelation of Mg^{2+} ions present in the outer membrane, has been shown to potentiate the action of antibacterials, e.g. phenolics, QACs, chlorhexidine, chloramine and many antibiotics against the organism.

Phenotypic variation in the cell-envelope composition of *Ps. aeruginosa* has been produced by manipulation of the growth conditions (Robinson *et al.*, 1974) and attempts have been made to correlate these changes with sensitivity to antibacterials. Melling *et al.* (1974) found that bacteria grown in continuous culture under conditions of carbon limitation were more sensitive than magnesium-limited cells to polymyxin, and that phosphate-limited cells were hypersensitive to this membrane-active agent. Although there were changes in the phospholipid and LPS content of these cells, no clear pattern emerged to link changes in antibacterial susceptibility with specific components of the outer membrane (Dean *et al.*, 1976). Gilbert & Brown (1978b) investigated the effect of nutrient limitation and growth rate on the sensitivity of *Ps. aeruginosa* to 3- and 4-chlorophenol. These substituted phenols increase the permeability of the cytoplasmic membranes to protons and thus uncouple oxidative phosphorylation from respiration. To assess sensitivity to these agents the rates of drug-induced proton translocation into cells were measured by following the rate of change of pH of the extracellular phase. Variation in the proton permeability is related to the concentration of the agent at the cytoplasmic membrane, so changes in sensitivity were interpreted as variations in the penetration of the agents through the outer membrane. Using these methods, Gilbert & Brown concluded that rapidly growing cells were generally more sensitive than slower-growing ones and that glucose-limited cells were more sensitive than magnesium-limited ones. It was also shown that uptake of the phenols by cell suspensions varied, sensitive bacteria absorbing more than resistant ones. This latter effect was demonstrable even after cells had been treated with solvent to remove readily extractable lipids (REL). Gross chemical analysis on the cells showed that their REL content did not change significantly with growth rate or nutrient limitation. These observations suggest that REL is not involved in altering the affinity of the cells to phenolic compounds. Using 2-keto-3-deoxyoctonic acid (KDO) as a marker they concluded that the LPS content was higher in the magnesium-limited cells, and that it decreased with increasing growth rates. LPS content correlated therefore with sensitivity, the less LPS present in the cells, the greater their sensitivity to chlorophenols. The uptake of the agents also correlated with cell LPS content. The LPS content thus appeared to determine the degree of penetration of the cell envelope by these chlorinated phenols.

Kropinski *et al.* (1978) used a genetic approach to study the effect of LPS on the resistance of *Ps. aeruginosa* to a variety of antibacterials including dyes, detergents, antiseptics and antibiotics. Of a collection of LPS-deficient mutants, only the roughest strain which had apparently lost all of the *O*-specific LPS side-chains and was also deficient in core constituents such as glucose and rhamnose, showed any increased sensitivity to sodium deoxycholate, hexadecylpyridinium chloride and benzalkonium chloride. By analogy with the deep rough mutants of *Sal. typhimurium*, it is possible that the loss of LPS in these strains could result in the relocation of more phospholipid at the outer membrane surface. It must be remembered, however, that phospholipids are apparently already exposed at the outer surface (Meadow, 1975).

4 MYCOBACTERIA

The sensitivity of *Mycobacterium* spp. to chemical agents has been reviewed by Croshaw (1971). In summary, mycobacteria, and especially the human tubercle bacillus, are considerably more resistant to acids, alkalis, QACs, chlorhexidine, dyes, halogens and heavy metals than are other vegetative bacterial cells. In addition to their intrinsic resistance, mycobacteria in clinical specimens are notoriously coated in mucous or necrotic caseous materials which inactivate disinfectants. Viable mycobacterial cells have thus been recovered from, for example, fibre-optic bronchoscopes after disinfection with an alcoholic iodophor (Nelson *et al.*, 1983) or glutaraldehyde (Wheeler *et al.*, 1989). Heat treatment should thus be used whenever possible for the disinfection of objects that may be contaminated with discharges from tuberculous patients (Bergan & Lystad, 1971). Only in circumstances where heat sterilization is not feasible should a chemical disinfectant be used, a clear soluble phenolic being chosen at a concentration suitable for heavily contaminated objects (Kelsey & Maurer, 1972).

Mycobacteria, of course, fail to take up many of the normal bacteriological dyes. Staining procedures such as that of Ziehl–Nielsen, where the arylmethane dye fuchsin, in phenolic solution as carbol fuchsin, is driven into the cells with heat, have to be used to stain these organisms. Once stained, the cells resist decolorization with acid-alcohol. This acid-fastness has been shown to be a function of their cell wall structure. The cell wall structure of mycobacteria has been reviewed in considerable detail (Barksdale & Kim, 1977; Petit & Lederer, 1978; Draper, 1982; Brennan, 1989). It appears that external to the cell cytoplasmic membrane is a sheet of peptidoglycan, and that this is covered by layers of rope-like peptidoglycolipids. These are peptidoglycans linked to arabinogalactan-mycolates and they are embedded in sulpholipids and trehalose-dimycolates. In the Ziehl–Nielsen stain, the fuchsin is believed to bind with the waxy mycolic acid residues of those lipid-rich layers and these complexes then resist decolorization with acid-alcohol. If these outer peptidoglycolipid layers of the wall are removed with alkaline ethanol then the cell loses its acid-fast character (Fisher & Barkesdale, 1973). It is probable that these lipid-rich, hydrophobic layers of the mycobacterial cell wall are also responsible for the resistance of these organisms to many chemical disinfectants.

The response of mycobacteria to biocides is considered in more detail in Chapter 10D.

5 BACTERIAL BIOFILMS AND RESISTANCE

In many natural habitats bacteria are able to adhere to and colonize available surfaces. The films of microbial growth that develop from these adhered cells are commonly mixed communities containing several different species. It is becoming increasingly clear that, in this mode of growth, bacteria exhibit characteristics that can be quite different from those of the same cells grown in suspension (Costerton *et al.*, 1987). These differences, sometimes referred to as sessile and planktonic growth modes, have important environmental, industrial and medical implications. Several groups have reported that bacteria growing in biofilms exhibit reduced sensitivities to antimicrobial agents when compared with cells of the same organism growing in the dispersed planktonic mode. Gwynne *et al.* (1981) showed that *Ps. aeruginosa*, *E. coli* and *Staph. aureus* adhering to glass culture vessels could survive in concentrations of β-lactam antibiotics that were bactericidal for the same cells growing in suspension. Marrie & Costerton (1981) demonstrated that *Serr. marcescens* growing on the walls of glass bottles could survive high concentrations (20,000 mg/l) of chlorhexidine. *Pseudomonas cepacia* growing on glass slides has also been shown to be protected against this antiseptic (Pallent *et al.*, 1983; Hugo *et al.*, 1986). The latter refers to early papers on surface colonization.

In an investigation of bladder instillations of antiseptics as a means of controlling urinary tract infections in patients with indwelling catheters, Stickler *et al.* (1987) used a physical model of the catheterized bladder to examine the effect of chlorhexidine (200 mg/l) on urinary pathogens. *Prov. stuartii*, *Ps. aeruginosa*, *Pr. mirabilis*, *E. coli*, *K. pneumoniae* and *Strep. faecalis* growing in urine in the bladder model rapidly recovered from the initial bactericidal effect of the antiseptic. During these experiments it was noticed that films of bacterial growth developed on the walls of the model, and cells in these biofilms appeared to be particularly resistant to the antiseptics and initiated the recovery of the cultures after the instillation. More recently biofilms of *E. coli* and other urinary tract pathogens established on silicon discs have also been shown to survive well in chlorhexidine (200 mg/l) for up to 2 h, whereas in urine suspension the cells were rapidly killed by this concentration of the antiseptic (Stickler *et al.*, 1989, 1991).

In many industrial processes, surfaces of storage tanks, pipelines and machinery can become colonized by microbial growths. Attempts to remove these unwanted growths with chemical biocides are often unsuccessful. Sharma *et al.* (1987), for example, have shown that a quaternary ammonium compound, a biguanide and an isothiazolone were less active against sessile than suspended cells of *Desulphovibrio desulfuricans*.

Concern has also been expressed about the biofilms in water-supply pipelines, and water circulation systems. *E. coli*, *Sal. typhimurium*, *Yersinia enterocolitica*, *Shigella sonnei*, and *K. pneumoniae* showed substantially reduced sensitivities to chlorination when adsorbed to carbon granules (Le Chevalier *et al.*, 1988). Similarly *Enterobacter cloacae* growing on particles sloughed off from a cast-iron pipe was also more resistant to disinfection than its planktonic sister cells (Herson *et al.*, 1987).

Costerton (1984) has observed that populations of bacteria growing in biofilms are embedded in an anionic polysaccharide matrix, and suggested that this glycocalyx affords considerable protection to the cells against antimicrobial agents. Little work has been published on the mechanism of antimicrobial resistance in biofilms. Nichols *et al.* (1988), however, have examined the hypothesis that the glycocalyx hindered the penetration of bactericidal molecules in the film. In this investigation they measured the ability of the antibiotic tobramycin to penetrate alginate gels which chemically resemble the exopolysaccharide of *Ps. aeruginosa* cells, and found that there was an initial inhibition of tobramycin diffusion, until all the gel binding sites were saturated. The antibiotic then diffused freely through the gel. It was calculated that the time required for the concentration of tobramycin at the base of a biofilm 100 μm thick to rise to 90% of the external concentration would increase from 27 s in the absence of any restriction to 77 s in the presence of 1% w/v extracellular polysaccharide. Such an effect is unlikely to be a major contribution to the 1000-fold reduction of sensitivity to tobramycin exhibited by mucoid biofilms of *Ps. aeruginosa* (Nichols *et al.*, 1989). In this case at least it would seem that restriction of penetration of the bactericide is not the sole cause of resistance.

Much of the work on resistance has been performed on biofilms with variable characteristics. It has also been pointed out that many experiments have not been controlled with respect to cell growth rate (Brown *et al.*, 1988). Differences in antimicrobial susceptibility have been reported between slow-growing sessile cells and rapidly growing suspended organisms. There is clearly a need to examine the resistance phenomenon in biofilms with defined standard characteristics of cell density, film thickness and bacterial growth rate.

6 DISINFECTION POLICIES AND INTRINSIC RESISTANCE

The recognition that the outer membrane of Gram-negative bacteria constitutes an effective barrier to the passage of so many antibacterial agents provides an opportunity for a rational approach to the design of new antiseptic and disinfectant preparations. The combination of an agent which opens up the outer membrane with compounds which attack, for example, the cytoplasmic membrane could produce a range of new formulations with improved activity against these refractile organisms. In this connection, Dankert & Schut (1976) and Russell & Furr (1977) have shown that the combination of EDTA with chloroxylenol potentiates the activity of this phenolic compound against *Ps. aeruginosa*. Russell & Furr, for example, showed that the EDTA–chloroxylenol mixture withstood a repeated challenge from daily doses of 10^6 viable cells/ml of *Ps. aeruginosa*. Even on day 48 no viable cells could be re-isolated from the disinfectant. Chloroxylenol alone, however, at an equivalent concentration, failed the test, cells being recovered from the disinfectant on day 2, and by day 12 the number of viable cells contaminating the solution was $>5 \times 10^6$/ml.

Kelsey & Maurer (1972) and Lowbury *et al.* (1975) called for hospitals to review their disinfection policies and to reduce the use of disinfectants in circumstances where heating or thorough cleaning will suffice (see also Chapter 10). This makes good economic sense and is also to be approved of on the general grounds that the more extensively an antibacterial agent is used, the more likely it will become that a resistant microbial flora will emerge. In our opinion, hospital Control of Infection Committees should also think carefully about their antiseptic or disinfectant policies in situations where intrinsically resistant bacteria are producing infections.

This view is based on observations on the mode of development of urinary tract infections in paraplegic patients enduring long-term intermittent bladder catheterization (Stickler *et al.*, 1971; O'Flynn & Stickler, 1972). Catheterization, which was performed three or four times daily, involved the washing of the periurethal area with chlorhexidine (600 mg/l) prior to insertion of the catheter. The effect of this repeated application of antiseptic on the bacterial flora of the urethral meatus was examined in a prospective study of patients from the date of injury and admission to the spinal unit up to the time they developed urinary tract infection. The urethral flora was examined daily before and after the application of the antiseptic, and the general pattern that emerged was that for the first few days after trauma the meatal skin carried a Gram-positive flora which was greatly reduced by the application of the antiseptic. A Gram-negative flora usually developed by about day 4 and proved to be more refractory to chlorhexidine. In particular *Pr. mirabilis*, *Ps. aeruginosa*, *Prov. stuartii* and *Klebsiella* spp. frequently survived the meatal cleansing and proceeded to infect the bladder. Many of these strains demonstrated an ability to grow in media containing 200 mg/l of chlorhexidine and some of the *Pr. mirabilis* and *Prov. stuartii* isolates from this source were shown to have MICs of up to 800 mg/l, well above the level of 10–50 mg/l originally reported to inhibit the growth of these Gram-negative species (Davies *et al.*, 1954).

In order to ascertain whether this resistance to chlorhexidine was a general phenomenon or was limited to special circumstances, Stickler & Thomas (1980) examined a large collection of isolates of Gram-negative bacilli causing urinary tract infections in patients from general practice, ante-natal clinics and six hospitals. It was observed that chlorhexidine resistance was not a widespread phenomenon. It was limited to *Pr. mirabilis*, *Ps. aeruginosa*, *Prov. stuartii* and *Serr. marcescens*, and the only major source of these resistant strains was another spinal unit where chlorhexidine was being used extensively in management of patients by long-term indwelling catheterization.

Analysis of the antibiotic sensitivities of the collection revealed a significant correlation between resistance to chlorhexidine and multiplicity of drug resistance, the chlorhexidine-resistant strains generally being resistant to five to seven of the antibiotics tested. These results led us to examine whether the correlation between antibiotic and antiseptic resistance had a basis in an association of the resistance genes. While a transferable resistance factor carrying the genetic information for resistance to commonly used antiseptics and antibiotics would constitute a formidable genetic package for nosocomial organisms, an investigation with strains of *Prov. stuartii* showed no evidence for the existence of such a genetic linkage, and it was suggested that chlorhexidine resistance was an intrinsic property of the cell walls of these organisms which denies the antiseptic access to its target site of the cytoplasmic membrane, or alternatively that chlorhexidine resistant strains happen to be efficient recipients for R-factors for some reason (Stickler *et al.*, 1983).

These observations suggest that an antiseptic policy involving the long-term and extensive use of chlorhexidine in clinical situations such as the catheterized urinary tract could well be counter-productive and lead to the selection of notoriously drug-resistant nosocomial pathogens (Stickler & Thomas, 1980). Some support for our contention was provided by the report (Walker & Lowes, 1985) of an outbreak of urinary infections in patients at a Southampton hospital. Here, urinary catheter management involved the use of chlorhexidine for perineal cleaning prior to catheterization. A gel containing chlorhexidine was used as a lubricant for the passage of the catheter, and chlorhexidine was included in the urine drainage bags and instilled into the bags every time they were emptied. The catheter–meatal junction was cleansed daily with chlorhexidine, after which a cream containing the antiseptic was applied to the periurethal area (Southampton Control of Infection Team, 1982). In the outbreak, 90 patients became infected with a chlorhexidine-resistant strain of *Pr. mirabilis* which was also resistant to sulphaphurazole, trimethoprim, ampicillin, mezlocillin, azlocillin, carbenicillin, gentamicin and tobramycin (Dance *et al.*, 1987). The epidemic strain was shown to survive the 'in-use' concentrations of chlorhexidine achieved in the urine reservoir bags (Walker & Lowes, 1985) and these authors considered that the epidemic strain may have been selected by the antiseptic policy, and recommended that the routine addition of chlorhexidine to the catheter bags be abandoned.

In the context of the use of antiseptics in preventing and controlling urinary tract infection, evidence is accumulating that the normal Gram-positive flora of the urethra has a role in protecting the urinary tract from enteric organisms (Kunin & Steele, 1985; Reid *et al.*, 1987). The antiseptics currently used in urethral disinfection are more active against the normal flora, and this may facilitate the colonization of the urethra by the Gram-negative pathogens. It would be most interesting to examine the long-term effects of antiseptic formulations that are selectively active on the urinary pathogens. It is our belief that the careful consideration of which antiseptic to use in special circumstances, and the implementation of the general disinfection policies formulated on the guidelines laid down by Kelsey & Maurer (1972), will help to reduce the accumulation of intrinsically resistant species in the hospital environment.

7 REFERENCES

Ames, G.F.L., Spudich, E.N. & Nikaido, H. (1974) Protein composition of the outer membrane of *Salmonella typhimurium*: effect of lipopolysaccharide mutations. *Journal of Bacteriology*, **117**, 406–416.

Angus, B.L., Carey, A.M., Caron, D.A., Kropinski, A.M.B. & Hancock, R.E.W. (1982) Outer membrane permeability in *Pseudomonas aeruginosa*: comparison of a wild-type with an antibiotic susceptible mutant. *Antimicrobial Agents and Chemotherapy*, **21**, 229–309.

Barksdale, L. & Kim, K.S. (1977) *Mycobacterium Bacteriological Reviews*, **41**, 217–372.

Benz, R. & Hancock, R.E.W. (1981) Properties of the large ion permeable pores formed from protein F of *Pseudo-*

monas aeruginosa in lipid bilayer membranes. *Biochimica et Biophysica Acta*, **646**, 298–308.

Bergan, T. & Lystad, A. (1971) Anti-tubercular action of disinfectants. *Journal of Applied Bacteriology* **34**, 751–756.

Berry, H. (1944) Antibacterial values of ethylene glycol mono-phenyl ether. *Lancet*, **ii**, 175–176.

Boggis, W., Kenward, M.A. & Brown, M.R.W. (1979) Effects of divalent metal cations in the growth medium upon sensitivity of batch-grown *Pseudomonas aeruginosa* to EDTA or polymyxin B. *Journal of Applied Bacteriology*, **47**, 477–88.

Brennan, P.J. (1989) Structure of Mycobacteria: recent developments in defining cell-wall carbohydrates and proteins. *Reviews of Infectious Diseases*, Supplement 2, S420–430.

Brown, M.R.W., Allison, D.G. & Gilbert, P. (1988) Resistance of bacterial biofilms to antibiotics: a growth related effect? *Journal of Antimicrobial Chemotherapy*, **22**, 777–780.

Brown, V.I. & Lowbury, E.J.L. (1965) Use of an improved agar medium and other culture methods for *Pseudomonas aeruginosa*. *Journal of Clinical Pathology*, **18**, 752–756.

Costerton, J.W. (1984) The aetiology and persistence of cryptic bacterial infections: a hypothesis. *Review of Infectious Diseases*, **6**, (Suppl. 3) S608–612.

Costerton, J.W., Cheng, K.J., Geesey, G.G. Ladd, T.T., Nickel, J.C., Dasgupta, M. & Marrie, T.J. (1987) Bacterial biofilms in nature and disease. *Annual Reviews of Microbiology*, **41**, 435–464.

Croshaw, B. (1971) The destruction of mycobacteria. In *Inhibition and Destruction of the Microbial Cell* (ed. Hugo, W.B.) pp. 420–450. London: Academic Press.

Dance, D.A.B., Pearson, A.D., Seal, D.V. & Lowes, J.A. (1987) A hospital outbreak caused by a chlorhexidine and antibiotic resistant *Proteus mirabilis*. *Journal of Hospital Infection*. **10**, 10–16.

Dankert, J. & Schut, I.K. (1976) The antibacterial activity of chloroxylenol in combination with ethylenediamine tetraacetic acid. *Journal of Hygiene*, **76**, 11–22.

Davies, G.E., Francis, J., Martin, A.R., Rose, F.L. & Swain, G. (1954) 1:6-di-4′-chlorophenyldiguanidohexane (Hibitane): laboratory investigation of a new antibacterial agent of high potency. *British Journal of Pharmacology and Chemotherapy*, **9**, 192–196.

Dean, A.C.R., Ellwood, D.C., Melling, J & Robinson, A. (1976) The action of antibacterial agents on bacteria grown in continuous culture. In *Continuous Culture 6: Applications and New Fields* (eds Dean, A.C.R., Ellwood, D.C., Evans, C.G.T. & Melling, J.) pp. 251–261. Society of Chemical Industry, London: Ellis Horwood Ltd.

Decad, G.M. & Nikaido, H. (1976) Outer membrane of Gram-negative bacteria XII. Molecular sieving function of cell wall. *Journal of Bacteriology*, **128**, 325–336.

Di Rienzo, J.M., Nakamura, K. & Inouye, M. (1978) The outer membrane proteins of Gram-negative bacteria: biosynthesis, assembly and functions. *Annual Review of Biochemistry*, **17**, 481–532.

Draper, P. (1982) The anatomy of mycobacteria. In *The Biology of the Mycobacteria* (eds Ratledge, C. & Stanford J.) pp. 9–52. London: Academic Press.

Ellwood, D.C. & Tempest, D.W. (1972) Environmental effects on bacterial walls. *Advances in Microbial Physiology* **7**, 83–117.

Fisher, C.A. & Barksdale, L. (1973) Cytochemical reactions of human leprosy bacilli and mycobacteria: ultrastructural implications. *Journal of Bacteriology*, **113**, 1389–1399.

Gilbert, P. & Brown, M.R.W. (1978a) Effect of R-plasmid RPI and nutrient depletion on the gross cellular composition of *Escherichia coli* and its resistance to some uncoupling phenols. *Journal of Bacteriology*, **133**, 1062–1065.

Gilbert, P. & Brown, M.R.W. (1978b) Influence of growth rate and nutrient limitation on the gross cellular composition of *Pseudomonas aeruginosa* and its resistance to 3-and 4-chlorophenol. *Journal of Bacteriology*, **133**, 1066–1072.

Gray, G.W. & Wilkinson, S.G. (1965) The action of ethylenedamine tetraacetic acid on *Pseudomonas aeruginosa*. *Journal of Applied Bacteriology*, **28**, 153–164.

Gustafsson, P., Nordstrom, K. & Normark, S. (1973) Outer penetration barrier of *Escherichia coli* K12: kinetics of the uptake of gentian violet by wild type and envelope mutants. *Journal of Bacteriology*, **116**, 893–900.

Gwynn, M.N., Webb, L.T. & Rolinson, G.N. (1981) Regrowth of *Pseudomonas aeruginosa* and other bacteria after the bactericidal action of carbenicillin and other β-lactam antibiotics. *Journal of Infectious Diseases*, **144**, 263–269.

Hamilton, W.A. (1970) The mode of action of membrane active antibacterials. *Federation of European Biochemical Societies Symposium*, **20**, 71–79.

Hamilton, W.A. (1971) Membrane active antibacterial compounds. In *Inhibition and Destruction of the Microbial Cell* (ed. Hugo, W.B.) pp. 77–93. London: Academic Press.

Hammond, S.M., Lambert, P.A. & Rycroft, A.N. (1984) The envelope of Gram-negative bacteria. *The Bacterial Cell Surface* pp. 57–118. Beckeham: Croom-Helm.

Hancock, R.E.W. & Nikaido, H. (1978) Outer membranes of Gram-negative bacteria: XIX Isolation from *Pseudomonas aeruginosa* PAO1 and use in reconstitution and definition of the permeability barrier. *Journal of Bacteriology*, **136**, 381–390.

Herson, D.S. McGonigle, B., Payer, M.A. and Baker, K.H. (1987) Attachment as a factor in the protection of *Enterobacter* from chlorination. *Applied and Environmental Microbiology*, **53**, 1178–1180.

Hugo, W.B. (1967) The mode of action of antiseptics. *Journal of Applied Bacteriology*, **30**, 17–50.

Hugo, W.B., Pallent, L.J., Grant, D.J.W., Denyer, S.P. & Davies, A. (1986) Factors contributing to the survival and a strain of *Pseudomonas cepacia* in chlorhexidine solutions. *Letters in Applied Microbiology*, **2**, 37–42.

Kamio, Y. & Nikaido, H. (1976) Outer membrane of *Salmonella typhimurium*: identification of proteins exposed on cell surfaces. *Biochimica et Biophysica Acta*, **464**, 589–601.

Kelsey, J.C. & Maurer, I.M. (1972) *The use of chemical disinfectants in hospitals*. Public Health Laboratory Service Monograph Series No. 2. London: HMSO.

Kenward, M.A., Brown, M.R.W. & Fryer, J.J. (1979) The influence of calcium or manganese on the resistance to EDTA, polymyxin B and cold shock and the composition of *Pseudomonas aeruginosa* grown in glucose-or magnesium-depleted batch culture. *Journal of Applied Bacteriology*, **47**, 489–503.

Klemperer, R.M.M., Ishmail, N.T.A. & Brown, M.R.W. (1980) Effects of R-plasmid RP1 and nutrient depletion on the resistance of *E. coli* to cetrimide, chlorhexidine and phenol. *Journal of Applied Bacteriology*, **48**, 349–357.

Kropinski, A.M.B., Chan, L. & Milazzo, F.H. (1978) Susceptibility of lipopolysaccharide-defective mutants of *Pseudomonas aeruginosa* strain PAO to dyes, detergents and antibiotics. *Antimicrobial Agents and Chemotherapy*, **13**, 494–499.

Kunin, C.M. & Steele, C. (1985) Culture of the surfaces of urinary catheters to sample urethral flora and study the effect of antimicrobial therapy. *Journal of Clinical Microbiology*, **21**, 902–908.

Le Chevalier, M.W., Cawthon, C.D. & Lee, R.G. (1988) Inactivation of biofilm bacteria. *Applied and Environmental Microbiology*, **54**, 2492–2494.

Leive, L. (1968) Studies on the permeability change produced in coliform bacteria by ethylenediamine-tetraacetate. *Journal of Biological Chemistry*, **243**, 2373–2380.

Leive, L. (1974) The barrier function of the Gram-negative envelope. *Annals of the New York Academy of Sciences*, **235**, 109–129.

Lowbury, E.J.L. (1975) Ecological importance of *Pseudomonas aeruginosa*: medical aspects. In *Genetics and Biochemistry of* Pseudomonas (eds Clarke, P.H. & Richmond, M.H.) pp. 37–65. London: John Wiley & Sons.

Lowbury, E.J.L., Ayliffe, G.A.J., Geddes, A.M. & Williams, J.D. (1975) *Control of Hospital Infection*. London: Chapman & Hall.

Marrie, T.J. & Costerton, J.W. (1981) Prolonged survival of *Serratia marcescens* in chlorhexidine. *Applied and Environmental Microbiology*, **42**, 1093–1102.

Meadow, P.M. (1975) Wall and membrane structures in the genus *Pseudomonas*. In *Genetics and Biochemistry of* Pseudomonas (eds Clarke, P.H. & Richmond, M.H.) pp. 67–98. London: John Wiley & Sons.

Melling, J., Robinson, A. & Ellwood, D.C. (1974) Effect of growth environment in a chemostat on the sensitivity of *Pseudomonas aeruginosa* to polymyxin B sulphate. *Proceedings of the Society for General Microbiology*, **1**, 61.

Muhlradt, P.F. & Golecki, J.R. (1975) Asymmetrical distribution and artificial reorientation of lipopolysaccharide in the outer membrane bilayer of *Salmonella typhimurium*. *European Journal of Biochemistry*, **51**, 343–352.

Nakae, T. (1976) Outer membrane of *Salmonella*: isolation of protein complex that produces transmembrane channels. *Journal of Biological Chemistry*, **251**, 2176–2178.

Nakae, T. & Nikaido, H. (1975) Outer membrane as a diffusion barrier in *Salmonella typhimurium*: penetration of oligo- and polysaccharides into isolated outer membrane and cells with degraded peptidoglycan layer. *Journal of Biological Chemistry*, **250**, 7359–7365.

Nelson, K.E., Larson, P.A., Schraufnaugel, D.E., & Jackson, J. (1983) Transmission of tuberculosis by flexible fibre bronchoscopes. *American Reviews of Respiratory Diseases*, **127**, 97–100.

Neu, H.C. & Chou, J. (1967) Release of surface enzymes in Enterobacteriaceae by osmotic shock. *Journal of Bacteriology*, **94**, 1934–1945.

Nicas, T.I. & Hancock, R.E.W. (1983) Outer membrane permeability in *Pseudomonas aeruginosa*. Isolation of a porin protein-F deficient mutant. *Journal of Bacteriology*, **153**, 281–285.

Nichols, W.W., Evans, M.J., Slack, M.P.E. & Walmsley, H.L. (1989) The penetration of antibiotics into aggregates of mucoid and non-mucoid *Pseudomonas aeruginosa*. *Journal of General Microbiology*, **135**, 1291–1303.

Nikaido, H. (1976) Outer membrane of *Salmonella typhimurium*. Transmembrane diffusion of some hydrophobic substances. *Biochimica et Biophysica Acta*, **433**, 118–132.

Nikaido, H. & Nakae, T. (1979) The outer membrane of Gram-negative bacteria. *Advances in Microbial Physiology*, **20**, 163–250.

Nikaido, H. & Vaara, M. (1985) Molecular basis of the permeability of the bacterial outer membrane. *Microbiological Reviews*, **49**, 1–32.

Nikaido, H., Takeuchi, Y., Ohnishi, S.I. & Nakae, T. (1977) Outer membrane of *Salmonella typhimurium*: electron spin resonance studies. *Biochimica et Biophysica Acta*, **465**, 152–164.

Nixdorff, K., Fitzer, H., Gmeiner, J. & Martin, H.H. (1977) Reconstitution of model membranes from phospholipid and outer membrane proteins of *Proteus mirabilis*. *European Journal of Biochemistry*, **81**, 63–69.

O'Flynn, J.D. & Stickler, D.J. (1972) Disinfectants and Gram-negative bacteria. *Lancet*, **i**, 489–490.

Pallent, L.J., Hugo, W.B., Grant, D.J.W. & Davies, A. (1983) *Pseudomonas cepacia* and infections. *Journal of Hospital Infection*, **4**, 9–13.

Petit, J.F. & Lederer, E. (1978) Structure and immunostimulant properties of mycobacterial cell walls. In *Relations between Structure and Function in the Prokaryotic Cell* (eds Stanier, R.Y., Rogers, H.J. & Ward, J.B.) Symposia of the Society for General Microbiology. Vol. 28, pp. 177–199. Cambridge: Cambridge University Press.

Reid, G., Cook, R.L. & Bruce, A.W. (1987) Examination of strains of lactobacilli for properties that may influence bacterial interference in the urinary tract. *Journal of*

Urology, **138**, 330–335.

Repaske, R. (1956) Lysis of Gram-negative bacteria by lysozyme. *Biochimica et Biophysica Acta*, **22**, 189–191.

Roantree, R.J., Kuo, T.T., MacPhee, D.G. & Stocker, B.A.D. (1969) The effect of various rough lesions in *Salmonella typhimurium* upon sensitivity to penicillins. *Clinical Research*, **17**, 157.

Roantree, R.J., Kuo, T.T. & MacPhee, D.G. (1977) The effect of defined lipopolysaccharide core defects upon antibiotic resistances of *Salmonella typhimurium*. *Journal of General Microbiology*, **103**, 223–234.

Robinson, A. & Tempest, D.W. (1973) Phenotypic variability of the envelope proteins of *Klebsiella aerogenes*. *Journal of General Microbiology*, **78**, 361–370.

Robinson, A., Melling, J. & Ellwood, D.C. (1974) Effect of growth environment on the envelope composition of *Pseudomonas aeruginosa*. *Proceedings of the Society for General Microbiology*, **1**, 61–62.

Rogers, H.J., Ward, J.B. & Burdett, I.D.J. (1978) Structure and growth of the walls of Gram-positive bacteria. In *Relations between Structure and Function in the Prokaryotic Cell* (eds Stainer, R.Y., Rogers, H.J. & Ward, J.B.) Symposia of the Society for General Microbiology, Vol. 28, pp. 139–176. Cambridge: Cambridge University Press.

Russell, A.D. (1971) Ethylenediamine tetraacetic acid. In *Inhibition and Destruction of the Microbial Cell* (ed. Hugo, W.B.) pp. 209–224. London: Academic Press.

Russell, A.D. & Furr, J.R. (1977) The antibacterial activity of a new chloroxylenol preparation containing ethylenediamine tetraacetic acid. *Journal of Applied Bacteriology*, **43**, 253–260.

Russell, A.D. & Furr, J.R. (1986a) The effects of antiseptics, disinfectants and preservatives on smooth, rough and deep rough strains of *Salmonella typhimurium*. *International Journal of Pharmaceutics*, **34**, 115–123.

Russell, A.D. & Furr, J.R. (1986b) Susceptibility of porin and lipopolysacchoride-deficient strains of *Escherichia coli* to some antiseptics and disinfectants. *Journal of Hospital Infection*, **8**, 47–56.

Russell, A.D. & Furr, J.R. (1987) Comparative sensitivity of smooth, rough and deep rough strains of *Escherichia coli* to chlorhexidine, quaternary ammonium compounds and dibromopropamidine isethionate. *International Journal of Pharmaceutics*, **36**, 191–197.

Russell, A.D. & Gould G.W. (1988) Resistance of Enterobacteriaceae to preservatives and disinfectants. *Journal of Applied Bacteriology Symposium Supplement*, **65**, 167S–195S.

Russell, A.D., Furr, J.R. & Pugh, W.J. (1985) Susceptibility of porin and lipopolysaccharide-deficient mutants of *Escherichia coli* to a homologous series of esters of p-hydroxybenzoic acid. *International Journal of Pharmaceutics*, **27**, 163–173.

Russell, A.D., Furr, J.R. & Pugh, W.J. (1987) Sequential loss of outer membrane lipopolysaccharides and sensitivity of *Escherichia coli* to antibacterial agents. *International Journal of Pharmaceutics*, **35**, 227–232.

Schlecht, S. & Westphal, O. (1970) Untersuchungen zur Typisierung von *Salmonella* R-formen, 4 mitteilung: Typisierung von *S. minnesota* R-mutanten mittels Antibiotica. *Zentralblatt fur Bakteriologie, Parasitenkunde Infektionskrankheiten und Hygiene (Abteilung I)*, **213**, 356–381.

Sharma, A.P., Battersby, N.S. & Stewart, D.J. (1987) Techniques for the evaluation of biocide activity against sulphate-reducing bacteria. In: *Preservatives in the Food, Pharmaceutical and Environmental Industries* (eds, Board, R.G., Allwood, M.C. & Banks, J.G.) pp. 165–175. Oxford: Blackwell Scientific Publications.

Smit, J., Kamio, Y. & Nikaido, H. (1975) Outer membrane of *Salmonella typhimurium*: chemical analysis and freeze-fracture studies with lipopolysaccharide mutants. *Journal of Bacteriology*, **124**, 942–958.

Southampton Control of Infection Team (1982) Evaluation of aseptic techniques and chlorhexidine on the rate of catheter-associated urinary-tract infection. *Lancet*, **i**, 89–91.

Stickler, D.J. & Thomas, B. (1976) Sensitivity of *Providencia* to antiseptics and disinfectants. *Journal of Clinical Pathology*, **29**, 815–823.

Stickler, D.J. & Thomas, B. (1980) Antiseptic and antibiotic resistance in Gram-negative bacteria causing urinary tract infection. *Journal of Clinical Pathology*, **33**, 288–296.

Stickler, D.J., Clayton, C.L. & Chawla, J.C. (1989) The resistance of urinary tract pathogens to chlorhexidine bladder washouts. *Journal of Hospital Infection*, **10**, 28–39.

Stickler, D.J., Wilmot, C.B. & O'Flynn, J.D. (1971) The mode of development of urinary infection in intermittently catheterized male paraplegics. *Paraplegia*, **8**, 243–252.

Stickler, D., Dolman, J. Rolfe, S. & Chawla J. (1990) Activity of antiseptics against *Escherichia coli* growing as biofilms on silicone surfaces. *European Journal of Clinical Microbiology*, **8**, 974–978.

Stickler, D.J., Dolman, J., Rolfe, S. & Chawla, J. (1991) Activity of some antiseptics against urinary tract pathogens growing on biofilms on silicone surfaces. *European Journal of Clinical Microbiology and Infectious Diseases*, **10**, 410–415.

Stickler, D.J., Thomas, B., Clayton, C.L. & Chawla, J. (1983) Studies on the genetic basis of chlorhexidine resistance. *British Journal of Clinical Practice, Symposium Supplement*, **25**, 23–30.

Sykes, G. (1958) *Disinfection and Sterilization*, 344 pp. London: E. & F.N. Spon Ltd.

Tamaki, S. & Matsuhashi, M. (1973) Increase in sensitivity to antibiotics and lysozyme on deletion of lipopolysaccharides in *Escherichia coli*, strains *Journal of Bacteriology*, **114**, 453–454.

Tempest, D.C. & Ellwood, D.C. (1969) The influence of growth conditions on the composition of some cell wall components of *Aerobacter aerogenes*. *Biotechnology and Bioengineering*, **11**, 775–783.

Thomas, B., Sykes, L. & Stickler, D.J. (1978) Sensitivity of urine grown cells of *Providencia stuartii* to antiseptics. *Journal of Clinical Pathology*, **31**, 929–932.

Trueman, J.R. (1971) The Halogens. In *Inhibition and Destruction of the Microbial Cell* (ed. Hugo, W.B.) pp. 137–183. London: Academic Press.

Verkleij, A., Van Alphen, L.V., Bijven, J. & Lutenberg, B. (1977) Architecture of the outer membrane of *Escherichia coli*: II. Freeze fracture morphology of wild-type and mutant strains. *Biochimica et Biophysica Acta*, **466**, 269–282.

Walker, E.M. & Lowes, J.A. (1985) An investigation into *in vitro* methods for the detection of chlorhexidine resistance. *Journal of Hospital Infection*, **6**, 389–397.

Wallhäusser, K.H. (1984) Antimicrobial preservatives used by the cosmetic industry. In *Cosmetic and Drug Preservation: Principles and Practice* (ed. Kabara, J.J.) pp. 605–745. New York: Marcel Dekker.

Wheeler, P.W., Lancaster, D. & Kaiser, A.B. (1989) Bronchopulmonary cross-colonization and infection related to mycobacterial contamination of suction valves of bronchoscopes. *Journal of Infectious Diseases*, **159**, 954–958.

Wilkinson, S.G. (1975) Sensitivity to ethylenediamine tetra-acetic acid. In *Resistance of Pseudomonas aeruginosa* (ed. Brown, M.R.W.) pp. 145–188. London: J. Wiley & Sons.

Woodruff, W.A., Parr, T.R. Jr., Hancock, R.E.W., Hanne, L., Nicas, T.J., & Inglewski, B. (1986) Expression in *Escherichia coli* and function of porin protein F of *Pseudomonas aeruginosa*. *Journal of Bacteriology*, **167**, 473–479.

Wright, N.E. & Gilbert, P. (1987) Influence of specific growth rate and nutrient limitation upon the sensitivity of *E. coli* towards chlorhexidine diacetate. *Journal of Applied Bacteriology*, **62**, 309–314.

Yoshimura, F. & Nikaido, H. (1982) Permeability of *Pseudomonas aeruginosa* outer membrane to hydrophilic solutes. *Journal of Bacteriology*, **152**, 636–642.

Yoshimura, F., Zalman, L.S. & Nikaido, H. (1983) Purification and properties of *Pseudomonas aeruginosa* porin. *Journal of Biological Chemistry*, **258**, 2308–2314.

B·PLASMIDS AND BACTERIAL RESISTANCE

1 INTRODUCTION

Bacterial resistance to biocides is essentially of two types: (a) intrinsic, a natural (innate), chromosomally controlled property of an organism; (b) acquired, resulting from genetic changes in a bacterial cell and arising either by mutation or by the acquisition of genetic material, e.g. via plasmids, from another cell. Intrinsic resistance has already been considered and this chapter will discuss acquired resistance associated with plasmids. Papers that have described this in detail are those by Russell (1985, 1990), Russell *et al.* (1986), Russell & Gould (1988), Heinzel (1988) and Russell & Chopra (1990). In addition, Chapter 10F, dealing with methicillin-resistant *Staphylococcus aureus* (MRSA) and biocides, should be consulted.

2 PLASMID-MEDIATED RESISTANCE

Plasmid-mediated resistance to non-chemotherapeutic agents has been most extensively studied with metals and especially mercury. Although non-mercury metals will form part of the discussion, it must be emphasized that, despite their biocidal activities, they do not have major practical applications as antibacterial agents. The role of plasmids in bacterial resistance to non-metallic biocides has not been widely investigated.

2.1 Heavy metal resistance

Genetic determinants of resistance to heavy metals are often found on plasmids and transposons, and this resistance may occur with high frequency. Additionally, there is sometimes, but not invariably, an association with antibiotic resistance.

2.1.1 Resistance to mercury

Mercuric chloride is a toxic agent and consequently is no longer widely used as a disinfectant. Organomercury compounds such as phenylmercuric nitrate (PMN) and acetate (PMA) are, however, widely used as preservatives in pharmaceutical products, and thiomersal in immunological preparations. Merbromin (mercurochrome) is a weak disinfectant.

Mercury resistance is plasmid-borne and not chromosomally mediated. It is transferred from donor cells to recipients by conjugation or transduction. Inorganic mercury and phenylmercury resistance is a common property of clinical isolates of *Staph. aureus* containing penicillinase plasmids (Novick & Roth, 1968; Novick & Bouanchaud, 1971). Plasmids in Gram-negative bacteria may also carry genes specifying resistance to antibiotics and in some instances cobalt (Co^{2+}), nickel (Ni^{+}), cadmium (Cd^{+}) and arsenate (AsO^{3+}) (Foster, 1983; Chopra, 1988; Silver & Misra, 1988). Mercury resistance is always inducible and is not the result of training or tolerance.

Plasmids conferring resistance to mercurials are of two types:

1 'narrow spectrum', which encode resistance to inorganic mercury (Hg^{2+}; Fig. 10.2) and to the organomercurials merbromin and fluorescein mercuric acetate in *Escherichia coli*. Other organomercury compounds are unaffected.

2 'broad spectrum', which specify resistance to

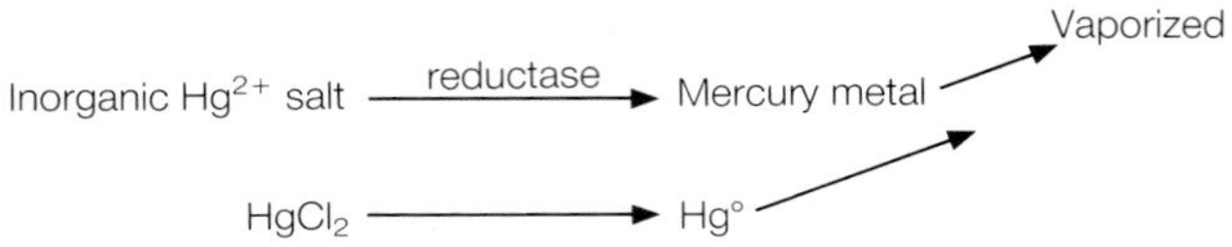

Fig. 10.2 Biochemical mechanism of resistance to inorganic mercury compounds.

Hg^{2+}, merbromin and fluorescein mercuric acetate and also to PMN, PMA, thiomersal, *p*-hydroxymercuribenzoate (PHMB), methylmercury and ethylmercury in *E. coli*.

Similar classes of plasmids occur with mercury-resistant strains of *Pseudomonas aeruginosa*, although the 'narrow spectrum' sub-class confers slight resistance to PHMB also (Clark *et al*., 1977). In *Staph. aureus*, only the 'broad-spectrum' sub-class is found (Table 10.2). The mechanism of resistance is shown in Fig. 10.3.

Considerable progress has been made in examining the genes responsible for various functions. The most widely studied plasmid is R-100, which confers Hg^{2+} but not organomercury resistance. The genetic map of the mercury resistance determinant, transposon Tn501, consists of the following genes: *merR* (regulatory gene), *merT* (Hg^+ transport), *merP* (the product is a periplasmic Hg^{2+}-binding protein), *merC* (uncertain function), *merA* (gene product is a subunit of mercuric reductase), *merB* (if present, the determinant of organomercury lyase) and *merD* (uncertain function) (Silver & Misra, 1988).

2.1.2 *Resistance to silver*

Of particular interest in the possible context of hospital infection is plasmid-mediated resistance to silver salts, since silver nitrate and silver sulphadiazine (AgSu) have been used topically for preventing infections in severe burns. In an early study, attempts to transfer silver resistance from silver-resistant (Ag^R) strains of *E. coli* and *Klebsiella* to silver-sensitive (Ag^S) strains of *E. coli* were unsuccessful (Gravens *et al*., 1969). McHugh *et al*. (1975) isolated a strain of *Salmonella typhimurium* from a burns unit, that was resistant to silver nitrate, mercuric chloride and various antibiotics; this resistance could be transferred to *E. coli* in *in vitro* mating experiments, although the authors pointed out the difficulty of transferring silver resistance from Ag^R to Ag^S strains. Nevertheless, plasmid-mediated Ag^+ resistance is determined by the very wide ratio (> 100:1) of MICs for Ag^R and Ag^S cells.

Silver reduction, analogous to inorganic mercury reduction (Fig. 10.2) is not the basis of resistance. The current hypothesis (Silver & Misra, 1988) is

Table 10.2 Plasmid-encoded resistance to mercury compounds*

Organism	Plasmid-encoded resistance to: Hg^{2+}	Plasmid-encoded resistance to: Organomercurials	Comment
Escherichia coli	+	+	Narrow- or broad-spectrum plasmids
Salmonella typhimurium	+	−	
Proteus spp.	+	−	
Providencia spp.	+	−	
Pseudomonas aeruginosa	+	+	Narrow- or broad-spectrum plasmids
Staphylococcus aureus	+	+	Broad-spectrum plasmids

* (1) Host cell background might affect pattern of resistance. (2) Although Hg^0 may be formed by volatilization from a number of organomercury substrates, this does not necessarily indicate that resistance is conferred. Seemingly, a threshold level of Hg^0 must be formed which, if exceeded, confers resistance. (3) Resistance to an organomercury compound does not necessarily involve volatilization of Hg^0: bacterial impermeability might be an alternative mechanism.

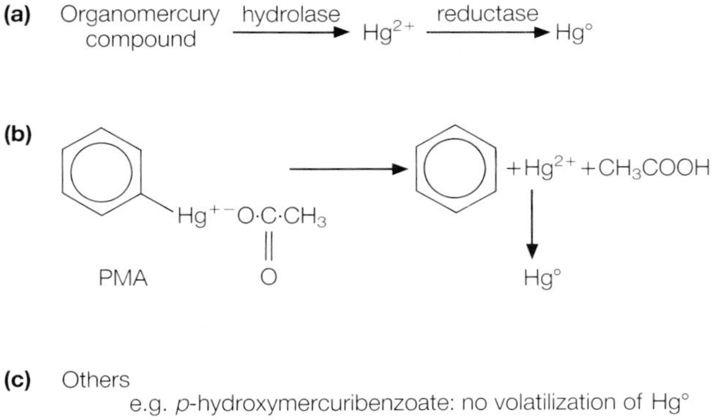

Fig. 10.3 Biochemical mechanisms of resistance to organic mercury compounds. (a) General pattern, (b) *Ps. aeruginosa* (broad spectrum plasmid), (c) other organomercury derivatives. Permeability barriers may play a role in the resistance of Gram-negative bacteria, and Hg^0 formation does not necessarily confer resistance. PMN, phenylmercuric nitrate.

that Ag^S cells bind silver so tightly that they extract it from silver chloride, whereas Ag^R cells do not compete successfully with Ag^+-halide complexes for Ag^+.

2.1.3 Resistance to other cations and to anions

Plasmid-encoded resistance to cations other than mercury and to anions has been demonstrated (Table 10.3). Resistances to arsenate (AsO^{-3}), arsenite (AsO^{3-}) and antimony (III) are encoded by an inducible operon-like system in both *E. coli* and *Staph. aureus*, and any one of the three ions induces resistance to all three. The mechanism of arsenate resistance involves an energy-dependent efflux of inhibitor, producing a reduced net accumulation (Silver *et al.*, 1989). This efflux system is mediated by an ATPase transport system.

At least four plasmid-determined systems confer cadmium (Cd^{2+}) resistance. The most widely studied are the *cadA* and *cadB* systems unique to staphylococcal plasmids (Smith & Novick, 1972; Silver & Misra, 1988). The *cadA* gene specifies an approximately 100-fold increase in Cd^{2+} resistance involving Cd^{2+} efflux via a specific efflux ATPase. These *cadA* and *cadB* systems also confer resistance to several other heavy metals. The third system has a *cadA* type mechanism but differs in conferring Cd^{2+} resistance only. The fourth system, found in an *Alcaligenes* strain, involves a plasmid locus simultaneously conferring resistance to Cd^{2+}, Zn^{2+} and Co^{2+}, but the mechanism is unknown.

Table 10.3 Plasmid-encoded resistance to cations and anions

Anion or cation	Plasmid-encoded resistance in
Ag^+	*E. coli*, *Salm. typhimurium*
Cd^{2+}	*Staph. aureus*
Co^{2+}	*E. coli*
Ni^+	*E. coli*
Zn^{2+}	*Staph. aureus*
Pb^{2+}	*Staph. aureus*
Cu^{2+}	*E. coli*
Arsenate, arsenite, antimony(III)	*E. coli*, *Staph. aureus*
CrO^{2-}	*Pseudomonas* strains, *Strep. lactis*
Tellurate, tellurite	*Alcaligenes* strains

2.2 Resistance to other biocides

The majority of the gentamicin R plasmids associated with MRSA strains also possess determinants encoding resistance to quaternary ammonium compounds (QACs) and other nucleic acid-binding (NAB) agents (Lyon & Skurray, 1987; Russell & Chopra, 1990). In laboratory experiments, resistance to some biocides (chlorhexidine, benzalkonium chloride, acriflavine and ethidium bromide) has been transferred from *Staph. aureus* to *E. coli* (Yamamota *et al.*, 1988); the resistance levels of the *E. coli* strain carrying recombinant plasmids were some 4–16-fold higher than the isogenic plasmid-free strains. The mechanism of resistance expressed in *E. coli* may be the presence of a biocide efflux system (Midgley, 1986, 1987).

The presence of the R TEM plasmid in *E. coli* or of the RP1 plasmid in *E. coli* or *Ps. aeruginosa* did not increase the resistance of cells to QACs, chlorhexidine, phenols or organomercurials

(Ahonkhai & Russell, 1979). Indeed, in some instances the plasmid$^+$ strains appeared to be rather more sensitive, although less so than claimed by Klemperer *et al.* (1980) and Michel-Briand *et al.* (1986). Sutton & Jacoby (1978) observed increased resistance to hexachlorophane (hexachlorophene) in *Ps. aeruginosa* harbouring the RP1 plasmid, although the mechanism is unclear. Curtis & Richmond (1974) found that a lysozyme-sensitive mutant of *E. coli* became lysozyme-resistant upon acquisition of RP1, suggesting cell surface modifications. The plasmid R124 has also been shown to modify cell surface changes and biocide response in *E. coli* (Roussow & Rowbury, 1984). About 15% of isolates of Gram-negative bacteria causing urinary tract infections in paraplegic patients show a high degree of resistance to QACs and chlorhexidine, as well as to antibiotics. These resistant species appear to have been selected as a consequence of the extensive use of cationic antiseptics but the possibility of a plasmid-linked association of antibiotic and antiseptic resistances has not been established (Stickler *et al.*, 1983). Attempts to transfer QAC and chlorhexidine resistance were unsuccessful.

Transferable resistance to formaldehyde and formaldehyde-releasing agents has been described in *Serratia marcescens* (Hall & Eagon, 1985; Candal & Eagon, 1984). The mechanism of resistance has not been involved, but possible mechanisms are (i) induction of surface changes in resistant cells, (ii) reduced uptake by resistant cells, (iii) formaldehyde metabolism.

3 CONCLUSIONS

Apart from mercury compounds and other heavy metals, plasmid-mediated resistance of Gram-negative bacteria to biocides does not appear to be an important mechanism of resistance (Nagai & Ogase, 1990). There is, nevertheless, evidence that some plasmids are responsible for producing surface changes in cells which, in turn, may modify sensitivity or resistance, and that the response depends not only on the plasmid but also on the host cells. In MRSA strains, certain plasmids are responsible for producing a low-level increase in resistance to QACs and other cationic biocides.

4 REFERENCES

Ahonkhai, I. & Russell, A.D. (1979) Response of RP1$^+$ and RP1$^-$ strains of *Escherichia coli* to antibacterial agents and transfer of resistance to *Pseudomonas aeruginosa*. *Current Microbiology*, **3**, 89–94.

Candal, E.J. & Eagon, R.G. (1984) Evidence for plasmid-mediated bacterial resistance to industrial biocides. *International Biodeterioration*, **20**, 221–224.

Chopra, I. (1988) Efflux of antibacterial agents from bacteria. *FEMS Symposium No. 44: Homeostatic Mechanisms of Micro-organisms*, pp. 146–158. Bath: Bath University Press.

Clark, D.L., Weiss, A.A. & Silver, S. (1977) Mercury and organomercurial resistance determined by plasmids in *Pseudomonas*. *Journal of Bacteriology*, **132**, 186–196.

Curtis, N.A.C. & Richmond, M.H. (1974) Effect of R-factor mediated genes on some surface properties of *Escherichia coli*. *Antimicrobial Agents and Chemotherapy*, **6**, 666–671.

Foster, T.J. (1983) Plasmid-determined resistance to antimicrobial drugs and toxic metal ions in bacteria. *Microbiological Reviews*, **47**, 361–409.

Gravens, M.L., Margraf, H.W., Gravens, C.K., Thomerson, J.E. & Butcher, H.R. (1969) Silver and intestinal flora. Roles in bacterial colonization of burn wounds. *Archives of Surgery*, **99**, 453–458.

Hall, E. & Eagon, R.G. (1985) Evidence for plasmid-mediated resistance of *Pseudomonas putida* to hexahydro-1,3,5-triethyl-*s*-triazine. *Current Microbiology*, **12**, 17–22.

Heinzel, M. (1988) The phenomena of resistance to disinfectants and preservatives. In *Industrial Biocides* (ed. Payne, K.R.) pp. 52–67. Chichester: John Wiley & Sons.

Klemperer, R.M.M., Ismail, N.T.A.J. & Brown, M.R.W. (1980) Effect of R-plasmid RP1 and nutrient depletion on the resistance of *Escherichia coli* to cetrimide, chlorhexidine and phenol. *Journal of Applied Bacteriology*, **48**, 349–357.

Lyon, B.R. & Skurray, R.A. (1987) Antimicrobial resistance of *Staphylococcus aureus*: genetic basis. *Microbiological Reviews*, **51**, 88–134.

McHugh, G.L., Hopkins, C.C., Moellering, R.C. & Swartz, M.N. (1975) *Salmonella typhimurium* resistant to silver nitrate, chloramphenicol and ampicillin. *Lancet*, **i**, 235–239.

Michel-Briand, Y., Laporte, J.M., Bassignot, A. & Plesiat, P. (1986) Antibiotic resistance plasmids and bactericidal effect of chlorhexidine on Enterobacteriaceae. *Letters in Applied Microbiology*, **3**, 65–68.

Midgley, M. (1986) The phosphonium ion efflux system of *Escherichia coli*: a relationship to the ethidium efflux system and energetic studies. *Journal of General Microbiology*, **132**, 3187–3193.

Midgley, M. (1987) An efflux system for cationic dyes and related compounds in *Escherichia coli*. *Microbiological Sciences*, **4**, 125–127.

Nagai, I. & Ogase, H. (1990) Absence of role for plasmids in resistance to multiple disinfectants in three strains of bacteria. *Journal of Hospital Infection*, **15**, 149–155.

Novick, R.P. & Bouanchaud, D. (1971) Extrachromosomal nature of drug resistance in *Staphylococcus aureus*. *Annals of the New York Academy of Sciences*, **182**, 279–294.

Novick, R.P. & Roth, C. (1968) Plasmid-linked resistance to inorganic salts in *Staphylococcus aureus*. *Journal of Bacteriology*, **95**, 1335–1342.

Roussow, F.T. & Rowbury, R.J. (1984) Effects of the resistance plasmid R124 on the level of OmpF outer membrane protein and on the response of *Escherichia coli* to environmental agents. *Journal of Applied Bacteriology*, **56**, 63–79.

Russell, A.D. (1985) The role of plasmids in bacterial resistance to antiseptics, disinfectants and preservatives. *Journal of Hospital Infection*, **6**, 9–19.

Russell, A.D. (1990) Mechanisms of bacterial resistance to biocides. *International Biodeterioration*, **26**, 101–110.

Russell, A.D. & Chopra, I. (1990) *Understanding Antibacterial Action and Resistance*. Chichester: Ellis Horwood.

Russell, A.D. & Gould, G.W. (1988) Resistance of Enterobacteriaceae to preservatives and disinfectants. *Journal of Applied Bacteriology Symposium Series*, **65**, 167S–195S.

Russell, A.D., Hammond, S.A. & Morgan, J.R. (1986) Bacterial resistance to antiseptics and disinfectants. *Journal of Hospital Infection*, **7**, 213–225.

Silver, S. & Misra, S. (1988) Plasmid-mediated heavy metal resistances. *Annual Review of Microbiology*, **42**, 717–743.

Silver, S., Nucifora, G., Chu, L. & Misra, T.K. (1989) Bacterial ATPases: primary pumps for exporting toxic cations and anions. *Trends in Biochemical Sciences*, **14**, 76–80.

Smith, K. & Novick, R.P. (1972) Genetic studies on plasmid-linked cadmium resistance in *Staphylococcus aureus*. *Journal of Bacteriology*, **112**, 761–772.

Stickler, D.J., Thomas, B., Clayton, J.C. & Chawla, J.A. (1983) Studies on the genetic basis of chlorhexidine resistance. *British Journal of Clinical Practice*, Symposium Supplement 25, pp. 23–28.

Sutton, L. & Jacoby, G.A. (1978) Plasmid-determined resistance to hexachlorophene in *Pseudomonas aeruginosa*. *Antimicrobial Agents and Chemotherapy*, **13**, 634–636.

Yamamoto, T., Tamura, Y. & Yokota, T. (1988) Antiseptic and antibiotic resistance plasmid in *Staphylococcus aureus* that possesses ability to confer chlorhexidine and acrinol resistance. *Antimicrobial Agents and Chemotherapy*, **32**, 932–935.

C·RESISTANCE OF BACTERIAL SPORES TO CHEMICAL AGENTS

1 INTRODUCTION

Bacterial spores are the most resistant life forms known, and procedures which result in their complete destruction will result in the inactivation of all other life forms with the possible exception of prions (Chapter 7).

Chemicals which destroy spores are known as sporicides and have the potential to act as sterilizing agents. In practice, chemical sterilization is rarely achievable at ambient temperatures, although for thermolabile materials it may be the only alternative to heat sterilization. Glutaraldehyde is a chemical agent sometimes used to sterilize equipment.

Compared to vegetative cells, spores may be as much as 100 000 times more resistant to chemicals (Phillips, 1952). Development of resistance to agents such as chlorhexidine occurs early in the sporulation process compared with glutaraldehyde resistance, which is a late event. During germination and outgrowth of spores resistance is lost and cells become sensitive to biocides.

In this chapter the resistance of spores to various chemical agents will be discussed. Factors affecting spore resistance and mechanisms of resistance will also be reviewed. Reviews of spore resistance are also given by Roberts & Hitchins (1969), Russell (1971, 1982, 1983, 1990), Gould (1983, 1985), Waites (1985), Quinn (1987), Russell *et al.* (1989) and Russell & Chopra (1990).

2 FACTORS AFFECTING RESISTANCE

When spores are exposed to chemical agents they may be inhibited, sublethally injured or irreversibly damaged. The relative resistance of spores grown in the laboratory and those occurring in their natural environments is unknown, but it is recognized that resistance of laboratory-grown spores may vary considerably depending not only on the chemical agent used but also on the bacterial species and strain, the method of spore production, preparation and storage and on the conditions used to study resistance. Although the factors affecting heat resistance have been extensively studied, fewer investigations have attempted to explain chemical resistance. The same factors appear to determine resistance to both heat and chemicals, but spores which are particularly resistant to heat are not especially resistant to phenol (Briggs, 1966), ethylene oxide (El-Bisi *et al.*, 1963), chlorine (Dye & Mead, 1972) or hydrogen peroxide (Toledo *et al.*, 1973).

2.1 Species and strain

Spores of different species show marked differences in resistance. Spores of *Bacillus stearothermophilus* were 10^3 times more resistant to hydrogen peroxide than those of *Clostridium botulinum* (Ito *et al.*, 1973) whilst spores of *Bacillus subtilis* were more resistant to chlorine than those of *B. cereus* and *Cl. bifermentans* (Cousins & Allan, 1967; Dye & Mead, 1972). Different strains of the same species may differ in their resistance; spore resistance of various strains of *B. subtilis* to hydrogen peroxide was found to vary by a factor of 10^4 (Waites & Bayliss, 1979b).

2.2 Sporulation media

Alterations in the constituents of the media on which spores are grown will alter their resistance to sporicidal agents. A chemically defined medium has been reported to produce spores of *B. subtilis* which are less variable in resistance to glutaraldehyde (Stark *et al.*, 1975; Forsyth, 1975) than those produced in soil extract medium used in the sporicidal test of the Association of Official Analytical Chemists (AOAC). Addition of glucose and metal salts to nutrient agar increased the resistance of spores of *B. subtilis* to hydrogen peroxide 10^4-fold (Waites & Bayliss, 1979a). Partly because of the problems of removing vegetative cells, sporulation media are designed to produce a high percentage of free spores and few vegetative cells or germinated spores (Gould, 1971) but it is possible that the conditions which produce sporulation in most of the population will produce spores with low resistance. Furthermore, spores produced on some media may have little resistance to one chemical but may be particularly resistant to others, whilst spores grown on different batches of the same media may differ in their resistance. Small changes in media preparation and harvesting times may thus alter resistance (Bomar, 1962).

2.3 Method of harvesting

In addition to dormant free spores, growth on most sporulation media produces vegetative cells, sporangial debris and germinated spores. Numerous methods have been devised to remove unwanted material and leave the dormant spore (Murrell, 1969), but all such methods may alter resistance and should be examined critically before routine use. In particular sonication, which has been used to remove sporangia from spores, may reduce resistance (St Julian *et al.*, 1967), while the two-phase system of Sacks & Alderton (1961), which separates free spores from germinated spores and vegetative cells, may initiate germination of a fraction of the spore population (Murrell & Warth, 1965). Nevertheless a reactive chemical will be rapidly neutralized by vegetative cell debris so that the spores in a suspension may appear more resistant than those in suspensions containing only spores.

2.4 Methods of storage

Spore resistance may change significantly during periods of prolonged storage (Forsyth, 1975; Waites & Bayliss, 1979a). Spores may be stored in glass-distilled water either refrigerated (although some strains of *Bacillus* may germinate during storage over long periods) or frozen. Alternatively spores may be stored freeze-dried, which may damage spores of some strains (Marshall *et al.*, 1963) or in ethanol (Molin & Östlund, 1976).

2.5 Conditions of test

In the laboratory, several types of tests are used to determine sporistatic and sporicidal activity. Sporistatic tests usually involve determination of minimum inhibitory concentrations, i.e. the minimum concentration required to prevent germination and/or outgrowth. Sporicidal activity is determined by measuring rates of kill or the time taken for complete destruction of a population. These tests are considered in detail in this volume by Reybrouck (Chapter 4) and also by Russell *et al.* (1991).

2.6 Recovery conditions

For a viable spore to be detected in bacteriological tests it must germinate and outgrow to form a vegetative cell, which must then multiply to produce visible growth.

In evaluating sporicidal activity neutralization of residual agent must be achieved at the moment of sampling to prevent continued action and possible sporistasis in the subculture medium. Methods for neutralization of antimicrobial agents are further discussed in Chapter 3, and by Bloomfield (1990).

When transferred to nutrient medium under optimum conditions, normal, untreated spores usually germinate rapidly within 20–30 min. For damaged spores the rate and extent of recovery will depend on the conditions used; damaged spores are particularly sensitive to recovery conditions which are less than optimal (Roberts, 1970; Futter & Richardson, 1970a,b) so that conditions for germination and growth must be carefully considered. Investigations have shown that post-treatment heat shock enhanced the revival of bacterial spores following treatment with HCl (Ortenzio, 1966), formaldeyhyde (Spicher & Peters, 1976, 1981) and glutaraldehyde (Gorman *et al.*, 1983a, Power *et al.*, 1988). Other agents which have been shown to affect spore revival include alkali (Power *et al.*, 1988, 1989, 1990; Dancer *et al.*, 1989) and lysozyme (Wyatt & Waites, 1975; Gorman *et al.*, 1983b; Gould, 1984). Revival of injured spores is reviewed in more detail by Russell (1990).

3 RESISTANCE TO CHEMICAL AGENTS

Chemical agents which destroy vegetative bacteria are described as disinfectants. Many highly active and widely used disinfectants such as the phenolics, quaternary ammonium compounds (QACS), alcohols, bisbiguanides, organic acids and esters, and mercurials have little or no sporicidal activity but are effective sporistatic agents, preventing germination and/or outgrowth of spores. Inhibition of spore germination and outgrowth is reviewed in more detail by Russell (1990).

Chemical agents which are sporicidal include glutaraldehyde and formaldehyde, chlorine and iodine, acids and alkali, hydrogen peroxide and other peroxygen compounds, ethylene oxide, β-propionolactone and ozone. To achieve sporicidal action with these compounds much higher concentrations and longer contact times are required compared with those used for destruction of vegetative cells. Table 10.4 lists chemicals in order of their sporicidal efficiency, although this must be considered as an approximation since the data were obtained under widely differing experimental conditions. The properties of these agents are reviewed in this section. The activity of sporicidal agents is also reviewed by Sykes (1970), Russell (1971, 1982, 1990), Roberts & Hitchins (1969), Block (1977) and Waites (1985).

3.1 Glutaraldehyde

Glutaraldehyde is an effective sporicidal agent. Its activity depends on pH, alkaline solutions being more effective (although less stable) than acid solutions. A 2% solution of glutaraldehyde will produce a 4-log reduction in spores of *Clostridium tetani* and *Bacillus anthracis* in 15–30 min (Rubbo *et al.*, 1967). Not all species of *Bacillus* are equally resistant to glutaraldehyde; *B. subtilis* and *B. pumilis* appear to be the most resistant (Rubbo *et al.*, 1967). With suspensions of *B. subtilis*, a contact period of 3 h with 2% alkaline glutaraldehyde produces a *ca.* 6-log reduction in viable count (Kelsey *et al.*, 1974; Gardner & Favero, 1985; Miner *et al.*, 1977). Babb *et al.* (1980) demonstrated that a 2–3 h contact period with 2% glutaraldehyde was required to produce sterilization of *B. subtilis* spores dried onto aluminium foil strips. Potentiation of glutaraldehyde by the use of cationic and anionic surfactant-divalent metal ion combinations and by the addition of sodium phenate and phenol has been described by Boucher (1975), Gorman & Scott (1979), Isenberg *et al.*, (1985) and Isenberg (1988). The properties of glutaraldehyde are reviewed in more detail by Gorman *et al.* (1980).

3.2 Formaldehyde

Formaldehyde is used in both liquid and gaseous forms. Formalin is an aqueous solution containing 34–38% formaldehyde; methanol is added to delay polymerization. Formaldehyde is sporicidal but at a slower rate than glutaraldehyde (Rubbo *et al.*, 1967). Mixtures of glutaraldehyde and formal-

Table 10.4 Resistance of spores to chemicals

Chemical	Organism	Kill	Time (h)	Concentration (% w/v)	Temperature (°C)	Reference
Peracetic acid vapour	*B. subtilis* var. *niger*	10^5	0.02	0.0001	25	Portner & Hoffman (1968)
HCl-vapour	*B. subtilis*	10^3	0.08	31*	20	Tuynenberg Muys *et al.* (1978)
Ethylene oxide	*B. subtilis*	10^2	0.7	0.07	40	Marletta & Stumbo (1970)
Hydrogen peroxide	*B. subtilis* var. *globigii*	10^3	0.17	25.8	24	Toledo *et al.* (1973)
Hypochlorous acid	*B. subtilis*	10^3	2.0	0.0†	10	Dye & Mead (1972)
Glutaraldehyde	*B. pumilis*	10^3	0.5	2.0	37	Thomas & Russell (1974)
Formaldehyde	*B. subtilis* var. *niger*	10^3	1.5	1.0	40	Trujillo & David (1972)
Propylene oxide	*B. subtilis* var. *niger*	10^3	17.0	0.1	37	Bruch & Koesterer (1961)
Sodium hydroxide	*B. subtilis*	10^3	24.5	5.0	40	Whitehouse & Clegg (1963)
Iodine (as an iodophor)	*B. subtilis*	10^2	>4.0	0.08	21	Cousins & Allan (1967)

* 0.25 ml in a 300 ml bottle.
† Free chlorine.

dehyde are found to be 10 times more effective than either chemical alone (Waites & Bayliss, 1984). The properties of other aldehydes are reviewed by Power & Russell (1990).

3.3 Halogens

Under most conditions, the sporicidal activity of halogens increases in the order bromine–iodine–chlorine (Marks & Strandskov, 1950), spores being more resistant to aqueous iodine than to iodophors (Cousins & Allan, 1967). The activity of halogen-releasing agents is strongly affected by pH, being more active at acid pH. Sodium hypochlorite at 100–200 ppm, pH 7–7.6, will produce a 4–5-log reduction in *B. subtilis* spores within 5 min (Death & Coates, 1979; Bloomfield & Arthur, 1989a). Babb *et al.* (1980) demonstrated that buffered solutions of NaOCl at 250 ppm (pH 7.0) and 1800 ppm (pH 10.0) produced sterilization of *B. subtilis* spores dried onto aluminum spore strips within 2 min and 60 min respectively. Bloomfield & Arthur (1989a) showed that spores are significantly more resistant to *N*-chloro compounds such as sodium dichloroisocyanurate, and particularly chloramine-T. Sodium hypochlorite may in turn be less rapidly sporicidal than chlorine dioxide (Ridenour *et al.*, 1949; Benarde *et al.*, 1967). Cousins & Allan (1967) demonstrated that *B. subtilis* spores were more resistant to chlorine than *B. cereus*. Generally spores of *Clostridium* spp. are more resistant to chlorine than are *Bacillus* spores. Death & Coates (1979) have shown that buffered methanol/sodium hypochlorite is more rapidly sporicidal than buffered hypochlorite alone. The sporicidal activity of both chlorine and iodine formulations is potentiated by the addition of 1–5% sodium hydroxide (Cousins & Allan, 1967; Bloomfield & Arthur, 1989b; Bloomfield & Megid, 1989). Heating of spores reduces their resistance to chlorine (Cousins & Allan, 1967).

3.4 Acid and alkali

Spores are resistant to acid pH, although prolonged incubation at pH 1.5 reduces their resistance (Sacks & Alderton, 1961). Some strains are resistant to constant boiling HCl at 20°C for up to 30 min but this extreme resistance is dependent on pre-drying of the spores (Ortenzio *et al.*, 1953). Gaseous HCl is rapidly sporicidal, producing sterility in seconds (Tuynenberg Muys *et al.*, 1978; Lelieveld, 1979). Alkalis are slowly sporicidal at elevated temperatures (von Bockelmann, 1974). Sodium hydroxide is found to sensitize spores of *Cl. perfringens* (Barach *et al.*, 1975; Labbé *et al.*, 1978) and *Cl. bifermentans* (Wyatt & Waites, 1975) to lysozyme and to the action of chlorine and iodine-releasing compounds (Cousins & Allan, 1967; Bloomfield & Arthur, 1989b; Bloomfield & Megid, 1989).

Sodium hydroxide also increases the germination rate of *Cl. bifermentans* (Waites *et al.*, 1972) and *B. megaterium* (Vary, 1973).

3.5 Hydrogen peroxide and other peroxygen compounds

The sporicidal properties of hydrogen peroxide have been extensively investigated (Ando & Tsuzuki, 1986a,b,; Bayliss & Waites, 1976, 1979; Toledo, 1975; Waites & Bayliss, 1979a; Waites *et al.*, 1976, 1979, 1988). Hydrogen peroxide is only slowly sporicidal at ambient temperatures, but at elevated temperatures activity is markedly increased. Toledo *et al.* (1973) demonstrated that at ambient temperatures a 25.8% solution produced a 99.99% kill of *B. subtilis* spores within 11 min, but at 76°C the kill time was reduced to 30 s. The action of hydrogen peroxide is potentiated not only by heat but also by transition metal ions or by UV irradiation (King & Gould, 1969; Wallen, 1976; Bayliss & Waites, 1976, 1979). This is thought to be associated with the production of highly reactive free hydroxyl radicals which are catalysed by heat, irradiation and metal cations such as Cu^{2+}. Peracetic acid is rapidly sporicidal (Baldry, 1983, 1988), a 0.1% solution producing a 99.9% kill of *B. subtilis* spores within 15 min (Bayliss *et al.*, 1981). Breakdown of peracetic acid produces acetic acid and oxygen and water, and leaves no residues. Peracetic acid is found to be more active than hydrogen peroxide and is only slightly affected by the presence of organic matter (Baldry, 1983, 1988).

3.6 Ethylene oxide

Ethylene oxide is an active sporicidal agent. In contrast with other sporicides, bacterial spores are generally only about 2–10 times more resistant to ethylene oxide than vegetative cells. Ethylene oxide sterilization is usually slow, taking up to 4 h and sometimes up to 18 h (Znamirowski *et al.*, 1960; Ernst, 1974, 1975; Phillips, 1977; Reich, 1980). Activity of ethylene oxide depends on a number of factors including temperature, contact time and water vapour. The sporicidal properties of ethylene oxide are reviewed in detail by Phillips (1977), Christensen & Kristensen (Chapter 20) and Caputo & Odlaug (1983).

3.7 Other sporicides

β-Propionolactone is an active sporicidal agent but is not widely used because of its allegedly carcinogenic effects. Its sporicidal activity is found to be a direct function of time, temperature, concentration and relatively humidity (Hoffman, 1971; Caputo & Odlaug, 1983).

Ozone is also an active sporicidal agent, but its use is limited by its instability (Hoffman, 1971; Foegeding, 1985; Foegeding & Fulp, 1988).

4 MECHANISMS OF RESISTANCE

4.1 Changes in resistance during spore formation and germination

Bacterial spores (as illustrated in Fig. 10.4) consist of an external protective spore coat, an intermediate cortex and an inner protoplast. The outer coat is made up of protein material, rich in cysteine, whereas the cortex is mainly peptidoglycan. The inner core is surrounded by a protoplast membrane and contains DNA, RNA and spore enzymes, together with a number of unique constituents such as dipicolinic acid.

During spore formation the protoplast contracts and loses water, possibly as a result of expansion of the cortex (Gould & Dring, 1975; Warth, 1978). During germination the cortex is degraded, the protoplast rehydrates and expands and the structure loses chemical and heat resistance. Evidence suggests that heat, and to a certain extent chemical, resistance is related to the dehydrated nature of the spore protoplast but the action of chemicals must be different from that of heat because they must penetrate the outer spore layers before they can exert their action.

A considerable amount of information is available about the way in which antibacterial agents affect vegetative bacterial forms (Russell, 1990). In contrast, mechanisms of sporicidal action are incompletely understood and may involve interaction at one or more sites within the spore coat, cortex or protoplast. Experimental evidence indicates

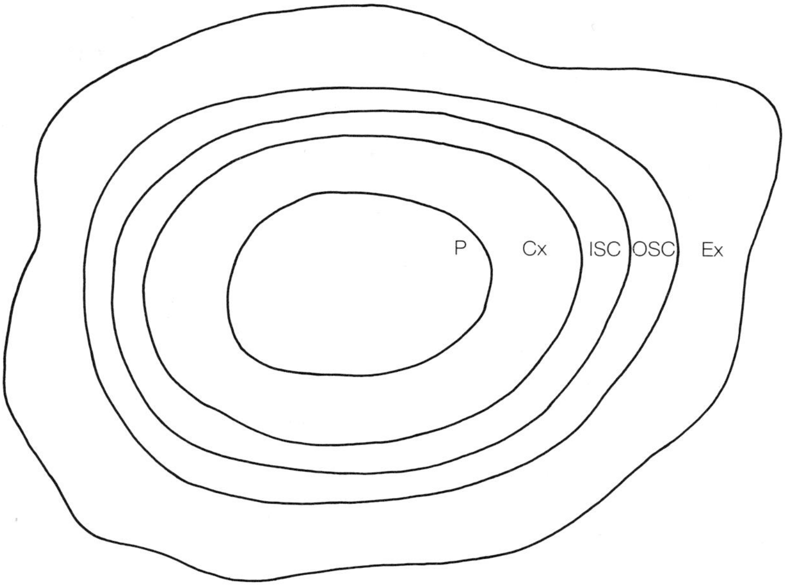

Fig. 10.4 Typical structure of the bacterial spore. Ex: exosporum; OSC: alkali-resistant outer spore coat; ISC: alkali-soluble inner spore coat; Cx: cortex; P: spore protoplast.

that development of resistance to antimicrobial agents during sporulation may result from changes in cell structure or function at the site of action, or may be due to alteration of permeability barriers which prevent access of the agent to its site of action.

Some insight into mechanisms of resistance can be gained by correlating the emergence of resistance to the stage of spore development. Investigations by Sousa *et al.* (1978), Gorman *et al.* (1984a) and Shaker *et al.* (1988) suggest that resistance to toluene and xylene is an early event compared with resistance to heat, chlorhexidine, alcohols and halogens. Resistance to phenols, chloroform, lysozyme and finally glutaraldehyde (Power *et al.*, 1988) appears only late in the sporulation process. In the following sections the relationship between spore structure and resistance is reviewed. These aspects are also reviewed by Waites (1985) and Russell (1983, 1990).

4.2 Spore coat and resistance

Experimental evidence suggests that the spore coat may be involved in resistance to many antimicrobial agents by preventing penetration of the agent to its site of action. Methods for studying the role of the spore coat generally involve the use of coatless or coat-defective spore forms. These are either coat-deficient mutant strains or more usually coat-extracted spores prepared by treatment with sodium hydroxide or with combinations of thioglycollic acid (TA), 2-mercaptoethanol (ME) or dithiothreitol, with urea and/or sodium dodecyl lauryl sulphate (SLS). Electron microscopy and chemical analyses of extracted spores indicate that the spore coat consists of two layers, an inner coat which is alkali-soluble and an outer coat which is alkali-resistant (Kulikovsky *et al.*, 1975; Labbé *et al.*, 1978; Nishihara *et al.*, 1981). Aronson & Fitz-James (1971), Vary (1973) and Gorman *et al.* (1983b) have demonstrated that treatment with disulphide-reducing agents produces extraction of both inner and outer spore coat protein which can range from 38% of total coat protein for urea-mercaptoethanol (UME) at pH 7.0 to 70% or more for dithiothreitol with urea and SLS (UDS).

Studies by Gould & Hitchins (1963) have shown that spores with intact coats are resistant to the lytic enzyme lysozyme, but spores treated with agents that alter the spore coat will germinate in its presence. Wyatt & Waites (1974) also showed that slow germination mutants of *Cl. bifermentens* which were resistant to disulphide-reducing agents appeared to have a reduced permeability to germinants such as alanine, and an altered coat structure.

Similar studies have been used to indicate the extent to which coat protein protects against the action of chemical agents. Aronson & Fitz-James (1976) found that spores of a *B. cereus* mutant which were lysozyme-sensitive were also more sensitive to octanol than the parent spores. Further work with temperature-sensitive mutants suggested that the outer layers of the coat were responsible for octanol resistance (Stelma *et al.*, 1978). Studies with coat-defective mutants also demonstrated the role of the spore coat in resistance to chloroform (Sousa *et al.*, 1978).

With ethylene oxide, on the other hand, somewhat conflicting results have been obtained. Dadd & Daley (1982) showed that resistance of *B. cereus* spores pretreated with dithiothreitol remained unchanged, whilst spores of a coat-defective mutant of *B. subtilis* were actually more resistant to ethylene oxide. In contrast, Marletta & Stumbo (1970) showed that urea + TA (UTA) treatment of *B. subtilis* spores reduced resistance to ethylene oxide, although this resistance was regained on storage. King & Gould (1969) showed that spores treated to allow lysozyme to initiate germination also regained lysozyme resistance during storage, probably as a result of oxidation of reduced disulphide bonds in their coats. Such changes may account for the recovery of resistance to ethylene oxide.

With hydrogen peroxide, sodium hydroxide and ethanol, Waites & Bayliss (1979b) showed that spores of *B. cereus* made sensitive to lysosyme by UME treatment were only slightly more sensitive than spores with intact coats, suggesting that the intact coat had little effect in this situation. Experiments with *Cl. bifermentans*, on the other hand, showed that intact spores were 500 times more resistant to hydrogen peroxide than spores pretreated with dithiothreitol (Bayliss & Waites, 1976).

Thomas & Russell (1974) showed that pretreatment with ME or TA had little or no effect on the resistance of *B. pumilus* spores to glutaraldehyde. On the other hand, Gorman *et al.* (1984b) and McErlean *et al.* (1980) indicated that pretreatment of *B. subtilis* spores with UME or UDS (producing 38% and 70% extraction of total coat protein respectively) caused a progressive increase in sensitivity to glutaraldehyde. Experiments by Munton & Russell (1970) and King *et al.* (1974) showed that, whereas under acid conditions glutaraldehyde resides at the spore surface, treatment of spores with glutaraldehyde under alkaline conditions (in the presence of bicarbonate) facilitated penetration of glutaraldehyde into the spores with increased activity. This suggests that alkaline but not acid glutaraldehyde causes disruption of spore coats.

Significant increases in sensitivity of *Cl. bifermentans*, *B. cereus* and *B. subtilis* spores to chlorine and iodine-releasing antibacterial agents following treatment with combinations of reagents causing extraction of spore coat protein have been demonstrated by Cousins & Allan (1967), Wyatt & Waites (1975), Waites *et al.* (1977), Bloomfield & Arthur (1989a,b), Waites & Bayliss (1979b), Gorman *et al.* (1983, 1984c, 1985) and Bloomfield & Megid (1989). Using agents which produced total coat protein extraction ranging from 10% for SLS alone to 70% for UDS, Gorman *et al.* (1983b) demonstrated that sensitivity to chlorine and chlorine/methanol mixtures was related to the extent of coat protein released.

From the results of these studies it is apparent that the intact coat plays some part in protecting the spore cortex and protoplast against the action of antibacterial agents, although the extent of this effect varies from one sporicide to another and between different spore species.

Investigations with agents such as hydrogen peroxide (Bayliss & Waites, 1976) and hypochlorite (Rode & Williams, 1966; Kulikovsky *et al.*, 1975; Wyatt & Waites, 1975; Foegeding & Busta, 1983) suggest that these agents may themselves cause disruption and extraction of spore coat material, thereby facilitating penetration to their site of action. Wyatt & Waites (1975) and Bayliss & Waites (1976) showed that treatment of *Cl. bifermentans*, *B. cereus* and *B. subtilis* spores with chlorine, and of *Cl. bifermentans* with hydrogen peroxide, produced solubilization of coat protein; gel electrophoresis of protein extracted with chlorine or hydrogen peroxide produced an identical electrophoretic band to that demonstrated by Vary (1973) from alkali extracts of *Cl. bifermentans*, but other less dense bands similar to those obtained from urea + dithiothreitol extracts (corresponding to outer coat protein material) were absent from chlorine and hydrogen peroxide extracts. Disruption of spore coat material by treatment with chlorine is also indicated by studies of Wyatt & Waites (1975) and Foegeding (1983) which showed that chlorine treatment of *B. subtilis*, *B. cereus*, *Cl. bifermentans* and *Cl. botulinum* spores increased their sensitivity to lysozyme.

Most recent investigations in our own laboratories (Bloomfield & Arthur, 1989a,b) suggest that results with extracted spores must be interpreted with care; experiments showed that treatment of *B. subtilis* spores with UDS produced substantial extraction of cortex peptidoglycan as well as coat protein, although the effects of other disulphide-reducing agents has not been investigated. The results as described in more detail below suggest that, although the coat may play a substantial part in resistance to chemical agents and heat, the cortex may also be involved.

4.3 Spore cortex and resistance

Experimental evidence increasingly suggests that agents such as glutaraldehyde, chlorine, hydrogen peroxide, octanol and butanol interact with spore cortex material, although the nature of this interaction varies considerably from one agent to another. Thus, Hughes & Thurman (1970) and Gorman *et al.* (1984b) report interaction of glutaraldehyde with the cortex of *B. subtilis* spores preventing degradation by lysozyme and nitrite. Waites *et al.* (1976, 1977), Gorman *et al.* (1984c) and Bloomfield & Arthur (1989a,b and unpublished), on the other hand, have shown that treatment with hydrogen peroxide or hypochlorite produces degradation of cortex material and, for hypochlorite (Wyatt & Waites, 1975), this treatment increases rather than decreases sensitivity to lysozyme.

For the various oxidizing agents such as hypochlorites and hydrogen peroxide, it seems unlikely that degradation of spore cortex is responsible for spore death *per se*, since lysozyme treatment alone under conditions producing cortex degradation does not result in significant spore death (Fitz-James, 1971; Bloomfield & Arthur, 1989a). Rather it would seem that cortex degradation facilitates penetration of these agents to their site of action on the underlying spore protoplast.

The significance of cortex degradation is further demonstrated by recent findings of Bloomfield & Arthur (1989a,b and unpublished); comparative studies with chlorine-releasing agents showed that although sodium hypochlorite (NaOCl), sodium dichloroisocyanurate (NaDCC) and chloramine-T solutions buffered to pH 7.4 had similar activity against vegetative cells of *B. subtilis* there was considerable variation in sporicidal activity, NaOCl (100 ppm, 5 min contact) showed significantly higher activity than NaDCC at 1000 ppm, whilst chloramine-T at 5000 ppm showed little or no activity after this contact time. Pretreatment of spores with NaOH to extract alkali-soluble coat protein increased sensitivity to NaOCl and particularly to NaDDC, but had little effect on chloramine-T. On the other hand, pretreatment of spores with UDS, and UDS followed by lysozyme, produced successive increases in sensitivity to all three agents. Chemical analysis of extracted spores confirmed that alkali treatment, whilst producing significant extraction of coat protein, had no measurable effect on cortex peptidoglycan. By contrast, treatment with UDS and UDS/lysozyme caused progressive extraction of cortex material (50% and 75% of total cortex material respectively) as well as coat protein. These results suggest that the increasing sensitivity to these chlorine-releasing agents is associated with progressive removal of spore coats and degradation of cortex peptidoglycan allowing access to the underlying protoplast. Whereas extraction of alkali-soluble coat protein alone produced substantial increases in sensitivity to NaOCl and NaDCC, degradation of both coat and cortex material was required to achieve significant activity with choramine-T. Further experiments (unpublished) have shown that NaOCl and NaDCC in the presence of NaOH themselves produce degradation of cortex peptidoglycan which may be responsible for their rapid sporicidal action under these conditions. By contrast, chloramine-T produced no degradation of peptidoglycan and was ineffective against normal and alkali-extracted spores, requiring extraction with UDS or UDS/

lysozyme to achieve activity.

From their experimental observations, Gould and co-workers (Gould, 1977; Gould & Dring, 1974, 1975) have postulated that spore cortex peptidoglycan is responsible not only for mechanical protection of the spore (as with vegetative cells) but also for maintaining dehydration of the spore protoplast. By maintaining a very low water level and a consequent high viscosity in the protoplast, diffusion of water-soluble antimicrobial agents into the protoplast is reduced. It may be, therefore, that rehydration of the spore protoplast following cortex degradation by the action of chlorine-releasing agents is required to facilitate diffusion of these agents to their site of action on the underlying protoplast.

From their observations of the action of chlorine/methanol mixtures, Death & Coates (1979) suggested that methanol potentiates the action of NaOCl by softening of spore coats allowing penetration to occur. The results described above suggest rather that the action of chlorine is to produce coat and cortex degradation, thereby facilitating diffusion of methanol to its site of action on the underlying protoplast.

For glutaraldehyde, on the other hand, current evidence suggests that interaction with the cortex may be directly responsible for spore death. Results by Thomas & Russell (1974) and Hughes & Thurman (1970) indicate that low concentrations of glutaraldehyde inhibit spore germination by interacting with and cross-linking amino groups in the cortex peptidoglycan. Further investigations (Thomas, 1977) suggest that at higher concentrations (10% alkaline glutaraldehyde) extensive irreversible interaction with spore outer layers produces a tough sealed structure such that germination can no longer occur and spore death results. Gorman *et al.* (1984b) showed that pretreatment with glutaraldehyde protects coatless spores of *B. subtilis* from the lytic action of lysozyme and sodium nitrite, and also reduces the solubilization of hexosamines from cortical fragments. If the sporicidal action of glutaraldehyde involves interaction with cortex peptidoglycan then it must follow that glutaraldehyde resistance will be determined by the extent to which this interaction is reversible or irreversible. Recent studies by Dancer *et al.* (1989) and Power *et al.* (1989, 1990) showed increased recovery of glutaraldehyde-treated spores by treatment with alkali (NaOH or $NaHCO_3$) but not with disulphide-reducing agents, lysozyme or with protease enzymes.

It is interesting to note that, whereas studies with glutaraldehyde suggest that interaction with spore outer layers produces sealing of spores, thereby preventing germination, the series of changes which occur following treatment with hypochlorite and hydrogen peroxide closely resemble those associated with spore germination, namely decrease in refractility whereby phase bright spores become phase dark (Wyatt & Waites, 1973, 1975; Waites *et al.*, 1976), degradation of cortex peptidoglycan (Gorman *et al.*, 1984c; Bloomfield & Arthur 1989a,b and unpublished), decrease in dry weight and optical density (Wyatt & Waites, 1973, 1975; Waites *et al.*, 1976).

There is evidence that other sporicidal agents may interact with the spore cortex. Imae & Strominger (1976), using mutants of *Bacillus sphaericus* which were defective in the synthesis of *meso*-diaminopimelate, showed that muramic lactam in the spore cortex increased linearly with an increase in the concentration of *meso*-diaminopimelic acid in the sporulation medium. When 25% of the maximum cortex concentration was produced the spores became resistant to both octanol and xylene, but 90% of the maximum cortex development was required for heat resistance. The time at which cortex synthesis occurs during spore formation also coincided with the ordered appearance of resistance to chloroform, methanol and octanol (Sousa *et al.*, 1978). Thus it would seem that a complete cortex is important in conferring resistance to these chemicals. However, an incomplete cortex may affect development of other spore components. Thus, Imae & Strominger (1976) showed that spores without cortices were irregularly shaped, suggesting that coats may also have been defective thereby reducing resistance.

For both glutaraldehyde and the various oxidizing agents there is evidence that changes in spore resistance can be achieved by conditions which modify their interaction with spore cortex material. Most particularly changes which alter the balance of cations and dipicolinic acid within the spore cortex and protoplast have been investigated. These aspects are discussed in the following section.

4.4 Osmoregulation and resistance

Gould & Dring (1974, 1975) have proposed that the heat resistance of spores probably results from dehydration of the spore protoplast which is brought about and maintained by the osmotic activity of expanded electronegative peptidoglycan within the spore cortex, the stability of the peptidoglycan being maintained by the presence of mobile positively charged counterions within the cortex. They found that coat-defective spores treated to allow penetration of multivalent cations showed increased sensitivity to heat, and suggested that, in this situation, the multivalent cations interacted with and cross-linked carboxyl groups of the peptidoglycan, causing it to contract, allowing partial rehydration and loss of heat resistance.

It was found that the presence of Cu^{2+} increased the lethal effect of hydrogen peroxide on spores of *Cl. bifermentans* but not of other species such as *B. subtilis* var. *niger* (Bayliss & Waites, 1976; Wallen, 1976; Waites *et al.*, 1979). Since the protoplasts of *Cl. bifermentans* bound Cu^{2+} but those of *B. subtilis* var. *niger* did not, even when incubated as ultrathin sections with Cu^{2+}, this suggests that the state of the protoplast and cortex may be important in determining the resistance of spores to hydrogen peroxide. Protoplasts of *Cl. bifermentans* bound UO^{2+} and Pb^{2+} more readily than those of other species (Waites *et al.*, 1972), suggesting differences in the availability of groups for binding. Spores of the same *Cl. bifermentans* species were also more sensitive to chlorine (Wyatt & Waites, 1975), to hydrogen peroxide (Bayliss & Waites, 1976) and to a combination of glutaraldehyde and formaldehyde (Hobler & Waites, unpublished) than those of other species, again suggesting that protoplast structure may be important in determining resistance to some chemicals.

Sacks & Alderton (1961) showed that titration with acid to produce H-form spores reduced heat resistance which was recovered by titration with Ca^{2+} to produce Ca-form spores. Gould & Dring (1975) have suggested that, in this situation, acid treatment displaces positively charged cations from the cortex by protonating peptidoglycan carboxyl groups, thus reducing cortex expansion and lowering osmotic pressure. They proposed that re-equilibration at high pH values reimposes expansion and increases the osmotic pressure exerted by the cortex, thereby reinstating heat resistance as is found experimentally.

Although further investigation is required, it is worth noting the results of Thomas & Russell (1975), McErlean *et al.* (1980) and Gorman *et al.* (1984b). These workers showed that stable Ca^{2+} forms of *B. subtilis* spores were more sensitive to glutaraldehyde, which appears to act by preventing cortical breakdown and spore germination, whereas NaOCl and NaOCl/methanol which cause cortical breakdown and destabilization of spores are more effective against unstable H-forms. Tawasatani & Shibasaki (1973) have shown that H-form spores were also more sensitive to propylene oxide than were normal or Ca-form spores.

At one time it was thought that dipicolinic acid played a significant role in the heat resistance of spores, but it has now been shown that mutants of *B. subtilis*, *B. cereus* and *B. megaterium* which contain no DPA and a low level of calcium retain full resistance to heat (Zytkovicz & Halvorson, 1972; Hanson *et al.*, 1972). It now seems more likely; as stated by Gould (1977), that calcium dipicolinate in the spore core plays a role in dormancy as a calcium buffer and a calcium store. It has been calculated (Gould, 1977) that the expanded cortex may exert an osmotic potential of as much as 2 MPa or more causing water to pass from the core to the cortex until the osmotic pressure is equalized. The water contents of the two compartments at equilibrium will therefore depend on the osmotic activity of the core. As far as is known the spore protoplast contains mainly macromolecules or insolubilized salts such as calcium dipicolinate or calcium salts of other weak acids such as glutamic and phosphoglyceric acids (Nelson *et al.*, 1969) which make only a small osmotic contribution thereby maintaining an equilibrium position in the direction of a high water content cortex surrounding a low water content core.

During germination, as the spore becomes sensitive to heat and other agents and loses its dormancy, calcium previously held by DPA in the core is mobilized in some way to neutralize negatively charged groups in the cortex; this in turn reduces the osmotic pressure and allows the protoplast to rehydrate.

In line with this it is found that hydrogen peroxide and chlorine-releasing agents produce leakage of Ca^{2+} and/or DPA from spores (Alderton & Holbrook, 1971; Dye & Mead, 1972; Gorman *et al.*, 1984c) whilst glutaraldehyde which appears to act by stabilization of the spore cortex does not (Thomas & Russell, 1974).

Balassa *et al.* (1979) have shown that a mutant of *B. subtilis* which did not synthesize dipicolinic acid during spore formation, and contained less Ca^{2+} than those of the parent spores, was also less resistant to phenol, pyridine and trichloroacetic acid than were the parent spores. When DPA was added to the sporulation medium it was taken up by the spores, which then became more resistant to these three agents. These results suggest that DPA in spore protoplasts may play some role in resistance to heat and chemical agents.

5 CONCLUSIONS

A review of the literature as presented in this chapter indicates that the mechanisms which account for the resistance of spores relative to that of vegetative bacterial forms against the action of antimicrobial agents are complex and only partially understood.

Most certainly it would appear that the spore coat plays an important part, by limiting penetration to the underlying cortex and protoplast, and that this situation applies even to agents which are known to be actively sporicidal.

It is found that sporicidal agents such as chlorine-releasing agents, hydrogen peroxide and possibly also glutaraldehyde applied under conditions in which they cause degradation of outer spore layers, are effective at relatively much lower concentrations, although these are generally in excess of those which kill vegetative cells. By contrast, for agents such as iodine, chloramine-T and NaDCC under conditions where they produce little or no coat protein extraction, concentrations and contact times required to achieve adequate penetration as required for destruction of spores are very considerably in excess of those which kill vegetative cells.

For antimicrobial agents such as chlorhexidine which have little or no sporicidal action it is suggested that these agents may be almost completely excluded from the spore. Shaker *et al.* (1988) have demonstrated that extraction of *B. subtilis* spores decreased resistance to chlorhexidine; whereas 25 μg/ml chlorhexidine produced only a 0.5-log reduction of intact spores within 2 h, the same concentration produced a 2-log reduction with UDS-treated spores.

Increasingly there is evidence to suggest that the spore cortex also plays a vital role in the resistance of spores to heat and chemical agents. It is suggested that this derives from the stable expanded spore cortex which maintains a stable dehydrated state and a consequent high viscosity within the spore protoplast. This thereby limits diffusion into the protoplast and initiates changes in the viable components of the protoplast, making them resistant to denaturation by heating. Experimental studies indicate that resistance imposed by the cortex may be overcome by interactions within the cortex or core which destabilize the cortex, facilitating diffusion of the antimicrobial agent into the sensitive protoplast. Alternatively the sporicide may interact to prevent cortex degradation, thereby preventing rehydration, germination and outgrowth of the spore. In this situation treatments which modify these interactions may be used to modify resistance to sporicidal agents.

ACKNOWLEDGEMENT

I would like to acknowledge Professor W.M. Waites, Department of Applied Biochemistry and Food Science, School of Agriculture, University of Nottingham, Sutton Bonnington, for his significant contribution to this chapter.

6 REFERENCES

Alderton, G. & Holbrook, W.V. (1971) Action of chlorine on bacterial spores. *Bacteriological Proceedings*, p. 12.

Ando, Y. & Tsuzuki, T. (1986a) The effect of hydrogen peroxide on spores of *Clostridium perfringens*. *Letters in Applied Microbiology*, **2**, 65–68.

Ando, Y. & Tsuzuki, T. (1986b) Changes in decoated spores of *Clostridium perfringens* caused by treatment with some enzymatic and non-enzymatic systems. *Letters in Applied Microbiology*, **3**, 61–64.

Aronson, A.I. & Fitz-James, P.C. (1971) Reconstitution of bacterial spore coat layers *in vitro*. *Journal of Bacteriology*, **108**, 571–578.

Aronson, A.I. & Fitz-James, P.C. (1976) Structure and morphogenesis of the bacterial spore coat. *Bacteriological Reviews*, **40**, 360–402.

Babb, J.R., Bradley, C.R. & Ayliffe, G.A.J. (1980) Sporicidal activity of glutaraldehyde and hypochlorites and other factors influencing their selection for the treatment of medical equipment. *Journal of Hospital Infection*, **1**, 63–75.

Balassa, G., Milhaud, P., Raulet, E., Silva, M.T. & Sousa, J.C.F. (1979) *A Bacillus subtilis* mutant requiring dipicolinic acid for the development of heat-resistant spores. *Journal of General Microbiology*, **110**, 365–379.

Baldry, M.G.C. (1983) The bactericidal, fungicidal and sporicidal properties of hydrogen peroxide and peracetic acid. *Journal of Applied Bacteriology*, **54**, 417–423.

Baldry, M.G.C. (1988) Disinfection with peroxygens. In *Industrial Biocides: Critical Reports on Applied Chemistry* (ed. Payne, K.R.) pp. 91–116. Chichester: John Wiley & Sons.

Barach, J.T., Flowers, R.S. & Adams, D.M. (1975) Repair of heat-injured *Clostridium perfringens* spores during outgrowth. *Applied Microbiology*, **30**, 873–875.

Bayliss, C.E. & Waites, W.M. (1976) The effect of hydrogen peroxide on spores of *Clostridium bifermentans*. *Journal of General Microbiology*, **96**, 401–407.

Bayliss, C.E. & Waites, W.M. (1979) The synergistic killing of spores of *Bacillus subtilis* by hydrogen peroxide and ultra-violet light irradiation. *FEMS Microbiology Letters*, **5**, 331–333.

Bayliss, C.E., Waites, W.M. & King, N.R. (1981) Resistance and structure of spores of *Bacillus subtilis*. *Journal of Applied Bacteriology*, **50**, 379–390.

Benarde, M.A., Snow, W.B. & Olivieri, V.P. (1967) Chlorine dioxide disinfection: temperature effects. *Journal of Applied Bacteriology*, **30**, 159–167.

Block, S.S. (ed.) (1977) *Disinfection, Sterilization and Preservation*. Philadelphia: Lea & Febiger.

von Bockelmann, I. (1974) The sporicidal action of chemical disinfectants. *S.I.K. Rapport*. No. 359, pp. 86–97.

Bloomfield, S.F. (1991) Methods for the assessment of antimicrobial activity. *Society of Applied Bacteriology Technical Series No. 27*, pp. 1–22 London: Academic Press.

Bloomfield, S.F. & Arthur, M. (1989a) Effect of chlorine-releasing agents on *Bacillus subtilis* vegetative cells and spores. *Letters in Applied Microbiology*, **8**, 101–104.

Bloomfield, S.F. & Arthur, M. (1989b) Studies in the mode of action of chlorine-releasing agents on *Bacillus subtilis* spores. *Journal of Applied Bacteriology*, **67**, xxii.

Bloomfield, S.F. & Megid, R. (1989) Comparative studies of the mode of action of chlorine and iodine antimicrobial agents. *Journal of Applied Bacteriology*, **67**, xxii.

Bomar, M. (1962) The relationship between the age of *Bacillus subtilis* spores and their resistance to ethylene oxide. *Folia Microbiologica Praha*, **7**, 259–261.

Boucher, R.M.G. (1975) On biocidal mechanisms in the aldehyde series. *Canadian Journal of Pharmaceutical Sciences*, **10**, 1–7.

Briggs, A. (1966) The resistance of spores of the genus *Bacillus* to phenol, heat and radiation. *Journal of Applied Bacteriology*, **29**, 490–504.

Bruch, C.W. & Koesterer, M.G. (1961) The microbicidal activity of gaseous propylene oxide and its application to powdered or flaked foods. *Journal of Food Science*, **26**, 428–435.

Caputo, R.A. & Odlaug, T.E. (1983) Sterilization with ethylene oxide and other gases. In *Disinfection, Sterilization and Preservation* (ed. Block, S.S.) 3rd Ed., pp. 47–64. Philadelphia: Lea & Febiger.

Cousins, C.M. & Allan, C.D. (1967) Sporicidal properties of some halogens. *Journal of Applied Bacteriology*, **30**, 168–174.

Dadd, A.H. & Daley, G.M. (1982) Role of the coat in resistance of bacterial spores to inactivation by ethylene oxide. *Journal of Applied Bacteriology*, **53**, 109–116.

Dadd, A.H., McCormick, K.E. & Daley, G.M. (1977) Increased bactericidal activity of ethylene oxide in the presence of methyl formate. *Journal of Applied Bacteriology*, **43**, xviii–xix.

Dancer, B.N., Power, E.G.M. & Russell, A.D. (1989) Alkali-induced revival of *Bacillus* spores after inactivation by glutaraldehyde. *FEMS Microbiology Letters*, **57**, 345–348.

Death, J.E. & Coates, D. (1979) Effect of pH on sporicidal and microbicidal activity of buffered mixtures of alcohol and sodium hypochlorite. *Journal of Clinical Pathology*, **32**, 148–153.

Dye, M. & Mead, G.C. (1972) The effect of chlorine on the viability of clostridial spores. *Journal of Food Technology*, **7**, 173–181.

El-Bisi, H.M., Vondell, R.M. & Esselen, W.B. (1963) Studies on the kinetics of the bactericidal action of ethylene oxide in the vapor phase. *Bacteriological Proceedings*, p. 13.

Ernst, R.R. (1974) Ethylene oxide sterilization kinetics. *Biotechnology Bioengineering Symposium*, **4**, 865–878.

Ernst, R.R. (1975) Sterilization by means of ethylene oxide. *Acta Pharmaceutica Suecica*, **12**, Supplement, 44–64.

Fitz-James, P.C. (1971) Formation of protoplasts from resting spores. *Journal of Bacteriology*, **105**, 1119–1136.

Foegeding, P.M. (1985) Ozone inactivation of *Bacillus* and *Clostridium* spores and the importance of the spore coat to resistance. *Food Microbiology*, **2**, 123–134.

Foegeding, P.M. & Busta, F.F. (1983) Proposed mechanism for sensitization by hypochlorite treatment of *Clostridium botulinum* spores. *Applied and Environmental Microbiology*, **45**, 1374–1379.

Foegeding, P.M. & Fulp, M.L. (1988) Comparison of coats

and surface-dependent properties of *Bacillus cereus T* prepared in two sporulation environments. *Journal of Applied Bacteriology*, **65**, 249–259.

Forsyth, M.P. (1975) A rate of kill test for measuring sporicidal properties of liquid sterilizers. *Developments in Industrial Microbiology*, **16**, 37–47.

Futter, B.V. & Richardson, G. (1970a) Viability of clostridial spores and the requirements of damaged organisms. I. Method of colony count, period and temperature of incubation, and pH value of the medium. *Journal of Applied Bacteriology*, **33**, 321–330.

Futter, B.V. & Richardson, G. (1970b) Viability of clostridial spores and the requirements of damaged organisms. II. Gaseous environment and redox potentials. *Journal of Applied Bacteriology*, **33**, 331–340.

Gardner, J.S. & Favero, M.S. (1985) Guideline for handwashing and hospital infection control. HHS publication No. 99–1117. Public Health Service, Centers for Disease Control, Atlanta, Georgia.

Gorman, S.P. & Scott, E.M. (1979) Potentiation and stabilization of glutaraldehyde biocidal activity utilizing surfactant divalent metal combinations. *International Journal of Pharmaceutics*, **4**, 57–65.

Gorman, S.P., Scott, E.M. & Russell, A.D. (1980) Antimicrobial activity, uses and mechanism of action of glutaraldehyde. *Journal of Applied Bacteriology*, **48**, 161–190.

Gorman, S.P., Hutchinson, E.P., Scott, E.M. & McDermott, L.M. (1983a) Death, injury and revival of chemically-treated *Bacillus subtilis* spores. *Journal of Applied Bacteriology*, **54**, 91–99.

Gorman, S.P., Scott, E.M. & Hutchinson, E.P. (1983b) The effect of sodium hypochlorite-methanol combinations on spores and spore forms of *Bacillus subtilis*. *International Journal of Pharmaceutics*, **17**, 291–298.

Gorman, S.P., Scott, E.M. & Hutchinison, E.P. (1984a) Emergence and development of resistance to antimicrobial chemicals and heat in spore of *Bacillus subtilis*. *Journal of Applied Bacteriology*, **57**, 153–163.

Gorman, S.P., Scott, E.M. & Hutchinson, E.P. (1984b) Interaction of *Bacillus subtilis* spore protoplast, cortex, ion-exchange and coatless forms with glutaraldehyde. *Journal of Applied Bacteriology*, **56**, 95–102.

Gorman, S.P., Scott, E.M. & Hutchinson, E.P. (1984c) Hypochlorite effects on spores and spore forms of *Bacillus subtilis* and on a spore lytic ensyme. *Journal of Applied Bacteriology*, **56**, 295–303.

Gorman, S.P., Scott, E.M. & Hutchinson, E.P. (1985) Effects of aqueous and alcoholic povidone-iodine on spores of *Bacillus subtilis*. *Journal of Applied Bacteriology*, **59**, 99–105.

Gould, G.W. (1971) Methods for studying bacterial spores. In *Methods in Microbiology* (eds Norris, J.R. & Ribbons, D.W.) Vol. 6A, pp. 326–381. London: Academic Press.

Gould, G.W. (1977) Recent advances in the understanding of resistance and dormancy in bacterial spores. *Journal of Applied Bacteriology*, **42**, 297–309.

Gould, G.W. (1983) Mechanisms of resistance and dormancy. In *The Bacterial Spore* Vol. 2 (eds Hurst, A. & Gould, G.W.) pp. 173–209. London and New York: Academic Press.

Gould, G.W. (1984) Injury and repair mechanisms in bacterial spores. In *The Revival of Injured Microbes* (eds Andrew, M.H.E. & Russell, A.D.) pp. 199–220. Society for Applied Bacteriology Symposium Series No. 12. London and New York: Academic Press.

Gould, G.W. (1985) Modifications of resistance and dormancy. In *Fundamental and Applied Aspects of Bacterial Spores* (eds Dring, G.J. Ellar, D.J. & Gould, G.W.) pp. 371–382. London and New York: Academic Press.

Gould, G.W. & Dring, G.J. (1974) Mechanisms of spore heat resistance. *Advances in Microbial Physiology*, **11**, 137–164.

Gould, G.W. & Dring, G.J. (1975) Heat resistance of bacterial endospores and concept of an expanded osmoregulatory cortex. *Nature, London*, **258**, 402–405.

Gould, G.W. & Hitchins, A.D. (1963) Sensitization of bacterial spores to lysozyme and to hydrogen peroxide with agents which rupture disulphide bonds. *Journal of General Microbiology*, **33**, 413–423.

Hanson, R.S., Curry, M.V., Gardner, J.V. & Halvorsen, H.O. (1972) Mutants of *Bacillus cereus* strain T that produce thermoresistant spores lacking dipicolinic acid and have low levels of calcium. *Canadian Journal of Microbiology*, **18**, 1139–1143.

Hoffman, R.K. (1971) Toxic gases. In *Inhibition and destruction of the microbial cell* (ed. Hugo, W.B.) pp. 225–258. London and New York: Academic Press.

Hughes, R.C. & Thurman, P.F. (1970). Cross-linking of bacterial cell walls with glutaraldehyde. *Biochemical Journal*, **119**, 925–926.

Imae, Y. & Strominger, J.L. (1976) Relationship between cortex content and properties of *Bacillus sphaericus* spores. *Journal of Bacteriology*, **126**, 907–913.

Isenberg, H.D. (1985) Clinical laboratory studies of disinfection with Sporicidin. *Journal of Clinical Microbiology*, **22**, 735–739.

Isenberg, H.D., Giugliano, E.R., France, K. & Alperstein, P. (1988) Evaluation of three disinfectants after in-use stress. *Journal of Hospital Infection*, **11**, 278–285.

Ito, K.A., Denny, C.B., Brown, C.K., Yao, M. & Seeger, M.L. (1973) Resistance of bacterial spores to hydrogen peroxide. *Food Technology*, **27**(11), 58–66.

Kelsey, J.C., MacKinnon, I.H. & Maurer, I.M. (1974) Sporicidal activity of hospital disinfectants. *Journal of Clinical Pathology*, **27**, 632–638.

King, J.A., Woodside, W. & McGucken, P.V. (1974) Relationship between pH and antibacterial activity of glutaraldehyde. *Journal of Pharmaceutical Sciences*, **63**, 804–805.

King, W.L. & Gould, G.W. (1969) Lysis of bacterial spores with hydrogen peroxide. *Journal of Applied Bacteriology*, **32**, 481–490.

Kulikovsky, A., Pankratz, H.S. & Sadoff, H.L. (1975) Ultrastructural and chemical changes in spores of *Bacillus cereus* after action of disinfectants. *Journal of Applied*

Bacteriology, **38**, 39–46.

Labbé, R.G., Reich, R.R. & Duncan, C.L. (1978) Alteration in ultrastructure and germination of *Clostridium perfringens* type A spores following extraction of spore coats. *Canadian Journal of Microbiology*, **24**, 1526–1536.

Lelieveld, H.L.M. (1979) The effect of pH on microbial growth and destruction. Society for Applied Bacteriology Technical Series No. 15 (eds Gould, G.W. & Corry, J.E.L.) pp. 71–98. London: Academic Press.

Marks, H.C. & Strandskov, F.B. (1950) Halogens and their mode of action. *Annals of the New York Academy of Sciences*, **53**, 163–171.

Marletta, J. & Stumbo, C.R. (1970) Some effects of ethylene oxide on *Bacillus subtilis*. *Journal of Food Science*, **35**, 627–631.

Marshall, B.J., Murrell, W.G. & Scott, W.J. (1963) The effect of water activity, solutes and temperature on the viability and heat resistance of freeze-dried bacterial spores. *Journal of General Microbiology*, **31**, 451–460.

McErlean, E.P., Gorman, S.P. & Scott, E.M. (1980) Physical and chemical resistance of ion-exchange and coat-defective spores of *Bacillus subtilis*. *Journal of Pharmacy and Pharmacology*, **32**, 32P.

Miner, N.A., McDowell, J.W., Wilcockson, G.W., Bruckner, N.I., Stark, R.C. & Whitmore, J. (1977) Antimicrobial and other properties of a new stabilized alkaline glutaraldehyde disinfectant sterilizer. *American Journal of Hospital Pharmacy*, **34**, 376–382.

Molin, G. & Östlund, K. (1976) Dry-heat inactivation of *Bacillus subtilis* var, *niger* spores with special reference to spore density. *Canadian Journal of Microbiology*, **22**, 359–363.

Munton, T.J. & Russell, A.D. (1970) Aspects of the action of glutaraldehyde on *Escherichia coli*. *Journal of Applied Bacteriology*, **33**, 410–419.

Murrell, W.G. (1969) Chemical composition of spores and spore structures. In *The Bacterial Spore* (eds Gould, G.W. & Hurst, A.) pp. 215–273. London: Academic Press.

Murrell, W.G. & Warth, A.D. (1965) Composition and heat resistance of bacterial spores. In *Spores III* (eds Campbell, L.L. & Halvorsen, H.O) pp. 1–24, Ann Arbor: American Society for Microbiology.

Nelson, D.L., Spudich, J.A., Donsen, P.P.M., Bertsch, L. & Kornberg, A. (1969) Biochemical studies of bacterial sporulation and germination. XVI Small molecules in spores. In *Spores IV* (ed. Campbell, L.L.) Bethesda, MD: American Society for Microbiology.

Nishihara, T., Yutsudo, T., Ichikawa, T. & Kondo, M. (1981) Studies on the bacterial spore coat. 8. On the SDS-DTT extract from *Bacillus megaterium* spores. *Microbiology and Immunology*, **25**, 327–331.

Ortenzio, L.F. (1966) Collaborative study of improved sporicidal test. *Journal of the Association of Official Analytical Chemists*, **49**, 721–726.

Ortenzio, L.F., Stuart, L.S. & Friedl, J.L. (1953) The resistance of bacterial spores to constant boiling hydrochloric acid. *Journal of the Association of Official Agricultural Chemists*, **36**, 480–484.

Phillips, C.R. (1952) Relative resistance of bacterial spores and vegetative bacteria to disinfectants. *Bacteriological Reviews*, **16**, 135–138.

Phillips, C.R. (1977) Gaseous sterilisation. In *Disinfection, Sterilization and Preservation* (ed. Block, S.S.) pp. 592–610. Philadelphia: Lea & Febiger.

Portner, D.F. & Hoffman, R.K. (1968) Sporicidal effect of peracetic acid vapour. *Applied Microbiology*, **16**, 1782–1785.

Power, E.G.M. & Russell, A.D. (1990) Sporicidal action of alkaline glutaraldehye: Factors influencing activity and a comparison with other aldehydes. *Journal of Applied Bacteriology*, **69**, 261–268.

Power, E.G.M., Dancer, B.N. & Russell, A.D. (1988) Emergence of resistance to glutaraldehyde in spores of *Bacillus subtilis* 168. *FEMS Microbiology Letters*, **50**, 223–226.

Power, E.G.M., Dancer, B.N. & Russell, A.D. (1989) Possible mechanisms for the revival of glutaraldehyde-treated spores of *Bacillus subtilis* NCTC 8236. *Journal of Applied Bacteriology*, **67**, 91–98.

Power, E.G.M., Dancer, B.N. & Russell, A.D. (1990) Effect of sodium hydroxide and two proteases on the revival of aldehyde-treated spores. *Letters in Applied Microbiology*, **10**, 9–13.

Quinn, P.J. (1987) Evaluation of veterinary disinfectants and disinfection processes. In *Disinfection in Veterinary and Farm Animal Practice* (eds Linton, A.H., Hugo, W.B. & Russell, A.D.) pp. 66–116. Oxford: Blackwell Scientific Publications.

Reich, R. (1980) Effect of sublethal ethylene oxide exposure on *Bacillus subtilis* spores and biological indicator performance. *Journal of the Parenteral Drug Association*, **34**, 200–211.

Ridenour, G.M., Ingols, R.S. & Armbruster, E.H. (1949) Sporicidal properties of chlorine dioxide. *Water and Sewage Works*, **96**, 279–283.

Roberts, T.A. (1970) Recovering spores damaged by heat, ionizing radiations or ethylene oxide. *Journal of Applied Bacteriology*, **33**, 74–94.

Roberts, T.A. & Hitchins, A.D. (1969) Resistance of spores. In *The Bacterial Spore* (eds Gould, G.W. & Hurst, A.) pp. 611–670. London: Academic Press.

Rode, L.J. & Williams, M.G. (1966) Utility of sodium hypochorite for ultrastructure study of bacterial spore integuments. *Journal of Bacteriology*, **92**, 1772–1778.

Rubbo, S.D. & Gardner, J.F. (1965) *A Review of Sterilization and Disinfection*. London: Lloyd-Luke.

Rubbo, S.D., Gardner, J.F. & Webb, R.L. (1967) Biocidal activities of glutaraldehyde and related compounds. *Journal of Applied Bacteriology*, **30**, 78–87.

Russell, A.D. (1971) The destruction of bacterial spores. In *Inhibition and Destruction of the Microbial Cell* (ed. Hugo, W.B.) pp. 451–612. London and New York: Academic Press.

Russell, A.D. (1982) *The Destruction of Bacterial Spores*. London: Academic Press.

Russell, A.D. (1983) Mechanisms of action of chemical

sporicidal and sporistatic agents. *International Journal of Pharmaceutics*, **10**, 127–140.

Russell, A.D. (1990) The bacterial spore and chemical sporicidal agents. *Clinical Microbiological Reviews*, **3**, 99–119.

Russell, A.D. & Chopra, I. (1990) *Understanding Antibacterial Action and Resistance*. Chichester: Ellis Horwood.

Russell, A.D., Dancer, B.N., Power, E.G.M. & Shaker, L.A. (1989) Mechanisms of bacterial spore resistance to disinfectants. *Proceedings of the 4th Conference Programme on Chemical Disinfectants*, Binghamton, New York. pp. 9–29.

Russell, A.D., Dancer, B.N. & Power, E.G.M. (1991) In Effects of chemical agents on bacterial sporulation, germination and outgrowth. *Mechanisms of Action of Chemical Biocides. Their Study and Exploitation*. Society of Applied Bacteriology. Technical Series No. 27 (eds Denyer, S.P. & Hugo, W.B.) pp. 23–24. Oxford: Blackwell Scientific Publications.

Sacks, L.E. & Alderton, G. (1961) Behavior of bacterial spores in aqueous polymer two-phase systems. *Journal of Bacteriology*, **82**, 331–341.

Shaker, L.A., Dancer, B.N., Russell, A.D. & Furr, J.R. (1988) Emergence and development of chlorhexidine resistance during sporulation of *Bacillus subtilis* 168. *FEMS Microbiology Letters*, **51**, 73–76.

Sousa, J.C.F., Silva, M.T. & Balassa, G. (1978) Ultrastructural effects of chemical agents and moist heat on *Bacillus subtilis*. II. Effects on sporulating cells. *Annales de Microbiologie*, **129B**, 377–390.

Spicher, G. & Peters, J. (1976) Microbial resistance to formaldehyde. I. Comparative quantitative studies in some selected species of vegetative bacteria, bacterial spores, fungi, bacteriophages and viruses. *Zentralblatt für Bakteriologie, Parasitenkunde, Infektionskrankheiten und Hygiene, I. Abteilung originale, Reihe B*. **163**, 486–503.

Spicher, G. & Peters, J. (1981) Heat activation of bacterial spores after inactivation by formaldehyde. Dependence of heat activation on temperature and duration of action. *Zentralblatt für Bakteriologie, Parasitenkunde, Infektionskrankheiten und Hygiene, I. Abteilung originale, Reihe B*. **173**, 188–196.

Stark, R.L., Ferguson, P., Garza, P. & Miner, N.A. (1975) An evaluation of the Association of Official Analytical Chemists sporicidal test method. *Developments in Industrial Microbiology*, **16**, 31–36.

Stelma, G.N., Aronson, A.I. & Fitz-James, P. (1978) Properties of *Bacillus cereus* temperature-sensitive mutants altered in spore coat formation. *Journal of Bacteriology*, **134**, 1157–1170.

St Julian, G., Pridham, T.G. & Hall, H.H. (1967) Preparation and characterization of intact and free spores of *Bacillus popilliae* Dutky. *Canadian Journal of Microbiology*, **13**, 279–285.

Sykes, G. (1970) The sporicidal properties of chemical disinfectants. *Journal of Applied Bacteriology*, **33**, 147–156.

Tawasatini, T. & Shibasaki, I. (1973) Change in the chemical resistance of heat sensitive and heat resistant bacterial spores against propylene oxide. *Journal of Fermentation Technology*, **51**, 824–891.

Thomas, S. (1977) Effect of high concentrations of glutaraldehyde upon bacterial spores. *Microbios Letters*, **4**, 199–204.

Thomas, S. & Russell, A.D. (1974) Studies on the mechanism of the sporicidal action of glutaraldehyde. *Journal of Applied Bacteriology*, **37**, 83–92.

Thomas, S. & Russell, A.D. (1975) Sensitivity and resistance to glutaraldehyde of the hydrogen and calcium forms of *Bacillus pumilus* spores. *Journal of Applied Bacteriology*, **38**, 315–317.

Toledo, R.T. (1975) Chemical sterilants for aseptic packaging. *Food Technology*, **29**(5), 102, 104, 105, 108, 110–112.

Toledo, R.T., Escher, F.E. & Ayres. J.C. (1973) Sporicidal properties of hydrogen peroxide against food spoilage organisms. *Applied Microbiology*, **26**, 592–597.

Trujillo, R. & David, T.J. (1972) Sporistatic and sporicidal properties of aqueous formaldehyde. *Applied Microbiology*, **23**, 618–622.

Tuynenberg Muys, G., Van Rhee, R. & Lelieveld, H.L.M. (1978) Sterilization by means of hydrochloric acid vapour. *Journal of Applied Bacteriology*, **45**, 213–217.

Vary, J.C. (1973) Germination of *Bacillus megaterium* spores after various extraction procedures. *Journal of Bacteriology*, **116**, 797–803.

Waites, W.M. (1985) Inactivation of spores with chemical agents. In *Fundamental and Applied Aspects of Bacterial Spores* (eds Dring, G.J., Ellar, D.J. & Gould, G.W.) pp. 383–396. London: Academic Press.

Waites, W.M. & Bayliss, C.E. (1979a) The preparation of bacterial spores for evaluation of the sporicidal activity of chemicals. *Society for Applied Bacteriology Technical Series* No. 15 (eds Gould, G.W. & Corry, J.E.L.) pp. 159–172. London: Academic Press.

Waites, W.M. & Bayliss, C.E. (1979b). The effect of changes in spore coat on the destruction of *Bacillus cereus* spores by heat and chemical treatment. *Journal of Applied Biochemistry*, **1**, 71–76.

Waites, W.M. & Bayliss, C.E. (1984) Damage to bacterial spores by combined treatments and possible revival and repair processes. In *The Revival of Injured Microbes* (eds Andrew, M.H.E. & Russell, A.D.) pp. 221–240. *Society for Applied Bacteriology Symposium Series*. No. 12. London and New York: Academic Press.

Waites, W.M., Bayliss, C.E., King, N.R. & Davies, A.M.C. (1979) The effect of transitional metal ions on the resistance of bacterial spores to hydrogen peroxide and to heat. *Journal of General Microbiology*, **112**, 225–233.

Waites, W.M., Harding, S.E., Fowler, D.R., Jones, S.H., Shaw, D. & Martin, M. (1988) The destruction of spores of *Bacillus subtilis* by the combined effects of hydrogen peroxide and ultraviolet light. *Letters in Applied Microbiology*, **7**, 139–140.

Waites, W.M., King, N.R. & Bayliss, C.E. (1977) The effect of chlorine and heat on spores of *Clostridium bifermentans*. *Journal of General Microbiology*, **102**, 211–213.

Waites, W.M., Wyatt, L.R. & Arthur, B. (1972) Effect of alkali treatment on the germination and morphology of spores of *Clostridium bifermentans*. In *Spores V* (eds Halvorsen, H.O., Hanson, R. & Campbell, L.L.) pp. 430–436. Washington, DC: American Society for Microbiology.

Waites, W.M., Wyatt, L.R., King, N.R. & Bayliss, C.E. (1976) Changes in spores of *Clostridium bifermentans* caused by treatment with hydrogen peroxide and cations. *Journal of General Microbiology*, **93**, 388–396.

Warth, A.D. (1978) Molecular structure of the bacterial spore. In *Advances in Microbial Physiology* (eds Rosen, A.H. & Morris, J.G.) Vol. **17**, pp. 1–45. London: Academic Press.

Wallen, S.E. (1976) Sporicidal action of hydrogen peroxide. Ph.D Thesis. University of Nebraska, Lincoln, Ne., USA.

Whitehouse, R.L. & Clegg, L.F.L. (1963) Destruction of *Bacillus cereus* spores with solutions of sodium hydroxide. *Journal of Dairy Research*, **30**, 315–322.

Wyatt, L.R. & Waites, W.M. (1973) The effect of hypochlorite on the germination of spores of *Clostridium bifermentans*. *Journal of General Microbiology*, **70**, 383–385.

Wyatt, L.R. & Waites, W.M. (1974) The effect of sodium hydroxide or dithiothreitol-urea on spores of germination mutants of *Clostridium bifermentans*. *Journal of General Microbiology*, **84**, 391–394.

Wyatt, L.R. & Waites, W.M. (1975) The effect of chlorine on spores of *Clostridium bifermentans*, *Bacillus subtilis* and *Bacillus cereus*. *Journal of General Microbiology*, **89**, 337–344.

Znamirowski, R., McDonald, S. & Roy, T.E. (1960) The efficiency of an ethylene oxide steriliser in hospital practice. *Canadian Medical Association Journal*, **83**, 1004–1006.

Zytkovicz, T.H. & Halvorsen, H.O. (1972) Some characteristics of dipicolinic acid-less mutant spores of *Bacillus cereus*, *Bacillus megaterium* and *Bacillus subtilis*. In *Spores V* (eds Halvorsen, H.O., Hanson, R. & Campbell, L.L.). Washington DC: American Society for Microbiology.

D · MYCOBACTERICIDAL AGENTS

1 INTRODUCTION

Mycobacteria are a fairly diverse group of acid-fast bacteria, the best-known and most important members of which are *Mycobacterium tuberculosis*, the aetiological agent of tuberculosis, and *M. leprae*, the causative agent of leprosy. An organism that is assuming greater clinical importance is *M. avium-intracellulare*, part of the *M. avium* and *M. intracellulare* (MAIS) complex, which is often associated with respiratory complications in AIDS patients (Collins, 1989; Guthertz *et al.*, 1989). Opportunistic pathogenic mycobacteria (Collins *et al.*, 1984) and potentially pathogenic mycobacteria (Goslee & Wolinsky, 1976) may be associated with water supplies.

1.1 Tuberculous and non-tuberculous mycobacteria

Included in the genus *Mycobacterium* are several intracellular bacterial parasites. *M. leprae* is an obligate intracellular pathogen, and species that cause progressive lung disease are *M. tuberculosis*, *M. bovis* and *M. avium*, which are facultative intracellular parasites. Species that are rarely pathogenic include *M. gordonae*, *M. fortuitum*, *M. terrae* and *M. smegmatis*, but there are many opportunistic species such as *M. intracellulare* (Collins, 1989; Grange *et al.*, 1990). The non-tuberculous mycobacteria are often referred to as atypical species.

Contrary to popular feeling, mycobacteria remain a public hazard, with tuberculosis itself still a major killer throughout the world. Added to this are the high isolation rate of mycobacteria from AIDS patients (Hanson, 1988), the prolonged chemotherapeutic treatment of tuberculosis patients and the above-average resistance of mycobacteria to biocides. Readers interested in obtaining further information about the clinical association of mycobacteria with disease should consult Wolinsky (1979), Ratledge & Stanford (1982), Wayne (1985), Damsker & Bottone (1985) and Collins (1989). Plasmids occur more frequently among clinical isolates of the MAIS complex than among environmental isolates (Jensen *et al.*, 1989).

1.2 Cell structure

Four closely related genera (*Corynebacterium*, *Mycobacterium*, *Nocardia* and *Rhodococcus*) make up the nocardioform actinomycetes. Most mycobacterial strains occur as unicellular rods but some develop as mycelial-producing organisms in which early fragmentation of the mycelium occurs during growth to produce either rods or branched rods. These organisms possess a distinctive cell wall, the composition of which is described below for mycobacteria.

1.3 Cell wall composition

Mycobacterial cell walls consist of several components. The 'covalent cell wall skeleton' (Fig. 10.5) comprises two covalently linked polymers, *viz.* peptidoglycan and a mycolate (Fig. 10.6) of arabinogalactan. Mycobacterial peptidoglycan contains *N*-glycolmuramic acid instead of the more widely found *N*-acetylmuramic acid, and differs in other ways also from more typical peptidoglycan. The arabinogalactan mycolate contains D-arabinose and D-galactose, ratio *ca.* 5:2, with about 10% of the arabinose residues esterified by a molecule of mycolic acid (Fig. 10.5). The general structure of mycolic acids is depicted in Fig. 10.6.

Other components of mycobacterial cell walls are the lipids and peptides. Lipids occur as free lipids, wax D (considered to be an autolysis product of the cell wall and immunologically identical with cell wall arabinogalactans) and 6,6′-dimycolates of α_1,α^1-D-trehalose, known as cord factors. The peptides can be removed by proteolytic enzymes. Further details are provided by Draper (1988).

2 RESPONSE TO BIOCIDES

2.1 Early findings

Early studies on the response of mycobacteria to biocides were reviewed by Croshaw (1971). This chapter will thus concentrate almost exclusively on subsequent work with merely an occasional citation to earlier findings. Croshaw's (1971) review can, in essence, be summarized as follows: mycobacteria are resistant to acids, alkalis, chlorhexidine, quaternary ammonium compounds (QACs), non-ionic and anionic surface-active agents, heavy metals and dyes, although many of these agents may inhibit mycobacterial growth without being mycobactericidal. Biocides that were listed by Croshaw (1971) as being mycobactericidal were ampholytic surfactants, e.g. 'Tego' compounds, ethylene oxide gas, iodine (more effective than hypochlorites), alcohols and especially phenolic compounds, notably cresol–soap formulations. Notable omissions from this list are formaldehyde and glutaraldehyde: conflicting results had been noted with the former although alcoholic solutions were more potent (Rubbo & Gardner, 1965; Rubbo *et al.*, 1967) and glutaraldehyde had been found by Bergan & Lystad (1971) to be surprisingly ineffective against tubercle bacilli. Spaulding (1972) proposed that acid-fast bacteria had a resistance to biocides intermediate between that shown by other non-sporing bacteria on the one hand and bacterial spores on the other. Hirsch (1954) demonstrated that formaldehyde (0.05%), sodium hypochlorite (< 0.05%) and potassium permanganate (0.005%) killed tubercle bacilli, whereas benzalkonium chloride (0.1%) did not. Unfortunately, Tween 80 was present as part of the testing procedure and it is possible that the non-ionic surfactant reduced considerably the effect of benzalkonium. Nevertheless, this compound has been used as a means of isolating *M. tuberculosis* (Patterson *et al.*, 1956).

Croshaw (1971) concluded that comprehensive data on the effects of biocides on mycobacteria were not available, that discrepancies existed (probably because of differences in technique in examining mycobactericidal activity), that many of the (then) newer disinfectants had not been examined and that most of the published work referred only to the tubercle bacillus. The important inference was made that a biocide effective against *M. tuberculosis* was not necessarily lethal to other mycobacteria. For an up-to-date assessment of mycobactericidal activity, see Best *et al.* (1990).

Several of these aspects will be reconsidered in the light of subsequent studies.

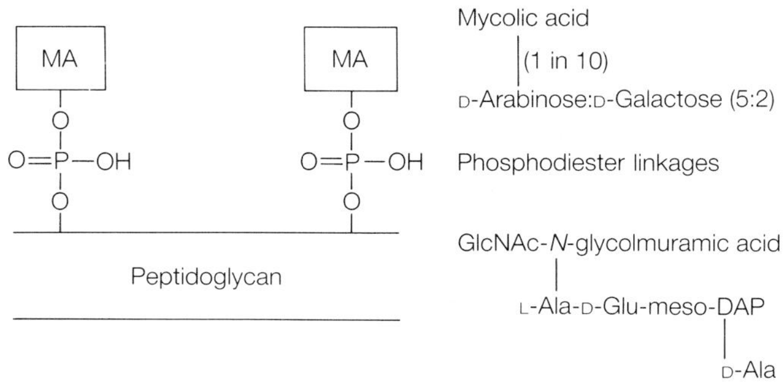

Fig. 10.5 Cell wall skeleton of mycobacteria. MA: mycolate of arabinogalactan.

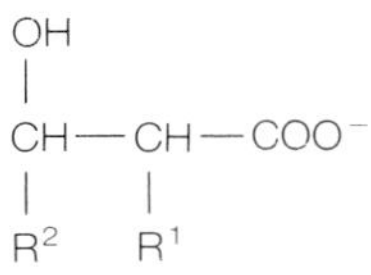

Fig. 10.6 General structure of mycolic acids. R^1 and R^2 are alkyl groups that may be saturated or unsaturated.

2.2 Recent concepts

The response of mycobacteria to biocides has been reviewed by Rubin (1983) and considered as part of an overall assessment of the sensitivity of microorganisms by Favero (1985), Gardner & Peel (1986) and Russell (1990, 1991).

Spaulding *et al.* (1977) recognize three levels of germicidal activity: (a) high-level activity, lethal to vegetative bacteria (including tubercle bacilli), spores, fungi, lipid-enveloped and non-lipid-enveloped viruses; (b) intermediate activity, lethal to all those listed in (a) except bacterial spores; (c) low activity, lethal only to vegetative bacteria (excluding tubercle bacilli), fungi and lipid-enveloped viruses.

Favero (1985) cites 2% glutaraldehyde, 8% formaldehyde in 70% alcohol, 6–10% stabilized hydrogen peroxide and gaseous ethylene oxide as being in category (a), with alcohol (70–90%), 0.5% iodine in 70% alcohol, 1% aqueous iodine, chlorine compounds and phenolics in category (b) and low-level disinfectants such as QACs and chlorhexidine in category (c). It is again noticeable, however, that the only mycobacterial species included in this scheme is the tubercle bacillus. This doubtless represents its clinical importance in the hospital environment, but other mycobacteria are also important pathogens and their sensitivity or resistance to biocides must also be considered. Depending on its concentration, alcohol is tuberculocidal (Smith, 1947) and might enhance the activity of other agents.

It is not the purpose of this paper to review the different types of test methods for evaluating mycobactericidal activity. This is the subject of a number of recent papers (Sonntag, 1978; Schleiser, 1979; AFNOR, 1981; Borneff *et al.*, 1981; Parkinson, 1981; AOAC, 1984; Lind *et al.*, 1986; Ascenzi *et al.*, 1986, 1987; F.M. Collins, 1986a,b; Quinn, 1987; van Klingeren & Pullen, 1987; Eigener, 1988; Isenberg *et al.*, 1988). Rather, it is the information obtained about mycobactericidal activity allied to the comparative sensitivity or resistance of various types of mycobacteria to a particular biocide that is important. It is also pertinent to point out, however, that conclusions as to efficacy may depend upon the technique employed, and that authors do not always discuss procedural problems (such as cell clumping) and ways of overcoming them.

Recent studies on mycobactericidal activity of various biocides have demonstrated that 2% alkaline glutaraldehyde is effective against *M. tuberculosis*, *M. smegmatis*, *M. fortuitum* and *M. terrae* (Collins & Montalbine, 1976; F.M. Collins, 1986a,b; van Klingeren & Pullen, 1987) although Carson *et al.* (1978) noted a variation in resistance of strains to formaldehyde and glutaraldehyde, and found that strains of *M. fortuitum* and *M. chelonei* in CDW (commercial distilled water) were very resistant to chlorine. The MAIS group undoubtedly presents a higher resistance to glutaraldehyde (Collins, 1986b; Hanson, 1988) than does *M. tuberculosis*. In accordance with earlier findings (Borick *et al.*, 1964; Borick, 1968; Miner *et al.*, 1977), this important biocide (Russell & Hopwood, 1976; Gorman *et al.*, 1980; Russell & Hugo, 1987) can now be considered as being a tuberculocidal agent (J. Collins, 1986; Cole *et al.*, 1990). Phenolics are also mycobactericidal (Richards & Thoen, 1979); chlorhexidine inhibits growth of some mycobacteria but is not lethal (Fodor & Szabo, 1980).

Nevertheless, it is still apparent that additional studies are necessary with typical and atypical mycobacterial strains and a wider range of agents. According to Ascenzi *et al.* (1986, 1987) a QAC has a similar tuberculocidal activity to 2% glutaraldehyde, and this claim requires re-investigation (cf. Merkal & Whipple, 1980). An interesting point made by these authors, however, was the influence of the recovery medium on the apparent numbers of survivors of glutaraldehyde-treated *M. bovis*.

Noteworthy omissions from the list of mycobactericidal agents are hydrogen peroxide and other peroxygens. These important biocides (Baldry & Fraser, 1988) are not mentioned by Rubin (1983) or Baldry & Fraser (1988) in connection with any mycobactericidal activity, although they are sporicidal (Russell, 1990).

A summary of the mycobactericidal activity or otherwise of different biocides is provided in Table 10.5. Differences of opinion are occasionally expressed by different authors. There is very little information available about the mechanisms of action of mycobactericides, and it must not be assumed that the pattern of inactivation is the same as with non-acid-fast, non-sporulating bacteria. This is an area in which extra data would be useful.

3 MECHANISMS OF BIOCIDE RESISTANCE

It is clear from the preceding section that mycobacteria are much more resistant than other non-sporing bacteria to a variety of biocides, but that differences in sensitivity exist between different mycobacterial species. Evidence was put forward several years ago (Chargaff *et al.*, 1931) that resistance to QACs was related to the lipid content of the cell wall, since *M. phlei* (with low total lipid) was more sensitive than *M. tuberculosis* which possessed a higher total cell lipid content. Croshaw (1971) quotes the work of T.H. Shen who, in 1934, found that the resistance of various species of mycobacteria was related to the content of waxy material in the wall.

Solvent-extractable free lipids account for about 25–30% of the weight of mycobacterial cell walls (Petit & Lederer, 1978) and it is likely that the

Table 10.5 Mycobactericidal activity of biocides as described by various authors

Antibacterial	Mycobacterial susceptibility (S) or resistance (R)	Comment	Reference*
Alcohol	S		1,2
	S	Reduced in presence of sputum	4
Chlorhexidine	R		1,3,4
Ethylene oxide	S		1,2,3
Formaldehyde	Moderately S		1
	S?		2
	S	In presence or absence of alcohol	3
	S	Alcoholic solutions	4
Glutaraldehyde†	Moderately S		1
	Generally S		2
	S		3
	S or R	Unproven (1971 ref.)	4
Hypochlorites	Moderately S		1
	S		3
	Moderately R		4
Iodophors†	S		1,2,3
	Moderately S	Rather more so than chlorine compounds	4
Phenols	S		1,2,3,4
QACs	R		1,2,3
	R	Highly inhibitory	4

* References: 1, Gardner & Peel (1986); 2, Rubin (1983); 3, Favero (1985); 4, Croshaw (1971)
† See text also.

lipid-rich, hydrophobic layers of the cell wall are responsible for acid-fastness (Fisher & Barksdale, 1973; Barksdale & Kim, 1977) and for resistance to many biocides (Middlebrook, 1965). These layers presumably act as a permeability barrier to the intracellular entry of many biocides (David *et al.*, 1988; Sareen & Khuller, 1990). Solutions containing a high concentration of soap or other suitable detergent are considered to penetrate the waxy coat (Hegna, 1977).

Nevertheless, many questions remain. (1) Why is glutaraldehyde tuberculocidal? Does alkaline glutaraldehyde penetrate the waxy cell wall or is its cross-linking effect on amino groups sufficient to explain its action? (2) How do other mycobactericidal agents pass through the wall? (3) Are differences in the amount and/or composition of lipid responsible for differing responses to biocides (as suggested by Chargaff *et al.*, 1931)? (4) Is it possible to use a permeabilizing agent (similar to ethylenediamine tetraacetate and Gram-negative bacteria) to enhance the mycobactericidal activity of various antibacterial agents? In this context, it is pertinent to note that spheroplasts and L-forms of mycobacteria can be produced under specified conditions (Willett & Thacore, 1966, 1967). These modified cell wall forms might be useful in studying mechanisms of mycobacterial resistance to biocides.

Mycobacteria are still important human pathogens (Section 4). Potent disinfectants that prevent the risk of spreading of infection are thus essential in the hospital environment, and possibly elsewhere. For details of mycobactericidal testing, see Ascenzi (1991).

4 CLINICAL AND MEDICAL USES OF MYCOBACTERICIDAL AGENTS

Disinfectants are widely used for various purposes in the hospital environment (Ayliffe *et al.*, 1984). In some specific instances, activity against mycobacteria is essential (Favero, 1985). Heat is undoubtedly the most effective method for destroying mycobacteria, which are not especially heat-resistant, and should always be employed if possible. Sterilization or disinfection by heat is not always practicable, however, notably when delicate items of equipment that would be damaged by heat are being used.

A classic example of this occurs with endoscopes. These must be decontaminated effectively and rapidly (Felmingham *et al.*, 1985; Ridgway, 1985). Collignon & Graham (1989) have pointed out that even resistant organisms such as mycobacteria and bacterial spores are likely to be killed by a disinfectant time for endoscopes of 5 min between patients, because of the low number present after effective cleaning. *M. tuberculosis* has been transmitted via a fibreoptic bronchoscope (Leers, 1980) but has not been reported via gastrointestinal endoscopes (Ridgway, 1985; Ayliffe, 1988). The disinfectant of choice is 2% alkaline glutaraldehyde, although this agent is by no means ideal. Uptake of glutaraldehyde to endoscopes can result (Power & Russell, 1989) and it is possible that—despite a subsequent rinse in sterile saline or water—release of aldehyde inside a patient could occur. Moreover, the disinfection period is often extremely short, to enable rapid turnover of a limited number of endoscopes in an endoscopy unit. Glutaraldehyde is also potentially toxic to personnel. Other biocides are usually unsuitable, because of (a) corrosive properties, e.g. chlorine disinfectants, or (b) lack of suitable antibacterial activity, e.g. chlorhexidine, and antiseptic-strength iodophors (Favero, 1985). The clear-soluble phenolics show activity against *M. tuberculosis* and are considered to be suitable for the disinfection of rooms occupied by patients with open tuberculosis.

George (1988) has listed the main requirements for preventing hospital-acquired tuberculosis as being (a) an occupational health scheme, (b) constant vigilance by staff and (c) the implementation of appropriate policies, *viz.* isolation of patients, control of infection and disinfection.

5 REFERENCES

AFNOR (1981) *Association Française de Normalisation.* Recueils de Normes Françaises des Antiseptiques et Désinfectants, 1st Ed.

AOAC (1984) *Official Methods of Analysis of the Association of Official Analytical Chemists*, 14th Ed. Washington, DC.

Ascenzi, J.M. (1991) Standardization of tuberculocidal testing of disinfectants. *Journal of Hospital Infection*, **18**, *Supplement A*, 256–263.

Ascenzi, J.M., Ezzell, R.J. & Wendt, T.M. (1986) Evaluation of carriers used in the test methods of the Association of Official Analytical Chemists. *Applied and Environmental Microbiology*, **51**, 91–94.

Ascenzi, J.M., Ezzell, R.J. & Wendt, R.M. (1987) A more accurate method for measurement of tuberculocidal activity of disinfectants. *Applied and Environmental Microbiology*, **53**, 2189–2192.

Ayliffe, G.A.J. (1988) Equipment-related infection risks. *Journal of Hospital Infection*, **11**, Supplement A, 279–284.

Ayliffe, G.A.J., Coates, D. & Hoffman, P.N. (1984) *Chemical Disinfection in Hospitals*. London: Public Health Laboratory.

Baldry, M.G.C. & Fraser, J.A.L. (1988) Disinfection with peroxygens. In *Industrial Biocides* (ed. Payne, K.R.) Critical Reports on Applied Chemistry, Vol. 23, pp. 91–116. Chichester: John Wiley & Sons.

Barksdale, L. & Kim, K.S. (1977) Mycobacterium. *Bacteriological Reviews*, **41**, 217–372.

Bergan, T. & Lystad, A. (1971) Antitubercular action of disinfectants. *Journal of Applied Bacteriology*, **34**, 751–756.

Best, M., Sattar, S.A., Springthorpe, V.S. & Kennedy, M.E. (1990) Efficacies of selected disinfectants against *Mycobacterium tuberculosis*. *Journal of Clinical Microbiology*, **28**, 2234–2239.

Borick, P.M. (1968) Chemical sterilizers (chemosterilizers). *Advances in Applied Microbiology*, **10**, 291–312.

Borick, P.M., Dondershine, F.H. & Chandler, V.L. (1964) Alkalinized glutaraldehyde, a new antimicrobial agent. *Journal of Pharmaceutical Sciences*, **53**, 1273–1275.

Borneff, J., Eggers, H.-J., Grün, L., Gundermann, K.-O., Kuwert, E., Lammers, T., Primavesi, C.A., Rotter, M., Schmidt-Lorenz, W., Schubert, R., Sonntag, H.-G., Spicher, G., Teuber, M., Thofern, E., Weinhold, E. & Werner, H.-P. (1981) Richtlinien für die Prüfung und Bewertung chemischer Desinfektionsverfahren. *Zentralblatt fûr Bakteriologie, Mikrobiologie und Hygiene*, **B172**, 534–562.

Carson, L.A., Petersen, J., Favero, M.S. & Aguero, S.M. (1978) Growth characteristics of atypical mycobacteria in water and their comparative resistance to disinfectants. *Applied and Environmental Microbiology*, **36**, 839–846.

Chargaff, E., Pangborn, M.C. & Anderson, R.J. (1931) The chemistry of the lipoids of tubercle bacilli. XXIII. Separation of the lipoid fractions from the Timothy bacillus. *Journal of Biological Chemistry*, **90**, 45–55.

Cole, E.C., Rutala, W.A., Nessen, L., Wannamaker, N.S. & Weber, D.J. (1990) Effect of methodology, dilution and exposure time on the tuberculocidal activity of glutaraldehyde-based disinfectants. *Applied and Environmental Microbiology*, **56**, 1813–1817.

Collignon, P. & Graham, E. (1989) How well are endoscopes disinfected between patients? *Medical Journal of Australia*, **151**, 269–272.

Collins, C.H., Grange, I.M. & Yates, M.D. (1984) Mycobacteria in water. *Journal of Applied Bacteriology*, **57**, 193–211.

Collins, F.M. (1986a) Kinetics of the tuberculocidal response by alkaline glutaraldehyde in solution and on an inert surface. *Journal of Applied Bacteriology*, **61**, 87–93.

Collins, F.M. (1986b) Bactericidal activity of alkaline glutaraldehyde solution against a number of atypical mycobacterial species. *Journal of Applied Bacteriology*, **61**, 247–251.

Collins, F.M. (1989) Mycobacterial disease, immunosuppression, and acquired immunodeficiency syndrome. *Clinical Microbiology Reviews*, **2**, 360–377.

Collins, F.M. & Montalbine, V. (1976) Mycobactericidal activity of glutaraldehyde solutions. *Journal of Clinical Microbiology*, **4**, 408–412.

Collins, J. (1986) The use of glutaraldehyde in laboratory discard jars. *Letters in Applied Microbiology*, **2**, 103–105.

Croshaw, B. (1971) The destruction of mycobacteria. In *Inhibition and Destruction of the Microbial Cell* (ed. Hugo, W.B.) pp. 429–449. London: Academic Press.

Damsker, B. & Bottone, E.U.J. (1985) *Mycobacterium avium-Mycobacterium intracellulare* from the intestinal tracts of patients with acquired immunodeficiency syndrome: concepts regarding acquisition and pathogenesis. *Journal of Infectious Diseases*, **151**, 179–181.

David, H.L., Rastogi, N., Seres, C.L. & Clement, F. (1988) Alterations in the outer wall architecture caused by the inhibition of mycoside C biosynthesis in *Mycobacterium avium*. *Current Microbiology*, **17**, 61–68.

Draper, P. (1988) Wall biosynthesis: a possible site of action for new antimycobacterial drugs. *International Journal of Leprosy*, **52**, 527–532.

Eigener, U. (1988) Disinfectant testing and its relevance in practical application. In *Industrial Biocides* (ed. Payne, K.R.) Critical Reports on Applied Chemistry, Vol. 23, pp. 37–51. Chichester: John Wiley & Sons.

Favero, M.S. (1985) Sterilization, disinfection and antisepsis in the hospital. In *Manual of Clinical Microbiology*, 4th Ed. (eds Lennette, E.H., Balows, A., Hausler, W.J. Jr & Shadomy, H.J.) pp. 129–137. Washington, DC: American Society for Microbiology.

Felmingham, D., Mowles, J., Thomas, K. & Ridgway, G.L. (1985) Disinfection of gastro-intestinal fibreoptic endoscopes. *Journal of Hospital Infection*, **6**, 379–388.

Fisher, C.A. & Barksdale, L. (1973) Cytochemical reactions of human leprosy bacilli and mycobacteria: ultrastructural implications. *Journal of Bacteriology*, **113**, 1389–1399.

Fodor, T. & Szabo, I. (1980) Effect of chlorhexidine gluconate on the survival of acid-free bacteria. *Acta Microbiologica*, **27**, 343–344.

Gardner, J.F. & Peel, M.M. (1986) *Introduction to Sterilization and Disinfection*. Edinburgh: Churchill Livingstone.

George, R.H. (1988) The prevention and control of mycobacterial infections in hospitals. *Journal of Hospital Infection*, **11**, Supplement A, 386–392.

Gorman, S.P., Scott, E.M. & Russell, A.D. (1980) Antimicrobial activity uses and mechanism of action of glutaraldehyde. *Journal of Applied Bacteriology*, **48**, 161–190.

Goslee, S. & Wolinsky, E. (1976) Water as a source of potentially pathogenic mycobacteria. *American Review of Respiratory Diseases*, **113**, 287–292.

Grange, J.M., Yates, M.D. & Broughton, E. (1990) The avian tubercle bacillus and its relatives. *Journal of Applied Bacteriology*, **68**, 411–431.

Guthertz, L.S., Damsker, B., Bottone, E.J., Ford, E.G., Midura, T.F. & Janda, J.M. (1989) *Mycobacterium avium* and *Mycobacterium intracellulare* infections in patients with and without AIDS. *Journal of Infectious Diseases*, **160**, 1037–1041.

Hanson, P.J.V. (1988) Mycobacteria and AIDS. *British Journal of Hospital Medicine*, **40**, 149.

Hegna, I.K. (1977) An examination of the effects of three phenolic disinfectants on *Mycobacterium tuberculosis*. *Journal of Applied Bacteriology*, **43**, 183–187.

Hirsch, J.G. (1954) The resistance of tubercle bacilli to the bactericidal action of benzalkonium chloride (Zephiran). *American Review of Tuberculosis*, **70**, 312–319.

Isenberg, H.D., Giugliano, E.R., France, K. & Alperstein, P. (1988) Evaluation of three disinfectants after in-use stress. *Journal of Hospital Infection*, **11**, 278–285.

Jensen, A.G., Bennedsen, J. & Rosdahl, V.T. (1989) Plasmid profiles of *Mycobacterium avium/intracellulare* isolated from patients with AIDS or cervical lymphadenitis and from environmental samples. *Scandinavian Journal of Infectious Diseases*, **21**, 645–649.

Leers, W.D. (1980) Disinfecting endoscopes: how not to transmit *Mycobacterium tuberculosis* by bronchoscopy. *Canadian Medical Association Journal*, **123**, 275–283.

Lind, A., Lundholm, M., Pedersen, G., Sundaeus, V. & Wahlen, P. (1986) A carrier method for the assessment of the effectiveness of disinfectants against *Mycobacterium tuberculosis*. *Journal of Hospital Infection*, **7**, 60–67.

Merkal, R.S. & Whipple, D.L. (1980) Inactivation of *Mycobacterium bovis* in meat products. *Applied & Environmental Microbiology*, **40**, 282–284.

Middlebrook, G. (1965) The mycobacteria. In *Bacterial and Mycotic Infections of Man* (eds Dubos, R.J. & Hirsch, J.G.) 4th Ed., pp. 490–530. London: Pitman Medical.

Miner, N.A., McDowell, J.W., Willcockson, G.W., Bruckner, I., Stark, R.L. & Whitmore, E.J. (1977) Antimicrobial and other properties of a new stabilized alkaline glutaraldehyde disinfectant/sterilizer. *American Journal of Hospital Pharmacy*, **34**, 376–382.

Parkinson, E. (1981) Testing of disinfectants for veterinary and agricultural use. In *Disinfectants: Their Use and Evaluation of Effectiveness* (eds Collins, C.H., Allwood, M.C., Bloomfield, S.F. & Fox, A.) pp. 33–36. London: Academic Press.

Patterson, R.A., Thompson, T.L. & Larsen, D.H. (1956) The use of Zephiran in the isolation of *M. tuberculosis*. *American Review of Tuberculosis*, **74**, 284–288.

Petit, J.-F. & Lederer, E. (1978) Structure and immunostimulant properties of mycobacterial cell walls. *Symposium of the Society for General Microbiology*, **28**, 177–199.

Power, E.G.M. & Russell, A.D. (1989) Glutaraldehyde: its uptake by sporing and non-sporing bacteria, rubber, plastic and an endoscope. *Journal of Applied Bacteriology*, **67**, 329–342.

Quinn, P.J. (1987) Evaluation of veterinary disinfectants and disinfection processes. In *Disinfection in Veterinary and Farm Animal Practice* (eds Linton, A.H., Hugo, W.B. & Russell, A.D.) pp. 66–116. Oxford: Blackwell Scientific Publications.

Ratledge, C. & Stanford, J. (eds) (1982) *The Biology of the Mycobacteria*. Vol. 1: *Physiology, Identification and Classification*. London: Academic Press.

Richards, W.D. & Thoen, C.O. (1979) Chemical destruction of *Mycobacterium bovis* in milk. *Journal of Food Protection*, **42**, 55–57.

Ridgway, G.L. (1985) Decontamination of fibreoptic endoscopes. *Journal of Hospital Infection*, **6**, 363–368.

Rubbo, S.D. & Gardner, J.F. (1965) *A Review of Sterilization and Disinfection*. London: Lloyd-Luke.

Rubbo, S.D., Gardner, J.F. & Webb, R.L. (1967) Biocidal activities of glutaraldehyde and related compounds. *Journal of Applied Bacteriology*, **30**, 78–87.

Rubin, J. (1983) Agents for disinfection and control of tuberculosis. In *Disinfection, Sterilization and Preservation* (ed. Block, S.S.) 3rd Ed. pp. 414–421. Philadelphia: Lea & Febiger.

Russell, A.D. (1990) The effect of chemical and physical agents on microbes: disinfection and sterilization. In *Topley & Wilson's Principles of Bacteriology and Immunity*, 8th Ed. (eds Linton, A.H. & Dick, H.M.) pp. 71–103. London: Edward Arnold.

Russell, A.D. (1991) Principles of antimicrobial activity. In *Disinfection, Sterilization and Preservation* (ed. Block, S.S.) 4th Ed. (In press.) Philadelphia: Lea & Febiger.

Russell, A.D. & Hopwood, D. (1976) The biological uses and importance of glutaraldehyde. *Progress in Medicinal Chemistry*, **13**, 271–301.

Russell, A.D. & Hugo, W.B. (1987) Chemical disinfectants. In *Disinfection in Veterinary and Farm Animal Practice* (eds Linton, A.H., Hugo, W.B. & Russell, A.D.) pp. 12–42. Oxford: Blackwell Scientific Publications.

Sareen, M. & Khuller, G.K. (1990) Cell wall composition of ethambutol susceptible and resistant strains of *Mycobacterium smegmatis* ATCC 607. *Letters in Applied Microbiology*, **11**, 7–10.

Schliesser, Th. (1979) Testing of chemical disinfectants for veterinary medicine. *Hygiene & Medizin*, **4**, 51–56.

Smith, C.R. (1947) Alcohol as a disinfectant against the tubercle bacillus. *Public Health Reports, Washington*, **62**, 1285–1295.

Sonntag, H.G. (1978) Desinfektionsverfahren bei tuberculose. *Hygiene & Medizin*, **3**, 322–325.

Spaulding, E.H. (1972) Chemical disinfection and antisepsis in the hospital. *Journal of Hospital Research*, **9**, 5–31.

Spaulding, E.H., Cundy, K.R. & Turner, F.J. (1977) Chemical disinfection of medical and surgical materials. In *Disinfection, Sterilization and Preservation*, 2nd Ed. (ed. Block, S.S.) pp. 654–684. Philadelphia: Lea & Febiger.

van Klingeren, B. & Pullen, W. (1987) Comparative testing of disinfectants against *Mycobacterium tuberculosis* and *Mycobacterium terrae* in a quantitative suspension test. *Journal of Hospital Infection*, **10**, 292–298.

Wayne, L.G. (1985) The 'atypical' mycobacteria: recognition and disease association. *Critical Reviews in Microbiology*, **12**, 185–222.

Willett, H.P. & Thacore, H. (1966) The induction by lysozyme of an L-type growth in *Mycobacterium tuberculosis*. *Canadian Journal of Microbiology*, **12**, 11–16.

Willett, H.P. & Thacore, H. (1967) Formation of spheroplasts of *Mycobacterium tuberculosis* by lysozyme in combination with certain enzymes of rabbit peritoneal monocytes. *Canadian Journal of Microbiology*, **13**, 481–488.

Wolinsky, E. (1979) Nontuberculous mycobacteria and associated diseases. *American Review of Respiratory Diseases*, **119**, 107–159.

E·LEGIONELLA

1 INTRODUCTION

Legionella first came to public prominence in 1977 when it was identified as the causative agent of an outbreak of pneumonia that had affected people in the vicinity of a Philadelphia hotel (McDade *et al.*, 1977). The disease had primarily affected delegates at an American Legions Annual Convention, and it is after these legionnaires that both the genus and the disease were named. *Legionella pneumophila* is the most notorious of the legionellae.

Following the initial identification, retrospective serological studies showed that it had been responsible for disease outbreaks going back to 1965 (Thacker *et al.*, 1978) and the new genus created was shown to contain species isolated as far back as 1947 (McDade *et al.*, 1979).

2 ISOLATION AND CULTIVATION

The organism was originally isolated by guinea pig inoculation followed by transfer to the yolk sac of fertile hens' eggs (McDade *et al.*, 1977). Later it was shown that the organism could be grown on bacteriological culture media (Feeley *et al.*, 1978). A major breakthrough, however, was the development of charcoal yeast extract agar (CYE) supplemented with L-cysteine and ferric pyrophosphate (Feeley *et al.*, 1979).

The charcoal probably functions in scavenging toxic oxygen radicals that are produced when the yeast extract agar is exposed to light. The addition of ACES buffer increases the buffering capacity of the medium to give buffered charcoal yeast extract agar (BCYE). The further addition of α-ketoglutarate improved recovery and gave faster initial growth rates. This medium is termed BCYEα agar (Edelstein, 1981).

The BCYE agars have proved very successful in the routine culturing of legionellae. For the examination of environmental samples, however, selective media have been developed. This has been achieved by including antibiotics in BCYE (Wadowski & Yee, 1981) to inhibit the growth of other environmental bacteria.

In addition, several selective techniques have been developed to increase the selectivity of the isolation procedure. These include an acid pretreatment of the sample using a pH 2.2 buffer for 5 min (Bopp *et al.*, 1981) and a heat treatment at 50°C for 30 min (Dennis *et al.*, 1984a). These methods have been shown to be successful but some variation is evident between techniques used (Roberts *et al.*, 1987).

3 TAXONOMY

The genus *Legionella* belongs to the family Legionellaceae and contains some 30 species, many of which can be subdivided into serogroups and subgroups (Harrison & Taylor, 1988). They are Gram-negative non-acid-fast motile rod-shaped bacteria. Most species are capable of liquefying gelatin and are catalase-positive (Isenberg, 1979). Some species exhibit autofluorescence (Hoffman, 1984), may be weakly oxidase-positive, hydrolyse sodium hippurate and produce a soluble brown pigment on Feeley–Gorman agar (Lattimer & Ormsbee, 1981). Many strains produce β-lactamase, which may explain why β-lactam antibiotics are not clinically effective (Thornsberry & Kirven, 1978). A range of these biochemical tests have been utilized in routine identification of the organism (Vesey *et al.*, 1988) but more typically isolates are identified by their characteristic fatty acid or ubiquinone composition (Wait, 1988) or by the use of specific serological methods such as indirect or direct immunofluorescence (Harrison & Taylor, 1988). DNA homology studies are also used in the classification of strains (Brenner *et al.*, 1984).

4 LEGIONELLA AND DISEASE

There are several clinically distinct diseases caused by *Legionella* species. These include Pontiac fever, Pittsburg pneumonia and the most serious, legionnaires' disease. Legionnaires' disease is a potentially severe pneumonia-type condition whereas Pontiac fever is a non-pneumonic, non-fatal illness of short duration. Pittsburg pneumonia appears similar to legionnaires' disease but is caused by *L. micdadei* (Rudin *et al.*, 1984). Susceptibility to legionnaires' disease is known to be enhanced by such factors as smoking, use of immunosuppressive drugs and alcoholism, and males are more susceptible than females (Anon, 1981). Once diagnosed, treatment for legionellosis is by erythromycin and rifampicin (Lattimer & Ormsbee, 1981). Infection occurs not by person-to-person spread but by inhalation of infected water droplets.

4.1 Occurrence

Legionellae are ubiquitous in aquatic habitats and have been regularly isolated from both man-made and natural environments (Fliermans *et al.*, 1979, 1981). The man-made systems include hot and cold water supplies (Hsu *et al.*, 1984), shower heads (Bollin *et al.*, 1985), whirlpool baths (Vogt *et al.*, 1987), specialist medical equipment (Moiraghi *et al.*, 1987), humidifiers (Tobin *et al.*, 1981) and cooling towers (Tobin *et al.*, 1981; Witherall *et al.*, 1984).

Several surveys in the United Kingdom have indicated the prevalence of the bacterium in water systems. One survey has reported the isolation of legionellae from 25 of 46 establishments examined. At these 46 sites, 86 discrete cooling water systems were identified, of which 34 were positive (Bartlett *et al.*, 1985). Other surveys outside the United Kingdom have confirmed the ubiquity of the organism in water systems (Ikedo & Yabuuchi, 1986; Tobin *et al.*, 1986).

5 CONTROL OF LEGIONELLA

Legionellae can enter both domestic waters and cooling systems by seeding from low-level contamination in feed-water supplies (Hsu *et al.*, 1984). The primary measures to control legionellosis therefore involve prevention of the organism growing and multiplying within the system, and minimizing the possibilities of producing and disseminating aerosols.

5.1 Domestic water systems

In domestic systems control of legionellae growth may be achieved by a combination of good design, construction and maintenance. This includes the use of suitable constructional materials which do not support the growth of legionella (Anon., 1989) and the elimination of dead-legs and stagnant areas. The water systems should be operated whenever possible at temperatures unfavourable to the growth of legionellae (Dennis *et al.*, 1984b). Cold water supplies should be maintained below 20°C and hot water calorifiers should reach a temperature of 60°C (Anon, 1987). Hot and cold water pipes should not run alongside one another, and hot water should reach the outlet at not below 50°C. Where these conditions cannot be met, or where there is a risk of scalding, point-of-use heating should be considered.

Potable water supplies are chlorinated in the United Kingdom but little if any residual chlorine is detectable at the point of use. Chlorine may be used to disinfect contaminated water systems or pasteurization may be considered in the case of hot water systems.

Reports vary on the efficacy of chlorine against legionellae, some sources stating that they are as sensitive to chlorine as *Escherichia coli* (Hsu *et al.*, 1984), whilst others report legionella to be more resistant than *E. coli* (Berg *et al.*, 1984, Kuchta *et al.*, 1983). *L. pneumophila* grown in continuous culture exhibits greater chlorine resistance than batch-grown organisms (Berg *et al.*, 1984) and resistant strains have been developed by culturing tap water adapted legionellae (Kuchta *et al.*, 1985). Legionellae have been isolated from systems treated with residual chlorine levels of 7.5 ppm (Tobin *et al.*, 1986) and even hyperchlorination has failed to eradicate *L. pneumophila* (Tobin *et al.*, 1980).

Ultraviolet light has been proposed as an alternative control method in hospital water distribution systems (Muraca *et al.*, 1987).

5.2 Recirculating water systems

These systems include cooling towers (which may be induced-draught (Fig. 10.7), forced-draught or natural-draught), evaporative condensers and humidification systems, and are all prone to microbial growth. Generally humidification systems are operated at temperatures below that required for

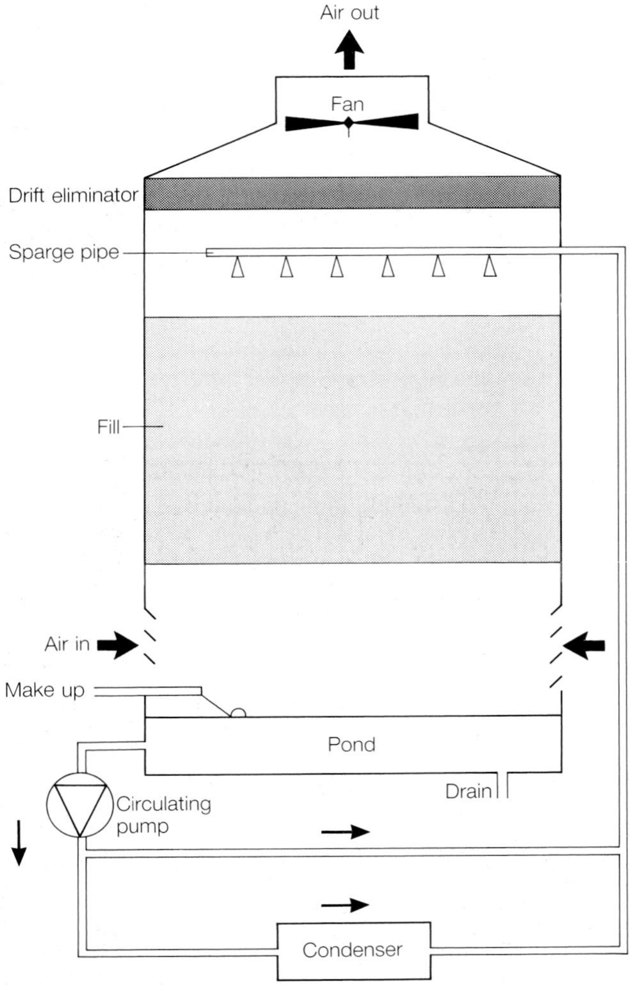

Fig. 10.7 Schematic diagram of an induced-draught cooling tower.

the growth of legionellae and biocides are not routinely used when the systems are in use, as the biocide would be introduced into the conditioned air. Biocides are, however, used in cooling towers and evaporative condensers to control biofouling (Fig. 10.8). This enables the efficient operation of the cooling system as biological growth and slimes can lead to reduced heat transfer, increased pumping costs, microbially induced corrosion and the degradation of water treatment chemicals such as corrosion inhibitors and descalants. Severe microbial growth can even produce structural damage: Figure 10.9 shows a cooling tower which has collapsed due to the sheer weight of biofouling.

Many of the industrial biocides used in recirculating water systems have been tested for activity against *L. pneumophila* in laboratory studies (Table 10.6). There is some evidence that *L. pneumophila* is less sensitive than *E. coli* to certain biocides, having a sensitivity similar to *Pseudomonas aeruginosa* (Hollis & Smalley, 1980; Cunliffe, 1990). Biocides tested for activity include chlorine (Skaliy *et al.*, 1980; Sorraco *et al.*, 1983; Kobayashi & Tsuzuki, 1984; Sawatari *et al.*, 1984), isothiazolinones (Skaliy *et al.*, 1980; Sorraco *et al.*, 1983; Sawatari *et al.*, 1984; Elsmore, 1986; McCoy *et al.*, 1986), quaternary ammonium compounds (Skaliy *et al.*, 1980; Grace *et al.*, 1981; Sorraco *et al.*, 1983; Elsmore, 1986), dibromonitrilo propionamide

Fig. 10.8 Photograph of tube and shell heat exchanger showing heavy microbial fouling.

Fig. 10.9 Photograph of part of an open recirculating evaporative cooling tower showing structural damage due to biofouling.

Table 10.6 Minimum inhibitory concentrations* of several water treatment biocides against *Legionella* species (Elsmore, 1986)[†].

Biocide	*L. pneumophila* NCTC 11192	NCTC 11378	NCTC 11405	NCTC 11417	Clinical isolate	Environmental isolate	*L. micdadei* NCTC 11371	*L. oakridgensis* Environmental isolate	*L. longbeachae* NCTC 11477	*L. gormanii* NCTC 11401	*L. bozmanii* *NCTC 11368*	*L. jordanis* NCTC 11533
2-Bromo-2-nitro-propane-1,3-diol (BNPD)	50	50	50	50	50	50	50	50	50	50	50	100
Blend of isothiazolinones	56	56	28	28	28	28	28	56	28	28	28	56
Methylene bisthiocyanate	100	50	100	50	50	50	100	100	50	50	25	100
Chlorinated phenolic thioether	20	20	20	20	20	20	20	20	20	20	20	20
2,2-Dibromo-3-nitrilo propionamide	800	800	400	200	200	200	800	200	100	200	200	400
Sodium dichlorophen	25	25	100	25	25	25	25	25	25	25	25	25
Cationic polyquaternary ammonium compound	800	800	800	800	800	800	400	400	400	400	800	400
Disodium mercaptobenzo-thiazole	72	72	>576	72	72	72	576	72	72	36	72	576
Dioctyl dimethylammonium chloride	50	50	50	50	50	50	25	50	50	50	25	50
2-(Thiocyanomethylthio) benzothiazole	30	60	240	30	60	30	60	60	30	30	30	60
Paracetic acid	200	200	200	200	200	200	200	200	200	200	200	200
Tetraalkyl phosphonium chloride	12.5	12.5	12.5	12.5	6.25	12.5	6.25	12.5	12.5	12.5	12.5	25

* Concentration expressed as ppm active ingredient.
[†] Results are from multipoint MIC test carried out in BCYE agar. Note that BCYE may inactivate some of the biocides tested, e.g. BNPD is antagonized by cysteine hydrochloride, a component of the medium.
NCTC, National Collection of Type Cultures.

(Skaliy *et al.*, 1980; Hollis & Smalley, 1980; Sorraco *et al.*, 1983; Elsmore, 1986), dichlorophen (Kobayashi & Tsuzuki, 1984; Elsmore, 1986), thiocarbamates (Hollis & Smalley, 1980; Skaliy *et al.*, 1980; Sorraco *et al.*, 1983), sodium pentachlorophenate (Sorraco *et al*, 1983), methylene bisthiocyanate (Grace *et al.*, 1981), 2-(thiocyanomethylthio) benzthiazole (Elsmore, 1986), *N*-alkyl-1,3-propanediamine (Grace *et al.*, 1981), bromochlorodimethylhydantoin (McCoy & Wireman, 1989), 2-bromo-2-nitropropane-1,3-diol (Sawatari *et al.*, 1984; Elsmore, 1986; Coughlin & Caplan, 1987), and several others.

The significance of the presence of biofilms in the testing of biocides is becoming more important. It has been shown that biofilms can provide protection to micro-organisms (LeChevalier *et al.*, 1988) and also that *L. pneumophila* can grow in biofilms (Colbourne & Dennis, 1988). In addition to suspension tests the use of biofilm generators and recirculating models has been examined for evaluating biocides against legionellae (Elsmore 1986; Coughlin & Caplan, 1987).

Extrapolation from these laboratory studies to in-use applications may not be realistic because of factors such as possible interaction with other water treatment chemicals and inactivation by large amounts of slime. This has been indicated by several workers who have shown that compounds which were deemed to be effective in a laboratory were less than effective in use (England *et al.*, 1982; Orrison *et al.*, 1981). To date, few extensive field studies have been published on the activity of biocides against *L. pneumophila* in recirculating water applications (Fliermans *et al.*, 1982; Kurtz *et al.*, 1982, 1984; Fliermans & Harvey, 1984; Grow *et al.*, 1984; Elsmore, 1986; Coughlin & Caplan, 1987; Elsmore *et al.*, 1987; Muraca *et al.*, 1988; Negron-Alvira *et al.*, 1988).

5.3 Assessment of activity

No standard method exists for the evaluation of biocides against legionellae. The report of the Expert Advisory Committee on biocides (Wright, 1989) recommends that 'The preparation of a standard procedure should be expedited for the assessment of the efficacy of biocides against legionellae.' In addition the report advocates field trials in cooling towers to establish the efficacy of different classes of biocides and the role of continuous or intermittent treatment.

5.4 Factors affecting biocide activity in recirculating water systems

Several factors can affect biocidal activity; these include pH, temperature, concentration and the presence of organic matter, e.g. slimes (see also Chapter 3). Figure 10.10 shows the effect of pH on the activity of one biocide (BNPD) against *L. pneumophila* NCTC 11192 in a suspension test. It is known that the stability of the compound is reduced at alkaline pH with the half-life decreasing from 1.5 years at pH 6 to 2 months at pH 8 (Croshaw & Holland, 1984). The relationship between activity and pH is more complex; Croshaw *et al.* (1964) reported that the activity of BNPD fell two to eight times when the pH was increased from 5.3 to 7 or 8. Tuttle *et al.* (1970) indicated that in certain circumstances BNPD was more active under alkaline conditions and at others it was less active. Moore (1978) stated that the activity of BNPD is not markedly affected by changes in pH over the range of 5–8. Moore & Stretton (1981), however, did indicate that BNPD was more active at higher pH values, based on extinction time experiments using *Ps. aeruginosa*. The results obtained may vary depending on the method used because, in long contact time tests, the increasing degradation of the BNPD under alkaline conditions may be an important factor. It seems probable that, in the case of *L. pneumophila*, the further the pH varies from the optimum pH for growth (pH 6.9), the organism may become stressed and is thus more susceptible to any biocide that may be used (States *et al.*, 1987). The majority of recirculating cooling systems are operated at alkaline pH to optimize corrosion inhibition programmes.

5.5 Resistance to biocides

It is a well-known fact that under conditions of continuous use micro-organisms can become resistant to certain biocides. The Expert Advisory Committee on biocides (Wright, 1989) advises the

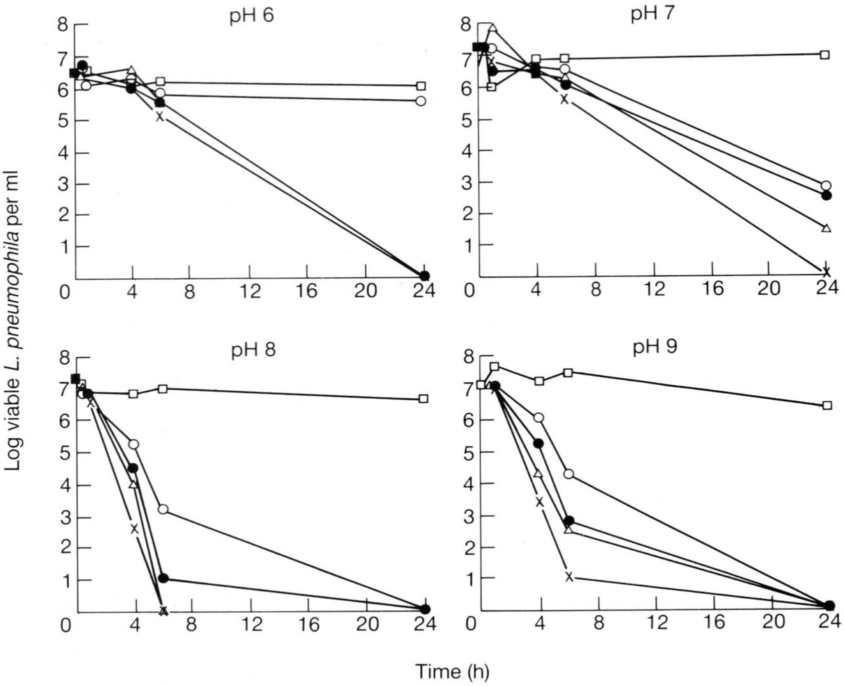

Fig. 10.10 Effect of pH on the activity of BNPD against *L. pneumophila* serogroup 1 (Elsmore, 1989). Tested in buffers of pHs of 6, 7, 8 and 9. □, Control (no BNPD); ○, 15 ppm BNPD; •, 25 ppm BNPD; △, 50 ppm BNPD; X, 100 ppm BNPD.

investigation of the possibility of resistance development by *Legionella* spp. to biocides. Furthermore, free-living amoebae have been involved with *L. pneumophila* from cooling water systems; when found within the cysts of *Acanthamoeba polyphaga*, the legionellae are protected and can survive exposure to high concentrations of chlorine (Kilvington & Price, 1990).

6 LEGIONELLA AND OTHER MICRO-ORGANISMS

It has been suggested that legionellae are more likely to be isolated from systems with high microbial counts (Elsmore *et al.*, 1989) and it would thus be prudent to maintain microbial counts as low as possible with biocide treatments active against a wide range of common water micro-organisms.

It has been postulated that the ability of legionellae to thrive in the natural environment is due to symbiotic-type relationships with other organisms. They have been associated with amoebae (Tyndall & Domingue, 1982; see also Section 5.5), cyanobacteria (Tison *et al.*, 1980), *Tetrahymena* (Fields *et al.*, 1984) and flavobacteria (Wadowski & Yee, 1983). It has therefore been suggested that if the overall microbial population can be controlled the growth of legionellae might be minimized (Anon, 1987).

7 CONCLUSION

Many biocides have been shown to be active against legionellae in the laboratory. With the development of standard test methods, more unified results will be obtainable for the assessment of biocide activity. However, direct extrapolation from these laboratory tests to in-use applications may not be valid due to interactions with water treatment chemicals and biofilms. Further testing should therefore be carried out to demonstrate if these factors will affect the activity of compounds in the field.

8 REFERENCES

Anon (1981) *Legionnaires' disease. Report on a WHO working group Euro Reports and Studies 72*, pp. 1–28. Copenhagen: World Health Organization.

Anon (1987) *Legionnaires' disease*, Guidance Note EH48 HSE, HMSO.

Anon (1989) *Water Fittings and Materials Directory*. Surrey: Unwin Brothers.

Bartlett, C.L.R., Hutchinson, J.G.P., Tillett, H.E., Turner G.C. & Wright, A.E. (1985) Final Report on a Public Health Laboratory Service Collaborative Study of *Legionella* species in Water Systems 1981–1985 (unpublished).

Berg, J.D., Hoff, J.C., Roberts, P.V. & Matin, A. (1984) Growth of *Legionella pneumophila* in continuous culture and its sensitivity to inactivation by chlorine dioxide. In *Legionella: Proceedings of the Second International Symposium* (eds Thornsberry, C., Ballows, A., Feeley, J.C. & Jakubowski, W.) pp. 68–70. Washington, DC: American Society for Microbiology.

Bollin, G.E., Plouffe, J.F., Para, M.F. & Hackman, B. (1985) Aerosols containing *Legionella pneumophila* generated by shower heads and hot water faucets. *Applied and Environmental Microbiology*, **50**, 1128–1131.

Bopp, C.A., Sumner, J.W., Morris, G.K. & Wells, J.G. (1981) Isolation of *Legionella* spp. from environmental samples by low-pH treatment and use of selective techniques. *Journal of Clinical Microbiology*, **13**, 714–719.

Brenner, D.J., Feeley, J.C. & Weaver, R.E. (1984) *Family VII Legionellaceae*. In Bergey's Manual of Systematic Bacteriology (eds Kreig, N.R. & Holt, J.G.) Vol. I, pp. 279–88. Baltimore: Williams & Wilkins.

Colbourne, J.S. & Dennis, P.J. (1988) Legionella: a biofilm organism in engineered water systems? In *Biodeterioration 7* (eds Houghton, D.R., Smith, R.N. & Eggins, H.O.W.) pp. 36–42. London: Elsevier.

Coughlin, M. & Caplan, G. (1987) Microbicidal efficacy of BNPD against *Legionella pneumophila. Cooling Tower Institute Annual Meeting Technical Paper TP 87–18*. New Orleans.

Croshaw, B. & Holland, V.R. (1984) Use of Bronopol as a cosmetic preservative. In *Cosmetic and Drug Preservation: Principles and Practice* (ed. Kabara, J.J.) pp. 31–62. New York: Marcel Dekker.

Croshaw, B., Groves, M.J. & Lessel, B. (1964) Some properties of Bronopol, a new antimicrobial agent active against *Pseudomonas aeruginosa. Journal of Pharmacy and Pharmacology*, **16**, 127T–130T.

Cunliffe, D.A. (1990) Inactivation of *Legionella pneumophila* by chloramine. *Journal of Applied Bacteriology*, **68**, 453–459.

Dennis, P.J., Bartlett, C.L.R. & Wright, A.E. (1984a) Comparison of isolation methods for *Legionella* spp. In *Legionella: Proceedings of the Second International Symposium* (eds Thornsberry, C., Ballows, A., Feeley, J.C. & Jakubowski, W.) pp. 294–296. Washington, DC: American Society for Microbiology.

Dennis, P.J., Green, D. & Jones, B.P.C. (1984b) A note on the temperature tolerance of *Legionella. Journal of Applied Bacteriology*, **56**, 349–350.

Edelstein, P.H. (1981) Improved semi-selective medium for isolation of *Legionella pneumophila* from contaminated clinical and environmental specimens. *Journal of Clinical Microbiology*, **14**, 298–303.

Elsmore, R. (1986) Biocidal control of Legionellae. *Israel Journal of Medical Sciences*, **22**, 647–654.

Elsmore, R. (1989) The activity of BNPD against *Legionella pneumophila* Serogroup 1: the influence of pH, inoculum level and test media. *International Biodeterioration*, **25**, 107–113.

Elsmore, R., Guthrie, W.G. & Parr, J.A. (1987) Laboratory and field experience with a bromonitroalkanol biocide in industrial water systems. *Speciality Chemicals*, **7**, 166–176.

Elsmore R., Corbett, R.J. & Channon, E.J. (1989) Relationship between the common water flora and isolation of *Legionella* species from water system. In *Airborne Deteriogens and Pathogens* (ed. Flannigan, B.) pp. 83–96. Kew: Biodeterioration Society.

England, A.C., Fraser, D.W., Mallison, G.F., Mackel, D.C., Skaliy, P. & Gorman, G.W. (1982) Failure of *Legionella pneumophila* sensitivities to predict culture results from disinfectant-treated air-conditioning cooling towers. *Applied and Environmental Microbiology*, **43**, 240–244.

Feeley, J.C., Gorman, G.W., Weaver, R.E., Mackel, D.C. & Smith, H.W. (1978) Primary isolation media for the Legionnaires' disease bacterium. *Journal of Clinical Microbiology*, **8**, 320–325.

Feeley, J.C., Gibson, R.J., Gorman, G.W., Langford, N.C., Rasheed, J.K., Mackel, D.C. & Baine, W.B. (1979) Charcoal-yeast extract agar: primary isolation medium for *Legionella pneumophila. Journal of Clinical Microbiology*, **10**, 437–411.

Fields, B.S., Shotts, E.B., Feeley, J.C., Gorman, G.W. & Martin, W.T. (1984) Proliferation of *Legionella pneumophila* as an intracellular parasite of the ciliated protoliferation *Tetrahymena pyriformis. Applied and Environmental Microbiology*, **47**, 467–471.

Fliermans, C.B. & Harvey, R.S. (1984) Effectiveness of 1-bromo-3-chloro-5,5-dimethylhydantoin against *Legionella pneumophila* in a cooling tower. *Applied and Environmental Microbiology*, **47**, 1307–1310.

Fliermans, C.B., Cherry, W.B., Orrison, L.H. & Thacker, L. (1979) Isolation of *Legionella pneumophila* from nonepidemic related aquatic habitats. *Applied and Environmental Microbiology*, **37**, 1239–1242.

Fliermans, C.B., Cherry, W.B., Orrison, L.H., Smith, S.J.,

Tison, D.L. & Pope, D.H. (1981) Ecological distribution of *Legionella pneumophila. Applied and Environmental Microbiology*, **41**, 9–16.

Fliermans, C.B., Bettinger, G.E. & Fynsk, A.W. (1982) Treatment of cooling systems containing high levels of *Legionella pneumophila*. *Water Research*, **16**, 903–909.

Grace, R.D., Dewar, N.E., Barnes, W.G. & Hodges, G.R. (1981) Susceptibility of *Legionella pneumophila* to three cooling tower microbiocides. *Applied and Environmental Microbiology*, **41** 233–236.

Grow, K.M., Wood, D.O., Coggin, J.H. & Leinbach, E.D. (1984) Environmental factors influencing growth of *Legionella pneumophila* in operating biocide treated cooling towers. In *Legionella: Proceedings of the Second International Symposium* (eds Thornsberry, C., Ballows, A., Feeley, J.C. & Jakubowski, W.) pp. 316–318. Washington, DC: American Society for Microbiology.

Harrison, T.G. & Taylor, A.G. (eds), (1988) *A Laboratory Manual for Legionella*. Chichester: John Wiley & Sons.

Hoffman, P. (1984) Bacterial physiology. In *Legionella: Proceedings of the Second International Symposium* (eds Thornsberry, C., Ballows, A., Feeley, J.C. & Jakubowski, W.) pp. 61–67. Washington, DC: American Society for Microbiology.

Hollis, C.G. & Smalley, D.L. (1980) Resistance of *Legionella pneumophila* to microbiocides. *Developments in Industrial Microbiology*, **21**, 265–271.

Hsu, S.C., Martin, R. & Wentworth, B.B. (1984) Isolation of *Legionella* species from drinking water. *Applied and Environmental Microbiology*, **48**, 830–832.

Ikedo, M. & Yabuuchi, E. (1986) Ecological studies on *Legionella* species. 1. Viable counts of *Legionella pneumophila* in cooling tower water. *Microbiology and Immunology*, **30**, 413–423.

Isenberg, H.D. (1979) Microbiology of Legionnaires' disease bacterium. *Annals of Internal Medicine*, **90**, 502–505.

Kilvington, S. & Price, J. (1990) Survival of *Legionella pneumophila* within cysts of *Acanthamoeba polyphaga* following chlorine exposure. *Journal of Applied Bacteriology*, **68**, 519–525.

Kobayashi, H. & Tsuzuki, M. (1984) Susceptibility of *Legionella pneumophila* to cooling tower microbiocides and hospital disinfectants. In *Legionella: Proceedings of the Second International Symposium* (eds Thornsberry, C., Ballows, A., Feeley, J.C. & Jakubowski, W.) pp. 342–343. Washington, DC: American Society for Microbiology.

Kuchta, J.M., States, S.J., McNamara, A.M., Wadowsky, R.M. & Yee, R.B. (1983) Susceptibility of *Legionella pneumophila* to chlorine in tap water. *Applied and Environmental Microbiology*, **46**, 1134–1139.

Kuchta, J.M., States, S.J., McGlaughlin, J.E., Overmeyer, J.H., Wadowsky, R.M., McNamara, A.M., Wolford, R.S. & Yee, R.B. (1985) Enhanced chlorine resistance of tap water-adapted *Legionella pneumophila* as compared with agar medium-passaged strains. *Applied and Environmental Microbiology*, **50**, 21–26.

Kurtz, J.B., Bartlett, C.L.R., Newton, U.A., White, R.A. & Jones, N. (1982) *Legionella pneumophila* in cooling water systems. *Journal of Hygiene, Cambridge*, **88**, 369–381.

Kurtz, J.B., Bartlett, C., Tillett, H. & Newton, U. (1984) Field trial of biocides in control of *Legionella pneumophila* in cooling water systems. In *Legionella: Proceedings of the Second International Symposium* (eds Thornsberry, C., Ballows, A., Feeley, J.C. & Jakubowski, W.) pp. 340–342. Washington, DC: American Society for Microbiology.

Lattimer, G.L. & Ormsbee, R.A. (eds) (1981) *Legionnaires' Disease*. New York: Marcel Dekker.

LeChevalier, M.W., Cawthon, C.D. & Lee, R.G. (1988) Factors promoting survival of bacteria in chlorinated water supplies. *Applied and Environmental Microbiology*, **54**, 649–654.

McCoy, W.F. & Wireman, J.W. (1989) Efficacy of bromochlorodimethylhydantoin against *Legionella pneumophila* in industrial cooling water. *Journal of Industrial Microbiology*, **4**, 403–408.

McCoy, W.F., Wireman, J.W. & Lashen, E.S. (1986) Efficacy of methylchloro/methylisothiazolone biocide against *Legionella pneumophila* in cooling in tower water. *Journal of Industrial Microbiology*, **1**, 49–56.

McDade, J.E., Shepard, C.C., Fraser, D.W., Tsai, T.F., Redus, M.A., Dowdle, W.R. & the Laboratory Investigation Team (1977) Legionnaires' disease: isolation of a bacterium and demonstration of its role in other respiratory disease. *New England Journal of Medicines*, **297**, 1197–1203.

McDade, J.E., Brenner, D.J. & Bozeman, F.M. (1979) Legionnaires' disease bacterium isolated in 1947. *Annals of Internal Medicine*, **90** 659–661.

Moiraghi, A., Castellani Pastoris, M., Barral, C., Carle, F., Sciacovel, A., Passarino, G. & Marforio, P. (1987) Nosocomial legionellosis associated with use of oxygen bubble humidifiers and underwater chest drains. *Journal of Hospital Infection*, **10**, 47–50.

Moore, K.E. (1978) Evaluating preservative efficacy in pharmaceutical and cosmetic products. PhD thesis, University of Technology, Loughborough, England.

Moore, K.E. & Stretton, J.R. (1981) The effect of pH, temperature and certain media constituents on the stability and activity of the preservative Bronopol. *Journal of Applied Bacteriology*, **51**, 483–494.

Muraca, P., Stout, J.E. & Yu, V.L. (1987) Comparative assessment of chlorine, heat, ozone and UV light for killing *Legionella pneumophila* within a model plumbing system. *Applied and Environmental Microbiology*, **53**, 447–453.

Muraca, P.W., Stout, J.E., Yu, V.L. & Lee, Y.C. (1988) Legionnaires' disease in the work environment: implications for environmental health. *American Industrial Hygiene Association Journal*, **49**, 584–590.

Negron-Alvira, A., Perez-Surez, I. & Huzen, T.C. (1988) *Legionella* spp. in Puerto Rico cooling towers. *Applied and Environmental Microbiology*, **54**, 2331–2334.

Orrison, L.H., Cherry, W.B. & Milan, D. (1981) Isolation of *Legionella pneumophila* from cooling tower water by filtration. *Applied and Environmental Microbiology*, **41**, 1202-1205.

Roberts, K.P., August, C.M. & Nelson, J.D. (1987) Relative sensitivities of environmental Legionellae to selective isolation procedures. *Applied and Environmental Microbiology*, **53**, 2704–2707.

Rudin, J.E., Wing, E.J. & Yee, R.B. (1984) An on-going outbreak of *Legionella micdadii*. In *Legionella: Proceedings of the Second International Symposium* (eds Thornsberry, C., Ballows, A., Feeley, J.C., Jakubowski, W.). pp. 227–229. Washington, DC: American Society for Microbiology.

Sawatari, K., Watanabe, K., Nakasato, H., Koga, H., Ito, N., Fujita, K., Shigeno, Y., Suzuyamá, Y., Yamaguchi, K., Saito, A. & Hara, K. (1984) Bactericidal effect of disinfectants against *Legionella pneumophila* and *Legionella bozmanii*. *Kansenshogaku Zasshi*, **58**, 130–136.

Skaliy, P., Thompson, T.A., Gorman, G.W., Morris, G.K., McEachern, H.V. & Machel, D.C. (1980) Laboratory studies of disinfectants against *Legionella pneumophila*. *Applied and Environmental Microbiology*, **40**, 697–700.

Sorraco, R.J., Gill, H.K., Fliermans, C.B. & Pope, D.H. (1983) Susceptibilities of algae and *Legionella pneumophila* to cooling tower biocides. *Applied and Environmental Microbiology*, **45**, 1254–1260.

States, S.J., Conley, L.F., Towner, S.G., Wolford, R.S., Stephenson, T.E., McNamara, A.M., Wadowsky, R.M. & Yee, R.B. (1987) An alkaline approach to treating cooling towers for control of *Legionella pneumophila*. *Applied and Environmental Microbiology*, **53**, 1775–1779.

Thacker, S.B., Bennet, J.V., Tsai, T.F., Fraser, D.W., McDade, J.E., Shephard, C.C., Williams, K.H., Stuart, W.H., Dull, H.B. & Eickhoff, T.C. (1978) An outbreak in 1965 of severe respiratory illness caused by the Legionnaires' disease bacterium. *Journal of Infectious Diseases*, **138**, 512–519.

Thornsberry, C. & Kirven, L.A. (1978) Beta-lactamase of the Legionnaires' bacterium. *Current Microbiology*, **1**, 51–54.

Tison, D.L., Pope, D.H., Cherry, W.B. & Fliermans, C.B. (1980) Growth of *Legionella pneumophila* in association with blue green algae (*Cyanobacteria*). *Applied and Environmental Microbiology*, **39**, 456–459.

Tobin, J.O'H., Beare, J., Dunnill, M.S., Fisher-Hoch, S., French, M., Mitchell, R.G., Morris, P.J. & Muers, M.F. (1980) Legionnaires' disease in a transplant unit: isolation of the causative agent from shower baths. *Lancet*, **ii**, 118–121.

Tobin, J.O'H., Swann, R.A. & Bartlett, C.L.R. (1981) Isolation of *Legionella pneumophila* from water systems: methods and preliminary results. *British Medical Journal*, **282**, 515–517.

Tobin, R.S., Ewan, P., Walsh, K. & Dutka, B. (1986) A survey of *Legionella pneumophilla* in water in 12 Canadian cities. *Water Research*, **20**, 495–502.

Tuttle, E., Phares, C. & Chiostri, R.F. (1970) Preservation of protein solutions with 2-bromo-2-nitro-1,3-propanediol (Bronopol). *American Perfumer and Cosmetics*, **85**, 87–89.

Tyndall, R.L. & Domingue, E.L. (1982) Cocultivation of *Legionella pneumophila* and free-living amoebae. *Applied and Environmental Microbiology*, **44**, 954–959.

Vesey, G., Dennis, P.J., Lee, J.V. & West, A.A. (1988) Further development of simple tests to differentiate the legionellas. *Journal of Applied Bacteriology*, **65**, 339–345.

Vogt, R.L., Hudson, P.J., Orciari, L., Heun, E.M. & Woods, T.C. (1987) Legionnaires' disease and a whirlpool-spa. *Annals of Internal Medicine*, **107**, 596.

Wadowski, R.M. & Yee, R.B. (1981) Glycine-containing selective medium for isolation of Legionellaceae from environmental specimens. *Applied and Environmental Microbiology*, **42**, 768–772.

Wadowski, R.M. & Yee, R.B. (1983) Satellite growth of *Legionella pneumophila* with an environmental isolate of *Flavobacterium breve*. *Applied and Environmental Microbiology*, **46**, 1447–1449.

Wait, R. (1988) Confirmation of the identity of Legionellae by whole cell fatty-acid and isoprenoid quinone profiles. In *A Laboratory Manual for Legionella* (eds Harrison, T.G. & Taylor, A.G.) pp. 69–101. Chichester: John Wiley & Sons.

Witherall, L.E., Novick, L.F., Stone, K.M., Duncan, R.W., Orciari, L.A., Jillson, D.A., Myers, R.B., & Vogt, R.L. (1984) *Legionella pneumophila* in Vermont cooling towers. In *Legionella: Proceedings of the Second International Symposium* (eds Thornsberry, C., Ballows, A., Feeley, J.C. & Jakubowski, W.) pp. 315–316. Washington, DC: American Society for Microbiology.

Wright, A.E. (1989) *Report of the Expert Advisory Committee on Biocides*. London: HMSO.

F · METHICILLIN-RESISTANT STAPHYLOCOCCI

1 INTRODUCTION

Staphylococcus aureus is a common cause of skin infections, osteomyelitis, wound infections and food poisoning (Shanson, 1989). In a national prevalence survey of hospitals in England and Wales it was isolated from 3% of urinary tract, 33% of wound and 6.5% of respiratory tract infections (Meers *et al.*, 1981). It is carried in the nose of 20–30% of the healthy population. For this reason patients, staff and visitors may all act unknowingly as sources of infection. Most strains are sensitive to antibiotics and resistant to penicillin only, but some are multi-resistant, epidemic in their spread and of high virulence (Phillips, 1988). Methicillin-resistant *Staph. aureus* (MRSA) have been recognized as a major cause of sepsis in UK hospitals (Cooke *et al.*, 1986) although not all MRSA strains are of increased virulence. For example, Lacey (1987) often found MRSA in burns in geriatric units without causing harm. In Ireland about 30% of all *Staph. aureus* isolated from blood culture were MRSA (Cafferkey *et al.*, 1988). Lyon & Skurray (1987) reported the isolation of strains of *Staph. aureus* resistant to over 20 antimicrobial agents. It has been estimated that the cost of treating infections caused by MRSA strains is about 68% higher than for sensitive strains. One patient in Seattle (Locksley *et al.*, 1982) showed it was possible to act as both a reservoir and a susceptible host. This, together with the mechanisms of gene transfer, presents a major challenge to the formulation of effective clinical control measures. Control includes a reduction in the movement of patients and staff both within and between hospitals, and screening of patients from 'infected' hospitals.

The term 'epidemic' methicillin-resistant *Staph. aureus* (EMRSA) is often used to denote the ease with which these strains can spread (Report, 1986, 1990). Patients particularly at risk are immunocompromised, debilitated ones or those with open sores.

In this chapter we shall consider the evolution of MRSA strains, the mechanisms of gene transfer, transferable resistance to antibiotics and biocides, and suitable hygienic control measures. Although antibiotics are outside the scope of this book it is impossible to consider the subject adequately without mention of them in relation to biocides.

2 EVOLUTION OF MRSA

This has still to be elucidated. However it is not unreasonable to expect that MRSA strains have evolved by the same mechanisms of mutation and gene transfer that exist in other species. The emergence of gentamicin-resistant plasmids illustrates the evolutionary potential of translocatable elements (Lyon & Skurray, 1987). This evolutionary progression is also believed to have occurred in the formation of the β-lactamase-heavy metal resistant plasmids (Shalita *et al.*, 1980).

Although there are examples of isolates resistant to penicillin via β-lactamase, which pre-date the use of the compound (Parker, 1983), the spread of the phenotype has most probably resulted from selection due to the widespread use of the antibiotic. This argument can be used to account for the emergence of gentamicin-, antiseptic- and disinfectant-resistant strains (Table 10.7). In addition cadmium has been reported to be selective for R^+ staphylococci (Kondo *et al.*, 1974). Staphylococci do not exist in isolation and appear to share a pool of plasmids with other skin flora, such as the streptococci (Murray, 1987). Similarities between plasmids encoding resistance to tetracycline, chloramphenicol and neomycin in *Staph. aureus* and *Staph. epidermidis* have been reported (Rosendorf & Kayser, 1974) as has identity between plasmids encoding gentamicin (Cohen *et al.*, 1982), cadmium (Cooksey & Baldwin, 1985) and antiseptic (Lyon & Skurray, 1987) resistance.

Table 10.7 Plasmid-encoded functions that could transfer to MRSA and EMRSA strains

Resistance phenotype	Transposable in staphylococci	Transposable in other organisms
Gentamicin	+	+
Gentamicin and kanamycin	+	+
Streptomycin and spectinomycin	+	+
Fusidic acid	–	–
Penicillin	+	+
Methicillin	+	+
Trimethoprim	+	+
Chloramphenicol	–	–
Tetracycline	+	+
Tobramycin	+	+
QACs	–	–
Ethidium bromide	–	–
Acridines	–	–
Diamidines	–	–
Mercury	+	+

+, In some cases, although transposition has not been formally demonstrated, genetic evidence suggests that this may be occurring; –, not yet been observed.

3 MECHANISMS OF TRANSFER

Each of the traditional processes of transfer (transduction, transformation and conjugation) has been described in *Staph. aureus*. However gene transfer *in vivo* remains to be demonstrated for all but transduction. For additional information, see Thompson (1986), Townsend *et al.* (1986) and Evans & Dyke (1988).

3.1 Transduction

Many clinical isolates possess more than one phage, as a prophage. This lysogenic state has been reported to influence the ability of the host cell to participate in gene exchange. Transduction was recognized early (Lacey, 1975) and assumed to be a major mechanism in the transfer of resistance genes. Calcium ions were found to promote, and chelating agents to interfere with, the transfer (Lacey, 1980). Both small plasmids and chromosomal genes can be transduced (Novick & Morse, 1968; Stiffler *et al.*, 1974; Kono & Sasatsu, 1976; Iordanescu, 1977). Transduction, via a cell free lysate, typically occurs at a frequency of 10^{-6} per recipient.

3.2 Transformation

Staph. aureus can be transformed by exogenous DNA, but cells are only competent for a short period, immediately prior to entry into the stationary phase (Rudin *et al.*, 1974; Pattee & Neveln, 1975). This is due to a transient absence of an exonuclease and consequently it is thought that transfer by this route will be low *in vivo*. This conclusion should perhaps be questioned until evidence is presented to demonstrate clearly that cells are not in this physiological state on skin for significant periods.

3.3 Conjugation

Different types of conjugation are known to exist in staphylococci. These are phage-mediated conjugation and plasmid-mediated conjugation. In addition, conjugative transposons have been discovered, which appear mechanistically to fall in the latter class.

3.3.1 Phage-mediated conjugation

Phage-mediated conjugation occurs in mixed cultures of lysogens and recipients (Lacey, 1980).

Transfer frequencies per recipient of plasmids can be very high, over 10^{-1}, and Barr *et al.* (1986) have recently shown that sub-inhibitory concentrations of β-lactam antibiotics induced a 100–1000-fold increase in plasmid transfer frequency. This process is deoxyribonuclease-insensitive (Schaeffler, 1982).

3.3.2 *Plasmid-mediated conjugation*

Plasmid-mediated conjugation is a surface preferred system of transfer in *Staph. aureus* (Archer & Johnson, 1983). It is different from phage-mediated transfer because cell contact is obligatory (Townsend *et al.*, 1986). Plasmids have not been identified in all cases of conjugal transfer. For example, El Solh *et al.* (1986) were unable to detect any plasmid DNA in recipients. This is perhaps indicative of conjugative transposons. Broad host range plasmids which can transfer resistance between staphylococci and streptococci are known (Buu-Hoi *et al.*, 1984). This and similarities between antibiotic resistances (Schaberg & Zervos, 1986) together suggest that genetic exchange occurs between these genera *in vivo*.

3.3.3 *Conjugative transposons*

Conjugative transposons (El Solh *et al.*, 1986) have been identified, although few of these non-plasmid transfer systems have been examined in any detail (Clewell & Gawron-Burke, 1986). These are transferable to and between staphylococci, and their resistances are expressed in a wide variety of Gram-positive bacteria; both properties make their investigation of clinical importance.

4 TRANSFERABLE RESISTANCE TO ANTIBIOTICS AND BIOCIDES

Transfer of penicillin and chloramphenicol resistance plasmids occurs in mixed cultures of *Staph. epidermidis* and *Staph. aureus* (Witte, 1977). Intraspecies transfer of gentamicin resistance plasmids can also occur on skin (Lacey, 1975; Noble & Naidoo, 1978). These plasmids can also mobilize smaller plasmids, encoding resistance to tetracycline, chloramphenicol and erythromycin (Naidoo, 1984). Although examples are still few in number, results (e.g. Bale *et al.*, 1988) suggest that frequent exchange of natural plasmids between natural bacteria will not be unusual.

Conjugative plasmid transfer can be enhanced by the exposure of mating cells to sub-inhibitory concentrations of β-lactam antibiotics (Barr *et al.*, 1986) and vancomycin (Al Masaudi *et al.*, in preparation).

The finding in a *Staph. aureus* isolate of a plasmid pSK1 (Tennent *et al.*, 1985) encoding resistance to ethidium bromide, acriflavine, benzalkonium chloride and other quaternary ammonium compounds, gentamicin, tobramycin, kanamycin and trimethoprim indicates the potential that transfer mechanisms have for aggregating phenotypes which increase the survival potential and opportunistic ability of staphylococci.

The term 'nucleic acid-binding (NAB) compound' has been adopted to describe those compounds that bind strongly to DNA (Townsend *et al.*, 1984a,b; Kigbo *et al.*, 1985). Cetyltrimethylammonium bromide (CTAB), a QAC, has been used (Townsend *et al.*, 1985) for the rapid isolation of plasmid DNA, although it must be pointed out that the concentration (0.5% w/v, 5000 μg/ml) of CTAB used for this purpose is very different, by a factor of 50–100, from those concentrations employed in sensitivity and resistance studies with MRSA strains.

Staph. aureus strains carry a variety of plasmids, many of which encode antibiotic resistance (Bigelow *et al.*, 1989). Resistance to acridines (Ac^R), ethidium bromide (Eb^R), QACs (Qa^R), and propamidine isothionate (PI^R) is mediated by a common determinant on a group of structurally related plasmids: see also below. Many of these plasmids carry the gentamicin, tobramycin and kanamycin resistance transposon *Tn*4001 and also encode resistance to the dihydrofolate reductase inhibitor, trimethoprim (Lyon *et al.*, 1984; Gillespie *et al.*, 1986; Skurray *et al.*, 1988). The prototype of this group of plasmids is pSK1; its genes have been cloned into an *E. coli* vector in which these resistances are then expressed (Tennent *et al.*, 1985). Yamamoto *et al.* (1988) have reported cloning chlorhexidine resistance into *E. coli*.

Townsend *et al.* (1984a) proposed that resistance

to CTAB and to the diamidine, propamidine ise-thionate (PI) was linked, and that these biocides acted as a selective pressure for the retention of plasmids encoding resistance to them. In the laboratory, CTAB could not be employed as a selective genetic marker because strains with plasmids carrying the R determinant were only about 3–4 times as resistant as plasmid-less strains (Table 10.8). With PI, however, there was up to a 32-fold difference in MIC values (Table 10.8). Cookson & Phillips (1988) found that resistance to aminoglycoside antibiotics and to PI, cetrimide (equivalent to CTAB) and ethidium bromide always transferred together. Cookson *et al.* (1990) have described transferable resistance to triclosan in MRSA strains.

There are at least three determinants determining biocide resistance in *Staph. aureus* isolates (Emslie *et al.*, 1985, 1986; Skurray *et al.*, 1988; Gillespie *et al.*, 1989, 1990). These are *qac*A, located on the pSK1 family of plasmids described above, encoding resistance to acridines, ethidium bromide, QACs and PI which is possibly translocatable; *qac*B, which is very similar; and *qac*C, which encodes resistance to QACs and low-level ethidium bromide, but is genetically unrelated to either the *qac*A or *qac*B determinants. The *qac*A determinant also specifies low-level resistance to chlorhexidine (Gillespie *et al.*, 1989).

These findings must, however, be put into perspective. Brumfitt *et al.* (1985) found that MRSA strains were only slightly more resistant to chlorhexidine than were MSSA ones. Al-Masaudi *et al.* (1988a) could find no difference in response to chlorhexidine, only a slight difference to QACs but a marked difference to dibromopropamidine isethionate (DBPI). Some of the findings quoted above also demonstrate only a slight increase in resistance to QACs (Lyon *et al.*, 1984; Townsend *et al.*, 1984a). Lacey *et al.* (1986) confirm much higher resistance of MRSA strains to PI and ethidium bromide but regard increases in resistance to QACs (2.67–4-fold) and chlorhexidine (2-fold) as being 'trivial'. In fact, Lacey & Kruczenyk (1986) are critical of the emphasis placed by the Australian workers on resistance to NAB agents in MRSA strains. This is because they are unlikely to be exposed to agents such as ethidium bromide,

Table 10.8 Effects of biocides on MRSA and MSSA strains

Biocide	MIC (µg/ml)		References*
	MSSA	MRSA	
Cetrimide/CTAB	1.6	6.25	1
	1.5	2.5–5	2
Chlorhexidine	2	4–8	3
	1.5	2–2.5	2
Benzalkonium chloride	<1	6	1
Acriflavine	30	340	4
Ethidium bromide	4	180	4
Propamidine isethionate	16	512	1
Parabens			
Methyl	2000	2000	
Ethyl	1000	1000	2
Propyl	400	400	
Butyl	125	125	
Phenols			
Phenol	2000	2000	
Cresol	750	1250	2
Chlorocresol	200	200	

* 1, Townsend *et al.* (1984a); 2, Al-Masaudi *et al.* (1988); 3, Brumfitt *et al.* (1985); 4, Gillespie *et al.* (1986).

whereas gentamicin resistance is considered to be a much more plausible selection pressure. Marples & Cooke (1988) pointed out that resistance to QACs is due to a plasmid-coded efflux system (Section 5) but added that resistance at this level probably has no clinical significance.

Furthermore, of the non-antibiotic agents described by the Australian workers, ethidium bromide is not used as an antiseptic or disinfectant, the acridines rarely, the diamidines are reserved for specific purposes (e.g. PI in the treatment of blepharitis and acute and chronic conjunctivitis, and pentamidine isethionate in the treatment of pneumonia caused by *Pneumocystis carinii*, particularly in AIDS patients), leaving just the QACs and chlorhexidine. Resistance to the former is not particularly marked and to the latter is slight, if any. The question must be raised, therefore, as to whether antiseptic resistance is of particular significance in terms of the potential for survival in the hospital environment (Gillespie *et al.*, 1986) or whether, as suggested by Lacey (1987), the MRSA strains have been selected by intense antibiotic usage in hospitals. It is particularly interesting to note that antiseptic resistance in clinical MRSA isolates has now been located on the chromosome (Rahman *et al.*, 1988; Gillespie *et al.*, 1989) thereby leading to the acquisition of genes to form a multi-resistant chromosome.

It is, perhaps, unfortunate that most studies have expressed resistance in terms of MIC values, because the factor of overriding importance must be the inactivation of MRSA in the clinical situation. To date only Haley *et al.* (1985) appear to have studied the bactericidal activity of antiseptics against MRSA and MSSA. MSSA strains were more sensitive to Phisohex (containing hexachlorophane) and *p*-chloro-*m*-xylenol, but showed the same response as MRSA strains to povidone-iodine and a chlorhexidine-based product.

Table 10.9 Plasmid-mediated resistance to cationic biocides in strains of *Staphylococcus aureus* and *Escherichia coli**

	P^+/P^-:MIC ratio	
Biocide	*Staph. aureus*	*E. coli*
Chlorhexidine gluconate	2	4–8
Benzalkonium chloride	2	4
Acriflavine	128	8
Ethidium bromide	64	16

* Based on the data of Yamamoto *et al.* (1988).
P^+, Plasmid-bearing strain; P^-, isogenic plasmid-less strain; P^+ *E. coli* strain, carries recombinant plasmid from *Staph. aureus*.

5 MECHANISMS OF BIOCIDE RESISTANCE

It is always of fundamental importance not only to record bacterial resistance to antibiotics and/or biocides but also to understand the mechanisms of such resistance. For convenience this section is sub-divided into two parts, the first of which deals with MRSA strains and the second, briefly, with other instances of staphylococcal resistance.

5.1 MRSA strains

Resistance of MRSA strains to cationic-type biocides may arise and may be plasmid-associated (Townsend *et al.*, 1983, 1984a,b; Lyon *et al.*, 1984, 1986; Jones & Midgley, 1985; Kigbo *et al.*, 1985; Emslie *et al.*, 1985, 1986; Gillespie *et al.*, 1986, 1989, 1990; Lyon & Skurray, 1987; Skurray *et al.*, 1988). Furthermore, recombinant plasmids have been transferred from *Staph. aureus* to *E. coli* (Tennent *et al.*, 1985; Yamamoto *et al.*, 1988; Table 10.9); these encode resistance to various cationic biocides, although often at fairly low levels.

There are various reasons that could possibly be put forward for biocide resistance in MRSA strains (see Table 10.10 for a summary). First, the surface of these cells could differ from MSSA cells. Al-Masaudi *et al.* (1988a) showed that MSSA strains were typically hydrophobic, a property likely to be determined by a protein or protein-associated molecule located at the cell surface. However, wide differences occurred with MRSA strains, different solvent systems produced different responses and there was little correlation when different methods of assessing hydrophobicity were employed. Secondly, there could be biocide inactivation systems present within MRSA but not MSSA strains: no evidence has been found to support this convention. Finally, reduced uptake of a biocide could result from an efficient efflux mechanism present in MRSA but not in MSSA strains. Evidence to substantiate this hypothesis has been produced by Jones & Midgley (1985) for ethidium bromide, thus explaining the earlier diminished uptake findings of Johnston & Dyke (1969), and for QACs. Jones & Midgley (1985) cloned a 1.1 kb DNA fragment (specifying resistance to ethidium bromide and QACs) from an MRSA strain into a plasmid vector in *E. coli*, but did not examine the Gram-negative cell to determine whether any plasmid-mediate cell envelope changes occurred. These authors reached two interesting conclusions, *viz.* that resistance to QACs and ethidium bromide had the same efflux basis as resistance to Cd^{2+}, tetracyclines, arsenate and arsenite; and that the

Table 10.10 Postulated mechanisms of resistance of MRSA strains to biocides

Class of biocide	Examples	Resistance mechanism	Comment
QAC	Cetrimide/CTAB Benzalkonium chloride	Efflux	Found in MRSA but not in MSSA strains; low-level resistance
Diamidines	Propamidine Dibromopropamidine	?	High-level resistance
DNA-intercalating agents	Acriflavine Acridine orange	Efflux?	
	Ethidium bromide	Efflux	Reduced uptake; high-level resistance
Biguanides	Chlorhexidine salts	Efflux?	Very low-level resistance only

primary target site of QACs and ethidium bromide must likewise be intracellular.

Little is known about the way in which biocides enter MRSA cells, although presumably this is achieved by passive diffusion across the cell wall. Interestingly the important topical antiseptic mupirocin is equally effective against MRSA and MSSA strains, whereas deep rough, but not wild-type, strains of Gram-negative bacteria are sensitive, indicating a barrier role in normal Gram-negative bacteria but not in MRSA or MSSA (Al-Masaudi *et al.*, 1988b).

5.2 Other staphylococcal resistance

Other resistance mechanisms of staphylococci to biocides have been described. *Staph. aureus* strains isolated from poultry-processing plants may be resistant to chlorine, either because they grow in macroclumps or because they produce an extracellular slime layer (Bolton *et al.*, 1988). Mucoid-grown *Staph. aureus* cells are less sensitive than non-mucoid ones to several commercial antiseptics and disinfectants; if the mucoid-grown cells are washed in saline or subcultured in BHI broth they become sensitive to these biocides, demonstrating that the extracellular slime layer, which forms a physical barrier around organisms, is an efficient resistant mechanism (Kolawole, 1984).

The staphylococci referred to by Bolton *et al.* (1988) and Kolawole (1984) are not MRSA strains. It is not known whether MRSA strains *in vivo* produce a slime layer or glycocalyx that could be a contributory factor in conferring resistance to antibiotics and/or biocides.

6 CONTROL OF MRSA STRAINS

It is necessary to know the significance in infectious terms of the re-emergence of MRSA strains. It is clear that hospital infections caused by these strains are increasing, and that they particularly affect patients in intensive-care units (Lejeune *et al.*, 1986). Gentamicin suddenly appeared in the UK in 1976, and methicillin- and gentamicin-resistant *Staph. aureus* (MGRSA) strains caused severe major hospital outbreaks (Shanson, 1986). The reasons for the re-emergence of MRSA strains are unclear: contributory factors may be the increased use of β-lactam antibiotics and the widespread use of gentamicin, leading to the selection of MGRSA strains. Australian workers have proposed that since resistance to NAB compounds was prevalent in the staphylococcal population long before the emergence of gentamicin resistance (Emslie *et al.*, 1985, 1986), antiseptic resistance is of particular significance in terms of the potential for their survival in the hospital environment (Gillespie *et al.*, 1986).

This, in turn, poses a problem in terms of control of infections caused by MRSA strains, since it suggests that antiseptics and disinfectants should not be employed. In fact, doubt has been cast on the efficacy of some antiseptic preparations. Shanson (1986), for instance, stated that colonized patient skin sites should be treated with antiseptics, but added that their clinical efficacy for eradicating MRSA had not been established. The uncertainties in the efficacy of topical antibiotic and antiseptic preparations were also pointed out in a Report (1986), although mupirocin gave good results, and antiseptic detergents for washing and daily bathing appeared to be satisfactory. Tuffnell *et al.* (1987) claimed that antiseptic body washing was of debatable use, but proposed that triclosan, a phenolic, which had prolonged surface action, was better for this purpose than hexachlorophane.

Various means of eradicating MRSA have been put forward. These include (Report, 1986; Shanson, 1986; Tuffnell *et al.*, 1987) the following: (a) antibiotic therapy, with the proviso that this be reserved for life-threatening conditions; (b) isolation of patients in a purpose-built, dedicated isolation unit; (c) use of disposable gloves and good handwashing with antiseptics, such as the chlorhexidine-based 'Hibiscrub' formulation, Lejeune *et al.* (1986) have commented on the utilization of a chlorhexidine detergent as an appropriate handwashing procedure. Of these, the single most important factor is listed in (b), together with reduction of staff and patient movement and the screening of patients from MRSA-infected hospitals.

One other point is worthy of comment. We have seen, and therefore should expect, new disease problems to arise coincidentally with the emergence of new strains with novel gene combinations. These are most likely to arise from gene transfer processes as the evolution of novel resistance genes is believed to be a very rare event. If resistance is acquired from co-resident strains it becomes important to understand the process of gene exchange. The key for control is thus to identify ways and means to inhibit and reduce gene transfer *in vivo*. In a competitive, challenging and changing environment bacteria have acquired mechanisms for the transfer and receipt of genes from a pool of associated organisms. The adoption of stringent and scientifically planned hygiene practices will no doubt show if infections may be controlled and if past practices and antimicrobial usage have acted to select for MRSA and EMRSA strains, or whether their emergence was due to other factors.

7 CONCLUSIONS

MRSA/EMRSA strains are capable of causing severe infections, particularly in debilitated patients. They have been found in many hospitals in several countries, possibly arising because of the selective pressure arising from the widespread use of antibiotics in hospitals. The comparatively low-level resistance to important biocidal agents such as chlorhexidine and QACs has been claimed to enhance the ability of MRSA strains to survive, but in the opinion of the present authors this has yet to be proven conclusively.

The other important message is that resistance to biocides may involve mechanisms as sophisticated as those encountered in resistance mechanisms to antibiotics.

8 REFERENCES

Al-Masaudi, S.B., Day, M.J. & Russell, A.D. (1988a) Sensitivity of methicillin-resistant *Staphylococcus aureus* strains to some antibiotics, antiseptics and disinfectants. *Journal of Applied Bacteriology*, **65**, 329–337.

Al-Masaudi, S.B., Russell, A.D. & Day, M.J. (1988b) Activity of mupirocin against *Staphylococcus aureus* and outer membrane mutants of Gram-negative bacteria. *Letters in Applied Microbiology*, **7**, 45–47.

Archer, G.L. & Johnson, J.L. (1983) Self transmissible plasmids in staphylococci that encode resistance to aminoglycosides. *Antimicrobial Agents and Chemotherapy*, **24**, 70–77.

Bale, M.J., Fry, J.C. & Day, M.J. (1988) Transfer and occurrence of large mercury resistance plasmids in river epilithon. *Applied and Environmental Microbiology*, **54**, 972–978.

Barr, V., Barr, K., Millar, M.R. & Lacey, R.W. (1986) β-Lactam antibiotics increase the frequency of plasmid transfer in *Staphylococcus aureus*. *Antimicrobial Agents and Chemotherapy*, **17**, 409–413.

Bigelow, N., Ng, L.-K., Robson, H.G. & Dillon, J.R. (1989) Strategies for molecular characterisation of methicillin and gentamicin-resistant *Staphylococcus aureus* in a Canadian nosocomial outbreak. *Journal of Medical Microbiology*, **30**, 51–58.

Bolton, K.J., Dodd, C.E.R., Mead, G.C. & Waites, W.M. (1988) Chlorine resistance of strains of *Staphylococcus aureus* isolated from poultry processing plants. *Letters in*

Applied Microbiology, **6**, 31–34.

Brumfitt, W., Dixson, S. & Hamilton-Miller, J.M.T. (1985) Resistance to antiseptics in methicillin and gentamicin resistant *Staphylococcus aureus*. *Lancet*, **i**, 1442–1443.

Buu-Hoi, A., Bieth, G. & Horaud, T. (1984) Broad host range of streptococcal macrolide resistance plasmids. *Antimicrobial Agents and Chemotherapy*, **25**, 289–91.

Cafferkey, M.T., Hone, R. & Keane, C.T. (1988) Sources and outcome for methicillin-resistant *Staphylococcus aureus* bacteremia. *Journal of Hospital Infection*, **11**, 136–143.

Clewell, D.B. & Gawron-Burke, C. (1986) Conjugative transposons and the dissemination of antibiotic resistance in streptococci. *Annual Review of Microbiology*, **40**, 635–659.

Cohen, M.L., Wong, E.S. & Falkow, S. (1982) Common R-plasmids in *Staphylococcus aureus* and *Staphylococcus epidermidis* during a nosocomial *Staphylococcus aureus* outbreak. *Antimicrobial Agents and Chemotherapy*, **21**, 210–215.

Cooke, E.M., Casewell, M.W., Emmerson, A.M., Gaston, M., de Saxe, M., Mayon-White, R.T. & Galbraith, N.S. (1986) Methicillin-resistant *Staphylococcus aureus* in the U.K. and Ireland. A questionnaire survey. *Journal of Hospital Infection*, **8**, 143–148.

Cooksey, R.C. & Baldwin, J.N. (1985) Program Abstract, 24th Interscience Conference on Antimicrobial Agents and Chemotherapy. Abstract No. 997.

Cookson, B.D. & Phillips, I. (1988) Epidemic methicillin-resistant *Staphylococcus aureus*. *Journal of Antimicrobial Chemotherapy*, **21**, Supplement C, 57–65.

Crossely, K., Leosch, D., Landesman, B., Mead, K., Chern, M. & Strate, R. (1979) An outbreak of infections caused by strains of *Staphylococcus aureus* resistant to methicillin and aminoglycosides: 1. Clinical studies. *Journal of Infectious Diseases*, **139**, 273–279.

El Solh, N., Allignet, J., Bismuth, R., Buset, B. & Fouace, J.M. (1986) Conjugative transfer of antibiotic resistance markers from *Staphylococcus aureus* in the absence of detectable extrachromosomal DNA. *Antimicrobial Agents and Chemotherapy*, **30**, 161–169.

Emslie, K.R., Townsend, D.E., Bolton, S. & Grubb, W.B. (1985) Two distinct resistance determinants to nucleic acid-binding compounds in *Staphylococcus aureus*. *FEMS Microbiology Letters*, **27**, 61–64.

Emslie, K.R., Townsend, D.E. & Grubb, W.B. (1986) Isolation and characterisation of a family of small plasmids encoding resistance to nucleic acid-binding compounds in *Staphylococcus aureus*. *Journal of Medical Microbiology*, **22**, 9–15.

Evans, J. & Dyke, K.G.H. (1988) Characterization of the conjugation system associated with the *Staphylococcus aureus* plasmid pJE1. *Journal of General Microbiology*, **134**, 1–8.

Gillespie, M.T., May, J.W. & Skurray, R.A. (1986) Plasmid-encoded resistance to acriflavine and quaternary ammonium compounds in methicillin-resistant *Staphylococcus aureus*. *FEMS Microbiology Letters*, **34**, 47–51.

Gillespie, M.T., Lyon, B.R. & Skurray, R.A. (1989) Gentamicin and antiseptic resistance in epidemic methicillin-resistant *Staphylococcus aureus*. *Lancet*, **i**, 503.

Gillespie, M.T., Lyon, B.R. & Skurray, R.A. (1990) Typing of methicillin-resistant *Staphylococcus aureus* by antibiotic resistance phenotype. *Journal of Medical Microbiology*, **31**, 57–64.

Haley, C.E., Marling-Cason, M., Smith J.W., Luby, J.P. & Mackowiak, P.A. (1985) Bactericidal activity of antiseptics against methicillin-resistant *Staphylococcus aureus*. *Journal of Clinical Microbiology*, **21**, 9911–992.

Hughes, J.M. (1988) Study on the efficiency of nosocomial infection conrol (S.E.N.I.C. Project): Results and implications for the future. *Chemotherapy*, **34**, 553–561.

Iordanescu, S. (1977) Relationships between cotransducible plasmids in *Staphylococcus aureus* NCTC 8325. *Journal of General Microbiology*, **96**, 227–281.

Jaffe, H.M., Sweeney, H.M., Nathan, C., Weinstein, R.A., Kabins, S.A. & Cohen, S. (1980) Identity and interspecific transfer of gentamicin-resistance plasmids in *Staphylococcus aureus* and *Staphylococcus epidermidis*. *Journal of Infectious Diseases*, **141**, 738–747.

Johnston, L.H., & Dyke, K.G.H. (1969) Ethidium bromide resistance, a new marker on the staphylococcal penicillinase plasmid. *Journal of Bacteriology*, **100**, 1413–1414.

Jones, I.G. & Midgley, M. (1985) Expression of a plasmid borne ethidium resistance determinant from *Staphylococcus* in *Escherichia coli*: evidence for an efflux system. *FEMS Microbiology Letters*, **28**, 355–357.

Kigbo, E.P., Townsend, D.E., Ashdown, N. & Grubb, W.B. (1985) Transposition of penicillinase determinants in methicillin-resistant *Staphylococcus aureus*. *FEMS Microbiology Letters*, **28**, 39–43.

Kolawole, D.O. (1984) Resistance mechanisms of mucoid-grown *Staphylococcus aureus* to the antibacterial action of some disinfectants and antiseptics. *FEMS Microbiology Letters*, **25**, 205–209.

Kondo, I., Ishidawa, T. & Nakahara, H. (1974) Mercury and cadmium resistances mediated by the penicillinase plasmid in *Staphylococcus aureus*. *Journal of Bacteriology*, **117**, 1–7.

Kono, M. & Sasatsu, M. (1976) Association of a penicillin resistance gene with a tetracycline resistance plasmid ($P_{TP\text{-}2}$) in *Staphylococcus aureus*. *Antimicrobial Agents and Chemotherapy*, **9**, 706–712.

Lacey, R.W. (1975) Antibiotic resistant plasmids of *Staphylococcus aureus* and their clinical importance. *Bacteriological Reviews*, **39**, 1–32.

Lacey, R.W. (1980) Evidence for two mechanisms for plasmid transfer in mixed cultures in *Staphylococcus aureus*. *Journal of General Microbiology*, **119**, 423–435.

Lacey, R.W. (1987) Multi-resistant *Staphylococcus aureus*: a suitable case of inactivity? *Journal of Hospital Infection*, **9**, 103–105.

Lacey R.W. & Kruczenyk, S.C. (1986) Epidemiology of antibiotic resistance in *Staphylococcus aureus*. *Journal of*

Antimicrobial Chemotherapy, **18**, Supplement C, 207–214.

Lacey, R.W., Barr, K.W., Barr, V.E. & Inglis, T.J. (1986) Properties of methicillin-resistant *Staphylococcus aureus* colonizing patients in a burns unit. *Journal of Hospital Infection*, **7**, 137–148.

Lejeune, B., Buzit-Losquim, F., Simitzis-Le Flohic, A.M., Le Bras, M.P. & Aliz, D. (1986) Outbreak of gentamicin-methicillin-resistant *Staphylococcus aureus* infection in an intensive care unit for children. *Journal of Hospital Infection*, **7**, 21–25.

Locksley, R.M., Cohen, M.L., Quinn, T.C., Tomkins, L.S., Coyle, M.B., Kirihara, J.M. & Counts, G.W. (1982) Multiply antibiotic resistant *Staphylococcus aureus*: introduction, transmission and evolution of nosocomial infection. *Annals of Internal Medicine*, **97**, 317–324.

Lyon, B.R. & Skurray, R. (1987) Antimicrobial resistance of *Staphylococcus aureus*: genetic basis. *Microbiological Reviews*, **51**, 88–137.

Lyon, B.R., May, J.W. & Skurray, R.A. (1984) In 4001: a gentamicin- and kanamicin-resistance transporon in *Staphylococcus aureus*. *Molecular and General Genetics*, **193**, 554–556.

Lyon, B.R., Tennent, J.M., May, J.W. & Skurray, R.A. (1986) Trimethoprim resistance encoded on a *Staphylococcus aureus* gentamicin resistance plasmid: cloning and transposon mutagensis. *FEMS Microbiology Letters*, **33**, 289–192.

Marples, R.R. & Cooke, E.M. (1988) Current problems with methicillin-resistant *Staphylococcus aureus*. *Journal of Hospital Infection*, **11**, 371–392.

Mayon-White, R.T., Ducal, G., Kereselidze, G. & Tikomirov, E. (1988) An international survey of the prevalence of hospital acquired infection. *Journal of Hospital Infection*, **11**, Supplement A, 43–48.

Meers, P.D. Ayliffe, G.A.J., Emerson, A.M., Leigh, P.A., Mayon-White R.T., Mackintosh, C.A. & Strange, J.L. (1981) National survey of infection in hospitals. *Journal of Hospital Infection*, **2**, Supplement.

Murray, B.E. (1987) Plasmid-mediated β-lactamase in *Enterococcus faecalis*. In *Streptococcal Genetics* (eds Feretti, J.V. and Curtiss, R. III,) pp. 83–86. Washington DC: American Society for Microbiology.

Naidoo, J. (1984) Interspecific co-transfer of antibiotic resistance in staphylococci *in vivo*. *Journal of Hygiene, Cambridge*, **95**, 59–66.

Noble, W.C. & Naidoo, J. (1978) Evolution of antibiotic resistance in *Staphylococcus aureus*: the role of the skin. *British Journal of Dermatology*, **98**, 481–489.

Novick, R.P. & Morse, S.I. (1968) *In vivo* transmission of drug resistance factors between strains of *Staphylococcus aureus*. *Journal of Experimental Medicine*, **125**, 45–59.

Parker, M.T. (1983) The significance of phage-typing patterns in *Staphylococcus aureus*. In *Staphylococci and Staphylococcal Infections*, Vol. 1: *Clinical and Epidemiological Aspects* (eds Easmon, F.S. & Adlam, C.) pp. 33–62. London: Academic Press.

Pattee, P.A. & Neveln D.E.S. (1975) Transformation analysis of three linkage groups in *Staphylococcus aureus*. *Journal of Bacteriology*, **124**, 201–211.

Phillips, I. (1988) Introduction: hospital infection in the 1990's. *Journal of Hospital Infection*, **11**, Supplement A, 3–6.

Rahman, M., Nando, J. & George, R.C. (1988) New generic location of gentamicin-resistance in methicillin-resistant *Staphylococcus aureus*. *Lancet*, **ii**, **2**, 1256.

Report (1986) Guidelines for the control of epidemic methicillin resistant *Staphylococcus aureus*. *Journal of Hospital Infection*, **7**, 193–201.

Report (1990) Revised guidelines for the control of epidemic methicillin-resistant *Staphylococcus aureaus*. *Journal of Hospital Infection*, **16**, 351–377.

Rosendorf, L.L. & Kayser, F.H. (1974) Transduction and plasmid deoxyribonucleic acid analysis in a multiply antibiotic resistant strain of *Staphylococcus epidermidis*. *Journal of Bacteriology*, **120**, 697–686.

Rudin, L., Sjostrom, J-E., Lindberg, M. & Phillipson, L. (1974) Factors affecting the competence of transformation in *Staphylococcus aureus*. *Journal of Bacteriology*, **118**, 155–164.

Schaberg, D.R. & Zervos, M.J. (1986) Intergeneric and interspecies gene exchange in Gram-positive cocci. *Antimicrobial Agents and Chemotherapy*, **30**, 817–32.

Schaeffler, S. (1982) Bacteriophage-mediated acquisition of antibiotic resistance in *Staphylococcus aureus* type 88. *Antimicrobial Agents and Chemotherapy*, **21**, 460–467.

Shalita, Z., Murphy, E. & Novick, R.P. (1980) Penicillinase plasmids of *Staphylococcus aureus*: structural and evolutionary relationships. *Plasmid*, **3**, 291–311.

Shanson, D.C. (1986) Staphylococcal infection in hospitals. *British Journal of Medicine*, **35**, 312–320.

Shanson, D.C. (1989) *Microbiology in Clinical Practice*, 2nd Ed. London: Wright.

Skurray, R.A., Rouch, D.A., Lyon, B.R., Gillespie, M.T., Tennant, J.M., Bryne, M.E., Meserotti, L.J. & May, J.W. (1988) Multiresistant *Staphylococcus aureus*: genetics and evolution of epidemic Australian strains. *Journal of Antimicrobial Chemotherapy*, **21**, Supplement C, 19–38.

Stiffler, P.W., Sweeney, H.M. & Cohen, S. (1974) Cotransduction of plasmids mediating resistance to tetracycline and chloramphenicol in *Staphylococcus aureus*. *Journal of Bacteriology*, **120**, 934–944.

Tennent, J.M., Lyon, B.R., Gillespie, M.T., May, J.W. & Skurray, R.A. (1985) Cloning and expression of *Staphylococcus aureus*, plasmid-mediated quaternary ammonium resistance in *Escherichia coli*. *Antimicrobial Agents and Chemotherapy*, **27**, 79–83.

Thompson, R. (1986) R plasmid transfer. *Journal of Antimicrobial Chemotherapy*, **18**, Supplement C, 13–23.

Thornsberry, C. (1988) The development of antimicrobial resistance in staphylococci. *Journal of Antimicrobial Chemotherapy*, **21**, Supplement C, 9–16.

Townsend, D.E., Ashdown, N., Greed, L.C. & Grubb, W.B. (1983) Plasmid-mediated resistance to quaternary ammonium compounds in methicillin-resistant *Staphylo-*

coccus aureus. *Medical Journal of Australia*, **ii**, 310.

Townsend, D.E., Ashdown, N., Bradley, J.M., Pearman, J.W. & Grubb, W.B. (1984a) 'Australian' methicillin-resistant *Staphylococcus aureus* in a London hospital? *Medical Journal of Australia*, **ii**, 339–340.

Townsend, D.E., Ashdown, N., Greed, L.C. & Grubb, W.B. (1984b) Transposition of gentamicin resistance to staphylococcal plasmids encoding resistance to cationic agents. *Journal of Antimicrobial Chemotherapy*, **14**, 115–134.

Townsend, D.E., Ashdown, N., Bolton, S. & Grubb, W.B. (1985) The use of cetyltrimethylammonium bromide for the rapid isolation from *Staphylococcus aureus* of relaxable and non-relaxable plasmid DNA suitable for *in vitro* manipulation. *Letters in Applied Microbiology*, **1**, 87–94.

Townsend, D.E., Bolton, S., Asdown, N., Taheri, S. & Grubb, W.B. (1986) Comparison of phage mediated and conjugative transfer of staphylococcus plasmid *in vitro* and *in vivo*. *Journal of Medical Microbiology*, **22**, 107–114.

Tuffnell, D.J., Croton, R.S., Hemingway, D.M., Hartley, M.N., Wake, P.N. & Garvey, R.J.P. (1987) Methicillin-resistant *Staphylococcus aureus*; the role of antisepsis in the control of an outbreak. *Journal of Hospital Infection*, **10**, 255–259.

Wenzel, R.P. (1987) Towards a global perspective of nosocomial infections. *European Journal of Clinical Medicine*, **6**, 341–343.

Witte, W. (1977) Transfer of drug resistance-plasmids in mixed cultures of staphylococci. *Zentrablatt für Bakteriologie, Parasitenkunde Infektionskrankheiten Hygiene, I, Abteilung Originale Reihe A*, **237**, 147–159.

Yamamoto, T., Tamura, Y. & Yokama, T. (1988) Antiseptic and antibiotic resistance plasmid in *Staphylococcus aureus* that possesses ability to confer chlorhexidine and acrinol resistance. *Antimicrobial Agents and Chemotherapy*, **32**, 932–935.

Chapter 11
Good Manufacturing Practice

1 INTRODUCTION

A good hygienic standard is one of the prime targets in the pharmaceutical, cosmetic and food industries. As well as protecting the consumer it has an economic basis in the prevention of product loss due to microbial spoilage (Hargreaves, 1990).

Raw materials including water supplies are one of the main sources of micro-organisms and can result in the contamination of the environment and manufacturing plant. Contamination may also arise from poor hygienic practices by process operators and a failure to follow cleaning and disinfection procedures. Microbial contamination can be controlled by the selection of raw materials and by following the principles of good manufacturing practice (GMP), i.e. providing suitable premises, equipment and environment with trained personnel to operate approved procedures.

Of equal importance to selecting raw materials with a good microbial quality is the control of the environment to create unfavourable conditions for microbial growth. To achieve this, both cleaning and disinfection must be approached on a technological basis with trials to evaluate the ability of detergents to remove soil residues since this will affect the efficiency of the disinfection stage. Cleaning and disinfection should be regarded as a part of the manufacturing process, with written procedures and an adequate time allotted for them to be carried out correctly.

2 CLEANING AGENTS

There is a wide choice of cleaning agents available, including alkalis, both mineral and organic acids, and cationic, anionic or non-ionic surfactants. Careful selection is necessary to ensure that the chosen agent fulfils the following criteria; it must:

1 suit the surface to be cleaned, and not cause corrosion;

2 remove the type of soil present without leaving any sort of residue;

3 be compatible with the water supply.

A suitable detergent must have adequate wetting properties to enable the solvent, usually water, to contact all areas by reducing the surface tension and permitting penetration into all cracks, pinholes and porous materials. In addition it should disperse any aggregates of soil into small particles, and retain any insoluble material in suspension in order that the soil may be easily flushed from the surface. The detergent itself must be able to be rinsed away without leaving a deposit on the surface.

Ideally only soft water should be used for cleaning, but where this is impracticable it is important that any alkaline detergent used is compatible with the local water supply, or that water conditioning or sequestering agents are added. If very hard water is used it may be necessary to incorporate an acid rinse into the cleaning cycle to prevent scale. This is of particular importance in the dairy industry to reduce the problems of 'milkstone'. This use, and that as a general cleaner, form the main functions of acid detergents.

In selecting an alkaline detergent, the active alkalinity is an important criterion if it is required to deal with fat-containing residues by saponification into a 'soap', or to neutralize acidic constituents. By counterbalancing the active alkalinity against the alkali demand, the optimum pH for soil removal and to protect the surface from corrosion can be achieved.

Each type of surface-active agent (see also Chapter 2) has different properties: anionics, salts of complex organic acids, are good detergents but poor bactericides; non-ionics, organic compounds but not salts, have good wetting powers; cationics, salts of complex organic bases, are good bactericides but have poorer detergent properties. Cationic and anionic compounds must not be used together, but their two properties are combined in amphoteric compounds.

Cleaning agents are often more effective when used hot, but temperatures of 65°C should not be exceeded when removing fat-containing films since the emulsion formed with the detergent is destroyed. This temperature restriction also applies to some alkaline detergents when used with hard water. Acid cleaners are normally used cold.

Detergents should be evaluated before their introduction as part of a cleaning cycle. A study of their physical properties, such as solubility in water, active alkalinity reaction, buffering ability, sequestering power and stability in both the dry and liquid forms, will give some guide as to their suitability for a given task, but the final test must be an assessment of the efficiency of removing soil from surfaces. In addition to visual and chemical tests for residues, a fluorescent dye may be introduced with the soil before application of the detergent, and the surface examined with ultraviolet (UV) light after cleaning. Many foodstuffs are, however, naturally fluorescent in UV light and it is often standard practice to include the examination of equipment with a specially designed lamp as a post-cleaning check.

It is sometimes useful to combine a cleaning and sanitizing stage, but this is only successful where light soiling occurs and a relatively low level of microbial contamination has to be removed. It also has the advantage of providing a bactericide in the wash water, a factor which is often a source of contamination in itself. Not all detergents and disinfectants are compatible, and this must be checked if novel combinations are used. Three main types are commercially available and include:

1 alkaline detergents formulated with chlorine-liberating compounds;

2 alkaline detergents formulated with quaternary ammonium compounds (QACs) or non-ionic surfactants;

3 acid detergents with iodophors.

Detailed accounts of detergency and cleaning practice in the food (Parker & Litchfield, 1962) and dairy (Anon., 1959a) industries have been published.

2.1 Control of cleaning agents

The effectiveness of in-place cleaning depends upon control of the detergent concentration, and this may be carried out by testing samples at both the start and end of the circulation period. If the detergent concentration is lower than that established in trials, then all the soil may not be removed; if it is higher, it may require additional rinsing to remove it from the plant, as well as being wasteful. One of the most useful tests is the titratable alkali or acid content.

Regular inspections should be carried out on all equipment, especially behind O-rings, gaskets and rubber diaphragms where soil may remain. As described previously inspection with an UV lamp is useful if the soil contains materials fluorescent under such conditions.

3 DISINFECTION AND STERILIZATION

The choice of disinfecting non-disposable equipment and instruments is usually between heat and a chemical agent. Heat is the more reliable and is the first choice for industrial plant used for aseptic preparation and filling operations, but it is usually both too expensive and impracticable for use with large-scale industrial machinery, and chemical agents are employed. Where necessary buildings, interiors and fittings are treated chemically, but a wider range of techniques are available for the sterilization of water, air and raw materials.

3.1 Chemical disinfectants

The choice of disinfectant is governed by the material or surface to be treated, and in some instances by the type of contaminating micro-organism present. The types of disinfectants and their properties are described in Chapter 2, but Table 11.1 shows some of their industrial applications.

3.1.1 Control and monitoring of chemical disinfectants

With the exception of some halogen-containing preparations, most sterilizing agents are stable chemically in the undiluted state for normal storage periods. Inorganic halogens such as sodium hypochlorite solution deteriorate on storage and must be assayed both on receipt and just before use if stored.

Written instructions should be available for the preparation or dilution of all disinfectants and they should state the source of the water to be used. It is important that water of good microbiological quality is used to dilute disinfectants, particularly those which may support the growth of waterborne organisms, e.g. QACs. Disinfectants prepared for use should be stored for the minimum possible time and be clearly labelled with the date of preparation and expiry, as well as the contents and the dilution factor. Diluted batches should not be 'topped up' with fresh solutions, but the containers should be emptied and cleaned before refilling. In the case of disinfectants which are vulnerable to colonization by some groups of micro-organisms such as biguanides and QACs, the containers should be washed and either heat-sterilized or treated with an active chemical agent before re-use. This also applies to sprays and other dispensing equipment.

The methods for evaluating chemical disinfectants were given in Chapter 4, and their selection and practical applications were considered in Chapter 2.

In addition to the selection of a disinfectant for a given task, regular 'in-use' tests should be made. These may take the form of examining the surface disinfected for residual micro-organisms, a facet which is considered later in this chapter, or they

Table 11.1 The industrial applications for chemical disinfectants

Disinfectant	Food industry	Pharmaceutical and cosmetic industry
Halogens, e.g. sodium hypochlorite, chlorine gas, iodophors	Water supplies, equipment, packaging, working surfaces	Water supplies, equipment packaging, working surfaces
Quaternary ammonium compounds (QACs)	Equipment, building interior fittings, working surfaces	Equipment, building interior fittings, working surfaces
Phenols and related compounds	Not in common use	Building interior fittings, skin disinfectant
Alcohols: ethanol or isopropanol	Working surfaces, equipment. Useful for small-scale treatment after maintenance during a production run	Working surfaces, equipment. Useful for small-scale treatment after maintenance during a production run
Amphoteric compounds	Skin disinfectant, equipment	Skin disinfectant, equipment
Hydrogen peroxide	Used hot for plastic packaging in the dairy industry. Some raw materials	Not in common use
Biguanides	Skin disinfectant	Skin disinfectant
Aldehydes		
Liquid or vaporized formaldehyde, glutaraldehyde	Not in common use	Process water, some equipment
Gaseous	Fumigation of poultry houses	Fumigation of clean or aseptic processing areas, packaging
Ethylene oxide	Some raw materials	Raw materials, finished products, packaging

may involve testing a sample of the disinfectant in which instruments or equipment are being treated, for the presence of micro-organisms. A detailed account of the test devised by Kelsey and Maurer giving dilution levels and the inactivating agents required for some disinfectants is given by Maurer (1985).

Gaseous disinfection is dependent both upon the environmental conditions and the concentration of the agent. When ethylene oxide is used, the temperature and the humidity must both be monitored (Chapter 20) and at least ten biological indicators, carrying spores of *Bacillus subtilis* (Beeby & Whitehouse, 1965) placed in the load. The spores may be dried onto aluminium or paper strips which after the cycle are tested for viable cells. Some commercial preparations are available in which the spore-bearing strip and medium for bacterial testing are contained in a single, double-walled unit which is convenient for the process operator to handle. Formaldehyde gas requires a relative humidity of 80–90% to be effective, and monitoring is usually carried out by checking the residual surviving micro-organisms on the surface of the treated materials.

Records should be kept of all monitoring carried out on chemical disinfection processes, and in the pharmaceutical industry these may be required to be kept with batch records of the product treated.

3.2 Disinfection and sterilization by heat

Heat may be used with or without the aid of moisture to disinfect or sterilize. The advantage of the pressure of moisture is that lower temperatures are required.

3.2.1 Dry heat

Temperatures in excess of 160°C throughout a hot-air oven are usually recommended for dry heat sterilization. This is used for sterilizing equipment and some dry powders in both the cosmetic and pharmaceutical industries. It is usually necessary for sterilizing ovens to be equipped with a fan to distribute heat evenly, and careful packing of the load is important to prevent local cold spots. The temperature should be recorded from a probe sited at the potentially coolest part of the load. An inlet air sterilizing filter should be fitted to prevent contamination as the load cools. Equipment or instruments sterilized by this method must be wrapped or suitably protected to prevent contamination on removal from the oven.

Containers used for parenteral pharmaceutical preparations are often sterilized at temperatures higher than those required to kill micro-organisms, in order to destroy any pyrogenic residues present.

3.2.2 Moist heat

Moist heat may be used in the form of steam under pressure in an autoclave at temperatures which destroy all micro-organisms (see Chapter 18A, B) or in the form of hot water or a water-and-steam mixture which kills only a limited range. Additionally, low-temperature steam with formaldehyde has some applications as a sterilizing agent (Chapter 18A). Correctly operated, hot-water pasteurization kills all but the most heat-resistant of bacterial cells in the vegetative phase, but it does not destroy bacterial spores.

The minimum useful temperature for hot-water pasteurization is 65°C which, with a 10-min holding time, may be used for pasteurizing some small items such as containers and for laundering fabric components. The minimum hold period decreases as the temperature increases, and where temperatures in excess of 80°C are possible the time may be reduced to a 1-min hold. It is important that all hot-water pasteurizing equipment is emptied during a standstill to reduce the risk of bacterial colonization (Hambraeus *et al.*, 1968). For large items of equipment, however, steam is more practicable and may be used to treat tanks, pipelines and other equipment whose surface is free from organic residues. If heavy soiling is present, there is the risk of baking it onto the surface and providing a protective layer of insulation around the micro-organisms. The monitor the process, the temperature of the steam condensate should be measured. For an efficient process this should reach 95°C and be maintained for a minimum period of 5 min to destroy vegetative cells. One advantage of this method is that the equipment is rinsed with sterile water.

Moist heat at temperatures of 121°C and above is used extensively in the pharmaceutical industry to sterilize equipment, instruments and heat-stable fluids. To ensure sterilization, equipment and instruments must be wrapped in a porous material which allows air to be drawn out and steam to penetrate in, but protects the item from recontamination after sterilization. The temperature must be recorded throughout the cycle by a probe sited in the coolest part of the load or chamber; in practice this is usually the chamber drain. The pressure may also be recorded, but must not be used to control the process. Precautions must be taken to prevent recontamination of the sterilizer load as it cools: this usually involves the installation of a pre-sterilized filter on the air inlet.

In the food industry, moist heat is used extensively for processing and sterilizing. For the latter, a balance has to be calculated to destroy the microbial load with minimal damage to the nutritional and organoleptic properties, and the additive value of all heat considered equivalent in minutes to 121.1°C (250°F), i.e. F or F_0 value, is used. The processing temperature and time thus vary with the type of food, its microbial load and, if being processed in the final container, the size and heat penetration properties of the container. For products which are processed by UHT and aseptically filled, the temperature and time will depend upon acidity (pH), viscosity and presence of particulate matter. There are legal requirements for the conditions of UHT processing of milk and milk-based products.

3.2.3 Monitoring of heat sterilization processes

Four main methods are used to monitor both moist

and dry heat sterilization processes. These are:

1 Sterility tests, which are tests on the sterilized product or material to detect the presence of micro-organisms. For pharmaceutical products this is usually performed in accordance with the European or United States Pharmacopoeias.

2 Biological indicator tests, which involve determining the viability, after processing, of paper strips impregnated with spores of *Bacillus stearothermophilus* (for moist heat) or a specific non-toxic strain of *Clostridium tetani* (dry heat). These indicators are placed in sealed envelopes or specially designed tubes in the load.

3 Physical tests, which are tests using copper–constantan thermocouples sited in various positions in the load to monitor the temperature. Special fittings are available for determining the temperatures inside containers, and for use with rotating moist-heat sterilizers as well as the stationary type. They have the advantage of showing both the temperature reached and the duration of hold in the load. They are very important in dry-heat sterilizing areas to ensure that the correct temperature is reached in all areas, and in some steam sterilizers to ensure that temperature layering due to the presence of residual air does not occur.

4 Chemical indicators, of which various types are available, including the following: Browne's tubes which are both temperature- and time-related; and heat-sensitive tapes which usually indicate only that a certain temperatures has been reached, but not the duration of hold, and do not therefore constitute proof of sterilization. Paper sterilization bags printed with a heat-sensitive indicator are, however, a useful visual guide to the operator in industry that the contents have been through a heat process.

More detailed accounts of sterilization control are given by Russell (1980) and Denyer (1987), and in Chapter 20.

4 BUILDING AND FITTINGS

Ideally the premises should be purpose-built to a sanitary design with modern easy-to-clean materials, and sited in surroundings which are free from potential harbourages for rodents, birds and insects. Buildings and sites which do not meet these requirements may be brought up to current standards by rigorous pest-control systems and renovation of interior finishes. Regardless of the age of the building, to maintain a good standard of hygiene a well-planned and adequate waste disposal system is essential.

4.1 Plant design

The design of a plant with regard to the separation of different functions and prescribed routes of movement for personnel, raw materials and waste influences the control of micro-organisms. The following are some examples of operations which can influence the microbial quality of the environment and their siting should be considered at the planning stage.

4.1.1 Large steam usage

Processes which generate or involve large steam usage, which results in high humidity, must be sited away from the production or filling of dry materials preserved by their lack of available water, since moisture in the form of condensate may spoil the product.

4.1.2 Waste disposal system

This must be designed to prevent the effluent from a potentially contaminated area from flowing through a cleaner one.

4.1.3 Dust generation

Operations which generate dust are usually a potential source of airborne contamination. They include the dispensing of raw materials, in particular flours, sugars and other dried materials from natural sources; packaging involving card or paperboard, and the soiled linen side of the laundry. These should be physically separated and have different dust control and air supply systems from functions which require a low microbial count.

4.1.4 Raw materials

Raw materials which have a high microbial count

should not pass through areas where clean operations are in process. In areas where a low microbial count is essential it may be desirable to dedicate fork-lift trucks to serve them and not risk the introduction of contamination from an all-purpose fleet. In addition, unless specified, pallets may not be restricted to use in factories where hygiene is at a premium and may introduce both micro-organisms and insects.

4.1.5 Staff

Staff working in a potentially contaminated or dusty area should not have access to cleaner areas without first washing and changing their clothing. In areas where aseptic work is carried out, it is usual to provide a separate changing room—fitted with sanitary washing facilities such as foot- or elbow-operated taps and hot-air hand-drying machines—through which the staff may pass by a series of airlocks before reaching the work area. The entry into a clean area may be delineated by the use of a contamination control mat, but this must be selected with care to ensure it does remove micro-organisms, as well as acting as a psychological barrier (Meddick, 1977).

4.2 Floors and drains

To minimize microbial contamination all floors must be easy to clean, impervious to water and laid on a flat surface. In some areas it may be necessary for the floor to slope towards a drain, in which case the gradient should be such that no pools of water form. Any joints in the floor, necessary for expansion, should be adequately sealed. The floor-to-wall junction should be coved.

The finish of the floor will often relate to its use or the process being carried out; in areas where little moisture or product is liable to be spilt, polyvinyl chloride welded sheeting may be satisfactory, but in wet areas, or where frequent washing is necessary, brick tiles or concrete with a hard finish of terrazzo or other ground and polished surfaces are superior. Where concrete is used as a flooring material it must be adequately sealed with an epoxy resin or substitute to protect it against food acids and alkaline cleaning compounds. Likewise, Portland cement joints cannot be used in food and dairy plants due to their erosion by food and cleaning acids. Corrosion-resistant resin cements can, however, be used. Whilst easier to clean, excessively smooth finishes must be avoided in wet areas where they may become very slippery.

In areas where very dirty or heavily contaminated materials are being handled, a high proportion of drains to floor area is necessary, and any such drains should be vented to the outside air and provided with rodent screens. Deep-seal traps (P-, V- or S-shaped but not bell-type) should be fitted to all floor drains and be easily accessible for cleaning. Adequate sealing arrangements must be made in dry- and cold-storage areas where water seals in traps evaporate without replenishment, and a regular inspection is important.

As mentioned earlier, the effluent from a contaminated area must not flow through a cleaner area, and drains should be avoided in locations where aseptic operations are carried out. If drains have to be installed, they must be fitted with effective vented traps, preferably with electrically operated heat-sterilizing devices. Where floor channels are necessary they should be open, shallow, easy to clean and connected to drains outside the critical area. Routine microbiological checks should be made on all drainage systems in such areas.

4.3 Walls and ceilings

To reduce microbial colonization the internal surfaces of walls and ceilings must be smooth and impervious to water, and the wall-to-ceiling joint coved to minimize dust collection. The surface should be washable and of a type which will not support mould growth. A modern material which meets this requirement is laminated plastic, but where a wall is plastered, it can be improved by a coat of hard gloss paint, which seals the nutrients present in the plaster from microbial attack more effectively than a softer matt finish. The addition of up to 1% of a fungistatic agent such as pentachlorophenol, 8-hydroxyquinoline or salicylanilide is also an advantage. In areas of high humidity, painted surfaces are likely to peel, and glazed bricks or tiles adequately sealed are the best finish. Where a considerable volume of steam is used, ventilation at ceiling level is important. Claddings of aluminium or stainless steel have been found to be satisfactory for cold-storage room walls, and thermal cellular glass insulation blocks are suitable for the construction of partitions or non-load-bearing walls.

To aid cleaning, all electrical cables and other services should be installed either in deep cavity walls or in a false ceiling where they are accessible for maintenance but do not collect dust. All pipes which pass through walls or ceilings must be well sealed and flush. Wall and false ceiling cavities must be included in the rodent and pest control.

Equipment or storage systems should be positioned to allow access to walls and ceilings for cleaning. In warehouse areas, pallets should be stacked away from walls to permit cleaning and adequate rodent control.

4.4 Doors, windows and fittings

Wherever possible, doors and windows should fit flush with the walls, and dust-collecting ledges should be eliminated. Where wood is used in the construction, a hard gloss finish is the easiest to clean. Doors should be well-fitting to reduce the entry of micro-organisms, except where a positive air pressure is maintained. Where positive pressure systems are required due to the critical nature of the work, they should be fitted with indicator gauges which must be checked regularly.

Windows in manufacturing areas should serve only to permit light entry and should not be used for ventilation. If, however, they are necessary for ventilation, they must be fitted with insect-proof meshes. An adequate air-control system other than windows must be supplied to all areas where aseptic techniques or operations vulnerable to microbial contamination are being carried out.

Overhead pipes in all manufacturing areas must be sited away from equipment to prevent condensation and possible contaminants from falling into the product. Unless neglected, stainless-steel pipes support little microbial growth, but lagged pipes always present a problem unless the lagging is well sealed with a waterproof outer membrane and treated regularly with a chemical disinfectant.

Recommendations of the building and standards of interior fittings recommended for the production of pharmaceutical products are given in the *Guide to Good Pharmaceutical Manufacturing Practice* (Anon., 1977).

4.5 Cleaning and disinfection

Walls, ceilings and fittings usually only require a hot-water and detergent wash to remove nutrients, which may encourage microbial growth, and dust, which might harbour it. Care must be taken not to scratch plaster surfaces since this may release additional nutrients to support mould growth. Where chemical disinfection is required, the surface must be cleaned thoroughly unless a detergent sanitizing agent is used. Suitable disinfectants include QACs and, except in food factories, phenolics.

The cleaning of floors depends both upon their construction and use, but in all instances, vacuum cleaning using an industrial sanitary model, which filters the exhaust air to remove micro-organisms before discharging it into the atmosphere, is preferable to the use of a broom which scatters dust and micro-organisms. If vacuum cleaning is not possible, damp cleaning may be used. Where brooms are used, they should be made from synthetic materials which can be heat sterilized.

In processing areas, the floors usually require a hot-water and detergent scrub, which includes all drainage channels and drains. This, followed by a hot-water rinse, is usually sufficient. Where greasy materials are present, drains require regular treatment with an alkali to eliminate residues which may support microbial growth. Where a disinfectant is required, a formulated halogen, a QAC or a phenolic may be used.

Fittings, furnishings and equipment external surfaces should be damp-cleaned with hot water containing a detergent. The detergent acts not only as a cleaning agent but also as a wetting agent for shiny surfaces. Disinfection is usually only necessary where neglect has permitted visible microbial colonization or where aseptic processes are being carried out. Suitable disinfectants include QACs, phenols, alcohols and formaldehyde, but a check on the compatibility with the surface material should be made before use.

With overhead fittings where regular cleaning is

impracticable, a thin smear of liquid paraffin may be used to coat fixtures after cleaning and act as a dust trap. This must, however, be cleaned off and a fresh coat applied on a planned basis.

The techniques for monitoring the microbiological state of building interiors and fittings are similar to those used for equipment, and will be described in Section 6.4.

4.6 Pest control

Pest control, preferably by denying access, is imperative to the maintenance of a good standard of hygiene. Insect control may be by prevention of access, i.e. insect-proof screens on all windows, doors and air intake fans which are used for ventilation, air currents or plastic strips for fork-lift truck access, and insectocutors sited at strategic points in the factory. The latter should, ideally, be sited outside manufacturing areas to attract flying insects before they reach the processing plant. Where they are sited inside manufacturing areas, it is important that they are placed to prevent insects attracted by them from flying over open vessels, or unprotected food materials. Inspection of raw materials, before acceptance, may reduce infestation in warehouses or manufacturing areas. If insecticides need to be used, either to eliminate infestation or as a prophylactic, only those approved for food use may be used, and all precautions should be taken to ensure they do not gain access to products, raw materials or packaging materials.

Rodents may be successfully controlled by prevention of access and baiting. All door fittings, pipe entry ports, etc. should be checked to ensure that they fit flushly, and rodent-proof strips should be fitted where necessary. Drains should be fitted with rodent-proof traps, and all service ducts baited and inspected regularly for rodent infestation.

Bird access, and soiling of the site and roofs, is often more difficult to control. Access may be prevented by maintaining the building in good condition, and by frequent inspection of the site, in particular warehouse and roof spaces to ensure no access points are present. For preference automatically opening doors should be used for fork-lift truck access, but in lieu of this, plastic strips may provide a deterrent. Soiling of roofs, particularly where nutritional powder emissions occur, is very difficult to control, and hygienic measures to ensure they are regularly sanitized, which also controls insect populations, should be carried out. Wherever possible, staff who need access to roofs should not re-enter a building, and if it is necessary to do so, should change their shoes. Over-shoes can be used, or a foot bath of disinfectant may be used to sanitize the boots or shoes of operatives who have to walk outside the building where bird soil contamination may be present.

5 AIR

The number of airborne micro-organisms is related to the activity in the environment, the amount of dust disturbed and the microbial load of the material being handled. Thus an area containing working machinery and an active personnel will have a higher microbial count than one with a still atmosphere. Some industrial processes which handle contaminated materials, particularly in the dry form, increase the air count; these include dispensing, blending and the additon to open vessels.

The control of the microflora of the air is desirable in all manufacturing areas and can be improved by air conditioning (Lidwell & Noble, 1975). Some processes do, however, require a very low microbial air count, and these include the manufacture and packaging of parenteral and ophthalmic preparations in the pharmaceutical and cosmetic industries, and aseptic filling and packaging in the food industry.

5.1 Disinfection

The microbial air count may be reduced by filtration (Chapter 21), chemical disinfection (Chapter 2) and to a limited extent by UV light (Chapter 19B). Filtration is the most commonly used method, and filters may be composed of a variety of materials, such as cellulose, glass wool, fibre-glass mixtures or polytetrafluoroethylene (PTFE) with resin or acrylic binders. For the most critical aseptic work it may be necessary to remove all particles in excess of 0.1 μm in size, but for many operations a standard of less than 100 particles per cu. ft. (3.5/l) of

0.5 μm or larger (class 100) is adequate. Such fine filtration is usually preceded by a coarser filter stage, or any suspended matter is removed by passing the air through an electrostatic field. To maintain efficiency, all air filters must be kept dry, sinc micro-organisms may be capable of movement along continuous wet films and may be carried through a damp filter.

Filtered air may be used to purge a complete room, or it may be confined to a specific area and incorporate the principle of laminar flow, which permits operations to be carried out in a gentle current of sterile air. The direction of the air flow may be horizontal or vertical, depending upon the type of equipment being used, the type of operation and the material being handled. It is important that there is no obstruction between the air supply and the exposed product, since this may result in the deflection of micro-organisms or particulate matter from a non-sterile surface and cause contamination.

Chemical disinfectants are of limited use as sterilants due to their irritant properties, but both atomized propylene glycol, at 0.05–0.5 mg/l, and QACs at 0.075% may be used. For areas which can be effectively sealed, formaldehyde gas is useful.

In the food industry a combination of hydrogen peroxide and filtration is used to sterilize air feeds to aseptic filling machines. Ultraviolet irradiation at wavelengths between 280 and 240 nm may be used to reduce the air count. Additional information is provided in Chapter 2.

5.2 Compressed air

Compressed air has many applications which bring it into direct contact with the product, examples being the conveyance of suspensions or dry powders, fermentations and some products such as ice-cream and whipped dairy confections that contain air as an integral part of the structure. Unless the air is pre-sterilized by filtration or a combination of heat and filtration, micro-organisms will be introduced into the product.

5.3 Monitoring air for microbial content

Air-flow gauges are essential in all areas where aseptic work is performed. In laminar flow units they are necessary for checking that the correct flow rate is obtained, and in complete suites to ensure that a positive pressure from clean to less-clean areas is always maintained.

The integrity of the air-filtration system must be checked regularly. One method is by counting the particulate matter both in the working area and across the filter surface. For foodstuffs and some pharmaceuticals which are aseptically filled, it is usual to carry out a count prior to the start of the operation. For systems which have complex ducting, or where the surface of the terminal filter is recessed, smoke tests using a chemical of known particulate size such as dioctylphthalate (DOP) may be introduced just after the main fan and monitored at each outlet. This test has a twofold application, since the integrity of the terminal filter is checked and any leaks in the ducting are detected.

The particulate air count, whilst rapid and useful, does not replace a count of the viable airborne micro-organisms. Common methods for checking this include:

1 The exposure of Petri dishes containing a nutrient agar to the atmosphere for a given length of time. This relies upon micro-organisms or dust particles bearing them to settle upon the surface.

2 The use of a slit sampling machine, which is essentially a device for drawing a measured quantity of air from the environment and impinging it upon either a revolving Petri dish containing a nutrient medium or a membrane filter which may then be incubated with a nutrient medium. This method provides valuable information in areas of low microbial contamination, particularly if the sample is taken close to the working area.

The microbial content of compressed air may be assessed by bubbling a known volume through a nutrient broth, which is then filtered through a membrane. The membrane is incubated on nutrient agar and a total viable count made.

A detailed account of air disinfection and sterilization and methods used for its monitoring was given by Sykes (1965).

6 EQUIPMENT

All equipment must be designed and constructed so that all internal contact points and the external surfaces may be cleaned.

Whilst many metals are suitable for the construction of parts which are not in direct contact with the product, copper, lead, iron, zinc, cadmium and antimony must be avoided for contact surfaces. The choice for contact surfaces includes stainless steel, except where corrosive acids are present, titanium, glass and (if excessive heat is not required) plastics. Cloth or canvas belts should not come into contact with the product since they are absorbent and difficult to clean. Plastics and cloths of synthetic fibres are superior.

Each piece of equipment has its own peculiar area where micro-organisms may proliferate, and knowledge of its weak points may be built up by regular tests for contamination. The type and extent of growth will depend upon the source of the contamination, the nutrients available and the environmental conditions, in particular the temperature and pH.

The following points are common to many pieces of equipment, including some used in hospitals, and serve as a general guide to appraising the cleaning programme for the equipment and reducing the risk of microbial colonization.

1 All equipment should be easy to dismantle and clean.

2 All surfaces which are in contact with the product should be smooth, continuous and free from pits. All sharp corners should be eliminated and any junctions welded. Any internal welds should be polished out. There must be no dead ends. All contact surfaces must be inspected on a routine basis for signs of damage: this is very important in the case of lagged equipment, double-walled and lined vessels, since any cracks or pinholes in the surface may allow the product to seep into an area where it is protected from cleaning and sterilizing agents, and where micro-organisms may grow and contaminate subsequent batches of product.

3 There should be no inside screw threads, and all outside threads should be accessible for cleaning.

4 Coupling nuts on all pipework and valves should be capable of being taken apart and cleaned.

5 Agitator blades should preferably be of one piece with the shaft and accessible for cleaning. Careful post-cleaning checks are usually necessary if the blade shaft is packed into a housing.

6 Rotary seals are superior to packing boxes since packing material is usually difficult to sterilize and often requires a lubricant which may gain access to the product.

7 The product must be protected from any lubricant used on moving parts.

8 Valves should be specially selected for the purpose they are to fulfil, and the type of cleaning designed to clean and sterilize all contact parts of the valve. The dairy industry has traditionally used the plug type of valve, incorporated with a cleaning system which will contact all surfaces. With the introduction of aseptic transfer and filling systems a bellows type of valve, with a steam barrier protection, has been favoured. The pharmaceutical and some food manufacturing industry processes successfully use a diaphragm type of valve. All valves must be well maintained and have a cleaning system which reaches all contact surfaces. With diaphragm type valves it is essential to ensure that the diaphragm is in good condition and the product cannot seep behind it, and in very wet areas it is protected so that water from hoses does not enter by the 'dirty' side of the diaphragm.

9 All pipelines should slope away from the product source and all process and storage vessels should be self-draining. Run-off valves should be as near to the tank as possible. Sampling through the run-off valve should be avoided, since any nutrients left in the valve may encourage microbial growth which could contaminate the complete batch. A separate sampling hatch or cock is preferable.

10 If a vacuum-exhaust system is used to remove air or steam from a preparation vessel, it is necessary to clean and disinfect all fittings regularly. This prevents residues which may be drawn into them from supporting microbial growth which may later be returned to the vessel with condensate.

11 Multipurpose and mobile equipment requires carefully planned cleaning programmes if used for, or moved into, areas where products of different vulnerability to microbial growth are made.

6.1 Instruments and tools

Any instruments or tools which may be used on product, contact parts of equipment, or for measuring or sampling the product, should be made of hygienic, non-corrosive material and be as simple in design and construction as possible. Tools with hollow handles should be avoided, and one-piece instruments are easier to clean than those with a separate handle. If joints are necessary, their welds should be polished out smooth. For some tasks such as sampling, pre-sterilized disposable instruments may be preferred.

6.2 Cleaning utensils

These should be as simple in construction as possible, and easy to clean. Stainless-steel bowls and buckets are ideal since they can be heat sterilized and their surfaces do not readily scratch or pit. Heat-resistant plastics are also suitable, but types which will not withstand autoclaving, and those of galvanized iron, are unsuitable. Likewise, brooms and mops should be of the type which can be heat sterilized. For preference, cleaning cloths should be disposable. If this is impracticable they must withstand boiling. Colquitt & Maurer (1969) found that all cloths and mops used for wet work had to be disinfected by heat, chemical treatment being ineffective. Scrubbing machines with badly designed tanks which cannot be emptied or heat sterilized have been found to cause contamination in hospitals (Thomas & Maurer, 1972).

6.3 Cleaning and disinfection

Equipment should be cleaned as soon as possible after use and disinfected just before it is used again. If there is a considerable time lag between uses, the equipment should be washed, disinfected and stored dry. It should then be disinfected again before use. Tanks, pumps, heat-exchange units and other equipment must be drained if standing idle and, if possible, pipelines 'cracked' open at the couplings to remove any moisture. Plant may be cleaned in place, dismantled and cleaned manually, or more commonly a combination of both methods is used. Standard cleaning procedures usually incorporate preflushing, washing, rinsing and disinfecting cycles, and it is important that a written procedure is available which states the concentration of all the agents to be used and the duration of the recycling period.

Sections of pipework are often specially designed for cleaning in place and are welded where possible to form continuous lengths and specially designed, crevice-free unions are used where coupling is necessary. An illustrated account of such fittings is given in Anon (1959b). Cleaning agents are forced through the system at a velocity of not less than 1.5 m (5 ft)/s through the largest pipe diameter of the system. The speed of flow coupled with the action of a suitable detergent removes both the soil residues and any micro-organisms which may be present, by its scouring action. It is, however, usual to pass a chemical disinfectant through the system after cleaning. Any cross-connections, T-pieces or blank ends must be carefully considered since they both decrease the efficiency of the system and provide harbours for micro-organisms.

In-place cleaning systems are also available for both plate and tubular types of heat-exchange units, pumps, some homogenizers and other equipment. However, valves. T-piece fittings for valves and gauges have to be cleaned manually. Tanks and reaction vessels may be cleaned and sterilized by the use of rotary sprays which are sited at the point in the vessel where the maximum wall area may be treated. Spray balls with a hole or jet pattern specifically designed for the individual vessel are the most efficient. Some fixtures such as agitators, pipe inlets and outlets, and vents may be blind to the spray pattern and require manual cleaning. Because of the relatively large-capacity storage tanks and pumps required for a totally automatic cleaning in-place system, it usually has to be fitted when the equipment is installed, but smaller local systems are available and can be accommodated into existing buildings and plant.

The nature of many products or plant design often renders cleaning in place impracticable, and the plant has to be dismantled for soaking and cleaning either manually or in an automatic washing machine.

Some applications for ultrasonic waves of frequencies of 30 000–40 000 Hz converted to mechanical vibrations have been found for the removal of heavy grease and food soils from small pieces of equipment which are difficult to clean, such as valves and parts with small orifices. Combination of ultrasonics with different disinfectants such as benzalkonium chloride (Shaner, 1967) and hydrogen peroxide (Ahmed & Russell, 1975) have been found to be suitable for the cold sterilization of instruments.

Equipment may be disinfected using agents such as halogens, QACs, phenolics (except for the food industry), formaldehyde, hot water and steam, or may be sterilized by moist or dry heat or exposure to ethylene oxide. Irradiation by gamma rays (Chapter 19A) is also suitable but is usually applied to disposable equipment only.

6.4 Monitoring the cleaning and disinfection of buildings and equipment

The efficiency of cleaning procedures can be assessed by chemical and microbiological tests but these often only confirm the findings of a visual inspection for soil residues. The effectiveness of the disinfection of a visually clean surface can only be established, however, by testing for the presence of micro-organisms.

There are three main methods for testing surfaces:

1 Collecting a sample of the final rinse water from an automatic cleaning cycle or rinsing the surface with a sterile diluent, and testing for the presence of micro-organisms.

2 Using a contact agar surface to replicate the flora present; this has the advantage of being quantitative, but the disadvantage of being suitable for flat planes only of hard surfaces. When this technique is used, residual nutrients may be left on the surface. Where presumptive mould growth is visible, clear vinyl tape may be used for transferring it from the surface to a microscope slide for detailed examination.

3 Using calcium alginate wool or cotton-wool swabs on the test surface and transferring to a suspending medium which is then examined for the presence of micro-organisms. In the case of calcium alginate wool swabs, quarter-strength Ringer solution containing 1.0% (w/v) sodium hexametaphosphate, which solubilizes the wool of the swab and releases the micro-organisms present, is used. Trimarchi (1959) found calcium alginate swabs to be superior to raw-cotton swabs for the examination of cutlery. This technique has the disadvantage that unless a measuring guide is used it is not quantitative, but the advantage that it may be used for any surface including curved pipes and orifices. It does not leave any residue, and for many processes the plant does not have to be recleaned and resterilized.

Modern rapid methods for the detection of micro-organisms by changes in impedance, conductivity of the media, bioluminescence or by immuno-assays can prove to be very cost-effective if used for monitoring the hygienic quality of the manufacturing environment, as well as for perishable raw materials.

A comparative study of the different methods for sampling surfaces for microbial contamination was made by Favero *et al.* (1968) and Nishannon & Pohja (1977).

7 WATER

The microbial quality of water is important because of its multiple use as a constituent of products, for washing both food and chemicals, for blanching, cooling and cleaning purposes. Micro-organisms indigenous to water are usually Gram-negative, saprophytic bacteria which are nutritionally undemanding and often have a low optimum growth temperature. Other bacteria may be introduced by soil erosion and contamination with decaying plant matter or sewage, which results in a more varied but undesirable flora and frequently includes enterobacteria.

7.1 Raw or mains water

The quality of water from the mains supply varies both with the source and the local authority responsible, and whilst it is free from pathogens and faecal contaminants such as *Escherichia coli*, it may contain other micro-organisms including *Pseudomonas aeruginosa*. Whilst bacteria tend to settle out on prolonged storage and in reservoirs, the reverse is true of industrial storage tanks where the intermittent throughput ensures that unless treated the contents serve as a source of infecton. In the summer months the count may rise rapidly and 10^5-10^6 per ml is not unknown. Collins (1964) found 98% of micro-organisms in industrial stored waters to be Gram-negative bacteria.

Regular microbiological monitoring is essential for all water supplies, and freedom from enterobacteria is essential for all water used to formulate products, to wash food or chemicals and for all plant-cleaning water. The tolerance of waterborne organisms such as pseudomonads will depend upon their ability to grow in and spoil the product.

Water used for cooling heat-processed products in cans or bottles, or for spray-cooling fluids in autoclaves, must be of a good microbial quality to eliminate the risk of post-processing contamination due to imperfect seals or seams.

The microbial count of mains water will be reflected in both the softened and de-ionized water prepared from it.

7.2 Softened water

This is usually prepared either by a base-exchange method using sodium zeolite, by a lime-soda ash process, or by the addition of sodium hexametaphosphate. Where chemical beds are used they must be treated regularly to preclude microbial colonization. Where brine is used to regenerate chemical beds, additional flora such as *Bacillus* spp. and *Staphylococcus aureus* may be introduced.

If softened water is used as the cooling agent for a canning or retorting plant, a disinfectant pretreatment to reduce the bacterial count will be necessary. Where it is used as a coolant in a heat-exchange system the microbial count will rise rapidly unless precautions are taken, and any faults or leaks arising in the heat-exchange plates or the wall of a jacketed vessel may result in the contamination of the product.

Disinfection is also necessary for water used for washing equipment whether the process is manual or automatic in-place cleaning.

7.3 De-ionized or demineralized water

De-ionized water is prepared by passing mains water through synthetic anion- or cation-exchange resin beds to remove ions. Thus any bacteria in the mains water will also be present in the de-ionized water, and beds which are not regenerated frequently with strong acid and alkaline solutions rapidly become contaminated. De-ionized water is commonly used for the formulation of pharmaceutical and cosmetic products and for the dilution of disinfectants.

7.4 Distilled water

As it leaves the still, distilled water is free from micro-organisms, and any contamination that occurs is either the result of a fault in the cooling system or in storage or distribution. If there is a fault in the cooling system, the water is usually unsatisfactory chemically as well. The flora of distilled water usually consists of Gram-negative bacteria, and since it is introduced after processing it is often a pure culture and counts of up to 10^6 organisms per ml have been recorded. Distilled water is used in the pharmaceutical industry for the preparation of oral and parenteral products. For parenteral products it is usually prepared in a specially designed glass still and a post-distillation sterilization stage is included within 4 h or collecting. Water prepared in this manner is often stored at temperatures in excess of 65°C until required, to prevent both bacterial growth and the production of pyrogenic substances which may accompany it.

7.5 Water treated by reverse osmosis

This plays a similar role to distilled water in the pharmaceutical and cosmetic industry. The process is the reverse of natural osmosis with the membrane acting as a molecular filter and retaining salts, bacteria and pyrogens. Water may, however, become contaminated either in a storage vessel or the distribution system.

7.6 Storage and distribution systems

If micro-organisms colonize a storage vessel, it then acts as a microbial reservoir and contaminates all water passing through it. It is therefore important that the contents of all storage vessels are tested regularly. Reservoirs of micro-organisms may also build up in booster pumps, water meters and unused sections of pipeline. Where a high positive pressure is absent or cannot be continuously maintained, outlets such as cocks and taps may permit bacteria to enter the system.

Burman & Colbourne (1977) carried out a survey on the ability of plumbing materials to support growth. They found that both natural and synthetic rubbers used for washers. O-rings and diaphragms were susceptible but for jointing, packing and lubricating materials, polytetrafluoroethylene (PTFE) and silicone-based compounds were superior to those based on natural products such as vegetable oils or fibres, animal fats and petroleum-based compounds. Some plastics, in particular plasticized polyvinyl chlorides and resins used in the manufacture of glass-reinforced plastics, are prone to microbial colonization.

7.7 Disinfection of water

The two main methods for treating water are by chemicals (Davis, 1959) or filtration, but UV irradiation has been used successfully with relatively low flow rates. Sodium hypochlorite or chlorine gas is the most common agent used, and the concentration employed depends both upon the dwell time and the chlorine demand of the water. For most purposes a free chlorine level of 0.5–5 parts/10^6 with a 20-min dwell time is sufficient, but for cooling processed cans or bottles, 4–10 parts/10^6 with a similar dwell time is recommended. Pipelines, outlets, pumps and meters may be treated with 50–250 parts/10^6 but it is usually necessary to use a descaling agent first in areas of hard water.

Distilled and de-ionized water systems may be treated with sodium hypochlorite or formaldehyde solution 1% (v/v). With de-ionized systems it is usually necessary to exhaust or flatten the beds with brine before sterilization with formaldehyde, to prevent inactivation to *para*-formaldehyde.

Membrane filtration is useful where the usage of water is moderate and a continuous circulation of water can be maintained. Thus, with the exception of the water drawn off the water is continually returned to the storage tank and refiltered. Control of bacteria in non-domestic water supplies has been reviewed by Chambers & Clarke (1968).

7.8 Monitoring

One of the most useful techniques for checking the microbial quality of water is by membrane filtration, since this permits the concentration of a small number of organisms from a large volume of water. The practical details are described by Windle Taylor & Burman (1964). When chlorinated water supplies are tested it is necessary to add an inactivating agent (see Russell *et al.*, 1979) such as sodium thiosulphate to the sample before testing. Although an incubation temperature of 37°C may be necessary to recover some pathogens or faecal contaminants from water, many indigenous species fail to grow at this temperature, and it is usual to incubate at 20–26°C for their detection.

8 RAW MATERIALS

Raw materials account for a high proportion of the micro-organisms introduced into processing factories and the selection of materials of a good microbial quality aids in the control of contamination levels in the environment.

Together with establishing a realistic but acceptable microbiological standard, the aspects of storage handling and processing must be considered.

8.1 Source

Raw agricultural products support a wide range of micro-organisms, including pathogenic types, and can lead to a variety of contamination problems. Treated or refined products may have a higher level of contamination than raw materials due to handling, or the balance of flora may be changed in relation to the refining process. Thus heat-treated materials may have a high bacterial spore load. Semi-synthetic and synthetic materials are usually of a good microbial quality with only casual contaminants present.

8.2 Monitoring

Four main factors must be taken into consideration when monitoring the microbial quality of raw materials:

1 If the material meets the quality demanded by

statutory requirements (if any).
2 If pathogenic organisms are present.
3 If spoilage organisms are present.
4 If the level of microbial contamination is consistent with good hygienic practice.

If pathogenic micro-organisms or their toxins are present, they must be destroyed either by a pre- or in-process sterilization stage. Precautions must be taken to prevent cross-contamination of other raw materials or finished products, particularly those which do not receive an in-process sterilization stage, by process operators or the use of common equipment or preparation surfaces.

When spoilage micro-organisms are present they must be eliminated before or during manufacture. If this is not possible, either an alternative source free from such organisms must be sought, or a preservative capable of preventing their growth added. The relationship between a product and its spoilage organisms is often quite specific, e.g. the load of spore-forming bacteria is of importance in the canning of low and medium acid foods due to their heat tolerance, but is usually less significant in the manufacture of antacid pharmaceutical preparations with a neutral-to-alkaline reaction where Gram-negative bacteria pose more serious spoilage problems. The presence of some micro-organisms in raw materials presents a threat to the whole factory environment. An example is the fungus *Neurospora sitophila* which, if present in materials used in a bakery, can spread rapidly throughout the plant.

Changes in the hygienic standard of the supplier can be detected by regular microbiological monitoring. This may take the form of a total count of bacteria or moulds, or the specific testing for organisms whose presence indicates an unsatisfactory standard of hygiene. In the water and dairy industry the presence of *E. coli* is regarded as evidence of faecal contamination, and the presence of other coliform bacteria as an index of unsatisfactory hygiene. Studies by Hartman (1960) and Raj *et al.* (1961) indicated that in the case of frozen foods enterococci were more relevant than coliform bacteria as an index of hygienic standard. The subject of microbiological standards in food and the value of indices of sanitary quality was reviewed by Jay (1970).

Staff handling raw materials with pathogens present must have adequate training to prevent both cross-contamination and self-infection.

9 PACKAGING

Packaging material has a dual role and acts both to contain the product and to prevent the entry of micro-organisms of moisture which may result in spoilage. In addition, it may be an essential barrier against light or oxygen, the entry of which may lead to the deterioration of the product.

For the purpose of sterilization, packaging components may be classified as being of two main types: those which require a pre-sterilizaton stage before they are used, and those which are sterilized simultaneously with the product, e.g. process cans.

Some packaging materials such as plastic containers, moulded plastics, cellulose and foil films have smooth surfaces free from interstices and harbour few micro-organisms if the standard of hygiene in the production plant and storage areas is good. Others such as paper, cardboard, tin cans and cork usually have a higher level of surface flora. Some materials are contaminated by their own packaging or during storage, e.g. glass bottles which are sterile on leaving the furnace but later become contaminated.

When dry materials are being packed it is often possible to eliminate a pre-sterilization stage for the packaging, but for dried pharmaceutical products required to pass a test for sterility, the packaging must be pre-sterilized. Unless the product is well preserved a sterilization stage is usually necessary for liquid and semi-solid materials.

Packaging may be treated by both moist and dry heat, irradiation or chemical disinfection. Chemical disinfectants usually selected include sodium hypochlorite, QACs, hydrogen peroxide and, in gaseous form, ethylene oxide or formaldehyde.

In addition to microbiological tests on packaging materials, checks must be made to ensure that the pack is correctly sealed and screw caps have an adequate torque to prevent both leakage of product and entry of micro-organisms.

The product and packaging may be sterilized as a complete assembly by irradiation, ethylene oxide gas and both moist and dry heat. Quality control checks for such operations must include an evaluation of the process as well as a test for sterility.

Where both the product and container are sterilized by moist heat and the cycle includes a water-cooling stage, checks must be made on the container before processing. In the case of process cans with double-overlap seams, it is usual to measure the percentage overlap of the seam, seam tightness and freespace, and countersink depth, as well as checking for faults in the seams at both ends of the can. If the balance of the measurements is incorrect and the seam overlap too low, or the seam too loose, cooling water and possibly micro-organisms may be drawn into the can. If the seams are too tight then damage such as cutovers or split droops may occur and again may permit the entry of post-processing contaminants. The complete subject of monitoring process cans was reviewed by Put *et al.* (1972). As with glass containers, it is important to check that the container has the correct level of vacuum before processing since a failure may result in either a 'peaked' or 'panelled' can, the distortion of which weakens the seam and may lead to post-process contamination.

10 STAFF HYGIENE AND PROTECTIVE CLOTHING

All personnel should receive a basic training in hygiene. This should include personal hygiene and an understanding of operator-borne contamination, as well as precautions necessary to prevent cross-infection, and the importance of cleaning and disinfection routines.

The type of clothing worn is influenced by the process but in all instances clean, non-fibre-shedding overalls and hair covering are necessary in all manufacturing areas. Where products are handled, gloves must be worn and for some processes face masks are necessary. For aseptic manufacturing, pre-sterilized clothing such as single- or two-piece trouser suits, footwear, hair covering (beards included), face masks and gloves are necessary. These should be changed on a regular basis, with fresh garments at least once a day.

11 DOCUMENTATION AND RECORDS

As mentioned earlier, written procedures should be available for all cleaning and disinfection operations, for both buildings and equipment, and for the monitoring of the efficiency of such processes. In some organizations it has been found to be advantageous to incorporate these stages into the manufacturing process sheet which has to be signed by the operator as each is completed. This not only ensures that the cleaning and disinfection is carried out, but also makes it an integral part of the manufacturing process and provides a permanent record. This system is not applicable to all processes and independent records may be necessary.

All tanks and equipment should bear a label with respect to their current state, e.g. 'in use', or 'clean but not sterilized' or 'clean and sterilized'. This is very important in the case of operations carried out by different shifts of operators. The monitoring of disinfection and sterilization processes is often a joint exercise between the production and quality assurance personnel, but comprehensive records must be maintained by both parties, and ideally held at a central location.

The concept of good manufacturing practice is embodied in the British Standards Institute Quality Assurance Standard BS5750, and its European equivalent, ISO 9000–90004/EN29000–EN29004, the UK Medicines Act and its subsequent Code of Practice. The EEC is currently in the process of preparing regulations on hygienic codes of practice for handling food products, and regulations for food manufacturing areas.

12 REFERENCES

Ahmed, F.I.K. & Russell, C. (1975) Synergism between ultrasonic waves and hydrogen peroxide in the killing of micro-organisms. *Journal of Applied Bacteriology*, **39**, 31–40.

Anon (1959a) Cleaning of dairy equipment. In *In-place Cleaning of Dairy Equipment* (ed. Davis, J.G.) pp. 1–8. Society of Dairy Technology.

Anon (1959b) Methods and equipment for in-place cleaning. In *In-place Cleaning of Dairy Equipment* (ed. Davis, J.G.) pp. 16–34. Society of Dairy Technology.

Anon (1977) *Guide to Good Pharmaceutical Manufacturing Practice*, London: HMSO.

Beeby, M.M. & Whitehouse, C.E. (1965) A bacterial spore test piece for the control of ethylene oxide sterilisation. *Journal of Applied Bacteriology*, **28**, 349–360.

Burman, N.P. & Colbourne, J.S. (1977) Techniques for the assessment of growth of micro-organisms on plumbing materials used in contact with potable water supplies. *Journal of Applied Bacteriology*, **43**, 137–144.

Chambers, C.S.W. & Clarke, N.A. (1968) Control of bacteria in non-domestic water supplies. *Advances in Applied Microbiology*, **8**, 105–143.

Collins, V.G. (1964) The freshwater environment and its significance in industry. *Journal of Applied Bacteriology*, **27**, 143–150.

Colquitt, H.R. & Maurer, J.M. (1969) Hygienic mop maintenance in hospitals. *British Hospital Journal and Social Service Review*, **79**, 2177.

Davis, J.G. (1959) The microbiological control of water in dairies and food factories. *Proceedings of the Society for Water Treatment and Examination*, **8**, 31–54.

Denyer, S.P. (1987) Sterilization control and sterility testing. In *Pharmaceutical Microbiology* (eds Hugo, W.B. & Russell, A.D.), 4th Ed. pp. 446–458. Oxford: Blackwell Scientific Publications.

Favero, M.S., McDade, J.J., Robertson, J.A., Hoffman, R.K. & Edward, R.W. (1968) Microbiological sampling of surfaces. *Journal of Applied Bacteriology*, **31**, 336–343.

Hambraeus, A., Bengtsson, S. & Laurell, G. (1968) Bacterial contamination in a modern operating suite. 4. Bacterial contamination of clothes worn in the suite. *Journal of Hygiene, Cambridge*, **80**, 175–181.

Hargreaves, D.P. (1990) Good manufacturing practice in the control of contamination. In *Guide to Microbiological Control in Pharmaceuticals* (eds Denyer, S.P. & Baird, R.M.), pp. 68–86. Chichester: Ellis Horwood.

Hartman, P.A. (1960) Enterococcus: coliform ratio in frozen chicken pies. *Applied Microbiology*, **8**, 114–116.

Jay, J.M. (1970) Indices of food sanitary quality, and microbiological standards. In *Modern Food Microbiology*, pp. 140–193. Van Nostrand Reinhold Company.

Lidwell, O.M. & Noble, W.C. (1975) Fungi and clostridia in hospital air: the effect of air conditioning. *Journal of Applied Bacteriology*, **39**, 251–261.

Maurer, I.M. (1985) *Hospital Hygiene*, 3rd Ed. London: Edward Arnold.

Meddick, H.M. (1977) Bacterial contamination control mats: a comparative study. *Journal of Hygiene, Cambridge*, **79**, 133–140.

Nishannon, A. & Pohja, M.S. (1977) Comparative studies of microbial contamination of surfaces by the contact plate and swab methods. *Journal of Applied Bacteriology*, **42**, 53–63.

Parker, M.E. & Litchfield, J.H. (1972) Effective detergency and cleaning practice. In *Food Plant Sanitation*. pp. 223–263. New York: Reinhold.

Put, H.M.C., Van Doren, H., Warner, W.R. & Kruiswick, J.T.H. (1972) The mechanism of microbiological leaker spoilage of canned foods: A review. *Journal of Applied Bacteriology*, **35**, 7–27.

Raj, H., Weibe, W.J. & Liston, J. (1961) Detection and enumeration of faecal indicator organisms in frozen sea food. *Applied Microbiology*, **9**, 295–308.

Russell, A.D. (1980) Sterilisation control and sterility testing. In *Pharmaceutical Microbiology* (eds Hugo, W.B. & Russell, A.D.) 2nd Ed. pp. 317–324. Oxford: Blackwell Scientific Publications.

Russell, A.D., Ahonkhai, I. & Rogers, D.T. (1979) Microbiological applications of the inactivation of antibiotics and other antimicrobial agents. *Journal of Applied Bacteriology*, **46**, 207–245.

Shaner, E.O. (1967) Acoustic-chemical procedures for the ultrasonic sterilization of instruments, a status report. *Journal of Oral Therapy*, **3**, 417–422.

Sykes, G. (1965) Air disinfection and sterilization. In *Disinfection and Sterilization, Theory and Practice*. 2nd Ed. pp. 253–288. London: E. & F.N. Spon.

Thomas, M.E.M. & Maurer, I.M. (1972) Bacteriological safeguards in hospital cleaning. *British Hospital Journal and Social Service Review*, **82**, Institutional Cleaning Supplement 6.

Trimarchi, G. (1959) The bacteriological control of food utensils in public service. Methods for the determination of the bacterial content. *Igiene Moderna*, **52**, 95–111.

Windle Taylor, E. & Burman, N.P. (1964) The application of membrane filtration techniques to the bacteriological examination of water. *Journal of Applied Bacteriology*, **27**, 294–303.

Chapter 12
Problems of Disinfection in Hospitals

1 INTRODUCTION

Infection has always been a problem in hospitals and before the introduction of antiseptic techniques by Lister (1868), mortality following surgery was often high. John Bell (1801) wrote about the 'hospital sore', describing it as an epidemic ulcer occurring in all hospitals, but particularly in the larger ones. He described how difficult it was for young surgeons in the Hotel Dieu in Paris when they saw many of their patients dying of hospital 'gangrene'. Following Lister's use of antiseptics in surgery (see Chapter 1), a gradual evolution has occurred in aseptic, sterilization, and disinfection techniques. Most hospitals now have a complete central sterile supply service for instruments, dressings and many other items, and operating theatres usually have a mechanical ventilation system providing filtered air. Nevertheless, although mortality has been considerably reduced, morbidity remains and approximately 10% of patients in hospital at any one time have acquired an infection (Meers *et al.*, 1981, Mayon-White *et al.*, 1988).

The main hospital-acquired infections are of the

urinary tract, operation or traumatic wounds, and the respiratory tract. Most of the infections are endogenous in origin. The elderly, newborn, and the seriously ill are particularly likely to acquire a hospital infection, as are diabetics, leukaemics or patients undergoing radiotherapy or receiving treatment with steroids or immuno-suppressive drugs. Infection is also more likely to follow the more complex surgical procedures of today and is associated with the more extensive use of intravenous infusions, urinary catheterization and respiratory ventilation. Patients are often crowded together in the same environment and some are admitted for the treatment of an existing infection. Hospital staff provide many opportunities for transfer of infection by successive close contact with infected and susceptible patients. The use of antibiotics has been associated not only with more effective treatment of infection, but also with the emergence of antibiotic-resistant organisms and their spread. In recent years methicillin-resistant *Staphylococcus aureus* (MRSA) have spread in the hospitals of many countries, eg. Australia, USA, Eire and more recently in some parts of England (Keane & Cafferkey, 1984). These epidemic strains have been difficult to control (Report 1986; Duckworth *et al.*, 1988). Antibiotic-resistant strains of Gram-negative bacilli (e.g. *Pseudomonas aeruginosa, Klebsiella* spp., *Serratia marcescens* and *Acinetobacter calcoaceticus*) continue to cause problems, particularly in high-risk units such as intensive care and burns. Although the nature of the hospital population and host susceptibility are more important factors contributing to infection than the inanimate environment, disinfection still has a role in the prevention of spread.

Disinfectants tend to be used indiscriminately, and a Public Health Laboratory Service Committee (1965) described a wide range of disinfectants in use in hospitals at that time. Although recommendations were made by the committee, the situation had shown little improvement by 1969 (Ayliffe *et al.*, 1969). Disinfectants were often used unnecessarily, and not used at all in situations where they could have been of value. Many of the products were unsuitable for hospital use, but were usually acceptable if they possessed a characteristic 'disinfectant' or 'antiseptic' smell. Dilutions of disinfectants were rarely measured, and concentrations were often inadequate and associated with bacterial contamination (Kelsey & Maurer, 1966; Prince & Ayliffe, 1972). Although disinfectant policies have been introduced in most hospitals, implementation is still often unsatisfactory (Cadwallader, 1989). However, the increasing use of complicated medical equipment, often heat-labile, and the presence of potentially hazardous infections, such as hepatitis B (HBV) and human immunodeficiency virus (HIV) infections, has increased the need for effective and well-defined disinfection procedures.

2 REASONS FOR INCORRECT USE OF DISINFECTANTS

The hospital staff responsible for buying and using environmental disinfectants are often poorly trained in control of infection techniques and have little knowledge of microbiology. They are often advised by representatives of disinfectant manufacturers and the advice is usually based on the results of laboratory tests and is not necessarily related to hospital conditions (Maurer, 1985). The misuse of disinfectants is often based on the following ill-defined concepts or misconceptions: all bacteria are more or less equally infective or at least undesirable; all bacteria spread in the air and since the air is in contact with all surfaces in the hospital, all surfaces must be regularly disinfected; disinfection of ceilings, walls and floors will therefore reduce the spread of infection; bacteria on a surface remain viable until killed by a disinfectant; all disinfectants are more or less equally effective, irrespective of concentrations, and no bacteria will survive in a disinfectant solution; if a surface is treated with a disinfectant, bacteria will continue to be killed even after the surface has dried.

These misconceptions led to the daily disinfection of all surfaces without any attempt to establish priorities based on the behaviour of different types of bacteria in the environment or the routes of spread of infection. Although much more relevant to the transfer of infection, the insides of tubing and medical equipment were frequently neglected in favour of floors, walls and ceilings.

3 A RATIONAL APPROACH TO DISINFECTION: A DISINFECTANT POLICY

Every hospital should have a disinfectant policy. The principles of preparing such a policy were described by Kelsey & Maurer (1972) and Ayliffe *et al.* (1984) and essentially consist of: listing the purposes for which disinfectants are used; eliminating their use when sterilization rather than disinfection is the object, where heat can be used or where thorough cleaning is adequate, or where disposable equipment can be economically used; selecting one or two disinfectants for most of the remaining uses. In order to produce a realistic policy, the reason for disinfection should be considered in detail. Risks of infection from equipment or the environment should be categorized, priorities allocated and resources made available on the basis of this assessment.

3.1 Objective

When deciding whether or not disinfection is necessary, it is important to consider the reason for the procedure. The objective is to prevent infection, but in more practical terms may be defined as 'the reduction of microbiological contamination to such a level that an infective dose is unlikely to reach a susceptible site on a patient'. However, an infective dose cannot easily be determined due to the variability in virulence of organisms and resistance of the host. In some instances, one virus-containing particle or a single tubercle bacillus will initiate an infection, but for most organisms a much larger number is necessary (Barkley & Wedum, 1977). In experiments with *Staph. aureus* in man, over 10^6 organisms are required to cause a local infection following intradermal injection, but in the presence of a suture only 10^2 organisms are required (Elek & Conen, 1957). An assessment of the value of disinfection in terms of a reduction in clinical infection would be very useful but is rarely possible. Trials would need to be large and the results could still be inconclusive because of the large number of interrelating factors although occasional studies have failed to show differences in infection rates between wards using environmental disinfectants and those using detergents only (Danforth *et al.*, 1987). Nevertheless, a rational decision can be made in most situations. For instance, chemical disinfection of an operating-room floor is probably unnecessary, because the bacteria-carrying particles already on the floor are unlikely to reach an open wound in sufficient numbers to cause an infection (Ayliffe *et al.*, 1967; Hambraeus *et al.*, 1978). Cleaning alone, followed by drying, will considerably reduce the bacterial population.

The standards of hygiene expected by patients and staff must also be considered. Even when these standards are illogical, failure to meet them may erode confidence and could cause unnecessary anxiety.

3.2 Categories of risk to patients and treatment of equipment and environment

The objective must be considered carefully in any situation and categories of risk determined (Spaulding, 1977; Rutala, 1990) and the appropriate treatment applied (Ayliffe & Gibson, 1975). Three categories of risk may be considered—high, intermediate or occasional, and low (Ayliffe *et al.*, 1976).

3.2.1 High risk

These are items of equipment or substances in close contact with a break in the skin or mucous membrane or introduced into a sterile body area. Items in this category should be sterilized by heat if possible, or, if heat-labile, may be treated with ethylene oxide, low-temperature steam and formaldehyde, or possibly commercially by irradiation. Liquid chemical 'sterilants' should be used only if other methods are unsuitable. This category includes surgical instruments, urinary and other catheters, parenteral fluids, syringes and needles, surgical gloves and other equipment used in surgical operations or aseptic techniques.

3.2.2 Intermediate or occasional risks

These are items of equipment or substances in close contact with intact skin or mucous membranes. Intact skin is usually impervious to bacteria, and infection by this route is uncommon in normal individuals. Although items in this category will usually require disinfection, it is not always necessary if the patient is not particularly susceptible to infection or the item is unlikely to be contaminated with pathogens. The risk is increased if the contaminating organisms are particularly virulent, highly infectious, the ensuing infection is likely to be difficult to treat, or the patient is unusually susceptible. In these circumstances it may be preferable to transfer these items to the high-risk category. Respiratory and anaesthetic equipment, gastrointestinal endoscopes, wash-bowls, bedding, bedpans, etc., are included in this category.

3.2.3 Low risk

These are items of equipment or substances or environmental surfaces not in close contact with the patient or his immediate environment. Items in this category are either unlikely to be contaminated with significant numbers of potential pathogens, or transfer to a susceptible site on the patient is unlikely. Cleaning will usually be adequate, and the category includes walls, ceilings, floors and other sites not in close contact with the patient. Cleaning may also be sufficient when recontamination is rapid and where disinfection would provide little additional benefit. Disinfection may be required rather than cleaning alone for removing contaminated spillage and for terminal disinfection in isolation units for infectious diseases. Pouring disinfectants into sinks and drains is wasteful and of little value in the prevention of hospital infection (Maurer, 1985).

3.3 Requirements of chemical disinfectants

All the requirements or desirable properties of disinfectants are not attainable by any single agent and a choice must be made depending on the particular use. Requirements are described in more detail in European publications (Reber *et al.*, 1972; Schmidt, 1973).

1 The disinfectant should preferably be bactericidal and its spectrum of activity should include all the common non-sporing pathogens, including tubercle bacilli. Virucidal activity is an increasing requirements for routine disinfection. Narrow-spectrum agents, such as quaternary ammonium compounds (QACs) or pine fluids, may select *Pseudomonas* spp. or other resistant Gram-negative bacilli, which are potentially hazardous to highly susceptible patients.

2 Disinfectants used on surfaces should be rapid in action since bactericidal activity ceases when the surface is dry.

3 The disinfectant should not be readily neutralized by organic matter, soaps, hard water or plastics.

4 Toxic effects should be minimal, and in-use dilutions of disinfectants should be, if possible, relatively non-corrosive. Confused or mentally defective patients may accidentally swallow a disinfectant solution. Many of the environmental disinfectants in routine use are both toxic and corrosive, and care is required in their use and storage. Employers in the UK are now responsible for assessing health risks and measures to protect the health of workers from toxic hazards (Control of Substances Hazardous to Health Regulations, 1988).

5 The disinfectant should not damage surfaces or articles treated. This property may vary with the particular situation, the criteria for selecting a disinfectant for a toilet are obviously different from those for selecting one for an expensive endoscope.

6 Costs should be acceptable and supplies assured.

3.4 The choice of a method of disinfection

3.4.1 Heat

Heat is the preferred method of disinfection for all medical equipment. Heat penetrates well, is predictably effective and is readily controlled. Steam at high pressure (e.g. 134°C for 3 min) will sterilize, and although a sporicidal effect may not necessarily be required, steam is the most reliable method of microbial decontamination. Heat-labile equipment, e.g. ventilator and anaesthetic tubing and used surgical instruments, may be decontaminated in a washing machine which reaches an appropriate temperature for disinfection, e.g. 70°C for 2 min, 80°C for 1 min, over 90°C (Collins & Phelps, 1985).

Low-temperature steam (73°C for 10 min) (see Chapter 18A) or immersion in water at 70–100°C

Table 12.1 Decontamination of equipment

Method	Temperature (°C)	Time (min)	Level of decontamination
Heat			
Autoclave	134	3	Sterilization
	121	15	Sterilization
Low-temperature steam	73	10	Disinfection
Low-temperature steam and formaldehyde	73	60–180	Sterilization
Boilers	100	5–10	Disinfection
Pasteurizers	70–100	Variable	Disinfection
Washing machines			
Bed-pans	80	1	Cleaning and Disinfection
Linen	65	10	Cleaning and Disinfection
	71	3	Cleaning and Disinfection
Others	65–100	Variable	Cleaning and Disinfection
Chemical			
Ethylene oxide	55	60–360	Sterilization
2% glutaraldehyde	RT	4–60	Disinfection
		>180	Sterilization
70% alcohol	RT	4–10	Disinfection

RT, room temperature.

for 5–10 min is effective in killing vegetative organisms and should inactivate most viruses, including HIV (Table 12.1).

3.4.2 Chemical

A clear soluble phenolic and a chlorine-releasing agent preparation (Chapter 2) should be sufficient for most environmental disinfection. Clear soluble phenolics are comparatively cheap, not readily neutralized, and are active against a wide range of organisms, although not usually against viruses. They are suitable for environmental disinfection, but not for skin or for equipment likely to come into contact with skin or mucous membranes, or in food-preparation or storage areas. Chlorine-releasing agents are very cheap, active against a wide range of organisms including viruses, but are readily neutralized and tend to damage some metals and materials. They are relatively non-toxic when diluted and are useful in food-preparation areas. Powders or tablets containing sodium dichloroisocyoanurute (NaDCC) are stable when dry and are useful for environmental decontamination (Bloomfield & Uso, 1985; Coates, 1988). Chlorine-releasing agents are increasingly used for routine disinfection and for removal of spillage, but can cause rapid deterioration of materials. Glutaraldehyde may occasionally be required for the decontamination of medical equipment if heat cannot be used. It is relatively non-corrosive and will kill spores with prolonged exposure (3–10 h: see Babb *et al.*, 1980), but it is potentially toxic. Irritant rashes and respiratory symptoms are being increasingly reported in staff using glutaraldehyde (Burge, 1989). An alternative non-toxic disinfectant is required which has similar virucidal properties. Possible alternatives are hydrogen peroxide, other peroxygen compounds and peracetic acid. Seventy per cent ethyl or 60% propyl alcohol is a rapid and effective method for disinfecting skin, trolleys and the surfaces of medical equipment. Compounds of low toxicity such as chlorhexidine or povidone-iodine (both of which were considered in Chapter 2) may be required for disinfecting skin or mucous membranes, and occasionally for inanimate items likely to contact skin or mucous membranes.

3.5 Implementation of the disinfectant policy

Although most hospitals have a policy, implementation is often rather inefficient. All hospital staff should be aware of the policy and of problems likely to arise if there are any major departures from that policy.

3.5.1 Organization

The infection control committee and team have the responsibility for preparing the policy and ensuring that the correct disinfectants and methods are used (Lowbury *et al.*, 1981). The microbiologist, pharmacist and infection control nurse should be members of the committee. The nursing and domestic staff, who are mainly responsible for the actual practice of disinfection, are also advised through their own organization, but responsibilities and priorities are often poorly defined. Information is not always passed to the workers who use the disinfectants.

3.5.2 Training

A logical and effective approach to disinfection requires trained staff. They should have some knowledge of microbiology, mechanisms of transfer of infection and properties of disinfectants. Alternatively, operatives should follow defined schedules and be supervised by trained staff. Decisions are still made too often by staff without adequate training.

3.5.3 Distribution and dilution of disinfectants

Since inaccurate dilution is one of the main causes of failure of disinfection, this aspect requires careful consideration. It is preferable to deliver disinfectants to departments at the use-dilution, but this is not always possible or convenient. If not possible, suitable dispensers are required and the staff must be trained in their use.

3.5.4 Testing of disinfectants

Official tests are available in some countries, e.g. Germany, France, USA, Switzerland and Holland, but not in the UK (see Chapter 4). The Kelsey–Sykes capacity test has been generally accepted in the UK and use-dilutions are commonly based on this test (Kelsey & Maurer, 1974). However, an internationally accepted test or series of tests is required. A reproducible quantitative suspension test (Council of Europe, 1987) would fulfil this role if agreement between countries could be reached.

Virucidal tests are also required and are being investigated (Tyler & Ayliffe, 1987; Sattar *et al.*, 1989; Tyler *et al.*, 1990). Tests should preferably be carried out by a reliable independent organization, and results supplied to hospitals by the manufacturers. The manufacturer should also provide evidence of other properties of the disinfectant, such as the range of susceptible organisms, toxicity and corrosiveness. Surface disinfection tests on tiles or linen are often used for hospital disinfectants in Europe but not in the UK or USA. In-use tests are useful when a new disinfectant is introduced, and possibly routinely at intervals of 6–12 months (Kelsey & Maurer, 1966; Prince & Ayliffe, 1972). These tests should detect the possible emergence of resistant strains as well as inadequate dilutions or loss of activity of the disinfectant.

3.5.5 Costs

Excessive costs may be due to unnecessary use, incorrect concentrations, or inappropriate disinfectants being used. The cost of the disinfection procedure, as well as the cost of the agent, should be considered.

4 PROBLEMS WITH CERTAIN MICRO-ORGANISMS

4.1 Bacterial spores

A process which kills spores is usually required for articles in the high-risk category (see Section 3.2.1). Liquid preparations such as glutaraldehyde, or occasionally formaldehyde, may be used but are generally less reliable than heat; penetration is often poor, thorough rinsing is required before use, and recontamination with micro-organisms can occur during the rinsing process. Two per cent alkaline glutaraldehyde requires a minimum exposure time of 3 h for an adequate sporicidal action, or up to 10 h on the basis of the AOAC test (Spaulding *et al.*, 1977). However, some spores e.g. *Clostridium difficile* appear to be killed by glutaraldehyde in a much shorter time (Dyas & Das, 1985). A number of glutaraldehyde preparations are now available and these show some variation in activity, stability and corrosiveness. Repeated use of a glutaraldehyde solution is common practice mainly due to expense. The length of time a solution is repeatedly used should depend on the extent of contamination with organic matter or dilution during use and not on stability alone. Buffered hypochlorite solutions are rapidly sporicidal but have the disadvantage of corroding instruments (Death & Coates, 1979).

4.2 Hepatitis, human immunodeficiency and 'slow' viruses

Hepatitis A (HAV), B (HBV), C (HBC) and other non-A, non-B viruses have not been grown *in vitro*, and reliable laboratory tests for inactivation are not available. Limited studies in chimpanzees have indicated that HBV is inactivated by temperatures of 98°C for 2 min, but lower temperatures were not investigated. Glutaraldehyde, 70% ethanol, hypochlorite solutions and iodophors also inactivate the virus, e.g. different authors quote 0.1% glutaraldehyde (24°C) in 5 min, 2% glutaraldehyde in 10 min, 70% isopropanol in 10 min, 80% ethanol in 2 min (Bond *et al.*, 1983, Kobayashi *et al.*, 1984). A study with the duck hepatitis B model showed that the virus was inactivated by 2% glutaraldehyde preparations in 2.5–10 minutes (Murray *et al.*, 1991).

Human immunodeficiency virus (HIV) is an enveloped virus and is readily inactivated by heat and commonly used antiviral disinfectants (Resnick *et al.*, 1986; Kurth *et al.*, 1986). It is inactivated by 2% glutaraldehyde in 1 min, but 70% ethanol has shown variable results in surface tests (Hanson *et al.*, 1989b; Van Bueren *et al.*, 1989). The inconsistent results were probably due to variability of penetration of dried organic material, and it is likely that 70% ethanol is effective against HIV on clean surfaces.

Hepatitis B virus particles are usually present in larger numbers than HIV in blood, and infection is more readily transmissible, but thorough washing of equipment with a detergent to remove blood and body secretions will minimize the risk of infection from these viruses. However, the use of a hypochlorite solution or powder should be effective in rapidly decontaminating blood spillage before cleaning, and is recommended particularly if the spillage is from an infected or high-risk patient (Ayliffe *et al.*, 1984; Coates, 1988: Bloomfield, *et al.*, 1990).

The agents causing Creutzfeldt–Jacob disease, kuru and scrapie are termed 'slow' viruses, although they have not been identified and are highly resistant to heat, glutaraldehyde and formaldehyde. Present evidence suggests that these viruses are inactivated by exposure to 134°C moist heat in 18 min (i.e. six cycles of 3 min), hypochlorites (10 000 ppm $AvCl_2$ for 30 min) and by 1 N sodium hydroxide (see Chapter 7).

4.3 Mycobacteria

These are more resistant to chemical disinfectants than most other non-sporing organisms, but are sensitive to heat. Heat is the preferred method of treating contaminated equipment, but ethylene oxide or low-temperature steam may sometimes be appropriate for heat-labile equipment. Glutaraldehyde (2%) is a less satisfactory alternative and the exposure time should be increased to at least 20–60 min (Bergan & Lystad, 1971; Hardie, 1985; Best *et al.*, 1990). The clear soluble phenolics are active against tubercle bacilli and are suitable for disinfection of rooms occupied by patients with open tuberculosis. Quaternary ammonium compounds and chlorhexidine show poor activity against tubercle bacilli. The resistance of mycobacteria to disinfectants is considered in Chapter 10D.

5 CONTAMINATED DISINFECTANT SOLUTIONS

Solutions contaminated with Gram-negative bacilli are a particular hazard in hospital and infections originating from them have been reported (Lee & Fialkow, 1961: Bassett *et al.*, 1970; Speller *et al.*,

1971). Contamination is usually due to inappropriate disinfectants (Sanford, 1970; Centre for Disease Control, 1974), the use of weak solutions (Prince & Ayliffe, 1979), or 'topping-up' of containers. The problem can usually be avoided by thorough cleaning and drying of the container before refilling but an additional biocide is sometimes necessary (Burdon & Whitby, 1967).

6 TREATMENT OF THE ENVIRONMENT AND EQUIPMENT

In many instances it is still difficult to decide on the appropriate method of decontamination, even after taking into consideration the objective and risk category of the item concerned. Cleaning alone may be adequate for most routine purposes, but disinfection may be required for the same item during outbreaks of infection. However, it is useful to remember that the risk of transmitting infection on an article which has been thoroughly washed and dried is very small (Nyström, 1981). Thorough cleaning also removes potential bacterial nutrients as well as bacteria themselves. Methods of decontamination of equipment are summarized in Table 12.1. The variable temperatures and exposure times are due to procedural differences and often to practical requirements. Infection risks have been reviewed by Ayliffe (1988).

Some of the problem areas in hospital are described in this section, but for more information see Lowbury *et al.* (1981), Block (1983), Maurer (1985), Bennett & Brachman (1986), Gardner & Peel (1986), Wenzel (1987) and Rutala (1990).

6.1 Walls, ceilings and floors

Walls and ceilings are rarely heavily contaminated provided the surface remains intact and dry (Wypkema & Alder, 1962). In our own studies using contact plates, bacterial counts on walls were in the range of 2–5 per 25 cm^2 and counts of 10 were unusually high. The organisms are mainly Gram-positive, coagulase-negative cocci, with occasional aerobic or anaerobic spore-bearing organisms, and rarely *Staph. aureus*. The number of bacteria does not appear to increase even if walls are not cleaned, and frequent cleaning has little influence on bacterial counts. Table 12.2 shows bacterial counts from an unwashed operating theatre wall over a 12–week period. No increase in contamination occurred over this period. Routine disinfection is therefore unnecessary, but walls should be cleaned when dirty.

Table 12.2 Bacterial contamination of walls in an operating theatre

Time of sampling after washing (weeks)	Mean counts from 10 contact plates (25 cm^2)	
	Total	*Staph. aureus*
1 day	2.8	0
1	5.0	0
3	3.4	0.2
5	4.6	0.2
12	1.2	0

Data from Ayliffe *et al.* (1967).

Floors are more heavily contaminated than walls and a mean count of 380 organisms per 25 cm^2 was obtained from ward floors in a study by the authors. As on the walls and other surfaces, most of the bacteria are from the skin flora of the occupants of the room. A small proportion, usually less than 1%, are potential pathogens such as *Staph. aureus*. The number of bacteria in the room environment tends to be related to the number and sex of people in the ward and their activity (Williams *et al.*, 1966; Noble & Somerville, 1974). Provided these factors remain relatively unchanged, the bacterial population on a surface will usually reach a plateau in a few hours. At this stage the rate of deposition and death remain constant (See Fig. 12.1). Routine disinfection could be of some value if the height of this plateau is reduced, although an effect on clinical infection is still unlikely. Wet cleaning will reduce the number of organisms by about 80% and the addition of a disinfectant may increase the reduction of over 95%. In a busy hospital ward, recontamination is rapid and bacterial counts may reach the pre-cleaning or predisinfection level in 1–2 h (Vesley & Michaelsen, 1964; Ayliffe *et al.*, 1966). The transient reduction obtained does not appear to justify the routine use of a disinfectant. There is also evidence that skin organisms on the

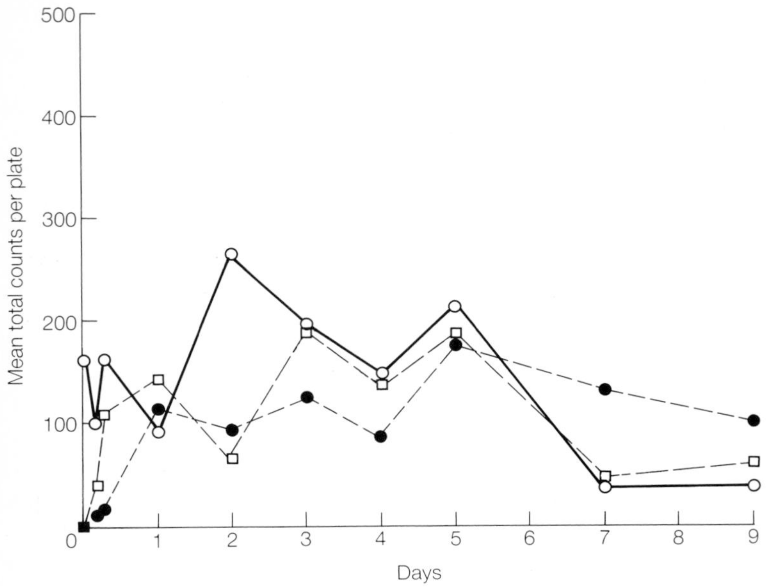

Fig. 12.1 Mean total counts taken on impression plates at intervals after cleaning the floor in a female surgical ward during the course of nine days. ○—○, Floor; ●— —●, vinyl off floor; □—□, vinyl on floor.

floor are not readily re-suspended into the air (Ayliffe *et al.*, 1967; Hambraeus *et al.*, 1978). Disinfection may still be required in areas of high risk or if the number of potential pathogens is thought to be high, for instance in a room after discharge of an infected patient, but even in these circumstances disinfection of walls and ceilings is rarely necessary. Carpets are now sometimes found in hospitals and may be exposed to heavy contamination from spillage of food, blood or faeces. The carpets must be able to withstand disinfection and should have a waterproof backing and the fibres should preferably not adsorb water (Ayliffe *et al.*, 1974a; Collins, 1979). There is no evidence that carpets increase the risk of infection in clinical areas and further unpublished studies over a long period in a surgical ward confirm the original findings. Regular routine maintenance is required and many of the failures in use of carpets have been due to an unpleasant smell associated with inadequate cleaning. This particularly applies to certain wards, e.g. psychogeriatric where spillage is excessive but carpets are preferred for aesthetic reasons. Although the risk of infection is small, careful thought should be given before carpets are fitted in clinical areas or where spillage is likely to be considerable (Collins, 1979).

6.2 Air

Airborne spread of infection is less important than previously thought (Brachman, 1971), but recent evidence has demonstrated that airborne spread plays a major role in prosthetic surgery. A controlled trial showed that an ultra-clean air ventilation system in an operating theatre, associated with the wearing of bacteria-impermeable clothing and an exhaust-ventilated hood by the operating team, reduced the deep wound infection rate in prosthetic surgery for hip and knee joints (Lidwell *et al.*, 1983). Outbreaks of *Aspergillus* infection have been reported in immunosuppressed patients, probably acquired by the airborne route, mainly during building demolition or structural renovation. This risk may be reduced by nursing susceptible patients in rooms supplied with HEPA filtered air (Rogers & Barnes, 1988; Walsh & Dixon, 1989). Legionnaire's disease is caused by the spread of legionellae from cooling towers, showers and water supplies or other aerosol-producing systems (Bartlett *et al.*, 1986). It does not spread from person to person. Prevention is possible by regular maintenance of systems, use of biocides and improved design to avoid static water (see Chapter 10E). In the event of an outbreak, hyperchlorination or heating of the hot water supply to an appropriate temperature for preventing the growth of legionellae may be introduced. However, hyperchlorination may corrode the water storage and supply systems, and excessive heating of water may cause scalding, particularly in children and old people. Disinfection of the air has been reviewed elsewhere (see Sykes, 1965), but is now rarely considered necessary in hospital. Thorough cleaning of surfaces and disinfection is thought to be more reliable than 'fogging', which is the production of a disinfectant aerosol (Centre for Disease Control, 1972). Fumigation of the environment with formaldehyde is only considered necessary after occupation by highly dangerous and infectious diseases such as Lassa fever (Department of Health & Social Security, 1986). Methods of air disinfection and air sterilization are considered in Chapters 2, 11 and 20.

6.3 Baths, wash-bowls and toilets

Bath water contains large numbers of bacteria including potential pathogens (Ayliffe *et al.*, 1975a). Many bacteria remain on the surface of the bath after emptying and may be transferred to the next patient. Thorough cleaning with a detergent after each use is usually sufficient, but disinfection is necessary in maternity or surgical units, or other areas where patients with open wounds use the same bath. Hypochlorite solutions or powders are commonly recommended for disinfection (Boycott, 1956; Alder *et al.*, 1966; Lowbury *et al.*, 1981). Abrasive powders may damage certain bath surfaces & non-abrasive hypochlorite powders should be used. Wash-bowls are often stacked so that a small amount of residual water remains in each after emptying, and Gram-negative bacilli may grow to large numbers overnight (Joynson, 1978). Routine disinfection is usually unnecessary, but thorough cleaning and drying is always required. Toilets are an obvious infection risk during outbreaks of gastro-intestinal infection. Disinfection of the seat of the toilet is probably of some value in these circumstances, but for routine purposes cleaning is usually sufficient. Risks of infection from aerosols after flushing are usually small (Newsom, 1972).

6.4 Bed-pans and urinals

These are required for patients confined to bed, but are used less often than formerly because of early mobilization of patients after surgical operations. After use, the contents require disposal and the container must be decontaminated, particularly if the patient is suffering from an enteric or urinary tract infection. Although bed-pan washers without a disinfecting heat cycle are commonly used with no evidence of cross-infection, a heat (either steam or hot water) process is now recommended on all machines (Ayliffe *et al.*, 1974b; Collins & Phelps, 1985). This is the preferred method of decontamination, and chemical methods should be avoided if possible. Immersion of bed-pans or urinals in tanks of disinfectant has been associated with the selection and growth of Gram-negative bacilli in the solution (Curie *et al.*, 1978). Macerators are an alternative to heat disinfection of metal or polypropylene pans and are satisfactory if well maintained, but possible disadvantages, particularly drainage requirements, should be considered before installation (Gibson, 1973a,b). They have the advantage of saving nursing time by disposing of several pans in one cycle and avoiding the necessity of handling pans after disinfection. Disposable urinals may not be acceptable in urological wards.

6.5 Crockery and cutlery

Hand-washed crockery and cutlery are frequently heavily contaminated after processing, but bacterial counts decrease considerably on drying. The addition of a disinfectant to the wash water is unreliable as a disinfection process (Department of Health & Social Security, 1986). Washing in a machine at a minimum temperature of 60°C with a final rinse at 80°C or more, followed by a drying cycle, is a satisfactory disinfection process (Maurer, 1985). Table 12.3 shows the difference in contamination of plates after hand and machine washing. If a suitable washing machine is not available, disposable crockery and cutlery may be used for patients with open tuberculosis and some other communicable infections, although the risks from washed and dried crockery and cutlery are minimal.

Table 12.3 Bacterial contamination of crockery (plates) after washing

Method of washing	No. of plates	No. of plates in range: bacteria per 25 cm^2		
		0–10	11–1000	>1000
Machine	72	67 (93%)	2	3
Hand	108	40 (37%)	46	22

6.6 Cleaning equipment

Floor mops are often heavily contaminated with Gram-negative bacilli. Although the opportunities for these organisms to reach a susceptible site on a patient are small, the presence of a large reservoir of Gram-negative bacilli is undesirable. Mops should be periodically disinfected, preferably by heat. Mop heads washed by a machine will usually be adequately disinfected, but soaking overnight in disinfectant is not recommended. Some phenolics may be partially inactivated by plastic floor mops (Leigh & Whittaker, 1967; Maurer, 1985). Moisture retained in mop buckets, trapped in the tanks of scrubbing machines or retained in the reservoir of spray cleaners can aso encourage the growth of Gram-negative bacteria (Medcraft *et al.*, 1987). If the fluid used is capable of supporting bacterial growth, the equipment should be dried and stored dry. Poorly maintained or badly designed scrubbing machines, carpet cleaners, or spray cleaning equipment can produce contaminated aerosols. Staff should understand the need to decontaminate equipment for use in a certain area, but only in cases where there is a specific risk of infection.

6.7 Laundry and waste disposal

Hospital linen can be a potential source of infection until disinfected by heat in a washing machine in the laundry. After removal from the bed or patient, it should be placed in a bag or container which is impervious to bacteria. Washing, chemical disinfection or unnecessary sorting should be avoided in the wards or other clinical areas. All used linen could be transferred to a washing machine without handling if sorting in the laundry was unnecessary. However, sorting is still required since linen bags often contain items such as forceps, needles, scissors and pens, which may cause serious damage to the washing machine. The infection risk of contaminated linen to sorting staff is minimal provided protective clothing is worn and hygienic techniques are good. Nevertheless, it is recommended that linen from patients with infections which might spread to staff should be sealed in a specifically coloured water-soluble bag (e.g. red), transferred unopened into the washing machine and disinfected by heat.

Three categories of linen are recognized in the United Kingdom—'used', 'infected' and 'heat-labile'. 'Infected' linen consists of linen from patients with open tuberculosis, HBV, HIV, salmonella and shigella infections and from other communicable diseases as specified by the Infection Control Team (Department of Health & Social Security, 1987). Linen from patients with HBV or HIV infection is unlikely to be a hazard unless bloodstained, and even then the infection risk would still be slight provided it is handled with gloves. It may be convenient in hospitals to treat all linen from these patients as 'infected' but it is not necessary in the community. Special arrangements, e.g. autoclaving before washing, may be required for particularly hazardous infections such as viral haemorrhagic fevers (Department of Health & Social Security, 1986). All other heat-stable linen is categorized as 'used'. It should also be disinfected by heat in a washing machine. The recommended temperatures are 65°C for 10 min or preferably 73°C for 3 min, after allowing for adequate heat penetration of the load. Heat penetration may not always be satisfactory, but few organisms remain after the completion of the normal drying process (Collins *et al.*, 1987).

Another problem is the increased use of clothing made from man-made fibres, which are distorted if subjected to the usual hospital laundry washing temperatures. If disinfection is required, hypochlorites in low final concentrations (125 parts/10^6 available chlorine) added to the rinse water are effective following a low-temperature washing process. Apart from this exception, chemical disinfection of linen is rarely required. If decontamination of heat-labile clothing from a patient with a transmissible infection is required, low-temperature steam is a more reliable process. Low-temperature steam and formaldehyde adequately disinfects woollens and blankets. A residual effect is obtained with the formaldehyde (Alder *et al.*, 1971), but since most hospital blankets are cotton, and can be exposed to an adequate disinfection temperature during the washing process, this method is rarely used routinely.

Other possible problems include the re-use of rinse water and tunnel or continuous-batch washers. Water from a final rinse may be used for preliminary sluicing of subsequent loads to avoid wastage of water. When stored overnight or during a weekend, small numbers of residual Gram-negative bacilli and aerobic spore-bearing organisms may multiply to large numbers. These may not be destroyed during the heating cycle and could cause infections in compromised patients. Surviving aerobic spore-bearing organisms on linen have caused infections on rare occasions. Similar problems of overnight growth of organisms can occur in tunnel or continuous-batch washers. Such machines should be drained or emptied overnight and linen should be heat-disinfected the following day.

The handling of waste requires a similar policy to that of laundry, but sorting is never required and the potential hazard to staff is even less. If sealed in a plastic bag or other appropriate container, waste can be safely transported throughout the hospital and to the site of final disposal. Needles and other 'sharps' should be disposed of in approved puncture-resistant containers (Department of Health & Social Security, 1982).

Hospital waste can be divided into two main categories, domestic and clinical. Clinical waste at present is further categorized into five groups in the United Kingdom—A: soiled dressings, materials from infected patients and human and animal tissues; B: discarded needles and other disposable 'sharp' equipment; C: laboratory and postmortem waste; D: certain pharmaceutical and chemical waste; E: used disposable bed-pan liners and urine containers, incontinence pads and stoma bags (Health Services Advisory Committee, 1982). Incineration is recommended for all these five groups, although group E cannot be classified as 'infectious'.

Hospital waste disposal is causing problems in many countries. Although incineration is desirable, it is expensive and may be responsible for considerable environmental pollution. There is no epidemiological evidence to suggest that hospital waste is any more infectious than community waste (Hedrick, 1988) and no infections from hospital waste (apart from needles) have been reported. However, it seems reasonable to categorize 'sharps', 'microbiological' and 'pathology' waste, and waste heavily contaminated with blood and other body fluids as 'infectious', and it should be incinerated. Human tissues are incinerated for aesthetic reasons. Clinical waste from patients with HBV, HIV, HCV, salmonella, shigella infections and open tuberculosis should be treated as 'infectious' and incinerated. Other clinical waste, i.e. category E, is not hazardous and surgical dressings, which are mainly contaminated with organisms unlikely to harm healthy people, should preferably be incinerated, but deep landfill is adequate. Clinical waste could usefully be divided into two further categories, i.e. 'infected' or 'non-infected' similar to that of laundry.

6.8 Babies' incubators

Surfaces of incubators are rarely heavily contaminated, but there is always a risk of transfer of infection from one baby to the next. Thorough cleaning and drying of surfaces, seals and humidifier is important and is usually sufficient for routine treatment. If disinfection is considered necessary in addition to cleaning, spraying with 70% alcohol or wiping over with a hypochlorite solution (125 parts/10^6 of available chlorine) is adequate (Ayliffe *et al.*, 1975b).

6.9 Respiratory ventilators and associated equipment

The accumulation of moisture and the warm conditions in ventilators and associated equipment is often associated with the growth of Gram-negative bacilli, particularly *Ps. aeruginosa* and *Klebsiella* spp. There is some experimental evidence that organisms are able to reach the patient from contaminated ventilator tubing (Babington *et al.*,

1971), and that infection can subsequently occur (Phillips & Spencer, 1965). Nebulization of contaminated droplets has caused lung infections (Sanford & Pierce, 1979). Apart from a contaminated nebulizer, the greatest infection risk is from the part of the circuit nearest to the patient. Changing the reservoir bag, tubing and connectors every 48 h is an important measure in the prevention of infection (Craven *et al.*, 1982). Ventilators are difficult to clean and disinfect, and most available methods are not entirely satisfactory (Phillips *et al.*, 1974; Lowbury *et al.*, 1981). The use of filters or heat moisture exchangers to isolate microbiologically the machine from the patient is a better method of preventing contamination of the machine and of subsequent cross-infection. The amount of condensate associated with water humidification is minimal if a heat moisture exchanger is used, and the circuitry can be changed less frequently, e.g. between patients. Less condensate is also produced with most neonatal ventilating systems and a change of circuitry every 7 days would appear to be adequate (Cadwallader *et al.*, 1990). Nevertheless, careful surveillance and monitoring of infection rates are necessary if a reversion to less frequent changing of circuits is introduced. Many ventilators now have autoclavable circuits. Nebulizers should preferably be capable of withstanding disinfection by heat, but if not should be chemically disinfected or cleaned and dried every day (Sanford & Pierce, 1979).

6.10 Anaesthetic equipment

Patients are usually connected to anaesthetic machines for a shorter period of time than to respiratory ventilators in intensive-care units, and machines are rarely heavily contaminated providing that the associated tubing is regularly changed. It is obviously preferable to provide each patient with a decontaminated circuit, but this could be expensive. Since contamination is usually not great, sessional replacement is an acceptable compromise provided decontaminated face-masks, endotracheal tubes, and airways are available for each patient during a session of about nine or ten operations. The corrugated tubing should be disinfected with low-temperature steam, or in a washing machine which reaches a temperature of 70–80°C (Bennett *et al.*, 1968; Collins & Phelps, 1985). Chemical disinfection with glutaraldehyde is less reliable (George, 1975), but if used the equipment should be rinsed at least three times. A disposable circuit may be preferred if a patient with known tuberculosis is anaesthetized.

6.11 Endoscopes

Flexible fibreoptic endoscopes are expensive and unable to withstand heat sterilization or even disinfection with low-temperature steam at 70–80°C. The channels are narrow and difficult to clean. The time for processing between patients is short, often not more than 15 min, and a compromise method of disinfection is required. The risk of transmission is low, particularly after thorough cleaning (Hanson *et al.*, 1989a). However, salmonella and pseudomonas infections have been acquired from inadequately disinfected endoscopes (O'Connor & Axon, 1983; Ayliffe, 1988). Acquisition of HBV infections is rare (Birnie *et al.*, 1983; Frank & Daschner, 1989b) and HIV infection has not been reported. Nevertheless, a virucidal agent is required and glutaraldehyde remains the disinfectant of choice. Glutaraldehyde does not damage the endoscope, but is unpleasant to use, is irritant to the skin and is often responsible for skin lesions and pulmonary symptoms in the staff of endoscopy units (Burge, 1989). This can be reduced by the use of automatic, enclosed, cleaning and disinfection machines and improved local ventilation (Babb *et al.*, 1984; Babb & Bradley, 1989). Endoscopes containing rubber or certain plastics may absorb glutaraldehyde (Power & Russell, 1989), although alternative agents are available and most are either less effective, damaging or show uncertain activity against viruses (Ayliffe *et al.*, 1986). Exposure to 2% glutaraldehyde or 70% ethanol for 4 min has been recommended in the United Kingdom (British Society of Gastroenterology, 1988), but some other countries recommend a 10–20-min exposure. Prolongation of the cleaning and disinfection time implies a necessity for more endoscopes or a reduction in the numbers of patients examined per session.

Cleaning has been considerably improved by the availability of fully immersible endoscopes with easy access to channels and valves, and by the use of automatic cleaning machines (Babb & Bradley, 1991a,b). These machines are expensive, but clean all channels. There is also a risk of recontamination of endoscopes if the water tank of the machine is not disinfected at the end of each session. Gram-negative bacilli in these tanks have been responsible for infection and are a particular hazard in ERCP procedures (Allen *et al.*, 1987).

After cleaning, residual moisture remains in the channels of the endoscope. Gram-negative bacilli, especially *Ps. aeruginosa*, may grow in these channels and in the water bottle over the next few days. Thorough disinfection is therefore required before, as well as after, the endoscopy session.

It is particularly important to disinfect the water bottle and accessories such as biopsy forceps and brushes. Autoclaving is preferred if the accessories will withstand the heat. If the instrument has been used on a patient with a known transmissible infection such as HBV, HIV, tuberculosis, salmonella or cryptosporidial infection, thorough cleaning and exposure to 2% glutaraldehyde for a longer period is often recommended. Treatment with ethylene oxide before the endoscope is used on another patient is preferable if suitable equipment is available. Nevertheless, thorough cleaning alone should considerably reduce the risk of spread of unknown infections during routine between-patient cleaning.

Bronchoscopes are more likely to be contaminated with mycobacteria than are other endoscopes, but reports of infection are rare (Nelson *et al.*, 1983).

After cleaning, bronchoscopes are usually exposed to 2% glutaraldehyde for 20–30 min and for 1 h following a known mycobacterial infection. Some strains of mycobacteria, e.g. *M. chelonei*, may be present in the water supply and contaminate the bronchoscope during rinsing. These could cause infection in highly susceptible patients and if present in bronchial washings may cause diagnostic problems. To eliminate these organisms an antibacterial filter in the water supply is required, although a final rinse with 70% alcohol may be a cheaper alternative.

Rigid fibreoptic endoscopes are sometimes autoclavable but may be sterilized with ethylene oxide, low-temperature steam and formaldehyde, or exposure to 2% glutaraldehyde for 3 h. There is usually inadequate time for these procedures and high-level disinfection with 2% glutaraldehyde is commonly used. Most spores will be removed by cleaning, and infection due to an inadequately sterilized endoscope is rare (Johnson *et al.*, 1982). Arthroscopes and laparoscopes are included in the high-risk category of equipment and preferably should be sterilized. Cystoscopes are in the intermediate-risk category and can be disinfected.

7 DISPOSABLE OR 'SINGLE-USE' EQUIPMENT

The use of disposables has increased considerably. Although there is little evidence that these have reduced infection rates, time spent by staff on reprocessing has been saved. Disposable equipment should be used, providing the costs are comparable with reprocessing, and the potential infection risk is established before the additional expense is accepted. Reprocessing should be considered if adequate cleaning is possible and the materials are not damaged by the process, e.g. ethylene oxide or irradiation. Responsibility for re-use after reprocessing is not accepted by manufacturers, and it is in their interest to market as many 'single-use' items as possible.

'Disposables' could usefully be defined as 'single-use', if they are never reprocessed, or 'limited-use' if they are processed several times before discarding. A distinction could also be made between high-risk items which must be sterilized and intermediate and low-risk items which are unlikely to be an infection hazard, and which could either be cleaned and dried or disinfected before re-use. Health services should encourage the use of non-disposable equipment whenever costs of disposables are excessive.

Equipment such as airways, respiratory circuits, suction bottles and humidifiers can easily and safely be reprocessed often at a lower cost than similar disposable products. Expensive items, such as cardiac catheters, are more of a problem as they are difficult to clean and if damaged or broken could cause major problems when introduced into the patient. Nevertheless, it has been shown that re-use of cardiac catheters does not increase the risk of infection (Daschner, 1989b). The responsibility of re-use of equipment is that of the clinician using it. However, the manufacturer should provide information on the materials, e.g. whether damaged by certain processes or whether toxic products are produced, and the sterile services manager, advised by the microbiologist, is responsible for ensuring that the sterilization process is effective and the packaging appropriate. The widespread use of disposables has also increased the need for incineration, which is likely to increase atmospheric pollution and is a further reason for a re-assessment of the necessity for 'single-use' items.

8 CONCLUSIONS

The increased use of invasive techniques in a hospital population consisting of both infected and highly susceptible patients has increased the risk of spread of infection. Disinfection has a role in reducing these risks, but in the past too great a reliance has been placed on chemical methods, often used in an indiscriminate, illogical and inefficient manner. Heat is the preferred method of microbial decontamination, but the continued use of complex, heat-sensitive equipment means that less satisfactory alternatives are still required. Manufacturers should be encouraged to produce equipment which can be readily cleaned and will withstand heat at least to 70–80°C, or preferably autoclaving at high temperature. A limited range of chemical disinfectants should be available and techniques of application should be standardized according to a well-defined policy. Allocation of resources for disinfection should be related to risks of infection and priorities decided according to the principles already described. All grades of staff should be trained in methods of disinfection and other control of infection techniques to an agreed level depending on their role in the hospital.

ACKNOWLEDGEMENT

We wish to thank the Editor of the *Journal of Hygiene* for permission to publish Fig. 12.1.

9 REFERENCES

Alder, V.G., Boss, E., Gillespie, W.A. & Swann, A.J. (1971) Residual disinfection of wool blankets treated with formaldehyde. *Journal of Applied Bacteriology*, **34**, 757–763.

Alder, V.G., Lockyer, J.A. & Clee, P.G. (1966) Disinfection and cleaning of baths in hospital. *Monthly Bulletin of the Ministry of Health and Public Health Laboratories Service*, **25**, 18–20.

Allen, J.I., O'Connor, A.M., Olson, M.M., Gerding, D.N., Schauholzer, C.J., Meier, P.B., Vennes, J.A & Silvis, S.E. (1987) Pseudomonas infection of the biliary system resulting from use of contaminated endoscope. *Gastroenterology*, **92**, 759–763.

Ayliffe, G.A.J. (1988) Equipment-related infection risks. *Journal of Hospital Infection*, **11** (Supplement A), 279–284.

Ayliffe, G.A.J. & Gibson, G.L. (1975) Antimicrobial treatment of equipment in the hospital. *Health & Social Services Journal*, **85**, 598–599.

Ayliffe, G.A.J., Collins, B.J. & Lowbury, E.J.L. (1966) Cleaning and disinfection of hospital floors. *British Medical Journal*, **ii**, 442–445.

Ayliffe, G.A.J., Collins, B.J. & Lowbury, E.J.L. (1967) Ward floors and other surfaces as reservoirs of hospital infection. *Journal of Hygiene, Cambridge*, **65**, 515–536.

Ayliffe, G.A.J., Brightwell, K.M., Collins, B.J. & Lowbury, E.J.L. (1969) Varieties of aseptic practice in hospital wards. *Lancet*, **ii**, 1117–1120.

Ayliffe, G.A.J., Babb, J.R. & Collins, B.J. (1974a) Carpets in hospital wards. *Health & Social Services Journal*, **84**, Supplement (October 5th), 12–13.

Ayliffe, G.A.J., Collins, B.J. & Deverill, C.E.A. (1974b) Tests of disinfection by heat in a bed-pan washing machine. *Journal of Clinical Pathology*, **27**, 760–763.

Ayliffe, G.A.J., Babb, J.R, Collins, B.J., Deverill, C. & Varney, J. (1975a) Disinfection of baths and bathwater. *Nursing Times, Contact* (September 11th) pp. 22–23.

Ayliffe, G.A.J., Collins, B.J. & Green, S. (1975b) Hygiene of babies' incubators. *Lancet*, **i**, 923.

Ayliffe, G.A.J., Babb, J.R. & Collins, B.J. (1976) Environment hazards—real and imaginary. *Health & Social Services Journal*, **86**, Supplement 3 (June 26th), 3–4.

Ayliffe, G.A.J., Coates, D. & Hoffman, P.N. (1984) *Chemical Disinfection in Hospitals*. London: Public Health Laboratory Service.

Babb, J.R., Bradley, C.R. & Ayliffe, G.A.J. (1980) Sporicidal activity of glutaraldehydes and hypochlorites and other factors influencing their selection for the treatment of medical equipment. *Journal of Hospital Infection*, **1**, 63–75.

Babb, J.R., Bradley, C.R. & Ayliffe, G.A.J. (1984) Comparison of automated systems for the cleaning and disinfection of flexible fibreoptic endoscopes. *Journal of Hospital Infection*, **5**, 213–216.

Babb, J.R. & Bradley, C.R. (1991a) Decontamination of

flexible fibreoptic endoscopes. *Gastroenterology Today*, **1**, 25–27.

Babb, J.R. & Bradley, C.R. (1991b) The mechanics of endoscope disinfection. *Journal of Hospital Infection*, **18**, Supplement A, 130–135.

Babington, P.C.B., Baker, A.B. & Johnson, H.H. (1971) Retrograde spread of organisms from ventilator to patient via the expiratory limb. *Lancet*, **i**, 61–62.

Barkley, W.E. & Wedum, A.G. (1977) The hazard of infectious agents in microbiological laboratories. In *Disinfection, Sterilization and Preservation* (ed. Block, S.) 2nd Ed. Philadelphia: Lea & Febiger.

Bartlett, C.L.R, Macrae, A.D. & Macfarlene, J.D. (1986) *Legionella Infections*. London: Arnold.

Bassett, D.C.J., Stokes, K.J. & Thomas, W.R.G. (1970) Wound infection with *Pseudomonas multivorans*. *Lancet*, **i**, 1188–1191.

Bell, J. (1801) *The Principles of Surgery*. Edinburgh: Printed for T. Cadell, jun. & W. Davies (Strand); T.N. Longman & O. Rees (Paternoster Row); W. Creech, P. Hill and Manners & Miller.

Bennett, J.V. & Brachman, P.S. (eds.) (1986) 2nd Ed. *Hospital Infections*. Boston: Little Brown & Company.

Bennett, P.J., Cope, D.H.P. & Thompson, R.E.M. (1968) Decontamination of anaesthetic equipment: a one-step washing machine for processing anaesthetic equipment and tubing. *Anaesthesia*, **23**, 670–675.

Bergan, T. & Lystad, A. (1971) Antitubercular action of disinfectants. *Journal of Applied Bacteriology*, **34**, 751–756.

Best, M., Sattar, S.A., Springthorpe, V.S. & Kennedy, M.E. (1990) Efficacies of selected disinfectants against *Mycobacterium tuberculosis*. *Journal of Clinical Microbiology*, **28**, 2234–2239.

Birnie, G.G., Quigly, E.M., Clements, G.B., Follet, E.A.C. & Watkinson, G. (1983) Endoscopic transmission of hepatitis B virus. *Gut*, **24**, 171–174.

Block, S. (ed) (1983) *Disinfection, Sterilization and Preservation*, 3rd Ed. Philadelphia: Lea & Febiger.

Bloomfield, S.F. & Uso, E.E. (1985) The antibacterial properties of sodium hypochlorite and sodium dichloroisocyanurate as hospital disinfectants. *Journal of Hospital Infection*, **6**, 20–30.

Bloomfield, S.F., Smith-Burchnell, C.A. & Dalgleish, A.G. (1990) Evaluation of hypochlorite-releasing disinfectants against the human immunodeficiency virus. *Journal of Hospital Infection*, **15**, 273–278.

Bond, W.W., Favero, M.S., Petersen, N.J. & Ebert, J.W. (1983) Inactivation of hepatitis B virus by intermediate to high level disinfectant chemicals. *Journal of Clinical Microbiology*, **18**, 535–538.

Boycott, J.A. (1956) A note on the disinfection of baths and basins. *Lancet*, **ii**, 678–679.

Brachman, P.S. (1971) In *Proceedings of the International Conference on Nosocomial Infections 1970*, pp. 189–192. Chicago: American Hospital Association.

British Society of Gastroenterology (1988) Cleaning and disinfection of equipment for gastrointestinal flexible endoscopy: interim recommendations of a working party. *Gut*, **29**, 1134–1151.

Burdon, D.W. & Whitby, J.L. (1967) Contamination of hospital disinfectants with *Pseudomonas* species. *British Medical Journal*, **ii**, 153–155.

Burge, P.S. (1989) Occupational risks of glutaraldehyde. *British Medical Journal*, **299**, 342.

Cadwallader, H. (1989) Setting the seal on standards. *Nursing Times*, **85**, 71–72.

Cadwallader, H.L., Bradley, C.R. & Ayliffe, G.A.J. (1990) Bacterial contamination and frequency of changing ventilator circuitry. *Journal of Hospital Infection*, **15**, 65–72.

Center for Disease Control (1972) *Fogging, an ineffective measure*. National Nosocomial Infections Study, Third Quarter 1972, pp. 19–22.

Center for Disease Control (1974) *Disinfectant or infectant: The label doesn't always say*. National Nosocomial Infections Study, Fourth Quarter 1973, pp. 18–23.

Coates, D. (1988) Comparison of sodium hypochlorite and sodium dichloroisocyanurate disinfectants. Neutralization by serum. *Journal of Hospital Infection*, **11**, 60, 67.

Collins, B.J. (1979) How to have carpeted luxury. *Health & Social Service Journal*, September Supplement.

Collins, B.J. & Phelps, M. (1985) Heat disinfection and disinfector machines. *Journal of Sterile Services Management*, **3**, 7–8.

Collins, B.J., Cripps, N. & Spooner, S. (1987) Controlling microbial decontamination levels. *Laundry & Cleaning News*, pp. 30–31.

Council of Europe (1987) Test methods for the antibacterial activity of disinfectants. Strasburg: Council of Europe.

Craven, D.I., Connolly, M.G., Lichtenberg, D.A., Primeau, P.J. & McCabe, W.R. (1982) Contamination of mechanical ventilators with tubing changes every 24 or 48 hours. *New England Journal of Medicine*, **306**, 1505–1509.

Curie, K., Speller, D.C.E., Simpson, R., Stephens, M. & Cooke, D.I. (1978) A hospital epidemic caused by a gentamicin-resistant *Klebsiella aerogenes*. *Journal of Hygiene, Cambridge*, **80**, 115–123.

Danforth, D., Nicolle, L.E., Hume, K., Alfierie, N. & Sims, H. (1987) Nosocomial infections on nursing units with floors cleaned with a disinfectant compared with detergent. *Journal of Hospital Infection*, **10**, 229–235.

Dean, A.G. (1977) Transmission of *Salmonella typhi* by fibre-optic endoscopy. *Lancet*, **ii**, 134.

Death, J.E. & Coates, D. (1979) Effect of pH on sporicidal and microbiocidal activity of buffered mixtures of alcohol and sodium hypochlorite. *Journal of Clinical Pathology*, **32**, 148–153.

Department of Health & Social Security (1986) *Health Service Catering Manual, Hygiene*. London: HMSO.

Department of Health & Social Security (1982) Specification for containers for disposal of needles and sharp instruments. TSS/S/330.015.

Department of Health & Social Security (1986) *The Control of Viral Haemorhagic Fevers*. London: HMSO.

Department of Health & Social Security (1987) *Hospital Laundry Arrangements for Used and Infected Linen*. London: HMSO.

Duckworth, G.J., Lothian, J.L.R. & Williams, J.D. (1988) Methicillin-resistant *Staphylococcus aureus*: report of an outbreak in a London teaching hospital. *Journal of Hospital Infection*, **11**, 1–15.

Dyas, A. & Das, B.C. (1985) The activity of glutaraldehyde against *Clostridium difficile*. *Journal of Hospital Infection*, **6**, 41–45.

Elek, S.D. & Conen, P.E. (1957) The virulence of *Staphylococcus pyogenes* for man. *British Journal of Experimental Pathology*, **38**, 573–586.

Frank, U. & Daschner, F. (1989a) Disinfection in gastrointestinal endoscopy. *Endoscopy*, **21**, 276–278.

Frank, U. & Daschner, F. (1989b) Cost-effectiveness in hospital infection control—lessons for the 1990's. *Journal of Hospital Infection*, **13**, 325–336.

Gardner, J.F. & Peel, M.M. (1986) *Introduction to Sterilization and Disinfection*. Edinburgh: Churchill Livingstone.

George, R.H. (1975) A critical look at chemical disinfection of anaesthetic apparatus. *British Journal of Anaesthesia*, **47**, 719–721.

Gibson, G.L. (1973a) Bacteriological hazards of disposable bed-pan systems. *Journal of Clinical Pathology*, **26**, 146–153.

Gibson, G.L. (1973b) A disposable bed-pan system using an improved disposal unit and self-supporting bed-pans. *Journal of Clinical Pathology*, **26**, 925–928.

Hambraeus, A., Bengtsson, S. & Laurell, G. (1978) Bacterial contamination in a modern operating suite 3. Importance of floor contamination as a source of airborne contamination. *Journal of Hygiene, Cambridge*, **80**, 169–174.

Hanson, P.J.V., Clarke, J.R., Nicholson, G., Gazzar, B., Gaya, H., Gor, D., Chadwick, M.V., Shah, N., Jeffries, D.J. & Collins, J.V. (1989a) Contamination of endoscopes used in AIDS patients. *Lancet*, **ii**, 86–88.

Hanson, P.J.V., Gor, D., Jeffries, D.J. & Collins, J.V. (1989b) Chemical inactivation of HIV on surfaces. *British Medical Journal*, **298**, 862–864.

Hardie, I.D. (1985) Mycobactericidal efficacy of glutaraldehyde based biocides. *Journal of Hospital Infection*, **6**, 436–438.

Health Service Advisory Committee (1982) *The Safe Disposal of Clinical Waste*. London: HMSO.

Hedrick, E.R. (1988) Infectious waste management—will science prevail? *Infection Control and Hospital Epidemiology*, **9**, 488–490.

Johnson, L.L., Schneider, D.A., Austin, M.D., Goodman, F.G., Bullock, J.M. & DeBrain, J.A. (1982) Two per cent glutaraldehyde: a disinfectant in arthroscopy and arthroscopic surgery. *Journal of Bone and Joint Surgery*, **64a**, 237–239.

Joynson, D.H.M. (1978) Bowls and bacteria. *Journal of Hygiene, Cambridge*, **80**, 423–425.

Keane, C.I. & Cafferkey, M. (1984) Re-emergence of methicillin-resistant *Staph. aureus* causing severe infection. *Journal of Hospital Infection*, **9**, 6–16.

Kelsey, J.C. & Maurer, I.M. (1966) An in-use test for hospital disinfectants. *Monthly Bulletin of the Ministry of Health and the Public Health Laboratory Service*, **25**, 180–184.

Kelsey, J.C. & Maurer, I.M. (1972) *The Use of Chemical Disinfectants in Hospitals*. Public Health Laboratory Service, Monograph no. 2. London: HMSO.

Kelsey, J.C. & Maurer, I.M. (1974) An improved Kelsey-Sykes test for disinfectants. *Pharmaceutical Journal*, **213**, 528–530.

Kobayashi, H., Tsuzuki, M., Koshimizu, K., Toyama, H., Yoshihara, N., Shikata, T., Abe, K., Mizuno, K., Otomo, N. & Oda, T. (1984) Susceptibility of hepatitis B virus to disinfectants or heat. *Journal of Clinical Microbiology*, **20**, 214–216.

Kurth, R., Werner, A., Barrett, N. & Dorner, F. (1986) Stability and inactivation of the human immunodeficiency virus. *Aids-forschnung*, **ii**, 601–607.

Lee, J.C. & Fialkow, P.J. (1961) Benzalkonium chloride—source of hospital infection with Gram-negative bacteria. *Journal of the American Medical Association*, **177**, 708–710.

Leigh, D.A. & Whittaker, C. (1967) Disinfectants and plastic mop-heads. *British Medical Journal*, **iii**, 435.

Lidwell, O.M., Lowbury, E.J.L., Whyte, W., Blowers, R., Stanley, S. & Lowe, D. (1983) Airborne contamination of wounds in joint replacement operations: the relationship to sepsis rates. *Journal of Hospital Infection*, **4**, 111–131.

Lister, J. (1868) An address on the antiseptic system of treatment in surgery. *British Medical Journal*, **ii**, 53–56; 101–102.

Lowbury, E.J.L., Ayliffe, G.A.J., Geddes, A.M. & Williams, J.D. (1981) *Control of Hospital Infection: A Practical Handbook*, 2nd Ed. London: Chapman & Hall (Revised edition in press).

Maurer, I. (1985) *Hospital Hygiene*. 3rd Ed. London: Edward Arnold.

Mayon-White, R.T., Ducel, G.I., Kereselidze, T. & Tikomirov, E. (1988) An international survey of the prevalence of hospital-acquired infection. *Journal of Hospital Infection*, **11** (Supplement A), 43–48.

Medcraft, J.W., Hawkins, J.M., Fletcher, B.N. & Dadswell, J.V. (1987) Potential hazard from spray cleaning of floors in hospital wards. *Journal of Hospital Infection*, **9**, 151–157.

Meers, P.D., Ayliffe, G.A.J., Emmerson, A.M., Leigh, D.A., Mayon-White, R.T., Mackintosh, C.A. & Stronge, J.L. (1981) Report on the national survey of infection in hospitals, 1980. *Journal of Hospital Infection*, **2** (Supplement), 1–53.

Murray, S.M., Freiman, J.S., Vickery, K., Lim, D., Cossart, Y.E. & Whiteley, R.K. (1991) Duck hepatitis B virus: a model to assess efficacy of disinfectants against hepadnavirus activity. *Epidemiology and Infection*, **106**, 435–443.

Nelson, K.E., Larson, P.A., Schraufnagel, D.E. & Jackson, J. (1983) Transmission of tuberculosis by flexible fibrebronchoscopes. *American Review of Respiratory Diseases*, **127**, 97–100.

Newsom, S.W.B. (1972) Microbiology of hospital toilets. *Lancet*, **ii**, 700–703.

Noble, W.C. & Somerville, D.A. (1974) *Microbiology of Human Skin*. London: Saunders.

Nÿstrom, B. (1981) Disinfection of surgical instruments. *Journal of Hospital Infection*, **2**, 363–368.

O'Connor, H.J. and Axon, A.T.R. (1983) Gastrointestinal endoscopy, infection and disinfection. *Gut*, **24**, 1067–1077.

Phillips, I., King, A., Jenkins, S. & Spencer, G. (1974) Control of respirator-associated infection due to *Pseudomonas aeruginosa*. *Lancet*, **ii**, 871–873.

Phillips, I. & Spencer, G. (1965) *Pseudomonas aeruginosa* cross-infection due to contaminated respirators. *Lancet*, **ii**, 1325–1327.

Power, E.G.M. & Russell, A.D. (1989) Glutaraldehyde: its uptake by sporing and non-sporing bacteria, rubber, plaster and an endoscope. *Journal of Applied Bacteriology*, **67**, 329–342.

Prince, J. & Ayliffe, G.A.J. (1972) In-use testing of disinfectants in hospitals. *Journal of Clinical Pathology*, **25**, 586–589.

Public Health Laboratory Service (1965) Committee on the testing and evaluation of disinfectants. *British Medical Journal*, **i**, 408–413.

Reber, H., Fleury, C., Gaschen, M., Hess, E., Regamey, R., Ritler, P., Tanner, F. & Vischer, W. (1972) Bewertung und Prüfung von Disinfektionsmitteln und Verfahren. Basel: Auftrag der schweizerischen Mikrobiologischen Gesellschaft.

Report of a combined working party of the Hospital Infection Society and the British Society for Antimicrobial Chemotherapy (1986) Guidelines for the control of epidemic methicillin-resistant *Staphylococcus aureus*. *Journal of Hospital Infection*, **7**, 193–201.

Report of a combined working party of the Hospital Infection Society and the British Society for Antimicrobial Chemotherapy (1990). Revised guidelines for the control of epidemic methicillin-resistant *Staphylococcus aureus*. *Journal of Hospital Infection*, **16**, 351–377.

Resnick, L., Veren, K., Salahuddin, S.Z., Troudeau, S. & Markham, P.D. (1986) Stability and inactivation of HTLV/LAV under clinical and laboratory environments. *Journal of the American Medical Association*, **255**, 1887–1891.

Rogers, T.R. & Barnes, R.A. (1988) Prevention of airborne fungal infection in immunocompromised patients. *Journal of Hospital Infection*, **11** (Supplement A), 15–20.

Rubala, W.A. (1990) APIC guidelines for selection and use of disinfectant. *American Journal of Infection Control*, **18**, 99–117.

Sanford, J.P. (1970) Disinfectants that don't. *Annals of Internal Medicine*, **72**, 282–283.

Sanford, J.P. & Pierce, A.K. (1979) In *Hospital Infections* (eds Bennett, J.V. & Brachman, P.S.) pp. 255–286. Boston: Little, Brown & Company.

Sattar, S.A., Springthorpe, V.S., Karim, Y. & Loro, P. (1989) Chemical disinfection of non-porous inanimate surfaces experimentally contaminated with four human pathogenic viruses. *Epidemiology and Infection*, **102**, 493–505.

Schmidt, B. (1973) Das 2. Internationale Colloquium uber die Wertbestimmung von Disinfektionsmitteln in Europa. *Zentralblatt für Bakteriologie, Parasitenkunde, Infektionskrankheiten und Hygiene 1. Abteilung Originale Reihe B*, **157**, 411–420.

Spaulding, E.H., Cundy, K.R. & Turner, F.J. (1977) Chemical disinfection of medical and surgical materials. In *Disinfection, Sterilization and Preservation*, (ed. Block, S.) 2nd Ed. Philadelphia: Lea & Febiger.

Speller, D.C.E., Stephens, M.E. & Viant, A.C. (1971) Hospital Infection by *Pseudomonas capacia*. *Lancet*, **i**, 798–799.

Sykes, G. (1965) *Disinfection and Sterilization*. 2nd Ed. London: E. & F.N. Spon.

Tyler, R. & Ayliffe, G.A.J. (1987) A surface test for virucidal activity: a preliminary study with herpes virus. *Journal of Hospital Infection*, **19**, 22–29.

Tyler, R., Ayliffe, G.A.J. & Bradley, C.R. (1990) Virucidal activity of disinfectants: studies with the poliovirus. *Journal of Hospital Infection*, **15**, 339.

Van Bueren, J., Cooke, E.M., Mortimer, P.P. and Simpson, R.A. (1989) Inactivation of HIV on surfaces by alcohol. *British Medical Journal*, **299**, 459.

Vesley, D. & Michaelsen, G.S. (1964) Application of a surface sampling method technique to the evaluation of the bacteriological effectiveness of certain hospital housekeeping procedures. *Health Laboratory Science*, **1**, 107.

Walsh, T.J. & Dixon, G.M. (1989) Nosocomial aspergillus: environmental microbiology, hospital epidemiology, diagnosis and treatment. *European Journal of Epidemiology*, **5**, 131–142.

Wenzel, R.P. (1987) *Prevention and Control of Nosocomial Infections*. Baltimore and London: Williams & Wilkins.

Williams, R.E.O., Blowers, R., Garrod, L.P. & Shooter, R.A. (1966) *Hospital Infection—Causes and Prevention*. London: Lloyd-Luke.

Wypkema, W. & Alder, V.G. (1962) Hospital cross-infection and dirty walls. *Lancet*, **ii**, 1066–1068.

Chapter 13
Special Problems in Hospital Antisepsis

1 INTRODUCTION

Long before the discovery of bacteria and the introduction of antiseptic surgery a variety of substances had been used to prevent putrefaction of meat and to preserve the bodies of the dead. It was also realized before the era of bacteriology that wound sepsis and the lesions of some infectious diseases resembled the process of putrefaction. The word antiseptic* seems to have been used first in a book on the plague, published in 1721, which contains the following sentence: 'This phenomenon shows the motion of the pestilential poison to be putrefactive; it makes the use of antiseptics a reasonable way to oppose it' (Place: quoted by Thompson, 1934). The application of antiseptics, including alcohol, was also recommended by a number of surgeons in the 18th century.

The word *antiseptic* has acquired the special meaning of an antimicrobial agent which is sufficiently free from injurious effects to be applied to surfaces of the body or to exposed tissues, though not suitable for treatment of infection by systemic administration (i.e. not an antimicrobial chemotherapeutic agent). An antiseptic may be regarded as a special kind of disinfectant, and some would dispense with the word antiseptic altogether, pointing out that one speaks of 'disinfection of the skin by antiseptics'; others would restrict the word *disinfectant* for those antimicrobial agents which are too irritant, toxic or corrosive to be applied to surfaces or tissues of the body, but suitable for disinfection of equipment or of the inanimate environment. The term *antimicrobial chemotherapeutic agent* includes antibiotics, and the word *antibiotic* is often used, for convenience, to describe all antimicrobials which can, with safety, be administered systemically. Some antibiotics (i.e. antimicrobial agents produced by micro-organisms) are too toxic for systemic use but have been used for

* Greek, σήψις = sepsis = putrefaction: σήπτικος = septikos = putrefactive.

topical application (e.g. neomycin), and might therefore be classified as antiseptics. It is important, however, to note that some toxic antibiotics, such as neomycin, can be absorbed in toxic amounts when applied on open wounds and burns; their topical use should therefore be restricted to surfaces, such as the anterior nares, from which they will not be absorbed into the bloodstream.

The scientific foundations of *antisepsis* (i.e. the topical application of antiseptics, associated with chemical disinfection of inanimate objects, for the prevention of wound infection) were laid by Ignaz Semmelweis and Joseph Lister. In 1847 (before the era of scientific bacteriology) Semmelweis (1861) introduced the practice of hand disinfection with chlorinated lime for persons working in labour wards of the Vienna Maternity Hospital. As a result there was a large reduction in mortality due to puerperal sepsis (from 18.7% in 1847 to 1.27% in 1848), much of which had apparently been due to virulent bacteria carried from the dissecting and autopsy rooms on the hands of doctors and medical students who assisted in deliveries; significantly, the incidence of puerperal sepsis before Semmelweis's innovation had been much lower in women attended by nurses than in those attended by medical staff or students. The role of doctors in transmitting puerperal sepsis had been demonstrated still earlier by Oliver Wendell Holmes (1842).

Some twenty years later, with Pasteur's recent discoveries of microbial infection in mind, Joseph Lister recognized the microbial causation of fulminant wound infection ('hospital gangrene') and introduced the practice of antisepsis in surgery. This involved the use of a 1 in 20 aqueous solution of phenol to kill bacteria on instruments, dressings and other materials used in operations or in handling traumatic wounds (e.g. open fractures), and also for disinfection of the operation site, the surgeon's hands and (in the initial period) the air. Lister's successful use of these methods (Lister, 1867, 1909) stimulated surgeons in many countries to adopt the antiseptic method, and within a few years hospital gangrene became an apparently extinct disease. Surgery could at last develop in many directions and on lines which had been technically possible before that time, though impractical because of the virtual inevitability of fulminant infection.

At the end of the 19th century Listerian antisepsis was displaced by *aseptic* methods, i.e. the use of heat-sterilized rather than phenol-disinfected instruments, dressings and other equipment used at operations, together with such additional safeguards as the use of sterile rubber gloves, face masks and theatre clothes (Walter, 1948). This was a technical advance of the greatest importance, both in providing facilities for true *sterilization* (destruction of bacterial spores as well as vegetative bacteria) and in the avoidance of phenol which had severe irritant effects (and would not be called an 'antiseptic' today). The revolutionary advance in control of surgical infection, however, had come with Lister's antiseptic method; asepsis merely strengthened the defences. At first it seemed that asepsis and antisepsis were antithetic approaches, but it was soon apparent that antiseptic methods were still required for disinfection of the skin, for application to tissues and for the treatment of heat-labile equipment; the word *asepsis* acquired a wider meaning, and *antisepsis* — now seen as a component of aseptic method — acquired a narrower meaning of disinfection or prophylactic treatment of skin and other living tissues with antiseptics.

The arrival of the antibiotics and of other chemotherapeutic agents did not eliminate the need for antiseptics. The factors which make antibiotics selectively active against microbes and relatively harmless to human tissues are also responsible for differences in their activity against different types of microbe, and for the emergence of resistant variants of many bacterial species to most antibiotics. Mutants of bacteria resistant to the commonly used antiseptics — alcohols, halogens, chlorhexidine — do not emerge. When applied to unbroken skin these agents act against a wide range of vegetative organisms with little risk of toxic absorption or of inactivation by organic matter. The situation is different in open wounds, but on these, too, there is a role for certain antiseptics which could not be used for systemic therapy; there are also limited indications for topical application of certain antibiotics to open wounds and for their injection or instillation into abscesses, hollow viscera and body cavities.

In this chapter the term *antisepsis* will be used in the sense of application of antimicrobial agents to the unbroken skin or mucous membrane, to burns and to open wounds for the purpose of preventing sepsis by removing or excluding microbes from these areas. These are essentially hospital practices stemming from the principles and practices of Semmelweis and Lister. In the time of those pioneers the main problems in the use of antimicrobial agents were to establish their effectiveness and to avoid toxic effects. Today there is a third problem, preventing the emergence of resistant variants, which has acquired special importance in hospitals. Although this applies essentially to antibiotics and chemotherapeutic agents, some antiseptics [e.g. chlorhexidine, quaternary ammonium compounds (QACs), dyes] are selective in their range of activity, and this gives a selective advantage to resistant organisms when these antiseptics are used in hospital practice.

2 DISINFECTION OF THE SKIN

2.1 Purposes

The skin and the mucous membranes are effective barriers against invasion of the tissue by micro-organisms, but they carry on their outer surfaces a rich microbial flora which normally presents no hazard to the person whose skin it is, or to other healthy people. The circumstances in which it is desirable to do more than keep the surface socially clean with soap and water are:

1 to protect a patient's tissues against his own skin flora when the skin is incised at surgical operations, or penetrated for infusions, injections or removal of blood and other fluids;

2 to protect patients with open traumatic or surgical wounds, or otherwise at special risk of infection, from micro-organisms on the hands of surgeons when they operate, and of nurses and others who handle patients in the wards;

3 occasionally, to reduce the numbers of staphylococci shed into the air by a disperser of *Staphylococcus aureus* from the surface of his body, if his presence in areas where there are patients is unavoidable.

2.2 Micro-organisms of the skin

The micro-organisms on the skin can be roughly classified under two headings, as *resident flora* and *transient flora* (Price, 1938). The *resident organisms*, i.e. the indigenous skin flora, multiply and persist on the skin; they are mainly non-pathogenic organisms or potential 'opportunist' pathogens, especially micrococci, coryneform bacilli and *Propionibacterium acnes* (Evans *et al.*, 1950; Noble, 1981), though occasionally *Staph. aureus* and, in damaged or persistently immersed skin, Gram-negative bacilli may become residents. The *transient flora* include any micro-organisms which are deposited but do not multiply on the skin; in hospital the transient flora include bacteria transmitted by various channels from other patients, including such wound pathogens as *Staph. aureus* and *Pseudomonas aeruginosa*. Some bacteria (e.g. *Streptococcus pyogenes*) are rapidly killed by unsaturated fatty acids of the skin (Burtenshaw, 1942; Ricketts *et al.*, 1951), and others—notably the Gram-negative bacilli—lose most of their numbers on evaporation of the fluid in which they were deposited (Ricketts *et al.*, 1951). Such organisms are therefore more transient in their presence than staphylococci and micrococci, which are much more resistant to unsaturated fatty acids and to desiccation. The dividing line between transients and residents is not sharp, and a transient organism may sometimes become resident (see also Noble, 1981).

2.3 Methods of reducing the skin flora

Micro-organisms on the skin can be reduced in numbers by:

1 removing them physically, mainly on desquamating epithelial scales, with soap or some other detergent and water (skin cleansing);

2 killing them on the skin, through the application of bactericidal agents (skin disinfection).

The skin cannot be sterilized (i.e. rendered free from all microbial flora, including bacterial spores), and for that reason it is one of the few remaining weak links in the network of modern aseptic practice. It is therefore important to use the most effective of the available methods of reducing the skin flora, but also to choose methods appropriate for the particular infective hazards, which are greater in some places, such as an operating theatre or an intensive-care unit, than in others, such as a general medical ward. In some situations, e.g. a general ward, transient organisms carried by staff from one patient to another present the greater hazard, while in other situations, especially operating theatres, resident organisms may be more important as agents of infection, because surgeons' hands are less likely to transmit bacteria from patient to patient, and because the patient's susceptibility to commensal organisms is enhanced at operations. Methods appropriate for the removal of resident organisms are different from those appropriate for removing transients, as the transients are much more easily removed by cleansing with a detergent and water, and also more easily killed by antiseptics. Methods for removal or killing of the transient flora of hands have been described by some authors as *hygienic* hand disinfection, while those suitable for removal or killing of the resident flora are described as *surgical* hand disinfection (Rotter *et al.*, 1974). In some operations, e.g. colorectal surgery, there is a much greater hazard of self-infection with faecal organisms than of cross-infection, or infection from the patient's skin; the most effective skin disinfection of surgeon and patient can do little or nothing to reduce this hazard.

2.4 Assessing the effectiveness of skin disinfection

It might seem that the value of skin disinfection could best be measured by showing how effectively it can prevent the development of sepsis (i.e. clinical infection). Semmelweis's demonstration that disinfection of the hands of accoucheurs led to a lower mortality from puerperal sepsis (Section 1) is still the most striking evidence of this type. Larson (1988) has reviewed the published literature from 1879 to 1986 on the effect of handwashing and disinfection by health-care personnel on the incidence of clinical infection. Some of the strongest bacteriological evidence has come from studies on the transfer of serotypes of *Klebsiella* spp. in an intensive-care unit (Casewell & Phillips, 1977; Casewell, 1981): following the introduction of antiseptic handwashing the rate of hospital-acquired infection with endemic types was significantly reduced. Maki & Hecht (1982) found that the incidence of infection in an intensive-care unit was almost halved when antiseptic hand preparations were used, compared with the findings when hands were washed with unmedicated soap. Striking evidence in support of skin antisepsis has been reported from neonatal units; e.g. the reduction in staphylococcal skin sepsis following the introduction of hexachlorophane preparations (e.g. Plueckhahn & Banks, 1963; Gezon *et al.*, 1964), and the return of higher infection rates when hexachlorophane was withheld following the published reports of its toxicity (Kaslow *et al.*, 1973; Hyams *et al.*, 1975). Studies on healthy naval cadets have shown a large reduction (40–50%) in skin infection where antiseptic soap was used in place of unmedicated soap (Leonard, 1967). Black *et al.*, (1981) reported a reduced incidence of diarrhoea in a day-care centre following the introduction of non-antiseptic handwashing. Khan (1982) showed a reduced incidence of shigellosis in Bangladesh families which observed a prescribed handwash routine.

There are major difficulties in using clinical criteria for assessment of the value of skin disinfection in surgery. Statistical evaluation of its effects would require concurrent prospective comparison with controls, but this would involve withholding skin disinfection from patients in the control series, which would be inadmissible on ethical grounds. Because of the generally low incidence of wound sepsis after clean operations, very large numbers of patients are required in attempts to evaluate skin disinfection by comparisons of sepsis rate before and after changes in disinfection routines. In view of the impracticability of assessing the clinical value of disinfecting the surgeon's hands and the patient's operation site, it has become customary to assess the relative merits of alternative methods of skin disinfection by measuring their ability to reduce the numbers of bacteria, both resident and transient, on the skin. Because of the ease of sampling from the hands, much of this research has been done using the hands as the test area.

2.4.1 *Tests for removal or killing of resident flora*

Handwash sampling and other contact sampling methods. Price (1938) devised a test in which the numbers of bacteria on the skin before and after cleansing or disinfection were assessed from viable counts on a series of standard handwashings before, and a series of similar washings after, the cleansing or disinfecting procedure. In most subsequent studies simpler methods have been used, which show the yield of bacteria on standard handwash sampling before and after disinfection (e.g. Quinn *et al*., 1954; Lowbury *et al*., 1960). Contact sampling by impression plate or finger streak plate has been used by some workers (e.g. Smylie *et al*., 1973). An indirect method of assessment, which shows the yield of bacteria from the surgeon's hands at the end of an operation, is the viable count of bacteria in washings from the inside of gloves worn by the surgeon (Lowbury & Lilly, 1960; Dineen, 1978). The numbers of bacteria emerging through holes deliberately pricked through the finger tips of rubber gloves have been used (Lowbury & Lilly, 1960) as a method of demonstrating the value of hand disinfection in protecting operation wounds against bacterial contaminants.

In the assessment of methods for disinfection of operation sites other than hands, and also by bathing, contact plates have often been used (Davies *et al*., 1977, 1978). A more thorough sampling for resident flora on such sites has been obtained by the use of rotating brush and sampling fluid held against the skin in a truncated cylinder (Price, 1951).

Though contact plate sampling is a relatively crude method which disregards the deeper flora, and may be invalidated by confluent growth, a comparison by parallel sampling of finger streak and bowl handwash sampling techniques showed a fairly good correspondence between the two methods in results of skin disinfection by alternative agents (Ayliffe *et al*., 1975).

To obtain a statistical assessment of the relative merits of different methods of skin disinfection, it is convenient to use a Latin square experimental design, in which each of a group of volunteers uses each of the agents being studied and a non-bactericidal control (e.g. soap and water). All the agents are tested on each of a series of experimental days, which are separated from each other by an interval of a week or more, to allow the equilibrium level of the skin flora to have been restored by the beginning of each experiment (Lowbury *et al*., 1960).

Skin biopsy viable counts. Skin biopsies taken after pre-operative disinfection have been used by Walter (1938), Gardner & Seddon (1946), Murphy *et al*. (1951), Myers *et al*. (1956) and Selwyn & Ellis (1972), for assessment of skin disinfection. A surprisingly large proportion of such samples (23/24) were found by Myers *et al*. (1956) to be free from detectable bacteria after 4 min pre-operative treatment with 0.5% aqueous chlorhexidine. This method has the advantage of sampling the full thickness of the skin; its disadvantages are:
1 the very small area of skin which can be sampled by biopsies;
2 the ethical unacceptability of pre-treatment sampling, which makes it impossible to measure, in the human skin, the reduction in numbers of bacteria or the proportion of samples rendered apparently sterile.

2.4.2 *Tests for removal or killing of transient flora*

Colebrook & Maxted (1933), Gardner & Seddon (1946) and Gardner (1948) allowed bacterial cultures to dry on the skin of volunteers and then applied antiseptics, swab-sampling after an appropriate interval to show the numbers of bacteria present before and after disinfection. Story (1952) developed this method, using a penicillin-resistant staphylococcus and a selective medium containing penicillin; the numbers of bacteria were assessed by viable counts of washings taken from the inoculated areas, in a truncated cylinder held firmly against the skin, by rubbing with a glass rod and using a measured volume of sampling fluid containing neutralizers to prevent the effects of 'carry-over' of antiseptic to the culture medium (see also Chapters 3 and 4). Destruction of 99.9% or more of the applied organisms in 20 s by 2% iodine in 70% ethanol was reported by Gardner. Lowbury *et al*. (1960, 1964a) used a method similar to that of Story (1952), but in later studies (see below) the influence of different methods of applying the bacterial cultures was studied (Lilly & Lowbury, 1978). Rotter and his colleagues (1974) developed a method in which the test organisms are applied by immersion of the hands, after thorough cleansing, in a suspension of the bacteria; before and after treatment with antiseptics or with a control fluid viable bacterial counts were obtained from finger samples, and the effectiveness of disinfection was expressed as a 'log reduction factor' (i.e. logarithm of the pre-treatment count minus the logarithm of the post-treatment count). Ayliffe *et al.* (1978) described a standardized test procedure for assessing 'hygienic' hand disinfection against several different test organisms, using a technique, modified from the standard German (formerly West German) method (DGHM, 1972), in which fingertips were inoculated with bacterial cultures, and viable counts of finger washings in broth were obtained after various forms of antiseptic or non-antiseptic treatment. A Latin square design was used for the experiments, as in earlier studies on the resident flora (Lowbury *et al.*, 1960). For prevention of carry-over, the broth used for washings contained neutralizers (0.75% lecithin–Tween mixture, containing 50 g Tween 80 and 5 g lecithin, with 1% sodium thiosulphate).

2.5 Pre-operative disinfection of the surgeon's hands ('surgical hand disinfection')

The importance of pre-operative cleansing and disinfection of the surgeon's hands was vividly demonstrated by Devenish & Miles (1939), who found that up to 24% of rubber gloves worn by members of the surgical team had pinhole punctures when the gloves were examined at the end of operations. Through these holes, and also through the sleeves of cotton theatre gowns, bacteria could be introduced into operation wounds, and if these included virulent *Staph. aureus*, post-operative sepsis was likely to occur. The authors described an outbreak of infection due to such contamination.

In a series of studies at the Birmingham Accident Hospital, a handwash test was used for the assessment of the reduction in yield of bacteria from the skin after cleansing or disinfection. Volunteers moistened their hands in bowls containing 100 ml of Ringer's solution containing neutralizers (1% Lubrol W, 0.5% lecithin, 1% Tween 80 and, in some experiments, 1% sodium thiosulphate), and rubbed palm against palm, right palm over left dorsum, left palm over right dorsum, and with fingers interlaced, each procedure three times, followed by thorough rinsing. Pour plates of nutrient agar with neutralizers were used for viable counts, and tests for 'carry-over' of antiseptic to culture plates were made (Lowbury *et al.*, 1960, 1963, 1964b; Lilly and Lowbury, 1971; Lowbury and Lilly, 1973; Lowbury *et al.*, 1974).

The preparations tested were of two types:

1 antiseptic detergent solutions, creams or soaps, by the use of which it was envisaged that the combined effects of disinfection and cleansing could be obtained;

2 alcohol, or alcoholic or aqueous solutions of antiseptics.

Antiseptic detergent preparations (see Chapter 2) containing 4% chlorhexidine, 10% povidone-iodine (an iodophor), 3% hexachlorophane or 2% Irgasan DP 300 (triclosan: 2,4,4′-trichlor-2′-hydroxydiphenylether) were used, with additions of running warm water from a tap, in a 2-min vigorous handwash without a brush, completely covering hands and wrists. Alcoholic preparations studied were ethyl or isopropyl alcohol at 70% or 95%, with 1% added glycerol to prevent excessive drying of the skin; they were used with and without the inclusion of chlorhexidine gluconate (0.5%) or of phenolic compounds. Two aliquots of 5 ml of these fluids were poured into the cupped hands and rubbed vigorously over the entire surface of the hands and wrists, allowing the skin to dry while rubbing. Aqueous solutions were similarly rubbed on to the skin, but were rinsed off, and the hands were then dried on a sterile towel.

Table 13.1 summarizes some of the findings in these studies. Soap and water caused very little reduction in the yield of bacteria from the skin after one standard surgical hand preparation or after six such procedures, three on one day and three on the next. Varying degrees of disinfection were obtained with antiseptics. Of the detergent antiseptic preparations, the 4% chlorhexidine detergent solution, 'Hibiscrub', gave the largest reduction on a single application, but after six applications similar results were obtained with

Table 13.1 Assessments of alternative methods of surgical hand disinfection and cleansing

Manner of use	Preparation	Means of percentage reduction in skin sample counts of viable bacteria: After one treatment	After six treatments (2 days)
Detergent used with running water	4% chlorhexidine ('Hibiscrub')	86.7 ± 3.0	99.2 ± 0.2
	10% providone-iodine ('Disadine')	68.0 ± 6.8	99.7 ± 0.7
	3% hexachlorophane ('Disfex')	46.3 ± 9.7	91.9 ± 3.8
	2% Irgasan DP 300 ('Zalclense')	11.2 ± 19.9	95.8 ± 1.8
Non-detergent, with no added water during use	0.5% chlorhexidine in 95% ethanol	97.9 ± 1.1	99.7 ± 0.1
	0.1% phenolic in 95% ethanol ('Desderman')	91.8 ± 4.6	99.5 ± 0.2
	0.5% chlorhexidine in water	65.1 ± 8.7	91.8 ± 2.4
Soap and water (control)	Experiment 1	3.3 ± 8.3	25.9 ± 5.1
	Experiment 2	12.3 ± 2.2	17.7 ± 3.7

povidone-iodine and Irgasan DP 300. In view of the poor results obtained with soap and water, the benefits of combining detergent action with disinfection are doubtful. The necessity to dilute the antiseptic with water from a tap when this method is used reduces its disinfectant efficiency by diluting the antiseptic. It is therefore not surprising that the best results were obtained with alcohol, and with alcoholic solutions rubbed to dryness on the hands (Lowbury *et al.*, 1974). These also led to a more rapid attainment of a low equilibrium level of bacteria on the skin. Repeated disinfection brings about a progressive reduction in the skin flora, as judged by the yield of bacteria on sampling, until a low equilibrium level is reached (Fig. 13.1). This level varies with the effectiveness of the antiseptic, lower equilibrium levels being obtained with more effective antiseptics (Fig. 13.2) (Lilly *et al.*, 1979a). If a more effective antiseptic, e.g. alcoholic chlorhexidine, is used on skin which has been disinfected to equilibrium level by a detergent antiseptic (e.g. 'Hibiscrub' or 'Ster-Zac'), a further reduction to the equilibrium level of alcoholic chlorhexidine is obtained ('two-phase' disinfection). There is no further reduction, however, when a less effective antiseptic is used after one which is more effective; indeed there may be an increase, and if a non-antiseptic detergent is used to wash the hands after the low equilibrium level with alcoholic chlorhexidine has been reached, there is a large increase in the yield of bacteria on sampling the skin (Fig. 13.3). These findings agree with the view that the low equilibrium level represents the balance between killing of bacteria on the surface by the antiseptic and emergence of deeper resident organisms to the surface by the friction used in applying the solution. It also illustrates how far we are from being able to sterilize the skin.

2.6 Residual action of antiseptic on skin

Certain non-volatile antiseptics leave an active residue on the skin after rinsing and drying, or after deposition from alcoholic solution. This was demonstrated by allowing bacterial suspensions to dry on the skin after it had been cleansed with soap and water or disinfected, and sampling 1 h later for survival of the deposited bacteria in these areas. Large numbers of the deposited bacteria were present in areas which had previously been cleansed with bar soap or disinfected with a volatile antiseptic (alcohol), but very few were present in areas previously disinfected with chlorhexidine, hexachlorophane or povidone-iodine (Lowbury *et al.*, 1964b; Lowbury & Lilly, 1973). Residues of hexachlorophane can be neutralized by blood seeping into gloves through puncture holes (Cole & Bernard, 1964) but a residue of chlorhexidine

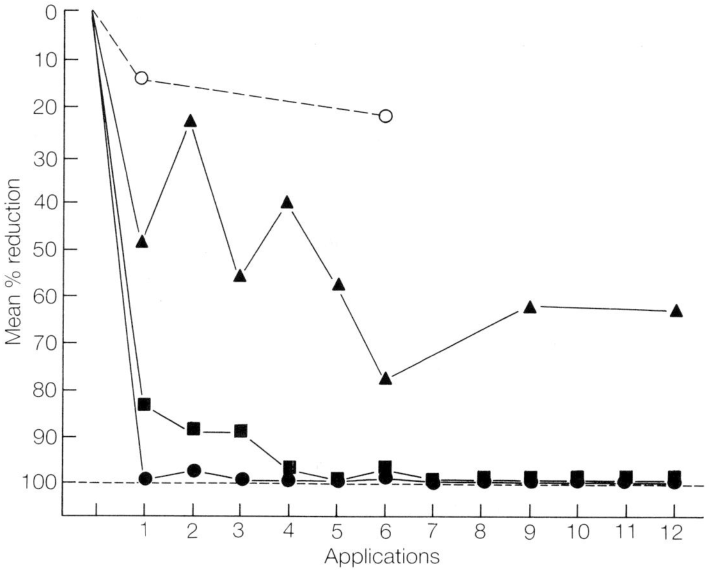

Fig. 13.1 Mean percentage reduction in viable bacteria on hands following disinfection. ▲—▲, 0.3% chlorocresol; ■—■, Hibiscrub; ●—●, 95% ethanol; ○—○, soap and water.

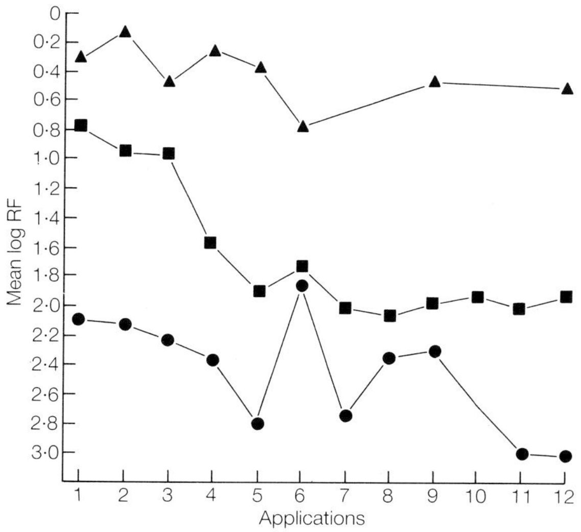

Fig. 13.2 Reduction in viable bacteria on hands following disinfection—mean logarithmic reduction factors. ▲—▲, 0.3% chlorocresol; ■—■, Hibiscrub; ●—●, 95% ethanol.

appears to be unaffected by the presence of blood on the skin (Lowbury & Lilly, 1974).

It is hard to assess the usefulness of residual action by antiseptics deposited on the skin. A study in which volunteers wore gloves for 3 h after having their hands disinfected with various antiseptics showed that the numbers of bacteria present at that time were smaller than those present on the skin immediately after disinfection with the same antiseptics (Lowbury *et al.*, 1974); in other words, there was a further fall in the numbers of bacteria on the skin of the surgeon's gloved hands during the course of an operation. This would seem to be due to continued action by residues of antiseptic, but, surprisingly, a similar effect was obtained with 70% ethyl alcohol, which evaporated completely before gloves were put on. As a hypothesis to explain this we suggested that many bacteria damaged by the alcohol would die if left on the skin, but could be resuscitated if they were immediately inoculated on a culture medium. This view was supported by an experiment in which bacteria, exposed briefly to alcohol or to water on a membrane filter, were cultured for viable counts immediately and after a 3-h delay (Lilly *et al.*, 1979b); the further reduction in viable counts of bacteria extracted from membrane filters held for 3 h was twice as great when the bacteria had been exposed to alcohol as when they had not been so exposed.

2.7 Disinfection of operation sites

Like the surgeon's hands, the patient's operation

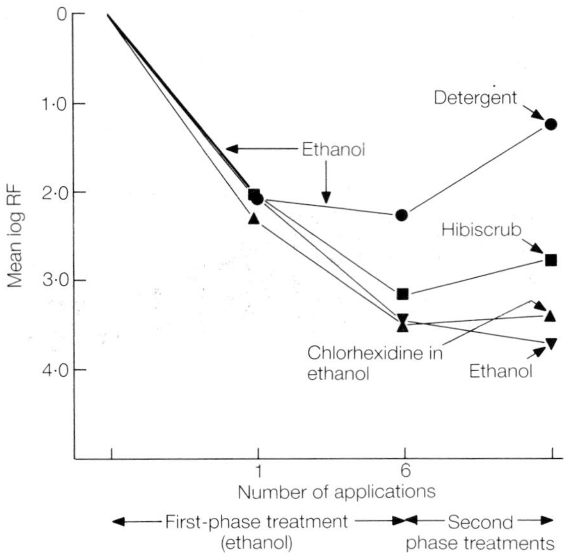

Fig. 13.3 Mean logarithmic reduction factors (RF) of bacteria in samplings from hands after one and after six treatments with 95% ethanol, and after an immediate further treatment with: 95% ethanol, ▼—▼; 0.5% chlorhexidine in 95% ethanol, ▲—▲; Hibiscrub, ■—■; a non-antiseptic detergent (the base of Hibiscrub), ●—●.

site requires 'surgical' disinfection, directed against the resident as well as the transient flora; often it requires maximum disinfection in a single treatment (e.g. in emergency surgery), without benefit from the progressive effects of repeated application.

By the use of a technique similar to that used for assessing disinfection of the surgeons' hands, the author and his colleagues (Lowbury *et al.*, 1960, 1964a,b) compared alternative methods of disinfecting the skin as in preparation of the operation site. The greatest reduction in yield of bacteria (about 80%) was obtained with 1% iodine in 70% ethanol and with 0.5% chlorhexidine in 70% ethanol: these were significantly greater than the reductions obtained by application of 70% ethanol, Lugol's iodine solution, or aqueous 0.5% chlorhexidine.

The antiseptic solution was applied with friction, on gauze swabs, over two hands in a period of 2 min. The 80% reduction obtained with 0.5% chlorhexidine in 70% alcohol was very poor compared with the reduction of about 99% obtained by use of the same solution for disinfection of the surgeons' hands, as described above. This discrepancy is due to the fact that disinfection, obtained by hand-to-hand friction on carrying out the surgical handwash, is more effective than that obtained by the use of gauze as an applicator, the usual method for operation site disinfection. This was shown by a comparison of the two methods of application—by gauze or by the gloved hand—of several different antiseptics (Lowbury and Lilly, 1975). Table 13.2 shows consistently larger reductions obtained by gloved hand application than by the conventional gauze application of the antiseptics; it also shows a larger reduction when a smaller area—one hand rather than two—was the experimental 'operation site' disinfected in 2 min with a gauze applicator.

The role of friction in obtaining good disinfection was further illustrated by the poorer results of disinfection obtained when an antiseptic solution was sprayed on to the skin than when it was rubbed on with gauze (Lowbury *et al.*, 1964b).

2.8 Disinfection of the hands of nurses, physiotherapists, etc.

To prevent the transfer of bacteria from one patient to another on the hands of staff in the wards it is necessary to use methods effective against the transient flora ('hygienic' hand disinfection). Early studies (e.g. Gardner & Seddon, 1946; Story, 1952; Lowbury *et al.*, 1960, 1964a) showed that a very large proportion of the bacteria deposited superficially on the skin were removed or destroyed either by washing or by disinfection with commonly used antiseptics. More recent studies, by Lilly & Lowbury (1978) (Table 13.3), have shown that bacterial suspensions rubbed onto the skin were much less effectively removed by washing with soap and water than were suspensions of the same organisms deposited and allowed to dry on the skin. By contrast, disinfection with 95% ethanol was as effective against rubbed-on bacteria as against those deposited without friction, and much more effective against both types of transient flora than was a single soap and water wash. An apparent paradox was the feebler effect of washing with an antiseptic detergent and water ('Hibiscrub') against

Table 13.2 Comparison of gauze applicator and gloved hand for disinfection of operation site*

Antiseptic	Mean percentage reduction in estimated skin bacteria after disinfection of: One hand: With gloved hand	One hand: With gauze	One hand: *P*	Two hands (with gauze: results of earlier studies)
0.5% chlorhexidine in 70% ethanol	98.8 ± 0.8	90.7 ± 2.1	<0.01	81.3 ± 2.6 (1960); 84.9 ± 1.4 (1964) 79.6 ± 3.6 (1971); 80.8 ± 4.1 (1973) 81.5 ± 3.4 (1974)
0.5% chlorhexidine in 95% ethanol	99.9 ± 0.02	93.5 ± 2.15	<0.02	—
0.5% chlorhexidine in distilled water	83.5 ± 5.8	53.7 ± 5.2	<0.01	60.7 ± 6.0 (1960)
10% povidone iodine in 70% ethanol	99.7 ± 0.14	86.9 ± 5.9	<0.1 >0.05 Not sig.	74.4 ± 5.2 (1971)
Distilled water (control)	25.1 ± 6.5	−4.1 ± 19.1	>0.1 Not sig.	14.7 ± 5.7 (1960) 8.5 ± 9.8 (1964) 4.7 ± 10.3 (1971)

* See Lowbury & Lilly (1975).

Table 13.3 Transient skin bacteria: influence of their mode of deposition on the effectiveness of cleansing and disinfection*

Mode of deposition of bacterial suspension on skin	Mean percentage survival after: Cleansing with soap and water	Disinfecting with 70% ethanol
Spread and allowed to dry	2.0	0.3
Rubbed in	29.6	0.3

* See Lilly & Lowbury (1978).

bacteria applied without friction than against bacteria rubbed onto the skin; but this was probably due to the shorter exposure to undiluted antiseptic of bacteria on the surface than of those which were rubbed into deeper layers, for 'Hibiscrub' applied without addition of water was equally effective against rubbed-on and against dried-on bacteria.

A study on the hands of nurses working in the wards of two hospitals showed, in both hospitals, that a larger proportion of nurses still carried *Staph. aureus* and Gram-negative bacilli after washing with soap and water than after applying 70% ethanol and rubbing to dryness (Ayliffe *et al.*, 1975). Ethanol disinfection has the additional advantage of requiring no towel and no sink, and would seem to be the most suitable method for hand cleansing by ward staff, especially where high-infection-risk patients are under care.

Any form of hand disinfection, and in particular the use of alcohol or alcoholic solutions which evaporate quickly, requires a conscious effort to cover the whole surface of hands and wrists (also forearms for pre-operative disinfection). An experiment in which dye was used as a marker in alcohol used for routine hand disinfection by nurses revealed that areas of skin, and especially the tips of fingers and thumbs, were commonly left untreated (Taylor, 1978).

2.9 Standardization of disinfectant testing

The need for internationally agreed criteria in the assessment of antiseptic and disinfectant preparations led to the formation in 1970 of the Committee on Standardization of Disinfectants in Europe; after the disbandment of this Committee, in 1978, its work was taken over by the the Council of Europe. Disinfection of the skin was one of the topics examined by the Committee. Methods for assessment of surgical disinfection of the types discussed above (Sections 2.5 and 2.6) were generally accepted, but there was some disagreement over the recommendations for testing hygienic hand disinfection. A method introduced by Rotter *et al.* (1974) was adopted as the official test by the Austrian and German Societies for Hygiene and Microbiology, and by the Federal Office of Health, Berlin, and in several European countries. Further studies were made by Rotter *et al.* (1986, 1988) and by Ayliffe *et al.* (1988), using slightly different techniques. Before binding standards can be established it is desirable that a wider range of test organisms, including Gram-positive cocci, mycobacteria and viruses, and different modes of application of test organisms should be examined. It is also important that disagreements on the inclusion of physical removal (by washing) of test organisms as a component of disinfection should be resolved; this is a particularly important consideration in the elimination of viral contaminants, some of which (Chapter 12) are likely to be resistant to chemical disinfection (see Ayliffe, 1989).

2.10 Disinfection in the bath

It is customary for patients to have a bath before operations. If the bath is an ordinary one, with soap and water, it can give little, if any, protection against endogenous contamination of the operation wound with skin bacteria. Nor can a bath with soap and water reduce the numbers of staphylococci that a disperser disseminates into the air. Some benefit, however, may come from the use of an antiseptic in the bath.

Davies *et al.* (1977) compared the use of detergent preparations of chlorhexidine, povidone-iodine and hexachlorophane with soap as a non-antiseptic control detergent. Four baths were taken by a group of volunteers on four successive days, and contact plate counts were obtained before and after bathing and drying. Immersed areas (inside of thigh) showed an appreciable drop in yield of skin flora after bathing with the chlorhexidine preparation, and smaller reductions were obtained with the other antiseptic agents; sites which were not continuously immersed (e.g. the chest) showed a much smaller reduction in bacterial counts on bathing with the chlorhexidine preparation.

It is not surprising, in view of the importance of friction on application, that the chlorhexidine detergent preparation, 'Hibiscrub', was much less effective in the bath than in disinfection of the hands, for the time during which any skin area was actually rubbed with the antiseptic preparation in the bath was short compared with the time that a comparable area of skin was rubbed with antiseptic during a 2-min hand disinfection.

Some studies have been reported on the clinical value of pre-operative antiseptic baths. In their major study on surgical wounds, Cruse & Foord (1973) reported a reduced post-operative infection rate following the introduction of pre-operative antiseptic showers. Ayliffe *et al.* (1983), by contrast, in a study on 5536 patients in three hospitals, found no significant difference in post-operative infection of patients who had bathed pre-operatively with a chlorhexidine detergent solution and those who had used unmedicated soap. Similar findings were reported by Leigh *et al.* (1983). In both studies antiseptic bathing caused a reduction in the skin bacteria. Brandberg *et al.* (1980) and Hayek *et al.* (1987) found less wound infection in patients who had taken antiseptic baths or showers than in control patients who had used unmedicated soap, but Rotter *et al.* (1988) found no such difference in large randomized controlled trials. The failure to reduce post-operative infection by a procedure which causes some reduction in skin bacteria is possibly due to the greater importance in clean operative surgery of airborne transmission in the operating theatre (Lidwell *et al.*, 1987).

2.11 Elimination of bacterial spores by skin disinfection

The spores of *Clostridium tetani* and of the gas gangrene clostridia are resistant to alcohols, chlorhexidine and most other antiseptics; the halogens have some activity against spores, but require a longer period of contact than that which is practicable for routine operation-site disinfection to achieve a useful effect against spores. *Cl. perfringens (welchii)* is often abundant on the skin of buttocks and perineum due to faecal contamination, and operations involving muscle with poor arterial circulation in this area (e.g. amputation of a leg in a patient with diabetic gangrene) carry a special hazard of endogenous gas gangrene (Parker, 1969; Ayliffe & Lowbury, 1969). Another situation in which there may be a hazard of infection due to clostridial spores is in operations on the hands of patients with ingrained dirt (e.g. gardeners, car mechanics).

An experiment in which a suspension of *Bacillus subtilis* spores was laid on the skin of volunteers showed that a reduction of over 99% in the numbers of spores could be obtained by application of a compress soaked in 10% aqueous povidone-iodine for 15–30 min (Lowbury *et al.*, 1964b). It may be assumed that the spores of clostridia are present as transient flora, though probably more adherent than were the suspensions allowed to dry on the surface for the above-mentioned experiment. There is, however, evidence that naturally occurring clostridia can be reduced by application of a povidone-iodine compress for 30 min before an operation that carries such a risk (Ayliffe & Lowbury, 1969; Drewett *et al.*, 1972). Though sporicidal treatment of the skin may have some value in such cases, systemic prophylaxis with penicillin is undoubtedly more important.

2.12 Disinfection of the nares

The squamous epithelium of the anterior nares is a site of carriage of *Staph. aureus* in 20–30% of normal people and in a higher proportion of nurses and others working in hospital wards. Some of these people are 'persistent carriers'. Nasal carriage of *Staph. aureus* is normal in such people, and the application of antimicrobials can do no more than bring about a temporary reduction or, possibly, removal of *Staph. aureus* from this site. Such treatment may be desirable in nurses or other members of clinical staff or patients who are carrying an epidemic strain which has caused an outbreak of staphylococcal sepsis. The application of cream containing mixtures of neomycin or framycetin with chlorhexidine, bacitracin, gramicidin or other antimicrobial agents to the anterior nares several times a day has been found to reduce or remove staphylococci from the area in many carriers (e.g. Rountree *et al.*, 1956; Stratford *et al.*, 1960), but this may require treatment for 14 days or longer. When the treatment is stopped, another strain of *Staph. aureus* is likely to colonize the nares if the subject has moved away from the environment where the epidemic strain was prevalent.

Nasal disinfection by antibiotics is undesirable because it encourages the emergence of resistant strains, and should be reserved for special situations, e.g. in removal of an epidemic strain from a ward. Gentamicin is as effective as neomycin, and has been considered appropriate for use when the strain of *Staph. aureus* is resistant to neomycin (Williams *et al.*, 1967); but gentamicin and its analogues, unlike neomycin, are of unique importance as antibiotics for systemic use, and should not be used as nasal antiseptics because of the risk of emergent resistance. A cream containing 1% chlorhexidine, though less effective than neomycin–chlorhexidine or gentamicin–chlorhexidine cream, has some value and would be more acceptable as a nasal antiseptic (Williams *et al.*, 1967). Mupirocin, an antibiotic suitable for topical but not for systemic use, has recently been found highly effective in removing *Staph. aureus* from the nares of carriers, and is probably the topical agent of choice (Casewell & Hill, 1986). Mupirocin-resistant *Staph. aureus* has been reported (Cookson *et al.*, 1990).

2.13 Disinfection of mucous membranes

Because of the diluent effects of saliva, alcohol is not effective as an antiseptic of the oral mucous membrane (Cawson & Curson, 1959). An aqueous solution of iodine and potassium iodide, or of an iodophor, has therefore been in common use for pre-operative disinfection of the oral mucosa. Selwyn *et al.* (1979) have reported the effectiveness of agents containing 1% chlorhexidine and of higher concentrations of chlorhexidine (10% and 15%) in a slow-release formulation ('Orabase'); the 1% gel gave an excellent immediate reduction in microbial count, which was relatively transient;

'Orabase' gave a slightly smaller but more sustained reduction. On repeated application of the 'Orabase' preparations, a cumulative decontaminant effect was found. Samples (on cotton-wool or polyester swabs) showed concentrations of chlorhexidine inhibitory to a wide range of Gram-positive and Gram-negative organisms for over 3 h. Duignan & Lowe (1975) reported that povidone-iodine surgical scrub (containing povidone-iodine) and the chlorhexidine–cetrimide mixture 'Savlon', at a dilution of 1 in 200, caused a similar considerable reduction in the numbers of potential pathogens including *Bacteroides* spp. Because of the high resistance of the oral mucous membrane to infection by contaminants from the mouth, it has become common practice for antiseptics not to be applied before routine dental procedures. Systemic chemotherapy with benzyl-penicillin or phenoxymethyl-penicillin is usually effective in removing *Streptococcus pyogenes* from the throat in patients with acute tonsillitis, but recurrence is likely unless the course is continued for about 10 days.

3 ANTISEPSIS IN BURNS

Prophylaxis of burns against infection involves the use of first- and second-line defences (i.e. measures used, respectively, to prevent contamination of the burn wound and to prevent invasion of tissues and bloodstream from a colonized wound; see Fig. 13.4). Topical application of antimicrobial agents is a component of the first line of defence, and it has been shown to have a valuable role in protecting the patient at a stage when infection presents a special hazard.

As a therapeutic measure against established infection, the topical application of antimicrobials has a less well-established role. Controlled trials in the 1950s showed that topical application of a cream containing penicillin was effective in removing *Strep. pyogenes* (Jackson *et al.*, 1951a), while a cream containing polymyxin E had some value in removing *Ps. aeruginosa* (Jackson *et al.*, 1951b). However, systemic chemotherapy (with erythromycin or a β-lactamase-stable penicillin) was more effective than topical penicillin against *Strep. pyogenes*, and the latter (as well as oral fucidin) has been shown to have considerable therapeutic value against *Staph. aureus* (Lowbury & Miller, 1962; Lowbury *et al.*, 1962). Gram-negative bacilli are not readily dislodged by systemic chemotherapy even with antibiotics active against them *in vitro*, but topical application of mafenide (Lindberg *et al.*, 1965) and of silver sulphadiazine cream (Fox, 1968) appears to have some therapeutic effect against *Ps. aeruginosa*. Gentamicin may be even more effective (Stone *et al.*, 1965), but the likelihood of emergence of

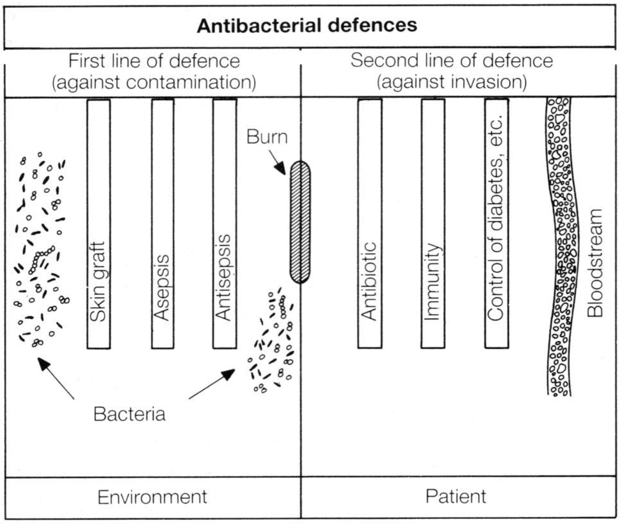

Fig. 13.4 First and second lines of defence against infection in patients with burns.

gentamicin-resistant variants makes the topical application of this antibiotic (combined with systemic therapy) a measure to be adopted only in patients likely to die from the infection and in whom other measures have failed; such patients should be treated under source isolation to prevent the transfer to other patients of gentamicin-resistant variants, should they appear on the patients' burns. In most patients, systemic therapy is the method of choice. Even if this does not succeed in removing the bacteria from the burn wound, it may prevent their invasion of the tissues and the bloodstream; this is the main objective. *Strep. pyogenes* is notorious for its ability to destroy skin grafts; preventing this complication is the main objective of chemotherapy against *Strep. pyogenes* today, when systemic invasion by that organism in patients with burns has become a rarity. Even when chemotherapy has been successful in removing *Ps. aeruginosa* from bloodstream and burns, the organism may have caused irreparable clinical damage before treatment has taken its bacteriological effect (Jones *et al.*, 1966). Because of the difficulties in therapy for established pseudomonas infection of patients with severe burns, special emphasis is placed on the use of effective prophylactic measures.

3.1 Topical chemoprophylaxis

Lister did not include burns among the wounds for which he advocated topical chemopropylaxis with phenol; there is only one paper on antisepsis for burns — a short one on the use of boric acid — in his *Collected Papers* (Lister, 1909). Some of Lister's followers tried antisepsis with phenol on burns (Pirrie, 1867; Maylard, 1892), but the method was abandoned because of the toxic effects of phenol.

During the early part of the century the role of infection in burns was overshadowed by other hazards, notably hypovolaemic shock and toxaemia attributed to the absorption of toxins produced in tissues when they were heated (e.g. Avdakoff, 1876; see Sevitt, 1957). With the development in the 1940s and 1950s of effective ways of preventing hypovolaemic shock, infection, especially with *Ps. aeruginosa* and other Gram-negative bacilli, came to be widely recognized as the major cause of death in severely burned patients; at the same time the symptoms formerly attributed to toxaemia were seen, in most cases, to be due to bacterial infection. Systemic chemotherapy and chemoprophylaxis had limited value because of the emergence and predominance in burns units of antibiotic-resistant bacteria. Colebrook and his colleagues in Birmingham introduced a number of aseptic and hygienic measures, including the topical application of penicillin to protect the burns against *Strep. pyogenes*, which was at that time a major infective hazard. Following these innovations there was a considerably lower incidence of *Strep. pyogenes* infection than Colebrook had reported from his previous studies in Glasgow, where these measures were not used (Colebrook *et al.*, 1948).

Following Colebrook's preliminary study, Jackson *et al.* (1951a,b) carried out controlled trials in the Birmingham Burns Unit, which demonstrated highly significant prophylaxis by penicillin cream (1000 units per g) against *Strep. pyogenes*, and a significant, though somewhat smaller, prophylactic effect of a cream containing polymyxin E (1 mg per g) against *Ps. aeruginosa*. Neither organism developed resistance to the antibiotic which was being used to keep it out of the burns. The clinical results, including results of skin grafting and healing time, were better in the patients treated with the antibacterial creams than in the control series. These trials were followed by assessments of a number of other topical applications, including a cream containing neomycin, polymyxin and chlorhexidine (Cason & Lowbury, 1960) and a tulle gras dressing containing neomycin and chlorhexidine (Lowbury *et al.*, 1962); both were highly effective in prophylaxis against various bacteria, including *Staph. aureus*. Ototoxic effects of neomycin were not recorded in these trials, but with the knowledge now available about that hazard it is important to ban the use of neomycin and homologous antibiotics in topical application to burns. It is important, too, that penicillin and other antibiotics which have an important role in systemic chemotherapy and a tendency to cause the emergence of resistance in pathogenic bacteria and allergy in patients should not be used for topical application. The antimicrobial tulle gras preparation, which produced relatively dry conditions on the burn wound, was especially effective against Gram-negative bacilli, but its use was associated with considerable delay in separation of slough, probably through suppression by the antimicrobial agents of bacteria that produce proteolytic enzymes.

This dilemma was largely resolved on the reintroduction by Moyer *et al.* (1965) of silver-nitrate, at a concentration of 0.5% for topical antimicrobial prophylaxis; it had formerly been used in much higher concentration, often with tannic acid, to produce a firm coagulum which was thought to trap hypothetical burn toxins and prevent toxaemia. A controlled trial of 0.5% silver-nitrate compresses on severely burned patients in the Birmingham Burns Unit confirmed Moyer's opinion of its value as a prophylactic agent (Cason *et al.*, 1966); *Ps. aeruginosa* was found in about 70% of the swab samplings from burns in the control series, but in only 3% of those taken from burns kept continuously moist with compresses of 0.5% silver nitrate from as soon as possible after the injury until healing or skin-grafting operations. This bacteriological effect was associated with a large reduction in the incidence of *Ps. aeruginosa* septicaemia (Cason & Lowbury, 1968) and a reduced mortality in the Burns Unit (Bull, 1971). The results were surprising, in view of the precipitation of silver chloride which was bound to occur when sodium chloride in the exudate mixed with the silver nitrate solution; but the dressings soaked in silver nitrate were acting as a chemical barrier, killing bacteria that settled on the outside or the edges of the dressing where there was an excess of unprecipitated silver nitrate (Ricketts *et al.*, 1970). There was some delay in separation of slough from silver-nitrate-treated burns, but this appeared to be less than it was with neomycin–chlorhexidine tulle gras, probably because of the moist surface under silver nitrate. Treatment with silver-nitrate compresses had some disadvantages, in particular, inadequate prophylaxis against many Gram-negative bacilli which are less sensitive than *Ps. aeruginosa* (notably *Klebsiella* spp.), discomfort (though not pain) and the need for supplements of calcium, sodium and potassium to rectify losses and imbalance resulting from the application of a hypotonic solution. Alternative chemoprophylactic applications were needed. One which was highly effective was 11% mafenide (sulfamylon) acetate cream, applied at least once a day and left to dry without dressing cover (Lindberg *et al.*, 1965). Though effective, this treatment caused severe pain on areas of partial skin-thickness loss, and sometimes resulted in a metabolic acidosis (which was reversible on stopping the use of mafenide). A controlled trial, in which we compared the use of mafenide cream, silver-nitrate compresses and exposure treatment without an antimicrobial application, showed that mafenide and silver nitrate had prophylactic effects, leading to a much lower incidence and density of bacteria (apart from miscellaneous coliform bacilli) on the burn surface than was found in patients treated by exposure without antimicrobials (Lowbury *et al.*, 1971; Table 13.4). Since the surface of burns treated by exposure is likely to show far fewer Gram-negative bacilli than those present under the dry eschar (Lowbury *et al.*, 1954), the difference in bacterial colonization of burns treated with or without topical antimicrobials is probably much greater than routine swab sampling suggested.

A more satisfactory topical prophylactic agent, silver sulphadiazine, was developed by Fox (1968). Controlled trials in Birmingham showed it to have overall prophylactic effects in severely burned patients which were comparable with those of silver-nitrate compresses; its action against *Klebsiella* spp. and some other Gram-negative bacilli was much greater than that of silver nitrate, but it was rather less active than silver nitrate against *Staph. aureus*, and slightly less active against *Ps. aeruginosa* and *Proteus* spp. Mortality was slightly (but not significantly) lower in the patients treated with silver sulphadiazine, and there was a significantly lower mean morning and evening temperature in these patients than in those who were dressed with silver-nitrate compresses (Lowbury *et al.*, 1976). Unfortunately, the use of silver sulphadiazine led—after some years—to the emergence of a very high incidence of plasmid-determined transferable sulphonamide resistance among the enterobacteria in the Burns Unit (Bridges & Lowbury, 1977). Because of this preponderance of sulphonamide-resistant strains, the use of silver sulphadiazine and of all sulphonamides

Table 13.4 Comparison of three alternative methods of local treatment for severe burns*

Antiseptic	Numbers and percentages of burn swab samples yielding: No bacterial growth	No growth or very scanty growth	*Staph. aureus*	*Ps. aeruginosa*	*Proteus* spp.	Coliform bacilli	Total: Swabs	Total: Burns
0.5% Silver-nitrate compresses	288 (35%)	386 (47%)	62 (7.5%)	44 (5.3%)	36 (4%)	298 (36%)	821	92
11.2% Mafenide acetate cream	54 (13%)	110 (13.5%)	111 (27%)	19 (4.6%)	36 (4%)	182 (44%)	413	53
Exposure method in warm, dry air	11 (2%)	17 (3%)	318 (61%)	75 (14%)	145 (28%)	210 (40%)	518	81

* See Lowbury *et al.* (1971).

in the unit was suspended, and a cream containing 0.5% silver nitrate and 0.2% chlorhexidine gluconate was used for topical prophylaxis; this cream, prepared in the hospital pharmacy, had been shown in a controlled trial to have prophylactic powers similar to those of silver sulphadiazine cream (Lowbury *et al.*, 1976). As a result of this policy, the proportions of sulphonamide-resistant enterobacteria fell to those which had prevailed formerly, and there was an associated fall in resistance to several antibiotics, to which the sulphonamide-resistance plasmid coded a linked resistance. No resistance to silver nitrate or to chlorhexidine occurred while silver nitrate–chlorhexidine cream was used.

Experience has shown that applications of antibiotics, such as gentamicin, may be highly effective as routine prophylactic agents, but their use for this purpose must be scrupulously avoided, because resistant variants are likely to emerge and, once present in a ward, are very hard to eliminate; while they are present, the antibiotic(s) against which resistance has developed must be removed from the list of drugs available for the treatment of infections. If it is considered clinically desirable to treat a patient with a topical antibiotic (except polymyxin, to which *Ps. aeruginosa*, at least, does not develop resistance), the patient should be source-isolated, and repeated cultures should be taken from his burns for early detection of resistant variants.

Other antimicrobial agents, including povidone-iodine (Georgiade & Harris, 1972) and cerium nitrate (Monafo *et al.*, 1976) have been tried, but have proved less effective in controlled trials than silver sulphadiazine or silver nitrate–chlorhexidine creams (Babb *et al.*, 1977; Bridges *et al.*, 1980).

In a controlled trial, a cream containing 2% phenoxetol and 0.2% chlorhexidine was found, (on burns of up to 15% of the body surface) to have antibacterial prophylactic effects comparable with those of silver nitrate–chlorhexidine cream, and showed significantly greater activity against *Staph. aureus*; unlike preparations containing silver nitrate, phenoxetol–chlorhexidine cream did not cause electrolyte imbalance (Lawrence *et al.*, 1982). Lawrence (1977) has also shown that dressing of small burns in an outpatient department with a chlorhexidine-medicated tulle gras had significant prophylactic action against infection with *Staph. aureus*.

3.2 Comment

Though topical antimicrobial prophylaxis has proved highly effective, and been shown capable of saving the lives of severely burned patients, there is a disturbingly small number of antimicrobial agents that are found acceptable for this purpose. None is entirely free from potential toxic or sensitizing effects, and none covers the whole range of potential pathogens and opportunist organisms. The more selectively the agents attack micro-organisms while sparing the host tissues, the greater is the likelihood that strains with intrinsic or acquired resistance will emerge. It is also important that topical antimicrobials should not interfere with natural immunity or with immunological responses to vaccines which have been developed as an effective prophylactic measure in the second line of defence. Agents that interfere with the phagocytic and bactericidal properties of neutrophils could interfere with these defences. However, the fact that topical antimicrobial prophylaxis has been shown to bring about a reduced morbidity and mortality in patients with severe burns shows that, on balance, the method is beneficial and deserves to be a component of burn management.

3.3 Topical mupirocin therapy for infection of skin, burns and leg ulcers

Mupirocin ('pseudomonic acid'), an antibiotic suitable for topical use, is particularly active against Gram-positive cocci, but moderately active also against some Gram-negative bacilli; its activity is mainly bacteriostatic, but it is bactericidal against the more sensitive organisms at concentrations attainable on topical application. Its antimicrobial mechanism is different from that of other antibiotics, and it appears to be free from toxic or sensitizing effects when applied topically.

An ointment containing 2% of mupirocin has been found clinically promising and very effective in removing infecting organisms from a variety of skin infections, from burns and from leg ulcers. It has advantages over neomycin, and seems to be about as effective a topical antimicrobial agent as fusidic acid, which should not be used for this purpose because of its value in systemic therapy against *Staph. aureus* (Symposium 1984). However, occasional strains of coagulase-negative staphylococci and *Staph. aureus* have shown resistance to mupirocin (Cookson *et al.*, 1990). Mupirocin-resistant strains have been reported following application to burns and the skin (Aycliffe, personal communication).

4 REFERENCES

Avdakoff, X.Y. (1876) *St. Petersburg Medizinische Wochenschrift*. Quoted by Stockis, E. (1896) in *Archives Internationales de Pharmacodynamie et de Therapie*, **2**, 201.

Ayliffe, G.A.J. (1989) Standardization of disinfectant testing. *Journal of Hospital Infection*, **13**, 211–216.

Ayliffe, G.A.J. & Lowbury, E.J.L. (1969) Sources of gas gangrene in hospital. *British Medical Journal*, **ii**, 333–337.

Ayliffe, G.A.J., Babb, J.R., Bridges, K., Lilly, H.A., Lowbury, E.J.L., Varney, J. & Wilkins, M.D. (1975) Comparison of two methods for assessing the removal of total organisms and pathogens from the skin. *Journal of Hygiene, Cambridge*, **75**, 259–274.

Ayliffe, G.A.J., Babb, J.R. & Quoraishi, A.H. (1978) A test for 'hygienic' hand disinfection. *Journal of Clinical Pathology*, **31**, 923–928.

Ayliffe, G.A.J., Noy, M.F., Babb, J.R., Davies, J.G. & Jackson, J. (1983) A comparison of pre-operative bathing with chlorhexidine detergent and non-medicated soap in the prevention of wound infection. *Journal of Hospital Infection*, **4**, 237–244.

Ayliffe, G.A.J., Babb, J.R., Davies, J.G. & Lilly, H.A. (1988) Hand disinfection: a comparison of various agents in laboratory and ward studies. *Journal of Hospital Infection*, **11**, 226–243.

Babb, J.R., Bridges, K., Jackson, D.M., Lowbury, E.J.L. & Ricketts, C.R. (1977) Topical chemoprophylaxis: trials of silver phosphate chlorhexidine, silver sulphadiazine and povidone iodine preparations. *Burns*, **3**, 65–71.

Black, R.E., Dykes, A.C., Anderson, K.E., Wells, J.G., Sinclair, S.P., Gary, G.W., Hatch, M.H. & Gangarosa, E.J. (1981) Handwashing to prevent diarrhoea in day-care centers. *American Journal of Epidemiology*, **113**, 445–451.

Brandberg, A., Holm, J., Hammarsten, J. & Schersten, T. (1980) Post operative wound infections in vascular surgery: effect of preoperative whole body disinfection by shower-bath with chlorhexidine soap. In *Problems in the Control of Hospital Infection. Royal Society of Medicine, International Congress and Symposium Series*, **23** (eds Newsom, S.W.B. & Caldwell, A.D.S.) pp. 71–75. London: Academic Press and Royal Society of Medicine.

Bridges, K. & Lowbury, E.J.L. (1977) Drug resistance in relation to use of silver sulphadiazine cream in a burns unit. *Journal of Clinical Pathology*, **31**, 160–164.

Bridges, K., Cason, J.S., Jackson, D.M., Kidson, A., Lowbury, E.J.L. & Wilkins, M.D. (1980) Topical chemoprophylaxis with cerium (cerous) nitrate cream. *Burns*, **6**, 231–234.

Bull, J.P. (1971) Revised analysis of mortality due to burns. *Lancet*, **ii**, 1133–1134.

Burtenshaw, J.M.L. (1942) The mechanism of self-disinfection of the human skin and its appendages. *Journal of Hygiene, Cambridge*, **42**, 184–210.

Casewell, M.W. (1981) The role of hands in nosocomial Gram-negative infection. In *Skin Microbiology: Relevance to Clinical Infection* (eds Maibach, H. & Aly, R.) pp. 192–202. New York: Springer-Verlag.

Casewell, M.W. & Hill, R.L.R. (1986) Elimination of nasal carriage of *Staph. aureus* with mupirocin ('pseudomonic acid'). *Journal of Antimicrobial Chemotherapy*, **17**,

365–372.

Casewell, M. & Phillips, I. (1977) Hands as route of transmission of *Klebsiella* species. *British Medical Journal*, **2**, 1315–1317.

Cason, J.S., Jackson, D.M., Lowbury, E.J.L. & Ricketts, C.R. (1966) Antiseptic and aseptic prophylaxis for burns: use of silver nitrate and of isolators. *British Medical Journal*, **ii**, 1288–1294.

Cason, J.S. & Lowbury, E.J.L. (1960) Prophylactic chemotherapy for burns: studies on the local and systemic use of combined therapy. *Lancet*, **ii**, 501–507.

Cason, J.S. & Lowbury, E.J.L. (1968) Mortality and infection in extensively burned patients treated with silver nitrate compresses. *Lancet*, **i**, 651–654.

Cawson, R.A. & Curson, I. (1959) The effectiveness of some antiseptics on the oral mucous membrane. *British Dental Journal*, **106**, 208–211.

Cole, W.R. & Bernard, H.R. (1964) Inadequacies of present methods of surgical skin preparation. *Archives of Surgery*, **89**, 215–222.

Colebrook, L. & Maxted, W.R. (1933) Antisepsis in midwifery. *Journal of Obstetrics and Gynaecology of the British Empire*, **40**, 966–990.

Colebrook, L., Duncan, J.M. & Ross, W.P.D. (1948) The control of infection in burns. *Lancet*, **i**, 893–899.

Cookson, B.D., Lacey, R.W., Noble, W.C., Reeves, D.S., Wise, R. & Redhead, R.J. (1990) Mupirocin-resistant *Staphylococcus aureus*. *Lancet*, **i**, 1095–1096.

Cruse, P.J.E. & Foord, R. (1973) A five year prospective study of 23,649 surgical wounds. *Archives of Surgery*, **107**, 206–210.

Davies, J., Babb, J.R., Ayliffe, G.A.J. & Ellis, S.H. (1977) The effect on the skin flora of bathing with antiseptic solutions. *Journal of Antimicrobial Chemotherapy*, **3**, 473–481.

Davies, J., Babb, J.R. Ayliffe, G.A.J. & Wilkins, M.D. (1978) Disinfection of the skin of the abdomen. *British Journal of Surgery*, **65**, 855–858.

Deutsche Gesellschaft für Hygiene und Mikrobiologie (DGHM) (1972) *Richtlinien für die Prüfung chemischer Desinfektions-mittel. Vol.* **3**, Stuttgart: Aufl. G. Fischer.

Devenish, E.A. & Miles, A.A. (1939) Control of *Staphylococcus aureus* in an operating theatre. *Lancet*, **i**, 1088–1094.

Dineen, P. (1978) Handwashing degerming: a comparison of povidone iodine and chlorhexidine. *Clinical Pharmacology and Therapeutics*, **23**, 63–67.

Drewett, S.E., Payne, D.J.H., Tuke, W. & Verdon, P.E. (1972) Skin distribution of *Clostridium welchii*: use of iodophor as sporicidal agent. *Lancet*, **i**, 1172–1173.

Duignan, N.M. & Lowe, P.A. (1975) Pre-operative disinfection of the vagina. *Journal of Antimicrobial Chemotherapy*, **1**, 117–120.

Evans, C.A., Smith, W.M., Johnson, E.A. & Giblett, E.R. (1950) Bacterial flora of normal human skin. *Journal of Investigative Dermatology*, **15**, 305–324.

Fox, C.L. (1968) Silver sulphadiazine — a new topical therapy for pseudomonas in burns. *Archives of Surgery*, **96**, 184–188.

Gardner, A.D. (1948) Rapid disinfection of clean unwashed skin. *Lancet*, **ii**, 760–763.

Gardner, A.D. & Seddon, H.J. (1946) Rapid chemical disinfection of clean unwashed skin. *Lancet*, **i**, 683–686.

Georgiade, N.G. & Harris, W.A. (1972) Open and closed treatment of burns with povidone iodine. In *Medical and Surgical Antisepsis with Betadine Microbicides* (eds Polk, H.L. & Ehrenkranz, N.J.) pp. 113–120. Miami: University of Miami.

Gezon, H.M., Thompson, D.J., Rogers, K.D., Hatch, T.F. & Taylor, P.M. (1964). Hexachlorophene bathing in early infancy: effect on staphylococcal disease and infection. *New England Journal of Medicine*, **270**, 379–386.

Hayek, L.J., Emerson, J.M. & Gardner, A.M.N. (1987) A placebo-controlled trial of the effect of two preoperative baths or showers with chlorhexidine detergent on post operative wound infection rates. *Journal of Hospital Infection*, **10**, 165–172.

Holmes, O.W. (1842) The contagiousness of puerperal fever. *New England Quarterly Journal of Medicine and Surgery*, **1**, 503–530.

Hyams, P., Counts, G.W., Monkus, E., Feldman, R., Kicklighter, J.L. & Gonzalez, C. (1975) Staphylococcal bacteremia and hexachlorophene bathing. *American Journal of Disease in Children*, **129**, 595–599.

Jackson, D.M., Lowbury, E.J.L. & Topley, E. (1951a) Chemotherapy for *Streptococcus pyogenes* infection of burns. *Lancet* **ii**, 705–710.

Jackson, D.M., Lowbury, E.J.L. & Topley, E. (1951b) *Pseudomonas pyocyanea* in burns: its role as a pathogen, and the value of local polymyxin therapy. *Lancet*, **ii**, 137–147.

Jones, R.J., Jackson, D.M. & Lowbury, E.J.L. (1966) Antiserum and antibiotic in the prophylaxis of burns against *Pseudomonas aeruginosa*. *British Journal of Plastic Surgery*, **19**, 43–57.

Kaslow, R.A., Dixon, R.E., Martin, S.M., Mallison, G.F., Goldman, D.A., Lindsey, J.D., Rhame, F.S. & Bennett, J.W. (1973) Staphylococcal disease related to hospital nursery bathing practices — a nationwide epidemiologic investigation. *Pediatrics*, **51**, 418–425.

Khan, M.U. (1982) Interruption of shigellosis by handwashing. *Transactions of the Royal Society of Tropical Medicine & Hygiene*, **76**, 164–168.

Larson, E. (1988) A causal link between handwashing and risk of infection. Examination of the evidence. *Infection Control Hospital Epidemiology*, **9**, 28–36.

Lawrence, J.C. (1977) The treatment of small burns with a chlorhexidine medicated tulle gras. *Burns*, **3**, 239–244.

Lawrence, J.C., Cason, J.S. & Kidson, A. (1982) Evaluation of phenoxetol–chlorhexidine cream as a prophylactic antibacterial agent in burns. *Lancet*, **i**, 1037–1040.

Leigh, D.A., Stronge, J.L., Marriner, J. & Sedgwick, J. (1983) Total body bathing with 'Hibiscrub' (chlorhexidine) in surgical patients: a controlled trial. *Journal of Hospital Infection*, **4**, 229–235.

Leonard, R.R. (1967) Prevention of superficial cutaneous infections. *Archives of Dermatology*, **95**, 520–523.

Lidwell, O.M., Elson, R.A., Lowbury, E.J.L., Whyte, W., Blowers, R., Stanley, S.J. & Lowe, D. (1987) Ultraclean air and antibiotics for prevention of post operative infection. *Acta Orthopaedica Scandinavica*, **58**, 4–13.

Lilly, H.A. & Lowbury, E.J.L. (1971) Disinfection of the skin: an assessment of some new preparations. *British Medical Journal*, **iii**, 674–676.

Lilly, H.A. & Lowbury, E.J.L. (1978) Transient skin flora: their removal by cleansing or disinfection in relation to their mode of deposition. *Journal of Clinical Pathology*, **31**, 919–922.

Lilly, H.A., Lowbury, E.J.L. & Wilkins, M.D. (1979a) Limits to progressive reduction of resident skin bacteria by disinfection. *Journal of Clinical Pathology*, **32**, 382–385.

Lilly, H.A., Lowbury, E.J.L., Wilkins, M.D. & Zaggy, A. (1979b) Delayed antimicrobial effects of skin disinfection by alcohol. *Journal of Hygiene, Cambridge*, **82**, 497–500.

Lindberg, R.B., Moncrief, J.A., Switzer, W.E., Order, S.E. & Mills, W. (1965) The successful control of burn wound sepsis. *Journal of Trauma*, **5**, 601–616.

Lister, J. (1867) Antiseptic principle in the practice of surgery. *British Medical Journal*, **ii**, 246–248.

Lister, J. (1909) *Collected Papers*. Oxford: Clarendon Press.

Lowbury, E.J.L., Babb, J.R., Bridges, K. & Jackson, D.M. (1976); Topical chemoprophylaxis with silver sulphadiazine and silver nitrate chlorhexidine cream; emergence of sulphonamide-resistant Gram-negative bacilli. *British Medical Journal*, **i**, 493–496.

Lowbury, E.J.L., Cason, J.S., Jackson, D.M. & Miller, R.W.S. (1962) Fucidin for staphylococcal infection of burns. *Lancet*, **ii**, 478–480.

Lowbury, E.J.L., Crockett, D.J. & Jackson, D.M. (1954) Bacteriology of burns treated by exposure. *Lancet*, **ii**, 1151–1153.

Lowbury, E.J.L., Jackson, D.M., Lilly, H.A., Bull, J.P., Cason, J.S., Davies, J.W.L. & Ford, P.M. (1971) Alternative forms of local treatment for burns. *Lancet*, **ii**, 1105–1111.

Lowbury, E.J.L. & Lilly, H.A. (1960) Disinfection of the hands of surgeons and nurses. *British Medical Journal*, **i**, 1445–1450.

Lowbury, E.J.L. & Lilly, H.A. (1973) Use of 4% chlorhexidine detergent solution ('Hibiscrub') and other methods of skin disinfection. *British Medical Journal*, **i**, 510–515.

Lowbury, E.J.L. & Lilly, H.A. (1974) The effect of blood on disinfection of surgeons' hands. *British Journal of Surgery*, **61**, 19–21.

Lowbury, E.J.L. & Lilly, H.A. (1975) Gloved hand as applicator of antiseptic to operation sites. *Lancet*, **ii**, 153–156.

Lowbury, E.J.L., Lilly, H.A. & Ayliffe, G.A.J. (1974) Preoperative disinfection of surgeons' hands: use of alcoholic solutions and effects of gloves on skin flora. *British Medical Journal*, **iv**, 369–374.

Lowbury, E.J.L., Lilly, H.A. & Bull, J.P. (1960) Disinfection of the skin of operation sites. *British Medical Journal*, **ii**, 1039–1044.

Lowbury, E.J.L., Lilly, H.A. & Bull, J.P. (1963) Disinfection of hands: removal of resident bacteria. *British Medical Journal*, **i**, 1251–1256.

Lowbury, E.J.L., Lilly, H.A. & Bull, J.P. (1964a) Disinfection of the hands: removal of transient organisms. *British Medical Journal*, **ii**, 230–233.

Lowbury, E.J.L., Lilly, H.A. & Bull, J.P. (1964b) Methods of disinfection of hands and operation sites. *British Medical Journal*, **ii**, 531–536.

Lowbury, E.J.L. & Miller, R.W.S. (1962) Treatment of infected burns with BRL 1621 (cloxacillin). *Lancet*, **ii**, 640–641.

Lowbury, E.J.L., Miller, R.W.S., Cason, J.S. & Jackson, D.M. (1962) Local prophylactic chemotherapy for burns treatment with tulle gras and by the exposure method. *Lancet*, **ii**, 958–963.

Maki, D.G. & Hecht, J. (1982) Antiseptic-containing handwashing agents reduce nosocomial infection. *Proceedings of 22nd Interscience Conference on Antimicrobial Agents & Chemotherapy*, p. 303A, Miami Beach.

Maylard, A.E. (1892) The antiseptic treatment of burns. *Glasgow Medical Journal*, **37**, 1–8.

Monafo, W.W., Tandon, S.N., Ayrazian, W.H., Tuchschmidt, J., Skinner, A.M. & Deitz, F. (1976) Cerium nitrate—a new topical antiseptic for extensive burns. *Surgery*, **80**, 465–473.

Moyer, C.A., Brentano, L., Gravens, D.L., Margraf, H.W. & Monafo, W.W. (1965) Treatment of large burns with 0.5% silver nitrate solution. *Archives of Surgery*, **90**, 812–867.

Murphy, J.J., Dull, J.A., Gamble, J., Fultz, C., Kretzler, H., Ellis, H., Nichols, A., Kucharczuk, J. & Zintel, H.A. (1951) Evaluation of preoperative skin preparation. *Surgery, Gynecology and Obstetrics*, **93**, 581–588.

Myers, G.E., Mackenzie, W.C. & Ward, K.A. (1956) The effect of a new antiseptic, 1,6-di-4′-chlorophenyldiguanidohexane, on skin flora. *Canadian Journal of Microbiology*, **2**, 87–93.

Noble, W.C. (1981) In *Microbiology of Human Skin* (eds Noble, W.C. & Somerville, D.A.) 2nd Ed. London: Lloyd-Luke.

Parker, M.T. (1969) Postoperative gas gangrene. *British Medical Journal*, **iii**, 671–676.

Pirrie, W. (1867) On the use of carbolic acid in burns. *Lancet*, **ii**, 575.

Plueckhahn, V.D. & Banks, J. (1963) Antisepsis and staphylococcal disease in the new-born child. *Medical Journal of Australia*, **2**, 519–523.

Price, P.B. (1938) The bacteriology of normal skin: a new quantitative test applied to a study of the bacterial flora and the disinfectant action of mechanical cleansing.

Journal of Infectious Disease, **63**, 301–318.
Price, P.B. (1951) Fallacy of a current surgical fad—the three-minute pre-operative scrub with hexachlorophene soap. *Annals of Surgery*, **134**, 476–485.
Quinn, H., Voss, J.G. & Whitehouse, H.S. (1954) A method for the *in vivo* evaluation of skin sensitizing soaps. *Applied Microbiology*, **2**, 202–204.
Ricketts, C.R., Squire, J.R., Topley, E. & Lilly, H.A. (1951) Human skin lipids with particular reference to the self-sterilizing power of the skin. *Clinical Science*, **10**, 89–111.
Ricketts, C.R., Lowbury, E.J.L., Lawrence, J.C., Hall, M. & Wilkins, M.D. (1970) Mechanisms of prophylaxis by silver compounds against infection of burns. *British Medical Journal*, **ii**, 444–446.
Rotter, M. (1988) Are models useful for testing hand antiseptics? *Journal of Hospital Infection*, **11**, Supplement A, 236–243.
Rotter, M., Mittermayer, H. & Kundi, M. (1974) Untersuchungen zum Modell der künstlich kontaminierten Hand: Vorschlag für eine Prüfmethode. *Zentrablatt für Bakteriologie, Parasitenkunde, Infektionskrankheiten und Hygiene, Abt. 1: Orig.*, **B159**, 560–581.
Rotter, M., Koller, W., Wewalka, G., Werner, H.P., Ayliffe, G.A.J. & Babb, J.R. (1986) Evaluation of procedures for hygienic hand-disinfection: controlled parallel experiments on the Vienna test model. *Journal of Hygiene, Cambridge*, **96**, 27–37.
Rotter, M.L., Larsen, S.O., Cooke, E.M., Dankert, J., Daschner, F., Greco, D., Grönroos, P., Jepson, O.B., Lydstad, A. & Nyström, B. (1988) A comparison of the effects of preoperative whole-body bathing with detergent alone and with detergent containing chlorhexidine gluconate on the frequency of wound infections after clean surgery. *Journal of Hospital Infection*, **11**, 310–320.
Rountree, P.M., Heseltine, M., Rheuben, J. & Shearman, R.P. (1956) Control of staphylococcal infection of the newborn by the treatment of nasal carriers in the staff. *Medical Journal of Australia*, **1**, 528–532.
Selwyn, S. & Ellis, H. (1972) Skin bacteria and skin disinfection reconsidered. *British Medical Journal*, **i**, 136–140.
Selwyn, S., Anderson, I.S. & Rogers, T.R. (1979) Quantitative studies on the decontamination of skin and mucous membranes in relation to immunodeficient patients: in *Clinical and Experimental Gnotobiotics, Zentralblatt für Bakteriologie*, Supplement 7, pp. 281–284.
Semmelweiss, I.P. (1861) *Die Aetiologie, der Begriff und die Prophylaxis des Kindbettfiebers*. Pest, Vienna and Leipzig: C.A. Hartleben.
Sevitt, S. (1957) *Burns: Pathology and Therapeutic Applications*. London: Butterworth.
Smylie, H.G., Logie, J.R.C. & Smith, G. (1973) From Phisohex to Hibiscrub. *British Medical Journal*, **iv**, 586–589.
Stone, H.H., Martin, J.P., Huger, W.E. & Kolb, L. (1965) Gentamicin sulphate in the treatment of pseudomonas sepsis in burns. *Surgery, Gynecology and Obstetrics*, **120**, 351–352.
Story, P. (1952) Testing of skin disinfectants. *British Medical Journal*, **ii**, 1128–1130.
Stratford, B., Rubbo, S.D., Christie, R. & Dixson, S. (1960) Treatment of the nasal carrier of *Staphylococcus aureus* with framycetin and other antibacterials. *Lancet*, **ii**, 1225–1227.
Symposium (1984) Mupirocin—a novel topical antibiotic. *International Congress and Symposium Series*, No. 80. London: Royal Society of Medicine.
Taylor, L.J. (1978) An evaluation of hand-washing techniques. *Nursing Times*, **74**, 108–110.
Thompson, C.J.S. (1934) *Lord Lister*, p. 45. London: J. Bale and Danielson.
Walter, C.W. (1938) The use of a mixture of coconut oil derivatives as a bactericide in the operating room. *Surgery, Gynecology and Obstetrics*, **67**, 683–688.
Walter, C.W. (1948) *The Aseptic Treatment of Wounds*. New York: Macmillan.
Williams, J.D., Waltho, C.A., Ayliffe, G.A.J. & Lowbury, E.J.L. (1967) Trials of five antibacterial creams in the control of nasal carriage of *Staphylococcus aureus*. *Lancet*, **ii**, 390–392.

Chapter 14
Recreational Waters and Hydrotherapy Pools

1 INTRODUCTION

Bathing pools of whatever size, and whether used for recreation or for hydrotherapy, need to be efficiently treated with a suitable disinfectant. This is necessary not only to give protection against cross-infection between bathers, but also to keep the pool aesthetically acceptable for use. Failure to control the growth of bacteria and algae will result in a pool being rendered unusable because of the development of discoloration, turbidity or disagreeable odour. Uncontrolled microbial growth can damage grouting between the tiles lining a pool, and may contribute to unsightly discoloration or corrosion of metal fittings.

2 AVAILABLE DISINFECTANTS

A recent report (Anon, 1990) has summarized the choice and application of disinfectants for hydrotherapy pools. However, the principles governing the application of disinfectants to recreational pools of all sizes, and even to spa pools (*jacuzzi*), are substantially the same, as is the range of agents from which to choose a suitable disinfectant.

Many different agents have been proposed for the disinfection of swimming pools. Halogens remain dominant, having the advantage that they not only kill micro-organisms, including viruses, but also oxidize organic material deriving from the bodily secretions of bathers. Among the halogens, chlorine gas and elementary bromine have been superseded by other chlorine and bromine derivatives. Thus there remain for consideration sodium and calcium hypochlorite, the chloroisocyanurates and the halogenated dimethylhydantoins. The characteristics of these halogen compounds have been reviewed in two joint reports by the Department of the Environment (DoE) and the National Water Council (NWC) (Anon, 1981a,b). In addition a polymeric biguanide ('Baquacil' ICI, see Chapter 2) is also a safe and effective agent, although with certain limitations on its use.

2.1 Hypochlorites

Of the hypochlorites, sodium hypochlorite is the one most widely used. It is cheaper than the calcium salt. Although less stable on prolonged storage it is more readily prepared at working dilutions. Hypochlorites can also be prepared *in situ* by electrolysis. Successful plants for achieving this are available, although not widely used. This approach is the subject of a further DoE/NWC publication (Anon, 1983). A difficulty that can attend the use of sodium hypochlorite is the production of toxic chloramines and haloforms. These are not only the cause of disagreeable chlorinous odours, but may also give rise to a painful chemical conjunctivitis. More serious pulmonary sensitization has occasionally been encountered (Penny, 1983). These drawbacks can be avoided by careful attention to the details of the disinfection process. It is particularly important to keep the level of active chlorine high, since active chlorine is not in itself malodorous or harmful, whereas low levels fail to bring about complete oxidation of organic residues from which toxic chloramines and haloforms may be formed. The disinfectant action of hypochlorites can be significantly enhanced by the addition of ozone. This entails the provision of a reliable ozone-generating plant, as well as involving additional safety precautions to offset the potential toxicity of the ozone. Two major advantages of this combination are that much lower levels of free chlorine are needed in the pool, and that the ozone may be helpful in preventing the colonization of filter beds by pseudomonads (Anon, 1983).

2.2 Chloroisocyanurates

The chloroisocyanurates, trichloroisocyanuric acid and sodium dichloroisocyanurate (Chapter 2), are convenient to use, safe to handle and readily soluble in water. Although more expensive than sodium hypochlorite, isocyanurates are reported to be more stable under exposure to ultraviolet irradiation from bright sunlight. This can be of some practical value for open-air pools in countries with sunny climates, but has little relevance to indoor pools in the United Kingdom. A disadvantage for this group is that the gradual accumulation of cyanuric acid interferes with the dissociation of chloroisocyanurates and reduces their microbicidal activity. The difficulty can be resolved only by rejecting a proportion of the water in the pool and replacing it with fresh water from the public mains. Notwithstanding this, isocyanurates can prove satisfactory for the treatment of hydrotherapy pools and other pools of small to medium capacity.

2.3 Halogenated dimethylhydantoins

Halogenated dimethylhydantoins, of which 1-chloro-3-bromo-5,5′-dimethylhydantoin is an example, are expensive. As with chloroisocyanurates activity can be impaired by the accumulation of dimethylhydantoin during prolonged use, and can be restored only by replacing a part of the pool water with a fresh supply. Although halogenated dimethylhydantoins are free from the problems of chlorinous odours and chemical conjunctivitis associated with hypochlorites, their use is now known to give rise to disabling contact dermatitis, which is sometimes severe (Rycroft & Penny, 1983).

2.4 Polymeric biguanide

A polymeric biguanide ('Baquacil', ICI) is used for the most part in small, private, open-air pools, operating seasonally and faced with very small bathing loads. If used in pools with filters in the circulating system, polymeric biguanide calls for filters of substantially increased capacity to allow for the accumulation of debris which would be oxidized by halogen-based disinfectant systems and ozone. A supplementary algicide is recommended.

3 CHOICE OF DISINFECTANT

Sodium hypochlorite is still the simplest and cheapest effective disinfectant currently available. Its use and limitations are well understood as a result of many years accumulated experience. The difficulties that may be encountered in its use, and the methods for avoiding or resolving them, are widely known.

In choosing a disinfecting system for a pool much will depend upon the size of the pool, the nature and weight of the expected bathing load, the first cost of equipment and installation and the continuing cost of running and maintenance. Whatever the agent, or combination of agents, finally chosen success depends substantially upon ensuring that active disinfectant is present in the pool continuously in adequate concentration, and that the pH in the pool is carefully maintained within limits shown by experience to be optimal. If the pH is too low there is a danger of evoking skin or eye reactions among bathers. If the pH is too high the efficiency of the disinfectant will be impaired. Chlorine levels and pH should be monitored continuously, with automatic systems for their immediate correction when necessary.

3.1 Pool design

In addition, much importance attaches to certain features of pool design and to careful monitoring of the chemistry of the pool and its overall appearance, backed by efficient management.

Design should be such as to secure an even distribution of disinfectant throughout the pool. The circulating pumps must be capable of operating continuously, even when the pool is not in use, and must have sufficient output to ensure a short turnover time. For a hydrotherapy pool this should be between 1 and 1½ h, with longer periods for larger recreational pools. Fresh disinfectant should be introduced into the circuit at a point just before the filters. A sampling point should be provided to enable samples of water to be taken immediately after it leaves the filters. If covers are to be used when the pool is not in use these must be designed to avoid 'dead spaces' not reached by disinfectant, where microbial growth can continue unchecked.

3.2 Pool management and monitoring

In the last analysis no pool, however well designed and equipped, will run satisfactorily unless it is efficiently managed and monitored. For pools disinfected with hypochlorite the automatic records of chlorine and pH should be supplemented by daily estimations of free and combined chlorine in order to detect any rise in the level of combined chlorine. This gives warning of the possible emergence of the toxic chloramines and haloforms already mentioned as associated with chlorinous odours and conjunctivitis. Pools treated with chloroisocyanurates or chlorobromodimethylhydantoin will require examination for cyanuric acid or dimethylhydantoin, respectively. The pool itself must be inspected at least daily for the appearance of turbidity, discoloration or unpleasant odour. A record should be kept of the daily bathing load and of such periodic operations as back-flushing the filters or exchanging a part of the pool water for fresh water, together with any untoward events that may occur. Hydrotherapy pools are prone to be confronted periodically by the involuntary release of stools or urine by handicapped patients. Records must not only be kept carefully, but studied regularly. Written policies should be provided for anticipated deviations from the norm. It is the responsibility of management to see that appropriate action is taken when necessary. One person should be placed in overall charge of the pool, with delegation of specified duties to named individuals. Those to whom duties are assigned must be given any necessary preliminary training to a level appropriate to their responsibility and understanding.

4 REFERENCES

Anon (1981a) *Swimming Pool Disinfection Systems using Sodium Hypochlorite and Calcium Hypochlorite*. London: HMSO.

Anon (1981b) *Swimming Pool Disinfection Systems using Calcium Hypochlorite, Chloroisocyanurates, and Halogenated Dimethylhydantoin*. London: HMSO.

Anon (1983) *Swimming Pool Disinfection Systems using Ozone with Residual Chlorination*. London: HMSO.

Anon (1990) *Hygiene for Hydrotherapy Pools*. London: Public Health Laboratory Service.

Penny, P.T. (1983) Swimming pool wheezing. *British Medical Journal*, **287**, 461–462.

Rycroft, R.J.G. & Penny, P.T. (1983) Dermatoses associated with brominated swimming pools. *British Medical Journal*, **287**, 462.

PART 2
PRESERVATION

Chapter 15
Preservation of Pharmaceutical and Cosmetic Products

1 INTRODUCTION

Despite the diversity of pharmaceutical and cosmetic products many of the problems involved in their protection against microbial spoilage are shared. For instance, the topical preparations and emulsions used medically have many formulation components in common with those used for cosmetics, although the latter usually incorporate a wider range of ingredients. Similarly there has been shared experience concerning the hazards which might attend the use of preparations contaminated with micro-organisms. Thus, Crompton (1963) reported that 33% of eye ointments tested in Australia were contaminated and later, Kuehne & Ahearn (1971) found that 12% of used eye cosmetics contained fungi with cultures detectable from the eyelids and conjunctivas of those women who had used the cosmetics. The dangers of using contaminated creams in British hospitals, highlighted by Noble & Savin (1966) and Savin (1967) were followed by a survey of microbial contamination of cosmetics and toiletries in the UK (Jarvis *et al.*, 1974). Although micro-organisms were detected in a wide range of cosmetics used topically, there was no evidence of these causing skin infections.

There can be little doubt that much of the impetus for studying the role of micro-organisms in pharmaceuticals stems from the work of Kallings *et al.* (1966) upon salmonellosis originating from raw materials used in tablets. Since then a variety of publications has dealt with the incidence of micro-organisms in oral preparations (Pederson & Ulrich, 1968; White *et al.*, 1968; Beveridge, 1975; Baird, 1985a,b). The preservation of oral dosage forms can be set against the background of shared experience with the food industry in much the same way that preservation of topical formulations and cosmetics is linked. Mossel (1971) has discussed in detail the complex changes associated with microbial proliferation in foods and the role of preservatives and, as will be shown later, the study of the ecology of the spoilage process can also be valuable when considering pharmaceutical and cosmetic preparations.

The range of products in which preservatives are or might be used is shown in Table 15.1. In many cases, particularly cosmetic preparations, the preservative is operating within a complex formulation such that its efficacy could be significantly modified. Thus, the preservation of eye-drops, which are essentially aqueous solutions, represents a very different problem from that presented by a cosmetic cream containing ingredients as diverse as oils, emulsifiers, humectants and perfume. Equally,

Table 15.1 Examples of preserved cosmetic and pharmaceutical preparations

Product	Preservative†	Concentration range (%w/v)
Solutions for injections*	Phenol	0.5
	Cresol	0.3
	Chlorocresol	0.1
	Phenylmercuric nitrate	0.001
Eye-drops*	Phenylmercuric nitrate or acetate	0.002
	Chlorhexidine acetate	0.01
	Benzalkonium chloride	0.01
Eye make-up	Methyl parabens (hydroxybenzoate esters)	0.1–0.2
	Germall[R]	0.1–0.5
Creams and cleansing	Parabens	0.1–0.2
	Phenonip[R]	0.5–1.0
	Dowicil[R]	0.1
Facial masks	Germall[R]	0.1
Shampoos	Bronopol[R]	0.2–0.5
	Germall[R]	0.1
	Dowicil[R]	0.1–0.2
Hair conditioners	Germall[R]	0.1
Liquid oral medicines	Chloroform	0.25
	Benzoic acid	0.1
	Methyl parabens	0.1
	Alcohol	12.0–20
	Sulphur dioxide	400 parts/10^6

* See Chapter 18C for further information.
†[R] Manufacturer's trade name. Names and addresses of the manufacturers are provided in Table 15.2.

of course, an entirely different level of antimicrobial potential might be demanded of the separate preservative systems since the former are used clinically and the latter on the intact skin of healthy individuals.

2 PRINCIPAL FACTORS MODIFYING PRESERVATIVE EFFICACY

2.1 pH

The ionic status of many preservatives is important in that activity is influenced by the presence of ionic and non-ionic species. The quaternary ammonium compounds (QACs), for instance, are cation-active and so are favoured by an increase in pH, whereas weak acid preservatives, such as benzoic and sorbic acids, active principally as unionized molecules, require an ambient pH level below their pK_a value, i.e. below 4, to be efficient (see also Chapters 2 and 3). The poor antimicrobial activity of the ionized species of organic acids has been attributed to their low lipid solubility and this feature is shared with phenols, although here the relevant pK_a values are much higher (*c.* 10.0). Knowledge of the pK_a of the preservative allows the calculation of the fraction undissociated at any given pH and hence the protection afforded at that pH (equation 15.1).

$$\text{Fraction of undissociated preservative} = \frac{1}{1 + \text{antilog}\,(\text{pH} - \text{p}K_a)} \qquad (15.1)$$

It is useful to remember that at pH values numerically equal to the pK_a value an acid preservative will be 50% dissociated. An example of this is the use of benzoic acid to preserve a liquid medicine such as the Paediatric Kaolin Mixture of the *British Pharmaceutical Codex* (1973). Freshly prepared mixtures have a pH of about 3.5, which would result in some 83% of the acid preservative being present in the active undissociated form so that theoretically the formulation is adequately preserved. There is, of course, oversimplification in this approach in that the light kaolin present in the mixture will decrease the activity of the benzoic acid during the shelf-life of the medicine (McCarthy, 1971), whereas additional preservative capacity is present in the form of chloroform. Another effect of pH upon preservatives is on stability. This is exemplified by Bronopol (2-bromo-2-nitropropane-1,3-diol) used in cosmetics and toiletries, particularly shampoos, which decomposes at alkaline pH (Bryce *et al.*, 1978).

2.2 Oil–water partition

The behaviour of a preservative in a simple oil–water system can be predicted from its oil–water partition coefficient for the oil concerned at any given temperature and the oil-to-water ratio (equation 15.2: Bean *et al.*, 1965).

$$C_w = C \frac{\phi + 1}{K_w^o \phi + 1} \tag{15.2}$$

where C_w = preservative concentration in water. C = total preservative concentration, K_w^o = oil–water partition coefficient, ϕ = oil/water ratio.

Although it is stating the obvious to say that the preservative should be chosen to ensure adequate protection of the aqueous phase of any formulation, nevertheless this guideline is often neglected. Baird (1974) highlights the dilemma for Calamine Cream BPC, an old-established pharmaceutical preparation. The formula contains no preservative, and microbial contamination was reported in samples manufactured industrially and in the hospital pharmacy. Early attempts to overcome this problem had included the addition of chlorocresol, which due to its high oil–water partition into vegetable oil (K_w^o = 117) was ineffective. The problem was resolved by substituting a mineral oil (liquid paraffin) for the vegetable oil (arachis oil) and using a preservative (phenoxyethanol) with low affinity for the mineral oil (K_w^o = 0.12).

A difficulty associated with this rational approach is resistance on the part of prescriber or user to changes in formulation. In the example given, it was pointed out that many dermatologists had a preference for vegetable oils for skin creams. This type of requirement for a pharmaceutical or cosmetic preparation virtually disqualifies most of the phenols and the esters of *p*-hydroxybenzoic acids as preservatives (Table 15.2).

An additional influence of lipophilic character upon preservative behaviour is the interaction between preservatives and micro-organisms. Thus, although the correlation between biological activity and concentration of preservative in the aqueous phase is of major importance, the degree of interaction between microbial cells and preservatives should not be ignored. Indeed, it has been suggested by Hansch & Clayton (1973) that traditional ideas of the role of solubility in the aqueous phase must be modified in a situation in which drugs may be bound with varying degrees of firmness by the variety of macromolecules which make up living cells. Thus in the case of the antifungal activity of esters of *p*-hydroxybenzoic acid, the consequent oil–water partition increasing with chain length has two effects. First, the higher the ester, the more effective it is with concentration up to the solubility- limiting chain length of six carbon atoms. Second, the higher the ester the less effective it is on a water saturation basis (McRobbie & Parker, 1974). The first relationship is that demonstrated by Ferguson (1939) in that limited solubility of the higher members of a congeneric series can impose a limit upon the linear correlation between activity and lipophilic character. The second relationship is indicative of the ester molecules being immobilized by spore lipids such that sensitive sites within the spore are protected. In a similar way the resistance of bacteria to antimicrobial agents has been linked to the cellular lipid content (Hugo & Franklin, 1968) and degree of uptake of *p*-hydroxybenzoate esters by bacterial cells related to partition into lipids (Furr & Russell, 1972). A practical significance of this is that if organisms become established in situations in which lipid formation is promoted, their resistance to a

Table 15.2 Characteristics of preservatives used in creams

Preservative†	Mineral oil K_w^o	Vegetable oil K_w^o	B*	pH effect
Chlorocresol	1.5	117.0	High	Active pH 5–8
Methyl parabens	0.02	7.5	High	Active pH 5–8
Propyl parabens	0.5	80.0	High	Active pH 5–8
Butyl parabens	3.0	280.0	High	Active pH 5–8
Cetyltrimethylammonium bromide	<1.0	<1.0	High	Less active below pH 5
Bronopol[R]	0.043	0.11	Low	Unstable above pH 5
Dowicil[R]	<1.0	1.0	Low	Active pH 5–8
Germall[R]	<1.0	<1.0	Low	Active pH 5–8
Phenonip[R]	>1.0	>1.0	Medium	Active pH 5–8
Phenylmercuric nitrate	<1.0	<1.0	Low	Active pH 5–8

* B = ratio of total to free preservative in typical non-ionic surfactant–water system.
†R Manufacturer's trade name:
Bronopol: 2-nitro-2-bromo-1,3-propanediol (Boots Pure Drug Co. Ltd., Nottingham, England)
Dowicil: 1-(3,chloroallyl)-3,5,7-triaza-1-azoniaadamantane chloride (Dow Chemical Co., London, England)
Germall: family of substituted imidazolidinyl urea compounds (Sutton Laboratories Inc., Rosella, USA)
Phenonip: a combination of parabens (esters of *p*-hydroxybenzoic acid) and phenoxyethanol (Nipa Laboratories, Treforest, Pontypridd, Wales)

variety of antimicrobial agents will increase. Thus, bacteria grown in the presence of glycerol, which increases their lipid content, showed enhanced resistance to QACs and to the higher, lipophilic alkyl phenols (Hugo & Franklin, 1968). Bradley *et al.* (1975) reported an accumulation of extracellular lipids by *Pseudomonas aeruginosa* when grown in the presence of common cream components such as glycerol, cetostearyl alcohol, polyethylene glycols and soft paraffin. The presence of such 'fattened' or lipid-rich cells as contaminants in pharmaceutical or cosmetic creams adds a further dimension to the problems of preservation.

2.3 Emulsified systems

It is well established that a wide range of emulgents used in cosmetic and pharmaceutical formulations can influence the activity of preservatives. A group of emulsifiers which have found an ever-increasing use in the production of elegant, stable preparations comprises the non-ionic surfactants, and these compounds pose a particular problem in their inactivation of preservatives. A variety of mathematical models has been used to predict the distribution of a preservative between the oily, aqueous and micellar components of emulsified systems. A typical model is that of Kazmi & Mitchell (1971, 1976) (equation 15.3).

$$C = C_w\ 1 + \frac{nK[M]}{1 + K(C_w)} + K_w^o\ \phi \div (\phi + 1) \qquad (15.3)$$

where C = total concentration of preservative, C_w = concentration of preservative in aqueous phase, ϕ = oil/water ratio, K_w^o = oil–water partition coefficient of the preservative, K = association constant of the binding of a molecule of preservative to an independent binding site on the surfactant M, n = number of binding sites on the surfactant, M = concentration of surfactant.

Kazmi & Mitchell (1976) have used this approach and extended it to include more than one preservative or surfactant, and Garrett (1966) proposed a general equation for preservative binding in a system containing several types of macromolecules.

In order to obtain the relevant data to satisfy an equation of the type shown, which would be a logical first step in estimating the preservative concentration required to protect a complex system, time-consuming experimental work is required. A wide variety of techniques is available to obtain such parameters (Parker & Barnes, 1967) and their application has provided insight into the mechanisms of interaction between preservatives and macromolecules. Thus, Donbrow & Rhodes (1966) used UV data to point to the localizing of benzoic acid within the palisade layer of the cetomacrogol micelle, whilst Corby & Elworthy (1971) similarly identified precise sites of solubilization for a variety of preservatives within the cetomacrogol micelle by utilizing UV nuclear magnetic resonance (NMR), viscometry and solubility techniques.

For practical purposes, it is useful to estimate directly the free preservative levels in complex formulations using dialysis cells (Kazmi & Mitchell, 1971, 1978a) or dissolution measurements (McCarthy, 1974; Parker, 1978) and the capacity of such systems to retain adequate protection despite preservative loss (Kazmi & Mitchell, 1978b); furthermore at some stage it is essential to evaluate the formulation against a direct microbial challenge.

2.4 Influence of colloids and suspended solids

A wide range of hydrocolloids is used in pharmaceutical and cosmetic products as stabilizers, dispersants or thickeners and suspended solids are therapeutically active ingredients in many medicines. In particular, silicates, both simple salts and complex clays, will adsorb and inactivate preservatives. Yousef *et al.* (1973) found that degrees of interaction were in the following decreasing order: veegum, magnesium trisilicate, bentonite, talc and kaolin. The efficacy of chlorbutol, chlorhexidine, methyl *p*-hydroxybenzoate and phenylmercuric nitrate was completely nullified by magnesium trisilicate, bentonite and veegum, and magnesium trisilicate and veegum, respectively. This type of inactivation presents a problem to the formulator of cosmetic solid preparations such as 'make-up' products or the various matt applications which might contain talc, kaolin, titanium dioxide, zinc oxide and chalk together with a variety of natural and synthetic pigments. Liquid medicines which can prove difficult to preserve due to suspended solids include antacids and sulphonamide preparations. Clark & Armstrong (1972) showed that in Paediatric Kaolin Mixture, BPC, the preservative used (benzoic acid) was adsorbed by the suspended light kaolin. This phenomenon was linked to pH as this influenced the overall charge upon kaolin particles such that the adsorption capacity of the kaolin markedly diminished above pH 5.0. The formulator here is presented with the dilemma that if the pH is increased to reduce preservative adsorption then concentration of undissociated acid, the active species, will fall. Thus, although the presence of chloroform as an additional preservative represents some degree of residual protection, the use of an alternative preservative such as methyl *p*-hydroxybenzoate is indicated. Sulphadimidine exerts a similar attraction for benzoic acid, resulting in the removal of this preservative from solution in sulphonamide mixtures by undissolved sulphadimidine (Beveridge & Hope, 1967). Other work has shown that for chloroform, in addition to volatilization there is an apparent reduction in the content of available preservative in formulations containing insoluble solids including kaolin, magnesium trisilicate and rhubarb (Lynch *et al.*, 1977).

The thickening or suspending agents used in pharmaceuticals and cosmetics including tragacanth, alginates, methylcellulose and polyvinylpyrrolidone are variously reported to diminish preservative efficacy. The reports are, however, contradictory in that gum tragacanth has been found to actually increase the activity of benzyl alcohol and methyl *p*-hydroxybenzoate (Yousef *et al.*, 1973). The alginates, being anionic in nature, will interact with any cation-active antimicrobial agents (Richardson & Woodford, 1964), but should show little reaction with the esters of *p*-hydroxybenzoic acid. Neither methyl cellulose nor polyvinylpyrrolidine significantly reduces the activity of the paraben esters (Yousef *et al.*, 1973). Interaction with solids can present a particular problem in the preservation of tablets in which active ingredients, fillers and disintegrants might all react with any added preservative. This presents an interesting problem in processing in that preservatives may be added as a dry mix in formulations which can be directly compressed into tablets or, when wet granulation is required, dissolved in the granulation water. Alternatively, the final granules may be sprayed with preservative solution, whilst rotating in a coating pan. Fassihi *et al.* (1978) examined these various methods of preservative incorporation. They found that although the dry-mix technique gave the highest levels of preservative (esters of *p*-hydroxybenzoic acid) in the finished tablets, as measured by chromatographic techniques, the tablets produced from granules which had been sprayed with preservative solution were the most resistant to microbial challenge. It is likely that in the dry-mix situation there is little interaction between preservative and tablet ingredients such that final measured levels of preservative are high. In the spray technique losses of preservative can occur during spraying due to interaction with tablet components in the moist state. These losses are, however, offset by the greater availability of the preservative for activity when coated externally onto the granules. This might be anticipated, since microbial spoilage of tablets is usually due to surface growth and preservative coated onto granules would more readily migrate to a surface situation than if it were incorporated into the core.

2.5 Preservative interaction with containers

The ubiquitous role of plastics in the packaging of both pharmaceutical and cosmetic products has brought in its wake a variety of problems involving leaching of additive from containers into their contents, and loss of formulation components by interaction with the container or permeation through it (Autian, 1963). An obvious consequence of this in the context of preservatives is that they are likely to be lost from formulations packed in plastic containers or with plastic closures. McCarthy (1971) examined the behaviour of a wide range of preservative solutions during storage in brown glass, polyvinylchloride, polyethylene and polypropylene containers at ambient temperatures during periods of up to 12 weeks. In general, polyethylene was the least suitable material, allowing substantial loss of phenolics such as chlorocresol and dichlorophenol and of dehydroacetic acid, although loss of the widely used *p*-hydroxybenzoates was negligible. The other plastics presented fewer problems, although sorbic acid and dichlorophenol were rapidly lost from polypropylene. Glass was the most stable of the materials tested, with amber glass providing the bonus of protection from light. Even here, however, there was a substantial loss of sorbic acid from solutions. McCarthy found that solubilization of phenolic preservatives in Tween (polysorbate) 80 reduced losses to polyethylene containers.

The multiplicity of factors which influence preservative–plastic interaction makes it difficult to assess information published by individual laboratories. Dean (1978) has emphasized that differences between grades of plastic, surface characteristics, thickness, degree of crystallinity/amorphous levels and presence of fillers, plasticizers, etc., all have their effects. Added to these is the contribution of the formulation itself, particularly if wetting agents are involved. The extent of the problem can be determined only by tests with the finally packed products. It has long been known that rubber, by virtue of its complex composition, will interact with many formulation components including preservatives, and the *British Pharmacopoeia* (1973) directs that rubber closures should be pre-treated with the relevant antimicrobial agents, in order to minimize the loss from injection and eye-drop solutions: see Chapters 3 and 18C for additional information. The synthetic rubbers, such as butyl and brominated butyl, exhibit a low affinity for preservatives and have good ageing characteristics and low permeability to moisture and oxygen. Their utilization as closures for multidose injection packs is restricted because of the lack of durability under repeated piercing.

3 ECOLOGY AND PRESERVED SYSTEMS

Once micro-organisms have become established within a preparation it is unlikely that the invasion will be restricted to a single species. Thus, the typical spoilage process is a dynamic one with initial invaders altering the environment such that secondary invaders can become established and similarly even tertiary forms. It is usual in this type of spoilage succession that the pioneer organisms, having altered the environment, lose their nutritional advantages and are eliminated. A classic example of this type of succession of micro-organisms is seen when raw milk is examined during spoilage (Fig. 15.1). The indigenous species,

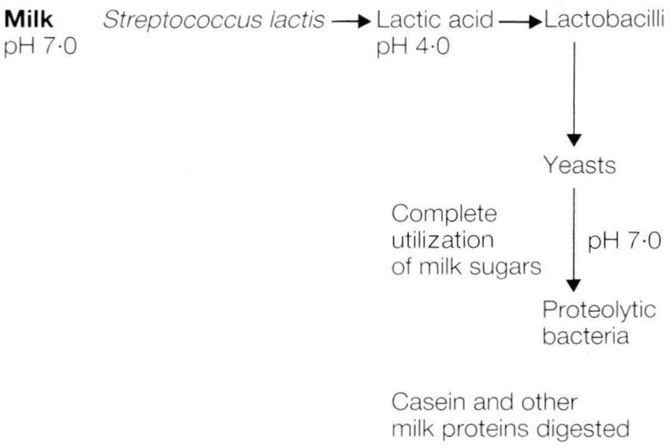

Fig. 15.1 Microbial spoilage succession in milk.

Streptococcus lactis, utilizes the milk sugars producing lactic acid and consequently lowering the pH. The conditions so created favour the establishment of acidophilic yeasts at the expense of the pioneering streptococcus. The yeasts eventually exhaust the carbohydrates and are themselves eliminated as these nutrients disappear and the pH rised. Conditions are now suitable for the tertiary proteolytic invaders, probably pseudomonads, which thrive at higher pH levels and utilize the milk proteins. A similar example of a spoilage succession is seen in pharmaceutical syrups, elixirs or cosmetic day creams with a high sugar content. In such formulations the water availability (a_w) is so low that only osmophilic yeasts can become established. If this happens the yeasts will utilize sugar, so lowering the osmotic tension and creating conditions of water availability which will allow secondary invaders (Fig. 15.2). The importance of the container for sugar-rich formulations has been highlighted by reports of Syrup BP fermenting during storage in plastic containers with production of sufficient gas to cause considerable deformation (Appleton *et al.*, 1972). Thus, although the heat involved in the preparation of the syrup, together with the low intrinsic water activity of the final product, would minimize normal microbial spoilage, any permeation of water vapour through the walls of the containing vessel could alter the osmotic status of the product, thereby allowing microbial proliferation.

A further consequence of the establishment of primary invaders in a formulation is a reduction of the efficiency of the preservative system. This may be affected by microbial breakdown of the preservatives and there are many examples of a variety of genera capable of this activity (Beveridge & Hugo, 1964; Hugo & Foster, 1964; Dagley, 1971; Beveridge, 1975; Hugo, 1991). Alternatively, change in ambient pH due to microbial activity can result in a deficiency of the active species of the preservative e.g. benzoic acid (equation 15.1). It is of value here to consider common spoilage associations in foodstuffs of the kind shown in Fig. 15.1. Thus, carbohydrates in a formulation will exert a 'protein-sparing' action due to acid release during glycolysis inhibiting proteolytic organisms (Mossel, 1971) and potentiating those preservatives active at low pH.

4 POTENTIATION OF PRESERVATIVE ACTIVITY

The variety of factors which influence preservative effectiveness, together with an ever-growing complexity of formulation components, are combining to create a situation in which the use of a single preservative to protect preparations is un-

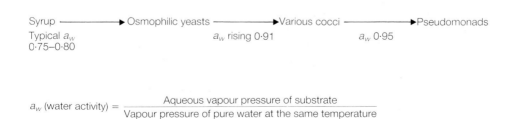

$$a_w \text{ (water activity)} = \frac{\text{Aqueous vapour pressure of substrate}}{\text{Vapour pressure of pure water at the same temperature}}$$

Fig. 15.2 Microbial spoilage succession in syrups.

realistic. It is more rational to explore the development of preservative combinations designed to have wider and more sustained powers of protection.

Garrett (1966) has discussed the justifications for using combinations of preservatives. These may be listed as follows:

1 the spectrum of antimicrobial activity is increased;

2 the toxic effects of the concentration level of one preservative alone required to give the equivalent effect of the mixture may be averted;

3 the development or modification of the resistance of an organism to one preservative alone may be prevented;

4 a synergistic effect (an activity of a combination of preservatives which exceeds that attributable to any component when present at a concentration equivalent to that of the total combination) may be achieved;

5 any economic savings or factors which ease formulation problems such as solubility may be attained.

It is important to bear these criteria in mind when examining the many examples of preservative combinations extant. For example, one review of preservatives in combination (Parker, 1973) cited formulations in which six preservatives were used to protect products rich in macromolecules such as make-up foundations, liners and cream shadow preparations. To justify such a complex mix it would be necessary to demonstrate that the component preservatives behaved independently both in respect of mechanism of antimicrobial action and in binding to macromolecules. These requirements would have been met by a combination of only three preservatives in the case cited. As opposed to such *ad hoc* mixtures, the following examples have a theoretical basis:

1 Hexachlorophane and esters of *p*-hydroxybenzoic acid. This represents a widening of the antimicrobial spectrum and allows the hexachlorophane to be used in low concentrations to minimize toxicity. Alternatives to hexachlorophane in this combination could be trichlorocarbanilide or 'Irgasan' (2,4,4′-trichloro-2′-hydroxy-diphenylether) (see Chapter 2).

2 Esters of *p*-hydroxybenzoic acid and 'Germall' (an imidazolidine urea compound: see Chapter 2). In such mixtures the readily water-soluble imidazolidinyl compound can be combined with one of the lipophilic parabens to give protection throughout a complex formulation.

3 QACs (benzalkonium chloride, cetyltrimethylammonium bromide, cetylpyridinium chloride) with esters of *p*-hydroxybenzoic acid. The addition of parabens widens the antimicrobial spectrum and presents a fundamentally different mode of activity.

It is interesting to consider some of the combinations of paraben esters which have been used over the years, ranging from 'Solution for Eyedrops' of older editions of the *British Pharmaceutical Codex* (methyl and propyl esters) to the various commercial mixtures marketed as 'Nipasterile®', 'Nipacombin®' and 'Nipastat®'. It is unlikely that in these mixtures any higher degree of saturation or higher thermodynamic activity in the aqueous phase can be attained than would be the case if a single ester was used (Evans, 1965). Thus, the synergism reported for such mixtures may be attributed to some difference in mechanism of action of the constituent esters (Gerrard *et al.*, 1962).

An alternative to the use of combinations of preservatives is to add potentiating agents, substances not usually used as antimicrobial agents *per se*, which enhance antimicrobial efficacy (Table 15.3). These agents act in a variety of ways ranging from the use of propylene glycol to increase the solubility of lipophilic preservatives and to reduce their loss to micelles to the widespread use of ethylenediamine tetraacetate (EDTA) in contact-lens solutions to interfere with permeability and metal ion balance and so augment bactericidal effects (Hart, 1984). Both phenylethyl alcohol (PEA) and phenoxyethanol (phenoxetol) potentiate antimicrobial activity by interfering with membrane permeability and by this mechanism have significant activity in their own right. Phenoxetol is used in combination with paraben esters in the commercially available 'Phenonip®', a liquid preparation useful in a variety of cosmetic formulations (Parker *et al.*, 1968). Synergy in preservative combinations has been reviewed (Denyer *et al.*, 1985).

Table 15.3 Potentiation of preservative activity

Potentiator	Preservative	Reference(s)
Phenoxyethanol (Phenoxetol)	Parabens	German patent 856043 British patent 566139
	Aminacrine hydrochloride	Clausen & Raugstad (1965)
Phenylethylalcohol	Benzalkonium chloride	Richards & McBride (1971)
	Chlorbutol	
	Chlorhexidine	
	Chlorocresol	Denyer *et al.* (1986)
	Parabens	
	Phenylmercuric nitrate	
	Aminacrine hydrochloride	Sheikh & Parker (1972) Parker (1977)
Ethylenediamine tetraacetic acid	Benzalkonium chloride	Brown & Richards (1965)
	Aminacrine hydrochloride	Sheikh & Parker (1972)
	Bronopol Cetrimide Chlorhexidine Germall Parabens Sorbic acid	Denyer & King (1988)
Propylene glycol	Parabens	Prickett *et al.* (1961)
	Sorbates	Woodford & Adams (1972)

5 STANDARDS AND PRESERVATION

The role of the preservative system in the preparation is closely linked with any microbial standards which apply to that preparation. Thus, solutions for injection and ophthalmic preparations such as eye-drops and contact-lens solutions are required to be sterile, and when these are used in multidose containers the preservative should be capable of maintaining this condition during a prescribed period of use. For pharmaceuticals given orally or used topically, a variety of standards are extant (Table 15.4) ranging from a numerical limit upon all organisms, as in the *Swedish Pharmacopoeia*, to the exclusion of named forms as in the *United States Pharmacopoeia* XXI, which requires freedom from *Escherichia coli* for oral solutions and from *Pseudomonas aeruginosa* and *Staphylococcus aureus* for topical preparations. In its guidelines upon the microbiological attributes of non-sterile pharmaceutical products, the *USP* states that the significance of micro-organisms in these products should be evaluated in terms of the use, nature and potential hazard to the user of the product. Both the American and British pharmacopoeias apply microbial standards to named substances such as gelatin which is required to be free from both *E. coli* and *Salmonella* spp. in given sample sizes. Additionally, named preparations, such as Alumina and Magnesium Oral Suspension USP and Aluminium Hydroxide Gel BP, are required to be free from *E. coli* in the former and pseudomonads in the latter. The exclusion type of standard, of course, is primarily achieved by the careful screening of ingredients, whereas limits upon total microbial content will be fostered in their achievement by the use of an adequate preservative.

A working party, set up by the Pharmaceutical Society of Great Britain, to examine the problem of microbial contamination in pharmaceuticals for oral and topical use, recommended that the final formulation should be capable of reducing or preventing the increase of such contamination (Sykes, 1971). They found that in the absence of

Table 15.4 Types of microbial standards applicable to pharmaceutical preparations

Products	*British Pharmacopoeia* 1988	*United States Pharmacopoeia* XXI	*European Pharmacopoeia*, draft proposals
Injections*	Sterile	Sterile	Sterile
Ophthalmic preparations*	Sterile	Sterile	Absence of revivable organisms in 1 g or 1 ml
Oral dosage forms	Exclusion of named organisms from some ingredients and preparations e.g. thyroid: free from *Salmonella* in 10 g and *E. coli* in 1 g; aluminium hydroxide: gel free from pseudomonads in 1 ml	All oral solutions and suspensions free from *E. coli*. A limit on total aerobic count of non-specified viable organisms for some preparations, e.g. Milk of Magnesia: 100 cells per ml. Exclusion of named organisms from certain ingredients and preparations e.g. natural plant and animal products free from *Salmonella*.	Limiting level of revivable organisms 10^3 to 10^4 aerobic bacteria/g or ml, 10^2 yeasts or moulds/g or ml. Exclusion of specified micro-organisms, e.g. absence of *E. coli* in 1 g or 1 ml, absence of *Salmonella* in 1 g or 1 ml, other enterobacteria not above 10^2/g or ml.
Topical preparations	Nil	All topical preparations free from *Ps. aeruginosa* and *Staph. aureus*.	Limiting level of revivable organisms 10^2 in 1 g or ml. Exclusion of *Ps. aeruginosa*, *Staph. aureus* and enterobacteria.

* See also Chapter 18C.

preservatives, liquid medicines in common use could support appreciable levels of bacteria, usually of the pseudomonas–achromobacter–alcaligenes types, originating from the water used. The working party were also adamant in their rejection of any limit imposed upon total microbial count on the grounds that reproducibility of such counts was poor, that it varied with culture medium used, temperature of incubation and other factors, and that the count would depend upon period and conditions of storage of the products.

Preservatives in cosmetic preparations have a less crucial, though by no means less demanding, task than those in pharmaceuticals. Thus, cosmetics will only be in contact with healthy tissues and should not upset the microbial balance with preservative systems powerful enough to destroy the commensals which afford protection against pathogenic forms. Within this context the cosmetic must not infect the consumer and must be resistant to microbial spoilage. The guidance issued by the Council of the Society of Cosmetic Chemists of Great Britain (1970) upon the hygienic manufacture and preservation of toiletries and cosmetics recommends that 'relevant known pathogenic micro-organisms be absent from cosmetics and that those preparations intended for use on newborn infants, for direct instillation into the conjunctival sac or for use on broken skin, should be sterile at the time of manufacture'. Spooner (1977) has reviewed the voluntary and regulatory situation pertaining to microbiological limits and guidelines for cosmetic products. In general, as with pharmaceuticals, there is the dual approach of seeking numerical limits and excluding specific organisms. The guidelines published by the Cosmetic, Toiletry and Fragrance Association (CTFA) of America in 1973 set a general numerical limit of 1000 organisms per g or ml with a strict limit of 500 organisms per unit weight for baby products or those for ophthalmic use; harmful organisms were required to be absent from all cosmetics. In Australia, more severe limits have been proposed by the Cosmetic and Toiletry Manufacture Association, with a general numerical limit of less than 100 organisms per g or ml and less than 10 organisms for eye cosmetics. The Toiletry Preparations Federation of the UK advise numerical limits of less than 1000 colony-forming units per gram for aerobic bacteria and for yeasts and moulds and less than 10 colony-forming units for baby and ophthalmic products.

The exclusion of harmful organisms as a general requirement hinges upon the definition of the term 'pathogenic', and certain genera have been proposed by the Society of Cosmetic Chemists, viz. *Clostridium, Salmonella, Pseudomonas, Escherichia, Klebsiella, Proteus, Streptococcus, Shigella* and coagulase-positive *Staphylococcus*.

To be satisfied that a preservative system will protect the product and maintain any predetermined microbiological standards, it is necessary to evaluate the preservative in the context of what is required of it. This is essentially a two-stage process, the first being a preliminary screening to find a preservative of suitable antimicrobial spectrum and the second a challenge test upon the final formulated product. The time-honoured methods of assessing antimicrobial activity by broth-dilution techniques or agar-plate diffusion have the merits of being simple to perform. They do, however, provide limited information in that only inhibitory values are obtained and, of course, even with authentic spoilage isolates represent an artificially lenient test. A useful adaptation of this type of test is to employ various measuring instruments in place of the eye to detect turbidity or some other index of cell development which occurs early in the growth cycle, and so obtain information within hours rather than days. Thus, rapid evaluation techniques have been based upon growth indices as diverse as bioluminescence, heat production, electric charge, gas production, enzyme action, refractility and turbidity (Parker, 1984; Leech, 1988). Such methods may allow for the effects of some formulation components to be determined (Parker, 1971).

The assessment of simply inhibitory or bacteriostatic activity does enjoy some official support in that the *British Pharmaceutical Codex* (1973) recommends for multidose injections 'the inclusion of a bactericide at a concentration sufficient to prevent the growth of micro-organisms'. This approach has some merits in that if the contaminating or challenge forms were bacterial spores it is quite possible that a lethal end-point could not be attained. In general, however, the most satisfactory performance required is that the preservative will kill micro-organisms. Even here, however, details may range from removing samples for inoculation into recovery media after fixed time intervals of preservative action to obtaining a full description of the course of inactivation of organisms by a viable counting technique. The former technique is typified by lethal end-point measurements, as used in Rideal–Walker types of test, whereas the latter has been advocated, particularly for eye-drops and contact-lens solutions, where not only killing power but speed of activity are important (Davies, 1978).

The characteristics of the preservative as determined by these initial investigations provide guidance as to the choice of a suitable antimicrobial agent but the final vindication of this choice can only come from challenge tests upon the formulated product. The rationale of such tests is to determine whether the preparation will, during storage and use, remain microbiologically acceptable. The type of microbiological standard applied should determine the nature of the challenge test with, for example, sterile solutions being capable of retaining this state and cosmetic preparations allowing no proliferation beyond acceptable limits. The *British Pharmacopoeia* (1973) defined in vague terms the required bactericidal performance of a solution for injection against microbial challenge by stating that the bactericide used should be capable of sterilizing the injection within 3 h of an inoculation with 10^6

Table 13.5 Challenge-testing procedures

	British Pharmacopoeia 1988	*United States Pharmacopoeia* XXI	Society of Cosmetic Chemists (UK)	Toilet Goods Association
I*	Applied to parenteral, ophthalmic, topical and oral liquid preparations. *A. niger*, *C. albicans*, *Ps. aeruginosa*, *Staph. aureus* and other typical contaminants allowed	Applied to parenteral, otic, nasal and ophthalmic products. *A. niger*, *C. albicans*, *E. coli*, *Ps. aeruginosa*. *Staph. aureus* and other typical contaminants allowed	Creams and lotions: *Staph. aureus*, *Strep. faecalis*, *Ps. aeruginosa*, *Ps. fluorescens*, *E. coli*, *Klebsiella* spp., *Proteus* spp., *A. niger*, *Penicillium* spp., *Cladosporum* spp., *Alternaria* spp., *Fusarium* spp., *Mucor* spp., *Rhizopus* spp., *Phoma* spp., *Trichoderma* spp., *Verticillium* spp., *C. albicans*, *Sacch. cerevisiae*. Eye cosmetics: *Ps. aeruginosa*, *Ps. fluorescens*, *Micrococcus luteus*, *Strep. faecalis*, Fresh saliva Shampoos: Spoilage isolates *Pseudomonas* spp. Toothpaste: Spoilage isolates	General cosmetics: *A. niger*, *C. albicans*, *E. coli*, *Ps. aeruginosa*, *Staph. aureus*, *B. subtilis*, *P. luteum*. Spoilage isolates
II*	10^6 per ml or g. Single challenge, separate portions for each micro-organism	10^5–10^6 per ml. Single challenge	10^6–10^7 per ml or g. Number of challenges may be varied	10^6 per ml or g. Two challenges may be made at 7-day intervals
III*	Injections and ophthalmic preparations—bacteria reduced by factor of 10^3 within 6 h and none recoverable at 24 h. Yeast and moulds reduced by factor of 10^2 within 7 days and no increase thereafter. Topical preparations—as above but 48 h allowed for reduction of bacterial count. Oral liquid preparations—as above but 48 h allowed for reduction of bacterial count and 14 days for moulds	Bacteria reduced to 0.1% of initial count by 14th day. Yeasts and moulds remain at or below initial count during 14 days. Count of each test organism remains at or below designated levels during 28 days	Shampoos self-sterilizing in 7 days. Creams and lotions should show drastically reduced count. Eye cosmetics should be bactericidal to *Ps. aeruginosa*	No formal recommendation, but no final judgement for 28 days

* I = Challenge organisms: II = number of challenging organisms; III = endpoint.

vegetative bacteria per ml. The *United States Pharmacopoeia* XXI is less ambiguous and provides details of tests designed to measure the preservative efficacy of systems protecting multidose parenteral, otic, nasal and ophthalmic products in the original unopened container. A challenge of five micro-organisms is specified, *Candida albicans*, *Aspergillus niger*, *E. coli*, *Ps. aeruginosa* and

Staph. aureus, each of a defined American Type Culture Collection strain. The preservative system is deemed effective if the number of viable vegetative organisms is reduced to not more than 0.1% of the initial inoculum (10^5–10^6 viable cells/ml) and the viable count of the yeast and mould remains unchanged or falls during the first 14 days after addition to the preparation under test. Additionally, the level of each test organism must remain at or below these designated levels for a total of 28 days from the beginning of the test. Samples are taken for plate counting every 7 days during the 28-day test period.

The *British Pharmacopoeia* 1988 details a testing procedure very much in line with that of the *USP*. The challenge micro-organisms listed are *C. albicans*, *A. niger*, *Ps. aeruginosa* and *Staph. aureus* with other such as *E. coli* and *Z. rouxii* allowed for oral liquids and syrups respectively. Details are provided of type, maintenance and subculturing of the organisms. Variation in the end-point required is allowed according to the product tested, with multidose injections and ophthalmic preparations having to reduce the bacterial challenge by a factor of not less than 10^3 within 6 h, whereas topical and oral liquid forms are allowed 48 h to achieve a similar reduction. As with the *USP* the performance demanded of the preserved systems against moulds and yeasts is less stringent, the reduction factor being 10^2 within 7 days of challenge but with no increase thereafter. In all cases samples are taken for viable counting periodically during 28 days. The test protocol proposed for the *European Pharmacopoeia* is similar but somewhat less stringent for topical preparations.

Guidance for the testing of preserved cosmetics has been provided by the Society of Cosmetic Chemists of Great Britain (1970). The test is in essence more severe than that of the *USP* in that spoilage isolates are recommended together with a wide range of bacteria, including a spore former, and moulds and yeasts. In addition there is provision for rechallenge of the product under test to provide further information on the stability of the preservative system. Advice is further given on adapting the test for different types of cosmetic product such as shampoos, toothpastes, creams or lotions and eye preparations (Table 13.5). Finally, long-term storage tests are recommended before finally approving the preservative system for use in a particular product. The Toilet Goods Association (1970) describes a challenge test which also includes product contaminants and allows for a rechallenge 7 days after the viable count of the original inoculum has been reduced to an acceptable level.

The criticisms of these challenge tests are many (Cowen & Steiger, 1976; Moore, 1978) and centre upon the choice of challenge organisms, number of challenges, microbial load in challenge, preparation of micro-organisms, ambient temperature of test, end-point stipulated, sampling and recovery techniques. It is inevitable that any or all of these factors can be criticized, or any defined test, such as that of the *USP*, and these can usually be overcome only by designing different tests for different products and circumstances of usage.

In general there has been a tendency to try to design a single test to meet all situations. This results in large numbers of different types of challenge organism being specified at high count levels and often with a rechallenge to assess the capacity of the preparation to deal with in-use contamination. There is probably a case for simplifying challenge tests as much as possible by using, say, two test organisms only, *viz.* a bacterial and a yeast or mould culture relevant to the spoilage situation at a modest level, around 10^4 cells per g or ml of preparation under test, with no more than one rechallenge within a month. This type of test should be adequate for cosmetic and non-sterile pharmaceutical preparations in which the preservative system would be expected to reduce the challenge count by 99.9% for the vegetative test form, and prevent any proliferation of the mould. For multidose injections and ophthalmic products there is a case for insisting upon a shorter time limit for activity as in the BP specification of 6 h. There can be little doubt that increasing pressures for complete safety in use can do nothing but reduce the number of antimicrobial compounds acceptable as preservatives. This, together with the ever more stringent requirements for microbiological standards, places greater emphasis upon the care taken in manufacture and the skills of the formulator.

ACKNOWLEDGEMENT

The author wishes to acknowledge 'Cosmetics and Toiletries—USA' for permission to reproduce Figs 15.1 and 15.2 and Table 10.5.

6 REFERENCES

Appleton, J.D., Midcalf, B. & Best, D. (1972) Stability of syrup. *Pharmaceutical Journal*, **208**, 569.

Autian, J. (1963) Plastics in pharmaceutical practice and related fields. *Journal of Pharmaceutical Sciences*, **52**, 2–23.

Baird, R.M. (1974) A proposed alternative to Calamine Cream, B.P.C. *Pharmaceutical Journal*, **213**, 153–154.

Baird, R.M. (1985a) Microbial contamination of pharmaceutical products made in a hospital pharmacy: a nine year study. *Pharmaceutical Journal*, **231**, 54–55.

Baird, R.M. (1985b) Microbial contamination of non-sterile pharmaceutical products made in hospitals in the North East Thames Regional Health Authority. *Journal of Clinical and Hospital Pharmacy*, **10**, 95–100.

Bean, H.S., Heman-Ackah, S.M. & Thomas, J. (1965) The activity of antibacterials in two-phase systems. *Journal of the Society of Cosmetic Chemists*, **16**, 15–27.

Beveridge, E.G. (1975) The microbial spoilage of pharmaceutical products. In *Microbial Aspects of the Deterioration of Materials* (eds Gilbert, R.J. & Lovelock, D.W.) pp. 213–235. London: Academic Press.

Beveridge, E.G. & Hope, I.A. (1967) Inactivation of benzoic acid in sulphadimidine mixture for infants B.P.C. *Pharmaceutical Journal*, **198**, 457–458.

Beveridge, E.G. & Hugo, W.B. (1964) The resistance of gallic acid and its alkyl esters to attack by bacteria able to degrade aromatic ring structures. *Journal of Applied Bacteriology*, **27**, 304–311.

Bradley, T.J., Holdom, R.S. & Khan, N.H. (1975) Factors in the production and composition of extracellular lipids of *Pseudomonas aeruginosa* NCTC 2000. *Microbios*, **14**, 121–134.

British Pharmaceutical Codex (1973) London: Pharmaceutical Press.

British Pharmacopoeia (1973, 1988) London: HMSO.

Brown, M.R.W. & Richards, R.M.E. (1965) Effects of ethylenediamine tetra-acetate on the resistance of *Pseudomonas aeruginosa* to antibacterial agents. *Nature, London*, **207**, 1391–1393.

Bryce, D.M., Croshaw, B., Hall, J.E., Holland, V.R. & Lessel, B. (1978) The activity and safety of the antimicrobial agent Bronopol (2-bromo-2-nitropropan-1,3-diol). *Journal of the Society of Cosmetic Chemists*, **29**, 3–34.

Clark, C.D. & Armstrong, N.A. (1972) Influence of pH on the adsorption of benzoic acid by kaolin. *Pharmaceutical Journal*, **209**, 44–45.

Clausen, O. & Raugstad, K. (1965) The bactericidal combination effect of propylene glycol β-phenyl ether plus aminacrine hydrochloride. *Norges Apotek Tidskrift*, **73**, 16, 365–370.

Corby, T.C. & Elworthy, P.H.E. (1971) Identification of the site of solubilization of various compounds by cetomacrogol. *Journal of Pharmacy and Pharmacology*, **23**, 495–525.

Cosmetic Toiletry and Fragrance Association (1973) Evaluation of methods for determining preservative efficiency. *Cosmetic, Toiletry and Fragrance Association Journal*, **5**, 1–4.

Council of the Society of Cosmetic Chemists (1970) The hygienic manufacture and preservation of toiletries and cosmetics. *Journal of the Society of Cosmetic Chemists*, **21**, 719–800.

Cowen, R.A. & Steiger, B. (1976) Antimicrobial activity—a critical review of test methods of preservative efficiency. *Journal of the Society of Cosmetic Chemists*, **27**, 467–481.

Crompton, D.O. (1963) Sterility of eye medicaments. *Lancet*, **ii**, 150.

Dagley, S. (1971) Catabolism of aromatic compounds by microorganisms. In *Advances in Microbial Physiology*. (eds Rose, A.H. & Wilkinson, J.F.) Vol. 6, pp. 1–46. London: Academic Press.

Davies, D.J.G. (1978) Agents as preservatives in eye-drops and contact lens solutions. *Journal of Applied Bacteriology*, **44**, SXIX-SXXVIII.

Davison, A.L. (1988) Preservative efficacy testing of non-sterile pharmaceuticals, cosmetics and toiletries and its limitations. In *Microbial Quality Assurance in Pharmaceuticals, Cosmetics and Toiletries* (eds Bloomfield, S.F., Baird, R.M., Leak, R.E. & Leech, R.) pp. 119–128. Chichester: Ellis Horwood.

Dean, D.A. (1978) Some recent advances in the packaging of pharmaceuticals. *Drug Development and Industrial Pharmacy*, **4**, v–vi.

Denyer, S.P. & King, R.O. (1988) Development of preservative systems. In *Microbial Quality Assurance in Pharmaceuticals, Cosmetics and Toiletries*. (eds Bloomfield, S.F., Baird, R.M., Leak, R.E. & Leech, R.) pp. 156–170. Chichester: Ellis Horwood.

Denyer, S.P., Hugo, W.B. & Harding, V.D. (1986) The biochemical basis of synergy between the antibacterial agents, chlorocresol and 2-phenylethanol. *International Journal of Pharmaceutics*, **29**, 29–36.

Denyer, S.R., Hugo, W.B. & Harding, V.D. (1985) Synergy in preservative combinations. *International Journal of Pharmaceutics*, **25**, 245–253.

Donbrow, M. & Rhodes, C.T. (1966) Spectroscopic examination of the solubilisation of benzoic acid by a non-ionic surfactant. *Journal of Pharmacy and Pharmacology*, **18**, 424–428.

Evans, W.P. (1965) Applicability of the Ferguson principle to systems of mixed preservatives. *Journal of Pharmacy and Pharmacology*, **17**, 217–221.

Fassihi, A.R., Parker, M.S. & Dingwall, D. (1978) The preservation of tablets against microbial spoilage. *Drug*

Development and Industrial Pharmacy, **4**, 515–527.

Ferguson, J. (1939) The use of chemical potentials as indices of toxicity. *Proceedings of the Royal Society B*, **127**, 387–404.

Furr, J.R. & Russell, A.D. (1972) Uptake of esters of *p*-hydroxybenzoic acid by *Serratia marcescens* and by fattened and non-fattened cells of *Bacillus subtilis*. *Microbios*, **5**, 237–246.

Garrett, E.R. (1966) A basic model for the evaluation and prediction of preservative action. *Journal of Pharmacy and Pharmacology*, **18**, 589–601.

Gerrard, H.N., Parker, M.S. & Bullock, K. (1962) The fungistatic activity of methyl and propyl hydroxybenzoates and a mixture of these against *Penicillium spinulosum*. *Journal of Pharmacy and Pharmacology*, **14**, 103–107.

Hansch, C. & Clayton, J.M. (1973) Lipophilic character and biological activity of drugs. Part II. *Journal of Pharmaceutical Sciences*, **62**, 1–21.

Hart, J.R. (1984) Chelating agents as preservative potentiators. In *Cosmetic and Drug Preservation: Principles and Practice* (ed. Kabara, J.J.) pp. 323–337. Cosmetic Science and Technology Series, Vol. 1. New York: Marcel Dekker.

Hugo, W.B. (1991) The degradation of preservatives by microorganisms. *International Biodeterioration*, **27**, 185–194.

Hugo, W.B. & Foster, J.H.S. (1964) Growth of *Pseudomonas aeruginosa* in solutions of esters of *p*-hydroxybenzoic acid. *Journal of Pharmacy & Pharmacology*, **16**, 209.

Hugo, W.B. & Franklin, I. (1968) Cellular lipid and anti-staphylococcal activity of phenols. *Journal of General Microbiology*, **52**, 365–372.

Jarvis, B., Reynolds, A.J., Rhodes, C.R. & Armstrong, M. (1974) A survey of microbiological contamination in cosmetics and toiletries in the UK (1971). *Journal of the Society of Cosmetic Chemists*, **25**, 563–575.

Kallings, L.O., Ringertz, O., Silverstone, L. & Ernerfeldt, F. (1966) Microbial contamination of medical preparations. *Acta Pharmaca Suecica*, **3**, 219–228.

Kazmi, S.J.A. & Mitchell, A.G. (1971) Dialysis method for determining preservative distribution in emulsions. *Journal of Pharmaceutical Sciences*, **60**, 1422–1424.

Kazmi, S.J.A. & Mitchell, A.G. (1976) The interaction of preservative and non-ionic surfactant mixtures. *Canadian Journal of Pharmaceutical Sciences*, **11**, 10–17.

Kazmi, S.J.A. & Mitchell, A.G. (1978a) Preservation of solubilised and emulsified systems. I. *Journal of Pharmaceutical Sciences*, **67**, 1260–1265.

Kazmi, S.J.A. & Mitchell, A.G. (1978b) Preservation of solubilised and emulsified systems. II. *Journal of Pharmaceutical Sciences*, **67**, 1266–1271.

Kuehne, J.W. & Ahearn, D.G. (1971) Incidence and characterization of fungi in eye cosmetics. *Developments in Industrial Microbiology*, **12**, 173–177.

Leech, R. (1988) New methodology for microbiological quality assurance. In *Microbial Quality Assurance in Pharmaceuticals, Cosmetics and Toiletries*. (eds Bloomfield, S.F., Baird, R.M., Leak, R.E. & Leech, R.) pp. 195–216. Chichester: Ellis Horwood.

Lynch, M. Lund, W. & Wilson, D.A. (1977) Chloroform as a preservative in aqueous systems. *Pharmaceutical Journal*, **219**, 507–510.

McCarthy, T.J. (1971) Aspects of preservative inactivation. *South African Pharmaceutical Journal*, **6**, 21–28.

McCarthy, T.J. (1974) Determination of preservative availability from creams and emulsions. *Pharmaceutisch Weekblad*, **109**, 85–91.

McRobbie, D.I. & Parker, M.S. (1974) Some aspects of the antifungal activity of esters of *p*-hydroxybenzoic acid. *International Biodeterioration Bulletin*, **10**, 109–112.

Microbiological Purity of Non-Compulsorily Sterile Pharmaceutical Preparations (1976) (Second joint report of the Committees of Official Laboratories and Drug Control Services, and the Section of Industrial Pharmacists FIP, July 1975). *Pharmaceutica Acta Helvetiae*, **51**, 33–40.

Moore, K.E. (1978) Evaluating preservative efficacy by challenge testing during the development stage of pharmaceutical products. *Journal of Applied Bacteriology*, **44**, SXLIII–SLV.

Mossel, D.A.A. (1971) Physiological and metabolic attributes of microbial groups associated with foods. *Journal of Applied Bacteriology*, **34**, 95–118.

Noble, W.C. & Savin, J.A. (1966) Steroid cream contaminated with *Pseudomonas aeruginosa*. *Lancet*, **i**, 347–349.

Parker, M.S. (1971) The rapid screening of preservatives for pharmaceutical and cosmetic preparation. *International Biodeterioration Bulletin*, **7**, 47–53.

Parker, M.S. (1973) Some aspects of the use of preservatives in combinations. *Soap, Perfumery and Cosmetics*, **46**, 223–225.

Parker, M.S. (1977) Potentiation of antifungal agents. *Bulletin of the British Mycological Society*, **11**, 142–143.

Parker, M.S. (1978) The preservation of cosmetic and pharmaceutical creams. *Journal of Applied Bacteriology*, **44**, SXXIX–SXXXIV.

Parker, M.S. (1984) Preservative Systems for Cosmetics. In *Cosmetic and Drug Preservation: Principles and Practice* (ed. Kabara, J.J.) pp. 389–402. Cosmetic Science and Technology Series, Vol. 1. New York: Marcel Dekker.

Parker, M.S. & Barnes, M. (1967) The interaction of non-ionic surfactants with preservatives. *Soap, Perfumery and Cosmetics*, **40**, 163–170.

Parker, M.S., McCafferty, M. & McBride, S. (1968) Phenonip, a broad spectrum preservative. *Soap, Perfumery and Cosmetics*, **41**, 647–650.

Pederson, E.A. & Ulrich, K. (1968) Microbial content in non-sterile pharmaceuticals. *Dansk Tidsskrift for Farmaci*, **42**, 71–83.

Prickett, P.S., Murray, H.L. & Mercer, N.H. (1961) Potentiation of preservatives (parabens) in pharmaceutical formulations by low concentrations of propylene glycol. *Journal of Pharmaceutical Sciences*, **50**, 316–320.

Richards, R.M.E. & McBride, R.T. (1971) Phenylethanol enhancement of preservatives used in ophthalmic preparations. *Journal of Pharmacy and Pharmacology*, **23**,

Supplement 141S–146S.

Richardson, G. & Woodford, R. (1964) Incompatibility of cationic antiseptics with sodium alginate. *Pharmaceutical Journal*, **192**, 527–528.

Savin, J.A. (1967) The microbiology of topical preparations in pharmaceutical practice. 1: Clinical aspects. *Pharmaceutical Journal*, **199**, 285–288.

Sheikh, M.A. & Parker, M.S. (1972) The influence of ethylenediamine tetra-acetate and phenylethanol upon the fungistatic action of aminacrine hydrochloride. *Journal of Pharmacy and Pharmacology*, **24**, Supplement 158S.

Spooner, D.F. (1977) Microbiological aspects of the European Economic Community Directives. *Cosmetics and Toiletries*, **92**, 42–51.

Sykes, G. (1971) Microbial contamination in pharmaceuticals for oral and topical use: Society's working party report. *Pharmaceutical Journal*, **207**, 400–402.

Toilet Goods Association Test (1970) A guideline for the determination of adequacy of preservation of cosmetic and toiletry formulations. *Toilet Goods Association Cosmetic Journal*, **2**, 20–23.

United States Pharmacopoeia (1985) Twenty-first revision. United States Pharmacopoeias Convention, Inc.

White, M., Bowman, F.W. & Kirschbaum, A. (1968) Bacterial contamination in some non-sterile antibiotic drugs. *Journal of Pharmaceutical Sciences*, **57**, 1061–1063.

Woodford, R. & Adams, E. (1972) Effects of ethanol and propylene glycol, and a mixture of potassium sorbate with either, on *Pseudomonas aeruginosa* contamination of an oil-in-water cream. *American Perfumery and Cosmetics*, **87**, 53–56.

Yousef, R.T., El-Nakeeb, M.A. & Salama, S. (1973) Effect of some pharmaceutical materials on the bactericidal activities of preservatives. *Canadian Journal of Pharmaceutical Sciences*, **18**, 54–56.

Chapter 16
Chemical Food Preservatives

1 INTRODUCTION

Expansion in industrial production and distribution of foods, development of more perishable food products, advances in food processing and distribution, acceptance of convenience foods and reduction in numbers of people involved in food production, coupled with increases in total world population and changes in lifestyles, have resulted in an increased potential for mishandling of foods during various stages of processing, storage, distribution and preparation for consumption. Consequently, food preservation has attained greater significance in the survival and well-being of the human race. Furthermore, food safety and utilization of chemicals in food processing and preservation have become important concerns for consumers, health professionals and regulators. Recent recognition of potential public health problems from psychrotrophic pathogenic micro-organisms, however, has emphasized the need for appropriate preservation of perishable foods.

Some methods of food processing and preservation have been used by humans since their early days of existence. These methods include drying (dehydration), salting, smoking and fermentation. Preserved foods could then be used during periods of shortages such as the winter months when crop production and hunting were limited. As the human population increased, food preservation became more important and added objectives were to diminish food waste and to maintain the wholesomeness and safety of food.

Improvements in food preservation by heat, storage at low temperature, packaging in modified atmosphere environments, and drying have increased their application in recent years. However, there are many foods where such processes cannot be applied or where their useful application is limited. In these instances, preservation by the application of chemical compounds increases in importance. During the past century some specific and well-identified compounds have been used for food preservation. In general terms, chemical preservation can include a variety of compounds employed in the processing of foods. In this text, compounds that are introduced into the food during processing and before consumption with the objective of preventing or delaying microbial spoilage and development of pathogenic micro-organisms are considered in some detail. Additional chemicals reported as having the potential to inhibit microbial growth in food systems, or contributing to preservation, are also presented.

2 FOOD SPOILAGE AND PRESERVATION

Microbial proliferation and associated chemical and enzymatic activities in a food may cause changes in the general appearance, colour, flavour, texture, consistency and nutritive value of the product. Certain micro-organisms may also affect the public's health when they multiply and grow in a food. Food that has experienced undesirable microbial growth becomes unfit for consumption and is considered a loss, thus contributing to our worldwide food shortage. Other unwanted consequences of such growth are health problems for individuals consuming the food and adverse effects to private and national economies.

The main objectives of food preservation are to extend the shelf-life, retain wholesomeness and ensure the safety of our food supply by delaying or preventing microbial decomposition and by inhibiting or suppressing the growth of pathogenic micro-organisms. Physical control processes such as dehydration (drying), low-temperature storage (refrigeration-freezing) and heat processing (Chapter 18D) constitute approved and widely used methods of food preservation. Application of such processes, however, is limited to certain types of food products, and the degree of such application is also limited in certain instances. Changes in product identity and functionality, energy requirements of the processes, available technology, method reliability and consumer acceptance are some major factors limiting the application of the physical control methods. Irradiation treatments can also be considered as physical control methods in food preservation. Their main application, however, is restricted to medical fields (Chapter 19A) since in most countries even approved food uses are not widely applied due to labelling, health and potentially economic concerns.

In many instances, however, the above physical methods of food preservation are being used in combination with a variety of chemical compounds. Such combinations allow these processes or agents to be used at lower intensity or concentration, and retain good keeping quality with only minor changes in product properties. In certain instances chemical compounds may be used alone as food preservatives without concomitant physical treatment.

The inhibition or inactivation of undesirable microbial proliferation by chemical compounds in a food system is chemical food preservation, and is the subject of this chapter. Other deteriorative changes in food resulting from chemical or enzymatic reactions may also be retarded or prevented through use of chemical preservatives. Such deterioration may include alterations of flavour, odour, colour, appearance, texture and nutritive value.

Chemical food preservatives are incorporated into food products either directly through addition or by their development during processing of the food. Some chemical compounds have been used accidentally or intentionally in the preservation of foods for many centuries. These traditional preservatives include common salt, sugars, spices, acids and components of smoke, and are introduced through processes such as fermentation, salting (curing) and smoking. Meat and fish products were widely preserved by such processes in ancient times.

During the 20th century the use of chemical food preservatives has been regulated by government authorities and only specific compounds have been allowed. Earlier, the use of chemicals in food was often considered adulteration, because they were used to increase the volume of the product or to conceal poor quality by improving the colour (Jarvis & Burke, 1976; Young, 1989).

3 REGULATORY ASPECTS OF CHEMICAL FOOD PRESERVATION

The use of chemical compounds in food preservation is regulated by the appropriate authorities of each country, such as the Food and Drug Administration (FDA) in the USA. For information about UK legislation, see Jones & Flowerdew (1982). Internationally, the Food and Agriculture Organization (FAO) and the World Health Organization (WHO) are concerned with chemical food preservatives. These organizations also establish the acceptable daily intake (ADI) of food preservatives. For a substance or compound to be considered as a legal food preservative its safety must be demonstrated by its manufacturer. In the USA the Food Additives Amendment to the Food, Drug and Cosmetic Act of 1938 and subsequent revisions specify the conditions and the process under which any substance may be approved as a chemical additive. Assuming the safety of the compound is established, a regulation will be issued specifying applications, amounts used and any other necessary conditions to protect the public well-being. Chemical food preservatives approved for use in the USA are designated by the Federal Food, Drug and Cosmetic Act of 1938 as amended. The use of additives and preservatives in foods is controlled by legislation in most countries. Details on legislation on preservatives in several countries can be found in Jarvis & Burke (1976) and Ahlborg *et al.* (1977). Information on food preservative regulations may be obtained from individual countries. Such information is especially useful when preparing food products for export markets. In the USA Title 21, parts 180–189 and other parts of the Code of Federal Regulations (1989) list chemicals permitted for use as preservatives in foods and conditions for their use.

Certain food additives, including some chemical preservatives (benzoate, propionate, sorbate, parabens) are *generally recognized as safe* (GRAS) and are exempted from the Food Additive Regulations in the USA. However, the additive's intended use must fall within its spectrum of activity, it must be approved for the food product, and the principles of good manufacturing practices must be employed when no limits in the use concentration are set in the GRAS list. Every chemical food preservative used in the USA must be listed on the label of the product. For specific information about the rules and legislation concerning the use of chemical food preservatives in a certain country the appropriate domestic authorities should be contacted.

The major arguments against the use of chemical compounds as food preservatives are that they are harmful to the consumer, they reduce the nutritional quality of foods, they make faulty food appear normal, and their use could be eliminated if good manufacturing procedures are followed. The regulatory authorities of each country are responsible for preventing the above abuses and hazards. These authorities will generally approve the use of chemicals as food preservatives only when the following conditions are fulfilled:

1 there should be a need for preservation of the food concerned;

2 the chemical must be proven capable of perform-

ing the described preservative action under the specific conditions of the described food product;
3 the compound suggested as a food preservative must be non-toxic;
4 it must be proven safe and non-carcinogenic, at concentrations well above intended use levels;
5 it must not change the identity of the food by altering its flavour, appearance, etc.;
6 its application to the food must be practicable and its properties (e.g. solubility) should not interfere with such application;
7 its cost should not be prohibitive;
8 it should be readily available;
9 its total consumption (including consumption from other uses) should not exceed specified safe levels.

These requirements have set some strict controls in the approval of chemical substances to be used as food preservatives (Ingram *et al.*, 1964; Kimble, 1977). Most of the initial preservatives, some of which are of proven effectiveness and safety by long customary or empirical accidental use, are still applied despite well-known limitations. Few new preservatives have been approved in recent years due to the existence of strict controls and requirements. In some cases it is even difficult to extend the application of commonly used preservatives to food products other than those currently approved and regulated. Such an example is potassium sorbate, which is widely used in foods but was not approved for use in cured meat products in the USA.

4 SELECTION OF CHEMICAL FOOD PRESERVATIVES

No single, currently available, food preservative satisfies all the requirements of the ideal, and is capable of being used in a wide range of food products. The preservative action of all chemical food preservatives is affected by a variety of factors (Ingram *et al.*, 1964; Mossel, 1975; Jarvis & Burke, 1976; Branen & Davidson, 1983). Such factors should be closely evaluated when a food preservative is to be selected for a specific food. The antimicrobial activity of individual compounds varies, and is in part dependent upon the types of micro-organisms likely to be encountered and the nature of the food to be preserved. It is highly desirable that the antimicrobial spectrum of a preservative be wide. Its activity should not inhibit the growth of one kind of micro-organism and as a consequence permit the growth of another, possibly pathogenic, type. In many instances one group of micro-organisms suppresses the growth of another. If the first group is inhibited, the second may predominate and cause problems not encountered previously. Therefore the range of acitivity of the selected compound should include the full complement of unwanted micro-organisms that may occur in the specific products. In certain instances, such as in lactic-acid fermentations, it is desirable to choose a preservative that suppresses unwanted growth but does not interfere with the organisms responsible for the desirable fermentation. Incorporation of a preservative in a food product should guard against the development of resistant strains, especially in the species against which it is used. For example, some mould and yeast species have developed resistance to benzoate and sorbate (Marth *et al.*, 1966; Sofos, 1989a). Concern over development of resistant strains has been the primary reason for reluctance of regulatory authorities to allow use of antibiotics in food preservation.

The physical and chemical properties of the preservative and their relationship to the specific food product constitute a major factor in the efficacy of the compound. Factors such as solubility, pK_a (dissociation constant), toxic levels and chemical reactivity are of considerable significance (see also Chapters 2, 3 and 15) and should be carefully examined before a compound is considered as a viable means of preservation in a specific system (Table 16.1). The preferential solubility of parabens (esters of *p*-hydroxybenzoic acid) in lipids is considered the main reason for their extensive performance in aqueous culture media and their low performance in lipid-containing food systems. The antimicrobial activity of weak acid preservatives is attributed mostly to their undissociated form (see Chapters 2 and 3, and Fig. 2.7 in Chapter 2). Thus, the pK_a value of a particular compound will predict its efficacy in a food system with a specified pH level. Different compounds of the same class may differ in antimicrobial activity as well as physical and chemical properties. The

Table 16.1 Some properties of commonly used chemical food preservatives

Agent	Chemical formula	Water solubility (g/100 ml, 25°C)	pK_a	Effective against
Lactic acid	$CH_3CHOHCOOH$	High	3.1	
Citric acid	$CH_2COOHCOHCOOHCH_2COOH$	High	3.1	
Acetic acid	CH_3COOH	High	4.75	
Sodium diacetate	$CH_3COONa \cdot CH_3COOH \cdot \frac{1}{2}H_2O$	100.0	4.75	
Sodium benzoate	C_6H_3COONa	50.0	4.2	Bacteria, yeasts, moulds
Sodium propionate	CH_3CH_2COONa	100.0	4.9	
Potassium sorbate	$CH_3CH{=}CHCH{=}CHCOOK$	139.2	4.75	
Methyl paraben	HO-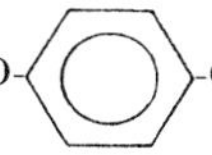-$COOCH_3$	0.25	8.5	
Sodium nitrite	$NaNO_2$	66.0	—	Bacteria, yeasts, moulds
Sulphur dioxide	SO_2	85.0	—	

most useful alternative should be chosen in such instances. Since the potassium salt of sorbic acid is more soluble in water than is the acid itself, the salt is preferred in spray or brine applications. However, in applications made directly into the products the acid form may be used. The antimicrobial activity of parabens increases with chain length, but paraben solubility in water decreases simultaneously. In this case a mixture of two or more compounds can improve effectiveness and can be used where activity over a wider pH range is required or a broader spectrum of micro-organisms must be controlled.

The most commonly used chemical food preservatives are weak acids or their salts or esters. Acidity is the main means of preservation in fermented products such as sauerkraut, pickles, yoghurt and fermented meats. The method of preserving foods by increasing their acidity, either naturally by fermentation or by addition of acids, has been in use for thousands of years. In certain instances the effect of acids may be combined with other factors such as heat processing, dehydration (a_w), or other chemical compounds (McCulloch, 1945; von Schelhorn, 1951; Freese *et al.*, 1973). Acidity also potentiates the preservative action of the salts of weak mineral acids such as nitrite and sulphite which are common preservatives. The preservative action of weak acids is twofold. The concentration of free hydrogen ions (H^+) is increased, and the undissociated form of the acid directly affects the micro-organisms. The growth and survival of micro-organisms during processing and storage are affected by the pH of the product. Low pH not only inhibits microbial growth; it also reduces microbial heat resistance during processing. The major effect of organic acid preservatives is the result of the toxic effect of their undissociated molecule. The pK_a values of most organic food preservatives, except parabens, are below pH 5.0 (Table 16.1). This is very important considering that the optimum pH range for the growth of most bacteria is between 5.5 and 7.0, whereas yeasts and moulds can grow at pH values as low as 2.0.

In general, pH not only directly influences the growth and survival of micro-organisms, but also the effects of the most commonly used preservatives are dependent on it. A low pH generally favours effective preservation. This is either due to its direct effect on the micro-organisms (especially bacteria) or due to the increased effectiveness of most preservatives at lower pH values. It is fortunate that most foods fall towards the acid side of the pH range where the available preservatives are generally effective. Table 16.2 lists some of the commonly used chemical food preservatives, their levels of incorporation and acceptable daily intake by humans. More details on these aspects are found in the text.

The above-mentioned properties of the compound should be considered in relation to the general composition, physical and chemical properties, storage and distribution of the food. The consideration of pH was identified earlier as a major determinant in selecting a preservative. Other components of the system may possess their own antimicrobial activity or act synergistically with the proposed preservative. Destruction or injury of micro-organisms during heat processing of the product, along with product dehydration and a lower water activity (a_w), may supplement the effect of preservatives and decrease the concentrations required for product stability. Cured meat products are a dramatic example of such complex interactions in food preservation (Ingram, 1974, 1976; Lechowich *et al.*, 1978; Sofos *et al.*, 1979c; Sofos & Busta, 1980). The microflora of the product also influence the selection of a food preservative. The types of micro-organisms present will determine which compound or compounds is/are most effective under the given conditions, and the extent of contamination will dictate what concentrations should be employed.

The complex requirements that a compound must meet in order to be approved as a food preservative, as well as the complexity of foods and the variety of influential factors, demonstrate the difficulty in selecting the appropriate preservative for a given system. This selective process may well be long and tedious. It is further complicated by the fact that only a few compounds are currently in use as preservatives; the number of alternative preservatives has not increased in recent years; tighter restrictions are being imposed by regulatory authorities; all available chemical food preservatives have certain disadvantages; the demand for

Table 16.2 Common uses of chemical food preservatives

Agent	Acceptable daily intake (mg/kg body weight)	Commonly used levels (%)	Food products of common usage
Lactic acid	No limit	No limit	Olives, salad dressings, mayonnaise, desserts, bakery goods
Citric acid	No limit	No limit	Carbonated beverages, fruit juices, wines
Acetic acid	No limit	No limit	Salad dressings, mayonnaise, olives, sauces, pickled meats, vegetables
Sodium diacetate	15	0.3–0.5	Bread and bakery goods
Sodium benzoate	5	0.03–0.2	Pickles, beverages, salads, syrups, fish, preserves, jams, jellies, margarine
Sodium propionate	10	0.1–0.3	Bread and bakery products, cheese products, fruits, vegetables
Potassium sorbate	25	0.05–0.2	Dairy products, baked goods, fruits, vegetables, soft drinks, margarine, pickled products, jams, jellies, meat and fish products
Methyl paraben	10	0.05–0.1	Fruit products, pickles, syrups, baked goods, creams, preserves, pastes
Sodium nitrite	0.2	0.01–0.02	Cured meats, cheese, fish
Sulphur dioxide	0.7	0.005–0.2	Wines, fruit juices, syrups, meat and fish products

food preservation is greater today than at any other time in history; and listing of chemical additives on product labels is unacceptable from a marketing standpoint.

5 COMBINATIONS AND INTERACTIONS OF PRESERVATIVES

Preservation of food products containing chemical food preservatives is usually based on the combined or synergistic activity of several additives, intrinsic product parameters (e.g. composition, acidity, water activity), and extrinsic factors (e.g. processing temperature, storage atmosphere and temperature). Use of this approach should continue in the future (Wagner & Moberg, 1989) because it minimizes undesirable changes in product properties and reduces concentration of additives and extent of processing treatments. The concept of combinations of preservatives and treatments to preserve foods is frequently called the hurdle or barrier concept (Leistner, 1978). Combinations of additives and preservative systems provide unlimited preservation alternatives for application in food products to meet consumer demands for healthy and safe foods.

6 APPLICATION OF CHEMICAL FOOD PRESERVATIVES

Chemical food preservatives are applied to foods as direct additives in the formulation, or develop during processes such as fermentation. Certain preservatives have been used either accidentally or intentionally for centuries, and include sodium chloride (common salt), sugar, acids, alcohols and components of smoke. In addition to preservation, these compounds contribute to the quality and identity of the products, and are applied through processing procedures such as salting, curing, fermentation and smoking.

Application of chemical food preservatives may be through direct addition in the formulation; spraying with or immersing in a solution; dusting with a powder; through application of an organic carrier such as ethanol, vegetable oil, or propylene glycol applied to the coating or packaging material that comes in contact with the surface of the food; or as an ingredient of multicomponent formulations applied in a single action.

Selection of the method of application is based on the properties of the preservative, processing procedures, convenience in processing, and type of food product. Properties of chemical food preservatives such as solubility and volatility are major determinants of the method of application. One important consideration in spray or dipping applications is to use adequate concentrations in order to achieve sufficient uptake by the food for its preservation, without exceeding legal limits or sensory thresholds. Often the method of application is selected on the basis of ease by which the preservative can be added through existing processing and packaging procedures.

7 TRADITIONAL CHEMICAL FOOD PRESERVATIVES

7.1 General

Substances which have been added to foods for centuries, and have traditionally contributed to their stability and safety, include common salt, sugar, smoke and spices. Their initial introduction into foods is lost in history, but they still continue to constitute basic adjuncts to our food supply. Their application may have started accidentally; evidently the first and foremost reason for their use was their effects on flavour. However, with time, their antimicrobial activity was also noticed. Their preservative action is either direct, indirect or through interactions between the preservatives as well as with other components of the food system, or other additives (Prescott & Proctor, 1937; Jensen, 1954; Reddish, 1957; Lueck, 1980; Branen & Davidson, 1983; Sofos, 1984).

7.2 Common salt

Sodium chloride, or common salt, is widely employed as a flavouring or preservative agent and its use dates to ancient times (Jensen, 1954). Common foods preserved with salt include meat and fish products, butter, margarine, cheeses and brined vegetables. It is the main ingredient of curing mixtures or brines. The use of salt in meat preservation led to the accidental and subsequent intentional use of nitrate and nitrite (Section 12) in meat curing (Binkerd & Kolari, 1975; Sofos *et al.*, 1979c). The preservative system of cured meats consists of salt, nitrite and other factors such as mild heat processing, low-temperature storage, smoking in certain instances, sugar, etc. (Sofos *et al.*, 1979c; Sofos & Busta, 1980).

The molecular weight of sodium chloride is 58.44 and it is a very water-soluble, white, cubic crystal. The compound is a dietary constituent that in excessive amounts may retard the growth and shorten the lifespan of laboratory animals (Meneely *et al.*, 1953). It should be noted that the acute toxicity dose (LD_{50}) of this traditional, widely and often freely used substance is half (5 g/kg body weight) that of sorbic acid, i.e. it is twice as toxic.

As stated, salt has been used for centuries and it continues to be an approved substance for use in foods. In recent years, however, there is a trend for reduction or elimination of sodium chloride and other sodium-containing substances in food formulations. This trend has arisen from evidence linking dietary sodium intake with development of hypertension in certain sensitive individuals (Sofos, 1984). One proposed method for reduction of sodium chloride amounts used in food processing is its partial replacement with potassium chloride or phosphates (Sofos, 1984, 1986a,b).

A 10% sodium chloride concentration reduces the water activity (a_w) of the system to levels below 0.935, a situation which is inhibitory to all types of *Clostridium botulinum* (Schmidt, 1964). Lower salt levels act synergistically with other preservatives including nitrite, sorbate and benzoate (Sofos, 1984). Due to the reduced a_w, the effects of salt on micro-organisms are related to preservation by drying, in conjunction with which salt is frequently used. Increased salt concentrations result in high osmotic pressures which cause dehydration of the micro-organisms existing in the food. Halophilic bacteria and osmophilic micro-organisms in general, however, are capable of proliferating in the presence of high salt concentrations and if present may result in food spoilage (Tanner, 1944; Walker, 1977). *Listeria monocytogenes* can also survive storage in high sodium chloride concentrations (Papageorgiou & Marth, 1989). Antimicrobial effects of sodium chloride may include dehydration, interference with enzymes and their action, plasmolysis, or cellular toxicity of high sodium or chloride concentrations (Sofos, 1984).

Various micro-organisms exhibit varying tolerances to sodium chloride, with mesophilic Gram-negative rods and psychrotrophic bacteria being the most sensitive, since they tolerate only 4–10% of the compound. Spore-forming and lactic acid-producing bacteria tolerate 4–16% sodium chloride, while halophiles (i.e. salt-loving) need relatively high salt concentrations for growth. The resistance of yeasts and moulds varies, with some species being extremely tolerant to salt (Banwart, 1989).

7.3 Sugars

Sugars (glucose, fructose, sucrose and syrups) are widely used as sweeteners, fermentable materials, flavourings, etc. They are usually highly soluble in water and sweet-tasting. Sucrose ($C_{12}H_{22}O_{11}$) is the most commonly used disaccharide with a molecular weight of 342.30. In recent years sucrose is being replaced in food formulations with high fructose corn syrup solids or non-nutritive sweeteners. In many instances sugars exhibit antimicrobial activity in food systems directly through increased osmotic pressure; through interactions with other components and processing of the food or indirectly by serving as substrates in food fermentations.

A 50% sugar concentration decreases a_w to 0.935, which is inhibitory to growth of *Cl. botulinum*. Increased sugar concentrations result in high osmotic pressures which prevent growth and multiplication of bacteria, since the moisture of the food is being tied up by the sugar, and becomes unavailable to the organism. Direct inhibition of micro-organisms, however, requires high concentrations of sugar. Examples of foods preserved by high sugar concentrations include jellies, preserves, syrups, juice concentrates, condensed milk and a variety of candies (sweets). Bacteria are generally less tolerant to increased osmotic pressure (or reduced a_w) than yeasts and moulds. Certain species of yeast, especially those belonging to the genera *Zygosaccharomyces* and *Torulopsis*, and the mould *Aspergillus glaucus*, are very osmotolerant or saccharophilic. Such organisms may develop and spoil foods even in the presence of high sugar concentrations.

Interactions of sugar with other ingredients or preservatives, and processes such as drying and heating, are of more practical importance in food preservation than using high concentrations of sugar, which is limited to only certain applications. In products where fermentation is important for preservation and flavour development, native or added sugars constitute the substrate for production of acid, alcohol, and other antimicrobial agents, which results in indirect food preservation by sugar (Christiansen *et al.*, 1975; Smith & Palumbo, 1981).

Small concentrations of sugars are necessary for the growth of many spoilage and pathogenic micro-organisms (Hobbs, 1976). In addition, through their osmotic effects, sugars may increase the heat resistance of moulds and other organisms (Doyle & Marth, 1975). Sugar–metal ion complexes, especially iron, may influence bacterial growth and control (Charley *et al.*, 1963; Sams & Carroll, 1966; Tompkin, 1978). Xylitol is not, or is only slowly, fermented by many food-borne micro-organisms, but it may have a unique antimicrobial activity (Makinen & Soderling, 1981).

7.4 Smoke

Smoking of certain products, such as meat and fish, is an ancient practice which is still being used in many places. Smoke from wood, besides contributing to flavour, may have preservative activity through heating and drying and also through the introduction into the product of certain chemical components of smoke (Maga, 1988). Phenolic compounds, formaldehyde, acetic acid and creosote may lower the pH of the smoked product. They are also likely to be active in other ways in preventing spoilage, since they prevent spore formation and control growth of certain micro-organisms (Sink & Hsu, 1977; Maga, 1988). Even though smoking continues to be one of the basic methods of food preservation, its action is mostly a surface phenomenon, since the components do not penetrate deeply into the product (Christiansen *et al.*, 1968; Tatini *et al.*, 1976).

Direct addition of refined liquid smoke flavourings to food products has been increasing in recent years. In addition to their flavouring properties, these preparations offer some advantages over the use of traditional open-fire wood smoking (Hollenbeck, 1979; Sofos & Maga, 1988). Liquid smoke is easier to apply uniformly and the concentrations used can be controlled for uniformity in flavour, colour and preservative action (Eklund *et al.*, 1982). Furthermore, use of liquid smoke minimizes pollution because crude tar production and polycyclic aromatic hydrocarbon carcinogens have been removed (White *et al.*, 1971). Compositional differences in liquid smokes, however, will result in differences in antimicrobial activity depending on the type of wood used to produce the preparations (Boyle *et al.*, 1988; Sofos *et al.*, 1988). Liquid smoke preparations also appear inhibitory to *L. monocytogenes* (Messina *et al.*, 1988).

7.5 Spices

Many spices, seasonings and essential oils are used in food processing, mainly as flavouring ingredients. Some of these flavouring components of processed foods contain substances with bacteriostatic or even bactericidal activity. Many scientific investigations have shown the antimicrobial activity of spices and their essential oils (Shelef, 1984; Deans & Ritchie, 1987). Information on the antimicrobial activity of spices, plant materials and their components can be found in several research publications (Bullerman, 1974; Beuchat, 1976; Huhtanen, 1980; Zaika, 1988), reviews (Shelef, 1984) and books (e.g. Davidson *et al.*, 1983).

The amounts of spices commonly introduced into the food are generally small and antimicrobial action of their components may be synergistic with the total preservative system in the product. Future research on the subject, however, may lead to identification and probably manufacture of new preservatives with regulatory, industrial and consumer acceptance.

7.6 Other

Various other naturally occurring compounds have demonstrated antimicrobial activity and may play key roles in preservation of natural foods (Davidson *et al.*, 1983). Such compounds are found in various foods but especially in milk and eggs. They include lysozyme, lactoperoxidase, lactotransferrin, casein, fatty acids, conalbumin and others. However, very little use has been made of these food components as intentional chemical food preservatives (Banks *et al.*, 1986; Beuchat & Golden, 1989).

The naturally occurring enzyme lysozyme, or muramidase, which is present in many biological systems, including several foods (e.g. milk and egg white), has been suggested as a preservative for other foods and beverages. The maximum antimicrobial activity of lysozyme is at pH 7.0 and it degrades the cell wall of susceptible bacteria, but it is expensive (Hughey & Johnson, 1987; Busta & Foegeding, 1983). Lysis of bacteria occurs through hydrolysis of the beta linkage between muramic acid and glycosamine of the glycopolysaccharides in the bacterial cell wall (Beuchat & Golden, 1989). The enzyme inactivates or prevents growth of *L. monocytogenes* in several foods (Hughey *et al.*, 1989).

Lactoperoxidase occurs in high amounts in milk and other body fluids, and combines with thiocyanate, other halides and with hydrogen peroxide to produce the lactoperoxidase antimicrobial system (Davidson *et al.*, 1983; Reiter & Harnulv, 1984; Beuchat & Golden, 1989). The components of the system occur naturally or are formed through microbial action (i.e. hydrogen peroxide) in milk. The system has been used in some developing countries in the preservation of milk (Medina *et al.*, 1989), and has a potential in preserving infant formulas (Banks & Board, 1985). The system was also inhibitory against the pathogenic bacteria *L. monocytogenes* (Earnshaw & Banks, 1989; Denis & Ramet, 1989), *Campylobacter jejuni* (Borch *et al.*, 1989), and *Salmonella typhimurium* (Earnshaw *et al.*, 1990). It should be noted, however, that the inhibitory activity of the lactoperoxidase system is neutralized by other enzymes (e.g. catalase), heating, reducing agents, and with storage time (Davidson *et al.*, 1983). It has been suggested, however, that this and other natural systems should be developed and applied in food preservation (Banks *et al.*, 1986).

Another system, which is related to the lactoperoxidase system, and which is supposed to be safe and highly antimicrobial, is the so-called glucose oxidase/glucose system. Actually this system acts as a source of hydrogen peroxide, which can be used in the lactoperoxidase system (Dziezak, 1986; Tiina & Sandholm, 1989).

8 ACIDULANTS AND OTHER PRESERVATIVES FORMED IN OR ADDED TO FOODS

8.1 General

Several common and naturally occurring acids and other compounds are added or are formed in foods through fermentation and other microbial processes. In addition to their preservative properties they act as flavouring agents, buffers, synergists to antioxidants, modifiers of certain properties and curing adjuncts (Gardner, 1972). Furthermore, many food preservatives are more active under acidic conditions at low pH values; thus, the acidulants enhance their antimicrobial activity. Moreover, acidic conditions facilitate destruction of micro-organisms by heat, permitting shorter sterilization or processing times, which are less detrimental to the quality of the product. Acidic conditions also prevent or delay spore germination and bacterial growth, and most lipophilic, weak acid preservatives are more effective at lower pH which increases their undissociated portion, the effective form. Inhibition of microbial growth, however, is variable with type of acidulant among other factors (Sorrells *et al.*, 1989).

Acidification is required by law for products such as canned figs, artichokes and several fruits and vegetables in some countries. A pH value of 4.6 or less is still required for the canning of certain foods in order to prevent growth of, or toxin production by, *Cl. botulinum*, even though botulinum toxin may be formed at pH values below 4.6 under certain conditions (Sugiyama & Sofos, 1988). Acidulants are also very important in cases where the lipophilic, weak acid preservatives are added as salts for increased solubility. In products of high pH (>5.5), an acidulant should be included (except for parabens) if no adverse effect on product characteristics and quality is encountered.

In addition to common acids (e.g. lactic, acetic, malic, fumaric, citric, etc.) the antimicrobial activity of ethyl alcohol, hydrogen peroxide and bacteriocins is discussed in this section.

8.2 Lactic acid

Lactic or 2-hydroxypropanoic acid ($CH_3CHOHCOOH$) is the main product of many food fermentations. It is formed by microbial degradation of sugars in products such as cheese, sauerkraut, pickles, olives, and fermented meat products (Daeschel, 1989). The acid produced in such fermentations decreases the pH to levels unfavourable for growth of spoilage organisms such as putrefactive anaerobes and butyric-acid-producing bacteria. Yeasts and moulds that can grow at such pH levels can be controlled by the inclusion of other preservatives such as sorbate and benzoate (Lueck, 1980; Sofos, 1989a).

The main species of bacteria that produce lactic acid belong to the genera *Lactobacillus*, *Lactococcus*, *Leuconostoc* and *Pediococcus*, but some mould species and certain other bacteria are also capable of producing lactic acid. Other end-products produced by lactic-acid bacteria during food fermentations include acetic acid, ethyl alcohol, carbon dioxide, diacetyl, bacteriocins and mannitol. The lactic acid produced by fermentation of added sugars (glucose, sucrose) should decrease the pH to levels sufficient to inhibit *Cl. botulinum* growth and toxin production. This process was allowed in the USA for the production of bacon, where it promotes faster nitrite depletion and botulinal protection due to lower pH levels (United States Department of Agriculture, 1979).

Lactic acid has a pK_a of 3.83, is highly water-soluble, and is usually manufactured by a fermentation process. Being a natural constituent of foods and an end-product of anaerobic hydrolysis, it is one of the oldest food preservatives, and is of low toxicity and non-mutagenic. Thus, it is a GRAS substance, and the FAO has set no limit for the acceptable daily intake of the acid and several of its salts. Sodium, calcium and potassium lactates are also classified as GRAS in the USA. Besides being an acidulant and exhibiting preservative action due to decreased pH, lactic acid may also be used as a flavouring agent in Spanish-type olives and in frozen desserts, or as an emulsifier in leavened bakery products (Gardner, 1972). Some lactic acid derivatives are also employed as direct food acidulants. Glucono-δ-lactone also is a permitted acidulant in certain meat products. This compound, following ring opening to give gluconic acid, functions in a similar manner to added lactic acid.

Lactic acid is also used as a preservative in combination with carbon dioxide, in certain carbonated beverages. Its food-grade DL-form is available as aqueous solutions which are colourless and odourless. It is very soluble in water and its taste is acrid. Lactic acid inhibits bacteria, including spore-formers such as putrefying anaerobes and butyric acid producers (Woolford, 1975; Wong & Chen, 1988). Lactic and acetic acid solutions have been recommended as sprays for decontamination of animal carcasses after slaughter (Smulders *et al.*, 1986; Adams & Hall, 1988). Lactic, as well as citric acid, inhibit formation of mycotoxins, such as aflatoxins and sterigmatocystin (Reiss, 1976), although at certain concentrations, lactic acid stimulates formation of aflatoxin (El-Gazzar *et al.*, 1987). In addition to the acid, sodium lactate is used in poultry meat products in the USA as a flavouring agent and flavour enhancer at levels of 1–3%. The compound also enhances product shelf-life by inhibiting spoilage and pathogenic bacteria (Debevere, 1989; Maas *et al.*, 1989).

8.3 Acetic acid

Acetic (ethanoic) acid (CH_3COOH) is produced through the oxidation of alcohol by bacteria of the genus *Acetobacter* and *Gluconobacter* (Desrosier, 1970). In the form of vinegar (i.e. 4% or more acetic acid) it constitutes one of the oldest preservatives and flavouring agents. Substrates for vinegar production include grapes, cider, wine, a variety of sugars and malt. Generally, two successive bioconversions, the first alcoholic (anaerobic fermentation) and the second acetic (aerobic oxidation) are employed (Jacobs, 1958; Reed, 1982).

Acetic acid is a general preservative inhibiting many species of bacteria, yeasts and to a lesser extent moulds (Ingram *et al.*, 1956; Chichester & Tanner, 1972), and is classified as GRAS in the USA. It is also a product of the lactic-acid fermentation, and its preservative action even at identical pH levels is greater than that of lactic acid. The main applications of vinegar (acetic acid) include products such as mayonnaise, salad dressings, pickles, olives, sauces and ketchup (catsup) (Prescott & Proctor, 1937). The use of propionates has replaced acetic acid as a rope-inhibiting agent in bread.

Besides acetic acid (vinegar), several related compounds (acetates) yield acetic acid and are used in food processing. The selection of the compound is dictated by flavour and economic reasons (Chichester & Tanner, 1972). Acetates (calcium acetate, sodium diacetate) have been reported effective against rope and mould in bread. Sodium diacetate has the advantage of not introducing off-flavours in bread when used as a mould and rope inhibitor. The antimicrobial activity of acetic acid and potassium acetate is reported to increase at lower pH values (pK_a = 4.76) where the amount of the undissociated acid is greater. Peracetic acid ($CH_3 \cdot COOOH$) is an oxidized derivative of acetic acid, and it decomposes to acetic acid and oxygen in the presence of organic substrates. The compound has been recommended as a disinfectant of food contact surfaces.

8.4 Other acidulants

Several other acids, some of which are also natural components of various food products, may be produced or added to foods for reasons mentioned in Section 7.1. Malic, or 1-hydroxy-1,2-ethanedicarboxylic acid ($COOHCH_2CHOHCOOH$) is the predominant natural acid in apples, peaches, cherries, grapes, apricots, bananas, carrots, broccoli, potatoes, peas and rhubarb. It is also found in citrus fruits, figs, tomatoes and beans (Gardner, 1972). In the USA it is a GRAS substance used primarily to acidify and preserve salad dressings, including mayonnaise, fruit preserves, sherbets, jams, jellies and beverages. It has pK_a values of 3.4 and 5.1 and it inhibits bacteria and yeasts (Banwart, 1989).

Citric acid ($COOHCH_2C(OH)(COOH)$-CH_2COOH) is the main acid in citrus fruits and is widely used in carbonated beverages and as an acidifying agent of foods because of its unique flavour properties. It has an unlimited acceptable daily intake, pK_a values of 3.1, 4.8 and 6.4, and is highly soluble in water. The acid and several of its salts are considered GRAS in the USA. The ability of many micro-organisms to metabolize citrate, and its low pK_a values, make it a less effective antimicrobial agent than other acids (Doores, 1983).

Fumaric acid (*trans*-butenedioic, COOHCH: CHCOOH) is of low solubility and has a strong acidic taste (Doores, 1983). It is used in gelatin desserts, pie fillings, biscuit doughs, wines and fruit drinks.

Dehydroacetic acid ($C_8H_8O_4$, pK_a 5.27) inhibits yeasts and moulds more than it does bacteria, and it is effective against secondary fermentations in alcoholic beverages. Sodium dehydroacetate was found to be twice as effective as sodium benzoate at pH 5.0 against *Saccharomyces cerevisiae*, and 25 times more effective against *Penicillium glaucum* and *Aspergillus niger* (Banwart, 1989). In the USA the compound or its sodium salt is approved for use to treat cut or peeled squash, and as a fungistat in cheese wrappers (Doores, 1983).

Formic acid (HCOOH) is a colourless, transparent liquid with a pungent odour and is miscible in water. Its pK_a value is 3.75 and it has an LD_{50} value of 1–2 g/kg body weight (Lueck, 1980). High concentrations may irritate the skin and mucous membranes, but its sodium and potassium salts are of lower acute toxicity. The acid is readily absorbed through the skin, mucous or intestinal membranes, and is a normal constituent of human blood and other tissues involved in transfer of one-carbon substrates. Use of formic acid as a food preservative is permitted in some countries, but not in the UK or the USA. Its antimicrobial activity is more potent against yeasts and to a lesser degree against bacteria.

Tartaric acid ($COOH(CHOH)_2COOH$) is the common acid of grapes and is manufactured from waste products of the wine industry. The compound is a GRAS substance in the USA, and it is used in fruits, jams, jellies, preserves, sherbets and beverages. Cream of tartar (monopotassium tartrate) is used in the baking industry.

Adipic acid ($COOH(CH_2)_4COOH$) is a low solubility, non-hygroscopic acid, useful as an acidulant in dry, powdered food products. Its antimicrobial activity is attributed only to reduced pH. The compound is classified as GRAS in the USA, when used according to good manufacturing practices as a buffering or neutralizing agent (Doores, 1983). Specific food uses include baking powders, powdered fruit beverages, candies, biscuits and gelatin desserts. It may also be used in canned vegetables, as a sequestrant in oils, and to improve the melting characteristics of processed cheeses (Gardner, 1972).

Succinic acid ($COOH(CH_2)_2COOH$) and its anhydride are used mostly as acidulants in bakery products. The compound has pK_a values of 4.2 and 5.6, and is considered GRAS in the USA. Succinic acid has reduced microbial loads on poultry carcasses, but it impairs appearance of the product (Cox *et al.*, 1974).

Caprylic or octanoic acid ($CH_3(CH_2)_6COOH$) has a pK_a value of 4.9, and is used mostly as a mould inhibitor in cheeses or cheese wrappers. The compound is a colourless oil of slight solubility in water, which is GRAS in the USA. It may be used as a flavouring adjuvant in cheese, baked foods, fats, oils, frozen dairy desserts, gelatins, puddings, meat products, snack foods and soft candy (Doores, 1983).

Glutaric acid ($COOH(CH_2)_3COOH$) occurs naturally in foods and has pK_a values of 4.3 and 5.2. The compound has been suggested for use as a food acidulant (Merten & Bachman, 1976).

Salicylic acid (*o*-hydroxybenzoic 2-hydroxybenzoic acid) is a white crystal of 138.12 molecular weight, and a solubility of 0.2% (w/w) in room-temperature water. The compound reacts with proteins and damages microbial cells (Lueck, 1980), but it is toxigenic and is not used as a food preservative. A few countries still permit its use at concentrations of 0.04–0.06%.

Boric acid (H_3BO_3) and borax ($Na_2B_4O_7 \cdot 10H_2O$) are white powders or crystals of 5% (w/v) solubility at room temperature. The pK_a value of boric acid is 9.14, which makes it almost completely undissociated in environments of even neutral pH. Because of their high toxicity the compounds are not permitted for food use in the USA.

Monohalogenacetic acids, which include monochloroacetic and monobromoacetic acid, are not permitted for use in foods, but in the past they were used, along with their esters, to stabilize juices and wines (Lueck, 1980). They are effective inhibitors of bacteria, moulds and especially yeasts (Busta & Foegeding, 1983).

Ascorbic acid ($C_6H_8O_6$) or vitamin C, its isomer isoascorbic or erythorbic acid, and their salts are highly soluble in water and safe to use in foods. The pK_a values are 4.17 and 11.57. At high concentrations (e.g. 0.05%), ascorbate enhances depletion of residual nitrite and reduces nitrosamine formation in cured meats, while at lower concentrations (e.g. 0.02%) it increases the anticlostridial activity of nitrite (Tompkin, 1978, 1983). Ascorbate alone has shown no major antimicrobial activity, although it has inhibited pseudomonads in liquid substrates (Banwart, 1989), and *Cl. botulinum* in cooked potatoes when used in combination with citric acid (Notermans *et al.*, 1985).

The inorganic acids, phosphoric (H_3PO_4) and hydrochloric (HCl) are strong acidulants, causing microbial inhibition due to increased hydrogen ion concentration, and are GRAS in the USA. Of these two GRAS inorganic acids, phosphoric is a common acidulant in carbonated beverages.

8.5 Ethyl alcohol

Ethyl alcohol or ethanol (CH_3CH_2OH) is a colourless liquid of 46.07 molecular weight, which is miscible with water. To be used as a food it is obtained from fermentation of sugar-containing liquid substrates. Consumption of 200–400 ml pure alcohol in a short period of time is hazardous for humans, while levels of 40–80 ml daily over longer periods of time may be tolerable. Use of alcohol for food preservation is not always regulated because the compound is a natural constituent of several food products. In many countries, however, the alcohol content of drinks may not be increased with addition of pure alcohol. In the USA, ethyl alcohol may be used as an antimicrobial agent on pizza crusts prior to final baking at levels not to exceed 2% (Busta & Foegeding, 1983).

Alcohol acts on micro-organisms through non-specific denaturation of proteins in the protoplast, when used at concentrations of 60–80%. Concentrations of 5–20% alcohol may have some inhibitory effect on micro-organisms due to reduction of water activity in the food (Shapero *et al.*, 1978). The non-specific protein denaturation of alcohol affects all types of micro-organisms, with the exception of bacterial spores, which are more resistant than vegetative cells. Products containing natural or added alcohol include wines, liquors, beers, other alcoholic beverages, flavour extracts and some intermediate moisture food products.

8.6 Hydrogen peroxide

Hydrogen peroxide or hydrogen dioxide (H_2O_2) is a water-miscible, colourless liquid of 34.01 molecular weight, and it is formed through hydrolysis of peroxides such as peroxidisulphuric acid. Concentrations of more than 30% are caustic, and it decomposes to oxygen and water in the presence of organic matter and metal ions, without being a toxicological hazard. It is useful as an oxidizing or bleaching agent.

The compound is approved for use as a food preservative in several countries, since when used in adequate amounts it inactivates micro-organisms (Stevenson & Shafer, 1983). Its antimicrobial activity is dependent on concentration, level of contamination, pH, temperature, and exposure time (Smith & Brown, 1980). The activity of hydrogen peroxide is more pronounced against bacteria than against yeasts or moulds. Aerobic, spore-forming and Gram-negative bacteria, however, are more resistant than *Staph. aureus* or clostridia (Walker & Harmon, 1965; Toledo *et al.*, 1973; El-Gendy *et al.*, 1980).

The antimicrobial activity of hydrogen peroxide is due to its intense oxidizing properties, but its effect is brief since it decomposes rapidly when exposed to organic matter. Uses of hydrogen peroxide include treatment of milk with 0.05% for manufacture of certain cheeses, and addition to egg whites for pasteurization at lower temperatures. Excess of the compound after treatment is inactivated by heat or by addition of catalase, which catalyses its conversion to water and oxygen. Other approved uses in the USA include starch, dried eggs, tripe, herring, wine, instant tea, etc. Hydrogen peroxide also inhibits microbial spoilage in fish marinades, and it can be used to decontaminate packaging materials for aseptic processing of juices and other foods. Care should be taken, however, to avoid oxidized flavours, bleached colours and loss of sensitive nutrients such as vitamin C.

Hydrogen peroxide is also produced and accumulates during growth of lactobacilli, which lack catalase, and inhibit other bacteria (Daeschel, 1989). In addition, hydrogen peroxide may react with other components to form microbial inhibitors such as the lactoperoxidase system. Growth of lactobacilli in milk produces hydrogen peroxide which reacts with thiocyanate with lactoperoxidase activity as the catalyst. The intermediary oxidation products formed inhibit micro-organisms (Banks *et al.*, 1986).

8.7 Bacteriocins

Bacteriocins are proteins or protein complexes with potent bactericidal activity (Daeschel, 1989). They are produced by a large and diverse assortment of Gram-positive and Gram-negative bacteria. Collectively, bacteriocins are a heterogeneous group of compounds with differing antibacterial activity, mode of action, and chemical properties relative to the bacteria which produce them. The most widely studied bacteriocins are the colicins derived from *Escherichia coli*. The lactic acid-producing bacteria also form bacteriocins, which became the subject of extensive investigation in the 1980s. Species of lactic acid bacteria recognized as producing bacteriocins include *Lactobacillus fermentum, L. helveticus, L. acidophilus, L. plantarum, Lactococcus lactis, Pediococcus acidilactici* and *P. pentosaceus* (Klaenhammer, 1988; Daeschel, 1989).

In general, bacteriocins have become popular subjects of investigation because they present the opportunity to preserve foods through natural means (Montville, 1989; Gombas, 1989; Hansen *et al.*, 1989). They can be present in foods subjected to fermentation or through growth of spoilage micro-organisms. Being proteins they are susceptible to digestive enzymes; thus, they are considered safe. Their susceptibility to enzymes and in most instances to heat, however, may limit their use to applications after thermal processing and denaturation of enzymes in foods. Among the micro-organisms inhibited by certain bacteriocins, several reports have included the fatal pathogen *L. monocytogenes* (Harris *et al.*, 1989; Spelhaug & Harlander, 1989). A common bacteriocin, which is permitted for use as a food preservative in several countries, is nisin.

Group N streptococci produce nisin, diplococcin and several other bacteriocins (Klaenhammer, 1988). The nisin family of polypeptides contains a high concentration of sulphur-containing amino acids, and the unique amino acids lanthionine, dehydroalanine, and β-methyl lanthanine (Hurst, 1981). Nisin is sensitive to α-chymotrypsin, but it is resistant to pronase and trypsin at 100°C for 10 min in acidic environments. Its stability to heat increases at higher pH values.

Nisin may be present naturally in milk and fermented dairy products, and it is permitted for use in foods in many countries, including the USA, UK, France, Finland, Belgium, Italy and India. Its main use is in the preservation of dairy products and especially processed cheeses. Amounts permitted or used in foods are in the range 100–500 mg/kg. The United States Food and Drug Administration has affirmed nisin preparation as a GRAS substance for use in pasteurized cheese spreads. The toxicity of nisin is low (Shtenberg & Ignat'ev, 1970), but it is not used in animal or human medicine.

Nisin is exclusively effective against Gram-positive bacteria, while yeasts and moulds are not inhibited, and some may even degrade the compound. Its activity is greater against bacterial spores than against vegetative cells, and it may even inhibit spore germination (Gupta *et al.*, 1972). It is usually used in combination with heat because it enhances bacterial spore sensitivity to heat and inhibition of outgrowth of surviving spores. Bacteria inhibited by nisin include species of *Bacillus* and *Clostridium* and *L. monocytogenes* (Daeschel, 1989).

In processed cheeses where nisin finds its major application it inhibits butyric acid bacteria and clostridia (Somers & Taylor, 1987). Another potential use is in canned products where, through its sensitizing effect, it may reduce the intensity of heat treatments needed to inactivate bacterial spores. Nisin has also been tested as an alternative to nitrite for inhibition of *Cl. botulinum* in meat products. Its activity, however, was variable and depended on factors such as pH and properties of the substrate (Rayman *et al.*, 1981, 1983; Scott & Taylor, 1981a,b; Taylor *et al.*, 1985).

Subtilin is one of the longest-known polypeptide bacteriocins. It is produced by *Bacillus subtilis*. Its water-solubility is low and it is not permitted for use in foods or in medicine in the USA. It is of low toxicity since it is decomposed by digestive enzymes (Andersen & Michener, 1950), and like nisin it is resistant to heat treatments commonly used in food processing. The compound is effective against Gram-positive bacteria, including clostridia and thermophiles, as well as against some Gram-negative bacteria (Banwart, 1989). Depending on the concentration used it may act as a bacteriostatic or a bactericidal agent. Its stability to heat and activity against clostridial spores should make it useful in reducing the intensity of thermal processes used in canned foods (Chichester & Tanner, 1972).

Additional bacteriocins produced by species and strains of lactic acid bacteria were identified in the 1980s and include lactocin and helviticin (*L. helveticus*), lactacin B and F (*L. acidophilus*), plantaricin A (*L. plantarum*), Las 5 and diplococcin (*S. cremoris*), and pediocins (*P. acidilactici* and *P. pentosaceous*) (Klaenhammer, 1988; Daeschel, 1989).

8.8 Other

Diacetyl ($C_4H_6O_2$; 2,3-butanedione) is chemically synthesized from methyl ethyl ketone, and is approved for use as a food flavouring and adjuvant in the USA. The compound is also synthesized biologically by heterofermentative lactic acid bacteria, providing the buttery odour or flavour in certain fermented dairy products (Daeschel, 1989). Diacetyl is also found in wine, brandy and coffee. As an antimicrobial agent, diacetyl was found to inhibit yeasts, Gram-negative and non-lactic Gram-positive bacteria. The compound was inactive against lactics and clostridia (Jay, 1982). However, in combination with reduced thermal processes it is effective at inactivating or inhibiting germinating bacterial spores (Tatini, 1989). Although it is a GRAS compound, its usefulness as a food preservative is questionable because of its flavour and the relatively large amounts needed for inhibition. It may also be useful as a sanitizer of equipment.

Another biologically derived antimicrobial, identified in the 1980s, is named reuterin, and it is believed to be a low molecular weight non-protein, which is highly soluble, and pH neutral. Reuterin is produced by the heterofermentative *Lactobacillus reuterii*, and it appears to be a broad-spectrum antimicrobial acting against certain Gram-negative and Gram-positive bacteria, yeasts, moulds and protozoa, including pathogens (Daeschel, 1989). Additional studies are needed on the efficacy, safety and formation before reuterin is approved for use as a food preservative.

9 COMMONLY USED LIPOPHILIC ACID FOOD PRESERVATIVES

9.1 General

Organic lipophilic acids, such as benzoic, propionic and sorbic acids, are among the most common compounds used in food preservation. Some of these weak acids are found in natural food products, e.g. benzoic acid in cranberries and sorbic acid in rowanberries (Lueck, 1976, 1980; Sofos, 1989a). The antimicrobial activity of lipophilic acids increases with chain length, but solubility restrictions limit their use to those of shorter chain length and greater solubility (benzoic, propionic, sorbic). Organic acids of chain length greater than C_{10} or C_{11} are very effective against pathogenic bacteria (Roth & Halvorson, 1952) but their potential use is restricted because of their low solubility.

The antimicrobial efficacy of these acids is optimal in an acidic environment since their pK_a values are generally between pH 3 and 5 (Sauer, 1977). At lower pH values the amount of undissociated acid is greater, and this is believed to be the major contributor (Eklund, 1980) to antimicrobial activity (see also Chapter 2). In foods of higher pH, the lipophilic acid preservatives may be used in combination with an acidulant, if feasible. In general, their application is limited to foods with pH values of less than 6.0 or 5.5. The esters of *p*-hydroxybenzoic acid (parabens) have a pK_a value of 8.5 permitting their use in foods with pH values around neutrality.

It is believed that the protonated (i.e. undissociated, uncharged) acid diffuses through the cell membranes into the cytoplasm where it dissociates under the neutral pH of the cell interior. Inhibition of growth is then believed to be due to acidification of the cytoplasm. The dissociated acid, however, has also shown antimicrobial activity (Eklund, 1980, 1983, 1985; Sofos, 1989a; Doores, 1983). Prior exposure to sub-inhibitory levels may increase resistance of yeasts, moulds and bacteria to these preservatives (Sofos, 1989a; Warth, 1977, 1985; Goodson & Rowbury, 1989).

Besides chain length, the antimicrobial activity of lipophilic acids increases with the degree of unsaturation and the *cis*-isomers are more effective than the *trans*-isomers (Kodicek, 1956). However, as mentioned previously, the better solubility, lower toxicity and more acceptable taste of short-chain lipophilic acids are major reasons contributing to their selection as antimicrobial agents.

9.2 Benzoic acid

Benzoic (phenylformic or benzenecarboxylic) acid (C_6H_5COOH), in the form of its sodium salt, constitutes one of the most common chemical food preservatives. It is a white granular or crystalline powder with a sweet or somewhat astringent taste. The solubility of benzoic acid in water is low (0.35 g in 100 ml) but increases with a rise in temperature. The widely used sodium salt, sodium benzoate, a white powder or flake, has an increased solubility in water (50 g in 100 ml) and in alcohol (1.3 g in 100 ml), but is insoluble in ether (Chichester & Tanner, 1972; Kimble, 1977), in other organic non-polar solvents, and in lipids.

Sodium benzoate has a molecular weight of 144.11 and a pK_a of 4.2. The maximum pH for antimicrobial activity is 4.5, while it is most effective in the pH range 2.5–4.0 (Cruess & Richert, 1929). At pH values above 4.5 its antimicrobial activity diminishes (at pH 6.0 its activity is 100 times less than at 4.0) and the introduction of an acidulant or other preservative should be considered.

Benzoic acid is more toxic to rats than is sorbic acid, but man apparently has a high tolerance. Benzoate does not accumulate in the human body since it is conjugated with glycine or gluconic acid to produce hippuric acid or benzoyl glucuronide which are excreted (Deuel *et al.*, 1954b; Chichester & Tanner, 1972). Benzoyl CoA is an intermediate in the detoxification process formed at the expense of ATP. Benzoate is not mutagenic in *Salmonella* or *Drosophila*, but it may interact with nucleosides and DNA *in vitro* (Njagi & Gopalan, 1980). In the USA, benzoic acid and sodium benzoate are GRAS substances. In other countries they are more widely used in foods than in the USA (Chichester & Tanner, 1972).

Sodium benzoate is the form used most widely in food preservation, due to its higher solubility in water. It is a common preservative in acid or acidified foods such as carbonated and still beverages, fruit juices, salad cream, syrups, jams and jellies, margarine, sauerkraut, pickles, olives, relishes, pie fillings, preserves, fish, mincemeat and fruit cocktails. It is used at concentrations ranging from 0.03% to 0.10% in the USA, and it is a natural component in many berries, cinnamon, ripe cloves, plums and prunes (Chipley, 1983).

Yeasts are inhibited by benzoate to a greater extent than are moulds and bacteria. Osmotolerant yeasts, however, may be resistant to benzoate and limit the shelf-life of intermediate-moisture foods (Jermini & Schmidt-Lorenz, 1987; Warth, 1977, 1985, 1988, 1989). Such yeast species include *Zygosaccharomyces bailii*, which can become resistant to benzoate, as well as sorbate, through an inducible, energy-requiring system which transports the compound out of the cell. Food-poisoning bacteria and spore-formers are inhibited by 0.01–0.02% undissociated benzoic acid, while spoilage bacteria show higher resistance. Benzoate also inhibits *L. monocytogenes* (El-Shenawy & Marth, 1988a). As with other lipophilic acids the antimicrobial activity of benzoate is due to its undissociated molecule. There is evidence that benzoate inhibits in part nutrient uptake through acidification of the cytoplasm (Eklund, 1980), and it interferes with enzymatic activity (Bosund, 1962; Chipley, 1983).

Benzoate is probably the dominant and most widely used food preservative, and its low cost is one of its advantages. In cases where it introduces a noticeable flavour to products such as beverages, a lower level of benzoate in combination with another preservative (sorbate, parabens) may be considered (Jermini & Schmidt-Lorenz, 1987). To avoid product discoloration due to benzoate, sulphurous acid may be introduced to retard oxidative changes. In such cases, however, sedimentation may increase, since both compounds influence the colloidal balance of juices (Kimble, 1977). Besides direct addition to the product, other means of application such as dipping of product and coating of packaging films have been suggested for benzoate, especially in the preservation of fish (Dunn, 1947).

9.3 Propionic acid

Propionic acid (CH_3CH_2COOH) is an aliphatic, monocarboxylic acid, and is the next higher homologue from acetic acid. Characteristically, it is produced during the manufacture of Swiss-type cheeses. The micro-organisms responsible for its production belong to the genus *Propionibacterium*. Propionic acid has a strong odour, and usually the sodium and calcium salts are used as food preservatives because the acid itself is somewhat corrosive. The sodium salt is more water-soluble than the calcium salt, their solubilities at 100°C being 150 and 55.8 g per 100 ml water, respectively. The salts are white, free-flowing powders with a slightly cheese-like flavour. In Swiss cheese, where as much as 1% propionic acid may be produced, the preservative contributes to the flavour of the cheese and retards mould growth. The *Propionibacterium* also produces gas which forms the characteristic 'eyes' (cavities) of Swiss cheese.

The main application of propionates is in the baking industry, where they are used to suppress the growth of bacteria (*Bacillus mesentericus*) causing ropiness in bread and the growth of moulds in bread and cakes (O'Leary & Kralovec, 1941;

Cathcart, 1951; Matz, 1960; Seiler, 1964). Bakery products in which propionates are used as preservatives include breads, fruit cakes, cheesecake, chocolate cake, pie fillings and pie crusts. Other applications are the control of surface mould growth on cheese, fruits, vegetables, tobacco and malt extract (Olson & Macy, 1945; Jacobs, 1947; Ingram *et al.*, 1956; Chichester & Tanner, 1972; Gardner, 1972). Propionate inhibits microbial growth through interference with nutrient transport functions (Eklund, 1980), and inhibition of enzymes. Calcium propionate appears to be more inhibitory to aflatoxin formation than to mould growth (Lueck, 1980). Propionic acid was also more effective than acetic acid against *Aspergillus parasiticus* (Rusul *et al.*, 1987) and it inhibited *L. monocytogenes* at pH 5.0 (El-Shenawy & Marth, 1989).

The effectiveness of propionates in controlling mould growth is generally greater than that of sodium benzoate, but the propionates have minimal activity against yeasts. Actually, many yeasts metabolize propionate, which makes it useful in the preservation of yeast-leavened bakery products since it does not interfere with the fermentation. Propionates also have marginal effectiveness against bacteria, excluding *B. mesentericus* where they show unique effectiveness. As with other lipophilic acids, their effect increases at lower pH levels since their pK_a value is 4.9 (Cruess & Richert, 1929; Cruess & Irish, 1932; Olson & Macy, 1945). Their optimum pH level is around 5.0 and in some foods they can be used at pH values up to 6.0. The type and amount of propionate to be employed depends upon the product and its acidity (Chichester & Tanner, 1972; Kimble, 1977). Propionate is considered safe to use since it is metabolized like any fatty acid, and levels as high as 0.38% may be used in food applications (Chichester & Tanner, 1972). Propionic acid and its calcium and sodium salts are considered to be GRAS substances in the USA.

Both the calcium and sodium salts mix well with emulsifying agents and the basic dough ingredients. However, calcium propionate is preferred in yeast-raised bread as a means of calcium enrichment, while the sodium salt is better in cakes since calcium ions may interfere with chemical leavening. As a mould inhibitor, in addition to being directly added to the product, propionate may also be applied to wrappers and packages.

9.4 Sorbic acid

Sorbic acid is a straight-chain, *trans–trans*-unsaturated fatty acid, 2,4-hexadienoic acid, of the following chemical formula: $CH_3—CH{=}CH—CH{=}CH—COOH$. It was first discovered by A. W. Hoffman, from the reaction of rowanberry oil with strong alkali. Its chemical structure was determined between 1870 and 1890 and it was first synthesised in 1900 (Lueck, 1976, 1980). Details on sorbate food preservatives can be found in a book by Sofos (1989a).

The carboxylic group of sorbic acid reacts similarly to other carboxylic groups and it yields sorbate salts and esters which in dry form are remarkably stable to oxidation. Aqueous solutions, however, are relatively unstable and degrade by first-order reaction kinetics (Sofos, 1989a). Because of their high aqueous solubility, salts of sorbic acid, especially potassium sorbate, are important food preservatives. The acid, which is more soluble in lipid materials than in water, is a white, crystalline powder with a weak acrid odour and acid taste. Its solubility is better in alcohol and in anhydrous acetic acid than in water. The water-solubility of sorbic acid is only 0.16% w/v at 20°C, but it increases with temperature and in buffered solutions with pH values above 4.4. Solubility, stability, uptake, diffusion and partition of sorbate in foods are important processes which affect its antimicrobial activity (Sofos, 1989a).

Potassium sorbate, a white, fluffy powder, is very soluble in water (over 50%) and when added to acidic foods it is hydrolysed to the acid form. Sodium and calcium sorbates also have preservative activities, but their application is limited compared to that for the potassium salt, which is employed because of its stability, general ease of preparation and water-solubility.

Sorbic acid is generally considered non-toxic and is metabolized, as are the longer chain fatty acids (Deuel *et al.*, 1954a,b), by β- and ω-oxidation. Among other common food preservatives the WHO has set the highest acceptable daily intake (25 mg/kg body weight) for sorbic acid (Lueck,

1980). The LD_{50} for sorbic acid is 7–11 g/kg body weight, while that for sodium sorbate is 6–7 g. High levels of sorbic acid (>1%) may irritate mucous membranes of highly sensitive individuals, but no mutagenic, teratogenic or carcinogenic effects have been observed in laboratory animals when used at reasonable levels. A report on potential allergenic reactions from consumption of sorbate-treated bacon in the USA has not been confirmed (Sofos, 1989a).

Sorbic acid and its salts are practically tasteless and odourless in foods, when used at reasonable levels (< 0.3%), and their antimicrobial activity is generally adequate. They were first recommended as preservatives by Gooding (1945) and their application has expanded to include a variety of products.

In the USA sorbates are classified as GRAS, at maximum permissible levels in various foods of 0.05–0.3%. Like all other lipophilic acid preservatives, sorbate is more effective in its undissociated form. Since its pK_a value is 4.76, the activity is higher at lower pH values (Gooding *et al.*, 1955; Bell *et al.*, 1959). The maximum pH for sorbate activity is 6.0–6.5, while that for propionate is 5.0 and for benzoate 4.5 (see also Chapter 2). These higher pH levels for sorbate activity, compared to other preservatives, extend its use to foods with higher pH values. It can sometimes replace benzoate, partially or totally, in order to avoid possible off-odour and extend the range of micro-organisms inhibited. Even at low pH levels (2.5–4.0) sorbate has a broader spectrum of activity compared to that of benzoate and propionate (Smith & Rollin, 1954; Gooding *et al.*, 1955; Sofos & Busta, 1981, 1983).

Sorbic acid and its salts inhibit growth of yeasts and moulds and many bacteria. Their effect against bacteria, however, is not as comprehensive as that against yeasts and moulds, but it was found to inhibit several pathogens, including *Cl. botulinum* (Sofos, 1989a), *L. monocytogenes* (El-Shenawy & Marth, 1988b), and *Yersinia enterocolitica* (Tsay & Chou, 1989). Sorbic acid is used to inhibit yeasts in situations such as cucumber fermentations where it allows growth of the catalase-negative, lactic-acid-producing bacteria (Phillips & Mundt, 1950; Jones & Harper, 1952; Costilow *et al.*, 1956, 1957).

Sorbates are used for mould and yeast inhibition in a variety of foods including cheese products, baked goods, fruits and vegetables, wines, soft drinks, fruit juices, pickles, sauerkraut, syrups, jellies, jams, preserves, salad cream, margarine and certain meat and fish products.

Evidence exists that some strains of moulds, bacteria and yeasts are more resistant or can metabolize sorbic acid (Melnick *et al.*, 1954; Troller, 1965; Warth, 1977, 1985; Sofos, 1989a). Since high concentrations of contamination of certain micro-organisms may degrade sorbate, and result in product defects, it should be expected to preserve products only when manufactured under sanitary conditions. It should not be considered as being a replacement for good manufacturing practices. This, of course, applies to all chemical food preservatives. Under certain conditions, mycotoxin formation by certain moulds has been enhanced in the presence of sorbate (Liewen & Marth, 1985; Sofos, 1989a).

Sorbate may be added directly to the product or to the food surface by dipping, spraying, dusting or by impregnating the wrappers and packaging materials. The method of application is determined by the form of sorbate used, the objective of the application and the food product to be preserved. There are certain exceptions to the application of sorbate. Since it is an effective yeast inhibitor, it may cause problems if it is used in yeast-raised bakery products. No such problem exists, however, when sorbate is used to preserve chemically leavened or unleavened items. Alternatives that may be used in yeast-leavened products include use of reduced sorbate levels, increased level of yeast inoculum, extension of fermentation time, application of sorbate sprays after baking, or use of slow-releasing sorbate preparations (Sofos, 1989a).

After the extensive research on sorbate in the 1950s, a new wave of investigations was initiated in the 1970s in an effort to expand its applications. Sorbic acid and potassium sorbate were found effective against *Staph. aureus* in bacon; *Pseudomonas putrefaciens*, *Ps. fluorescens*, *Aspergillus parasiticus* and *Penicillium commune* on laboratory media; *Vibrio parahaemolyticus* in fish; yeasts and moulds in hams; *Salmonella* spp. in fresh poultry; and *Bacillus* spp. in the rice filling of Karelain pastry

(Raevuori, 1976; Robach, 1978, 1979; Robach & Hickey, 1978; Robach & Ivey, 1978; Bullerman, 1979; Kemp *et al.*, 1979; Pierson *et al.*, 1979). Other workers found that it extended the shelf-life of poultry parts and fish sausage (Amano *et al.*, 1968; Wada *et al.*, 1975; Cunningham, 1979). In general, several studies found that sorbate inhibited spoilage and pathogenic bacteria in various types of meat and poultry products (Robach & Sofos, 1982; Sofos, 1989a).

Sorbate was examined extensively as a preservative of meat products after a report showed that potassium sorbate delayed toxin production by *Cl. botulinum* in an uncured sausage product (Tompkin *et al.*, 1974). Earlier reports had indicated that not only was sorbic acid ineffective against clostridia, but also that it could be used as a selective agent for such organisms (Emard & Vaughn, 1952; York & Vaughn, 1954, 1955; Hansen & Appleman, 1955). The above conclusions were probably the result of the low solubility of sorbic acid in aqueous media and the pH levels at which the studies were performed. Consequently, the observation by Tompkin *et al.* (1974) of activity against clostridia stimulated additional research.

The need for elimination or reduction of nitrite in cured meat products due to concern over potential carcinoginic properties and the necessity to find a replacement with antibotulinal activity, coupled with the promising results of the Tompkin report, stimulated the new-found interest in sorbate as an antibotulinal agent. The lack of new preservatives, the drawbacks of the existing ones and the properties of sorbate contributed to the expansion of the research beyond cured meats to other microbial species and food products. These studies on sorbate as an antibotulinal agent in meat products, either by itself or with low nitrite levels (40–80 parts/10^6), demonstrated effectiveness in meat products such as wieners, bacon and comminuted pork (Ivey & Robach, 1978; Ivey *et al.*, 1978; Sofos *et al.*, 1979a,b,c,d, 1980a,b). However, the use of sorbate as a direct additive to all meat products in the USA was not permitted.

Reports of mutagenic effects due to possible nitrite–sorbate reactions have not been verified in realistic food systems (Kada, 1974; Hayatsu *et al.*, 1975; Namiki & Kada, 1975; Sofos, 1981, 1989a). The only approved use in meats in the USA, to date, is the dipping of casings for dry sausages to prevent growth of surface moulds.

Several studies have reported on synergistic antimicrobial effects and interactions of sorbate with salt, sugar and other compounds, as well as processing and storage conditions (Gooding *et al.*, 1955; Robach, 1979; Restaino *et al.*, 1982; Beuchat, 1981a,b,c, 1982; Roland & Beuchat, 1984; Sofos, 1985, 1989a). Taking advantage of such interactions should be useful in minimizing levels of additives and processes in order to enhance product shelf-life while maintaining sensory quality. Antimicrobial effects of sorbate derivatives have also been described; sorbohydroxamic acid, sorbic aldehyde and other derivatives are more effective than sorbic acid over a wider pH range against several micro-organisms (Dudman, 1963; Troller & Olsen, 1967; Sofos, 1989a).

Sorbic acid retards bacterial spore germination (loss of heat resistance) in comminuted meat systems and culture media (Sofos *et al.*, 1979b,d, 1986). The action of sorbate on bacterial spore germination appears to occur during the connecting reactions which follow triggering or initiation in the germination process. This inhibitory effect appears to involve spore membranes or protease enzymes involved in germination (Sofos *et al.*, 1986). Inhibition of metabolic function in vegetative cells has been associated with alterations in membranes in the morphological structure of the cells, and inhibition of cell transport processes and enzymes (Sofos, 1989a). It is likely that more than one mechanism of inhibition may be involved under various conditions.

10 ESTERS USED AS FOOD PRESERVATIVES

10.1 General

In addition to acids and their salts, esters of various acids have been proposed, tested or are in use as chemical preservatives in foods. Esters with antimicrobial activity include those of *para*hydroxybenzoic acid, maleic acid, dicarbonic acid and sucrose fatty acid esters.

10.2 Esters of *para*-hydroxybenzoic acid

The methyl, ethyl, propyl, butyl and heptyl esters of *p*-hydroxybenzoic acid ($C_6H_4(OH)COOH$), also known as parabens, parasepts, or PHB esters, find use as preservatives in pharmaceutical, cosmetic, and food products (Chapter 15). They are generally white, free-flowing powders. They have properties similar to those of benzoic acid, but the chemical modification improves their usefulness. Their water-solubility decreases as the number of carbon atoms in the ester group increases, whereas their solubility in ethanol, propylene glycol and oil increases with increasing numbers of carbon atoms in the ester group (Chichester & Tanner, 1972). The water-solubility of the methyl ester is 0.25% (w/w) at 25°C. The methyl and propyl esters are GRAS in the USA and they can be used in food preservation at an upper total limit of 0.1%. Heptyl paraben is also approved to inhibit microbiological spoilage in malt beverages (up to 12 parts/10^6) and non-carbonated soft drinks (up to 20 parts/10^6) in the USA. The ethyl and butyl esters are also approved for certain uses in other countries. The toxicity of parabens is low with an acute toxicity dose (LD_{50}) ranging from 180 to over 8000 mg/kg body weight depending on the form and method of administration (Matthews *et al.*, 1956; Chichester & Tanner, 1972; Lueck, 1980). The acceptable average daily intake is set at 10 mg/kg body weight.

Parabens inhibit or prevent the growth of a variety of yeasts, moulds and bacteria. They are more effective against yeasts and moulds than against bacteria, especially Gram-negative bacteria (Ingram *et al.*, 1964; Davidson, 1983). They may be used as preservatives in baked goods (except yeast-leavened products), fruit products, jams, jellies, preserves, pickles, olives, syrups, beverages, creams and pastes (Neidig & Burrell, 1944; von Schelhorn, 1951; Jermini & Schmidt-Lorenz, 1987). Products in which parabens have been tested experimentally include meats, margarine, soy sauce, maple syrup, beer and butter (Frank & Willits, 1961). In meat products in the USA they may be used as mould inhibitors by dipping the casings of dry sausages in a 3.5% solution. They were also proposed as antibotulinal agents in a five-compound patent suggested as an alternative to nitrite in the USA (Sweet, 1975). However, they appear to be ineffective against *Cl. botulinum* in meat (Deibel, 1979), while Robach & Pierson (1978) found the methyl and propyl esters to be very effective antibotulinal agents in laboratory media. Their antimicrobial activity has been demonstrated against a variety of species including *E. coli, Staph. aureus, B. subtilis, Salmonella typhi, L. monocytogenes, Sacch. cerevisiae, Rhizopus nigrificans, A. niger*, etc. (Fung *et al.*, 1985; Payne *et al.*, 1989). Propyl paraben, at 0.03–0.05%, inhibited *Sal. typhimurium* and *Staph. aureus* (Pierson *et al.*, 1980). Inhibition of nutrient transport appears to be the primary mode of antimicrobial action by parabens (Eklund, 1980), as demonstrated with *E. coli, Ps. aeruginosa* and *B. subtilis*. Parabens have also inhibited bacterial spore germination (Parker, 1969), as well as respiration (Shiralkar & Rege, 1978), protease secretion (Venugopal *et al.*, 1984), and synthesis of DNA, RNA and protein (Nes & Eklund, 1983).

An advantage of parabens over other chemical food preservatives is their high pK_a value (8.5) which extends their spectrum of activity to foods with pH values near neutrality. Their antimicrobial activity increases with the number of carbon atoms in the ester group while the activity of branched-chain esters is low (Huppert, 1957; Dymicky & Huhtanen, 1979). Since solubility decreases with chain length, the lower esters are more often used in practice. However, a more common procedure is a combination of the methyl and propyl esters to include both good antimicrobial activity and solubility. In slightly acid foods, and where problems of flavour may arise, parabens can be combined with benzoate, which also is less expensive. In many cases, benzoate is preferred to parabens since yeasts and moulds can grow at acidic pH values where benzoate is more effective. Thus, the main application of parabens is at higher pH values (above 6.8 or 7.0) where the other preservatives are ineffective.

10.3 Other esters

Di- or poly-carbonic acid esters (R_1O—CO—O—CO—OR_2), include diethyl and dimethyl esters. The diethyl ester of dicarbonic acid is known as diethyl pyrocarbonate (DEDC or DEPC), while the dimethyl ester is known as dimethyl dicarbonic acid (DMDC). The compounds have been reviewed by Ough (1983a). DMDC has a molecular weight of 134.1, and its water-solubility is 3.65%. DEDC (molecular weight 162.1) is of lower water-solubility (0.6%), while both are miscible with ethanol. Both compounds are colourless liquids with faint fruity odours. In water solutions DMDC and DEDC hydrolyse to methanol and ethanol, respectively, and carbon dioxide. Hydrolysis is faster for DMDC than DEDC and proceeds more rapidly in acidic conditions.

DEDC and DMDC are both fungicidal for yeasts, as well as bactericidal. Activity against moulds is expressed in the presence of concentrations higher than those needed for yeasts and bacteria (Ough, 1983a). The antimicrobial activity is more potent at higher temperatures and pH values below 4.0 (Chichester & Tanner, 1972). The antimicrobial activity of these esters is due to their interaction with microbial enzyme nucleophilic groups (Genth, 1964; Ough, 1983a).

The dicarbonates should decompose in foods before consumption; therefore the safety of their reaction products may be of more concern than the original compounds. DEDC and DMDC, however, irritate the skin and mucous membranes and thus eye contact should be avoided. Details on toxicology and safety of the dicarbonic acid esters are presented by Ough (1983a).

DEDC has been used as a yeast inhibitor in wines, non-carbonated beverages, fruit juices, fermented malt beverages and beer. The compound acts as a sterilant, so the product should be maintained free of subsequent contamination. Potential toxicity of products of their hydrolysis and decomposition, such as methanol and ethyl carbonate, has resulted in banning most of their uses in the USA and other countries. DMDC is still permitted in the USA as an inhibitor of yeasts in wines at levels of up to 0.02%. The FAO/WHO Expert Committee on Food Additives has recommended that human daily intake of ethyl carbonate, a carcinogen resulting from reaction of ammonia with DEDC, should not exceed 10 μg/day.

Esters of fumaric (*trans*-butenedioic) acid, such as monomethyl fumarate (methyl fumarate) and dimethyl fumarate, have exhibited inhibitory activity against fungi and *Cl. botulinum* (Huhtanen *et al.*, 1981). At levels of 0.15–0.2% these compounds were suggested as alternatives to nitrite in preservation of bacon (Doores, 1983). In addition, the *n*-mono-alkyl maleates and fumarates esterified with C_{13} to C_{18} alcohols have exhibited antimicrobial activity (Dymicky *et al.*, 1987).

Sucrose fatty acid esters are approved emulsifiers in the USA derived from sucrose esterified with a mixture of palmitic and stearic acids. There is evidence that these esters in combination with sorbate or propionate may provide added antimycotic activity at pH levels higher than the optimum for either inhibitor alone (Sofos, 1989a). The compounds have also inhibited heat-damaged as well as unheated bacteria spores (Tsuchido *et al.*, 1983). Also some aliphatic esters of phenylalanine have been reported as bacterial and mould inhibitors in foods and beverages at levels as low as 0.005% (Kiritaguchi *et al.*, 1973).

Monoglycerides of lauric acid are known as monolaurin or lauricidin, classified as GRAS emulsifiers in the USA. Monolaurin has shown antimicrobial activity against psychrotrophic as well as spore-forming and pathogenic bacteria (e.g. *Clostridium sporogenes, Cl. botulinum, Cl. perfringens* and *Staph. aureus*), moulds and osmophilic yeasts (Kabara, 1981, 1983, 1984). The compound has been proposed as a component of multicompound antimicrobial systems in foods (Kabara, 1981).

11 GASEOUS CHEMICAL FOOD PRESERVATIVES

11.1 General

Several gases or vapours are used in food processing either as antimicrobial agents, or for other purposes exhibiting indirect antimicrobial activity. Gases such as carbon dioxide, sulphur dioxide, epoxides and chlorine have been used commercially as antimicrobial food preservatives or water disinfectants. Nitrogen and oxygen, frequently used in packaging of food products, have no direct adverse effect on micro-organisms and are not considered as chemical food preservatives. Nitrogen can be used as a cryogenic agent, or inert gas in controlled atmosphere storage, and may indirectly affect some micro-organisms, especially through elimination of oxygen (Huffman, 1974). Oxygen levels may be reduced in storage of fruits, vegetables and meat, mainly for physiological reasons (Clark & Lentz, 1973). Other biocidal gases mostly used in medicine will not be included in this discussion, neither will carbon monoxide and acetaldehyde, also shown to possess potential food preservative action (Clark *et al.*, 1976).

11.2 Sulphur dioxide and sulphites

Sulphur dioxide (SO_2) has been used for many centuries as a fumigant and especially as a wine preservative (Amerine & Joslyn, 1951; Joslyn & Braverman, 1954; Hammond & Carr, 1976; Banks *et al.*, 1987). It is a colourless, suffocating, pungent-smelling, non-flammable gas and is very soluble in cold water (85 g in 100 ml at 25°C) and in organic solvents. Sulphur dioxide and the various sulphites dissolve in water, and at low pH levels yield sulphurous acid, bisulphite and sulphite ions. The various sulphite salts contain 50–68% active sulphur dioxide. A pH-dependent equilibrium is formed in water and the proportion of SO_2 ions increases with decreasing pH values. At pH values less than 4.0 the antimicrobial activity reaches its maximum (Wyss, 1948). Sulphur dioxide is used as a gas or in the form of its sulphite, bisulphite and metabisulphite salts, which are powders. The gaseous form is produced either by burning sulphur or by its release from the compressed, liquefied form. The sulphites, including sodium sulphite, sodium hydrogen sulphite, sodium metabisulphite, potassium metabisulphite and calcium sulphite, are easier to handle and use than the gas or liquid forms of SO_2.

Metabisulphites are more stable to oxidation than bisulphites, which in turn show greater stability than sulphites. They are GRAS substances in the USA, but levels of application in wines are restricted to 350 mg/l by the Bureau of Alcohol, Tobacco and Firearms. Sulphites are not permitted or recommended for preservation of foods considered as important sources of vitamin B_1 (thiamine), because they destroy this nutrient.

Consumption of sulphur dioxide and sulphites does not result in their accumulation in the body because they are rapidly oxidized to sulphate and excreted in the urine. The LD_{50} values of various sulphiting agents for different animals vary from 40 to 2000 mg/kg in equivalent amounts of SO_2 (Ough, 1983b). Sulphites are not mutagenic, while SO_2 has shown mutagenic effects in bacterial tests (Mukai *et al.*, 1970; Hayatsu & Miura, 1970). Sulphites have also been linked to triggering of asthma attacks and other acute responses in a small number of susceptible individuals. This has led to a decreased use of the compounds in foods, special labelling requirements (e.g. salads, wines), and concerns about foods with no ingredient labels, such as vegetable salads treated with sulphites in restaurants to prevent browning (Walker, 1985; Institute of Food Technologists, 1986).

The antimicrobial action of sulphur dioxide against yeasts, moulds and bacteria is selective, with some species being more resistant than others (Clark & Takacs, 1980). In water, SO_2 forms sulphurous acid (H_2SO_3) with pK_a values of 1.8 and 7.2. These forms are more inhibitory to microbial growth than sulphite ions. Thus, it is not surprising that the undissociated acid was 1000 times more effective than sulphite and bisulphite ions against *E. coli*, 100–500 times more effective against yeasts (*Sacch. cerevisiae*), and 100 times more effective against moulds (*A. niger*) (Cruess & Irish, 1932; Joslyn & Braverman, 1954; Ingram *et al.*, 1956). Antimicrobial activity is influenced by pH, concentration, SO_2 binding, and duration of contact.

Due to its high reactivity, SO_2 can interact with various cell components and produce lethal or inhibitory effects. Cell components interacting with SO_2 include thiol groups in proteins, enzymes, vitamins, cofactors, nucleotides, nucleic acids and lipids (Woodzinski *et al.*, 1978; Clark & Takacs, 1980; Lueck, 1980; Ough, 1983b). Acting on proteins, SO_2 cleaves disulphide bonds, changing the conformation of enzymes and their active sites. In addition, SO_2 inhibits enzymes by binding enzyme intermediates or end-products, which upsets the equilibrium of various reactions. Causing lipid peroxidation, SO_2 may interfere with membrane functions.

Sulphur dioxide and sulphites are used in the

preservation of a variety of food products. In addition to wine these include dehydrated fruits and vegetables, fruit juices, acid pickles, salads, syrups, and meat and fish products in certain countries. In fruits they control the growth of moulds such as *Botrytis* and *Cladosporium* in order to extend the processing period of products such as grapes, cherries and other berry fruits. In fruit juices they prevent undesirable fermentations during processing and storage. When used in excessive amounts, however, sulphites induce off-flavours and product discoloration. In wine-making, sulphites are added to the expressed juice (must) of grapes to destroy the naturally occurring undesirable flora before the desirable fermentative yeasts are added (Amerine & Joslyn, 1951; Joslyn & Braverman, 1954). The condition of the grapes, type of wine, pH, sugar concentration and contamination determine the amount (50–100 parts/10^6) of sulphite to be used in wine-making (Amerine & Joslyn, 1951). In wine preservation, sulphite is also important for cleaning the equipment; it prevents undesirable changes and bacterial spoilage during storage; and it may serve as an antioxidant and clarifying agent.

Sulphites are not permitted for use in fresh and processed meats in the USA. However, they are used as sausage preservatives in the UK, as dried fish and shrimp preservatives in France, and were shown to delay *Cl. botulinum* growth and toxin production in meat (Tompkin *et al.*, 1980). They are also used to prevent 'black spot', a discoloration caused by oxidation, in shrimp in the USA. The reason that they are prohibited from meats in the USA is that they destroy thiamine, and may restore the colour of old meat, which could be misleading to the consumer. Their use in fresh sausage in the UK is to delay the growth of yeasts, moulds and Gram-negative mesophilic bacteria. This is associated with the fact that sulphites favour the development of acid-producing bacteria (*Lactobacillus* spp. and *Microbacterium thermosphactum*), especially under refrigerated storage (Dyett & Shelley, 1966). Studies showing inhibition of proteolytic breakdown in meat have been reported by Block & Bevis (1963), Block & Taylor (1964) and Pearson (1970). The most commonly used form in sausage is sodium metabisulphite at a maximum concentration of 450 parts/10^6 as SO_2. In addition to its antimicrobial effects, sulphur dioxide is added to foods for its antioxidant and reducing properties, and to prevent enzymatic and non-enzymatic browning reactions.

11.3 Carbon dioxide

Carbon dioxide (CO_2) is a colourless, odourless, non-combustible gas, acidic in odour and flavour. In commercial practice it is sold as a liquid under pressure (58 kg per cm^2) or solidified as dry ice. The gas is readily soluble in water (171 ml per 100 ml at 0°C) and in the liquid phase of foods where carbonic acid is formed. Lung exposure in humans to atmospheres of more than 10% CO_2 causes unconsciousness. Amounts of 30–60% (v) CO_2 in the presence of 20% (v) oxygen cause rapid death to animals (Lueck, 1980). Inhalation of lower concentrations over long periods of time may also be dangerous. The compound, however, is virtually not subject to food law regulations. The antimicrobial activity of carbon dioxide is dependent on concentration, the micro-organisms under consideration, their stage during growth, the a_w of the system, and the temperature of storage. Depending on these factors, CO_2 may have no effect, may have a stimulatory effect, may inhibit growth, or may be lethal to micro-organisms (King & Nagel, 1967; Parekh & Solberg, 1970; Foegeding & Busta, 1983c). Low concentrations of CO_2 may stimulate microbial growth, but concentrations of 100% have killed species of *Bacillus, Aerobacter, Flavobacterium* and *Micrococcus*, while species of *Proteus, Lactobacillus* and *Cl. perfringens* were only inhibited (Ogilvy & Ayres, 1951, 1953; Parekh & Solberg, 1970). Carbon dioxide at atmospheric pressure inhibited spore germination of *Bacillus cereus* spores, but enhanced germination of clostridia (Enfors & Molin, 1978). Concentrations of CO_2, of 10 and 25 atmospheres, however, inhibited germination of *Cl. sporogenes* and *Cl. perfringens*, respectively. Generally, CO_2 concentrations of 5–50% are inhibitory to most yeasts, moulds and bacteria (Hales, 1962; Smith, 1963). High CO_2 concentrations increase the lag phase and generation time of micro-organisms (Tomkins, 1932). However, increasing concentrations do not increase activity indefinitely. From a concentration of 5 to about 25–50%, inhibitory action increases almost linearly, but at higher concentrations activity increases only slightly or not at all (Ogilvy & Ayres, 1951, 1953; Clark & Lentz, 1969, 1973). With decreasing temperatures both CO_2 solubility and antimicrobial activity increase (Golding, 1945).

Carbon dioxide is used as a solid (dry ice) in many countries as a means of low-temperature storage and transportation of food products. Besides keeping the temperature low, as it sublimes, the gaseous CO_2 inhibits growth of psychrotrophic micro-organisms and prevents spoilage of the food. Foods in which CO_2 controls psychrotrophic spoilage include meats and meat products, poultry, eggs, fish and fruits and vegetables. Although the inhibitory activity of CO_2 against psychrotrophic organisms is well accepted, it is, in fact, variable among groups, genera and species. Moulds are generally most sensitive while yeasts (fermentative) are more resistant, and Gram-positive bacteria are more resistant than Gram-negative types (Tomkins, 1932; Ogilvy & Ayres, 1953). Among bacteria, meat spoilage organisms such as pseudomonads, micrococci and bacilli are very sensitive to CO_2, while acid-producing organisms (lactobacilli) are generally resistant (Ogilvy & Ayres, 1953; King & Nagel, 1975; Gill & Tan, 1979).

Gaseous CO_2 is used as a direct additive in the storage of fruits and vegetables, meats and beverages. In vacuum-packaged meats, CO_2 inhibits the growth of aerobic spoilage organisms while the growth of lactobacilli is encouraged. Handling of meat in this fashion has been a very important innovation in meat storage and transportation. A concentration of 10–20% CO_2 is usually common in the controlled/modified-atmosphere storage of fresh meats. Higher concentrations may cause undesirable odours and the increase in antimicrobial activity is only marginal (Clark & Lentz, 1969; Silliker *et al.*, 1977).

In the controlled/modified-atmosphere storage of fruits and vegetables, the correct combination of O_2 and CO_2 delays respiration and ripening as well as retarding mould and yeast growth. The final result is an extended storage of the products for transportation and for consumption during the off-season. The amount of CO_2 (5–10%) is determined by factors such as nature of product, variety, climate and extent of storage (von Schelhorn, 1951; Smith, 1963).

Use of increased CO_2 levels in modified atmosphere storage of foods has been increasing because the appropriate gaseous composition minimizes chemical and biological product decomposition (Finne, 1982; Rowe, 1988; Baker & Genigeorgis, 1990). One major safety concern with products preserved under modified atmosphere storage is whether pathogens will outgrow spoilage organisms and render the product unsafe for human consumption before any visible signs of spoilage (Ito & Bee, 1980; Genigeorgis, 1985; Post *et al.*, 1985; Garcia *et al.*, 1987; Hintlian & Hotchkiss, 1987). This concern is especially valid for seafood stored under modified atmospheres which may allow production of toxin by non-proteolytic, psychrotrophic strains of *Cl. botulinum*.

Carbon dioxide finds a major application in carbonated soft drinks and mineral waters. It serves a dual purpose, having both an antimicrobial and an effervescing effect. Levels of 3–5 atm of CO_2 are common since they strongly inhibit or destroy spoilage and pathogenic micro-organisms. The antimicrobial action of CO_2 in carbonated beverages increases with CO_2 pressure and decreases with sugar content (Insalata, 1952). The presence of CO_2, along with exclusion of oxygen, prevents oxidative deterioration in beer and ale. The inhibitory effect of CO_2 is a direct antimicrobial action as well as an indirect effect due to a decrease in pH caused by carbonic acid formation from CO_2 (Koser & Skinner, 1922; Hays *et al.*, 1959). Another application of CO_2 is the preservation of eggs during refrigerated storage with a concentration of 2.5% CO_2. During World War II it was used extensively in the preservation of vegetables such as carrots, and it has been shown to increase the shelf-life of milk.

11.4 Epoxides

Ethylene (C_2H_4O) and propylene (C_3H_6O) oxides are organic epoxides or cyclic ethers possessing antimicrobial properties. In their molecule an oxygen atom is linked to two adjacent carbon atoms of the same chain. Ethylene oxide (Chapters 2 and 20) is a colourless, non-corrosive gas at ambient temperatures, which liquefies at 10.8°C, and freezes at −111.3°C. It is highly reactive and as a liquid it is miscible in water and organic solvents. It is flammable, and at concentrations of more than 700 parts/10^6 the gas form has an ether-like odour. Low concentrations (3%) of ethylene oxide are explosive in air and this constitutes a drawback in its handling and application. Mixtures of 10–20% ethylene oxide with 80–90% carbon dioxide are non-flammable and are recommended for use. Mixtures of ethylene oxide and fluorinated hydrocarbons or methyl formate have also been available for commercial application. Ethylene oxide does not lose its antimicrobial activity in such mixtures, which are commonly used as sterilizing agents (Mayr & Suhr, 1972). Ethylene oxide at 0.1–0.2 g per litre of air may be fatal to humans (Lueck, 1980). Concentrations higher than 100 mg/kg result in lung and eye irritations and may cause nausea and mental disorientation.

Propylene oxide has similar properties to ethylene oxide but it is less volatile and its antimicrobial activity is lower. It is a flammable, colourless gas that liquefies at 34.5°C and freezes at −110°C. It is less reactive and less penetrating than ethylene oxide and has a narrower explosive range (2–22%). The toxicity of propylene oxide has been reported to be only one-third that of ethylene oxide (Bruch, 1961).

Ethylene oxide gas penetrates most organic materials without causing any damage. This is advantageous since it can be used for sterilization of sensitive materials. Its breakdown products include glycol and ethylene chlorohydrin (Bruch, 1972; Wesley *et al.*, 1965). The epoxides are removed from the food by evacuating the chamber accompanied by agitation and gentle heating. The remaining glycols are considered as generally non-toxic, and thus epoxides are allowed for use in certain food products.

The epoxides are antimicrobial in both aqueous and gaseous phases (Marletta & Stumbo, 1970). Ethylene oxide is the simplest and the most widely used epoxide. As a gas it has been used widely to decontaminate several dried-food products. Such products include dried fruits, corn starch, potato flour, corn, wheat, barley, dried eggs, gelatin, gums and cereals (Whelton *et al.*, 1946; Pappas & Hall, 1952; Mayr & Kaemmerer, 1959; Bruch & Koesterer, 1961). Questions about the safety of ethylene chlorohydrin, a product of ethylene oxide hydrolysis, have limited the application of ethylene oxide in recent years only to spices. The regulatory authorities of the USA have set a gas residue limit in spices of only 50 parts/10^6, and other countries have similar rules and requirements. Approval of irradiation treatments to disinfect spices in the USA was aimed at reducing dependence on epoxides for such applications. Besides potential toxicity, the use of ethylene oxide is also restricted because of its adverse effect on the stability of essential vitamins and amino acids (Windmueller *et al.*, 1959). Breakdown of propylene oxide yields propylene glycol, which is a harmless and widely used humectant. In many countries propylene oxide is not allowed for use in food products, but in others, such as the USA, it has in many respects replaced ethylene oxide. In the USA propylene oxide may be used to control micro-organisms and insects in products such as cocoa, spices, starch, nuts and gums. Such application is allowed only in products that are going to be further processed, and a residue limit of 300 parts/10^6 has been set.

Both epoxides, ethylene and propylene, have been widely used for equipment sterilization, and they have both been reported to kill a variety of yeasts, moulds, bacteria and viruses (Whelton *et al.*, 1946; Phillips & Kaye, 1949; Pappas & Hall, 1952; see also Chapter 20).

Ethylene oxide is most effective against yeasts and moulds, while vegetative cells and spores of bacteria are less susceptible. The antimicrobial action is a function of time, concentration, temperature, relative humidity and penetration of the gas through the treated material. Propylene oxide is less active as a sterilizing agent and less penetrating than ethylene oxide. Generally, the same factors that affect ethylene oxide activity are also important in propylene oxide application (Skinner & Hugo, 1976). However, propylene oxide concentrations (800–2000 mg/l) double those for ethylene oxide are necessary for similar sterilization effects (Bruch, 1961). Both epoxides are alkylating agents and their sterilizing effect is believed to be related to this property (Winarno & Stumbo, 1971; Chapter 2).

11.5 Ozone

Ozone (O_3) is a water-soluble, unstable, blue gas, which has a pungent, characteristic odour, and occurs freely in nature. Maximum amounts tolerated by humans are 0.04 mg/kg, while concentrations of 0.1 mg/kg are objectionable because they cause eye, nose, throat and mucous membrane irritation. Ozone is produced commercially by passing electrical discharges or ionizing radiation through air or oxygen (Nagy, 1959). When exposed to air and water it decomposes rapidly and forms oxygen. Thus, it is usually generated at the point of its use.

Yeasts and moulds are not as sensitive to ozone as are bacteria, while bacterial spores are more resistant than vegetative cells (Foegeding, 1985). Of bacteria, Gram-negative species are less sensitive than Gram-positives. Lethal effects from ozone are due to its strong oxidizing activity, which may affect sulphydryl groups of enzymes and cell wall lipids. This may result in loss of enzymatic activity and leakage of vital cell components. The antimicrobial activity of ozone is affected by pH, stage of microbial growth, temperature, relative humidity, and organic matter present in the substrate (Clark & Takacs, 1980).

Applications of ozone in various countries have included sterilization and removal of off-odours, flavours and colours from water. In the USA, ozone is approved as an antimicrobial for bottled water. In addition, it is used as a maturing agent in wines and ciders, and to sterilize beverage containers (Torricelli, 1959). Ozone can also preserve eggs and other foods, and it inactivates mycotoxins.

11.6 Chlorine

The various forms of chlorine (see Chapter 2) constitute the most widely used chemical sanitizer in the food industry. These chlorine forms include chlorine (Cl_2), sodium hypochlorite (NaOCl), calcium hypochlorite ($Ca(OCl)_2$), and chlorine dioxide (ClO_2) gas. These compounds are used as water adjuncts in processes such as product washing, transport, and cooling of heat-sterilized cans; in sanitizing solutions for equipment surfaces; and in washing treatments to reduce microbial loads on the surface of meat, poultry, and seafood (Cords, 1983). Elemental chlorine is highly corrosive, causes severe inflammation of the skin and mucous membranes, and inhalation of air with more than 20 parts/10^6 chlorine for 15 min may be fatal (Lueck, 1980).

Owing to its strong penetrating ability and oxidizing effect, adequate chlorine concentrations result in rapid inactivation of micro-organisms. It has been reported that chlorine disrupts bacterial spore coats damaging germination mechanisms, prevents outgrowth of germinated spores, and causes leakage of spore contents (Foegeding, 1983; Foegeding & Busta, 1983a,b). Since chlorine is highly reactive, depending on concentration, its antimicrobial activity is reduced or eliminated in the presence of organic matter. The antimicrobial activity of chlorine is higher at neutral or slightly acidic pH values, where the active form (HOCl) is present in higher concentrations. Heat also increases the antimicrobial activity of chlorine, which is active against all types of micro-organisms, including *L. monocytogenes* (El-Kest & Marth, 1988a,b,c). Important applications of chlorine and its compounds include disinfection of drinking water and sanitation of food processing equipment.

12 NITRITE AND NITRATE

Nitrite (NO_2^-) or nitrate (NO_3^-) sodium and potassium salts have been used in meat processing for many centuries. Their use started accidentally from their presence as impurities of common salt (NaCl) that was used to preserve meats in ancient times (Binkerd & Kolari, 1975; Sofos *et al.*, 1979c). Desert salts and salts from coastal areas contain nitrates of potassium and calcium which are products of nitrifying bacteria. Potassium nitrate is known as saltpetre or nitre; calcium nitrate from caves (wall saltpetre) was used by ancient people in the curing of meat (Binkerd & Kolari, 1975). Observations that these nitrate impurities caused a reddening effect on meat led to the regular use of nitrate in meat curing in order to achieve uniform colour. At the end of the 19th century it was shown that nitrite, and not nitrate, was responsible for cured-meat colour fixation through reaction with the haem proteins, haemoglobin and myoglobin.

At the beginning of the 20th century the use of nitrite in meat curing was officially permitted in the USA and other countries, and its functions were defined.

Nitrite added to meat or fish products possesses both chemical and antimicrobial properties. As mentioned above, it reacts with haem proteins to fix the characteristic cured meat colour, and this constitutes the original reason for nitrite addition to meat products. Other nitrite functions include a not very well-defined effect on the flavour of cured meat products, a mild antioxidant effect that prevents rancidity and 'warmed-over' flavour in such products and finally an antimicrobial effect, especially against *Cl. botulinum*. During this century, nitrite and nitrate salts (especially sodium or potassium) have been regularly used in meat processing in many countries. Experience and research have demonstrated the above properties, and regulatory authorities have approved their use in meat-curing mixtures. Nitrate is not believed to have a direct effect on the above properties; it functions only as a source of nitrite (Binkerd & Kolari, 1975; Christiansen *et al.*, 1973, 1974), and most of its uses have been discontinued. The good safety record against botulism of commercially processed cured meat products is believed to be related to nitrite addition (Silliker *et al.*, 1958; Silliker, 1959; Ingram, 1974; Roberts, 1975; Sofos *et al.*, 1979c; Sofos & Busta, 1980). Other factors (heat processing, product pH and composition, microbial contamination, refrigeration, NaCl concentration), however, are also important. Besides meats, nitrite and nitrate are sometimes used in fish and cheese processing.

In general, concentrations of more than 100 parts/10^6 are necessary for botulinal control. It has been indicated, however, that lower nitrite concentrations (40–80 parts/10^6) may be sufficient for antimicrobial activity when sorbate (Ivey & Robach, 1978; Ivey *et al.*, 1978; Sofos *et al.*, 1979a,b,c,d, 1980a,b; Sofos, 1989a), or sugar and a starter culture (Tanaka *et al.*, 1980, 1985) are included in the formulations. The antimicrobial effects of nitrite were observed early in its regular use against several bacterial genera (*Achromobacter, Aerobacter, Escherichia, Flavobacterium, Micrococcus,* and *Pseudomonas*) (Tarr, 1941a,b, 1942). The most important antimicrobial action of nitrite, however, is against *Cl. botulinum*, which produces highly potent neurotoxins, and its value as an insurance factor contributing to the botulinal safety of cured meat products has been demonstrated in a number of studies (Sofos *et al.*, 1979c; Sofos & Busta, 1980). Presence of nitrite in a meat system, however, does not inhibit botulinal outgrowth indefinitely. The safety of the product is the result of interactions among the variety of factors mentioned above. Among these factors, nitrite is a very important one since it has a direct antibotulinal effect and it also interacts with most of the other factors. The eventual result is an extended botulinal-safety of the product (Silliker, 1959; Roberts, 1975; Sofos *et al.*, 1979c; Roberts *et al.*, 1981; Robinson *et al.*, 1982).

The effect of nitrite is not the same against all genera and species of micro-organisms. Some bacteria (salmonellae, lactobacilli, bacilli, *Cl. perfringens*) are more resistant to nitrite than *Cl. botulinum* (Castellani & Niven, 1955; Grever, 1974). Studies have indicated that *L. monocytogenes* appears to be relatively resistant to inhibition by nitrite (Buchanan *et al.*, 1989; Junttila *et al.*, 1989). Increased nitrite concentrations, however, may eliminate such resistance. Inhibitory effects of nitrite have been demonstrated against *Staph. aureus, Cl. perfringens*, salmonellae, and total spoilage flora in culture media and meat products (Gough & Alford, 1965; Buchanan & Solberg, 1972; Bayne & Michener, 1975; Riha & Solberg, 1975a,b; Sauter *et al.*, 1977). These nitrite effects are generally greater under vacuum packaging than aerobic conditions (Barber & Deibel, 1972; Herring, 1973; Labots, 1977). However, the major application of nitrite as a chemical food preservative is that of an antibotulinal agent in cured meat products.

A vast amount of research has demonstrated the chemical and antimicrobial activities of nitrite. When added to meat, it is involved in a variety of chemical reactions (Cassens *et al.*, 1979). The rate of these reactions is affected by product pH, temperature, composition and microbial contamination, and influences the depletion of the compound. As the pH of the environment decreases, nitrite depletion is increased through increased production of nitrous acid and nitric oxide, which constitute the reactive forms of nitrite. Nitrite concentrations (15–50 parts/10^6) lower than those for antimicrobial activity are necessary for chemical effects (colour, flavour).

No precise mechanism of antimicrobial activity by nitrite has been presented, but several theories have been proposed. Tompkin (1983) presented a chronological review of research which has contributed to our understanding of the antimicrobial activity of nitrite. Possible explanations of the antimicrobial activity of nitrite (Sugiyama & Sofos, 1988) include reactions of nitrite with food components and formation of antibotulinal compound(s), such as the Perigo factor(s) (Benedict, 1980; National Research Council, 1981, 1982). This, however, is considered as unimportant because it forms at higher temperatures (e.g. >105°C) and loses its activity in presence of meat particles. Other possible explanations are based on the premise that nitrite or its derivatives nitrous acid and nitric oxide act directly on the organism and/or restrict the availability to the organism of an essential nutrient (Vahabzadeh *et al.*, 1983; Kim *et al.*, 1987; Sugiyama & Sofos, 1988).

During the past decade a series of reports has demonstrated the occurrence of carcinogenic *N*-nitroso compounds (nitrosamines) in some cured meat products (e.g. bacon) when cooked under certain conditions (e.g. >171°C). More than 65 nitrosamines have been reported as being carcinogenic (Magee & Barnes, 1967). Excellent reviews on nitrosamine formation, their importance and occurrence in meat products as well as other foods are given by Sebranek & Cassens (1973), Crosby & Sawyer (1976) and Gray & Randall (1979). Nitrosamine incidence and level of occurrence in meat products have decreased in recent years through research and product control, and in the USA the appropriate authorities have set maximum levels of acceptance monitored by strict regulations.

The effects of minute amounts of nitrosamines on human health, and their importance relative to higher concentrations of nitrate, nitrite and nitrosamines from other food sources (e.g. vegetables) are unknown. The importance of nitrite in botulism control, as well as the extremely deleterious effects of botulinal toxins, have caused regulatory authorities to be cautious on the subject. No major changes in nitrite regulations have been imposed and a compromise solution balancing botulism and nitrosamine risks and benefits may prevail. Such a compromise might be a reduction of ingoing nitrite levels coupled with simultaneous inclusion of other preservatives or an increase in levels of existing product components (e.g. salt).

In 1979, nitrite itself was implicated as being a direct carcinogen in laboratory animals. Newberne (1979) published results, which remain unconfirmed, indicating increased carcinogenicity with nitrite consumption. Ignoring the nitrosamine–nitrite–carcinogenicity controversy, nitrite used under existing regulations is not considered a health hazard. At high concentrations, however, nitrite is toxic, with a lethal dose of 300–500 mg/kg of body weight. Since it oxidizes haemoglobin to methaemoglobin at these high intakes, the condition of methaemoglobinemia occurs, which can result in death due to oxygen shortage. The nitrite issue has caused an extensive debate among scientists, consumers, producers and regulatory authorities in several countries, especially in the USA, but the debate has subsided in recent years. The acceptable daily intake of nitrite set by the FAO is 0–0.2 mg/kg. The subject of nitrite in foods has been summarized in an overview paper published by the Institute of Food Technologists (1987).

Of the various compounds and process modifications tested as alternatives to nitrite in cured meat products during the 1970s and early 1980s, only the use of a starter culture (e.g. *Pediococcus acidilactici*) along with sugar and 80 mg/kg nitrite was permitted by the United States Department of Agriculture for use in bacon. This product is organoleptically acceptable and gives rise to substantially fewer nitrosamines when fried. Furthermore, if the bacon is temperature-abused, the starter culture grows and produces lactic acid from the added sugar, which reduces the pH and inhibits *Cl. botulinum* (Tanaka *et al.*, 1985).

13 ANTIBIOTICS

13.1 General

Antibiotics were frequently tested and used in food preservation in the 1950s and 1960s but in recent years their application has been either restricted or prohibited. Marth (1966) gave an excellent review of the literature on antibiotics published during that period. Other reviews on the subject have been presented by Fukusumi (1972) and Katz (1983). In the USA, on 6 September 1967, the FDA prohibited such use and introduced specifications to eliminate residues in food products carried over from treated animals. Their main uses included preservation of meat, poultry, fish, milk and its products, fresh fruits and vegetables and canned foods.

The major reason that the use of antibiotics in food preservation was restricted or prohibited was the development and discovery of antibiotic-resistant strains of micro-organisms in certain instances. Microbial resistance to antibiotics is the result of genetic mutation or of selection of existing resistant organisms. If antibiotic-resistant strains of micro-organisms colonize the digestive tract of man and animals, the antibiotics used in medicine may then become ineffective. Continuous use of antibiotics as food preservatives meant that micro-organisms were exposed to sub-lethal doses of these drugs, and development of resistant strains might also result in loss of their value in food preservation.

The discovery of antibiotic-resistant micro-organisms caused concern over the use of antibiotics as growth stimulators in farm animals (Levy, 1987). In the late 1950s it was discovered that sensitive bacteria can acquire resistance to various unrelated groups of antibiotics by plasmid-mediated transfer (Watanabe, 1963) of resistance genes from resistant bacteria. Transferable resistance can take place not only between members of the same species but also among different species (Hahn, 1976; see also Chapters 10B, F). The transfer of R factors from non-pathogenic to pathogenic bacteria may result in the failure of antibiotics to act as therapeutic agents in humans. In the UK the Swann Committee (Anon, 1969), and in the USA the FDA Task Force (Anon, 1972), reported that the use of antibiotics in farm animals may result in the development of antibiotic-resistant bacteria which could be transferred from animals to humans. In order to avoid such undesirable consequences the use of antibiotics in farm animals should be restricted to those which do not show cross-resistance with therapeutically important antibiotics.

Following these discoveries the use of antibiotics came under attack, and they were prohibited or restricted in most countries. The only antibiotic still remaining in some use as a food preservative in certain countries is the dyene macrolide natamycin (pimaracin).

The primary use of antibiotics was to extend the refrigerated storage stability of fresh meat, poultry and fish (Goldberg, 1964). The main antibiotics used for the above purpose were oxytetracycline and chlortetracycline. These tetracycline-type antibiotics have the advantage of inhibiting both Gram-positive and Gram-negative bacteria. In general, however, antibiotics are of selective antimicrobial activity, and they differ from common chemical food preservatives in that their activity is not always pH-dependent, and that they demonstrate much higher activities than common preservatives applied at similar concentrations (Chichester & Tanner, 1972). Another potential use of antibiotics in food preservation is to reduce the intensity of thermal processing requirements for canned foods.

The presence of antibiotics in foods today is generally due to their use in animal feeds at sub-therapeutic levels to improve efficiency of production and reduce costs (Franco *et al.*, 1990). The presence of antibiotic residues in foods such as milk and meat is not permitted in the USA and other countries. The subject, however, has become controversial and has led to trade restrictions among various countries.

13.2 Tetracyclines

Two tetracycline antibiotics which have been used as food preservatives are oxytetracycline (Terramycin) and chlortetracycline (Aureomycin). Their basic structure consists of a four-membered (tetracaine) ring with characteristically distributed polar side groups. They are weakly basic, poorly soluble in water (Kurytowicz, 1976), and stable to temperatures up to boiling.

Low concentrations of the compounds are broad-spectrum bacteriostatic agents, while higher concentrations become lethal. Tetracyclines inhibit binding of aminoacyl tRNA to the acceptor site on the 30S ribosomal subunit. The lethal action of high concentrations may be due to linkage with Mg^{++} in ribosomes. The result of these reactions is inhibition of protein synthesis and interference with enzymatic cellular activity (Fey & Kersten, 1972; Franklin & Snow, 1989).

Tetracyclines were used to extend the shelf-life of fresh meat, poultry and fish (Michener *et al.*, 1959; Goldberg, 1964). Common applications included immersing fresh poultry or fish in tetracycline solutions of 3–100 mg/kg for 0.6–2 h, followed by refrigerated or ice storage (Kohler *et al.*, 1955; Lee *et al.*, 1967; Boyd & Southcott, 1968).

13.3 Natamycin

Natamycin or pimaricin is a metabolic product of *Streptococcus natalensis*, which is active as an antifungal agent against yeasts and mycotoxin-producing moulds. The compound is a dyene macrolide ($C_{33}H_{47}NO_{13}$) which forms white crystalline needles and is of low solubility (0.005%) in water and alcohol. Macrolides are characterized by a large lactone ring which is glycosidically linked to rare sugars. It is, however, highly soluble in acetic acid, glycol and glycerol (Clark *et al.*, 1964; Lueck, 1980). Its LD_{50} is 0.45–4.7 mg/kg body weight, depending on animal species (Levinskas *et al.*, 1966).

Although it is active against yeasts and moulds, natamycin is inactive against bacteria, viruses and actinomycetes. In addition, some moulds, such as *A. flavus*, inactivate the compound with enzymes they produce. This, of course, is a problem only when the antibiotic is applied to foods after mould growth is initiated. Inhibition depends on concentration (Rusul & Marth, 1988b), and it appears to be due to interaction with cell membranes which results in loss of cellular components (Lueck, 1980).

Natamycin has been used as a surface treatment in cheese, and such use has also been proposed for sausage products to inhibit growth of mycotoxin-producing moulds (Bullerman, 1977; Holley, 1981). It has also been used as an antifungal agent in fruits, juices and poultry. Methods of application include direct mixing into the food, spraying, dusting, dipping, or through treatment of the packaging material. The FAO acceptable daily intake for natamycin is 0.3 mg/kg body weight. Its use is permitted in certain western European countries as a preservative of cheese, but not in the UK and Germany. In the USA, natamycin may be applied to the surface of cheese cuts and slices to inhibit moulds. The procedure of application involves dipping or spraying with solutions of 0.02–0.03%.

13.4 Tylosin

Another macrolide antibiotic is tylosin, which is produced by *Streptomyces fradiac*. Its water-solubility is low and it is not permitted for use in foods in the USA. The LD_{50} was reported to be 12 g/kg body weight (Shibasaki, 1970). Tylosin is effective against Gram-positive bacteria, including clostridia, and its antimicrobial spectrum is greater than that of bacteriocins such as nisin and subtilin (Poole & Malin, 1964; Suzuki *et al.*, 1970). The compound is more heat-stable than nisin and has been tested in canned foods as an adjuvant to thermal processing (Denny *et al.*, 1961). Tylosin has prevented toxin production by *Cl. botulinum* in smoked fish (Segmiller *et al.*, 1965).

14 INDIRECT CHEMICAL FOOD PRESERVATIVES

14.1 General

Chemical substances added to foods with the objective of inhibiting microbial growth for extension of product shelf-life and assurance of consumer safety from pathogenic micro-organisms may be classified as direct chemical foods preservatives. In contrast, indirect chemical food preservatives may be called the chemical additives added to foods as processing aids or to improve chemical and sensory qualities, but which may also contribute to inhibition of microbial growth. Such indirect chemical food preservatives are phenolic antioxidants, phosphates, and ethylenediamine tetraacetic acid.

14.2 Phenolic antioxidants

Derivatives of phenol have been known as antiseptic agents for a long time (Hugo, 1979; Davidson,

1983). Some phenolic compounds approved for use in foods include the parabens, which are used as antimicrobials, and phenolic compounds approved for use as antioxidants in foods. Additional phenolic compounds occur naturally in foods or are introduced through food processing. Common antioxidants with potential antimicrobial activity include butylated hydroxyanisole (BHA), butylated hydroxytoluene (BHT), tertiary butylhydroquinone (TBHQ) and propyl gallate (PG).

Butylated hydroxyanisole ($C_{11}H_{16}O_2$; 2- and 3-isomer of tertiary-butyl-4-hydroxyanisole) has exhibited antimicrobial properties against various microorganisms, including *A. parasiticus, Sacch. cerevisiae, Cl. perfringens, Sal. typhimurium, Staph. aureus, E. coli* and *V. parahaemolyticus* (Davidson, 1983; Raccach, 1984; Rusul & Marth, 1988a,b). Inhibitory concentrations have varied with substrate, pH and type of micro-organism, but they exceed 0.01%. It should be noted, however, that most tests on the antimicrobial activity of this and other phenolic antioxidants have involved aqueous culture media, while in food systems their inhibitory effects may be reduced drastically (Dawson *et al.*, 1975).

Butylated hydroxytoluene ($C_{15}H_{24}O$; 2,6-di-tertiary-butyl-*p*-cresol) has also exhibited antimicrobial properties in culture media and at concentrations greater than 0.01%. Among the organisms inhibited are *Cl. botulinum* and *Staph. aureus*, while *Salmonella senftenberg* was not inhibited by 1% BHT (Davidson, 1983). In general, BHT is less effective as an antimicrobial agent than other phenolic antioxidants.

Tertiary butylhydroquinone (TBHQ) was inhibitory against bacteria and yeasts at concentrations of even less than 0.01% (Davidson, 1983). The antimicrobial activity of propyl gallate (PG) appears to be limited.

14.3 Phosphates

Several phosphate compounds, such as sodium acid pyrophosphate ($Na_2H_2P_2O_7$), sodium tripolyphosphate ($Na_5P_3O_{10}$), sodium hexametaphosphate ($(NaPO)_{13}$-Na_2O) and tetrasodium pyrophosphate ($Na_4P_2O_7$) are approved for use in processed foods in the USA and other countries. Their contribution to various food products relates to water retention, binding, emulsification, coagulation, texture, colour and flavour (Tompkin, 1984; Sofos, 1986a, 1989b; Wagner, 1986). In processed meat products, especially in formulations with reduced sodium chloride, phosphates improve water and fat retention, meat particle cohesion, texture, colour and flavour.

The influence of phosphates on microbial growth is variable and depends on individual type and concentration, substrate, pH, microbial contamination, heat treatment, chemical additives and storage conditions. It is believed that their antimicrobial activity is due to chelation of metal ions useful in microbial metabolism. It has also been suggested that phosphates inhibit enzymes involved in transport functions, metabolism and activation of microbial toxins (Wagner, 1986; Sofos, 1989b).

14.4 Ethylenediamine tetraacetic acid

Ethylenediamine tetraacetic acid (EDTA) or versene ($(HOOCCH_2)_2{-}NCH_2CH_2N{-}(CH_2COOH)_2$) and its salts are chelating agents used as synergists of antioxidants in foods. The compounds are approved for use in foods in the USA and other countries. Chelation of trace metal ions by EDTA results in inhibition of certain microorganisms including *Cl. botulinum* (Winarno *et al.*, 1971; Tompkin, 1978). Several studies have reported inhibition of microbial growth and extension of shelf-life in products, such as fish (Kuusi & Loytomaki, 1972; Wilkinson, 1975; Levin, 1967; Russell, 1971; Russell & Fuller, 1979; Ward & Ashley, 1980; Bulgarelli & Shelef, 1985).

15 OTHER ANTIMICROBIAL COMPOUNDS

A variety of compounds have either found some limited use as chemical food preservatives, have been suggested for use, or their use has been discontinued.

Low molecular weight glycols, such as propylene glycol ($CH_3CHOHCH_2OH$) and butylene glycol ($CH_3CHOHCHOHCH_3$), are permitted for use in foods as water activity-reducing humectants, which also retard microbial growth. They find major application in intermediate moisture foods to inhibit fungi (McIver *et al.*, 1978).

Diphenyl, biphenyl, or phenylbenzene ($C_6H_5C_6H_5$) is a permitted food additive in the UK and other countries, because it inhibits a large number of micro-organisms, and especially moulds (e.g. *Penicillium italicum* and *P. digitatum*). The compound is applied to wrapping materials to preserve citrus fruits during storage and transportation (Hopkins & Loucks, 1947; Lueck, 1980).

The compound, *N*-trichloromethylmercapto-4-cyclohexene-1,2-dicarboximide (Captan; $C_9H_8Cl_3NO_2S$) has found application as a fungistat for raisin grapes. Cinnamylphenol and cinnamic aldehyde, components of cinnamon, have exhibited antimicrobial properties and may preserve products such as fruit juices. Glutaraldehyde ($HOC(CH_2)_3CHO$) may inactivate viruses and it is a natural component of various foods (Saitanu & Lund, 1975).

The compound *o*-phenylphenol (*o*-hydroxybiphenyl, orthoxenol, Dowicide 1, SOPP, 2-phenylphenol, $C_6H_5C_6H_4OH$) denatures microbial cell wall components and inhibits enzymes (Lueck, 1980). Concentrations of 0.001–0.005% inhibit moulds, while higher concentrations are needed for inhibition of bacteria. The compound may preserve citrus fruits by immersion for 0.5–1 min in a 0.5–2% solution.

Potassium bromate ($KBrO_3$) increases the oxidation–reduction potential of systems, which causes some antimicrobial activity. An application, which has been discontinued because of off-flavours, involved use of up to 0.04% bromate to inhibit butyric and anaerobic bacteria in processed cheeses (Lueck, 1980). Quaternary ammonium chloride combinations are permitted in the USA to be used as antimicrobial agents in raw sugar-cane juice, added prior to clarification when further processing of the sugar-cane juice must be delayed. Calcium chloride, potassium chloride, potassium hydroxide, potassium and sodium carbonates, sodium bicarbonate and sodium hypophosphite are also listed as GRAS in the USA, and may exhibit antimicrobial activity. Sodium bicarbonate was found to inhibit aflatoxin formation in corn (Montville & Goldstein, 1989), yeasts in apple juice (Curran & Montville, 1989), and bacteria and yeasts in culture media (Corral *et al.*, 1988).

Fluorides (NaF, KF) act on enzymes and inhibit micro-organisms, but they are toxic, and their use for preservation of dairy products, meat, beer and wine has been discontinued. Wine has been stabilized with allyl isothiocyanate ($CH_2{=}CHCH_2NCS$), but it has an undesirable odour.

Thiourea (H_2NCSNH_2) has been applied on the surface or on wrappers to protect citrus fruit from mould spoilage, but its use is prohibited in the USA because of toxicity. Tobacco and some foods have been preserved with 8-oxyquinoline (C_9H_7NO), 8-hydroxyquinoline, or hydroxybenzopyridine (Lueck, 1980). The amino acid glycine (NH_2CH_2COOH) has inhibited several bacteria (Hammes *et al.*, 1973).

Nitrofuran derivatives, such as furyl furamide ($C_{11}H_8O_5N_2$; AF-2) and nitrofuryl acrylamide (nitrofuran 2) inhibit electron transfer of aerobic bacteria, but have been reported as mutagenic and carcinogenic (Sugiyama *et al.*, 1975; Takayama & Kuwabara, 1977). Furyl furamide was at first permitted and used to preserve tofu and meat in Japan, but it was soon disallowed.

Thiabendazole ($C_{10}H_7N_3S$) is considered safe at concentrations permitted for preservation of citrus fruits, apples and bananas in several countries. The compound is an effective fungistatic agent (Robinson *et al.*, 1964; Rizk & Isshak, 1974).

Hexamethylenetetramine ($C_6H_{12}N_4$) was used as a preservative in several countries of Europe, but its use was discontinued because it is mutagenic (Natvig *et al.*, 1971; Hurni & Ohder, 1973). Silver, as the silver ion, Ag^+, generated because metallic silver yields Ag^+ in solution, has been used to disinfect drinking water, vinegar, fruit juices, drinks and wine. It is active against bacteria and to a lesser extent against yeasts and moulds, but it is inactivated by suspended matter, proteins, chlorides and calcium ions (Lueck, 1980).

A variety of other compounds have demonstrated antimicrobial activity in model or food systems either alone or in combination with other additives or processing factors. Such compounds include hinokitiol (*m*-isopropyltropolon, 2-hydroxy-4-isopropylol, or 2,4,6-cycloheptatriene), idoacetamide, chloroacetamide, lactulose, xylitol, etc. (Davidson *et al.*, 1983) and volatile oils (Deans & Ritchie, 1987).

16 MECHANISMS OF CHEMICAL FOOD PRESERVATION

The objective of chemical food preservation is the prevention or delay of microbiologically induced changes in a food product. In some instances, and under certain circumstances, some physical control methods of food preservation (e.g. heat) or chemical compounds (e.g. alkylating agents) may result in product sterilization by actually killing the indigenous microbial flora. Frequently, the initial microbial population remains viable in the product, but its proliferation is inhibited or retarded by the chemical compounds added to the product as food preservatives. In certain instances, chemical food preservatives are applied in combination with physical control processes.

Extension of product wholesomeness is the practical objective of food preservation regardless of means or processes employed in each case. Accomplishment of this task is one of the most important factors employed in the selection of chemical food preservatives.

Although the final effect of every compound used in chemical food preservation is one and the same (microbial death or retardation of microbial proliferation), the specific effects and the mechanisms through which they are accomplished may vary between compounds and other conditions. The mechanisms of chemical food preservation may differ between compounds used as preservatives, food systems being preserved, micro-organisms to be controlled, other constituents of the system, and between culture media and actual foods. The complexity of food systems, the diversity of microbial species and the extensive interactions, are major reasons why the mechanisms of food preservation in most instances are not well defined. Several reviews of pertinent information exist in the literature (Wyss, 1948; Bosund, 1962; Oka, 1964; Hugo, 1967, 1976a,b; Vinter, 1970; Freese *et al.*, 1973; Warth, 1977; Freese & Levin, 1978; Sofos *et al.*, 1986; Sofos, 1989a; Denyer & Hugo, 1990), but many effects still remain unexplained and, in most instances, definite answers are still lacking (see also Chapter 9).

Determination of specific mechanisms of microbial inhibition will facilitate the search for new preservatives, may explain the development of resistant microbial strains, and may result in selection of ideal chemical food preservatives. As mentioned in other sections of this chapter, a very important factor in chemical food preservation is the pH of the system. A high level of acidity may directly inhibit microbial growth, or it may facilitate the action of lipophilic acid preservatives by increasing the proportion of their more effective undissociated form. Of the commonly used chemical food preservatives only the esters of *p*-hydroxybenzoic acid have a high pK_a value, 8.5, and are effective at higher pH values, >7.0.

The growth of most micro-organisms reaches an optimum at pH values near neutrality (7.0). The pH range for growth, however, is different among microbial groups, genera, etc. In general, bacteria do not grow well at pH levels below 4.5, while yeasts and moulds are more resistant to acidity and some can even grow at pH values below 2.0. The range of pH values in which certain micro-organisms can grow is also affected by environmental factors such as oxygen tension, other microbial species present, storage temperature, a_w, heat processing, gas atmosphere, nutrient availability and means of acidification.

The internal pH of microbial cells may be considerably affected by the pH of their environment. Acidification of the interior of the cell can result in growth inhibition. Such inhibition, however, varies among microbial species, since different species exhibit different tolerances toward internal acidity (Neal *et al.*, 1965; Hunter & Segel, 1973; Freese *et al.*, 1973). In the case of acid preservatives, especially lipophilic acids, a lowering of the pH of the medium can have a dual effect. One is direct acidification, and the second an increase in the effective undissociated form as the pH approaches the pK_a value of the compound. Chemical food preservatives, in general, exert their antimicrobial activity through some type of a reaction with components of the microbial cell (Oka, 1964). This reaction may be interfering with cell membranes and their permeability, with the genetic apparatus of the cell, or with enzymatic or other chemical activities within the cell (Wyss, 1948). Oka (1964) classified the antimicrobial effect of food preservatives into two groups. One group shows antimicrobial activity dependent on the sorption of the compound onto the cell surface, whereas the antimicrobial activity of the second group is dependent upon cell permeability. Freese *et al.* (1973) indicated that lipophilic acid preservatives uncouple substrate transport and oxidative phosphorylation from the electron transport system by making the cytoplasmic membrane freely permeable to protons, thereby destroying part of the protonmotive force (Chapter 9). They further suggested that, as a result, growth inhibition occurs through inhibition of active cellular uptake of compounds such as amino acids, organic acids and phosphate. The authors also reported that sulphite and nitrite, on the other hand, inhibit growth but not transport. Bosund (1962) indicated that growth inhibition of micro-organisms by compounds such as benzoate is the result of interference with the metabolism of substrates such as acetate which is required for the formation of energy-rich compounds. Such action blocks cell metabolism. Several studies have suggested that microbial inhibition by sorbic acid and similar compounds is the result of inhibition of certain dehydrogenase enzymes (Sofos, 1989a).

The controversy over the use of nitrite in meat curing and the potential health hazards associated with such use demonstrate the need for knowledge of the mechanisms of chemical food preservation. Definite answers on the mechanism of nitrite inhibition of botulism are still lacking (Sofos *et al.*, 1979c; Benedict, 1980). On the basis of indirect but conclusive evidence, Tompkin (1978) suggested that nitrite may be reacting with an iron-containing compound (ferredoxin) within the germinated botulinal cell and consequently could interfere with energy metabolism to prevent outgrowth and toxin production.

The above highlight only a few of the theories presented to explain the effectiveness of some chemicals used in preventing microbial growth in food systems. Final conclusions are yet to be reached and the subject is still open. It is very likely, however, that more than one mechanism is involved in inhibition of micro-organisms by chemical food preservatives.

17 REFERENCES

Adams, M.R. & Hall, C.J. (1988) Growth inhibition of food-borne pathogens by lactic and acetic acids and their mixtures. *International Journal of Food Science and Technology*, **23**, 287–292.

Ahlborg, U.G., Dich, J. & Eriksson, H.-B. (1977) Data on food preservatives. *Var Foda*, **29**, 41–96.

Amano, K., Shibasaki, I., Yokoseki, M. & Kawabata, T. (1968) Preservation of fish sausage with tylosin, furylfuramide and sorbic acid. *Food Technology*, **22**, 881–885.

Amerine, M.A. & Joslyn, M.A. (1951) *Table Wines: The Technology of Their Production*. Berkeley, California: University of California Press.

Andersen, A.A. & Michener, H.D. (1950) Preservation of foods with antibiotics. I. The complementary action of subtilin and mild heat. *Food Technology*, **4**, 188–189.

Anon (1969) Swann Report: *Report of the Joint Committee on the Use of Antibiotics in Animal Husbandry and Veterinary Medicine*. London: HMSO.

Anon (1972) Report of the Commissioner of the Food and Drug Administration by the FDA Task Force on the use of antibiotics in animal feeds. Rockville, Maryland, USA: United States Department of Health, Education and Welfare, Food and Drug Administration.

Baker, D.A. & Genigeorgis, C. (1990) Predicting the safe storage of fresh fish under modified atmospheres with respect to *Clostridium botulinum* toxigenesis by modeling length of the lag phase of growth. *Journal of Food Protection*, **53**, 131–140.

Banks, J.G. & Board, R.G. (1985) Preservation by the lactoperoxidase system (LP-S) of a contaminated infant formula. *Letters in Applied Microbiology*, **1**, 81–85.

Banks, J.G., Board, R.G. & Sparks, N.H.C. (1986) Natural antimicrobial systems and their potential in food preservation of the future. *Biotechnology and Applied Biochemistry*, **8**, 103–147.

Banks, J.G., Nychas, G.J. & Board, R.G. (1987) Sulphite preservation of meat products. In *Preservatives in the Food, Pharmaceutical and Environmental Industries* (eds. Board, R.G., Allwood, M.C. & Banks, J.G.) Society for Applied Bacteriology Technical Series No. 22, pp. 17–33. Oxford: Blackwell Scientific Publications.

Banwart, G. (1989) *Basic Food Microbiology*, 2nd Ed. Westport, Connecticut: AVI Publishing Co.

Barber, L.E. & Deibel, R.H. (1972) Effect of pH and oxygen tension on staphylococcal growth and enterotoxin formation in fermented sausage. *Applied Microbiology*, **24**, 891–898.

Bayne, H.G. & Michener, H.D. (1975) Growth of *Staphylococcus* and *Salmonella* on frankfurters with and without sodium nitrite. *Applied Microbiology*, **30**, 844–849.

Bell, T.A., Etchells, J.L. & Borg, A.F. (1959) Influence of sorbic acid on the growth of certain species of bacteria, yeast and filamentous fungi. *Journal of Bacteriology*, **77**, 573–580.

Benedict, R.C. (1980) Biochemical basis for nitrite-inhibition of *Clostridium botulinum* in cured meat. *Journal of Food Protection*, **43**, 877–891.

Beuchat, L.R. (1976) Sensitivity of *Vibrio parahaemolyticus* to spices and organic acids. *Journal of Food Science*, **41**, 899–902.

Beuchat, L.R. (1981a) Combined effects of solutes and food preservatives on rates of inactivation of and colony formation by heated spores and vegetative cells of molds. *Applied and Environmental Microbiology*, **41**, 472–477.

Beuchat, L.R. (1981b) Influence of potassium sorbate and sodium benzoate on heat inactivation of *Aspergillus flavus*, *Penicillium puberulum* and *Geotrichum candidum*. *Journal of Food Protection*, **44**, 450–454.

Beuchat, L.R. (1981c) Effects of potassium sorbate and sodium benzoate on inactivating yeasts heated in broths containing sodium chloride and sucrose. *Journal of Food Protection*, **44**, 765–769.

Beuchat, L.R. (1982) Thermal inactivation of yeasts in fruit juices supplemented with food preservatives and sucrose. *Journal of Food Science*, **47**, 1679–1682.

Beuchat, L.R. & Golden, D.A. (1989) Antimicrobials occurring naturally in foods. *Food Technology*, **43**(1), 134–142.

Binkerd, E.F. & Kolari, O.E. (1975) The history and use of nitrate and nitrite in the curing of meat. *Food and Cosmetics Toxicology*, **13**, 655–661.

Block, S.S. & Bevis, J. (1963) Investigation of chemical agents for the canning preservation of meat. *Developmental and Industrial Microbiology*, **4**, 201–212.

Block, S.S. & Taylor, J., Jr (1964) Storage tests of bisulfite-preserved canned beef. *Developmental and Industrial Microbiology*, **6**, 277–283.

Borch, E., Wallentin, C., Rosen, M. & Bjorck, L. (1989) Antibacterial effect of the lactoperoxidase/thiocyante/hydrogen peroxide system against strains of *Campylobacter* isolated from poultry. *Journal of Food Protection*, **52**, 638–641.

Bosund, I. (1962) The action of benzoic and salicylic acids on the metabolism of microorganisms. *Advances in Food Research*, **11**, 331–353.

Boyd, J.W. & Southcott, B.A. (1968) Comparative effectiveness of ethylenediaminetetraacetic acid and chlortetracycline for fish preservation. *Journal of the Fisheries Research Board, Canada*, **25**, 1753.

Boyle, D.L., Sofos, J.N. & Maga, J.A. (1988) Inhibition of spoilage and pathogenic microorganisms by liquid smoke from various woods. *Lebensmittel Wissenschaft und Technologie*, **21**, 54–58.

Branen, A.L. & Davidson, P.M. (eds) (1983) *Antimicrobials in Foods*. New York: Marcel Dekker.

Bruch, C.W. (1961) Gaseous sterilization. *Annual Review of Microbiology*, **15**, 245–262.

Bruch, C.W. (1972) Sterilization of plastics: toxicity of ethylene oxide residues. In *Industrial Sterilization* (eds Phillips, G.B. & Miller, W.S.) pp. 49–77. Durham, North Carolina: Duke University Press.

Bruch, C.W. & Koesterer, M.G. (1961) The microbicidal activity of gaseous propylene oxide and its application to powdered or flaked foods. *Journal of Food Science*, **26**, 428–435.

Buchanan, R.L. & Solberg, M. (1972) Interaction of sodium nitrite, oxygen, and pH on growth of *Staphylococcus aureus*. *Journal of Food Science*, **37**, 81–85.

Buchanan, R.L., Stahl, H.G. & Whiting, R.C. (1989) Effects and interactions of temperature, pH, atmosphere, sodium chloride, and sodium nitrite on the growth of *Listeria monocytogenes*. *Journal of Food Protection*, **52**, 844–851.

Bulgarelli, M.A. & Shelef, L.A. (1985) Effect of ethylenediamine-tetraacetic acid (EDTA) on growth from spores of *Bacillus cereus*. *Journal of Food Science*, **50**, 661–664.

Bullerman, L.B. (1974) Inhibition of aflatoxin production by cinnamon. *Journal of Food Science*, **39**, 1163–1165.

Bullerman, L.B. (1977) Incidence and control of mycotoxin producing molds in domestic and imported cheeses. *Annals of Nutritional Alimentation*, **31**, 435–446.

Bullerman, L.B. (1979) Effects of potassium sorbate on mycotoxin production and growth of *Aspergillus parasiticus*, *Penicillium commune* and *Penicillum patulum* in broth substrates. Presented at the 39th Annual Meeting of the Institute of Food Technologists, 10–13 June, St Louis, Missouri. Abstract No. 454.

Busta, F.F. & Foegeding, P.M. (1983) Chemical food preservatives. In *Disinfection, Sterilization & Preservation* (ed. Block, S.S.) 3rd Ed. pp. 656–694. Philadelphia: Lea & Febiger.

Cassens, R.G., Greaser, M.L., Ito, T. & Lee, M. (1979) Reactions of nitrite in meat. *Food Technology*, **33**, 48–57.

Castellani, A.G. & Niven, C.F., Jr (1955) Factors affecting the bacteriostatic action of sodium nitrite. *Applied Microbiology*, **3**, 154–159.

Cathcart, W.H. (1951) Baking and bakery products. In *The Chemistry and Technology of Food and Food Products* (ed. Jacobs, M.B.) Vol. II, 2nd Ed. pp. 1195–1203. New York: Interscience Publications.

Charley, P.J., Sarkar, B., Stitt, C.F. & Saltman, P. (1963) Chelation of iron by sugars. *Biochimica et Biophysica Acta*, **69**, 313–321.

Chichester, D.F. & Tanner, F.W. (1972) Antimicrobial food additives. In *Handbook of Food Additives* (ed. Furia, T.E.) 2nd Ed. pp., 115–184. Boca Raton, Florida: CRC Press.

Chipley, J.R. (1983) Sodium benzoate and benzoic acid. In *Antimicrobials in Foods* (eds Branen, A.L. & Davidson, P.M.) pp. 11–35. New York: Marcel Dekker.

Christiansen, L.N., Deffner, J., Foster, E.M. & Sugiyama, H. (1968) Survival and outgrowth of *Clostridium botulinum* type E spores in smoked fish. *Applied Microbiology*, **16**, 133–137.

Christiansen, L.N., Johnston, R.W., Kautter, D.A., Howard, J.W. & Aunan, W.J. (1973) Effect of nitrite and nitrate on toxin production by *Clostridium botulinum* and on nitrosamine formation in perishable canned comminuted cured meat. *Applied Microbiology*, **25**, 357–362.

Christiansen, L.N., Tompkin, R.B., Shaparis, A.B., Kueper, T.V., Johnston, R.W., Kautter, D.A. & Kolari, O.E. (1974) Effect of sodium nitrite on toxin production by *Clostridium botulinum* in bacon. *Applied Microbiology*, **27**, 733–737.

Christiansen, L.N., Tompkin, R.B., Shaparis, A.B., Johnston, R.W. & Kautter, D.A. (1975) Effect of sodium nitrite on *Cl. botulinum* growth in a summer-style sausage. *Journal of Food Science*, **40**, 488–490.

Clark, D.S. & Lentz, C.P. (1969) Microbiological studies in poultry processing plants in Canada. *Canadian Institute of Food Science and Technology Journal*, **2**, 33–36.

Clark, D.S. & Lentz, C.P. (1973) Use of mixtures of carbon dioxide and oxygen for extending shelf-life of pre-packaged fresh beef, *Canadian Institute of Food Science and Technology Journal*, **6**, 194–196.

Clark, D.S. & Takacs, J. (1980) Gases as preservative. In *Microbial Ecology of Foods*. Volume I: *Factors Affecting Life and Death of Microorganisms*. International Commission on Microbiological Specifications of Foods, pp. 170–192. New York: Academic Press.

Clark, D.S., Lentz, C.P. & Roth, L.A. (1976) Use of carbon monoxide for extending shelf-life of pre-packaged fresh beef. *Canadian Institute of Food Science and Technology Journal*, **9**, 114–117.

Clark, W.L., Shirk, R.J. & Kline, E.F. (1964) Pimaracin, a new food fungistat. In *Microbial Inhibitors in Food* (ed. Molin, N.) pp. 167–184. Stockholm: Almquist & Wiksell.

Cords, B.R. (1983) Sanitizers: halogens and surface-active agents. In *Antimicrobials in Foods* (eds Branen, A.L. & Davidson, P.M.) pp. 257–298. New York: Marcel Dekker.

Corral, L.G., Post, L.S. & Montville, T.J. (1988) Antimicrobial activity of sodium bicarbonate. *Journal of Food Sciences*, **53**, 981–982.

Costilow, R.N., Coughlin, F.M., Robach, D.L. & Ragheb, H.S. (1956) A study of acid-forming bacteria from cucumber fermentations in Michigan. *Food Research*, **21**, 27–33.

Costilow, R.N., Coughlin, F.M., Robbins, E.K. & Hus, W.-T. (1957) Sorbic acid as a selective agent in cucumber fermentations. II. Effect of sorbic acid on the yeast and lactic acid fermentation in brined cucumbers. *Applied Microbiology*, **5**, 373–379.

Cox, N.A., Mercuri, A.J., Juven, B.J., Thompson, J.E. & Chew, V. (1974) Evaluation of succinic acid and heat to improve the microbiological quality of poultry meat. *Journal of Food Science*, **39**, 985–987.

Crosby, N.T. & Sawyer, R. (1976) *N*-nitrosamines: a review of chemical and biological properties and their estimation in foodstuffs. *Advances in Food Research*, **22**, 1–71.

Cruess, W.V. & Irish, J.H. (1932) Further observations on the relation of pH value to toxicity of preservatives to microorganisms. *Journal of Bacteriology*, **23**, 163–166.

Cruess, W.V. & Richert, P.H. (1929) Effects of hydrogen ion concentration on the toxicity of sodium benzoate to microorganisms. *Journal of Bacteriology*, **17**, 363–371.

Cunningham, F.E. (1979) Shelf-life and quality characteristics of poultry parts dipped in potassium sorbate. *Journal of Food Science*, **44**, 863–864.

Curran, D.M. & Montville, T.J. (1989) Bicarbonate inhibition of *Saccharomyces cerevisiae* and *Hansenula wingei* growth in apple juice. *International Journal of Food Microbiology*, **8**, 1–9.

Daeschel, M.A. (1989) Antimicrobial substances from lactic acid bacteria for use as food preservatives. *Food Technology*, **43**(1), 164–167.

Davidson, P.M. (1983) Phenolic compounds. In *Antimicrobials in Foods* (eds Branen, A.L. & Davidson, P.M.) pp. 37–74. New York: Marcel Dekker.

Davidson, P.M., Post, L.S., Branen, A.L. & McCurdy, A.R. (1983) Naturally occurring and miscellaneous food antimicrobials. In *Antimicrobials in Foods* (eds Branen, A.L. & Davidson, P.M.) pp. 371–419. New York: Marcel Dekker.

Dawson, L.E., Stevenson, K.E. & Gertonson, E. (1975) Flavor, bacterial and TBA changes in ground turkey patties treated with antioxidants. *Poultry Science*, **54**, 1134–1139.

Deans, S.G. & Ritchie, E. (1987) Antibacterial properties of plant essential oils. *International Journal of Food Microbiology*, **5**, 165–180.

Debevere, J.M. (1989). The effect of sodium lactate on the shelf life of vacuum-packed coarse liver paté. *Fleischwirtschaft International*, **3**, 68–69.

Deibel, R.H. (1979) Parabens. Presented at the Meat Industry Research Conference, 29–30 March. Washington, DC: American Meat Institute.

Denis, F. & Ramet, J.-P. (1989) Antibacterial activity of the lactoperoxidase system on *Listeria monocytogenes* in trypticase soy broth, UHT milk and French soft cheese. *Journal of Food Protection*, **52**, 706–711.

Denny, C.B., Sharpe, L.E. & Bohrer, C.W. (1961) Effects of tylosin and nisin on canned food spoilage bacteria. *Applied Microbiology*, **9**, 108–110.

Denyer, S.P. & Hugo, W.B. (1991) Eds. *Mechanisms of Action of Chemical Biocides: their Study and Exploitation*. Society for Applied Bacteriology, Technical Series No. 27. Oxford: Blackwell Scientific Publications.

Desrosier, N.W. (1970) *The Technology of Food Preservation*. Westport, Connecticut: AVI Publishing Company.

Deuel, H.J., Jr, Alfin-Slater, R., Weil, C.S. & Smyth, H.F., Jr (1954a) Sorbic acid as a fungistatic agent for foods. 1. Harmlessness of sorbic acid as a dietary component. *Food Research*, **19**, 1–12.

Deuel, H.J., Jr, Calbert, C.E., Anisfeld, L., McKeehan, H. & Blunder, H.D. (1954b) Sorbic acid as a fungistatic agent for foods. II. Metabolism of β-unsaturated fatty acids with emphasis on sorbic acid. *Food Research*, **19**, 13–19.

Doores, S. (1983) Organic acids. In *Antimicrobials in Foods* (eds Branen, A.L. & Davidson, P.M.) pp. 75–108. New York: Marcel Dekker.

Doyle, M.P. & Marth, E.H. (1975). Thermal inactivation of

conidia from *Aspergillus flavus* and *Aspergillus parasiticus*. II. Effects of pH and buffers, glucose, sucrose and sodium chloride. *Journal of Milk and Food Technology*, **38**, 750–758.

Dudman, W.F. (1963) Sorbic hydroxamic acid, an antifungal agent effective over a wide pH range. *Applied Microbiology*, **11**, 362–367.

Dunn, C.G. (1947) Chemical agents give quality improvement in fisheries. *Food Technology*, **1**, 371–384.

Dyett, E.J. & Shelley, D. (1966) The effects of sulphite preservative in British fresh sausage. *Journal of Applied Bacteriology*, **29**, 439–446.

Dymicky, M. & Huhtanen, C.N. (1979) Inhibition of *Clostridium botulinum* by *p*-hydroxybenzoic acid *n*-alkyl esters. *Antimicrobial Agents and Chemotherapy*, **15**, 798–801.

Dymicky, M., Bencivengo, M., Buchanen, R.L. & Smith, J.L. (1987) Inhibition of *Clostridium botulinum* 62A by fumarates and maleates and relationship of activity to some physicochemical constants. *Applied and Environmental Microbiology*, **53**, 110–113.

Dziezak, J.D. (1986) Antioxidants—the ultimate answer to oxidation. *Food Technology*, **40**, 94–103.

Earnshaw, R.G. & Banks, J.G. (1989) A note on the inhibition of *Listeria monocytogenes* NCTC 11994 in milk by an activated lactoperoxidase system. *Letters in Applied Microbiology*, **8**, 203–205.

Earnshaw, R.G., Banks, J.G., Francotte, C. & Defrise, D. (1990) Inhibition of *Salmonella typhimurium* and *Escherichia coli* in an infant milk formula by an activated lactoperoxidase system. *Journal of Food Protection*, **53**, 170–172.

Eklund, M.W., Pelroy, G.A., Paranjpye, R., Peterson, M.E. & Teeny, F.M. (1982) Inhibition of *Clostridium botulinum* types A and E toxin production by liquid smoke and NaCl in hot-process smoke-flavored fish. *Journal of Food Protection*, **45**, 935–940.

Eklund, T. (1980) Inhibition of growth and uptake processes in bacteria by some chemical food preservatives. *Journal of Applied Bacteriology*, **48**, 423–432.

Eklund, T. (1983) The antimicrobial effect of dissociated and undissociated sorbic acid at different pH levels. *Journal of Applied Bacteriology*, **54**, 383–389.

Eklund, T. (1985) The effect of sorbic acid and esters of p-hydroxybenzoic acid on the protonmotive force in *Escherichia coli* membrane vesicles. *Journal of General Microbiology*, **131**, 73–76.

El-Gazzar, F.E., Rusul, G. & Marth, E.H. (1987) Growth and aflatoxin production of *Aspergillus parasiticus* NRRL 2999 in the presence of lactic acid and at different initial pH values. *Journal of Food Protection*, **50**, 940–944.

El-Gendy, S.M., Nassib, T., Abed-El-Gellel, H. & Nanafy, N-El-Hoda (1980) Survival and growth of *Clostridium* species in the presence of hydrogen peroxide. *Journal of Food Protection*, **43**, 431–432.

El-Kest, S.E. & Marth, E.H. (1988a) Inactivation of *Listeria monocytogenes* by chlorine. *Journal of Food Protection*, **51**, 520–524.

El-Kest, S.E. & Marth, E.H. (1988b) *Listeria monocytogenes* and its inactivation by chlorine: a review. *Lebensmittel Wissenschaft und Technologie*, **21**, 346–351.

El-Kest, S.E. & Marth, E.H. (1988c) Temperature, pH, and strain of pathogen as factors affecting inactivation of *Listeria monocytogenes* by chlorine. *Journal of Food Protection*, **51**, 622–625.

El-Shenawy, M.A. & Marth, E.H. (1988a) Sodium benzoate inhibits growth of or inactivates *Listeria monocytogenes*. *Journal of Food Protection*, **51**, 525–530.

El-Shenawy, M.A. & Marth, E.H. (1988b) Inhibition and inactivation of *Listeria monocytogenes* by sorbic acid. *Journal of Food Protection*, **51**, 842–847.

El-Shenawy, M.A. & Marth, E.H. (1989) Behavior of *Listeria monocytogenes* in the presence of sodium propionate. *International Journal of Food Microbiology*, **8**, 85–94.

Emard, L.O. & Vaughn, R.H. (1952) Selectivity of sorbic acid media for the catalase-negative lactic acid bacteria and clostridia. *Journal of Bacteriology*, **63**, 487–494.

Enfors, S.-O. & Molin, G. (1978) The influence of high concentrations of carbon dioxide on the germination of bacterial spores. *Journal of Applied Bacteriology*, **45**, 279–285.

Fey, G. & Kersten, H. (1972) Fluorescence analysis of tetracycline binding to ribosomes. *Advanced Antimicrobial Antineoplastic Chemotherapy*, **1**, 827.

Finne, G. (1982) Modified- and controlled-atmosphere storage of muscle foods. *Food Technology*, **36**(2), 128–133.

Foegeding, P.M. (1983) Bacterial spore resistance to chlorine compounds. *Food Technology*, **37**(11), 100–104, 110.

Foegeding, P.M. (1985) Ozone inactivation of *Bacillus* and *Clostridium* spore populations and the importance of spore coat to resistance. *Food Microbiology*, **2**, 123–134.

Foegeding, P.M. & Busta, F.F. (1983a) Hypochlorite injury of *Clostridium botulinum* spores alters germination responses. *Applied and Environmental Microbiology*, **45**, 1360–1368.

Foegeding, P.M. & Busta, F.F. (1983b) Proposed mechanism for sensitization by hypochlorite treatment of *Clostridium botulinum* spores. *Applied and Environmental Microbiology*, **45**, 1374–1379.

Foegeding, P.M. & Busta, F.F. (1983c) Effect of carbon dioxide, nitrogen and hydrogen gases on germination of *Clostridium botulinum* spores. *Journal of Food Protection*, **46**, 987–989.

Franco, D.A., Webb, J. & Taylor, C.E. (1990) Antibiotic and sulfonamide residues in meat: implications for human health. *Journal of Food Protection*, **53**, 178–185.

Frank, H.A. & Willits, C.O. (1961) Prevention of mold and yeast growth in maple syrup by chemical inhibitors. *Food Technology*, **15**, 1–3.

Franklin, T.J. & Snow, G.A. (1989) *Biochemistry of Antimicrobial Action*, 4th Ed. London: Chapman & Hall.

Freese, E. & Levin, B.C. (1978) Action mechanisms of preservatives and antiseptics. *Developments in Industrial*

Microbiology, **19**, 207–227.

Freese, E., Sheu, C.W. & Galliers, E. (1973) Function of lipophilic acids as antimicrobial food additives. *Nature, London*, **24**, 321–325.

Fukusumi, E. (1972) Preservatives in the future. Properties and uses. *Shokuhin Kogyo*, **15**, 40–45.

Fung, D.Y.C., Lin, C.C.S. & Gailani, M.B. (1985) Effect of phenolic antioxidants on microbial growth. *CRC Critical Reviews in Microbiology*, **12**(2), 153–183.

Garcia, G.W., Genigeorgis, C. & Lindroth, S. (1987) Risk of growth and toxin production by *Clostridium botulinum* nonproteolytic types B, E, and F in salmon fillets stored under modified atmospheres at low and abused temperatures. *Journal of Food Protection*, **50**, 330–336.

Gardner, W.H. (1972) Acidulants in food processing. In *Handbook of Food Additives* (ed. Furia, T.E.) 2nd Ed. pp. 225–270. Boca Raton, Florida: CRC Press.

Genigeorgis, C.A. (1985) Microbial and safety implications of the use of modified atmospheres to extend the storage life of fresh meat and fish. *International Journal of Food Microbiology*, **1**, 237–251.

Genth, H. (1964) On the action of diethylpyrocarbonate on microorganisms. In *Proceedings of the 4th International Symposium on Food Microbiology*, pp. 77–84. Goteborg.

Gill, C.O. & Tan, K.H. (1979) Effect of carbon dioxide on growth of *Pseudomonas fluorescens*. *Applied and Environmental Microbiology*, **38**, 237–240.

Goldberg, H.S. (1964) Non-medical use of antibiotics. *Advances in Applied Microbiology*, **6**, 91–117.

Golding, N.S. (1945) The gas requirements of molds. IV. A preliminary interpretation of the growth rates of four common mold cultures on the basis of absorbed gases. *Journal of Dairy Science*, **28**, 737–750.

Gombas, D.E. (1989) Biological competition as a preserving mechanism. *Journal of Food Safety*, **10**, 107–117.

Gooding, C.M. (1945) Process of inhibiting growth of molds. US Patent 2 379 294.

Gooding, C.M., Melnick, D., Lawrence, R.L. & Luckmann, E.H. (1955) Sorbic acid as a fungistatic agent for foods. IX. Physicochemical considerations in using sorbic acid to protect foods. *Food Research*, **20**, 639–648.

Goodson, M. & Rowbury, R.J. (1989) Resistance of acid-habituated *Escherichia coli* to organic acids and its medical and applied significance. *Letters in Applied Microbiology*, **8**, 211–214.

Gough, B.J. & Alford, J.A. (1965) Effect of curing agents on the growth and survival of food-poisoning strains of *Clostridium perfringens*. *Journal of Food Science*, **30**, 1025–1028.

Gray, J.I. & Randall, C.J. (1979) The nitrite/*N*-nitrosamine problem in meats: an update. *Journal of Food Protection*, **42**, 168–179.

Grever, A.B.G. (1974) Minimum nitrite concentrations for inhibition of clostridia in cooked meat products. In *Proceedings of the International Symposium on Nitrite in Meat Products* (eds Krol, B. & Tinbergen, B.J.) pp. 103–109. Wageningen: Pudoc.

Gupta, K.G., Sidhu, R. & Yadav, N.K. (1972) Effect of various sugars and their derivatives upon the germination of *Bacillus* spores in the presence of nisin. *Journal of Food Science*, **37**, 971–972.

Hahn, F.E. (1976) ed. *Antibiotics and Chemotherapy*. Vol. 20: *Acquired Resistance of Micro-organisms to Chemotherapeutic Drugs*. Basel Muchen: S. Karger A.G.

Hales, K.C. (1962) Refrigerated transport on shipboard. *Advances in Food Research*, **12**, 147–152.

Hammes, W., Schleifer, K.H. & Kandler, O. (1973) Mode of action of glycine on the biosynthesis of peptidoglycan. *Journal of Bacteriology*, **116**, 1029–1053.

Hammond, S.M. & Carr, J.G. (1976) The antimicrobial activity of SO_2—with particular reference to fermented and non-fermented fruit juices. In *Inhibition and Inactivation of Vegetative Microorganisms* (eds Skinner, F.A. & Hugo, W.B.) pp. 89–110. Society for Applied Bacteriology Symposium Series No. 5. London: Academic Press.

Hansen, J.D. & Appleman, M.D. (1955) The effect of sorbic, propionic, and caproic acids on the growth of certain clostridia. *Food Research*, **20**, 92–96.

Hansen, J.N., Banerjee, S. & Buchman, G.W. (1989) Potential of small ribosomally synthesized bacteriocins in design of new food preservatives. *Journal of Food Safety*, **10**, 119–130.

Harris, L.J., Dreschel, M.A., Stiles, M.E. & Klaenhammer, T.R. (1989) Antimicrobial activity of lactic acid bacteria against *Listeria monocytogenes*. *Journal of Food Protection*, **52**, 384–387.

Hayatsu, H. & Miura, A. (1970) The mutagenic action of sodium bisulfite. *Biochemical and Biophysical Research Communications*, **39**, 983–988.

Hayatsu, H., Chung, K.G., Kada, T. & Nakajima, T. (1975) Generation of mutagenic compound(s) by a reaction between sorbic acid and nitrite. *Mutation Research*, **30**, 417–419.

Hays, G.L., Burroughs, J.D. & Warner, R.C. (1959) Microbiological aspects of pressure packaged foods. II. The effect of various gases. *Food Technology*, **13**, 567–570.

Herring, H.K. (1973) Effect of nitrite and other factors on the physico-chemical characteristics and nitrosamine formation in bacon. In *Proceedings of the Meat Industry Research Conference*, pp. 47–60. Washington, D.C.: American Meat Institute.

Hintlian, C.B. & Hotchkiss, J.H. (1987) Comparative growth of spoilage and pathogenic organisms on modified atmosphere-packaged cooked beef. *Journal of Food Protection*, **50**, 218–223.

Hobbs, G. (1976) *Clostridium botulinum* and its importance in fishery products. *Advances in Food Research*, **22**, 135–185.

Hollenbeck, C.M. (1979) Liquid smoke flavoring-status of development. *Food Technology*, **33**(5), 88–92.

Holley, R.A. (1981) Prevention of surface mold growth on Italian dry sausage by natamycin and potassium sorbate. *Applied and Environmental Microbiology*, **41**, 422–429.

Hopkins, E.F. & Loucks, K.W. (1947) The use of diphenyl

in the control of stem-end rot and mold in citrus fruits. *Citrus Industry*, **28**, 5–11.

Huffman, D.L. (1974) Effect of gas atmospheres on microbial quality of pork. *Journal of Food Science*, **39**, 723–725.

Hughey, V.L. & Johnson, E.A. (1987) Antimicrobial activity of lysozyme against bacteria involved in food spoilage and food-borne disease. *Applied and Environmental Microbiology*, **53**, 2165–2170.

Hughey, V.L., Wilger, P.A. & Johnson, E.A. (1989) Antibacterial activity of hen egg white lysozyme against *Listeria monocytogenes* Scott A in foods. *Applied and Environmental Microbiology*, **55**, 631–638.

Hugo, W.B. (1967) The mode of action of antibacterial agents. *Journal of Applied Bacteriology*, **30**, 17–50.

Hugo, W.B. (1976a) The inactivation of vegetative bacteria by chemicals. In *Inhibition and Inactivation of Vegetative Bacteria* (eds Skinner, F.A. & Hugo, W.B.) pp. 1–11. Society for Applied Bacteriology Symposium Series No. 5. London: Academic Press.

Hugo, W.B. (1976b) Survival of microbes exposed to chemical stress. In *The Survival of Vegetative Microorganisms* (eds Gray, T.G.R. & Postgate, J.R.) pp. 383–413. 26th Symposium, Society of General Microbiology. Cambridge: Cambridge University Press.

Hugo, W.B. (1979) Phenols: a review of their history and development as antimicrobial agents. *Microbios*, **23**, 83–85.

Huhtanen, C.N. (1980) Inhibition of *Clostridium botulinum* by spice extracts and aliphatic alcohols. *Journal of Food Protection*, **43**, 195–196.

Huhtanen, C.N., Dymicky, M. & Trenchard, H. (1981) Methyl and ethyl esters of fumaric acids as substitutes for nitrite for inhibiting *Clostridium botulinum* spore outgrowth in bacon. Presented at the Annual Meeting of the Institute of Food Technologists, June, Atlanta, Georgia.

Hunter, D.R. & Segel, I.H. (1973) Effect of weak acids on amino acid transport by *Penicillium chrysogenum*: evidence for a proton or charge gradient as the driving force. *Journal of Bacteriology*, **113**, 1184–1192.

Huppert, M. (1957) The antifungal activity of homologous series of parabens. *Antibiotics and Chemotherapy*, **7**, 29–36.

Hurni, H. & Ohder, H. (1973) Reproduction study with formaldehyde and hexamethylenetetramine in beagle dogs. *Food and Cosmetic Toxicology*, **11**, 459–462.

Hurst, A. (1981) Nisin. In *Advances in Applied Microbiology*, Vol. 27 (eds Perlman, D. & Laskin, A.I.) pp. 85–123. New York: Academic Press.

Ingram, M. (1974) The microbiological effects of nitrite. In *Proceedings of the International Symposium of Nitrite in Meat Products* (eds Krol, B. & Tinbergen, B.J.) pp. 63–75. Wageningen: Pudoc.

Ingram, M. (1976) The microbial role of nitrite in meat products. In *Microbiology in Agriculture, Fisheries, and Food* (eds Skinner, F.A. & Carr, J.G.) pp. 1–18. London: Academic Press.

Ingram, M., Ottaway, F.J.H. & Coppock, J.B.M. (1956) The preservative action of acid substances in foods. *Chemistry and Industry*, **42**, 1154–1163.

Ingram, M., Buttiaux, R. & Mossel, D.A.A. (1964) General microbiological considerations in the choice of antimicrobial food preservatives. In *Microbial Inhibitors in Food* (ed. Molin, N.) pp. 381–392. Stockholm: Almquist & Wiksell.

Insalata, N.F. (1952) CO_2 versus beverage bacteria. *Food Engineering*, **24**(7), 84–85, 190.

Institute of Food Technologists (1986) Sulfites as food ingredients. *Food Technology*, **40**(6), 47–52.

Institute of Food Technologists (1987) Nitrate, nitrite and nitroso compounds in foods. *Food Technology*, **41**(4), 127–134, 136.

Ito, K.A. & Bee, G.R. (1980) Microbiological hazards associated with new packaging techniques. *Food Technology*, **34** (10), 78–80.

Ivey, F.J. & Robach, M.C. (1978) Effect of potassium sorbate and sodium nitrite on *Clostridium botulinum* growth and toxin production in canned comminuted pork. *Journal of Food Science*, **43**, 1782–1785.

Ivey, F.J., Shaver, K.J., Christiansen, L.N. & Tompkin, R.B. (1978) Effect of potassium sorbate on toxinogenesis of *Clostridium botulinum* in bacon. *Journal of Food Protection*, **41**, 621–625.

Jacobs, M.B. (1947) *Synthetic Food Adjuncts*. New York: D. Van Nostrand.

Jacobs, M.B. (1958) Vinegar. In *The Chemical Analysis of Foods and Food Products*, 3rd Ed. pp. 614–616. Princeton, New Jersey: D. Van Nostrand.

Jarvis, B. & Burke, C.S. (1976) Practical and legislative aspects of the chemical preservatives of food. In *Inhibition and Inactivation of Vegetative Microbes* (eds Skinner, F.A. & Hugo, W.B.) pp. 345–367. London: Academic Press.

Jay, J.M. (1982) Antimicrobial properties of diacetyl. *Applied and Environmental Microbiology*, **44**, 525–532.

Jensen, L.B. (1954) *Microbiology of Meats*. Champaign, Illinois: Garrard Press.

Jermini, M.F.G. & Schmidt-Lorenz, W. (1987) Activity of Na-benzoate and ethyl-paraben against osmotolerant yeasts at different water activity values. *Journal of Food Protection*, **50**, 920–927.

Jones, A.H. & Harper, G.S. (1952) A preliminary study of factors affecting the quality of pickles on the Canadian market. *Food Technology*, **5**, 304–308.

Jones, N.R. & Flowerdew, D.W. (1982) *Food Additives: Descriptions, Functions and UK Legislation*, 3rd Ed. Leatherhead: British Food Industries Research Association.

Joslyn, M.A. & Braverman, J.B.S. (1954) The chemistry and technology of the pretreatment and preservation of fruit and vegetable products with sulfur dioxide and sulfites. *Advances in Food Research*, **5**, 97–160.

Junttila, J., Hirn, J., Hill, P. & Nurmi, E. (1989) Effect of different levels of nitrite and nitrate on the survival of *Listeria monocytogenes* during the manufacture of fermented sausage. *Journal of Food Protection*, **52**, 158–161.

Kabara, J. (1981) Food-grade chemicals for use in designing food preservative systems. *Journal of Food Protection*, **44**, 633–647.

Kabara, J.J. (1983) Medium-chain fatty acids and esters. In *Antimicrobials in Foods* (eds Branen, A.L. & Davidson, P.M.) pp. 109–140. New York: Marcel Dekker.

Kabara, J.J. (1984) Inhibition of *Staphylococcus aureus* in a model agar–meat system by monolaurin: a research note. *Journal of Food Safety*, **6**, 197–201.

Kada, T. (1974) DNA-damaging products from reaction between sodium nitrite and sorbic acid. *Annual Report of the National Institute of Genetics (Japan)*, **24**, 43–44.

Katz, S.E. (1983) Antibiotic residues and their significance. In *Antimicrobials in Foods* (eds Branen, A.L. & Davidson, P.M.) pp. 353–370. New York: Marcel Dekker.

Kemp, J.D., Langlois, B.E., Solomon, M.B. & Fox, J.D. (1979) Quality of boneless dry-cured ham produced with or without nitrate, netting or potassium sorbate. *Journal of Food Science*, **44**, 914–915.

Kim, C., Carpenter, C.E., Cornforth, D.P., Mettanant, O. & Mahoney, A.W. (1987) Effect of iron form, temperature, and inoculation with *Clostridium botulinum* spores on residual nitrite in meat and model systems. *Journal of Food Science*, **52**, 1464–1470.

Kimble, C.E. (1977) Chemical food preservatives. In *Disinfection, Sterilization, and Preservation* (ed. Block, S.S.) 2nd Ed. pp. 834–858. Philadelphia, Pennsylvania: Lea & Febiger.

King, A.D. & Nagel, C.W. (1967) Growth inhibition of *Pseudomonas* by carbon dioxide. *Journal of Food Science*, **32**, 575–579.

King, A.D. & Nagel, C.W. (1975) Influence of carbon dioxide upon the metabolism of *Pseudomonas aeruginosa*. *Journal of Food Science*, **40**, 362–366.

Kiritaguchi, S., Maraki, M., Mizoguchi, T. & Shida, A. (1973) *Fungicide for Food and Drink*. Japanese Patent 7 303–371.

Klaenhammer, T.R. (1988) Bacteriocins of lactic acid bacteria. *Biochimie*, **70**, 337–349.

Kodicek, E. (1956) The effect of unsaturated fatty acids, of vitamin D and other sterols on Gram-positive bacteria. In *Biochemical Problems of Lipids* (eds Popjak, G. & LeBreton, E.) pp. 401–406. London: Butterworths.

Kohler, A.R., Miller, W.H. & Broquist, H.P. (1955) Aureomycin chlortetracycline and the control of poultry spoilage. *Food Technology*, **9**, 151–154.

Koser, S.A. & Skinner, W.W. (1922) Viability of the colon–typhoid group in carbonated water and carbonated beverages. *Journal of Bacteriology*, **7**, 111–121.

Kurytowicz, W.A. (Ed.) (1976) *Antibiotics: A Critical Review*. Warsaw: Polish Medical Publishers.

Kuusi, T. & Loytomaki, M. (1972) On the effectiveness of EDTA in prolonging the shelf-life of fresh fish. *Zoological Lebensmittel-Untersuch Forschungsanstalt*, **149**, 196–204.

Labots, H. (1977) Effect of nitrite on development of *Staphylococcus aureus* in fermented sausage. In *Proceedings of the Second International Symposium on Nitrite in Meat Products* (eds Tinbergen, B.J. & Krol, B.) pp. 21–27. Wageningen: Pudoc.

Lechowich, R.V., Brown, W.L., Diebel, R.H. & Somers, I.I. (1978) The role of nitrite in the production of canned cured meat products. *Food Technology*, **32**, 45–58.

Lee, J.S., Willett, C.L., Robinson, S.M. & Sinnhuber, R.D. (1967) Comparative effects of chlortetracycline, freezing and γ-radiation on microbial populations of ocean perch. *Applied Microbiology*, **15**, 368–372.

Leistner, L. (1978) Microbiology of ready to serve foods. *Fleischwirtschaft*, **58**, 2088–2111.

Levin, R.E. (1967) The effectiveness of EDTA as a fish preservative. *Journal of Milk and Food Technology*, **30**, 277–283.

Levinskas, G.J., Ribelin, W.E. & Shaffer, C.B. (1966) Acute and chronic toxicity of pimaricin. *Toxicology and Applied Pharmacology*, **8**, 97–109.

Levy, S.B. (1987) Antibiotic use for growth promotion in animals: ecologic and public health consequences. *Journal of Food Protection*, **50**, 616–620.

Liewen, M.B. & Marth, E.H. (1985) Growth and inhibition of microorganisms in the presence of sorbic acid: a review. *Journal of Food Protection*, **48**, 364–375.

Lueck, E. (1976) Sorbic acid as a food preservative. In *International Flavors and Food Additives*, **7**(3), 122–124, 127.

Lueck, E. (1980) *Antimicrobial Food Additives*. Berlin: Springer-Verlag.

Maas, M.R., Glass, K.A. & Doyle, M.P. (1989) Sodium lactate delays toxin production by *Clostridium botulinum* in cook-in-bag turkey products. *Applied and Environmental Microbiology*, **55**, 2226–2229.

Maga, J.A. (1988) *Smoke in Food Processing*. Boca Raton, Florida: CRC Press.

Magee, P.N. & Barnes, J.M. (1967) Carcinogenic nitroso-compounds. *Advances in Cancer Research*, **10**, 163–246.

Makinen, K.K. & Soderling, E. (1981) Effect of xylitol on some food-spoilage microorganisms. *Journal of Food Science*, **46**, 950–951.

Marletta, J. & Stumbo, C.R. (1970) Some effects of ethylene oxide on *Bacillus subtilis*. *Journal of Food Science*, **35**, 627–631.

Marth, E.H. (1966) Antibiotics in foods—naturally occurring, developed and added. *Residue Reviews*, **12**, 65–161.

Marth, E.H., Capp, C.M., Hasenzahl, L., Jackson, H.W. & Hussong, R.V. (1966) Degradation of potassium sorbate by *Penicillium* species. *Journal of Dairy Science*, **49**, 1197–1205.

Matthews, C., Davidson, J., Bauer, E., Morrison, J.L. & Richardson, A.P. (1956) *p*-Hydroxybenzoic acid esters as preservatives. II. Acute and chronic toxicity in dogs, rats, and mice. *Journal of the American Pharmaceutical Association, Scientific Edition*, **45**, 260–267.

Matz, S.A. (1960) Minor ingredients. In *Bakery Technology and Engineering*, pp. 231–232. Westport, Connecticut: AVI Publishing Company.

Mayr, G. & Kaemmerer, H. (1959) Fumigation with ethylene oxide. *Food Manufacture*, **34**, 169–170.

Mayr, G.E. & Suhr, H. (1972) Preservation and sterilization of pure and mixed spices. *Proceedings of the Conference on Spices*. pp. 201–207. London: Tropical Products Institute.

McCulloch, E.C. (1945) *Disinfection and Sterilization*, 2nd Ed. Philadelphia: Lea & Febiger.

McIver, R., Noren, P. & Tatini, S.R. (1978) Influence of certain food preservatives on growth and production of enterotoxins by *Staphylococcus aureus*. Annual Meeting of the American Society of Microbiology. Abstract No. 187.

Medina, M., Gaya, P. & Nunez, M. (1989) The lactoperoxidase system in ewe's milk: levels of lactoperoxidase and thiocyanate. *Letters in Applied Microbiology*, **8**, 147–149.

Melnick, D., Luckmann, F.H. & Gooding, C.M. (1954) Sorbic acid as a fungistatic agent for foods. VI. Metabolic degradation of sorbic acid in cheese by molds and the mechanism of mold inhibition. *Food Research*, **19**, 44–58.

Meneely, G.R., Tucker, R.G., Darby, W.J. & Auerbach, S.H. (1953) Chronic sodium chloride toxicity: hypertension, renal and vascular lesions. *Annals of Internal Medicine*, **39**, 991–998.

Merten, H.L. & Bachman, G.L. (1976) Glutaric acid: a potential food acidulant. *Journal of Food Science*, **41**, 463–464.

Messina, M.C., Ahmad, H.A., Marchello, J.A., Gerba, C.P. & Paquette, M.W. (1988) The effect of liquid smoke on *Listeria monocytogenes*. *Journal of Food Protection*, **51**, 629–631.

Michener, H.D., Thompson, F.A. & Lewis, J.C. (1959) Search for substances which reduce the heat resistance of bacterial spores. *Applied Microbiology*, **7**, 166–173.

Montville, T.J. (1989) The evolving impact of biotechnology on food microbiology. *Journal of Food Safety*, **10**, 87–97.

Montville, T.J. & Goldstein, P.K. (1989) Sodium bicarbonate inhibition of aflatoxigenesis in corn. *Journal of Food Protection*, **52**, 45–48.

Mossel, D.A.A. (1975) *Microbiology of Foods and Dairy Products*. Utrecht: University of Utrecht, Faculty of Veterinary Medicine.

Mukai, F., Hawryluk, I. & Shapiro, R. (1970) The mutagenic specificity of sodium bisulfite. *Biochemical and Biophysical Research Communications*, **39**, 983–988.

Nagy, R. (1959) Application of ozone from sterilamp in control of mold, bacteria and odors. In *Ozone Chemistry and Technology* (ed. Leedy, H.A.) Advanced Chemical Series No. 21. Washington, DC: American Chemical Society.

Namiki, M. & Kada, T. (1975) Formation of ethylnitrolic acid by the reaction of sorbic acid with sodium nitrite. *Agricultural and Biological Chemistry (Japan)*, **39**, 1335–1336.

National Research Council (1981) *The Health Effects of Nitrate, Nitrite and* N-*nitroso Compounds*. Washington, DC: National Academy Press.

National Research Council (1982) *Alternatives to Current Use of Nitrite in Foods*. Washington, DC: National Academy Press.

Natvig, H., Andersen, J. & Rasmussen, E.W. (1971) A contribution of the toxicological evaluation of hexamethylenetetramine. *Food and Cosmetics Toxicology*, **9**, 491–500.

Neal, A.L., Weinstock, J.O. & Lampen, J.O. (1965) Mechanisms of fatty acid toxicity for yeast. *Journal of Bacteriology*, **90**, 126–131.

Neidig, C.P. & Burrell, H. (1944) The esters of para-hydroxybenzoic acid as preservatives. *Drug and Cosmetic Industry*, **54**, 408–415.

Nes, I.F. & Eklund, T. (1983) The effect of parabens on DNA, RNA and protein synthesis in *Escherichia coli* and *Bacillus subtilis*. *Journal of Applied Bacteriology*, **54**, 237–242.

Newberne, P.M. (1979) Nitrite promotes lymphoma incidence in rats. *Science*, **204**, 1079–1081.

Njagi, G.D.E. & Gopalan, H.N.B. (1980) DNA and its precursors might interact with the food preservatives, sodium sulphite and sodium benzoate. *Experientia*, **36**, 413–414.

Notermans, S., Dufrenne, J. & Keybets, M.J.H. (1985) Use of preservatives to delay toxin formation by *Clostridium botulinum* (type B, strain okra) in vacuum-packed, cooked potatoes. *Journal of Food Protection*, **48**, 851–855.

Ogilvy, W.S. & Ayres, J.C. (1951) Post-mortem changes in stored meats. II. The effect of atmosphere containing carbon dioxide in prolonging the storage life of cut-up chicken. *Food Technology*, **5**, 97–102.

Ogilvy, W.S. & Ayres, J.C. (1953) Post-mortem changes in stored meats. V. Effects of carbon dioxide on microbial growth on stored frankfurters and characteristics of some microorganisms isolated from them. *Food Research*, **18**, 121–130.

Oka, S. (1964) Mechanism of antimicrobial effect of various food preservatives. In *Microbial Inhibitors in Food* (ed. Molin, N.) pp. 1–15. Stockholm: Almquist & Wiksell.

O'Leary, D.K. & Kralovec, R.D. (1941) Development of *B. mesentericus* in bread and control with calcium acid phosphate and calcium propionate. *Cereal Chemistry*, **18**, 730–741.

Olson, J.C., Jr & Macy, H. (1945) Observations on the use of propionate-treated parchment in inhibiting mold growth on the surface of butter. *Science*, **28**, 701–710.

Ough, C.S. (1983a) Dimethyl dicarbonate and diethyl dicarbonate. In *Antimicrobials in Foods* (eds Branen, A.L. & Davidson, P.M.) pp. 299–325. New York: Marcel Dekker.

Ough, C.S. (1983b) Sulfur dioxide and sulfites. In *Antimicrobials in Foods* (eds Branen, A.L. and Davidson, P.M.) pp. 299–325. New York: Marcel Dekker.

Papageorgiou, D.K. & Marth, E.H. (1989) Behavior of *Listeria monocytogenes* at 4 and 22°C in whey and skim milk containing 6 or 12% sodium chloride. *Journal of Food Protection*, **52**, 625–630.

Pappas, H.J. & Hall, L.A. (1952) Control of thermophilic bacteria. *Food Technology*, **6**, 456–458.

Parekh, K.G. & Solberg, M. (1970) Comparative growth of *Clostridium perfringens* in carbon dioxide and nitrogen atmospheres. *Journal of Food Science*, **35**, 156–159.

Parker, M.S. (1969) Some effects of preservatives on the development of bacterial spores. *Journal of Applied Bacteriology*, **32**, 322–328.

Payne, K.D., Rico-Munoz, E. & Davidson, P.M. (1989) The antimicrobial activity of phenolic compounds against *Listeria monocytogenes* and their effectiveness in a model milk system. *Journal of Food Protection*, **52**, 151–153.

Pearson, D. (1970) Effect on various spoilage values of the addition of sulphite and chlortetracycline to beef stored at 5°C. *Journal of Food Technology*, **6**, 141–147.

Phillips, C.R. & Kaye, S. (1949) The sterilizing action of gaseous ethylene oxide. *American Journal of Hygiene*, **50**, 270–279.

Phillips, G.F. & Mundt, J.O. (1950) Sorbic acid as inhibitor of scum yeast in cucumber fermentations. *Food Technology*, **4**, 291–293.

Pierson, M.D., Smoot, L.A. & Stern, N.J. (1979) Effect of potassium sorbate on growth of *Staphylococcus aureus* in bacon. *Journal of Food Protection*, **42**, 302–304.

Pierson, M.D., Smoot, L.A. & van Tassel, K.R. (1980) Inhibition of *Salmonella typhimurium* and *Staphylococcus aureus* by butylated hydroxyanisole and the propyl ester of *p*-hydroxybenzoic acid. *Journal of Food Protection*, **43**, 191–194.

Poole, G. & Malin, B. (1964) Some aspects of the action of tylosin on *Clostridium* species PA 3679. *Journal of Food Science*, **29**, 475.

Post, L.S., Lee, D.A., Solberg, M., Furgang, D., Specchio, J. & Graham, C. (1985) Development of botulinal toxin and sensory deterioration during storage of vacuum and modified atmosphere packaged fish fillets. *Journal of Food Science*, **50**, 990–996.

Prescott, S.C. & Proctor, B.E. (1937) *Food Technology*. New York: McGraw-Hill.

Raccach, M. (1984) The antimicrobial activity of phenolic antioxidants in foods: a review. *Journal of Food Safety*, **6**, 141–170.

Raevuori, M. (1976) Effect of sorbic acid and potassium sorbate on growth of *Bacillus cereus* and *Bacillus subtilis* in rice filling of Karelian pastry. *European Journal of Applied Microbiology*, **2**, 205–213.

Rayman, M.K., Aris, B. & Hurst, A. (1981) Nisin: a possible alternative or adjunct to nitrite in the preservation of meats. *Applied and Environmental Microbiology*, **41**, 375–380.

Rayman, K., Malik, N. & Hurst, A. (1983) Failure of nisin to inhibit outgrowth of *Clostridium botulinum* in a model cured meat system. *Applied and Evironmental Microbiology*, **46**, 1450–1452.

Reddish, G.F. (1957) *Antiseptics, Disinfectants, Fungicides, and Chemical and Physical Sterilization*. 2nd Ed. Philadelphia: Lea & Febiger.

Reed, G. (ed.) (1982) *Prescott and Dunn's Industrial Microbiology*, 4th Ed. Westport, Connecticut: AVI Publishing Co.

Reiss, J. (1976) Prevention of the formation of mycotoxins in whole wheat bread by citric acid and lactic acid (mycotoxins in foodstuffs, IX). *Experientia*, **32**, 168–169.

Reiter, B. & Harnulv, G. (1984) Lactoperoxidase antibacterial system: natural occurrence, biological functions and practical applications. *Journal of Food Protection*, **47**, 724–732.

Restaino, L., Lenovich, L.M. & Bills, S. (1982) Effect of acids and sorbate combinations on the growth of four osmophilic yeasts. *Journal of Food Protection*, **45**, 1138–1142.

Riha, W.E., Jr & Solberg, M. (1975a) *Clostridium perfringens* inhibition by sodium nitrite as a function of pH, inoculum size and heat. *Journal of Food Science*, **40**, 439–442.

Riha, W.E., Jr & Solberg, M. (1975b) *Clostridium perfringens* growth in a nitrite-containing defined medium sterilized by heat or filtration. *Journal of Food Science*, **40**, 443–445.

Rizk, S.S. & Isshak, Y.M. (1974) Thiabendazole as a post harvest disinfectant for citrus fruits. *Agricultural Research Review*, **52**, 39–46.

Robach, M.C. (1978) Effect of potassium sorbate on the growth of *Pseudomonas fluorescens*. *Journal of Food Science*, **43**, 1886–1887.

Robach, M.C. (1979) Influence of potassium sorbate on growth of *Pseudomonas putrefaciens*. *Journal of Food Protection*, **42**, 312–313.

Robach, M.C. & Hickey, C.S. (1978) Inhibition of *Vibrio parahaemolyticus* by sorbic acid in crab meat and flounder homogenates. *Journal of Food Protection*, **41**, 699–702.

Robach, M.C. & Ivey, F.J. (1978) Antimicrobial efficacy of potassium sorbate dip on freshly processed poultry. *Journal of Food Protection*, **41**, 284–288.

Robach, M.C. & Pierson, M.D. (1978) Influence of *p*-hydroxybenzoic acid esters on the growth and toxin production of *Clostridium botulinum* 10755A. *Journal of Food Science*, **43**, 787–789.

Robach, M.C. & Sofos, J.N. (1982) Use of sorbates in meat products, fresh poultry and poultry products. *Journal of Food Protection*, **44**, 614–622.

Roberts, T.A. (1975) The microbial role of nitrite and nitrate. *Journal of Science, Food and Agriculture*, **26**, 1755–1760.

Roberts, T.A., Gibson, A.M. & Robinson, A. (1981) Prediction of toxin production by *Clostridium botulinum* in pasteurized pork slurry. *Journal of Food Technology*, **16**, 337–355.

Robinson, A., Gibson, A.M. & Roberts, T.A. (1982) Factors controlling the growth of *Clostridium botulinum* types A and B in pasteurized, cured meats. V. Prediction of toxin production: non-linear effects of storage temperature and salt concentration. *Journal of Food Technology*, **17**, 727–744.

Robinson, H.J., Phares, H.F. & Graessle, O.E. (1964) Antimycotic properties of thiabendazole. *Journal of Investigative Dermatology*, **42**, 479–482.

Roland, J.O. & Beuchat, L.R. (1984) Biomass and patulin production by *Byssochlamys nivea* in apple juice as affected by sorbate, benzoate, SO_2 and temperature. *Journal of Food Science*, **49**, 402–406.

Roth, N.G. & Halvorson, H.O. (1952) The effect of oxidative rancidity in unsaturated fatty acids on the germination of bacterial spores. *Journal of Bacteriology*, **63**, 429–435.

Rowe, M.T. (1988) Effect of carbon dioxide on growth and extracellular enzyme production by *Pseudomonas fluorescens* B52. *International Journal of Food Microbiology*, **6**, 51–56.

Russell, A.D. (1971) Ethylenediaminetetraacetic acid. In *Inhibition and Destruction of the Microbial Cell* (ed. Hugo, W.B.) pp. 209–224. London: Academic Press.

Russell, A.D. & Fuller, R. (eds) (1979) *Cold-tolerant Microorganisms in Spoilage and the Environment*. Society for Applied Bacteriology Technical Series No. 13. London and New York: Academic Press.

Rusul, G. & Marth, E.H. (1988a) Food additives and plant components control growth and aflatoxin production by toxigenic aspergilli: a review. *Mycopathologia*, **101**, 13–23.

Rusul, G. & Marth, E.H. (1988b) Growth and aflatoxin production by *Aspergillus parasiticus* in a medium at different pH values and with or without pimaricin. *Zoological Lebensmittel Untersuch Forschungsanstalt*, **1897**, 436–439.

Rusul, G., El-Gazzar, F.E. & Marth, E.H. (1987) Growth and aflatoxin production by *Aspergillus parasiticus* NRRL 2999 in the presence of acetic or propionic acid and at different pH values. *Journal of Food Protection*, **50**, 909–914.

Saitanu, K. & Lund, E. (1975) Inactivation of enterovirus by glutaraldehyde. *Applied Microbiology*, **29**, 571–574.

Sams, W.M., Jr & Carroll, N.V. (1966) Prediction and demonstration of iron chelating ability of sugars. *Nature, London*, **212**, 404–405.

Sauer, F. (1977) Control of yeasts and molds with preservatives. *Food Technology*, **31**(2), 62–65.

Sauter, E.A., Kemp, J.D. & Langlois, B.E. (1977) Effect of nitrite and erythorbate on recovery of *Clostridium perfringens* spores in cured pork. *Journal of Food Science*, **42**, 1678–1679.

Schmidt, C.F. (1964) Spores of *Clostridium botulinum*: formation, resistance, germination. In *Botulism, Proceedings of a Symposium* (eds Lewis, K.H. & Cassel, K.) pp. 69–82. Washington, DC: US Department of Health, Education, and Welfare, Public Health Service, No. 999–FP-1.

Scott, V.N. & Taylor, S.L. (1981a) Effect of nisin on the outgrowth of *Clostridium botulinum* spores. *Journal of Food Science*, **46**, 117–120, 126.

Scott, V.N. & Taylor, S.L. (1981b) Temperature, pH and spore load effects on the ability of nisin to prevent the outgrowth of *Clostridium botulinum* spores. *Journal of Food Science*, **46**, 121–126.

Sebranek, J.G. & Cassens, R.G. (1973) Nitrosamines: a review. *Journal of Milk and Food Technology*, **36**, 76–91.

Segmiller, J.L., Xezones, H. & Hutchings, I.J. (1965) The efficacy of nisin and tylosin lactate in selected heat-sterilized food products. *Journal of Food Science*, **30**, 166–171.

Seiler, D.A.L. (1964) Factors affecting the use of mould inhibitors in bread and cake. In *Microbial Inhibitors in Food* (ed. Molin, N.) pp. 211–220. Stockholm: Almquist & Wiksell.

Shapero, M., Nelson, D.A. & Labuza, T.P. (1978) Ethanol inhibition of *Staphylococcus aureus* at limited water activity. *Journal of Food Science*, **43**, 1467–1469.

Shelef, L.A. (1984) Antimicrobial effects of spices. *Journal of Food Safety*, **6**, 29–44.

Shibasaki, I. (1970) Antibacterial activity of tylosin on Hiochi-bacteria. *Journal of Fermentation Technology*, **48**, 110–115.

Shiralkar, N.D. & Rege, D.V. (1978) Mechanism of action of *p*-hydroxybenzoates. *Indian Food Packer*, **32**, 34–41.

Shtenberg, A.J. & Ignat'ev, A.D. (1970) Toxicological evaluation of some combinations of food preservatives. *Food and Cosmetic Toxicology*, **8**, 369–380.

Silliker, J.H. (1959) The effect of curing salts on bacterial spores. In *Proceedings of the Meat Industry Research Conference*, pp. 51–60. Washington, DC: American Meat Institute.

Silliker, J.H., Greenberg, R.A. & Schack, W.R. (1958) Effect of individual curing ingredients on the shelf stability of canned comminuted meats. *Food Technology*, **12**, 551–554.

Silliker, J.H., Woodruff, R.E., Lugg, J.R., Wolfe, S.K. & Brown, W.D. (1977) Preservation of refrigerated meats with controlled atmospheres: treatment and post-treatment effects of carbon dioxide on pork and beef. *Meat Science*, **1**, 195–204.

Sink, J.D. & Hsu, L.A. (1977) Chemical effects of smoke processing on frankfurter manufacture and storage characteristics. *Journal of Food Science*, **42**, 1489–1491.

Skinner, F.A. & Hugo, W.B. (eds) (1976) *Inhibition and Inactivation of Vegetative Microbes*. London: Academic Press.

Smith, D.P. & Rollin, N. (1954) Sorbic acid as a fungistatic agent for foods, VII. Effectiveness of sorbic acid in protecting cheese. *Food Research*, **19**, 59–65.

Smith, J.L. & Palumbo, S.A. (1981) Microorganisms as food additives. *Journal of Food Protection*, **44**, 936–955.

Smith, Q.J. & Brown, K.L. (1980) The resistance of dry spores of *Bacillus subtilis* var. *globigii* (NCIB 8058) to solutions of hydrogen peroxide in relation to aseptic packaging. *Journal of Food Technology*, **15**, 169–179.

Smith, W.H. (1963) The use of carbon dioxide in the transport and storage of fruits and vegetables. *Advances in Food Research*, **12**, 96–118.

Smulders, F.J.M., Barendsen, P., van Logtestijn, J.G.,

Mossel, D.A.A. & van der Marel, G.M. (1986) Review: Lactic acid: considerations in favour of its acceptance as a meat decontaminant. *Journal of Food Technology*, **21**, 419–436.

Sofos, J.N. (1981) Nitrite, sorbate and pH interaction in cured meat products. In Proceedings of the 34th Annual Reciprocal Meat Conference, pp. 104–120. Chicago, Illinois: National Live Stock and Meat Board.

Sofos, J.N. (1984) Antimicrobial effects of sodium and other ions in foods: a review. *Journal of Food Safety*, **6**, 45–78.

Sofos, J.N. (1985) Improved cooking yields of meat batters formulated with potassium sorbate and reduced levels of NaCl. *Journal of Food Science*, **50**, 1571–1575.

Sofos, J.N. (1986a) Use of phosphates in low-sodium meat products. *Food Technology*, **40**(9), 52–69.

Sofos, J.N. (1986b) Antimicrobial activity and functionality of reduced sodium chloride and potassium sorbate in uncured poultry products. *Journal of Food Science*, **51**, 16–19, 23.

Sofos, J.N. (1989a) *Sorbate Food Preservatives*. Boca Raton, Florida: CRC Press.

Sofos, J.N. (1989b) Phosphates in meat products. In *Development in Food Preservation–5* (ed. Thorne, S.) pp. 207–252. Amsterdam: Elsevier.

Sofos, J.N. & Busta, F.F. (1980) Alternatives to the use of nitrite as an antibotulinal agent. *Food Technology*, **34**(5), 244–251.

Sofos, J.N. & Busta, F.F. (1981) Antimicrobial activity of sorbate. *Journal of Food Protection*, **44**, 614–622.

Sofos, J.N. & Busta, F.F. (1983) Sorbates. In *Antimicrobials in Foods* (eds Branen, A.L. & Davidson, P.M.) pp. 141–175. New York: Marcel Dekker.

Sofos, J.N. & Maga, J.A. (1988) Composition and antimicrobial properties of liquid spice smokes. In *The Shelf-life of Foods and Beverages* (ed. Charalambas, G.) pp. 453–472. Amsterdam: Elsevier.

Sofos, J.N., Busta, F.F., Bhothipaksa, K. & Allen, C.E. (1979a) Sodium nitrite and sorbic acid effects on *Clostridium botulinum* toxin formation in chicken frankfurter-type emulsions. *Journal of Food Science*, **44**, 668–675.

Sofos, J.N., Busta, F.F. & Allen, C.E. (1979b) Sodium nitrite and sorbic acid effects on *Clostridium botulinum* spore germination and total microbial growth in chicken frankfurter emulsions during temperature abuse. *Applied and Environmental Microbiology*, **37**, 1103–1109.

Sofos, J.N., Busta, F.F. & Allen, C.E. (1979c) Botulism control by nitrite and sorbate in cured meats: a review. *Journal of Food Protection*, **42**, 739–770.

Sofos, J.N., Busta, F.F. & Allen, C.E. (1979d) *Clostridium botulinum* control by sodium nitrite and sorbic acid in various meat and soy protein formulations. *Journal of Food Science*, **44**, 1662–1667.

Sofos, J.N., Busta, F.F. & Allen, C.E. (1980a) Influence of pH on *Clostridium botulinum* control by sodium nitrite and sorbic acid in chicken emulsions. *Journal of Food Science*, **45**, 7–12.

Sofos, J.N., Busta, F.F., Bhothipaksa, K., Allen, C.E., Robach, M.C. & Paquette, M.W. (1980b) Effects of various concentrations of sodium nitrite and potassium sorbate on *Clostridium botulinum* toxin production in commercially prepared bacon. *Journal of Food Science*, **45**, 1285–1292.

Sofos, J.N., Maga, J.A. & Boyle, D.L. (1988) Effect of ether extracts from condensed wood smokes on the growth of *Aeromonas hydrophila* and *Staphylococcus aureus*. *Journal of Food Science*, **53**, 1840–1843.

Sofos, J.N., Pierson, M.D., Blocher, J.C. & Busta, F.F. (1986) Mode of action of sorbic acid on bacterial cells and spores. *International Journal of Food Microbiology*, **3**, 1–17.

Somers, E.B. & Taylor, S.L. (1987) Antibotulinal effectiveness of nisin in pasteurized process cheese spreads. *Journal of Food Protection*, **50**, 842–848.

Sorrells, K.M., Enigl, D.C. & Hatfield, J.R. (1989) Effect of pH, acidulant, time, and temperature on the growth and survival of *Listeria monocytogenes*. *Journal of Food Protection*, **52**, 571–573.

Spelhaug, S.R. & Harlander, S.K. (1989) Inhibition of foodborne bacterial pathogens by bacteriocins from *Lactococcus lactis* and *Pediococcus pentosaceous*. *Journal of Food Protection*, **52**, 856–862.

Stevenson, K.E. & Shafer, B.D. (1983) Bacterial spore resistance to hydrogen peroxide. *Food Technology*, **37**(11), 111–114.

Sugiyama, H. & Sofos, J.N. (1988) Botulism. In *Developments in Microbiology–4* (ed. Robinson, R.K.) pp. 77–120. London: Elsevier.

Sugiyama, T., Goto, K. & Uenaka, H. (1975) Acute cytogenetic effect of 2-(2-furyl)-3-(5-nitro-2-furyl)-acrylamide (AF-2, a food preservative) on rat bone marrow cells *in vivo*. *Mutation Research*, **31**, 241–246.

Suzuki, M., Okazaki, M. & Shibasaki, I. (1970) Mode of action of tylosin. *Journal of Fermentation Technology*, **48**, 525–532.

Sweet, C.W. (1975) Additive composition for reduced particle size meats in the curing thereof. US Patent No. 3 899 600.

Takayama, S. & Kuwabara, N. (1977) The production of skeletal muscle atrophy and mammary tumors in rats by feeding 2-(2-furyl)-3-(5-nitro-2-furyl) acrylamide. *Toxicology Letters*, **1**, 11–16.

Tanaka, N.E., Traisman, E., Lee, M.H., Cassens, R.C. & Foster, E.M. (1980) Inhibition of botulinum toxin formation in bacon by acid development. *Journal of Food Protection*, **43**, 450–457.

Tanaka, N., Meske, L., Doyle, M.P., Traisman, E., Thayer, D.W. & Johnston, R.W. (1985) Plant trials of bacon made with lactic acid bacteria, sucrose and lowered sodium nitrite. *Journal of Food Protection*, **48**, 679–686.

Tanner, F.W. (1944) *The Microbiology of Foods*, 2nd Ed. Champaign, Illinois: Garrard Press.

Tarr, H.L.A. (1941a) The action of nitrites on bacteria. *Journal of Fisheries Research Board, Canada*, **5**, 265–275.

Tarr, H.L.A. (1941b) Bacteriostatic action of nitrites.

Nature, London, **147**, 417–418.

Tarr, H.L.A. (1942) The action of nitrites on bacteria; further experiments. *Journal of Fisheries Research Board, Canada*, **6**, 74–89.

Tatini, S.R. (1989) Process for control of food pathogens. US Patent No. 4871563.

Tatini, S.R., Lee, R.Y., McCall, W.A. & Hill, W.M. (1976) Growth of *Staphylococcus aureus* and production of enterotoxins in pepperoni. *Journal of Food Science*, **41**, 223–225.

Taylor, S.L., Somers, E.B. & Krueger, L.A. (1985) Antibotulinal effectiveness of nisin–nitrite combinations in culture medium and chicken frankfurter emulsions. *Journal of Food Protection*, **48**, 234–239.

Tiina, M. & Sandholm, M. (1989) Antibacterial effect of the glucose oxidase–glucose system on food-poisoning organisms. *International Journal of Food Microbiology*, **8**, 165–174.

Toledo, R.T., Escher, F.E. & Ayres, J.C. (1973) Sporicidal properties of hydrogen peroxide against food spoilage organisms. *Applied Microbiology*, **26**, 592–597.

Tomkins, R.G. (1932) The inhibition of the growth of meat-attacking fungi by carbon dioxide. *Journal of the Society of Chemical Industry*, **51**, 261T–264T.

Tompkin, R.B. (1978) The role of mechanism of the inhibition of *C. botulinum* by nitrite—is a replacement available? In *Proceedings of the 31st Annual Reciprocal Meat Conference*. pp. 135–147. Chicago, Illinois: National Live Stock and Meat Board.

Tompkin, R.B. (1983) Nitrite. In *Antimicrobials in Foods* (eds Branen, A.L. & Davidson, P.M.) pp. 205–256. New York: Marcel Dekker.

Tompkin, R.B. (1984) Indirect antimicrobial effects in foods: phosphates. *Journal of Food Safety*, **6**, 13–28.

Tompkin, R.B., Christiansen, L.N., Shaparis, A.B. & Bolin, H. (1974) Effects of potassium sorbate on salmonellae, *Staphylococcus aureus*, *Clostridium perfringens*, and *Clostridium botulinum* in cooked, uncured sausage. *Applied Microbiology*, **28**, 262–264.

Tompkin, R.B., Christiansen, L.N. & Shaparis, A.B. (1980) Antibotulinal efficacy of sulfur dioxide in meat. *Applied and Environmental Microbiology*, **39**, 1096–1099.

Torricelli, A. (1959) Sterilization of empty containers for food industry. In *Ozone Chemistry and Technology* (ed. Leedy, H.A.) Advanced Chemistry Series No. 21. Washington, DC: American Chemical Society.

Troller, J.A. (1965) Catalase inhibition as a possible mechanism of the fungistatic action of sorbic acid. *Canadian Journal of Microbiology*, **11**, 611–617.

Troller, J.A. & Olsen, R.A. (1967) Derivatives of sorbic acid as food preservatives. *Journal of Food Science*, **32**, 228–231.

Tsay, W.I. & Chou, C.C. (1989) Influence of potassium sorbate on the growth of *Yersinia enterocolitica*. *Journal of Food Protection* , **52**, 723–726.

Tsuchido, T., Takano, M. & Shibasaki, I. (1983) Inhibitory effect of sucrose esters of fatty acids on intact and heated bacterial spores. *Journal of Antibacterial and Antifungal Agents*, **11**, 567–573.

United States Department of Agriculture (1979) Acid producing micro-organisms in meat products for nitrite dissipation. *Federal Register*, 13 February, **44**, 9372–9373.

Vahabzadeh, F., Collinge, S.K., Cornforth, D.P., Mahoney, A.W. & Post, F.J. (1983) Evaluation of iron binding compounds as inhibitors of gas and toxin production by *Clostridium botulinum* in ground pork. *Journal of Food Science*, **48**, 1445–1451.

Venugopal, V., Pansare, A.C. & Lewis, N.F. (1984) Inhibitory effect of food preservatives on protease secretion by *Aeromonas hydrophila*. *Journal of Food Science*, **49**, 1078–1081.

Vinter, V. (1970) Germination and outgrowth: effect of inhibitors. *Journal of Applied Bacteriology*, **33**, 50–59.

von Schelhorn, M. (1951) Control of microorganisms causing spoilage in fruit and vegetable products. *Advances in Food Research*, **3**, 429–482.

Wada, S., Nonaka, J., Koizumi, C., Konuma, H. & Suzuki, A. (1975) The preservative effects of sorbic acid for fish sausage. *Journal of the Food Hygiene Society of Japan*, **17**, 95–100.

Wagner, M.K. (1986) Phosphates as antibotulinal agents in cured meats: a review. *Journal of Food Protection*, **49**, 482–487.

Wagner, M.K. & Moberg, L.G. (1989) Present and future use of traditional antimicrobials. *Food Technology*, **43**(1), 143–147, 155.

Walker, G.C. & Harmon, L.G. (1965) Hydrogen peroxide as a bactericide for *Staphylococcus* in cheese milk. *Journal of Milk and Food Technology*, **28**, 36–40.

Walker, H.W. (1977) Spoilage of food by yeasts. *Food Technology*, **31**(2), 57–61, 65.

Walker, R. (1985) Sulphiting agents in foods: some risk/benefit considerations. *Food Additives and Contaminants*, **2**, 5–24.

Ward, R.L. & Ashley, C.S. (1980) Comparative study on the mechanisms of rotavirus inactivation by sodium dodecyl sulfate and ethylenediaminetetraacetic acid. *Applied and Environmental Microbiology*, **39**, 1148–1153.

Warth, A.D. (1977) Mechanism of resistance of *Saccharomyces bailli* to benzoic, sorbic and other weak acids used as food preservatives. *Journal of Applied Bacteriology*, **43**, 215–230.

Warth, A.D. (1985) Resistance of yeast species to benzoic and sorbic acids and to sulfur dioxide. *Journal of Food Protection*, **48**, 564–569.

Warth, A.D. (1988) Effect of benzoic acid on growth yield of yeasts differing in their resistance to preservatives. *Applied and Environmental Microbiology*, **54**, 2091–2095.

Warth, A.D. (1989) Relationships among cell size, membrane permeability, and preservative resistance in yeast species. *Applied and Environmental Microbiology*, **55**, 2995–2999.

Watanabe, T. (1963) Infective heredity or multiple drug resistance in bacteria. *Bacteriological Reviews*, **27**, 87–115.

Wesley, F., Rourke, B. & Darbishire, O. (1965) The formation of persistent toxic chlorohydrins in foodstuffs by fumigation with ethylene oxide and with propylene oxide. *Journal of Food Science*, **30**, 1037–1042.

Whelton, R., Phaff, H.J., Mark, E.M. & Fisher, C.D. (1946) Control of microbiological food spoilage by fumigation with epoxides. *Food Industry*, **18**, 23–25; 174–176; 318–319.

White, R.H., Howard, J.W., Barnes, C.J. (1971) Determination of polycyclic aromatic hydrocarbons in liquid smoke flavors. *Journal of Agricultural Food Chemistry*, **19**, 143–145.

Wilkinson, G.S. (1975) Sensitivity to ethylenediaminetetraacetic acid. In *Resistance of Pseudomonas aeruginosa* (ed. Brown, M.R.W.) pp. 145–188. London: J. Wiley & Sons.

Winarno, F.G. & Stumbo, C.R. (1971) Mode of action of ethylene oxide on spores of *Clostridium botulinum* 62A. *Journal of Food Science*, **36**, 892–895.

Winarno, F.G., Stumbo, C.R. & Hayes, K.M. (1971) Effect of EDTA on the germination and outgrowth from spores of *Clostridium botulinum* 62A. *Journal of Food Science*, **36**, 781–785.

Windmueller, H.G., Ackerman, C.J., Bakerman, H. & Mickelson, O. (1959) Reaction of ethylene oxide with nicotinamide and nicotinic acid. *Journal of Biological Chemistry*, **234**, 889–894.

Wong, H.-C. & Chen, Y.-L. (1988) Effects of lactic acid bacteria and organic acids on growth and germination of *Bacillus cereus*. *Applied and Environmental Microbiology*, **54**, 2179–2184.

Woodzinski, R.S., Labeda, D.P. & Alexander, M. (1978) Effect of low concentrations of bisulfite-sulfite and nitrite on microorganisms. *Applied and Environmental Microbiology*, **35**, 718–723.

Woolford, M.K. (1975) Microbiological screening of food preservatives, cold sterilants, and specific antimicrobial agents as potential silage additives. *Journal of the Science of Food and Agriculture*, **26**, 229–237.

Wyss, O. (1948) Microbial inhibition by food preservatives. *Advances in Food Research*, **1**, 373–393.

York, G.K. & Vaughn, R.H. (1954) Use of sorbic acid enrichment media for species of *Clostridium*. *Journal of Bacteriology*, **68**, 739–744.

York, G.K. & Vaughn, R.H. (1955) Resistance of *Clostridium parabotulinum* to sorbic acid. *Food Research*, **20**, 60–65.

Young, J.H. (1989) *Pure Food: Securing the Federal Food and Drugs Act of 1906*. Princeton, New Jersey: Princeton University Press.

Zaika, L.L. (1988) Spices and herbs: their antimicrobial activity and its determination. *Journal of Food Safety*, **9**, 97–118.

Chapter 17
Preservation in Specialized Areas
A·METAL WORKING FLUIDS

1 THE MICROBIOLOGY OF METAL WORKING FLUIDS

Microbial contamination of cutting oil emulsions has been studied for almost 40 years (see Lee & Chandler, 1941; Tant & Bennett, 1956; Hill, 1977) and the economic consequences have been well documented. These oil-in-water (o/w) emulsions are stabilized with a variety of anionic and non-ionic emulsifying agents and the hydrocarbon content in use varies from *ca.* 1% to 15%, depending on the application. They are used to cool and lubricate a wide range of metal working processes. Other chemicals in the formulation may control viscosity, corrosiveness, extreme pressure lubricity, smell, foaming, colour and microbial infestation. Bennett (1974) has reviewed this field of biodeterioration, and Hill (1984a) and Rossmore (1985) have added more recent information. Cutting oils are usually sold as concentrates which are then diluted with water by the user. Many formulations are inherently susceptible to microbial attack, which is all too frequent an occurrence; the organisms are free-living in the water phase and metabolize the ingredients migrating from the oil phase. Fluid malfunctions are associated with microbial proliferation, particularly emulsion instability and corrosiveness. There may also be unpleasant odours, particularly following plant shut-downs (even over a weekend) and there is growing concern about incipient health problems (Hill, 1983).

Cutting oil formulations are normally alkaline (*ca.* pH 8–9), and as they are circulated and hence aerated in use, the initial microbial contamination is normally by aerobic Gram-negative bacteria, particularly *Pseudomonas* spp. However, oxygen deficiencies occur as the flora increase, and it has been found that many of these bacteria are facultative, some by virtue of their ability to reduce nitrite, a cost-effective corrosion inhibitor. After some time, tank bottoms may be sufficiently anaerobic to allow sulphate reducing bacteria to proliferate (Isenberg & Bennett, 1959; Hill *et al.*, 1986).

During the past two decades, traditional o/w emulsions have been substantially replaced by 'synthetic' and 'semi-synthetic' metal working fluids (MWF). The former are true solutions and are nominally oil-free. The latter contain some oil, typically as a micro-dispersion. These formulations are also sold as concentrates and are diluted with water by the user. In many formulations glycols have figured as partial replacements for oil. These fluids also suffer microbial contamination, but with a tendency to be more prone to fungal attack. Most of the strictures appropriate to conventional cutting oils apply.

When preservatives (usually referred to as biocides in the metal-working industry) are being considered to control microbial proliferation, it is necessary to determine their activity towards the initial invading organisms. Preliminary information can be derived from the minimum inhibitory concentrations (MICs) to a range of organisms published in the biocide suppliers' data sheets. It has been found in practice that some of the commonly used biocides, particularly those functioning by virtue of a formaldehyde release mechanism, have little activity against yeasts and fungi, and these organisms may present a serious secondary infection hazard after the more vigorously growing bacteria have been suppressed. To guard against this contingency, a mixture of biocides may be indicated. Occasionally the pH of a formulation contaminated with bacteria may fall sufficiently to favour a natural secondary contamination with fungi but frequently modern MWFs are inherently prone to fungal infection, even at alkaline pH. As regards the temperatures likely to be encountered during use, it has been found that the bulk temperature of machine tool fluids is just above ambient, although there are obviously locally heated areas at the work-piece. Oil emulsions are used in substantial volumes to cool and lubricate rolling mills; here the bulk temperature is much higher, *ca*. 40–65°C, and a different microbial flora can be expected.

2 SELECTION OF BIOCIDES

2.1 Preservation of MWF concentrates and fluids diluted for use

Whilst it is obvious that effective biocides must exert their activity in the in-use water phase, they are commonly added to the concentrate at manufacture and must disperse in the water phase when this is added by the user. Relative solubility in oil and water is hence an important property of the biocide if the concentrate is an oil phase; the final relative volume of oil to water also influences the all-important equilibrium concentration in the aqueous phase (Carlson & Bennett, 1960). This is illustrated hypothetically in Table 17.1(A). The practice of adding biocide to a concentrate is still controversial, as the formulator must assume a dilution ratio over which he has no control. Too great a dilution will result in an ineffective aqueous biocide concentration, whilst too little will be wasteful and in some cases hazardous if the excessive biocide concentration is irritant to the skin or lungs.

Table 17.1 Theoretical biocide concentrations in aqueous phase of oil-in-water emulsions

A. *Oil concentrate assumed to contain 1000 parts/10⁶ biocide*						
Relative oil:water solubilities of biocide	1:1		1:10		10:1	
Mixture ratios, oil concentrate:water	1:100	1:10	1:100	1:10	1:100	1:10
Biocide (parts/10^6) in aqueous phase at equilibrium	10	91	10	99	9	50
B. *1000 parts/10^6 biocide assumed to be added to total mix*						
Relative oil:water solubilities of biocide	1:1		1:10		10:1	
Mixture ratios, oil concentrate:water	1:100	1:10	1:100	1:10	1:100	1:10
Biocide (parts/10^6) in aqueous phase at equilibrium	1000	1000	1010	1090	918	550

Preserved concentrates are expected to have a long shelf-life and any biocide incorporated must be selected on this basis. Some are never suitable for preserving concentrates.

As an alternative, biocides can be added 'tank-side' by the user when the concentrate is diluted for use, and then the water-solubility of candidate materials has to be considered. Again there are critics of this procedure as target concentrations (often 1000 parts/10^6) are rarely achieved. Volumes of fluid in use are rarely known with certainty, measuring equipment is sometimes a bucket and the conduct of the operation is relegated to unskilled staff. The mix ratio and relative solubilities, however, have less effect (see Table 17.1(B)) than adding biocide to the concentrate.

Some aspects of this problem are discussed by Carlson & Bennett (1960).

Fortunately a new strategy has been developed to assay the in-use concentrations of biocide (Hill *et al.*, 1986) and this will be discussed in Section 3.

2.2 Cleaning up microbially contaminated systems

The delivery of cutting fluids to the work-face follows two systems. In one, each machine has its individual reservoir and pump; top-up to replace evaporation and 'drag-out' (fluid lost by splashing and adherence to the work-piece) can be calculated and carried out for each individual sump, or ready-mixed fluid can be drawn from a central mixing tank. In the other system the fluid is held in a large central reservoir and distributed by a system of pipes to the work-faces of the machines in the shop, being returned by open or closed conduits to the central holding tank.

Biocides have an important valid application as part of the cleansing process which should be applied to cutting oil distribution systems between changes of fresh fluid. This procedure is aimed at breaking the sequence of reinfection. In this respect the principles of good manufacturing practice applied to the pharmaceutical and food industries should also be applied here. Methods of doing this are given in detail in the Institute of Petroleum's *Code of Practice for Metalworking Fluids* (1978/1990). In brief two basic procedures are used:

1 Discard the original fluid; rinse the reservoirs and distributing systems with water and/or cleanser if necessary; clean manually; circulate aqueous biocide, rinse with water if necessary; re-charge with new MWF.

2 Add a high concentration of detergent–biocide to the residual fluid; circulate for *ca.* 6 h; reject this and re-fill with fresh cutting fluid.

There are obviously many variations to these procedures and the method adopted is very much governed by the time and labour available and the facilities at hand for disposing of the volumes of liquid produced. Descending pipework poses a particular problem and it may be necessary to back-up or even reverse the flow, so that pipes can be expected to be completely filled with biocide solution. Floors and stonework around machine tools may become so impregnated with infected fluid that they too will have to be scrubbed and sterilized.

The biocide formulation used should ideally possess the following properties: it should be quick-acting; have a broad spectrum of biological activity at the pH and temperature of the fluid; have detergent properties; must not be inactivated by slimes or the chemicals in the cutting fluids; possess good skin tolerance; should not be corrosive; should be disposable.

2.3 Preservation of fluids in use

Biocides intended for tank-side addition to the dilute MWF fluid, i.e. addition to MWF at the works, will need to have different properties from those added by the fluid manufacturer before delivery to the works. They need not be quick-acting, although they must obviously be capable of coping with continuous re-contamination from outside sources such as carry-over from other microbially contaminated systems, detritus, contaminated rust-preventive and hydraulic oils, contaminated dilution water and air-borne contamination. Of prime importance is their compatibility with the formulation components, particularly oil emulsifying agents. This can readily be checked by an oil droplet size analysis of the emulsion after biocide addition, and a method of doing this with the Coulter particle counter was described by Hill (1976). This method detects the coalescence of small droplets to give larger droplets if the emulsifying system is compromised. A typical example is given in Fig. 17.1. In practice, coalescence would soon result in 'cream' formation, i.e. mechanical separation of components by gravity, and ultimately a layer of unemulsified oil would appear on the surface, indicating that the emulsion had 'cracked', i.e. that the emulsion structure had collapsed. For some applications, such as aluminium rolling, the emulsion stability is critically poised and a change to greater stability is also functionally unacceptable. Hence the biocide should not 'break' or 'tighten' the emulsion.

The biocide should not inactive the anticorrosive components of the formulation, which it might do by direct inactivation or indirectly by lowering the pH; rust inhibitors work best in alkaline conditions. Other chemical incompatibilities, with dyes, odour masks, extreme pressure additives and copper passivators may be experienced.

If the user adds a biocide after microbial proliferation has occurred, scums of dead organisms may aggregate at the surface and plug filters. These additions cannot improve a partially spoilt emulsion but they prevent its further deterioration.

3 INACTIVATION AND DEPLETION OF BIOCIDES

Chemical incompatibilities work in both directions, and it is very common to find that the biocide is inactivated by an emulsion constituent. One obvious incompatibility is found between an anionic emulsion and a cationic biocide, and this is the prime reason why quaternary ammonium compounds (QACs, quats) are little used in machine-tool cooling fluids. Many biocides are not persistent and lose their activity progressively in MWF, often within a few days and particularly at above ambient temperature. This is of particular concern where fluids are mixed in bulk centrally, as any biocide incorporated may be ineffective by the time the fluid has been filled into the machine tool container. Even stable biocides will deplete, as in most cases they are irreversibly bound to those organisms which they have killed.

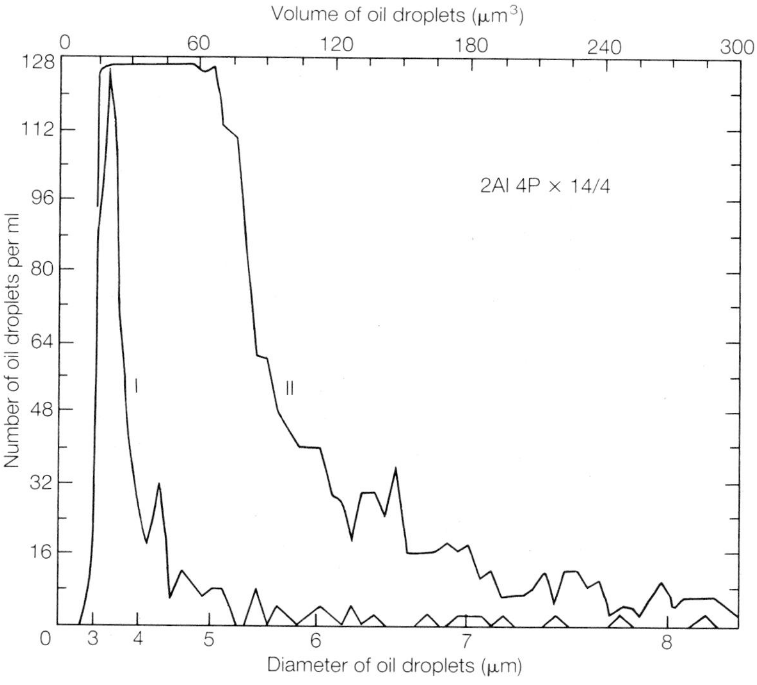

Fig. 17.1 'Oversize' droplet size analysis of an oil emulsion treated with biocide 'P' after 1(I) and 2(II) days. Analysis has been performed by a Coulter Counter 2B fitted with a P64 Analyser and Plotter; a 2000-fold division of the sample was passed through a 70-μm orifice. The emulsion has become less stable.

It cannot be emphasized too strongly that biocide activity can be dramatically decreased by relatively small reductions in concentration, especially if the biocide has a high concentration exponent, η (see Chapter 3).

Many users resort to the process of topping-up the biocide level, sometimes on hit-or-miss time intervals, sometimes when obvious spoilage is occurring (much too late to be of any value) and sometimes by monitoring the systems. Traditional physico-chemical biocide assays are far too complex for shop-floor use, and it has been more practicable to estimate regularly the bacterial population of the fluids using 'Dip-slides' (Hill, 1975), as illustrated in Fig. 17.2. Similar tests are available for yeasts and fungi. There is no agreed population level at which addition of further biocide is indicated, but many believe that 10^5 bacteria per ml is a reasonable upper limit. One must accept that modern 'bio-stable' fluids may continue to function adequately at higher levels of microbial contamination.

Hill (1984b) described a new concept for on-site use, the Sig Test. The most useful versions industrially are those which rapidly and semi-quantitatively detect nitrite-utilizing and sulphide-generating bacteria. Hence to some extent the significance of the organisms is emphasized, as well as their numbers. Rapid depletion of nitrite impairs the anticorrosive properties of some grinding fluids. Generation of sulphide, especially the volatile hydrogen sulphide (sulphurated hydrogen), is directly corrosive as well as being of an offensive odour and a health hazard.

Fig. 17.2 Easicult TTC Dip-slide unused (right) and after dipping into an infected oil emulsion and incubating (left). The microbial population is *ca.* 10^5/ml.

Any method which relies on a microbiological threshold being reached before more biocide is added can be criticized in that this permits some spoilage to occur. An alternative strategy is to repeatedly monitor biocide concentration.

The advantages of this strategy are that biocide concentration is frequently adjusted and spoilage is averted, not 'corrected'. If coupled to microbiological tests a realistic 'target' biocide concentration can be established and maintained. In large complex systems we have some guarantee that a biocide has been dosed at the correct concentration and is adequately dispersed. Experience indicates that different target concentrations may be desirable for the same biocide in different systems.

Simple colorimetric assays for formaldehyde released from donor biocides have been available for some years, but do not seem to be widely used. One problem is that such biocides exert their antimicrobial activity due both to formaldehyde release and inherent properties of the parent molecule. The technique is suitable for on-site use.

Chemical and physical assays for other biocides usually necessitate initial extraction and/or concentration followed by assay using procedures such as HPLC. The determination may not correlate with known antimicrobial activity, particularly if more than one active agent is present or where biocide activity is potentiated by a formulated component. The techniques are not suitable for on-site use.

There are, of course, a variety of biological techniques for assaying antimicrobial activity, all involving the inhibition of growth of a sensitive micro-organism. Hill (1982) proposed a biological method of assaying biocides in MWF which involved challenging aliquots of the preserved MWF at various storage or in-use time intervals with a standard inoculum of *Pseudomonas aeruginosa* and determining the survivors over a 6 h period. The procedure was relative rather than absolute; comparison of the various survival curves could reveal biocide depletion or inactivation.

A much simpler biological assay was proposed for MWF by Hill *et al.* (1986) and for fuel water bottoms by Hill in 1987. The assay organism was a member of the *Bacillus* sp. The spores of this organism, plus dried nutrients and a tetrazolium salt as a growth indicator, were carried on a pad mounted on a 5 × 55 mm plastic strip. This was dipped briefly into the fluid to be assayed, and incubated overnight at 37°C. Reduction of the tetrazolium to a red formazan accompanied spore germination and growth, and thus gave an obvious indication of the presence or absence of a chemical inhibitor. The strip could be calibrated against known biocides and biocide mixtures; the MIC so determined could then be utilized to assay unknown biocide concentrations in a fluid in use by testing a range of dilutions and establishing the greatest dilution which just contained the MIC. A simple calculation yields the concentration of biocide present.

The device used is referred to as a Biocide Monitor (Echa Microbiology Ltd, Cardiff Workshops, Cardiff). The assay organism is much more sensitive to biocides than are normal spoilage organisms, and hence the MIC determined for the device against a specific biocide is much lower than the target concentration of that biocide.

Using this device it is relatively easy to determine whether target biocide concentrations have been achieved and are being maintained.

Example

A MWF is preserved with Biocide X; the MIC of the Biocide Monitor for Biocide X is 100 ppm; the target concentration is 1000 ppm. A sample is taken and a range of dilutions tested with the Biocide Monitor. Results are:

Dilution:	1/7	1/8	1/9	1/10	1/11
Colour of pad:	White	Red	Red	Red	Red
Biocide concentration:	>700	<800	<900	<1000	<1100

Thus the concentration in the MWF is between 700 and 800 ppm, and a top-up of 250–300 ppm would be appropriate.

A better knowledge of the target concentration is accumulated if microbiological tests are also used, for example to test which organisms are controlled at different biocide concentrations.

The Biocide Monitor is not a universal tool for detecting all biocides/preservatives. The assay organism will be relatively resistant to some antimicrobial agents. The strain currently used exhibits a sensitivity gap to many phenolics and some QACs, particularly those with low water-solubility, and hence cannot be used to monitor their concentration.

3.1 Changes in microflora

There is some evidence that resistant strains of bacteria appear, but in most cases actual biocide assays indicate that the dosage is, in fact, inadequate (Hill *et al.*, 1986). It is, however common to find, as stated earlier, substantial secondary yeast and fungal contamination occurring even at high pH. This, of course, will necessitate a change in the biocide regime, usually by addition of an antifungal agent. Some machine shops consider it prudent to alternate biocides routinely.

4 THE IDEAL LONG-TERM BIOCIDE

The desirable properties of a preservative for both the concentrated and diluted emulsion may be summarized as follows:

1 speed of kill sufficient to cope with recontamination;
2 broad spectrum of biological activity at the pH and temperature of the cutting fluids;
3 not inactivated by the cutting fluid formulation;
4 more soluble in water than oil;
5 good skin and inhalation tolerance;
6 no detrimental effect on functional properties of the cutting fluids;
7 safe to handle and easy to measure;
8 disposable.

5 HEALTH HAZARDS FROM BIOCIDES

There is considerable concern about possible health hazards from biocides, and undoubtedly there are occasions when skin irritation has been experienced. The evidence for direct irritancy is not always good, however, and there are clear indicators that substantial overdosing has often been involved, or that the observed effect was due to a complex reaction involving both biocide and fluid. The use of fluids, especially with high-speed tools, may create a fine mist in the atmosphere. The permitted Time Weighted Average concentration of oil in the atmosphere is 5 mg/m^3 (UK Health and Safety Executive, 1990); if this arose from a 2% cutting oil emulsion containing 1000 parts/10^6 biocide, it would also represent 0.025 mg/m^3 of biocide in the atmosphere. This inference should be borne in mind when contemplating biocide inhalation toxicity.

5.1 Combination processes

To reduce possible hazards from biocide use or misuse, methods of reducing the concentration required should be mentioned. Increasing activity by heat is one possibility, and rendering microbes more permeable to biocides with sub-lethal doses of ultrasound is another. Both are no more than laboratory curiosities at the moment. When fluids are held in a central tank, a pasteurization procedure can be applied to the bulk fluid. In-line pasteurization can also be used (Elsmore & Hill, 1985); possibly a low dose of biocide would extend the downstream effect.

A large proportion of biocides used in MWF owe at least part of their activity to the release of formaldehyde. Considerable concern has been documented in the USA [DHEW (NIOSH) Publication No. 77–126 (1976)] which has led to restrictions on the use of formaldehyde, particularly in Scandinavian countries.

Some MWF contain both nitrite and amine, and it is now well known that these can combine slowly to form carcinogenic nitrosamines. Less well known is that formaldehyde significantly promotes this reaction. A few biocides are themselves nitrosating agents and also release formaldehyde.

In the UK the Control of Substances Hazardous to Health Regulations (1988) lay a duty on employers to conduct 'risk assessments' for hazardous chemicals, and this must include biocides. It thus becomes obligatory to avoid overdosing to the point of creating a risk; hence monitoring biocide concentration assumes greater importance. In assessing the risk one should not neglect the exposure to high concentrations of biocide of those handling preserved MWF concentrates or making tank-side biocide additions. The special case of enhancing nitrosamine formation must also be considered.

6 BIOCIDES FOR METAL WORKING FLUIDS

The range of biocides for this purpose is extensive, and a list of compounds that have been or are used is given in Table 17.2 (see also Wheeler & Bennett, 1953; Bennett, 1974; Rossmore, 1981). Their general properties and chemical structures are considered in Chapter 2 of this volume.

Cresylic acid was an early-used preservative for cutting oils, but its objectionable smell and irritancy, and environmental considerations, have persuaded most formulators to seek alternatives. Some of these have been phenolic, although there

Table 17.2 Examples of compounds* used in the preservation of cutting oil emulsions

2-Phenylphenol
2-Benzyl-4-chlorophenol
2,4,6-Trichlorophenol
Dichlorophane
2,2′-Thiobis (3,4,6-trichlorophenol)
6-Acetoxy-2,4-dimethyl-1,3-dioxane (GivGard DXN)
1,3-Di (hydroxymethyl)-5,5-dimethyl-2,4-dioxoimidazole (Dantoin, DMDMH-55)
N,N-Methylenebis-5′-(1-hydroxymethyl-2,5,-dioxo-4-imidazolidinyl urea (Germall 115)
5-Chloro-2-methyl-4-isothiazolin-3-one } (Kathone 886 MW)
2-Methyl-4-isothiazolin-3-one } (Kathone 886 MW)
cis-1-(3-chlorallyl-3,5,7-triaza-1-azonia) adamantane chloride (Dowicil 200)
Hexahydro-1,3,5-triethyl-*s*-triazine
1,3-Dichloro-5-dimethyldioxomimidazole (Halane)
1,2-Benzisothiazolin-3-one
4-(2-nitrobutyl)-morpholine
Tris(hydroxymethyl) nitro-methane
Sodium-2-pyridinethiol-1-oxide
4,4-Dimethyloxazolidine

* For further information on many of these compounds, see Chapter 2.

has been a substantial environmental lobby to restrict phenolic discharges. The formaldehyde releasers (Chapter 2), have found more and more use in all areas of preservation including cutting fluids. The triazines, e.g. hexahydro-1,3,5-triethyl-*s*-triazine, imidazoles and hexamine derivatives are examples. Isothiazolones, oxazolidines and dioxanes are also widely used.

As in all cases when newer compounds are being considered, formulators should ensure that toxicological and environmental hazards are evaluated as well as in-use efficacy, and compatibility with product ingredients. Genuinely new antimicrobial agents are in short supply. There is sound logic in seeking enhanced activity and spectrum for preservative systems for MWF by using combinations of two or more biocides chosen from those whose toxicology is well understood.

7 OTHER EMULSIFIED FLUIDS

It should be noted that, for some applications, water-in-oil (w/o) emulsions are used, particularly where flame resistance is important (e.g. steel mill hydraulic fluids). It has been found that incorporation of preservative into the aqueous phase before emulsifying this with the oil is a feasible approach. If a biocide must be added after the emulsion has been made, it must have sufficient oil-solubility to disperse in the continuous oil phase and sufficient water-solubility to pass from there into the entrained water droplets.

8 DISPOSABILITY

With or without preservatives, cutting fluids (whatever the type) have a finite life determined by solids content, chemical and physical change, performance failure and sometimes merely by their acquisition of an objectionable smell. At this point they must be disposed of in a manner which will satisfy national and local bye-laws relating to pollution and waste disposal. This could be by approved dumping, or by approved effluent discharge, often to the local authority sewerage. There is no consistent policy for approving discharges; dilution as a result of mixing with other discharges is important. Normally a requirement to separate the emulsion phases chemically and remove the oil layer before discharging the aqueous phase would be anticipated. However, local authorities frequently require assurance that if biocides are present in any product they are not present in the discharge at a concentration which could inhibit biological sewage treatment processes. In some cases the 'cracking' process already referred to inactivates the biocide, or alters its solubility so that it passes into the oil phase. In other cases a practical course of action is to dilute the discharge; fortunately most of the common biocides are biodegradable at appropriate dilution. In practice the dilemma is considerably eased by anticipating the disposal date and stopping biocide additions during the latter part of the fluid's life. Dutka & Gorrie (1989) have evaluated techniques for monitoring toxic discharges and commented favourably on the Biocide Monitor (Section 3).

9 CONCLUSIONS

The management of MWF systems for maximum functional life frequently necessitates the use of biocides. Many factors have to be considered for their selection and for designing a treatment regime, and it is only in recent years that the necessary technical knowledge and competence have become available. Environmental and health considerations are rightly playing an increasing role in this field.

10 REFERENCES

Anon (1976) Criteria document: *Recommendations for an Occupational Exposure Standard for Formaldehyde*. US Department of Health Education and Welfare (National Institute for Occupational Safety and Health). Publication No. 77–126.

Anon (1988) *The Control of Substances Hazardous to Health Regulations*. London: HMSO.

Anon (1990) *Occupational Exposure Standards*. Health and Safety Executive, UK. (Also OSHA IMIS 5010, USA.)

Bennett, E.O. (1974) The deterioration of metal cutting fluids. *Progress in Industrial Microbiology*, **13**, 121–150.

Carlson, V. & Bennett, E.O. (1960) The relationship between the oil–water ratio and the effectiveness of inhibitors in oil-soluble emulsions. *Lubrication Engineering*, **16**, 572–574.

Dutka, B.J. & Gorrie, J.F. (1989) Assessment of toxicant

activity in sediments by the Echa Biocide Monitor. *Environmental Pollution*, **57**, 1–7.

Elsmore, R. & Hill, E.C. (1985). The ecology of pasteurised metal-working fluids. *International Biodeterioration*, **22**, 101–109.

Hill, E.C. (1975) Biodeterioration of petroleum products. In *Microbiological Aspects of the Deterioration of Materials* (eds Gilbert, R.J. & Lovelock, D.W.) pp. 127–136. London: Academic Press.

Hill, E.C. (1976) Evaluation of biocides for use with petroleum product. *Process Biochemistry*, **11**, 36–48.

Hill, E.C. (1977) Microbial infection of cutting fluids. *Tribology International*, **10**, 49–54.

Hill, E.C. (1982) The current state of the art on chemical and physical antimicrobial measures. In *Proceedings: Lubrication in Metal-working* (ed. Bartz, W.J.) Vol. II, pp. 82.1–82.4. Esslingen: Technische Akademie.

Hill, E.C. (1983) Microbial aspects of health hazards from water-based metal-working fluids. *Tribology International*, **16**, 136–140.

Hill, E.C. (1984a) Biodegradation of petroleum products. In *Petroleum Microbiology* (ed. Atlas, R.M.) pp. 579–617. London: Macmillan.

Hill, E.C. (1984b) Microorganisms—numbers, types, significance, detection. In *Monitoring and Maintenance of Aqueous Metal-working Fluids* (eds Hill, E.C. & Chater, K.W.A.) pp. 97–112. Chichester: John Wiley & Sons.

Hill, E.C. (1987) Fuels. In *Microbial Problems in the Offshore Oil Industry* (eds Hill, E.C., Shennan, J.L. and Watkinson, R.J.) pp. 219–229. Chichester: John Wiley & Sons.

Hill, E.C., Hill, G.C., Robbins, D.A. & Williams, E. (1986) Sulphide generation in metal-working fluids and its control. In *Additives for Lubricants and Operational Fluids* (ed. Bartz, W.J.) Vol. II, pp. 10.1–10.7. Esslingen: Technische Akademie.

HM Factory Inspectorate Threshold Limit Values (1976) Health and Safety Executive, Technical Data Note 2/75.

Institute of Petroleum (1990) *Code of Practice for Metal-working Fluids*, 2nd Ed. London: Heyden.

Isenberg, D.L. & Bennett, E.O. (1959) Bacterial deterioration of emulsion oils. II. Nature of the relationship between aerobes and sulphate-reducing bacteria. *Applied Microbiology*, **7**, 121–125.

Lee, M. & Chandler, A.C. (1941) A study of the nature, growth and control of bacteria in cutting compounds. *Journal of Bacteriology*, **41**, 373–386.

Rossmore, H.W. (1981) Antimicrobial agents for water-based metal-working fluids. *Journal of Occupational Medicine*, **23**, 247–254.

Rossmore, H.W. (1985) Microbial degradation of water-based metal-working fluids. In *Comprehensive Biotechnology* (ed. Moo Young, M.) Vol. 14, pp. 249–269. Oxford: Pergamon Press.

Tant, C.O. & Bennett, E.O. (1956) The isolation of pathogenic bacteria from used emulsions. *Applied Microbiology*, **4**, 332–338.

Wheeler, H.O. & Bennett, E.O. (1953) Bacterial inhibitors for cutting oils. *Applied Microbiology*, **4**, 122–126.

B · FUELS AND LUBRICANTS

1 THE MICROBIAL PROBLEM

The previous section (Chapter 17A) discussed the use of biocides in petroleum products in which the major phase was water and the justification for the use of biocides was to prevent spoilage and malfunction.

In this section the problems discussed occur in oil–water mixtures in which water is the minor component (usually *ca.* 0.1%), present as a contaminant.

In most fuel contamination problems (Hill, 1978a), the lower layer of contaminated water (or water bottom, as it is called) is in contact with the oil phase for a short time, as fuel is used and replaced every few hours while the contaminated water bottom remains. The fuel invariably contains additives which enhance its nutritional status. One cannot expect much chemical change to occur in fuel if the contact time with contaminated water is short and the problem with contaminants thus involves fouling and corrosion of tanks and pipes. Early recognized problems occurred in aircraft which employed kerosene as propellant; it is now known that microbial contamination occurs widely in paraffin, diesel fuel, gas oil and tractor vaporizing oil. Long-term strategic fuel storage in rock caverns has been identified as a potential microbial problem. The Institute of Petroleum, London, was concerned enough to sponsor, in 1986, a task force to consider fuel problems, to commission a video and to organize a symposium.

Within the fuel storage space in the aircraft wings, a water bottom is formed; water, dissolved in fuels, is deposited from solution as the fuel cools in flight and also condenses from humid air within the cold wing structure. Fuel is turned over on every flight, but the water bottom is drained irregularly. Obviously, growth cannot occur to any significant extent when the fuel is cold and microbial problems are experienced only in warm, under-utilized aircraft. More luxuriant growth can be anticipated if water bottoms persist in ground storage installations or in supersonic aircraft (Hill & Thomas, 1975).

The organisms isolated in water bottoms are Gram-negative bacteria (particularly *Pseudomonas* spp.), yeasts and fungi. Of the latter, *Hormoconis (Cladosporium) resinae* is considered of most significance. The main problems are fouling, water entrainment and corrosion pitting. In stagnant tanks, hydrogen sulphide from sulphate in salt water residues and sulphur-containing fuel components may be evolved and contribute to corrosion.

In the 1980s most problems occurred in diesel and gas oil installations, particularly in ships. There is no 'cold cycle' as there is in aircraft, the water phase is usually salt not fresh, the turnover is less frequent and 'housekeeping' is generally less satisfactory. In salt water caverns temperatures are more likely to be higher, *c.* 50–55°C. Not surprisingly the microbial ecology differs from location to location and does not follow that found in aircraft.

In the case of lubricants, the oil phase is more nutritious as it may contain 20% of additives, some of them incorporating the vital elements nitrogen and phosphorus. Hence the contamination becomes more prolific, and although the infection may initially be restricted to a water bottom, infected water droplets eventually become dispersed in the oil phase. The problem takes the form of fouling, spoilage and corrosion. Ships' engine lubricants are particularly prone to infection (Hill, 1978b,c) as they are inevitably water-contaminated and maintained at *ca*. 38–50°C. Turbine lubricating oils are also prone to water contamination and hence susceptible to infection; microbial problems have also been experienced in a variety of 'straight' oils, even rust protective oils.

2 ANTIMICROBIAL MEASURES IN FUELS

2.1 General

Undoubtedly a major factor in the success of antimicrobial measures can be summarized as 'good housekeeping'. The aviation industry has been educated to appreciate the microbial nature of fouling and corrosion, and has significantly improved the design of both ground and aircraft fuel installations to minimize water accumulation. This has been coupled with the introduction of better routines for water draining and fuel testing.

Unfortunately the message has spread rather more slowly to other users of light fuel oils such as railway engineers and ship owners. Indeed, in ships it is accepted that a water bottom will inevitably be present in fuel storage tanks because they are often at the lowest point in the hull, and some vessels have fuel installation systems in which, as the fuel is used, sea-water is taken into the tanks to preserve the trim of the vessel.

2.2 Aircraft

Three positive antimicrobial approaches have been taken. First, antimicrobial pellets (usually formulations of strontium chromate) have been dispersed across the inside face of the lower wing plank. These can only be active when positioned to be in contact with free water and this condition is difficult to guarantee. The antimicrobial effectiveness of some formulations has been questionable (Rubridge, 1975). Secondly, biocides have been incorporated into the surface coatings which are used in the wings to protect the metal and render the structure fuel tight. This approach has not progressed much beyond disappointing laboratory trials. Thirdly, antimicrobials have been added to the fuel. These can, of course, be added at any stage during fuel storage and distribution; if added too early in the distribution system they leach out into every water bottom encountered and little may be left to protect the aircraft. Hence some operators favour the incorporation of metered biocide each time the aircraft is fuelled. Others add biocide only at major groundings when the aircraft could be most at risk.

The desirable properties of a fuel biocide are listed below. It must:

1 be combustible, with no residual ash;
2 not interfere with the fuel properties or the combustion process, or any other aspect of engine performance;
3 be soluble in fuel at −40°C (it must be borne in mind that the fuel cools during long flights in subsonic aircraft);
4 be active against Gram-negative bacteria and fungi at low concentration;
5 present no health hazard during handling or combustion;
6 be soluble (or very miscible) in fuel, but preferentially soluble in water;
7 not be corrosive;
8 achieve a total 'kill' during one flight.

No such ideal biocide has been developed for commercial use; two biocides achieved early market penetration, although deficient in some of the listed characteristics. These are Biobor JF and ethyleneglycol mono-methyl ether (EGME). They both exhibit 'antifreeze' properties and thus are particularly suitable for use in aircraft where ice formation in water contamination is of operational concern.

2.2.1 Biobor JF

Biobor JF (US Borax & Chemical Corp.), a mixture of two organo-boron compounds, is favoured for intermittent treatment. It leaves an ash on combustion and takes several days to be completely effective biologically. It therefore tends to be used for 'shock' treatment at times when an aircraft is considered to be at risk (such as when grounded for major maintenance), or when microbial contamination is suspected. It has had somewhat grudging approval by engine builders who tend to permit semi-continuous use at 135, and occasional use at 270 parts/10^6.

2.2.2 EGME (ethyleneglycol mono-methyl ether)

EGME has had more widespread acceptance, particularly by military operators. It is completely combustible, but again is only slowly biocidal. However, many military aircraft require anti-icing additives in the fuel to prevent ice formation from the entrained water, and hence EGME at *ca.* 0.15% is used to provide both anti-icing and antimicrobial properties. Civilian aircraft are more likely to possess fuel heaters to prevent ice crystal formation and hence the continuous use of an anti-icing additive is not justified. EGME affects the flash point of the fuel and there are moves to replace it with the diethylene derivative. Its major deficiency, however, is that at low concentrations it is readily metabolized by micro-organisms and hence, if used intermittently, there is a real risk that growth will be promoted if there is an interval between additions. This has actually occurred in some instances. Fortunately, military users normally stipulate that each fuel load should contain EGME.

It has already been pointed out that in oil/water systems the relative volumes of the two phases are of some importance. As a rule of thumb, neither of these biocides is likely to be very effective when the ratio of water to fuel is greater than 1:400.

2.2.3 Other biocides

Considerable research has gone into devising better biocides for aircraft, and some have been evaluated in depth. Diethylene glycol has been sanctioned for aircraft use; some alternative biocides are used occasionally for flushing out contaminated aircraft tanks. Soluble chromates have been added to heavily contaminated water bottoms in ground aviation fuel storage tanks, but there are serious engine problems if these become entrained in the fuel.

The consequences of using inappropriate biocides are perhaps less severe in marine and land transportation, and a variety of biocides have been formulated and tested with varying degrees of success. Some based on isothiazolines, oxazolidines and morpholines are in commercial use. Unlike the aircraft biocides they do not exhibit antifreeze properties and will function at higher ratios of water contamination. Diesel engine builders are generally prepared to accept their use more readily than aircraft engine builders. Two strategies are practised, fuel preservation (all fuel used is protected) and fuel disinfection (biocide application only when a functional problem is perceived). In the latter strategy speed of action (6 h or less for 'kill') is imperative; some manual cleaning or even de-sludging may be necessary.

There are no standard methods for testing biocides in fuel but Rossmore *et al.* (1988) have drawn attention to the various factors which affect efficacy.

2.3 Ships and oil-rigs

Many navies operate gas-turbine ships and find it impossible to eliminate water from the fuel storage tanks. These tanks may be an integral part of the double-bottom structure. Not surprisingly gas turbine ships use similar fuel to turbine-engined aircraft. Microbial contamination is often substantial, particularly where the surrounding sea temperature is high. The fuel is pumped up to a service tank and from there fed to the engines and stripped of water by a coalescer unit. Malfunction of this is the usual symptom of microbial contamination. Improved housekeeping is only of limited value; some naval operators with problems have added Biobor to all fuel used, but this expedient is not effective if water content is high. Engine builders may also have reservations on this strategy.

In some turbine ships, and in some oil-rig fuel storage facilities, fuel is displaced upwards, as it is used, by sea-water. Most attempts at antimicrobial measures under these circumstances have met with only limited success. Measures are usually aimed at adding a biocide to the sea-water as it is admitted, but as this water is discharged again on refuelling, often into harbour waters, any biocide must be environmentally acceptable. A temporary solution has been to discharge this biocide containing sea-water into shore tanks for disposal.

In the past decade there has been a remarkable upsurge in the occurrence of microbial problems in diesel-engined ships. Severe fuel line and injector fouling have brought ships to a halt throughout the world. Distillate fuels have changed in chemical composition and additive content, and are more supportive of microbial growth. Even heavy fuel oils have been found to be contaminated.

Ship operators have been reluctant to use fuel preservatives and have favoured a disinfection strategy, activated by a positive fuel test or a visual assessment. Few biocides have the speed and spectrum of activity for this application.

2.4 Trains and road vehicles

System fouling, filter plugging and serious malfunction of diesel engine injectors have also been recognized as microbial phenomena in road and rail vehicles. The problems are usually resolved by good housekeeping and additions of biocides when operational difficulties are experienced. In general, the procedures follow those described for diesel ships. In many cases the operators have their own storage tanks and these must be included in decontamination procedures.

2.5 Heating oils

Although microbial contamination of heating oils is commonplace, associated fouling and corrosion are rarely considered to be of enough significance to warrant antimicrobial measures, other than improved housekeeping.

2.6 Monitoring

'Dip-slides' can be used to evaluate contamination in fuel tank water bottoms but results are erratic if they are used on the fuel phase. The Biocide Monitor (see Chapter 17A, Section 3) is a useful device for assaying biocide concentration in water under biocide-treated fuel.

3 ANTIMICROBIAL MEASURES IN LUBRICANTS

3.1 Good housekeeping

As in fuels, emphasis is placed on water elimination, but this cannot approach the success achieved in aviation fuels. As indicated in Section 1, slow-speed diesel engine crankcase oils are particularly prone to microbial contamination. Lubricating oils tend to entrain water, and this is only partially resolved by the normal de-watering procedures of heating and centrifuging. Batch renovation, which involves heating the whole oil charge to 70–80°C for one or two days, is less common than hitherto but was undoubtedly beneficial for its sterilizing as well as its water-separating function. Considerable data on heating as a key procedure in 'good-housekeeping' have been published (Hill & Genner, 1981). High-speed engine lubricants cannot suffer microbial spoilage as the oil temperature achieved effectively pasteurizes the system.

Most large engines have a 'purifier' to remove water which continuously heats and centrifuges a slip-stream of the main lubricant charge. If the heater temperature is kept above 70°C and the flow regulated to achieve a 30 s 'contact' time this slip-stream is continuously decontaminated. Despite this knowledge major crankcase oil problems still occur.

3.2 Cleaning-up contaminated engine systems

At an early stage it must be decided whether the lubricating oil charge is to be dumped or retained as still serviceable. If it is to be retained, a procedure would be to pump most of the charge up for batch heat sterilization, add oil-soluble biocide to the remainder of the charge and circulate this in the engine for 12–24 h. This would then be dumped and hand cleaning carried out. The heat-sterilized oil would then be returned to the engine via the purifier and topped up, and re-spiked with additive oils if considered necessary. If the oil has deteriorated substantially, and is considered unserviceable, the whole oil charge can be dosed with an oil-soluble biocide and circulated to sterilize the system before hand cleaning. It is much preferred to carry out these procedures with hot oil.

In the majority of incidents, microbial proliferation would also take place in the engine cooling waters (cylinder and piston) and it has been postulated (Hill, 1978b) that these are the major source of both contaminating water and degradative microbes. These systems would therefore be dumped, flushed with aqueous biocide, hand cleaned and re-filled. The cooling waters are invariably treated in use with corrosion-inhibiting chemicals, particularly nitrite–borate formulations or soluble oils, and these support microbial growth.

3.3 Sterilizing oils in use

Engine oil infections are often detected at an early stage by on-board testing with Dip-slides, possibly after minor indications of oil malfunction. Experience has shown that growth of micro-organisms in the lubricating oil is at first confined to a water pocket at the bottom of the sump, and ships' engineers frequently detect this stage of the spoilage sequence. It can usually be successfully treated by pouring down the sounding pipe of the sump a biocide possessing water and oil solubility. The amount of biocide is estimated from a knowledge of the likely numbers of micro-organisms in the pocket, and the volume of the pocket.

In some circumstances, particularly where the ship is at sea experiencing some malfunction, and microbes have been detected throughout the oil system, it may be considered prudent to treat the whole of the oil charge in use with an oil-soluble biocide. Detailed information of this procedure is available to ship owners from the General Council of British Shipping, and some appropriate biocides are listed in their publications TR/069 of 1978 and TR/104 of 1983.

The biocide used must be selected with great care as it is imperative that it does not impair the functional properties of the lubricant. In brief it must not affect the 'wear' properties of the lubricant, its water-shedding capabilities or its aggressiveness. Some procedures for carrying out these tests have been given by Hill (1978c). Any biocide application will result in the release into the oil of dead microbial sludges, which may block filters.

It is not normal to add biocides to crankcase lubricants as preservatives as persistence is poor at the high temperatures of the engine. Some hydraulic oils and low-temperature lubricants may have a preservative added. However, oil formulators prefer to re-formulate to improve biostability.

3.4 Other straight mineral oils

Microbial growth in turbine oils and hydraulic oils is not uncommon, and the treatment procedures would generally follow those suggested for ships' lubricating oil, always paying due regard to minimum interference with the functional properties of the oil.

4 REFERENCES

Hill, E.C. (1978a) Biodegradation of hydrocarbons in industrial use. In *Developments in Biodegradation of Hydrocarbons*, Vol. 1 (ed. Watkinson, R.J.) pp. 201–225. London: Applied Science Publishers.

Hill, E.C. (1978b) *Microbial aspects of corrosion, equipment malfunction and systems failure in the marine industry*. Technical Research Report TR/069. General Council of British Shipping. Reprinted 1983 as TR/104.

Hill, E.C. (1978c) Microbial degradation of marine lubricants—its detection and control. *Transactions, Institute of Marine Engineers*, **90**, 197–216.

Hill, E.C. & Genner, C. (1981) Avoidance of microbial infection and corrosion in slow speed diesel engines by improved design of the crankcase oil system. *Tribology International*, **14**, 67–74.

Hill, E.C. & Thomas, A. (1975) Microbiological aspects of supersonic aircraft fuel. In *Proceedings of the 3rd International Biodegradation Symposium* (eds Sharpley, J.M. & Kaplan, A.M.) pp. 157–174. London: Applied Science Publishers.

Rossmore, H.W., Wireman, J.W., Rossmore, L.A. & Riha, V.F. (1988) Factors to consider in testing biocides for distillate fuels. In *Distillate Fuel: Contamination, Storage and Handling*, ASTM STP 1005 (eds Chesnau, H.L. & Doris, M.M.) pp. 95–104.

Rubridge, T. (1975) Inadequacy of a strontium chromate formulation for control of fungal growth in a kerosene/water system. *International Biodeterioration Bulletin*, **11**, 133–135.

Smith, R.N. (ed.) (1986) *Microbiology of Fuels*. London: Institute of Petroleum.

C·PRESERVATION OF PAPER AND PULP

1 INTRODUCTION

Raw materials for use in the paper and board industry are usually stored under dry conditions, until required in the manufacturing process. The nature and degree of microbial contamination will largely depend upon such physical characteristics as moisture content, temperature and pH. Certain grades of sulphite pulps and moist groundwood pulps have a 50% moisture content, whilst the moisture content of kraft and the majority of sulphite pulps lies between 10% and 15%.

The development of microbial contaminants may be controlled to some extent by conditions and period of storage. Deterioration is less likely to occur in chemical than in groundwood pulps. However, if chemical pulps are stored badly, for example in exposed stacks, discolouration and decay do occur, and in this sense the deterioration may be comparable with that of groundwood pulps. For this reason, wrapping was introduced. Pulps may have a considerable bacterial content, but the fungal content has proved to be a more reliable indicator of storage properties of pulps (Russell, 1957; Hughes, 1968). The two principal forms of fungal attack on pulps are cellulolytic, which weaken the fibres mechanically, and disfigurative (discolorative) caused by a variety of common airborne fungi (see Table 17.3).

The growth of basidiomycete fungi in pulps, producing as they do cellulases, results in shorter fibres with poor strength properties and consequently a final product of poor strength. In addition, there is a greater fibre loss to effluent, which is uneconomical. Even if cellulolytic activity is low, the discoloration caused by non-basidiomycete fungi will produce a darker than normal product (e.g. growth of *Paecilomyces* spp. in pulps has resulted in loss of brightness in the finished products). In addition, if the fungal hyphae, irrespective of their source, bind the fibres together and interfere with the beating process, the paper product will be non-uniform and will appear speckled. Prolonged beating will raise production costs; therefore as an alternative it may be necessary to use such infected pulps as secondary fibres in the production of boards.

Table 17.3 Some examples of cellulolytic and disfigurative fungi recovered from a range of mechanical and chemical pulps

Cellulolytic	Disfigurative
Alternaria spp.	*Aleurisma* spp.
Aspergillus fumigatus	*Aspergillus niger*
Basidomycetes spp.*	*Aureobasidium (Pullularia)* spp.†
Ceratostomella spp.†	*Botrytis* spp.
Cladosporium spp.	*Mucor* spp.
Epicoccum spp.	*Paecilomyces* spp.
Fusarium spp.	*Penicillium cyclopium*
Geotrichum spp.	*Penicillium roqueforti*
Gliocladium spp.	
Monilia spp.	
Phoma spp.	
Stemphylium spp.	
Trichoderma spp.	

* Basidiomycete fungi are the major cellulolytic fungi, but also produce red stains on pulp.
† *Ceratostomella* spp. and *Aureobasidium (Pullularia)* spp. produce blue stains on pulp.

Resistance to microbial attack was an inherent property of papers and boards produced from a pure cellulose furnish (initial raw materials) combined with good-quality fresh water. Modern techniques of paper production utilize chemically treated wood fibres and employ surface sizes, colours and coatings which are mainly carbohydrates or proteins. Nutrients are further increased by the re-use of backwaters (i.e. process water drained from the wire of the paper machine during sheet formation, containing small concentrations of fibre and filler, etc.) and recycled fibre. The moisture content of paper and board products is rarely sufficient to encourage bacterial attack; these same products can frequently, however, provide infecting fungal spores with both their moisture and nutrient requirements, and at normal temperatures paper is not among the more resistant of materials. For example, when relative humidity (r.h.) is >70% fungal spores may germinate, and certain *Aspergillus* spp. germinate at r.h. <70%. Papers and boards are relatively heterogeneous and usually contain additives such as rosin, wax, starch, gelatin and various other organic and inorganic substances, all of which may act as additional nutrients. Hence, spoilage other than cellulolytic may occur due to fungal attack on the additives. This in turn can give rise to additional disfigurative spoilage.

The elimination of sources of infection during manufacture, handling and storage of pulps and paper and board products will reduce the microbial problem. However, it is necessary to impart some protection to those items which are susceptible to microbial attack and which also need to be preserved. To date this has been achieved mainly by the incorporation of fungicides into pulps, papers and boards, but the latter may also be protected by physical barriers.

2 PULPS

In the wood-pulping process, wood fibres are separated. The use of pulps with high lignin content leads to products with poor strength and colour properties. The necessary removal of lignin may be achieved by chemical processing.

2.1 Chemical pulps

There are two major types of chemical pulp—acid sulphite and kraft. The former is made using a cooking liquor of calcium bisulphite and sulphurous acid, whilst the kraft or sulphate process utilizes sodium hydroxide and sodium sulphite. Kraft pulps are stronger, darker and less easily bleached than acid sulphite pulps.

2.2 Mechanical pulps

One of the mechanical methods of pulping involves the pressing of logs against grinders, such that the heat generated by friction softens the lignin in the middle lamella and thereby facilitates fibre separation. The groundwood pulps produced from this process are more susceptible to fungal deterioration than the chemical pulps, which have undergone a cooking process and therefore have a lower nutrient content; furthermore, the chemical and heat treatment will act as a sterilant (Sanborn, 1955).

2.3 Thermomechanical and chemithermomechanical pulps

Thermomechanical (TMP) and chemithermomechanical (CTMP) pulps offer alternatives to chemical or mechanical pulps. Essentially the TMP process involves atmospheric pre-steaming of wood chips followed by washing and preheating to 125°C prior to pressurized refining. Unbleached pulp yields fall in the range 95–99%. In the CTMP process the chip-washing stage is replaced by chemical impregnation with sodium sulphite solution and the pulp is then treated as in the TMP process. Yields are in the lower range 90–95% (Anon, 1985). Hardwoods require different chemical treatment, because they swell more readily in alkali than do softwoods, and therefore caustic sodium sulphite solutions are used for impregnation (Moore, 1987).

The pulp produced by TMP pulping has superior burst, tensile and tear strength over groundwood pulp. Another advantage is that the power required for refining is reduced. However, the total energy demand is increased, because of the need to generate steam.

It is the chemical pretreatment which gives CTMP the advantage over TMP. The sulphonation provides more selective fibre separation, and better fibre flexibility. In addition, resins can be readily removed from CTMP, rendering the pulps more suitable for making absorbent grades (Moore, 1986).

2.4 Sources of contamination

Mechanical pulps can become infected at a very early stage in their production. For example, the fungal contaminants of a pulpwood may be found in the resultant groundwood pulp. The condition of the process water (whitewater) and the degree to which it is re-used will further influence levels of contamination. Higher grinding temperatures will, however, impart some protection to the pulp produced; for example, if grinding is carried out at 79.5°C then the pulp has been found to remain free from red rot fungi for a longer period than a pulp processed at 65°C (Russell, 1957).

Biological slimes are accumulations of micro-organisms, mainly bacteria and fungi together with fibre and organic and inorganic debris, which bind in viscous masses and attach to various sections of pulp and paper machines. The control of biological slimes is as important within a pulp mill as within a paper or board mill. In addition, pulps which are heavily infected during production will not store well. If pulp and paper operations are integrated, then slushed pulp (along with any contamination) will be pumped from the pulp mill directly to the paper mill.

In contrast to chemical pulps, which tend to be stored indoors, groundwood pulps are often stored in exposed stacks. Clean conditions of storage are of prime importance for all types of pulp, and any contaminated stacks must be isolated in order to prevent the spread of infection. As always, airborne infection is a constant problem and one which is difficult to control.

2.5 Methods of preservation

2.5.1 Fungicides and their methods of application

It is desirable that the applied fungicide should have a toxicity to basidiomycetes, and also to the staining and spotting fungi, although the latter may be considered less important. In addition, adequate protection is generally required for about nine months.

The physical and chemical characteristics of fungicides applied as preservatives to pulps should include good solubility and an affinity for the fibre, resistance to leaching and stability at increasing temperatures. The simplest and most economical method, in terms of effort in application, is to add the agent to the pulp slurry at the beaters. If the compound is not water-soluble, then it must be readily dispersed in water, so that it may be precipitated onto the fibre and be retained (Heron & Sproule, 1957). Although concentration of initial application may influence retention, chemical losses tend to be higher when applications are made at the slurry stage. Powders and suspensions are less convenient to handle, and techniques of application such as spraying or immersion are also less desirable. The incorporation of a fungicide into pulps may be most conveniently achieved by metering the diluted agent into a stock chest feeding the wet lap (pulp) presses (Russell, 1957). Chemical losses and therefore costs are also reduced, but the reduction of undesirable quantities of toxic chemicals in effluent discharges is a more important factor from an environmental point of view.

Fungicides currently used in the field of pulp preservation are dichlorophen, benzothiazoles, copper-8-hydroxyquinolinolate, chlorophenols (mainly pentachlorophenol, although very much less is used now) and to a lesser extent polymeric biguanides and salicylanilide (Anon, 1974, 1989a). The incorporation of fungicides has proved to be the most reliable method of preservation.

Environmental pressures and a greater awareness of industrial health hazards have resulted in the elimination of the use of mercurials in the pulp and paper industry. However, even when used, mercurials were not entirely successful, as evidenced by the frequent occurrence of *Penicillium roqueforti* in pulps treated with phenylmercuric acetate, and their use had to be supplemented with the other agents such as oxine (8-hydroxyquinoline).

2.5.2 Drying

For many years groundwood pulps and sulphite pulps of high moisture content (50%) were shipped, even at the risk of mildew formation, because early drying methods resulted in a serious deterioration of quality (e.g. strength losses).

A pulp-drying machine is very similar to a paper machine with wet stock metered onto a moving wire to facilitate sheet formation and then feeding presses and drying cylinders, which may be supplemented by hot-air chambers. Both moist and dry pulps are cut into sheets at the end of the pulp machine and baled ready for transport. In the mid-1960s a new method of drying wood-pulp emerged, called flash-drying. After mechanical removal of water, the pulp is dried in a fluffed state in a stream of hot air and combustion gases, and thus water in the fibre evaporates instantaneously. Flash-dried pulp can be easily compressed into bales or pelleted. Apart from the resistance to fungal attack (moisture content <10%), there are obvious savings in transport and handling costs.

3 PAPER AND BOARD PRODUCTS

Approximately 50% of the fibrous raw material currently used in the paper and board industry in the United Kingdom is derived from waste papers (Anon, 1989b). Coupled with a high degree of water re-use, recycled fibre contributes significantly to the levels of solubles which are dried back into paper and board products. Despite this, the major isolates from reels leaving paper or board machines are members of the heat-resistant, sporing bacteria, *Bacillus* spp. (Chapter 18B), whilst the fungi, which are not heat-resistant, are absent. Modern papers and boards with a surface size of starch provide attractive substrates for a range of contaminating fungi, which may damage or disfigure them.

The degree of fungal attack is governed by temperature and moisture under conditions of usage. The majority of infecting organisms will thrive at temperatures of 10–30°C. If r.h. is >75%, growth is more varied and dense. As a result of airborne contamination, penicillia are the most common spoilage organisms. However, the *Aspergillus glaucus* series will flourish in conditions in which the moisture content is inadequate for the growth of most other fungi (Evans, 1957). Unfortunately, the control of temperature and moisture conditions does not overcome the problems of microbial deterioration either easily or economically, and therefore fungicides are used. Many products of today are intended for a short life and are not expected to withstand adverse conditions of r.h. for prolonged periods. Generally, the fungicidal treatment of a product is adequate, if microbial growth is not apparent, under its normal conditions of usage.

3.1 Methods of preservation

3.1.1 Fungicides and their method of application

Fungicides applied to paper and board products require the same basic properties as those agents applied to pulp, but in addition they must not have any adverse effects upon the products to which they are applied. These effects include properties such as strength, colour and printability. If an odour is imparted to the product this may affect consumer reaction adversely. For one or more of these reasons, many agents have been found to be unsuitable, even though they have good antimicrobial properties (Conkey & Carlson, 1969). Formaldehyde has long been used as a preservative for starch-based adhesives, but growing concern about the health effects resulting from occupational exposure has led to its replacement by a range of other substances. These microbicides range from organobromine to organosulphur compounds and other substances such as barium metaborate (Caulkins, 1987; Keddy, 1988). It has been noted that organosulphur-based biocides can cause a drop in sheet base brightness when high addition levels are necessary to control microbial growth on machine (Sanford, 1986).

Early methods of application ranged from the addition of agents at the beater stage to treatments of formed sheets by roll sizes or spraying (Hughes, 1957). The incorporation of agents into coatings is also practised along with traditional methods of application. The most economical application for a stated usage of product is normally sought. However, the effectiveness and safety of use of preservatives are far more critical factors than cost, bearing in mind the small quantities used. Soluble agents of low vapour pressure and good heat stability are easily added at the beater stage. In the past, organomercurials and sodium pentachlorophenate were applied in this way. These have been replaced, to some extent, by the use of products containing solubilized copper-8-quinolinolate, which can be converted to an insoluble compound capable of filtering out on to the fibres. Such agents are intended to give a higher retention by fibre on the machine and therefore greater permanence in the finished paper or board. However, the solubilized agent or suspension cannot be entirely eliminated from the backwater system, and although it may assist in slime control as a side-effect, it will eventually flow to effluent. Other important factors which must be considered before agents are applied at this stage include capacity to corrode machinery and the production of toxic vapours.

It may not be necessary to treat all the stock which is incorporated into a board product. However, the heavier board machines offer greater flexibility in application, as it is possible to select out the stock source feeding a single vat or group of vats producing a particular layer. In such multi-vat machines the plies (layers) are formed on top of each other on a single moving felt, which feeds the drying section. The middle plies may be of cheaper stock (e.g. waste paper) with a bleached chemical pulp forming the outer layers.

For many years paper and lightweight boards for wrapping tableted soap were made incorporating chlorophenates into the whole of the stock. The desire to eliminate problems of odour, colour and irritation associated with chlorophenates which were widely used, has resulted in the development and use of new chemical preservatives such as benzothiazoles.

Apart from soap wrappers which protect the package and content, many other papers require a permanent treatment. These include certain grades of book papers, map papers and wallpapers, although the latter may also employ a treated adhesive. Seed-germination papers require some degree of mould-proofing, but agents must not be present in sufficient quantities to be toxic to the seedlings.

Chemical preservatives can be added to the finished sheet when it is partially dried, for example by roll sizing or spraying. These methods have the advantage that the chemicals used are not lost to effluent and therefore they are more cost-effective. However, they do not result in a product with the same degree of permanence as the beater applications, and unless carefully chosen, the agents will interact with the size. Thus, an agent is required which is soluble or easily emulsified in water, which firmly attaches to the fibres and which is non-dusting when dry.

Alternatively, a treated coating may be applied either to a treated or an untreated base paper. A suitable agent for use in coating materials must be compatible with the binder, be heat-stable and have a low vapour pressure if a reasonable life is required. An example of the undesirable interaction of preservative with binder is the loss of the adhesive power of a glue.

The quantities and types of preservatives will vary according to the nature of the coating colours, sizes and adhesives to be used. Preservation of paper and boards relies, to some extent, upon the use of chlorophenols, but environmental pressures and hazards of handling are now phasing out their use within the industry. Other agents currently employed as preservatives include dichlorophen, benz*iso*thiazolones, benzothiazoles, sodium metaborate and more recently the dithiocarbamates.

It is well recognized that acidity accelerates paper degradation and therefore alkaline papers offer certain advantages over acid papers. More recent papermaking techniques have solved some of the early manufacturing and conversion problems. Alkaline papers constitute more than 65% of Europe's paper production, and products range from bonds to book papers, reprographic and offset grades (Vincent, 1989). The choice of sizing agent is specific to the process and the alkaline-compatible synthetic sizing used in alkaline papermaking (i.e. alkylketene dimer of alkenyl succinic anhydride) enhances resistance of sheet to brittleness and yellowing, which is particularly important when the product is for archival use (Johnson, 1986). Effective biocide programmes for alkaline papers are based on chlorine dioxide. Production costs are cut by conversion in mills where expensive pulps are used and those where water systems are more closed (Sanford, 1986).

Consideration of safety issues is now more prominent than ever before, and careful attention should be paid not only to the choice of biocide but in particular to its method of application.

3.1.2 Physical barriers

Barrier coating may also be used, provided that the rigidity induced by the treatment is desirable in the product. Unlike a metal foil, which is inert, a wax film is susceptible to microbial attack at the wax/fibre interface, in conditions of high r.h. However, waxed papers were often used in food packagings (e.g. bread wrap), where chemical preservation is prohibited or restricted. These have been replaced by the greaseproof papers and glassines, and now fine polythene bag wrappings are the norm for bread wrap. A number of non-flexible food packages also utilize plastic laminates such as polyethylene. Even map papers may be laminated with plastic today.

Barrier coatings are used in industry, for example building materials such as certain insulation; for example, underfelts for floor coverings, and roofing products which may incorporate bitumen. However, bitumen impregnation is often inadequate and therefore mould-proofing agents must also be included (Herschler, 1955). The industrial usage of paper and board products requires that they retain their strength characteristics, and therefore resistance to microbial deterioration is even more important.

There is a continuing increase in the use of plastics, particularly for food packaging. However, difficulties arise in recycling such products, and therefore the development of safe and efficient chemical preservatives suitable for incorporation into paper and board products will still be necessary.

4 REFERENCES

Anon (1974) Industrial uses of pesticides. In *The Non-agricultural Uses of Pesticides in Great Britain*. Department of the Environment, Pollution Paper No. 3, pp. 61–63. London: HMSO.

Anon (1985) The manufacture, physical properties and end uses of high yield pulps. *Paper Technology and Industry*, **26**, No. 6, pp. 258–266.

Anon (1989a) *Report of the Expert Advisory Committee on Biocides* London: HMSO DHSS.

Anon (1989b) *British Paper & Board Industry Federation Reference Book*.

Caulkins, D. (1987) Selecting acceptable preservatives for corrugating adhesives. *Technical Association of the Pulp and Paper Industry*, **70**, No. 6, pp. 194–195.

Conkey, J.H. & Carlson, J.A. (1969) Relative toxicity of biostatic agents suggested for use in the pulp and paper industry: 1968 Review. *Technical Association of the Pulp and Paper Industry*, **52**, 2311–2318.

Evans, D.M. (1957) The use of fungicides in paper, board and packaging materials. *Proceedings of the Technical Section of the British Paper and Board Makers' Association*, **38**, 279–291.

Heron, P.N. & Sproule, J.StG. (1957) The chemical nature of fungicidal agents employed in the pulp and paper industry. *Proceedings of the Technical Section of the British Paper and Board Makers' Association*, **38**, 199–220.

Herschler, R.J. (1955) Preservation of paper products. *Microbiology of Pulp and Paper*. Technical Association of the Pulp and Paper Industry Monograph Series No. 15, pp. 169–181.

Hughes, R.L. (1957) The application of mouldproofing agents to paper and board. *Proceedings of the Technical Section of the British Paper and Board Makers' Association*, **38**, 273–277.

Hughes, R.L. (1968) Microbiological deterioration in the paper, printing and packaging industries. *Proceedings of the 1st International Biodeterioration Symposium*, pp. 281–290. Amsterdam: Elsevier.

Johnson, R.G. (1986) U.S. Alkaline fine papermaking to experience slow but steady growth. *Pulp & Paper*, **60**, No. 12, pp. 66–67.

Keddy, I (1988) Microbiological control in paper systems. *Paper Southern Africa*, **8**(4), 37, 39–40.

Moore, G.K. (1986) CTMP—A new generation of cellulose fibres. *Fibre Developments for Paper, Board & Nonwoven Applications,* PIRA Paper & Board Division Seminar PB/CSM-86/13.

Moore, G.K. (1987) Mechanical systems. *Introduction to Paper and Papermaking Processes*. PIRA Paper & Board Division Teach-In, 4–5 March PB/CSM/87/1.

Russell, P. (1957) Problems concerning the infection of groundwood pulp. *Proceedings of the Technical Section of the British Paper and Board Makers' Association*, **38**, 241–254.

Sanborn, J.R. (1955) Preservation of pulps. *Microbiology of Pulp and Paper*. Technical Association of the Pulp and Paper Industries Monograph Series No. 15, pp. 75–96.

Sanford, T.A. (1986) Chlorine dioxide controls deposits in alkaline systems. *Southern Pulp & Paper*, **48**(7), 20–21.

Vincent, G.G. (1989) Alkaline papers gain acceptance. *Graphic Arts Monthly*, **61**, No. 6, pp. 70, 74.

D·TEXTILE AND LEATHER PRESERVATION

1 INTRODUCTION

Biodeterioration of textile and leather materials refers to a decrease in value of such materials or a reduction in the ability of such products to fulfil the function for which they were intended, due to the biological activities of macro- and/or micro-organisms. It encompasses all biological processes which adversely affect the textile and leather processing industries.

Under suitable environmental conditions during textile and leather processing, microbial growth and proliferation may occur on exposed or stored leather or textile substrates, which in turn may result in a variety of spoilage phenomena (e.g. odour production, fibre tendering, strength loss, variegate pigmentation, etc.), and a subsequent devaluation of the substrate. Textile and leather materials may be affected by both aesthetic biodeterioration and chemical assimilatory/dissimilatory biodeterioration. For example, microbes may be found growing on otherwise undamaged textile substrates utilizing dirt and other extraneous substances, which leads to the development of an unpleasant aesthetic appearance (such as pigment staining) and which seriously detracts from its value. Alternatively, the substrate itself may be utilized as a source of nutrient and/or suffer biochemical damage due to the excretion of waste products.

Reported incidences of biodeterioration in the textile and leather industries are characterized by their sporadic nature. The primary agents of biological attack of such materials are bacteria, fungi and insects. A range of factors are known to affect the incidence and severity of product spoilage (see Table 17.4).

A diverse range of chemicals, antimicrobial agents or biocides, are applied to textile substrates

Table 17.4 Factors affecting substrate biodeterioration

Type of substrate
Presence of auxiliaries
Dyeing
pH
Degree of chemical damage
Water activity
Materials in contact
Stage of processing
Length of storage
Light exposure
Mechanical damage
Biodeteriogen distribution
Presence of biocides
Temperature

at different stages of manufacture to prevent microbial degradation and/or insect attack. Biocides may be applied as rot-proofing treatments, to provide temporary protection during processing, or as hygienic finishes. Table 17.5 gives a representative list of the major biocides which are currently used in the UK textile industry.

Some guidance on the selection of textile preservatives is available. British Standard 2087 (Anon, 1981b) Parts 1 and 2 (and Amendments 4195 and 4195b) deal with methods of treatment and application of a range of textile preservatives with a guide to the selection of suitable processes and methods of determining the biocide content of

Table 17.5 Biocides used in the textile industry

Producer	Trade name	Active ingredient
Givaudan (Brenntag (UK) Ltd)	GivGard D X N	6-Acetoxy-2,4-dimethyl-1,3-dioxane
Rohm & Haas	Kathon LM	2-*n*-Octyl-4-isothiazolin-3-one
Hickson & Welch Ltd	Ultrafresh DM50	Tri-*n*-butyltin maleate
Schill & Seilacher	Afrotin ZNK 10 & ZNL	Aqueous dispersal of zinc pyridinthione
Hansa/Goldschmidt	Hansa CID BF	Heterocyclic blend
Bayer	Preventol GD	(2,2′-Dihydroxy-5,5′-dichloro)-diphenyl methane
	Preventol Trial Product OC 3040	(2,2′-Dihydroxy-5,5′-dichloro)-diphenyl methane
	Preventol O extra	2-Phenylphenol
	Preventol ON extra	Sodium 2-phenylphenolate
	Preventol R80 & R50	Quaternary ammonium salts
Catomance	Mystox 8	Copper 8-hydroxyquinolinolate
	Mystox	Pentachlorophenyl laurate
Thor Chemicals (UK) Ltd	Konservan SN	Organic tin combination
Durham Chemicals Ltd	Nuodex zinc naphthenate	Zinc naphthenate
	Nuodex copper naphthenate	Copper naphthenate
Ciba-Geigy	Fungitex ROP	Dichlorophen
Sandoz (Sanitized AG)	Sanitized BSC (TB 8327)	Thiobendazole
	Sanitized RT-8711	Prepolymerized halogenated organic compounds
	Sanitized DET 8530	Quaternary ammonium compounds
Boots	Myacide	2-Bromo-2-nitropropane-1,3-diol
	Myacide SP	2,4-Dichlorobenzyl alcohol
BP Chemicals	Cunilate	Copper 8-hydroxyquinolinolate
(Honeywill & Stein Maiten International)	2419–75	
Hoechst		
NIPA	Nipastat	Parabens
Protex		
Rudolf Chemicals	Rustol HEC	Fatty acid salts of quaternary compounds
	HED	Organo-tin
Albright & Wilson	Tolcide C30	2′(Thiocyanomethylthio) benzothiazole
	Tolcide PS3	Quaternary phosphonium salt + surfactant
K & K Greef Ltd (Progiven)	Biocide PB940	2,2′-Dihydroxy-5,5′dichlorodiphenyl monosulphide
	Esterol 100 CD	PCPL
	Biocide CBA	Synergistic formulation based on halogen- and nitrogen-containing heterocyclic compounds
British Sanitized Ltd	Actifresh RT-87-11	Alkaline mixture of halogenated organic compounds
ICI	Densil P	Dithio-2,2′-bis(benzmethylamide)

treated fabrics. The standard is currently being revised.

Related products/formulations are used in the leather industry; for example, *p*-nitrophenol has been used for military purposes but may in some instances cause discoloration problems. A list of biocides used in the leather industry is presented in Table 17.6.

Formaldehyde has been used during the pre-tanning process although its use is being reviewed in the light of environmental considerations. Leather may be initially protected from microbial attack by the use of sodium chloride — the 'salting' process. At the tannery, the leather is soaked to remove the salt and additional antimicrobial agents, e.g. myacide may be applied. Antifungal agents may be applied to the leather in the 'wet blue' state before dyeing. Similarly, additional fungicide may be applied for increased protection during the dyeing process.

The use of selected biocides in the textile and leather industries is currently attracting intense scrutiny because of environmental considerations. For example, within European legislation, Directive 76/769/EEC covers the laws, regulations and administrative provisions of member states relating to restrictions on the marketing and use of certain dangerous substances and preparations. The ninth amendment of this directive relates specifically to pentachlorophenol (PCP) and its compounds. A pentachlorophenol prohibition order (PCP−V) dated 12 December 1989 has now been introduced in Germany which bans the sale of products, including textiles, which contain more than 5 parts per million of PCPs. The new regulation will also apply to carpets, as one example, which are sold at retail level after 22 March 1990 which are exported to Germany. Other member states will no doubt be affected. Similar developments have occurred affecting products used for the

Table 17.6 Biocides used in the leather industry

Producer	Trade name	Active ingredients
Buckman	Busan 30	30% TCMTB 2-(thiocyanomethylthio) benzothiazole
	Busan 52	32% Dithiocarbamate + 8% 2-mercaptobenzothiazole
	Busan 85	50% Dithiocarbamate
	Busan 86	25% Dithiocarbamate + 20% 2-mercaptobenzothiazole
	Busan 1009	10% TCMTB + 10% 2-Mercaptobenzothiazole
	Busan 1058	24% Thione
ABM	Glokill 77	Triazine
ICI	Vantoc CL	50% Quat: Benzylalkyldimethylammonium chloride
	Vantocil IB	20% Polymeric biguanide hydrochloride
	Proxel TN	BIT: Benz-isothiazoline/triazine Mix
	Proxel LB/LC/LD	BIT: Benzo-isothiazoline in various solvents
Boots	Myacide AS	100% Bronopol: 2-bromo-2-nitropropane-1,3-diol
	Myacide S25	20% Bronopol, 4% TCMTB
Abbott	Amical	Di-iodomethyl-*p*-tolyl sulphone
ABM	Nercolan FR	Not quoted: mixed phenolics (cresols)
Bayer	Preventol WB	Not known: mixed phenolics
	Preventol CR	20% TCMTB: 2-(thiocyanomethylthio) benzothiazole
Albright & Wilson	Tolcide MN10	10% MBT methylene bisthiocyanate
	Tolcide FSM	10% MBT + 10% TCMTB
Catomance	Mystox E10	10% Phenolic: dichlorophen + 2-phenylphenol
	Mystox WFA	30% Phenolic 2-phenylphenate (Na)
Catomance	Mystox LB	Unknown: Quat/Phenol mix
J. Robinson	PNP	100% *p*-nitrophenol
Albright & Wilson	Slimicide MC	10% Methylene bisthiocyanate
	Dazomet	100% Thione

mothproofing of wool textiles.

Formaldehyde treatment may be applied, normally in the country of production, to natural keratin fibres to prevent problems of anthrax contamination.

2 RECOGNITION OF SUBSTRATE BIODETERIORATION

The importance of, and difficulties associated with, the recognition of biodeterioration of raw materials and manufactured products have been well documented (Eggins & Oxley, 1980). The following methods have been found most useful in detecting microbial growth on textiles. Similar methods may be applied to leather products. Microbial spoilage may be readily apparent due to severe pigmentation and fibre tendering. A characteristic fusty odour may be associated with fungal growth and/or bacterial degradation. Detection at this stage normally implies that significant microbial growth has occurred. Sellotape application may, in some instances, be used to recover microbial fragments directly from textile fibres prior to examination. Direct microscopic examination may reveal extensive fibre damage due to bacterial activity, or fungal growth on the surface or within the fibre.

Supporting staining methods have been recommended for assisting the detection of microbial activity on substrates: these include cotton blue-lactophenol; methylene blue G acidified with acetic acid; carbol-fuchsin; safranin; bromthymol blue, and the Pauly stain (McCarthy & Greaves, 1988). Similarly, stained areas on wool produced by mildew sometimes fluoresce under UV light. However, as various optical brightening auxiliaries also fluoresce, the method is little used.

3 OVERVIEW OF TECHNIQUES FOR TESTING TEXTILE MATERIALS FOR RESISTANCE TO MICROBIAL ATTACK

Test methods for assessing the susceptibility of textile materials to microbial degradation, or assessing the efficacy of biocides applied to such materials, are generally based on the 'challenge testing' principle. These involve a method of deliberately infecting the substrate with suitable biodeteriogenic organisms, combined with a method of testing (usually visual assessment or tensile strength testing) the extent of spoilage. The method selected for testing purposes should reflect the nature of the biocide and its expected in-house performance (McCarthy, 1986).

The major testing procedures may be classified as follows.

3.1 Pure-culture technique

Samples of material are exposed to attack by a pure culture of a known micro-organism under controlled conditions. The processes used for sterilization may modify the substrate (e.g. keratin in wool). The results obtained reflect, of course, growth in a man-made environment.

3.2 Mixed-culture technique

The advantage of a mixed inoculum is the simultaneous exposure of test samples to a number of organisms which may possess different susceptibilities to biocides and varied metabolic requirements. However, toxic metabolites may accumulate in the growth medium.

3.3 Perfusion technique

This method allows the continuous replacement of nutrients and removal of waste metabolic products by perfusion during the incubation period.

3.4 Soil-burial method

This appears to be the most severe and widely used test method. Test strips are buried in soil in trays or beds under controlled conditions and assessed for loss of strength. Variations in microbial activity will occur with soils from different locations, with time of year, etc.

3.5 Soil-infection method

Test strips are inoculated by partially coating them with a soil suspension thickened with kieselguhr, incubated over water and tested after conditioning.

An aqueous suspension of horse dung adjusted to a pH of 5.5 to suppress bacterial growth has also been used. Alternatively a manure/soil mixture has been used.

4 LABORATORY TESTING TECHNIQUES FOR SUBSTRATE SUSCEPTIBILITY AND BIOCIDE EFFICACY

Methods selected for testing of textile materials for susceptibility to microbial attack, or to assess biocide performance, will be determined by the nature of the information required (e.g. problem-solving or testing to contract specification). For example, samples of biocide-treated yarn or fabric, as received from industrial sources, are normally tested 'as received' or after being subjected to various durability procedures. In some instances conventional chemical assay of the preservative will suffice. In other cases biological testing may be required.

4.1 Durability testing

The samples may be initially pre-treated as follows:

(a) Water leaching. Immerse the textile sample in a large beaker or flask of tap water flowing at a rate which will give approximately two or three volume changes per hour. Use an initial liquor ratio of 1:100 (w/w). Continue the process for 24 h. Air-dry the samples at room temperature on a 'washing-line' arrangement composed of two laboratory clamps and connecting string.

(b) Heat ageing. Expose the sample in a dry oven at between 100°C and 105°C for 24 h. Ensure that the oven is well ventilated.

(c) Light exposure. Expose the samples as specified in method BO2 of British Standard 1006 (Anon, 1978).

(d) Weathering. Expose the samples as specified in method BO4 of British Standard 1006 (Anon, 1978).

Durability trials are normally required only for very specialized applications (e.g. woollen felt for use in paper-making, military textiles, etc).

4.2 Application of biocides under laboratory conditions

For laboratory biocide applications, the following standard test cloths may be used:
1 100% worsted flannel (style 526) supplied by Testfabrics Inc., Middlesex, NJ, USA;
2 100% wool cloth supplied by the Society of Dyers and Colourists (SDC), Bradford, UK;
3 100% cotton control cloth to confirm inoculum viability supplied by the British Textile Technology Group, Manchester, UK.

Biocides may normally be applied to the test fabrics in an aqueous solution with a Jeffreys trial dyeing rig (or comparable laboratory dyeing equipment). The conditions in the test rig may be adjusted as appropriate to conform to conditions in an industrial dyeing winch or scouring set. The system of application will be determined by the nature of the biocide, the particular processing conditions (i.e. duration of process, temperature, etc.), the textile substrate and the degree of protection required. For comparing biocide efficacy, a uniform system (determined by the individual constraints of the industrial problem) is required.

Similarly, biocides may be applied using full-scale processing machinery:
1 application to yarn packages using a Morel conditioning machine;
2 direct application to yarn via a lick roller on conventional spinning machines;
3 incorporation into an oil emulsion applied to loose stock before carding and spinning, and
4 direct application via conventional dyeing machines and scouring sets.

4.3 Standard test methods

The most widely used and accepted testing standards employed by government and industry alike in determining antimicrobial effectiveness in textiles are those set forth by the American Association of Textile Chemists and Colorists (AATCC) and by the British Standards Institution (BSI). A wide variety of national and industrial test methods are currently under review by the ISO/TC38 Textiles Committee of the International Organization for Standardization (ISO).

The following discussion of the major standard methods aims to provide a practical summary of the techniques involved. For full detailed information the reader should refer to the standard texts as appropriate. For example, the foreword to British Standard 6085 states that the general purpose of these methods is to determine susceptibility of textiles to micro-organisms and to evaluate the resistance of treated textiles and textile-containing products to attack by micro-organisms. It may be slightly modified to cover leather materials. The standard specifies three areas of testing whereby specimens of the material under test are subjected to microbial attack by soil burial, mixed inoculation on an agar plate or in a saturated atmosphere. Biocide efficacy is observed as a significant reduction in strength loss compared with similar material without biocide addition, or prevention of visual surface discoloration.

4.3.1 BS 6085: 1981 (Anon, 1981a)*

(a) Soil burial. This is a very severe test for most textile materials. Fabric or yarn specimens (150 × 25 or 600 mm respectively) are buried to a depth of 30–50 mm in John Innes No. 1 potting compost in plastic or metal trays. A loose-fitting lid is required to maintain the moisture content of the soil between 20% and 30%. Glass plates are used to separate neighbouring fabric specimens in the trays. Ten specimens of the material under test are required and five of a cotton control cloth (which should show a strength loss of at least 80% after incubation) for each experiment. The prepared soil trays are placed in an incubator at 28 ± 1°C with a relative humidity (r.h.) of at least 95%. The cotton control cloths are removed after 7 days' incubation with particles of soil being removed by gentle agitation and brushing before rinsing with water. The specimens or fragments are then sterilized by soaking in 70% (v/v) ethanol for 4 h at ambient temperature, allowed to condition (at 20 ± 2°C and 65 ± 2 r.h.) and their residual tensile strength (compared with unexposed specimens) determined in accordance with BS 2576 (Anon, 1977) (fabric) or BS 1932: Part 1 (Anon, 1965). If a strength loss of > 80% has been achieved, incubate the remaining specimens for a full 28 days. Prepare the specimens for testing as above, and record as a percentage the observed strength loss between the exposed material and the unexposed controls.

(b) Mixed-inoculum agar plate test. The nine standard test biodeteriogens specified in the standard may be obtained from CAB International, Kew, UK. The cultures may be used only when they are between 14 and 28 days old. However, cultures less than 21 days old may be stored, securely stoppered, in a refrigerator at 4°C for up to 3 months prior to use. Add 15 g of agar (Bacto: Difco) per litre of mineral salts solution, and 0.05% (w/v) dioctyl sodium sulphosuccinate to form a mineral salts/wetting agent solution. Add 30 g per litre sucrose to the agar, if necessary, to encourage fungal growth. Gently add 10 ml of mineral salts/wetting agent to each of the nine culture slopes. With a sterile wire hook scrape the surface of the slope to liberate spores without unduly detaching mycelial fragments. Decant the nine suspensions into a 500 ml sterile flask containing a number of glass beads, and shake vigorously. Filter through a glass filter funnel containing sterile cotton wool to remove large clumps. If a large number of specimens are to be inoculated, pool the suspensions prepared from a number of fungal sets. Centrifuge the mixed spore suspension three times at 3500 *g*, discarding the supernatant and resuspending the spores in sterile mineral salts solution. Wet out the test specimens (2.5 × 2.5 mm for visual assessment—four specimens per sample) and controls by immersing the fabrics in water containing 0.05% (w/v) dioctyl sodium sulphosuccinate for several minutes. Place each fabric piece on individual mineral salt agar in Petri dishes and add 0.5 ml of the mixed inoculum to each side of the material. Work in a microbiological safety cabinet when manipulating the cultures. Autoclave and discard unused

* Update: BS 6085: 1981, BS 2087: 1981—revised standards 1991 circulated for public comment. BSI Committee to ratify standards held 2 July 1991.

spore suspensions at the end of the day. Assess the cotton controls after 14 days and the remaining specimens after 28 days. Strength loss may be assessed as above. Alternatively, assess specimens visually in accordance with the grading scale listed in the standard.

(c) Saturated atmosphere test. This procedure is intended for textiles that will not come into contact with fungi in the vegetative form, but may be contaminated with airborne spores before storage in humid conditions. Inoculate 1 ml of the mixed spore suspension (prepared as above) onto the cloth or related specimens and controls. Suspend the fabrics above free water (>90% r.h.) in sealed glass kilner jars. Incubate for 14 days and assess the cotton controls. If the controls are graded four or above (against the visual scale), continue the trial and assess the remaining specimens after 28 days.

4.3.2 AATCC Test Method 147–1988, 'Detection of antibacterial activity fabrics: parallel streak method' (Anon, 1988)

This method is adaptable for biocide-treated yarns, loose stock and most carpet samples, as well as fabric. The defined objective is the detection of bacteriostatic activity exhibited by textile fabrics. The bacterial species cited in the standard are given below. Similarly, details of maintenance of culture of the test organisms are presented in the standard.

Prepare AATCC bacteriostatis broth as described. Adjust the medium to pH 6.8 with sodium hydroxide. Add 15 g of Bacto (Difco) agar per litre, adjust to pH 7.0–7.2 with sodium hydroxide to prepare AATCC bacteriostatis agar. Prepare the challenge inoculum by transferring 1 ml of a 24-h broth culture (37°C) of a test organism to 9 ml sterile distilled water control. After adequate mixing with a 4 mm inoculating loop, transfer one loopful of diluted inoculum to AATCC agar in a Petri dish, making five approx. 7.5 cm long parallel streaks 1 cm apart without refilling the loop. Locate the textile specimen (normally 1–4 cm diameter) transversely across the inoculum streaks and ensure intimate contact. Small sterile glass weights may be used to prevent the material curling away from the agar. Incubate all samples at 37°C for 24 h.

Results may be evaluated in two ways: (a) growth-free zone—assess the width (in millimetres) of the growth-free zone surrounding the test specimens; (b) contact inhibition—lift the specimens from the agar surface and using a low-power binocular microscope, assess the percentage growth-free contact area. The latter method may be used to provide a rough estimate of biocide efficacy in that the count of the inoculum will decrease from initial contact on the nutrient agar to the end of the final streak, resulting in increasing degrees of sensitivity. *Staphylococcus aureus* and *Pseudomonas aeruginosa* may be selected as representative test organisms.

4.3.3 AATCC Test Method 30–1986, 'Fungicides. Evaluation of textiles: mildew and rot resistance of textiles' (Anon, 1986b)

This standard is again arranged in three sections. Test 1 presents a soil-burial method which may be used as an alternative to BS 6085: 1981. The agar plate–pure culture–sterile specimen method, which forms the basis of Test 2 is for cellulosic materials only. Test 3 is recommended for evaluation of textile specimens where surface-growing organisms are important. The method involves the growth of *Aspergillus niger* (ATCC 6275) on glucose mineral salts agar. Prepare a spore suspension from 10–14-day-old cultures of the test organism by scraping the fungal mycelia growing on agar slopes into a sterile flask containing 50 ml of sterile water and glass beads. Shake the flask thoroughly to prepare a spore suspension. Prepare the culture medium as described. Autoclave at 121°C for 15 min; wet the specimens (3 × 3 cm) in water containing 0.05% (w/v) dioctyl sodium sulphosuccinate (BDH); position on the poured medium in a Petri dish and inoculate the surface evenly with 1 ml of the spore suspension using a sterile dispenser. Incubate the inoculated and control specimens at 28°C for 14 days only. Examine the specimens visually and microscopically for evidence of the growth of *A. niger*. The initial specimens may be subjected to various pre-treatments before testing (e.g. leaching, weathering, exposure to dry heat). Test 1 may be used to demonstrate long term biocide proofing of material, whereas Test 3 may be used to assess biocides applied during processing to provide temporary antifungal protection during manufacture.

4.3.4 *AATCC Test Method 100–1986, 'Evaluation of antibacterial finishes on fabrics' (Anon, 1986c)*

This method presents four qualitative techniques for demonstrating bacteriostatic activity. Specimens of treated and control fabrics (3 × 3 cm) may be tested qualitatively for antibacterial efficacy by any one of the following methods: (a) AATCC agar plate method, (b) streak test, (c) Major's test, (d) Quinn test. For example, in the 'streak test', streak sufficient agar (AATCC bacteriostasis agar) in Petri dishes with either *Staph. aureus* or *Klebsiella pneumoniae*. Place individual treated or control specimens at right angles to the direction of streak. Examine for clear areas (no growth) either visually or with a low-power microscope.

Specimens showing activity are tested quantitatively. Prepare sufficient specimens (4.8 cm diameter) of the test substrate (and controls—made of the same material but untreated) to absorb 1 ml of test inoculum (note the number used). Apply 1 ml of an appropriate dilution of a 24-h culture of the test organism (one of the above) so that recovery at time 0 from the control or the sample is 1 to 2×10^5. Dilute using AATCC broth. Sterilize the samples before the inoculation using ethylene oxide or intermittent sterilization. Place the discrete sets of specimens in 0.237-litre (8 oz) sterile glass jars and apply 1 ml of the inoculum evenly to the specimens using a sterile dispenser. Include uninoculated but treated controls and seal the containers. For time 0 testing, add 100 ml of AATCC broth (or neutralizer solution if available) and shake vigorously for 1 min. Make serial dilutions in AATCC broth and plate (in duplicate) on Tryptone Glucose Extract agar (Difco). Incubate the remaining jars at 37°C for 18–24 h and plate out as above. Incubate all plates at 37°C for 48 h. Report bacterial counts as colony-forming units (c.f.u.) of bacteria per fabric sample (i.e. the number in the jar). Calculate percentage reduction of each test organism for each fabric treatment. Uninoculated samples should be sterile and increasing numbers of organisms should be observed on the inoculated, untreated control. The method is intended for biocide treatments which may not be detectable by agar plate techniques. However, it is cumbersome, time-consuming and difficult to reproduce. Work is in progress to replace the serial dilution evaluation stage with a membrane filter procedure which, it is hoped, will increase reproducibility and reduce the time necessary to perform the test.

The following method has been suggested for testing biocide-treated materials and may be applied directly to textiles and leather materials.

4.3.5 *Dow Corning corporate test method (CTM)-0923, 'Antimicrobial activity—dynamic test of surfaces' (McGee & White, 1984)*

The method is performed by enumeration of microbes in a flask of phosphate-buffered water, both before and after a pre-determined shaking period. The challenge inoculum is assessed spectrophotometrically before application and verified by viable counts based on the pour-plate procedure. Treated and untreated substrates, along with an inoculum-control flask containing only buffer and inoculum, are monitored to demonstrate that antimicrobial activity is a result of the treatment, and not a characteristic of some other material on the substrate or simply a moribund culture. McGee & White (1984) cite an example whereby 0.75 g of treated material was shaken for 1 h in a test system containing 7.5×10^5 to 1.5×10^6 viable cells of *K. pneumoniae* ATCC 4352 in phosphate buffer at room temperature. They stress that clear differentiation between treated and untreated samples must be obtained. The survival of the challenge organism is monitored with time.

4.3.6 *Bioluminescence techniques applied to biodeterioration*

Growth of micro-organisms on textile materials may be assessed by the firefly bioluminescence detection method and/or assay of adenosine triphosphate (ATP). For a quantitative assessment, prepare a mixed-spore suspension in accordance with BS 6085 (described above). Likewise prepare all fabric specimens (pre-weighed and of uniform size) in accordance with Section Three (agar plate test) of the standard. The initial stages of the test method were adopted to prepare standard contaminated conditions to encourage fungal growth. Incubate all specimens (three replicates per test material per assay time) at 28°C. At each time interval (normally 3-h intervals throughout the working day) assay the resultant microbial growth (McCarthy, 1989). A Biocounter M2010 (Lumac BV) and corresponding Lumac reagents (ATP standards, nucleotide-releasing reagents and luciferin–luciferase mixtures) may be used for ATP assays. Alternatively, samples may be boiled in trichloroacetic acid extract ATP from the samples (Lundin & Thore, 1975) or immersed in various novel extractants (McCarthy, 1989). Test 'time 0' samples immediately following addition of the mixed spore suspension. Inoculate all samples simultaneously and monitor growth of the inoculum at regular intervals over a period of 24–72 h (or longer if necessary). Express results as an 'activity index' with units of picograms of ATP/0.1 g of test substrate, derived as a mean result from the three replicates. The assay thus provides a rapid non-species-specific test for microbial growth, with significant increases in ATP levels on untreated wool materials. The presence of a biocide applied to fabrics will result in prevention of growth or the rapid killing of the organisms in the inoculum. A positive untreated control (with developing biomass) is required to demonstrate inoculum viability.

4.3.7 *Additional national standards*

Finally, various additional national standards have been introduced and may be used as alternatives to those described above, for example, Australian Standard 1157.1972 Part 2—Resistance of Textiles to Fungal Growth (Anon, 1972a). In Section One of this standard the method describes how sterile test specimens are inoculated with *A. niger* van Tieghem (Defence Standard Laboratory Culture Collection No. 72) and then incubated for 14 days. Assessments are then made of the extent of surface fungal growth. Similarly, the South African Bureau of Standards SABS Method 472 (Anon, 1967) describes tests for monitoring the effect on textiles of attack by *A. niger* SABS Culture No. 70. Alternatively, South African Bureau of Standards SABS Method 484 (Anon, 1972b) is concerned with resistance to the fungal attack by mixed culture. The Canadian Standard CAN2-4.2-M77 Method 28.2-1972, Method of test for resistance to microorganisms: surface-growing fungus test—pure culture, is again normally used to assess biocide efficacy. *A. niger* (USDA 215–4247) is used as the inoculum with growth assessed after 14 days. The extent of growth of the test organism on the specimens is determined together with any staining

5 LEATHER

Leather is a product made from skins. It is a proteinaceous, 'readily woven' material which finds extensive application in footwear, luggage and harness. The treatment to preserve the material and render it pliable and free from the malodour found with raw skins possibly started with simple drying followed by mechanical manipulation. This was followed by salt treatment, and finally the discovery that leather could be produced by soaking skins in the steep water from certain tree barks, a process called tanning, laid the foundation for the modern process.

Today leather is produced by soaking skins in an alkaline solution to saponify grease and make dehairing easy. Dehaired hides are tanned, coloured, oiled and finished by a variety of processes.

It is at risk of microbial attack during the processing of the skins, when bacteria are the chief source of trouble, and after finishing and making up, when mould growth can be a major hazard. For protection during processing, phenolics, including salicylanilide, 8-hydroxyquinoline and acetic acid, have been used. For preservation of the finished product 4-nitrophenol, 2-naphthol, 2,4-dimethyl-3-chlorophenol, salicylanilide and pentachlorophenol have been recommended. Conventional biocides are presented in Table 17.6.

Under cool conditions with well-protected skins,

sodium chlorite provides good protection of the skin but does not protect the soak liquor. An application rate of 0.1% sodium chlorite solution prevents the build-up of soak liquor bacteria for at least 24 h but is ineffective at higher temperatures. For prolonged soaking, where high temperatures are involved or where the raw stock is suspect, biocides based on Bronopol, methylene bisthiocyanate or triazine are recommended.

For examples of original publications on this subject see Jordan (1934), Money (1970) and Wessel *et al.* (1964), all listed in the General Bibliography.

6 CONCLUSIONS

Biocides may be applied to textile and leather substrates to prevent infection (e.g. anthrax), to minimize biodeterioration problems or as hygienic finishes. Commercial formulations of industrial biocides are available to both the textile and leather industries with appropriate methods of application and stated compatibility. Such lists will be subject to ever-increasing scrutiny as environmental pressures and resultant legislation evolve. Biocide efficacy may be confirmed by routine chemical assays or by specialized biological testing (primarily challenge testing).

7 REFERENCES

Anon (1965) Determination of breaking strength and extension. British Standard 1932, Part 1. London: British Standards Institution.

Anon (1967) Resistance to fungal attack by *Aspergillus niger* SABS culture No. 70. South African Standard Method 472. Pretoria: South African Bureau of Standards.

Anon (1972a) Resistance of textiles to fungal growth. Australian Standard 1157, Part 2. Sydney: Standards Association of Australia.

Anon (1972b) Method of testing for resistance to micro-organisms: surface-growing fungus test—pure culture. Canadian Standard CAN 2-4.2-M77. Ottawa: Canadian Government Specification Board.

Anon (1973) Resistance to fungal attack by mixed cultures. South African Standard Method 484. Pretoria: South African Bureau of Standards.

Anon (1981a) Methods of testing for determination of the resistance of textiles to microbiological deterioration. British Standard 6085. London: British Standards Institution.

Anon (1981b) Preservative treatments for textiles. British Standard 2087, Parts 1 and 2. London: British Standards Institution.

Anon (1986a) Methods for testing the strength of textiles: woven fabrics—determination of breaking strength and elongation (strip method). British Standard 2576. London: British Standards Institution.

Anon (1986b) AATCC Test Method 30–1986. Fungicides. Evaluation of textiles: mildew and rot resistance of textiles. AATCC Technical Manual. Triangle Park, NC: American Association of Textile Chemists and Colorists.

Anon (1986c) AATCC Test Method 100–1986. Evaluation of antibacterial finishes on fabrics. AATCC Technical Manual. Triangle Park, NC: American Association of Textile Chemists and Colorists.

Anon (1988) AATCC Test Method 147–1988. Detection of antibacterial activity of fabrics: parallel streak method. AATCC Technical Manual. Triangle Park, NC: American Association of Textile Chemists and Colorists.

Anon (1990) Methods of testing for colour fastness of textiles and leather. British Standard 1006. London: British Standards Institution.

Eggins, H.O.W. & Oxley, T.A. (1980) Biodeterioration and biodegradation. *International Biodeterioration Bulletin*, **16**, 53–56.

Lundin, A. and Thore, A. (1975) Comparison of methods for extraction of bacterial adenine nucleotides determined by firefly assay. *Applied Microbiology*, **30**, 713–721.

McCarthy, B.J. (1986) Preservatives for use in the wool textile industry. In *Preservatives in the Food, Pharmaceutical and Environmental Industries* (eds Board, R.G., Allwood, M.C. & Banks, J.G.) pp. 75–98. Oxford: Blackwell Scientific Publications.

McCarthy, B.J. (1989) Detection and enumeration of micro-organisms on textiles using ATP luminescence In *ATP Luminescence: Rapid Methods in Microbiology* (eds Stanley, P.E., McCarthy, B.J. & Smither, R.) pp. 81–86. Oxford: Blackwell Scientific Publications

McCarthy, B.J. & Greaves, P.H. (1988) Mildew—causes, detection methods and prevention. *Wool Science Review*, **65**, 27–48.

McGee, J. & White, W.C. (1984) Evaluation of surface bonded cationic antimicrobials. *Carpet and Rug Industry*, **12**, 24–41.

8 BIBLIOGRAPHY—GENERAL

Agarwal, P.N. & Nanda, J.N. (1972) Correlation of tropical room experiments with weathering exposure. In *Biodeterioration of Materials*, Vol. 2 (eds Walters, A.H. & Hueck-van der Plas, E.H.) pp. 179–184. London: Applied Science Publishers.

Armstrong, E.F. (1941) The rotproofing of sand bags. *Chemistry and Industry*, **60**, 668–674.

Bayley, C.H. & Weatherburn, M.W. (1947a) The effect of weathering on various rotproofing treatments applied to cotton tentage duck. *Canadian Journal of Research*, **25F**, 92–109.

Bayley, C.H. & Weatherburn, M.W. (1947b) The rot-proofing efficacy of metallic naphthenates. *Canadian Journal of Research*, **25F**, 209–220.

Benignus, P.G. (1948) Copper-8-hydroxyquinolinate, industrial preservative. *Industrial and Engineering Chemistry*, **40**, 1426–1429.

Block, S.S. (1953) Humidity requirements for mould growth. *Applied Microbiology*, **1**, 287–293.

Brinj, J.La. & Kauffman, H.R. (1972) Fungal testing of textiles: a summary of co-operative experiments carried out by the working group on textiles of the International Biodegradation Research Group (IBRG). In *Biodeterioration of Materials*, Vol. 2 (eds Walters, A.H. & Hueck-an der Plas, E.H.) pp. 208–217. London: Applied Science Publishers.

Burgess, R. (1924) Bacteriology and mycology of wool. *Journal of the Textile Institute*, **15**, T333–T383.

Burgess, R. (1928) Microbiology of wool. *Journal of the Textile Institute*, **19**, T315–T322.

Burgess, R. (1934) Causes and prevention of mildew on wool. *Journal of the Society of Dyers and Colourists*, **50**, 138–142.

Cavill, G.W.K., Phillips, J.N. & Vincent, J.M. (1949) Relation between fungistatic activity and structure in a series of simple aromatic compounds. *Journal of the Society of Chemical Industry*, **68**, 12–16.

Corry, J.E.L. (1973) The water relations and heat resistance of micro-organisms. *Progress in Industrial Microbiology*, **12**, 73–108.

Fargher, R.G., Galloway, LK.G. & Probert, M.E. (1930) The inhibitory action of certain substances on the growth of mould fungi. *Journal of the Textile Institute*, **21**, T245–T260.

Jordan, I.D. (1934) Troubles in leather manufacture caused by moulds. *Leather Trades Review* **67**, 197–198.

Kaplan, A.M., Mandels, M. & Greenberger, M. (1972) Mode of action of resins in preventing microbial degradation of cellulosic textiles. In *Biodeterioration of Materials*, Vol. 2. (eds Walters, A.H. & Hueck-van der Plas E.H.) pp. 268–278. London: Applied Science Publishers.

Lloyd, A.O. (1968) The evaluation of rot resistance of cellulosic textiles. In *Biodeterioration of Materials* (eds Walters, A.H. & Elphick, J.J.) pp. 170–177. Amsterdam: Elsevier.

Lollar, R.M. (1944) Mould resistant treatment for leather. *Journal of the American Leather Chemists Association*, **39**, 12–24.

Marsh, P.B., Greathouse, G.A., Bollenbacher, K. & Butler M.L. (1944) Copper soaps as rot proofing agents on fabrics. *Industrial and Engineering Chemistry*, **36**, 176–181.

Mills, J., Allsopp, D. & Eggins, H.O.W. (1972) Some new developments in cellulosic material testing using perfusion techniques. In *Biodeterioration of Materials*, Vol. 2 (eds Walters, A.H. & Hueck-van der Plas, E.H.) pp. 227–232. London: Applied Science Publishers.

Miller, G. (1972) Tributyltin oxide: some factors influencing its development and application as a preservative. In *Biodeterioration of Materials*, Vol. 2 (eds Walters, A.H. & Hueck-van der Plas, E.H.) pp. 279–285. London: Applied Science Publishers.

Money, C.A. (1970) Short term preservation of hides. *Journal of the American Leather Chemists Association*, **65**, 57–59.

Selby, K. (1968) Mechanism of biodegradation of cellulose. In *Biodeterioration of Materials* (eds Walters, A.H. & Elphick, J.J.) pp. 62–78. Amsterdam: Elsevier.

Turner, R.L. (1972) Important factors in the soil burial test applied to rotproofed textiles. In *Biodeterioration of Materials*, Vol. 2 (eds Walters, H.A. & Hueck-van der Plas, E.H.) pp. 218–226. London: Applied Science Publishers.

Wessel, C.J. Lee, R.W.H. & Janecka, H. (1964) Recent developments in the control of microbial growth on leather and fabrics. *Developments in Industrial Microbiology*, **5**, 36–49.

9 BIBLIOGRAPHY — WOOL

Allsopp, C. & Allsopp, D. (1983) An updated survey of commercial products used to protect materials against biodeterioration. *International Biodeterioration Bulletin*, **19**, 99–146.

Andersen, R.L. (1969) Biological evaluation of carpeting. *Applied Microbiology*, **18**, 180–187.

Anon (1950) The mildewing of wool: causes and prevention. *Wool Science Review*, **6**, 31–42.

Arnold, L.B. (1984) Antimicrobial activity of carpet. *Carpet and Rug Industry*, **12**, 22–27.

Batson, D.M., Tennisson, D.J. & Porges, N. (1944) Study of a soil burial method for determining rot-resistance of fabrics. *American Dyestuff Reporter*, **33**, 423–454.

Blowers, R. & Wallace, K.R. (1955) The sterilization of blankets with cetyl trimethylamine bromide. *Lancet*, **i**, 1250.

Bobkova, T.S., Zlochevskaya, I.V., Chekunova, L.N., Kirkina, L.I. & Monakhova, R.I. (1975) Use of a rapid method of soil testing for evaluation of the biodeterioration resistance of textile materials. *Vestnik Moskovskovo Universiteta Biologia, Pochvovedenie*, **30**, 55–59.

Brown, J.C. (1959) The determination of damage to wool fibres. *Journal of the Society of Dyers and Colourists*, **75**, 11–21.

Burgess, R. (1924) Studies on the bacteriology of wool. *Journal of the Textile Institute*, **15**, T575–583.

Burgess, R. (1934) The use of trypsin for the determination of the resistance of wool fibres to bacterial disintegration. *Journal of Applied Bacteriology*, **17**, 230–245.

Burgess, R. & Galloway, L.D. (1940) *Applied Mycology*

and Bacteriology, 2nd Ed. London: Leonard Hill.

Burgess, R. & Rimington, C. (1929) A technique for the microscopical examination of wool fibres. *Journal of the Royal Microscopic Society*, **49**, 341–347.

Church, B.D. & Loosli, C.G. (1953) The role of the laundry in the recontamination of washed bedding. *Journal of Infectious Diseases*, **93**, 65–74.

Cody, H.J., Smith, P.F., Blaser, M.J., LaForce, F.M. & Wang W.L. (1984) Comparison of methods for recovery of *Escherichia coli*, and *Staphylococcus aureus* from seeded laundry fabrics. *Applied and Environmental Microbiology*, **47**, 965–970.

Eggins, H.O.W. (1967) The economics of biodeterioration. *Environmental Engineering*, **29**, 15–16.

Eggins, H.O.W., Malik, K.A. & Sharp, R.F. (1968) Some techniques to investigate the colonisation of cellulosic and wood substrates. In *Proceedings of First International Biodeterioration Symposium* (eds Walters, A.H. & Elphick, J.J.) pp. 120–131. London: Elsevier.

Eggins, H.O.W. & Oxley, T.A. (1980) Biodeterioration and biodegradation. *International Biodeterioration Bulletin*, **16**, 53–56.

English, M.P. (1965) The saprotrophic growth of nonkeratinophilic fungi on keratinized substrata and a comparison with keratinophilic fungi. *Transactions of the British Mycology Society*, **48**, 219–235.

Fraser, R.D.B. & Gillespie, J. (1976) Wool structure and biosynthesis. *Nature London*, **261**, 650–654.

Garner, W. (1967) *Textile Laboratory Manual*, 3rd Ed., Vol. 6, p. 153. London: Heywood.

Geiger, W.B., Patterson, W.I., Mizell, L.R. & Harris, M. (1941) The nature of the resistance of wool to digestion by enzymes. *Journal of Research of the National Bureau of Standards*, **27**, 459–468.

Georgiewics, G. (1924) *Lehrbuch der Chemisten Technologie der Gespinstfasern Deuticke*. Leipzig and Vienna.

Gray, W.D. & Martin, G.W. (1947) Improvements on the soil-burial testing method. *Mycologia*, **39**, 358–369.

Grimm, H. & Kuhne, C. (1969) The standardization of earth rotting tests of the testing of rot-proofing finishes to cellulosic fibres. *Deutscher Textiltechnie*, **19**, 46–49.

Hirst, H.R. (1927) Ultra-violet radiation as an aid to textile analysis. *Journal of the Textile Institute*, **18**, 369–375.

Hughes, W.H., & Davies, R.R. (1970) Bacteria and cadmium-treated fabrics. *British Medical Journal*, **1**, 430.

Ilyichev, V.D. (1979) *Rtitzy-istochnik bioprovrezhdenii*, pp. 47–53. Moscow: Znanie.

Jain, P.C. & Agrawal, S.C. (1980) A note on the keratin decomposing capability of some fungi. *Transactions of the Mycology Society of Japan*, **21**, 513–517.

Kempton, A.G., Maisel, H. & Kaplan, A.M. (1963) Study of the deterioration of fungicide-treated fabrics in soil burial. *Textile Research Journal*, **33**, 87–93.

Lashen, E.S. (1971) New method for evaluating antimicrobial activity directly on fabric. *Applied Microbiology*, **21**, 771–773.

Latlief, M.A., Goldsmith, M.T., Friedl, J.L. & Stuart, L.S. (1951) Bacteriostatic, germicidal and sanitising action of quaternary ammonium compounds on textiles. I. Prevention of ammonia formation from urea by *Proteus mirabilis*. *Journal of Paediatrics*, **39**, 730–737.

Lemon, H.M. (1943) A method for collection of bacteria from air and textiles. *Proceedings of the Society of Experimental Biology and Medicine*, **54**, 293–301.

Lewis, J. (1981) Microbial biodeterioration. In *Economic Microbiology* (ed. Rose, A.H.) pp. 81–130. London: Academic Press.

Lloyd, A.D. (1955) A soil-infection method for the testing of textiles for resistance to microbiological attack. *Journal of the Textile Institute*, **46**, 653–661.

Lloyd, A.D. (1965) An adhesive tape technique for the microscopical examination of surfaces supporting mould growth. *International Biodeterioration Bulletin*, **1**, 10–13.

Mahall, K. (1982) Biodegradation of textile fibres as seen under the microscope—actual case histories. *International Textile Bulletin*, **4**, 280–292.

Majors, P. (1959) Evaluation of the effectiveness of antibacterial finishes for cloth. *American Dyestuff Reporter*, **48**, 91–93.

Mandels, G.R. & Siu, R.G. (1950) Rapid assay for growth: microbial susceptibility and fungistatic activity. *Journal of Bacteriology*, **60**, 249–262.

Mandels, G.R., Stahl, W. & Levinson, H. (1948) Structural changes to wool degraded by ringworm fungus (*Microsporum gypseum*). *Textile Research Journal*, **18**, 224–231.

McCarthy, B.J. (1983a) Biodeterioration in wool textile processing. In *Biodeterioration 5* (eds Oxley, T.A. & Barry, S.) pp. 519–527. Chichester: John Wiley.

McCarthy, B.J. (1983b) Bioluminescent assay of microbial contaminants on textile materials. *International Biodeterioration Bulletin*, **19**, 53–57.

McCarthy, B.J. (1984) Bioluminescent determination of microbial activity on textiles. In *Analytical Applications of Bioluminescence and Chemiluminescence* (eds Kricka, L.J., Stanley, P.E., Thorpe, G.H.G. & Whitehead, T.P.) pp. 46–49. London: Academic Press.

McGee, J.B. & Gettings, R.L. (1985) Method for the evaluation of immobilized antimicrobial agents. In *Book of Papers*. International Conference of the American Association of Textile Chemists and Colorists.

McGee, J. & White, W.C. (1984) Evaluations of surface bonded cationic antimicrobials. *Carpet and Rug Industry*, **12**, 24–41.

McQuade, A.B. & Sutherland, W.J.A. (1960) An improved device for sampling bacterial populations on blankets. *Journal of Hygiene*, **58**, 157–158.

McQuade, A.B. (1964) Microbiological degradation of wool. *Dermatologia*, **128**, 249–266.

Mebes, B. (1975) Hygiene finishing in the dyebath. *International Textile Bulletin*, **2**, 122.

Mulcock, A.P. (1965) *Peyronallaea glomerata*—a fungus growing with the fibres of the unshorn fleece. *Australian Journal of Agricultural Research*, **16**, 691–697.

Mulcock, A.P. (1965) The fleece as a habitat for micro-organisms. *New Zealand Veterinary Journal*, **13**, 87–93.

Nichols, P.S. (1970) Bacteria on laundered fabrics. *American Journal of Public Health*, **60**, 2175–2180.

Nopitsch, M. (1953) Micro-organic attack on textiles and leather. *CIBA Review*, No. 100, pp. 3582–3610.

Osborn, J.G.B. (1912) Moulds and mildews: their relation to the damaging of grey cloth and prints. *Journal of the Society of Dyers and Colourists*, **28**, 204–208.

Pauly, H. (1904) Ueber die konstitution des histidins (I). *Zeitschrift für Physiologische Chemie*, **42**, 508–518.

Puck, T.T., Robinson, O.H., Wise, H., Loosli, C.G. & Lemon, H.M. (1946) The oil treatment of bedclothes for the control of dust-borne infection. 1. Principles underlying the development and use of a satisfactory oil-in-water emulsion. *American Journal of Hygiene*, **43**, 91–104.

Quinn, H. (1962) A method for the determination of the antimicrobial properties of treated fabrics. *Applied Microbiology*, **10**, 74–78.

Race, E. (1946) Problems in the microbiology of protein fibres. *Journal of the Society of Dyers and Colourists*, **62**, 67–85.

Raschle, P. (1983) Contribution to the examination of the rot resistance of textiles. *International Biodeterioration Bulletin*, **19**, 13–17.

Ruehle, G. & Brewer, C. (1931) United States Food and Drug Administration, *Methods of Testing Antiseptics and Disinfectants*. Circular No. 198. Washington: US Department of Agriculture.

Safranek, W.W. & Goos, R.D. (1982) Degradation of wool by saprophytic fungi. *Canadian Journal of Microbiology*, **28**, 137–140.

Sankov, E.A., Suchkova, G.C. & Andreeva, K.I. (1972) Investigations of biological wool fibre damage by the dyeing method. *Technical Textiles Industry*, USSR, **4**, 152–153.

Seal, K. & Allsopp, D. (1983) Investigative biodeterioration. In *Biodeterioration 5* (eds Oxley, T. & Barry, S.) pp. 528–534. Chichester: John Wiley.

Sherrill, J.C. (1956) The evaluation of bacteriostatic reagents and methods of application to textile fabrics. *Textile Research Journal*, **26**, 342–350.

Thomas, J.C. & Van Den Ende, M. (1941) The reduction of dust-borne bacteria in the air of hospital wards by liquid paraffin treatment of bedclothes. *British Medical Journal*, **1**, 953.

Vigo, T.L. (1978) Antibacterial fibres. In *Modified Cellulosics*. Symposium of cellulose, paper and textiles, pp. 259–284. Division of the American Chemical Society.

Vigo, T.L. & Benjaminson, M.A. (1981) Antibacterial fibre treatments and disinfection. *Textile Research Journal*, **51**, 454.

Von Bergen, W. & Mauersberger, H.R., (1948) *American Wool Handbook*. USA Textile Book Publishers.

Walton, D.W.H. & Allsopp, D. (1977) A new test cloth for soil burial trials and other studies on cellulose decomposition. *International Biodeterioration Bulletin*, **13**, 112–115.

Wehrner, C. (1902) Stains on textiles caused by *Aspergillus fumigatus*. *Journal of the Society of Dyers and Colourists*, **18**, 112.

Wellman, R.H. & McCallan, S.E.A. (1945) Office of Strategic Research and Development Report 5683. Washington: US National Defense Research Communication.

Wiksell, J.C., Pickett, M.A. & Hartmann, P.A. (1973) Survival of micro-organisms in laundered polyester cotton sheeting. *Journal of Applied Bacteriology*, **25**, 431–435.

Wilkoff, L.J., Westbrook, L. & Dixon, G.L. (1969) Factors affecting the persistence of *Staphylococcus aureus* on fabrics. *Applied Microbiology*, **17**, 268–274.

E·PAINT AND PAINT FILMS

1 LIQUID EMULSION PAINTS

Liquid emulsion paints generally contain high proportions of water and inorganic pigments, plus organic constituents which may include polymer emulsion, emulsion stabilizers, thickeners, surfactants, dispersants, antifoams, coalescing agents, levelling and freeze–thaw stabilizing agents and colour tinters. Without experimentation it is not possible to predict whether any given material will be inhibitory or stimulatory to microbial growth (Briggs, 1977).

The components of an emulsion paint may be supplied, handled or stored in aqueous dispersion or solution. The factory environment is of course not sterile, storage and mixing tanks may be open to the air or, when closed, subject to considerable condensation. It is not uncommon for pipework and equipment to have numerous dead spots where old or diluted materials may accumulate, washings may be stored or recirculated, and ultimately the paint will most likely be distributed in metal cans which may retain a greasy lubricant coating and which will probably undergo temperature cycling during storage. For these reasons, various microbiological problems can occur, leading to deterioration or spoilage of liquid emulsion paint.

Probably the most common form of attack is on the cellulose ether thickening agent of the paint, resulting in a loss of viscosity (and perhaps sedimentation of the solid phase). Alternative mechanisms postulated involve either enzyme-catalysed hydrolysis (Floyd *et al.*, 1966; Winters *et al.*, 1974) or an oxidation process involving bacterial hydrogen peroxide (Winters & Goll, 1976). Other phenomena known to occur include gassing or frothing of paint, malodour and discoloration (perhaps with change in pH, rheological properties or dispersion stability).

There is considerable evidence to link both bacteria and fungi to emulsion paint spoilage (Bravery, 1988; Zyska *et al.*, 1988), and, as already indicated, the source of contamination may be a raw material, a factory process or practice, or a storage condition. Problems can best be avoided by a combination of uncontaminated raw materials, resistant formulation, good factory hygiene and effective use of chemical preservation, with particular emphasis being placed on the last in this sub-chapter.

1.1 Preservation of emulsion paints

Extensive use has been made of organo-mercurial preservatives such as phenylmercuric acetate, phenylmercuric dodecyl succinate and others, because these have wide-spectrum antimicrobial activity, are capable of inhibiting a large number of proteins by reaction with protein sulphydryl groups, especially in enzymes, and can be effective at low concentrations in paint (0.001–0.03% mercury). Such mercurial preservatives tend to be generally toxic, and the coatings industry has been actively phasing out their use.

As alternatives, a fairly large number of non-mercurial preservatives are available commercially (Wallhäusser & Fink, 1976; Smith, 1980); however, these have varying chemical, physical and toxicological properties and need to be matched to the formulation in which activity is required. Examples of types include organo-tins, formaldehyde and formaldehyde-releasing agents, quaternary ammonium compounds (QACs), phenolics, nitrogen and sulphur heterocycles and mixtures of various types. Many of these groups are considered in

Chapter 2. Successful use of non-mercurial preservatives, particularly, requires attention to the points listed below.

1.1.1 Spectrum of activity

Aqueous raw materials (e.g. pigment and extender slurries, polymer emulsion, etc.) present the first possible source of bacterial, fungal or enzyme contamination. Within the factory, containers of aqueous raw materials having been opened may be partially used then set aside for future use. Thickeners may be dissolved and then stored in solution. Mixing procedures will leave liquid or semi-solid accumulations in and on equipment, water and washings will collect and may be recirculated, and frequently condensation will dilute the preservative and possibly wash contamination into the paint. Such circumstances may encourage bacterial or fungal growth (e.g. *Pseudomonas aeruginosa*, *Ps. putida*, *Fusarium* spp., *Scopulariopsis* spp.) in or on susceptible materials (Miller, 1973; Keene & Springle, 1976; Briggs, 1978b).

An ideal preservative would have antibacterial, antifungal and enzyme-blocking action; however, only heavy-metal compounds appear to be capable of achieving the latter, and then only at impractical levels of addition. The first two requirements are attainable, except that where the liquid paint is concerned, activity is needed in the aqueous phase (requiring the preservative to be water-soluble), whilst in semi-solid paint accumulations water-insolubility may be advantageous to reduce leaching of the preservative by condensation water. Partitioning of preservative between oily and aqueous phases is also an important point to be considered in the preservation of certain pharmaceutical products (Chapter 15).

1.1.2 Preservative concentration and usage

Since contamination by micro-organisms (and/or their enzymes) can occur at various points before, during and even after paint manufacture, early use of an effective preservative concentration is essential. An initially high preservative concentration added to aqueous raw materials etc. allows for dilution to a final, economic level in the finished paint. Also, since further dilution will occur in washings and residues which may be re-used, the preservative should either tolerate some dilution or be boosted by further addition.

The 'use concentration' of a preservative is usually estimated by evaluations carried out in paint(s). However, the fully formulated paint is often not a particularly susceptible material (in fact it is quite possible for an emulsion paint formulation to be toxic or at least inhospitable to bacteria and fungi), suggesting that normal evaluation procedures may not adequately represent the range of in-use situations in which preservative action will be needed.

1.1.3 Preservative stability

A preservative being considered for use in a given paint formulation must be stable in the formulation. Despite this there are occasions when incompatibilities occur. For example, a mercury compound used with sulphide pigment such as lithapone may react to produce black mercury sulphide. It is quite common for emulsion paints to be alkaline (pH 8–9), and some preservatives will rapidly hydrolyse under this condition. Again, ammonia may be used to obtain alkalinity and this may react with certain phenolics or formaldehyde-releasing agents. Preservative partition between oil and water phases in the paint can markedly deplete the water phase (Pauli, 1973), although it is not known whether this renders the preservative ineffective. Drastic reduction in active concentration can, however, be caused by, for example, adsorption onto clay extenders or reaction with microbial protein introduced or derived from previous contamination (Smith, 1977; Briggs, 1978a). It seems probable that such deactivation processes which reduce preservative effectiveness may well have been mistakenly interpreted as an 'increase in resistance' of micro-organisms.

2 FILMS FROM EMULSION AND OIL PAINTS

Once applied to a surface, emulsion paints lose water by evaporation and the polymer particles coalesce to form a paint film which contains pigments plus residues of the various components and additives already mentioned. The presence of these may significantly influence microbial susceptibility of the film, at least whilst it remains relatively free from organic debris. Oil paints tend to be simpler in formulation, and though the paint film touch-dries quite quickly by solvent evaporation it will continue oxidation processes for some considerable time thereafter. The products of oxidation may significantly affect microbial susceptibility of the film (again whilst it remains relatively clean).

Given a suitably moist or humid condition, fungal spores present on the surface of a susceptible paint film will germinate to produce mycelial or colonial growth. The organic nutrients required by fungi may come from the paint film or from accumulation of organic debris (e.g. food residues, grease, soil, etc.). It has been reported that distinct colonization sequences tend to occur (Winters *et al.*, 1975) though equally a specific fungus is frequently observed to colonize a particular situation. Fungi commonly isolated include species of the genera *Alternaria*, *Aspergillus*, *Aureobasidium*, *Cladosporium* and *Penicillium*, but this depends on the situation (Skinner, 1972; Hirsch & Sosman, 1976). Where water and light are available (usually soiled exterior surfaces) algal as well as fungal growth may proliferate, and genera such as *Nostoc*, *Oscillatoria*, *Pleurococcus*, *Scytonema*, *Stichococcus* and *Trentapohlia* have been isolated. Variation in paint film composition, the nature of the substrate (e.g. wood, plaster, metal, brick, etc.), and the film's environment (e.g. interior, exterior, etc.) will help to determine whether growth occurs and the form it takes.

In the UK, the Clean Air Act has been responsible for revealing many problems of 'dirtiness' as microbial disfigurement. In addition certain modern building techniques and living habits (e.g. absence of cavity walls; use of poorly insulated pre-cast building slabs; restricted ventilation in kitchens, bathrooms and renovated properties; intermittent cooking and heating systems, particularly those which humidify internal air, etc.) tend to encourage conditions conducive to biological growth (Building Research Establishment, 1981). Thus considerable incentive may exist to try to protect a given surface against fungi or algae, for which application a biocidal paint film may be utilized (probably in conjunction with a disinfectant wash or surface sterilizing agent).

2.1 Paint film preservative

A paint film applied over a surface may be exploited as a reservoir of biocide (fungicide or algicide) in which a small quantity of active material can be distributed over a wide area. Provided suitable leaching and mobility characteristics are exhibited, continuous protection is possible for a considerable time (though it must be stressed that as detritus and soiling increase on the paint film so the biocide's ability to protect will be impaired).

Organo-mercurial compounds have been used extensively because of their wide-spectrum activity and relative cheapness; however, such compounds tend to be toxic to higher organisms, often volatile or water-sensitive, and may darken in industrial atmospheres due to mercury sulphide formation. Alternative fungicides include inorganic and organic compounds of zinc, barium, copper and tin, as well as a fair number of purely organic materials (Springle, 1979). Most of the organic biocides are halogen-, nitrogen- and/or sulphur-containing compounds (such as diidomethyl *p*-tolyl sulphone; *N*-(trichloromethyl)-thio-4-cyclohexene-1,2-dicarboximide; 2,4,5,6-tetrachloro-isophthalonitrile; 2-*n*-octyl-4-isothiazolin-3-one) and, especially with newer products, toxicity to mammals and fish tends to be minimized as much as possible, as does persistence in the environment.

Some fungicidal compounds, such as tetramethylthiuram disulphide and tributyl tin oxide, also possess algicidal properties and have been used for general protection of exterior paintwork. Other fungicides may well have this ability and, in addition, agricultural herbicides (e.g. triazines; chlorophenyl urea compounds) have found application. In selecting a film biocide it is advisable to consider the spectrum of action, toxicology, and all other technical data available.

An ideal film biocide would have wide-spectrum activity, low mammalian toxicity, resistance to both water leaching and UV degradation, compatibility with and stability in different paints and a competitive price. Commercial products have appeared which have suffered from various shortcomings, including retarding oxidative drying of oil paints such that they remain tacky; colouring white paints due to degradation intermediates or by reaction with metal ions such as copper or iron; disturbing the ionic balance of emulsion paints and causing precipitation; hydrolysing under the alkaline conditions (pH 7.5–9.5) in an emulsion paint and so losing biocidal effectiveness.

Interest in methods of evaluating biocide effectiveness developed along with the appearance of the chemicals themselves, and both natural exposure and laboratory testing have been employed (Springle, 1975; Post *et al.*, 1976; Hoffmann, 1977).

It has been suggested that only natural exposure can give meaningful assessment. This type of evaluation, however, tends to be expensive, time-consuming, uncontrolled in terms of exposure conditions and often markedly affected by climatic variations. Laboratory exposure conditions (inoculum, temperature, humidity, surface contamination, substrate, film pre-treatment, etc.) can be much more closely controlled, and it is possible to simulate an in-use condition of the paint film where this is known.

Laboratory testing can be used to eliminate much time-consuming and expensive natural exposure. Failure of a paint film to prevent growth under laboratory conditions is a definite indication of its limitation; however, a variety of conditions (involving water leaching, exposure to heat and UV light, and contamination of the surface by organic materials) will be needed to represent the range of situations met with in use. Standardization in test methodology is generally considered desirable, and a Paints Working Group operating within the International Biodeterioration Research Group (sponsored by the OECD, Paris) has been evaluating, towards this end, methodology for testing mould resistance of paint (Barry *et al.*, 1977; Bravery *et al.*, 1978). A new standard BS 3900: Part G6: 1989, has resulted from the collaboration.

3 ANTIFOULING PAINT FILMS

Surfaces submerged in the sea tend to accumulate a variety of marine organisms, for example bacteria, fungi, algae, barnacles, hydroids, sea-squirts, tube-worms and mussels. When the surface is part of a man-made structure this 'fouling' can have disastrous results by causing such problems as increased weight and size, impaired moving parts, blocked or restricted valves, pipework and conduits and increased frictional resistance. This last is of particular importance where ships' hulls are concerned, since the increased drag results in greater fuel consumption to maintain a given service speed, and ultimately means dry-docking the ship for cleaning and repair.

Ships, such as oil tankers, which operate fairly continuously with few lay-days, have a tendency to foul with algal forms such as *Enteromorpha* spp. and *Ectocarpus* spp., whereas ships operating in an intermittent manner with considerable lay-days (e.g. naval ships) tend to foul with animal rather than algal forms. Economic and military implications have stimulated much research into methods of controlling marine fouling. The most practicable and economic method relies on antifouling paint films from which chemical biocides are released into the water alongside the hull to keep the surface free of fouling for something between 0.5 and 3 years (at present) depending on the paint formulation and exposure conditions involved.

Paints have been developed to work by various mechanisms of biocide release (Furtado & Fletcher, 1987; Mihm & Loeb, 1988). Soluble matrix paints contain a sea-water-soluble binder component, such as rosin, which dissolves to release the toxicant. Continuous-contact paints contain a greater volume of biocide than the soluble matrix paints. The binder is insoluble, such as vinyl or chlorinated rubber, and holds the biocide particles closely packed and in continuous contact. Biocide deep within the paint reaches the surface as the biocide above it dissolves in sea-water. Diffusion coatings are intended to act as a solid solution of biocide in the binder, which provides a steady supply of biocide at the surface by diffusion through the film. Binders formed as organo-metallic co-polymers are a development in which the organo-metallic biocide (e.g. an organo-tin compound) is provided at the surface by slow hydrolysis of the paint film (Atherton, 1978; Mihm & Loeb, 1988). The basic intention of a great proportion of research into antifouling paints is concerned with the increase of performance life, either by controlling the rate of biocide release from the paint film or by controlling rate of transport away from the hull (van Londen *et al.*, 1975; Christie, 1978; Lorenz, 1978).

Types of biocides which have been used in antifouling paints include copper compounds (mainly cuprous oxide), organo-tin and organo-lead compounds, inorganic and organic compounds of mercury, arsenic and zinc, and organic compounds such as polychlorinated hydrocarbons, phenols, thiadiazoles, nitrothiazoles, dithiocarbamates, chloronaphthoquinones and chlorophenyl urea compounds (de la Court & de Vries, 1973; de la Court, 1977).

The impact of some of these biocides on man and the environment is a matter of concern, and is leading to the introduction of restrictions or controls on their usage by certain countries. Studies by various organizations including the Paint Research Association have shown that low-toxicity organic antifoulants can be used with some success. The present intention, however, seems to be to accumulate performance data and keep such materials as a reserve armoury of biocides.

ACKNOWLEDGEMENT

The authors wish to thank the Paint Research Association for permission to publish this chapter.

4 REFERENCES

Atherton, D. (1978) New developments in antifouling, a review of the present state of the art. *American Chemical Society, Division of Organic Coatings and Plastics Chemistry Preprints*, **39**, 380–385.

Barry, S., Bravery, A.F. & Coleman, L.J. (1977) A method for testing the mould resistance of paints. *International Biodeterioration Bulletin*, **13**, 51–57.

Bravery, A.F. (1988) Biodeterioration of paint—a state-of-the-art comment. In *Biodeterioration 7* (eds Houghton, D.R., Smith, R.N. & Eggins, H.O.W.) pp. 466–485. London: Elsevier Applied Science.

Bravery, A.F., Barry, S. & Coleman, L.J. (1978) Collaborative experiments on testing the mould resistance of paint films. *International Biodeterioration Bulletin*, **14**, 1–10.

Briggs, M.A. (1977) In-can preservation: the cellulase mechanism of paint spoilage. Paint Research Association Technical Report TR/4/77.

Briggs, M.A. (1978a) An investigation into the preservation of a china clay slurry. Paint Reseach Association Technical Report TR/6/78.

Briggs, M.A. (1978b) Comparison of factory practice and hygiene with the available test methods of preservative efficacy. Paint Research Association TR/8/78.

Building Research Establishment (1981) *Mould Growth in Buildings*. Proceedings of a joint BRE/Paint RA seminar.

Christie, A.O. (1978) Self-polishing antifouling—a new approach to long term fouling control and hull smoothness. *American Chemical Society, Division of Organic Coatings and Plastics Chemistry Preprints*, **39**, 585–589.

de la Court, F.H. (1977) Fouling resistant coatings: their functioning and future developments. *Proceeding of 3rd International Conference on Organic Coatings*, pp. 97–137.

de la Court, F.H. & de Vries, H.J. (1973) Advances in fouling prevention. *Progress in Organic Coatings*, **1**, 375–404.

Floyd, J.D., James, W.G. & Wirick, M.G. (1966) Viscosity stability of latex paints containing water-soluble cellulose polymers, *Journal of Paint Technology*, **38**, 398–401.

Furbado, S.E.J. & Fletcher, R.L. (1987) Test procedures for marine antifouling paints. In *Preservatives in the Food, Pharmaceutical and Environmental Industries* (eds. Board, R.G., Allwood, M.C. & Banks, J.G.) Society for Applied Bacteriology Technical Series No. 22, pp. 145–163. Oxford: Blackwell Scientific Publications.

Hirsch, S.R. & Sosman, J.A. (1976) A one-year survey of mould growth inside twelve homes. *Annals of Allergy*, **36**, 30–38.

Hoffmann, E. (1977) Techniques for the investigation of the biodeterioration of paints developed at CSIRO, Australia. *Journal of the Oil and Colour Chemists Association*, **60**, 127–136.

Keene, C.R. & Springle, W.R. (1976) In-can preservation. Paint Research Association Technical Report TR/2/76.

Lorenz, J. (1978) Protection against marine growth—the current situation. *Polymers, Paint and Colour Journal*, August pp. 737–747.

Mihm, J.W. & Loeb, G.I. (1988) The effect of microbial biofilms on organism release by an antifouling paint. In *Biodeterioration 7* (eds Houghton, D.R., Smith, R.N. & Eggins, H.O.W.) pp. 309–314. London: Elsevier Applied Science.

Miller, W.G. (1973) Incidence of microbial contamination of emulsion paint during the manufacturing process. *Journal of the Oil and Colour Chemists Association*, **56**, 307–312.

Pauli, O. (1973) Inter-phase migration of preservatives in latex paints. *Journal of the Oil and Colour Chemists Association*, **56**, 289–291.

Post, M.A., Iverson, W.P. & Campbell, P.G. (1976) Non-mercurial fungicides. *Modern Paint and Coatings*, September, **11**, 31–38.

Skinner, C.E. (1972) Laboratory test methods for biocidal paints. In *Biodeterioration of Materials*. Vol. 2, Part VIII, pp. 346–354, London: Applied Science Publishers.

Smith, A.L. (1980) *Guide to Preservatives for Water-Borne Paints*. Paint Research Association Technical Publication.

Smith, Q.J. (1977) In-can preservation: bacterial resistant strains. Paint Research Association Technical Report TR/2/77.

Springle, W.R. (1975) Testing biocidal paints. *Society for Applied Bacteriology Technical Series 8: Some Methods for Microbiological Assay*, pp. 191–201. London: Academic Press.

Springle, W.R. (1979) *Guide to Paint Film Fungicides*. Paint Research Association Technical Publication.

van Londen, A.M., Johnsen, S. & Govers, G.J. (1975) The case of long life antifoulings. *Journal of Paint Technology*, **47**, 62–68.

Wallhausser, K.H. & Fink, W. (1976) Konservierung von Dispersionen und Dispersionsfarben. *Farbe und Lacke*, **82**(2), 108–125.

Winters, H. & Goll, M. (1976) Non-enzymatic oxidative degradation of hydroxyethyl cellulose thickened latex paints. *Journal of Coating Technology*, **48**, 80–85.

Winters, H., Guidetti, G. & Goll, M. (1974) Growth of a typical paint bacterial isolate in aqueous emulsion paint. *Journal of Paint Technology*, **46**, 69–72.

Winters, H., Isquith, I.R. & Goll, M. (1975) A study of the ecological succession in the biodeterioration of a vinyl acrylic paint film. *Developments in Industrial Microbiology*, **17**, 167–171.

Zyska, J., Cheplik, Z.T., Kwiatkowska, D., Wichary, H.M. & Kozlowska, R. (1988) Fungal colonization of organic coatings in cotton mills. In *Biodeterioration 7* (eds Houghton, D.R., Smith, R.N. & Eggins, H.O.W.) pp. 486–492. London: Elsevier Applied Science.

F·PRESERVATION IN THE CONSTRUCTION INDUSTRY*

1 INTRODUCTION

A wide variety of materials of organic and inorganic origin is used in the construction industry. Two of the more important, wood with wood-based products, and paint, are considered individually in separate sections of this book (Chapters 17G and 17E, respectively). The present section will therefore be concerned principally with inorganic masonry materials such as stone, concrete, brick and asbestos cement, with some reference also to preservation requirements for adhesives, sealants and plastics.

2 MASONRY MATERIALS

Whether stone can be considered the building material first used by early man in constructing dwellings, enclosures, fortifications and the like is debatable. Certainly many natural stones are extremely durable and archaeological structures built in natural stone have survived thousands of years. However, natural stones vary widely in their composition and properties (Ashurst & Dimes, 1977). Broadly, igneous rocks such as granite are produced from molten magma. They are highly crystalline, silica-rich, dense and of low porosity. Sedimentary rocks are laid down by settlement of eroded particles under water. They include sandstones, consisting mainly of quartz grains bound with iron oxide or calcium carbonate, and limestones consisting mainly of calcium and magnesium carbonates. They are generally more porous than igneous rocks. Slate and marble building materials are of metamorphic rock produced by the action of secondary heat and pressure on igneous or sedimentary rocks.

Cementatious materials, such as concrete and mortar, are produced by mixing together in appropriate proportions an aggregate of natural sand and gravel with water and cement powder. The latter is a mixture of calcium silicates and aluminates produced by burning calcium carbonate from chalk or limestone with clay. The chemistry of cement setting is a complex process of recrystallization with water. The porosity and strength of concrete depends upon a number of complex factors including cement content, the cement: water ratio and the cement:aggregate ratio. The nature of the aggregate, compaction processes and the curing time and conditions all play a part. Bricks are produced by baking clays, mostly consisting of aluminium silicates and some calcium silicates. Variation in porosity and hardness results from differing clays, differing compaction and differing firing procedures.

* The views expressed are those of the author and do not necessarily correspond with the views of the Department of the Environment.

2.1 Durability and biological agencies

The principal degrading agency associated with stone and other masonry materials is the weather. Durability is correlated with the propensity of the stone to absorb and retain water, for the extent of damage depends upon the ability of the stone to resist the solubilizing effects of the water, as well as the stresses induced by freeze–thaw cycling and salt recrystallization induced by the presence of water. Indeed, it is the presence and availability of water which, as with any other ecological niche, is critical in permitting establishment of a population of organisms and, to a degree, in determining the composition of that population (Bravery & Jones, 1977). Studies on the processes of soil formation repeatedly confirm that biological agencies play a significant supporting role to weathering forces in the breakdown of natural stones. Thus a structure built in natural stone or other masonry material presents many of the same ecological 'niches' as occur in the exposed stone of natural cliffs, rock faces and pavements. Whilst the durability and integrity of a stone-built structure depends mainly on the resistance of its stone to weathering forces, there is no doubt that a similar sequence of colonizing organisms can be observed on stone buildings and similar patterns of biologically aided breakdown appear to occur. Furthermore, ecological observations on surfaces of man-made, inorganic materials including concrete, brick and asbestos cement (Lloyd, 1976; Figg *et al.*, 1987) reveal strikingly similar patterns under similar environmental conditions of pH, temperature, illumination, moisture and rates of drying.

Newly exposed surfaces of masonry materials may need preconditioning before any organism can establish itself. Regular wetting is essential, and studies have revealed that it is the duration of the period of wetness that is important rather than the frequency of wetting itself (Bravery & Jones, 1977). The pH, in particular that of new concrete and asbestos cement (which may be as high as 14), will have to be changed to within the pH range 3–9 (Figg *et al.*, 1987).

2.2 Organisms and the nature of the problems

At an early stage of exposure, new surfaces of masonry materials present little nutritional inducement so that early colonizers must have nutritional independence. Generally, the colonization sequence appears to commence with the establishment of autotrophic bacterial populations. In particular, species of sulphur-oxidizing bacteria such as *Desulphovibrio desulphuricans*, *Thiobacillus thio-oxidans* and *Thiobacillus thiroparus* have been isolated (Krumbein & Pochon, 1964; Sadurska & Kawalik, 1966; Pochon & Jaton, 1967; Jaton, 1972, 1973; Paleni & Curri, 1972; Milde *et al.*, 1983; Sand and Bock, 1987). These authors are among the leading authorities who have advanced theories on the sulphur-oxidative mechanism of bacterial action by which sulphuric acid is produced, which in turn has a direct degrading influence on the material. The decay of concrete in sewer pipes by sulphuric acid produced by *Thiobacillus concretivorus* has been cited by Hueck van der Plas (1968) and Todd (1974) and by Sand and Bock (1987).

Species of the autotrophic oxidizing bacteria *Nitrosomonas* and *Nitrobacter* have also been isolated from decayed stonework (Kauffman, 1952, 1960; Kauffman and Toussaint, 1954; Jaton, 1972, 1973; Eckhardt, 1985); from concrete (Kaltwasser, 1971) and from asbestos cement (Novotny *et al.*, 1973). It has been postulated that ammonia in rainwater and the air, produced by nitrifying bacteria, is oxidized to nitrate, which in turn reacts with calcium carbonate to produce the more soluble calcium nitrate. Subsequent solubilization of the calcium nitrate destroys the integrity of the stone.

Heterotrophic bacteria have been isolated from natural rocks and implicated in degradation by the organic acids they produce (Krumbein, 1983; Berthelin, 1983), solubilizing phosphates, silicates and ions of aluminium, iron and magnesium (Duff *et al.*, 1963; Sahinkaya & Gurbuzer, 1968; Aristovskaya & Kutuzova, 1968; Wood & Macrae, 1972; Dumitru *et al.*, 1976). Heterotrophic bacteria have received comparatively little attention until more recently, but they do appear to have significant decay capability (Eckhardt, 1985; Lewis *et al.*, 1985, 1987, 1988; May & Lewis, 1988).

Though extensively investigated, the role of bacteria in the degradation of stone and masonry remains contentious. However, since these species have been consistently isolated from decayed stonework, and they are known to be capable of producing metabolic acids, it seems reasonable to expect them to be of potential significance to the durability of such materials.

2.2.1 *Algae*

Algae, requiring only water and traces of mineral salts, are well able to colonize surfaces of masonry materials when conditions are suitable (Paleni & Curri, 1973: Richardson, 1973). When surfaces become sufficiently wet and remain so for sufficient periods of time, extensive populations of algae are quick to develop. Although the range of species may be large, among those that predominate are the green algae *Stichococcus*, *Pleurococcus*, *Trentepholia* and *Oscillatoria* (Grant, 1982). A number of species of the blue-green algae, the cyanophycetes, are often associated with natural stone and soil. Trotet *et al.* (1973) isolated various cyanophycetes from the surface of a concrete runway and suggested that the algae dissolved calcium carbonate, releasing residual particles of the aggregate to form a slippery mud under wet conditions. As proposed by Bachmann as early as 1915, it seems likely that acidic by-products of algal metabolism induce chemical changes in certain types of masonry materials, though there is in fact little direct evidence. Certainly the extensive sheets of algal growth that develop under wet conditions will retard subsequent drying of the water responsible for their growth, and this in turn will exacerbate water-induced damage of the underlying masonry. In addition, whilst the algal growth itself can be unsightly, the appearance is made even worse by the considerable quantities of fine inorganic dust, soot, etc. that become entrapped in the algal mass, particularly in urban environments (Grant, 1982).

2.2.2 *Fungi*

Colonization of external as well as internal surfaces by species of fungi depends upon nutritional preconditioning in which previously established populations of bacteria and algae may play a major part. Eutrophication also arises from organic debris deposited from wind and rain, and by bird-droppings, which may be considerable in certain situations of favoured bird-perching. Fungi have been extensively isolated from wet interior surfaces of plaster- or cement-rendered walls, particularly in relation to food processing, brewing and laundering premises (Flannigan, 1989). Among the commonest are species of *Penicillium*, *Cladosporium*, *Aspergillus* and *Alternaria*. (Bravery *et al.*, 1987; Hunter *et al.*, 1988; Grant *et al*, 1989). In such situations fungi are more significant as fouling organisms and for potential hazards to human health, rather than for any direct degradation. Their presence is indicative of undesirably high moisture levels resulting usually from condensation, damp penetration or leakage. Such moisture sources themselves indicate building faults or inadequate ventilation, heating and insulation (Bravery *et al.*, 1987).

Fungi have been studied less extensively in the exterior situation. Ionita (1971, 1974), Paleni & Curri (1972), Krumbein (1972) and Lepidi & Schippa (1973) have isolated a number of fungi from decaying stonework. Lepidi & Schippa (1973) indicated that hyphae were extensively distributed within the decayed stone but penetrated even into that which appeared sound. Production of organic acids by fungi, including oxalic and citric acids, is well known under laboratory conditions (Neculce, 1976) and the ability of such acids to solubilize constituents of stone has also been demonstrated (Webley *et al.*, 1963; Henderson & Duff, 1963; Gaur *et al.*, 1973). Though there is little direct evidence, certain fungi clearly have the potential to contribute to the degradation of masonry materials.

Fungi are also significant in the process of lichenization of algal growths on masonry. Studies on pre-washed asbestos cement panels have revealed lichenization within 12–18 months even in the urban environment of central London (A.O. Lloyd, personal communication). In the practical context it is the lichens themselves which are important, rather than the lichen-forming fungi.

2.2.3 *Lichens*

Lichens can apparently develop on almost any surface with the exception of metallic materials. Their development is well known to be sensitive to local environmental conditions and particularly to atmospheric levels of sulphur dioxide. Indeed, lichens have been used as indicators of air pollution in urban areas. Certainly the range of species occurring on masonry surfaces is much greater in the cleaner rural environment. The commonest species observed in urban situations are *Lecanora dispersa* and species of *Caloplaca* and of *Candelariella*, including particularly *C. aurella* and *C. vitellina*. Other species common on a variety of masonry materials, especially in rural areas, include *L. conizaeoides L. atra*, *L. muralis*, *Xanthoria parietina*, and species of *Physcia* including *P. caesia*, *P. grisea* and *P. orbicularis*.

Whilst lichen growths are sometimes considered of aesthetic appeal, mellowing the otherwise drab or stark appearance of concrete or stone, they may also have quite serious deleterious effects. In some situations they are distinctly disfiguring. They are also capable of withstanding prolonged periods of drought, resuming active growth when wet conditions return. Under drought conditions they desiccate and shrink markedly, inducing shear stresses at the interface with the masonry. Strong rhizoids, which can penetrate several millimetres even into basaltic granite (Lloyd, 1976), cause shearing and detachment of the outer millimetre or so of material, particularly near the centre of the lichen thallus. Retention of moisture in and on the surface of the structure is potentially degrading and the thalli, which are difficult to remove completely, can interfere with the bond required in the application of any subsequent recoating such as masonry paints (Whiteley & Bravery, 1982), renderings or concrete guniting. Extensive lichen growths on asbestos cement paving cause a slippery walking surface when wet (Barr, 1977), which can be extremely dangerous in gardens or on the maintenance inspection areas of roofs.

2.2.4 *Mosses, ferns and higher plants*

Mosses, ferns and higher plants may develop wherever there is a potential for root development. Commonest among the mosses are *Tortula muralis*, *Barbula cylindrica*, *Grimmia pulvinata*, *Camptothecium sericeum* and *Rhynchostegiella tenella*. *Asplenium* spp. are common among the ferns, whilst a wide variety of higher plants occur whose seed dispersal is by wind. Accumulations of fine soils are not an essential prerequisite, as rooting occurs directly into some highly porous stones such as tufa, or even into an artificial soil as may be provided by roofing chips.

The action of the earlier colonizers, combined with weathering forces, causes the erosion of small pockets and ledges in stonework and mixtures of organic and inorganic debris accumulate within them. Spores of mosses and ferns or airborne seeds of higher plants eventually arrive and germinate. Mosses and many ferns do not require extensive rooting support and can become established in profusion with only a very shallow hold on old buildings and structures. Higher plants are more variable, and whilst grasses and opportunist annuals may abound, even shrubs and trees can be remarkably tenacious. Once again such vegetation retains large quantities of moisture against the masonry surface. In addition, the stresses caused by powerful penetrating roots can induce physical failure of the materials and even serious instability of the building structure. Pavements, road surfaces and runways may be disrupted with serious economic and safety consequences.

2.3 Remedial and preventive measures

The presence of organic growths on masonry surfaces is not always regarded as undesirable and damaging, nor is it always necessary or practicable to remove them. The probability of significant biological colonization in relation to the quantities of concrete, brick and natural stone utilized in the 'construction industry', therefore, make pretreatment to preserve them chemically against future biological growths generally impracticable and uneconomic. Preservation of old stonework affected by chemical degradation is a specialized subject outside the scope of the present book. Incorporation of chemical toxicants into concrete, plaster and mortars has been proposed but it is not practised on a significant scale.

The potential problems associated with biological growths are being increasingly recognized, and measures to kill and remove contamination of undesirable organisms are being taken as part of normal maintenance procedures (British Standard Institution, 1982). In this sense then, sterilization of masonry materials is carried out on a growing scale, and chemical methods predominate both for interior and exterior situations.

2.3.1 Chemical control

The commonest approach involves chemical solutions as so-called toxic washes (Anon, 1982; Richardson, 1973; Allsopp & Allsopp, 1983). A number of different chemicals have been employed as sterilants and preservatives for masonry, both experimentally as well as in commercial practice (Tables 17.7 and 17.8). The main types approved for practice (Anon, 1990) (see also Chapter 2) are:

1 sodium hypochlorite (common bleach);
2 sodium pentachlorophenoxide;
3 sodium 2-phenylphenoxide;
4 boric acid;
5 quaternary ammonium compounds (QACs);
6 dodecylamine salicylate and lactate;
7 dichlorophen;
8 tri-*n*-butyl tin oxide;
9 halogenated organic compounds (e.g. sulphamides, thiophthalimides).

The simplest formulations usually contain one of the first seven compounds and are extensively used for initial toxic washing over large surface areas. More complex formulations are available, intended to be more permanent, and often contain mixtures of one or more of the chemicals with additives to improve water repellency.

In the main, toxic washes are made up in water on site and applied to flood-affected areas thoroughly using brushes or spraying and watering equipment. For exterior surfaces it is desirable wherever possible to apply the toxic wash some 3–14 days before attempting to remove the growths. The washes are more effective when applied to damp surface growths but should not be used immediately after heavy rain or prior to expected rainfall. After prolonged dry periods, growths should be wetted by hosing or spraying with water shortly before applying the toxic wash. Where growths are particularly dense or leathery, penetration and effectiveness of the fluids can be aided if growths are loosened or partially removed by abrading the surface during or immediately prior to treating. Dead and moribund growth is removed using stiff wire brushes, scrapers or powerful water jets. The cleaned surface should be inspected carefully for evidence of residual growths as certain lichen thalli can be extremely resistant. Residual growth can seriously impair the performance of any subsequent coatings and may also be capable of regeneration. A secondary application of the same, or a more permanent, toxic wash may then be appropriate.

The effective life of exterior toxic washes varies according to the nature of the formulation, the porosity of the surface and the degree of exposure to rain wash. On more porous surfaces somewhat sheltered from the most severe weathering influence, residual control may be obtained for 3 or 4 years. A good-quality, dense concrete surface in exposed conditions may remain protected for only 1 year or less. The application of a colourless water-repellent after the toxic wash has sometimes been advocated. In practice, variable absorptions can lead to a patchy appearance and there can be interference with subsequent applications of coatings. The measure of improved control frequently may not justify the additional costs of the water-repellent and its application. Regular applications of inhibitors may be necessary on prestige buildings or monuments, and care must then be taken to ensure that abrasion of the surfaces does not spoil architectural or artistic detail.

Chemical treatment of interior surfaces may often require special considerations relating to the needs and safety of the occupants of dwellings or the nature of operations in affected areas. Wall coverings and other furnishings may impose limitations whilst high condensation in bathrooms and swimming pools, in addition to surface contamination in kitchens, bakeries, breweries, etc., will make particular demands for permanence and safety of the products and the methods of applying

Table 17.7 Inorganic chemicals for controlling growths on masonry

Active chemical	Application rate/ concentration (%)	Product	Application*	Reference
Alkali fluorides			I	Nicot, 1951
Ammonium fluoride			I	Roizin, 1951
Barium metaborate			P	Drisko, 1973
Chromium trioxide			C	Forrester, 1959
Copper (metallic)			C	Forrester, 1959
Copper (II) aceto-arsenite (plus many other Cu compounds including oxychloride)	10		C	Robinson & Austin, 1951
Copper (II) carbonate			C	Gilchrist, 1953
Copper (II) carbonate ammonia in dilute	0.2 5		I	Rechenberg, 1972 Anon, 1982 Genin, 1973
Copper (II) cyanide or arsenate + copper (II) oxide			IE	Norddeutsche Affinerie, 1953
Copper (II) naphthenate			E	Stinson, 1956
Copper (II) 8-quinolinolate				Richardson & Ogilvy, 1955
Copper (II) oxide	0.2 (by wt in cement)		EC	Rechenberg, 1972 Lurie & Brookfield, 1948
Copper (II) sulphate	(2 in limewash) 0.1 (by wt in cement)		CE P	Aslam & Singh, 1971 Rechenberg, 1972 Kauffmann, 1960
Disodium octaborate tetrahydrate†	5 4–10	Polybor		Genin, 1973 Anon, 1982 Richardson, 1973
Iron fluoride			I	Roizin, 1951
Mercuric chloride (mercury (II) chloride)			E	Sadurska & Kawalik, 1966
Magnesium fluorosilicate‡	4–10	Lithurin	IE	Genin, 1973 Keen, 1976 Anon, 1982
Potassium permanganate				Rechenberg, 1972
Selenium metal			C	Gilchrist, 1953
Silver nitrate				Sadurska & Kawalik, 1966
Sodium fluoride				Roizin, 1951
Sodium hypochlorite	5	Bleach	CI	Rechenberg, 1972 Keen, 1976 Anon, 1972
Sodium salicylate	2		I	Rechenberg, 1972
Sodium silicofluoride			IC	Roizin, 1951 Gilchrist, 1953
Zinc fluorosilicate‡	4	Lithurin	IE	Genin, 1973 Keen, 1976 Anon, 1972
Zinc naphthenate			E	Stinson & Keyes, 1953
Zinc oxychloride			I	Anon, 1977 Savory, 1980

* C, cement additive; E, toxic wash (exterior use); I, toxic wash (interior use); P, plastics product.

† Borax Consolidated Ltd, Borax House, Carlisle Place, London SW1, UK.

‡ Laporte Industries Ltd, General Chemicals Division, Moorfields Road, Widnes WA8 OHE *and* Chemical Buildings Product Ltd, Cleveland Road, Hemel Hempstead, Herts HP2 7PH, UK.

Masonry biocides are controlled under the control of Resticides Regulations, 1986. Only approved products can be sold supplied, used, stored or advertised. Publication in this list does not imply approval.

Table 17.8 Organic chemicals used to control growths in the construction industry

Key to coding
A = adhesives
B = bitumen products
C = cement additive
E = toxic wash (exterior use)
F = fillers, stoppers, groutings
I = toxic wash (interior use)
J = jointing compounds, sealants, putty
O = wet state protection concrete additives
P = plastic products
R = rubbers (synthetic and natural)

Active chemical	Application rate/ concentration (%)	Product	Source of supply*	Application	Reference(s)
Aqueous cresol (cresylic acid)		Lysol		I	Rechenberg, 1972
					Keen, 1976
Alkoxysilane: 3 (trimethoxysilyl)-propyldimethyl-octadecyl ammonium chloride	0.1	Si-QAC	Dow Corning Corp.,	E	Isquith *et al.*, 1972
Benzimidazole derivative + chloracetamide	0.5–2	Mergal 592	Hoechst UK Ltd	PF	
1,2-Benzisothiazolin-3-one	0.01–0.1	Proxel AB, CRL, HL	ICI Organics	AO	
Benzyl-hemiformals mixture		Preventol D2	Bayer UK	A (liquids)	
Bis(trichloromethyl sulphone)		Chlorosulphone	Tenneco Organics Ltd	AO	
Chloracetamide + polyglycols + heterocyclic compounds	2–5	Mergal K6	Hoechst UK Ltd	EI	
	0.1–0.3			A	
Chloracetamine + quaternary ammonium compound + fluorides	0.1–0	Mergal AF	Hoechst UK Ltd	A	
Cresylic acids	2			R	Pitis, 1972
Copper 8-hydroxyquinolinolate				P	Kaplan *et al.*, 1970
Dichlorophen [2,2′-methylene-bis(4-chlorophenol)]	1 free phenol in isopropanol	Panacide	BDH	EC	Rechenberg, 1972
					Keen, 1976
2,3-Dichloro 1,4 naphthoquinone				I	Morgan, 1959
Diisocyanate				I	Sponsel, 1956
Dimethyl benzylammonium chloride		Hyamine 3500	Rohm & Haas (UK) Ltd	IE	
Dimethyl aminomethyl phenol				R	Anon., 1974
3,5-Dimethyl-tetra-hydro 1,3,5-2H-thiadiazine-2-thione			Tenneco Organics Ltd	AP	
Diquat 1-1 ethylene-2,2 dipyridiylium				ME	Rechenberg, 1972
Dithio 2,2-bis benzmethylamide	0.2–2	Densil P	ICI Organics	A	
Dithiocarbamates + benzimidazole derivatives	0.05–0.6	Mergal AT30	Hoechst UK Ltd	AFJ	
Dodecylamine salicylate	2–5	Nuodex 87	Durham Chemicals	EI	
Fluorinated sulphonamide	0.2	Acticide APA	Thor Chemicals Ltd	F	
Formaldehyde	5			IE	Rechenberg, 1972
	2				Keen, 1976

Continued

Table 17.8 (*contd*) Organic chemicals used to control growths in the construction industry

Key to coding
A = adhesives
B = bitumen products
C = cement additive
E = toxic wash (exterior use)
F = fillers, stoppers, groutings
I = toxic wash (interior use)
J = jointing compounds, sealants, putty
O = wet state protection concrete additives
P = plastic products
R = rubbers (synthetic and natural)

Active chemical	Application rate/ concentration (%)	Product	Source of supply*	Application	Reference(s)
Halogenated acid amide derivatives	0.1–0.3	Parmetol A23	Sterling Industrial	AO	
Halogenated acid amide derivatives + aldehyde + heterocyclic compounds	0.05–0.3	Parmetol K50	Sterling Industrial	O	
Halogenized acid amide derivatives + heterocyclic compounds	1.0–3.0	Parmetol DF12	Sterling Industrial	I	
Hexaminium salt	0.1–0.3	Preventol D1	Bayer UK	A	
2-Hydroxybiphenyl potassium salt	3–20	Acticide 50	Thor Chemicals Ltd	E	
2-Hydroxydiphenyl sodium salt		Preventol 0N	Bayer UK	A	
5-Hydroxymethoxmethyl 1-aza-3,7-dioxabicyclo (3,3,0) octane + other substituted oxazolidines		Nuosept 95	Durham Chemicals Tenneco Organics Ltd	AFO	
Lead phenolate and other lead salts of synthetic fatty acids				P	Wexler *et al.*, 1971
3-Methyl-4-chlorophenol		Preventol CMK	Bayer UK	A (powder) F	
Methylene-bisthiocyanate			Tenneco Organics Ltd	APFO	
2-Mercaptobenzthiazole	0.1–1	Mystox MB	Catomance Ltd	AO	
2-Mercaptobenzothiazole sodium salt	0.1–0.5	Nuodex 84	Nuodex UK Ltd; Tenneco Organics Ltd	A	
N-dimethyl-*N'*-phenyl-(*N'*-fluorodichloromethylthio) sulphamide	1.5–2	Preventol A4	Bayer UK Ltd	EIJ	
N(fluordichloromethylthio) phthalimide	1–2	Preventol A3	Bayer UK Ltd	EIPJ	
N(trichloromethylthiophthalimide		Folpet	Murphy Chemical Ltd (UK)	PEI	Kaplan *et al.*, 1970 Rechenberg, 1972
N(Trichloromethyl)thio-4-cyclohexene 1,2-dicarboximide	0.5–2.5	Captan	Murphy Chemical Ltd (UK)	P	Kaplan *et al.*, 1970
2,*n*-Octyl-4-isothiazolon-3-one		Kathan 893	Rohm & Haas UK Ltd	EI	
Organic acid amine	1–5	Nuodex 87	Nuodex Ltd UK	EI	
Organic-ethoxy compound	0.1–0.5	Acticide BG	Thor Chemicals	AFO	
	0.3–0.8	THP		AO	

Organo-mercury				I	Nicot, 1951
				R	Zyska *et al.*, 1972
Organo-tin	0.2–0.5	Acticide FPF	Thor Chemicals	AF	
Ortho-phenyl phenol				E	
10,10′-Oxybisphenoxarsine				P	Darby & Kaplan, 1968
					Cadmus, 1976
Oxyquinoline					Nicot, 1951
Oxyquinoline sulphate					Nicot, 1951
Paraquat		Gramoxone		E	Powell, 1975
Penthachlorophenol	2	Mystox G	Catomance Ltd	ECR	Kaplan *et al.*, 1970
	0.1–0.3			A (starch pastes)	Rechenberg, 1972
					Gilchrist, 1953
					Purkiss, 1972
					Zyska *et al.*, 1972
Pentachlorophenyl laurate	1–3.5	Mystox LPL LSL	Catomance Ltd	APOR	Zyska *et al.*, 1972
Phenoxy fatty acid polyester	0.4–1.5	Preventol B2	Bayer (UK) Ltd	JB	
Phenyl mercury acetate			Tenneco Organics Ltd	A	
Phenyl mercury nonane	0.05–0.3	Aciticide MPM	Thor Chemicals	AO	
Phenyl mercury oleate					Drisko, 1973
Quaternary ammonium compounds	1	Gloquat C	ABM Chemicals: Glover (Chemicals) Ltd	E	Keen, 1976
				I	Genin, 1973
					Anon., 1972
					Richardson, 1973
					Nicot, 1951
		Preventol R	Bayer UK Ltd		
	0.3–0.2	Vantoc HL., CL., IB	ICI Organics		
Quaternary ammonium salt: di-isobutyl phenoxyethoxyethyl dimethylbenzyl ammonium chloride monohydrate		Hyamine 10x	Rohm & Haas	IE	Paleni & Curri, 1972
Quaternary ammonium salt: di-isobutyl phenoxyethoxyethyl dimethylbenzyl ammonium chloride monohydrate	0.5	Hyamine 1622	Rohm and Haas	IE	Paleni & Curri, 1972
Quaternary ammonium compound + lauryl pentachlorphenate		Mystox QL.	Catomance Ltd	E	Barr, 1977
Quaternary ammonium salt with tri-*n*-butyl tin oxide		Thaltox Q Stannicide AQ	Wykamol Limited: Thomas Swan & Co Ltd	E	Genin, 1973, Keen, 1976 Richardson, 1973.
Salicylamide	5–8		Bayer UK Ltd	JP (cable insulation)	Cadmus, 1976

Continued

Table 17.8 (*contd*) Organic chemicals used to control growths in the construction industry

Key to coding
A = adhesives
B = bitumen products
C = cement additive
E = toxic wash (exterior use)
F = fillers, stoppers, groutings
I = toxic wash (interior use)
J = jointing compounds, sealants, putty
O = wet state protection concrete additives
P = plastic products
R = rubbers (synthetic and natural)

Active chemical	Application rate/ concentration (%)	Product	Source of supply*	Application	Reference(s)
Sodium 2-phenylphenoxide	2 2.5	Brunsol con[c]	Stanhope Chemical Products Ltd	E	Genin, 1973 Rechenberg, 1972 Keen, 1976
	5	Mystox WFA	Catomance Ltd	EI	
Sodium pentachlorophenoxide	2 0.2 on wt of cement	Santobrite	Monsanto Ltd	EI C	Genin, 1973 Rechenberg, 1972 Keen, 1976 Sponsel, 1956
		Preventol PN	Bayer UK Ltd	AFJ	
	2	Brunobrite	Stanhope Chemical Products Ltd	E	Anon, 1972
Sodium salicylanide	1–5 0.5–1.5	Shirlan NA	ICI Ltd	I A	Keen, 1976
2,4,5,6-Tetrachloro-isophthalonitrile	0.5–1.5	Nopcocide N96	Diamond Shamrock UK	APJ	
2,4,5-Tetrachloro-isophthalonitrile (aq.)	0.3–1.8	Nopcocide N54D	Diamond Shamrock UK	AP	
3,3,4,4-Tetrachloro-tetrahydrothiophene 1,1-dioxide		Nopcocide 170	Diamond Shamrock UK	EI	
Thiadiazine	0.1–1.0	Thion 66	Thor Chemicals	A	
Thinned tar oil					Rechenberg, 1972 Keen, 1976
Tri-*n*-butyl-tin acetate	0.005–1			C P	Bartl & Velecky, 1971 Cadmus, 1976
Tri-*n*-butyl tin oxide	1	Stannicide M Stannicide A	Thomas Swan & Co. Ltd	IEO	Drisko, 1973 Richardson, 1973 Sadurska & Kawalik, 1966

Tri-*n*-butyl tin oxide + non-ionic emulsifier		Stannicide O	Thomas Swan & Co. Ltd		
Trifluoromethyl-thiophthalimide					Rechenberg, 1972
α,α-Trithiobis (*N,N*-dimethylthioformalite)				I	Morgan, 1959
Zinc dithiocarbamate + benzimadazole derivatives	0.5–1.0	Mergal S88	Hoechst UK Ltd	AFJ	
Zinc-8-hydroxyquinolinolate			Ward Blenkinsop	A	

* ABM Chemicals, Woodley, Stockport, Cheshire, UK.
Bayer (UK) Ltd, Bayer House, Richmond, Surrey TW9 1SJ, UK.
BDH, Poole, Dorset BN12 4NN, UK.
Catomance Ltd, 94 Bridge Road East, Welwyn Garden City A17 1JW, UK.
Diamond Shamrock (UK), 147 Kirkstall Road, Leeds LS3 1JN, UK.
Dow Corning Corporation, Laboratory Division, Stone, Stafford ST15 0BG, UK.
Durham Chemicals, Birtley, Co. Durham DH3 1QX, UK.
Glovers (Chemicals) Ltd, Wortley Low Mills, Whitehall Road, Leeds LS12 4RF, UK.
Hoechst (UK) Ltd, Hoechst House, Salisbury Road, Hounslow TW4 6JH, UK.
ICI Ltd, P.O. Box 19, Templar House, 81–87 High Holborn, London WC1V 6NP, UK.
ICI Organics, Blackley, Manchester M9 3DA, UK.
Monsanto Ltd, Monsanto House, 10–18 Victoria Street, London, SW1H 0NQ, UK.
Murphy Chemicals Ltd, Wheathampstead, St Albans, Herts., UK.
Nuodex (UK) Ltd, Birtley, Co. Durham DH3 1QX, UK.
Rohm & Haas (UK) Ltd, Lennig House, 2 Mason Avenue, Croydon CR9 2NB, UK.
Stanhope Chemical Products, 94 Bridge Road East, Welwyn Garden City A17 1JW, UK
Sterling Industrial, Chapeltown, Sheffield S30 4YP, UK.
Thomas Swan & Co., Ltd, Consett, Co. Durham DH8 7ND, UK.
Tenneco Organics Ltd, Rockingham Works, Avonmouth, Bristol B11 0YT, UK.
Thor Chemicals Ltd, Ramsgate Road, Margate, Kent, UK.
Ward Blenkinsop, Empire Way, Wembley, London HA9 0LX, UK.
Wykamol Ltd, Tingewick Rd, Buckingham, Bucks, MK18 1AN

Masonry biocides and other specific use of pesticides are controlled under the Control of Pesticides Regulations, 1986. Only approved products can be sold, supplied, used, stored or advertised. Publication in this list does not imply approval.

them. Domestic bleach, QACs, dodecylamine salicylate and lactate, as well as dichlorophen, are widely favoured as toxic washes for removing growths on internal surfaces. Growths are washed with a soft brush or absorbent cloth liberally soaked in the sterilant solution containing also a small quantity of liquid soap to wet the spores. With growths showing prolific sporing, special care is needed to minimize release of spores into the atmosphere, and respiratory protection must be worn. After cleaning, application of a more permanent and penetrating formulation was often advocated, traditionally based on sodium pentachlorophenoxide or sodium 2-phenylphenoxide. There is no published evidence as to whether penetrating formulations or indeed the sometimes specified subsequent 'barrier' formulations are necessary. In particularly severe cases of microbial contamination they may be beneficial. Certainly, the use of penetrating wall sterilants usually based on sodium pentachlorophenoxide or sodium 2-phenylphenoxide, QACs and zinc oxychloride plaster are used for eliminating the mycelium of the dry rot fungus *Serpula lacrymans* from within masonry (Anon, 1977; Savory, 1980). In dealing with internal mould contamination it is desirable to reduce the concentration of spores in the atmosphere. Increasing ventilation reduces both spore concentration and the high humidity which might otherwise facilitate regrowth (Bravery, 1987). Use of disinfectant sprays, even as an adjunct to such measures, is of doubtful value since potential health risks arise as much from inhalation of the particulate matter in the air (dead or alive) as from any risk of live infections.

Rates of application of chemical solutions, both for interior and exterior use, vary according to the formulations of the different products, and manufacturers' guidance should be followed. Dense growth will require considerably increased amounts of fluid, though with certain materials the dilution may be adjusted. Most commercially available products contain active ingredients at 0.5–5.0% by weight after dilution and are designed for dilution in water at ratios from 1:9 to 1:20 applied at coverage rates of the order of 1.5–2.5 m^2/l (75–120 sq. ft/gallon). Products are also available in which active chemicals are incorporated into pastes or gels, and these can be useful on vertical surfaces or to provide longer-lasting and deeper-penetrating protection.

Development of improved and safer chemical control agents and requirements for efficacy data for approval purposes have led to a need for standardized, accelerated methods of test. Available techniques have been assessed (Grant & Bravery, 1981a,b) and new methods proposed (Grant & Bravery, 1987).

An alternative chemical approach which has been attempted for certain special applications is that of incorporating toxicants as additives into cementacious materials. Incorporation of pentachlorophenol, copper carbonate, sodium fluorosilicate or even selenium (Gilchrist, 1953) was unsuccessful, despite the compounds being effective in aqueous solution. Keen (1976) has suggested that copper powder (1%), copper sulphate (0.1%) or sodium pentachlorophenate (0.2%) may be effective as additives to concrete, but copper II oxide is not only ineffective but may interfere with normal setting. Robinson & Austin (1951) examined in the laboratory more than 20 compounds of copper, lead and arsenic for their fungicidal effectiveness when incorporated into concrete. They concluded that 10% of copper aceto-arsenite was four times as effective as copper oxychloride cement. Although the strength of the concrete was slightly reduced the process could be economical for special-risk applications such as flooring in showers, locker rooms of swimming pools, kitchens, etc. In similar studies, Bartl & Velecky (1971) found that incorporation of low concentrations of tributyl tin acetate into cement and plaster effectively prevented fungal growth. There is no published information on the effectiveness of additives in preventing fouling in practice. Critical factors will be the rates of leaching, the availability of the toxicant to the colonizing organisms and the effects of the toxicants on particular properties of the cement or concrete.

Safety considerations. Biocides used for preservation in the construction industry are pesticides in the context of the definitions given in the Food and Environment Protection Act 1985 (FEPA). The Control of Pesticides Regulations 1986 (CPR) enacted under the powers of FEPA require that only approved pesticide products shall be sold, supplied, used, stored or advertised. As yet not all non-agricultural uses of pesticides are subject to equal scrutiny under the provisions of CPR. Masonry biocides certainly are, and the products approved for this use are listed in the MAFF/HSE Manual current at any time (currently '*Pesticides 1991*'; see Anon, 1991).

Applications of preservative products in the construction industry are also subject to control under the Control of Substances Hazards to Health Regulations 1988. These Regulations lay down essential requirements and a step-by-step approach for the control of hazardous substances and for protecting people exposed to them. The Regulations set out essential measures that employers (and employees) have to take. The basic principles of the COSHH Regulations are:

1 to introduce appropriate measures to control the risk;
2 to ensure control measures are used;
3 to monitor the exposure of workers and keep their health under surveillance;
4 to inform, instruct and train employees about risks and precautions.

Specific sources of safety guidance are available relating to particular applications but precautions of particular importance are:

1 wear protective gloves, clothes, boots, caps, eye and respiratory protection when mixing and applying toxic products;
2 do not allow waste fluids, drift, spray or run-off to contact adjacent personnel, vegetation, water courses, drainage or sewerage disposal systems or to enter other premises;
3 dispose of waste containers, washings and contaminated growth safely, as agreed with manufacturers of products and waste disposal authorities;
4 never allow untrained personnel to handle toxic products.

Some products may contain chemicals corrosive to flashings, gutters and damp-proof courses, or which may be harmful to certain types of natural stone. Advice and assurances from manufacturers and contractors should be sought at an early stage in specifying work.

Chemical herbicides. Herbicides are sometimes employed for the control of higher plants in certain constructional situations such as roadways, pavements and the like. It is beyond the scope of the present chapter to consider herbicides in detail. The reader is referred to a short account of higher plants as deteriogens by Allsopp & Drayton (1976) in which three main types of chemical control are recognized:

1 contact herbicides having a corrosive action on plant tissues;
2 systemic herbicides which enter through aerial parts and are translocated within the plant;
3 soil-sterilants which poison the soil and are taken up into the plant through the roots.

Herbicides are available with a range of specificity of target plant species and growth-regulating chemicals are also used in plant control. They are all strictly controlled under the Control of Pesticides Regulations 1986, and only approved products can be used.

Aquatic control. In special circumstances, control of vegetation may be required under water, e.g. water drainage and supply structures, retaining walls and weirs. Keen (1976) proposes three approaches including the use of admixtures, antifouling paints and treatment of the water with algicides. All the systems have serious limitations because of the high rates of loss by leaching. Toxicity to animal and plant life and effects on potability of water also impose limitations. The use of admixtures is considered earlier in this chapter, and antifouling paints are considered elsewhere in the book. A code of practice is available on the use of herbicides in water courses and lakes (Anon, 1975).

2.3.2 Non-chemical methods of control

One classic principle of controlling deterioration of materials by organisms is to adjust the environmental conditions to limit growth (Chapter 3). In the context of constructional masonry materials the source of inoculum is always present, whilst nutritional requirements and oxygen are likewise rarely limiting. Thus water supply becomes the only critical factor capable of providing a potential means of control. Exposure of exterior surfaces to rainfall is largely inevitable, but there is scope for ensuring that water is not concentrated or focused on to particular parts of structures by features of the design and construction, or by inadequate consideration of maintenance needs. Ledges, sills, parapets and similar architectural features can cause localized shedding of water in streaks or sheets, facilitating algal and lichen growth. Poor arrangements for water dispersal from structures or blocked gutters and damaged flashings may permit localized downwash. Regular removal of accumulated dust, silt, leaves and other debris from horizontal surfaces, troughs and gutters can minimize the risk of growth from higher plants.

Interior surfaces are inevitably exposed to the risk of microbial contamination, with water again being the only potential limiting factor. Rising damp, direct water penetration and particularly condensation are the main sources of excessive moisture. Rectification of faults in the waterproofing of the structure is necessary to prevent the first two sources, whilst elimination of condensation can be much more complex. Requirements will include a combination of improvements in insulation with appropriate installation of vapour barriers, increased ventilation and/or heating. Impermeable wall coverings and non-absorptive paint can often exacerbate the problem of condensation. Restoring absorptive surfaces or the use of anti-condensation paints can be beneficial.

Heat sterilization. Heat sterilization has been used in the eradication of the dry rot fungus *Serpula lacrymans* from walls. However, the system has fallen from favour due to the often unacceptably high risk of fire, the high cost and the impracticability of producing sufficiently high temperatures throughout the thickness of the wall. Blow-lamp burning can, however, be a convenient method to remove surface growth and colonization if used safely, and paraffin-powered flame guns are commonly used for clearing unwanted higher plant vegetation from verges, parking spaces, waste ground and the like.

3 POLYMERIC MATERIALS, ADHESIVES AND ADDITIVES

A variety of polymeric materials is used in the construction industry as damp-proofing compounds, sealants, gaskets, adhesives, plastics, wall and floor coverings.

Many of these compounds are manufactured, stored, transported and applied in a 'wet' state as emulsions or suspensions with water, and in this form are highly vulnerable to bacterial, actinomycete or fungal infection. Even in the solid or 'dry' state many of these materials may be subject to intermittent or permanent dampness with the attendant risk of colonization by mixed populations of bacteria and mould fungi.

3.1 Water-based mixtures

3.1.1 Problems

Within the scope of this chapter it is not possible to consider in detail the nature, use and microbial susceptibility of the full range of water-based products used in building and construction. It is possible, however, to simplify matters by considering together the problems of all such materials, because of the similarity in the colonizing microflora and in the basic mechanism of deterioration.

Many cement and concrete additives, adhesives and waterproofing compounds are supplied as mixtures of the active organic chemicals with emulsifiers and surfactants in water, sometimes called 'multiple-phase systems' (Purkiss, 1972). These are vulnerable to forms of microbial fermentation similar to those occurring in emulsion paints, cutting oils and fuel oil systems. Common among the large numbers of organisms implicated are *Escherichia coli*, *Pseudomonas fluorescens* and *Ps. aeruginosa*, *Micrococcus* spp., *Bacillus subtilis*, *Streptococcus* spp., *Proteus rettgeri*, *Enterobacter* spp. and species of fungi from the genera *Cladosporium*, *Penicillium*, *Paecilomyces* and *Aspergillus*.

Purkiss (1972) has proposed a generalized mechanism of attack of multiple-phase systems in which the micro-organisms growing in the water phase oxidize emulsifiers and surfactants inducing instability of the emulsion. Droplet fusion begins to occur and the organisms may then attack the oil phase itself. Continuing attack leads to continually increasing droplet size, culminating in separation of the system. In addition, generation of gases as by-products of metabolism can cause pressurizing, even bursting, of containers.

3.1.2 *Preservation*

The specific chemical constituents, solvents, emulsifiers and surfactants in the various formulations demand particular properties of any preservative agent, thus generalizations are difficult. Biocides need to be compatible with the particular formulation, of low volatility, non-corrosive, have a broad spectrum of action, and have suitable chemical stability and water solubility; in particular the partition coefficients are important. Many emulsions are stabilized at alkaline pH values; thus the biocides must remain stable at pH 8–9. Above all they must not interfere with the ultimate function of the formulation. The problem of microbial growth in water-based emulsion systems is now widely accepted and most commercial products contain biocides to prevent in-can spoilage. Some products can confer protection also in the subsequent dry state, though normally the concentration of biocides is increased or an alternative is added which does not lose its activity when the formulation dries or sets. Table 17.8 indicates some of the main chemicals used experimentally and commercially for the different applications.

3.2 Plastics, rubbers, sealants and bitumen

3.2.1 *Problems*

Natural and synthetic polymers are used as vapour barriers, damp-proof courses, waterproofing products, coatings and sheatings for pipework and cables, rainwater and foul-water pipework, gaskets for pipework and components as well as jointing and sealing materials between components, cast concrete sections and for glazing and filling purposes. In almost all of these service situations the materials are exposed to natural microbial infection from the air, water, sewage, etc., and almost all become wet because of the very nature of their function.

Studies on the fundamental susceptibility to microbial attack of polymer materials and their constituents are numerous (Klausmeier, 1966; Darby & Kaplan, 1968; Dubok *et al.*, 1971; Osmon *et al.*, 1972; Pankhurst *et al.*, 1972; Cadmus, 1976; Zyska, 1981). A recent comprehensive and detailed review has been published by Seal (1988).

Natural and vulcanized rubbers are regarded as generally susceptible to attack by actinomycetes, bacteria and fungi, though they vary in degree (Zobell & Grant, 1942; Zobel & Beckwith, 1944; Rook, 1955; Zyska, 1981; Williams, 1982; Tsuchii *et al.*, 1985). Synthetic rubbers appear to show even more variability in susceptibility to microbes. Polyisoprenes (Tsuchii *et al.*, 1979) and polyisobutadienes (Tsuchii *et al.*, 1978, 1984) show vulnerability to limited degradation by soil bacteria, whilst most of the available experimental evidence indicates that styrene–butadiene co-polymers are resistant (Blake *et al.*, 1955; Dickenson, 1969; Potts, 1978). However, the presence of specific compounding ingredients can decrease the natural resistance of these materials. Acrylonitrile–butadiene rubbers are significantly less susceptible again than styrene–butadienes (Zobell & Beckwith, 1944; Potts *et al.*, 1973). Chloroprene rubbers are considered relatively inert to microbial attack, probably due to the extent of cross-linking and the presence of sulphur (Heap & Morrell, 1968; Dubok *et al.*, 1971; Cundell & Mulcock, 1973). As with other polymer formulations, however, the presence of microbiologically susceptible plasticizers can induce susceptibility (Heap & Morrell, 1968).

Polyurethanes are widely used in construction as adhesives, thin sheet, cable sheathings and more particularly as rigid and flexible foams. Generally polyurethanes are susceptible to microbial attack by bacteria and particularly by fungi (Darby & Kaplan, 1970; Kaplan *et al.*, 1970; Wales & Sagar, 1985; Seal & Morton, 1986). Susceptibility is correlated strongly with esterase activity of particular micro-organisms (Shuttleworth, 1987) and the nature of the constituent components of the polyurethane (Darby & Kaplan, 1968; Seal & Morton, 1986).

Polysulphide rubbers are used extensively as sealants, mastics and tank linings, and are accepted as being very resistant to microbial attack. Silicone rubbers are extremely inert, though contamination with low molecular weight hydrocarbons can permit microbial colonization (Heap & Morrell, 1968). Zobell & Beckwith (1944) observed utilization of silicone rubber by marine microbes, possibly for this reason. Of the two main types of polyesters, aromatic polyesters are regarded as resistant to the growth of micro-organisms (Potts, 1978) whilst aliphatic polyesters have been shown to be biodegradable (Potts *et al.*, 1973; Shuttleworth, 1987). Polyamides are the nylons, which are not used significantly in construction, though in any case are generally regarded as resistant to microbial attack.

Polyethylenes have been extensively studied and microbial susceptibility shown to be related to molecular weight (Potts *et al.*, 1973). Low molecular weight oligomers appear to be utilizable by microbes, but fractions above MW 1000 are non-biodegradable. Direct studies of polyethylenes in soil burial have shown only 1–3% mass loss over periods of 1–8 years (Colin *et al.*, 1981) which was believed to reflect the extent of low molecular weight contaminants in the polymer. Hence it has been concluded that high molecular weight polyethylene is resistant to microbial attack (Seal, 1988).

The chemistry of polystyrene provides a highly resistant structure. However, it has been proposed that susceptibility to micro-organisms could occur by aromatic ring degradation mechanisms (Seal, 1988). Certainly the styrene dimers, trimers and tetramers can be biodegraded (Tshuchii *et al.*, 1977). Whilst mechanisms have been proposed for polystyrene biodeterioration, it is not generally regarded as of major practical significance in construction.

Clearly microbial resistance of polymers can relate to molecular size, as well as to the amounts and types of primary components, stabilizers, plasticizers, etc. The variation in resistance to attack of some common plasticizers is given in Table 17.9, from data supplied by Seal (personal communication). Studies with building sealants (Bravery *et al.*, 1977) revealed that in the field a one-part polysulphide sealant was very susceptible to mould, whilst the two-part polysulphide and acrylic types were less susceptible; a silicone type was almost completely resistant. Three different polyurethane types were resistant, moderately resistant and susceptible, respectively. In laboratory tests *Epicoccum purpureum* caused significant loss in tensile strength of a polysulphide and a polyurethane sealant prior to weathering, whilst the other main fungal species isolated from the field tests, *Cladosporium herbarum*, *Mucor racemosus* and *Botrytis cinerea*, only significantly affected the polyurethane. The susceptibility sometimes changed after weathering. Pankhurst *et al.* (1972) concluded that polymers without additives were usually inert, though susceptibility increased with increasing complexity of the material. Polyethylene, polypropylene, epoxy and coal-tar resins were all likely to prove resistant in a soil environment although bitumen was susceptible. The susceptibility of bitumen for building insulation or coatings of pipes, cables and road surfaces is acknowledged by Pitis & Stanci (1977). Changes caused by microbial attack included asphaltene content, flexibility, surface appearance, resin and oil content.

Evidence as to the susceptibility of polymer materials to microbial attack appears sometimes conflicting. For example Dunkeley (1964) and Dickenson (1965) have contended that natural rubber in pipe rings is resistant to microbial growth despite the evidence of Heederik (1966) and Hills (1967). Cadmus (1976) states that synthetic polymers are generally very resistant, though susceptibility may increase in certain use situations, such as environments with aggressive microbial populations or in contact with susceptible materials. Klausmeier (1966) offers an explanation for the sometimes conflicting opinions and apparent variations in susceptibility and performance of polymer materials by proposing that certain micro-organisms can attack only if additional nutrient is present. This phenomenon is called 'co-metabolism' and additional external sources of carbon may be very important. Prediction of likely performance in a given service situation and the potential need for biocidal preservation are complicated by these considerations. The evidence does, however, support the need for specifications

Table 17.9 Relative resistance of some plasticizers to biodegradation*

Decreasing resistance to biodegradation ↓	Tricresyl phosphate, diiso-octyl phthalate, dinonyl phthalate, didecyl phthalate
	Dioctyl phthalate
	Dibutyl phthalate
	Dinonyl adipate
	Dioctyl adipate
	Dimethyl sebacate
	Diiso-octyl adipate
	Diiso-octyl sebacate
	Butyl stearate
	Dioctyl sebacate
	Dihexyl adipate
	Dibutyl sebacate
	Dicapryl adipate
	Dibenzyl sebacate
	Polypropylene sebacate
	Methyl ricinoleate
	Butyl ricinoleate
	Butoxyethyl stearate
	Zinc ricinoleate

* Based on Petri dish tests using 24 fungi and measuring growth (colony diameters) on agar contaning mineral salts and plasticizer (after Seal, personal communication).

to take account of possible biological hazards in service and require assessments to be made of the durability of given materials under conditions representative of those likely to be encountered.

Experience in the methodology needed for such biological testing of polymer materials is already extensive (Walters, 1977).

3.2.2 Preservation

Susceptible plastics, rubbers and bitumens can be successfully preserved (Kaplan *et al.*, 1970; Pitis, 1972; Zyska *et al.* 1972) although biocides and the methods of their application must be carefully selected to be compatible both with the mix during production and with the finished product.

Zyska *et al.* (1972) studied fungicides incorporated into rubber plasticizers and concluded that organo-mercury compounds were barely effective at 2%, pentachlorophenol was effective at above 2.5% but more than 5% of pentachlorophenol laurate was needed. Cresylic acids at 2% were found effective by Pitis (1972), but efficacy varied according to the type of plasticizer used. Compatibility with the mix and residual effectiveness of the biocide have been referred to by Cadmus (1976), who found poor stability with organo-tin acetate and salicylate as well as inactivation by UV radiation and hydrolysis. Biocides for polymer materials need some mobility in order to be effective, either by their own vapour pressure or by combination with one of the other constituents such as the plasticizer (Cadmus, 1976). Captan and folpet, though effective fungicides, tend to be thermally unstable and sometimes do not control surface growths when incorporated into PVC. Darby & Kaplan (1968) indicate that incorporation of biocides is more difficult in urethanes than in vinyl systems. Both they and Cadmus (1976), however, cite 10,10′-oxybisphenoxarsine as having good compatibility, thermal stability and effectiveness. A number of organo-metallic, organo-arsenical and organo-sulphur compounds were found useful by Darby & Kaplan (1968). Wexler *et al.* (1971) demonstrated the compatibility and effectiveness of lead phenolate or lead salts of other low-molecular-weight synthetic fatty acids in protecting PVC insulating materials.

A number of chemicals assessed as biocides for the protection of polymer materials are included in

Table 17.9, coded to indicate the respective fields of use.

A consequence of continuing extensive studies on the physiological and metabolic mechanisms of microbial attack of polymers is that the improved understanding creates the opportunities for development of microbiologically resistant polymers. This approach, whilst reducing dependence on toxic preservatives, brings with it the dilemma of disposing of extremely inert polymers.

4 CONCLUSIONS

A wide variety of biological problems are encountered in the construction industry capable of inducing significant, even serious, financial loss or wastage. The increasing awareness of the range of problems, organisms and materials involved has generated developments in the chemical industry to produce or adapt biocides for these specific control purposes. In many situations, little is known of the nature of the organisms and their mechanisms of attack, so that chemical control procedures are necessarily pragmatic. Sometimes, although the incidence of micro-organisms is recognized, their significance has not been fully investigated.

Many of the materials subject to attack, as well as the biocides themselves, are produced from oil and are energy-intensive to manufacture. Maintenance and repair work occasioned by inadequate performance of materials in service is increasingly expensive, so major cost savings are possible from a better understanding of the significance of biological agencies of deterioration, and of strategies for their control. Specifications for building materials and procedures must increasingly take account of potential biodeterioration and demand adequate resistance or protection of materials, as well as require designs which minimize the development of conditions conducive to the growth of potentially deteriogenic organisms.

5 REFERENCES

Allsopp, C. & Allsopp, D. (1983) An updated survey of commercial products used to protect materials against biodeterioration. *International Biodeterioration Bulletin*, **19**, 99–145.

Allsopp, D. & Drayton, I.D.R. (1976) The higher plants as deteriogens. *Proceedings of the 3rd International Biodeterioration Symposium* (eds Sharpley, J.M. & Kaplan, A.M.) pp. 357–364, London: Applied Science Publishers.

Anon (1974) *Latex preservation. Dimethylaminomethyl phenol*. Annual Report of the Rubber Research Institute of Malaya 1972, pp. 128–129.

Anon (1975) *Code of practice for the use of herbicides on weeds in water courses and lakes*. Ministry of Agriculture, Fisheries and Food. July 1975.

Anon (1977) *Decay in buildings: recognition, prevention and cure*. Building Research Establishment, Princes Risborough Laboratory. Technical Note No. 44.

Anon (1982) *Control of lichens, moulds and similar growths*. Building Research Establishment, Digest No. 139, London: HMSO.

Anon (1991) *Pesticides 1991*. MAFF/HSE Reference Book No 500. London: HMSO.

Aristovskaya, R.V. & Kutuzova, R.S. (1968) Microbial factors in the extraction of silicon from slightly soluble natural compounds. *Soviet Soil Science*, **12**, 1653–1659.

Ashurst, J. & Dimes, F.G. (1977) *Stone in Building: its Use and Potential Today*. London: Architectural Press.

Aslam, M. & Singh, S.M. (1971) Copper sulphate as an algicide in limewash. *Paintindia*, **21**, 21–22.

Bachmann, E. (1915) Kalklösende Algen. *Berichte der Deustchen Botanische Gesellschaft*, **33**, 45–57.

Barr, A.R.M. (1977) *Comparative studies on the inhibition of lichen and algal growth on asbestos paving slabs*. International Biodegradation Research Group. Constructional Materials Working Group. April 1977.

Bartl, M. & Velecky, R. (1971) The fungicidal effect of organic tin in cements, limes and plasters. *Cement Technology*, **51**, 54–57.

Berthelin, J. (1983) Microbial weathering processes. In *Microbial Geochemistry* (ed. Krumbein W.L.) pp. 223–262. Oxford: Blackwell Scientific Publications.

Blake, J.T., Kitchin, D.W. & Pratt, O.S. (1955) Microbiological deterioration of rubber insulation. *Applied Microbiology*, **3**, 35–39.

Bolokova, T.S., Zlotsevskaya, I.V., Rudakova, A.K. & Tsekunova, L.N. (1971) *Destruction of Industrial Materials by Microorganisms*. Moscow: Izdatelstro Moskovskogo Universiteta.

Bravery, A.F. & Jones, S.C. (1977) Occurrence of biological growths on concrete dams in North Scotland. Unpublished paper. Department of the Environment, Princes Risborough Laboratory. Summary in Biodeterioration Society Newsletter (3) 1977.

Bravery, A.F., Jones, R.J.R. & Jones, S.C. (1977) Susceptibility to mould growth of some jointing materials. Unpublished report. Building Research Establishment, Princes Risborough Laboratory. Aylesbury, Bucks.

Bravery, A.F., Grant, C. & Sanders, C.H. (1987) Controlling mould growth in housing. *Proceedings of a Conference on*

Unhealthy Housing. University of Warwick, December. Institute of Environmental Health Officers.

British Standards Institution (1982) Cleaning and surface repairs of buildings Part 1. Natural stone, cast stone and clay and calcium silicate. Brick masonry. BS 6270.

Cadmus, E.L. (1976) Biodeterioration in the United States: A review. *Proceedings of the 3rd International Biodegradation Symposium* (eds Sharpley, J.M. & Kaplan, A.M.) pp. 343–346. London: Applied Science Publishers.

Colin, G., Cooney, J.D., Carlsson, D.J. & Wiles, D.M. (1981) Deterioration of plastic films under soil burial conditions. *Journal of Applied Polymer Science*, **26**, 509–519.

Cundell, A.M. & Mulcock A.P. (1973) The measurement of the microbiological deterioration of vulcanised rubber. *Material und Organismen*, **8**, 1–15.

Darby, R.T. & Kaplan, A.M. (1968) Fungal susceptibility of polyurethanes. *Applied Microbiology*, **16**, 900–905.

Dickenson, P.B. (1969) Natural rubber and its traditional use in underground pipe sealing rings. *Journal of the Rubber Research Institute of Malaya*, **22**, 165–175.

Drisko, R.W. (1973) *Control of algal growths on paints at tropical locations*. US Dept Commerce, National Technical Information Service. Naval Civil Engineering Laboratory, California, December 1973.

Dubok, N.N., Angert, L.G. & Ruban, G.I. (1971) Study of the fungus resistance of rubbers, mix ingredients and vulcanisates. *Soviet Rubber Technology*, 17–20.

Duff, R.B., Webley, D.M. & Scott, R.O. (1963) Solubilisation of minerals and related materials by 2-ketogluconic acid-producing bacteria. *Soil Science*, **95**, 105–114.

Dumitru, L., Popea, F. & Lazar, I. (1976) Investigations concerning the presence and role of bacteria in stone deterioration of some historical monuments from Bucharest, Jassy and Cluj-Napoca. *Proceedings of the 6th Symposium on Biodeterioration and Climatisation*, p. 67. Bucharest, Rumania: Institul de Cercetari Pentru Industria Electrotechnica.

Dunkeley, W.E. (1964) Die Verwendungsdauer des Kautschuks in Rohren und Leitungen. *Kautschuk–Fontschritt und Entwicklung*, **17**, 98–102.

Eckhardt, F.E.W. (1985) Mechanisms of the microbial degradation of minerals in sandstone monuments, medieval frescos and plaster. *Proceedings of the 5th International Congress on Deterioration and Conservation of Stone* (ed. Felix, G.) pp. 643–652. Lausanne Presses Polytechniques Romandes.

Figg, J., Bravery, A.F. & Harrison, W. (1987) *Covenham Reservoir Wave Wall—a full scale experiment on the weathering of concrete*. American Concrete Institute. SP-100, pp. 460–492.

Flannigan, B. (1989) Airborne micro-organisms in British houses: factors affecting their numbers and types. In *Airborne Deteriogens and Pathogens* (ed. Flannigan, B.) Biodeterioration Society Occasional Publications No. 6, Kew: CAB International.

Forrester, J.A. (1959) Destruction of concrete caused by sulphur bacteria in a purification plant. *Surveyor*, **118**, 881–884.

Gaur, A.C., Madad, M. & Ostwal, K.P. (1973) Solubilisation of phosphatic compounds by native microflora of rock phosphates. *Indian Journal of Experimental Biology*, **11**, 427–429.

Genin, G. (1973) Control of lichens, fungi and other organisms. *Paint Pigments Vernis*, **49**, 3–6.

Gilchrist, F.M.C. (1953) Microbiological studies of the corrosion of concrete sewers by sulphuric acid-producing bacteria. *South African Industrial Chemist*, **7**, 214–215.

Grant, C. (1982) Fouling of terrestrial substrates by algae and implications for control—a review. *International Biodeterioration Bulletin*, **18**, 57–65.

Grant, C. & Bravery, A.F. (1981a) Laboratory evaluation of algicidal biocides for use on constructional materials. 1. An assessment of some current test methods. *International Biodeterioration Bulletin*, **17**, 113–123.

Grant, C. & Bravery, A.F. (1981b) Laboratory evaluation of algicidal biocides for use on constructional materials 2. Use of the vermiculite bed technique to evaluate a quarternary ammonium biocide. *International Biodeterioration Bulletin*, **17**, 125–131.

Grant, C. & Bravery, A.F. (1987) Evaluation of biocides for use on building materials. In *Preservatives in the Food, Pharmaceutical and Environmental Industries* (eds Board, R.G., Allwood, M.C. and Banks, J.G.) pp. 133–144. Oxford: Blackwell Scientific Publications.

Grant, C., Hunter, C.A., Flannigan, B. & Bravery, A.F. (1989) The moisture requirements of moulds isolated from domestic dwellings. *International Biodeterioration*, **25**, 259–284.

Heap, W.M. & Morrell, S.H. (1968) Microbiological deterioration of rubbers and plastics. *Journal of Applied Chemistry*, **18**, 189–193.

Heederik, J.P. (1966) Prüfen von Betonrohren in den Niederlanden. *Beton-Zeitung*, **32**, 635.

Henderson, M.E.K. & Duff, R.B. (1963) The release of metallic and silicate ions from minerals, rocks and soils by fungal activity. *Journal of Soil Science*, **14**, 236–246.

Hills, D.A. (1967) The degradation of natural rubber pipe-joint rings. *Rubber Journal*, **149**, 12–15; 17–77.

Hueck-Van der Plas, E.H. (1968) The microbiological deterioration of porous building materials, *International Biodeterioration Bulletin*, **4**, 11–28.

Hunter, C.A. & Bravery A.F. (1989) Requirements for growth and control of surface moulds in dwellings. In *Airborne Deteriogens and Pathogens* (ed. Flannigan, B.) pp. 174–182. Biodeterioration Society Occasional Publications No. 6. Kew: CAB International.

Hunter, C.A., Grant, C., Flannigan, B. & Bravery, A.F. (1988) Mould in buildings: the air spora of domestic dwellings. *International Biodeterioration*, **24**, 81–101.

Ionita, I. (1971) Contributions to the study of the biodeterioration of works of art and historic monuments, III. Species of fungi isolated from stone monuments. *Revue Roumaine de Biologie—Serie Botanique*, **16**, 433–436.

Ionita, I. (1974) The involvement of fungi in the stone degradation process of some historical monuments. *Proceedings of the Symposium on Biodeterioration Science (Roumania)*, **4**, 117–122.

Isquith, A.J., Abbot, E.A. & Walters, P.A. (1972) Surface-bonded antimicrobial activity of an organo-silicon quaternary ammonium chloride. *Applied Microbiology*, **24**, 859–863.

Jaton, C. (1972) Microbiological changes in the monolithic church of Aubeterre sur Dronne. *Revue d'Ecologie et de Biologie du Sol*, **9**, 471–477.

Jaton, C. (1973) Microbiological aspects of the alteration of stonework of monuments. *Proceedings of the 1st International Symposium on the Deterioration of Building Stones*, pp. 149–154. La Rochelle. Centre de Recherches et d'Etudes Oceanographiques.

Kaltwasser, H. (1971) Destruction of concrete by nitirification. *European Journal of Applied Microbiology and Technology*, **3**, 185–192.

Kaplan, A.M., Greenberger, M. & Wendt, T.M. (1970) Evaluation of biocides for treatment of polyvinyl chloride film. *Polymer Engineering Science*, **10**, 241–246.

Kauffmann, J. (1952) Rôles des bactéries nitrifiantes dans l'alteration des pierres calcaires des monuments. *Compte-rendu*, **234**, 2395–2397.

Kauffmann, J. (1960) Corrosion et protection des pierres calcaires des monuments. *Corrosion et Anticorrosion*. **8**, 87–95.

Kauffman, J. & Toussaint, P. (1954) Corrosion des pierres: nouvelles experiences montrant le rôle des bactéries nitrifiantes dans l'alteration des pierres calcaires des monuments. *Corrosion et Anticorrosion*, **2**, 240–244.

Keen, R. (1976) *Controlling algae and other growths on concrete*. Advisory Note 45–020. London: Cement and Concrete Association.

Kerner-Gang, W. (1977) Evaluation techniques for resistance of floor coverings to mildew. In *Biodeterioration Investigation Techniques* (ed. Walters, A.H.) pp. 95–104. London: Applied Science Publishers.

Klausmeier, R.E. (1966) The effects of extraneous nutrients on the biodeterioration of plastics. In *Microbiological Deterioration in the Tropics*. SCI Monograph 23, pp. 232–243. London: Society for Chemical Industry.

Krumbein, W.E. (1972) The role of micro-organisms in the genesis, diagenesis and degradation of rocks. *Revue d'Ecologie et de Biologie du Sol*, **9**, 283–319.

Krumbein, W.E. (1983) *Microbiol Geochemistry*. Oxford: Blackwell Scientific Publications.

Krumbein, W.E. & Pochon, J. (1964) Bacterial ecology of altered stones of monuments. *Annales de l'Institut Pasteur*, **107**, 724–732.

Lepidi, A.A. & Schippa, G. (1973) Some aspects of the growth of chemotrophic and heterotrophic microorganisms on calcareous surfaces. *Proceedings of the 1st International Symposium on the Biodeterioration of Building Stones*, pp. 143–148. La Rochelle: Centre de Reserches et d'Études Oceanographiques.

Lewis, F., May, E. & Bravery, A.F. (1985) Isolation and enumeration of autotrophic and heterotrophic bacteria from decayed stone. In *Proceedings of the 5th International Congress on Deterioration and Conservation of Stone* (ed. Felix, G.) pp. 255–278. Lausanne: Presses Polytechniques Romandes.

Lewis, F., May, E., Daley, B. & Bravery, A.F. (1987) The role of heterotrophic bacteria in the decay of sandstone from ancient monuments. In *Biodeterioration of Constructional Materials* (ed. Morton, L.H.G.) pp. 45–53. Biodeterioration Society Occasional Publication No. 3. Preston: Lancashire Polytechnic.

Lewis, F., May, E. & Greenwood, R. (1988) A laboratory method for assessing the potential of bacteria to cause decay of building stone. In *6th International Congress on Deterioration and Conservation of Stone*. Torun, Poland, pp. 48–58. Vol. 2 Supplement. Torun, Nicholas Cupernicus University Press.

Lloyd, A.O. (1976) Progress in studies of deteriogenic lichens. *Proceedings of the 3rd International Biodegradation Symposium* (eds Sharpley, J.M. & Kaplan, A.M.) pp. 395–402. London: Applied Science Publishers.

Lurie, H.I. & Brookfield, E. (1948) Copper impregnated concrete floors. *South Africa Medical Journal*, **22**, 487–489.

May, E. & Lewis, F. (1988) Strategies and techniques for the study of bacterial populations on decaying stonework. In *6th International Congress on Deterioration and Conservation of Stone*, Torun, Poland, pp. 59–70. Vol. 2 Supplement. Torun, Nicholas Cupernicus University Press.

Milde, K., Sand, W., Wolff, W. & Bock, E. (1983) Thiobacilli of the corroded concrete walls of the Hamburg sewer system. *Journal of General Microbiology*, **129**, 1327–1333.

Morgan, O.D. (1959) Chemical control of algae and other nuisance growths on greenhouse benches, pots and potting soil. *Plant Disease Reporter*, **43**, 660–663.

Neculce, J. (1976) Some aspects of fungi in stone biodeterioration. *Proceedings of the 6th Symposium on Biodeterioration and Climatisation*, pp. 117–123. Bucharest, Rumania: Institul de Cercetari Pentru Industria Electrotechnica.

Nette, I.T., Pomortserva, N.V. & Kozlova, E.I. (1959) Deterioration of rubber by microorganisms. *Microbiologiya*, **28**, 881.

Nicot, J. (1951) Degradation des murs de plâtre par les moissisures. *Revue Mycologique*, **16**, 168–172.

Nordeutsche Affinerie (1953) Preventing the development of animal and plant life on water-soaked surfaces. German patent 870 340. *Chemical Abstracts*, **52** (1958), 20775f.

Novotony, J., Wasserbauer, X.Y. & Zadak, Z. (1973) Influence of the biological factors on the destruction of asbestos-cement roofing of stables. *Symposium on the Deterioration of Building Stones*, pp. 155–156. La Rochelle: Centre de Recherches et d'Études Oceanographiques.

Osmon, J.L., Klausmier, R.E. & Jamison, E.I. (1972) Rate

limiting factors in biodeterioration of plastics. *Proceedings of the 2nd International Biodeterioration Symposium*, pp. 66–75, London: Applied Science Publishers.

Paleni, A. & Curri, S. (1972) Biological aggression of works of art in Venice. *Proceedings of the 2nd International Biodeterioration Symposium*, pp. 392–400. London: Applied Science Publishers.

Paleni, A. & Curri, S. (1973) The attack of algae and lichens on stone and means of their control. *Proceedings of the 1st International Symposium on the Deterioration of Building Stones*, pp. 157–166. La Rochelle: Centre de Recherches et d'Études Oceanographiques.

Pankhurst, E.S., Davies, M.J. & Blake, H.M. (1972) The ability of polymers or materials containing polymers to provide a source of carbon for selected micro-organisms. *Proceedings of the 2nd International Biodeterioration Symposium*, pp. 76–90. London: Applied Science Publishers.

Pitis, I. (1972) Mycological protection of rubber for industrial products. *Proceedings of the 2nd International Biodeterioration Symposium*, pp. 294–300. London: Applied Science Publishers.

Pitis, I. & Stanci, A. (1977) Testing of biodeteriorated bitumens. In *Biodeterioration Investigation Techniques*. (ed. Walters, A.H.) pp. 23–40. London: Applied Science Publishers.

Pochon, J. & Jaton, C. (1967) The role of microbiological agencies in the deterioration of stone. *Chemistry and Industry*, 1587–1589.

Potts, J.E. (1978) Biodegradation. In *Aspects of Degradation and Stabilisation of Polymers* (ed. Jellinck, H.H.G.) pp. 617–657. Amsterdam: Elsevier.

Potts, J.E., Glendinning, R.A., Ackart, W.B. & Niegisch, W.D. (1973) The biodegradability of synthetic polymers. In *Polymers and Ecological Problems* (ed. Guillet, J.E.) pp. 61–79. New York: Plenum Press.

Powell, J.M. (1975) Use of gramoxone to control mosses and liverworts in greenhouse pots. Bi-monthly Research Note, Vol. 31, No. 5, Sept.–Oct. Department of the Environment of Canada.

Purkiss, B.E. (1972) Biodeterioration of multiple phase systems. *Proceedings of the 2nd International Biodeterioration Symposium*, pp. 99–102. London: Applied Science Publishers.

Rechenberg, W. (1972) The avoidance and control of algae and other growths on concrete. *Betontechnische Berichte*, **22**, 249–251.

Richardson, B.A. (1973) Control of biological growths. *Stone Industries*, **8**, 2–6.

Richardson, J.H. & Ogilvy, W.S. (1955) Antimicrobial penetrant sealers. *Applied Microbiology*, **3**, 277–288.

Robinson, R.F. & Austin, C.R. (1951) Effect of copper-bearing concrete on moulds. *Industrial and Engineering Chemistry*, **43**, 2077–2082.

Roizin, M.B. (1951) A whitewash that prevents moulding in storage houses for fruit, vegetables and potatoes. *Doklady Vshesoyuznoy Akademii Nauk imeni V.I. Lenina*, **16**, 39–41. In *Chemical Abstracts*, **46** (1952), 224.

Rook, J.J. (1955) Microbiological deterioration of vulcanised rubber. *Applied Microbiology*, **3**, 302–309.

Sadurska, I. & Kawalik, R. (1966) Experiments on control of sulphur bacteria active in biological corrosion of stone. *Acta Microbiologica Polonica*, **15**, 199–202.

Sahinkaya, H. & Gurbuzer, E. (1968) Study of rock-phosphate dissolving micro-organisms. Abstracts communications: National Conference of General and Applied Microbiology, Bucharest, p. 98.

Sand, W. & Bock, E. (1987) Simulation of biogenic sulphuric acid corrosion of concrete—importance of hydrogen sulphide, thiosulphate, and methylmercaptane. In *Biodeterioration of Constructional Materials* (ed. Morton, L.H.G.) pp. 29–36. Biodeterioration Society Occasional Publication No. 3. Preston: Lancashire Polytechnic.

Savory, J.G. (1980) Treatment of outbreaks of dry rot *Serpula lacrymans*. *Newsletter, British Wood Preservation Association*, News sheet No. 160, May 1980.

Schwartz, A. (1963) *Microbial corrosion of plastics and their compounds*. Arbeit Deutscher Akademie der Wissenschaften zu Berlin No. 5.

Seal, K.J. (1988) The biodeterioration and biodegradation of naturally occurring and synthetic plastic polymers. *Biodeterioration Abstracts*, **2** (4), 295–317.

Seal, K.J. & Morton, L.H.G. (1986) Chemical materials. In *Biotechnology*, Vol. 8: *Microbial Degradation* (ed. Schonborn, W.). Verlagsgesellschaft, Weinheim: 583–606.

Shuttleworth, W.A. (1987) Biodegradation of polycaprolactone polyurethane by *Gliocladium roseum*. Ph.D. thesis, Cranfield Institute of Technology, UK.

Sponsel, K. (1956) Vermeidung von Pilz-und Schimmelbildung in Textilbetrieben. *Zeitschrift für die gesamte Textil-Industrie*, **58**, 596–597.

Stinson, R.F. (1956) Algal growth and the performance of flowering plants in clay pots treated with copper naphthenate. *Proceedings of the American Society of Horticultural Science*, **68**, 564–568.

Stinson, R.F. & Keyes, G.G. (1953) Preliminary report on copper and zinc naphthenate treatments to control algae on clay flower pots. *Proceedings of the American Society of Horticultural Science*, **61**, 569–572.

Todd, J.J. (1974) Blow your problems. *Environment Pollution Management, Classe Chemie, Geologie und Biologie*, **4**, 79–81.

Trotet, G., Dupuy, P. & Grossin, F. (1973) A biological nuisance caused by cyanophycetes. *Proceedings of the 1st International Symposium on the Deterioration of Building Stones*, pp. 167–170. La Rochelle: Centre de Recherches et D'Études Oceanographiques.

Tsuchii, A., Suzuki, T. & Takahara, Y. (1978) Microbial degradation of liquid polybutadiene. *Agricultural and Biological Chemistry*, **43**, 1217–1222.

Tsuchii, A., Suzuki, T. & Takahara, Y. (1979) Microbial degradation of *cis*-1,4-polyisoprene. *Agricultural and Biological Chemistry*, **43**, 2441–2446.

Tsuchii, A., Suzuki, T. & Fukuoka, S. (1984) Bacterial

degradation of 1,4-type polybutadiene. *Agricultural and Biological Chemistry*, **48**, 621–625.

Tsuchii, A., Suzuki, T. & Takeda, K. (1985) Microbial degradation of natural rubber vulcanizates. *Applied and Environmental Microbiology*, **50**, 965–970.

Wales, D.S. & Sagar, B.F. (1985) The mechanism of polyurethane biodeterioration. In *Biodeterioration and Biodegradation of Plastics and Polymers*. Proceedings of the Annual Meeting of the Biodeterioration Society (ed. Seal, K.J.) pp. 56–59. Kew: CMI.

Walters, A.H. (1977) *Biodeterioration Investigation Techniques*. London: Applied Science Publishers.

Webley, D.M., Henderson, M.E.K. & Taylor, I.F. (1963) The microbiology of rocks and weathered stones. *Journal of Soil Science*, **14**, 102–112.

Wexler, T., Ortenberg, E. & Pitis, I. (1971) New fungistatic agents and their behaviour in PVC mixtures. *Chimica Industriale, Chimica Generale*, **104**, 201–206.

Whiteley, P. & Bravery, A.F. (1982) Masonry paints and cleaning methods for walls affected by organic growths. *Journal of the Oil and Colour Chemists Association*, **65**, 25–27.

Williams, G.R. (1982) The breakdown of rubber polymers by micro-organisms. *International Biodeterioration*, **18**, 31–36.

Wood, P.A. & Macrae, I.C. (1972) Microbial activity in sandstone deterioration. *International Biodeterioration Bulletin*, **8**, 25–27.

Zobell, C.E. & Beckwith, J.D. (1944) The deterioration of rubber products by micro-organisms. *Journal of the American Water Works Association*, **36**, 439–453.

Zobell, C.E. & Grant, C.W. (1942) The bacterial oxidation of rubber. *Science*, **96**, 379–380.

Zyska, H. (1981) Rubber. In *Microbial Biodeteriorations; Economic Microbiology* Vol. 6 (ed. Rose, A.H.) pp. 323–385. London: Academic Press.

Zyska, B.J., Rytych, B.J., Zankowicz, L.P. & Fudalej, D.S. (1972) Microbiological deterioration of rubber cables in deep mines and the evaluation of some fungicides in rubber. *Proceedings of the 2nd International Biodeterioration Symposium*, pp. 256–267. London: Applied Science Publishers.

G · WOOD PRESERVATION

1 INTRODUCTION

Wood is destroyed, or deteriorates, by action of fungi, bacteria, insects, chemical and physical agents, including, weather, fire and mechanical wear. Economically, decay by fungi or insects is most serious and wood preservation is primarily aimed at their prevention.

Some fungi feed on wood substances (cellulose, hemicellulose and lignin), thereby causing massive decay (wet rot or dry rot). Other fungi and some bacteria have a more limited ability to attack wood, and cause deterioration but not massive decay (sap stain fungi discolour and reduce impact resistance, bacteria increase permeability). Yet other fungi (moulds) feed on material within the cells without affecting the main structure.

Insects simply eat the wood; attack in temperate climates is mainly by the larvae of coleoptera (beetles) but in the tropics and sub-tropics isoptera (termites) are major destroyers of wood.

Wood preservation is the protection of wood from decay by treatment with chemicals. Both the preservative used and the process used to apply it are important in determining the degree of protection.

2 DETERIORATION

2.1 Fungi

Fungi require food, warmth and water to grow. Wood is food, warmth is almost any ambient temperature, so that the liability of wood to fungal decay parallels its liability to get wet. Buried in, or in contact with, the ground, wood will certainly get wet, infection is immediate and continuous, decay is certain. It is most rapid in the wet, warm tropics. Outdoors, exposed to the weather, wood will get wet intermittently; drying out is very varied, so that while wood in this situation is always at risk, occurrence is variable, especially when partly protected by design, or when a surface finish restricts drying more than wetting. Inside a building, wood should remain dry unless there is faulty design or construction, or failure in the integrity of the outer skin, damp-proofing, plumbing and the like, coupled with lack of maintenance. Experience shows that decay due to one or more of these causes is sufficiently frequent, or of such consequences with some components, to justify preservation. Accordingly the need to protect wood inside a building is based on experience.

2.1.1 Fungal decay

The fungi causing massive wood decay are basidiomycetes. Decay may be wet rot or dry rot. Wet rot is by far the most common form of decay, both inside buildings and outside. Many species cause wet rot, some are brown rots, some white rots (Table 17.10). Optimum wood moisture content for different species of wet rot fungi range from 30–40% (*Coniophora puteana*) to 50–70% (*Paxillus panuoides*) (Bech-Andersen, 1985). The moisture content was based on the dry weight of wood. Growth is substantially confined to the wet part of any piece of wood.

Dry rot in the UK is caused by a single, somewhat unique species, *Serpula lacrymans*, with an optimum moisture content for growth of 20–30%, and not growing above 55% (Bech-Andersen, 1985). It produces sufficient water to sustain further growth, is able to transport water and nutrients over some distance and so is able to spread into drier wood and over non-nutrient bases such as masonry to infect timber distant from the first outbreak (Coggins, 1976; Jennings, 1981; Bravery & Grant, 1985). In damp walls these strands can survive for a long time, possibly as long as 9 years. The need to kill them, so that they do not regrow to start a new outbreak, adds considerably to the difficulties and cost of eradicating dry rot.

Serpula is important in the UK; it has some importance in parts of continental Europe, locally in parts of North America and in Honshu province in Japan (Doi, 1983) and in parts of southern

Table 17.10 Wood decay fungi

Latin name	Common name	Woods attacked	Occurrence
Wet rots			
Brown rots			
Coniophora puteana	Cellar fungus	Softwoods and hardwoods	Widely, especially in wood soaked by water leakage
Amyloporia xantha	—	Softwoods	Common especially in warmer parts of buildings (*Amyloporia xantha*, *Poria placena*, *Fibroporia vaillantii*)
Poria placena	—	Softwoods	
Fibroporia vaillantii	White pore or mine fungus	Softwoods	
Paxillus panuoides			
White rots			
Phellinus contiguus	—	Softwoods and hardwoods	External joinery
Donkioporia expansa	—	Hardwoods especially oak	Near leaks or in beam ends, with death watch beetle
Pleurotus osteatus	Oyster fungus	Hardwoods	Chipboard, etc.
Asterostroma spp.	—	Softwoods	E.g. skirting boards, generally limited spread, exceptionally very wide
Dry rot			
Brown rot			
Serpula lacrymans	Dry rot fungus	Any	In buildings only

Australia (Thornton, 1989). It has a low upper temperature threshold for growth and is consequently unknown in the tropics and places with summer temperatures above about 27°C (Hegarty, *et al.*, 1986). Growth ceases at this temperature, and death occurs if subjected to temperatures above 35°C (Miric & Willitner, 1984), even for only a few hours.

Infected, decayed wood generally looks dry; hence the name. Appearance alone is not, however, an indication of dry rot, any decayed timber that becomes dry, cracks and looks dry. In countries outside Britain other fungi may be referred to as dry rot if the decayed timber has this appearance.

Dry rot occurs only in buildings and, while less common than wet rot, individual outbreaks are usually more extensive and more expensive to eradicate.

Some fungi destroy cellulose preferentially, leaving the lignin largely intact. Decayed wood is brown and these fungi are called brown rots. White rots also attack the lignin leaving the wood white or light coloured (Table 17.10).

The micromorphology of the two types of fungi is different. In both, the hyphae penetrate into the lumen and lie on the inner cell wall. With white rot lysis occurs along the line of contact, while with brown rot erosion of the cell wall is more general (Levy, 1987). This is due to the extent to which the enzymes diffuse away from the hyphae (Green, 1980).

With timber buried in the soil, or in very wet conditions, decay is commonly by microfungi (ascomycetes, fungi imperfecti). While these destroy wood substance, attack is confined to a zone near the wood surface and only develops deeper as the outer layers are destroyed. Such decay is referred to as soft rot (Savory, 1955). Because of the severity of the conditions decay is none the less rapid.

Soft rot hyphae penetrate into the cell wall and form cavities in the centre of the cell wall. Some soft rot fungi can, at high temperatures (35–40°C), grow at moisture contents down to 15% (Morton & Eggins, 1976).

Under abnormal conditions, such as are found in the ground below the water table, destruction may be due to bacteria and anaerobic fungi (Boutelje & Goransson, 1971).

Decay, in some situations, is the result of a complex process of a succession of organisms, involving many species of fungi and other micro-organisms with competition between different species and with stimulation or inhibition of one by another.

Typically, new timber is initially invaded by a random range of bacterial and fungal spores. Early bacterial development causes little damage but opens up the way to fungal invasion. The first fungi to develop are the micro-fungi, soft rot, moulds and sap stainers. Commonly these are then overtaken by the basidiomycetes. Many accounts give overall details or examine specific aspects (Findlay & Savory, 1954; Savory, 1954; Levy, 1965, 1987; Butcher, 1971; Dickinson & Levy, 1979; Levy & Dickinson, 1980, Smith, 1980; Carey, 1981, 1982).

2.1.2 Non-decaying fungi

Some fungi grow on wood without causing any great decay. These are moulds and blue stain.

Moulds such as *Penicillium* spp., *Aspergillus* spp. and *Cladosporium* spp. feed on free sugars or surface dirt of damp wood; they are unsightly but cause no real damage. Moulds occur both indoors and outdoors. Outdoor timber may also support slime moulds, known collectively as myxomycetes.

Blue stain or sap stain is the name given to fungi which grow in sapwood causing discoloration. Hyphae permeate throughout the sapwood, penetrating cell walls through very fine boreholes but do little harm other than to discolour the wood. The impact strength may be reduced but the timber is suitable for all but the most demanding uses (Cartright & Findlay, 1958). The discoloration reduces the value of new timber and mars the appearance of transparent finishes. For sap staining fungi to grow, moisture content must be above fibre saturation but below complete saturation, i.e. with both air and water in the lumen. Over 260 species have been reported as causing sap stain; some continue growth below freezing (Land *et al.*, 1985). Some sap stained woods were sought after to form decorative inlay for cabinet making. Sap stain commonly develops in freshly felled timber while it is drying out, but if timber in service reaches similar moisture contents it may also be attacked. Common species in the two situations are different. Those most common in service are *Aureobasidium pullulans*, *Schlerophoma pithyophila*, *Diplodia* spp. and *Cladosporium* spp. Most commonly these grow under paints and other surface finishes, and the most noticeable effect is on the finish.

2.2 Insects

Throughout the world, seasoned wood in use is liable to be attacked by insects. Only a few species attack wood; in all parts of the world the larvae of some beetles (coleoptera) live in and feed on wood. Adults emerge from wood solely to mate and lay eggs, often flying away to spread infestation (Hickin, 1963).

In the UK and much of the temperate regions the most important species are: the common furniture beetle or woodworm *Anobium punctatum* (De Geer), death watch beetle, *Xestobium rufovillosum* (De Geer), lyctus or powder post beetles, *Lyctus linearis* (Goeze), *L. brunneus* (Stephens) and other *Lyctus* spp. and the house longhorn beetle *Hylotrupes bajulus* (Linneaus). All these occur in northern Europe and America, in South Africa, Australia, New Zealand and elsewhere but their relative importance varies.

In the UK the woodworm is by far the most common, most older houses being infested to some extent. Death watch is the most notorious; it favours old, damp hardwoods such as are most common in churches and other historic buildings. It knocks its head on the wood to attract a mate, and this sound has given rise to morbid superstitions of an approaching death. House long-horn has a very limited distribution in the UK, being common only around Camberley. It is more widespread in continental Europe, and also occurs in South Africa.

Different woods differ in their susceptibility to insect attack, but use and location are less significant than with fungi. Structural timber, furniture, tool handles, anything made of wood may become infested, and while very dry wood is less likely to be attacked than damp, moisture content is not critical, most economic damage being to wood that is 'ordinarily' dry.

Weevils may attack timber when it is wet and slightly decayed, and perhaps sometimes when it is not. Generally these are regarded as minor pests but in parts of the UK, they are becoming more common (Hum, *et al.*, 1980).

Many more beetles and some other insects, including wasps, attack fallen wood in the forest; occasionally these insects may attack timber in use. Pinhole borers attack newly felled wood, but attack dies out as soon as the wood is seasoned. Boreholes, usually surrounded by a dark stain, caused by symbiotic fungi, may be seen in such woods.

In the tropics by far the most damaging timber pests are termites. There are about 1500 species of termite, several hundred of which attack wood (Harris, 1971; Hickin, 1971). Termites are social insects building nests with thousands, or even millions, of individuals. Main groups are: (i) subterranean termites building nests in the ground and foraging for wood; (ii) dry wood termites building nests in wood; and (iii) damp wood termites inhabiting old stumps and damp wood.

Ants (*Camponotus* spp.) damage sound wood in nest-building in some countries, e.g., Sweden (Butovitsch, 1976), Canada and the USA (Hickin, 1985).

2.3 Marine

Timber in the sea is subject to fungal attack by marine species and is also subject to damage by marine borers such as *Teredo* spp. (shipworm) and *Limnoria* (gribble) (Ray, 1959; Jones & Eltringham, 1968).

2.4 Weather

On exposure to the weather, wood is subject to a variable cocktail of physical, chemical and biological agents (Hilditch & Woodbridge, 1985; Hilditch, 1987). These cause deterioration at the surface and may pave the way for deeper decay.

Principal agents are radiation from the sun, wetting by rain or dew changes in atmospheric humidity, changing temperature, wind and windborne particles, atmospheric chemicals and fungal, algal and bacterial infection.

Wood exposed to the weather constantly goes through wetting and drying cycles, these changes causing repeated shrinking and swelling. Changes are greater near the surface than at depth, thereby setting up strains that lead to physical separation of fibres. There may also be direct degradation of the wood substance by water. Light, both ultraviolet and visible, causes breakdown of both cellulose and lignin. Protection against the weather is by use of paints, wood stains and similar finishes (Hilditch & Crookes, 1981).

3 PRESERVATION

The main sectors of timber preservation are:

1 Preventative (pre-)treatment, being the treatment of timber before it is installed to prevent decay or insect attack.

2 Remedial or curative treatment, being the treatment of timber in place, in buildings or elsewhere to cure decay or insect attack and to prevent recurrence.

Industrial pre-treatment and remedial treatment by specialists are major, world-wide industries. There is also substantial treatment of timber, for either purpose, by private individuals ('do-it-yourself', DIY), craftsman or tradesman and on estates and farms.

3.1 Prevention

In principle there are two approaches to preserving wood: to impregnate the whole of the wood with a preservative or to impregnate the outer zone of each piece so as to create a toxic barrier, or 'cordon sanitaire', around the rest of the wood. In practice, because of the resistance of wood to liquid penetration, it is seldom if ever possible to treat the whole of the wood, and a compromise has to be accepted with maximum achievable penetration giving a thick toxic barrier. The effectiveness of such a treatment depends on its resistance to fungal penetration, its life and integrity. For many situations more limited penetration provides adequate protection, allowing use of less preservative and more convenient or economical treatment methods.

Wood has two parts, heartwood and sapwood. Heartwood is the inner part of the tree trunk, and in some but not all species, contains resins and extractives that give it a high natural durability. With most species heartwood is difficult to impregnate. Sapwood, which is the outer part of the trunk in which sap moves in the living tree, is of low natural durability. Treatability of sapwood is species-specific, some readily accepting treatment, others not. For specific uses, both treatability and natural durability must be considered. Essentially, if the sapwood is permeable and the heartwood durable, the timber can be treated for use in a high-hazard situation, but if the sapwood is impermeable and the heartwood perishable then the timber cannot be treated for any but low-hazard situations.

Theoretically any preservative can be applied by almost any method. However, when the intrinsic properties of the preservative, the achievement of the different methods of application and economics are all taken to account the market splits along technical lines (Table 17.11).

3.1.1 Industrial

Current practice for preventative pretreatment in industry falls into several groups (Anon, 1986c):

1 The application of creosote under pressure. This is the main treatment for railway sleepers and transmission poles; it is also used for some farm and estate timbers.

2 Application of water-borne salts under pressure. This process competes with creosote in the treatment of poles and posts but is also used to treat building timbers. It is little used on dimensioned timbers such as window frames and other joinery because of the risk of distortion.

3 Double-vacuum or double-vacuum pressure treatment with organic solvent preservatives is mainly used for window frames and other dimensioned components, including prefabricated roof trusses, where the absence of any dimensional effect is the main consideration.

4 Some industrial pretreatment is by simple immersion of timber in an organic solvent preservative.

3.1.2 Trade and amateur

DIY, trade maintenance or craft construction uses organic solvent preservatives or, for fences

Table 17.11 Fields of use

	Preservative		
Application	Creosote	Water-borne	Organic solvent
Pressure	Sleepers, posts and poles	Posts and poles	Not used in UK, poles in USA
Double-vacuum/ double-vacuum + pressure	Not used	Not used	Building timbers, especially external joinery
Immersion	Fence panels	Not used	Building components, garden timbers
Spray	Amateur	Not used	Remedial, amateur
Brush	Amateur	Not used	Amateur

and similar uses, creosote. Application is mostly by brush, sometimes by spray or immersion. These are the least effective of the methods of treatment but, using organic solvent preservatives which have superior penetrating powers, adequate protection for all but the most demanding situations can be obtained.

Whenever timber is worked, treatment cannot be effectively carried out until after working is complete. Other methods of treatment are not practically available for many wooden items made by this group.

3.2 Eradication

Most dwellings, and many other buildings worldwide, are part wood and at some time in their life will suffer insect attack or decay. Commonly this is of limited extent, and repair, depending on the type and extent of deterioration, is a combination of replacement and curative treatment.

The basic principles of eradicating insect attack and decay are quite different.

3.2.1 Insects

For the eradication of insects, organic solvent preservatives containing an insecticide with contact and stomach action are mainly used. These are applied to the surface of the infected timber, into which they penetrate typically 4–10 mm. In badly infested wood much deeper penetration will occur through the galleries bored by the insect larvae.

Any larvae within the zone of penetration are killed immediately, both solvent and insecticide having effect. Some kill below this zone may result from fumigant action but insects deep inside the wood are not killed at the time of application. Kill will follow when, as is necessary to complete their life cycle, the larvae tunnel towards the surface.

The technique is effective for eradication of insects in 'ordinary' size timbers but can be less than fully effective with large timbers.

Several other methods may be used selectively, including drilling and injection of fluid and the use of pastes. These pastes are applied thickly to the surface and then penetrate slowly over several days or weeks. This technique is also used against fungi.

There is some, but increasing, use of insecticidal emulsions for woodworm eradication. Penetration is less than with solvent products and they are less effective, but have the major advantages of being free from solvent odour and fire risk.

Remedial treatments are carried out by many specialist firms, by the building trade and by private individuals (DIY). Professional application is mostly by spray, but DIY usage is more often by brush. Often insect attack is, in the initial stages, very localized. Local treatment by the householder is fully adequate and considerably cheaper.

3.2.2 Fungi

To speak of eradicating fungal attack from timber is somewhat misleading. Preservatives of the sort used for preventative treatment will kill any fungus when they contact it. However, to achieve sufficient penetration to kill all the fungal mass pervading infected wood is not practical except (and then not always reliably) where decay and infection is only shallow, or by using special techniques, only suitable for museums.

Eradication of fungal decay from a building is a combination of measures: (a) to cut out decayed and infected timber and remove or eradicate any other source of infection; (b) to eliminate the dampness, without which decay would not have occurred; (c) to apply preservative to remaining sound timbers as an additional safeguard against re-occurrence; (d) to replace, with pre-treated timber, timbers that have been cut out.

In taking these measures there is a major difference between wet rot and dry rot. With wet rot, infection spreads little if at all beyond the visible decay. With dry rot there may be some infection of the wood beyond the obvious, and there is commonly massive growth over and into walls, often for some metres from the wood. Treatment of dry rot must therefore include sterilization of the wall. This is done by irrigating the infected parts with fungicide, mostly in aqueous solution.

4 WOOD PRESERVATIVES

Wood preservatives are liquids with fungicidal and/or insecticidal components which will remain active over many years so as to give long-term protection. The common types are categorized (Anon, 1975) as: tar oil (creosote), water-borne, and organic solvent. For the last two the liquid in which the preservative components are dissolved is water or an organic solvent, respectively.

4.1 Creosote

Creosote is obtained by distillation of coal tar, which in turn is obtained by the destructive distillation of coal. Creosote is the fraction collected between about 200°C and 400°C.

Originally the prime processing of coal was to produce coal gas for lighting and heating. Creosote was one of several by-products. Currently processing is mainly to produce smokeless fuels or blast furnace coke.

The exact composition of creosote varies with the coal from which it is obtained and the process used for its manufacture. Essentially it is a mixture of tar acids, tar bases and neutral materials. Tar acids are mixed, phenol, cresol, xylenols and higher homologues. Tar bases include pyridine, quinoline, acridine, etc. Neutral compounds are mainly hydrocarbons such as naphthalene, anthracene, fluorene (diphenylene methane) and phenanthracene (van Groenou *et al.*, 1951; McNeil, 1952).

Commercially creosote is available in heavy grades that must be applied hot, and in low viscosity grades that can be applied cold by brush or dip (Anon, 1973a). The difference between the two is mainly in the proportion boiling above 355°C.

Despite having been in use since at least 1838 (Bethell, 1838), creosote is still one of the most effective preservatives known. It is also one of the cheapest, but is a dark variable brown, is oily and has a strong odour. These make it unacceptable for building and many other uses. Its main uses are for the pressure treatment of wooden railway sleepers, telegraph and fence posts (Anon, 1973b) and for dip treatment of fence panels and DIY retreatment of them, with some use on farm and estate timbers.

4.2 Water-borne

Many water-soluble inorganic salts are effective fungicides. Used as timber preservatives they are liable to be leached out if the timber is put into a wet location. Water-borne preservatives in use today follow developments from the 1930s based on the use of mixtures of salts that, after impregnation into the wood, undergo a change so that the residual preservative is insoluble and therefore leach-resistant. Most fall into one of two groups. Foremost are those using dichromate, which causes a reaction with the wood, and those based on ammonia, evaporation of which leaves a residue insoluble in water.

Water attaches to the wood cellulose by hydrogen

bonding, these bondings cause the cell wall to expand, and the whole wood to swell as it gets wet and shrink as it dries. Treatment with water-borne preservatives may therefore cause distortion.

Water-borne preservatives do not naturally penetrate readily into seasoned timber, and are therefore applied only by pressure processes. Because of the amount of water absorbed (150–300 litres per cubic metre, 150–300 l/m^3) timber needs redrying for some uses. The cost and/or time of drying can be a restriction on its use.

4.2.1 *Copper chrome arsenate*

The most widely used water-borne preservative is copper chrome arsenate (CCA), known in America as chromated copper arsenate. It consists of a mixture of copper, arsenic and dichromate salts, for example:

Copper sulphate ($CuSO_4 \cdot 5H_2O$)	32–35%
Sodium dichromate ($Na_2Cr_2O_7 \cdot 2H_2O$)	41–45%
Arsenic pentoxide ($As_2O_5 \cdot 2H_2O$)	26–20%
	(Anon, 1987a)
or	
Chromium trioxide (CrO_3)	65.5%
Cupric oxide (CuO)	18.1%
Arsenic pentoxide (As_2O_5)	16.4%
	(Anon, 1981)

Argument has gone on for years over the relative merits of the two types and on the effect of changes in the ratio of components. There does not seem to be any good evidence of significant differences between products of the first (salt) type and those of the second (oxide) type in their effectiveness in preserving wood. The electrical conductivity of wood treated with salt-type formulations is much higher and the rate of corrosion of metals (under conditions where both types cause corrosion) is also higher with salt-type (Cross *et al.*, 1989). Variation in ratios, especially of copper:dichromate, have a modifying effect on fixation (Wallace, 1964).

Some countries place restrictions on the use of arsenic-containing preservatives in buildings and some other places. Many alternatives have been proposed; several are used in various parts of the world but few, if any, fully match in performance (Tillott & Coggins, 1981).

Preservatives that fix by dichromate reaction, but that do not contain arsenic, include CCB (Wolman, 1958), based on copper, dichromate and boric acid, typically 34% $CuSO_4 \cdot 5H_2O$, 38% $K_2C_2rO_7$, 26% H_3BO_3 (Wolman, 1975). Chromium is now also regarded as hazardous.

4.2.2 *Ammoniacal preservatives*

Preservatives fixing by evaporation of ammonia are less used, but include ammoniacal copper arsenate (ACA) made by dissolving cuprous oxide and arsenic pentoxide in approximately equal amounts (calculated as Cu_2O and As_2O_5) in ammonia solution in the presence of air (Anon., 1974a). Other compositions have used, in addition to copper and ammonia, pentachlorophenol (Hagar, 1954), caprylic acid (Hagar, 1972) or various branched-chain carboxylic acids (Hilditch, 1977a).

4.3 Organic solvent preservatives

Organic solvent preservatives are solutions of an active ingredient in an organic liquid, currently almost always petroleum-derived. There are two types. One type uses a light volatile paraffinic solvent with boiling range typically 140–270°C which, after application, dries leaving a clean, paintable surface (Anon, 1979a). The other type is based on a non-volatile solvent similar to gas oil or diesel oil, boiling range 180–370°C (Anon, 1979b).

Organic solvents penetrate more readily than any other type, enabling use of less onerous methods of application. They do not form any bond to wood so that treatment does not cause any dimensional change. Thus they are used for the treatment of wood that has already been shaped (Hilditch, 1964). Organic solvent products also have the advantage of being clean and quick-drying, but they are the most expensive of the preservatives. Use is therefore mainly where these features are of most benefit.

In addition to the main solvent, auxiliary solvents are needed with some active ingredients to give stable solutions. Aromatic solvents, some esters and alcohols have been used. Crystalline active ingredients also require an anti-bloom agent to stop formation of crystals on the surface during drying; non-volatile esters, oils and resins are used.

Depending on the specific intended use of the preservative the active ingredient is a fungicide or an insecticide, or both. Fungicides in use in the past 25 years are: pentachlorophenol 5%, tributyl tin oxide 1%, a combination of the two (1.75% and 0.44%, respectively) and copper naphthenate, 2% or 2.75% Cu (Anon, 1979a). New materials that have appeared on the market in the last 5 years are Acypetacs–zinc and trihexyleneglycol biborate (Anon, 1986a). Lindane has been the main insecticide, but is now being partly superseded by synthetic pyrethroids such as permethrin and cypermethrin.

4.3.1 Copper and zinc naphthenate

The copper and zinc salts of naphthenic acid were first used as wood preservatives in Denmark in 1911 under the trade name 'Cuprinol'. Naphthenic acid is a mixture of saturated cyclic carboxylic acids occurring naturally in crude petroleum.

In the UK both naphthenates have long been used in DIY and industrial preservatives (Bulman, 1955; Hilditch, 1964, 1977b). In the USA copper naphthenate in heavy oil is used for pressure preservation of heavy structural timbers (Barnes & Hein, 1988); it gives good service, especially in soil. For this and similar uses it is increasingly replacing pentachlorophenol because of environmental considerations.

In recent years metal salts of synthetic organic acids, especially those produced by the 'oxo' and 'Koch' processes, have been developed (Sparks, 1978; Hilditch *et al.*, 1983). These are cleaner and more consistent than the naphthenates but otherwise have broadly similar properties. Acypetacs–zinc is a combination of the zinc salts of C_8–C_{10} oxo and Koch acids (Hilditch *et al.*, 1978).

4.3.2 Pentachlorophenol

Pentachlorophenol (PCP) was developed from 1930 (Carswell & Nason, 1938) and has become more used than any other active ingredient for organic solvent preservatives. Application is by any of the main processes—double-vacuum, immersion, brush or spray for pre-treatment of building components, and for remedial treatment of wet or dry rot. In the USA it is also used for pressure treatment of heavy constructional timbers. It gives excellent results even in the ground (Cockroft, 1974).

The sodium salt of PCP in water is used to treat green timber to prevent sap staining between felling and seasoning, and for wall sterilization in dry rot control. PCP and its salts have many other uses, and as a combined result has become widely distributed in the environment (Rango Rao, 1977; Anon, 1987b). Consequently restrictions are now being placed on its use in some countries for some purposes (Anon, 1991).

4.3.3 Tributyl tin oxide

Tributyl tin oxide (TBTO) came into use as a wood preservative in the 1960s (Richardson, 1988) and from 1968 became the most widely used preservative for the treatment of window joinery in the UK. The main advantage of TBTO for this purpose is ready acceptance, without any adverse effect of paint. TBTO does not perform well in soil contact and its adequacy in other situations, including joinery, has been questioned. Established instances of failure in service are, however, few.

TBTO was also extensively used in marine antifouling paints; pollution of waters and its effects on fish resulted in its prohibition for this use, and restrictions of its use as a wood preservative have recently been introduced in the UK (following some restriction elsewhere).

4.3.4 Lindane

Lindane is the pure gamma-isomer of hexachlorocyclohexane (HCH) (Biegel, 1988). It is a powerful insecticide with good persistence, and is extensively used in wood preservatives at 0.5% for prevention, or 1% for eradication.

Lindane is called gamma benzene hexachloride (BHC) in the USA and elsewhere. This has given rise to confusion with benzene, to which it is unrelated. Confusion also exists between the pure lindane and crude mixed isomers.

Lindane has become widely distributed in the

environment as a result of agricultural use, and there is concern about its effects on marine life and on human health. There is controversy around its use as a wood preservative, in particular because of its fatal effect on bats, which often roost in places that are treated to eradicate woodworm.

Other chlorinated hydrocarbon insecticides such as dieldrin, aldrin and chlordane have been used in wood preservatives, but their use is now minimal because of concern about their health and environmental effects.

4.3.5 Synthetic pyrethroids

Permethrin, cypermethrin and deltamethrin belong to a group of synthetic chemicals related to the naturally occurring pyrethrum. They have become widely used in place of lindane in wood preservatives (Carter, 1984).

5 PRESERVATION PROCESSES

Several methods are used to apply preservatives, ranging from a prolonged treatment under pressure, to force deep penetration, to a simple short dip or brush treatment, resulting in relatively shallow penetration (Hunt & Garratt, 1953; Nichols, 1973; Wilkinson, 1979; Anon, 1986c).

5.1 Pressure processes

Timber is placed in a closed vessel, the vessel is flooded with preservative, a pressure of around 14 bar is applied to the liquid and held for typically 4 hours, to force preservative into the wood.

There are two basic types of process—full-cell and empty-cell. In the full-cell process the pressure is released, preservative pumped out of the treatment vessel and the timber taken out. In the empty-cell process a second vacuum is applied to draw out some of the preservative. The two processes achieve similar penetration but the empty-cell process uses less preservative and leaves a cleaner surface. There are several varieties of both processes, some using an initial vacuum to increase preservative uptake.

As with all processes, the achievement is different with different timbers. With a readily treatable timber such as European redwood or Scots pine, (*Pinus sylvestris*) all sapwood will be fully penetrated and there will be some penetration into the heartwood. Preservative usage is high, typically 300 litres per cubic metre (300 l/m^3) for full-cell treatment and 150 l/m^3 for empty-cell. Because of this high usage, with potentially high cost, only water-borne preservatives and creosote are applied by these processes. With impermeable woods such as spruce (*Picea abies*) penetration may be only a few millimetres.

With either creosote or CCA both processes are very effective, giving service lives in the 50–100-year range.

5.2 Double-vacuum/double-vacuum pressure processes

Timber is placed in a closed vessel and a vacuum drawn to pull air out of the wood. The vessel is filled with preservative and the vacuum released. Preservative is drawn into the timber. After a short period for completion of absorption, a second vacuum is applied to draw some preservative out. The amount used is reduced, leaving a cleaner, quicker drying treatment. The process is used for light or medium treatment of permeable softwoods such as European redwood, for example, in window frames.

For treatment of less permeable woods, or for higher levels of treatment in permeable ones, further absorption is forced by applying a positive pressure of between 1 and 2 bar held for 15–60 min (double-vacuum pressure process).

Only organic solvent-type preservatives are applied by this process; fluid usage is typically 25–50 l/m^3.

5.3 Immersion treatment

Timber is simply immersed totally in the preservative fluid. Organic solvent preservatives and creosote are applied this way.

The efficiency of the process is totally dependent on the immersion time. As generally practised this is 3–10 min; at this level the process is somewhat less effective than double-vacuum, but is still adequate for many purposes. Extended to several hours, as used on some estates and by amateurs, and provided the right products are used, the process gives long-term protection even to timbers in ground contact.

5.4 Brush and spray

Topical application with a brush or spray uses less preservative and achieves less penetration than other methods. It is thus the least effective. Spraying is extensively used for professional, remedial treatment of timbers *in situ*. Brushing, and to a lesser extent spraying, is used for both preventative and remedial treatment by amateurs. Using organic solvent preservatives of low viscosity creosote, and providing care is taken to ensure application to all surfaces of the wood, adequate protection is obtained for most purposes where there is no ground contact. Where there is exposure to the weather, exposed surfaces should be periodically re-treated.

Brushing is also used to treat cut ends and other worked surfaces on timber treated by other processes prior to working.

5.5 Miscellaneous methods

Several other methods are used to apply wood preservatives in specific situations. These include the following procedures.

Hot and cold soak, whereby timber is heated in a bath of preservative and, while still in the bath, allowed to cool; the contraction of air in the wood sucks in preservative. This method was much used for butt treatment of fence posts.

Injection of preservative directly into the timber is used for remedial treatment of large timbers in insect eradication, e.g. death watch or termites, of early decay in window frames, for ground line treatment of transmission and other poles. Several techniques are used.

Pastes, either of water-diffusible salts or of organic solvent preservatives (bodied mayonnaise emulsions), are applied to the surface of the wood. They provide a reservoir of preservative that will continue to penetrate into the timber for several days or more. Both pastes and injection techniques aim at getting deep penetration into timbers in existing structures where pressure and similar methods are inapplicable.

Some timber is treated while green (unseasoned) by diffusion or sap displacement methods. The two commonest are boron diffusion, whereby wood is dipped in a bath of hot, concentrated solution of borax and boric acid, lifted out and stacked under cover, to prevent drying until the borax has diffused throughout the timber. This is one of the few techniques that achieves full penetration even into heartwood, but because the borax remains water-soluble it cannot be used in wet situations or be exposed to the weather. The second of the common methods is the Boucherie process. This is used in France and some other countries to treat green poles for use as transmission posts. One end of the pole is capped and preservative (copper sulphate solution) is fed into the cap from a tank at the top of a tower. Over a few days the solution will diffuse down the length of the pole.

6 TESTING

Testing of a wood preservative involves demonstrating the chemical's ability to kill or inhibit wood-destroying organisms and to demonstrate that this activity will be retained by the treated wood in service over many years. Further testing must determine the effect, if any, that treatment will have on all the properties of wood and any working or further processing, finishing, etc. to which the treated wood may be subjected. Extensive testing to evaluate health and environmental risks, in using the preservative or treated wood, is now essential.

Present practices in fungal testing have been reviewed (Hilditch & Mendes, 1987). The commonest laboratory test is to treat small blocks of wood with serial concentrations of preservative and then expose them to assault by single species of wood-destroying fungi. Separate tests with different species must be done to give a useful picture. Standard methods (Anon, 1982, 1985a) must be used when testing is for official approval, although many variations in block size and culture conditions are used for other purposes.

Similar principles are followed in testing for effectiveness against insects (Anon, 1989a,b,c,d).

To get an indication of permanence either fungal or insect tests may be preceded by submitting the wood blocks to artificial leaching (Anon, 1989f) or evaporation (Anon, 1989e).

Such tests examine the resistance of wood preservatives to specific, single assault. They in no way mimic the multiple assault or complex succession of organisms that are encountered in real situations (Levy, 1987; Hilditch & Mendes, 1987). No accelerated laboratory test yet devised does this in full. Some approach is made in tests similar to those already described, but these incubate the treated wood in natural, not sterile, soil. These tests have much value but have the major disadvantage of poor reproducibility.

Laboratory tests as currently used examine the effectiveness of chemicals, not of the total treatment. To evaluate properly the practical performance of a treatment—depending, as it does, partly on the chemicals employed and partly on the method of application used—field tests in which treated timber is exposed to natural conditions are essential. There are two disadvantages: firstly, the time, 15–25 or more years, and secondly, the fact that any one test relates only to the specific conditions under which it is carried out.

Commonest of the field tests is the burial of stakes (Anon, 1974b) while a variety of tests have been used for natural evaluation under out-of-ground situations (Hilditch & Mendes, 1987).

Tests are based on practical principles as much as on scientific rules. They seek to reflect performance under specific real conditions, for which the basic scientific details have yet to be fully elucidated.

7 SAFETY

Wood preservatives are designed to kill or prevent development of wood-destroying fungi or insects, and the question of adverse effects on other organisms—including higher plants, animals and man—has become important. Detailed studies on some have led to proposals to restrict their use (Anon, 1988) and in most developed countries there is some control on what may be used (Anon, 1985b, 1986b).

Long experience shows harmful effects to occur only when there is gross disregard for even simple precautions such as should be taken in using any chemical. Nonetheless, as understanding of the more subtle relations between human health and the environment evolves, there is need to introduce new materials with less effect on non-target organisms. Much current development has this as a cornerstone.

Considerations include both the chemicals used and the design of plant and methods for their application.

Currently, much development effort is aimed a determining more exactly the risks associated with specific chemicals used in wood preservation at all stages from manufacture through use to the long-term use of treated timber.The search is also being actively pursued for materials that are without potential risk.

8 CONCLUSION

For the construction of dwellings and many other structures there is no sensible alternative to wood. Wood decay is natural and unavoidable. The practice and science of wood preservation are well established. Yet many current materials and practices are facing challenge resulting from the general concern about the indiscriminate use of chemicals, especially as pesticides. To take the science and practice of wood preservation forward, a higher level of research into all aspects of use, and towards the development of new materials, is essential. The basis for this input exists.

9 REFERENCES

Anon (1973a) British Standard 144: 1973. Specification for coal tar creosote for the preservation of timber. London: British Standards Institution.

Anon (1973b) British Standard 913: 1973. Specification for wood preservation by means of pressure creosoting. London: British Standards Institution.

Anon (1974a) Standard 080 wood preservation. P5–72 Standards for water-borne preservatives. Rexdale, Ont.: Canadian Standards Association.

Anon (1974b) Standard D–1758–74. Standard method of evaluating wood preservatives by field test with stakes. Philadelphia, PA: American Society for Testing and Materials.

Anon (1975) British Standard BS 1282: 1975. Guide to

the choice, use and application of wood preservatives. London: British Standards Institution.

Anon (1979a) British Standard BS 5707: 1979 Part 1. Solutions of wood preservatives in organic solvent. Part 1. Specification for solutions for general purpose applications, including timber that is to be painted. London: British Standards Institution.

Anon (1979b) British Standard BS 5707: 1979, Part 2. Solutions of wood preservatives in organic solvent. Specification for pentachlorophenol wood preservative for use on timber that is not required to be painted. London: British Standards Institution.

Anon (1981) Standard P5–81 Standards for waterborne preservatives. Washington, DC: American Wood-Preserver's Association.

Anon (1982) British Standard BS 6009: 1982. Wood preservatives. Determination of toxic values against wood destroying basidiomycetes cultured on an agar medium. London: British Standards Institution.

Anon (1985a) British Standard BS 6559: 1985. General introductory document on European (or CEN) methods of test for wood preservatives. London: British Standards Institution.

Anon (1985b) Food and environmental protection act 1985, Chapter 48. London: HMSO.

Anon (1986a) Standard 2.0, Specification for biocides. London: British Wood Preserving Association.

Anon (1986b) Pesticides. The Control of Pesticides Regulations 1986. Statutory Instrument 1986, No. 1510. London: HMSO.

Anon (1986c) *Timber Preservation*. London: Timber Research and Development Association and British Wood Preserving Association.

Anon (1987a) British Standard 4072: Part 1: 1987. Wood preservation by means of copper/chrome/arsenic compositions. Part 1. Specification for preservatives. London: British Standards Institution.

Anon (1987b) *Environmental Health Criteria. 71: Pentachlorophenol*. Geneva: World Health Organization.

Anon (1989a) British Standard BS 5436: 1989. Wood preservatives: determination of eradicant action against larvae of *Anobium punctatum* (De Geer) (laboratory method). London: British Standards Institution.

Anon (1989b) British Standard BS 5218: 1989. Wood preservatives: determination of the toxic values against *Anobium punctatum* (De Geer) by larval transfer (laboratory method). London: British Standards Institution.

Anon (1989c) British Standard BS 5434: 1989. Wood preservatives: determination of preventative action against recently hatched larvae of *Hylotrupes bajulus* (Linnaeus) (Laboratory method). London: British Standards Institution.

Anon (1989d) British Standard BS 5435: 1989. Wood preservatives: determination of toxic values against larvae of *Hylotrupes bajulus* (Linnaeus) (laboratory method). London: British Standards Institution.

Anon (1989e) British Standard BS 5761 Part 1: 1989. Wood preservatives: accelerated aging of treated wood prior to biological testing. Part 2: Evaporative aging procedure. London: British Standards Institution.

Anon (1989f) British Standard BS 5761 Part 2: 1989. Wood preservatives: accelerated aging of treated wood prior to biological testing. Part 2: Leaching procedure. London: British Standards Institution.

Anon (1991) Council Directive 91/173/EEC 21 March 1991 amending for the ninth time Directive 76/769/EEC. Restrictions on the marketing and use of certain dangerous substances and preparations. *Official Journal of the European Communities*, L85, S April 1991. pp. 34–36. Luxembourg: Office for Official Publications.

Barnes, H.M. & Hein, R.W. (1988) Treatment of steam-conditioned Pine Poles with copper naphthenate in hydrocarbon solvent. *Record of the 1988 Annual Convention of the British Wood Preserving Association*, pp. 3–24. London: British Wood Preserving Association.

Bech-Andersen, J. (1985) Basische Baustoffe und begrenzte Feuchtigkeit-Verhaltnisse Antworten auf die Frage, wasum der echte Nausschwamm nur in Hausern vorkommt. *Material und Organismen*, **20**, 301–309.

Bethell, J. (1838) British patent 7731/1838: Rendering wood, cork and other articles more durable etc. London: Her Majesty's Patent Office.

Biegel, W. (ed.) (1988) *Lindane; Answers to Important Questions*. Brussels: Centre International d'Etudes du lindane.

Boutelje, J.B. & Goransson, B. (1971) Decay in wood construction below the ground water table. In *Biodeterioration of Materials* (eds Walters, A.H. & Hueck-van der Plas, E.H.) Vol. 2, pp. 311–318. London: Applied Science Publishers.

Bravery, A.F. & Grant, C. (1985) Studies on the growth of *Serpula lacrymans* (Schumacher ex Fr.) Gray. *Material und Organismen*, **20**, 171–191.

Bulman, R.A. (1955) The development and use of naphthenates for timber preservation. *Record of the 1955 Annual Convention of the British Wood Preserving Association*, pp. 36–46. London: British Wood Preserving Association.

Butcher, J.A. (1971) Analysis of the fungal population in wood. In *Biodeterioration of Materials* (eds Walters, A.H. & Hueck-van der Plas, E.H.) Vol. 2, pp. 319–325. London: Applied Science Publishers.

Butovitsch, V.V. (1976) Uber vorkommen und schadwirkung der rossameisen *Camponotus herculeanus* und *C. ligniperda* in Gebauden in Schweden. *Material und Organismen*, **11**, 160–170.

Carey, J.K. (1981) Colonisation of wooden joinery. In *Biodeterioration* (eds Oxley, T.A. & Barry, S.) Vol. 5, pp. 13–25. Chichester: John Wiley & Sons (this paper was presented in 1981, but published in 1983).

Carey, J.K. (1982) Assessing the performance of preservative treatments for window joinery. *Holz als Roh-und Werkstoff*, **40**, 269–274.

Carswell, T.S. & Nason, H.K. (1938) Properties and uses of pentachlorophenol. *Industrial and Engineering Chemistry*, **30**, 622–626.

Carter, S.W. (1984) The use of synthetic pyrethroids as wood preservatives. *Record of the 1984 Annual Convention of the British Wood Preserving Association*, pp. 32–41. London: British Wood Preserving Association.

Cartright, K.St.G. & Findlay, P.F.K. (1958) *Decay of Timber and its Prevention*. London: HMSO.

Cockroft, R. (1974) *The Performance of Pentachlorophenol in a Stake Test in the United Kingdom*. Watford: Building Research Establishment, Department of the Environment.

Coggins, C.R. (1976) Growth patterns of *Serpulia lacrimans*, the dry rot fungus. *Record of the 1976 Annual Convention of the British Wood Preserving Association*, pp. 73–83. London: British Wood Preserving Association.

Cross, J.N., Bailey, G. & Schofield, M.J. (1989) Performance of metal fastenings in CCA treated timber. *Record of the 1989 Annual Convention of the British Wood Preserving Association*, pp. 3–6. London: British Wood Preserving Association.

Dickinson, D.J. & Levy, J.F. (1979) Mechanisms of decay and its prevention. *Record of the 1979 Annual Convention of the British Wood Preserving Association*, pp. 33–37. London: British Wood Preserving Association.

Doi, S. (1983) The evaluation of survey of dry rot damage in Japan. Document IRG/WP/1179. Stockholm: International Research Group on Wood Preservation.

Findlay, W.P.K. & Savory, J.G. (1954) Decomposition of wood by lower fungi. *Holz als Roh-und Werkstoff*, **12**, 293–296.

Green, N.B. (1980) The biochemical basis of wood decay micro-morphology. *Journal of the Institute of Wood Science*, **8**, 221–228.

van Groenou, H.B., Rischen, H.W.L. & van den Berge, J. (1951) *Wood preservation during the last 50 years*. Leiden: A.W. Sijthoff Uitgeversmaatschappij N.V.

Hagar, B.O. (1954) British patent 808 277: Improvements in or relating to preserving agents for timber or other organic material. London: Her Majesty's Patent Office.

Hagar, B.O. (1972) British patent 1 379 095: Improvements relating to materials and processes applicable to treatment of wood and similar materials. London: Her Majesty's Patent Office.

Harris, W.V. (1971) *Termites, Their Recognition and Control*, 2nd Ed. London: Longman.

Hegarty, B., Buckwald, G., Cymorek, S. & Willeitner, H. (1986) Der Echte Hausschwamm – immer noch ein Problem? *Material und Organismen*, **21**, 87–99.

Hickin, N.E. (1963) *The Insect Factor in Wood Decay*. London: Hutchinson.

Hickin, N.E. (1971) *Termites: A World Problem*. London: Hutchinson.

Hickin, N.E. (1985) *Pest Animals in Buildings*. London: George Godwin.

Hilditch, E.A. (1964) Modern developments in organic solvent wood preservers. *Record of the 1964 Annual Convention of the British Wood Preserving Association*, pp. 41–53. London: British Wood Preserving Association.

Hilditch, E.A. (1977a) British Patent 1,574,939: Compositions containing preservative metals and their use for preservation of wood and like materials and as a fungicide. London: Her Majesty's Patent Office.

Hilditch, E.A. (1977b) Wood preservative naphthenates. *Timber Trades Journal*, 22 October.

Hilditch, E.A. (1987) Protecting wood against the weather. In *Wood and Cellulosics* (eds Kennedy, J.F., Phillips, G.O. & Williams, P.A.) pp. 545–552. Chichester: Ellis Horwood.

Hilditch, E.A. & Crookes, J.V. (1981) Exterior wood stains, varieties performance and appearance. *Record of the 1981 Annual Convention of the British Wood Preserving Association*, pp. 59–67. London: British Wood Preserving Association.

Hilditch, E.A. & Mendes, F. (1987) Wood preservation – fungal testing. In *Preservatives in the Food, Pharmaceutical and Environmental Industries* (eds Board, R.G., Allwood, M.C. & Banks, J.G.) Society for Applied Bacteriology Technical Series No. 22, pp. 115–131. Oxford: Blackwell Scientific Publications.

Hilditch, E.A. & Woodbridge, R.J. (1985) Progress in timber finishing in Great Britain. *Journal of the Oil and Colour Chemists Association*, **68**, 217–228.

Hilditch, E.A., Hambling, R.E., Sparks, C.R. & Walker, D.A. (1978) European Patent 5361. Anti-fungal compositions and methods of preserving materials therewith. London: European Patent Office.

Hilditch, E.A., Sparks, C.R. & Worringham, J.H.M. (1983) Further developments in metal soap-based preservatives. *Record of the 1983 Annual Convention of the British Wood Preserving Association*, pp. 61–72. London: British Wood Preserving Association.

Hum, M., Glasser, A.E., & Edwards, R. (1980) Wood-boring weevils of economic importance in Britain. *Journal of the Institute of Wood Science*, **8**, 201–207.

Hunt, G.M. & Garratt, G.A. (1953) *Wood Preservation*. New York: McGraw-Hill.

Jennings, D.H. (1981) Recent studies on translocation in the dry rot fungus *Serpula lacrimans*. *Record of the 1981 Annual Convention of the British Wood Preserving Association*, pp. 19–25. London: British Wood Preserving Association.

Jones, E.B.G. & Eltringham, S.K. (1968) *Marine Borers and Fouling Organisms of Wood*. Paris: Organisation for Economic Cooperation and Development.

Land, C.J., Banhidi, Z.G. & Albertsson, A-C. (1985) Surface discoloring and blue staining filamentous fungi on outdoor softwood in Sweden. *Material und Organismen*, **20**, 133–156.

Levy, J.F. (1965) The soft rot fungi, their mode of action and significance in the degradation of wood. In *Advances in Botanical Research* (ed. Preston, R.D.) pp. 323–357. London: Academic Press.

Levy, J.F. (1987) The natural history of the degradation of wood. *Philosophical Transactions of the Royal Society, London*, **A321**, 423–433.

Levy, J.F. & Dickinson, D.J. (1980) Wood protection research at Imperial College. *Record of the 1980 Annual Convention of the British Wood Preserving Association*, pp. 67–73. London: British Wood Preserving Association.

McNeil, D. (1952) Some notes on the chemical composition of coal tar creosote. *Record of the 1952 Annual Convention of the British Wood Preserving Association*, pp. 147–161. London: British Wood Preserving Association.

Miric, M. & Willitner, H. (1984) Lethal temperatures for some wood destroying fungi with respect to heat. Document IRG/WP/1229. Stockholm: International Research Group on Wood Preservation.

Morton, L.H.G. & Eggins, H.O.W. (1976) The effect of moisture content in wood on the surface growth and penetration of fungi. *Material und Organismen*, **11**, 279–294.

Nichols, D.D. (1973) *Wood Preservation and its Prevention by Preservative Treatment*, 2 vols. Syracuse, NY: Syracuse University Press.

Rango Rao, K. (ed.) (1977) *Pentachlorophenol. Chemistry, Pharmacology and Environmental Toxicology*. New York: Plenum Press.

Ray, D.L. (ed.) (1959) *Marine Boring and Fouling Organisms*. Seattle, WA: University of Washington Press.

Richardson, B.A. (1988) *Organotin Wood Preservatives: Activity and Safety in Relation to Structure*. Proceedings, American Wood-Preserver's Association 1988, pp. 56–69. Stephensville MD: American Wood-Preserver's Association.

Savory, J.G. (1954) Breakdown of timber by ascomycetes and fungi imperfecti. *Annals of Applied Biology*, **41**, 336–347.

Savory, J.G. (1955) The role of microfungi in the decomposition of wood. *Record of the 1955 Annual Convention of the British Wood Preserving Association*, pp. 3–20. London: British Wood Preserving Association.

Smith, D.N.R. (1980) Study of decay of preservative-treated wood in soil. *Journal of the Institute of Wood Science*, **8**, 194–200.

Sparks, C.R. (1978) A new brand of metallic chemical for use in wood preservation. *Record of the 1978 Annual Convention of the British Wood Preserving Association*, pp. 48–51. London: British Wood Preserving Association.

Thornton, J.D. (1989) The restricted distribution of *Serpula lacrymans* in Australian buildings. Document IRG/WP/1382. Stockholm: International Research Group on Wood Preservation.

Tillott, R.J. & Coggins, C.R. (1981) Non-arsenical waterborne preservatives — a review of performance and properties. *Record of the 1981 Annual Convention of the British Wood Preserving Association*, pp. 32–48. London: British Wood Preserving Association.

Wallace, E.M. (1964) Factors affecting the permanence of wood preservatives and some of the problems arising therefrom. *Record of the 1964 Annual Convention of the British Wood Preserving Association*, pp. 131–150. London: British Wood Preserving Association.

Wilkinson, J.G. (1979) *Industrial Timber Preservation*. London: Associated Business Press.

Wolman (1958) Allgemeine Holzimpragnierung Dr Wolman GmbH. British patent 911 519. Wood preserving agents. London: Her Majesty's Patent Office.

Wolman (1975) Dr Wolman Gmbh. British patent 1,531,868. Wood Preservative solution containing a dye. London: Her Majesty's Patent Office.

H·PRESERVATION OF MUSEUM SPECIMENS

1 INTRODUCTION

Conservation, the science of preserving artefacts in a museum, can be defined as 'the means by which the true nature of an object is preserved'. The true nature of an object includes evidence of its origins, its original construction, the materials of which it is composed and information as to the technology used in its manufacture (UKIC, 1984). Conservation is, however, frequently confused with restoration, which is not directly concerned with preservation, but with improvements to the appearance of a deteriorated object.

Museums, libraries and historic houses can contain a wide range of historic and aesthetic objects collected from activities in the sciences and arts, and this diversity is reflected in the many branches of conservation. Practitioners are often generalists treating and preserving collections of natural history, archaeology, social history, fine and decorative art and even buildings. Conservation practice draws on the knowledge and experience of many disciplines, adapting them and using them to their best effect. As a preservation science in its own right, it has only developed in any substance since the 1950s and come of age in the last few years.

The aim of conservation, which is to preserve objects for perpetuity, is patently unachievable. The size and variety of collections often only allows a broad preservation policy to slow down deterioration, and only in significant cases—such as the Lindow Bog Man, preserved in a peat bog since its ritual burial there in the first century, or the *Mary Rose*, the flagship of Henry VIII excavated and lifted from Portsmouth Harbour in 1982—can detailed and specific remedial action be taken.

2 DEGRADATION OF HISTORIC AND ARTISTIC MATERIAL

It is known that materials deteriorate through a number of complex mechanisms. In the case of aesthetically appreciated objects, that deterioration may not be degradation but a surface despoiling such as mould growth or soiling. However, the major factors causing deterioration are a combination of chemical, physical and biological agents that, although their actions are interlinked, can be considered separately (Thomson, 1986).

2.1 Environmental destructive factors

2.1.1 Temperature

Most artefacts are by their very nature relatively stable at normal ambient temperatures. However, temperature changes can affect some objects through a number of mechanisms such as phase change, expansion/contraction cycles, etc. Wax-faced dolls and entomological specimens embedded in wax have been damaged irreparably by the radiant heat of spotlights, while poorly glazed pottery can develop 'crazing' caused by the incompatible expansion coefficients. Temperature also affects the rate of reactions according to the Arrhenius equation:

$$k = A \exp(-E/RT)$$

where k is the rate constant, R the gas constant, T the temperature, A the frequency factor, and E the activation energy.

As a general rule of thumb, a 10°C rise in temperature is considered to double the rate of chemical reaction (see also Chapter 3). As a consequence, vulnerable material is stored at low temperature, with costume and other textiles often stored at around 15°C, while colour photographs are recommended to be stored at 2°C. Low-temperature storage inhibits the growth of biological systems and thus is effective in controlling insect pests, fungal growth and small pest mammals such as mice. Chemical activity, such as metal corrosion, light-catalysed oxidation of organic polymers (paints, varnishes, plastics, rubbers, wood-based materials, etc.), is slowed down. As an economic preservative tool it has much to recommend it for long-term care; however, its effective use is often counteracted by the higher temperatures demanded by visitors and researchers.

2.1.2 Humidity

Relative humidity (r.h.) is defined as:

$$\frac{\text{The amount of water in a given quantity of air}}{\text{The maximum amount of water which that air can hold at that temperature}} \times 100\%$$

and this is thus expressed as a percentage. It represents the degree of saturation of the air at a particular temperature. All organic materials under normal circumstances contain loosely bound water in their structures that is in dynamic equilibrium with the r.h. of the surrounding air. To a lesser degree most porous inorganic materials, such as pottery, stone and some metals, are in the same equilibrium.

A rise or fall in the r.h. of the micro-climate surrounding an object induces it to gain or lose moisture to restore the equilibrium. In most organic materials the absorption of atmospheric moisture is within the fibrous structure of the cells. For instance, in wood (Fig. 17.3) the cellular fibre saturation point is reached at approximately a 25% equilibrium moisture content which corresponds to a relative humidity of around 100% r.h. Below the fibre saturation point, the effect of fluctuating moisture content tends to cause dimensional changes in organic materials (Hoadley, 1978).

Where movement is restricted, either by the anisotropy of the material and/or by the method of construction, the cellular structure becomes permanently damaged and cracks, splits, shakes, warps, etc. can develop, through plastic deformation (Buck, 1972). Low humidities (40% r.h.) are especially damaging as the loss of moisture causes embrittlement of the structure. High humidities (65–70% r.h.) are associated with

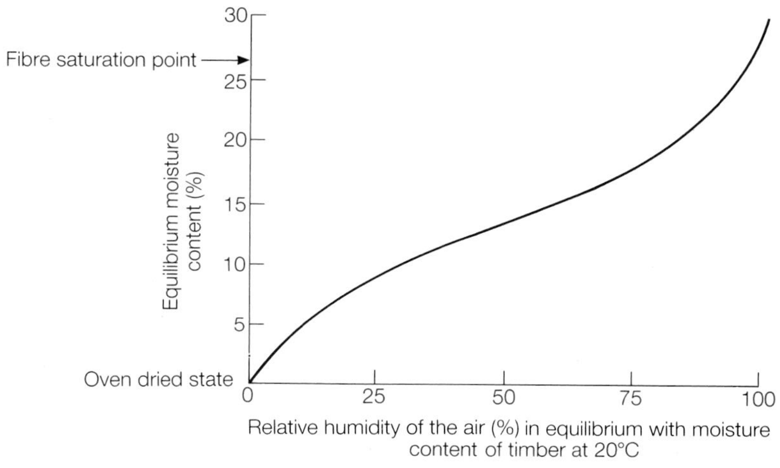

Fig. 17.3 The relationship between relative humidity and moisture content of wood.

enhanced biological action through bacterial, fungal and insect attack, and chemical deterioration is also increased.

Porous inorganic materials such as some stonework and pottery can be damagingly affected by fluctuating humidities. Absorbed hygroscopic salts can concentrate on or near the surface, causing disfiguring salt growths or spalling (splintering and cracking) of the surface layers (Torraca, 1988).

Current conservation practice in assessing suitable storage environments considers a number of factors, scientific and pragmatic. A knowledge of the environmental history of the object is important as it may have achieved a long-term stability by acquiring an equilibrium with seemingly non-ideal conditions. The long-term preservation of fine furniture in damp castles, for instance, would be jeopardized by re-siting that furniture into stores at lower humidities to inhibit the possibilities of biological growth.

Very low humidities are recognized as slowing down many chemical and biological deteriogens, and thus might be considered advantageous. However, other factors such as the concomitant increase in fragility through embrittlement at low humidities thus increasing the danger of mechanical damage, may legislate against its use.

A common economically acceptable compromise solution for determining storage conditions is to use environmentally buffered stores and displays which avoid large fluctuations in conditions and maintain a r.h. of the annual mean inside level. In the UK and other temperate climates this is usually 50–60% r.h.; in tropical climates 60–70% r.h., and in cooler, northern countries such as Canada, 40–50% r.h. Where special conditions are required, air-conditioning, or mechanical humidification/dehumidification systems can be used for large areas, while small, well-sealed show-cases and storage containers can be well controlled using hygroscopic materials such as silica gel. The silica gel is preconditioned to provide a moisture reservoir which will effectively maintain the container in which it is put, at a specified humidity.

2.1.3 Light

Visible light and the associated infrared and ultraviolet (UV) radiations are major deteriogens of museum objects, though their actions vary. Infrared radiation (radiant heat) causes damage through its heating effect leading to temperature damage. The shorter wavelengths of visible light and UV radiation cause chemical damage, notably oxidative reactions and breakdown of polymeric materials through a number of complex pathways believed to be based on peroxide and free-radical formation (Brill, 1980). Thus, where R is an organic molecule excited by light energy, h is Planck's constant and $h\nu$ the energy of photon of light of frequency ν,

$$R + h\nu \rightarrow R^*$$

free-radical formation ensues:

$$R^* \rightarrow R^0$$

Reaction with oxygen follows to form the highly reactive, strongly oxidizing peroxy radical:

$$R^0 + O_2 \rightarrow RO_2{}^0$$

The observed deterioration from light attack is familiar as fading of dyestuffs and pigments, embrittlement and breaking of textile threads, and the yellowing of newspapers.

Light-induced damage is limited by dark storage and low-level lighting illuminance of displays. Commonly used limits are: (i) a maximum of 50 lux illuminance for sensitive material such as textiles, watercolours; (ii) a maximum of 200 lux illuminance for less sensitive material such as polychromed wood, oil paintings. Normally, all UV radiation is eliminated by careful choice of illuminants and by UV screening.

2.1.4 Pollution

Museums and their contents are at a heightened risk from pollution damage because of the extreme length of exposure. Chronic deterioration may become apparent only after considerable periods of time have elapsed, even with low pollution levels (Baer & Banks, 1985).

Particulate pollution from combustion products such as smoke and soot is normally acidic and hygroscopic, and can be oily and sticky. It causes deterioration through soiling and chemical attack, particularly on carbonate rocks (limestone, marble) where the damage is evident as surface blackening and increased erosion. Drying plaster and cement can produce aerosols of alkaline particles which are known to attack oil-painting varnishes.

Gaseous pollution is divided between that generated externally, such as the oxides of sulphur and nitrogen, and that generated locally within the museum. The protective envelope of containers, showcases and buildings limits the effect of external pollutants but can contain and intensify the damaging effect of indoor sources. Sulphur dioxide from space heating can tarnish metals, damage paints, pigments and dyes, and weaken organic materials such as paper, leather and textiles. Hydrogen sulphide from rubber, some plastic and dyes and from wool can tarnish metals and photographic emulsions. Ozone from electrical discharges in machinery (e.g. some photocopiers) can cause colour changes in pigments, degrade cellulose, etc.

Damage from pollution is limited by excluding external sources by having well-sealed buildings, filtered air-handling systems, protected storage and display conditions; by minimizing pollution sources by removing non-vented heating systems, sealing surfaces with non-emitting coatings and by testing all storage and display materials for their stability; and by the rational use of absorbers, corrosion inhibitors, etc. such as charcoal-weave cloth as a local absorbent of pollutant gases.

3 PRESERVATION OF ORGANIC ARCHAEOLOGICAL MATERIAL

Historical material from buried environments presents particular conservation problems on its excavation, owing to the rapid change in ambient conditions. Objects are frequently mechanically damaged before burial, and invariably some aerobic decomposition has taken place through insect or microbial attack.

Insects cause mechanical damage to organic materials, especially wood tissues. The principal insect classes responsible for damage in seasoned wood are the Anobiidae, Cerambycidae, Lyctidae and Curculionidae. The larval stage of the insects attacks the wood by extensive boring into the interior sapwood or heartwood, reducing it to a fine powder.

Micro-organisms including the Basidiomycotina, Ascomycotina, Deutoromycotina and bacteria can colonize and decompose wood, primarily if conditions of temperature, moisture content and pH are suitable. Mould fungi of the Ascomycotina type are not responsible for biodeterioration, being essentially surface colonies. However, soft rot fungi and brown rot fungi can break down cellulose and brown rot fungi can also break down lignin, eventually causing the total decomposition of the wood. Other organic materials are similarly degraded (Young, 1988).

On burial in an anaerobic environment insect attack ceases and fungal attack is strongly inhibited. It is thought that some bacterial action can continue, but at a very low level. Objects maintain their dimensional stability through bulking, i.e. filling, by water. On excavation, objects are normally in a highly fragile state and in danger of collapsing on desiccation. The abnormal shrinkage noted in drying out biodegraded waterlogged objects is due to cell collapse when the bulking water is removed (Kaarik, 1974).

Immediate conservation treatment for excavated waterlogged material is water immersion or spraying in holding-tanks. Further biodegradation can be retarded by the use of biocides, but where this may hinder future analysis (for ^{14}C dating) chilled water is preferred. Treatments for preservation involve dehydrating the wood without cell collapse to consolidate the object sufficiently for handling. Early treatments involved dehydration with acetone followed by impregnation with resin—an expensive, dangerous and often unsuccessful technique. Present methods concentrate on freeze-drying followed by consolidation with polyethylene glycol (PEG, a water-soluble synthetic wax of various molecular weights). Timbers from the *Mary Rose* were treated by initial washing followed by pre-treatment with Disodium Edetate to remove iron salts precipitated within the wood. The wood is then immersed in baths of PEG 3400 (PEG of average molecular weight 3400) of increasing concentrations over a period of months until a 50% solution is reached. Excess water is sublimated out of the wood by freeze-drying at $-20°C$, when the wood is removed and stored at a relative humidity of 50–60%.

Other organic materials are treated similarly. Lindow Man, a first century human body excavated from a waterlogged peat bog in 1984, was initially placed in cold storage to minimize biodeterioration. After cleaning and microbiological monitoring to determine the presence of pathogens or deteriogens, the body was consolidated in an 15% aqueous solution of PEG 400 and then freeze-dried (Omar *et al.*, 1989).

4 PRESERVATION OF NATURAL HISTORY COLLECTIONS

Museums have a long tradition of collecting natural history material, and tried-and-tested methods of preservation have grown up, based on desiccation or on fluid immersion. Recently, stricter legislation on the use of biocides, and a greater awareness of the degradation effects of some preservatives on objects, has led to a re-evaluation of methods (Stansfield, 1984).

4.1 Preservation through desiccation

Drying of organisms may be sufficient to ensure their long-term preservation by lowering the moisture content below that necessary to support fungal and bacterial deteriogens. The drying mechanisms follow a number of courses.

4.1.1 Taxidermy

Birds and animals have traditionally been preserved by the taxidermist's art in removing the skin (and other structural and relevant material such as bones, skull and claws) of an animal. The skin is defleshed and all fat removed, and then is preserved either by desiccation (through natural drying or with desiccants) or, in the case of larger mammals, by pickling or tanning. The treated skin is then mounted over a framework in a life-like pose. Further attack by biodeteriogens is prevented by fungicides and insecticides.

4.1.2 Freeze-drying

Owing to the expense and time required for the specialist art of taxidermy, small birds and mammals are increasingly preserved by freeze-drying. Advantages are the preservation of internal organs and the dry preservation of specimens previously only preservable by total fluid immersion.

4.1.3 Desiccation

Entomological collections and other suitable natural history material such as egg shells, mollusc shells and herbariums are regularly preserved by drying-out under normal ambient relative humidities. Occasionally biocides are used to prevent any further biodegradation.

4.1.4 Total immersion

Natural history material that is difficult to preserve is normally maintained by immersion in a preserving fluid. Traditionally, soft-bodied mammals, invertebrates and botanical material have been preserved in formaldehyde solution or ethanol. Recently, the use of propylene phenoxetol solution has been advanced as a safer alternative preservative, because it is non-flammable and maintains the colour of specimens.

5 CONCLUSIONS

The traditional methods of museum preservation tended to concentrate on the use of adhesives, consolidants, protective surface coatings and the ubiquitous use of biocides. The inevitable deterioration was masked by heavy restoration methods disguising or replacing damaged areas. Modern conservation techniques stress the importance of static conditions with the objects in equilibrium with their environment. Intrusive preservation methods are evaluated for their effect on the object, as well as their toxicity or hazardous nature, and the treatments are designed to be as far as possible invisible and reversible. Old damage and deterioration is accepted as part of the history of the object, and conservation is concerned with the long-term preservation of objects for future generations.

6 REFERENCES

Baer, N.S. & Banks, P.N. (1985) Indoor air pollution: effects on cultural and historic materials. *International Journal of Museum Management and Curatorship*, **4**, 9–20.

Brill, T.B. (1980) *Light: its Interaction with Art and Antiquities*. London: Plenum Press.

Buck, R.R. (1972) Some applications of rheology to the treatment of panel paintings, *Studies in Conservation*, **17**, 1–11.

Hoadley, R.B. (1978) The dimensional response of wood to variation in relative humidity. *Conservation of Wood in Painting and the Decorative Arts*, **IIC** (Oxford Congress), 1–6.

Kaarik, A.A. (1974) Decomposition of wood. In *Biology of Plant Litter Decomposition* (eds Dickinson, C.H. & Pugh G.F.) pp. 129–174. London: Academic Press.

Omar, S., McCord, M. & Daniels, V. (1989) The conservation of bog bodies by freeze-drying. *Studies in Conservation*, **34**, 101–109.

Stansfield, G. (1984) Conservation and storage: biological collections. *Manual of Curatorship*, pp. 289–295. London: Butterworths/Museum Association.

Thomson, G. (1986) *The Museum Environment*. London: Butterworths.

Torraca, G. (1988) *Porous Buildings Materials*. Rome: ICCROM.

United Kingdom Institute for Conservation (1984) *Guidance for Conservation Practice*. London: UKIC.

Young, A.M. (1988) *An Assessment of the Fungal Populations within the Timbers of the Tredunnock Boat*, University of Wales, B.Sc. archaeological conservation thesis.

PART 3
STERILIZATION

Chapter 18
Heat Sterilization

A·STERILIZATION AND DISINFECTION BY HEAT METHODS

1 INTRODUCTION

Of all the methods available for sterilization and disinfection, heat, and particularly moist heat, is the most reliable and the most widely used. If enough heat is applied, all forms of microbial life are destroyed and sterilization is effected.

The definition of the term 'sterilization' is the complete destruction or removal of all living micro-organisms (sporing and non-sporing bacteria, viruses, fungi and protozoa). The term 'disinfection' has been defined as the removal or destruction of harmful micro-organisms, not usually including bacterial spores (Maurer, 1984).

Heat methods using saturated steam under pressure or hot air are the classic sterilizing agents, they are the most reliable and comparatively easy to use and control. Disinfection or decontamination by heat at temperatures below 100°C is an appropriate choice in many instances, except in the presence of living tissues and where the material may be damaged at disinfection temperatures. Moist heat processes at temperatures below 100°C in combination with formaldehyde can also be employed for sterilizing some heat-sensitive materials (Section 4.5).

1.1 The relative efficiencies of dry and moist heat

When applying heat sterilization techniques it is necessary to know the reasons for differentiating between dry and moist heat and the limitations of these two agents because the lethal processes are not the same. Under conditions of moist heat, for example saturated steam, destruction of micro-organisms is achieved by the irreversible denaturation of enzymes and structural proteins. The temperature at which denaturation occurs varies inversely with the amount of water present, as demonstrated in the data for the coagulation of the protein egg albumin (Perkins, 1960), viz:

Egg albumin + 50% water coagulates at 56°C
Egg albumin + 25% water coagulates at 74–80°C
Egg albumin + 0% water coagulates at 160–170°C

In dry heat processes the variable moisture content is obviously a limiting factor and the primary lethal process is considered to be oxidation of cell constituents (Ernst, 1977). Thus sterilization methods involving dry heat require a higher temperature and a longer exposure time than is required for moist heat (Fig. 18.1).

1.2 Heat resistance of micro-organisms

The thermal death times of micro-organisms vary depending on the innate heat resistance of the strain, the temperature of the treatment and the recovery conditions, in particular the culture medium and temperature of incubation. While it may be safe to assume that vegetative bacteria do not survive exposure to moist heat for 10 min at 80°C and 15 min at 73°C, bacterial spores require exposure to much higher temperatures. The enhanced thermal resistance of the bacterial spore has been related to structural components, particularly dipicolinic acid (DPA) which is chelated with calcium ions in the complex spore wall, and is absent from vegetative cells (Church and Halvorsan, 1959; Levinson *et al.*, 1961). The rate of degradation of the calcium–DPA complex on heating has been related to the thermal death rate of spores, with heat-resistant strains losing DPA less rapidly than heat-sensitive strains (Grecz *et al.*, 1972). The more recent theory of osmoregulation is discussed in Chapter 18B.

The variation in response of different bacterial spores to exposure to moist or dry heat is demonstrated by comparing the spores of *Bacillus stearothermophilus* and *B. subtilis* var. *niger*. In saturated steam at 121°C, 10^6 spores of *B. subtilis* are destroyed in <1 min whereas 10^5 spores of *B. starothermophilus* require 12-min exposure under the same conditions. However, *B. subtilis* var. *niger* is more resistant to dry heat (under the same high temperature conditions) than is *B. stearothermophilus* (Ernst, 1977).

Variations in thermal death times can also be expected because of differences in exposure conditions. In medical, surgical and veterinary practice, micro-organisms are frequently embedded in organic debris such as dried blood, sputum, faeces, skin scales or dried, encrusted serous materials which will insulate the organism from the effects of heat, thus prolonging thermal death times of vegetative cells and spores. In these situations thorough cleaning of the item is essential prior to heat sterilization.

The thermal death times of fungi and protozoa

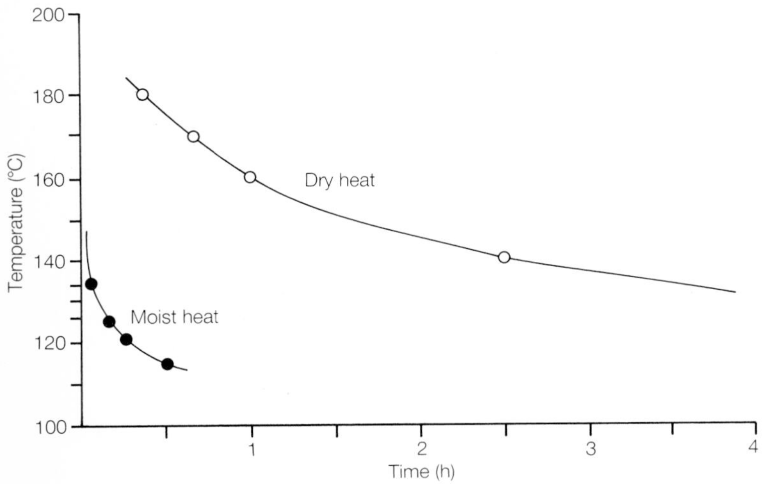

Fig. 18.1 Thermal death curves for *Bacillus stearothermophilus* exposed to moist or dry heat.

are similar to those of non-sporing bacteria. Most viruses are inactivated at 60°C within 20 min, although longer exposure periods and higher temperatures are required for more resistant virus particles such as polio and possibly hepatitis B (Sykes, 1965). The infectious agent of Creutzfeldt–Jakob disease is considered to be of such high heat resistance that the standard sterilization cycle is extended from 3 min to 18 min at 134°C (Advisory Group, 1981; see also Chapter 7). However, for highly infectious organisms including some viruses it should be noted that the safest method of destroying any micro-organism is by incineration.

2 STERILIZATION BY DRY HEAT

The value of heat in the form of fire has been known for many centuries as a means of preventing the spread of disease. Incineration, defined by Lawrence (1968) as 'to burn or reduce to ashes', is an efficient and effective method of killing harmful micro-organisms and disposing of contaminated materials where destruction of the article is of no concern. Incinerators are used to destroy contaminated waste materials from hospital and community sources, for example used surgical dressings, disposable hypodermic syringes and needles and pathological waste materials. Dry heat in the form of the Bunsen burner flame is used in laboratories to sterilize inoculating wires and loops, and to provide rapid decontamination of the necks of culture vessels by 'flaming', although the reliability of this method is uncertain.

2.1 Hot air sterilizers

The method of sterilization by use of hot air in ovens is simple in principle, dry heat having the advantages of penetrating power and lack of corrosive properties. Diffusion and penetration of heat into the load are achieved slowly because of the relative inefficiency of air as a heat medium. The equilibration of heat may be accelerated by forced air circulation using a fan, which will additionally overcome the tendency for stratification in the chamber. The slow rates of heat absorption and microbial killing by hot air combine to make this a time-consuming method, the total process time including the time taken for the free chamber space to achieve temperature, the time for all parts of the load to achieve temperature, the sterilizing time and the cooling time. The recommended sterilizing times at different temperatures are given in Table 18.1.

It is recommended that hot air ovens should be automatically controlled and fitted with door locks, and should comply with British Standard 3421 (published in 1961) and in the United Kingdom with Health Technical Memorandum (HTM) No. 10 (1980, see Appendix). The load should be packed in the oven chamber in such a way that sufficient space remains between articles to allow hot air circulation. Improved heat transfer may be achieved by supporting heavy instruments in a metal cradle to assist heat transfer by conduction.

The high temperatures needed to achieve dry heat sterilization have a damaging effect on many materials. This method should therefore be used only for those thermostable materials which cannot be sterilized by steam because of deleterious effects or failure to penetrate. Such materials include oils and some oily injections, powders and glassware.

2.2 Infrared radiation

Infrared radiation has been used as a method of sterilizing small items of surgical equipment which are passed on a slowly moving belt through the path of the rays. The method was developed successfully for the sterilization of glass hypodermic

Table 18.1 Recommended minimum holding periods for thermal sterilization at different temperatures

Process	Temperature (°C)	Holding time‡ (min) for sterilization
Dry heat*	160	120
	170	60
	180	30
Moist heat (saturated steam)†	121	15
	126	10
	134	3

* European Pharmacopeia (1990).
† Medical Research Council (1959).
‡ Holding times are for loads that have been brought to the required temperature before sterilizing time commences.

syringes (approximately 600 per day) for a hospital central sterile supply service (Darmady *et al.*, 1957). However, with the commercial development of pre-sterilized and pre-packaged plastic syringes and needles, in the late 1960s, use of glass syringes rapidly declined and the method has not had widespread application.

Infrared radiation transmits heat directly to those surfaces of the load exposed, with penetration achieved slowly by conduction. One limitation of the method therefore is that it may only be applied successfully to small numbers of simple instruments. Care must be taken to ensure that no instrument impedes the direct path of the rays to any other part of the load. Under carefully controlled conditions, sterilization is achieved more rapidly using infrared radiation than by hot air in electrically heated ovens, the most resistant bacterial spores being destroyed at 180°C for 15 min (Sykes, 1965).

3 STERILIZATION BY MOIST HEAT

3.1 Steam under pressure

The basic principle of sterilization by steam under pressure is to expose the materials to be processed to dry saturated steam at the required temperature and pressure for the necessary length of time. The minimum recommended standard for sterilization is exposure to steam at approximately 1 bar gauge pressure, equivalent to 121°C for 15 min. The pressure serves as a means of controlling the temperature at which steam is produced from boiling water.

Saturated steam is a much more efficient means of destroying micro-organisms than either boiling water or dry heat. At an equivalent temperature of 100°C there is at least seven times as much available heat from saturated steam as from boiling water (Ernst, 1977). The presence of air in steam affects the sterilizing efficiency by changing the pressure–temperature relationship, for example at 1 bar gauge pressure, saturated steam within a closed chamber has a temperature of 121°C provided that all the air is first removed from the chamber. With only half the air removed, the temperature of the resulting air–steam mixture at the same pressure is only 112°C. Thus, the presence of air in packages of porous materials, e.g. surgical dressings, will hinder the penetration of steam and prevent sterilization of the complete load (Alder & Gillespie, 1957).

3.2 Autoclaves and their design

The process of steam sterilization is carried out in a pressure vessel called an autoclave, of which there are various types in the following categories.

1 The small upright non-jacketed autoclave (laboratory bench type). The air within this type of autoclave is expelled under pressure through a valve in the lid of the autoclave by the turbulent mixture of steam, generated by boiling water in the chamber, and air. Small electrically heated steam sterilizers, with a similar air expulsion system, designed for steam sterilization of unwrapped instruments and utensils, are used in medical and dental community practice.

2 The downward displacement autoclave. This is usually jacketed, horizontal and cylindrical in shape. The air is removed by downward displacement by steam through an automatic air and condensate discharge valve at the base of the autoclave chamber. There are three main types: (a) laboratory autoclaves; (b) hospital autoclaves for sterilizing unwrapped surgical instruments, bowls, etc., for use in operating theatres; (c) autoclaves for sterilizing fluids in sealed containers, used, for example, in hospital pharmacy departments. These autoclaves are commonly fitted with rapid cooling devices.

3 The porous-load high-temperature steam sterilizer. This is used mainly for such porous materials as towels, surgical gowns, dressings, etc., or for trays packed with instruments and porous materials, e.g. swabs, towels, drapes, etc., for use in operating theatres. The sterilizer is equipped with a vacuum system to ensure a high degree of air removal.

3.3 The non-jacketed laboratory autoclave

The laboratory autoclave is a simple piece of apparatus for boiling water under pressure. It has a vertical non-jacketed metal chamber with a metal lid fastened with clamps. A rubber gasket is fitted between the lid and the chamber. An air and steam discharge valve, pressure gauge and adjustable safety valve are fitted in the lid. Water in the base of the autoclave is heated externally by gas or internally by an electric immersion heater or steam coil. Oates *et al.* (1983) have described the development of an automatically controlled laboratory autoclave system incorporating a number of safety features. (See also Appendix, Section 6: BS 2646 (1988), Autoclaves for sterilization in laboratories.)

In the operation of the autoclave, sufficient water is placed in the bottom of the autoclave, the chamber is loaded with the materials to be sterilized and the lid is clamped down, ensuring that the air and steam discharge valve is open. The safety valve is adjusted to the required pressure and the water is heated. When the water boils, steam issues from the discharge valve and carries the air from the chamber with it. The removal of air may be tested by attaching one end of a length of tubing to the discharge valve and placing the other end in a vessel of cold water. Steam from the discharge valve will condense in the water and any air will rise through the water as bubbles, to the surface. When the issue of bubbles ceases it may be assumed that the air has been removed from the chamber space and only saturated steam is present. The steam should be allowed to escape freely for 3 min from the discharge valve to ensure that as much air as possible has been removed. The discharge valve is then closed and the tubing removed. The steam pressure will rise until the required level is reached and the safety valve emits steam.

After time has been allowed for the temperature of the load inside the chamber to reach steam temperature, the sterilizing period is timed with pressure maintained for the required period (Table 18.1). At the end of the sterilizing period the heater is turned off and the pressure gauge allowed to fall to zero (atmospheric pressure). The air and steam discharge valve is opened very gently to test for any residual pressure in the chamber. If the valve is opened when the chamber in still under pressure, fluids, e.g. culture media, could start to boil explosively and glass bottles may even burst. The contents of the autoclave should be allowed to cool down sufficiently until they are relatively safe to handle. The cooling-down period may be several hours depending on the size of container in the load. It is dangerous to remove a bottle of fluid or agar medium for immediate inspection; the quick change in temperature may crack a glass container, allowing the hot liquid to be ejected. The operator should wear a visor and protective gloves when opening the lid of the autoclave to remove its contents.

It is strongly advised that laboratory media and fluids in sealed containers are sterilized only in autoclaves which have a door interlock to prevent the autoclave being opened until the load has cooled sufficiently (80°C). The door interlock may act by means of a simulator or time lock. The use of rapid-cooling systems is advocated, for example internal chamber sprays of cold water for bottled fluids (Wilkinson *et al.*, 1960) and methods of 'dry cooling' for laboratory media.

Laboratory discard autoclaves used for sterilization of infected and potentially infected waste, particularly from clinical laboratories, should be monitored using thermocouples inserted into standard loads to ascertain the time taken for the load to reach the required temperature, usually 121°C for not less than 15 min (*Code of Practice for the Prevention of Infection in Clinical Laboratories and Post-mortem Rooms*, DHSS, 1978). In order to ensure that no pathogen waste is carried over into the condense drain prior to full exposure to the sterilizing stage, it is recommended that all condensate produced during the cycle be retained for the full time and temperature required to effect sterilization before discharging to the drain. For dangerous pathogens some arrangement to prevent the escape of organisms in the discharge effluent from the drain should be considered.

3.4 The non-jacketed, electrically heated bench-top sterilizer

The non-jacketed, electrically heated bench-top sterilizer which does not require a mains steam supply, provides a versatile means of sterilizing metal instruments and utensils in small clinics and laboratories. There are, however, several disadvantages which represent the major problems for heat sterilization processes. The method of removing air from the chamber is inefficient and particularly unsatisfactory for the sterilization of porous articles. The steam supply is not 'dry' and readily condenses on the surface of the load, causing severe wetting of porous materials (fabrics, paper, etc.). There is no means of drying the load after sterilization, which is essential to prevent rapid recontamination of articles wrapped in paper or cloth and stored before use. Downward displacement and porous high load pressure sterilizers have been developed to overcome these difficulties.

3.5 The quality of steam for autoclaves

Before considering the methods of operating more specialized autoclaves, attention must be given to the quality of steam that is used, which must be both 'saturated' and 'dry'. The temperatures and pressures of steam normally used for sterilization procedures involving moist heat, which are shown in Table 18.1, apply only to saturated steam. The word 'saturated' in this context means that steam is at a phase where it is holding all the water that it can, in the form of transparent vapour. It does not contain water droplets, and is therefore described as being 'dry'; if it meets an object cooler than itself it is at the point of condensing. Under these conditions the steam is described as being at the phase boundary.

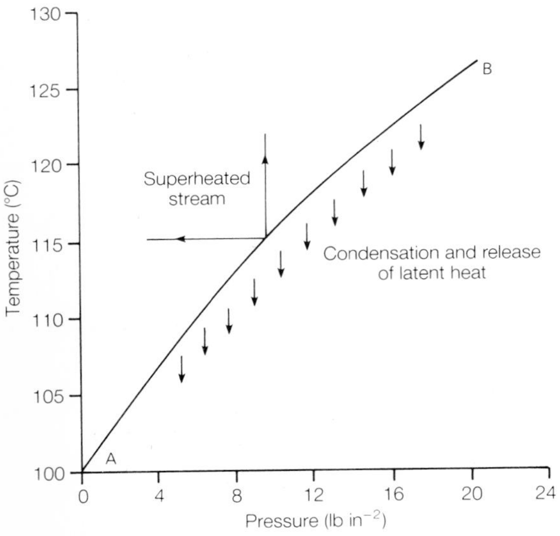

Fig. 18.2 Temperature and pressure relationship for saturated steam.

The phase boundary is maintained at a particularly relationship of temperature and pressure, as shown in Fig. 18.2. The line A–B is the phase boundary for saturated steam and indicates the conditions of temperature and pressure required to maintain it. If higher temperatures are required, then higher pressures must be employed to maintain the steam at the phase boundary. If at any given pressure the temperature is reduced, for example by contact with cooler surfaces such as an unheated chamber wall or door, metal objects, bottles of cooler fluid and entrapped air, then condensation will result and the steam will release its latent heat until the object is brought to the same temperature as the steam. On the other hand, should the temperature rise and the pressure remain constant, the steam will be 'superheated', i.e. it will be at a temperature above that of saturated steam and will condense less readily. Saturated steam gives up its heat at constant temperature, whereas superheated steam gives up its heat with loss of temperature. As steam becomes more superheated it behaves more like hot air and is therefore less effective as a sterilizing medium than saturated steam at the same pressure.

It is important that steam should be 'dry', i.e. free from water droplets. Steam flowing along main steam pipes from a separate boiler to supply autoclaves may contain droplets of water which can be removed by engineering devices such as separators and traps. The main reason for keeping the steam dry, particularly when applied to materials such as towels and surgical dressings in hospital autoclaves, is to prevent the soaking of porous materials, thus impeding the penetration of steam into the article as well as prolonging the drying period after sterilization. A lengthy drying process at raised temperatures may cause damage to some materials, for example, rubber.

3.6 Removal of air from autoclaves

The method of removing air from autoclave chambers by venting air and steam through a discharge valve at the top of the chamber, as in the case of the laboratory bench-type autoclave, is both time-consuming and uncertain. A better method of air removal is to take advantage of the difference in density of air relative to steam to displace the air downwards and out of the chamber through a discharge pipe at the lower part of the chamber. This method is termed 'downward displacement'. A more certain way of removing the air is to extract it from the chamber by strong vacuum systems or pressure/vacuum pulsing (Alder & Gillespie, 1957; Perkins, 1960). High-vacuum systems are also time-saving (Knox & Penikett, 1958), a preliminary vacuum of 20 mmHg (absolute) for removing air enabling saturated steam to penetrate a test package and to achieve a sterilizing temperature in 1 min.

3.7 Downward displacement autoclaves

The general design of downward displacement or gravity displacement autoclaves is shown in Fig. 18.3. A pressure-operated safety device ensures that the door cannot be opened while the chamber is under pressure. Steam is admitted into the chamber in such a way that it is deflected upwards by a baffle. The steam, being less dense than the cool air within the chamber, fills the chamber from the top downwards. Condensation of steam occurs on cooler surfaces such as the chamber door, with the air and condensate forced out of the drain positioned in the lowest part of the chamber by gravity displacement. The drain contains a thermometer to measure the temperature of the effluent and an automatic 'near-to-steam' trap.

The automatic steam trap is termed 'near-to-steam' because it operates at a temperature just (approximately 2°C) below that of saturated steam. It is an engineering device designed to ensure that only saturated steam is retained inside the chamber and that air and condensed steam, which are at temperatures below that of saturated steam, are automatically discharged from the drain.

The drain from the autoclave discharge is sited in such a way that there is a gap between the outer end of the drain pipes and the opening of the waste pipe connected to the effluent system in the building where the autoclave is situated. This ensures that no contaminated water can 'back-siphon' from the waste pipe into the autoclave chamber.

When the thermometer fitted to the chamber drain records the temperature of saturated steam at the operating pressure, it is assumed that the

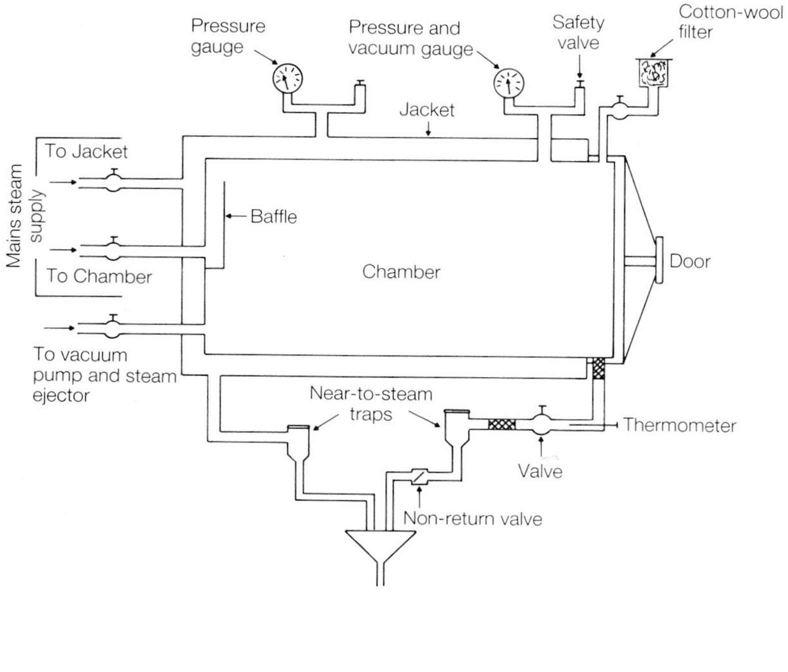

Fig. 18.3 Downward displacement autoclave.

chamber is at the proper temperature for sterilization. The sterilization period then commences according to the recommended holding times (Table 18.1).

After the sterilizing period has been completed, the valve which controls the steam entering the chamber is closed and the autoclave is allowed to cool until the pressure gauge records atmospheric pressure. The air-to-chamber inlet valve is opened and the contents of the chamber are allowed to cool. The cooling times can vary according to the nature of the contents, e.g. large bottles of agar take several hours to cool to about 80°C. Following an adequate cooling time, the door of the autoclave is opened carefully and the contents are removed by the operator, who should wear protective gloves and a visor. The time taken for a standard load to cool to 80°C should be determined by thermocouple testing and a suitable time lock fitted to ensure that the door cannot be opened prematurely.

The performance of downward displacement autoclaves should be monitored routinely by temperature and automatic control tests with quarterly thermocouple tests as described in HTM 10 (1980). Sterilizers should be thermocoupled on standard loads to establish the heat-up time required to achieve the recommended temperature–pressure relationship and this time should be added to the selected sterilizing time at the temperature chosen. Bottled fluid sterilizers are additionally monitored with thermocouples in test bottles sited in different parts of the chamber. Accelerated cooling of fluids in sealed containers may be achieved by use of a cooling water spray (Wilkinson *et al.*, 1960). Again, it is essential that the door of the sterilizer cannot be opened until the temperature of the contents has fallen below 80°C (BS 3970, Part 2). This is best achieved by machines with an automatic cycle.

Downward displacement autoclaves are widely used for the sterilization of non-porous articles whose surfaces are freely exposed to steam, for example metal instruments and containers, hence the term 'bowl and instrument machine', commonly used in hospital practice. Laboratory media in unsealed vessels, water and pharmaceutical products and laboratory discards are also processed in downward displacement autoclaves. Sterilizers for fluids in sealed containers are widely used in pharmacy departments and industrial establishments. However, for all downward displacement autoclaves the process time is prolonged by the time required to remove air, to heat the load and, when necessary, to dry the load at the end of the cycle. Insufficient drying favours recontamination of materials subsequently in contact with non-sterile surroundings, and for porous materials there is the uncertainty as to whether air has been completely removed. Sterilizers for porous loads have therefore been developed which overcome these difficulties.

3.8 Sterilizers for porous loads

The porous load sterilizer is fitted with a vacuum system to ensure that air and non-condensable gases are removed from the chamber and load prior to the admission of steam for the sterilizing period and to dry the load after sterilization. The process of air removal is achieved by a single high-vacuum evacuation of the chamber or, as in modern machines, by a pulsing, automatic multistage process in which the evacuation of the chamber alternates with the admission of steam. An important advantage of this type of system over the conventional downward displacement autoclave is that steam admitted into the chamber for the sterilizing period penetrates almost instantaneously into all parts of the load, which is rapidly and evenly heated even when tightly packed. The British Standard 3970 Part 3 (1990) requires the load to be in contact with steam at the sterilizing temperature for a fixed hold period; for example 134°C for a minimum of 3 min. The total cycle time should not exceed 35 min in this instance.

Devices are fitted to detect leakages of air into the chamber through faulty pipe connections and door seals, and for faulty air removal systems by the monitoring of the partial air pressure inside the chamber. The full operation of the autoclave is carried out under an automatic control system.

The porous load sterilizer is widely used for processing porous items which are capable of surviving short periods of exposure to high-pressure steam, for example dressings, fabrics and equipment made of rubber such as tubing. It is also the method of choice for metal instruments and utensils which are wrapped in paper or other porous materials and which will be stored before use. The speed and efficacy of the process has resulted in the porous load sterilizer generally replacing the downward displacement autoclaves in hospitals, even for the sterilization of unwrapped instruments.

The efficiency of the porous load sterilization cycle depends on the removal of sufficient air and non-condensable gases from the chamber and load before steam is admitted during the 'sterilizing' stage. Air trapped within the load would prevent penetration of part of the load by steam and consequently sterilizing conditions may not be achieved (Alder & Gillespie, 1957). A daily asessment of the correct functioning of the porous load sterilizer is essential and may be achieved by a combination of test records and observations which are described in detail in HTM 10 (1980). These include:

1 temperature record chart for each load (daily);
2 indicating thermometer (daily);
3 air detection function test (quarterly);
4 Bowie–Dick test (daily);
5 leak rate test (weekly);
6 thermocouple tests (quarterly).

3.8.1 Bowie–Dick test

The principle of the test (see also Chapter 22) is to prove whether or not steam penetration of the test pack has been rapid and even, and that air and other non-condensable gases have not entered the test pack (Bowie *et al.*, 1963).

The original Bowie–Dick test was based on the use of adhesive indicator tape, in the shape of a St Andrew's cross, fixed onto a piece of paper and placed in the centre of a standard pack comprising huckaback towels. In current UK practice, indicators conforming to the Department of Health specification may be either in the form of tape or of a pre-prepared sheet. The indicator shows a colour change on exposure to steam, related to the time of exposure, temperature and moisture content. The test pack is sterilized on its own as the first run of the day, thus ensuring a rigorous test system. If all the air has been removed, the steam will penetrate rapidly and completely, and the indicator will show an even colour change. If all the air has not been removed before the steam is admitted for the sterilizing stage, air will collect at the centre of the pack as a 'bubble'. The colour of the indicator in proximity to the bubble will be paler than elsewhere along its length because of the lower temperature and reduced moisture level, and this will be observed when the indicator is removed at the end of the cycle.

The details of the test procedure, which should be followed precisely, are given in HTM 10 (1980). At each daily Bowie–Dick test run the temperature record chart and indicating thermometer should be monitored, and the results recorded in a log book.

3.8.2 Leak rate test and air detection function

The presence of air in the chamber and load prevents complete penetration of the load by steam and thus precludes sterilization. In addition, air leaking into the chamber at the end of the sterilization stage is a potential source of contamination as it will not have passed through a bacterial filter. The leakage of air into the chamber should not exceed a maximum value specified by BS 3970 Part 3 (1990).

The leak rate test involves the drawing of a vacuum followed by closure of all valves leading to the chamber, stopping the means of drawing a vacuum and observing the chamber pressure for a timed period. The maximum leak rate, when tested in accordance with BS 3970 Part 3 (1990) should not exceed 1.3 mbar/min.

The air detector function test establishes that the air detector will abort a cycle if air and other non-condensable gases are retained sufficient to cause the temperature at the centre of the Bowie–Dick test pack to be 2°C lower than the temperature measured in the chamber drain (BS 3970 Part 3, 1990).

The measurement of physical parameters such as temperature provides a rapid, reliable and simple means of assessing the efficiency of high-pressure steam sterilizers in direct correlation with established characteristics for sterilization, and is therefore preferred routinely to biological testing methods using bacterial spores and test pieces or chemical indicators.

3.9 Other moist heat sterilization processes

3.9.1 Heat plus bactericide

Aqueous solutions or suspensions of pharmaceutical products unstable at higher temperatures may be sterilized in sealed containers with the addition of a bactericide at 98–100°C for 30 min. Recommended bactericides for eye-drops include benzalkonium chloride, chlorhexidine acetate and phenylmercurie acetate (*British Pharmaceutical Codex*, 1973; *Pharmaceutical Codex*, 1979). Further information is provided in Chapter 18C. The method is no longer an official one for the sterilization of injections.

3.9.2 Low-temperature steam (at sub-atmospheric pressure) with formaldehyde

The sporicidal effect of adding formaldehyde to low-temperature steam, at sub-atmospheric pressure, was first demonstrated for *Bacillus anthracis* in a 70°C process by Esmarch (1902). The importance of optimal relative humidity and the prior evacuation of the chamber before admission of formaldehyde and steam to achieve adequate penetration of the load was described by Nordgren (1939). However, it was not until the 1960s that low-temperature steam processes with or without formaldehyde were developed for routine hospital use in the UK (Alder *et al.*, 1966; Gibson & Johnstone, 1967).

Using an apparatus modified from a standard high-pressure autoclave, Alder *et al.* (1971b) found that vegetative bacteria were killed after 5 min exposure to saturated steam at 80°C. When formaldehyde gas, generated from heated formalin, was added prior to the admission of unsaturated steam (60–90% RH) the process was sporicidal. Test spores of *B. stearothermophilus* dried in serum and saline on filter paper strips were killed in 2 h, although spores entrapped in the threads of assembled nuts and bolts survived. Further work showed that the operating temperature could be reduced from 80°C to 73°C, thus minimizing damage to heat-sensitive equipment without loss of sporicidal efficiency (Mitchell & Alder, 1975).

The sporicidal action of the combination of low-temperature steam and formaldehyde has been repeatedly demonstrated, although the optimum conditions and interpretation of available data are hampered by the wide range of cycle characteristics used in practice (Gibson, 1980).

Early work was done using autoclaves which drew a single high vacuum prior to the admission of formaldehyde vapour into the chamber. In this multistage process, emphasis was placed on the initial penetration of the load by three pulses of formaldehyde, each from 2 ml heated formalin/0.03 m^3, followed by the introduction of a relatively high concentration of the gas from 8 ml heated formalin/0.03 m^3 followed by unsaturated steam (60–90% RH) and then by saturated steam to 73%, which was held for 2 h (Alder *et al.*, 1971b). The development of the cycle which remained in routine hospital use for 10 years was described in detail by Alder (1987) and Gardner & Peel (1991).

The original method was carried out in a modified autoclave as shown in Fig. 18.4. The modifications included a reservoir and heat exchanger for the formalin: this was attached to the steam inlet pipe for injecting formaldehyde into the chamber through a valve. It was necessary to maintain the jacket temperature at least 5°C higher than the chamber temperature to reduce condensation. A steam jacket was found to be more reliable for this purpose than electrically heated thermal tape in ensuring that all areas of the chamber wall were heated, including the rear wall and chamber door. With the conventional type of autoclave, where the jacket surrounds the top, sides and base of the chamber (Figs 18.3 and 18.4), uneven heating occurs particularly on the door surface and possibly at the rear wall, and condensation occurs at the door surface and door seal. An autoclave designed with a jacket covering all areas of the chamber wall including the door and rear wall might well reduce temperature differences and uneven heating of chamber wall areas for LTS and LTS/F processes.

When first developed, using an injection of formaldehyde followed by steam, the method was successful for surface sterilization but the extent of penetration into narrow-bore tubing was uncertain. Further development showed that if the chamber and load were saturated first with formaldehyde gas from heated formalin by a pulsing method

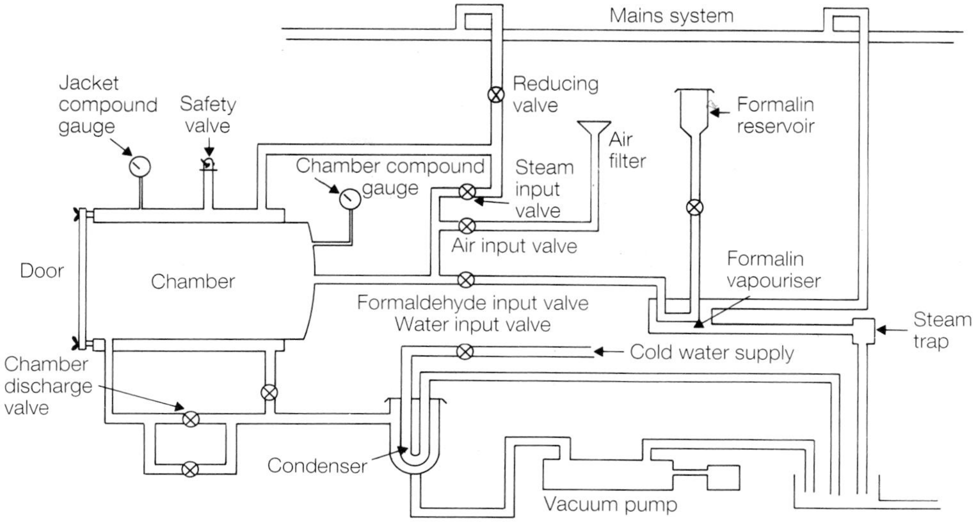

Fig. 18.4 Diagram of autoclave modified for use with sub-atmospheric steam and formaldehyde.

following a 'dry' evacuation of air, and the steam added to the gas, a deep penetration of gaseous mixture occurred. Bacterial spores were killed inside narrow-bore tubing and simulated test pieces (Alder, 1968; Alder *et al.*, 1971b; Mitchell & Alder, 1975).

The development of 'multiple pulsing' with steam to achieve improved air removal in porous load sterilizers led to the parallel development of LTS/F sterilizers, in which formalin vapour was introduced into the chamber with the series of air removal steam pulses. This method effectively utilized a lower concentration of formaldehyde and is typical of the machines currently available in the UK (Pickerill, 1975; Gibson, 1977).

In contrast, Weymes (1977) has developed a LTS/F process for porous loads which operates at a lower temperature and requires repeated pulsing of small amounts of formalin vapour. An initial vacuum below 50 mmHg is achieved, followed by a series of deep pulses of steam and formaldehyde (1 ml formalin/0.03 m^3), between 50 mmHg abs. and 200 mmHg abs. at 65°C. For disinfection purposes, five pulses with formalin vapour are recommended, and for sterilization, 15 pulses. Each of these periods is followed by five pulses of steam without formalin vapour. The final removal of formaldehyde is achieved by three pulses of vacuum/air between atmospheric pressure and 50 mmHg (Weymes, 1977).

The measurement of physical parameters associated with sterilization by steam and formaldehyde is impracticable, and routine testing therefore relies on assessing the ability of the process to kill bacterial spores. The spore test organism, *B. stearothermophilus*, impregnated on to paper discs, is placed in a test piece designed to simulate the challenge of intricate endoscopy equipment. Various test pieces have been described; probably the most widely used is that of Line & Pickerill (1973) consisting of a helix of stainless-steel tubing connected to a brass capsule. The details of spore test pieces and procedures are given in Chapter 22. The reported conditions for the cultures of exposed spore strips show considerable variation in length of time of incubation (from 3 to 14 days), in temperature (50–60°C) and culture media (Alder *et al.*, 1966; Alder, 1968; Line & Pickerill, 1973; Gibson, 1977). An incubation time of 14 days at 56°C in tryptone soya broth is now recommended (Cripps *et al.*, 1976) until the reliability of the machine is known. Selection of the most suitable medium for the recovery of spores is of considerable importance, an indicator dye commonly used in culture medium being inhibitory to the recovery of heat-damaged spores (Cook & Brown, 1960; Bühlmann *et al.*, 1973).

Conflicting reports as to the effectiveness of LTS/F as a sterilizing process are probably related to fundamental differences in cycle characteristics and the lack of a standard spore challenge and test method (Alder & Gillespie, 1961; Alder *et al.*, 1971b; Pickerill, 1975; Cripps *et al.*, 1976; Weymes, 1977). Considerable variability in the resistance of different strains of *B. stearothermophilus* to exposure to LTS/F has been reported, and further reflects the need for standardization of the spore strain used, method of preparation and number of organisms present (Blake *et al.*, 1977), to ensure a realistic challenge.

Guidance on commissioning, recommissioning and routine testing of LTS/F was issued by the Department of Health (HEI 95, 1980). Current work is in progress to produce a British Standard specification for the LTS/F sterilizer requirements and performance testing, including the biological indicator.

Polymerization of formaldehyde, with subsequent condensation and deposition as a white powder on surfaces, will impede the penetration of formaldehyde. A flush-through process with water after each LTS/F cycle is therefore essential to prevent blockage of fine delivery tubing and valves. The minimum amount of formaldehyde compatible with a successful spore test result should be used, thus lessening the tendency for polymer deposition and reducing the likelihood of residual formaldehyde vapour in the load and chamber which would constitute a hazard both to the operator and in the immediate use of processed equipment (Weymes *et al.*, 1975; Cripps *et al.*, 1976; Handlos, 1979).

4 DISINFECTION BY MOIST HEAT

4.1 Disinfection by moist heat at 100°C

Many surgical and laboratory instruments can be decontaminated by boiling in water for 5–10 mins. Non-sporing organisms and some spores will be killed, but more resistant bacterial spores will survive. The method has been used as a rapid emergency procedure when high-temperature processes were unavailable, but its routine use in medical and surgical practice has been discouraged (Health circular 67/13). Instruments processed by this method may not be stored because of possible rapid recontamination.

4.2 Repeated steaming at 100°C (Tyndallization)

This method was devised as a means of sterilizing fluids which would be damaged at higher temperatures, for example culture media containing carbohydrates or serum. The materials are processed by steaming in a closed chamber for 30–45 min on each of three successive days, the principle being that on the first day vegetative bacteria are killed and any bacterial spores that survive will germinate in the nutrient medium overnight, producing vegetative forms that are killed by the second and third steamings.

4.3 Pasteurization

The process of pasteurization is widely used in the food industry for the destruction of microorganisms which could be harmful and cause undesirable spoilage. The method originates from the observation of Louis Pasteur that spoilage of wines was prevented by heating the wine to temperatures between 50°C and 60°C. The most widespread application today is in the pasteurization of milk, for which the statutory requirements are that the milk should be retained at a temperature of not less than 62.8°C and not more that 65.6°C for at least 30 min, and be immediately cooled to a temperature of not more than 10°C: *or* retained at a temperature of not less than 71.7°C for at least 15 s and be immediately cooled to a temperature of not more that 10°C (Food and Drugs Act, 1977, No. 1033). It is not a sterilization process; thermoduric organisms and spores survive the treatment.

Another application is in the preparation of whole bacterial cell vaccines. A pasteurization method has also been used to decontaminate some heat-sensitive instruments, for example cystoscopes, by immersion in a water-bath at 75°C for 10 min or 80°C for 5 min (Gillespie & Mitchell, 1967). The method has been shown to be as satisfactory for disinfection purposes as boiling water (Francis, 1959), and is less likely to damage the components of the cystoscope, particularly by agitation from bubbles. A thermostatically controlled water-bath is used which should be large enough to avoid an undue decrease in temperature when the cold metal instrument is immersed in it. The use of a timing interlock is recommended.

Pasteurizers are also used for the decontamination of freshly expressed human milk and infant formula feeds. Care must be taken to use simulator bottles and thermocouples to ensure that all parts of the bottle, particularly the neck, attain the recommended temperature for the required period of time.

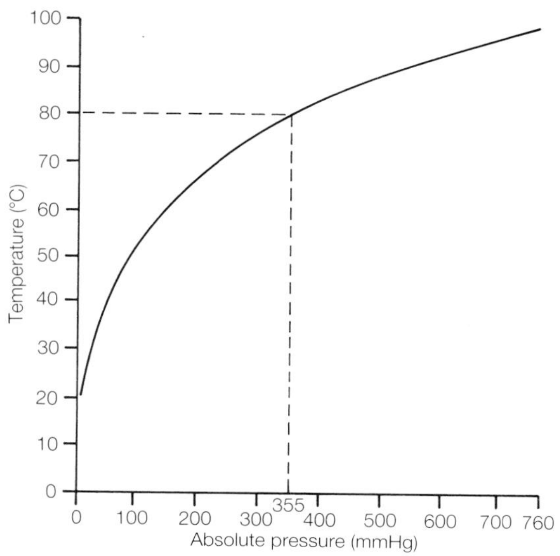

Fig. 18.5 The temperature of saturated steam at pressure below atmospheric.

4.4 Disinfection by moist heat in washer–disinfectors

Several types of washer–disinfector have been developed to clean and make microbiologically safe contaminated re-usable equipment such as surgical instruments, bed-pans, urinals or anaesthetic tubing. During continuous operation the machine must achieve a required minimum surface temperature on the load for a required time, such as 80°C for 1 min or 70°C for 3 min (Central Sterilising Club, 1986).

4.5 Low-temperature steam (at sub-atmospheric pressure)

The use of low-temperature steam (LTS) at subatmospheric pressure was developed for the disinfection of heat-sensitive equipment, the method being used initially for the disinfection of woollen blankets (Alder & Gillespie, 1961). The principle of the method is based on the fact that, if steam is admitted to a previously evacuated autoclave chamber, the temperature of the steam can be accurately maintained by controlling the pressure inside the chamber. The relationship between the temperature of saturated steam and pressure below atmospheric is shown in Fig. 18.5. Saturated steam at sub-atmospheric pressure, for example at 80°C, is a much more efficient disinfecting agent than water at the same temperature. In the evacuated chamber, steam condenses giving up latent heat energy while the sensible heat of the material exposed stays at 80°C. Thus, at temperatures well below that of boiling water, non-sporing organisms can be destroyed more rapidly without incurring damage to heat-sensitive equipment.

Disinfectors operating at sub-atmospheric pressures in the order of 350 mbar have been developed to disinfect heat-sensitive medical products by the use of dry saturated steam at low temperature (73°C) in the absence of formaldehyde. The equipment is intended for treating both wrapped and unwrapped instruments and for those materials unsuitable for treatment at temperatures greater than 80°C. The operating cycle has usually been provided as an alternative cycle on equipment designed for sterilization by LTS/F, although this has led to many difficulties in practice. Equipment providing a single LTS cycle has been encouraged by the publication of a new British Standard on the specification and performance requirements for low-temperature steam disinfectors (BS 3970 Part 5: 1990).

The cycle stages for the LTS process are as follows:

Stage 1 — Pre-heating. It is necessary to ensure that the walls and door of the chamber are preheated to minimize condensation and eliminate cold spots known to occur where there are masses of metal such as the chamber head-ring.

Stage 2—Air removal. Sufficient air is removed from the chamber, by pumped evacuation usually with the assistance of a number of steam pulses to assist the purging of traces of air from the load. A vacuum of 100 mbar or less is required.

Stage 3—Air ingress monitoring, to ensure that air does not leak back into the chamber during the disinfection stage at a rate greater than 5 mbar/min and thereby preclude attainment of disinfecting conditions.

Stage 4—Steam admission, until the temperature attained throughout the load is 73 ± 2°C.

Stage 5—Disinfection. The temperature throughout the chamber and load is held at 73°C for a hold period not less than 10 min.

Stage 6—The steam is removed from the chamber by vacuum to dry the load by evaporation of condensate.

Stage 7—Admission of air. Filtered air is admitted to the chamber to establish atmospheric pressure.

An efficient vacuum system is an essential component of the LTS cycle, both to ensure adequate steam penetration for the disinfection stage and to enable removal of moisture from the load in the final stages. In the original development (Alder & Gillespie, 1961), a 'dry' evacuation method was used which employed an Edwards type oil pump; subsequently a water ring pump reinforced with a strong steam eject-type vacuum pump working simultaneously was also found to be effective. This facility confers a major advantage of LTS over other heat disinfection processes, in enabling intricate wrapped instruments to be reliably heat-disinfected and released dry for immediate use or storage as required.

Low-temperature steam at 73–80°C is a useful method for disinfecting a wide range of heat-sensitive materials for hospital use, including various types of rigid endoscopes (cystoscopes), plastic articles, tubing and face-masks of anaesthetic apparatus and woollen blankets. It kills non-sporing organisms (most bacterial pathogens), is economical, speedy and can be automated easily. It offers a consistent and effective disinfection/decontamination process for heat-sensitive equipment and is increasingly regarded as an essential item of equipment in the Hospital Sterilization and Disinfection Unit (HSDU).

5 USE OF MICROWAVES

Microwave radiation, a form of electromagnetic energy generated within ovens at a typical frequency of 2450 MHz, has been extensively studied as an alternative energy source for sterilization. While some controversy remains about the nature of the microbicidal action (thermal and non-thermal effects), there have also been conflicting reports of sterilizing efficacy for micro-organisms in the dry or wet state (Goldblith & Wang, 1967; Lechowitch *et al.*, 1969; Vela & Wu, 1979).

Microwave sterilization processes have been proposed for a range of medical products including dental handpieces, vials for parenteral solutions and laboratory applications (Latimer & Matsen, 1977; Rohrer & Bulard, 1985; Lohmann & Manique, 1986). However, it has been demonstrated that microwave heating produces only a small and variable decrease in the number of bacterial spores present (Cowan & Allen, 1985) and extensive modification of the oven would be required to permit processing of certain materials such as metals. In a detailed comparison of microwave sterilization in the dry state with a conventional dry-heat oven, it was concluded that the only advantage was in a slightly shorter heat-up time. The D-values in both heating systems for *Bacillus subtilis* were identical (Jeng *et al.*, 1987). There is currently no fully validated and reliable sterilization or disinfection process utilizing microwaves accepted for hospital practice in the UK.

6 APPENDIX

Guidance to hospital authorities in respect of choice, installation, testing, commissioning and maintenance of steam sterilizers for unwrapped instruments and porous loads, and hot air sterilizers is given in the Health Technical Memorandum (HTM) No. 10 (Department of Health, 1980). A revision of HTM10 is currently under preparation. The British Standards Institution has published standards in respect of sterilizers and disinfectors for laboratory, pharmaceutical and medical use, including:

BS 2646 (1988) Autoclaves for sterilization in laboratories. Part 1: Specification for design and construction.

BS 3421 (1961) Specification for performance of electrically heated sterilizing ovens.

BS 3970 (1990) Sterilizing and disinfecting equipment for medical products. Part 1: Specification for general requirements; Part 3: Specification for steam sterilizers for wrapped goods and porous loads; Part 4: Specification for transportable steam sterilizers for unwrapped instruments and utensils; Part 5: Specification for low-temperature steam disinfectors.

Work is currently in progress in the European Standards Committee CEN/TC102 to produce a common European standard for steam sterilizers in 1992. The series of standards (ENs) will include the specification requirements and testing of large sterilizers for wrapped instruments and porous loads, for small transportable sterilizers, for biological and chemical indicators and for single-use and re-usable packaging materials.

7 REFERENCES

Advisory Group on the Management of Patients with Spongiform Encephalopathy (Creutzfeldt–Jakob Disease (CJD)) (1981) Report to the Chief Medical Officers of the Department of Health and Social Security, The Scottish Home and Health Department and the Welsh Office. London: HMSO.

Alder, V.G. (1968) *Sterilization by low temperature steam and formaldehyde under subatmospheric pressure at 80°C* (ed. Sneath, P.M.A.) pp. 141–155, COSPAR (Committee of Space Research) Technique Manual Series No. 4. Paris: COSPAR Secretariat.

Alder, V.G. (1987) The formaldehyde/low temperature steam sterilizing procedure. *Journal of Hospital Infection*, **9**, 194–200.

Alder, V.G. & Gillespie, W.A. (1957) The sterilization of dressings. *Journal of Clinical Pathology*, **10**, 299–306.

Alder, V.G. & Gillespie, W.A. (1961) Disinfection of woollen blankets in steam at subatmospheric pressure. *Journal of Clinical Pathology*, **14**, 515–518.

Alder, V.G., Boss, E., Gillespie, W.A. & Swann, A.J. (1971) Residual disinfection of wool blankets treated with formaldehyde. *Journal of Applied Bacteriology*, **34**, 757–763.

Alder, V.G., Brown, A.M. & Gillespie, W.A. (1966) Disinfection of heat-sensitive material by low-temperature steam and formaldehyde. *Journal of Clinical Pathology*, **19**, 83–89.

Alder, V.G., Gingell, J.C. & Mitchell, J.P. (1971) Disinfection of cystoscopes by subatmospheric steam and formaldehyde at 80°C. *British Medical Journal*, **iii**, 677–680.

Blake, G.C., Cornick, D.E.R. & Vidie, J. (1977) Testing of low temperature steam-formaldehyde with *B. stearothermophilus* spores. *Hospital Engineering*, **22**, 19–21.

Bowie, J.H., Kelsey, J.C. & Thompson, G.R. (1963) The Bowie and Dick autoclave tape test. *Lancet*, **1**, 586–587.

British Pharmaceutical Codex (1973)

Bühlmann, X., Gay, M. & Schiller, I. (1973) Test objects containing *Bacillus stearothermophilus* spores for the monitoring of antimicrobial treatment in steam autoclaves. Results obtained with commercial preparations and with the authors' own test objects. *Pharmaceutica Acta Helvetica*, **48**, 223–224.

Central Sterilizing Club (1986) Working Party Report on 'Washer/Disinfection Machines'. Central Sterilizing Club.

Church, B.D. & Halvorson, H. (1959) Dependence of heat resistance of bacterial endospores in their dipicolinic acid content. *Nature, London*. **183**, 124–125.

Cook, A.M. & Brown, M.R.W. (1960) Preliminary studies of the heat resistance of bacterial spores on paper carriers. *Journal of Pharmacy and Pharmacology*, **12**, 116T–118T.

Cowan, M.E. & Allen, J. (1985) Microwave processing of dehydrated culture media. *Medical Laboratory Sciences*, **42**, 156–160.

Cripps, N., Deverill, C.E.A. & Ayliffe, G.A.J. (1976) Problems with low-temperature steam and formaldehyde sterilizers. *Hospital Engineering* (International Federation Issue). **19**, 30–31.

Darmady, E.M., Hughes, K.E.A. & Tuke, W. (1957) Sterilization of syringes by infra-red radiation. *Journal of Clinical Pathology*, **10**, 291–298.

Ernst, R.R. (1977) Sterilization by heat. In *Disinfection, Sterilization and Preservation* (ed. Block, S.S.) 2nd Ed. pp. 481–739. Philadelphia: Lea & Febiger.

Esmarch, E. (1902) Die Wirking von Formalinwässer/dämpfen in Disinfectionsapparat. *Hygenische Rundschau*, **12**, 961–970.

European Pharmacopeia (1990).

Francis, A.E. (1959) Disinfection of cystoscopes by pasteurisation. *Proceedings of the Royal Society of Medicine*, **52**, 998–1000.

Gardner, J.F. & Peel, M.M. (1991) *Introduction to Sterilization, Disinfection and Infection Control*. Edinburgh: Churchill Livingstone.

Gibson, G.L. (1977) Processing urinary endoscopes in a low-temperature steam and formaldehyde autoclave. *Journal of Clinical Pathology*, **30**, 269–274.

Gibson, G.L. (1980) Processing heat-sensitive instruments and materials by low-temperature steam and formaldehyde. *Journal of Hospital Infection*, **1**, 95–101.

Gibson, G.L. & Johnston, H.P. (1967) Practical sterilization by low-temperature steam with formaldehyde. *British Hospital Journal and Social Services Review*, 1208–1215.

Gibson, G.L., Johnston, H.P. & Turkington, V.E. (1968)

Residual formaldehyde after low temperature steam and formaldehyde sterilization. *Journal of Clinical Pathology*, **21**, 771–775.

Gillespie, W.A. & Mitchell, J.P. (1967) Sterilization and Disinfection of Cystoscopes. In *Notes on Sterilization*. No. 1.: The Association of Clinical Pathologists.

Goldblith, S.A. & Wang, D.I.C. (1967) Effect of microwaves on *Escherichia coli* and *Bacillus subtilis*. *Applied Microbiology*, **15**, 1371–1375.

Grecz, N., Tang, T. & Rajan, K.S. (1972) In *Spores V*. (eds Halwassan, H.O., Hanson, R. & Campbell, L.L.) Fifth International Spore Conference, pp. 53–60. Washington: American Society for Microbiology.

Handlos, V. (1979) Formaldehyde sterilization, 2. Formaldehyde steam sterilization, the process and its influence on formaldehyde residuals. *Archives for Pharmaci og Chimi, Scientific Edition*, **7**, 1–11.

HEI 95/80. Departmental advice on some aspects of disinfection and sterilization (1980) Issue 88, Item 95/80, 26–33. Health Equipment Information. London: HMSO.

HTM (1980) *Health Technical Memorandum, No. 10, Sterilizers* (under revision). London: DHSS.

Hurrell, D.J., Line, S.J. & Cutts, D.W. (1983) Isolating samples in the chamber of a steam–formaldehyde steriliser. *Journal of Applied Bacteriology*, **55**, 135–142.

Jeng, D.K.H., Kaczmarek, K.A., Wodworth, A.G. & Balasky, G. (1987) Mechanism of microwave sterilization in the dry state. *Applied and Environmental Microbiology*, **53**, 2133–2137.

Knox, R. & Penikett, E.J.K. (1958) Influence of initial vacuum on steam sterilization of dressings. *British Medical Journal*, **1**, 680–682.

Latimer, J.M. & Matsen, J.M. (1977) Microwave oven irradiation as a method for bacterial decontamination in a clinical microbiology laboratory. *Journal of Clinical Microbiology*, **6**, 340–342.

Lawrence, C.A. (1968) In *Disinfection, Sterilization and Preservation* (eds Lawrence, C.A. & Block, S.S.) p. 12. Philadelphia: Lea and Febiger.

Lechowitch, R.V., Beuchat, L.R., Fox, K.I. & Webster, F.H. (1969) Procedure for evaluating the effects of 2450 mega-hertz microwaves upon *Streptococcus faecalis* and *Saccharomyces cerevisiae*. *Applied Microbiology*, **17**, 106–110.

Levinson, H.S., Hyatt, M.T. & Moore, F.E. (1961) Dependence of the heat resistance of bacterial spores on calcium: dipicolinic acid ratio. *Biochemical and Biophysical Research Communications*, **5**, 417–421.

Line, S.J. & Pickerill, J.K. (1973) Testing a steam formaldehyde sterilizer for gas penetration efficiency. *Journal of Clinical Pathology*, **26**, 716–720.

Lohmann, S. & Manique, F. (1986) Microwave sterilization of vials. *Journal of Parenteral Science and Technology*, **40**, 25–30.

Marcos, D. & Wiseman, D. (1979) Measurement of formaldehyde concentrations in a subatmospheric steam-formaldehyde autoclave. *Journal of Clinical Pathology*, **32**, 567–575.

Maurer, I.M. (1984) *Hospital Hygiene*. 3rd Ed. London: Edward Arnold.

Medical Research Council (1959) Sterilization by steam under increased pressure. A report to the Medical Research Council by the Working Party on Pressure-Steam Sterilizers. *Lancet*, **i**, 427–435.

Mitchell, J.P. & Alder, V.G. (1975) The disinfection of urological endoscopes. *British Journal of Urology*, **47**, 571–576.

Nordgren, G. (1939) Investigations on the sterilisation efficiency of gaseous formaldehyde. *Acta Pathologica et Microbiologica Scandinavica*, Supplement xi. 1–165.

Oates, K., Deverill, C.A., Phelps, M. & Collins, B.J. (1983) The design of a laboratory autoclave system. *Journal of Hospital Infection*, **4**, 181–190.

Perkins, J.J. (1960) *Principles and Methods of Sterilization*. 2nd Ed. Springfield: Charles C. Thomas.

Pharmaceutical Codex (1979).

Pickerill, J.K. (1975) Practical system for steam-formaldehyde sterilizing. *Laboratory Practice*, **24**, 401–404.

Rohrer, M.D. & Bulard, R.A. (1985) Microwave sterilization. *Journal of the American Dental Association*, **110**, 194–198.

Sykes, G. (1965) *Disinfection and Sterilization*. 2nd Ed. London: E. & F.N. Spon.

Vela, G.R. & Wu, J.F. (1979) Mechanism of lethal action of 2450 MHz radiation on microorganisms. *Applied Microbiology*, **37**, 550–553.

Weymes, C. (1977) Low temperature steam and formalin. *ASSA Journal*, **6**(2), 8, 10.

Weymes, C., White, J.D. & Harris, C. (1975) *Studies in the use of low concentrations of formaldehyde with steam at subatmospheric pressures as a method of sterilizing non-porous heat sensitive items*. Greater Glasgow Health Board, Sterilization Research Centre. No. 4.

Wilkinson, G.R., Peacock, F.G. & Robins, E.L. (1960) A shorter sterilizing cycle for solutions heated in an autoclave. *Journal of Pharmacy and Pharmacology*, **12**, 197T–202T.

B·DESTRUCTION OF BACTERIAL SPORES BY THERMAL METHODS

1 INTRODUCTION

A variety of different thermal methods is applied in large-scale sterilization processes. These methods include autoclaving using saturated steam or high-pressure water (Ernst, 1968: Brennan *et al.*, 1969), high-temperature–short-time sterilization using steam injection or heat-exchanging systems (Ashton, 1977) and continuous sterilization with either superheated steam (metal cans: Denny & Matthys, 1975; Quast *et al.*, 1977) or short-wave infrared radiation (glass vessels: Molin, 1976). The various heating methods have many technical differences, but as far as bacterial spores are concerned they are relatively similar. However, apart from the time/temperature cycle there is one major difference, namely whether the method is based on moist (wet) heat or on dry heat. Moist heat is by definition a condition where the water activity (a_w) is 1.0 and dry heat thus represents all conditions where the a_w is less than 1.0 (Pflug & Schmidt, 1968).

The heat inactivation kinetics of bacterial spores are strongly dependent on whether the spores are exposed to moist or dry heat.

Whatever heat sterilization method is used, the most important consideration when evaluating the effectiveness of a specific heating cycle is the a_w value. The inactivation rate of spores exposed to heat in a certain sterilization process can thus be calculated on the basis of heat resistance data achieved from inactivation studies at a defined a_w. The heat resistance of the spores is not, however, solely influenced by the a_w, but also by a number of other parameters. These parameters, on the other hand, are not necessarily directly linked to a specific sterilization method, but rather to the nature of the substrate or material with which the spore is associated.

In the present review an account of the various parameters which influence the heat resistance of bacterial spores is given and discussed in the light of current ideas concerning the heat inactivation mechanisms of spores.

2 KINETICS

Micro-organisms are generally considered to be heat-inactivated in geometric regression where in each equal successive time interval the same fraction of remaining viable cells is destroyed. This process can be described in equation (13.1):

$$\log N_T = -\frac{T}{D} + \log N_0 \qquad (13.1)$$

where N_0 is the initial viable cell number, D is the microbial inactivation rate (the time needed to reduce the population by 90% at a certain temperature) and N_T is the viable cell number after T minutes of heating. If the logarithmic number of surviving cells is plotted versus time, the resulting curve ('survivor curve' or 'inactivation curve') is a straight line.

Furthermore, the relationship between the inactivation rate and temperature can be represented by a straight line (thermal resistance curve). This empirically found phenomenon was first observed by Bigelow (1921). The temperature coefficient, D_r, of Bigelow is described in equation (13.2):

$$\log D_r = \frac{1}{z}(T_0 - T) + \log D_{r_0} \qquad (13.2)$$

where T_0 is the initial temperature, D_{r_0} is specified and T is the new temperature corresponding to D_r. As seen from equation (13.2), the z value is a measure of the slope of the straight line and the number of degrees (°C) of temperature change necessary to change to D-value by a factor of 10.

The logarithmic order of inactivation and the temperature coefficient model of Bigelow are in general considered to be valid for both moist and dry heat inactivation of bacterial spores.

Deviations from the logarithmic order of inactivation are frequently reported in the literature. The course of the non-linear inactivation curves has been explained by experimental artefacts (Stumbo, 1965), the multiple critical sites theory (Rahn, 1943; Moats, 1971) and heterogeneity of spore heat resistance (Han, 1975; Han *et al.*, 1976; Sharpe & Bektash, 1977). Nevertheless, it should be borne in mind when inactivation data are evaluated that the logarithmic inactivation model imposes a number of restrictions on an experimental programme. According to Pflug (1973) these are:

1 the spores of the sample being evaluated must be genetically, chemically and physically uniform;

2 the conditions of the heat-inactivation tests must be constant on a test-to-test basis;

3 the overall handling procedures, the media, incubation temperature and the recovery method must be constant.

Common types of deviations from linearity are a shoulder or a sudden drop at the beginning of the inactivation curve and a 'tailing' of the later portion of the curve. All types have been reported in both moist and dry heat-inactivation studies, e.g. in moist heat by Russell (1971, 1982) and in dry heat by Fox & Pflug (1968), Alderton & Snell (1969) and Staat & Beakley (1969). Tailing has been extensively discussed by Cerf (1977).

Several workers have pointed out that the linear relationship obtained between the inactivation rate and temperature is an approximation only valid in narrow temperature ranges (Rahn, 1945; Amaha, 1953; Levine, 1956) and the Arrhenius analysis is sometimes proposed as an alternative to the temperature coefficient model of Bigelow. Deviations from the model of Bigelow have been reported to occur in moist heat by for example, Wang *et al.* (1964) and Edwards *et al.* (1965a) at temperatures >120°C, and in dry heat at temperatures >160°C by Oag (1940). However, in dry heat at low a_w, Molin (1977c) showed that the thermal resistance curve of *Bacillus subtilis* spores was straight (constant z-value) in the temperature interval of 37–190°C. This supports the accuracy of the Bigelow model at conditions of low a_w values. With moist heat, on the other hand, neither the Bigelow model nor the Arrhenius model seems to fit when applied over a wide temperature range (Davies *et al.*, 1977; Jonsson *et al.*, 1977).

3 INHERENT HEAT RESISTANCE

3.1 Moist heat

The heat resistance varies between spores of different species and strains. The magnitude of this genetically determined variation is often difficult to estimate due to the influence of a wide spectrum of other parameters critical to the apparent heat resistance (see below). However, the order of magnitude of the moist heat resistance for a range of organisms is indicated in Table 18.2.

It has been shown by Warth (1978) that the heat resistance of the spores of different *Bacillus* spp. increased with an increasing optimum growth temperature for the vegetative cells of the organism. Thus, the spores of organisms with a high optimum temperature (55–67°C), e.g. *B. coagulans*, *B. stearothermophilus* and *B. caldolyticus*, had the

Table 18.2 Some D- and z-values for spores heated in phosphate buffer (pH 7) or in water

Organism	Strain	Investigated temperature range (°C)	D-value (min)	z-value (°C)	Reference
B. cereus 1	—	104–121	$D_{121} = 0.03$	9.9	Bradshaw *et al.*, 1975
B. cereus 2	—	116–129	$D_{121} = 2.4$	7.9	
B. coagulans	604	115–125	$D_{120} = 2.3$	7.2	Daudin & Cerf, 1977
B. globisporus	ATCC 23301	85–90	$D_{90} = 11$	7.8	Michels & Visser, 1976 Bender & Marquis, 1985
B. megaterium	ATCC 19213	85–100	$D_{92} = 1$	6.3	
B. psychrosaccharolyticus	ATCC 23296	81–90	$D_{90} = 4.5$	8.5	
B. stearothermophilus	NCIB 8923	115–130	$D_{120} = 5.8$	13	Schofield & Abdelgadir, 1974
B. stearothermophilus	NCIB 8919	115–130	$D_{120} = 5.3$	11	
B. stearothermophilus	NCIB 8924	115–130	$D_{120} = 1.0$	8.9	
B. stearothermophilus	ATCC 7953	111–125	$D_{121} = 2.1$	8.5	Jonsson *et al.*, 1977
B. stearothermophilus	—	110–121	$D_{121} = 3.4$	7.6	Pflug & Smith, 1977
B. stearothermophilus	ATCC 7953	110–120	$D_{118} = 10$	5.7	Bender & Marquis, 1985
B. subtilis	5230	77–121	$D_{121} = 0.5$	14	Fox & Eder, 1969
B. subtilis	NCIB 8054	85–95	$D_{90} = 4.8$	9.3	Härnulv & Snygg, 1972
B. subtilis var. *niger*	—	90–100	$D_{94} = 10$	6.6	Bender & Marquis, 1985
C. aerofoetidum	NCTC 505	80–95	$D_{90} = 139$	6.8	Roberts *et al.*, 1966a
C. botulinum	—	104–127	$D_{101} = 5.5$	8.5	Stumbo *et al.*, 1950
C. botulinum	62A	104–113	$D_{113} = 1.7$	11	Alderton *et al.*, 1976
C. botulinum	—	110–115	$D_{110} = 1.2$	10	Odlaug *et al.*, 1978
C. histolyticum	NCIB 503	70–90	$D_{90} = 12$	10	Roberts *et al.*, 1966b
C. perfringens	NCTC 8238	80–100	$D_{90} = 120$	9	Roberts, 1968
C. perfringens	NCTC 8797	80–100	$D_{90} = 15$	12–24	
C. perfringens	NCTC 8798	80–100	$D_{90} = 36$	16	
C. perfringens	NCTC 3181	80–100	$D_{90} = 5.0$	6	
C. perfringens	NCTC 8084	80–100	$D_{90} = 4.5$	7	
C. perfringens	NCTC 8798	99–116	$D_{101} = 2.3–3.3$	10–12	Bradshaw *et al.*, 1977
C. perfringens	NCTC 10240	99–116	$D_{101} = 1.4–5.2$	9.5–12	
C. sporogenes	PA 3679	104–132	$D_{101} = 37$	9.8	Stumbo *et al.*, 1950
C. sporogenes	NCTC 532	70–90	$D_{90} = 34$	13	Roberts *et al.*, 1966b
C. sporogenes	NCTC 532	105–115	$D_{103} = 43$	9.0	Pflug & Smith 1977

highest moist heat resistance. *B. stearothermophilus* is also a commonly used indicator organism for the biological controlling of moist heat sterilization processes (Kereluk & Gammon, 1973; Heintz *et al.*, 1976). However, the calculated *z*-values (Table 18.2) indicate that *Clostridium* spp. are often the most heat-resistant spores at higher inactivation temperatures (>140°C). The D_{100} values between different species were found to span 600-fold or 3000-fold by Beaman *et al.* (1982) and Beaman & Gerhardt (1986), respectively. In both cases, *B. stearothermophilus* was the most resistant species while *B. cereus* spores were amongst the most heat-sensitive ones.

It should be noted that the genetic variation in moist heat resistance between different strains of the same species may be of a considerable magnitude. For example, Roberts (1968) found that the D_{90} value for seven strains of *Clostridium perfringens* had a maximum variation of 48 times (*z* value 4 times) and Bradshaw *et al.* (1975) reported the D_{121} value of two strains of *B. cereus* to vary by a factor of 78 (*z* value 1.2).

3.2 Dry heat

Some data taken from the literature concerning the dry heat resistance of spores of different organisms are shown in Table 18.3.

As can be seen, the variations in data for the same species, in some cases even within the same investigation, are so large that it is almost impossible to draw any conclusions about the significance of the differences in heat resistance between the different species and strains. For example, the *z* values reported for *B. subtilis* var. *niger* spores vary from 13°C to 139°C. This can be compared to the variation in *z* value of 6.8°C to 24°C in moist heat, including all organisms listed in Table 18.2. The main reason for the large discrepancy in the dry heat resistance data may be that the different studies have been performed at different a_w values. The a_w is fixed for all inactivation studies in moist heat, but can have an infinite number of values between 0.0 and 1.0 in dry heat. However, in a standardized test system, Molin (1977a) attempted to evaluate the magnitude of the inherent genetic differences in dry heat resistance between nine different *Bacillus* strains (including seven different species). The highest *D* values were recorded for *B. subtilis* var. *niger* spores and the lowest for *B. cereus* spores. The difference was about 10-fold in the whole temperature range investigated. The highest *z*-value (31°C) was obtained for *B. coagulans* and the lowest (19°C) for a strain of *B. stearothermophilus*. It should be pointed out that the difference in dry heat resistance between the different *Bacillus* spores tested in this investigation was relatively small compared with the variations reported in the literature, especially with respect to the *z*-value.

Generally, *B. subtilis* var. *niger* is considered to be a suitable indicator organism for the biological control of dry heat sterilization processes (Bruch *et al.*, 1963; Craven *et al.*, 1968; Costin & Grigo, 1974).

4 PRE-HEATING HISTORY

4.1 Sporulation medium

Components of the sporulation medium which affect spore formation include carbohydrates, amino acids, fatty acids, cations and phosphates. The effects of these are reflected in the number of spores produced and also in the properties of the spores, for example, their heat resistance. The influence of these and other nutrients on moist heat resistance has been thoroughly reviewed by Roberts & Hitchins (1969) and Russell (1971, 1982).

An attempt to estimate the importance of medium composition on the dry heat resistance of *B. subtilis* spores was made by Molin & Svensson (1976). *B. subtilis* spores were investigated on 20 different media. The yield varied by a factor of 10^6 and the variation of the D_{160} value was about 10-fold. However, the main part of the tested media gave spores with a D_{160} value in the range of 40–150s, i.e. the heat resistance changed by a factor of about 4.

4.2 Sporulation temperature

The moist heat resistance of *Bacillus* spores, as seen from the *D*-value, has in some investigations been found to increase when the spores were pro-

Table 18.3 Some *D*- and *z*-values for spores inactivated by dry heat

Organism	Strain	Investigated temperature range (°C)	*D*-value (min)	*z*-value (°C)	Reference
B. cereus	NCIB 9373	140–160	$D_{160} = 0.03$	22	Molin, 1977a
B. coagulans	NCIB 9365	140–170	$D_{160} = 0.18$	31	
B. megaterium	NCIB 9376	150–170	$D_{160} = 0.06$	21	
B. polymyxa		145–182	$D_{177} = 0.1$	28	Collier & Townsend, 1956
B. polymyxa	NCIB 8158	150–170	$D_{160} = 0.27$	22	Molin, 1977a
B. pumilus	NCTC 10337	150–180	$D_{160} = 0.23$	25	
B. stearothermophilus	1518	160–180	$D_{177} = 0.1$	26	Collier & Townsend, 1956
B. stearothermophilus	1518	121–160	$D_{160} = 0.35$	24	Bruch *et al.*, 1963
B. stearothermophilus	NCA 1518	100–125	$D_{160} = 3.2–27$	14–22	Alderton & Snell, 1969
B. stearothermophilus		100–160	$D_{160} = 5$	40	Niepokojczycka & Zakrzewski, 1972
B. stearothermophilus	ATCC 7953	150–170	$D_{160} = 0.08$	19	Molin, 1977a
B. stearothermophilus	NCTC 10339	150–180	$D_{160} = 0.16$	26–29	
B. subtilis	5230	121–160	$D_{160} = 1.4–1.7$	18	Pheil *et al.*, 1967
B. subtilis	5230	124–140	$D_{110} = 47–95$	17–55	Fox & Pflug, 1968
B. subtilis	5230	95–152	$D_{112} = 10$	17	Fox & Eder, 1969
B. subtilis	NCIB 8054	105–145	$D_{112} = 12–150$	13–19	Härnulv & Snygg, 1972
B. subtilis	NCIB 8054	150–170	$D_{160} = 0.25$	23	Molin 1977a
B. subtilis	ATCC 6633	120–180	$D_{160} = 0.43$	23	Molin & Östlund, 1975
B. subtilis	1–12	95–110	$D_{110} = 2–100$	10–70	Kooiman & Jacobs, 1977
B. subtilis var. *niger*		121–160	$D_{160} = 1.8$	27	Bruch *et al.*, 1963
B. subtilis var. *niger*		105–160	$D_{125} = 78–3200$	13–32	Angelotti *et al.*, 1968
B. subtilis var. *niger*		200–300	$D_{210} = 0.02–0.03$	29, 139	Bruch & Smith, 1968
B. subtilis var. *niger*		115–135	$D_{125} = 2–220$	13–22	Wang, 1968
B. subtilis var. *niger*		120–150	$D_{150} = 0.23–0.35$	18–23	Filho, 1975
B. subtilis var. *niger*	ATCC 9372	120–190	$D_{160} = 0.3–0.8$	22	Molin & Östlund, 1976
B. xerothermodurans	ATCC 27380	125–150	$D_{150} = 150$	15	Bond & Favero, 1975
C. sporogenes	PA 3679	148–177	$D_{177} = 0.1$	60	Collier & Townsend, 1956
C. sporogenes	PA 3679	124–160	$D_{160} = 1.0–3.9$	18–21	Augustin & Pflug, 1967
C. sporogenes	PA 3679	121–160	$D_{160} = 1.9–2.4$	22	Pheil *et al.*, 1967

duced at higher temperatures (El-Bisi & Ordal, 1956; Lechowitch & Ordal, 1960; Cook & Gilbert, 1968b). El-Bisi & Ordal (1956) showed that although the *D* value increased at increasing growth temperatures, the *z*-value decreased.

Yokoya & York (1965) and Rey *et al.* (1975) tested the influence of incubation temperature on *B. coagulans* and *Cl. perfringens* respectively, but noted no effect on the heat resistance. Sugiyama (1951) studied *Clostridium botulinum* spores and reported that the highest resistance was obtained at a sporulation temperature of 37°C. On the other hand, Beaman & Gerhardt (1986) demonstrated that an increasing sporulation temperature causes reductions in protoplast water content between limits of *ca.* 57% and 28% (wet weight basis), thereby increasing sporal heat resistance. Futhermore, a heat shock of dormant spores does not necessarily break the dormancy in all exposed spores (so-called heat activation). Some spores may become only partly activated, which can actually increase their resistance by a factor of 2.6 (Beaman *et al.*, 1988).

It should be noted that the reports mentioned deal with the influence of incubation temperature on the moist heat resistance of spores. There is a lack of data concerning the relations between sporulation temperature and dry heat resistance of spores.

4.3 Chemical state

The 'chemical state' of bacterial spores can be manipulated by *in-vitro* chemical pre-treatments between a heat-sensitive and a heat-resistant state (Alderton & Snell, 1963; Alderton *et al.*, 1964; Ando & Tsuzuki, 1983; Bender & Marquis, 1985). The change in resistance, under certain circumstances, may also occur during the course of heat treatment.

The bacterial spore has a reversible cation exchange system, which when loaded with Ca^{2+} ions, gives a spore of high resistance (resistant state) and when loaded with hydronium ions gives a spore of low resistance (sensitive state). The change in moist heat resistance (*D*-value) between spores of the two states can be more than 10-fold (Alderton *et al.*, 1976). The phenomenon has also been shown to exist in dry heat (Alderton & Snell, 1969, 1970).

It should be stressed that even if the *D*-values at lower temperatures are decreasing by mineralization with hydronium ions, the *z*-value of H-spores is higher (Bender & Marquis, 1985). Thus, the difference in heat resistance between spores of the two chemical states decreases with increasing inactivation temperature.

5 HEATING CONDITIONS

5.1 Water activity

The heat resistance of bacterial spores is generally considerably higher in dry heat ($a_w < 1.0$) than in moist heat ($a_w = 1.0$). It was shown by Murrell & Scott (1966) that the heat resistance (*D* value) of *B. megaterium* spores heated at constant water activities varied by a factor greater than 1000 in the water activity range of 0.0–1.0. The highest *D*-value was reported at a_w values of 0.2–0.4. These findings have since been confirmed by Angelotti *et al.* (1968), Alderton & Snell (1970) and Härnulv & Snygg (1972) in studies on spores of *B. subtilis* var. *niger*, *B. stearothermophilus* and *B. subtilis* (NCIB 8054), respectively. It was further shown by Brannen & Garst (1972) that even in very dry systems ($a_w < 0.013$) changes in the water activity influenced the heat resistance of *B. subtilis* spores. Brannen & Garst found that in the a_w range of 6×10^{-5} to 1×10^{-2} the highest *D* value was obtained at 1×10^{-2} and the lowest at 7×10^{-4}.

The investigations mentioned above have been carried out at constant a_w values. Such constant conditions in a_w can hardly be achieved in dry heat sterilization under actual working conditions where the a_w is changing with temperature and treatment time during the course of the heat exposure. Thus, in a system with no control of a_w, the available amount of water present in the spores during heating is dependent on the initial water content of the spores, the water level of the heating environment and the desiccation (or sorption) rate of the spores during the heat treatment. The desiccation rate, which has been shown to be critical for heat resistance (Angelotti, 1968), is strongly dependent on whether the heating system is open or closed, i.e. if the spores are enclosed within a limited space or if they are surrounded by an 'infinite' space. The influence of the water content of spores heated in open systems has been studied by Hoffman *et al.* (1968), Fox & Pflug (1968) and Drummond & Pflug (1970), amongst others.

Hoffman *et al.* showed that the D_{160} value was changed about three times depending on whether the spores before heating were equilibrated to the relative humidity (r.h.) of 11% or 85%. The difference in D-value increased with decreasing temperature. It has also been shown that spores equilibrated to a high moisture content generally have a higher dry heat resistance in open systems, as seen from the D-value, than spores equilibrated to a low initial water content (Hoffman *et al.*, 1968; Drummond & Pflug, 1970).

It has been proposed by Alderton & Snell (1970) that anomalous discrepancies in z-values obtained in some dry heat inactivation studies, e.g. Angelotti *et al.* (1968) and Bruch & Smith (1968), are due to changes in water activity of the spores during heating. Thus, the obtained D-values in such a system are dependent not only on the temperature but also on the a_w, which is changing with the temperature and either diminishing or reinforcing the temperature effect on the inactivation rate.

5.2 pH and ionic environment

It is well documented that factors such as pH, buffer components, sodium chloride and cations in the suspending menstruum, can influence the heat resistance of bacterial spores (Roberts & Hitchins, 1969; Russell, 1971, 1982). For example, the resistance of *B. stearothermophilus* spores heated in acetate buffer was successively increased from a pH value of 3.0 (D_{100} = 23 min) to one of 6.0 (D_{100} = 14 h). At a pH value of over 8.0 the resistance started to decrease again (Anderson & Friesen, 1974). According to Löwik & Anema (1972), the z-value is independent of pH.

Phosphates generally seem to decrease the moist heat resistance of spores (Cook & Gilbert, 1968b; Adams, 1973; Steinbuch, 1977), the magnitude of influence depending on the spore strain, Adams (1973) found that the heat resistance (D_{100}) of three different *Clostridium* spp. was, respectively, 1.4, 2.0 and 41 times higher in water than in 60 mM sodium phosphate buffer (pH 7).

Sodium chloride in smaller concentrations is reported to have a weak sensitizing effect (Anderson *et al.*, 1949) or no effect at all (Roberts *et al.*, 1966b). In contrast, Härnulv & Snygg (1972) demonstrated that the D_{95} value of *B. subtilis* spores decreased by a factor of about 6 when heated in 26% NaCl (a_w = 0.78), compared with water vapour at the same a_w.

Ca^{2+} ions have been reported to protect spores from moist heat (Steinbuch, 1977) which contradicts earlier findings by Sugiyama (1951). However, in the light of newer findings on the importance of the chemical state of spores, it is obvious that Ca^{2+} ions can improve the heat resistance of insufficiently Ca-loaded spores. Bender & Marquis (1985) showed that the heat resistance of remineralized H-spores increased in the order K < Mg < Mn < Ca. Remineralization with Na^+ ions yielded spores with an even lower heat resistance than the H-spores.

5.3 Organic substances

Proteins (e.g. serum albumin) and carbohydrates (e.g. sucrose) are known to increase the heat resistance of bacterial spores (Amaha & Sakaguchi, 1954; Roberts & Hitchins, 1969; Russell, 1971; Smelt *et al.*, 1977). However, under certain conditions some sugars seem to have the ability to decrease the heat resistance. The D_{160} value of *B. subtilis* spores in dry heat was decreased by a factor of 3 when heated in the presence of glucose or fructose. On the other hand, the D_{160} value of the same spores was increased to the same degree in sucrose (Molin, 1977b).

Furthermore, the concentration of viable spores at the start of heat exposure may affect the measured D-value. This has been shown in both moist heat (Casolari, 1974) and in dry heat (Molin & Östlund, 1976).

Spores heated in the presence of lipids have a higher heat resistance than spores heated in pure phosphate buffer (Molin & Snygg, 1967; Senhaji & Loncin, 1977). It has been argued that this effect is due solely to a reduction in a_w by the added lipid (Russell, 1971). This assumption was also supported by a numerical simulation of results obtained from spores heated in soya bean oil (Senhaji, 1977). However, when the effect of different lipids on the spore resistance was measured in dry heat, i.e. all spores were heated at the same low a_w regardless of their being enclosed in lipid or not, it was shown that the different lipids increased the heat resistance in the order: olive oil < triolein < soya bean oil < tricaprin < trilaurin (Molin, 1977b). Spores heated in the presence of tricaprin or trilaurin had a significantly higher heat resistance than the controls (clean spores), while spores heated in soya bean oil had about the same resistance as the controls. It may be pointed out that in the above study only the *D*-values were influenced by the lipids. The *z*-value was not affected.

5.4 Gas atmosphere

The effect of various gas atmospheres on the dry heat resistance of spores has been studied by Pheil *et al.* (1967) and Filho (1975), amongst others. These studies show only a minor influence of the gas atmosphere (CO_2, O_2 or N_2) on heat resistance. Thus, it seems that no significant advantages, with respect to the inactivation rate, are to be gained by exchanging the air with, for instance O_2 or CO_2, in dry heat sterilization processes.

5.5 Supporting material

Spores exposed to dry heat on carriers of different materials can show differences in heat resistance (Bruch *et al.*, 1963; Angelotti *et al.*, 1968; Bruch & Smith, 1968). Bruch *et al.* (1963), for example, found that the *D*-value of spores heated on three different carriers decreased in the order: sand > glass > paper. Angelotti *et al.* (1968) and Alderton & Snell (1970) suggested that drastic differences in heat resistance between spores applied on (or in) different materials, are due to differences in the a_w of the micro-environment of spores during heating, and not to any unknown characteristic of the material.

6 RECOVERY

6.1 Medium

Heat-damaged spores are sometimes more exacting in their growth requirements than are unheated spores. The composition of the recovery medium may thus affect the apparent resistance of heat-treated spores. The influence of the recovery medium on the moist heat resistance of bacterial spores is complex, but has been relatively well studied (reviewed by Roberts & Hitchins, 1969; Roberts, 1970; Russell, 1971, 1982).

Little information is available concerning the effect of the composition of the recovery medium on the dry heat resistance of spores. Augustin & Pflug (1967) reported that the apparent dry heat resistance of *Clostridium* spores varied on different recovery media. The D_{149} value varied with a factor of about two between seven different media tested. The *z*-value varied in the range of 18.3–21.7°C. The corresponding values in moist heat were a factor of three (D_{121} value) and 9.6–11°C (*z* value).

6.2 Temperature

Data on the influence of incubation temperature on the recovery of heat-damaged spores are scanty. There are indications that the recovery of moist heat-treated spores are more effective at temperatures somewhat below the optimum growth temperature of the organism (Williams & Reed, 1942; Edwards *et al.*, 1965b; Cook & Gilbert, 1968a; Futter & Richardson, 1970).

The temperature interval giving maximum recovery seems to be narrower for heated than for unheated spores. There are also indications that it is not the germination that is critical for recovery, but the outgrowth (Prentice & Clegg, 1974).

7 MECHANISMS OF HEAT INACTIVATION AND SPORE RESISTANCE

The mechanism(s) of heat inactivation of bacterial spores is (are) often linked to the mechanisms of heat resistance of spores. Different theories for the latter subject have been thoroughly discussed by, for example, Roberts & Hitchins (1969), Russell (1971), Gould (1977) and Gerhardt & Murrell (1978). Spore heat resistance is today best explained by a multi-component theory. This theory consists of four major components: (1) An inherent molecular component related to the temperature optima for spore-forming organisms, i.e. organisms with high temperature optimum of growth produce the most heat-resistant spores, while those with low optima produce the least resistant ones (Warth, 1978). (2) Heat resistance arises from dehydration of of the protoplast (Beaman *et al.*, 1984;

Koshikawa *et al.*, 1984; Nakashio & Gerhardt, 1985). This dehydration may be explained by theories as, for example, the 'osmoregulatory expanded cortex' theory (Gould & Dring, 1975) or 'anisotrophic swollen cortex by enzymatic cleavage' theory (Warth, 1977). (3) The third component of the spore heat resistance is associated with mineralization (see chemical state above). (4) The relationship between the dipicolinic acid and calcium content of the spore (Mallidis & Scholefield, 1987). It appears that the dehydration of the protoplast is the most important parameter for the heat resistance and that, for example, thermal adaptation and increased mineralization also cause reductions in protoplast water content (Beaman & Gerhardt, 1986). However, it may be difficult to understand fully the mechanisms of the extreme heat resistance of the bacterial spore before the fundamental principles of heat inactivation mechanisms of micro-organisms are known.

The heat inactivation of micro-ogranisms is generally believed to be due to denaturation of critical proteins and of RNA and DNA in the cell. It is believed that denaturation of proteins and nucleic acids is related to the breakage of the intramolecular hydrogen bonds which are responsible for the geometric structure of the molecules. A critical number of these bonds must be broken before denaturation takes place. The thermal death of micro-organisms has been discussed, in general terms, by Rahn (1945), Charm (1958), Pflug & Schmidt (1968) and Corry (1973) amongst others.

Brannen (1970) presented experimental evidence in favour of the assumption that the principal mechanism for moist heat inactivation of spores is DNA denaturation. This, however, somewhat contradicts the findings of Flowers & Adams (1976), who suggest that the site of injury is the spore structure destined to become the cell membrane or cell wall.

The resistance of spores to dry heat differs considerably from the resistance to moist heat concerning both inactivation rate (D-value) and temperature coefficient (z-value). The differences indicate that the critical protein denaturation follows different pathways in the two systems.

Dry heat inactivation has generally been considered to be primarily an oxidation process (Rahn, 1945; Sykes, 1965; Ernst, 1968; Wang, 1968). However, this contradicts the findings of Pheil *et al.* (1967) that showed the dry heat resistance of spores to be somewhat higher in oxygen than in air. Similar results have been reported by Rowe & Koesterer (1965) and Fox & Pflug (1968), who compared the resistance in air with that in nitrogen, i.e. the resistance in air was higher than that in nitrogen.

Considering the strong influence of a_w on the dry heat resistance of spores, a possible explanation of dry heat inactivation could be the removal of bound water critical for maintaining the helical structure of proteins. This belief is stressed in investigations that show that a certain level of water is necessary for the maintenance of heat stability in spores. If the spores were strongly desiccated by high vacuum drying, they would be sensitized to heat (Soper & Davies, 1971, 1973). Furthermore, it has been shown that *B. subtilis* spores heated at lower a_w are inactivated in accordance with a constant z-value (23°C) over the temperature interval of 37–190°C (Molin, 1977c). Thus, in a dry environment the spores were inactivated at growth temperature (D_{37} = 44 d) and this inactivation followed the same inactivation model as the one valid at high temperatures (140–190°C).

8 REFERENCES

Adams, D.M. (1973) Inactivation of *Clostridium perfringens* type A spores at ultra high temperatures. *Applied Microbiology*, **26**, 282–287.

Alderton, G., Ito, K.A. & Chen, J.K. (1976) Chemical manipulation of the heat resistance of *Clostridium botulinum* spores. *Applied and Environmental Microbiology*, **31**, 492–498.

Alderton, G. & Snell, N. (1963) Base exchange and heat resistance in bacterial spores. *Biochemical and Biophysical Research Communications*, **10**, 139–143.

Alderton, G. & Snell, N. (1969) Chemical states of bacterial spores: dry-heat resistance. *Applied Microbiology*, **17**, 745–749.

Alderton, G. & Snell, N. (1970) Chemical states of bacterial spores: heat resistance and its kinetics at intermediate water activity. *Applied Microbiology*, **19**, 565–572.

Alderton, G., Thompson, P.A. & Snell, N. (1964) Heat adaptation and ion exchange in *B. megaterium* spores. *Science*, **143**, 141–143.

Amaha, M. (1953) Heat resistance of Cameron's putrefactive anaerobe 3679 in phosphate buffer (*Clostridium sporogenes*). *Food Research*, **18**, 411–420.

Amaha, M. & Sakaguchi, K.-I (1954) Effects of carbohydrates, proteins, and bacterial cells in the heating media on the heat resistance of *Clostridium sporogenes*. *Journal of Bacteriology*, **68**, 338–345.

Anderson, E.E., Esselen, W.B. & Fellers, C.R. (1949) Effect of acids, salt, sugar, and other food ingredients on thermal resistance of *Bacillus thermoacidurans*. *Food Research*, **14**, 499–510.

Anderson, R.A. & Friesen, W.T. (1974) The thermal resistance of *Bacillus stearothermophilus* spores: The effects of temperature and pH of the heating medium. *Pharmaceutica Acta Helvetiae*, **49**, 295–298.

Ando, Y. & Tsuzuki, T. (1983) Mechanism of chemical manipulation of the heat resistance of *Clostridium perfringens* spores. *Journal of Applied Bacteriology*, **54**, 197–202.

Angelotti, R. (1968) Protective mechanisms affecting dry-heat sterilization. In *Sterilization Techniques for Instruments and Materials as Applied to Space Research* (ed. Sneath, P.H.A.) COSPAR Technique Manual Series, No. 4, pp. 59–74. Paris: COSPAR Secretariat.

Angelotti, R., Maryanski, J.H., Butler, T.F., Peeler, J.T. & Campbell, J.E. (1968) Influence of spore moisture content on the dry-heat resistance of *Bacillus subtilis* var. *niger*. *Applied Microbiology*, **16**, 735–745.

Ashton, T.R. (1977) Ultra-high-temperature treatment of milk and milk products. *World Animal Review*, **23**, 37–42.

Augustin, J.A.L. & Pflug, I.J. (1967) Recovery patterns of spores of putrefactive anaerobe 3679 in various subculture media after heat treatment. *Applied Microbiology*, **15**, 266–276.

Bigelow, W.D. (1921) The logarithmic nature of thermal death time curves. *Journal of Infectious Diseases*, **29**, 528–536.

Beaman, T.C. & Gerhardt, P. (1986) Heat resistance of bacterial spores correlated with protoplast dehydration, mineralization, and thermal adaptation. *Applied and Environmental Microbiology*, **52**, 1242–1246.

Beaman, T.C., Greenamyre, J.T., Corner, T.R., Pankratz, H.S. & Gerhardt, P. (1982) Bacterial spore heat resistance correlated with water content, wet density, and protoplast/sporoplast volume ratio. *Journal of Bacteriology*, **150**, 870–877.

Beaman, T.C., Koshiikawa, T., Pankratz, H.S. & Gerhardt, P. (1984) Dehydration partioned within core protoplast accounts for heat resistance of bacterial spores. *FEMS Microbiology Letters*, **24**, 47–51.

Beaman, T.C., Pankratz, H.S. & Gerhardt, P. (1988) Heat shock affects permeability and resistance of *Bacillus stearothermophilus* spores. *Applied and Environmental Micriobiology*, **54**, 2515–2520.

Bender, G.R. & Marquis, R. (1985) Spore heat resistance and specific mineralization. *Applied and Environmental Microbiology*, **50**, 1414–1421.

Bond, W.W. & Favero, M.S. (1975) Thermal profile of a *Bacillus* species (ATCC 27380) extremely resistant to dry heat. *Applied Microbiology*, **29**, 859–860.

Bradshaw, J.G., Peeler, J.T. & Twedt, R.M. (1975) Heat resistance of ileal loop-reactive *Bacillus cereus* strains isolated from commercially canned food. *Applied Microbiology*, **30**, 943–945.

Bradshaw, J.G., Peeler, J.T. & Twedt, R.M. (1977) Thermal inactivation of ileal loop-reactive *Clostridium perfringens* type A strains in phosphate buffer and beef gravy. *Applied and Environmental Microbiology*, **34**, 280–284.

Brannen, J.P. (1970) On the role of DNA in wet heat sterilisation of micro-organisms. *Journal of Theoretical Biology*, **27**, 425–432.

Brannen, J.P. & Garst, D.M. (1972) Dry heat inactivation of *Bacillus subtilis* var. *niger* spores as a function of relative humidity. *Applied Microbiology*, **23**, 1125–1130.

Brennan, J.G., Butters, J.R., Cowell, N.D. & Lilly, A.E.V. (1969) *Food Engineering Operations*. Amsterdam, London, New York: Elsevier.

Bruch, C.W., Koesterer, M.G. & Bruch, M.R. (1963) Dry-heat sterilization: Its development and application to components of exobiological space probes. *Developments in Industrial Microbiology*, **4**, 334–342.

Bruch, M.K. & Smith, F.W. (1968) Dry heat resistance of spores of *Bacillus subtilis* var. *niger* on kapton and teflon film at high temperatures. *Applied Microbiology*, **16**, 1841–1846.

Casolari, A. (1974) Non-logarithmic behaviour of heat-inactivation curves of P.A. 3679 spores. *Proceedings, IV International Congress of Food Science and Technology*, **3**, 86–92.

Cerf, O. (1977) A review: tailing of survival curves of bacterial spores. *Journal of Applied Bacteriology*, **42**, 1–19.

Charm, S.E. (1958) The kinetics of bacterial inactivation by heat. *Food Technology*, **12**, 4–8.

Collier, C.P. & Townsend, C.T. (1956) The resistance of bacterial spores to superheated steam. *Food Technology*, **10**, 477–481.

Cook, A.M. & Gilbert, R.J. (1968a) Factors affecting the heat resistance of *Bacillus stearothermophilus* spores. I. The effect of recovery conditions on colony count of unheated and heated spores. *Journal of Food Technology*, **3**, 285–293.

Cook, A.M. & Gilbert, R.J. (1968b) Factors affecting the heat resistance of *Bacillus stearothermophilus* spores. II. The effect of sporulating conditions and nature of the heating medium. *Journal of Food Technology*, **3**, 295–302.

Corry, J.E.L. (1973) The water relations and heat resistance of microogranisms. *Progress in Industrial Microbiology*, **12**, 75–108.

Costin, I.D. & Grigo, J. (1974) Bioindikatoren zur Autoklavierungskontrolle Einige theoretische Aspekte und praktische Erfahrungen bei der Entwicklung und Anwendung. *Zentralblatt für Bakteriologie, Parasitenkunde, Infektionskrankheiten und Hygiene. Abteilung I.*

Originale, **A227**, 483–521.

Craven, C.W., Stern, J.A. & Ervin, G.F. (1968) Planetary quarantine and space vehicle sterilization. *Astronautics and Aeronautics*, **6**, 18–48.

Daudin, J.D. & Cerf, O. (1977) Influence des chocs thermiques sur la destruction des spores bacteriennes par la chaleur. *Lebensmittel-Wissenschaft und Technologie*, **10**, 203–207.

Davies, F.L., Underwood, H.M., Perkin, A.G. & Burton, H. (1977) Thermal death kinetics of *Bacillus stearothermophilus* spores at ultra high temperatures. I. Laboratory determination of temperature coefficients. *Journal of Food Technology*, **12**, 115–129.

Denny, C.B. & Matthys, A.W. (1975) *NCA tests on dry heat as a means of sterilization of containers, lids, and a closing unit for aseptic canning*. Final report No. RF 4614. Washington DC: National Canners Association.

Drummond, D.W. & Pflug, I.J. (1970) Dry-heat destruction of *Bacillus subtilis* spores on surfaces: Effect of humidity in an open system. *Applied Microbiology*, **20**, 805–809.

Edwards, J.L., Jr, Busta, F.F. & Speck, M.L. (1965a) Thermal inactivation characteristics of *Bacillus subtilis* spores at ultrahigh temperatures. *Applied Microbiology*, **13**, 851–857.

Edwards, J.L., Jr, Busta, F.F. & Speck, M.L. (1965b) Heat injury of *Bacillus subtilis* spores of ultrahigh temperatures. *Applied Microbiology*, **13**, 858–864.

El-Bisi, H.M. & Ordal, Z.J. (1956) The effect of sporulation temperature on the thermal resistance of *Bacillus coagulans* var. *thermoacidurans*. *Journal of Bacteriology*, **71**, 10–16.

Ernst, R.R. (1968) Sterilization by heat. In *Disinfection, Sterilization and Preservation* (eds Lawrence, C.A. & Block, S.S.) pp. 703–740. Philadelphia: Lea & Febiger.

Filho, L.P.G. (1975) Die Thermische Abtötung von Sporen von *Bacillus subtilis* var. *niger* ATCC 9372 in Gasphasen mit einer Wasseraktivität < 1.0. *Lebensmitel-Wissenschaft und Technologie*, **8**, 29–33.

Flowers, R.S. & Adams, D.M. (1976) Spore membrane(s) as the site of damage within heated *Clostridium perfringens* spores. *Journal of Bacteriology*, **125**, 429–434.

Fox, K. & Eder, B.D. (1969) Comparison of survivor curves of *Bacillus subtilis* spores subjected to wet and dry heat. *Journal of Food Science*, **34**, 518–521.

Fox, K. & Pflug, I.J. (1968) Effect of temperature and gas velocity on the dry-heat destruction rate of bacterial spores. *Applied Microbiology*, **16**, 343–348.

Futter, B.V. & Richardson, G. (1970) Viability of clostridial spores and the requirements of damaged organisms: I, Method of colony count, period and temperature of incubation, and pH value of the medium. *Journal of Applied Bacteriology*, **33**, 321–330.

Gerhardt, P. & Murrell, W.G. (1978) Basis and mechanism of bacterial spore resistance. *Spore Newsletter*, **6** (March), 1–21.

Gould, G.W. (1977) Recent advances in the understanding of resistance and dormancy in bacterial spores. *Journal of Applied Bacteriology*, **42**, 297–309.

Gould, G.W. & Dring, G.J. (1975) Role of expanded cortex in resistance of bacterial endospores. In *Spores VI* (eds Gerhardt, P., Costilow, R.N. & Sadoff, H.L.) pp. 541–546. Washington DC: American Society for Microbiology.

Han, Y.W. (1975) Death rates of bacterial spores: nonlinear survivor curves, *Canadian Journal of Microbiology*, **21**, 1464–1467.

Han, Y.W., Zhang, H.I. & Krochta, J.M. (1976) Death rates of bacterial spores: mathematical models. *Canadian Journal of Microbiology*, **22**, 295–300.

Härnulv, B.G. & Snygg, B.G. (1972) Heat resistance of *Bacillus subtilis* spores at various water activities. *Journal of Applied Bacteriology*, **35**, 615–624.

Heintz, M.-T., Urban, S., Schiller, I., Gay, M. & Bühlman, X. (1976) The production of spores of *Bacillus stearothermophilus* with constant resistance to heat and their use as biological indicators during the development of aqueous solutions for injection. *Pharmaceutica Acta Helvetiae*, **51**, 137–143.

Hoffman, R.K., Gambill, V.M. & Buchanan, L.M. (1968) Effect of cell moisture on the thermal inactivation rate of bacterial spores. *Applied Microbiology*, **16**, 1240–1244.

Jonsson, U., Snygg, B.G., Härnulv, B.G. & Zachrisson, T. (1977) Testing two models for the temperature dependence of the heat inactivation rate of *Bacillus stearothermophilus* spores. *Journal of Food Science*, **42**, 1251–1252, 1263.

Kereluk, K. & Gammon, R. (1973) A comparative study of biological indicators for steam sterilization. *Developments in Industrial Microbiology*, **15**, 411–419.

Kooiman, W.J. & Jacobs, R.P.W.M. (1977) The heat resistance of *Bacillus subtilis* 1–12 in relation to the water activity during pre-equilibration and during exposure to heat. In *Spore Research 1976* (eds Barker, A.N., Wolf, J., Ellar, D.J., Dring, G.J. & Gould, G.W.) pp. 477–485. London, New York, San Francisco: Academic Press.

Koshikawa, T., Beaman, T.C., Pankratz, H.S., Nakashio, S., Corner, T.R. & Gerhardt, P. (1984) Resistance, germination, and permeability correlates of *Bacillus megaterium* spores successively divested of integument layers. *Journal of Bacteriology*, **159**, 624–632.

Lechowitch, R.V. & Ordal, Z.J. (1960) The influence of sporulation temperature on the thermal resistance and chemical composition of endospores. In *Bacteriological Proceedings*, pp. 44–45. Society of American Bacteriologists.

Levine, S. (1956) Determination of the thermal death rate of bacteria. *Food Research*, **21**, 295–301.

Löwick, J.A.M. & Anema, P.J. (1972) Effect of pH on the heat resistance of *Clostridium sporogenes* spores in minced meat. *Journal of Applied Bacteriology*, **35**, 119–121.

Mallidis, C.G. & Scholefield, J. (1987) Relation of the heat resistance of bacterial spores to chemical composition and structure I. Relation to core components. *Journal of Applied Bacteriology*, **62**, 65–69.

Michels, M.J.M. & Visser, F.M.W. (1976) Occurrence and

thermoresistance of spores of pyschrophilic and psychrotrophic aerobic sporeformers in soils and food. *Journal of Applied Bacteriology*, **41**, 1–11.

Moats, W.A. (1971) Kinetics of thermal death of bacteria. *Journal of Bacteriology*, **105**, 165–171.

Molin, G. (1976) Infra-red sterilization of glass packaging for aseptic processing. *22nd European Meeting of Meat Research Workers*, Congress Documentation, Vol. II, J8:3–7.

Molin, G. (1977a) Inherent genetic differences in dry heat resistance of some *Bacillus* spores. In *Spore Research 1976* (eds Barker, A.N., Wolf, J., Ellar, D.J., Dring, G.J. & Gould, G.W.) pp. 487–500, London, New York, San Francisco: Academic Press.

Molin, G. (1977b) Dry-heat resistance of *Bacillus subtilis* spores in contact with serum albumin, carbohydrates or lipids. *Journal of Applied Bacteriology*, **42**, 111–116.

Molin, G. (1977c) Inactivation of *Bacillus* spores in dry systems at low and high temperatures. *Journal of General Microbiology*, **101**, 227–231.

Molin, G. & Östlund, K. (1975) Dry-heat inactivation of *Bacillus subtilis* spores by means of infra-red heating. *Antonie van Leeuwenhoek Journal of Microbiology and Serology*, **41**, 329–335.

Molin, G. & Östlund, K. (1976) Dry-heat inactivation of *Bacillus subtilis* var. *niger* spores with special reference to spore density. *Canadian Journal of Microbiology*, **22**, 359–363.

Molin, N. & Snygg, B.G. (1967) Effect of lipid materials on heat resistance of bacterial spores. *Applied Microbiology*, **15**, 142–146.

Molin, G. & Svensson, M. (1976) Formation of dry-heat resistant *Bacillus subtilis* var. *niger* spores as influenced by the composition of the sporulation medium. *Antonie van Leeuwenhoek Journal of Microbiology and Serology*, **42**, 387–395.

Murrell, W.G. & Scott, W.J. (1966) The heat resistance of bacterial spores at various water activities. *Journal of General Microbiology*, **43**, 411–425.

Nakashio, S. & Gerhardt, P. (1985) Protoplast dehydration correlated with heat resistance of bacterial spores. *Journal of Bacteriology*, **162**, 571–578.

Niepokojezycka, E. & Zakrzewski, K. (1972) Alumina-attached spores of *Bacillus stearothermophilus* for the control of sterilization process. *Acta Microbiologica Polonica* (Ser. B), **4**, 141–153.

Oag, R.K. (1940) The resistance of bacterial spores to dry heat. *Journal of Pathology and Bacteriology*, **51**, 137–141.

Odlaug, T.E., Pflug, I.J. & Kautter, D.A. (1978) Heat resistance of *Clostridium botulinum* type B spores grown from isolates from commercially canned mushrooms. *Journal of Food Protection*, **41**, 351–353.

Pflug, I.J. (1973) Heat sterilization. In *Industrial Sterilization* (eds Phillips, G.B. & Miller, W.S.) pp. 239–282. Durham, North Carolina: Duke University Press.

Pflug, I.J. & Schmidt, C.F. (1968) Thermal destruction of microorganisms. In *Disinfection, Sterilization and Preservation* (eds Lawrence, C.A. & Block, S.S.) pp. 63–105. Philadelphia: Lea & Febiger.

Pflug, I.J. & Smith, G.M. (1977) Survivor curves of bacterial spores heated in parenteral solutions. In *Spore Research 1976* (eds Barker, A.N., Wolf, J., Ellar, D.J., Dring, G.J. & Gould, G.W.) pp. 501–525. London, New York, San Francisco: Academic Press.

Pheil, C.G., Pflug, I.J., Nicholas, R.C. & Augustin, J.A.L. (1967) Effect of various gas atmospheres on destruction of microorganisms in dry heat. *Applied Microbiology*, **15**, 120–124.

Prentice, G.A. & Clegg, L.F.L. (1974) The effect of incubation temperature on the recovery of spores of *Bacillus subtilis* 8057. Journal of Applied Bacteriology, **37**, 501–513.

Quast, D.G., Leitao, M.F.F. & Kato, K. (1977) Death of *Bacillus stearothermophilus* 1518 spores on can covers exposed to superheated steam in a Dole aseptic canning system. *Lebensmittel-Wissenschaft und Technologie*, **10**, 198–202.

Rahn, O. (1943) The problem of the logarithmic order of death in bacteria. *Biodynamica*, **4**, 81–130.

Rahn, O. (1945) Physical methods of sterilization of microorganisms. *Bacteriological Reviews*, **9**, 1–47.

Rey, C.R., Walker, H.W. & Rohrbaugh, P.L. (1975) The influence of temperature on growth, sporulation and heat resistance of spores of six strains of *Clostridium perfringens. Journal of Milk and Food Technology*, **38**, 461–465.

Roberts, T.A. (1968) Heat and radiation resistance and activation of spores of *Clostridium welchii. Journal of Applied Bacteriology*, **31**, 133–144.

Roberts, T.A. (1970) Recovering spores damaged by heat, ionizing radiations or ethylene oxide. *Journal of Applied Bacteriology*, **33**, 74–94.

Roberts, T.A., Gilbert, R.J. & Ingram, M. (1966a) The heat resistance of anaerobic spores on aqueous suspension. *Journal of Food Technology*, **1**, 227–235.

Roberts, T.A., Gilbert, R.J. & Ingram, M. (1966b) The effect of sodium chloride on heat resistance and recovery of heated spores of *Clostridium sporogenes* (PA 3679/S_2). *Journal of Applied Bacteriology*, **29**, 549–555.

Roberts, T.A. & Hitchins, A.D. (1969) Resistance of spores. In *The Bacterial Spore* (eds Gould, G.W. & Hurst, A.) pp. 611–670. London, New York: Academic Press.

Rowe, J.A. & Koesterer, M.G. (1965) Dry heat resistance of *Bacillus subtilis* under several heated gaseous environments. In *Bacteriological Proceedings*, p. 8. Society of American Bacteriologists.

Russell, A.D. (1971) The destruction of bacterial spores. In *Inhibition and Destruction of the Microbial Cell* (ed. Hugo, W.B.) pp. 451–612. London: Academic Press.

Russell, A.D. (1982) *The Destruction of Bacterial Spores*. London: Academic Press.

Scholefield, J. & Abdelgadir, A.M. (1974) Heat resistance characteristics of spores of rough and smooth variants of *B. stearothermophilus*. *Proceedings of the IV International Congress of Food Science and Technology*. Vol. 3,

pp. 71–78.
Senhaji, A.F. (1977) The protective effect of fat on the heat resistance of bacteria (II). *Journal of Food Technology*, **12**, 217–230.
Senhaji, A.F. & Loncin, M. (1977) The protective effect of fat on the heat resistance of bacteria (I). *Journal of Food Technology*, **12**, 203–216.
Sharpe, K. & Bektash, R.M. (1977) Heterogeneity and the modelling of bacterial spore death: the case of continuously decreasing death rate. *Canadian Journal of Microbiology*, **23**, 1501–1507.
Smelt, J.P.P.M., Santos Da Silva, M.J. & Haas, H. (1977) The combined influence of pH and water activity on the heat resistance of *Clostridium botulinum* types A and B. In *Spore Research 1976* (eds Barker, A.N., Wolf, J., Ellar, D.J., Dring, G.J. & Gould, G.W.) pp. 469–476. London, New York, San Francisco: Academic Press.
Soper, C.J. & Davies, D.J.G. (1971) The effect of high vacuum drying on the heat response of *Bacillus megaterium* spores. In *Spore Research 1971* (eds Barker, A.N., Gould, G.W. & Wolf, J.) pp. 275–288. London, New York: Academic Press.
Soper, C.J. & Davies, D.J.G. (1973) The effects of rehydration and oxygen on the heat resistance of high vacuum treated spores. *Journal of Applied Bacteriology*, **36**, 119–130.
Staat, R.H. & Beakley, J.W. (1969) Dry heat inactivation characteristics of *Bacillus subtilis* var. *niger* spores. In *Bacteriological Proceedings*. Vol. **17**, p. 17. Society of American Bacteriologists.
Steinbuch, E. (1977) The acid sensitization of heat resistant bacterial spores. In *Spore Research 1976* (eds Barker, A.N., Wolf, J., Ellar, D.J., Dring, G.J. & Gould, G.W.) pp. 451–468. London, New York & San Francisco: Academic Press.
Stumbo, C.R. (1965) *Thermobacteriology in Food Processing*. New York: Academic Press.
Stumbo, C.R., Murphy, J.R. & Cochran, J. (1950) Nature of thermal death time curves for P.A. 3679 and *Clostridium botulinum. Food Technology*, **4**, 321–326.
Sugiyama, H. (1951) Studies on factors affecting the heat resistance of spores of *Clostridium botulinum. Journal of Bacteriology*, **62**, 81–96.
Sykes, G. (1965) *Disinfection and Sterilization*, 2nd Ed. London: Chapman & Hall.
Wang, D.I.C. Scharer, J. & Humprey, A.E. (1964) Kinetics of death of bacterial spores at elevated temperatures. *Applied Microbiology*, **12**, 451–454.
Wang, J.-S (1968) Alternation of dry heat resistivity of *Bacillus subtilis* var. *niger* by intracellular and extracellular water. Thesis. Massachusetts Institute of Technology. Boston.
Warth, A.D. (1977) Molecular structure of the bacterial spore. *Advances in Microbial Physiology*, **17**, 1–45.
Warth, A.D. (1978) Relationship between the heat resistance of spores and the optimum and maximum growth temperatures of *Bacillus* species. *Journal of Bacteriology*, **124**, 699–705.
Williams, O.B. & Reed, J.M. (1942) The significance of the incubation temperature of recovery cultures in determining spore resistance to heat. *Journal of Infectious Diseases*, **71**, 225–227.
Yokoya, F. & York, G.K. (1965) Effect of several environmental conditions on the "thermal death rate" of endospores of aerobic, thermophilic bacteria. *Applied Microbiology*, **13**, 993–999.

C · MEDICAL APPLICATIONS OF THERMAL PROCESSES

1 PARENTERAL PRODUCTS

All parenteral products must be sterile when administered. Whenever possible, aqueous injections are terminally sterilized by autoclaving, the exception being products containing heat-labile drugs. Pharmacopoeial methods in Europe recommend moist-heat sterilization at a minimum temperature of 121°C maintained throughout the load during a holding period of 15 min. Other combinations of time and temperature can be used, but the crucial requirement is that the cycle delivers an adequate level of 'lethality' to the product. In practice, many manufacturers apply the F_0 principle (see Chapter 18D) to autoclave processing, an F_0 of 8 being the usual minimum lethality acceptable. However, in some instances of poor heat tolerance of a product, an F_0 value as low as 4 can be employed. It is essential in all cases to ensure a low pre-sterilization bio-burden and absence of heat-resistant spores, especially when the F_0 approach is employed. In addition to the requirement for sterility, all parenteral products must be free from excessive numbers of particles and be non-pyrogenic (see Groves, 1973, for a detailed discussion of these issues).

The modern approach to parenterals is to consider not only the injection (formulation, sterility, etc.) but also the safest means of delivery to the patient. Consequently, there have been significant developments in the packaging of parenterals to improve this safe delivery. Because this has led to the wider use of plastic materials to fabricate such delivery systems, the applicability of thermal processing has been compromised in many instances. It is important to ensure that the introduction of less heat-stable packaging does not sustantially reduce the sterility assurance of the final product.

1.1 Small-volume injections

Parenteral preparations of potent heat-stable drugs are distributed into, and sterilized in, glass or plastic ampoules. Glass ampoules are made by extrusion of tubular borosilicate glass. They may be made under clean-room conditions and supplied sealed ready for filling, resealing and sterilization. The most critical operation during the preparation of glass ampoules is the ampoule-sealing process (Brizell & Shatwell, 1973). To detect leakage the most convenient method is to immerse ampoules in a heat-stable dye solution during autoclaving. Any seal failure will lead to loss of air from the ampoule during heating-up and consequent ingress of dye during cooling, which is easily seen on inspection. For a detailed analysis of leak testing, see Anon. (1986). Injections can also be manufactured in polyethylene ampoules, using the Rommelag process, in which the ampoule is formed, filled, sealed and heat-sterilized in one continuous process (Sharpe, 1988).

1.2 Multidose injections

A small number of injections are still required in multidose containers, comprising glass vials with an aluminium ring holding the rubber closure tightly on the bottle neck. Multidose injections must include a preservative unless the drug is intrinsically antimicrobial (Allwood, 1978). However, none of the multidose injections, that remain acceptable to Licensing Authorities, such as insulin, some vaccines and heparins, are heat-sterilized.

1.3 Fat emulsions

It is possible to prepare a stable fat emulsion for parenteral administration which is sterilized by autoclaving. Such emulsions consist of 10–20% oil in water, stabilized by lecithin. The droplet size is in the range 0.2–0.4 μm mean diameter. These emulsions are used as an energy source in parenteral nutrition (fat contains more than twice the calorie content of carbohydrates, compared on a weight basis, yet does not increase the tonicity of the injection). Emulsions can also be used as a vehicle for poorly water-soluble drugs such as fat-soluble vitamins and the intravenous anaesthetic propofol. It is also possible to use fat emulsions to target drugs to particular organs such as the liver.

1.4 Oily injections

Thermostable drugs prepared in anhydrous vehicles intended for parenteral administration are sterilized by dry heat, using a cycle of 180°C for 30 min, or its equivalent time/temperature combination (*British Pharmacopoeia*, 1988). As with aqueous injections, the F_0 approach is now commonly applied to the sterilization of anhydrous products. These oily injections are normally packed in single-dose ampoules.

1.5 Large-volume parenterals

Large-volume aqueous injections (>100 ml) have a variety of clinical uses (Allwood, 1987). Such preparations are prepared in glass or plastic containers. The manufacturing process for large volume parenterals (LVPs) is designed to ensure that a particle- and pyrogen-free solution with low microbial content is filled into clean containers. Controls designed to achieve this end, however, may be nullified by poor container design or manufacture. Therefore the choice, quality and method of manufacture of the packaging is critical to the quality of the finished product.

1.5.1 Rigid containers

Rigid containers manufactured from lime soda or borosilicate glass have been widely used for large-volume sterile fluids in the past, but have now been largely superseded by plastic containers. However, glass bottles are still used for some products, such as amino acid infusions, some blood substitutes and agents such as the hypnotic, chlormethiazole. Such products are sterilized by autoclaving. Although soda glass is cheap and readily moulded, it is prone to damage by thermal shock, and to surface attack by alkaline solutions, resulting in flaking of the glass surface. Borosilicate glass is more resistant to thermal and chemical shock. Bottles are closed using a rubber (elastomer) plug secured by an aluminium ring which holds the rubber plug tightly onto the bottle rim. The major microbial risk to a product autoclaved in a glass bottle sealed with a rubber plug results from seal failure under the physical stress exerted on the closure during the autoclaving cycle. For a typical glass infusion container, the combined effect of steam under pressure and air at 121°C, together with the compression of the head-space due to water expansion, creates a pressure in the bottle of approximately 2.9 bar (56 p.s.i) greater than the chamber pressure. This internal pressure exerts considerable stress on the rubber closure, already softened by the high temperature. Seal failure can occur because of poor manufacturing tolerances of the bottle neck or rim, inadequate torque applied to the rubber plug by the aluminium cap, incorrect hardness of rubber or poor closure design. The consequence of seal failure is air loss from the bottle during the heating-up stage of autoclaving (Allwood *et al.*, 1975) and subsequent ingress of water during spray-cooling (Beverley *et al.*, 1974). The entry of spray-cooling water poses the greatest risk since it may contain viable micro-organisms

(Coles & Tredree, 1972). Even if the spray-cooling water is sterile, it remains contaminated with particulate matter, trace metals and pyrogens. The incidence of closure failure may be reduced by improved closure design (Hambleton & Allwood, 1976a). There is little evidence to suggest that an insert-type closure offers greater seal effectiveness than flat liners of the correct thickness and rubber hardness. The bottle neck quality and variations in neck dimensions are a especially important factors. The degree of torque applied to the rubber closure via the aluminium crimp-on cap is also significant. Glass containers are no longer considered the most suitable container for parenterals, especially as plastic containers are now available that provide a product more cheaply with less risk of contamination and lower particulate levels.

1.5.2 *Flexible containers*

The choice of a suitable plastic to package LVPs is largely governed by the thermal stability of the material. However, a number of factors must be considered. These include the ease of production of a suitable design which is particle- and pyrogen-free, easily filled under clean-room conditions and does not impart significant quantities of extractibles, leached from the material of the container itself to the contents. For example, it is well recognized that plasticizers in polyvinyl chloride (PVC), such as phthalate salts, can leach from poor-quality film into aqueous solutions (Hambleton & Allwood, 1976b). Plastic containers can be formed into a completely sealed pouch or bottle before autoclaving. Therefore, there is no danger of spray-cooling water or air entering the contents during autoclaving, provided there is no seam failure or pinholing (these faults are normally detected by leakage of the contents). Since plastic films become more flexible on heating, the pressure increase in the container during autoclaving is far less than in a rigid container. However, in order to prevent flexible plastic containers from bursting, it is essential that autoclaving be conducted in an air–steam mixture to counterbalance pressure differences (Schuck, 1974). Plastic LVP containers are discussed by Petrick *et al.* (1977) and Turco & King (1987). The most commonly used plastics for sterile products are PVC, polyethylene and polypropylene. The relative merits of each are discussed by Hambleton & Allwood (1976b) and Turco & King (1987). One significant point of relevance to sterilization is that PVC-fabricated packs can be placed in an outer wrap before autoclaving. Also, PVC is able to withstand higher temperatures (up to 115–117°C) than polyethylene (112–114°C).

2 NON-PARENTERAL STERILE FLUIDS

Sterile fluids suitable for clinical use are required in increasing quantity. These include non-injectable water, for use in theatres and wards when sterile fluids are required to wash open wounds for peritoneal dialysis, fluids for antiseptic solutions in ready-to-use dilution in critical risk areas, and for diluents for drugs used in nebulizers. All of these applications required the sterile fluid to be packaged in such a way that it can be used without becoming contaminated. For example, non-injectable water is required in a rigid bottle that allows pouring of a sterile liquid; antiseptic solutions should be transferable to a sterile container at the bedside without contamination. Peritoneal fluids must be packaged in order to allow convenient delivery into the peritoneum via suitable administration sets. This requires a flexible-walled container that collapses on emptying.

Most producers manufacture non-injectable water in rigid polypropylene bottles. The bottle may be sealed using a screw cap, with tear-off hermetic overseal, or a snap-break closure of a fully moulded container. Peritoneal dialysis fluids are packaged in flexible PVC pouches or rigid polypropylene bottles. Smaller-volume antiseptic solutions and nebulizer solutions may be packaged in plastic ampoules, PVC or laminate sachets. All these preparations should be autoclavable.

3 OPHTHALMIC PREPARATIONS

All ophthalmic preparations must be sterile to avoid the introduction of infecting micro-organisms on to the surface of the eye. Under certain circumstances, such as post-operatively or after trauma, the cornea and conjunctiva are very susceptible to infection. Eye-drops are available in single and multidose presentations. The former method of packaging is clearly preferable, since the risks inherent in repeated-use preparations are removed. Traditionally, eye-drops have been prepared in glass containers (see below), although it is now far more common to use plastic. Single-dose packs are available in which the solutions can be sterilized by autoclaving in air-ballasted autoclaves. These solutions can therefore be formulated without a preservative. One example is the 'Minim' (Smith & Nephew Ltd), in which the package is made from polypropylene film with a removable cap for ease of use. This is placed in an outer wrap prior to autoclaving. Each 'Minim' contains 0.5 ml.

For reasons of convenience and economy, many eye-drops are still prepared in multidose glass or plastic eye-dropper bottles. The glass bottles consist of amber, fluted neutral or surface-treated glass, with phenolic (bakelite) plastic screw caps and a neutral glass dropper. They are sealed with a natural or synthetic rubber teat which serves the dual role not only of sealing the cap to the neck of the bottle but also of providing a bulb for the dropper tube. This pattern of container has been available for many years, but was not originally designed to be autoclaved. During autoclaving, the teat softens and balloons, the cap may become distorted and therefore allow air to leak out of the container. This usually leads to a vacuum in the head space which encourages the ingress of non-sterile air during cooling and storage. In fact, the *British Pharmaceutical Codex* (1973) and the *Pharmaceutical Codex* (1979) indicate that eye-drops may be sterilized at 98–100°C or 115–116°C. The former process is based on the presence of a preservative in the eye-drop solution which, it is assumed, should be sporicidal at 98–100°C. The recommended preservatives are phenylmercuric nitrate or acetate (0.002% w/v), chlorhexidine acetate (0.01% w/v) or benzalkonium chloride (0.01% w/v). Only the mercurial compounds have been shown to possess sporicidal action under these conditions (Berry *et al.*, 1938). Therefore, it is now recommended (1988) that eye-drops be sterilized by autoclaving whenever the stability of therapeutic agents permits. Only then do the antimicrobial agents fulfil the role for which they were originally intended. Most types of rubber absorb preservatives (see Allwood, 1978). It is therefore necessary to compensate for this loss by pre-equilibrating rubber closures with the particular preservative in the formulation. Benzalkonium chloride may be incompatible with natural rubber (Anon, 1966) and therefore synthetic rubber teats should be substituted, silicone rubber being recommended. However, moisture loss through silicone rubber occurs rapidly during storage, thus limiting the shelf-life of such a package (Shaw *et al.*, 1972). This is sometimes overcome by supplying the dropper separately from the bottle, the dropper being applied to the bottle immediately before use. Eyedrops are also commonly prepared in plastic dropper bottles, using filter-sterilized solutions and aseptic processing into pre-sterilized containers.

The sealing of eye-dropper bottles during autoclaving can be improved by substituting metal for bakelite caps (Richards *et al.*, 1963). Other suggestions have been made for improving this type of packaging (Norton, 1962). Similar problems relate to containers for eye lotions except that the closure does not incorporate a rubber teat. Eye lotions are normally treated as single-dose items and a preservative is not included. In contrast, contact-lens solutions, as well as being prepared as sterile preparations preferably terminally sterilized by autoclaving, contain antimicrobial combinations to act as preservatives since they are multidose preparations (Davies, 1978).

4 DRESSINGS

4.1 Dressing sterilizers

There are two types of autoclave cycles (see also Chapter 18A) that can be employed to sterilize dressings. In both cases the essential requirements are for total removal of air from the load and the prevention of excessive condensation within the dressing packs during the cycle. If air is not removed, sterilizing conditions throughout the load will not be attained. If excessive condensation occurs, the dressing will become unusable. Condensation may also interfere with heat penetration.

Autoclaves for dressing sterilization are described in British Standard BS 3970.

4.1.1 *Gravity (downward) displacement autoclaves*

The cycle is designed so that steam under pressure flows downwards through the chamber, pushing air before it down the drain which is left open until the drain thermometer records the sterilizing temperature. Air removal may be accelerated by the repeated application of a vacuum down to 20 mmHg prior to steam entry (Wilkinson & Peacock, 1961). One such system has been described by Knox & Pickerill (1964). The drain temperature should correspond to the appropriate theoretical chamber pressure, assuming the chamber contains pure steam. The time required for a complete cycle is relatively long. The 'penetration time' is to allow steam to displace air and penetrate all parts of the chamber and dressings. Sterilization consists of the holding time, based on the temperature of sterilization, and a safety period (or 'margin of safety'). Fifty per cent of the holding time has been recommended (Anon, 1959). Finally, there is the cooling–drying phase. It is usual practice to remove the steam and enhance the drying rate of the load by applying a vacuum down to 20 mmHg, after which warm air, sterilized by passing through appropriate filters, enters the chamber. It is important to prevent non-sterile air entering through faulty filters, non-return valves or outlet drain lines. The total cycle time is of the order of up to 60 min, sterilizing at 134°C, made up of minima of 20-min pre-vacuum, 20-min sterilizing and 20-min drying time, plus heating-up times. The method is now considered obsolete.

4.1.2 *High-vacuum autoclaves*

The essential difference between downward displacement and high-vacuum air removal is the use of a far greater vacuum applied in the chamber to remove almost all of the air in the air space and trapped within the dressing packs. It is essential that air leaks into the chamber are prevented (Fallon, 1961). This vacuum must be below 20 mmHg absolute, which will remove more than 95% of the air in the chamber and load almost instantaneously. As the initial pressure is very low, steam is less likely to condense on the load material during the initial heating-up phase. This also depends on packing, and will vary in mixed loads; in fact, to ensure complete air removal from the load it is usual to employ a rapid pulsing evacuation procedure before the final heating-up stage, taking 6–8 min in all. The holding time of 3–4 min at 134°C, a saturated steam pressure equivalent to 2.2 bar or 32 p.s.i., is followed by steam removal by condenser or vacuum, and drying, which can be shortened to 3–4 min for most loads packaged in paper or linen. Therefore, the total cycle time is about 28–35 min.

Whichever autoclave cycle is employed, it is essential to ensure that the steam is dry and saturated, containing $\ngtr 5\%$ by weight of water as condensed droplets. If the steam is too wet it will soak dressings, causing them to trap air. The other danger to be avoided is superheating. This can be caused by the lagging of reducing valves, by exothermic reactions related to greases in valves etc., by too high a jacket temperature or by retention of air in the load. Superheating can also occur within the load from the heat of hydration of very dry ($<1\%$ moisture content) cotton fabrics (Bowie, 1961; Sykes, 1965). This can be avoided by allowing fabrics to equilibrate with normal levels of humidity ($>50\%$ r.h.) before sterilization.

4.2 Surgical dressings

It is essential that surgical dressings are sterile. Most dressings are sterilized by moist heat. Correct packaging of each item is vital to allow sterilization and avoid contamination during application. The nature of the packaging must allow complete steam penetration into the dressing as well as post-sterilization drying, and must be designed to allow the item to be removed aseptically. In general, all dressings are double-wrapped so that items can be taken through a contamination barrier into a clean area during which the dressing and its immediate packaging remain sterile. Also, items are usually packed individually or in dressing kits [all the required items for one procedure are packed into one outer wrapping (Hopkins, 1961)]. Fortunately, packaging developments have proceeded apace with improvements in autoclave technology. Improvements in the design of the autoclave cycle have allowed the use of improved packaging materials and methods of packing. Thus introduction of the high pre-vacuum autoclave cycle has not only provided a much shorter cycle period and improved sterilization performance, but also provided greater flexibility in the use of packaging techniques.

Any packaging material must allow steam and air to penetrate but still maintain its resistance to heat and breakage, especially when wet (Hunter *et al.*, 1961). It should be an adequate barrier to prevent entry of dust or micro-organisms during storage. There is a considerable choice of material available, including metal, calico (muslin), cardboard, paper and plastic films. Traditionally, stainless-steel dressing drums have been used for the routine packing of dressings. However, these have now been superseded, especially with the use of high pre-vacuum autoclaves although metal boxes are being re-introduced. It is now usual practice to pack each item in paper, and then overwrap it in paper or fabric; alternatively, they may be placed in cardboard boxes (Hopkins, 1961), although other packaging materials are also available. In general, steam- and air-permeable paper packs are relatively easily sterilized, either by gravity or high pre-vacuum steam control. In addition, the material is cheap and readily disposed of, and each pack is sealed with self-adhesive autoclave tape. Cardboard cartons can serve as outer rigid containers and are re-usable. It is, however, important to maintain the steam in a dry state during autoclaving or the cardboard will disintegrate. Fabrics, such as calico, are suitable for gravity steam penetration and the material often proves to be a reasonably effective air filter. However, fabrics are less resistant to bacterial penetration than paper (Standard *et al.*, 1973). They are re-usable but require laundering. Some plastic film materials can be employed provided the material is steam-penetrable. Cellophane is often suitable for small items but tends to become brittle during autoclaving and therefore cannot be used in high-temperature autoclaves. The method of packing is often critical, especially in gravity displacement autoclaves. Packs must be arranged so that the critical steam flow is not impeded between dressings. The use of high pre-vacuum cycles largely overcomes the problem of steam penetration, provided the packing is sufficiently loose to allow good air and steam circulation inside and between packs and packaging material.

5 USES OF DRY HEAT STERILIZATION

Dry heat as a means of sterilization is reserved for those products and materials that contain little or no water and cannot be saturated with steam during the heating cycle. It is used for dry powdered drugs, heat-resistant containers (but not rubber items), certain terminally sterilized preparations, some types of surgical dressings and surgical instruments. The instruments include metal scalpels, other steel instruments and glass syringes (although most syringes now consist of plastic and are disposable). The advantage offered by dry heat sterilization of syringes is that they can be sterilized fully assembled in the final container (Anon., 1962). The difficulties associated with autoclaving syringes include lack of steam penetration, enhanced by the protective effect of lubricant, and the need to assemble them after sterilization. Examples of pharmaceutical products subjected to dry heat sterilization include implants, eye ointment bases, oily injections (usually sterilized in ampoules) and other oily products (silicone used for catheter lubrication, liquid paraffin, glycerine). Dressings sterilized by dry heat include paraffin gauze and other oily impregnated dressings.

The recommended treatment is maintenance of the item at 180°C for 30 min. This may be limited by the heat stability of the particular item and therefore some dispensation is accepted, e.g. human fibrin foam is sterilized at 130°C for 3 h. Sutures may be sterilized at 150°C for 1 h in a non-aqueous solvent. However, after this treatment the suture material must be transferred to aqueous tubing fluid to render the material flexible and restore its tensile strength. Ionizing radiation is now the preferred method of sterilization of sutures, as it minimizes the loss of tensile strength.

6 REFERENCES

Allwood, M.C. (1978) Antimicrobial agents in single- and multi-dose injections. *Journal of Applied Bacteriology*, **44**, Svii–Sxiii.

Allwood, M.C. (1987) Sterile pharmaceutical products. In *Pharmaceutical Microbiology* (eds Hugo, W.B. & Russell, A.D.) 4th Ed. pp. 417–432. Oxford: Blackwell Scientific Publications.

Allwood, M.C., Hambleton, R. & Beverley, S. (1975) Pressure changes in bottles during sterilization by autoclaving. *Journal of Pharmaceutical Sciences*, **64**, 333–334.

Anon (1959) *Medical Research Council, Report by Working Party on Pressure-Steam Sterilization*. London: HMSO.

Anon (1962) *The Sterilization, Use and Care of Syringes*. MRC Memorandum No. 14. London: HMSO.

Anon (1966) Pharmaceutical Society Laboratory Report P/66/7.

Anon (1986) *The Prevention and Detection of Leaks in Glass Ampoules*. Technical Monograph No. 1. Swindon: Parenteral Society Publications.

Berry, H., Jensen, E. & Siller, F.K. (1938) The sterilization of thermolabile substances in the presence of bactericides. *Quarterly Journal of Pharmacy*, **11**, 729–735.

Beverley, S., Hambleton, R. & Allwood, M.C. (1974) Leakage of spray cooling water into topical water bottle. *Pharmaceutical Journal*, **213**, 306–308.

Bowie, J.H. (1961) The control of heat sterilisers. In *Sterilization of Surgical Materials*, pp. 109–142. London: Pharmaceutical Press.

British Pharmacopoeia (1988) London: HMSO.

British Pharmaceutical Codex (1973) London: Pharmaceutical Press.

Brizell, I.G. & Shatwell, J. (1973) Methods of detecting leaks in glass ampoules. *Pharmaceutical Journal*, **211**, 73–74.

Coles, J. & Tredree, R.L. (1972) Contamination of autoclaved fluids with cooling water. *Pharmaceutical Journal*, **209**, 193–195.

Cox, P.H. & Spanjers, F. (1970) The preparation of sterile implants by compression. *Overdurk Mit Pharmaceutisch Weekblad*, **105**, 681–684.

Davies, D.J.G. (1978) Agents as preservatives in eye drops and contact lens solutions. *Journal of Applied Bacteriology*, **44**, Sxix–Sxxxiv.

Fallon, R.J. (1961) Monitoring of sterilization of dressings in high vacuum pressure-steam sterilizers. *Journal of Clinical Pathology*, **14**, 666–669.

Fallon, R.J. & Pyne, J.R. (1963) The sterilization of surgeons' gloves. *Lancet*, **i**, 1200–1202.

Groves, M.J. (1973) *Parenteral Products*. London: Heinemann.

Hambleton, R. & Allwood, M.C. (1976a) Evaluation of a new design of bottle closure for non-injectable water. *Journal of Applied Bacteriology*, **41**, 109–118.

Hambleton, R. & Allwood, M.C. (1976b) Containers and closures. In *Microbiological Hazards of Infusion Therapy* (eds Phillips, I., Meers, P.D. & D'Arcy, P.F.) pp. 3–12. Lancaster: MTP Press Ltd.

Hopkins, S.J. (1961) Central sterile supply in Cambridge Hospitals. In *Sterilization of Surgical Materials*, pp. 153–166. London: Pharmaceutical Press.

Hunter, C.L.F., Harbord, P.E. & Riddett, D.J. (1961) Packaging papers as bacterial barriers. In *Sterilization of Surgical Materials*, pp. 166–172. London: Pharmaceutical Press.

Knox, R. & Pickerill, J.K. (1964) Efficient air removal from steam sterilized dressing without the use of high vacuum. *Lancet*, **i**, 1318–1321.

Norton, D.A. (1962). The properties of eye-drop bottles. *Pharmaceutical Journal*, **189**, 86–87.

Petrick, R.J., Loucas, S.P., Cohl, J.K. & Mehl, B. (1977) Review of current knowledge of plastic intravenous fluid containers. *American Journal of Hospital Pharmacy*, **34**, 357–362.

Pharmaceutical Codex (1979) London: Pharmaceutical Press.

Richards, R.M.E., Fletcher, G. & Norton, D.A. (1963) Closures for eye drop bottles. *Pharmaceutical Journal*, **191**, 655–660.

Schuck, L.J. (1974) Steam sterilization of solutions in plastic bottles. *Developments in Biological Standards*, **23**, 1–5.

Sharpe, J.R. (1988) Validation of a new form-fill-seal installation. *Manufacturing Chemist and Aerosol News*, **59**, 22,23,27,55.

Shaw, S., Hayward, J. & Edlongton, M. (1972) Eye drop bottles. *Journal of Hospital Pharmacy* (April), 108.

Standard, P.G., Mallison, G.F. & Mackel, D.C. (1973) Microbial penetration through three types of double wrappers for sterile packs. *Applied Microbiology*, **26**, 59–62.

Sykes, G. (1965) *Disinfection and Sterilization*. 2nd Ed. London: E. & F.N. Spon.

Turco, S. & King, R.E. (1987) *Sterile Dosage Forms*, 3rd Ed. Philadelphia: Lea & Febiger.

Wickner, H. (1973) Hospital pharmacy manufacturing of sterile fluids in plastic containers. *Svensk Farmaceutisk Tidskrift*, **77**, 773–777.

Wilkinson, G.R. & Peacock, F.G. (1961) The removal of air during autoclave sterilization of fabrics using low pressure steam. *Journal of Pharmacy and Pharmacology*, **13**, 67T–71T.

D·APPLICATIONS OF THERMAL PROCESSING IN THE FOOD INDUSTRY

1 INTRODUCTION

1.1 Aims of thermal processing

The aims of the thermal processing of foods are to eliminate mainly the vegetative forms of micro-organisms by pasteurization processes and to eliminate both vegetative cells and endospores by sterilization processes. These remain the basis of large and important food processing industries around the world.

If an otherwise unpreserved food is to be microbiologically stable during indefinite storage at ambient temperatures, all micro-organisms in the food that are capable of growth must be eradicated, and reinfection from extraneous sources prevented. If the ambient temperatures include those that are experienced under tropical conditions the thermal process must be sufficient to inactivate spores of thermophilic bacteria such as *Bacillus stearothermophilus* and *Clostridium thermosaccharolyticum* that might otherwise germinate and multiply under these conditions. Such thermophilic bacteria produce the most heat-resistant types of spores, so that the required thermal process is severe. If the food is to be distributed in non-tropical regions where temperatures do not exceed about 40°C for significant periods of time, complete eradication of thermophiles is not necessary since they cannot grow, and milder thermal processing is adequate. Such foods therefore need not be sterile. However, they should be heated sufficiently to be free from the spores of spoilage and toxinogenic micro-organisms capable of growth under the particular environmental conditions. This is sometimes referred to as 'commercial sterility'. If foods are formulated in such a way that spoilage and toxinogenic spore-formers are unable to multiply, for example by reduction of pH value or of water activity, or by the addition of preservatives, then it may be unnecessary to inactivate their spores. Thus even milder, heat processing (pasteurization), will be adequate to ensure stability and safety. Finally, for some foods that are unpreserved, yet stored for only limited periods of time or at low temperatures prior to consumption, pasteurization may likewise be sufficient. Whereas requirements for sterilization are thus clearly defined (see below), requirements for pasteurization are less well-defined and much more dependent on product characteristics and intended storage.

1.2 Heat inactivation kinetics

The basic essentials of the thermal processing of foods were clearly set out by Smelt & Mossel (1982) in the first edition of this book. Some of the procedures for delivering heat and for controlling heat processing, and the variety of packaging options, have continued to develop since then, but the important fundamentals of thermal processing remain the same, and are therefore summarized below.

The numbers of viable spores in a population of a single strain of micro-organism heated at constant temperature are generally regarded to decrease exponentially with time (Fig. 18.6a), often assumed to result from 'single-hit' kinetics. The slope of this

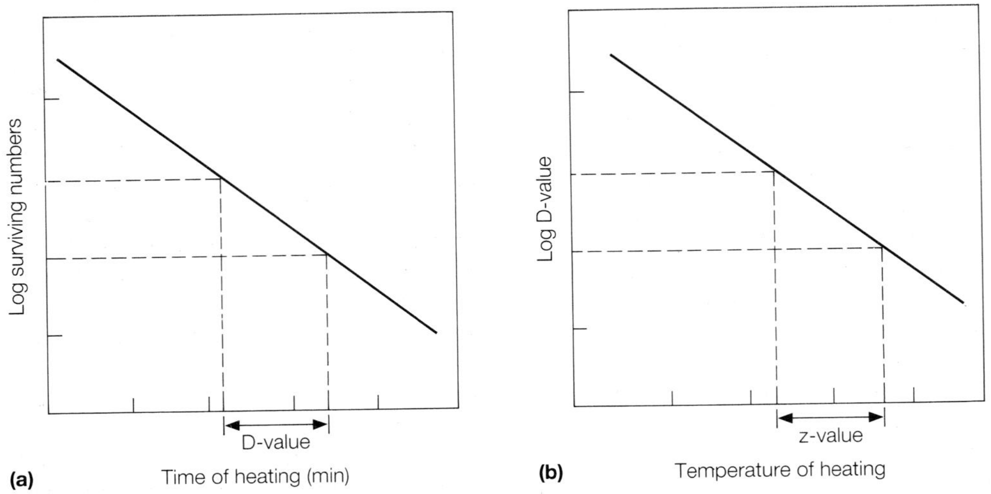

Fig. 18.6 Idealized heat inactivation curves of bacterial spores showing: (a) logarithmic decline in numbers of survivors during heating at constant temperature, and derivation of '*D*-value'; (b) logarithmic decline in *D*-value with rise in temperature, and derivation of '*z*-value'.

inactivation curve is usually designated '*D*' in minutes. The rate of inactivation increases with temperature in such a way that *D* is commonly observed to decrease exponentially with rise in temperature also, and the slope of this curve is usually designated '*z*' in degrees (Fig. 18.6b): see also Chapter 18B.

These relationships form the basis for the thermal processing of foods despite the fact that very many experimental observations have cast doubts on the universal validity of the simple relationships indicated in Fig. 18.6. Indeed, all of the various curves summarized in Fig. 18.7 have been reported for different organisms heated under different circumstances, and various explanations of the 'deviations from linearity' have been given (Roberts & Hitchins, 1969; Pflug & Holcomb, 1977; Russell, 1982; Gould, 1989). For example, it has been suggested that curves with shapes like *b* in Fig. 18.7 result from 'multi-hit' inactivation processes (Moats *et al*., 1971). Alternatively, the presence of many clumps in a suspension may result in such a delay before numbers of colony forming units (c.f.u.) begin to fall. An initial rise (curve *c*) or shoulder may result if the spores require to be heat-activated before they can germinate and so form colonies. Tailing (*d*) is

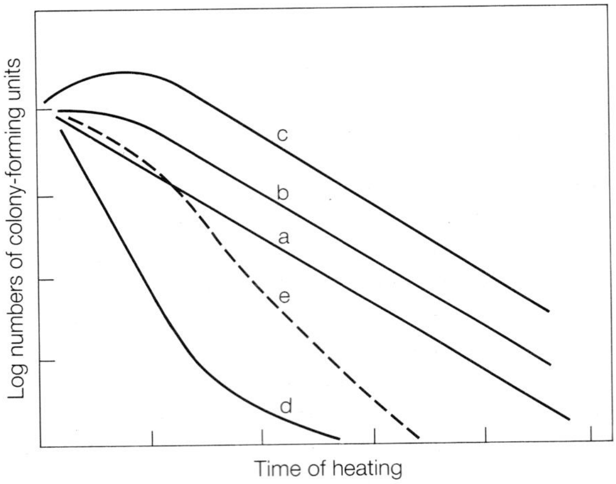

Fig. 18.7 Experimentally derived heat inactivation curves (b-e) that differ from the 'classic' kinetics in Fig. 18.6. For proposed explanations, see text (from Gould, 1989).

often observed, and may result from the presence of small numbers of large clumps in the suspension, from variability of individual spore resistances within the population (Sharpe & Bektash, 1977; Cerf, 1977), or from an increase in resistance during the heating process itself ('heat adaptation': Han *et al.*, 1976). Mixtures of these effects will be expected to generate curves with shapes like the commonly observed *e*.

At very high UHT (ultra-heat treatment) temperatures, when inactivation rates are very high also, accurate data are difficult to obtain. Consequently, there has been a tendency to extrapolate to very small values of *D*, assuming a constant *z* over the whole temperature range (Fig. 18.6b). The most confidently obtained data suggest that this has not led to underestimation of required heat processing, and theoretical considerations indicate that any deviations within the practically usable range of temperatures should be small (McKee & Gould, 1988).

In spite of the many observed deviations from exponential kinetics, the simple relationships summarized in Fig. 18.6 still form the basis for the calculation of thermal processes in the food industry, and with an excellent track record of efficacy and safety.

2 THERMAL PROCESSING

2.1 General requirements

For food sterilisation processes the basic rationale remains the requirement to reduce the chance of survival of spores of mesophilic strains of *Clostridium botulinum* by a sufficiently large factor. The decision as to what is a 'sufficiently large factor' still derives from the studies of Esty & Meyer (1922), who proposed standards for sterilization equivalent to a reduction in spore numbers by a factor of about 10^{12}, and by Hicks (1961), who put forward arguments to show that destruction of spores of *Cl. botulinum* by this extent (the '12*D* concept') was necessary to ensure an acceptable degree of safety for low-acid thermally processed foods.

Since the *z*-value (Fig. 18.6) allows comparison of the lethal effects of heating at different temperatures, it is useful, for practical purposes, to choose a standard temperature to which the effects of other temperatures can be related. This is done with the *F*-value, which expresses a heat treatment in terms of the equivalent effect of a stated number of minutes at some standard temperature, for a particular *z*-value. A reference temperature of 121.1°C (250°F) and a *z* of 10°C (18°F) for mesophilic *Cl. botulinum* spores are adopted by the food thermal processing industries and, under these conditions, *F* is designated F_0. Based on the heat inactivation kinetics of *Cl. botulinum* spores in phosphate buffer, an F_0-value of 2.45 min is accepted as the heat treatment necessary to achieve a 10^{12}-fold reduction in numbers. In some foods, *D*-values somewhat higher than those in buffers are found (Murrell & Scott, 1966; Verrips & Kwast, 1977; Alderton *et al.*, 1980), so the required F_0 is commonly taken as 3.0 to ensure the expected lethality.

In pasteurization processes, '*P*-values', analogous to *F*-values, but with reference temperatures more relevant to the lower heat processes (e.g. 60°C or 71°C: Shapton *et al.*, 1971; Wojchiechowski, 1981) are sometimes used. There have been arguments in favour of abandoning this parameter and using *D*- and/or *F*-values instead (Corry, 1974; Verrips & Kwast, 1977; Smelt & Mossel, 1982). However, for non-sterilizing heat processes *where the* D- *and* z-*values of a particular target micro-organism are confidently known*, it would seem appropriate to retain the use of *P*-values, if only to ensure clear distinction from the parameters used in conventional thermal processing for sterility.

2.2 Process calculation

For foods processed in hermetically sealed containers, temperatures are measured using thermocouples during heating and cooling at the slowest heating point within containers within the retort. Calculation of *F*-value delivered is estimated from the lowest integrated time–temperature curve registered, and the required, minimal, F_0 is based on this. A consequence is that the majority of the food in a batch is normally substantially overprocessed. Biological indicators (e.g. spores of *B. stearothermophilus*; Pflug *et al.*, 1980) can be used to check the validity of processes.

Guidelines for the setting of processes are adequately covered in several standard texts (see Stumbo, 1973; Hersom & Hulland, 1980; Pflug, 1982a,b), but all rely on integration to determine the total F-value of the process, having chosen the values of D and z.

In the graphical method the lethal rate per minute, at a particular temperature, is represented by length on the vertical axis of 'F-reference paper' (Fig. 18.8). Time is plotted linearly on the horizontal axis.

The area beneath the curve is then a measure of the F-value, which can be calculated simply by multiplication by the appropriate scale factor (see inset to Fig. 18.8). (For example, the area within the rectangle delineated by the ordinate 121.1°C on the vertical axis and a length of 1 min on the horizontal axis, corresponds, by definition, to an F_0-value of 1 min). The cumulative areas of the rectangles represent the cumulative lethality of the process and, as illustrated in Fig. 18.8, when the appropriate scale factor is applied, give the F_0 of the process.

In the addition method, the lethal rate per minute at each specific temperature is read from a table (Table 18.1), and the F_0-value of the process calcu-

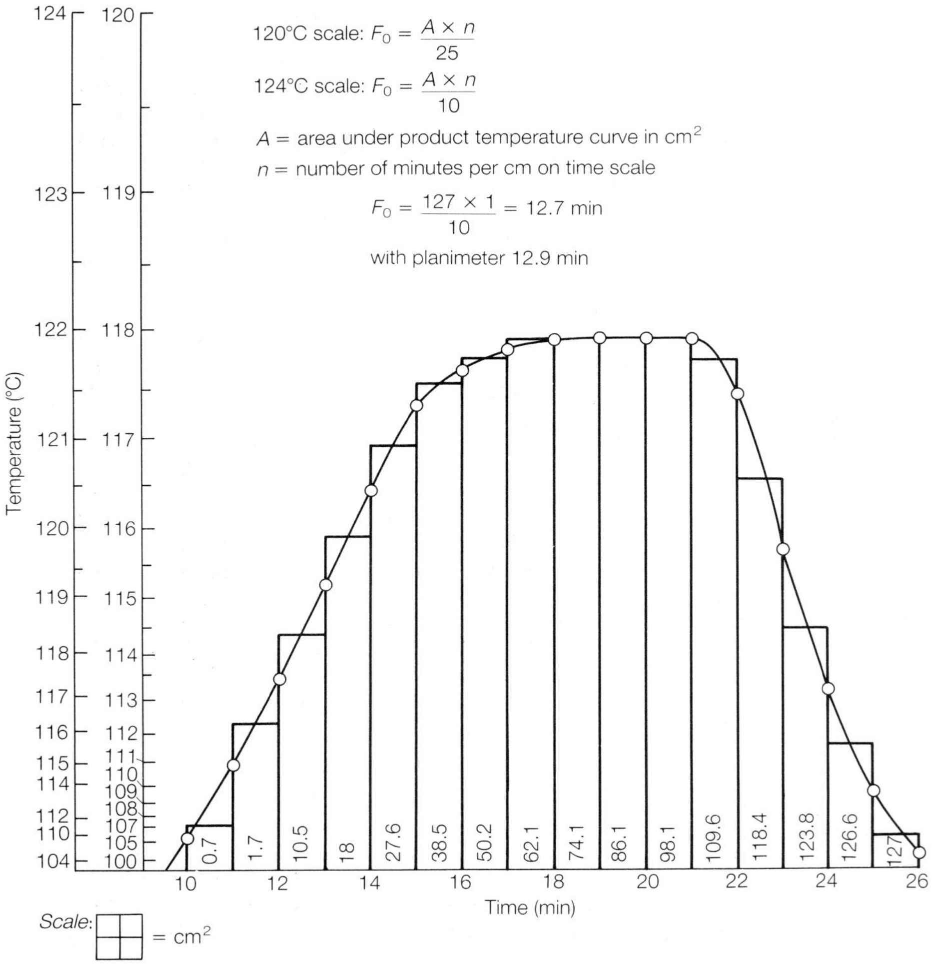

Fig. 18.8 Graphical determination of F_0 value from measured temperatures (○) during a thermal process. The figures within the rectangles represent the *cumulative* areas, and therefore *cumulative* lethality of the process when adjusted by the appropriate scale factor: see inset (from Smelt & Mossel, 1982).

Table 18.4 Lethal rates for thermal processing of foods

T	*LR*	*T*	*LR*	*T*	*LR*	*T*	*LR*
88.0	0.001	109.4	0.068	115.4	0.269	120.0	0.774
92.0	0.001	109.7	0.073	115.5	0.275	120.1	0.791
93.0	0.002	110.0	0.077	115.6	0.281	120.2	0.809
95.0	0.002	110.2	0.080	115.7	0.287	120.3	0.828
95.2	0.003	110.4	0.084	115.8	0.294	120.4	0.848
96.5	0.003	110.6	0.088	115.9	0.301	120.5	0.868
96.7	0.004	110.8	0.093	116.0	0.308	120.6	0.888
97.5	0.004	111.0	0.097	116.1	0.315	120.7	0.909
97.8	0.005	111.2	0.102	116.2	0.322	120.8	0.930
98.3	0.005	111.4	0.107	116.3	0.330	120.9	0.951
98.5	0.006	111.6	0.112	116.4	0.338	121.0	0.974
99.0	0.006	111.8	0.117	116.5	0.346	121.1	0.998
99.4	0.007	112.0	0.122	116.6	0.354	121.2	1.022
99.7	0.007	112.1	0.124	116.7	0.362	121.3	1.046
100.0	0.008	112.2	0.128	116.8	0.370	121.4	1.070
100.6	0.009	112.3	0.131	116.9	0.379	121.5	1.094
101.1	0.010	112.4	0.134	117.0	0.388	121.6	1.118
101.4	0.011	112.5	0.137	117.1	0.397	121.7	1.144
101.7	0.011	112.6	0.141	117.2	0.406	121.8	1.172
102.0	0.012	112.7	0.144	117.3	0.416	121.9	1.199
102.2	0.013	112.8	0.148	117.4	0.426	122.0	1.227
102.5	0.014	112.9	0.151	117.5	0.436	122.1	1.256
102.8	0.015	113.0	0.154	117.6	0.446	122.2	1.286
103.0	0.016	113.1	0.158	117.7	0.456	122.3	1.317
103.3	0.017	113.2	0.162	117.8	0.466	122.4	1.347
103.6	0.018	113.3	0.166	117.9	0.477	122.5	1.377
103.9	0.019	113.4	0.170	118.0	0.488	122.6	1.408
104.2	0.020	113.5	0.174	118.1	0.499	122.7	1.441
104.4	0.022	113.6	0.178	118.2	0.511	122.8	1.475
104.7	0.023	113.7	0.182	118.3	0.523	122.9	1.510
105.0	0.024	113.8	0.186	118.4	0.536	123.0	1.546
105.3	0.026	113.9	0.190	118.5	0.549	123.1	1.582
105.6	0.028	114.0	0.194	118.6	0.562	123.2	1.619
105.9	0.030	114.1	0.198	118.7	0.574	123.3	1.657
106.1	0.032	114.2	0.203	118.8	0.587	123.4	1.695
106.4	0.034	114.3	0.208	118.9	0.601	123.5	1.732
106.7	0.036	114.4	0.213	119.0	0.615	123.6	1.770
107.0	0.038	114.5	0.218	119.1	0.630	123.7	1.809
107.2	0.041	114.6	0.223	119.2	0.645	123.8	1.858
107.5	0.043	114.7	0.228	119.3	0.660	123.9	1.900
107.8	0.046	114.8	0.234	119.4	0.675		
108.0	0.049	114.9	0.239	119.5	0.691		
108.3	0.053	115.0	0.245	119.6	0.707		
108.6	0.056	115.1	0.251	119.7	0.723		
108.9	0.060	115.2	0.257	119.8	0.740		
109.2	0.064	115.3	0.263	119.9	0.757		

The table shows the lethal rates (LR) at temperatures (T) from 88°C to 123.9°C assuming a z-value of 10°C. (Data from Smelt & Mossel, 1982 and the *Laboratory Manual for Food Canners & Processors*, National Food Processors Association Research Laboratories: Westport, Connecticut: AVI Publishing Co.)

lated from the sum of the lethal effects (rates) multiplied by the appropriate time factor in minutes.

The precision of the two methods is similar, and has been improved mainly by better accuracy in temperature recording and by user-friendly computer-aided integration of lethality (Tucker & Clark, 1989; Tucker, 1990). This has made the evaluation of thermal processes far less time-consuming, and allowed greater confidence. Changing z-values and reference temperatures allows use of the programmes for pasteurization processes and also allows determination and control of cook values (see below). Graphical representation still has the advantages of clearly indicating the relevant importance of the heating, holding and cooling phases, and of ensuring that any error in temperature recording is immediately obvious, but modern thermal processing computer programs also have built-in automatic checking for 'rogue' values.

Process *control* has likewise become increasingly precise with the use of modern temperature recorder–controllers that have been developed to the point that they become complete process controllers themselves (Hamilton, 1990).

2.3 Heat delivery and product quality

The temperature coefficients of many of the chemical reactions that cause quality loss of foods — by leading to changes in taste, texture, and appearance and to losses of nutritional value — are such that it is almost invariably advantageous to process foods at as high a temperature as possible for, consequently, as short a time as possible. For example, Ohlsson (1980a) found 'z-values' as high as 33°C for the deterioration of various parameters of product quality, and used the data he derived to define the optimum processes for quality retention in foods thermally processed in flat containers (Ohlsson, 1980b) and in cylindrical cans (Ohlsson, 1980c). Higher temperature – shorter time processing is of course less easy to achieve in container-packed than in free-flowing foods, so that liquid products such as milk, custards, sauces and soups have benefited most substantially from HTST or UHT processing.

2.4 Process hygiene

Post-process contamination of thermally treated foods may occur through defective packaging, defects in sealing or damage to otherwise intact packs. Since so-called 'leaker' spoilage results from the access of micro-organisms to the food from the external environment, the types of organisms involved may be very diverse.

Spoilage resulting from leakage through seams is the most important (Segner, 1979) and avoidance demands a high degree of post-process hygiene. In particular, the major contributing factor to leaker spoilage is unhygienic handling of processed packs whilst they are still wet, so that clean handling immediately following processing, and especially during cooling, when pressure changes may encourage leaks, is particularly important. A dependable, non-destructive, in-line leak detection method is still not widely available, but a variety of 'biotest' methods (challenging packs with high concentrations of micro-organisms externally: see Michels & Schram, 1979) allow statistical estimates of the incidence of potential leakers to be made.

3 RECENT DEVELOPMENTS

Most of the recent developments in the thermal processing of foods have continued to address further improvements in product quality (1) by reducing heat-induced damage to the organoleptic properties of foods by aiming for higher temperature–shorter time processing; (2) by using new forms of packaging that allow more rapid, and more uniform, heat transfer into packed foods during processing, and (3) by delivering heat in new ways, and controlling processes more effectively so as to achieve more *uniform* heating, and so avoid the extreme overprocessing that often occurs within batches of conventionally thermally processed foods.

Progress with the first of these, aseptic processing and packaging, has been substantial. The high temperature–short time heat process is usually delivered to the food in plate or tubular heat exchangers if the products are liquid or viscous, and in scraped surface heat exchangers if the product contains particulates, and these can be processed at sizes up to about 1.5 cm in diameter. Typically, temperatures may be within the range 135–145°C and holding times less than 5 s. The technique, however, is complex, so that successful application requires a high degree of discipline and operator skill.

Since it is not possible to measure continuously the temperature within a food particle as it moves through a flowing system, the F_0 delivered to the centre of the particle must be estimated from the thermal properties and residence times within the system then, ideally, verified using biological methods (Dignan *et al.*, 1989). Such methods have involved the use of 'biological thermocouples', consisting of spores sealed into small glass bulbs (Hersom & Shore, 1981) or entrained within gel particles, such as beads of calcium alginate (Dallyn *et al.*, 1977).

Most of the aseptic filling systems used with UHT or HTST processes make use of hydrogen peroxide to sterilize the packs or packaging materials prior to dosing of the sterilized product. These procedures can regularly achieve inactivation of spores on packaging by factors in excess of 10^8-fold.

Overall, rigorous control of the total system is essential. This is illustrated by the statistics quoted by Warwick (1990), who found, in a survey of 120 users of aseptic systems in Europe, that nearly 50% of installations experienced more than one non-sterile pack per 10 000. Most of the non-sterile packs did not result from failure of the thermal process *per se* to deliver the required level of inactivation of spores.

Although, as pointed out in Section 1.2, good thermal death time data at UHT temperatures are difficult to obtain, experiments using *Cl. botulinum* spores at temperatures over 140°C have been undertaken, and recent studies (Brown & Gaze, 1988) indicate that at these temperatures the inactivation kinetics are close to those that would be expected by extrapolation from lower temperatures.

Most failures result from problems in 'downstream' equipment and procedures, e.g. from mechanical or electrical failures, contaminated packaging, seal failures, etc.

The major changes in packaging that allow improved, more uniform, heat penetration into products, and new attractive forms of presentation of foods to the consumer, have involved the development of new thermally processable flexible pouches and polypropylene rigid containers. Cartons and thermoformed containers are the most-used forms of packaging for aseptically processed foods, but any type of pack that can be hermetically sealed can be used. The materials from which containers are constructed now include aluminium, tin-free steel, aluminium foil, a wide variety of plastics and foil–plastic combinations in addition to glass and tin plate (Bean, 1983).

Processing times can obviously be reduced by the use of thinner packs, such as flexible pouches or shallow trays, containing viscous or solid foods that heat predominantly by conduction. Such packs do not have the strength of conventional cans or glass jars, so that specially careful pack handling techniques are employed, and various types of outer overwraps or cartons are used to protect the packs and help to avoid recontamination during distribution (Turtle & Anderson, 1971). There is currently a very rapid increase in the variety of such packs that are available and coming on to the market (Aggett, 1990).

In the future, new heat-delivery methods for thermally processed foods will no doubt come into even wider use. Procedures investigated include a number of alternatives to traditional steam heating, including direct application of flame to containers, heating by microwave energy or by passing alternating electric currents through foods ('ohmic heating'). In particular, much development work is under way on the large-scale use of microwaves and on the ohmic heating procedures that allow rapid, controlled delivery of heat, and improved product quality.

Already the first commercial applications of ohmic heating coupled with aseptic packaging have commenced (Goddard, 1990). There is the attraction of overcoming the slow transfer of heat to the centre of particles that is inherent in conventional heating, so allowing the inclusion of larger food pieces in aseptically packed products. Developments like these, which aim to raise the quality of products by minimizing heat damage to the food components, whilst at the same time maintaining the correct F_0 and consequent inactivation of the target bacterial spores, will be the most important changes in the thermal processing of foods in the near future.

4 REFERENCES

Aggett, P. (1990) New niche for processables. *Food Manufacture*, **65**(6), 43–46.

Alderton, G., Chen, J.K. & Ito, K.A. (1980) Heat resistance of the chemical resistance forms of *Clostridium botulinum* 62A over the water activity range 0 to 0.9. *Applied and Environmental Microbiology*, **40**, 511–515.

Bean, P.G. (1983) Developments in heat treatment processes for shelf-stable products. In *Food Microbiology: Advances and Prospects* (eds Roberts, T.A. & Skinner, F.A.) pp. 97–112. London: Academic Press.

Brown, K.L. & Gaze, J.E. (1988) High temperature resistance of bacterial spores. *Dairy Industries International*, **53**(10), 37–39.

Cerf, O. (1977) Trailing of survival of bacterial spores. *Journal of Applied Bacteriology*, **37**, 31–43.

Corry, J.E.L. (1974) The effect of sugars and polyols on the heat resistance of Salmonellae. *Journal of Applied Bacteriology*, **37**, 31–43.

Dallyn, H., Falloon, W.C. & Bean, P.G. (1977) Method for the immobilization of bacterial spores in alginate gel. *Laboratory Practice*, **26**, 773–775.

Dignan, D.M., Berry, M.R., Pflug, I.J. & Gardine, T.D. (1989) Safety considerations in establishing aseptic processes for low-acid foods containing particulates. *Food Technology*, **43**(3), 118–112, 131.

Esty, J.R. & Meyer, K.F. (1922) The heat resistance of the spores of *B. botulinus* and allied anaerobes. XI. *Journal of Infectious Diseases*, **31**, 650–663.

Goddard, R. (1990) Developments in aseptic packaging. *Food Manufacture*, **65**(10), 63–66.

Gould, G.W. (1989) Heat-induced injury and inactivation. In *Mechanisms of Action of Food Preservation Procedures* (ed. Gould, G.W.) pp. 11–42. London: Elsevier.

Hamilton, R. (1990) Heat control in food processing. *Food Manufacture*, **65**(6), 33–36.

Han, Y.W., Zhang, H.I. & Krochta, J.M. (1976) Death rates of bacterial spores: mathematical models. *Canadian Journal of Microbiology*, **22**, 295–300.

Hersom, A.C. & Hulland, E.D. (1980) *Canned Foods: Thermal Processing and Microbiology*, 7th Ed. London: Churchill Livingstone.

Hersom, A.C. & Shore, D.T. (1981) Aseptic processing of foods comprising sauce and solids. *Food Technology*, **35**(5), 53–62.

Hicks, E.W. (1961) Uncertainties in canning process calculations. *Journal of Food Science*, **26**, 218–226.

McKee, S. & Gould, G.W. (1988) A simple mathematical model of the thermal death of microorganisms. *Bulletin of Mathematical Biology*, **50**, 493–501.

Michels, M.J.M. & Schram, B.L. (1979) Effect of handling procedures on the post-process contamination of retort pouches. *Journal of Applied Bacteriology*, **47**, 105–111.

Moats, W.A., Dabbah, R. & Edwards, V.M. (1971) Interpretation of non-logarithmic survivor curves of heated bacteria. *Journal of Food Science*, **36**, 523–526.

Murrell, W.G. & Scott, W.J. (1966) The heat resistance of bacterial spores at various water activities. *Journal of General Microbiology*, **43**, 411–425.

Ohlsson, T. (1980a) Temperature dependence of sensory quality changes during thermal processing. *Journal of Food Science*, **45**, 836–839, 847.

Ohlsson, T. (1980b) Optimal sterilization temperature for flat containers. *Journal of Food Science*, **45**, 848–852, 859.

Ohlsson, T. (1980c) Optimal sterilization temperatures for sensory quality in cylindrical containers. *Journal of Food Science*, **45**, 1517–1522.

Pflug, I.J. (1982a) *Textbook for an Introductory Course in the Microbiology and Engineering of Sterilization Processes*. Minneapolis: Environmental Sterilization Laboratory.

Pflug, I.J. (1982b) *Selected Papers on the Microbiology and Engineering of Sterilization*, 4th Ed. Minneapolis: Environmental Sterilization Laboratory.

Pflug, I.J. & Holcomb, R.G. (1977) Principles of thermal destruction of microorganisms. In *Disinfection, Sterilization and Preservation* (ed. Block, S.S.) pp. 933–994. Philadelphia: Lea & Febiger.

Pflug, I.J., Smith, G., Holcomb, R. & Blanchet, R. (1980) Measuring sterilizing values in containers. *Journal of Food Protection*, **43**, 119–123.

Roberts, T.A. & Hitchins, A.D. (1969) Resistance of spores. In *The Bacterial Spore* (eds Gould, G.W. & Hurst, A.) pp. 611–670. London: Academic Press.

Russell, A.D. (1982) *The Destruction of Bacterial Spores*. London: Academic Press.

Segner, W.P. (1979) Mesophilic aerobic spore forming bacteria in the spoilage of low acid canned foods. *Food Technology*, **33**(1), 55–59, 80.

Shapton, D.A., Lovelock, D.W. & Laurito-Longo, R. (1971) The evaluation of sterilization and pasteurization processes from temperature measurements in degrees Celsius (°C). *Journal of Applied Bacteriology*, **34**, 491–500.

Sharpe, K. & Bektash, R.M. (1977) Heterogeneity and the modelling of bacterial spore death: the case of continuously decreasing death rate. *Canadian Journal of Microbiology*, **23**, 1501–1507.

Smelt, J.P.P.M. & Mossel, D.A.A. (1982) Applications of thermal processing in the food industry. In *Principles and Practice of Disinfection, Preservation and Sterilisation* (eds Russell, A.D., Hugo, W.B. & Ayliffe, G.A.J.) pp. 478–512. London: Blackwell Scientific Publications.

Stumbo, C.R. (1973) *Thermobacteriology and Food Processing*, 2nd Ed. New York: Academic Press.

Tucker, G.S. (1990) Evaluating thermal processes. *Food Manufacture*, **65**(6), 39–40.

Tucker, G.S. & Clark, P. (1989) *Computer Modelling for the Control of Sterilisation Processes*, Technical Memorandum No. 529. Campden Food & Drink Research Association.

Turtle, B.I. & Alderson, M.G. (1971) Sterilisable flexible packaging. *Food Manufacture*, **45**, 23, 48.

Verrips, C.T. & Kwast, R.H. (1977) Heat resistance of *Citrobacter freundii* in media with various water activities. *European Journal of Applied Microbiology*, **4**, 225–231.

Warwick, D. (1990) Aseptics: the problems revealed. *Food Manufacture*, **65**(6), 49–50.

Wojchiechowski, J. (1981) Charakteristik und Bewertung der technologischen Verwendbarkeit thermobakteriologischer Pasteurisierungstests von Fleischkonserven 2. Mitteilung: Charakteristik der Hitzewiderstandigkeit der Aerobier, Pasteurisierungswert und Kritische Punkte von Halbkonserven. *Fleischwirtschaft*, **61**, 437–442.

Chapter 19
Radiation Sterilization

A · IONIZING RADIATION

1 INTRODUCTION

Sterilization by means of ionizing radiation, viz. gamma, Röntgen or electron irradiation, is a low-temperature sterilization method which can be used where heat sterilization would cause unacceptable damage to products. Radiation sterilization is a favourable alternative to ethylene oxide or formaldehyde sterilization in a number of cases. However, for economic reasons the method is suitable for large-scale sterilization only.

Radiation sources powerful enough to be used for sterilization purposes outside the laboratory have been available since the Second World War. Such sources are either a radioactive isotope or a machine that accelerates electrons. In a gamma-radiation plant the source is either cobalt-60 (^{60}Co) or caesium-137 (^{137}Cs). In electron-radiation plants the sources are machines that accelerate electrons to high energy levels (5–10 MeV).

Strict national and international rules for the use of radiation sources have existed as long as the sources have been available, and the rules, regulations and recommendations have been regularly updated (e.g. IAEA Technical Report Series and ICPR publications). The use of ionizing radiation for sterilization has been promoted and supported by the International Atomic Energy Agency (IAEA), and this support has been most valuable and efficient.

When large radiation sources became available the potential benefits of the use of these sources for the destruction of micro-organisms were obvious. The irradiation could penetrate the products and kill the micro-organisms without associated problems of heat exchange, pressure differences or hindrances by diffusion barriers. The radiation would cause a moderate rise in temperature and be efficient at ambient temperature, and even at temperatures below zero. The loss of food caused by micro-organisms and pests is a problem of such magnitude that a technology with potential for a new method of food preservation attracted many scientists, and research programmes were established even before large radiation sources could be achieved outside the military establishment. Practical value of the investments in food irradiation (see Section 7) has been low, and of little significance compared with the total effort spent on the subject. However, the scientific value of the large amount of data on radiation chemistry and biology obtained during food irradiation research cannot be questioned. Many of the publications dealing with food irradiation form parts of the basic knowledge necessary for the present utilization of ionizing radiation for sterilization of medical products.

In 1956–58 a group of scientists in the USA demonstrated that surgical sutures could be sterilized by electron irradiation (Artandi & Van Winkle, 1959). Thus it was in the field of sterilization of medical products that radiation sterilization was first demonstrated to be a significant practical advantage, superior to other sterilization methods where contaminating micro-organisms may be difficult to reach with toxic chemicals or the products cannot tolerate the temperature necessary for heat sterilization. Soon after this successful application of the method to catgut sutures, groups of researchers in the USA, UK, Denmark and several other countries followed the track of the pioneers by applying radiation techniques to various medical products (IAEA, 1967a,b). The successful applications were mainly in the field of medical devices composed of plastics. The chemical and toxicological problems connected with radiation sterilization of pharmaceuticals were in general too complex to justify the research and development necessary to achieve official approval of a radiation-sterilized drug. In contrast to pharmaceuticals, heat-sensitive medical devices presented few, if any, toxicological problems not already possessed by the unirradiated products. Radiation sterilization was an elegant alternative to sterilization by toxic gases, where problems associated with pressure equilibration and diffusion (Chapter 20) were constantly complicating the development of medical equipment made from the growing number of artificial polymers and required for the various new and device-demanding fields pertaining to medicine and surgery. From a microbiological point of view the benefit of radiation sterilization compared to ethylene oxide sterilization was most pronounced for complex devices for single use, e.g. oxygenators for heart–lung machines and the various tubing systems for infusion. However, in the production of less complex devices like syringes, needles, catheters and scalpels, it could also be of significant benefit in avoiding the severe limitations in the design of the product itself and its package which were required if sterilization were to be carried out by means of toxic gases. In Europe, where the technology connected with gas sterilization of medical devices was not as well developed as in the USA, radiation sterilization achieved rapid growth in the 1960s, and from the early years of the 1970s this development was also marked in the USA. At present, increasing difficulties with the toxicity of ethylene oxide (Chapter 20) are promoting the use of the available alternative, ionizing radiation.

2 RADIATION ENERGY

Ionizing radiation used for sterilization of medical products penetrates not only the products to be sterilized but the contaminating micro-organisms as well. The penetrating radiation lets loose its energy, forming tracks of ionized and excited atoms and molecules. The binding energy of a covalent chemical bond is generally below 12 eV (1 eV is equivalent to 1.6×10^{-19} Joule) while the energy of the sterilizing radiation used is several orders of magnitude higher. Therefore an immense variety of chemical reactions is possible, both in the products themselves and in micro-organisms, as a result of irradiation.

The basic physical and chemical processes by which ionizing radiation interacts with matter are complex (see McLaughlin & Holm, 1973; Silverman & Sinskey, 1977; Wilski, 1987, 1990). The changes in the products after the administration of a required dose for sterilization can be difficult, if not impossible, to predict. Minor differences in the composition of the products can cause important differences in the reactions they may undergo. The margin between insignificant changes and unacceptable damage to the product can be narrow, and sometimes the harmful effects of radiation on physical properties can be noticed only days or weeks after irradiation. The total absorbed energy determines the extent of the changes, and thus the damage caused by irradiation is additive. It is clear, therefore, that the chemical composition of medical devices to be sterilized by radiation is of the utmost importance.

Many of the plastics suitable for single-use medical devices can tolerate radiation doses several times higher than the dose necessary for sterilization. However, many other plastics are damaged by doses lower than those normally used for sterilization, and several radiation-sterilized medical devices cannot be resterilized without an unacceptable risk of damage. Changes in mechanical properties, in colour or in odour, are not uncommon when plastic devices are radiation-sterilized, and, therefore, even when the relatively simple chemical systems in the medical devices are to be irradiated, experience is necessary to attain acceptable results (Skiens, 1980).

The complex chemical changes caused by absorbed radiation energy are, in general, a hindrance to the use of radiation sterilization of pharmaceuticals. The necessary toxicological examinations are costly even when the pharmacologically active ingredients are relatively resistant to radiation. However, for decontamination of some contaminated raw materials for the pharmaceutical industry, such as products of animal or plant origin for manufacture of hormones, enzymes or alkaloids, irradiation can be an advantageous alternative to other methods for inactivation of micro-organisms. Precautions against microbial contamination of clean production premises can be necessary even when these precautions add further chemical and toxicological problems to the complex production processes. The chemical changes can be kept to acceptable levels because the dose necessary to reduce the number of organisms to the requested standard can be much lower than that needed for sterilization.

In the preservation by radiation of food for human consumption, the induced chemical changes in the products have been, and still are, by far the most important hindrance to the industrial use of the method. Changes in odour, taste and colour, even after small doses, are, for many products, prohibitive. Precautions to prevent these changes (Section 7) will add to the costs of the process, and the margin is often narrow between a dose high enough to secure a significant prolongation of the shelf-life and a dose low enough to ensure that the radiation does not render the product unacceptable.

Interaction between radiation and matter within living cells is the desired effect of the process of radiation sterilization. The effects of radiation on living cells are described by the summation of direct effects on vital centres in the cells and indirect effects on the same centres caused by chemical changes outside these centres, mainly in water, secondarily transferred to the vital centres. Most of the effects of radiation on bacteria and viruses known today can be explained by direct and indirect effects on DNA (or RNA) modified by a number of repair systems in the living cells. Damage to DNA and to the various repair systems may, however, not be the only important reactions in the inactivation of living cells by radiation. Damage to the cell membrane or to other structures necessary for the interaction of enzyme systems may also be involved in the process. Repair of damaged DNA in micro-organisms is dealt with by Bridges (1976), Moseley & Williams (1977) and Moseley (1984): see also Chapter 19B.

3 LARGE RADIATION SOURCES

Excellent reviews on large radiation sources have been published (e.g. Jefferson, 1973; Gaughran & Goudie, 1974; Beck & Morrissey, 1986; Beers, 1990). For large-scale radiation sterilization, two types of source are used: in gamma radiation plants the source is a radioactive isotope, whereas in electron radiation plants the source is a machine that accelerates electrons to high energy levels.

3.1 ^{60}Co- and ^{137}Cs-sources

Radioactive cobalt is a by-product from the nuclear reactor and can be produced by exposure of naturally occurring cobalt (^{59}Co) to neutrons, in a reactor. The radiation from ^{60}Co consists of two photons (1.33 and 1.17 MeV, respectively) and one electron. The radiation is reduced by a factor of two after 5.3 years, or about 10% each year.

Radioactive caesium (^{137}Cs) is a fission product and must be separated from spent fuel elements from a nuclear reactor. The radiation from ^{137}Cs consists of one photon (0.66 MeV) and one electron and the half-life is approx. 30 years.

The majority of radionucleide facilities are based on ^{60}Co. Only a few industrial radiation facilities using ^{137}Cs have been put into operation.

The environment and personnel at the plant are protected against irradiation by concrete shielding, and when not in use the source is submerged in water, making admittance to the irradiation chamber possible. The irradiation of a product is performed either as a batch operation or as a continuous irradiation procedure. In a batch irradiation procedure, the product is placed close to the source, and its position changed at regular intervals until all parts are irradiated with the intended dose. In the continuous process, a mechanical transport system conveys the product into and out of the irradiation chamber, shifting the position of the product relative to the source during the irradiation exposure to ensure that all parts of the product receive the same dose. By varying the exposure time, different doses can be given.

The intensity of radiation from ^{60}Co and ^{137}Cs decreases exponentially as it penetrates a product. For a density of 1 g cm^{-3}, the layer needed to reduce the intensity to 50% is approx. 10 cm for ^{60}Co, and 6 cm for ^{137}Cs. The strength of the source in an industrial gamma-radiation plant is normally $1-4 \times 10^{16}$ Bq (200–1000 kCi). The irradiation from the isotope is continuous, and the loss of source strength is, as mentioned above, about 10% per year in a ^{60}Co plant. Reloadings in order to adjust the radiation capacity to the expected production level are therefore required.

3.2 Electron accelerators

There are several commercially available types of electron accelerators (Jefferson, 1973; McKeown, 1990). Commonly, machines giving from 5 to 10 MeV electrons are used for radiation sterilization. At energy levels lower than 5 MeV the electron penetration is generally insufficient. About 0.5 cm of water or materials of equal density can be penetrated per MeV. At energies higher than 10 MeV, problems with induced radioactivity in the products start becoming significant.

As in the gamma plant, the environment and the personnel at the plant are protected against the radiation from the electron accelerator by concrete shielding. The scattered electrons are not the only source of radiation in the electron accelerator plant. Part of the electron beam will inevitably strike material of sufficient density to generate Röntgen rays. Therefore the concrete shielding surrounding the accelerators is about the same size as for the cobalt sources. As in the continuous irradiation operation in an automatic gamma plant, the products are conveyed through the irradiation field from the electron accelerator by means of a package conveyer. The conveyor system is relatively simple because the products are normally irradiated from one or two sides only. The dose rate in the electron accelerator is high compared to that in the gamma plant. The exposure times necessary for the doses normally used for sterilization are measured in seconds in the accelerator plant, in hours in the gamma plant.

Röntgen rays are an electromagnetic radiation, as are gamma rays. Provided their energy is high enough, penetration can be sufficient for sterilization. Electron radiation can be converted to Röntgen rays if the electron beam strikes a metallic target of high atomic number. When products with too high a density for the electron beam are to be dealt with at the electron accelerator plant, use can be made of the conversion of electron radiation to Röntgen rays. As much as 30% of the energy in an electron beam can be utilized as Röntgen rays.

3.3 Radiation dose

In order to be sure that a radiation sterilization procedure meets the prescribed requirements with regard to absorbed dose, the dose distribution in the products must be reasonably homogeneous. The source parameters, the source-to-product geometry and the product conveyor speed will define the absorbed dose. The dose in a certain position in the product can be measured by means of a dosimeter. No product can in practice be irradiated completely homogeneously. Some parts of a product will receive a minimum dose, determining the minimum biocidal effect, and other parts a maximum dose, determining the maximum degrading effect on the product. During a validation of the irradiation process of a certain product, the zones or locations of minimum and maximum dose must be identified by placing dosimeters in or at samples of the product, placed in the same packages and with the same irradiation geometry as will be used in the sterilizing processing. Several reliable dosimetry systems are available, some of them calibrated by national, regional or international organizations (for more comprehensive information refer to Holm, 1968, 1973; McLaughlin *et al.*, 1989). Recommendations for industrial process control measures have been published (IAEA, 1967a, 1975; Frohnsdorff & Peter, 1977; AAMI, 1984; EUCOMED, 1988; UK Panel, 1989).

4 RADIATION RESISTANCE OF MICRO-ORGANISMS

Informative surveys of radiation resistance of micro-organisms have been published (IAEA, 1973; Gaughran & Goudie, 1977).

The result of a sterilization procedure depends on the amount of energy transferred to the contaminating micro-organisms relative to the number and the resistance of these micro-organisms. The dose–response curve for a mixed population of micro-organisms is not a straight line in semilogarithmic system (Fig. 19.1). When a high level of safety against surviving organisms is to be ensured, a small fraction of the population will be the most significant because of a relatively high resistance. For sterilized medical products it is generally accepted that a high safety margin is necessary, e.g. the standard for sterilized medical products recommended by the health authorities in the Nordic countries is not more than one colony-forming unit per million product units (National Board of Health and Welfare, Sweden, 1976; *Danish Standards for Pharmaceutical Products*, 1979). In the late 1980s a sterility assurance level (SAL) of 10^{-6} was generally accepted as indicating a proper safety margin for sterilization of medical products (Ph. Eur., 1983; AAMI, 1984; EUCOMED, 1988).

In general, multicellular organisms are more sensitive to radiation than are unicellular organisms. Gram-negative bacteria are more sensitive

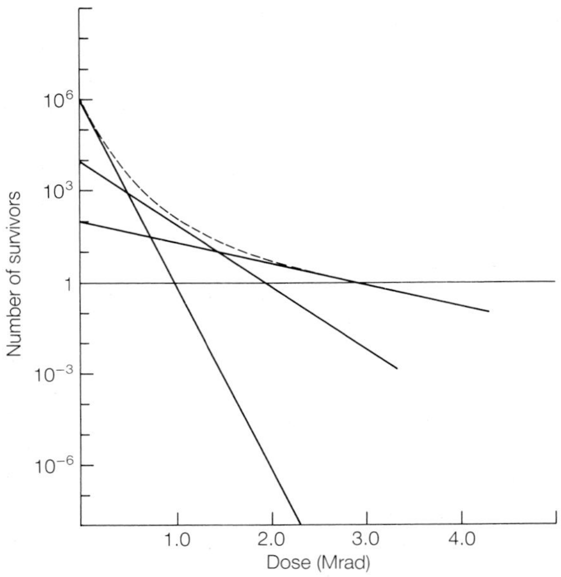

Fig. 19.1 An inactivation curve for a mixed population of micro-organisms (dashed line) is not a straight line in a semilogarithmic system. The curve demonstrated is a summation of a number of examinations of dust samples from production areas and of the microflora collected from medical devices (from Christensen, 1977). The three lines symbolize that the curve is a result of inactivation of numerous strains with different radiation resistance (1.0 Mrad = 10 kGy).

than Gram-positive, and bacterial spores are more resistant than vegetative forms. The most radiation-resistant fungi are about as resistant as those bacterial spores having moderate radiation resistance, and the viruses in general are more resistant than bacteria. Some viruses are among the living systems with the highest radiation resistance known (for detailed information for special purposes see IAEA's *Manual on Radiation Sterilization*, 1973, and Ingram, 1975).

Micro-organisms with a low resistance will not survive an exposure to a dose of radiation efficient enough to have a measurable influence on a very resistant micro-organism even when the number of sensitive cells is high. It must, however, be noted that enzymes, pyrogens, toxins and antigens of microbial origin are in general very radiation-resistant compared to living cells. Therefore the number of micro-organisms present prior to a radiation sterilization is of importance when dealing with medical products, regardless of the radiation resistance of the contaminating population.

The radiation resistance of micro-organisms is basically genetically determined. The conditions for the organisms prior to, during, and after irradiation treatment also, however, affect resistance. The presence of water and oxygen will enhance the radiation damage. Very dry conditions also may increase sensitivity of some endospores (Ley, 1973). Protection or sensitization due to environmental agents must be considered, the environmental influence being well recognized in the food irradiation field. It is, however, not always taken into account when dealing with radiation sterilization of medical products. Small numbers of micro-organisms per product unit or per gram of a medical product manufactured in a controlled and clean area do not necessarily mean that the micro-environment for contaminating organisms is less protecting than the micro-environment for organisms from an open, less clean area. In controlled areas for the manufacture of medical products the major part of the microbial contamination is from the personnel working in the area. Human skin does not release bacteria as individual cells but in clumps or aggregates (Noble, 1975). Furthermore, these clumps will be associated with organic matter, e.g. epidermal fragments and sebum. Cells at the centre of these aggregates will be protected by surrounding cells and by the associated debris. When possible, the actual resistance of micro-organisms on and in the products should be taken into account when the dose necessary for sterilization is evaluated. When this resistance is unknown and cannot be measured directly, it is recommended that the highest *D*-values for the resistant organisms consistent with the physical and chemical conditions be used in the evaluation.

In food irradiation research (investigated several years prior to the utilization of radiation sterilization for medical products), much interest was focused on *clostridium botulinum* (Schmidt *et al.*, 1962), because this dangerous toxin-producing and spore-forming species was shown to be among the most radiation-resistant bacteria.

In 1956 a very radiation-resistant bacterial strain was isolated (Anderson *et al.*, 1956). This organism

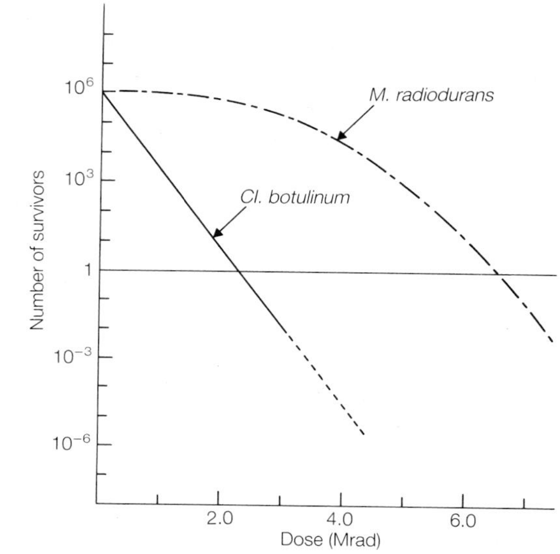

Fig. 19.2 Inactivation curves for dried preparations of two strains of bacteria, *Micrococcus radiodurans*, strain R_1 and *Clostridium botulinum*, type A, respectively, with high resistance against radiation. The strains were irradiated in a ^{60}Co-cell (1.0 Mrad = 10 kGy).

Deinococcus radiodurans (*Micrococcus radiodurans*) (Brooks & Murray, 1981) was, at the dose levels discussed for sterilization, more resistant to radiation than any known spore-forming organism (Fig. 19.2). However, the heat resistance was low. The growth rate on various culture media was relatively slow. No harmful effects from this organism were known apart from its ability to spoil irradiated food. *D. radiodurans* was therefore generally regarded as a curiosity of much scientific interest, but of little significance in radiation sterilization.

Radiation-resistant non-sporing bacteria may occur as contaminants (from airborne dust, hands, handling equipment, working surfaces or raw materials) in or on medical products requiring sterilization. Their presence is of no consequence if the final sterilization process is by heat. Their presence cannot be ignored if a radiation sterilization process is to be used and the minimum dose must be calculated with due regard to all types of microorganisms likely to be present on or in the actual product prior to sterilization.

Many bacterial spores isolated from dust and soil

will have D values between 2.0 and 3.0 kGy, when irradiated in dried preparation and conglomerated with small amounts of organic matter. However, a few spore-forming strains with higher resistance are known, viz. some clostridia (Schmidt *et al.*, 1962) and a few *Bacillus* strains (Christensen, 1974a). Surprisingly, a number of non-spore-forming bacteria with resistance comparable to, or higher than, the commonly occurring endospores are known, and may often be present in some environments (Iizuka & Ito, 1968; Kristensen, 1974; Christensen, 1977; Maxcy & Rowley, 1977; Christensen & Kristensen, 1981). Gram-positive cocci, non-spore-forming rods (Christensen *et al.*, 1967) and even pyrogen-producing Gram-negative rods (Christensen, 1974b) with high radiation resistance have been selected from unsterilized medical devices or from dust collected in the areas where medical devices are manufactured. In Fig. 19.3, several characteristic dose–response curves for various bacteria with high radiation resistance are shown. In all cases the micro-organisms were irradiated in air-dried preparations in the presence of albumin to simulate the assumed protection encountered under conditions of normal contamination. The demonstrated radiation resistance in this model is assumed to be representative of the maximum resistance likely to be exhibited in an industrial radiation sterilization process for medical devices as used today.

As mentioned earlier, fungi are less resistant to radiation than the commonly occurring spores of *Bacillus* strains (Fig. 19.4). However, some strains may be resistant enough to be of significance in radiation sterilization, because the level of initial fungal contamination may be high in some products submitted to a radiation sterilization regimen (Österberg, 1974; Ingram, 1975; Kristensen, 1981).

Viruses may have a high resistance to radiation, and D values of about 5 kGy have been described (Sullivan *et al.*, 1971, 1973) and for the scrapie agent the extremely high D-value of about 50 kGy is indicated (Gibbs *et al.*, 1978). Taking into account that 'slow viruses' might be the cause of some still unexplained human diseases, there are good reasons to hesitate before products in which

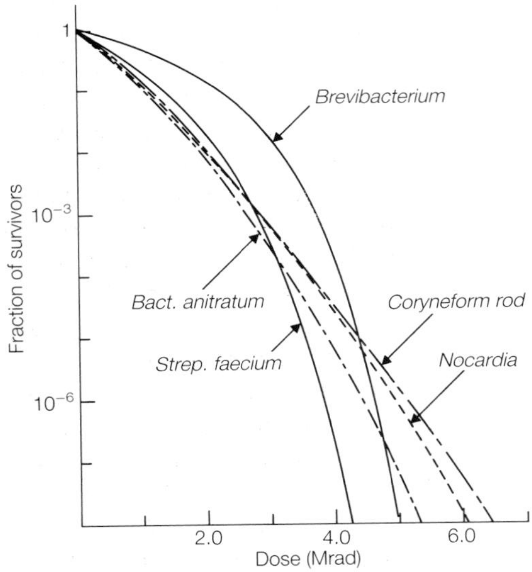

Fig. 19.3 Characteristic inactivation curves for some selected strains of micro-organisms with unusually high radiation resistance. Dried preparations of the micro-organisms were irradiated in a ^{60}Co-cell (1.0 Mrad = 10 kGy).

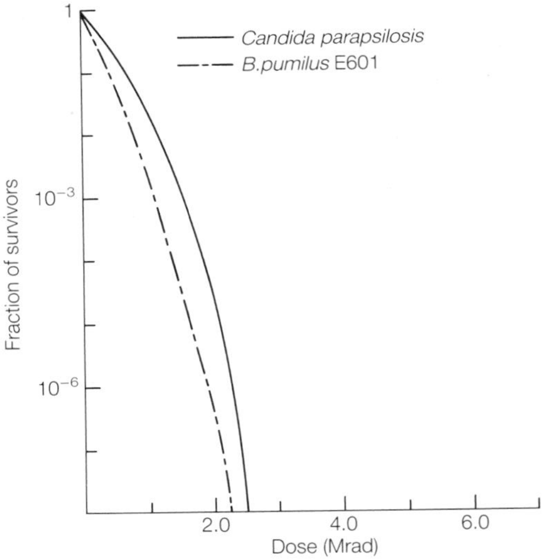

Fig. 19.4 The inactivation curve for *Candida parapsilosis* is a summation of several nearly identical strains. For comparison, an inactivation curve for spores of *Bacillus pumilus* strain E601 is shown. Dried preparations of the micro-organisms were irradiated in a ^{60}Co-cell (from Kristensen, 1981) (1.0 Mrad = 10 kGy).

viruses might form part of the microbial contamination are sterilized by radiation. Resterilization of medical equipment used at hospitals is not to be recommended unless the risk of virus contamination can be eliminated.

Statements concerning the radiation resistance of a species of micro-organisms should always be regarded as relative. Differences in the inherent radiation resistance between strains of bacteria of the same species are significant (Christensen *et al.*, 1967; Ley, 1973; Christensen, 1974b) and there has been much discussion as to whether the most resistant strains are extremes in a normal variation within a species or population, or mutants induced by the irradiation (Goldblith, 1967; Idziak, 1973). Very resistant substrains can be selected deliberately from irradiated cultures (Witkin, 1946, 1947; Erdman *et al.*, 1961; Christensen & Kjems, 1965). The increased mutation rate induced by irradiation is, of course, of no significance when sterilizing doses are applied. The phenomenon may, however, be important if, in the future, radiation is used on a large scale for decontamination under conditions where there is the possibility of growth of survivors after irradiation.

5 CHOICE OF DOSE FOR STERILIZATION OF MEDICAL PRODUCTS

In most countries (including the UK) a dose of 25 kGy, either as minimum or average absorbed dose, is considered a suitable sterilizing dose, regardless of the type of medical products being sterilized (UK Panel on Gamma and Electron Irradiation, 1987). This standpoint, reflected in several pharmacopoeias, may, however, be without sufficient flexibility to comply with current demands for safety in connection with the use of sterilized medical products. In the first version of the *Recommended Code of Practice for Radiation Sterilization of Medical Products* (IAEA, 1967a) and in the official recommendations in the Scandinavian countries (National Board of Health and Welfare, Sweden 1976: *Danish Standards for Pharmaceutical Products*, 1979) the minimum dose depends on the number and resistance of microbial contaminants on the products prior to irradiation. A similar evaluation is expressed in recommendations from the Association for Advancement of Medical Instrumentation, in the USA (1984).

The industrial use of radiation sterilization of medical products was introduced for sutures by the Ethicon company in the USA in 1956. Based on data on the radiation sensitivity of a large collection of different strains of micro-organisms, it was concluded that at a level of contamination of $<10^3$ colony-forming units per suture unit, radiation doses considerably lower than 25 kGy would sterilize the product. An average dose of 25 kGy was recommended to allow a safety margin (Van Winkle *et al.*, 1967; Artandi, 1973). More than 20 years' experience with radiation-sterilized surgical sutures have confirmed that, from a practical point of view, this choice of dose was sound. Therefore, based on experience gained with radiation-sterilized sutures, the dose of 25 kGy was recommended for a wide variety of medical products and was generally regarded as being equivalent to the standard heat sterilization regimens, viz. 121°C for 15 min with saturated steam and 160°C for 2 h with dry heat (e.g. Ph. Eur., 1983). This conclusion is not necessarily correct, however, since it does not take into account the many examples of bacteria and viruses with a radiation resistance much higher than the most resistant organisms which formed the basis for the choice of 25 kGy as sterilizing dose.

It can be questioned whether a standard for sterilized medical products should be based on a maximum probability of one colony-forming unit (c.f.u.) per million product units, or whether more than one level is to be preferred, based on a classification of products according to the risk involved if microbial contamination occurs. A maximum probability of one surviving organism per 10^3 or 10^4 product units may be defensible for many of the single-use devices now sterilized by radiation. Two facts might support such a choice of standard. In nearly all procedures where sterilized devices are used, microbial contamination from the environment, from the physician or nurse, or from the patient, can be estimated as being more frequent than one episode per 10^3. Furthermore, if virus contamination can be excluded, nearly all micro-organisms with very high resistance are fortunately not particularly dangerous to man. In fact, most of these organisms are harmless unless they occur in large numbers. Most types of micro-organisms can be dangerous when conditions for multiplication exist prior to, or in connection with, their subsequent use in surgery or medicine, and many normally harmless bacteria and fungi can be dangerous when a patient's resistance against infection is lowered. However, the risks connected with possible growth of micro-organisms and with decreased resistance against infections in a number of patients can perhaps be eliminated by a reasonable classification of sterilized devices and supplies, with different standards for the various classes. In such a system, ordinary syringes, needles, catheters, etc., could be placed on a quality level equal to the level required for aseptically prepared pharmaceuticals. An official system of that kind would probably not be very different from the unofficial systems already followed at various institutions and companies in internal sterilization and quality control.

If the official standard for all sterilized medical products is not more than one organism per 10^6 product units, *viz.* a sterility assurance level (SAL) of 10^{-6}, the use of a 25 kGy dose for sterilization, without a routine control of the number and the resistance of the contaminating micro-organisms on the product prior to sterilization, can hardly be justified. Highly resistant micro-organisms exist and are often present as ordinary contaminants.

In a controlled manufacturing area with a mechanized automatic production process, the number of contaminating organisms per product unit prior to sterilization (the 'bioburden': Miller & Bérubé, 1977) can be kept at a low average level without the sporadic high contamination levels so common on products exposed to handling by humans. It is likely that even with the standard $1{:}10^6$ as an official requirement, a sterilizing dose lower than 25 kGy could be justified for a product with low average contamination and without much variation in the contamination level. The choice of dose should, of course, be based on data from the routine control on the numbers and resistance of the microbial contamination. However, when the bioburden is low the number of samples necessary for collecting valid data on the radiation resistance of a representative segment of the relevant microbial population will be large, and may be too large to be realistic.

If a choice of dose based on an estimate of the resistance of the microbial contamination is preferred, a large safety margin is necessary. The experience with other products manufactured in other environments might be too optimistic, and the most unfavourable conditions for sterilization, *viz.* a high frequency of organisms with high resistance, must be taken into account.

The dose of 25 kGy as well as the dose of 35 kGy recommended in the Scandinavian countries when the number of contaminating organisms prior to irradiation does not exceed 50 per product unit (Public Health Service of Denmark, 1972; National Board of Health, Sweden, 1976; *Danish Standards for Medical Products*, 1979), is primarily based on experience gained with radiation sterilization of products manufactured under good hygienic conditions and therefore at low levels of contamination. The possibility of direct measurements of the radiation resistance of the contamination was not taken into account when these recommendations were given. Today such measurements are possible (see Sections 6.1 and 6.2).

6 MICROBIOLOGICAL CONTROL OF RADIATION STERILIZATION

Inactivation factors (IFs) for various micro-organisms at radiation doses normally used for sterilization are very high for most micro-organisms, including common pathogenic bacteria. However, for some bacteria and viruses these IFs are small compared to those for *all* types of micro-organisms when heat or gas sterilization is used *lege artis*. Therefore a limitation of the possibilities of microbial contamination of the products before sterilization is at least as important when radiation is used as it is in connection with other methods.

Several official guidelines for good manufacturing practice exist (e.g. *Basic Standards*, EFTA, 1983; FDA, *Medical Devices*, 1984; *Guide to GMP*, EEC and EFTA, 1989). The various methods of establishing a controlled area for production of sterile medical products will not be dealt with here (see Chapter 22). It should, however, be mentioned that the microbial contamination on most of the medical devices commonly sterilized by radiation originates from contact with a contaminated environment, e.g. surfaces, hands, cooling water and, last, but not least, air. In some cases simple precautions can be efficient against contamination with little extra cost. When, for example, the airborne dust forms a significant part of the microbial contamination, the devices can be enclosed in plastic boxes or bags during delays in the assembly or packaging processes. The time of exposure to the contaminated air is of importance, as are the number of organisms per unit volume of air.

6.1 Total counts of microbial contaminants prior to radiation

The average number of c.f.u. per product unit, and the deviations from the average, can give an objective picture of the efficiency of the precautions taken to avoid contamination. In radiation sterilization these data are also important for evaluating the dose necessary to achieve a defined level of survival probability for organisms following irradiation, i.e. the SAL. The relationship between the absorbed dose and the inactivation of micro-organisms is relatively well defined, and the minimum absorbed dose can be measured with acceptable accuracy by physical and chemical methods. Even more important for the choice of dose, however, is the resistance of the contaminating population. As mentioned above, a relatively large safety margin is necessary if the resistance must be estimated rather than measured. Coincidence of unfavourable conditions must be taken into account, and a relatively high number of organisms with relatively high resistance per product unit must be the basis for the evaluation. The present basis for such an evaluation in Denmark is demonstrated in Fig. 19.5, in which the curve is a summation of a number of examinations of dust samples from production areas and of the microflora collected from medical devices. All irradiations were performed in a ^{60}Co-cell.

Taking into account that the radiation resistance of an isolated culture of micro-organisms in a dried laboratory preparation rich in organic compounds probably indicates a maximum resistance compared to the *in situ* resistance, the minimum dose for radiation sterilization of ordinary medical devices with a bioburden of 10^2 c.f.u. (average initial count or total aerobic count) should be 30 kGy, and the minimum dose corresponding to a bioburden of one c.f.u. should be 24 kGy when a SAL level of 10^{-6} is requested (Fig. 19.5). These estimated doses for devices produced in the Scandinavian countries are in reasonable harmony with the sterilizing dose of 25 kGy recommended by Van Winkle *et al.*, (1967) and by the UK Panel on Gamma and Electron Irradiation (1987).

The published data on the composition of contaminating micro-organisms and the frequency of occurrence of highly radiation-resistant micro-organisms have been obtained from northern Europe or North America (Tiwary & Maxcy, 1972; Ley *et al.*, 1972; Christensen, 1974a; Osterberg, 1974; Christensen, 1977; Whitby, 1979; Christensen & Kristensen, 1981). Therefore, investigations are needed when a new radiation plant is built in an area where no experience with

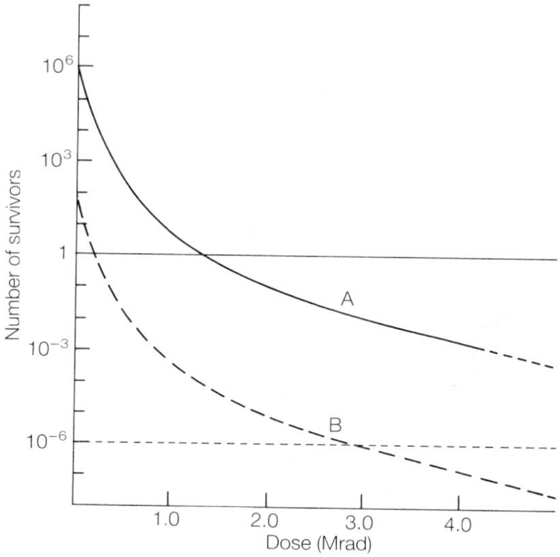

Fig. 19.5 The curve A is a summation of a number of examinations of dust samples from production areas and of the microflora collected from medical devices. The dotted line B is parallel to A, based on the assumption that the radiation resistance is independent of the density of organisms in the samples (from Christensen, 1977) (1.0 Mrad = 10 kGy).

the radiation resistance of the microbial contamination in relevant environments has been collected previously.

6.2 Evaluation of the radiation resistance of contaminants

A good approximation to a constant contamination level, without the sporadic high peaks in numbers of contaminants so often found when the environmental control in production premises is inefficient, is a condition for obtaining valid information about the radiation resistance of the microbial contamination by examining product units collected at random. It is not possible to ensure that a sporadic and infrequent contamination is represented among the samples examined (e.g. Council of the Pharmaceutical Society of Great Britain, 1963).

Provided that a reasonably low level of contamination without extreme variations has been established, a membrane filtration technique for counting micro-organisms prior to sterilization gives the opportunity for a continuous screening of the radiation resistance of the isolated micro-organisms (Christensen, 1974a; Österberg, 1974; Christensen & Kristensen, 1981).

Another possibility of evaluating the resistance of the contaminating population is the use of a sterility test technique on product units irradiated with doses much lower than the routine dose (Tallentire *et al.*, 1971; Tallentire, 1973; Tallentire & Khan, 1977; AAMI, 1984; Davis *et al.*, 1987; Doolan *et al.*, 1988). This method provides information as to the number of survivors after irradiation with sub-process doses. Provided that sufficient numbers of samples are examined, evaluation of the SAL obtained with the routine dose is possible.

The small amount of information obtained so far with the two methods does not allow for a comparison of their routine values.

Both methods can at best indicate a dose range corresponding to the required SAL, and the minimum dose for routine sterilization must be based on a qualified estimate.

Evaluation of the radiation resistance of the bioburden on a certain medical device based on selection and dose–response analyses of the most resistant of the micro-organisms picked up by routine total aerobic count analyses, probably produces an overestimation compared to the *in situ* resistance. The reason for this is that although the average total count and the frequency of occurrence of resistant organisms are minimum values, the resistance measured by irradiation of a laboratory preparation rich in organic compounds probably represents a maximum value. The minimum dose necessary for a required SAL is calculated with the minimum values on a logarithmic scale for numbers of organisms and the maximum value for resistance as a D or D-6 value on an equidistant scale for dose (Christensen & Kristensen, 1981).

In doses assessed by irradiating product units with incremental doses and performing sterility testing on the irradiated samples, the dose necessary for a SAL of 10^{-3} can be determined if the samples included in the primary validation and the revalidations provide a sufficient number of micro-organisms to be representative for the bioburden on the product just prior to routine irradiation. However, if a SAL of 10^{-6} is required, extrapolation is unavoidable and then the simplification obtained by assuming that the dose–response curves for all micro-organisms are linear causes an error. Doses for products with small bioburdens will be too low, and doses for products with large bioburdens will probably be too high (Davis *et al.*, 1984).

6.3 Standardized microbiological preparations

Microbiological preparations can be used to demonstrate the microbiological efficiency of the doses delivered in a radiation plant. When the environmental conditions for the micro-organisms before, during and after exposure to radiation are defined, the relationships between the IFs for pure cultures of micro-organisms and the absorbed doses are also defined. The inactivation curves obtained after irradiation of the same standard preparation of micro-organisms are therefore, in principle, the same after irradiation under similar conditions at different plants. Differences can be explained either by dosimetry failures or by failures in the microbiological procedures.

Since the first version of the IAEA's *Code of*

Practice for Radiation Sterilization was published in 1967 (IAEA, 1967a) it has been regarded as a condition for radiation sterilization of medical products that the manufacturer or the radiation plant should have access to a qualified dosimetrist and a qualified microbiologist. In a microbiological efficiency measurement by means of standardized microbiological preparations, irradiated at different radiation facilities and with the dose-response curves compared, reliable dosimetry as well as an accurate microbiological counting technique must be used if identical curves are to be obtained (Emborg *et al.*, 1971). Figure 19.6 demonstrates the inactivation curves for three spore-forming strains commonly used for examinations of biological efficiency.

In the 1980s, international cooperation in dosimetry was intensified and improved (IAEA, 1985a; UK Panel, 1989; McLaughlin *et al.*, 1989) and therefore the value of the less accurate intercomparisons by standardized microbiological preparations was decreasing. A nominal absorbed dose

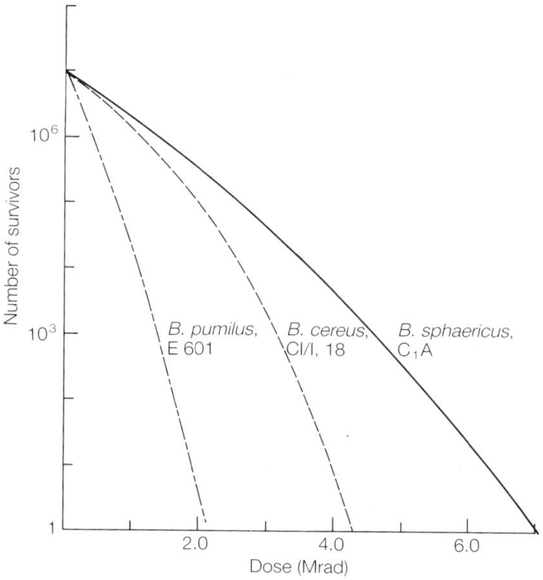

Fig. 19.6 Inactivation curves for three strains of spore-forming bacteria irradiated in dried preparations in a ^{60}Co-cell. At various dose levels these strains can be used for examination of the microbiological efficiency of the measured dose (1.0 Mrad = 10 kGy).

delivered at any radiation facility can and should be documented and made traceable to primary standards. When needed, the International Atomic Energy Agency can provide an *International Dose Assurance Service* (Nam, 1989). Preparations of micro-organisms can still, however, when needed, provide a relevant measure of the integrated effect of the absorbed dose and process-related variations in temperature, humidity or oxygen concentration.

6.4 Biological indicators

Biological indicators are designed to indicate, by growth of the test strain, that the safety margin of a sterilization procedure is too narrow. Such a warning system is a 'go—no go' test. In radiation sterilization physical and chemical dosimetry are mandatory. Therefore, in general, biological indicators have no place in routine radiation sterilization.

Should, however, the use of a biological indicator be required, it is essential for the value of the indicator system that the resistance of the indicator units be adjusted to the required dose. The biological indicator shall give growth of all or nearly all units after a dose not less than about 80% of the required minimum dose, if the reliability of the process is to be assessed by means of the indicator. This will give an inconvenient probability of some units showing growth also, when the absorbed dose is at the required minimum.

6.5 Sterility tests on the finished products

Sterility tests (e.g. *European Pharmacopoeia*) on sterilized medical products are still mandatory in several countries. It is, however, well known (Chapter 22) that sterility tests under optimal conditions can only reveal gross contamination (e.g. Council of the Pharmaceutical Society of Great Britain, 1963). When the test is mandatory it has, of course, the legal value also for radiation sterilized products. However sterility tests have no value in the quality control of radiation-sterilized products, unless the packages are insufficient, the control of the contamination prior to irradiation is neglected, the dosimetry is very inaccurate, or the frequency of the occurrence of radiation-resistant organisms is unknown. If a radiation sterilization process for a certain product is validated *lege artis*, a sterility test on the finished product cannot give further information about the SAL, when the actual minimum dose delivered is known.

7 FOOD IRRADIATION

The applications of ionizing radiation, to avoid destruction of food by pests, to achieve a prolonged storage lifetime to obtain a selective kill of harmful micro-organisms, or to prevent the natural decrease in quality of potatoes and onions caused by sprouting, were promising projects some 40 years ago. At present few of these projects actually exist as industrial realities. Several difficulties in the use of ionizing radiation for food preservation were discovered to be more serious than expected for the practical application of the technique. The taste and smell of the food products were often changed by the doses necessary to attain a prolonged storage time. The enzymes were not destroyed by irradiation, at least not by doses which could be used without spoiling the products. Sterilization could be difficult to achieve because of significant differences in the radiation resistance of micro-organisms. A destruction of harmful organisms in food products was, in a number of cases, not of any practical value unless the products could be protected against recontamination. The public health authorities in many countries evaluated irradiation as being an additive to the food products in a manner analogous to various chemical additives and requested a complicated and time-consuming testing of wholesomeness of all irradiated food products for human consumption. These difficulties, and probably a number of economic and political difficulties as well, have hindered the use of food irradiation on a large scale. However, this has not eliminated the idea of radiation as a method for food preservation, neither have they dashed the optimism of the scientists involved. Publications demonstrating the potential benefits are still to be found each year e.g. *International acceptance of irradiated food*; *Decontamination of animal feeds by irradiation* (IAEA, 1979a, 1985b), and procedures with full technical details have been published for the combined use of heat treatment in order to inactivate enzymes, low temperature and vacuum for minimizing the changes in taste caused by irradiation at ambient temperature and in the presence of oxygen and a sterilizing dose of radiation (Brynjolfsson, 1978; IAEA, 1981).

In the early 1980s, WHO and FAO approved the use of radiation for treatment of food with doses lower than an average 10 kGy (WHO, 1981, FAO and WHO, 1984). This official international recognition caused renewed interest in the method (IAEA, 1989). Decontamination of most food products for human consumption by means of radiation must obviously be combined with efficient precautions against recontamination and against growth of surviving organisms, if the method is to find general application. Irradiation of potatoes for sprout inhibition for sprout inhibition has been tried on a large scale in Japan (Umeda, 1978) and may be of importance in equalizing the supply of potatoes for the market throughout the year. Of other procedures of practical value, decontamination of spices by radiation as a substitute for decontamination by toxic gases, and the sterilization or decontamination of food for laboratory animals can be mentioned. Summaries on radiation microbiology relative to food irradiation have been published by Ingram (1975) and by Josephson & Peterson (1982–83).

8 REFERENCES

Anderson, A.W., Nordan, H.C., Cain, R.F., Parrish, G. & Duggan, D. (1956) Studies on a radio-resistant micrococcus. I. Isolation, morphology, cultural characteristics and resistance to gamma radiation. *Food Technology*, **10**, 575–578.

Artandi, C. & Van Winkle, W. (1959) Electron-beam sterilization of surgical sutures. *Nucleonics*, **17**, 86–90.

Artandi, C. (1973) Sutures. In *Manual on Radiation Sterilization of Medical and Biological Materials*. Technical Report Series No. 149. STI/DOC/10/149. pp. 173–187. Vienna: IAEA.

Association for the Advancement of Medical Instrumentation (1984). *Guidelines for Gamma Radiation Sterilization of Medical Devices*. AAMI, 1901 North Ford Myer Drive, Suite 602, Arlington, VA 22209, USA

Basic Standards of Good Manufacturing Practice for Pharmaceutical Products (1983) Convention for the mutual recognition of inspections in respect of the manufacture of pharmaceutical Products. Document PH 3/83. Geneva: The EFTA Secretariat.

Beck, J.A. & Morrissey, R.F. (1986) An overview of radiation sterilization technology. In *Sterilization of Medical Products*. (eds Gaughan, E.R.L., Morrissey, R.F. & Wang, J.) IV, Montreal, Canada: Johnson & Johnson Polyscience Publications Inc.

Beers, E. (1990) Innovations in irradiator design. *Radiation Physics and Chemistry*, **35**, 539–546.

Bridges, B.A. (1976) Survival of bacteria following exposure to ultraviolet and ionising radiation. In *The Survival of Vegetative Microbes* (eds Gray, T.R.G. & Postgate, J.R.) pp. 183–208. Cambridge: Cambridge University Press.

Brooks, B.W., & Murray R.G.E. (1981) Nomenclature for '*Micrococcus radiodurans*' and other radiation-resistant cocci: *Deinococcaceae* fam. nov. and *Deinococcus* gen. nov., including five species. *International Journal of Systematic Bacteriology*, **31**, 353–360.

Brynjolfsson, A. (1978) Progress in food irradiation in United States of America. In *Food Irradiation Information*, No. 9, Dec. 1978, pp. 66–99. Publ.: International Project in the Field of Food Irradiation. Institut für Strahlen Technologie, Postfach 36–40. D–7500 Karlsruhe, Federal Republic of Germany.

Christensen, E.A. & Kjems, E. (1965) The radiation resistance of substrains from *Streptococcus faecium* selected after irradiation of two different strains. *Acta Pathologica et Microbiologica Scandinavica, B*, **63**, 281–290.

Christensen, E.A., Holm, N.W. & Juul, F.A. (1967) Radiosterilization of medical devices and supplies. In *Radiosterilization of Medical Products*. STI/PUB/157. pp. 265–286. Vienna: IAEA.

Christensen, E.A. (1974a) The selection of test strains and the choice of methods for preparation of biological monitors for control of radiation sterilization. In *Experiences in Radiation Sterilization of Medical Products*. Proceedings of working group meeting. Risö, June 1972. Technical Report No. 159, pp. 67–87. Vienna: IAEA.

Christensen, E.A. (1974b) Radiation-induced mutants with increased resistance against ionizing radiation. In *Experiences in Radiation Sterilization of Medical Products*. Proceedings of working group meeting, Risö, June 1972. Technical Report No. 159, pp. 29–36. Vienna: IAEA.

Christensen, E.A. (1977) The role of microbiology in commissioning a new facility and in routine control. In *Sterilization by Ionizing Radiation* (eds Gaughran, E.R.L. & Goudie, A.J.) Vol. II, pp. 50–64. Montreal, Quebec, Canada: Multiscience Publishers Ltd.

Christensen, E.A. & Kristensen, H. (1981) Radiation resistance of microorganisms from the air in clean premises. *Acta Pathologica et Microbiologica Scandinavica, B*, **89**, 293–301.

Council of the Pharmaceutical Society of Great Britain (1963) Round Table Conference on Sterility Testing. Conclusions, p. Fl. London.

Danish Standards for Pharmaceutical Products (1979) Public Health Service of Denmark. (In Danish.)

Davis, K.W., Strawderman, W.E. & Whitby, J.L. (1984) The rationale and a computer evaluation of a gamma irradiation sterilization dose determination method for medical devices using a substerilization incremental dose sterility test protocol. *Journal of Applied Bacteriology*, **57**, 31–50.

Doolan, P.T., Halls, N.A. & Tallentire, A. (1988) Subprocess irradiation of naturally contaminated hypodermic needles. *Radiation Physics and Chemistry*, **31**, 699–703.

EEC Guide to Good Manufacturing Practice for Medical Products (1989) Brussels: Commission of the European Communities, Directorate-General for Internal Market and Industrial Affairs.

Emborg, C., Christensen, E.A., Eriksen, W.H. & Holm, N.W. (1971) Control of the microbiological efficiency of radiation sterilization plants by means of *B. sphaericus*, strain C_1A and *Str. faecium*, strain A_2I. Progress Report, IAEA Research Contract No. 973/R1/RB. IAEA Contractors Coordination Meeting, Risö.

Erdman, I.E., Thatcher, F.S. & MacQueen, K.F. (1961) Studies on the irradiation of microorganisms in relation to food preservation. II. Irradiation resistant mutants. *Canadian Journal of Microbiology*, **7**, 207–215.

European Confederation of Medical Suppliers Associations (1988). *Recommendations for the Sterilization of Medical Devices and Surgical Products*. EUCOMED, 551 Finchley Road, Hampstead, London NW3 7BJ, England.

FAO and WHO (1984) Codex general standard for irradiated foods and recommended international code of practice for the operation of radiation facilities used for the treatment of foods. Codex Alimentarius Commission, Vol. XV, first edition. Rome: Food and Agriculture Organization of the United Nations, World Health Organization.

FDA, *Medical Devices* (1984) Code of Federal Regulations, parts 800 to 895. US Food and Drug Administration, Bureau of medical devices. Washington, DC: US Government Printing Office.

Frohnsdorff, R.S.M. & Peter, K.H. (1977) The control of radiation sterilization facilities. *Radiation Physics and Chemistry*, **10**, 55–60.

Gaughran, E.R.L. & Goudie, A.J. (1974) *Sterilization by Ionizing Radiation: Technical Developments in Prospects of Sterilization by Ionizing Radiation*. Vol. I. Montreal, Quebec, Canada: Multiscience Publishers Ltd.

Gaughran, E.R.L. & Goudie, A.J. (1977) *Sterilization by Ionizing Radiation: Sterilization of Medical Products by Ionizing Radiation*. Vol. II. Montreal, Quebec, Canada: Multiscience Publishers Ltd.

Gibbs, C.F., Carleton Gajdusek, D. & Latarjet, R. (1978) Unusual resistance to ionizing radiation of the viruses of kuru, Creutz-feldt-Jakob disease and scrapie. *Proceedings of the National Academy of Sciences, USA*, **75**, 6268–6270.

Goldblith, S.A. (1967) General principles of radiosterilization. In *Radiosterilization of Medical Products*. STI/PUB/157. pp. 3–22. Vienna: IAEA.

Guide to good manufacturing practice for pharmaceutical products, (1989) Convention for the Mutual Recognition of Inspections in respect of the Manufacture of Pharmaceutical Products. Document PH 5/89. Geneva: EFTA Secretariat.

Holm, N.W. (1968) Dosimetry in radiosterilization of medical products. Appendix to the thesis. Danish Research Establishment, Risö.

Holm, N.W. (1973) Dosimetry. In *Manual on Radiation Sterilization of Medical and Biological Materials*. STI/DOC/10/149. pp. 99–109. Vienna: IAEA.

IAEA (1967a) *Radiosterilization of medical products*. Proceedings of a Symposium, Budapest, June 1967 and Recommended Code of Practice. STI/PUB/157. Vienna: IAEA.

IAEA (1967b) *Radiosterilization of medical products, pharmaceuticals and bioproducts*. Technical Reports Series No. 72, STI/DOC/10/72. Vienna: IAEA.

IAEA (1973) *Manual on radiation sterilization of medical and biological materials*. Technical Reports Series No. 149. STI/DOC/10/149. Vienna: IAEA.

IAEA (1974) *Experiences in radiation sterilization of medical products*. Proceedings of the working group meeting, Risö, June, 1972. Technical Reports Series No. 159. Vienna: IAEA.

IAEA (1975) *Radiosterilization of medical products*. Proceedings of the Symposium on Ionizing Radiation for Sterilization of Medical Products and Biological Tissues, Bombay, December 1974. Vienna: IAEA.

IAEA (1979a) *Decontamination of animal feeds by irradiation*. Proceedings from an advisory group meeting on radiation treatment of animals feed organized by the joint FAO/IAEA division of atomic energy in food and agriculture, Sofia. October, 1977. Vienna: IAEA.

IAEA (1979b) *International acceptance of irradiated food: legal aspects*. Report of a joint FAO/IAEA/WHO advisory group on international acceptance of irradiated food. Wageningen, December 1977. Vienna: IAEA.

IAEA (1981) Combination processes in food irradiation. Proceedings of a Symposium. Colombo, November 1980. STI/PUB/568. Vienna: IAEA.

IAEA (1985a) High-dose dosimetry. Proceedings of a Symposium. Vienna, October 1984, STI/PUB/671. Vienna: IAEA.

IAEA (1985b) Food irradiation processing. Proceedings of a Symposium. Washington, DC, March 1985. STI/PUB/695. Vienna: IAEA.

IAEA (1989) Acceptance, control of and trade in irradiated food. Conference Proceedings. Geneva, December 1988. STI/PUB/788. Vienna: IAEA.

ICRP publication (1977) International Commission on Radiological Protection publication. No. 26. Annals of the ICRP, Vol. 1, No. 3.

Iizuka, H. & Ito, H. (1968) Effect of gamma irradiation on the microflora of rice. *Cereal Chemistry*, **45**, 503–511.

Idziak, E.S. (1973) Radiation sensitivity of microorganisms. Effect on radiations on microorganisms. In *Proceedings of the U.S.P. Conference on Radiation Sterilization*. Washington D.C., October 1972. *International Journal of Radiation Sterilization*, **1**, 45–59.

Ingram, M. (1975) *Microbiology of foods pasteurised by ionizing radiation*. Report of a joint FAO/IAEA consultants meeting on microbiological aspects of food irradiation. Vienna, December 1974. West Germany: Institut für Strahlentechnologie. Karlsruhe.

Jefferson, S. (1973) Facilities required for radiosterilization. In *Manual on Radiation Sterilization of Medical and Biological Materials*. STI/DOC/10/149. pp. 89–94. Vienna: IAEA.

Josephson, E.S. & Peterson, M.S. (1982, 1983) *Preservation of Food by Ionizing Radiation*, Vols I, II and III. Boca Raton, Florida: CRC Press.

Kristensen, H. (1974) Isolation of radiation resistant microorganisms from the environment of Cobalt^{60} sources. Preliminary results. In *Experiences in Radiation Sterilization of Medical Products*. Proceedings of the working group meeting. Risö, June 1972. Technical Report No. 159, pp. 43–49. Vienna: IAEA.

Kristensen, H. (1981) Radiation resistance of *Candida parapsilosis*. *Acta Pathologica et Microbiologica Scandinavica, B*, **89**, 303–309.

Ley, F.J. (1973) The effect of ionizing radiation on bacteria. In *Manual on Radiation Sterilization of Medical and Biological Materials*. STI/DOC/10/149. pp. 37–63. Vienna: IAEA.

Ley, F.J., Winsley, B., Harbord, P., Keall, A. & Summers, T. (1972) Radiation sterilization: Microbiological findings from sub-process dose treatment of disposable plastic syringes. *Journal of Applied Bacteriology*, **35**, 53–61.

Maxey, R.B. & Rowley, D.B. (1977) Radiation resistant vegetative bacteria in a proposed system of radappertization of meats. Presented at IAEA/FOA International Symposium on Food Preservation by Irradiation, Wageningen, Netherlands, November 1977.

McKeown, J. (1990) Technology review of accelerator facilities. *Journal of Radiation Physics and Chemistry*, **35**, 606–611.

McLaughlin, W.L. & Holm, N.W. (1973) Physical characteristics of ionizing radiation. In *Manual on Radiation Sterilization of Medical and Biological Materials*. STI/DOC/10/149. pp. 5–12. Vienna: IAEA.

McLaughlin, W.L., Boyd, A.W., Chadwick, K.H., McDonald, J.C. & Miller, A. (1989). *Dosimetry for Radiation Processing*. London: Taylor & Francis.

Miller, W.S. & Berube, R. (1977) Environmental control and bioburden in manufacturing process. In *Sterilization by Ionizing Radiation* (eds Gaughran, E.R.L. & Goudie, A.J.) Vol II. pp. 33–45. Montreal, Quebec, Canada: Multiscience Publishers Ltd.

Moseley, B.E.B. (1984) Radiation damage and its repair in non-sporulating bacteria. In *The Revival of Injured Microbes* (eds Andrew, M.H.E. & Russell, A.D.) Society for Applied Bacteriology Symposium Series No. 12, pp. 147–174. London: Academic Press.

Moseley, B.E.B. & Williams, E. (1977) Repair of damaged DNA in bacteria. *Advances in Microbial Physiology*, **14**, 99–156.

Nam, J.W. (1989) High-dose standardization and dose assurance. *Radiation Physics and Chemistry*, **34**, 399–401.

National Board of Health and Welfare, Sweden (1976) *Guidelines for control of the sterility of industrially sterilized single-use medical devices, May 1976*. (In Swedish; version in English available).

Noble, W.C. (1975) Dispersal of skin microorganism. In *Proceedings of the Nordic Association for Contamination Control*. 1975 Symposium. Contamination Control to Benefit Man and Product, Goethenburg. April 1975, p. 111–123.

Österberg, B.O. (1974) Radiation sensitivity of the microbial flora present on suture material prior to irradiation. *Acta Pharmaceutica Suicica*, **11**, 53–58.

Ph. Eur. (1983) *European Pharmacopoeia*, 2nd Ed. IX.1. Maisonneuve: Council of Europe.

Ph. Eur. (1986) *European Pharmacopoeia*, 2nd Ed. Test for sterility. V. 2.1.1. Maisonneuve: Council of Europe.

Public Health Service of Denmark (1972). Recommendations concerning medical utensils, A–2, April 1972 (In Danish).

Schmidt, C.F., Nank, W.K. & Lechowich, R.W. (1962) Radiation sterilization of food. II. Some aspects of growth, sporulation and the radiation resistance of spores of *Clostridium botulinum* type E. *Journal of Food Science*, **27**, 77–84.

Silverman, G.J. & Sinskey, A.J. (1977) Sterilization by ionizing irradiation. In *Disinfection. Sterilization and Preservation* (ed. Block, S.S.) 2nd Ed., pp. 542–561. Philadelphia: Lea & Febiger.

Skiens, W.E. (1980) Sterilizing radiation effects on selected polymers. *Radiation Physics and Chemistry*, **15**, 47–57.

Sullivan, R., Fassolitis, A.C., Larkin, E.P., Read, R.B. & Peeler, J.T. (1971) Inactivation of thirty viruses by gamma radiation. *Applied Microbiology*, **22**, 61–65.

Sullivan, R., Scarpino, V.P., Fassolitis, A.C., Larkin, E.P. & Peeler, J.T. (1973) Gamma radiation inactivation of coxsackievirus B-2. *Applied Microbiology*, **26**, 14–17.

Tallentire, A. (1973) Aspects of microbiological control of radiation sterilization. *International Journal of Radiation Sterilization*, **1**, 85–103.

Tallentire, A., Dwyer, J. & Ley, F.J. (1971) Microbiological quality control of sterilized products: Evaluation of a model relating the frequency of contaminated items with increasing radiation treatment. *Journal of Applied Bacteriology*, **34**, 521–534.

Tallentire, A. & Khan, A.A. (1977) The sub-process dose in defining the degree of sterility assurance. In *Sterilization by Ionizing Radiation*, Vol II (eds Gaughran, E.J.L. & Goudie, A.J.) pp. 65–80. Montreal, Quebec, Canada: Multiscience Publishers Ltd.

Tiwary, N.P. & Maxy, R.B. (1972) Moraxella-acinetobacter as contaminants of beef and occurrence in radurized product. *Journal of Food Science*, **37**, 901–903.

UK Panel on Gamma and Electron Irradiation (1987) Radiation sterilization dose. *Radiation Physics and Chemistry*, **29**, 87–88.

UK Panel on Gamma and Electron Irradiation (1989) Code of practice for the validation and routine monitoring of sterilization by ionizing radiation. *Radiation Physics and Chemistry*, **33**, 245–249.

Umeda, K. (1978) The first potato irradiator in Japan—the successes and setbacks encountered during three years commercial operation. In *Food Irradiation Information*. No. 8. pp. 31–41. Publ. International project in the field of food irradiation. West Germany: Institut für strahlentechnologie, Karlsruhe.

Van Winkle, W., Borick, P.M. & Fogarty, M. (1967) Destruction of radiation resistant microorganisms on surgical sutures by ^{60}Co-irradiation under manufacturing conditions. In *Radiosterilization of Medical Products*. STI/PUB/157. pp. 169–180. Vienna: IAEA.

Whitby, J.L. (1979) Radiation resistance of microorganisms comprising the bioburden of operating room packs. *Radiation Physics and Chemistry*, **14**, 285–288.

Whitby, J.L. & Storey, D.G. (1982) Effect of incremental doses of radiation on viability of the microbial population of synthetic operating room gowns. *Applied and Environmental Microbiology*, **43**, 528–533.

WHO (1981) *Wholesomeness of Irradiated Food*. Report of a joint FAO/IAEA/WHO Expert Committee. World Health Organization. Technical Report Series 659. WHO: Geneva.

Wilski, H. (1987) The radiation-induced degradation of polymers. *Radiation Physics and Chemistry*, **29**, 1–14.

Wilski, H. (1990) Radiation stability of polymers. *Radiation Physics and Chemistry*, **35**, 186–189.

Witkin, E.M. (1946) Inherited differences in sensitivity to irradiation in *E. coli*. *Proceedings of the National Academy of Sciences, USA*, **32**, 59–68.

Witkin, E.M. (1947) Genetics of resistance to radiation in *E. coli*. *Genetics*, **32**, 221–248.

B · ULTRAVIOLET RADIATION

1 INTRODUCTION

Ultraviolet (UV) radiation has a wavelength range between about 328 and 210 nm (3280 and 2100 Å). Its maximum bactericidal effect is listed as 240–280 nm (Sykes, 1965), 265 nm (Thimann, 1963; Morris, 1972; Schechmeister, 1983) and 254–280 nm (McCulloch, 1945). Modern mercury-vapour lamps emit more than 90% of their radiation at 253.7 nm (Morris, 1972), which is at, or near to, the maximum for microbicidal activity. The quantum of energy liberated is low, so that UV radiation has less penetrating ability and is less effective as a microbicidal agent than other radiations (Gardner & Peel, 1986).

There are several reviews dealing with the action and uses of UV radiation, notably those of Hollaender (1955); Smith & Hanawalt (1969); Roberts & Hitchins (1969); Russell (1971, 1982, 1990a,b, 1991); Morris (1972); Howard-Flanders (1973); Bridges (1976); Witkin (1969, 1976); Moseley & Williams (1977); Hanawalt *et al.* (1979); Alper (1979); Harm (1980); Haseltine (1983); Schechmeister (1983); Moseley (1984); Gould (1983, 1984, 1985); Phillips (1987) and Thurman & Gerba (1988). This chapter will compare the susceptibility of different types of micro-organisms to UV radiation, examine the factors influencing these responses, discuss the theoretical aspects of inactivation and repair and finally will consider the practical uses of UV light as a sterilizing or disinfecting agent. Additional information will be found in chapters dealing with viruses (Chapter 6), unconventional agents (Chapter 7) and protozoa (Chapter 8).

2 SURVIVAL CURVES

Survival curves of bacteria or bacterial spores exposed to UV light are generally of two types:
1 a straight-line response (Fig. 19.7), as noted with *Salmonella typhimurium* (Moseley & Laser, 1965), *Escherichia coli* B_{S-1} (Haynes, 1966) and the *E. coli* K12 strain AB2480 $uvr^- rec^-$ (Tyrell *et al.*, 1972);
2 an initial shoulder, followed by exponential death (Fig. 19.7), as found with vegetative cells (a very slight shoulder) and dormant spores (much greater initial shoulder) of *Bacillus megaterium* (Donnellan & Stafford, 1968). A large initial shoulder has also been noted for UV-irradiated *E. coli* B/r (Haynes, 1964, 1966), *E. coli* K12 strain, AB1157 $uvr^+ rec^+$ (Tyrrell *et al.*, 1972) and *Staphylococcus aureus* and *Micrococcus lysodeikticus* (Haynes, 1964). The classic example, however, is undoubtedly *Deinococcus radiodurans*, which is highly resistant

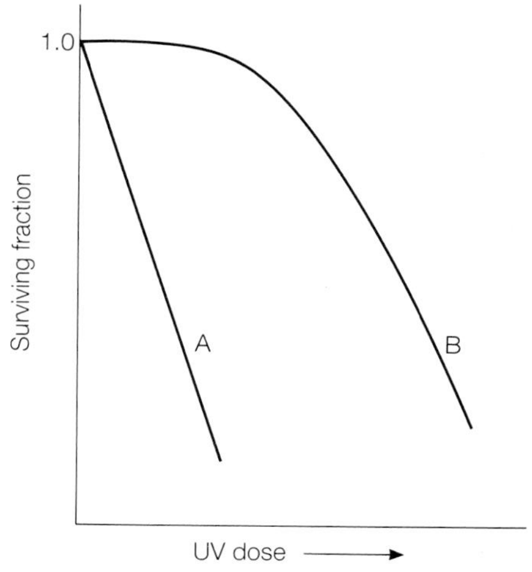

Fig. 19.7 Survival curves for UV-exposed bacteria. A: some non-sporulating bacteria (not *D. radiodurans*); B: bacterial spores and *D. radiodurans*.

to both UV and ionizing radiations; survival curves for this organism against both types of radiation have large initial shoulders, with high extrapolation numbers (Moseley & Laser, 1965; Moseley, 1967). Organisms that are resistant to UV radiation may possess efficient repair processes and thus can survive quite high doses: see Section 3.8. Ability to repair UV-induced damage to DNA is probably the single most important factor in determining microbial response to UV light.

3 FACTORS INFLUENCING ACTIVITY OF UV RADIATION

Ultraviolet radiation has several uses but unfortunately is also subject to several limitations. It is important, therefore, to consider the various factors that affect its activity.

3.1 Type of organism

According to McCulloch (1945), Gram-negative rods are the most easily killed by UV light, followed (in this order) by staphylococci, streptococci and bacterial spores, with mould spores being the most resistant. This early classification is inevitably somewhat out of date, because it takes no account of viruses, protozoa and prions or of non-sporulating bacteria that possess the ability to repair UV-induced injury. *Legionella pneumophila* and other species of legionellae are very sensitive to low doses of UV light (Table 19.1).

Bacterial spores are generally more resistant to UV radiation than are vegetative cells (Sykes, 1965; Ashwood-Smith & Bridges, 1967; Russell, 1982, 1991) although the degree of sporulation can influence the sensitivity (Section 5).

Viruses are also inactivated by UV light (Morris & Darlow, 1971); they are less resistant than bacterial spores but are often more resistant than non-sporulating bacteria (Morris, 1972). UV radiation at doses below 5×10^3 J/m^2 may not eliminate all infectious human immunodeficiency virus (HIV; Report, 1990). Unenveloped animal viruses are

Table 19.1 Relative resistances of micro-organisms to ultraviolet radiation*

Resistance level	Examples of micro-organisms
High	Prions *Deinococcus radiodurans* *Bacillus subtilis/B. globigii* spores† *Sarcina lutea*‡
Intermediate	*M. sphaeroides* *Salmonella typhimurium* *Saccharomyces* spp. *Streptococcus lactis* Protozoa
Low	Legionellae HIV? Vaccinia virus *Escherichia coli* *Staphylococcus aureus* *Proteus vulgaris* Brewer's yeast T3 coliphage

* Based on Morris (1972), Johansen & Myhrstad (1978), Latarjet (1979), Rice & Hoff (1981), Gilpin (1984), Chang *et al.* (1985), Knudsen (1985), Muraca *et al.* (1985), Rodgers *et al.* (1985), Committee (1986), Farr *et al.* (1988), Department of Health (1989) and Report (1990).

† *B. pumilus* E601 (ATCC 27142) spores are considered to be highly UV-resistant and to be suitable organisms for monitoring the effectiveness of UV radiation (Abshire *et al.*, 1980).

‡ High resistance is possibly the result of a screening effect produced by cell aggregates.

more resistant to UV light than enveloped ones (Watanabe *et al.*, 1989), but conventional virus types are considerably more susceptible than the unconventional or so-called slow viruses, the prions. Creutzfeldt–Jakob disease (CJD) agent is highly resistant to UV radiation (Committee, 1986; Rappaport, 1987); the agents of kuru and scrapie are likewise insusceptible (Latarjet, 1979). Morphological changes induced in human rotaviruses have been described (Rodgers *et al.*, 1985).

Protozoa such as *Giardia lamblia* cysts are more UV-resistant than non-sporulating bacteria (Rice & Hoff, 1981).

Examples of relative susceptibilities to UV radiation are provided in Table 19.1.

3.2 Inoculum size

As would be expected, the greater the inoculum size, the greater is the UV dose necessary to effect an equivalent lethality (Morris, 1972).

3.3 Stage of growth or germination

Tyrrell *et al.* (1972) investigated the variation in UV sensitivity of four K12 strains (AB2480 *uvr*$^-$ *rec*$^-$, AB1886 *uvr*$^-$ *rec*$^-$, AB2463 *uvr*$^+$ *rec*$^-$ and AB1157 *uvr*$^+$ *rec*$^+$) of *E. coli* as a function of their growth phase. The smallest changes in sensitivity were found in the double mutant, the excision-deficient and recombination-deficient AB2480 *uvr*$^-$ *rec*$^-$ and in the excision-deficient mutant AB1886 *uvr*$^-$ *rec*$^+$. With the recombination-deficient mutant, AB2463 *uvr*$^+$ *rec*$^-$, UV sensitivity increased during the early exponential growth phase, and decreased after 5 h. With the mutant (AB1157 *uvr*$^+$ *rec*$^+$) possessing the full complement of repair genes, a sharp decrease in UV sensitivity was observed in the early exponential phase, followed by a large increase and later a decrease.

At certain times in their germination, spores of *Bacillus cereus* (Stuy, 1956), *B. subtilis* (Irie *et al.*, 1965; Stafford & Donnellan, 1968; Donnellan & Stafford, 1968) and *B. megaterium* (Stafford & Donnellan, 1968; Donnellan & Stafford, 1968) become much more resistant to UV radiation. This phase is followed by one in which the sensitivity to UV light of the germinating spores increases, and eventually these forms become more sensitive than the dormant spores. The possible reasons for this phenomenon are discussed later (Section 5).

3.4 Type of suspension

B. subtilis spores are more resistant to UV radiation when tested in the form of a 'dust suspension' than when they are exposed as an aerosol (Sykes, 1965). Likewise, a small but significant increase in UV irradiation is required for a 90% or 98% disinfection level of dried droplets, as opposed to wet droplets, of *B. globigii* spores and of non-sporulating organisms (Morris, 1972).

3.5 Effect of organic matter

Morris (1972) has shown that the presence of peptone, egg, milk and especially blood and serum means that the UV dose required for 90% inactivation of *Serratia marcescens* increased markedly when compared with buffer suspensions of this organism. Thus, surfaces infected with these fluids would need greater UV irradiation to ensure disinfection.

3.6 Effect of temperature

Most organisms (a notable exception is *D. radiodurans*) appear to be supersensitive to UV radiation at low temperatures (Ashwood-Smith & Bridges, 1967), although this increase in sensitivity occurs only when the bacteria are frozen; under such conditions the number of thymine dimers is reduced considerably. Another thymine-containing photoproduct accumulates which appears to be less susceptible to repair by the bacterial cell (see Sections 3.8, 4.1, 4.2 and 4.3).

3.7 Wavelength of UV radiation

Ultraviolet lamps are normally employed at 253.7 nm. There is, however, a peak of activity at 250–280 nm with negligible activity above a wavelength of 300 nm (Setlow & Boling, 1965).

3.8 Repair processes

Many bacterial species can, under appropriate conditions, repair the damage induced by UV radiation. The repair processes involve light repair (photoreactivation) and dark repair (excision and recombination) and organisms capable of repairing damage are obviously likely to be more resistant to UV radiation than those that lack these repair systems. The isolation of mutants which are defective in one or more of these systems has been responsible for a much better understanding of the nature of UV-induced damage at the molecular level, and of the ways in which organisms achieve repair. These aspects are considered in more detail later (Sections 4.2 and 4.3).

4 EFFECT OF UV RADIATION ON NON-SPORULATING BACTERIA

4.1 Target site and inactivation

The major target site for UV radiation is undoubtedly DNA. Several types of damage have been found to occur in UV-treated bacteria: low numbers of phosphodiester strand breaks and DNA intrastrand cross-links occur at high UV doses. Nucleic acid–protein cross-links are also induced, but their significance in microbial inactivation is uncertain. The most important event is the accumulation of photoproducts (Bridges, 1976; Moseley, 1984).

In vegetative bacteria and yeasts, purine and pyrimidine dimers are formed between adjacent molecules in the same strand of DNA. This is exemplified in Fig. 19.8 by the formation of thymine dimers (T͡T), the most widely studied phenomenon, in UV-irradiated DNA. Ultraviolet radiation is absorbed most strongly by nucleic acids, especially the wavelength (253.7 nm) which forms the output of most lamps (Bridges, 1976).

Another type of photoproduct (5,6-dihydroxydihydrothymine, Fig. 19.9a) is found in *D. radiodurans*. In bacterial spores, yet another photoproduct (5-thyminyl-5,6-dihydrothymine, TDHT; Fig. 19.9b) is induced. This is considered in more detail later (Section 5).

Unless removed, these photoproducts form noncoding lesions in DNA and cell death occurs. In the frozen state, UV-treated non-sporulating bacteria accumulate a photoproduct (presumably TDHT; see Fig. 19.9b) which appears to be identical to that found in the DNA of UV-exposed bacterial spores. TDHT is not repairable in nonsporing organisms and under such conditions the cells are supersensitive to UV radiation. The yield of cyclobutane-type dimers is greatly reduced and photoreactivation (PR, see Section 4.1) is ineffective.

4.2 Repair mechanisms

In *Escherichia coli*, most of the inducible genes that code for DNA repair proteins belong to one of two major regulatory networks that are induced as a consequence of DNA injury. These are (i) the SOS network, controlled by the RecA and LexA proteins, and (ii) the adaptive response network, controlled by the Ada protein (Walker, 1985).

The SOS network controls the expression of genes whose products play roles in, for example,

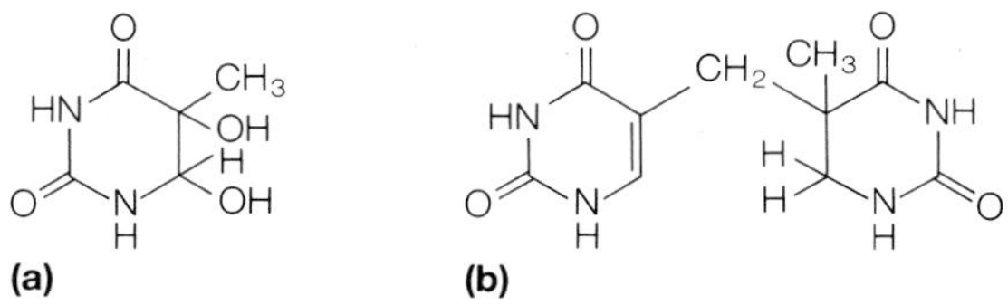

Fig. 19.9 (a) 5,6-dihydroxydihydrothymine; (b) 5-thyminyl-5,6-dihydrothymine (TDHT).

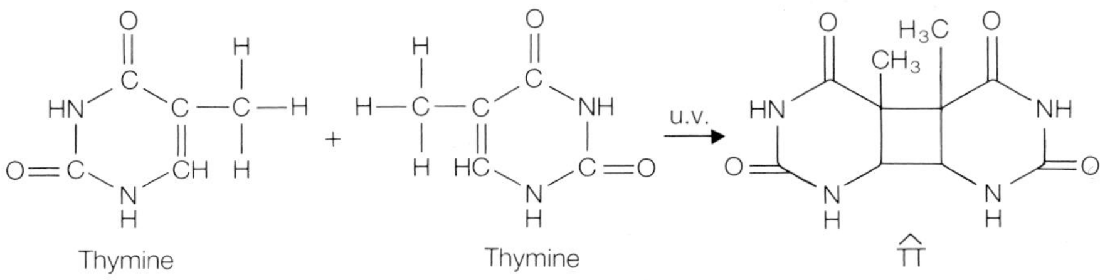

Fig. 19.8 Formation of thymine dimer (T͡T) in UV-irradiated DNA.

excision repair, daughter-strand gap repair and double-strand break repair. When *E. coli* is exposed to agents (UV and other) that damage DNA or interfere with DNA replication, a diverse set of physiological responses, the SOS responses, is induced. These include an increased capacity to reactivate UV-irradiated phage, the induction of mutations, filamentous growth and the increased capacity to repair double-strand breaks. SOS responses pertinent to the repair of UV-induced injury are considered in Section 4.3.

The adaptive response network differs from the SOS. *E. coli* cells exposed to low concentrations of methylating mutagens become resistant to the mutagenic and lethal effects of higher concentrations. This induced resistance results from the formation of a set of induced repair processes independent of the SDS network and controlled by production of the *ada* gene. UV light and most of the other agents that induce an SOS response do not induce the adaptive response. For detailed information on revival and repair, see Andrew & Russell (1984).

Repair mechanisms in non-sporulating bacteria exposed to UV radiation are of three major types. These are: (a) light repair (photoreactivation) in which a photoreactivating enzyme (photolyase; Sancar & Sancar, 1988) becomes activated when UV-treated cells are exposed to light of a higher wavelength; (b) dark repair (excision) in which the non-coding lesion is excised and replaced; (c) dark repair (post-replication recombination) which involves recombination between two sister DNA strands.

4.3 Radiation mutants of *Escherichia coli*

Several radiation-sensitive and resistant mutants of *E. coli* have been described over the years. The sensitive mutants have a block in one or more of the pathways involved in DNA repair. Some of the best known types of these mutants are described briefly below.

1 *phr* gene: *phr*$^-$ mutants lack the ability to photoreactivate, because the photo-reactivating (PR) enzyme is absent. Kelner (1949a,b) found that the exposure of UV-irradiated *Streptomyces griseus* or *E. coli* to suitable visible light, below 510 nm, resulted in the recovery of a large portion of the cells from what would otherwise have been death. This phenomenon, photoreactivation, has since been defined (Jagger, 1958) as the reversal with near-UV or visible light of UV-radiation damage to a biological system, or as the restoration of UV-radiation lesions in a biological system with light of wavelength longer than that of the damaging radiation. The process of photoreactivation is depicted in Fig. 19.10, from which it can be seen (Fig. 19.10a) that the PR enzyme brings about a monomerization *in situ* of the thymine dimers resulting in repair of the damage to DNA (Fig. 19.10b).

In *E. coli*, the DNA photolyase binds equally well to UV-irradiated supercoiled and relaxed, double-stranded DNA; the enzyme does not un-

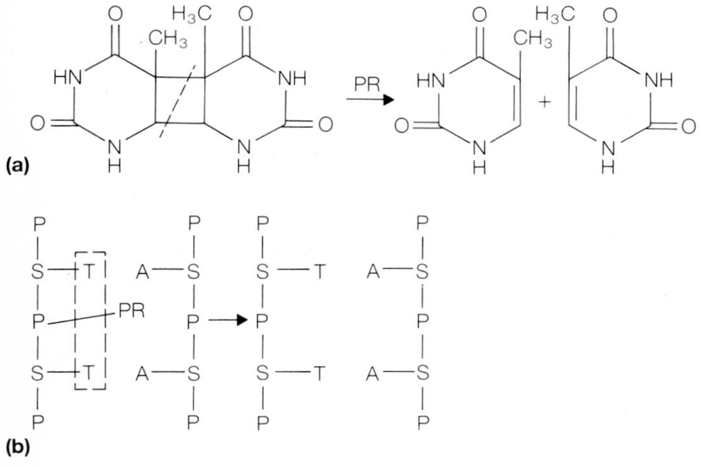

Fig. 19.10 Photoreactivation (PR) by photoreactivating enzyme: (a) monomerization of thymine dimer; (b) formation of T͡T in DNA and photoreversal. P, phosphate; S, sugar; T, thymine; A, adenine.

wind the helix to a significant degree upon binding (Sancar & Sancar, 1988).

It must be added that there is a wide divergence among bacteria in their PR capability. Bacterial spores cannot be photoreactivated, whereas vegetative cells of bacilli can (Stuy, 1955). Sporulating cultures of *B. cereus* completely lose their PR ability at the same time as UV resistance increases (Romig & Wyss, 1957).

As pointed out in Section 4.1, bacteria in the frozen state are usually more sensitive to UV radiation, because of a reduction in the yield of cyclobutane-type pyrimidine dimers and the formation of TDHT, a photoproduct insusceptible to the action of DNA photolyase.

2 *uvr* gene: mutants *uvrA*$^-$ and *uvrB*$^-$ lack the UV-specific endonuclease involved in dark repair and are unable to excise pyrimidine dimers from their DNA or from irradiated phage. They are thus unable to carry out host-cell reactivation of UV-irradiated phage and in addition to being *uvr*$^-$ mutants they are thus also termed *Hcr*$^-$. These mutants do not, however, show an increased sensitivity to ionizing radiation. Mutations in *uvrA*, *uvrB* or *uvrC* genes render cells extremely sensitive not only to UV radiation but also to mitomycin C, nitrous acid and other genotoxic agents (Sancar & Rupp, 1983; Sancar & Sancar, 1988). *uvrD* also interferes with the excision repair of pyrimidine dimers, but differs from the other three *uvr* mutations in that a mutation at the *uvrD* locus can also cause a considerable increase in spontaneous mutation rate (Walker, 1985).

3 *polA* gene: polymerase-deficient mutants lack the activity of DNA polymerase I and show a 10-fold increase in sensitivity to UV radiation and a three-fold increase in sensitivity to ionizing radiation (Bridges, 1976). These mutants are also *Hcr*$^-$.

The excision mechanism (dark repair) for the removal of UV-induced thymine dimers is a multi-enzyme process which involves (Fig. 19.11) a single-strand incision by a UV-specific endonuclease in the region of $\widehat{TT}$, an excision of the dimer and adjacent bases (by means of the exonucleolytic activity of DNA polymerase I or a UV-specific exonuclease), a repolymerization with DNA polymerase I of the single-strand gap using the complementary strand as a template, and finally a

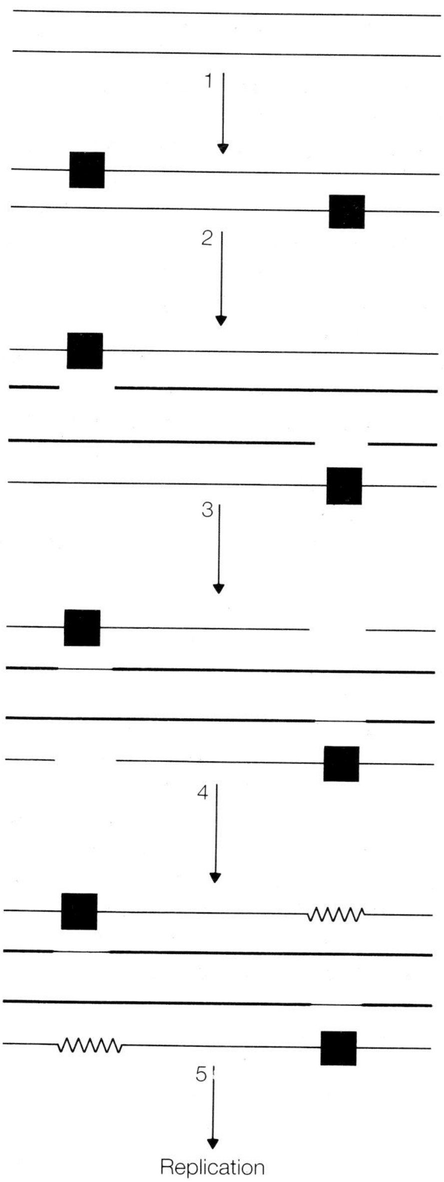

Fig. 19.11 Excision-repair mechanism (dark repair). Stage 1, induction of thymine dimer (■) in UV-irradiated DNA; Stage 2, incision by dimer-specific endonuclease; Stage 3, excision and repair replication by DNA polymerase I; Stage 4, sealing of gap by polynucleotide ligase.

joining of the single-strand break by means of a polynucleotide ligase. Thus, mutants such as *uvr*$^-$ and *pol*$^-$ which lack some part of the dark-repair (excision) mechanism show an increased sensitivity to UV light.

4 *rec* gene: this gene is lacking in recombination-deficient mutants. *recA* mutants show no genetic recombination, whereas mutants lacking *recB* or *recC* genes have a lowered genetic recombination. For a general review of recombination, see Cox & Lehman (1987).

In post-replication recombination repair, DNA replication continues normally until it reaches an unexcised dimer which is a non-coding lesion, and so a gap is left opposite. Replication then recommences at a new initiation site some distance from the dimer. Since cyclobutane-type dimers are likely to occur in both parental strands, the gaps left opposite them will also be present in both daughter strands and so full coding potential is lacking in all four DNA strands. Thus, soon after synthesis, the new DNA strands occur in relatively short pieces, whereas after further incubation the pieces become longer until they eventually attain the normal length. This disappearance of the gaps is attributed to crossovers (Witkin, 1976). Post-replication repair is eliminated by *recA* mutations which abolish this crossing over.

The most sensitive of all mutants to UV radiation are the *uvr*$^-$ *recA*$^-$ double mutants which lack both of the dark-repair (excision and recombination) mechanisms.

5 *exr(lex)* gene: an important *recA*$^+$-dependent pathway is known as error-prone repair. A characteristic effect of UV radiation is the induction of mutants among the survivors, these mutants arising as errors during post-treatment repair of DNA damage. Bacteria lacking the *exr* gene show no radiation mutagenesis, since the *exr* mutant blocks this error-prone pathway active in post-replication repair (Setlow & Carrier, 1972). There is increased DNA degradation in these strains, which show an increased sensitivity to UV radiation (15-fold) and to ionizing radiation (three-fold); see Bridges (1976).

6 *lon (fil)* gene: some strains of *E. coli*, e.g. strain B, show a loss in viability when exposed to UV radiation even though growth and nucleic acid synthesis are normal. The cells form long, non-septate filaments which eventually lyse. Radiation-sensitive mutants, designated *lon*$^-$, produce filaments and are about ten times as sensitive to UV light and three times as sensitive to ionizing radiation (Bridges, 1976). The first radiation-resistant mutant (B/r) of *E. coli* B possesses a suppressor (designated *sul*) for *lon*.

For further information on the various repair processes, the interested reader should consult Fig. 19.12 and the following references: Boyce & Howard-Flanders, 1964; Howard-Flanders & Boyce, 1966; Howard-Flanders, 1973; Hanawalt & Setlow, 1975; Bridges, 1976; Witkin, 1976; Haseltine, 1983; Moseley, 1984; Walker, 1985; Cox & Lehman, 1987 and Sancar & Sancar, 1988.

4.4 *Deinococcus radiodurans*

D. radiodurans is the organism most resistant to ionizing and UV radiations. It appears to possess a remarkable ability to repair damage inflicted on its DNA by both types of radiation (Bridges, 1976), especially by excision repair, although why this is more efficient than with other organisms is currently unknown.

It is of interest to note that whereas most bacteria in the frozen state become more sensitive to UV radiation (Section 3.6), *D. radiodurans* shows no difference in sensitivity at temperatures down to −60°C and actually becomes more resistant between −60°C and −196°C, presumably because it can repair damage resulting from the formation of another thymine photoproduct (Ashwood-Smith & Bridges, 1967).

5 EFFECT OF UV RADIATION ON BACTERIAL SPORES

5.1 Inactivation and repair

It was pointed out above (Sections 3.1 and 3.3) that bacterial spores are more resistant than vegetative bacteria to UV radiation, and that at certain times during germination spores become much more resistant.

When bacterial spores are irradiated, thymine-containing photoproducts (5-thyminyl-5,6-

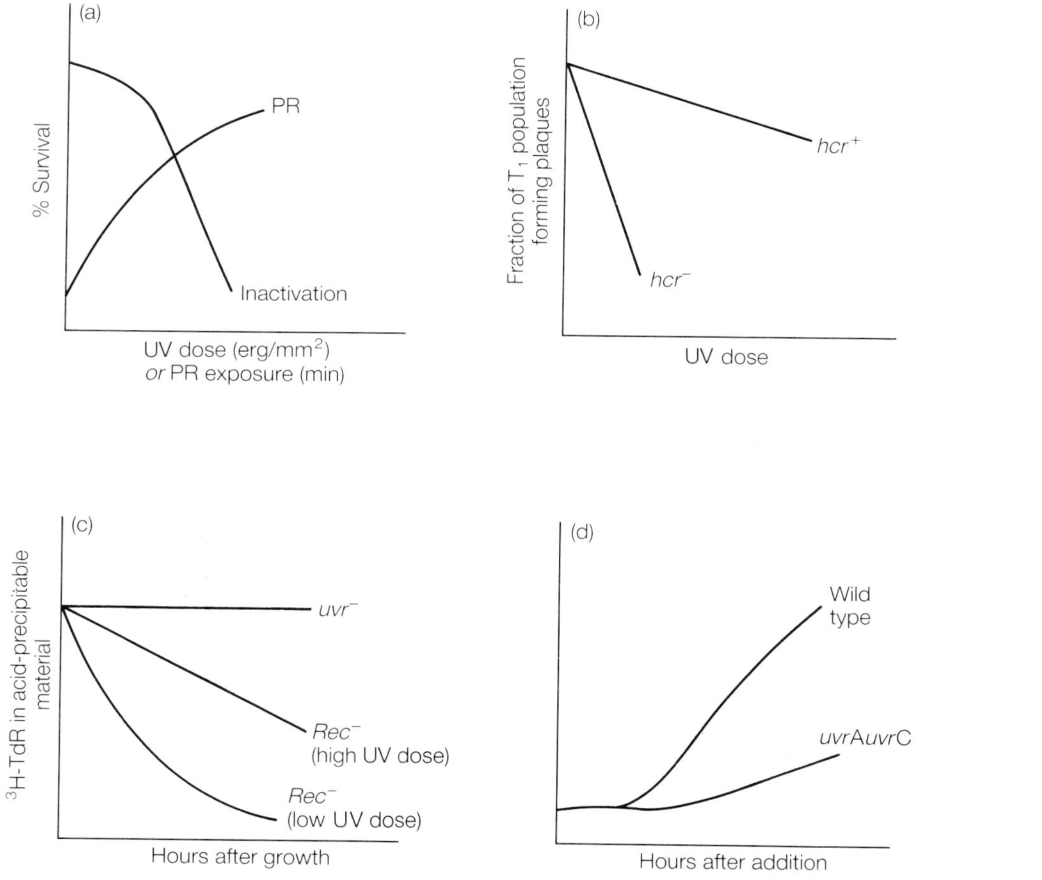

Fig. 19.12 Summary of responses to UV radiation. (a) Photoreactivation (PR); (b) Host-cell reactivation (*hcr*); (c) Post-irradiation DNA degradation; (d) Post-irradiation DNA synthesis. rec^- ... recombination-deficient strains; uvr^- ... mutant lacking UV-specific endonuclease. In (c), the organisms are grown in media containing ^{3}H-thymidine (^{3}H-TdR), then irradiated and subsequently suspended in unlabelled medium containing thymine to minimize re-incorporation of any ^{3}H-TdR released. In (d), the irradiated cells are transferred to a suitable medium containing ^{3}H-TdR; the ordinate scale (y-axis) is as depicted for (c).

dihydrothymine; Varghese, 1970; see Fig. 19.9b and postulated formation in Fig. 19.13) accumulate which are different from the thymine-containing cyclobutane dimers (Fig. 19.7) produced in vegetative cells (Donnellan & Setlow, 1965). In spores, these non-cyclobutane photoproducts do not disappear after a photoreactivation process, but are eliminated from DNA by a dark-repair mechanism which is different from that found for thymine dimers in non-sporulating bacteria (Donnellan & Stafford, 1968).

During germination of *B. megaterium* spores (Stafford & Donnellan, 1968) the peak resistance to UV light occurs at 3 min, and at this point the amount of thymine-containing photoproducts is only a fraction of that found in vegetative cells or dormant spores. During the germination, the amount of spore photoproduct falls rapidly but for the 3-min period there is little or no vegetative cell photoproduct (thymine dimer) formation. After this 3-min period, spore photoproduct falls slightly but $\widehat{UT}$ and $\widehat{TT}$ dimers rapidly begin to appear, coinciding with an increase in UV sensitivity. The changes in sensitivity during germination have

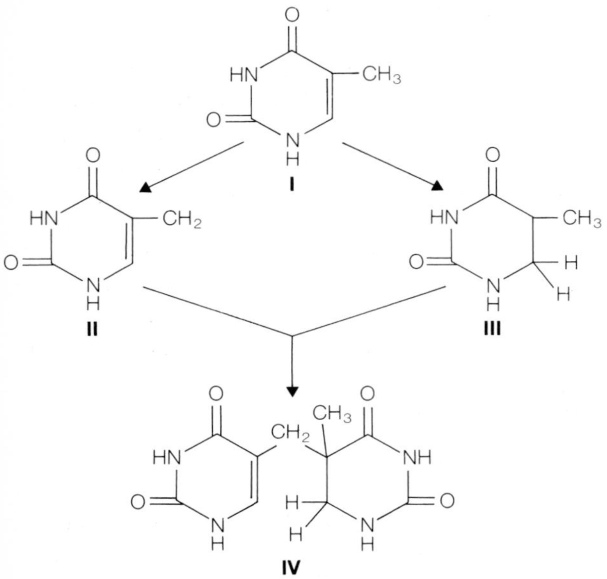

Fig. 19.13 Postulated formation of spore photoproduct (5-thyminyl 5,6-dihydrothymine; TDHT) (after Varghese, 1970). I, thymine; II, thyminyl radical; III; thymyl radical; IV, TDHT.

been explained (Stafford & Donnellan, 1968) in terms of:

1 changes in spore-type and cyclobutane type photoproducts;

2 absence of both types at 3 min being responsible for the extreme resistance of spores at that point.

The transition in UV resistance from dormant spores to vegetative cell over an extended time scale was re-investigated by Nokes & Powers (1977), who found that the major peak of UV resistance occurred after about 60-min incubation at 25°C, with a secondary peak of resistance at *c*. 20 min. It was suggested that the reason for this latter phenomenon was linked to DNA conformation, since the DNA in spores, in germinating spores and in vegetative cells may exist in different environments—at one extreme the 'dry' DNA of spores and at the other the 'wet' DNA of vegetative cells.

The spore photoproduct (TDHT, Figs. 19.9b and 19.13) is, in fact, identical to a photoproduct that accumulates in hydrolysates of DNA exposed dry or as a frozen solution to UV radiation (Rahn & Hosszu, 1968; Varghese, 1970). The sensitivity of spore core DNA to UV light varies with the water content of the core (Germaine *et al.*, 1973).

It was stated earlier (Sections 3.6 and 4.4) that vegetative cells (except *D. radiodurans*) in the frozen state were supersensitive to UV light, and (Section 3.6) that another photoproduct, presumably TDHT, accumulated which was less susceptible to repair. The logical question is, therefore, why spores in which TDHT is induced by UV radiation should be so much more resistant to UV than non-sporing organisms. Clues are provided from the studies of Munakata & Rupert (1972, 1974) who showed that UV-sensitive mutants of UV-resistant *B. subtilis* spores formed the same thymine-containing photoproduct (TDHT) and to the same extent for a given UV dose as the resistant spores; thus the ability to remove TDHT must be linked to resistance. Two genetically controlled mechanisms were described for this removal; the first involved the early elimination of TDHT during germination, although vegetative growth was not required; the second, demonstrated in a mutant lacking the first mechanism, required further development towards the vegetative cell for operation, and was an excision–resynthesis mechanism. TDHT was not removed in spores of high UV sensitivity in which both mechanisms were blocked (Munakata & Rupert, 1972). During germination, spores possessing the 'spore repair' process can change the TDHT into a harmless product. This appears to be a direct, enzymatic dark repair whereby TDHT is converted to thymine with the result that the DNA backbone is left intact (Van Wang & Rupert, 1977).

5.2 UV and hydrogen peroxide

Although bacterial spores are more resistant to UV light and to hydrogen peroxide than non-sporulating bacteria, simultaneous treatment of spores with far-UV radiation and peroxide produces a greatly enhanced rate of kill (Bayliss & Waites, 1979a,b; Waites & Bayliss, 1984; Waites *et al.*, 1988). The most effective wavelength is around 270 nm, and it has been postulated that the action of the UV radiation in the combination is not directly on spore DNA but rather on the production of free hydroxyl radicals from hydrogen peroxide (Waites *et al.*, 1988).

6 PRACTICAL USES OF UV RADIATION

Ionizing radiations such as X-rays, γ-rays and high-speed electrons (β-rays) strip off electrons from the atoms of the material through which the radiations pass and essentially all the chemical effects are produced by these stripped-off electrons. In contrast, UV light causes excitation of atoms, i.e. there is an alteration of electrons within their orbits but insufficient energy is possessed for electron ejection to produce an ion; UV radiation is not, therefore, an ionizing radiation. Ultraviolet radiation has little penetrative power through solids and is extensively absorbed by glass and plastics. Sterilization is achieved only by irradiation levels beyond the limits of practicability (Morris, 1972; Gardner & Peel, 1986).

It would nevertheless be incorrect to state that UV radiation serves no useful purpose as a disinfection procedure. It has been employed in the disinfection of drinking water (Sykes, 1965; Angehrn, 1984), as a possible means of obtaining pyrogen-free water (Cook & Saunders, 1962) and especially in air disinfection, notably in hospitals (wards and operating theatres), in aseptic laboratories and in ventilated safety cabinets in which dangerous micro-organisms are being handled (Morris, 1972).

In air disinfection of rooms, UV irradiation is directed towards the upper portion of the rooms to protect any personnel working in these areas. In contrast to this indirect irradiation, continuous irradiation from wall- or ceiling-fixed UV lamps can be employed, but any personnel present must wear protective clothing and adequate eye shields. One of the best methods of achieving air sterilization is to use a combination of air filtration and UV radiation.

The value of UV irradiation of operating theatres has been shown to be rather uncertain, the overall infection rate being unaffected, although some reduction in the sepsis of clean wounds has been noted (National Research Council, 1964). A possible reduction in the cross-infection of chicken pox has been claimed with the use of UV barriers over doors (McMath & Hussain, 1960).

An important offshoot of molecular biological aspects of excision–repair mechanisms in bacteria has been a better understanding of a disease (xeroderma pigmentosum) in humans, characterized by an abnormal sensitivity of the skin to sunlight and the likely development of malignant tumours. In a most interesting review of the repair processes for photochemical damage in mammalian cells, Cleaver (1974) has likened such people to uvr^- and Hcr^- bacterial mutants. DNA repair in mammalian cells has also been dealt with comprehensively by Hanawalt *et al.* (1979).

7 CONCLUSIONS

This brief chapter has dealt with the factors influencing the activity of UV radiation and its actions, uses and limitations. There is no doubt that UV light is much less useful as a sterilizing/disinfecting agent than ionizing radiation, but it is nevertheless of some value in air disinfection. Molecular biology studies, especially on repair processes, have yielded exciting new information with at least one important application to human welfare.

8 REFERENCES

Abshire, R.L., Bain, B. & Williams, T. (1980) Resistance and recovery studies on ultraviolet-irradiated spores of *Bacillus pumilus*. *Applied and Environmental Microbiology*, **39**, 695–701.

Alper, T. (1979) *Cellular Radiobiology*. Cambridge: Cambridge University Press.

Andrew, M.H.E. & Russell, A.D. (Eds) (1984) *The Revival of Injured Microbes*. Society for Applied Bacteriology Symposium Series No. 12. London: Academic Press.

Angehrn, M. (1984) Ultraviolet disinfection of water. *Aqua*, **2**, 109–115.

Ashwood-Smith, M.J. & Bridges, B.A. (1967) On the sensitivity of frozen micro-organisms to ultraviolet radiation. *Proceedings of the Royal Society of London, Series B*, **168**, 194–202.

Bayliss, C.E. & Waites, W.M. (1979a) The synergistic killing of spores of *Bacillus subtilis* by hydrogen peroxide and ultraviolet light irradiation. *FEMS Microbiology Letters*, **5**, 331–333.

Bayliss, C.E. & Waites, W.M. (1979b) The combined effects of hydrogen peroxide and ultraviolet light irradiation on bacterial spores. *Journal of Applied Bacteriology*, **47**, 263–269.

Boyce, R.P. & Howard-Flanders, P. (1964) Release of ultraviolet light-induced thymine dimers from DNA in *E. coli* K12. *Proceedings of the National Academy of Sciences, USA*, **51**, 293–300.

Bridges, B.A. (1976) Survival of bacteria following exposure to ultraviolet and ionizing radiations. In *The Survival of Vegetative Microbes* (eds Gray, T.G.R. & Postgate, J.R.) 26th Symposium of Society for General Microbiology. pp. 183–208. Cambridge: Cambridge University Press.

Bridges, B.A., Ashwood-Smith, M.J. & Munson, R.J. (1967) On the nature of the lethal and mutagenic action of ultraviolet light on frozen bacteria. *Proceedings of the Royal Society of London, Series B*, **168**, 203–215.

Chang, J., Ossoff, S., Lobe, D., Dorfman, M., Dumais, C., Qualls, R. & Johnson, J. (1985) UV inactivation of pathogenic and indicator organisms. *Applied and Environmental Microbiology*, **49**, 1361–1365.

Cleaver, J.E. (1974) Repair processes for photochemical damage in mammalian cells. *Advances in Radiation Biology*, **4**, 1–75.

Committee (1986) Committee on Health Care Issues, American Neurological Association. Precautions in handling tissues, fluids and other contaminated materials from patients with documented or suspected Creutzfeldt-Jakob disease. *Annals of Neurology*, **19**, 75–77.

Cook, A.M. & Saunders, L. (1962) Water for injection by ion-exchange. *Journal of Pharmacy and Pharmacology*, **14**, 83T–86T.

Cox, M.M. & Lehman, I.R. (1987) Enzymes of general recombination. *Annual Review of Biochemistry*, **56**, 229–262.

Department of Health (1989) *Report of the Expert Advisory Committee on Biocides*. London: HMSO.

Donnellan, J.E. & Setlow, R.B. (1965) Thymine photoproducts but not thymine dimers found in ultraviolet-irradiated bacterial spores. *Science, New York*, **149**, 308–310.

Donnellan, J.E. & Stafford, R.S. (1968) The ultraviolet photochemistry and photobiology of vegetative cells and spores of *Bacillus megeterium*. *Biophysical Journal*, **8**, 17–28.

Farr, B.M., Gratz, J.C., Tartaglino, J.C., Getchell-White, S.I. & Groschel, D.H.M. (1988) Evaluation of ultraviolet light for disinfection of hospital water contaminated with legionella. *Lancet*, **2**, 669–672.

Gardner, J.F. & Peel, M.M. (1986) *Introduction to Sterilization and Disinfection*. Edinburgh: Churchill Livingstone.

Germaine, G.R., Goggiola, E. & Murrell, W.G. (1973) Development of ultraviolet resistance in sporulating *Bacillus cereus* T. *Journal of Bacteriology*, **116**, 823–831.

Gilpin, R.W. (1984) Laboratory and field applications of UV light disinfection on six species of *Legionella* and other bacteria in water. In *Legionella: Proceedings of the Second International Symposium* (eds Thornsberry, C., Balows, A., Feeley, J.C. & Jakubowski, W.) pp. 337–339. Washington, DC: American Society for Microbiology.

Gould, G.W. (1983) Mechanisms of resistance and dormancy. In *The Bacterial Spore* (eds Hurst, A. & Gould, G.W.) Vol. 2, pp. 173–209. London: Academic Press.

Gould, G.W. (1984) Injury and repair mechanisms in bacterial spores. In *The Revival of Injured Microbes* (eds Andrew, M.H.E. & Russell, A.D.) Society for Applied Bacteriology Symposium Series No. 12, pp. 199–220. London: Academic Press.

Gould, G.W. (1985) Modification of resistance and dormancy. In *Fundamental and Applied Aspects of Bacterial Spores* (eds Dring, D.J., Ellar, D.J. & Gould, G.W.) pp. 371–382. London: Academic Press.

Hanawalt, P.C. & Setlow, R.B. (1975) *Molecular Mechanisms for the Repair of DNA*. New York: Plenum Press.

Hanawalt, P.C., Cooper, P.K., Ganesan, A.K. & Smith, C.A. (1979) DNA repair in bacteria and mammalian cells. *Annual Review of Biochemistry*, **48**, 783–836.

Harm, W. (1980) *Biological Effects of Ultraviolet Radiation*. IUPAB Biophysics Series I. Cambridge: Cambridge University Press.

Haseltine, W.A. (1983) Ultraviolet light repair and mutagenesis revisited. *Cell*, **33**, 13–17.

Haynes, R.H. (1964) Role of DNA repair mechanisms in microbial inactivation and recovery phenomena. *Photochemistry and Photobiology*, **3**, 429–450.

Haynes, R.H. (1966) The interpretation of microbial inactivation and recovery phenomena. *Radiation Research Supplement*, **6**, 1–29.

Hollaender, A. (1955) *Radiation Biology*, Vol. 2. New York: McGraw-Hill.

Howard-Flanders, P. (1973) DNA repair and recombination. *British Medical Bulletin*, **29**, 226–235.

Howard-Flanders, P. & Boyce, R.P. (1966) DNA repair and genetic recombination studies of mutants of *Escherichia coli* deficient in these processes. *Radiation Research, Supplement*, **6**, 156–184.

Irie, R., Yano, N., Morichi, T. & Kembo, H. (1965) Temporary increase in U.V. resistance in the course of spore germination of *Bacillus subtilis*. *Biochemical and Biophysical Research Communications*, **20**, 389–392.

Jagger, J. (1958) Photoreactivation. *Bacteriological Reviews*, **22**, 99–142.

Johansen, E.S. & Myhrstad, J.A. (1978) Factors influencing the use of u.v. irradiation as a water disinfectant. *NIPH Annual*, **1**, 3–10. (National Institute of Public Health, Oslo, Norway.)

Kelner, A. (1949a) Effect of visible light on the recovery of *Streptomyces griseus* conidia from ultraviolet irradiation injury. *Proceedings of the National Academy of Sciences, U.S.A.*, **35**, 73–79.

Kelner, A. (1949b) Photoreactivation of ultraviolet-irradiated *Escherichia coli* with special reference to the dose-reduction principle and to ultraviolet-induced mutation. *Journal of Bacteriology*, **58**, 511–532.

Knudsen, G.B. (1985) Photoreactivation of UV-irradiated *Legionella pneumophila* and other *Legionella* species. *Applied and Environmental Microbiology*, **49**, 975–980.

Latarjet, R. (1979) Inactivation of the agents of scrapie,

Creutzfeldt–Jakob disease and kuru by radiations. In *Slow Transmissible Diseases of the Nervous System* (eds Prusiner, S.B. & Hadlow, W.J.) Vol. 2, pp. 387–407. London: Academic Press.

McCulloch E. (1945) *Disinfection and Sterilization*. London: Kimpton.

McMath, W.E.T. & Hussain, K.K. (1960) Investigation of ultraviolet radiation in the control of chicken pox cross-infection. *British Journal of Clinical Practice*, **14**, 19–21.

Morris, E.J. (1972) The practical use of ultraviolet radiation for disinfection purposes. *Medical Laboratory Technology*, **29**, 41–47.

Morris, E.J. & Darlow, H.M. (1971) Inactivation of viruses. In *Inhibition and Destruction of the Microbial Cell* (ed. Hugo, W.B.) pp. 637–702. London: Academic Press.

Moseley, B.E.B. (1967) Repair of ultraviolet radiation damage in sensitive mutants of *Micrococcus radiodurans*. *Journal of Bacteriology*, **97**, 647–652.

Moseley, B.E.B. (1984) Radiation damage and its repair in non-sporulating bacteria. In *The Revival of Injured Microbes* (eds Andrew, M.H.E. & Russell, A.D.) Society for Applied Bacteriology Symposium Series No. 12, pp. 147–174. London: Academic Press.

Moseley, B.E.B. & Laser, H. (1965) Similarity of repair of ionizing and ultraviolet radiation damage in *Micrococcus radiodurans*. *Journal of Bacteriology*, **97**, 647–652.

Moseley, B.E.B. & Williams, E. (1977) Repair of damaged DNA in bacteria. *Advances in Microbial Physiology*, **16**, 99–156.

Munakata, N. & Rupert, C.S. (1972) Genetically controlled removal of 'spore photoproduct' from deoxyribonucleic acid of ultraviolet-irradiated *Bacillus subtilis* spores. *Journal of Bacteriology*, **111**, 192–198.

Munakata, N. & Rupert, C.S. (1974) Dark repair of DNA containing 'spore photoproduct' in *Bacillus subtilis*. *Molecular and General Genetics*, **130**, 239–250.

Muraca, P., Stout, J.E. & Yu, V.L. (1985) Comparative assessment of chlorine, heat, ozone and light for killing *Legionella pneumophila*, within a modern plumbing system. *Applied and Environmental Microbiology*, **53**, 447–453.

National Research Council (1964) Post-operative wound infection. *Annals of Surgery*, Supplement No. 2.

Nokes, M.A. & Powers, E.L. (1977) Sensitivity of bacterial spores to UV during germination and outgrowth. *Photochemistry and Photobiology*, **25**, 307–309.

Phillips, J.E. (1987) Physical methods of veterinary disinfection and sterilisation. In *Disinfection in Veterinary and Farm Animal Practice* (eds Linton, A.H., Hugo, W.B. & Russell, A.D.) pp. 117–143. Oxford: Blackwell Scientific Publications.

Rahn, R.O. & Hosszu, J.L. (1968) Photoproduct formation in DNA at low temperatures. *Photochemistry and Photobiology*, **8**, 53–63.

Rappaport, E.B. (1987) Iatrogenic Creutzfeldt–Jakob disease *Neurology*, **37**, 1520–1522.

Report (1990) *HIV–The Causative Agent of AIDS and Related Conditions*. Second Revision of Guidelines. Advisory Committee on Dangerous Pathogens.

Rice, E. & Hoff, J. (1981) Inactivation of *Giardia lamblia* cysts by ultraviolet irradiation. *Applied and Environmental Microbiology*, **42**, 546–547.

Roberts, T.A. & Hitchins, A.D. (1969) Resistance of spores. In *The Bacterial Spore* (eds Gould, G.W. & Hurst, A.) pp. 611–670. London: Academic Press.

Rodgers, F.G., Hufton, P., Kurzawska, E., Molloy, C. & Morgan, S. (1985) Morphological response of human rotavirus to ultraviolet radiation, heat and disinfectants. *Journal of Medical Microbiology*, **20**, 123–130.

Romig, W.R. & Wyss, O. (1957) Some effects of ultraviolet radiation on sporulating cultures of *Bacillus cereus*. *Journal of Bacteriology*, **74**, 386–391.

Russell, A.D. (1971) The destruction of bacterial spores. In *Inhibition and Destruction of the Microbial Cell* (ed. Hugo, W.B.) pp. 451–612. London: Academic Press.

Russell, A.D. (1982) *The Destruction of Bacterial Spores*. London: Academic Press.

Russell, A.D. (1990a) Bacterial spores and chemical sporicidal agents. *Clinical Microbiology Reviews*, **3**, 99–119.

Russell, A.D. (1990b) The effects of chemical and physical agents on microbes: disinfection and sterilization. In *Topley & Wilson's Principles of Bacteriology, Virology and Immunity*, 8th ed., Vol. 1 (eds Linton, A.H. & Dick, H.M.) pp. 71–103. London: Edward Arnold.

Russell, A.D. (1991) Theoretical aspects of microbial inactivation. In *Sterilization Technology* (eds Morrissey, R.F. & Phillips, G.B.) (In press.) New York: Van Nostrand Rheinhold.

Sancar, A. & Rupp, W.D. (1983) A novel repair enzyme: uvrABC excision nuclease of *Escherichia coli* cuts a DNA strand on both sides of the damaged region. *Cell*, **33**, 249–260.

Sancar, A. & Sancar, G.B. (1988) DNA repair enzymes. *Annual Review of Biochemistry*, **57**, 29–67.

Schechmeister, I.L. (1983) Sterilization by ultraviolet irradiation. In *Disinfection, Sterilization and Preservation*, 3rd edn. (ed. Block, S.S.) pp. 106–124. Philadelphia: Lea & Febiger.

Setlow, J.K. & Boling, M.E. (1965) The resistance of *Micrococcus radiodurans* to ultraviolet radiation. II Action spectra for kiling, delay in DNA synthesis and thymine dimerization. *Biochimica et Biophysica Acta*, **108**, 259–265.

Setlow, R.B. & Carrier, J.K. (1972) The disappearance of thymine dimers from DNA: an error-correcting mechanism. *Proceedings of the National Academy of Sciences, USA*, **51**, 226–231.

Smith, K.C. & Hanawalt, P.C. (1969) *Molecular Photobiology, Inactivation and Recovery*. London: Academic Press.

Stafford, R.S. & Donnellan, J.E. (1968) Photochemical evidence for confirmation changes in DNA during germination of bacterial spores. *Proceedings of the National Academy of Science, USA*, **59**, 822–828.

Stuy, J.H. (1955) Photoreactivation of ultraviolet-inactivated bacilli. *Biochimica et Biophysica Acta*, **17**, 206–211.

Stuy, J.H. (1956a) Studies on the mechanism of radiation inactivation of micro-organims. II. Photoreactivation of some bacilli and of the spores of two *Bacillus cereus* strains. *Biochimica et Biophysica Acta*, **22**, 238–240.

Stuy, J.H. (1956b) Studies on the mechanism of radiation inactivation of micro-organisms. III. Inactivation of germinating spores of *Bacillus cereus. Biochimica et Biophysica Acta*, **22**, 241–246.

Sykes, G. (1965) *Disinfection and Sterilization*. 2nd Ed. London: E. & F.N. Spon.

Thimann, K. (1963) *The Life of Bacteria*. 2nd Ed. New York: Macmillan.

Thuman, R.B. & Gerba, C.P. (1988) Molecular mechanisms of viral inactivation by water disinfectants. *Advances in Applied Microbiology*, **33**, 75–105.

Tyrrell, R.M., Moss, S.H. & Davies, D.J.G. (1972) The variation in u.v. sensitivity of four K12 strains of *Escherichia coli* as a function of their stage of growth. *Mutation Research*, **16**, 1–12.

Van Wang, T.-C. & Rupert, C.S. (1977) Evidence for the monomerization of spore photoproduct to two thymines by the light-independent 'spore repair' process in *Bacillus subtilis. Photochemistry and Photobiology*, **25**, 123–127.

Varghese, A.J. (1970) 5-thyminyl-5,6-dihydrothymine from DNA irradiated with ultraviolet light. *Biochemical and Biophysical Research Communications*, **38**, 484–490.

Waites, W.M. & Bayliss, C.E. (1984) Damage to bacterial spores by combined treatments and possible revival and repair processes. In *The Revival of Injured Microbes* (eds Andrew, M.H.E. & Russell, A.D.) Society for Applied Bacteriology Symposium Series No. 12, pp. 221–240. London: Academic Press.

Waites, W.M., Harding, S.E., Fowler, D.R., Jones, S.H., Shaw, D. & Martin, M. (1988) The destruction of spores of *Bacillus subtilis* by the combined effects of hydrogen peroxide and ultraviolet light. *Letters in Applied Microbiology*, **7**, 139–140.

Walker, G.C. (1985) Inducible DNA repair systems. *Annual Review of Biochemistry*, **54**, 425–457.

Watanabe, Y., Miyata H. & Sato, H. (1989) Inactivation of laboratory animal RNA-viruses by physicochemical treatment. *Experimental Animals* **38**, 305–311.

Witkin, E.M. (1969) Ultraviolet-induced mutation and DNA repair. *Annual Review of Genetics*, **3**, 525–552.

Witkin, E. (1976) Ultraviolet mutagenesis and inducible DNA repair in *Escherichia coli. Bacteriological Reviews*, **40**, 869–907.

Chapter 20
Gaseous Sterilization

1 INTRODUCTION

Only two gases (ethylene oxide and formaldehyde) find extensive use in the sterilization of medical products. Both are alkylating agents, and the inactivating effect on micro-organisms is considered to be a result of the alkylation of proteins, DNA and RNA (Russell, 1976). Other toxic gases such as methyl bromide, β-propiolactone and propylene oxide have been used for special sterilization purposes (for information see Russell, 1976), but are in general little used as routine methods for sterilization of medical products (Phillips, 1977).

The need for alternative sterilization procedures when the two heat sterilization methods, saturated steam under pressure (autoclaving) and dry heat, cannot be used because of damaging effects on the products, has been obvious from the early days of asepsis in surgical practice. Among the many methods used of decontamination of heat-sensitive products were a number of procedures employing formaldehyde: a treatment with gaseous formaldehyde and water vapour became accepted as a sterilization method, because this method inactivated viruses and bacterial spores as well as vegetative bacteria and fungi. In various modifications formaldehyde sterilization was, and in several countries still is, used as a supplement to heat sterilization methods at hospitals, clinics, health centres, etc. It was generally considered that this method was less reliable than thermal methods. Therefore, formaldehyde sterilization was used only when heat sterilization was impossible because of unacceptable damage to the products, and the method was deemed to be an efficient disinfection procedure rather than one of sterilization.

Prior to, and during, the Second World War, treatment with ethylene oxide gained acceptance as a decontamination method. In the food industry ethylene oxide was used for fumigation of various heat-sensitive products, e.g. spices, and after the comprehensive study by Phillips & Kaye (1949) it gradually became accepted for sterilization of certain medical products also.

With the rapid growth in the industrial production of presterilized medical devices, ethylene oxide sterilization became a popular sterilization method, not only in factories, but also in hospitals, clinics and laboratories. Unfortunately, it was not always looked upon with the same scepticism and distrust as formaldehyde procedures. The toxicity of ethylene oxide and the complexity of the sterilization procedure should, however, have been good reasons for restrictions on its use in hospitals and for concern as to the microbiological efficiency of some of the procedures in common use.

From about 1960 sterilization by means of ionizing radiation (Chapter 19A) became a realistic alternative to ethylene oxide sterilization for some heat-sensitive medical equipment. Comparisons of the advantages and disadvantages of the two methods were followed by a slow but steady rise in the number of publications with a critical attitude to ethylene oxide sterilization in general and to the use of the gas in small hospital sterilizers in particular. In the 1980s, it was realized that ethylene oxide and formaldehyde are carcinogens as well as mutagens, and strict limitations upon the release to the environment, on the permitted concentration in working areas and for residues of the two toxic gases in medical products, are now in force in the industrialized countries.

The type of products sterilized by the two gaseous sterilization methods and the difficulties associated with them are similar. Historically, formaldehyde sterilization is the older. However, the volume of medical materials sterilized by ethylene oxide far exceeds that sterilized by formaldehyde. Therefore, sterilization by means of ethylene oxide will be described first.

2 STERILIZATION BY ETHYLENE OXIDE

Several good reviews which deal with ethylene oxide sterilization have been published (Bruch, 1961; Steiger & Synek, 1973; Ernst, 1975; Phillips, 1977; Morrissey, 1985; Christensen, 1986).

2.1 Physical and chemical properties of ethylene oxide

At atmospheric pressure and ambient temperature, ethylene oxide ($(CH_2)_2O$) is a colourless gas with an uncharacteristic aromatic odour, not unpleasant to most people. At low temperature ethylene oxide is a liquid, with a boiling point at atmospheric pressure of 10.8°C. The acute toxicity is at the same level as ammonia, the acute symptoms being irritation of the conjunctiva and respiratory tract, headache, dizziness and vomiting. The liquid phase and the gas dissolved in natural or synthetic polymers, e.g. leather, rubber, plastics, can cause severe irritations of the skin. Anaphylactic reactions are rare, but have been reported (Poothullil *et al.*, 1975; Dolovich & Bell, 1978). The gas is mutagenic and carcinogenic (Ehrenberg *et al.*, 1974; Hogstedt *et al.*, 1978, 1979; OSHA, 1983) and precautions should always be taken to protect personnel and patients against exposure to it.

Pure ethylene oxide is explosive and inflammable between about 3% and 100% gaseous volume in mixtures with air. The risk of explosions can be eliminated by the use of ethylene oxide in mixtures with carbon dioxide or fluoridated hydrocarbons (Steiger & Synek, 1973). In the correct mixtures the resulting gas can be mixed with air in all proportions without being inflammable. For industrial use a mixture with carbon dioxide is generally preferred because of the lower cost of the diluent and the high vapour pressure of the mixture, thereby facilitating the filling procedure of large sterilization chambers. Mixtures with fluoridated hydrocarbons are preferred for the small sterilizers in hospitals, laboratories, etc., because of the much lower total pressure associated with the same concentration of ethylene oxide. Fluoridated hydrocarbons have a destructive effect on the ozone layer protecting the biosphere against the ultraviolet radiation from the sun. This was realized in the late 1980s, and severe restrictions on the use of, and in particular the release of, fluoridated hydrocarbons will in the 1990s influence the use of these gases in sterilizers.

Ethylene oxide polymerizes slowly, and mainly in the liquid phase. The process releases some heat and is accelerated by catalysts such as copper oxide. In mixtures with carbon dioxide and fluoridated hydrocarbons the ability to polymerize is decreased. The solid polymer may give rise to blockages in the tubing system of the sterilizers: it is not susceptible to detonation and is soluble in hot water.

As mentioned earlier, the smell of ethylene oxide is not unpleasant. The threshold of the smell is estimated to be about 700 parts/10^6 (Jacobson *et al.*, 1956). As the safe maximum concentration of ethylene oxide in the air in the working area is estimated to be lower than one part/10^6 (Bruch, 1977; Glaser, 1977; OSHA, 1983), there is a significant danger that operators of ethylene oxide sterilizers and persons involved in transport and storage of ethylene oxide-sterilized products may be unaware of being exposed to harmful concentrations. This necessitates sufficient ventilation in the appropriate areas, and atmospheric concentrations of ethylene oxide must be monitored in the working areas. In daily routine work the exposure to ethylene oxide ought to be a fair approximation to zero. However, short-time exposures to concentrations of about 10 parts/10^6 may be difficult to avoid even with excellent safety precautions.

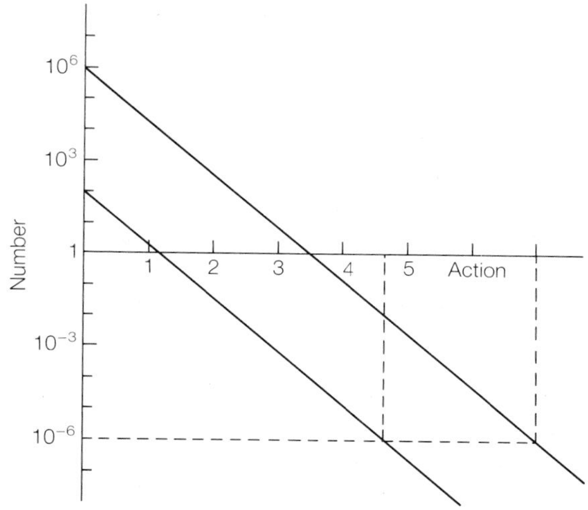

Fig. 20.1 Exponential (logarithmic) order of death of pure cultures of bacteria. When plotted semilogarithmically the data give straight lines. The dotted lines indicate the exposure necessary to obtain an inactivation factor of 10^6 if the initial populations are 10^2 and 10^6 viable units, respectively.

2.2 Microbicidal action and parameters for the sterilizing process

2.2.1 Microbial spectrum

Ethylene oxide inactivates all types of micro-organisms, including endospores of bacteria and viruses (Phillips, 1977). The action is influenced by the concentration of ethylene oxide, temperature, duration of exposure and water content of the micro-organisms. The relationship between these parameters and the inactivation of micro-organisms has been examined by Phillips (1949) and Kaye & Phillips (1949) and further elucidated by many other authors (Gilbert *et al.*, 1964; Christensen, 1964; Doyle & Ernst, 1968; Bruch & Bruch, 1970; Kereluk, 1970; Kristensen, 1970; Dadd & Daley, 1980, 1982; Caputo & Odlaug, 1983).

Provided the toxic gas has unhindered access to the micro-organisms and the water content in the organisms is sufficient, the inactivation is a classic first-order reaction, the dose–response curve for a pure culture being a straight line in a semilogarithmic system (Fig. 20.1). Nonlinear dose–response curves do occur. Differences in resistance to ethylene oxide between various micro-organisms exist. These differences are not, however, of great significance in the application of the sterilization method to medical products. The resistance of bacterial spores is only about 5 times greater than the resistance of the vegetative forms (Phillips, 1949).

A doubling of the concentration of ethylene oxide will reduce the exposure time necessary to achieve the same inactivation factor by a factor of two. However, at high concentrations, the benefit of a further increase in concentration is reduced (Ernst, 1974). The temperature coefficients (Q_{10} values) vary from 3 to 2 for ethylene oxide concentrations from about 400 mg/l to about 100 mg/l (Ernst, 1974).

2.2.2 Relative humidity

The role of moisture in the inactivation of micro-organisms by ethylene oxide was examined by Kaye & Phillips (1949). An optimal microbicidal effect was demonstrated at about 30% relative humidity (r.h.) with a greatly reduced effect at lower r.h. and a smaller reduction at higher humidity. These data, obtained in laboratory experiments, form the basis for misunderstandings and conflicting opinions because a high r.h., close to 100%, is required in the majority of sterilization procedures in practice if a reliable procedure is to be established. The data illustrating the relationship between the r.h. and the inactivating effect of ethylene oxide are not incorrect; however, ideal conditions with free access of ethylene oxide and water vapour to the micro-organisms are not often found outside laboratory experiments and are difficult to establish even in the laboratory. The molecules of ethylene oxide must, of course, penetrate to the vital macromolecules (proteins, nucleic acids; see Chapter 2) in the micro-organisms and the necessary water molecules have to be at the vital site before the inactivating chemical reactions can take place. In a sterilizer loaded with plastic medical devices wrapped in envelopes with a paper back and a polyethylene front, and packed in multi-unit containers of cardboard, a part of the ethylene oxide and water vapour will be absorbed by the plastic, the cellulose, or other materials in the load. The ability to absorb water will vary from one load to another, even when the sterilizer is loaded with the same product on each occasion, unless great care is taken to ensure that the water content in materials of paper, textiles and the like are independent of the variations in temperature and humidity in the environment. The routine sterilization procedures will typically include an evacuation of the air from the sterilization chamber in order to facilitate a fast and equal distribution of ethylene oxide and water vapour. The vacuum will remove some water from the products to be sterilized and also from the contaminating organisms. Furthermore, the typical routine sterilization procedure will include a rise from ambient temperature to about 55°C with the related decrease in r.h. Consequently, some extra water must be added to the sterilization chamber and the load in order to achieve an r.h. high enough to obtain a reliable killing effect of the ethylene oxide throughout the load. The penetration of ethylene oxide and water vapour takes time, and an equilibrium between the gas concentration and the water vapour in the free space in the sterilization chamber and the amount of gas and water in the products to be sterilized is not always established within a routine sterilization cycle. It is, therefore, often preferable that the r.h. in the sterilization chamber should be as near to 100% as possible without causing harmful effects to the products.

Of special importance for the proper use of ethylene oxide in the large-scale sterilization of single-use medical devices is the fact that dried micro-organisms can have a very high resistance to ethylene oxide and can be very difficult to rehydrate by means of water vapour (Phillips, 1961; Gilbert *et al.*, 1964). Dust from various environments may contain a few highly resistant c.f.u. in about 10^5 total organisms (Fig. 20.2) (Kristensen, 1970; Christensen & Kristensen, 1979). It is not only bacterial spores that may acquire an extremely high resistance to ethylene oxide. Gram-positive cocci (Gilbert *et al.*, 1964; Nyström, 1975; Christensen & Kristensen, 1979) and other non-spore-forming organisms and fungi (Christensen & Kristensen, 1979) can also be resistant under the same conditions. This phenomenon can be explained by the inclusion of micro-organisms in small crystals (Abbott *et al.*, 1956) or in amorphous substances. Free water can release the trapped organisms and change the apparent resistance from

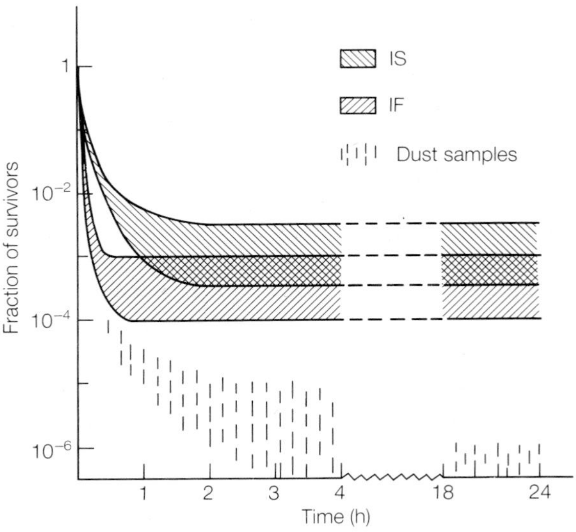

Fig. 20.2 Inactivation of micro-organisms in samples of dust and two biological indicators with spores of *Bacillus subtilis* absorbed on sand (IS) and on cotton fibres (IF) during a suboptimal exposure to ethylene oxide (450 mg/l) and water vapour (r.h. 60%) (from Christensen & Kristensen, 1979).

high to normal very rapidly. However, dried micro-organisms can be exposed to a r.h. above 30% for many hours without their resistance being altered (Phillips, 1961; Gilbert *et al.*, 1964). The occurrence of highly resistant micro-organisms in airborne contamination can be explained by the significant temperature differences in the environments which normally exist in industrialized societies. Central heating systems, parts of machines, electric bulbs, etc., create areas with a relatively high temperature and consequently a low r.h.

The combined effects of:

1 an impediment to free access of gas and water vapour to the organisms contaminating medical products of complex structure and wrapped in paper and/or plastic;

2 the competition for the available water (and gas) between paper, textiles, plastics, etc., and the micro-organisms;

3 the occurrence of dried micro-organisms, probably protected in crystals

explain the exposure times used for ethylene oxide sterilization in routine procedures in hospitals and factories. Under controlled experimental conditions, inactivation factors for the test strains of bacteria in use as biological indicators can be 10^6 or higher after 20-min exposure to, for example, about 600 mg ethylene oxide per litre at 55°C and 60% r.h. (USP, 1990a). With the same parameters the routine procedures normally take at least 4 h and sometimes even 18 h.

With the realization that from 12 to about 50 times longer exposure time is needed for a 10^6 reduction in the number of viable spores under practical sterilization conditions, compared to what is obtainable under ideal conditions, it is understandable that the differences in genetically determined resistance between various kinds of micro-organisms are of little significance for the practical use of ethylene oxide as a sterilant.

2.2.3 *Prolonged incubation*

From a practical point of view the inactivation effect of ethylene oxide on micro-organisms seems to be irreversible. Damage to micro-organisms cannot be neutralized or repaired after exposure. However, some repair processes may occur (Michael & Stumbo, 1970; Russell, 1976), and may be the reason for some variation in lag phase when organisms surviving an exposure to ethylene oxide are cultivated on agar plates. The fact that a prolonged incubation in sterility tests on ethylene oxide sterilized products sometimes reveals a few samples with growth after a period of several weeks without visible growth in the cultures (Brewer & Briggs Phillips, 1968) is not in conflict with the general statement that the inactivation effect is irreversible. In the cases examined, the organisms in these delayed 'positive' cultures did not possess an exceptionally high resistance or an unusual shape of inactivation curve when examined as pure cultures. Explanations for such delayed growth after exposure to ethylene oxide can be given. Thus, a cell may be embedded in porous material, be hidden in a narrow fissure or be surrounded by amorphous or crystalline compounds. Such a location can prevent the sterilizing agent from reaching the cell and later, in the incubation period of the sterility test, delay the penetration of the culture media to the cell. Spore dormancy might be a further explanation for the late occurrence of some of the positive cultures after ethylene oxide treatment. Finally, organisms which multiply slowly do exist.

The occurrence of delayed growth after intended sterilization is by no means a phenomenon exclusively observed after ethylene oxide treatment, even though it might be more common after ethylene oxide and formaldehyde procedures than after heat and radiation methods. As might be expected from the above, the probability of the occurrence varies with the type of product being sterilized.

In the experience of the authors, the delayed growth visible only after more than 2 weeks of incubation is relatively common in experimental work with ethylene oxide-treated samples of fertilized soil and samples of dust. It is therefore not surprising that this phenomenon also occurs in connection with gas sterilization of complex medical devices, because a part of the contamination could have originated from dust, e.g. from transport crates or an open window close to working areas in the production premises for medical devices. This kind of contamination should not, of course, take place during the manufacture of medical products. However, such failures can occur and are, most probably, more common than the delayed growth in sterility tests.

2.3 Choice of sterilization procedure and design of the products to be sterilized

All sterilization methods have advantages and disadvantages. Ethylene oxide is toxic and explosive and the reliability of the antimicrobial effect depends on a strict control of several parameters (concentration of the toxic gas, temperature, r.h. and time of exposure). The sterilization method is complex and in fact only reliable when used by specialists. The method does, however, possess some important advantages. Deleterious effects to medical products are very rare, when the toxicity added to the products is not taken into account. The risk from harmful effects of toxic residues can be eliminated by correct treatment, handling and storage of sterilized products. It has to be mentioned, however, that ethylene chlorohydrin (boiling point 128.8°C at atmospheric pressure) may remain when ethylene oxide is evaporated after the aeration procedures normally used. Some occurrences of damage to plastics and rubber can be explained by unintentional exposure to fluid ethylene oxide in primitive sterilization equipment, and can be avoided by means of improved technology. Provided that a sufficient humidity can be ensured, ethylene oxide can also sterilize at ambient temperature.

In hospitals a method for sterilization at moderate temperatures is needed. The majority of the heat-sensitive devices and instruments can be disinfected instead of sterilized, because only the endospores of bacteria can survive a *lege artis* hot water or saturated steam disinfection at temperatures from 80°C to 100°C. However, a group of sterilization tasks not amenable to these processes remain, and must be achieved either by means of toxic chemicals in solutions or in the gaseous phase. Some optical instruments and some electrical devices are very sensitive to heat and/or chemicals. Equipment which is not routinely sterilized or disinfected, and therefore not designed to tolerate a sterilization, can become contaminated with dangerous pathogenic organisms, or it may be needed for a patient kept under aseptic conditions. In such cases a gas sterilization procedure, reliable and not too complex, is needed. At hospitals in Denmark, Norway and Sweden formaldehyde sterilization is preferred, whereas in the United States and in most countries in western Europe ethylene oxide sterilization is generally preferred.

When the choice between ethylene oxide and formaldehyde was made in the Scandinavian countries, between 30 and 20 years ago, two aspects of gas sterilization were considered, *viz.* reliable control of microbiological efficiency, and toxicological hazards. Hospital staff in these countries were familiar with formaldehyde treatment of heat-sensitive devices (Nordgren, 1939) and a routine control by means of biological indicators was established (Møller & Volkert, 1952; Christensen *et al.*, 1969). Toxicological problems with formaldehyde were well known and often serious. However, it was, in general, regarded as a significant advantage that the characteristic and unpleasant smell of formaldehyde could give a warning against unacceptable toxicological risks. A dangerous concentration of the toxic gas could not be kept in the working area without the personnel responsible for the sterilization procedures being aware of the risk.

The then available ethylene oxide sterilizers for use in hospitals could not, in general, inactivate the biological indicator routinely used (e.g. Winge-Hedén, 1963; Christensen, 1964; Nyström, 1970), and the toxicological hazards associated with ethylene oxide were used as an argument against the method. The concentration of ethylene oxide in a working area can be several times higher than the acceptable level without being noticed by personnel in that area (Jacobson *et al.*, 1956; Hine & Rowe, 1963; Glaser, 1979).

The notable advantages of ethylene oxide (it is a more flexible method, because it could be used also at ambient temperature without too much polymerization, and has a superior ability to penetrate into complex structures) were not regarded as justification for its use as a sterilant in the hospitals. At present only a single or a few centres in each of the three Scandinavian countries has ethylene oxide sterilizers available for the hospitals. In the few cases where ethylene oxide sterilization cannot be substituted by another method, the contaminated equipment is sent to these centres.

For large-scale industrial sterilization, the advantages of ethylene oxide sterilization by far outweigh the disadvantages. The method can be used for sterilization of temperature-sensitive plastic and rubber products. The damage to the products is negligible, and when a sterilization failure occurs, a resterilization procedure can be instituted.

Until the early 1970s, the toxicity of ethylene oxide had raised very few problems in connection with the industrial sterilization of medical products. In general, the time period between sterilization and actual usage was so long that residues of ethylene oxide, which could otherwise have had serious harmful effects on patients, had dissipated before the products were used. The acute and subacute toxicity of ethylene oxide and its degradation products for personnel dealing with this sterilization procedure and the initial storage of the sterilized products, when considerable amounts of ethylene oxide are released from the products, were estimated and dealt with differently in the various countries, according to the national regulations (Bruch, 1973; Glaser, 1977; Environmental Protection Agency, 1978; OSHA, 1983).

The difficulties and costs involved in the control of microbiological efficiency have always been correlated with the official standard for sterilized medical products. If the standard is based solely on a spot test on the final products (sterility testing) (WHO, 1960; Ph. Eur., 1986; USP, 1990a), then only gross failure of the sterilization process can be detected (Council of the Pharmaceutical Society of Great Britain, 1963). When, however, the standard is based on a statistical evaluation of the probability of micro-organisms surviving on or in the sterilized product (such as a maximum of one colony-forming unit in a total of one million product units, a sterility assurance level of 10^{-6}) or on the use of biological indicators with a defined resistance, based on an official reference biological indicator (e.g. Christensen *et al.*, 1969; Ph. Nord., 1970; UK Department of Health and Social Security, 1975a; Ph. Eur., 1983; USP, 1990), then the control of microbiological efficiency becomes complicated as well as costly. In return, the microbiological quality assurance resulting from a gas-sterilized product may, however, equal that of heat-sterilized products. Sterility testing is discussed in detail in Chapter 22.

Regardless of the costs directly involved in the sterilization process, the cost for:
1 protection of personnel;
2 protection of the environment in general;
3 reliable microbiological control both of the manufacturing conditions (to minimize the microbial contamination of the products prior to sterilization) and of the sterilization procedure itself
may lead to a tendency to change to other sterilization methods whenever possible.

Radiation sterilization (see Chapter 19A) is an obvious industrial alternative to gas sterilization. Formaldehyde sterilization is an alternative for the sterilization of heat-sensitive materials in hospitals and may, at least for some products, be an alternative to ethylene oxide for large-scale procedures as well.

For some products, however, e.g. pacemakers, an ethylene oxide sterilization is the only realistic possibility for reliable sterilization at present, and for complex, high-cost products sufficient control of the toxicological hazards and of the microbiological efficiency can, of course, be attained.

It is important that the products, as well as the packings and containers, to be sterilized by means of a toxic gas are designed with due regard to the sterilization method. A sufficient amount of water vapour and of the toxic gas must penetrate to all parts of the product. Equalization of differences in total pressure is a rapid process compared to equalization of differences in partial pressures by diffusion; therefore the products and packagings must be designed to permit an evacuation of the air and an intrusion of water vapour and toxic gas with a difference in total pressure as the main driving force. The permeability to gases of the packaging must be adequate whilst at the same time not reducing the ability to protect the product against microbial recontamination. The function of the product, e.g. the tightness of a syringe or a tap, must not be affected by the considerations necessary for the penetration of water vapour and sterilizing gas into the narrowest interstices of the product. These conflicting requirements restrict the use of gas sterilization.

2.4 Control of ethylene oxide sterilization procedures

Control measurements of sterilization procedures with ethylene oxide must ensure:

1 that the procedure has the necessary microbicidal effect, *viz*. that the product has been sterilized;

2 that the procedure is within specified limits with regard to gas concentration, temperature, r.h. and duration, in order to ensure that the procedure is defined and can be reproduced;

3 that working conditions for personnel have no unacceptable hazards;

4 that the sterilized product when released has no unacceptable toxic side-effects to patients.

2.4.1 General precautions

It is a condition for manufacture of sterilized medical products that one or another of the official rules for Good Manufacturing Practice (e.g. EEC, 1989; EFTA, 1989; USP, 1990b) are followed. Therefore, when large-scale ethylene oxide sterilization is used, the number of contaminating micro-organisms prior to sterilization, the so-called bioburden, can be expected to be kept within reasonable limits.

For small-scale use in hospitals and laboratories it is an accepted condition that standard procedures for sterilization are based on standard procedures for treatment of instruments and devices prior to sterilization. A fluctuation in numbers of micro-organisms can be expected, even when the hospital hygiene is unimpeachable. When necessary, the instruments must be disinfected; they should always be cleaned, and the wrapping should follow an appropriate routine.

The balance between gas concentration and water vapour in the sterilization chamber and the gas and water content of the load to be sterilized can be influenced significantly by the type of load because of differences in ability to absorb gas and water. Therefore, standard rules for loading the sterilizer should be followed. New instruments, new devices and new wrapping materials always require special attention, with intensified use of microbiological and toxicological measurements.

2.4.2 Measurements of physicochemical parameters

The physicochemical parameters for the sterilization procedure should be measured whenever possible in order to establish a reproducible and quantifiable process. The possible combinations of the significant variables with and without pre-humidification, one or more pre-vacuum periods and one or more post-vacuum periods, are so numerous that no standard requirements for the measurements of temperature, duration, gas concentration and r.h. can be given. However, unless data on the important parameters for each single process are available, each will be new and unique, and no guarantee of perfection can be established.

A typical procedure will have one or more pre-vacuum periods in order to remove the air from the load to be sterilized, then a humidification procedure followed by the filling of the chamber with ethylene oxide (pure or in mixture with carbon dioxide or freon). The sterilization time is the period from the attainment of the desired partial pressure of ethylene oxide until this partial pressure is decreased deliberately by removal of the mixture of gases from the sterilization chamber. Normally this is done by one or more evacuation periods in order to remove the products from the chamber without unreasonable toxic hazards for personnel.

The temperature and pressure in the sterilization chamber during such a cycle must be known, and in many routine procedures the partial pressure of both water vapour and ethylene oxide mixture can be measured. In other procedures only the total amounts of water and ethylene oxide mixture used in the procedure can be measured. As mentioned earlier (Section 2.2), however, the physicochemical parameters measured in the free space in the sterilization chamber are not *a priori* a reliable indication of the conditions in the micro-environment for the micro-organisms contaminating the load.

2.4.3 Biological indicators

The use of biological indicators is the only reliable way to ensure that the microbiological efficiency of ethylene oxide sterilization complies with an official standard for sterilized medical products, even when the official standard is based solely on a sterility test. Conventional sterility testing (see Chapter 22) reveals only gross contamination and as a control measurement of the efficiency of sterilization procedures it is inaccurate and troublesome, in particular when testing complex medical devices. From the information that the sterilized product complies with the minimum requirement (the sterility test) it cannot be deduced how much better than this necessary minimum the procedure has been, or how much variation in efficiency there is within a series of routine sterilization procedures.

The general standard for sterilized medical products (Ph. Eur., 1983; EUCOMED, 1988; USP, 1990a,b), a sterility assurance level (SAL) of 10^{-6}, is applicable for ethylene oxide-sterilized medical devices, and only the use of a reliable biological indicator system can ensure that the sterilized products comply with the required standard.

Biological indicators must be designed with due regard to official standards, and to the resistance of the microbial contamination on and in the product to be sterilized. Some information can be gained about the resistance of the micro-organisms in the actual environment by examining samples of dust or other reference samples from nature. Experience shows that the free access of ethylene oxide and water vapour to the organisms is by far the most important factor for inactivation. The construction of the products, the ability to absorb ethylene oxide and water by the components of the products and the local protection of micro-organisms are important details. Therefore, examination of a number of product units contaminated with high numbers of organisms with known high resistance to the sterilizing agent: inoculated product units (USP, 1990a) is necessary, to ensure that the construction of the product (including the wrapping) is suitable for that product to be sterilized by ethylene oxide.

When the standard for sterilized products is not more than one c.f.u. per million product units, an examination of the occurrence of extremely resistant organisms in the environment is important for the choice of resistance characteristics of the biological indicators to be used in the daily routine control. In Denmark the frequency of c.f.u. in dust which can be inactivated by ethylene oxide only when exposed to high relative humidities seems to be about one c.f.u. per 10^5 (Kristensen, 1970; Christensen & Kristensen, 1979). It is conceivable that the frequency of micro-organisms dried and protected by organic or inorganic substances, and therefore protected against rehumidification, is dependent on the climate. Taking the relatively cold and humid climate in Denmark into account, it might be expected that protected organisms would be more common in countries with a dry and hot climate and in countries where air-conditioning or central heating systems are used against extreme climatic conditions.

In nearly all cases the routine use of contaminated product units as biological indicator systems is too complicated and expensive. Therefore, in daily routine control, contaminated carriers are normally used as biological indicators. These carriers should, to a reasonable degree, simulate the conditions under which micro-organisms occur in the product to be sterilized. If the water-binding capacity of the carriers deviates significantly from that of the product, the resistance of the indicator may either be too high or too low. It is recommended that the type of indicator chosen shall have at least the same resistance as the artificially contaminated product units. Furthermore, the biological indicators should contain some deliberately protected and dried organisms, demonstrated to be rehumidified only when exposed to combinations of r.h. and times of exposure suitable for rehumidification of the 'resistant' fraction of micro-organisms in the airborne dust particles from a relevant environment (Christensen & Kristensen, 1979).

Variations in the preparation and standardization of biological indicator systems for gas sterilization are too numerous to be discussed here. It must, however, be mentioned that a declaration of the number of c.f.u. per test piece of the indicator is of no value without knowledge of the resistance under defined conditions. Even a well-known and stable test strain of a spore-forming organism can be prepared with different resistance characteristics over a broad range, e.g. organisms can be damaged by washing procedures or by storage in various chemicals, or be protected by various organic or inorganic compounds (Abbott *et al.*, 1956; Beeby & Whitehouse, 1965; Doyle & Ernst, 1968). A biological indicator system for gas sterilization should be described by the test strain, the number of c.f.u. per test piece and the inactivation curves for at least one set of exposure conditions with a sub-optimal r.h. and one with optimal r.h. Furthermore, an expiry date or an indication of the storage life-time with unchanged resistance characteristics is necessary. Because the major cost factor in the production of biological indicators is the continuous control of resistance from batch to batch and of the single batch during the time period the batch is in use, the use of commercially available indicator systems is necessary in small and medium-size gaseous sterilization procedures. Frequently, the use of less than optimal biological indicator systems is the result of attempts to find a commercially available indicator suitable for the control of specific products sterilized in an available sterilizer. In large-scale utilization of ethylene oxide sterilization such problems should be non-existent. An indicator system can be specifically designed for the purpose (Fig. 20.3).

2.4.4 *Precautions against toxicity*

Ethylene oxide should not be used for sterilization without due attention to its possible harmful effects to personnel operating the sterilizers and the subsequent aeration procedures, to the environment and, last, but not least, to the patients exposed to the sterilized products during therapy and care. The official and semi-official guidelines for its safe use in the sterilization of medical products (see p. 557) indicate that the use of ethylene oxide for sterilization is for specialists only.

It can be concluded that it is irresponsible to use ethylene oxide sterilization for medical products without reasonable safeguards against the known and the presumed toxic effects of the gas. The safety precautions should be at least as good as prescribed at present by national authorities. Whenever possible, sterilization by saturated steam or by dry heat is to be preferred to other sterilization methods. When possible in small-scale sterilization, ethylene oxide should be replaced by formaldehyde, or disinfection by steam or hot water should be used instead of gaseous sterilization. Industrially, radiation sterilization is, whenever possible, to be preferred to ethylene oxide. When ethylene oxide must be used for sterilization — and such occurrences still exist — exposure to personnel, to the environment and to patients should, in the authors' opinion, approximate to zero.

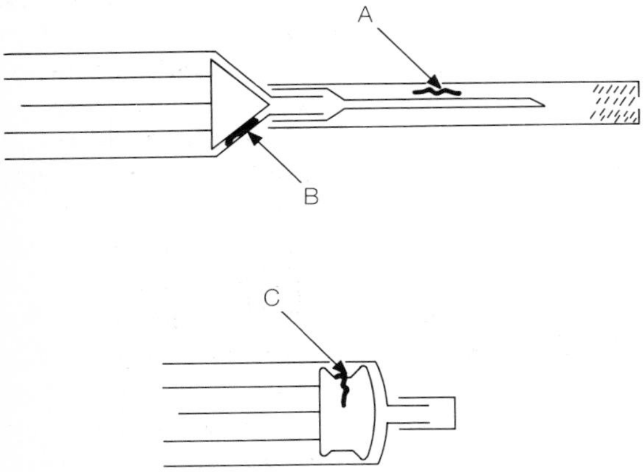

Fig. 20.3 A, B and C are typical loci difficult to reach by toxic gases and/or water vapour. Such loci are well suited for insertion of biological indicators (from Christensen & Kristensen, 1979).

2.5 Uses of ethylene oxide

Sterilization of medical devices and supplies has been, and still is, the most important use of ethylene oxide sterilization. However, various powdered drugs (Diding *et al.*, 1968; *British Pharmacopoeia*, 1973) and raw materials for the pharmaceutical industry can be sterilized or decontaminated by means of ethylene oxide.

As mentioned (p. 560), ethylene oxide sterilization can be used on occasions when materials and supplies not normally sterilized prior to use, but disinfected or cleaned, are required for a special purpose or have been contaminated accidentally with a dangerous infectious agent. Whenever the need arises for sterilization (or decontamination) of rarely used objects, regardless of the kind and size of the product, gaseous sterilization by means of ethylene oxide or other toxic gas should be among the methods to be considered. A cost–benefit risk analysis may show that ethylene oxide is to be preferred, e.g. in spacecraft sterilization in the United States.

The use of ethylene oxide for decontamination for sterilization in the food industry must be mentioned, but will not be evaluated here: appropriate information is provided in Chapter 16.

3 STERILIZATION BY FORMALDEHYDE

Disinfection and sterilization procedures with formaldehyde (H.CHO) as the active agent in aqueous solution or as a gas have been used for many years (Nordgren, 1939). Other papers describing formaldehyde sterilization have been published by Alder *et al.* (1966), Weymes & White (1975), Phillips (1977) and Christensen (1986).

3.1 Physical and chemical properties of formaldehyde

Formaldehyde gas is colourless and has a characteristic unpleasant odour. The smell threshold is estimated to be less than half of the acceptable maximum concentration in air. Formaldehyde gas is neither explosive nor inflammable. At ambient temperature the maximum partial pressure of formaldehyde gas is only a few mmHg, or about 1 mg formaldehyde per litre. The affinity of the gas for water is high, and at room temperature a solution of about 37% w/w formaldehyde can be obtained. Formaldehyde solution (formalin) contains 34.2–38.1% formaldehyde in water, together with stabilizers to prevent the formation of polymers. At temperatures below *c.* 80°C, formaldehyde gas polymerizes readily to various solid polymers, the most common of which is paraformaldehyde (see also Chapter 2).

Formaldehyde is an alkylating agent. Acute toxic symptoms are irritation of the conjunctiva and of the respiratory tract. Allergic reactions caused by formaldehyde are not uncommon (e.g. Hendrick & Lane, 1975). Formaldehyde is mutagenic and carcinogenic (Feldman, 1973; Marshall, 1987). The safe maximum concentration in the air in the working area is probably lower than one part/10^6.

3.2 Microbicidal action and parameters influencing the sterilizing process

Formaldehyde has an inactivating effect on all types of micro-organisms, including bacterial spores and viruses. The action is influenced by formaldehyde concentration, temperature, water content in the micro-organisms and duration of exposure.

Formaldehyde sterilization is often considered as being a method for decontaminating laboratories or hospital rooms when dangerous infections have contaminated an area, and as a somewhat primitive method for sterilization of outer surfaces. In the authors' experience, an evaluation of formaldehyde sterilization based solely on primitive procedures at room temperature is unsatisfactory. When advanced technology comparable to that used for ethylene oxide sterilization is used, the same degree of reliability with small-scale hospital formaldehyde sterilization can be obtained. For large-scale sterilization of medical devices a formaldehyde procedure may be less applicable because of the relatively high temperature necessary to minimize the condensation of paraformaldehyde on the products. An unquestionable advantage in hospitals is that, unlike ethylene oxide, formaldehyde is nonflammable and its presence in the environment is evidenced by its smell. It remains to be seen, however, whether large-scale formaldehyde sterilization with modern technology can be made efficient and competitive with ethylene oxide.

In principle, conditions for efficient sterilization by formaldehyde gas are the same as for ethylene oxide (Section 2.2), i.e. provided that access of the toxic gas and water vapour to the micro-organisms is unhindered, the microbicidal effect is rapid and reliable. A high r.h. is necessary for this rapid inactivation of micro-organisms. However, the extraordinary affinity of formaldehyde for water may give rise to failures in sterilization procedures, as excess free water can occasionally be present in the sterilization chamber. Further, the ability of formaldehyde to polymerize at temperatures below 80°C often gives rise to problems. Paraformaldehyde can be condensed in the tubes, vents and valves in the sterilizer, as the temperature at these locations is often lower than in the chamber, and consequently the gas concentration in the chamber may be lower than expected. When the sterilizer is used alternately for formaldehyde sterilization and saturated steam disinfection at about 80°C, the effect of the disinfection procedure can be much better than expected because formaldehyde is released from the paraformaldehyde in tubes and vents. In procedures at temperatures below 80°C, condensation of paraformaldehyde on the sterilized products often occurs, giving an irritant smell to the products and a toxicological hazard to personnel unless there is a long aeration period. In order to ensure even distribution of gas and water vapour throughout the load, and to minimize the condensation of polymers on the load, one or more evacuations, alternating with filling with saturated steam prior to the exposure to formaldehyde can be used. A temperature of 80°C is preferable. Temperatures of 60°C or 70°C are also acceptable but (as pointed out above), the tendency for polymerization onto the products is significantly higher than at 80°C. Alternating vacuum and steam after exposure to formaldehyde ensures a low content of the aldehyde in the sterilized products (Weymes & White, 1975; Handlos, 1979).

Exposure times used in formaldehyde sterilizers are traditionally shorter than the times used for ethylene oxide. In general, procedures are used where a full cycle with pre- and post-evacuation takes 1–2 h (e.g. Alder *et al.*, 1971). Efficient sterilization of endoscopes can be achieved with such a short exposure time. When, however, pressure equilibration or diffusion are likely to be impeded, longer exposure times in parallel with the times used in ethylene oxide sterilization may be necessary.

As mentioned previously, a high r.h. is necessary for reliable formaldehyde sterilization, and from 75% to 100% is desirable. Therefore, regardless of the temperature of the sterilizing process it is important that temperature differences within the area to be sterilized are avoided. One or more cool spots will cause condensation of water, concentration of formaldehyde in the water and formation of paraformaldehyde. The sterilizing effect on the relatively hotter parts of the area can be decreased or may even be insufficient because of too low r.h. or gas concentration.

The damaging effect of formaldehyde on micro-organisms is generally regarded as being irreversible. Recent observations, however, contradict this (Spicher & Peters, 1981). A surprisingly large proportion of bacterial spores 'inactivated' in aqueous formaldehyde solution at 20°C is reported as being reactivated by heat treatment. This phenomenon, normally carried out at temperatures above 60°C, is not important in formaldehyde sterilization. Delayed growth occurs in sterility tests on formaldehyde-sterilized products, and is possibly more common with this sterilization method than with ethylene oxide. This delayed-growth phenomenon is correlated with physicochemical protection of the organisms, as is the case with ethylene oxide. However, reactivation of spores could also be of significance. For sterilization by formaldehyde gas, genetically determined differences in resistance (Spicher & Peters, 1976) have so far been insignificant compared with the differences in resistance caused by dehydration and physicochemical protection of some of the micro-organisms contaminating medical products (see Sections 2.2.1 and 2.2.2).

3.3 Control of formaldehyde sterilization

3.3.1 Control measurements

To ensure that the procedure used is reproducible within reasonable limits, temperature, pressure variations (if any) and the duration of the various steps in the procedure should be recorded. Furthermore, the amount of formalin, or the amount of formaldehyde and water used in the procedure, should be known. It is, however, impossible to evaluate the microbicidal efficiency of the procedure on physicochemical data only. The complex interrelationships of the factors influencing the antimicrobial activity (gas concentration, r.h., duration of exposure, temperature), the affinity of formaldehyde for water, the formation of paraformaldehyde, and the possibility of depolymerization of paraformaldehyde, together necessitate the use of biological indicators when a reliable evaluation of the microbicidal efficiency is needed.

3.3.2 Biological indicators

As with other alkylating agents, water is necessary for activity. Therefore it is essential that the biological indicator system used should have a built-in ability to reveal insufficient humidity in the sterilization procedure. The test pieces of the indicator should contain dried micro-organisms protected against rehumidification at low and moderate r.h. This can be done by means of organic or inorganic compounds added to the spore preparation. This protection should, however, dissolve or disintegrate readily when the r.h. is *c.* 80% or higher.

The indicator system should either simulate any impedance likely to be encountered to pressure equilibration and diffusion in the products to be sterilized, or the test pieces of the indicator should be placed within the products in the locations most difficult to sterilize.

When formaldehyde procedures are used for sterilization purposes, the use of biological indicators in every load is to be recommended. For small-scale hospital use, however, where the aim is mainly a reliable disinfection rather than sterilization with the broad safety margin defined by the official requirement, the biological indicator is used at regular intervals, e.g. every 4 or 8 weeks, as well as when changes in the procedure or products take place, or whenever a single positive in the routine use of biological indicator control has indicated that the safety margin in the routine procedure may be too narrow.

Spores of *B. subtilis* and *B. stearothermophilus* can be used as test organisms in a biological indicator for formaldehyde sterilization. When an indicator specifically designed and calibrated for control of formaldehyde procedures cannot be obtained, the use of an indicator for ethylene oxide procedures as a substitute can be justified. Spores of *B. stearothermophilus* seem, however, to be the most resistant to formaldehyde among the commonly used test organisms, and in the Scandinavian countries experience with various formaldehyde sterilizers at hospitals during the 1980s resulted in simultaneous use of a *B. subtilis* indicator revealing insufficient humidification and a *B. stearothermophilus* indicator revealing too low a concentration of formaldehyde gas.

3.3.3 Precautions against toxicity

Condensation of paraformaldehyde on the sterilized products often occurs, and frequently the grey appearance of the surfaces and the irritant smell are accepted by hospital personnel as a relatively harmless phenomenon. This attitude to the warning given by the smell of formaldehyde is unacceptable. Allergy to formaldehyde is not uncommon, and the olfactory senses can be damaged permanently if exposed to formaldehyde in toxic concentrations. Therefore, even when the more severe damage caused by the acute and chronic toxicity of formaldehyde can be avoided by reasonable handling of both the sterilization procedure and the sterilized products, the irritant smell of formaldehyde should not be ignored. The sterilization procedure, possibly with an aeration period added, is not satisfactory unless the sterilized products can be used without unpleasant odour from the products or the wrapping materials. The presence of small amounts of formaldehyde may be registered by the very sensitive sense of smell and can be unavoidable, but a strong irritant smell is definitely unacceptable.

3.4 Formaldehyde-releasing agents

Aqueous solutions of formaldehyde (various concentrations) are the normal sources of gaseous formaldehyde for sterilization because high r.h. is a condition for reliable antimicrobial activity of the aldehyde. Paraformaldehyde, a polymer of formaldehyde, can, however, be used as a source for pure monomeric formaldehyde gas (Tulis, 1973). The necessary humidity should then be secured by other means.

Other sources for monomeric formaldehyde gas are melamine formaldehyde and urea formaldehyde (Russell, 1976). These resins release formaldehyde, the rate of release being temperature dependent.

Additional information is provided in Chapter 2.

3.5 Uses of formaldehyde

Gaseous formaldehyde in combination with water vapour is used for sterilization of heat-sensitive medical devices and supplies.

On the rare occasions when disinfection of rooms in hospitals or other premises is needed, gaseous formaldehyde at high r.h. can be efficient, provided temperature differences within the premises to be disinfected can be avoided. Another relevant use of formaldehyde gas is for *in-situ* decontamination of the air filters in biological safety cabinets for handling infected material and other dangerous biological substances.

Formaldehyde as a gas or in aqueous solutions is widely used as a disinfectant (Russell, 1976: see also Chapter 2).

4 REFERENCES

Abbott, C.F., Cockton, I. & Jones, W. (1956) Resistance of crystalline substances to gas sterilization. *Journal of Pharmacy and Pharmacology*, **8**, 709–719.

Alder, V.G., Brown, A.M. & Gillespie, W.A. (1966) Disinfection of heat-sensitive material by low-temperature steam and formaldehyde. *Journal of Clinical Pathology*, **19**, 83–89.

Alder, V.G., Gingell, J.C. & Mitchell, J.P. (1971) Disinfection of cystoscopes by subatmospheric steam and steam and formaldehyde at 80°C. *British Medical Journal*, **iii**, 677–680.

Beeby, M.M. & Whitehouse, C.E. (1965) A bacterial spore test piece for the control of ethylene oxide sterilization. *Journal of Applied Bacteriology*, **28**, 349–360.

Brewer, J.H. & Briggs Phillips, G. (1968) Proper use of biological indicators in sterilization. *Bulletin of the Parenteral Drug Association*, **22**, 157–169.

British Pharmacopoeia (1973) pp. 1163–1164. London: Pharmaceutical Press.

Bruch, C.W. (1961) Gaseous sterilization. *Annual Review of Microbiology*, **15**, 245–262.

Bruch, C.W. (1973) Sterilization of plastics: Toxicity of ethylene oxide residues. In *Symposium on Industrial Sterilization* (ed. Phillips, G.B. & Miller, W.S.) pp. 51–77. Durham, North Carolina: Duke University Press.

Bruch, C.W. (1977) Food and drug administration activities on ETO residuals. In *Ethylene Oxide—Update*. HIMA report 77–7. Washington DC: Health Industry Manufacturers Association.

Bruch, C.W. & Bruch, M.K. (1970) Gaseous disinfection. In *Disinfection* (ed. Benarde, M.A.) pp. 149–206. New York: Marcel Dekker.

Caputo, R.A. & Odlaug, T.E. (1983) Sterilization with ethylene oxide and other gases. In *Disinfection, Sterilization and Preservation* (ed. Block, S.S.) 3rd Ed. Y7–6Y. Philadelphia: Lea & Febiger.

Christensen, E.A. (1964) Newer methods of sterilization. *Ugeskrift for Laeger*, **126**, 330–339. (In Danish.)

Christensen, E.A. (1986) Gaseous methods of sterilization. In *Sterilization of Medical Products*, (eds Gaughran, E.R.L., Morrissey, R.F., Wang, J.) IV. Montreal, Canada: Johnson & Johnson, Polyscience Publications.

Christensen, E.A., Kallings, L.O. & Fystro, D. (1969) Microbiological control of sterilization procedures and standards for the sterilization of medical equipment. (Simultaneously published in *Ugeskrift for Laeger*, **131**, 2123 (Copenhagen); *Läkartidningen*, **66**, 5117 (Stockholm); *Tidsskrift for den Norske Laegeforening*, **89**, 1806 (Oslo)). (Version in English available.)

Christensen, E.A. & Kristensen, H. (1979) Biological indicators for the control of ethylene oxide sterilization. *Acta Pathologica et Microbiologica Scandinavica, Section B*, **87**, 147–154.

Council of the Pharmaceutical Society of Great Britain (1963) Round Table Conference on Sterility Testing. London, p.Fl.

Dadd, A.H. & Daley, G.M. (1980) Resistance of microorganisms to inactivation by gaseous ethylene oxide. *Journal of Applied Bacteriology*, **48**, 89–101.

Dadd, A.H. & Daley, G.M. (1982) Role of the coat in resistance of bacterial spores to inactivation by ethylene oxide. *Journal of Applied Bacteriology*, **53**, 109–116.

Diding, N., Wergeman, L., & Samulson, G. (1968) Ethylene oxide treatment of crude drugs. *Acta Pharmaceutica Suecica*, **5**, 177–182.

Dolovich, J. & Bell, B. (1978) Allergy to a product(s) of ethylene oxide gas. Demonstration of IgE and IgG antibodies and hapten specificity. *Journal of Allergy and Clinical Immunology*, **62**, 30–32.

Doyle, J.E. & Ernst, R.R. (1968) Influence of various pretreatments (carriers, desiccation and relative cleanliness) on the destruction of *Bacillus subtilis* var. *niger* spores with gaseous ethylene oxide. *Journal of Pharmaceutical Sciences*, **57**, 433–436.

EEC *Guide to Good Manufacturing Practice for Medical Products* (1989) Commission of the European Communities, Brussels: Directorate-General for Internal Market and Industrial Affairs.

EFTA *Guide to Good Manufacturing Practice for Pharmaceutical Products* (1989) Convention for the Mutual Recognition of Inspections in respect of the Manufacture of Pharmaceutical Products. Document PH 5/89. Geneva: EFTA Secretariat.

Ehrenberg, L., Hiesche, K.D., Osterman-Goldar, S. & Wennberg, I. (1974) Evaluation of genetic risks of alkylating agents. Tissue doses in the mouse from air contaminated with ethylene oxide. *Mutation Research*, **24**, 83–103.

Environmental Protection Agency, USA (1978) Ethylene oxide. *Federal Register*, **43**, 3799–3815.

Ernst, R.R. (1974) Ethylene oxide gaseous sterilization. In *Developments in Biological Standardization*. Vol. 23, pp. 40–50. Basel, Paris, London, New York: Karger.

Ernst, R.R. (1975) Sterilization by means of ethylene oxide. *Acta Pharmaceutica Suecica*, **12**, Supplement, 44–64.

European Confederation of Medical Suppliers Associations

(1988). Recommendations for the sterilization of medical devices and surgical products. EUCOMED, 551 Finchley Road, Hampstead, London NW3 7BJ, England.

Feldman, M. Ya. (1973) Reactions of nucleic acids and nucleoproteins with formaldehyde. In *Progress in Nucleic Acid Research and Molecular Biology*, Vol. 13 (eds Davidson, J.B. & Cohn, W.E.) pp. 1–49. New York: Academic Press.

Gilbert, G.L., Gambell, V.M., Spiner, D.R., Hofmann, R.K. & Phillips, C.R. (1964) Effect of moisture on ethylene oxide sterilization. *Applied Microbiology*, **12**, 496–509.

Glaser, Z.R. (1977) Special occupational review and control recommendations for the use of ethylene oxide as a sterilant in medical facilities. DHEW Document No. (NIOSH) 77–200. National Institute for Occupational Safety and Health. Washington, D.C.

Glaser, Z.R. (1979) Ethylene oxide: Toxicology review and field study results of hospital use. *Journal of Environmental Pathology and Toxicology*, **2**, 173–208.

Handlos, V. (1979) Formaldehyde sterilization. II. Formaldehyde-steam sterilization, the process and its influence on the formaldehyde residuals. *Archiv for Pharmaci og Chemi. Scientific Edition*, **7**, 1–11.

Hendrick, D.J. & Lane, D.J. (1975) Formalin asthma in hospital staff. *British Medical Journal*, **i**, 607–608.

Hine, C.H. & Rowe, V.K. (1963) Ethylene oxid. In *Industrial Hygiene and Toxicology*, Vol. II. Toxicology. (eds Fassett, D.W. & Irish, D.D.) 2nd Ed., pp. 1626–1634. New York: Interscience Publishers.

Hogstedt, C., Berndtsson, B.S., Rohlen, O., Axelson, O. & Ehrenberg, L. (1978) Death among employees occupied with ethylene oxide production. A prevalence-study 10 years after exposure. *Läkartidningen*, **75**, 3285–3287. (In Swedish.)

Hogstedt, C., Malmqvist, N. & Wadman, B. (1979) Leukaemia in workers exposed to ethylene oxide. *Journal of the American Medical Association*, **11**, 1132–1133.

Jacobson, K.H., Hackley, E.B. & Feinsilver, L. (1956) The toxicity of inhaled ethylene oxide and propylene oxide vapours. *Archives of Industrial Health*, **13**, 237–244.

Kaye, S. & Phillips, C.R. (1949) The sterilizing action of gaseous ethylene oxide. IV. The effect of moisture. *American Journal of Hygiene*, **50**, 296–306.

Kereluk, K., Gammon, R.A. & Lloyd, R.S (1970) Microbial aspects of ethylene oxide sterilization. III. Effects of humidity and water activity on the sporicidal activity of ethylene oxide. *Applied Microbiology*, **19**, 157–162.

Kristensen, H. (1970) Ethylene oxide resistance of microorganisms in dust compared with the resistance of *Bacillus subtilis* spores. *Acta Pathologica et Microbiologica Scandinavica, Section B*, **78**, 298–304.

Marshall, E. (1987) EPA indicts formaldehyde. *Science*, **236**, 381.

Michael, G.T. & Stumbo, C.R. (1970) Ethylene oxide sterilization of *Salmonella senftenberg* and *Escherichia coli*: death kinetics and mode of action. *Journal of Food Science*, **35**, 631–634.

Morrissey, R.F. (1985) Ethylene oxide sterilization. Process development and validation. In *Sterilization of Medical Products*, III (eds Harris, L.E. & Skopek, A.J.) Australia: Johnson & Johnson Pty Ltd.

Møller, V. & Volkert, M. (1952) Formaldehyde sterilizers. *Ugeskrift for Laeger*, **114**, 928–930. (In Danish.)

Nordgren, G. (1939) Formaldehyde sterilization. *Acta Pathologica et Microbiologica Scandinavica*, Supplement, 38–41.

Nyström, B. (1970) Ethylene oxide sterilization in hospitals. *Läkartidningen*, **67**, 4657–4663. (In Swedish).

Nyström, B. (1975) Differences between sterilization at hospitals and in industry. *Acta Pharmaceutica Suecica*, **12**, *Supplement*, 72–77.

Occupational Safety and Health Administration (OSHA). Occupational exposure to ethylene oxide (1983), *Federal Register*, **48**, 17284–17319.

Ph. Eur. (1983) *European Pharmacopeia*, 2nd Ed., Methods of Sterilization, IX.1. Maisonneuve: Council of Europe.

Ph. Eur. (1986) *European Pharmacopeia*, 2nd Ed., Test for Sterility, V.2.1.1. Maisonneuve: Council of Europe.

Pharmacopeae Nordica. Editio Danica (1970) Addendum, p. 603. Copenhagen: Nyt Nordisk Forlag.

Phillips, C.R. (1949) The sterilizing action of gaseous ethylene oxide. II. Sterilization of contaminated objects with ethylene oxide and related compounds, time, concentration and temperature relationship. *American Journal of Hygiene*, **50**, 280–289.

Phillips, C.R. (1961) The sterilizing properties of ethylene oxide. In *Symposium on Recent Developments in the Sterilization of Surgical Materials*. pp. 59–75. London: Pharmaceutical Press.

Phillips, C.R. (1977) Gaseous sterilization. In *Disinfection, Sterilization and Preservation* (ed. Block, S.S.) 2nd Ed. pp. 592–611. Philadelphia: Lea & Febiger.

Phillips, C.R. & Kaye, S. (1949) The sterilizing action of gaseous ethylene oxide. I. Review. *American Journal of Hygiene*, **50**, 270–279.

Poothullil, J., Shimizu, A., Day, R.P. & Dolovich, J. (1975) Anaphylaxis from the product(s) of ethylene oxide gas. *Annals of Internal Medicine*, **82**, 58–60.

Russell, A.D. (1976) Inactivation of non-sporing bacteria by gases. In *Symposium No. 5*. pp. 61–88. Society of Applied Bacteriology. London: Academic Press.

Spicher, G. & Peters, J. (1976) Microbial resistance to formaldehyde. I. Comparative quantitative studies in some selected species of vegetative bacteria, bacterial spores, bacteriophages and viruses. *Zentralblatt für Bakteriologie, Parasitenkunde, Infectionskrankheiten, und Hygiene, I. Abteilung Originale, Reihe B*, **163**, 486–508 (in German).

Spicher, G. & Peters, J. (1981) Heat activation of bacterial spores after inactivation by formaldehyde: dependence of heat activation on temperature and duration of action. *Zentralblatt für Bakteriologie, Parasitenkunde, Infectionskrankheiten und Hygiene, I. Abteilung Originale, Reihe B*, **173**, 188–196 (in German).

Steiger, E. & Synek, J. (1973) Sterilization durch äthylenoxide. In *Handbuch der Desinfektion und Sterilization*. Band II. Grundlagen der Sterilization. VEB. (eds Horn, V.H., Privora, M. & Weuffen, W.) pp. 181–215. Berlin: Verlag Volk und Gesundheit. (In German.)

Tulis, J.J. (1973) Formaldehyde gas as a sterilant. In *Industrial Sterilization* (eds Phillips, G.B. & Miller, W.S.) International Symposium, Amsterdam, 1972. Durham, North Carolina, USA: Duke University Press.

UK Department of Health and Social Security (1975a) *Sterilization of single use plastic products by ethylene oxide*. Scientific and Technical Branch, Supply Division. Requirements 20. London: HMSO.

UK Department of Health and Social Security (1975b) Guide to good manufacturing practice for sterile, single-use medical devices. Scientific and Technical Branch, Supply Division. Final draft July 1975.

USP XXII (1990a) Biological indicators, 171–173 and 1625–1626. United States Pharmacopeial Convention, Inc., 12601 Twinbrook Parkway, Rockville, MD 20852, USA.

USP XXII (1990b) Good Manufacturing Practice, 1671–1681. United States Pharmacopeial Convention, Inc., 12601 Twinbrook Parkway, Rockville, MD 20852, USA.

Weymes, C. & White, J.D. (1975) Studies in the use of low concentrations of formaldehyde with steam at subatmospheric pressures as a method of sterilizing nonporous heat-sensitive items. Glasgow Greater Health Board, Sterile Supply Service.

Winge-Hedén, K. (1963) Ethylene oxide sterilization without special equipment. *Acta Pathologica et Microbiologica Scandinavica, Section B*, **58**, 225–244.

World Health Organization (1960) General requirements for the sterility of biological substances. Technical Report Series Number 200, p. 13.

Chapter 21
Filtration Sterilization

1 HISTORICAL INTRODUCTION

It was stated in Chapter 1 that ancient historical writers recognized the clear and drinkable quality of water trickling through a river or lake bank, although the source was foul-tasting and clouded. Certain ancient purveyors of wine, Rhodian for example, were renowned for producing a crystal-clear product although, like other wise technologists, they did not make their secret available to others but it was believed that a filtration process was involved.

Early attempts to purify water were made by allowing it to percolate through beds of sand, gravel or cinders and a complex ecosystem developed on these filters. An increasing knowledge of bacteriology and an awareness of the involvement of water-borne bacteria (*Vibrio cholerae*, entobacteria) and pathogenic protozoa and worms, in disease and epidemics, eventually led to a more thorough study of filtration devices. Finally, the technology became such that filtration could be used to remove bacteria from solutions destined for parenteral administration to man and animals.

2 FILTRATION MEDIA

2.1 Unglazed ceramic filters

Chamberland, a colleague of Louis Pasteur, invented a thimble-like vessel made by sintering a moulded kaolin and sand mix. These so-called Chamberland candles were the first fabricated filters and represent another example of the inventive output from the Pasteur school (Chamberland, 1884). They were later to be made by the English firm of Doulton and other ceramic manufacturers, and were essentially of unglazed porcelain.

These are available in a variety of shapes and porosities and, apart from the traditional candle filter, ceramic filter discs are available for mounting in suitable holders. They were used extensively for clarification, and filtration grades suitable for sterilization were used in the pharmaceutical industry.

A typical modern version of the ceramic filter is the Pyrolith produced by Fairey Industrial Ceramics Ltd. This is made by mixing size-graded particles with fluxes and other additives, shaping and firing, during which chemical changes take place and a hard porcelain-type product is obtained. Various grades of porosity are obtainable; the grade PO has a maximum diameter of 15 μm and it has been validated down to a removal efficiency of 0.3 μm.

Porosity range in all these filters is achieved by varying the particle size of the constituents and the temperature of sintering or firing. Candle filters are closed with a glazed ceramic insert carrying a nozzle. The luting or affixing of this insert must be performed with care and this seal is often a point of weakness. These filters can, however, be used repeatedly provided the lute seal is checked and the filter cleansed by scrubbing, immersion in dilute hypochlorite solution or heating to dull redness. These filters enjoyed a great vogue in the pharmaceutical industry until the advent of membrane filters (Section 2.5) rendered them practically obsolete in this area.

For those who may find they still use these filters the paper of Royce & Sykes (1950) should be consulted; this deals with aspects of safety testing and correlates bubble pressure tests (Section 4.1) with microbiological filtration performance. It should also be borne in mind that ceramics are relatively powerful sorbers.

2.2 Filters of compressed diatomaceous earth

In 1891 Carl Nortmeyer in Germany produced a filter from compressed kieselguhr, a diatomaceous earth. These filters were to become known as Berkefeld filters—Berkefeld was the owner of the mine from which the earth was obtained. Later these filters were produced in the United States and were known as Mandler filters.

Kieselguhr filters are softer than the filters of unglazed porcelain and are seldom, if ever, used for pharmaceutical sterilization purposes today. However, such filters find wide application in water purifying systems and an ingenious extension of their efficacy (already alluded to on p. 58) is the incorporation of silver in the filter matrix so that the oligodynamic action of the metal enhances and complements the filtering facility of the kieselguhr.

The paper by Royce & Sykes (1950) deals also with the bacteriological performance of non-impregnated kieselguhr filters and their testing by the bubble pressure technique (Section 4.1).

Domestic water for drinking, whether piped on a large grid or obtained locally from wells, must attain a certain bacteriological standard. This aspect of water technology is beyond the scope of this book, but at the house level suspect water may be purified and cleared of pathogens by the use of kieselguhr devices or the porcelain filters already referred to (Section 2.1). Both on the national and local scale, chlorination is used as a back-up to promote maximum safety.

Diatomaceous earth, added to liquid products to form a suspended slurry, is widely used as a filter aid in the pharmaceutical industry. The slurry is deposited on porous supports and the liquid then passes through, leaving coarse particulate matter entrained within the retained filter cake. Such an approach is employed in rotary drum vacuum filters (Dahlstrom & Silverblatt, 1986), as used in antibiotic manufacture for instance, where the drum rotates within the slurry, pulling filtered liquid through the retained cake under vacuum, leaving the cell debris behind.

2.3 Fibrous pad filters

Early types were essentially pads of asbestos made by allowing a slurry of asbestos fibres to dry in suitable moulds. They were invented in Germany and were known as Seitz filters. For use, they are held in some form of support where they can be clamped and thus secured in the form of a filter funnel or in a filter press. Such a press may embody a dozen or more square pads.

These filters enjoyed a vogue in the pharmaceutical industry and in hospitals for the preparation of sterile solutions, possessing remarkably efficient particle-removal capability attributed to electrostatic interaction. The appearance of reports about the toxicity of asbestos, its possible carcinogenicity and the new much higher standards for particulate-free medicines for parenteral administration, have led to their becoming practically obsolete and their use is now banned by the United States Food and Drugs Administration (Casola, 1975; Elias, 1975).

Alternative developments have employed microfibres of borosilicate glass to create filters. These have found widespread application in filter presses and as prefilters for clarification of pharmaceutical solutions. It is usual to employ such filters with a membrane filter (Section 2.5) downstream to collect any shed fibres.

Other materials used in the construction of this type of filter include paper, nylon, polyester, cellulose acetate fibres and woven wool fibres.

2.4 Sintered or fritted ware

This type of filter was made by taking particles of glass or metal (stainless steel or silver), assembling them in suitable holders and subjecting them to a heat process so that the particles melted or softened on their faces and, on cooling, fused together. It is clear that a complete melting would defeat the object of the technology and this partial melting followed by surface fusion was called sintering or frittering. Such a process will give rise to a porous sheet of material which can then act as a filter (Smith, 1944). This process differs from the sintering process used in the manufacture of unglazed porcelain in that the latter contains several components and the process is accompanied by chemical changes in the constituents.

2.4.1 Sintered glass filters

Their invention is attributed to the German glass manufacturers Scholt u Gen. of Jena (Prausnitz, 1924).

Their application to bacteriology was described by Morton & Czarnatzky (1937) where a disc of porosity 3 surmounted by one of porosity 5 suitably retained in a funnel, was used to sterilize culture media. They also showed that broth cultures of several microbial species, including *Serratia marcescens*, were sterilized by passing through this system.

The pore size of sintered glass filters is controlled by the general particle size of the glass powder used to fabricate them. Bacteriological grades were given the number 5 by the German innovators, and the English manufacturers also used this code. The current British Standard no longer uses this code, and the equivalent grade is P1.6, with a maximum pore diameter of 1.6 μm (British Standard 1752, 1983). Their application in sterilization is now largely restricted to specialist situations involving highly corrosive or viscous liquids.

Sintered glass filters are easily cleaned using back-washing or oxidizing chemicals such as hypochlorite or nitric/sulphuric acid; they have low sorption properties and do not shed particles into the solution they are filtering. On the other hand, their size is constrained by their nature, they are fragile and relatively expensive.

2.4.2 Sintered metal filters

Metal particles can be fabricated into porous sheets by the same process as for glass. Bronze, cupronickel, stainless steel and silver have been used.

Sintered silver is a potential sterilizing filter combining as it does its filtering facility with its potential oligodynamic action.

2.5 Membrane filters

Membrane filter technology has had over 70 years in which to develop since the first description, by Zsigmondy & Bachmann in 1918, of a method suitable for producing cellulose membrane filters on a commercial scale. The full potential of membrane filters was not recognized until their successful application in the detection of contaminated water supplies in Germany during the Second World War (Gelman, 1965). Following their commercial exploitation in the 1950s and 1960s a number of large international companies evolved which now offer the potential user an ever-increasing but bewildering array of filters and associated equipment from which to choose. Undoubtedly, the role played by membrane filters continues to expand, both in the laboratory and in industry, and they are now routinely used in water analysis and purification, sterility testing and sterilization. Their future is assured, at least in the pharmaceutical industry, and unless other, as yet undiscovered, techniques emerge, since they represent the most suitable filtration medium presently available for the preparation of sterile, filtered parenteral products to a standard accepted by all the various regulatory authorities.

2.5.1 Methods of manufacture

There are three major methods of membrane filter manufacture currently employed on an industrial scale. These involve either a gelling and casting process, an irradiation-etch process or an expansion process. Each method produces membranes with their own particular characteristics.

1 Gelling and casting process. This is perhaps the most widely used process and all the major filter manufacturers offer filters prepared by this method. Cast polymeric membranes, as they are known, are principally derived from pure cellulose nitrate or mixed esters of acetate and nitrate although many other materials are available offering greater chemical resistance (Gelman, 1965). In essence, the process still utilizes the principles outlined by Zsigmondy & Bachmann in 1918, where the ester is mixed with a suitable organic solvent or combination of solvents and allowed to gel (Ehrlich, 1960). In the modern process a minute quantity of hydrophilic polymer may be present as a wetting agent, ethylene glycol may be added as a 'pore-former' and glycerol is often included to afford flexibility to the finished membrane. The mixture is then cast onto a moving, perfectly smooth stainless steel belt to give a film 90–170 μm thick (Fig. 21.1). By carefully controlling the temperature and relative humidity the solvents are slowly evaporated off leaving a wet gel of highly porous, three-dimensional structure which dries to give a membrane of considerable mechanical strength (Fig. 21.2). Pore size and other membrane characteristics are determined by the initial concentration of the cellulose ester, the mixing process, including

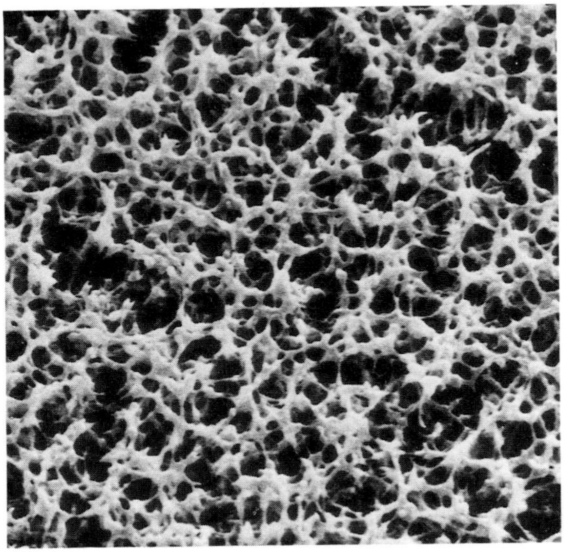

Fig. 21.2 Scanning electron micrograph (4000 ×) of the surface of a 0.22 μm pore size cast cellulose membrane filter (courtesy of Nuclepore Corporation).

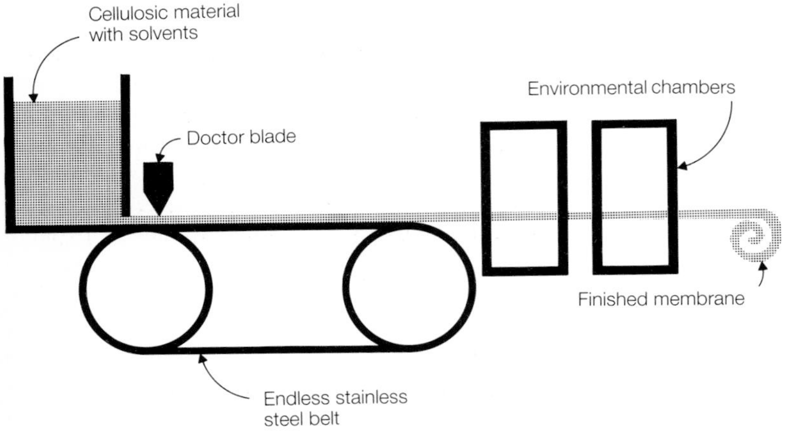

Fig. 21.1 Membrane manufacture — the casting process (courtesy of Nuclepore Corporation).

the solvents added, and the environmental drying conditions.

The casting process can be extended to other polymeric substances (e.g. nylon; Kesting *et al.*, 1983) where phase inversion may be achieved by wet, dry, or thermal methods.

2 Irradiation-etch process. Developed from the method of Fleischer *et al.* (1964) and originally patented with the Nuclepore Corporation, this process is operated in two stages. First, a thin film (5–10 μm thick) of polycarbonate or polyester material is exposed to a stream of charged particles in a nuclear reactor; this is followed by a second stage where the fission tracks made through the film are etched out into round, randomly dispersed cylindrical pores (Fig. 21.3). Pore density and pore size are controlled by the duration of exposure of the film within the reactor, and by the etching process, respectively. The finished 'nuclear-type' membranes are thin, transparent, strong and flexible (Fig. 21.4).

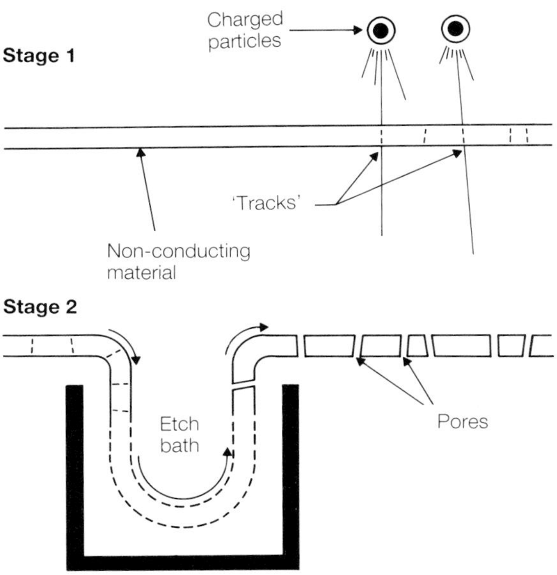

Fig. 21.3 Membrane manufacture—the irradiation-etch process (see text for details of Stages 1 and 2) (courtesy of Nuclepore Corporation).

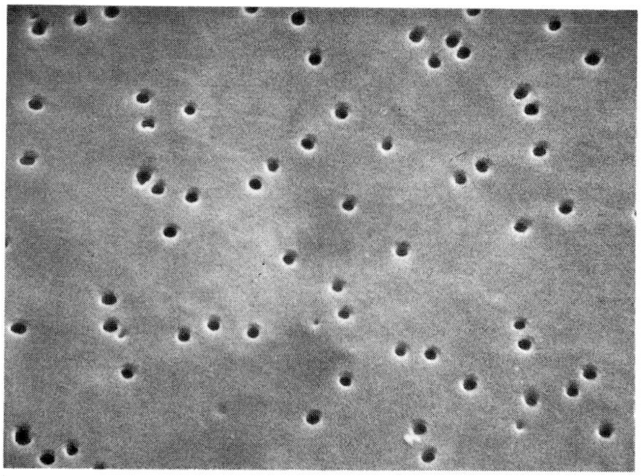

Fig. 21.4 Scanning electron micrograph (10 000 ×) of the surface of a 0.2-μm pore size polycarbonate 'nuclear-type' membrane filter (courtesy of Nuclepore Corporation).

3 Expansion process. Stretching and expanding of fluorocarbon sheets, e.g. polytetrafluoroethylene (PTFE), along both axes is sometimes undertaken to provide porous, chemically inert membranes. A support of polyethylene or polypropylene is usually bonded to one side of the membrane to improve handling characteristics. Their hydrophobic nature ensures that these filters are widely employed in the filtration of air and non-aqueous liquids.

An alternative method of production for PTFE filters is by a process that forms a continuous mat of microfibres fused together at each intersection to prevent shedding into the filtrate. These filters usually have no supporting layer to reduce their chemical resistance.

4 Other methods of filter construction. Other methods of manufacture include solvent leaching of one material from a cast mixture leaving pores, the production of bundles of hollow fibres, and porous anodic film construction. The latter filter type represents a recently introduced novel inorganic (aluminium oxide) membrane of highly organized and regular pore structure.

2.5.2 *The mechanisms of membrane filtration*

Membrane filters are often described as 'screen' filters and are thereby contrasted directly with filter media that are believed to retain particles and organisms by a 'depth' filtration process. By this simple definition, filters made from sintered glass, compressed fibre or ceramic materials, are classified as depth filters, while membranes derived from cast materials, stretched polymers and irradiated plastics are classified as screen filters. In essence, during depth filtration, particles are trapped or adsorbed within the interstices of the filter matrix, while screen filtration involves the exclusion (sieving out) of all particles larger than the rated pore size (Fig. 21.5).

Unfortunately, classification of membrane filters is not nearly as simple as this scheme might suggest. It is now recognized that the filtration characteristics of many membrane filters cannot be accounted for in terms of the sieve retention theory alone. In 1963, Megaw & Wiffen pointed out that although membrane filters would be expected to act primarily by sieve retention, they did possess the property of retaining particles that were much smaller than the membrane pore size, larger particles being trapped by impaction in the filter pores. (This aspect is discussed in more detail below). A more precise classification might be expected to take into consideration the considerable variation in membrane filter structure (see Section 2.5.1) and the subsequent influence that this may have on the mechanism of filtration.

The influence of membrane filter structure on the filtration process. Several studies have reported a marked difference between the pore structure of the upper and lower surfaces of cellulose membrane filters. Of particular note are the works of Preusser (1967), Denee & Stein (1971) and Marshall & Meltzer (1976). These workers have all shown one surface to have a greater porosity than the other. This phenomenon can be used to advantage in filtrations since it confers a depth-like filtration characteristic on the cellulose membranes when used with the more open side upstream. Particles can now enter the interstices of the filter, increasing the time to clogging. The variation in flow rate and total throughput resulting from the different directions of flow can exceed 50%. Most filter manufacturers recognize the asymmetry of their membranes; indeed several emphasize it in their technical literature and ensure that all filters are packed in the preferred flow direction (top to bottom). Highly anisotropic membranes with superior filtration characteristics to those of conven-

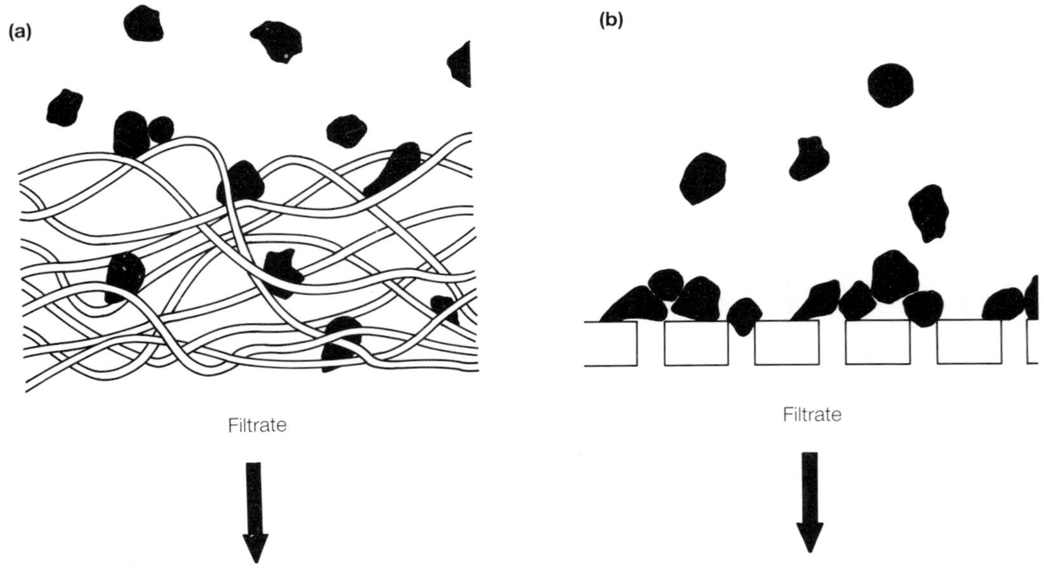

Fig. 21.5 Comparison between (a) depth; and (b) screen filtration.

tional mixed-ester membranes have been described (Kesting *et al.*, 1981; Wrasidlo & Mysels, 1984).

A membrane filter can be further characterized by its pore size distribution and pore numbers. Manufacturers give their membranes either a 'nominal' or 'absolute' pore size rating, usually qualified by certain tolerance limits. 'Nominal' pore size implies that a certain percentage of contamination above that size is retained, e.g. if the initial inoculum is 10^6 bacteria, a 99.999% retention efficiency for an organism above the pore size means that 10 bacteria pass into the filtrate (Wallhausser, 1976). Graphs depicting pore size distribution have been offered by several filter manufacturers (Fig. 21.6). It must be remembered that the techniques used to establish pore size vary from manufacturer to manufacturer and the values obtained are not necessarily comparable (Brock, 1983).

Jacobs (1972) described the distribution of pore diameters in graded ultrafilter membranes and discussed the maximum pore diameters (MPD) and average pore diameters (APD) of various commercially available membranes. The general ratio MPD/APD varies for membranes made by different companies, but for 0.2–0.22-μm and 0.45-μm-rated membrane filters the ratios were 3.5:5 and 2:3.3, respectively. More recent work has been unable to confirm a pore size distribution of ± 0.03 μm about a mean value as is claimed for certain 0.45-μm filters (Pall, 1975; Marshall & Meltzer, 1976). The Nuclepore Corporation state in their literature that the maximum pore diameter of their 'nuclear-type' filters lies within + 0% and − 20% of the rate pore size. Stamm (1971) has confirmed that this type of filter possesses a greater uniformity than its cellulose acetate counterpart, but 'nuclear-type' filters may not be entirely free from irregularities in pore size and shape (Pall, 1975; Alkan & Groves, 1978). A broader pore size distribution within a membrane filter is not necessarily considered a failing since it offers resistance to early clogging occasioned by too close a match between the dominant pore size and the prevailing particle size.

Cellulosic filters (available in a range of pore sizes from around 12 μm down to 0.025 μm) possess between 10^7 and 10^{11} pores per cm^2, the number increasing as the pore size decreases. This contrasts with the 10^5 to 6×10^8 pores per cm^2 offered by a similar size range of 'nuclear-type' filters. The number of pores and their size distribution will contribute to the overall porosity (void volume) of the filter system which is considered to be approximately 65–85% for cellulose filters (decreasing with decreasing pore size) and only 5–10% for the capillary pore 'nuclear-type' product. Overall fluid flow characteristics are similar for both types of filter (Ballew *et al.*, 1978), however, since the

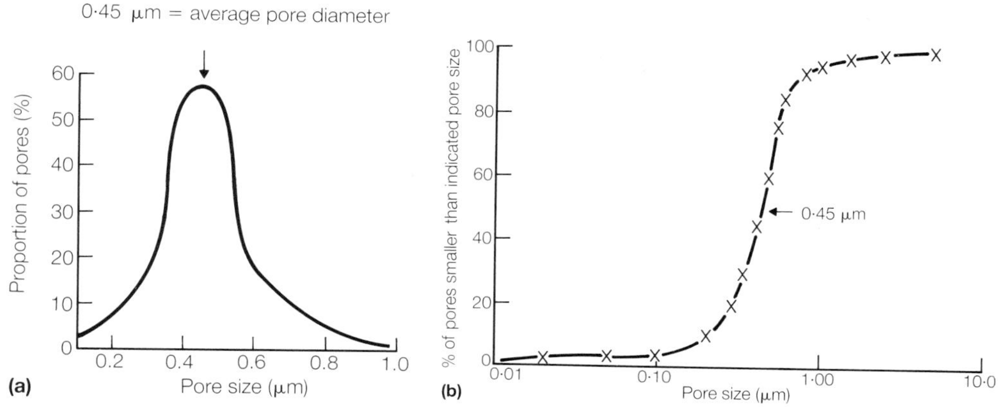

Fig. 21.6 Typical pore size distribution curves for some commercially available 0.45 μm rated cellulose membrane filters. (a) Schleicher & Schüll type BA85: (b) Oxoid Nuflow. These data were obtained from mercury intrusion tests. (Reproduced by courtesy of the companies concerned.)

greater thickness of cellulose filters (≃ 150 μm) and their tortuous pore system affords approximately 15 times more resistance to flow than the 10 μm-thick capillary pore filter.

There appears little justification for assuming a uniform pore structure, at least within the cast polymeric membranes, and the simple capillary pore model (Fig. 21.5) can no longer be used to describe correctly the typical membrane filter. Duberstein (1979) states that the bacterial removal efficiency of membrane filters depends on the membrane pore size distribution and on the thickness of the membrane; the latter is in disagreement with the sieve theory (see below) which relies solely on retention associated with the pore size of the surface pores. For the thin 'nuclear-type' membrane the contribution made by the thickness of the filter towards the retention process may be considered small, especially in the light of their relatively uncomplicated pore structure, and the term 'screen' filter may adequately describe this type of membrane (Heidam, 1981). The thicker cast polymeric membranes, as exemplified by the cellulose filters, however, offer characteristics between those of a true depth filter and those of a true screen filter and may best be described as membrane 'depth' filters. With these filters very small particles will be retained by adsorption but a point must be reached beyond which the smallest particle confronting any filter is larger than that filter's largest pore, in which case the sieve mechanism can adequately describe the filtration phenomenon.

By accepting this distinction within the group of membrane filters it is possible to understand why the useful lifetime of 'nuclear-type' filters can sometimes be extended by 'backflushing'. During any filtration process, as particles are removed from suspension and deposited on the filter, a gradual increase in pressure is required to maintain the same filtration rate. At a certain point this pressure becomes unacceptably high and the membrane can then be said to be effectively plugged. The reversal of fluid flow easily dislodges particles from the membrane surface, satisfactorily unplugging screen filters, but it cannot remove those particles trapped within the interstices of the membrane 'depth' filter, which generally remains blocked.

The removal of micro-organisms from liquids by filtration. It would be logical to assume that the pore size of sterilizing membrane filters is a major factor in determining whether bacteria are retained by the filter or can pass through into the filtrate. Such a premise is based on the sieve retention theory of filtration, with a direct relationship between the largest pore in the filter and the smallest particle present (Brooks, 1979). The bubble point method commonly used as an indication of pore size (Section 4; see also Rogers & Rossmore, 1970; Lukaszewicz *et al.*, 1978) is considered to be a useful guide to the ability of a filter element to remove bacteria, although it is deficient in some respects (Pall, 1975). Lukaszewicz & Meltzer (1979a) and Trasen (1979) likewise opine that this method serves as an index of retentivity.

Sterile filtration, the absolute removal of bacteria, yeasts and moulds, should by definition be able to deliver a sterile effluent independently of the challenge conditions, even when these are severe (Reti, 1977). In practice, this can be achieved by means of a 0.22 (or 0.2)-μm filter, although various authors have, in fact, shown that this filter is not absolute. Bowman *et al.* (1967) described the isolation of an obligate aerobe (cell diameter < 0.33 μm), then termed a *Pseudomonas* sp. ATCC 19146 (now known as *Ps. diminuta* ATCC 19146), which could pass through a 0.45-μm membrane filter (cf. below); this poses a severe challenge to sterilization by filtration. The idea that sterile filtration is independent of the challenge conditions is, in fact, no longer tenable. One of the prerequisites for successful filtration is an initial low number of organisms; as the number of *Ps. diminuta* in the test challenge increases, the probability of bacteria in the filtrate increases (Wallhausser, 1976). An early report (Elford, 1933) had likewise shown that a filter's ability to retain organisms decreased as the number of test organisms (in this case *Serr. marcescens*) increased and as the filter's pore size rating increased. Approximately 0–20 *Pseudomonas* organisms/litre can pass through even so-called absolute filters (Wallhausser, 1979); the extent of the passage of *Ps. diminuta* through membrane filters is encouraged by increasing pressures (Reti & Leahy, 1979). *Serr. marcescens* can also pass through a 0.2-μm filter, although to a much smaller extent than *Ps. diminuta* (Wallhausser, 1979). Mycoplasmas, which lack rigid cell walls and consequently have a more plastic structure than bacteria, can pass through 0.22-μm filters (Lukaszewicz & Meltzer, 1979b). Wallhausser (1979) emphasizes the pore size distribution of filter materials, which may be heterogeneous in form and composition, and the fact that pore size itself cannot be taken as an absolute yardstick for sterile filtration.

The foregoing thus suggests that sieve retention is only one mechanism responsible for sterile filtration. Other contributing factors include van der Waals' forces and electrostatic interactions (Lukaszewicz & Meltzer, 1979b). Tanny *et al.* (1979) showed that many *Ps. diminuta* cells could be removed from suspension by adsorptive sequestration using a 0.45-μm membrane filter, and postulated that an organism could actually enter the pore but is retained there by this mechanism. The retention mechanisms operating during membrane filtration are elegantly illustrated in the scanning electron micrographs of Todd & Kerr (1972), where the screen-filter action of a 'nuclear-type' filter is clearly contrasted with the depth-filter characteristics of a cellulose membrane filter. The dominance of adsorptive effects during the filtration of plasma proteins and influenza vaccine through 0.22-μm and 0.45-μm membrane filters, respectively, has been recognized (Hawker & Hawker, 1975; Tanny & Meltzer, 1978). 'Nuclear-type' filters show few adsorptive properties and this can be attributed to their thinness, lack of tortuous channels and hence purely sieve-like properties. Adsorptive sequestration is not an inherent quality of a filter, but rather describes the ability of that filter to capture organisms of a given size (Lukaszewicz *et al.* 1978; Lukaszewicz & Meltzer, 1979a). Depth-type filters, with a broad distribution of pore sizes, are believed to retain organisms largely by adsorption (Lukaszewicz & Meltzer, 1979a).

Specific developments in membrane filter materials have led to the creation of positively-charged filters (Hou *et al.*, 1980) with the capacity to remove viral, pyrogen and bacteriophage contaminants from liquids. These contaminants are retained by electrostatic attraction within the matrix of the filter; their dimensions would not allow removal by sieving. The efficiency of charged filters can be influenced by operational conditions (Carrazzone *et al.*, 1985).

Thus, sieve retention may yet be the most important mechanism whereby sterile filtration is achieved, but it is unlikely to be the sole contributory factor. Although many membrane filters can no longer be considered to act simply as sieves, their thinness and greater uniformity of pore size give them several advantages over conventional depth filters (Section 2.5.4), a fact that is widely exploited in filtration technology.

Perhaps the most widely accepted description of a membrane filter would be that it has a thin, continuous and homogeneous polymeric structure, from which no parts can be shed. As such it would comply with the definition laid down by the Federal Drugs Administration (FDA) in the United States for a non-fibre-releasing filter which 'after any appropriate pre-treatment such as washing or flushing, will not continue to release fibres into the drug product or component which is being filtered' (Elias, 1975). In addition, it would also meet the requirements for a sterilizing filter as laid down by the *United States Pharmacopoeia* (1990) and the *British Pharmacopoeia* (1988).

2.5.3 Membrane filters used for sterilization

A typical size distribution of particles within a fluid is illustrated in Fig. 21.7 where, despite the broad range of sizes, the highest concentration of particles exists in the submicron range. Superimposed upon the graph are curves comparing the reduced particulate burden of the filtrate following passage through a 1.0-μm nominal depth filter and a 1.0-μm absolute membrane filter.

The most suitable pore size for a sterilizing grade filter is chosen, in part, by considering the minimum dimension (frequently less than 1 μm) of the microorganism to be retained (Fig. 21.7). The efficient removal of all bacteria from contaminated solutions may sometimes require a 0.1-μm-rated membrane filter (Howard & Duberstein, 1980). Certainly the exclusion of mycoplasmas from certain tissue culture preparations is achieved by the use of such a filter (Lukaszewicz & Meltzer, 1979b). Experience has shown, however, that, under normal Good

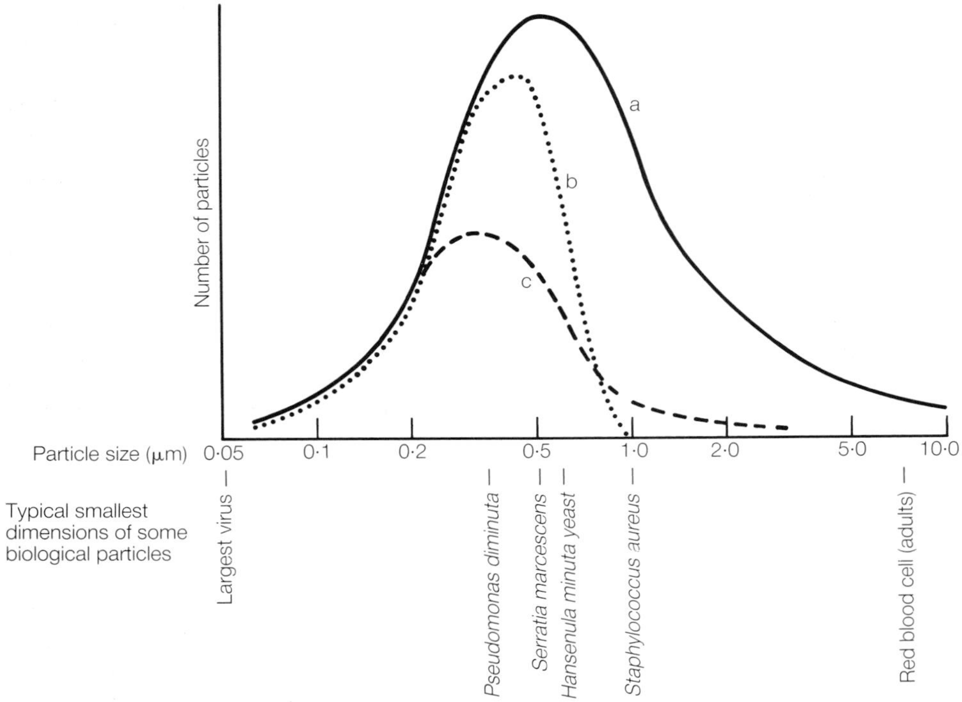

Fig. 21.7 A typical distribution of particle sizes within a fluid. (a) Unfiltered particle size distribution; (b) distribution after passage through a 1-μm absolute membrane filter; (c) distribution after passage through a 1-μm nominal depth filter.

Pharmaceutical Manufacturing Practice (GMP) conditions (*Guide*, 1983; Anon, 1989), the sterilization of pharmaceutical and blood products can be assured by their passage through a 0.2–0.22-μm membrane filter, but part of the process validation must include regular sterility tests (Wallhausser, 1977, 1979).

In other areas where the likely contaminants are known, or additional filtrative mechanisms are at play, a membrane filter of larger pore size may be considered sufficient to ensure sterility. For instance, the sterilization of air and gases during venting or pressurizing procedures can often be assured by passage through filters of 0.45–0.8-μm-rated pore size. The removal of yeast during the stabilization of beers and wines can be effected by a 0.6-μm membrane filter. In general, however, such filters are only employed in systems where a reduction in bacterial numbers and not complete sterilization is demanded. An ideal example of this is the routine filtration through a 0.45-μm-rated filter, of parenteral solutions that are later to be terminally sterilized. This reduces the likelihood of bacterial growth and pyrogen production prior to autoclaving.

An absolute filter cannot distinguish between particle types and, as a consequence, filtration sterilization will ensure the removal of all particles (in addition to micro-organisms) with dimensions in excess of the rated pore size. This is of obvious benefit in the pharmaceutical production of sterile parenteral fluids in which the presence of particulate matter can have serious consequences (Turco & Davis, 1973a).

Sterilizing membrane filters are available in discs ranging from 13 to 293 mm in diameter and are designed for assembly into filter holders of the types illustrated in Figs 21.8 and 21.9. Their filtrative capacities make them the ideal choice for the small- and medium-scale processes normally

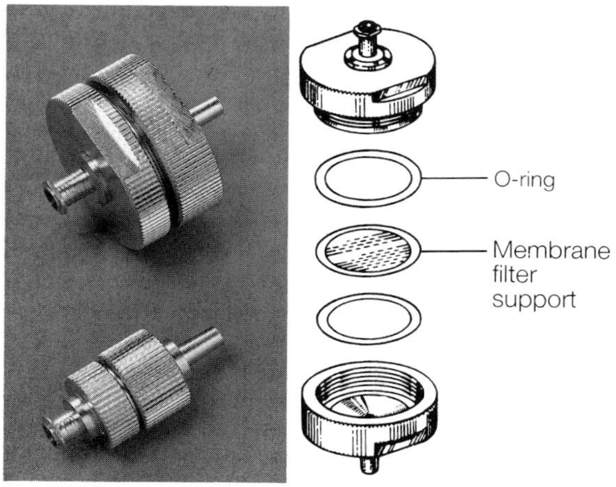

Fig. 21.8 13-mm and 25-mm stainless steel filter holders designed for filtering small volumes of fluid from a syringe (courtesy of Nuclepore Corporation).

Table 21.1 Effect of filter diameter on filtration volumes

Filter diameter (mm)	Effective filtration area* (cm^2)	Typical batch volume† (l)
13	0.8	0.01
25	3.9	0.05–0.1
47	11.3	0.1–0.3
90	45	0.3–5
142	97	5–20
293	530	20

* Taken from one manufacturer's data (Nuclepore Corporation) and to some extent dependent on the type of filter holder used. Values may well vary from manufacturer to manufacturer.
† For a low viscosity liquid.

encountered in the laboratory or hospital pharmacy (Table 21.1).

The flow rate of a clean liquid through a membrane filter (volume passed per unit time) is a function of that liquid's viscosity, the pressure differential across the filter and the filtration area and is given by

$$Q = C\frac{AP}{V} \qquad (21.1)$$

where Q = volumetric flow rate, A = filtration area, V = viscosity of the liquid, P = pressure differential across the membrane, C = resistance to fluid flow offered by the filter medium, governed in part by the size, tortuosity and number of pores.

The industrial manufacturer of sterile fluids needs to filter very large volumes and as a consequence demands a flow rate far beyond the capabilities of the largest available membrane disc. To provide the filtration area needed, multiple-plate filtration systems have been designed where up to

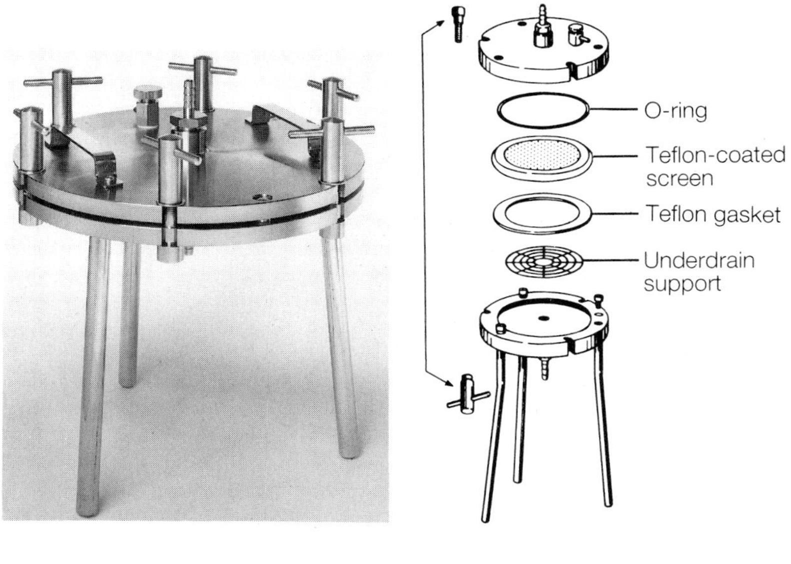

Fig. 21.9 293 mm stainless steel filter holder (courtesy of Nuclepore Corporation).

60 flat filter discs of 293 mm diameter, separated by screens and acting in parallel, can be used to provide a total surface area of 3.0 m^2. A typical multiple plate filtration system is illustrated in Fig. 21.10.

A second approach can be to use cartridge filters (Cole *et al.*, 1979). These are essentially hollow cylinders formed from a rigid perforated plastic core around which the membrane filter, supported by a suitable mesh and sometimes protected by a prefilter, is wound. An outer perforated plastic sleeve provides protection against back-pressure and is held in place by bonded end-caps. The cartridge filter combines the advantages of increased filtration area with ease of handling. Since the filter is no longer in the form of a fragile disc it can be easily installed in special holders. Multiple cartridge units are available that may contain up to twenty 79-cm filter tubes (of 5.7 cm diameter) giving a maximum filtration area of approximately 2.4 m^2.

A further development for use in large-scale filtration systems is the pleated membrane cartridge. Early devices were manufactured from a flexible acrylic polyvinylchloride co-polymer membrane incorporating a nylon web support (Conacher, 1976); other membranes have now evolved which can also be pleated without damage (Meltzer & Lukaszewicz, 1979) and the range of materials includes cellulose esters, PTFE, nylon, acrylic and polysulphone. The pleated configuration of the membrane ensures a far greater surface area for filtration than a normal cartridge filter of similar dimensions. For comparison, a single stan-

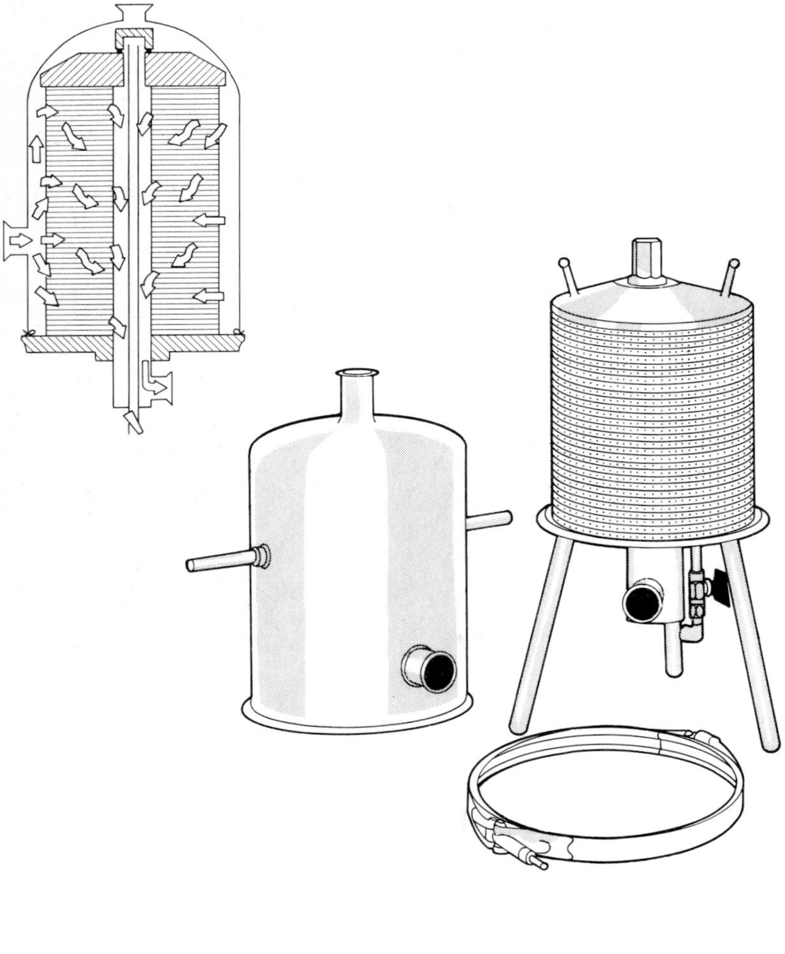

Fig. 21.10 A typical multiple-plate filtration system, the Nuclepore Hi Vol™ 30, with inset showing the fluid flow path during filtration (courtesy of Nuclepore Corporation).

dard pleated polycarbonate membrane cartridge of 24.8 cm length and 6.4 cm diameter, such as that illustrated in Fig. 21.11 can offer a filtration area approaching 1.7 m^2, approximately 30 times that afforded by a typical 293-mm membrane disc.

To ensure the widest application for their filters, manufacturers offer their membranes in a wide variety of constituent materials. This permits the selection of a suitable filter type for use with most of the commonly encountered solvent systems (Gelman, 1965; Brock, 1983). Extensive chemical compatibility lists are included in the catalogues of most manufacturers and further guidance can often be obtained through their technical support services. Subtle changes in filter structure do occur, however, when processing mixtures of liquids, the complex fluid presenting entirely different solvent properties to the membrane than could be predicted from compatibility studies involving the individual liquid components. In a number of instances these changes have resulted in filter failure, and compatibility tests should always be undertaken when mixed solvent systems are to be processed (Lukaszewicz & Meltzer, 1980). It is as well to remember, also, that any system is only as compatible as its least resistant component and attention must be paid to the construction materials of the filter holder, seals, tubing and valves.

Hydrophobic filters (e.g. PTFE) are available for the sterile aeration of holding tanks in the beverage industry, for the supply of fermentation tanks with sterilized gas, for the filtration of steam, and the removal of water droplets from an oily product. They can be used to filter aqueous solutions by first wetting the membrane with a low-molecular-weight alcohol such as ethanol. Hydrophobic-edged filters derived from cellulose nitrate or acetate whose rims have been impregnated to a width of 3–6 mm with a hydrophobic agent can also be obtained. These find wide application in filtrations requiring that no residual solution remains trapped under the sealing ring of the filter holder, e.g. during the sterility testing of antibiotics. They also have the advantage that air or gas trapped behind a filter can escape through the rim and thus prevent air-locks or dripping during a filtration process (Fig. 21.12).

To ensure the production of a sterile filtrate, the

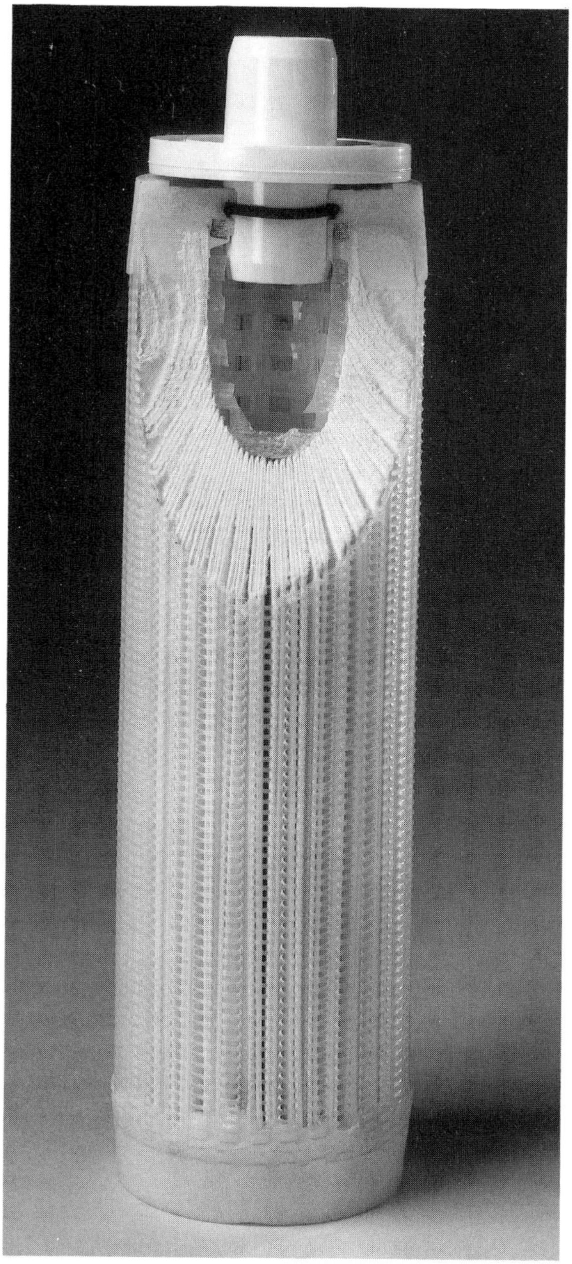

Fig. 21.11 Cutaway showing the construction of a pleated polycarbonate membrane cartridge filter (courtesy of Nuclepore Corporation).

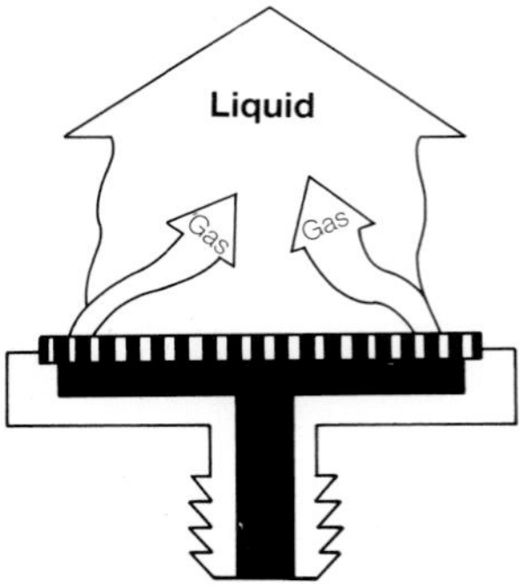

Fig. 21.12 A hydrophobic-edged membrane filter allows the passage of both fluid and gas.

final filter and its holder together with any downstream distribution equipment must be sterilized. To minimize aseptic manipulations it is customary to sterilize the membrane filter after mounting it in the filter holder. The sterilization method is usually selected from among the following: autoclaving, in-line steaming, dry heat, ethylene oxide and gamma irradiation. The choice depends largely upon the heat resistance of the filter and its ancillary equipment, and before embarking upon any sterilizing procedure it is first necessary to confirm their thermal stability. In extreme cases, chemical sterilization by immersion in a 2–3% formalin solution for 24 h may be the only satisfactory method.

Most filter types will withstand autoclaving conditions of 121°C for 20–30 min and, as a result, the routine autoclaving of assembled small-scale filtration equipment is common practice. Similarly, in-line steaming is a widely used process in which moist steam is forced through the assembled filter unit (and often the entire filtration system) under conditions sufficient to ensure an adequate period of exposure at 121°C or other appropriate temperature (Kovary *et al.*, 1983; Chrai, 1989). This method is of particular value in large systems employing cartridge filters. It has the added advantage that the complete system can be sterilized, thereby lowering the bacterial contamination upstream from the final bacteria-proof filter. If the sterilization temperature or time exceeds the limits which are imposed by the manufacturer, 'pore collapse' may occur with a subsequent reduction in membrane porosity. For this reason dry heat sterilization is rarely used since the conditions employed are often too severe. For convenience, certain membrane filters may be obtained in a pre-sterilized form, either individually packed or ready-assembled into filter holders as single-use devices. Sterility is, in this case, usually achieved by ethylene oxide treatment or gamma irradiation.

2.5.4 Advantages and disadvantages of membrane filters

Membrane filters have several advantages over conventional depth filtration systems, a conclusion emphasized by the technical literature supplied by the major membrane filter companies. Table 21.2 summarizes the more important characteristics of membrane filters and compares them with conventional depth filters. Several features require further discussion since they have considerable bearing on the quality of the final filtered product.

A problem usually associated only with conventional depth filters is that of 'organism growthrough'. If a bacterial filter is used over an extended period of time, bacteria lodged within the matrix can reproduce and successive generations will penetrate further into the filter, eventually emerging to contaminate the filtrate. The extent of this phenomenon will be a function of, at least in part, the nutritional status of the medium being filtered and the nutritional requirements of the contaminant. This problem is no longer considered to be exclusive to conventional depth filters and has been recognized to occur with some 0.45-μm membrane 'depth' filters (Section 2.5.2) (Rusmin *et al.*, 1975). For this reason it is recommended that the duration of filtration be as short as possible (Lukaszewicz & Meltzer, 1979a; *United States Pharmacopoeia* 1990).

Solute adsorption by filters is rarely a major problem in large-scale industrial processes, but it can be of greater consequence in the filtration of small volumes containing medicaments at high dilution. Conventional depth filtration media have been implicated in the adsorption of antibiotics from solution (Wagman *et al.*, 1975), while the thinner membrane filters appear to suffer less from this disadvantage (Rusmin & DeLuca, 1976).

Table 21.2 Characteristics of membrane and depth filters

Characteristic	Membrane	Depth
1 Filtration (retention) efficiency for particles > rated pore size (see Fig. 21.7)	100%	< 100%
2 Speed of filtration	Fast	Slow
3 Dirt handling capacity	Low	High
4 Duration of service (time to clogging)	Short	Long
5 Shedding of filter components (media migration)	No	Yes
6 Grow-through of micro-organisms	Rare (see text)	Yes
7 Fluid retention	Low	High
8 Solute adsorption	Low	High
9 Chemical stability	Variable (depends on membrane)	Good
10 Mechanical strength	Considerable (if supported)	Good
11 Sterilization characteristics	Good	Good
12 Ease of handling	Generally poor	Good
13 Disposability	Yes	Not all types
14 Leaching of extractables	Variable (depends on membrane)	Unlikely

Nevertheless, Naido *et al.* (1972) have reported the retention of appreciable quantities (11–17%) of benzalkonium chloride on a 0.45-μm cellulose membrane filter after passing 30 ml of an ophthalmic solution containing 0.02% w/v of the preservative through that filter. Denyer (unpublished results) has observed a similar loss (38%) of tetradecyltrimethylammonium bromide after filtration of 10 ml of a 0.001% w/v solution through a 0.22-μm cellulose membrane filter. Drug sorption has been reported by De Muynck *et al.* (1988), and a method for its control suggested by Kanke *et al.* (1983). Presumably, adsorption sites are rapidly saturated in these thin membranes and the passage of additional solution would probably occur without further loss. Nevertheless, it emphasizes the need to select the most compatible filter material and to discard, if at all possible, the first few millilitres of solution run through any filtration system. Flushing through to remove downstream particles is often an integral part of the filtration process anyway.

Care should be taken in the choice of filter in specialized operations. For instance, proteins (in particular those of high molecular weight) are readily removed from solution on passage through cellulose nitrate and mixed ester filters, and nylon (Hawker & Hawker, 1975; Olson *et al.*, 1977). This is not so evident for fluorocarbon and cellulose acetate filters which would therefore be more suitable for filtration of pharmaceutical protein preparations (Pitt, 1987). The conformational changes elicited in proteins by filtration through filter media have been highlighted by Truskey *et al.* (1987).

A further problem associated with some membrane filters is the leaching of extractives, some of which may be potentially toxic (Brock, 1983). Surfactants, glycerol and other extractable materials added during the manufacturing process may leach from these filters during use and limited flushing beforehand is recommended (Olson *et al.*, 1980). As an alternative to flushing, a leaching process has been recommended that requires boiling the new filter for 5–10 min in two changes of apyrogenic water. The level of extractable material ranges from 0% to 15% of the filter weight and varies according to filter type and filter manufacturer. Special low-water-extractability filters are available for use in highly critical applications involving sensitive biological systems, e.g. tissue culture work, or very small volumes of filtrate. Nuclear-type membranes yield no leachable material and need not be treated before use.

One problem associated with membrane filters of all types, and of considerable economic importance, is the rapidity with which they clog when a large volume of solution or highly contaminated fluid is processed. To overcome this it is possible to introduce a depth filter, as a pre-filter, into the system, the high 'dirt' handling capacity of which will remove much of the initial solids and complement the filtering efficiency of the final (sterilizing) membrane filter (Lukaszewicz *et al.*, 1981a). Such a pre-filter is generally constructed of bonded borosilicate glass fibre and is available from most manufacturers in sizes and grades compatible with their membrane filters. For use on a large scale, pre-filters are often supplied as cartridges. In the critical area of parenteral product filtration, cellulose webbing pre-filters that do not shed particles are available. By selecting the correct grade of pre-filter, the throughput characteristics for any membrane filtration assembly can be improved significantly (Fig. 21.13).

The correct matching of pre-filter grade with membrane pore-size rating does not, on its own, provide the most economical and efficient system. Consideration must also be given to the pre-filter/membrane surface-area ratio, since too small a pre-filter area will result in premature plugging with useable life still remaining in the membrane. Conversely, if the area of the pre-filter is too large

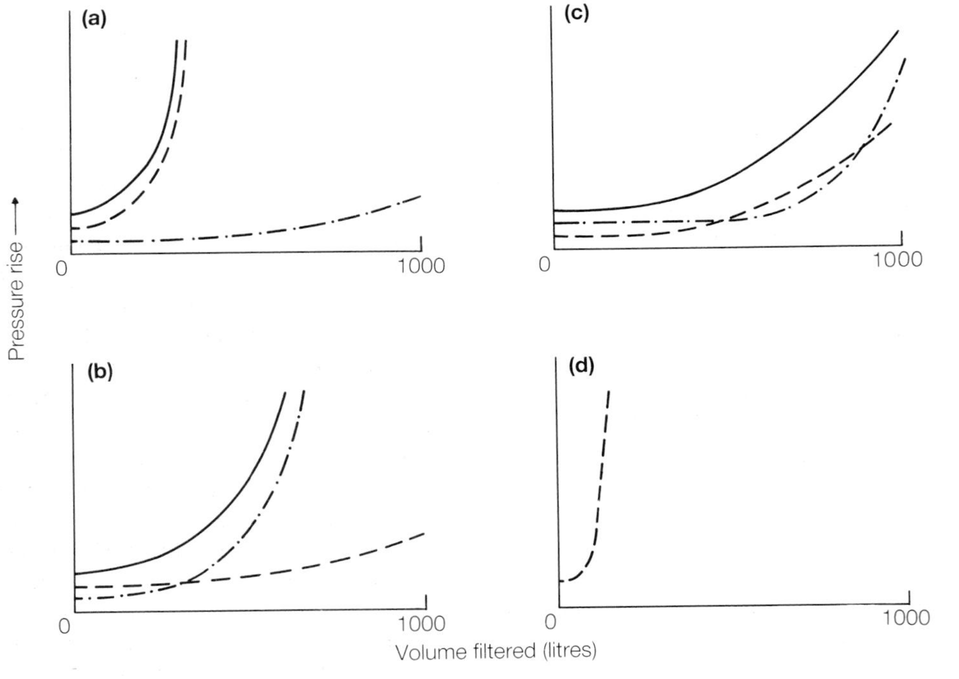

Fig. 21.13 Effect of pre-filter characteristics on the volume filtered and filtration pressure.——, combination of membrane filter + pre-filter; —·—·—·, pre-filter alone; – – – – –, membrane filter alone. (a) Pre-filter too coarse: insufficient preseparation, membrane filter clogs rapidly, pressure rises rapidly. (b) Pre-filter too fine: pre-filter clogs faster than membrane filter, poor effective filter life. (c) Correct pre-filter: pre-filter and membrane filter exhaust themselves approx. simultaneously, optimum effective filter life. (d) Membrane filter without pre-filter: rapid rise in pressure, short effective filter life. (Courtesy of Schleicher & Schull GMBH.)

then it will be left only partly used when the membrane becomes blocked. The ideal ratio will make for the most economic filtration and must be determined for each new system.

3 APPLICATIONS AND LIMITATIONS OF FILTRATION

3.1 Filtration sterilization

Sterilization by filtration is widely used industrially and in hospitals. In brief, it may be employed for the sterilization of thermolabile solutions and solids, as well as in the sterilization of air; the last-named is of particular importance in areas involving the aseptic production of many pharmaceutical products (*Guide*, 1983; Denyer, 1987; Fare, 1987; Stockdale, 1987; Anon., 1989) in surgical theatres and in hospital wards specially designed for patients with a low resistance to infection. It would, however, be erroneous to imply that filtration sterilization has no disadvantages or limitations, and these will also be considered where appropriate.

3.1.1 Sterilization of solutions

Wherever possible, solutions should be sterilized by heating in an autoclave. Some solutions are unstable when heated and consequently an alternative sterilizing procedure has to be sought. Ionizing radiation has been studied extensively, but unfortunately many substances which can be sterilized by this process in the solid state are unstable when irradiated in solution. Filtration is an obvious choice, although it must be added that another alternative for substances thermostable in the solid form but unstable in solution (even at ambient temperatures) is to sterilize the solid by dry heat and prepare the solution aseptically immediately before use.

Wallhausser (1979) has, however, queried whether filtration can, in fact, be regarded as being a true sterilization process. Admittedly, it will remove micro-organisms (see Section 2.5.2 for a discussion of the possible mechanisms of filtration), but the filtration process must then be followed by an aseptic transference of the sterilized solution to the final containers which are then sealed, and recontamination at this stage remains a possibility.

Persuasive arguments, based on a statistical appraisal of the information conventional sterility tests can supply, have been put forward for their abandonment as a means of monitoring thermal sterilization processes, the tendency now being to validate these processes by biological indicators (see Chapter 22 and Brown & Gilbert, 1977). Nevertheless, although there might be much scientific merit in their abandonment they do form an additional defence in the case of litigation following trauma from a suspected contaminated product, and sterility testing should always be carried out on samples of any batch prepared by an aseptic method. This would mean, in essence, that a solution which can be sterilized rapidly by filtration should ideally not be used until the test sample has passed the sterility test, which may take several days. In an emergency, however, it may well be that clinical judgement has to come down in favour of a hospital-prepared product which has not yet passed a test for sterility if failure to use it poses a greater risk to the patient.

Despite these criticisms, filtration sterilization is performed on a wide range of liquid preparations (Meltzer & Lukaszewicz, 1979) and routinely on liquid parenteral products (including sera) and on ophthalmic solutions. It is often the only method available to manufacturers of products that cannot be sterilized by thermal processes. Information as to the actual procedures may be found in the *British Pharmacopoeia* (1988), *United States Pharmacopoeia* (1990) and other national and international pharmacopoeias. It must be emphasized that membrane filters, and most often those derived from cellulose, are almost exclusively used in this context and that filtration with a filter of 0.22 (or 0.2)-μm pore size rather than one of 0.45 μm is recommended for this purpose (Walhausser, 1976).

Membrane filters find an equally important application in the small-scale intermittent preparation of sterile radiopharmaceuticals and intravenous additives. As a result of the special circumstances surrounding the preparation and use of such products, disposable, sterile filters attached to a syringe are generally used. Preparation of these products is best performed under laminar air flow conditions (Section 3.1.3).

The use of sterilizing grade filters in parenteral therapy is not confined to the production stage alone. In-line terminal membrane filtration has been widely advocated as a final safeguard against the hazards associated with the accidental administration of infusion fluids contaminated with either particles or bacteria (Ryan *et al.*, 1973; Turco & Davis, 1973a; Maki, 1976: Turco, 1978; Rapp *et al.*, 1979: Lowe, 1981). These filtration units, generally of 0.22 μm rating, may comprise an integral part of the administration set or form a separate device for introduction proximal to the cannula. In addition to affording some protection against particles and micro-organisms introduced during the setting-up of the infusion or while making intravenous additions (Davis *et al.*, 1970a,b; Davis & Turco, 1971; Myers, 1972; Holmes & Allwood, 1979) terminal filters also reduce the risk of an air embolism from air bubbles or when an intravenous infusion runs out (a wetted 0.22-μm membrane filter will not pass air at a pressure below 379 kPa (55 psi)). An early problem associated with in-line filters, *viz.* the formation of air locks stopping fluid flow, has now been largely overcome either by increasing the upstream chamber volume of the filter device, or more ingeniously, by incorporating a hydrophobic 0.2-μm membrane filter to permit the continuous venting of accumulated air (Wood & Ward, 1981). The properties of a wetted membrane filter have been further exploited in infusion burette devices where they act as an air shut-off 'valve' designed to operate following administration of the required volume.

In-line filter systems have been the subject of several studies which indicate that their use is not entirely without problems. Turco & Davis (1973b) have shown that, with certain fluids, infusion pumps may be needed to maintain adequate flow rates especially through a 0.22-μm in-line filter, while Miller & Grogan (1973) have highlighted the increased risk of microbial contamination accompanying the extra manipulations of the giving set associated with the inclusion of an in-line filter. It is likely that their use will be further restricted by the additional burden they impose upon the hospital budget. In-line membrane filters may ultimately be limited to patients receiving long-term intravenous infusion, total parenteral nutrition or dialysis, where the frequency and continuation of administration could compound the problems normally associated with these forms of therapy.

3.1.2 Sterilization of solid products

The *British Pharmacopoeia* (1988) lists four methods that may be used to sterilize powders: ionizing radiation, dry heat, ethylene oxide and filtration. The principle of the filtration process is that the substance to be sterilized is dissolved in an appropriate solvent, the solution filtered through a membrane filter and the sterile filtrate collected. The solvent is removed aseptically by an appropriate method (evaporation, vacuum evaporation, freeze-drying) and the sterile solid transferred into sterile containers that are then sealed. Such a method was originally used in the manufacture of sterile penicillin powder.

It appears likely that the probability of contamination occurring during the post-filtration (solid recovery) stage is higher than that described above for sterilizing solutions.

3.1.3 Air sterilization

Several methods can be used for reducing the viable microbial count in air (Sykes, 1965; Fifield, 1977). These include ultraviolet radiation (Chapter 19B), chemical aerosols (Chapter 2) and filtration. Air filtration has the greatest practical potential (Decker *et al.*, 1963) and air filters may be made of cellulose, glass wool or glass-fibre mixtures, or of PTFE with resin or acrylic binders (Underwood, 1987).

Depth filters, such as those made from fibreglass, are believed to achieve air sterilization because of the tortuous passage through which the air passes, ensuring that any micro-organisms present are trapped not only on the filter surface, but also within the interior. The removal of micro-organisms from air occurs as a result of interception, sedimentation, impaction, diffusion and electrostatic attraction (Fifield, 1977).

The quality of moving air is described by the maximum level of contamination permitted. In the United States, Federal Standard 209D recognizes six classes, *viz.* Class 1, Class 10, Class 100, Class

1000, Class 10 000 and Class 100 000, where the maximum numbers of particles 0.5 μm or larger are respectively 1/ft^3 (0.035/litre), 10/ft^3, 100/ft^3, 1000/ft^3, 10 000/ft^3 and 100 000/ft^3. Only Class 100 air or better is acceptable for aseptic (sterile area) purposes and the viable particle count is 0.1/ft^3 (0.0035/litre) (see Phillips & Runkle, 1972). In the United Kingdom, environmental cleanliness is stated in terms of size and maximum permitted number of airborne particles and ten lettered classes now exist (BS 5295:1989); classes F, J, K and L are essentially comparable to the classes 1, 2, 3 and 4 of the original BS 5295 (1976). Class F is the equivalent of Class 100 of the Federal Standard, with a particle count not exceeding 3500/m^3 for 0.5 μm size or greater. High efficiency particulate air (HEPA) filters are available that remove particles of 0.3 μm or larger (Wayne, 1975) and indeed for strict aseptic conditions, Phillips & Runkle (1972) state that they will remove particles much smaller than this. Passage of phage particles (0.1μm diameter) through ultrahigh-efficiency filters is remarkably low and it is considered that these filters provide excellent protection against virus aerosols (Harstad *et al.*, 1967).

An important type of air filtration incorporates the principle of laminar air flow (LAF). This was introduced by Whitfield in 1961 (Whitfield, 1967; Soltis, 1967; Whitfield & Lindell, 1969) and is defined as unidirectional air flow within a confined area moving with uniform velocity and minimum turbulence (Phillips & Brewer, 1968; Bowman, 1968; McDade *et al.*, 1969; Brewer & Phillips, 1971). Whitfield (1967) stated that the close control of airborne contamination was a difficult problem partly because of the non-uniform nature of the air flow patterns in a conventional clean room, partly because they did not carry particulate matter away from critical work areas and partly because airborne contamination was not removed as quickly from the room as it was brought in. He concluded that a uniform air flow pattern was needed to carry airborne contamination away from the work area. Laminar air flow was designed originally to remove dust particles from air by filtration but will also remove bacteria (Coriell & McGarrity, 1967). It was employed initially in the electronics and aerospace industries for the purpose of producing air with low particulate levels, necessary to prevent instrument and circuitry malfunction, but is now widely used by the pharmaceutical, cosmetic and other industries (Borick & Borick, 1972).

Laminar air flow can be used in the form of

1 LAF rooms with wall or ceiling units, the air flow originating through one wall or ceiling and exiting at the opposite end, to produce a displacement of air;

2 LAF units (see below) suitable for small-scale operations, such as the LAF bench used for aseptic processing and sterility testing (Phillips, 1975).

Thus airborne contamination is not added to the work space and any generated by manipulations within that area is swept away by the laminar air currents (Coriell, 1975). Nevertheless, there are limitations to the use of LAF, *viz.* it will not sterilize a contaminated product or area (Wayne, 1975). Laminar air flow controls only airborne particulate contamination and does not remove surface contamination (Phillips & Brewer, 1968; Brewer & Phillips, 1971). Correct techniques must be used, since poor aseptic technique can nullify LAF and holes in the HEPA filter, or air leaks in the system may allow contaminated air to enter the aseptic area (Coriell & McGarrity, 1970).

Filters that are used in LAF devices are HEPA filters mentioned above. These have been designed with a bacterial removal efficiency of greater than 99.99% (Mika, 1971; Phillips & Runkle, 1972) and often possess particle removal efficiencies in the order of 99.9997% against 0.3 μm particles, a standard sufficient for even the most exacting pharmaceutical purposes. Their life can be prolonged by employing low-efficiency filters upstream to intercept most of the larger particles and some smaller ones before they reach the expensive HEPA filters (Phillips & Runkle, 1972). HEPA filters are most efficient when air passes through them at an average velocity of 100 ft/min (30 m/min; Coriell, 1975).

Laminar air flow units providing Class 100 (Class F) clean air are of two types, horizontal and vertical, depending upon the direction of the air flow. In vertical LAF (Fig. 21.14), a supply fan passes air down through an ultrahigh-efficiency filter into the work area, and the air exhausts through a grated work surface often with the aid of a second fan. A slight negative pressure is maintained by adjusting

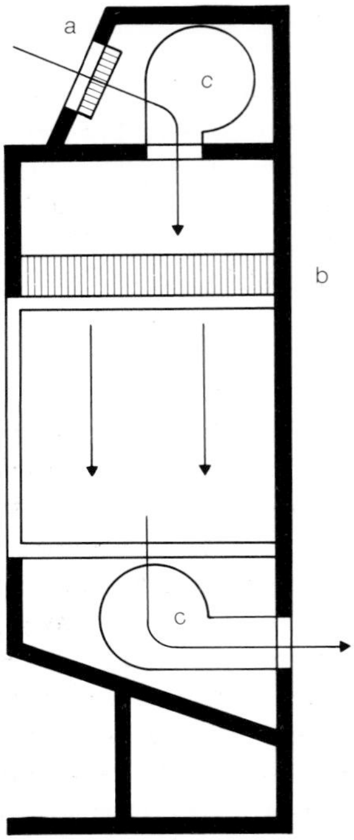

Fig. 21.14 Vertical laminar air flow unit. (a) Pre-filter; (b) HEPA filter; (c) fan.

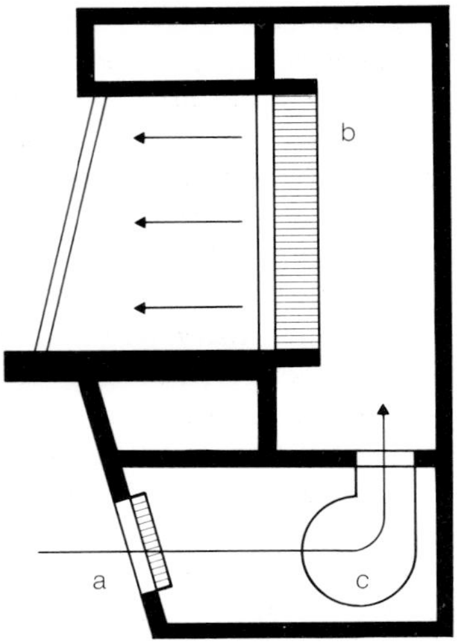

Fig. 21.15 Horizontal laminar air flow unit. (a) Pre-filter; (b) HEPA filter; (c) fan.

the fans to exhaust more air than is supplied; this causes ambient air to move from the operator towards the external periphery of the work area so that a protective curtain of air is created (Favero & Berquist, 1968). A vertical LAF of 100 ft/min maintains a Class 100 condition whereas 60 ft/min does not (Loughhead & Vellutato, 1969). In horizontal LAF (Fig. 21.15), air passes from back to front through a HEPA filter at an average velocity of 100 ft/min, travels horizontally with minimum turbulence and exits at the front of the unit (Coriell & McGarrity, 1968, 1970).

Laminar air flow units have three general areas of usefulness (Favero & Berquist, 1968; McDade *et al.*, 1968): (1) for product protection, e.g. in sterility testing or aseptic filling; for these purposes a standard horizontal LAF is suitable; (2) for personal protection, i.e. protection of personnel processing infectious material, where a horizontal LAF is obviously unsuitable; here, a vertical LAF is essential; (3) for product and personnel protection, in which case a vertical LAF must be employed. Examples of published work in these areas include those of Coriell (1975) who considers various applications; Bowman (1968), sterility testing; Elias & Vellutato (1966), drug contamination; Brewer & Phillips (1971), sterility testing and sterile filtration; Coriell & McGarrity (1968), prevention of infection during microbiological procedures; Loughhead & Vellutato (1969), parenteral production.

Additionally, LAF rooms have been used as follows:

1 for conferring protection to patients undergoing bone marrow transplants. In this procedure LAF in conjunction with a strict aseptic technique produces maximum protection against microbial contamination from the environment (Solberg *et al.*, 1971);

2 for conferring protection from the environment upon leukaemic patients undergoing immunosuppressive (radiomimetic) and anti-cancer drug therapy. Results suggest that the incidence of infection of leukaemic patients in LAF rooms is substantially less than treated elsewhere leukaemic patients (Bodey *et al.*, 1969);

3 for preventing cross-contamination in germ-free mice (van der Waaij & Andreas, 1971);

4 for aiding in the treatment of burns (Anon, 1975).

On a smaller scale the sterile filtration of air (and other gases) for venting, aeration or pressurizing purposes can often be accomplished through membrane filters. In line, these filters can also ensure the clarification and sterilization of medical gases. Most membranes used are deliberately of the hydrophobic type so that they will resist wetting by entrained water droplets which might otherwise cause an air lock. Hydrophobic filters of 0.2 μm have been used to replace the conventional airways needed with rigid infusion and irrigation containers. The hydrophobic material will support the solution but allow filtered sterile air to enter as the fluid is used.

During gas filtration, retentive mechanisms which have only a minor role in fluid filtration come to the fore (p. 588) and membrane 'depth' filters will often prevent the passage of particles and micro-organism far smaller than the stated pore dimensions. Filters of up to 1.2-μm pore size have been found suitable for the provision of sterile air. Nevertheless, at these larger pore sizes occasional problems with moisture condensation and subsequent grow-through of bacteria can occur, and Good Manufacturing Practice regulations generally require a 0.2–0.22-μm filter for air sterilization.

3.1.4 Microbiological safety cabinets

Microbiological safety cabinets are of three types: Class III, which provides the highest degree of containment for handling Category A pathogens; Class II (laminar flow recirculating cabinet), which protects both the work and the operator from contamination; and Class I (exhaust protective cabinet), which protects the worker against bacterial aerosols possibly generated when handling pathogenic material (Clark, 1980). The cabinets employ HEPA and pre-filters, and further information can be obtained by consulting British Standard 5726: 1979 and Newsom (1979a,b).

3.2 Non-sterilizing uses of membrane filtration

Apart from their use, described above, as a method of sterilization, filters—and especially membrane filters—have wide applications in other microbiological areas.

Membrane filtration in the sterility testing of antibiotics was first described by Holdowsky (1957) and this method is now commonly employed in sterility testing generally (Russell *et al.*, 1979; *British Pharmacopoeia*, 1988; *United States Pharmacopoeia*, 1990).

One method of determining the numbers of c.f.u. in bacterial suspensions or in fluids which may be contaminated by micro-organisms, is by means of membrane filtration. Basically, this procedure consists of filtering a suitable dilution of the suspension through a membrane filter, which retains the organisms and which is then transferred to the surface of an appropriate solid medium. This method has been used for the bacterial examination of water (Windle-Taylor & Burman, 1964). Suitable adaptations have been made to this procedure for determining the numbers of cells surviving treatment with antibiotics (Meers & Churcher, 1974) or disinfectants (Prince *et al.*, 1975). The amounts of disinfectants, for example benzalkonium chloride, phenylmercuric borate or chlorhexidine gluconate adsorbed on to most types of membrane filters are apparently small (Van Ooteghem & Herbots, 1969; cf. above and Naido *et al.*, 1972, however). Russell (1981) has described a method employing membrane filtration for demonstrating the inactivation of disinfectants by neutralizing agents. The *British Pharmacopoeia* (1988) recommends the use of membrane filtration in preservative efficacy tests when the preservative cannot be readily inactivated by dilution or specific neutralizing agents. A membrane filter technique has been described for the detection and enumeration of *E. coli* in food (Anderson & Baird-Parker, 1975) and again, in modified form, for the improved detection of damaged cells (Holbrook *et al.*, 1980). Membrane filtration combined with epifluorescent microscopy (known as the direct epifluorescent filtration technique; DEFT) has been employed for the rapid enumeration of contaminating microorganisms in the water industry (Hobbie *et al.*, 1977) dairy and food products (Pettipher, 1983), ultra-pure water (Mittelman *et al.*, 1983, 1985), and parenteral pharmaceutical products (Denyer & Ward, 1983; Denyer & Lynn, 1987).

A further analytical application for membrane filters is in the bacteriological sampling of moist surfaces using a simple contact technique (Craythorn *et al.*, 1980). In this method the sterile membrane (3–5-μm pore size) is placed in direct contact with a contaminated surface for 5 s and then removed, incubated in the conventional manner on the surface of a solid nutrient medium and the resultant colonies counted. A comparison with traditional contact sampling techniques indicates that the membrane filter method can be successfully employed for the quantitative bacteriological examination of contaminated clinical surfaces (Craythorn *et al.*, 1980).

Membrane-active antibiotics and disinfectants induce the release of intracellular constituents from bacteria (see Chapter 9). A procedure using membrane filters has been devised for determining the extent of this leakage (Brown *et al.*, 1969). It must be emphasized that, before use, the membrane must be boiled in water to release any surface-active agents which may be present in the membrane and which could interfere with the assessment of the leakage.

Membrane filtration has been adapted, by means of tangential flow filter systems, to provide an alternative to centrifugation for the small-scale harvesting of bacterial cultures (Tanny *et al.*, 1980; Brock, 1983). These filtration devices combine normal fluid flow through the membrane with a washing action, and as a result manage to keep the majority of filtered material in suspension, thereby preventing rapid clogging of the filter (Lukaszewicz *et al.*, 1981b). The technique is reported to have little effect on cell viability and offers a recovery efficiency of up to 75% (Tanny *et al.*, 1980). For the concentration of particularly delicate organisms, a 'reverse-flow' filtration system has been developed (Brock, 1983). Other applications of tangential filtration have been described by Genovesi (1983).

Jacobs (1972) describes the use of membrane filters for separating, by zone electrophoresis, individual macromolecular substances from their mixtures, such as the separation of protein fractions in serum or other biological fluids. Jacobs also reports the earlier application of graded collodion (gradocol) membranes (Elford, 1933) to determine the size of virus particles. Nucleic acid hybridization, immunoblotting, and protein electrophoresis all exploit membrane technology (Brock, 1983).

Ultrafilter membranes have been used in the purification of water by reverse osmosis (Pohland, 1980). This process may be defined as a reversal of the natural phenomenon of osmosis. If a solution of dissolved salts and pure water is separated by a semipermeable membrane, water will pass through the membrane into the salt solution. This is osmosis itself. Solutes dissolved in the water diffuse less easily and if their molecular weight is greater than 250 they do not diffuse at all. To reverse the process of osmosis, a pressure in excess of the osmotic pressure of the salt solution is applied and water is thereby forced out of this solution through the membrane in the reverse direction. Since the typical reverse osmosis membrane has pores approaching 2 nm in diameter, this process will remove bacteria, viruses and pyrogens and the purified water produced will be sterile and apyrogenic; it must, however, be added that contamination could occur after production. Ultrafiltration membranes are also exploited in haemodialysis.

4 THE TESTING OF FILTERS

4.1 Filters used in liquid sterilization

Confidence in the integrity and suitability of a filter for its intended task is of paramount importance in filtration sterilization, and this must ultimately rely upon stringent efficiency testing. Several direct and indirect methods have evolved by which the efficiency of such filters can be confirmed. The tests described below are most frequently applied to membrane filters but the underlying principles will apply equally well in the validation of most other filtration media (Section 2).

Obviously the most severe and direct test to which a bacteria-proof filter can be subjected is the bacterial challenge test (Bowman *et al.*, 1967). This involves filtration of a bacterial suspension through a sterile filter assembly with subsequent collection into nutrient medium and incubation of the filtrate. In the absence of passage of organisms no growth should be visible.

In the filter industry, such tests are employed for

validation purposes (Wallhausser, 1982). They generally use *Serr. marcescens* (minimum dimensions approximately 0.5 μm) and *Saccharomyces cereviseae* to challenge 0.45 μm and 0.8 μm pore size filters, respectively, while a more rigorous challenge is applied to the 0.2–0.22-μm-rated sterilizing filters. Such filters are defined as being capable of removing *Ps. diminuta* ATCC 19146 (minimum dimension approximately 0.3 μm) completely from suspension. A typical protocol would involve exposure of a sterile filter at a pressure of 276 kPa (40 psi) to a volume of culture medium containing 10^7/ml *Ps. diminuta* cells to result in a total challenge of approximately 10^9 organisms. The filtrate is either passed through a second 0.22-μm membrane disc, which is then placed on an agar plate and incubated for 2 days, or the effluent itself is collected in a sterile flask and incubated for up to 5 days. Any sign of growth would result in failure of the filter. A satisfactory filter would be expected to have a log removal factor of at least 7 (HIMA, 1982). Whilst recognizing that such a test should represent the severest challenge possible, Tanny & Meltzer (1979) recommend a realistic approach to selecting a suitable suspension concentration. Details of culture maintenance and handling and factors that govern the final test design have been considered by Reti & Leahy (1979) and Wallhausser (1982).

The bacterial retention tests described above are destructive tests and could not be used by the manufacturers of parenteral products to substantiate the efficacy and integrity of the membrane before and after use as required by a number of regulatory authorities (Olson, 1980). Similarly, the physical method of mercury intrusion, frequently used to determine pore size distribution (Marshall & Metzer, 1976), does not offer a satisfactory in-process test. What is required is a simple, rapid, non-destructive test that can be performed under aseptic conditions on sterile membranes to ensure the integrity of the membrane and the use of the correct pore size (Springett, 1981). With this aim in mind a considerable proportion of the industry's research effort has been directed towards validating existing indirect tests and establishing new ones.

The oldest and perhaps most widely used non-destructive test is the bubble point test (Bechold, 1908) which is the subject of BS 1752: 1983. To understand the principles behind this test it is necessary to visualize the filter as a series of discrete, uniform capillaries passing from one side to the other. When wetted the membrane will retain liquid in these capillaries by surface tension and the minimum gas pressure required to force liquid from the largest of these pores is a measure of the maximum pore diameter (d) given by

$$d = \frac{K \, \sigma \cos \theta}{P} \qquad (21.2)$$

where P = bubble point pressure, σ = surface tension of the liquid, θ = liquid to capillary wall contact angle, K = experimental constant.

The pressure (P) will depend in part upon the characteristics of the wetting fluid, which for hydrophilic filters would be water but for hydrophobic filters may be a variety of solvents (e.g. methanol, isopropanol).

To perform the test the pressure of gas upstream from the wetted filter is slowly increased and the pressure at which the largest pore begins to pass gas is the first bubble point (Fig. 21.16). In practice this value is frequently taken as the lowest pressure required to produce a steady stream of bubbles from an immersed tube on the dowstream side. The bubble point for a water-wet 0.22-μm-rated filter is 379 kPa (55 psi). An automated method for bubble point testing has been developed (Sechovec, 1989).

The inadequacies of the capillary pore model for describing the membrane structure have already been discussed (Section 2.5.2). The bubble point test is unlikely, therefore, to provide an exact indication of pore dimensions (Lukaszewicz *et al.*, 1978; Meltzer & Lukaszewicz, 1979). Instead its value lies in the knowledge that experimental evidence has allowed the filter manufacturer to correlate bacterial retentivity with a particular bubble point (see also tests on ceramic and kieselguhr filters (p. 572) and Royce & Sykes, 1950). Thus any sterilizing grade filter having a bubble point within the range prescribed by the manufacturer has the support of a rigorous bacterial challenge test regimen to ensure confidence in its suitability. In the words of one manufacturer, 'An observed bubble point which is significantly lower than the

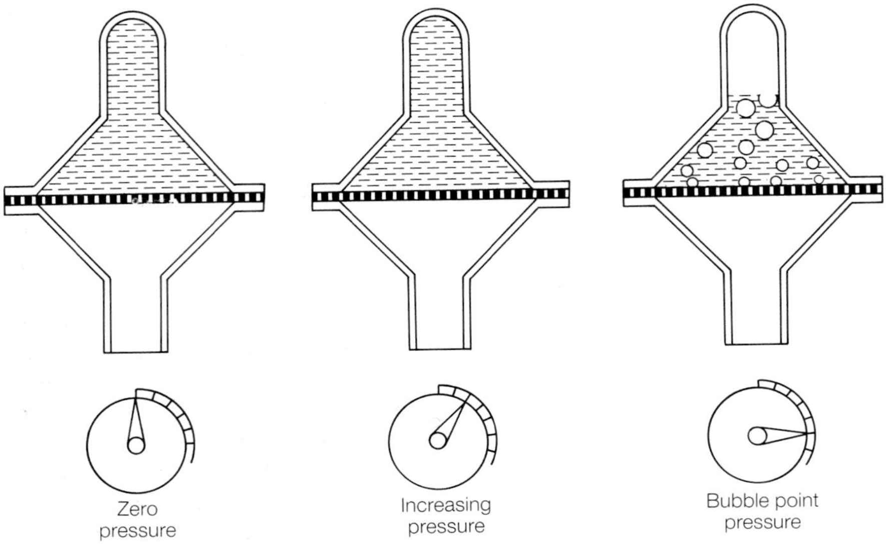

Fig. 21.16 Stages in the bubble point test.

bubble point specification for that particular filter indicates a damaged membrane, ineffective seals or a system leak. A bubble point that meets specifications ensures that the system is integral.'

Small volumes of fluid are often sterilized by passage through a filter unit attached to a hypodermic syringe. The following approximation to the bubble point test can be applied to such a system to confirm its integrity after use. If the syringe is part-filled with air then any attempt to force this air through the wet filter should meet appreciable resistance (the bubble point pressure). Any damage to the membrane would be immediately indicated by the unhindered passage of air.

The bubble point test has been criticized because it involves a certain amount of operator judgement and is less precise when applied to filters of large surface area (Trasen, 1979; Johnston *et al*, 1981; Springett, 1981). Johnston & Meltzer (1980) recognized an additional limitation to the accuracy of this test; commercial membranes often include a wetting agent (see Section 2.5.1, 'Methods of manufacture') which may well alter the surface tension characteristics of water held within the filter pores and hence the pressure at which bubbles first appear. This wetting agent is frequently extracted from the membrane during aqueous filtrations, rendering invalid any attempt to make an accurate comparison between before and after bubble point values (Johnston & Meltzer, 1980). These authors now propose an additional test based on the flow of air through a filter at pressures above the bubble point. The robust air-flow test examines the applied pressure/air-flow rate relationship and is amenable to both single-point and multiple-point determinations. This test is described as convenient to use and would, if several readings were taken at different applied air pressures, be more accurate than the single-point bubble point determination.

The passage of a gas through a wetted filter is not confined solely to bulk flow at applied pressures in excess of the bubble point: it can also occur at lower pressure values by a molecular diffusion process. With filters of small surface area this flow is extremely slow but it increases to significant levels in large area filters and provides the basis for a sensitive integrity test (Reti, 1977). This test finds its widest application in large-volume systems where the need to displace a large quantity of downstream water before the detection of bubbles makes the standard bubble point test impracticable. To perform this diffusion test, gas under pressure is applied at 80% of the bubble point pressure

(Reti, 1977; Olson *et al.*, 1981) for that particular wetted filter and the volumetric gas flow rate determined by measuring either the rate of flow of displaced water or the volume of gas passed in a specified time (Trasen, 1979). A marked increase in gas flow seen at lower pressures than would normally be expected for that filter type indicates a breakdown in the integrity of the system.

The diffusion test can also be combined with bubble point determination whereby changes in applied pressure can be measured against gas flow and a break observed at the first bubble point (Olson *et al.*, 1983; Emory, 1989). This approach can be used to assess pore size distribution: a narrow distribution would be indicated by a significant rise in gas flow at applied pressures only marginally above the bubble point, while a wide distribution would cause a more gradual increase in gas flow. This approach to integrity testing is amenable to automation and can give diffusion rate, first bubble point pressure, and pore size distribution (Olson *et al.*, 1983; Hofmann, 1984). The performance of an automated pressure hold/forward flow (Pall, 1975; Cole & Pauli, 1975; Price & Pauli, 1976; Schroeder & DeLuca, 1980; Springett, 1981) test system has been recently evaluated (Lee, 1989).

4.2 Filters used in air sterilization

The continuous production of high-quality filtered air by any HEPA filtration system (Section 3.1.3) can be assured by the application of rigorous efficiency tests to the filter, both at the time of installation and at intervals throughout its service life. When in constant use, a laminar air flow (LAF) unit may require 6-monthly testing in addition to the routine monitoring of air quality by mechanical sampling devices and settle plates (Kay, 1980).

Currently, one of the most exacting test methods available is the dioctyl-phthalate (DOP) smoke test (Gross, 1976, 1978). In this test DOP is vaporized upstream of the filter to produce an aerosol of particles which can be detected in the filtered air using a suitable photoelectric device. For efficiency testing by the filter manufacturer DOP smoke should be thermally generated to give mono-sized particles of approximately 0.3 μm diameter, but cold DOP aerosols of larger polydisperse droplet size (Caldwell, 1978) have been recommended for detecting small flaws and leaks that may develop in a filter during use (Gross, 1978). The passage of DOP particles is best examined in a LAF unit by using a small probe to scan the filter surface closely in an overlapping pattern (Gross, 1976). This will detect any areas of particular weakness such as pinholes or poor seals (McDade *et al.*, 1969). A HEPA filter is expected to have an overall minimum retention efficiency of 99.97% to hot DOP (Gross, 1978), this value being increased to 99.999% for ultra HEPA filters (Groves, 1973). Mika (1971) has suggested that filtration efficiency is at a minimum for airborne particles of 0.2–0.3 μm diameter and the bacterial retention properties of a HEPA filter (Section 3.1.3) may well be underrated by this test.

Alternatively, filters can be examined using the sodium flame test (BS 3928: 1969) in which a minimum retention efficiency of 99.995% is expected of all HEPA filters used to prepare air to Class F standard (BS 5295: 1989). An aerosol is produced from a sodium chloride solution, upstream of the filter, and rapid evaporation of these droplets then ensures that the air arriving at the filter contains minute particles of sodium chloride. Retention efficiency is evaluated by downstream sodium flame photometry. Other testing methods involve discoloration by atmospheric dust or weight gain during filtration, and are generally confined to filters of a coarser grade.

A bacterial aerosol challenge test has been developed to study the filtration efficiency of air and gas filters (Duberstein & Howard, 1978). Other workers (Harstad & Filler, 1969; Mika, 1971; Regamey, 1974) have suggested using phage particles, vegetative organisms and spores as a suitable challenge for HEPA filters. In the Public Health Laboratories at Porton Down, UK, a red pigmented strain of *Bacillus pumilus* (Jones, 1981) has been employed for filter testing. Typically, a bacterial challenge aerosol, produced from a suspension of resting spores in water ($1-2 \times 10^9$/ml), would be used in this test, and although no official standard is laid down, a HEPA filter would be expected to exhibit an efficiency of at least 99.9999% (Darlow, personal communication).

5 DESIGNING A FILTRATION SYSTEM FOR THE PREPARATION OF MEDICINAL PRODUCTS

Sterilization and clarification by filtration are routinely applied to a variety of liquids, which often differ markedly in their filtration characteristics. The first stage in designing any filtration system, therefore, is to classify the fluid to be processed according to the ease with which it can be filtered. The majority of aqueous solutions for intravenous, ophthalmic and irrigation purposes pass easily through a sterilizing grade membrane filter while at the other end of the spectrum, oils and fluids with a high particulate or protein content (e.g. vaccines, serum, plasma and tissue culture media) will, without exception, require some form of pretreatment before final processing. The early methods of pretreatment which included centrifugation and settling have largely been replaced by extensive pre-filtration (see Section 2.5.4 and Fig. 21.13) or by sequential filtration through a series of membrane filters of progressively smaller pore size. Often this series consists of a stack of membrane discs, separated by a support mesh, assembled together in a single filter holder. For ease of handling it is advisable to arrange the stack of filters in a separate holder from the final sterile, 0.22-μm, sterilizing filter. The serial filters can then be replaced when they become clogged without jeopardizing the sterility of the final filter. The successive filteration of serum through various grades of pre-filter followed by passage through 1.2, 0.8, 0.45 and 0.22-μm membranes provides a typical example of serial filtration. The pore size of the final filter is dictated by the need to provide a sterile product.

Small-volume parenteral, ophthalmic and other hospital-produced products are routinely passed through single disc filter systems capable of processing batches in the region of 500 l (Fig. 21.9). Bulk industrial production, however, with its larger volumes and attendant high capital investment, requires a more sophisticated approach to system design. Invariably, this will demand a pilot study where results obtained from flow decay tests performed on approximately 0.1% of the batch volume or with small-capacity filters, can be used to provide sufficient information for the scaling-up operation (Meltzer & Lukaszewicz, 1979). At least one major filter firm offers an on-site analysis programme culminating in a computer-assisted appraisal of the filtration process. Any system finally chosen must attempt to optimize total fluid throughput, flow rate and filter and pre-filter life.

The ancillary equipment required for an evolving filtration system is determined, at least in part, by the scale of the process. Large industrial systems will make many individual demands for specialized equipment, which may include pumps, holding tanks, cartridge filter holders and extensive stainless-steel plumbing. This combination of components is rarely found in small-scale hospital units.

Accumulated expertise has now clearly demonstrated that when selecting equipment for assembly into any filtration system, no matter what its size, the following important points must be taken into consideration:

1 Is filtration to be performed under positive or negative pressure? Vacuum filtration is well suited for small-scale analytical processes such as sterility testing but should not be used for production purposes. Positive pressure, provided by syringe, pump or nitrogen gas under pressure, offers the important advantages of high flow rates and easier bubble point testing, and also protects against the ingress of unsterile air and solvent evaporation. Equipment should be designed, therefore, to withstand the pressures employed during the filtration process.

2 Is filtration to be a batch or continuous process? In a continuously operating large-scale system, provision must be made to allow filter changes without interrupting the process. To do this a valve must be included to switch flow over to another unit fitted with a fresh filter.

3 The system must be amenable to regular maintenance and cleaning. If not, the filters may well be exposed to challenge levels in excess of their capabilities.

4 The amount of particulate contamination within a system is directly proportional to the number of valves, joints and junctions. It is considered advisable, therefore, to keep any system as simple as possible.

5 All valves shed particles during use and must be placed upstream of the final filter.

6 It is axiomatic that the final membrane filter must be placed at the last possible point in the system.

A system that pays attention to all these points should be capable of providing parenteral products of a standard acceptable to all the regulatory authorities. As a final cautionary word, however, the quality of the finished product does not depend solely upon the design and efficiency of the filtration system: it will also owe a great deal to the standard of the production environment, containers used and personnel employed and must, therefore, depend ultimately upon the continued observance of all Good Pharmaceutical Manufacturing Practice (GMP) requirements (Guide, 1983; Anon, 1989; BS 5295: 1989); see also Chapter 11.

6 REFERENCES

Alkan, M.H. & Groves, M.J. (1978) The measurement of membrane filter pore size by a gas permeability technique. *Drug Development and Industrial Pharmacy*, **4**, 225–241.

Anderson, J.M. & Baird-Parker, A.C. (1975) A rapid and direct plate method for enumerating *Escherichia coli* biotype 1 in food. *Journal of Applied Bacteriology*, **39**, 111–117.

Anon (1975) Clean areas aid treatment of burns. *Laboratory Equipment Digest*, December, pp. 51–52.

Anon (1989) The rules governing medicinal products in the European Community, Vol. IV: *Guide to Good Manufacturing Practice for Medicinal Products*. London: HMSO.

Ballew, H.W. & The Staff of Nuclepore Corporation (1978) *Basics of Filtration and Separation*. California: Nuclepore Corporation.

Bechold, H. (1908) Durchlässigkeit von ultrafiltern. *Zeitschrift für Physikalische Chemie*, **64**, 328–342.

Bodey, G.P., Freireich, E.J. & Frei, E. (1969) Studies of patients in a laminar air flow unit. *Cancer*, **24**, 972–980.

Borick, P.M. & Borick, J.A. (1972) Sterility testing of pharmaceuticals, cosmetics and medical devices. In *Quality Control in the Pharmaceutical Industry* (ed. Cooper, M.S.) Vol. I. pp. 1–38. New York & London: Academic Press.

Bowman, F.C. (1968) Laminar air flow for environmental control and sterility testing. *Bulletin of the Parenteral Drug Association*, **22**, 57–63.

Bowman, F.W., Calhoun, M.P. & White, M. (1967) Microbiological methods for quality control of membrane filters. *Journal of Pharmaceutical Sciences*, **56**, 222–225.

Brewer, J.H. & Phillips, G.B. (1971) Environmental control in the pharmaceutical and biological industries. *C.R.C. Critical Reviews in Environmental Control*, **1**, 467–506.

British Pharmacopoeia (1980) London: HMSO.

BS 1752: 1983. Laboratory sintered or fritted filters including porosity grading. London: British Standards Institution.

BS 3928: 1969. Method for sodium flame test for air filters (other than for air supply to I.C. engines and compressors). London: British Standards Institution.

BS 5295: 1989. Environmental cleanliness in enclosed spaces. London: British Standards Institution.

BS 5726: 1979. Specification for microbiological safety cabinets and amendments. London: British Standards Institution.

Brock, T.D. (1983) *Membrane Filtration: A Users Guide and Reference Manual*. Madison: Science Tech. Inc.

Brooks, N. (1979) Filter validation symposium. V. A synopsis of the PDA Panel on Filter Validation. *Journal of the Parenteral Drug Association*, **33**, 280–282.

Brown, M.R.W. & Gilbert, P. (1977) Increasing the probability of sterility of medicinal products. *Journal of Pharmacy and Pharmacology*, **27**, 484–491.

Brown, M.R.W., Farwell, J. & Rosenbluth, S.A. (1969) Use of membrane filters for measurement of 260 μm absorbing substances from bacterial cells. *Analytical Biochemistry*, **27**, 484–491.

Caldwell, G.H. Jr. (1978) Evaluation of high efficiency filters. *Journal of the Parenteral Drug Association*, **32**, 182–187.

Carazzone, M., Arecco, D., Fava, M. & Saucin, P. (1985) A new type of positively charged filter: preliminary test results. *Journal of Parenteral Science and Technology*, **39**, 69–75.

Casola, A.R. (1975) Federal regulations concerning use of asbestos filters in manufacturing parenteral drugs. *Bulletin of the Parenteral Drug Association*, **29**, 216–218.

Chamberland, C. (1884) Sur un filtre donnant de l'eau physiologiquement pure. *Compte rendu Hebdomadaire des Séances de l'Academie des Sciences*, **99**, 247–252.

Chrai, S.S. (1989) Validation of filtration systems: considerations for selecting filter housings. *Pharmaceutical Technology*, **13**, 85–96.

Clark, R.P. (1980) Microbiological safety cabinets. *Medical Laboratory World*, March, pp. 27–33.

Cole, J.C. & Pauli, W.A. (1975) Field experiences in testing membrane filter integrity by the forward flow test method. *Bulletin of the Parenteral Drug Association*, **29**, 296–304.

Cole, J.C., Farris, J.A. & Nickolaus, N. (1979) Cartridge filters. In *Filtration: Principles and Practice*, Part II (ed. Orr, C.) pp. 201–259. New York; Marcel Dekker.

Conacher, J.C. (1976) Membrane filter cartridges for fine particle control in the electronics and pharmaceutical industries. *Filtration and Separation*. May/June pp. 1–4.

Coriell, L.L. (1975) Laboratory applications of laminar air

flow. In *Quality Control in Microbiology* (eds Prior, J.E., Bertole, J. & Friedman, H.) pp. 41–46. Baltimore: University Park Press.

Coriell, L.L. & McGarrity, G.J. (1967) Elimination of airborne bacteria in the laboratory and operating room. *Bulletin of the Parenteral Drug Association*, **21**, 46–51.

Coriell, L.L. & McGarrity, G.J. (1968) Biohazard hood to prevent infection during microbiological procedures. *Applied Microbiology*. **16**, 1895–1900.

Coriell, L.L. & McGarrity, G.J. (1970) Evaluation of the Edgegard laminar flow hood. *Applied Microbiology*, **20**, 474–479.

Craythorn, JM., Barbour, A.G., Matsen, J.M., Britt, M.R. & Garibaldi, R.A. (1980) Membrane filter contact technique for bacteriological sampling of moist surfaces. *Journal of Clinical Microbiology*, **12**, 250–255.

Dahlstrom, D.A. & Silverblatt, C.E. (1986) Continuous vacuum and pressure filtration. In *Solid/Liquid Separation Equipment Scale-up* (eds Purchase, D.B. & Wakeman R.J.) pp. 510–557, London; Uplands Press, and Filtration Specialists.

Davis, N.M. & Turco, S. (1971) A study of particulate matter in IV infusion fluids—phase 2. *American Journal of Hospital Pharmacy*, **28**, 620–623.

Davis, N.M., Turco, S. & Sivelly, E. (1970a). A study of particulate matter in IV infusion fluids. *American Journal of Hospital Pharmacy*, **27**, 822–826.

Davis, N.M., Turco, S. & Sivelly, E. (1970b) Particulate matter in IV infusion fluids. *Bulletin of the Parenteral Drug Association*, **24**, 257–270.

Decker, H.M., Buchanan, L.M., Hall, L.B. & Goddard, K.R. (1963) Air filtration of microbial particles. *American Journal of Public Health*, **12**, 1982–1988.

De Muynck, C., De Vroe, C., Remon, J.P. & Colardyn, F. (1988) Binding of drugs to end-line filters: a study of four commonly administered drugs in intensive care units. *Journal of Clinical Pharmacy and Therapeutics*, **13**, 335–340.

Dence, P.B. & Stein, R.L. (1971) An evaluation of dust sampling membrane filters for use in the scanning electron microscope. *Powder Technology*, **5**, 201–204.

Denyer, S.P., (1987) Factory and hospital hygiene and good manufacturing practice. In *Pharmaceutical Microbiology* (eds. Hugo, W.B. & Russell, A.D.) 4th Edn. pp. 433–445. Oxford: Blackwell Scientific Publications.

Denyer, S.P. & Ward, K.H. (1983) A rapid method for the detection of bacterial contaminants in intravenous fluids using membrane filtration and epifluorescence microscopy. *Journal of Parenteral Science and Technology*, **37**, 156–158.

Denyer, S.P. & Lynn, R. (1987) A sensitive method for the rapid detection of bacterial contaminants in intravenous fluids. *Journal of Parenteral Science and Technology*, **41**, 60–66.

Duberstein, R. (1979) Filter Validation Symposium. II. Mechanisms of bacterial removal by filtration. *Journal of the Parenteral Drug Association*, **33**, 251–256.

Duberstein, R. & Howard, G. (1978) Sterile filtration of gases: a bacterial aerosol challenge test. *Journal of the Parenteral Drug Association*, **32**, 192–198.

Ehrlich, R. (1960) Application of membrane filters. *Advances in Applied Microbiology*, **2**, 95–112.

Elford, W.J. (1933). The principles of ultrafiltration as applied in biological studies. *Proceedings of the Royal Society*, **112B**, 384–106.

Elias, W.E. (1975) Panel discussion: Asbestos and glass fibre regulations. *Bulletin of the Parenteral Drug Association*, **29**, 215.

Elias, W. & Vellutato, A. (1966) Penicillin contamination of drugs: evaluation of test conditions by use of laminar flow. *Bulletin of the Parenteral Drug Association*, **20**, 193–198.

Emory, S.F. (1989) Principles of integrity-testing hydrophilic microporous membrane filters Part II. *Pharmaceutical Technology*, **13**, 36–46.

European Pharmacopoeia (1969) p. 54. Sainte-Ruffine: Maisonneuve.

European Pharmacopoeia (1971) Vol. II Test for sterility; Revised text, 1978, Paris: Maisonneuve.

Fare, G. (1987) Manufacture of Antibiotics. In *Pharmaceutical Microbiology*, (eds Hugo, W.B. & Russell. A.D) 4th Edn., pp. 151–162. Oxford: Blackwell Scientific Publications.

Favero, M.S. & Berquist, K.R. (1968) Use of laminar airflow equipment in microbiology. *Applied Microbiology*, **16**, 182–183.

Fifield, C.W. (1977) Sterilization filtration. In *Disinfection, Sterilization and Filtration* (ed. Block, S.S.) 2nd Ed. pp. 562–591. Philadelphia: Lea & Febiger.

Fleischer, R.L., Price, P.B. & Symes, E.M. (1964) Novel filter for biological materials. *Science*, **143**, 249–250.

Gelman, C. (1965) Microporous membrane technology: Part 1. Historical development and applications. *Analytical Chemistry*, **37**, 29A–37A.

Genovesi, C.S. (1983) Several uses for tangential-flow filtration in the pharmaceutical industry. *Journal of Parenteral Science and Technology*, **37**, 81–86.

Gross, R.I. (1976) Laminar flow equipment: performance and testing requirements. *Bulletin of the Parenteral Drug Association*, **30**, 143–151.

Gross, R.I. (1978) Testing of laminar flow equipment. *Journal of the Parenteral Drug Association*, **32**, 174–181.

Groves, M.J. (1973) *Parenteral Products*. London: William Heinemann Medical Books.

Guide to Good Pharmaceutical Manufacturing Practice (1983) London: HMSO.

Harstad, J.B., Decker, H.M., Buchanan, L.S. & Filler, M.E. (1967) Air filtration of submicron virus aerosols. *American Journal of Public Health*, **57**, 2186–2193.

Harstad, J.B. & Filler, M.E. (1969) Evaluation of air filters with submicron viral aerosols and bacterial aerosols. *American Industrial Hygiene Association Journal*, **30**, 280–290.

Hawker, R.J. & Hawker, L.M. (1975) Protein losses during sterilization by filtration. *Laboratory Practice*, **24**,

805–807, 818.

Heidam, N.Z. (1981) Review: aerosol fractionation by sequential filtration with Nuclepore filters. *Atmospheric Environment*, **15**, 891–904.

HIMA (1982) Microbiological evaluation of filters for sterilizing liquids Document No. 3, Vol. 4. Washington: Health Industry Manufacturers Association.

Hobbie, J.E., Daley, R.J. & Jasper, S. (1977) Use of Nuclepore filters for counting bacteria by fluorescence microscopy. *Applied and Environmental Microbiology*, **33**, 1225–1228.

Hofmann, F. (1984) Integrity testing of microfiltration membranes *Journal of Parenteral Science and Technology*, **38**, 148–158.

Holbrook, R., Anderson, J.M. & Baird-Parker, A.C. (1980) Modified direct plate method for counting *Escherichia coli* in foods. *Food Technology in Australia*, **32**, 78–83.

Holdowsky, S. (1957) A new sterility test for antibiotics: an application of the membrane filter technique. *Antibiotics & Chemotherapy*, **7**, 49–54.

Holmes, C.J. & Allwood, M.C. (1979) A review. The microbial contamination of intravenous infusions during clinical use. *Journal of Applied Bacteriology*, **46**, 247–267.

Hou, K., Gerba, C.P., Goyal, S.M. & Zerda, K.S. (1980) Capture of latex beads, bacteria, endotoxin and viruses by charge modified filters. *Applied and Environmental Microbiology*, **40**, 892–896.

Howard, G. Jr. & Duberstein, R. (1980) A case of penetration of 0.2 μm rated membrane filters by bacteria. *Journal of the Parenteral Drug Association*, **34**, 95–102.

Jacobs, S. (1972) The distribution of pore diameters in graded ultrafilter membranes. *Filtration and Separation*. September/October, 525–530.

Johnston, P.R. & Meltzer, T.H. (1980) Suggested integrity testing of membranes filters at a robust flow of air. *Pharmaceutical Technology*, **4**(11), 49–59.

Johnston, P.R., Lukaszewicz, R.C. & Meltzer, T.H. (1981) Certain imprecisions in the bubble point measurement. *Journal of Parenteral Science and Technology*, **35**, 36–39.

Jones, B.P.C. (1981) Personal Communication from Microbiological Safety Reference Laboratory, Porton Down. Salisbury, UK.

Kanke, M. Eubanks, J.L. & Deluca, P.P. (1983) Binding of selected drugs to a "treated" inline filter. *American Journal of Hospital Pharmacy*, **40**, 1323–1328.

Kay, J.B. (1980) Manufacture of pharmaceutical preparations. In *Textbook of Hospital Pharmacy* (eds Allwood, M.C. & Fell, J.T.) pp. 71–143. Oxford: Blackwell Scientific Publications.

Kesting, R., Murray, A., Jackson, K. & Newman, J. (1981) Highly antisotropic microfiltration membranes. *Pharmaceutical Technology*, **5**, 53–60.

Kesting, R.E., Cunningham, L.K., Morrison, M.C. & Ditter, J.F. (1983) Nylon microfiltration membranes: state of the art. *Journal of Parenteral Science and Technology*, **37**, 97–104.

Kovary, S.J., Agalloco, J.P. & Gordon, B.M. (1983) Validation of the steam-in-place sterilization of disc filter housings and membranes *Journal of Parenteral Science and Technology*, **37**, 55–64.

Lee, J.Y. (1989) Validating an automated filter integrity test instrument. *Pharmaceutical Technology*, **13**, 48–56.

Loughhead, H. & Vellutato, A. (1969) Parenteral production under vertical laminar air flow. *Bulletin of the Parenteral Drug Association*, **23**, 17–22.

Lowe, G.D. (1981) Filtration in IV therapy. Part 1: Clinical aspects of IV fluid filtration. *British Journal of Intravenous Therapy*, **2**, 42–52.

Lukaszewicz, R.C. & Meltzer, T.H. (1979a) Concerning filter validation. *Journal of the Parenteral Drug Association*, **33**, 187–194.

Lukaszewicz, R.C. & Meltzer, T.H. (1979b) Filter Validation Symposium. I. A co-operative address to current filter problems. *Journal of the Parenteral Drug Association*, **33**, 247–249.

Lukaszewicz, R.C. & Meltzer, T.H. (1980) On the structural compatibilities of membrane filters. *Journal of the Parenteral Drug Association*, **34**, 463–474.

Lukaszewicz, R.C., Johnston, P.R. & Meltzer, T.H. (1981a) Prefilters/final filters: a matter of particle/pore/size distribution. *Journal of Parenteral Science and Technology*, **35**, 40–47.

Lukaszewicz, R.C., Kuvin, A. Hauk, D. & Chrai, S. (1981b) Functionality and economics of tangential flow microfiltration. *Journal of Parenteral Science and Technology*, **35**, 231–236.

Lukaszewicz, R.C., Tanny, G.B. & Meltzer, T.H. (1978) Membrane filter characterizations and their implications for particulate retention. *Pharmaceutical Technology*, **2**(11), 77–83.

McDade, J.J., Sabel, F.L., Akers, R.L. & Walker, R.J. (1968) Microbiological studies on the performance of a laminar airflow biological cabinet. *Applied Microbiology*, **16**, 1086–1092.

McDade, J.J., Phillips, G.B., Sivinski, H.D. & Whitfield, W.J. (1969). Principles and applications of laminar flow devices. In *Methods in Microbiology* (eds Ribbons, D.W. & Norris, J.R.) Vol. 1, pp. 137–168. London & New York: Academic Press.

Maki, D.G. (1976) Preventing infection in intravenous therapy. *Hospital Practice*, **11**, 95–104.

Marshall, J.C. & Meltzer, T.H. (1976) Certain porosity aspects of membrane filters: their pore-distributions and anisotropy. *Bulletin of the Parenteral Drug Association*, **30**, 214–225.

Meers, P.D. & Churcher, G.M. (1974) Membrane filtration in the study of antimicrobial drugs. *Journal of Clinical Pathology*, **27**, 288–291.

Megaw, W.J. & Wiffen, R.D. (1963) The efficiency of membrane filters. *International Journal of Air and Water Pollution*, **7**, 501–509.

Meltzer, T.H. & Lukaszewicz, R.C. (1979) Filtration sterilization with porous membranes. In *Quality Control in the*

Pharmaceutical Industry (ed. Cooper, M.S.) Vol. 3, pp. 145–211, London: Academic Press.

Mika, H. (1971) Clean room equipment for pharmaceutical use. *Pharmaceutica Acta Helvetiae*, **46**, 467–482.

Miller, R.C. & Grogan, J.B. (1973) Incidence and source of contamination of intravenous nutritional infusion systems. *Journal of Paediatric Surgery*, **8**, 185–190.

Mittelman, M.W., Geesey, G.G. & Hite, R.R. (1983) Epifluoresence microscopy: a rapid method for enumerating viable and non-viable bacteria in ultra-pure water systems. *Microcontamination*, **1**, 32–37, 52.

Mittelman, M.W., Geesey, G.G. & Platt, R.M. (1985) Rapid enumeration of bacteria in purified water systems *Medical Device and Diagnostics Industry*, **7**, 144–149.

Morton, H.E. & Czarnetzky, E.J. (1937) The application of sintered (fritted) glass filters to bacteriological work. *Journal of Bacteriology*, **34**, 461–464.

Myers, J.A. (1972) Millipore infusion filter unit: interim report of a clinical trial. *Pharmaceutical Journal*, **208**, 547–549.

Naido, H.T., Price, C.H. & McCarty, T.J. (1972) Preservative loss from ophthalmic solutions during filtration sterilization. *Australian Journal of Pharmaceutical Sciences*, **NS1**, 16–18.

Newsom, S.W.B. (1979a) The Class II (Laminar Flow) biological safety cabinet. *Journal of Clinical Pathology*, **32**, 505–513.

Newsom, S.W.B. (1979b) Performance of exhaust-protective (Class I) biological safety cabinets. *Journal of Clinical Pathology*, **32**, 576–583.

Olson, W. (1980) LVP Filtration conforming with GMP. Communication prepared for Sartorius Symposium "50 Jahre Sartorius Membranfilter" held on 7th October 1980 at the Holiday Inn, Frankfurt.

Olson, W.P., Briggs, R.O., Garanchon, C.M., Ouellet, M.J., Graf, E.A. & Luckhurst, D.G. (1980) Aqueous filter extractables: detection and elution from process filters. *Journal of the Parenteral Drug Association*, **34**, 254–267.

Olson, W.P., Bethel, G. & Parker, C. (1977) Rapid delipidation and particle removal from human serum by membrane filtration in a tangential flow system. *Preparative Biochemistry*, **7**, 333–343.

Olson, W.P., Martinez, E.D. & Kern, C.R. (1981) Diffusion and bubble point testing of microporous cartridge filters: preliminary results of production facilities. *Journal of Parenteral Science and Technology*, **35**, 215–222.

Olson, W.P., Gatlin, L.A. & Kern, C.R. (1983) Diffusion and bubble point testing of microporous cartridge filters: electro mechanical methods. *Journal of Parenteral Science and Technology*, **37**, 117–124.

Pall, D.B. (1975) Quality control of absolute bacteria removal filters. *Bulletin of the Parenteral Drug Association*, **29**, 192–204.

Pettipher, G.L. (1983) *The Direct Epifluorescent Filter Technique for the Rapid Enumeration of Microorganisms*. Letchworth: Research Studies Press.

Phillips, G.B. (1975) Contamination control during the manufacture of medical products. *Acta Pharmaceutica Suecica*, **12** (Suppl.), 6–14.

Phillips, G.B. & Brewer, J.H. (1968) Recent advances in microbiological control. *Development in Industrial Microbiology*, **9**, 105–121.

Phillips, G.B. & Runkle, R.S. (1972) Design of facilities. In *Quality Control in the Pharmaceutical Industry* (ed. Cooper, M.S.) Vol. 1, pp. 73–99. New York and London: Academic Press.

Pitt, A.M. (1987) The non-specific protein binding of polymeric microporous membranes. *Journal of Parenteral Science and Technology*, **41**, 110–113.

Pohland, H.W. (1980) Seawater desalination by reverse osmosis. *Endeavour* (New Series), **4**, 141–147.

Prausnitz, P.H. (1924) Fritted glass filter discs. *Industrial and Engineering Chemistry*, **16**, 370.

Preusser, H.J. (1967) Elektronenmikroskopische Untersuchungen an Oberflachen von Membranfiltern. *Kolloidzeifschrift und Zeitschrift für Polymere*, **218**, 129.

Price, J.M. & Pauli, W.A. (1976) Utilization of new integrity test for membrane filter cartridges. *Bulletin of the Parenteral Drug Association*, **30**, 45–48.

Prince, J., Deverill, C.M.A. & Ayliffe, G.A.J. (1975) A membrane filter technique for testing disinfectants. *Journal of Clinical Pathology*, **28**, 71–76.

Rapp, R.P., Bivins, B.A. & Deluca, P. (1979) Sepsis in rabbits following administration of contaminated infusions through filters of various pore sizes. *American Journal of Hospital Pharmacy*, **36**, 1711–1713.

Regamey, R.H. (1974) Application of laminar flow (clean work bench) for purifying the atmosphere. *Developments in Biological Standards*, **23**, 71–78.

Reti, A.R. (1977) An assessment of test criteria for evaluating the performance and integrity of sterilizing filters. *Journal of Parenteral Drug Association*, **31**, 187–194.

Reti, A.R. & Leahy, T.J. (1979) Filter Validation Symposium. III. Validation of bacterially retentive filters by bacterial passage testing. *Journal of the Parenteral Drug Association*, **33**, 257–272.

Rogers, B.G. & Rossmore, H.W. (1970) Determination of membrane filter porosity by microbiological methods. *Developments in Industrial Microbiology*, **11**, 453–458.

Royce, A. & Sykes, G. (1950) Aspects of sterilization by candle filtration. *Proceedings of the Society for Applied Bacteriology*, **13**, 146–151.

Rusmin, S. & Deluca, P.P. (1976) Effect of in-line intravenous filtration on the potency of potassium penicillin G. *Bulletin of the Parenteral Drug Association*, **30**, 64–71.

Rusmin, S., Althauser, M. & Deluca, P.P. (1975) Consequences of microbial contamination during extended intravenous therapy using in-line filters. *American Journal of Hospital Pharmacy*, **32**, 373–377.

Russell, A.D. (1981) Neutralization procedures in the evaluation of bactericidal activity. In *Disinfectants*. Society for

Applied Bacteriology Technical Series, No. 16 (eds Collins, C.H., Allwood, M.C., Fox, A. & Bloomfield, S.F.) pp. 45–59. London & New York: Academic Press.

Russell, A.D., Ahonkhai, I. & Rogers, D.T. (1979) Microbiological applications of the inactivation of antibiotics and other antimicrobial agents. *Journal of Applied Bacteriology*, **46**, 207–245.

Ryan, P.B., Rapp, R.P., Deluca, P.P., Griffin, W.O., Jr., Clark, J.D. & Clays, D. (1973) In-line final filtration-a method of minimizing contamination in intravenous therapy. *Bulletin of the Parenteral Drug Association*, **27**, 1–14.

Schroeder, H.G. & Deluca, P.P. (1980) Theoretical aspects of sterile filtration and integrity testing. *Pharmaceutical Technology*, **4**(11), 80–85.

Sechovec, K.S. (1989) Validation of an automated filter integrity tester for use in bubble point testing. *Journal of Parenteral Science and Technology*, **43**, 23–26.

Smith, I.P.C. (1944) Sintered glassware: its manufacture and use. *Pharmaceutical Journal*, **152**, 110–111.

Solberg, C.O., Matsen, J.M., Vesley, D., Wheeler, D.J., Good, R.A. & Meuwissen, H.J. (1971) Laminar airflow protection in bone marrow transplantation. *Applied Microbiology*, **21**, 209–216.

Soltis, C. (1967) Construction and use of laminar flow rooms. *Bulletin of the Parenteral Drug Association*, **21**, 55–62.

Springett, D. (1981) The integrity testing of membrane filters. *Manufacturing Chemist and Aerosol News*, February, 41–45.

Stamm, A.J. (1971) Maximum effective pore size of Nuclepore membrane filters. *Tappi*, **54**, 1909.

Stockdale, D. (1987) Clean rooms for aseptic pharmaceutical manufacturing. In *Aseptic Pharmaceutical Manufacturing Technology for the 1990s* (eds Olson, W.P. & Groves, M.J.) pp. 151–160. Prairie View: Interpharm Press.

Sykes, G. (1965) *Disinfection and Sterilization*. 2nd Ed. London: E. & F.N. Spon.

Tanny, G.B. & Meltzer, T.H. (1978) The dominance of adsorptive effects in the filtrative purification of a flu vaccine. *Journal of the Parenteral Drug Association*, **32**, 258–267.

Tanny, G.B. & Meltzer, T.H. (1979) A review of sterilization with membrane filters. *Pharmaceutical Technology International*, pp. 44–49.

Tanny, G.B., Mirelman, D. & Pistole, T. (1980) Improved filtration technique for concentrating and harvesting bacteria. *Applied and Environmental Microbiology*, **40**, 269–273.

Tanny, G.B., Strong, D.K., Presswood, W.G. & Meltzer, T.H. (1979) Adsorptive retention of *Pseudomonas diminuta* by membrane filters. *Journal of the Parenteral Drug Association*, **33**, 40–51.

Todd, R.L. & Kerr, T.J. (1972) Scanning electron microscopy of microbial cells on membrane filters. *Applied Microbiology*, **23**, 1160–1162.

Trasen, B. (1979) Filter Validation Symposium, IV. Non-destructive tests for bacterial retentive filters. *Journal of the Parenteral Drug Association*, **33**, 273–279.

Truskey, G.A., Gabler, R. DiLeo, A. & Manter, T. (1987) The effect of membrane filtration upon protein conformation. *Journal of Parenteral Science and Technology*, **41**, 180–193.

Turco, S. (1978) All about the microporous filter. *National Intravenous Therapy Association (NITA)*, **1**, 217–225.

Turco, S. & Davis, N.M. (1973a) Clinical significance of particulate matter; a review of the literature. *Hospital Pharmacy*, **8**, 137–140.

Turco, S. & Davis, N.M. (1973b) A comparison of commercial final filtration devices. *Hospital Pharmacy*, **8**, 141–160.

Underwood, E. (1987) Ecology of microorganisms as it affects the pharmaceutical industry. In *Pharmaceutical Microbiology* (eds Hugo, W.B. & Russell, A.D.) 4th Ed. pp. 343–359. Oxford: Blackwell Scientific Publications.

United States Pharmacopoeia (1990) Twenty-second revision. Rockville: United States Pharmacopoeial Convention Inc.

Van Der Waaij, D. & Andres, A.H. (1971) Prevention of airborne contamination and cross-contamination in germ-free mice by laminar flow. *Journal of Hygiene, Cambridge*, **69**, 83–89.

Van Ooteghem, M. & Herbots, H. (1969) The adsorption of preservatives on membrane filters. *Pharmaceutica Acta Helvetiae*, **44**, 610–619.

Wagman, G.H., Bailey, J.V. & Weinstein, M.J. (1975) Binding of aminoglycoside antibiotics to filtration materials. *Antimicrobial Agents and Chemotherapy*, **7**, 316–319.

Wallhausser, K.H. (1976) Bacterial filtration in practice. *Drugs Made in Germany*, **19**, 85–98.

Wallhausser, K.H. (1977) Germ-free filtration. *Journal de Pharmacie de Belgique*, **32**, 463–467.

Wallhausser, K.H. (1979) Is the removal of microorganisms by filtration really a sterilization method? *Journal of the Parenteral Drug Association*, **33**, 156–170.

Wallhausser, K.H. (1982) Germ removal filtration. In *Advances in Pharmaceutical Sciences* (eds Bean, H.S., Beckett, A.H. & Carless, J.E.) pp. 1–116. London: Academic Press.

Wayne, W. (1975) Clean rooms—letting the facts filter through. *Laboratory Equipment Digest*, December, 49.

Whitfield, W.J. (1967) Microbiological studies of laminar flow rooms. *Bulletin of the Parenteral Drug Association*, **21**, 37–45.

Whitfield, W.J. & Lindell, K.F. (1969) Designing for the laminar flow environment. *Contamination Control*, **8**, 10–21.

Windle-Taylor, F. & Burman, N.P. (1964) The application of membrane filtration techniques to the bacteriological examination of water. *Journal of Applied Bacteriology*, **27**, 294–303.

Wood, G.J. & Ward, M.E. (1981) The Pall Ultipor IV filter and air eliminator. *British Journal of Intravenous Therapy*,

2, 15–16.

Wolley, E.L. (1969) Dealing with impurities and pollution. *The Illustrated Carpenter and Builder*, No. 12.

Wrasidlo, W. & Mysels, K.J. (1984) The structure and some properties of graded highly asymmetrical porous membranes. *Journal of Parenteral Science and Technology*, **38**, 24–31.

Zsigmondy, R. & Bachmann, W. (1918) Über neue Filter. *Zeitschrift für Anorganische und Allgemeine Chemie*, **103**, 119–128.

Chapter 22
Sterility Assurance: Concepts, Methods and Problems

1 INTRODUCTION

The basic aim of all sterilizing treatments is to render an object or material completely free of all viable micro-organisms. The preceding chapters described the equipment and processes commonly used by industrial manufacturers and hospitals to accomplish this aim. This chapter will deal with the outcome, i.e. how effective were the sterilizing treatments? Sterility assurance means exactly that: can the operator be assured that an object or material which has been subjected to a sterilizing process (heat, gas, radiation, or filtration) is indeed sterile?

At first glance, the question does not pose an insurmountable challenge: a simple 'yes' or 'no' will do. A sample from a batch of the product in question can be cultured before and after the sterilization process. It can then be decided whether or not the process rendered the material 'completely free of all viable micro-organisms'. In fact, during the earlier days of bacteriology, before the field was invaded by statisticians and philosophers, this was the basic approach used. Today, however, it is reluctantly recognized that simple tests and simple answers are often meaningless and frequently misleading. Sterility assurance is now a complicated and sometimes controversial enterprise which requires a thorough understanding of microbiology, laboratory technology and statistics in order to perform and interpret 'sterility tests'. In addition, decisions that deal with 'microbial safety' and 'adequacy of sterilization' require some knowledge of law and, also, familiarity with the semantics that permeate the field.

2 THE MYSTIQUE OF STERILITY ASSURANCE

Though the technology of sterilization and sterility control is based on good scientific logic and empirical measurements, an aura of mystery and confusion may still prevail. Kelsey (1972) described this confusion with remarkable insight in a *Lancet* article entitled 'The myth of surgical sterility'. He pointed out that historical misconceptions, unreal expectations and semantic interpretations have seriously compromised the usefulness of the term 'surgical sterility', and suggested that a new terminology be developed. The ensuing years with emphasis, in the United States at least, on solving all problems by litigation, have only emphasized the wisdom of Kelsey's stand.

The myth and the mystery derive in part from the classic definition of sterility: *complete freedom from micro-organisms*. This is an absolute definition that must have comforted generations of bacteriologists, nurses and doctors living in a world fraught with uncertainty. From a practical point of view there is nothing wrong with the concept; it is certainly possible to reduce the microbial contamination on a device or in a product to a level so low that it cannot be detected by bacteriological tests, to a level low enough to qualify as 'free from micro-organisms'. The definition implies, however, that the new level is *zero*. This is an entirely different statement, one that is difficult to reconcile with what is known about microbial death processes. Theory dictates that *zero* counts are impossible to attain, and laboratory practice shows that they are impossible to ascertain. This is the paradox that engenders mystery. On the one hand it is claimed that sterility is dichotomous: an item is sterile or it is not; there is no such thing as 'partly sterile' or 'nearly sterile'; there are no compromises with the definition. On the other hand, in the world inhabited by statisticians we are forced to deal with 'fractions' of a microbe, greater or lesser probability of the presence of a microbe, confidence limits. The worst reality of all is that laboratories sometimes make mistakes—sometimes by not finding microbes that really are there, and sometimes by finding microbes that really weren't there in the original sample but which were added during the testing process itself.

Statisticians further disrupt the comfortable dichotomous world of textbook definitions by pointing out that microbiologists do not really test items that are to be used. Instead, they test *samples* from a batch and make inferences from their tested samples to the remaining material in that batch that *was itself not tested*!

Some of the complexity and controversy associated with sterility assurance is a result of the number and types of materials and products that are being sterilized today, and their diversity—from chicken soup to spacecraft. Just as there is no single, simple process that is suitable for sterilizing all of these items, there is no single, simple technology available to test their sterility. Moreover, sterilization and sterility testing are undertaken in many diverse places, e.g. laboratories, hospitals, pharmaceutical factories, food processing plants and private clinics. Historically, many of these enterprises have developed their own sterility standards and their own eclectic approaches to testing, accuracy and reliability. The very term 'sterile' may mean different things to bacteriologists working in a governmental regulatory agency, to hospital pharmacists, to surgeons, to the quality control director of a canning plant, and to an attorney involved in nosocomial infection litigation. This diversity has certainly enhanced our knowledge, but it has also contributed to the mystification referred to above. It seems that the simple phrase 'no bacteria detected' is a useful one.

Commercial purveyors of the chemical and biological indicators which monitor sterilizing processes have also added their share to the confusion. Extravagant claims of efficacy were often made for one or another of these indicators; conflicting information was provided about what they could and could not do; worst of all, veiled inferences and rumours abounded about what might happen to the health and life of patients whose hospital depended on a competitor's sterility indicator. Professional associations of hospital workers who tried to bring some sense to this field often issued ambiguous recommendations based on inadequately researched information, thus further contributing to the mystery. Governmental regulatory agencies did not help by insisting that legal validation of sterility be measured only by certain direct culturing tests that were quite impractical and questionably relevant for many of the devices and materials being tested.

It might be impossible to dispel completely the mystique of sterility control. Still, it should be emphasized that much of the confusion results not from the unknown, but rather from ignorance or disregard of scientific theory and probability statistics. The medical supply and pharmaceutical industries, the hospital world, and food-processing manufacturers have been sterilizing their devices, materials and products successfully for more than a century and have developed, both empirically and by design, a very useful armoury of quality assurance tests and programmes. This chapter will try to review the tests most commonly used, and the concepts on which they are based. Where appropriate, the pitfalls associated with these tests and their interpretation will be identified.

It must be added that this chapter is not a comprehensive compendium of methods for sterility assurance. It does not describe specific approaches for solving specific problems. The list of sterility tests, process monitoring systems and quality assurance protocols is a long one; this brief review can only cite examples and must omit methodological details. The interested reader is advised to become familiar with the official and quasi-official documents that describe relevant regulations, guidelines and test methods for specific products, and which can be obtained from the following sources:

Association for the Advancement of Medical Instrumentation, 3330 Washington Blvd, Arlington, VA 22201, USA.

British Pharmacopoeia Commission, Market Towers, 1 Nine Elms Lane, London SW8 5NQ, UK.

British Standards Institution, 2 Park Street, London W1A 2BS, UK.

Bureau of Medical Devices, US Food and Drug Administration, 5600 Fishers Lane, Rockville, MD 20857, USA.

Department of Health, 14 Russell Square, London WCIB 5EP, UK.

European Pharmacopoeia Commission, Council of Europe, BP 431 RS, 6700C Strasbourg Cedex, France.

Hospital Infections Programme, Centers for Disease Control 1600 Clifton Road NE, Atlanta, GA 30333, USA.

United States Pharmacopeial Convention, 12601 Twinbrook Parkway, Rockville, MD 20852, USA.

3 APPROACHES TO STERILITY ASSURANCE

3.1 Historical background

In the early days of bacteriology the autoclaves and steam chambers of Pasteur and Koch were used mostly to sterilize bacteriological culture media. In those days, sterility determination was deceptively easy and the interpretation of the results unequivocal. The sterilized media were simply allowed to stand (i.e. incubate) for several days prior to use. Sterile media remained clear; improperly sterilized media, or those flasks which had become recontaminated after cooling, became cloudy. The 'biological indicators' were the common contaminants present in the media prior to sterilization. The tests were not destructive: the only flasks discarded were those which showed growth; all the 'good' (uncloudy) ones were used. There was no problem about incubation period or storage limits: the observation period lasted until the last flask of medium was used.

The other major deployment of sterilizing apparatus in the 19th century was in the food industry. This was nearly as good a place as the bacteriology laboratory to monitor sterilizing processes by direct product observation. The food, with its indigenous biological indicators, spoilage micro-organisms, either spoiled or remained palatable during storage. If the product became spoiled, either the sterilizer or the sterilizing process was considered defective; if the product did not spoil the systems were considered satisfactory. Indeed, this might have been the first systematic sterility assurance programme in history. Several problems arose, however, with this product-testing system. Several heat-resistant food contaminants, including the notoriously toxicogenic *Clostridium botulinum*, do not provide overt evidence of spoilage. Fatalities due to this agent have been traced to ostensibly sterilized canned foods that passed visual inspection, even in recent years. Moreover, food manufacturers are in business to sell their product, not to store it. As a consequence the food industry developed more reliable and economic systems of sterility assurance than long-term product observation (see Chapter 18D).

By the end of the 19th century the sterilization practices of the bacteriology laboratory were being introduced into the hospital. The simple world of sterility monitoring became more technically difficult, statistically troublesome and increasingly expensive when it became necessary to develop sterility assurance tests for items that, unlike culture media and canned food, could not be directly examined for microbial growth. These developments were pioneered by hospital pharmacists who designed aseptic sampling and culturing procedures for assuring the sterility of parenteral products, surgical dressings, ligatures and sutures, eye-drops and ointments and other items. The protocols of the hospital pharmacy became the forerunners of the current official sterility tests adopted by the national pharmacopoeias.

Sterility testing in surgery and in the hospital supply industry took a different track (Kilmer, 1897). It is one thing to culture fluid aliquots from a flask of sterilized saline or short suture strands from a batch; it is quite another task to cut up a surgeon's gown aseptically or culture an electronic pacemaker. This led to empirical sterility assurance programmes based on 'test pieces'. Small items were inoculated with spore-forming organisms, placed in the centre of a surgical pack or tray of instruments, subjected to the normal sterilizing exposures and then cultured. If the inoculated test pieces (forerunners of the biological indicators in use today) showed no growth, the remaining items in the pack or tray were also considered sterile. Some hospitals, particularly in Europe, placed packets of garden soil into surgical packs and cultured them to verify the effectiveness of the sterilizing treatment. Hospitals also started using chemical indicators, a pellet which melts or a dye which changes colour at a defined temperature, to verify that the items placed in the autoclave actually were exposed to the desired sterilizing conditions. In the modern hospital today, sterile supply services still rely almost entirely on chemical and biological indicators for sterility assurance. In contrast, the medical supply industry, which provides presterilized single-use items to the hospital, conforms to much more rigorous sterility assurance programmes. To meet legal requirements, they depend on direct testing methods and process validation protocols.

Perhaps the most formidable challenge to sterility assurance was posed by NASA's programme to deliver a sterile automated life-detection laboratory, Viking, to the surface of Mars in 1976. This mission utilized all of the knowledge and quality assurance experience acquired by the sterilization industry during the previous century. The ultimate approach employed, *viz.* a process validation system, was similar to that currently used in the food and sterile medical device industry: careful design of a sterilizing treatment that would reduce the final contamination level on the Viking lander to a preselected level (less than 1×10^{-6}), scrupulous control before and during the sterilization treatment, and protecting the finished product from recontamination (Hall, 1971).

3.2 Basic approaches to sterility assurance

The sterility assurance field will become less complicated when it is recognized that there are really only two basic approaches that are used, and that all of the tests, devices and systems described in the literature fall into one of two categories (see also Denyer, 1987): (1) those that determine the status of a given product directly by some kind of microbiological assessment, either by inoculation into a suitable culture medium or by membrane filtration; (2) those that monitor the sterilization process itself, and make indirect inferences about the status of the product based on the treatment it has undergone.

Product-culturing approaches are conceptually simple but technically and statistically very rigorous. They are based on the absolute definition of sterility, *viz.* the complete absence of viable microorganisms. The results are as straightforward as the definition: growth, or a positive culture, means the object tested was not sterile; absence of growth implies a sterile product. By using a suitable number of samples from a batch, a statistical inference can be made about the sterility of the remaining objects from that batch.

Process-monitoring approaches are more indirect but often more reliable. They are based on the proposition that if the equipment is in proper working order and the product has actually been subjected to a sterilizing treatment that was validated as effective (by experience and/or theory) and if good manufacturing practices are followed, the product can be assumed to be sterile. Process monitoring approaches involve at least three related components:

1 equipment function tests that demonstrate the proper mechanical operations of the sterilizer;

2 exposure verification tests that demonstrate that the products actually were exposed to the required sterilizing treatments;

3 process validation practices that measure the bioload, verify the destruction kinetics, justify the design of the sterilizing treatment and ensure the proper pre- and post-handling of the products.

4 PRODUCT TESTING

Standard instructions for sterility testing of products and devices are provided in the respective British, European, and United States pharmacopoeias. These instructions form the basis of legal referee data. Anyone who requires sterility data for purposes of litigation, legal validation or regulatory purposes is advised to refer to the most recent edition of the relevant pharmacopoeia for detailed procedures. Though the most common application of these procedures is for sterile fluids (e.g. injections) and small items (e.g. sutures), the latest editions of these official compendia also provide instructions for sterility testing of devices and objects too large to be immersed or inoculated into culture flasks.

The official tests for sterility utilize at least two different types of culture media: soybean–casein digest medium for aerobic microbes and thioglycollate medium for anaerobes. Any dilution or rinse-elution fluids that are to be used in the tests are also described in detail. Before use, the culture media must be tested for their growth-promoting qualities, using a variety of specified aerobic and anaerobic test organisms. Similarly, several bacteriostatic and fungistatic tests are described to ensure that negative tests (i.e. sterile cultures) really mean that the product is sterile and are not merely negative because of carry-over of microbial inhibitors from the test item.

Much attention is paid by the pharmacopoeias to the number of items or amount of product to be tested. This is perhaps one of the most critical considerations in product testing. Obviously, the larger the number of contaminated items in a batch, the greater the probability that the contamination will be discovered. Similarly, the larger the number of samples tested from a marginally contaminated batch, the greater will be the probability of discovering any of the contaminated items and the consequent rejection of that batch. This relationship can be expressed by the following formula:

$$P = (1 - x)^y$$

where P = the probability of certifying a product batch as sterile, x = the proportion of contaminated units in a batch, and y = sample size (the number of randomly selected units tested).

Thus for example, if in a batch of 1000 sterilized items there remained 10 items that were still contaminated (1.0% or 0.01) and if 20 randomly selected items from that batch were tested according to the official methods under consideration, the probability of accepting the entire batch as sterile would be $(1-0.01)^{20} = 0.99^{20} = 0.82$. In other words, 82 times out of 100, all 20 of those random samples would yield negative cultures and the whole batch would be certified as sterile, even if the batch actually contained 10 contaminated items. The same formula could be used to show that 50 samples from that batch would reduce the probability of acceptance to 0.61 and 100 samples to 0.37, and that it would require more than 500 samples before the probability of accepting that batch could be reduced to less than 1 in 100. Similar calculations would demonstrate the probability of accepting or certifying as sterile batches containing different numbers of contaminated items (Bryce, 1956; Brewer, 1957).

Testing 500 items out of a batch of 1000 is time-consuming, expensive and impractical. Thus the official instructions in the respective pharmacopoeias provide practical guidelines about the numbers of replicates (usually between two and 20) that should be tested for sterility from any manufacturing run. The numbers depend on the size of the batch (i.e. less than 100, between 100 and 500, greater than 500, etc.) the nature of the product (i.e. parenteral solutions, surgical dressings, ophthalmic ointments, etc.) and its intended use (e.g. internally by injection, topically).

Detailed instructions are given for the actual performance of the sterility tests, whether by direct inoculation, membrane filtration or elution of surfaces followed by membrane filtration, as well as the aseptic precautions that must be taken by the operators. It is recommended that the tests be performed in sterile laminar air flow (LAF) cabinets to eliminate adventitious contaminants from the environment. Finally, detailed guidelines are provided for the interpretation and verification of test results: how to distinguish between true and false positives and true and false negatives.

Sterility assurance by direct product testing has become a painstaking and sophisticated enterprise. The state of the art requires specialized laboratories and carefully trained operators. Very few hospitals have the facilities for this kind of work and, as mentioned earlier, this kind of testing is carried out mainly in governmental regulatory laboratories and by the medical device/pharmaceutical industries.

Even with all of the precautions, however, it is not completely foolproof. Laboratory mistakes do happen and false positives lead to unjustified rejection of sterile goods while false negatives permit acceptance of contaminated items. Even without overt error, the statistical imperatives dictate that very high probabilities of safety can be provided but never of absolute assurance. Moreover, with the ever-increasing use by physicians and surgeons of expensive, complicated mechanical and electronic devices, the destructive nature of product-testing introduces an economic component into the sterility assurance field that was not there when these tests were developed and made official. It is to the great credit of governmental regulators, and the compilers of the pharmacopoeias, that these drawbacks are now being officially recognized and that process control approaches are being recommended, where applicable, for products that cannot be tested by direct culturing.

5 MONITORING THE STERILIZING PROCESS

5.1 Equipment function tests

Fundamental to sterility assurance is the proper design, construction, and operation of the sterilizer, be it steam, dry heat, gas, ionizing radiation or filtration. This usually involves some mechanical testing and becomes a major challenge, if only because of the diversity of equipment used and the variety of ways each of these devices can be tested. Moreover, the ability of a hospital sterile supply department to validate proper functioning of its equipment is quite different from the ability of a sterile product manufacturer to do the same thing. Much of the responsibility for equipment validation, therefore, lies in the hands of the equipment manufacturer. He/she is responsible for the design and construction of the autoclaves, irradiation chambers and filtration machinery. It should reasonably be expected that the apparatus will perform according to contracted (or advertised) specifications at the time of delivery and installation.

When new and remodelled steam and gas autoclaves are installed, it is important for the sterilizer operator to check the heat distribution throughout the chamber, the penetration of steam through a porous load, and the rate of heat transfer through solution containers before certifying the device for routine use. In some installations this is done by means of a recording potentiometer attached to a bimetallic thermocouple (usually copper–constantan). Thermocouples are inserted into representative packs and/or containers and the terminal ends are brought out under the door of the sterilizer or through a thermocouple gland installed especially for this purpose (Alder, 1976). The potentiometer measures not only the ultimate temperature reached in the most inaccessible parts of the chamber but also how quickly this temperature was attained and for how long it was maintained (temperature profile). Once the autoclaves are installed, these potentiometer tests are not done routinely, but mainly whenever there is any change in the routine operation, e.g. type of material being sterilized, type, shape, or size of pack, or type of wrapping material.

Thermocouples are good sensors of the conditions in the internal environment of the pack but they are cumbersome to use and require some technical skill. The Association for Advancement of Medical Instrumentation (AAMI) recommends that, in place of thermocouples, hospitals validate the performance of the autoclave with challenge test packs or test flasks containing biological indicators (AAMI 1983, 1985, 1988a). These packs, which must meet specified size dimensions and densities, contain materials that hospitals usually sterilize, such as towels, dressings, instruments and tubing, and are wrapped with the kind of materials routinely used in hospital sterile supply departments. Again, these packs are not recommended for routine monitoring, but rather to challenge the sterilizer performance after installation and/or after a change in department practices. Interestingly, the *US Pharmacopoeia* (1985) also recommends a biological indicator, *Pseudomonas diminuta*, for use as a qualifying challenge to certify the proper design and installation of filtration sterilization equipment.

Subsequent to validating the proper manufacture and installation of the sterilizing machinery, their routine mechanical operation is monitored during every sterilizing run by a variety of time-, temperature-, and pressure-recording devices and gauges strategically located within the sterilization chamber or exhaust lines. Similarly, automatic time–temperature controls which programme the whole sterilizing cycle are standard equipment on all pre-vacuum steam and gas sterilizers purchased by American hospitals. These controls will ensure automatic recycling of the load in the event that the desired conditions in the sterilizing chamber fall below any specified level during the sterilizing cycle. These mechanical sensors, of course, cannot compensate for mistakes made during the preparation, wrapping or loading of the packs. Such errors must be controlled by 'good manufacturing practices' or 'administrative' controls mentioned below. The prime purpose of thermometers and gauges is to effect economy and uniformity of results and to guard against human error in sterilizer operation. However, these sensors depend for their reliability on properly trained mechanics and service personnel, and also on frequent inspection and maintenance.

The instruments which monitor conditions within the sterilization chamber provide information immediately, provide permanent records as chart recordings or computer printouts and are, in the main, easy to interpret. They will verify that lethal conditions have been generated in their immediate vicinity and imply that the same conditions prevail in or on the items undergoing sterilization. It is quite evident, none the less, that they do not assure sterility of any given item. Perhaps their most important function is a negative one: if the desired lethal conditions have not been attained in the chamber, we are made aware of this quickly and without much doubt, and the products in the chamber will not be certified as sterile. Instead they will be scheduled for immediate re-sterilization, and the defective operation can be corrected without any unnecessary delay.

In the case of pre-vacuum and gas sterilizers, recording thermometers and pressure gauges must be supplemented with vacuum gauges. Further, since undetected air leaks constitute a threat to sterilization efficiency, a daily air-tightness test (vacuum leak) should be run. The maximum vacuum level normally occurring during a standard cycle should be drawn and the vacuum held for 10 min. If the loss of vacuum is more than 10 mm/10 min, the test has failed and the autoclave should not be used until the leak has been corrected. Another equipment function test that should be performed each day on vacuum autoclaves is the Bowie–Dick procedure. The instructions for performing this test (Bowie *et al.*, 1963; HTM (Health Technical Memorandum), 1980; AAMI, 1988a) must be adhered to diligently. Essentially, two strips of officially approved autoclave tape (Section 5.2.1) are applied to a sheet of paper in the form of an '×'; this is inserted into the centre of a test pack of cotton towels and the pack autoclaved. If the colour change throughout the tapes (both strips) is uniform, it is inferred that the steam penetrated through the pack uniformly and was not inhibited by any residual air pockets. If, on the other hand, the tape is paler in the centre than at the ends, it might be suspected that air was present in the pack and that the sterilizing cycle might have failed.

5.2 Exposure verification tests

The equipment function tests described above verify that the sterilizer is working and that lethal conditions are provided in the macro-environment of the sterilization chamber. However, the actual items to be sterilized are located in different positions within the chamber, and are themselves protected by a variety of wrapping and packaging materials designed to preserve their sterility after removal from the chamber. Thus it is necessary to verify that the lethal conditions of the chamber actually permeated to the micro-environments of the microbial contaminants which must be destroyed. This can be done either by thermocouples, described above, which are not suitable for routine process monitoring, or by various chemical (CI) and biological (BI) indicators (Sections 5.2.1 and 5.2.2, respectively).

The CI and BI in use today are the descendants of the historical 'test pieces' innovated by the early microbiologists to verify the proper working of their sterilizers. The major difference is that the pioneers in the field did not pay very much attention to quality control; one sample of garden soil was very much like any other, in their eyes. Today's CI and BI are manufactured under rigorously controlled conditions and meet exacting specifications (AAMI, 1986a,b). They are also very convenient to use, are relatively inexpensive, and are usually easy to interpret.

They are particularly useful for indicating sterilization failure, i.e. the non-attainment of sterilizing conditions within a given pack or container. In this respect they supplement the instruments that monitor chamber environments. If the recording thermometer shows proper equipment function but the CI/BI shows inadequate treatment, it might mean that the the steam or gas did not penetrate the packaging material, that the autoclave was incorrectly loaded, that the pack was too dense to allow thorough steam permeation or that the thermometer was malfunctioning.

It should not be necessary to point out that, despite their usefulness, popularity and almost universal acceptance, CI and BI test pieces do not by themselves verify the sterility of a product. They only verify that the product has been exposed to the sterilization treatment. They cannot be used to monitor the subsequent history of the product after removal from the sterilization chamber. In other words, the product may become recontaminated during handling and/or storage, but the test piece remains unchanged.

5.2.1 Chemical indicators (CIs)

The rationale underlying chemical monitoring of the sterilization process is based on the ability of heat, ethylene oxide and ionizing radiation to change the physical and/or chemical nature of a variety of chemical substances sufficiently to be detected by the naked eye or in a spectrophotometer. In certain cases the change involves a colour transformation; in others, a solid material melts or changes shape. It is possible to manufacture a device or test piece which contains just the right amount of such chemical or chemicals, so that the visible or spectrophotometric change will be evident only if the exposure exceeded a given threshold (intensity and/or duration) of heat, ethylene oxide or radiation. More than a dozen categories of such chemical monitors are available for verifying sterilizing processes (HIMA, 1978). They are arranged in Table 22.1 according to the sterilizing treatment they are designed to monitor.

Chemical indicators are used in hospitals and the sterilization industry for four basic functions:

(i) 'Throughput' indicators. These are used to distinguish between processed and unprocessed packs or containers, without any precise implication about sterilization. The classic example is indicator tape applied externally to packs destined for steam or ethylene oxide treatment. These indicators will help to identify, particularly in a busy production or storage area, which packs have gone through the autoclave and which are still awaiting their turn. It should always be remembered that external indicators have really only been exposed to the chamber environment, without the resistances imposed by package density or wrapping material. Thus they do not represent the conditions that prevailed within the pack itself.

(ii) Bowie–Dick indicators. These are used to

Table 22.1 Chemical indicators for sterility process monitoring*

Sterilization method	Type	Approach
Dry heat	1	Time–temperature integrated colour change ink on pressure-sensitive label stock. The label stock is made of a heat-resistant material and removable adhesive. The chemical reaction occurs within the temperature range of 148–182°C, the rate being a direct function of temperature. This system can therefore be used over a wide temperature range. It is easily removed from re-usable items and can be placed on each article to be sterilized. This indicator system cannot be used at temperatures above 200°C as the label will char and the adhesive will bond the label to the item being sterilized. This system can lose its adhesive qualities if stored under adverse conditions and must be affixed to a clean surface or it may become detached during processing.
	2	Temperature-sensitive ink on a pressure-sensitive label stock. This indicator system usually consists of white pigmented wax on a black absorbent paper. When the wax melts the white colour disappears, leaving a black background or making a previously imprinted legend appear. These waxes are temperature-specific and melting occurs within seconds of achieving a predetermined temperature. They can be used over a wide temperature range. They are easily removed from re-usable items and can be placed on each article to be sterilized. The indicator system can lose its adhesive qualities if stored under adverse conditions and must be affixed to a clean surface or it may become detached during processing.
	3	Temperature-sensitive pellets or crayons. The pellet will melt when a preset temperature is achieved. The crayon touched to an item will leave a mark if the item is at or above the melting point of the crayon. These indicators have a good shelf-life over a wide temperature range. They cannot be used on all materials and cannot be kept as a permanent record.
	4	Thermochromic inks and crayons. These indicators consist of either a thermochromic ink or crayon, which exhibits a colour change in a specific temperature range. These indicators demonstrate a good shelf-life over a wide temperature range and can be applied to any surface. They show distinctive temperature-dependent colour changes. They do not, however, monitor all dry heat sterilization temperature ranges. Some inks and crayons also show a colour reversal upon cooling. Also inks tend to settle and give erroneous results if not thoroughly mixed prior to use.
	5	Fusible pellet in glass tube. This type of indicator consists of a chemical having a specific melting point and sealed in a glass tube. The glass tubes usually have threads attached to assist in handling. Since the pellet is sealed in a glass tube, product contamination is minimized. These indicators have a good shelf-life over a wide temperature range.
Steam autoclaves	1	Fusible pellet in glass tube. This type of indicator consists of a chemical having a specific melting point and sealed in a glass tube. Certain of this type of indicator are designed to be time-specific. The glass tubes usually have threads attached to assist in handling. Since the pellet is sealed in a glass tube, product contamination is minimized. These indicators have a good shelf-life over a wide temperature range. They are, however, not directly moisture-responsive.

Continued

Table 22.1 (*contd*)

Sterilization method	Type	Approach
	2	Chemical ink indicators usually consist of various thermochromic inks printed on paper. When exposed to saturated steam, the ink undergoes a chemical reaction which changes its colour. In some types of printed ink indicators, presence of air pockets inhibits the colour change reaction. Certain of this type of indicator can monitor time, temperature and steam penetration. For proper storage, use and interpretation of results, manufacturer's instructions should be followed.
	3	Capillary device indicators consist of a wax-like pellet in contact with chromatography paper. These pellets gradually liquefy as temperature increases. The melted fluid then wicks along the chromatography paper to form a band whose length is dependent upon time and temperature.
Ethylene oxide	1	Chemical ink indicators consist of chemothermochromic inks printed on paper. When exposed to ethylene oxide, the ink undergoes a chemical reaction which results in colour change. The rate of colour development varies with time and temperature. Some indicators sense the presence of moisture. For proper storage, use and interpretation of results, manufacturer's instructions should be followed.
	2	Chemical resin with a chemical indicator contained in an open glass tube. When exposed to ethylene oxide, the resin absorbs the gas and the chemical indicator undergoes a chemical reaction and colour change.
Ionizing radiation	1	*Qualitative indicator*. Qualitative (go–no go) indicators are radiochromic chemicals impregnated in plastic. They come in the form of various self-adhesive tapes and dots and are used to indicate that an object has been irradiated. For the most part, a colour change occurs at relatively low doses and, therefore, these materials are used as part of the quality assurance programme to assure some exposure to radiation. Like other self-adhesive label stock, they adhere well only on clean surfaces and are prone to lose adhesive properties when stored incorrectly.
	2	*Quantitative liquid dosimeter*. Liquid indicators are usually considered the more accurate quantitative dosimeter. There are two major types: ferric ammonium sulphate and ceric sulphate, both of which are dissolved in dilute sulphuric acid. The dose received is determined from a spectrophotometric absorption in the UV region. Besides the disadvantages of manipulation and the need for a UV spectrophotometer, the indicators are sensitive to organic compounds and, more seriously, the response is dose-rate-dependent at the high dose rates achieved in electron beam sterilization. They are, however, very reliable and used extensively for ^{60}Co and ^{137}Cs irradiators. Ferric sulphate is useful only for doses up to 100 krad (1kGy) and ceric sulphate is useful for 0.5–5.0 Mrad (5–50 kGy). The solutions can be purchased in bulk or in ampoules.
	3	*Quantitative solid dosimeter*. Radiochromic solids come in a number of forms. The common ones are red polymethyl methacrylate, amber polymethyl methacrylate, nylon polyvinyl chloride, etc.

Table 22.1 (*contd*)

Sterilization method	Type	Approach
		Red and amber polymethyl methacrylates are produced in the form of a slide. The optical density change induced by radiation is read in either a special reader or with an adapted visible-light spectrophotometer. These dosimeters come in hermetically sealed packages and should not be removed until the dosimeter is to be read. The useful range for amber polymethyl methacrylate is 0.1–1.0 Mrad (1–10 kGy) and for red polymethyl methacrylate is 0.5–5.0 Mrad (5–50 kGy).
		Red polymethyl methacrylate is also supplied in the form of cubes and cylinders. These have a similar range and accuracy but must be read in special readers. They are less humidity dependent than the slide form, and are subject to some slow post-radiation fading.
		The nylon film dosimeters are also read in the special reader or by an adapted spectrophotometer. The nylon film must be protected from UV sources such as germicidal lights, certain fluorescent lights and particularly sunlight. The dose is obtained from a calibration curve over a range of 0.1–5.0 Mrad (50 kGy). They are reported to be stable.

* Permission for reprinting this material from HIMA Report 78–44 (1978) is gratefully acknowledged.

challenge pre-vacuum autoclaves with respect to air removal. These have been discussed in Section 5.1. Since the temperature–time exposures used in the Bowie–Dick test may be different from those required to achieve routine sterilization, these tests should not be considered as sterility tests.

(iii) Temperature specific indicators. Placed in the centre of a pack these verify that the pack is indeed one that had been autoclaved. They demonstrate whether or not a specific temperature was attained, but do not reveal for how long this temperature was maintained, the presence of dry air pockets or gas concentrations. They are mostly used to detect malfunctions of the sterilizer's temperature control instrumentation, or errors in packaging and loading.

(iv) Multi-parameter process indicators. These respond to the combined action of different components of the lethal process, e.g. heat and duration of treatment, gas concentration and exposure time. Examples of these are the 'Therm-A-Log-S' and 'Browne's tubes' used in autoclaves, 'Royce's sachets' used in gas sterilizers and the radiation dosimeters. The usefulness of these indicators is self-evident: they demonstrate quite convincingly whether or not sterilization conditions were maintained in the product's micro-environment for a sufficient period to render the product sterile. Their 'readout' is immediate, unlike that of the BI which must be incubated before interpretation.

However, it must be emphasized that all CIs, including the multi-parameter systems, have limitations of sensitivity and specificity. False-positive results (CI changing colour too soon) might lead to acceptance of non-sterile products, whereas false-negative results (CI not responding) will reject those which are truly sterile. Moreover, even the best CI is but a proxy for a microbial population.

The market-place is adequately supplied with commercial products from each of the categories described in Table 22.1. Information about the advantages and disadvantages of any CI, i.e. its sensitivity and specificity, the conditions it is designed to monitor, its ease of interpretation, reliability, stability and safety, can be obtained from a manufacturer and its competitors. The astute sterilizer operator will certainly take advantage of all of the information available before choosing a CI appropriate for the specific sterility assurance test needed.

5.2.2 Biological indicators (BIs)

Biological indicators probably come closest to being the ideal test pieces for verifying exposure of a product to a sterilizing process. Firstly, like CIs and thermocouples, they can be placed directly into a container, in intimate association with the product. Second, they are universal monitors, independent of the specific sterilization process being tested. Thirdly, they integrate all of the sterilizing parameters involved: time, germicidal intensity, environmental conditions, packaging, etc. Most important, they measure sterilization directly, not merely the physical and chemical conditions necessary for sterilization.

BIs in current use are the endospores of the following species:

1 For monitoring steam sterilization: *Bacillus stearothermophilus* (NCTC 10007) (NCIB 8157) (ATCC 7953) and *Clostridium sporogenes* (NCTC 8594) (NCIB 8053) (ATCC 7955).

2 For monitoring dry heat cycles: *Bacillus subtilis* var. *niger* (NCIB 8058) (ATCC 9372).

3 For monitoring exposure to ethylene oxide: *Bacillus subtilis* var *niger* (NCTC 10073) (ATCC 9372).

4 For monitoring ionizing radiation: *Bacillus pumilus* (NCTC 8241) (NCIB 8982) (ATCC 14884), *Bacillus cereus* (SS1 C 1/1) and *Bacillus sphaericus* (SS1 C1A).

The resistance specifications (*D* values) of these cultures and the minimum numbers of each that constitute a challenge dose (between 10^5 and 10^8 per BI) are provided in the *British Pharmacopoeia* (1988) and the *US Pharmacopoeia* (1985). Spores are usually the microbial forms most resistant to these processes (Russell, 1982).

BIs are available commercially, either as suspensions for inoculating test pieces, or on already inoculated carriers such as filter paper ('spore strips'), glass or plastic. The variety of products is shown in Table 22.2 (HIMA, 1978). After exposure to the sterilization process, either in a test pack or during a sterilizing run, the BIs are cultured in appropriate media and under suitable conditions for the growth of the respective species employed in the test (note that some are anaerobes and some are thermophiles). If no growth takes place after a long enough incubation period—designated by the manufacturer—it is assumed that sterilization has taken place. In other words, the designated sterilization exposure has been verified. If on the other hand, growth is detected, it is advised that the growth be examined microbiologically to see whether it was the original spore inoculum that germinated or whether adventitious contamination occurred during handling and culturing.

The BI provides another advantage in addition to merely verifying sterilization exposures in a pack. Since the spores employed are considerably more resistant than the usual contaminants found on or in items that are being sterilized and since the numbers of spores on the BI exceed by several magnitudes the usual contamination level (bioload) normally present on the product of interest, the judicious use of BI actually creates a 'worst possible' challenge case. By a process of more rigorous reasoning, it may be inferred that if the spore strip has been sterilized then every other item in that pack would also be sterile. In this respect, BI test data are often accepted with the same degree of confidence as data from direct product sterility tests. However, the inference cannot be made casually. The problems of false-positives and false-negatives cannot be overlooked. The BI must be placed in the proper position in the pack, the pack itself must be properly positioned in the sterilizing chamber, and a reasonable number of replicates must be evaluated before BIs can be relied upon to be the sole criteria of sterility assurance.

Above all, the quality control practices observed by the manufacturers of the BI must be taken into account. Spore strips inoculated with abnormally high or low challenge doses, or with extremely resistant or weakened spores, will yield misleading information. This in turn raises questions about quality control of items designed to measure the quality control of other items, and so on *ad infinitum*. The AAMI standards (1981, 1982,

Table 22.2 Biological indicators for sterility process monitoring*

Sterilization Method	Type	Approach
Dry heat	1	Paper strip inoculated with spores of *Bacillus subtilis*. Some commercial spore strips are impregnated with spores of both *B. subtilis* and *B. stearothermophilus* and these strips can be used as indicators for dry heat or other sterilization processes. It has been well documented that there is no interference between organisms. Use of this system requires aseptic culturing techniques. This system cannot be used with temperatures that may char the paper carrier.
	2	Product or simulated product inoculated with a known spore suspension of *B. subtilis*. The use of inoculated product may more closely simulate conditions of actual product sterilization. Selection of the indicator organism is based on microbiological considerations of product and process. Aseptic techniques must be adhered to with these systems. These systems may be used at any selected temperature.
Steam	1	Paper strip inoculated with spores of *B. stearothermophilus*. Some commercial spore strips are impregnated with spores of both *B. stearothermophilus* and *B. subtilis* and these strips can be used as indicators for steam or other sterilization processes. It has been well documented that there is no interference between organisms. Use of this system requires aseptic culturing techniques using soybean–casein digest medium or equivalent.
	2	Glass ampoule containing spores of *B. stearothermophilus* suspended in liquid culture medium. With this system, aseptic culturing techniques are not required. Although this system cannot directly monitor steam penetration, it is appropriate for monitoring sterilization of hermetically sealed aqueous products.
	3	Plastic self-contained unit containing a spore strip of *B. stearothermophilus* and a crushable glass ampoule of liquid culture medium. With this indicator system, aseptic culturing techniques are not required.
	4	Product or simulated product inoculated with a known spore suspension. The use of inoculated product may simulate more closely the conditions of actual product sterilization. Selection of indicator organism is based on microbiological considerations of product and process. For processes performed at 121°C or higher, spores of *B. stearothermophilus* are used, whereas for processes below 121°C, other spores may be utilized. Aseptic techniques must be adhered to with these systems.
Ethylene oxide	1	Paper strip inoculated with spores of *B. subtilis*. Some commercial spore strips are impregnated with both *B. subtilis* and *B. stearothermophilus* and these strips can be used as indicators for ethylene oxide and other sterilization processes. It has been well documented that there is no interference between organisms. Use of this system requires aseptic culturing techniques using soybean–casein digest medium or equivalent.
	2	Plastic self-contained units containing a spore strip of *B. subtilis* and a crushable glass ampoule of liquid culture medium. With this indicator system, aseptic culturing techniques are not required. Systems based on colour changes due to the pH of the culture medium must be compared against their controls and should be monitored frequently

Continued

Table 22.2 (*contd*)

Sterilization Method	Type	Approach
		during incubation times which exceed a manufacturer's recommendation.
	3	Product or simulated product inoculated with spores of *B. subtilis*. Aseptic techniques must be adhered to with these indicators.
Ionizing radiation	1	Paper strip inoculated with spores of *B. pumilus*. The use of the system recommends aseptic culturing technique using soybean–casein digest or equivalent.
	2	Product or simulated product inoculated with a known microbial suspension. The use of inoculated product may simulate more closely the conditions of actual product sterilization. Selection of indicator organisms is based on microbiological considerations of product and process. Aseptic technique must be adhered to with this system.

* Permission for reprinting this material from HIMA Report 78–44 (1978) is gratefully acknowledged.

1986a,b) are useful sources of information for the interested reader.

Most American hospitals use BIs to monitor their routine sterilizing cycles at least weekly, and in some of the larger institutions, daily. It appears that the Americans place a lot more confidence in BIs than do the British, who use them mainly to monitor ethylene oxide sterilization, a process that has never been accepted with enthusiasm in the UK. This is a dynamic field, however, and low-temperature steam/formaldehyde is also used in the UK and Europe.

Remarkable changes in attitude to sterility assurance practices have occurred in the past few years, and the most recent American and British pharmacopoeias devote more space to BIs than ever before. There is no doubt that improvement in the quality control of BI manufacture has played a role in this change. More acceptance will probably be forthcoming when the British turn to process validation as the 'gold standard' for sterility.

5.3 Process validation practices

The most reliable approach to sterility assurance is neither a culture test nor a mechanical sensor, nor even a BI/CI test piece. It is an approach based on microbial inactivation kinetics (see Chapter 18B, D) wherein a sterilization protocol is specifically designed to reduce the contamination level to a desired margin of safety and the manufacturing process is scrupulously controlled to conform to that protocol.

Theory predicts, and experiments verify, that the death of a microbial population exposed to such lethal treatments as heat, gas and radiation adheres to a logarithmic pattern throughout most of the treatment time. This pattern, the rate of destruction, is a reproducible phenomenon that depends on the microbe itself (its resistance), the intensity of the lethal treatment, and the physicochemical environment in which the process is taking place. If these factors are kept constant, and the original microbial population is known, it is possible to predict the number of survivors after a given period of exposure. Conversely, by manipulating the exposure period to a given treatment, then starting with a known number of organisms of a specified resistance, the ultimate survivor number can be reduced to any desired level.

For example: if the original contamination level of a product is 100 spores per gram and the decimal reduction time or *D*-value at 120°C of the most resistant spore is 1 min, heating that product for 1 min at 120°C will reduce the count to <10 c.f.u./g. A further period of 1 min at the same temperature will reduce the count to 10^0 (or 1) c.f.u./g. Further heating will continue to lower the count, and after

8 min the treatment will yield a product with a 'count' of 10^{-6} c.f.u./g or a one in a million chance that a viable spore still exists in 1 g of product.

This is the basis of sterility assurance by process validation. Since the count in the final product is much too low to be detected by routine product culturing tests, the product is released to the consumer on the basis of confidence in the process. The approach is sometimes called process-control release, parametric release or dosimetric release. The margin of safety or probability of finding a living survivor is known as SAL (sterility assurance level), or MSI (microbial safety index). The approach has been used by food processors for more than 60 years, and is the accepted modern method in factories that manufacture sterile devices and products for medical and surgical use. Essentially, it involves three basic operations: (a) selecting and validating a sterilization cycle that will yield the desired margin of safety; (b) monitoring the process to make sure that all of the parameters upon which the cycle design is based are kept constant; and (c) administrative control of the complete manufacturing process to meet legal requirements.

5.3.1 Selecting and validating a processing cycle

Specific guidelines for designing and validating a steam sterilization cycle can be found in AAMI (1987); for ethylene oxide in AAMI (1988b); and for gamma radiation in AAMI (1984). The acceptability of using this approach for sterility assurance is presented in *US Pharmacopoeia* XXI (*USP*, 1985); and an early but still useful overview of process validation was prepared by Bruch (1982).

A sterilization cycle is selected for a given product on the basis of three variables: the maximum level of contamination expected (the bioload or bioburden); the *D*-value of the most resistant spore-former found in the bioload; and the desired SAL or safety margin. The latter is selected by the manufacturer and will usually range between 10^{-6} for invasive devices and parenteral products and 10^{-3} for topical devices and products.

The bioload itself is determined by quantitative culturing of the specific product just before it is to be sterilized. This should be done frequently and systematically. Since the final bioload *after* sterilization is directly related to the initial bioload, it is axiomatic that errors in estimating this variable can invalidate the final sterility assurance.

D-values are also determined in the laboratory. Spore-formers isolated from the bioload are cultured and spore suspensions are subjected to fractional sterilization tests to determine their inactivation kinetics under treatment conditions.

Once the manufacturer has validated the bioload and its maximum resistance, a suitable sterilizing cycle is selected (precisely defined intensity and duration of exposure) which should achieve the desired SAL for the product under consideration. The manufacturer must then produce a detailed protocol describing the whole sterilization process, including pre-sterilization handling, packaging and post-sterilization handling. Finally, pilot sterilization tests will be conducted using actual or simulated products packaged in the wrappers or containers that will be used in the actual operation. These products will be inoculated with representative numbers (bioload mean + 3 standard deviations) of the most resistant spores liable to be encountered in this operation. Alternatively, the manufacturer may include within the package BIs containing larger inocula than those anticipated of spores with greater *D*-values than those already encountered. The pilot-sterilized products or the BIs are then cultured for viable survivors; if the selected cycle is adequate, repeated pilot tests will show no growth.

When the successful sterilizing protocol, used for the pilot studies, is followed during routine manufacturing operations, and if the parameters on which the protocol is based remain constant, it is reasonable to expect that the final product will have a contamination burden equal to or less than the one for which the manufacturer was aiming.

It should be pointed out that hospitals very rarely have the equipment and personnel to test for bioloads and *D*-values, and usually do not design different sterilizing protocols for specific products. Instead, hospital sterilization operations depend for their sterility assurance on an 'overkill' variation of the process validation practice described above. Their sterilization cycles and protocols are designed by the manufacturer to destroy 10^{12} spores of *B. stearothermophilus* (for steam) or *B. subtilis* (for ethylene oxide). These putative 'bioloads' are so much in excess of what would be found in any worst-possible case that any treatment designed to inactivate them would provide a comfortable margin of safety. Moreover, as mentioned, hospitals in the United States monitor their routine sterilization operations with BIs that provide a much greater challenge — both with respect to numbers and to resistance — than any bioload ever expected.

5.3.2 *Monitoring the sterilization process*

The key word in process validation is reproducibility. If the bioload (numbers and resistance) does not deviate significantly, if the containers and/or packaging remain unchanged, if the sterilization protocol is kept constant with respect to duration and intensity of exposure, if the equipment and the instruments function as designed, and if it can be demonstrated that the lethal treatment penetrated to the micro-environment where the spores are found, sterility will be assured with the margin of safety intended.

Reproducibility of sterilizing conditions can be assured by a proper monitoring system. This includes monitoring the equipment (described in Section 5.1) and the use of CIs and BIs to verify proper sterilization conditions in the actual product micro-environment (Section 5.2). Continued routine monitoring of the bioload and the *D*-values of resistant spores present on the product is also advised to verify the assumptions on which the sterilization protocol is based.

5.3.3 *Good manufacturing practices and administrative control*

In 1978 the American Food and Drug Administration (FDA) issued regulations known collectively as good manufacturing practices (GMP) which require manufacturers of sterile devices to adhere to a comprehensive quality control programme. The GMP, which deal essentially with the operational–managerial aspects of sterilization help focus attention on the subjective aspects of the enterprise, the area where human, rather than equipment and instrument, errors occur.

Among others, GMP provide guidelines to environmental sanitation and ventilation of the areas where sterile items are being manufactured. They cover personnel training, maintenance of equipment and calibration of instruments, as well as packaging, labelling, wrapping, handling and storage of sterile goods. Most of the emphasis of the GMP, however, is devoted to record-keeping and documentation. FDA inspectors will examine carefully all records pertaining to every aspect of sterilization, i.e. temperature recording charts, autoclave maintenance records, BI and CI readouts, laboratory data regarding bioloads and *D*-values, protocols and their validation and any product-testing results. The FDA does not dictate the methods and validation approaches to be followed by the manufacturer, but does place the burden of proof upon that company to demonstrate that the protocols used are valid, and that they achieve the levels of sterility and safety claimed on the product label.

In an industry which relies less and less on product testing to verify claims of sterility, and more and more on parametric release, the GMP, with their emphasis on protocol validation and detailed documentation of every step, are essential to the assurance of sterility and the ultimate safety of the consumer.

6 PERSPECTIVES IN STERILITY ASSURANCE

It might appear from the foregoing that the advances made in sterility assurance during recent decades have eliminated most concerns about the safety of current sterilization practices. To a large extent this is true; however, some serious inconsistencies remain and new problems seem to surface just when it is assumed that technology, reasoning, statistics and the most recent legal regulations have solved the problems raised by Kelsey in 1972.

6.1 Double standards

Bruch (1982) was among the first to recognize that American hospitals do not conform to the same standards of sterility assurance as do manufacturers of sterile devices. He pointed out that although hospitals meet licensing and accreditation standards, their sterilization operations are not subject to the rigorous supervision of the FDA who maintain a uniform national standard for all manufacturers engaged in interstate commerce. Hospitals do follow sterilization protocols designed to 'overkill' the bioburden on their instruments and packs, but in fact the actual bioburden is really unknown, and could be much higher than assumed. Moreover, the packaging materials that hospitals use to protect sterile materials from post-sterilization contamination do not meet the same specifications as those used by industry. Bruch did not imply that the sterile items processed in the hospital are less safe in that there is a greater risk of infection, but raised the question of equity: if industry is forced to comply with strict standards and statistically sophisticated monitoring programmes, why are hospitals who provide sterile items to the same patients not required to comply to the same standards? Does 'sterile' mean the same thing to everyone in the medical profession who uses the term?

As a case in point, it might be appropriate to mention a 'cold' sterilization approach, to sterilize heat-sensitive devices such as endoscopes with delicate optics when ethylene oxide sterilizers are either unavailable or contraindicated. The process involves immersion in a glutaraldehyde solution at room temperature for a specified length of time (see also Chapter 12). Neither the finished product nor the process is monitored by any objective test or instrument. The only control measure is 'administrative', i.e. adhering to protocols designed by the instrument manufacturer and the germicide purveyor.

In fact, glutaraldehyde sterilization has the sanction of the US Environmental Protection Agency on the basis of the AOAC Sporicide test (AOAC, 1984), and hospitals traditionally follow manufacturers' protocols without validating them (Section 5.3.1). However, it must be emphasized that in the case of steam and gas sterilization, hospitals use CIs and BIs to monitor equipment function and the attainment of sterilizing conditions; the monitoring is part of the protocol. In the case of glutaraldehyde immersion there are no chemical, biological or mechanical indicators available to monitor the process, nor does the hospital laboratory culture the processed product according to USP guidelines. CIs have been designed, however, for monitoring the stability of glutaraldehyde solutions (Power & Russell, 1988; Kleier *et al.*, 1989) but are not universally employed.

This subject was introduced to bring sterility assurance into perspective. Microbiologists sometimes get so involved in the complexities of product testing, and autoclave operators so caught up in their CIs and BIs, that it is often overlooked that hospitals use items *labelled* sterile without any independent verification of their status or the process. It is to be wondered whether all the concern felt about sterility assurance, and particularly the strict legal standards to which industry must conform, are really justified.

6.2 Quarantine and storage

Common sense would dictate that a sterilized item should not be released for patient use until sterility tests and/or process monitoring data indicate that the product meets the sterility assurance criteria established for it. Indeed, this is ordained by the FDA regulations under which industry operates, and poses no excessive burden on a factory which manufactures large quantities of product.

On the other hand, in hospitals with a limited inventory of expensive instruments, there is a certain amount of administrative pressure for rapid turnover. The problem may be complicated by the hospital's choice of the BIs used for monitoring the sterilization cycle. Some BIs require a week of incubation before a final decision can be made about the survival of any spores; other commercial BIs provide a readout in 48 h. Though both types are 'approved', there is some serious doubt as to whether they are equivalent to each other with respect to sensitivity. The choice is left to the value judgement of the individual hospital.

The problem is further compounded by the AAMI guidelines (1988a) for frequency of use of BIs. They should be used weekly; preferably on a daily basis; and for each load containing implantable devices. Once more the spectre of inconsistency in sterility definition and assurance is introduced.

Perhaps the most serious problem related to product quarantine concerns those items which are sterilized and released for use immediately, on the basis of a CI but without any opportunity for obtaining a readout from a cultured BI. This occurs when hospitals employ 'flash sterilization' of unwrapped instruments that are delivered directly to the operating theatre from the autoclave. AAMI guidelines (1986c) exist for this contingency, and the people who use it are fairly warned that this method should not be used, if time permits, as a substitute for the routine, wrapped pack which can be quarantined. However, without making any statement about the relative safety of this method it is another example of a weak link in the chain of quality control.

It is a paradox that the same hospitals which sterilize some items by 'flash autoclaving' (without any BIs or quarantine) and others by glutaraldehyde immersion (no monitors and no quarantine) are deeply concerned about 'expiry dates' of sterile packs. There is no doubt that properly sterilized materials can become re-contaminated if they are incorrectly packaged, mishandled, and/or stored. The problem, however, is not a question of time. A properly packaged sterile item will remain sterile as long as the wrapping material retains its integrity. A recent study of long-term storage by Klapes *et al.* (1987) verified this axiom and showed that the probability of contamination in freshly sterilized packs was no different, statistically, from packs which had been stored for periods up to a year.

6.3 Re-sterilizing single-use items

Rising health-care costs have prompted hospitals to turn to reprocessing and re-use of disposable devices as a cost-saving measure (Greene, 1986; Mayhall, 1986: see also Chapter 12). This practice raises legal, ethical and economic issues, as well as the familiar technical ones dealing with sterility assurance (Institute of Health Policy Analysis, 1984). There is no doubt that hospitals can sterilize such items to a sufficiently safe level to prevent infections. However, the question is not only one of infection control. There is a fundamental difference between re-sterilizing a syringe or a forceps and reprocessing a pacemaker or a cardiac catheter. The re-processing of many single-use items is essentially a re-manufacturing operation that requires a sophisticated quality control programme to ensure the functional reliability of the device, pyrogen control and toxicological safety—most of which are beyond the capability of the average hospital. The questions raised by Bruch (1982) about double standards are even more pertinent here than with respect to sterility assurance. Neither FDA nor AAMI publishes guidelines that turn a hospital into a sterile device manufacturer.

The best advice at present is to let the original manufacturer do the re-processing.

6.4 Confidence in *D*-values and inactivation kinetics

One of the first lessons taught in philosophy of science courses is the danger of extrapolating an experimentally determined data plot into the realm of the yet-unverified. Though this practice can lead to interesting speculations, and even significant breakthroughs, it should be done with the utmost caution when dealing with possible health consequences. Nevertheless, this is what is done when *D* values for bioloads are determined and sterilizing cycles then designed to achieve a safety margin far beyond the point where survivors can be assessed empirically. It is assumed that the rate of kill, determined from experimental measurements of survivors, will continue unchanged as a straight line, until that safety margin is reached. In actual practice, killing-curves often show deviations from straight lines (Cerf, 1977; Russell, 1982) and some notable tragedies have occurred when unwarranted confidence was placed on their extrapolation. The survival of live poliovirus in Salk's earlier vaccines is a case in point.

This is the reason why the process validation procedure is so rigorous, and why so much emphasis is placed on monitoring sterilization with BIs that contain excessive numbers of very resistant spores. Killing-curves, even with their shoulders and tails, are useful for predicting theoretical endpoints, but the final safety of the product must be based on more empirical data.

In this respect it is encouraging that the theoretical and statistical assumptions underlying sterility assurance are occasionally verified by empirical observations. Kereluk (1977) presented the results of a 'natural' experiment that was inadvertently performed in a surgical suture manufacturing operation that used gamma radiation for sterilizing the product. Sutures inoculated with approximately 10^4 *B. pumilus* spores as BIs were used to monitor the sterilization process which was designed to lower the bioload by 8 logs or an SAL of 10^{-4}. It would be impossible to detect this level by any laboratory assay; normally all the operator could verify would be that the BI showed no growth when cultured. However, in 12 years of this operation, 1016069 BIs were tested and 44 were found to be positive. This is equivalent to a SAL of 4.3×10^{-5} or just a little better than the theoretical design. In truth, on the 44 days when those positive BIs were discovered, the factory manager was convinced that a disastrous sterilizer failure had occurred, and one can imagine the escalating consternation the second time this happened. In retrospect, however, it was an object lesson in BI reliability and theory validation.

6.5 Sterility assurance, contamination and infection control

Notwithstanding the inconsistencies described above, it is evident that sterility assurance is now a fairly sophisticated enterprise that becomes more complicated, and expensive, as time progresses. It might be pertinent to query the relevance of all of these tests, regulations and protocols, particularly as they relate to the ultimate aim of sterility assurance, i.e. protection from infection (Greene, 1982).

A century ago, when sterility tests and process monitoring originated, most hospital infections were truly 'cross-infections' transmitted either directly from people or indirectly by contaminated fomites. Some infections, notably tetanus, could be attributed to spore-forming bacteria. In those days the only sure way to prevent infection transmission by fomites was to autoclave them, and the only way to verify that the fomite was truly safe was by the various tests described above.

Today, most hospital infections are autogenous, caused by microbes that live on or in the patient himself. Furthermore the major pathogens involved in nosocomial infections are staphylococci, streptococci, Gram-negative rods and non-spore-forming anaerobes, that can be killed by treatments much milder than those required for spores. Is it really necessary, therefore, in order to prevent infections today, to subject a device or product to a treatment that will kill 10^{12} hardy spores? The sterilization cycles commonly used today are so far biased toward 'overkill' that even sterilization 'failures' are often sufficient to render a surgical/medical device non-infectious. Most surgical packs that a hospital would reject as understerilized might actually be safe. This may account for our epidemiological acceptance of glutaraldehyde immersion, flash autoclaving and the 'double standards' of hospital sterility assurance. Even though some of these practices do not meet the rigorous standards imposed on industry, the latter standards are so high that there is an ample margin of safety available even to those who cannot match them.

In this regard it should be noted that sterilized devices and products are not completely blameless in infection transmission even today. Parenteral solutions, medications, saline and water have been repeatedly incriminated. Implants, porcine heart valves, lumbar puncture kits, as well as intraocular lenses, catheters, and transducers have caused sporadic infections. It must be emphasized however, that almost invariably the infection was due to human error rather than to sterilizer failure. Most of the problems involved post-sterilization recontamination, several the use of non-sterilized products mistakenly assumed to be sterile; none involved products or devices that met even the minimum standards of sterility assurance.

That might be the proper answer to the critics of today's sterility assurance regulations and practices. The enterprise as carried out in hospitals and by industry has been so successful in providing safety to the users of sterile devices that it is taken for granted. In the United States alone, millions upon millions of sterilized products, foods, pharmaceuticals and medical devices are used daily, all without any adverse result and with no expectation of one. The absolute confidence placed by the ultimate consumer in the safety of the sterilized item is the best reason for continuing in the same direction on the sterility assurance path.

7 REFERENCES

AAMI (1981) *Standard for BIER/Steam Vessels*. Arlington, Va: Association for the Advancement of Medical Instrumentation.

AAMI (1982) *Standard for BIER/EO Gas Vessels*. Arlington, Va: Association for the Advancement of Medical Instrumentation.

AAMI (1983) *Hospital Steam Sterilizers*. Arlington, Va: Association for the Advancement of Medical Instrumentation.

AAMI (1984) *Process Control Guidelines: Gamma Radiation Sterilization of Medical Devices*. Arlington, Va: Association for the Advancement of Medical Instrumentation.

AAMI (1985) *Good Hospital Practice: Performance Evaluation of Ethylene Oxide Sterilizers—Ethylene Oxide Test Packs*. Arlington, Va: Association for the Advancement of Medical Instrumentation.

AAMI (1986a) *Biological Indicators for Ethylene Oxide Sterilization Processes in Health Care Facilities*. Arlington, Va: Association for the Advancement of Medical Instrumentation.

AAMI (1986b) *Biological Indicators for Saturated Steam Sterilization Processes in Health Care Facilities*. Arlington, Va: Association for the Advancement of Medical Instrumentation.

AAMI (1986c) *Good Hospital Practice: Steam Sterilization Using the Unwrapped Method (Flash Sterilization)*. Arlington, Va: Association for the Advancement of Medical Instrumentation.

AAMI (1987) *Guideline for Industrial Moist Heat Sterilization of Medical Products*. Arlington, Va: Association for the Advancement of Medical Instrumentation.

AAMI (1988a) *Good Hospital Practice: Steam Sterilization and Sterility Assurance*. Arlington, Va: Association for the Advancement of Medical Instrumentation.

AAMI (1988b) *Guideline for Industrial Ethylene Oxide Sterilization of Medical Devices*. Arlington, Va: Association for the Advancement of Medical Instrumentation.

Alder, V.G. (1976) Sterilization and disinfection by physical methods. In *Microbiological Methods* (eds Collins, C.H. & Lyne, P.M.) pp. 69–91. London: Butterworths.

AOAC (1984) *Official Methods of Analysis*, 14th Ed. Washington, DC: Association of Official Analytical Chemists.

Bowie, J.H., Kelsey, J.C. & Thompson, G.R. (1963) The Bowie and Dick autoclave tape test. *Lancet*, **i**, 586.

Brewer, J.H. (1957) Sterility tests and methods for assuring sterility. In *Antiseptics, Disinfectants, Fungicides and Sterilization* (ed. Reddish, G.F.) 2nd Ed., pp. 158–174. Philadelphia; Lea & Febiger.

British Pharmacopoeia (1988) London: HMSO.

Bruch, C.W. (1982) Inhospital versus industrial sterility assurance: Is there a double standard? In *Inhospital Sterility Assurance—Current Perspectives*. AAMI Technology Assessment Report No. 4–82, pp. 19–23. Arlington, Va: Association for the Advancement of Medical Instrumentation.

Bryce, D.M. (1956) Tests for the sterility of pharmaceutical preparations. The design and interpretation of sterility tests. *Journal of Pharmacy and Pharmacology*, **8**, 561–572.

Cerf, O. (1977) Tailing of survival curves of bacterial spores. *Journal of Applied Bacteriology*, **42**, 1–19.

Denyer, S.P. (1987) Sterilisation control and sterility testing. In *Pharmaceutical Microbiology* (eds Hugo, W.B. & Russell, A.D.) 4th Ed., pp. 446–458. Oxford: Blackwell Scientific Publications.

Greene, V.W. (1982) Infection control methods and monitoring. In *In-hospital Sterility Assurance—Current Perspectives*. AAMI Technology Assessment Report No. 4–82, pp. 41–45. Arlington, Va: Association for the Advancement of Medical Instrumentation.

Greene, V.W. (1986) Reuse of disposable medical devices: historical and current aspects. *Infection Control*, **7**, 508–513.

Hall, L.B. (1971) *Planetary Quarantine*. New York: Gordon & Breach.

HIMA (1978) *Biological and Chemical Indicators* (ed. Worden, L.J.) Report No. 78–14. Washington: Health Industry Manufacturers Association.

HTM (1980) Health Technical Memorandum No. 10, Sterilizers (Under revision). London: DHSS.

Institute for Health Policy Analysis (1984) *Reuse of Disposable Medical devices in the 1980s*. Washington, DC: Georgetown University Medical Center.

Kelsey, J.C. (1972) The myth of surgical sterility. *Lancet*, **ii**, 1301–1303.

Kereluk, K. (1977) Microbiological control of sterilization processes. In *Sterilization of Medical Products* (eds Gaughran, E.R.L. & Kereluk, K.) pp. 43–68. New Brunswick, NJ: Johnson & Johnson.

Kilmer, F.B. (1897) Modern surgical dressings. *American Journal of Pharmacology*, **69**, 24–39.

Klapes, N.A., Greene, V.W., Langholz, A.C. & Hunstiger, C. (1978) Effect of long-term storage on sterile status of devices in surgical packs. *Infection Control*, **8**, 289–293.

Kleier, D.J., Tucker, J.E. & Averbach, R.E. (1989) Clinical evaluation of glutaraldehyde nonbiologic monitors. *Infection Control*, **20**, 271–277.

Mayhall, C.G. (1986) Types of disposable medical devices reused in hospitals. *Infection Control*, **7**, 491–494.

Power, E.G.M. & Russell, A.D. (1988) Assessment of 'Cold Sterilog Glutaraldehyde Monitor'. *Journal of Hospital Infection*, **11**, 376–380.

Russell, A.D. (1982) *The Destruction of Bacterial Spores*. London: Academic Press.

USP (1985) *The Pharmacopoeia of the United States of America XXI*. Rockville Md.: US Pharmacopoeial Convention.

Index

Page numbers in *italics* refer to figures and/or tables.